INDEX

TO THE

PICTORIAL HISTORY OF ENGLAND:

FORMING A

Complete Chronological Key

TO

THE CIVIL AND MILITARY EVENTS,

THE

LIVES OF REMARKABLE PERSONS,

AND THE

PROGRESS OF THE COUNTRY IN RELIGION, GOVERNMENT, INDUSTRY, ARTS AND SCIENCES,
LITERATURE, MANNERS, AND SOCIAL ECONOMY.

BY H. C. HAMILTON, ESQ.

OF HER MAJESTY'S STATE PAPER OFFICE.

LONDON:

WM. S. ORR & CO., AMEN-CORNER, PATERNOSTER-ROW.

1850.

PREFACE.

It having been suggested that an INDEX to the Eight Volumes of the "PICTORIAL HISTORY OF ENGLAND" would not only be exceedingly useful in regard to that work, but that, by adding the Date to each event, a single reference would at once render a satisfactory answer to a historical question, which might otherwise require a long research to elucidate,—the suggestion has been adopted; and, where the History itself proved deficient, a Date has been supplied from the most authentic sources. Thus a complete ALPHABETICAL HISTORY OF ENGLAND, and of everything that has concerned England from the earliest times, has been produced, which, it is hoped, will greatly enhance the value of the work.

H. C. H.

October, 1850.

INDEX

TO THE

PICTORIAL HISTORY OF ENGLAND.

The mark § prefixed to the Reference denotes that it will be found in the Second Series of Volumes, containing the reign of George III.—as for instance, Abaris i. 15, means that Abaris is to be found in vol. i. p. 15 of the First Series: Abbaye § ii. 394, means Vol. ii. p. 394 of the Second Series.

ABARIS an Irishman, his embassy to Athens from the Hyperboreans, i. 15.

Abbaye, prison of the, § ii. 394.

ABBOT, Dr. George, promoted to the primacy, 1611; iii. 45. His Presbyterian principles, ib. He coincides with the measures adopted by the English king against Vorstius, 47. Attends Prince Henry in his last moments, and takes his dying confession of faith, 1612; 51, 53. Crowns Charles I., 1626; 117. Is suspended, 124. Restored to his dignity, 130. His death, August 4, 1633; 157. His portrait, 433.

ABBOTT, Dr. Robert, chaplain to James I., elected to the bishopric of Salisbury, October 11, 1615. Died March 2, 1618; iii. 520.

ABERCROMBY, Sir Ralph, a distinguished British officer, born 1738; iv. 603. His service against the French in Holland, 1799; § iii. 547. He dies of wounds, March 28, 1801, received at the battle of Alexandria, 556°—558°.

ABERGAVENNY, Lady, pleads for the life of Mrs. Alicia Lisle, 1685; iii. 781.

Abjuration Bill, the, 1690; iv. 21.

Aboukir, battle of, gained by the French over the Turks, July 25, 1799; § iii. 547.

ACHAIUS, king of the Scoti, descended from Fergus the Dalriadian, espoused a Pictish princess, sister of king Constantine, i. 217. His successor was Alpin, and his grandson Kenneth II., or Mac Alpin, which warlike prince, on the death of Uven the Pictish monarch, slain in battle by the Danes, claimed the vacant crown in right of his grandmother, and governed both nations, 843, as king of the Scots and Picts, ib.

Acorns, beaten down for swine, i. 277.

Acre, siege of, 300,000 Christians perish at the, i. 495. Surrenders June 12, 1191; ib. View of the ramparts, ib. The Saracens agree to restore the wood of the Holy Cross, to set 1500 Christian captives at liberty, and pay 200,000 pieces of gold, ib. Siege of, by Bonaparte, 1799; § iii. 547, 548.

Acta, a settlement on the Isthmus of Darien, established by Paterson, regno William III., iv. 96.

ACTON, Sir Roger, a Lollard, 1414, executed, ii. 26.

Actresses first appear on the English stage in the 17th century, iii. 901.

Acts—see Parliament.

ADDINGTON, Henry—see Sidmouth.

ADDISON, Joseph, an eminent literary character, born May 1, 1672, author of the 'Campaign,' the 'Spec-

ADDISON, Joseph—tator,' and other productions, iv. 796. Appointed secretary to the Lords Justices, 1714; 302. Retires from office, 344. His death, June 17, 1719; ib. His portrait, 735.

ADELAIS, or Alice, daughter of Geoffrey duke of Louvain and niece of the reigning pope Calixtus II., married to Henry I., 1120; i. 416. She receives Matilda in Arundel Castle, 1139; 428.

ADELAIS, niece of king Stephen, married to Louis VII., 1160; i. 446.

ADELAIS, daughter of Louis VII., affianced wife of prince Richard. Henry refuses to consent to her marriage. Suspicions as to his conduct with regard to her, i. 477, 478. He offers to unite her to his son John, 1189, and appoint him his successor in Normandy. Her brother Philip refuses this proposal. 478.

Adjutators, alias Agitators, instituted by Cromwell, 1647; iii. 366.

ADRIAN IV., pope (Nicholas Breakspear, an Englishman and cardinal), elected December 3, 1154. Henry II. sends to congratulate him. He died August 30, 1159; i. 442.

ÆLFRIC, his Saxon Homilies, i. 301.

AGAR, Sir Anthony, 1558, slain in the capture of Calais by the Duke of Guise, ii. 534.

AGATHA, mother of Edgar Atheling, flies to Scotland, 1068; i. 369.

AGGAS, Ralph, an eminent surveyor and engraver, famous for his great plan of London in the reign of Elizabeth. He died in London, 1579; aged about sixty, iii. 577.

Aghrim, battle of, fought July 12, 1691; iv. 33.

Agincourt, or Azincourt, battle of, 25th October, 1415; ii. 30, et seq., 36. Song on the victory at Agincourt, 1415, and the music to the same, 233, 234. This is the first English part-music whereof we have any remains, iii. 564.

AGRICOLA, Cnæus Julius, 78, extended the Roman conquest to the Grampian Hills, i. 44. He gained the respect and regard of the Britons, promoted education, &c., 45. He built castles and ramparts wherever he carried his arms, ib. Agricola's Wall, from the Solway to the Tyne, ib. He constructed a chain of forts, 81, from the Clyde to the Forth, afterwards more solidly improved by Lollius Urbicus, 45, 47. He subdued the tribes of Galloway, 82, and in 83 he encountered the Caledonians to the north of the Forth, with varying success, 46.

B

AGRICOLA—
In his last campaign, 84, he totally defeated Galgacus on *Mons Grampius*, *ib.* His fleet sailed round the island; particulars given by Tacitus of this periplus, 47. Britain enjoyed a long period of repose, consequent on his firm and wise administration, *ib.* Agricola recalled by the emperor Domitian, *ib.*

Agriculture:—Corn in the Roman period was exported in large quantity from Britain, i. 106. Other exports, horses, cheese, chalk, &c. *ib.* The great bulk of the Saxon population engaged in producing food, 276. Ordinary divisions of rural employment soon after the conquest, 596. Reaping and gleaning, from an ancient MS., *ib.* Use of manures, &c., *ib.* Threshing and corn sacks, from an ancient MS., 597. Great improvements in agriculture effected by the industry of the monks, *ib.* Draining of the fens of Cambridgeshire and Lincolnshire commenced in the early Norman period, 598. Low state of agriculture in Scotland and Ireland, *ib.* Various particulars respecting the agriculture of this period, *ib.* Years of great scarcity, &c., 598, 599. Gardens, orchards, and vineyards, enumerated in the Conqueror's survey, 599. Description of agriculture from the reign of Edward I. to that of Richard II., 838—840. Produce, rents, tenancy, &c., 1420; ii. 189. Exportation of corn, regulations, statutes, 1425; 188. The wheeled plough, and oxen, *ib.* Value of land, years' purchase, &c., 189. Laws to retain emancipated serfs on the land: Statutes of labourers, 1351—1405, *ib.* Wages, *ib.* Increase of wool, sheep, and pasturage, 189, 190. Agriculture during the 17th century, ii. 803—806.

Agriculture:—(18th century). Introduction of turnips as a field-crop renders it unnecessary to allow the land to lie fallow, § i. 573. Drill husbandry, an important feature of the agriculture of East Kent, *ib.* Strong spirit of agricultural improvement; new processes of cultivation, § iii. 665.

Agriculture:—(19th century). Introduction of the Swedish turnip and mangold wurzel as winter provisions, § iv. 694-695.

AGUILAR, don Juan d', commanding a Spanish army in Ireland, fortified Kinsale, 1601; but Tyrone attempting to relieve him in that port, was defeated by Lord Mountjoy, ii. 693. Capitulation of Kinsale, the Spaniards allowed to embark for their own country, *ib.*

Air-pump, the, invented by Otto von Guericke, in the latter part of the seventeenth century, iv. 779.

AITKIN, James, *alias* John the Painter, a dangerous incendiary, tried and executed March, 1777; § i. 287—289.

Aix-la-Chapelle, treaty of, concluded April, 1668, between Charles II. and Louis XIV., iii. 706.

Aix-la-Chapelle, treaty of, concluded October 1748, between George II. and Louis XV., iv. 558.

ALAN, lord of Richmond, desirous of marrying Maud, daughter of Margaret sister of Edgar Atheling and wife of Malcolm, but dies before he could receive an answer from William II., i. 406.

ALAN, of Galloway, marries the eldest daughter of David, earl of Huntingdon, brother of William the Lion, and thus Dervorguil, his eldest daughter by this marriage, transmitted to her descendants the lineal right of succession to the throne, i. 700. Serious commotions in Galloway, 1233, upon his death, *ib.*

ALBAN, St., first British martyr, perished in the persecution of Diocletian, 286; i. 74.

ALBANO, Francisco, a Bolognese painter, born 1578, famous for his female figures and Cupids; Charles I. invites him over to England; he died at his native city in 1660; iii. 569.

Albany, view of, § i. 352.

ALBANY, duke of, brother of king Robert III., aspires to the Scottish succession, 1401; ii. 9. His great power, in the reign of Robert of Scotland, 11. Is supposed to have starved David, earl of Rothsay, in Falkland Castle, 1405; 19, 131. Prince James being captured at sea, and Robert dying in 1406, Albany, who was subservient to the English king, continued to govern Scotland, 19, 131. He and Douglas besiege Berwick and Roxburgh, 38. At his death his son Murdoch becomes regent, but made no effort to release king James from Windsor Castle, 49, 132. His armies entering England are defeated at Nesbit Moor, and Homildon Hill, by the Scotch Earl of March, and Hotspur, 11, 131. Albany in person marches to the border, but hearing of Henry IV.'s victory at Shrewsbury, returns, 131. A truce, 1405, 1412, with the English, 131, 132. Continued as regent, 1406, James I. being a captive at Windsor, *ib.* The Lord of the Isles defeated by Mar, 1411, at the battle of Harlaw, 132. This northern prince is compelled to acknowledge himself a vassal of the Scottish crown, *ib.* Murdoch, son of Albany, is exchanged for Henry Percy, the son of Hotspur, *ib.* In 1417, the regent broke the truce at the head of 60,000 Scots, advanced to Roxburgh and the borders, but retreated before an English force; this was named the "Foul Raid," 132. In consequence, the south of Scotland was laid waste in revenge, *ib.* Vendome, French envoy, obtains a force of 7,000 Scots, under Buchan, a son of the regent, to serve the dauphin Charles in France, *ib.* Earl of Douglas joins Buchan and Wigton, with 5,000 more Scots, *ib.* The regent died, aged eighty, in 1419, at Stirling, having governed thirty-four years, *ib.* His power had been upheld by the great nobles, and feudal tyranny in his time assumed its darkest aspect, *ib.* Their design was to revive the institution of a *dependent king*, *ib.*

ALBANY, duke of, Murdoch Stewart, son of the great duke of Albany, taken prisoner at Homildon Hill, ii. 131. Murdoch exchanged for Percy, son of Hotspur, 132. He succeeds his father as Regent of Scotland, 1419; *ib.* Having no talent, a state of anarchy ensued, until 1424, when James I. and his queen were crowned at Scone, *ib.* His trial, May 1428; 133. The duke, with his sons, Walter and Alexander Stewart, and his father-in-law, the earl of Lennox, executed at Stirling, *ib.* Their estates forfeited to the Crown, *ib.*

ALBANY, duke of, second son of James II., his ambition, ii. 135. In 1482, he returns from France, and treats under the style of Alexander, king of Scotland, with Edward IV., to whom he promises fealty as his liege lord, 115, 136. Richard of Gloucester invades Scotland, by virtue of this treaty, 114, 136. A short reconciliation with his brother, James III., but in a few months another revolution causes Albany to rebel and fly to England, 115, 136. Richard III., occupied at home, is unable to succour him, *ib.*

ALBANY, duke of, landed from France in 1515, and proclaimed regent, ii. 350. He compelled queen Margaret, at Stirling, to resign the care of her sons to certain peers, 351. Home rebels, and concerts measures with lord Dacre, *ib.* Home and Angus abandoned Margaret on the English border, and submitted to the popular regent, who restored them in honours and estates, *ib.* On the rebellion of Arran, Glencairn, Lennox, &c. Home again plots with lord Dacre, the agent of Wolsey, *ib.* Albany triumphed, forgave those lords, but executed Home and his brother, at Edinburgh, 351, 352. The regent hearing that Dacre was preparing to pass an English army into the lowland counties, went over to France for auxiliaries, 352. Queen Margaret hav-

ALBANY, duke of—
ing visited her brother Henry, 1516, and returned to Scotland, became incensed both with Dacre and king Henry for his unjust ambition, and recalled the regent, 353. The regent's declaration of war; his numerous army at Annan, prepared for an advance on Carlisle, 364. Dacre's force unable to resist the Scottish army; but queen Margaret is said to have contravened Albany's plans, *ib.* Wolsey's letter to Henry VIII., declaring this great expedition to have ended in a truce, September 1522, *ib.* Albany retired to France, in October, leaving the administration in the hands of Huntley, Arran, and Argyle, *ib.* He returns with soldiers, artillery, &c., which had been furnished to him by France, 429. The Scots accuse him of wishing to urge them into a war with England, *ib.* He marches to the Tweed with 40,000 men, but is compelled to retreat. The Scottish peers accuse him of being the cause of their disgrace, and compel him to dismiss the foreign auxiliaries. In the Spring of 1523, Albany returns in disgust to France, whence he marches with the French king into Italy, 1524; 359, 429. Allusions to, 361. Ruin of his party in Scotland, *ib.*

ALBEMARLE, William de Mandeville, earl of, 1179. Carries the crown at the coronation of Richard I., 1189; i. 483. Is joined with Pudsey in the regency of England, 485. He died 1190.

ALBEMARLE, George Monk, duke of, first a royalist, then a parliamentarian, iii. 432, takes possession of Berwick, Oct. 29, 1659. Is made commander-in-chief by the presbyterian majority in Parliament, Feb. 1660; 430°. His private negotiations with Charles II., *ib.* Letters from the king are sent to the houses of parliament: that to the commons contains the Declaration of Breda, 431°. Monk is created Duke of Albemarle, July 7, 1660; 664. His disgraceful conduct towards the marquess of Argyle, 681. His engagement with the Dutch admiral De Ruyter, 1666; 698. He died April, 1670.

ALBEMARLE, Christopher Monk, duke of, collects a force, 1685, to oppose the duke of Monmouth. He died 1688; iii. 773.

ALBEMARLE, Arnold Joost von Keppel, created Feb. 10, 1696; iv. 138. Burns several French magazines near Arras, 1705; 265. Is taken prisoner by marshal Villars; his death, 1718; 269.

ALBERIC, bishop of Ostia, the pope's legate in England in 1139; at his intercession a peace is concluded between Stephen and David king of Scotland, i. 426.

ALBERONI, Julius, a Spanish statesman and cardinal, born 1664. Became prime minister 1717; iv. 341. His dispute with the duke of Escalona, which ends in the banishment of the latter, 342-343. He contracts a marriage with the Princess Clementina, granddaughter of John Sobieski, king of Poland, 352. The French regent bribes the marquess Scotti to intrigue against him, 365. Alberoni is dismissed from his employments and banished Spain, Dec. 5, 1720, *ib.* He died in 1752.

ALBERT, archduke, succeeds to the government of the Spanish Netherlands, 1596. Takes Calais from Henri IV.; ii. 680. Marries the Infanta Donna Isabella Clara Eugenia, daughter of Philip II., who had a claim to the English succession on the death of Elizabeth through John of Gaunt, 685.

ALBERT, archbishop of York, rebuilds the cathedral after the fire in 767; i. 310.

ALBINEY, William d', commander of the forces of the barons at the taking of Rochester castle, i. 530. He defends it against the king, but at length is obliged to surrender, 1215, *ib.*

Albinn, the name for Scotland used by all the races of Gaels (the *white island*), i. 21. Innis-wen, or white island, another form for Britain among the Welsh, *ib.*

ALBINUS, Clodius, governor of Britain, his battle with the emperor Severus in France, i. 49. So many British soldiers of Albinus slain in this contest that the Scots and Picts invaded Britain, *ib.* Severus, in his old days, resolved to repress the invaders, and penetrated farther than any other Roman into the north of Caledonia, 207, *ib.*

Albion, son of Neptune, fabled to have taken Britain from the Celts. Annius appears to have been the inventor of this fable, i. 8.

Albion, the early name of England, as known to the Greeks and Romans, i. 21.

ALBRET, d', king of Navarre, attacked by the duke of Alva, retired to his principality of Bearn, 1512, and Ferdinand, the Catholic, acquired Navarre, ii. 321.

ALBRET, Henry d', king of Navarre, 1526; ii. 365.

ALBRET, d', prince of Bearn, 1486, seeks the hand of Anne of Brittany, ii. 292. He marched to the aid of her father Francis II., but had to capitulate to a French force, 292, 294. His vexation at Maximilian's secret marriage with the princess Anne, caused him to betray Nantes to the French, 296.

ALBRET, Jean d', constable of France, general of the French forces, 1415, at Agincourt, ii. 29, 31. Slain by the English archers, together with many illustrious knights, 32, 33.

Alcazar, battle of, 1578. Sebastian, king of Portugal, slain by the Moors, ii. 651.

Alchemy, its influence on the progress of medical science, i. 844, 845; doubts raised in the 15th century respecting the lawfulness of the study, ii. 307.

ALCUIN, Flaccus, a learned prelate of the 8th century, educated under Egbert, archbishop of York, and the venerable Bede; his school of St. Martin in the city of Tours, i. 307.

ALDERIC, William of, conspires to place Stephen count of Aumale on the throne, 1095, is taken and hanged, i. 400.

ALDRED, archbishop of York, translated from Worcester, 1061; i. 204, 360. His servants insulted by the Norman garrison at York, 369. Reprimands the king, *ib.* Dies Sept. 1069 of disappointment and grief, *ib.*

ALDRED, an early English historian, i. 542.

ALDRICH, Henry, dean of Christ Church, Oxford, 1689. His decision of the question as to the authenticity of the work on music ascribed to Henry VIII., iii. 562. He was architect of the Peckwater quadrangle, and the church of All Saints, at Oxford. His death took place in 1710; 750.

ALENÇON, duke of, returns from the army in Gascony, ii. 19. He confederates, 1409, with young Orleans and the count of Armagnac, against the duke of Burgundy, 21. His display of valour, 1415, in the mêlée at Agincourt; he strikes York to the ground with his battle-axe, and king Henry shielding that duke receives the second blow of Alençon, which knocked off part of the crown he wore on his helmet, 33. Alençon being surrounded by some English who close about their king, the French duke surrenders to the brave Henry, who was holding out his hand to receive him, but at that instant Alençon was slain, *ib.*

ALENÇON, duke of, his address to Talbot, prisoner at Patay, 1429; ii. 68.

ALENÇON, duke of, a suitor of queen Elizabeth, ii. 636. He became duke of Anjou, when his brother Henry, duke of Anjou, mounted the French throne, 649. *See* Anjou.

ALESSI, Guiseppe, heads a formidable insurrection in Italy against Philip IV., of Spain, iii. 395.

ALEXANDER I., 1107—1124, king of Scotland, son of Malcolm III., and brother of king Edgar of Scotland, began to reign January 8, 1107. Marries the lady Sibilla, illegitimate daughter of Henry I., i. 538. Cumberland is dismembered from the Scottish crown, being bequeathed by king Edgar to his younger

ALEXANDER I.—
brother David, *ib.* Alexander disclaims the assumed authority of the English archbishops over the Scottish church, 538—539. His death, April 27th 1124; *ib.*

ALEXANDER II., 1214—1249, king of Scotland, and son of William the Lion, when in his seventeenth year succeeded his father, and was crowned at Scone, December 10, 1214; i. 546. This young king takes part with the barons; John marches to oppose him, and lays waste all the country in his way, 530. Alexander retires, and John having advanced as far as Edinburgh returns, burning Haddington, Dunbar, and Berwick, *ib.* After the death of John, he continues to co-operate with prince Louis and the confederate English barons; Louis makes peace with Henry and he returns home, and shortly after effects his reconciliation with the Pope and the new English king, 700. He marries the princess Joan, Henry's eldest sister, June 25, 1221, and a long uninterrupted peace followed, *ib.* Disturbances in the Northern districts, *ib.* Alexander surrenders to Henry the town of Carlisle, 1217, *ib.* Agreement as to his claims to the counties of Northumland, Cumberland, and Westmoreland, 701. His wife Joan dies on the 4th of March, 1238, leaving no issue, and in the following year he married Mary, daughter of Ingelram de Couci, a great lord of Picardy, *ib.* Henry proclaims war with him, 1244, but a peace is concluded at Newcastle, 702. Alexander undertakes an expedition against Angus, lord of Argyle, for refusing to transfer to the Scottish crown the homage which he had been wont to render for certain of the western islands to the king of Norway, *ib.* He was engaged in this war when he was taken ill, and died in the island of Kerrary, on the 8th of July, 1249, *ib.* His amiable character, *ib.*

ALEXANDER III., 1249—1286, was born at Roxburgh, on the 4th of September, 1241, and was the only son of Alexander II., to whom he succeeded in 1249; i. 702. His nuptials with Margaret, daughter of king Henry, celebrated at York, with great magnificence, December 26, 1251; 703. Disturbed state of Scotland during his minority, occasioned by contentions for the management of affairs, between the powerful family of the Comyns, and the adherents of the English interest in Scotland. In 1260, Alexander and his wife pay a visit to king Henry, and in 1261, the queen of Scots was delivered of a daughter, at Windsor, who was named Margaret, 704. In 1263, the earl of Ross with other northern chiefs invade the Hebrides, which were under the dominion of Norway. Haco, the Norwegian king, prepares an expedition against Scotland; he is at first very successful, but in the autumn his ships are destroyed by the storms, and many of his men slain at the battle of Largs. Haco retires to Orkney and expires, December 15, 704-705. The Hebrides and the Isle of Man, with all other islands in the western and southern seas which Norway might hitherto have held or claimed, are made over in full sovereignty to Scotland, 705. After this, Scotland enjoyed twenty years of peace and prosperity, *ib.* In 1275, queen Margaret died, and in 1281 the princess Margaret was married to Eric, king of Norway, *ib.* In the following year, Alexander the king's only son (his brother David having died) married Margaret, daughter of Guy, earl of Flanders, *ib.* In 1283, the queen of Norway died, leaving only an infant daughter, *ib.* And on the 28th of January, 1284, her brother also died, leaving the succession to the infant daughter of Eric, 706. On the 5th of February, the parliament assembled at Scone, and acknowledged for their sovereign the Norwegian princess, *ib.* Alexander marries Joleta, daughter of the count of Dreux, April 15th, 1285. But with-

ALEXANDER III.—
in a year after his marriage, on the 16th of March, 1286, whilst riding in a dark night between Kinghorn and Burnt Island, his horse stumbled with him over a high cliff and he was killed, *ib.* At a meeting of the Estates at Scone on the 11th of April, a regency was appointed, and in 1289, Eric opens a negotiation with Edward on the affairs of his infant daughter and her kingdom; at Edward's request the Scottish regency sent three of its members to take part in a solemn deliberation at Salisbury, in which it was agreed that the young queen should be immediately conveyed to her own dominions or to England, *ib.* Edward proposes that she should be married to her cousin, his eldest son, with which the Scottish nation are highly delighted; July 18th, 1290, a treaty was concluded, and the proposed marriage finally arranged, 707. The princess was taken sick on her passage, and landing on one of the Orkney islands, died there, in her eighth year, *ib.*

ALEXANDER, emperor of Russia, 1801—1825. He succeeds to the throne on the death of his father, Paul I., March 24, 1801; § iii. 553*. For his wars with the French, *see* Bonaparte. Treaty of Tilsit, § iv. 296. The Russians defeated by the Turks before Silistria. and compelled to recross the Danube, 1809; 405-406. Alexander enters Paris with the allied army, March 31, 1814; § iv. 615*. He takes a conspicuous part in the arranging of a general peace, 616*-617*. Visits England after the signing of the treaty of Paris, 619*.

ALEXANDER III., acknowledged Pope by Louis and Henry I., i. 446. He enjoyed the pontificate from 1159 to 1181.

ALEXANDER V., pope (Peter surnamed Philargi, archbishop of Milan), elected June, 1409. He issues a sentence of excommunication against all men concerned in the murder of Scrope, archbishop of York, but Henry IV. sending a justification of his conduct he revokes the sentence. His death took place May 3, 1410; ii. 17.

ALEXANDER VI., pope, (Roderic Borgia, nephew of Calixtus III.) elected August 1492. Died, August 1502-3; ii. 311—318. His son, Cæsar Borgia, 311 —318.

ALEXANDER, archdeacon of Salisbury, nephew of the powerful Roger, bishop of Sarum, nominated to the see of Lincoln, April 15, 1123. Stephen orders his arrest, i. 426. He joins Matilda, 428. Having got together the scattered forces of Nigel, and being in alliance with the earls of Lincoln and Chester, he makes himself formidable to the king, who besieges the castle of Lincoln, when the earl of Gloucester advancing with 10,000 men a battle is fought, in which Stephen is taken prisoner, 430. Alexander died in 1147.

Alexandria, battle of, gained by general Abercromby March 21, 1801, over the French under Menou, § iii. 556*—558*.

ALFERE, ealderman of Mercia, declares for the secular clergy against Dunstan, 975, and expels all monks from his territory, i. 174. He leagues with Elfrida, mother of Ethelred, 175. Succeeded in his earldom by his son Alfric, 176.

ALFORD, Edward, appointed sheriff by Charles I.,1625; iii. 117. 534.

ALFRED THE GREAT (*Portrait of*, i. 246). He was the youngest and favourite son of Ethelwulf, and carried to Rome by that devout king of Wessex, where the pope anointed the prince with holy oil with his own hands, to the great umbrage of his three older brothers (previous to 857); i. 153, 156, 165. He succeeds Ethelred in 871 on the throne of their father Ethelwulf, 154. Was long in danger from the fierce Danes and Norsemen, and could scarcely maintain himself in his kingdom of Wessex, or find

ALFRED the Great—
security for his life, *ib.* His savage enemies, known since then as Normans in France and Italy, particularly described, *ib.* Their fleets and entrenched camps on the coasts, 155. District militia of the Saxons intercepting the marauding Danes on their return with booty to their ships, gave no quarter, *ib.* The Anglo-Saxon standard is driven to the S.W. of the island, Somersetshire, Devonshire, and Cornwall, 156. The king exhibits calmness and skill, 157. In Alfred's absence his troops meet the Danes (in 874) at Wilton, and put them to flight, but the Danes returning remain masters of the field, *ib.* His kingdom of Wessex evacuated by the Danes, and a peace concluded (in 874); *ib.* The Danes again design to ravage Wessex, and, in 875, surprise Wareham castle, Dorsetshire, *ib.* The Saxons having long neglected maritime affairs, king Alfred resolves to oppose the Northmen by sea; and his small fleet of frail vessels repulses seven Danish ships, one of which remains in Alfred's hands (876); *ib.* A new treaty, the Danes again evacuating Wessex, *ib.* Alfred makes their chiefs swear upon relics of Christian saints, as well as by their own gold bracelets, yet the next night they surprise him on his way to Winchester, and slay his horsemen, *ib.* The Danes desirous to attack him in his stronghold in the west, *ib.* A Danish fleet sailing from the Thames with reinforcements, *ib.* Half their ships are wrecked on the Hampshire coast, the rest are met near the Exe by Alfred's still infant fleet, and totally destroyed, *ib.* Alfred invests Exeter in person, when Guthrun, the Dane, by capitulation marches into Mercia, abandoning Wessex and Exeter, *ib.* On New Year's day, 878, this Danish king marches suddenly against Alfred, who escapes and is unable to defend himself; being thus surprised in Chippenham, that fortified residence is taken by the Danes and Wessex overrun, 158. Skirmishes ensue, and the king betakes himself to the woods and moors, *ib.* His hardships and hunger, whilst in such concealment, *ib.* Story of the king and loaves, that were scorching (in his care) while he was preparing a bow and arrows, *ib.* Concealed in the isle of Athelney, a small band of brave dependants remain near his quarters, and make the islet more inaccessible by good field-works, *ib.* Representation of the pilgrim's solicitation to the king, *ib.* St. Cuthbert in the ensuing night avows his errand, and demands of Alfred to remember him on his approaching prosperity, 159. Defeat of Hubba, a Danish king, on the Devonshire coast, *ib.* He is slain, and his magical banner captured, *ib.* Receiving so much encouragement, Alfred prepares his mind for the great struggle for the Heptarchy (878); *ib.* As a wandering minstrel he explores, during his songs and music, the tents of Guthrun's camp, notes well the indolence and negligence that prevailed, and overhears a part of their counsels, *ib.* He appoints a rendezvous for his warriors at Egbert's stone, east of Selwood forest, 160. Joy of his subjects on beholding their lost prince, *ib.* He surprises the Danes; his great victory of Ethandune (Slaughter-ford close to Yatton?) in 878; *ib.* After a most severe loss, Guthrun places the rest of his troops in a fortified position, *ib.* He is compelled to surrender, *ib.* Articles of pacification, Guthrun to embrace Christianity, *ib.* That being performed, Alfred grants the royal Dane a considerable territory, *ib.* Wise policy of the Saxon legislator; he hoped to cause a fusion of the two inimical races, and induce the Christianized Danes to guard those coasts they had often desolated, *ib.* Guthrun and his chiefs repair to Alfred at Aulre, near Athelney, where Alfred answers for him at the font, the Dane receiving the name of Athel-

ALFRED the Great—
stan, and the ceremony is completed at Wedmor, a royal town, *ib.* Guthrun departed loaded with magnificent presents, and remained a faithful vassal of the great Alfred, *ib.* The laws of the Danelagh assimilated to the Anglo-Saxon. Guthrun's subjects become industrious and civilized, *ib.* The same fine payable for the violent death of a Dane, as for that of an Englishman, *ib.* Other laws and statutes, 161. The Danes generally embrace Christianity, *ib.* Gold ornament, called ' *Alfred's Jewel,*' depicted, *ib.* This great king invites the monk Asser to reside at court for his own instruction, *ib.* The learned monk consents for better than half of each year; he receives two abbeys, a rich pall, incense, &c. *ib.* Their friendship only terminated with Alfred's death, who recorded his esteem for Asser in his will, *ib.* In 879, a vast host of Pagans cross the Strait and winter at Fullanham, or Fulham; in spring they descend the Thames *en route* for Ghent, *ib.* Having probably regained great portions of the Heptarchy, or states consolidated by his grandfather Egbert, the present monarch rebuilds and re-peoples London (882—886); 162. He appoints Ethelred, husband of his daughter Ethelfleda, earl, or ealderman of the Mercians, *ib.* In 882, Alfred's fleet took four of the Northmen's ships, *ib.* In 885, he takes sixteen Norman or Danish vessels, and attacks a Danish host at Rochester; takes a strong tower they had built, recovers all the captives, seizes all the horses they brought from France, and drives them to their ships, *ib.* The Pagans occupied in the siege of Paris and devastation of Flanders, leaving Alfred seven years in repose, *ib.* England was smiling with fields of corn, the pastures were covered with flocks, the fatted beeves occupied the stalls (in 890); *ib.* The Normans had created a dire famine on the continent, *ib.* In 893, the renowned sea-king Hasting, with his host, impelled by hunger arrives on the coast, *ib.* His fleet was 250 ships, full of brave and desperate soldiery, *ib.* They land on the banks of the river Limine, near Romney marsh, *ib.* They form a strong camp at Appledore in the Andredswold, *ib.* Their commander Hasting with another fleet of eighty ships ascends the Thames, and takes Milton near Sittingbourne, where he strongly entrenched himself, *ib.* Their ravages and foraging from the two camps last about one year, *ib.* Other marauding squadrons menace the coasts as a diversion, *ib.* Guthrun having died three years previously, his people in the Danelagh take up arms and add to the foes of Alfred, *ib.* The war that ensued between the celebrated sea-king and the still more celebrated English monarch endured for three years, *ib.* Statistics of Alfred's military force, *ib.* He divides the *fyrd*, or militia, of his kingdom into two divisions (as they were by law only bound to keep the field for a limited time), *ib.* Alfred keeps the half on foot, leaving the reserve half at their homes to defend their firesides and the towns, and attend to the needful agriculture, *ib.* In due time he relieves one of the divisions of the English militia by the other, and so forth, 162, 163. Alfred takes up a position in Kent, with a forest on one side and deep swamps on the other; he renders his front secure from every assault, 163. By this military stratagem he effectually separates the Danes in the advanced camp from the main body near the coast or in the weald, *ib.* Townspeople and villagers animated with the best spirit in the service of the wise monarch, *ib.* Hasting sends in hostages, and apparently sails with his main force, *ib.* The strong division in Alfred's rear break up suddenly from the entrenched camp, seeking a ford across the Thames to Essex, where Hasting by compact should meet

ALFRED the Great—
them, his sailing being a *ruse de guerre*, *ib.* Alfred's
vessels being incompetent to pursue the great sea-
king, he hotly follows this separated army, *ib.* He
completely defeats this corps, some perishing by
the sword (near Farnham), and numbers drowned,
163. The remnant march by Middlesex into Essex,
are pushed by Alfred beyond the river Coln, and
find a refuge in the isle of Mersey, *ib.* He might
have reduced this corps of Danes by famine, but is
constrained to march in defence of the west, *ib.*
He leaves a strong body to watch Essex, and mounting the troops he designed to lead, he reaches
Exeter by forced marches, *ib.* He forces the
Danes to raise the siege, and drives them to their
ships, *ib.* On his return, Ethelred, his son-in-law,
delivers to him the wife and sons of Hasting, *ib.*
He is counselled to command the execution of the
two sons, but being of a magnanimous spirit he
sends them with presents to Hasting, *ib.* The
Danish leader marching to the Severn, Alfred defeats him at Buttington, 163, 164. Hasting having
taken Chester, is compelled by Alfred's army and
fleet in the Mersey to withdraw into North Wales,
ib. In 896, this bitter contest is transferred to the
banks of the Lea; Hasting builds a fortress near
Ware, 164. Alfred constructs two fortresses on
either bank below that of the Danes. He cuts
three deep channels from the Lea to the Thames,
which so reduces the former river that the Danish
armament is left aground, *ib.* The London burgesses burn some of those vessels, and getting others
afloat, convey them in triumph to their city, *ib.*
Danish camp of Quatbridge (Quatford, near Bridgenorth?) *ib.* The Danes disperse suddenly, having
long held out against the active measures of the
great English monarch, *ib.* In the spring, 897,
Hasting sails with a defeated and greatly diminished
army to the Seine, and establishes himself in France,
164, 165. Alfred defeats at sea the Northumbrian
pirates, and those of the Danelagh, after the expulsion of Hasting, 165. Improved condition, build
and burthen of his ships, under the king's superintendence, 165, 166. His large galleys constructed
on a plan of his own invention, carrying sixty oars,
ib. He retains the Frieslanders in his naval service, 165. After an action off the Isle of Wight,
two Northumbrian ships being cast ashore, the
king, then at Winchester, condemns the crews to
be hanged, *ib.* The king continued the like severity
to the end of his reign, putting to death the crews
of twenty ships manned by Northumbrians, taken
in the space of his last three years, as pirates and
rebels, *ib.* Reflections on the further details of
Alfred's reign, *ib.* His early travels abroad re-
verted to, *ib.* Influence on his mind of the edifices
of Rome, and his residence in Paris, 165, 166. His
youthful predilection for the Anglo-Saxon ballads,
recited by the minstrels and glee-men, 166. Occasion of his learning to read, by which his mother
Osburgha awards him her illuminated manuscript
of Saxon poetry, *ib.* He increases his mental acquisitions, and gains a profound knowledge of Latin,
himself translating many Latin works into the
Anglo-Saxon vernacular, for the advantage of his
people, *ib.* He laments the decline of Latin learning, 305. He encourages Johannes Erigena, Grimbald, his early friend Asser, and other learned men
at his court, 161, 166, 305. His personal habits,
166. Clepsydras, &c. being unknown in England,
Alfred resorted to candles, the notches on which
marked the lapse of time, *ib.* These burning un-
steadily by reason of draughts, the king invents
and fashions lanthorns of horn, in which to shelter
them, *ib.* His early predilection for hunting and
field sports gives place at a maturer age to more dig-

ALFRED the Great—
nified pursuits, *ib.* He gathers information from
celebrated navigators of his time, and adds to his
geographical knowledge, 166, 167. He commits all
this to writing in the Anglo-Saxon tongue, 167.
His mission of Swithelm, bishop of Sherburn, over-
land, to Malabar and Coromandel, to visit certain
colonies of Christian Syrians, *ib.* His fame greatly
increased, and England thereby made known to the
East, *ib.* He improves the national architecture, *ib.*
Founds or rebuilds many towns, *ib.* Erects fortifications and strong castles, *ib.* Surveys the coasts
and rivers, *ib.* He establishes a well-ordered police
throughout his states, so that private property, and
even the highways, were rendered perfectly secure,
ib. Laws of the wise Alfred, 165, 167. The Witenagemot, 167. This monarch was inexorable to unjust magistrates and judges, whom he constantly
put to death, *ib.* He personally heard all appeals,
and revised important suits with great industry, *ib.*
Silver coins of, *ib.* Most severe maladies had long
afflicted this great prince, *ib.* His death in his fifty-
third year, Oct. 28, 901, and sepulture at Winchester in an abbey he had founded, *ib.* His character,
approached to ideal perfection in his age, *ib.* Praise
of him by the Norman historians, 168. Sir James
Mackintosh extols his institutions, *ib.* His supposed embassy to India, 266.
ALFRED (younger brother of Edward the Confessor),
inveigled from exile into England by a letter said
to be from his mother Emma, 1035, 1036, disem-
barks with many soldiers on the west bank of the
Thames, i. 184. Question as to who wrote this
treacherous missive, *ib.* Earl Godwin, strongly
suspected of treason towards the young Alfred,
convoys him to Guildford, and billets his band of
followers through the town, 185. King Harold's
forces set upon them in the night, and bind them,
ib. Next morning 600 followers of the prince are
tortured and massacred, each tenth man escaping
by an inverse species of decimation, *ib.* Alfred
is carried on a palfrey through London to Ely, is
there tried, and his eyes are put out, of which, in a
few days, he died, *ib.* Remarks on the guilt of this
action, *ib.* The queen Emma retires out of England to the court of Baldwin, earl of Flanders, *ib.*
Deep resentment of her brother, Edward the Confessor, for this foul deed, 187, 188.
ALFRIC, earl of Mercia, exiled by Ethelred, recalled,
981, on the invasions by Sweyn, i. 176. His revenge impels him to a covert design of treason, *ib.*
Having the command of the king's newly equipped
fleet, 992, he goes over to the Danes with many
ships, on the eve of expected battle, *ib.* His son
Elfgar blinded by command of the king, 176, 178.
After the massacre of the Danes in most parts of
England (1002), Sweyn arrives with a magnificent
fleet and mighty host, takes ample vengeance, 1003—
1006, and devastates the country and city with fire
and sword, 177, 178. A powerful Anglo-Saxon
army, sufficient to overpower king Sweyn, is
sent to intercept him, 178. The traitor Alfric
is again entrusted with the command, and just
as battle was to be joined, 1003, draws off the
English, Sweyn then embarking with immense
booty, *ib.*
ALGAR, son of earl Leofric, on the disgrace of Godwin,
1051, obtains Harold's government of East Anglia,
i. 194. Harold, succeeding to all his father's former
power, expels earl Algar, *ib.* The latter seeks aid
from his father-in-law Griffith, and with Welsh
forces takes Hereford and burns the minster, *ib.*
He repulses Raulf, earl of Hereford, who mounted
the Saxons, " against the custom of their country,"
ib. Is himself defeated by Harold, who pursues
him into the Welsh fastnesses, *ib.* On the death of

ALGAR—
Leofric, he has still sufficient power to secure himself in his father's earldom and government, *ib.* Being now a formidable rival to Harold, the latter marches against him, when Algar resorts to Ireland for aid from the Danish settlers on that coast, *ib.* He recovers his territory, and maintains himself by force of arms, *ib.* Earl Algar dies, 1059, his sons Morcar and Edwin inheriting each a portion of his lands and government, *ib.*

ALGITHA, sister of Morcar, marries Harold, and becomes queen of England, i. 208.

Alicant, taken by the allies, 1706; iv. 186. Retaken by the French, 1709; 236.

ALICE, princess, sister of Philip II., king of France, betrothed to earl John, i. 509.

ALIVERDY Khan, mussulman viceroy of the great Mogul, his death in 1756, when he was succeeded by his grandson Suraj-u-Dowlah, § ii. 39.

ALLAN, the Breton, Richemont, or Richmond, in Yorkshire, granted to him by the king, 1073; i. 374.

ALLECTUS, a Briton, 297, slays at York the emperor Carausius, i. 53. He succeeds him in the government of Britain, reigning three years, *ib.* His army comprised thus early many Saxons and Franks from the continent, *ib.* Attacked by the troops of Constantius, he falls in battle, 300, *ib.*

ALLEN, Ethan, an American Revolutionist, takes the Forts of Ticonderoga and Crown Point, 1775; § i. 217–218. He is taken prisoner by General Campbell, 219–220, 258.

ALLEN, archbishop of Dublin, surprised in 1535, and murdered by the partisans of the Fitzgerald then in rebellion, ii. 425.

ALLEN, Mr., author of the 'Vindication of the Ancient Independence of Scotland,' quoted, i. 533, 534, 537, 538, 580.

ALLIBONE, Sir Richard, one of the judges who sat on the trial of the petitioning bishops, 1688; iii. 792.

ALMAINE, Henry d', son of Richard, king of the Romans, is murdered by Simon and Guy de Montfort, 1271; i. 688.

Almanza, battle of, gained by the duke of Berwick, April 14, 1707; iv. 202.

ALMERIC, Master of the English Templars, attends the king at the signing of Magna Charta, 1215; i. 528.

Almonry, the, at Westminster, ii. 203.

ALPHEGE, archbishop of Canterbury, defends the city against the Danes, but is reduced by treachery, and loaded with fetters, early in the *ninth century*, i. 179. The invaders accustomed by Ethelred to take ransoms, demand gold of the primate for his life and liberty, *ib.* The archbishop resolved to give a solitary instance of heroism and patriotism, in a feeble reign, sternly refuses to pay for his life, *ib.* The Danish oppressors make a great feast, and send for Alphege once more to comply with their demand, *ib.* They assault him with the bones and drinking horns, with missiles collected in a heap, until he falls exhausted, *ib.* A pirate, whom he had recently baptized, kills this English Saint with his battle-axe, 1009; *ib.*

ALRED, archbishop of York, supposed to have crowned Harold, i. 204.

Alton, battle of, 1265; i. 688.

Alum, this commodity had been frequently sought in England, without success. In 1566, Elizabeth granted letters patent to Cornelius de Vos and other Germans to dig for alum and copperas, as well as for gold, &c. Lord Mountjoy having discovered copperas ore, the patent was, 1565, assigned to him, ii. 811.

ALVA, duke of. took Pamplona, 1512; deprived king Albret of Navarre, who retired to his principality of Bearn, ii. 321. Paul IV. sends him, in 1555, to take upon himself the government of Naples, 531. Philip II. makes him regent of the Netherlands,

ALVA, duke of—
621, 626. General alarm lest he should land in England, 639. He is recalled by Philip, and succeeded by Zuniga, the Commendator of Requesens, 649.

ALWIN, bishop of Winchester, I. 188.

ALWIN, of East-Anglia, a powerful noble, 975, gives support to Dunstan against the secular clergy, i. 174.

ALZEVEDO, Dom Antonio d', ambassador from Lisbon, at the court of George II., iv. 416.

AMADEUS VIII., the retired duke of Savoy, being called to the pontifical dignity in 1439, by the Council of Basil, exchanges his temporal style for the spiritual title of Felix V., ii. 138, but the cardinals at Rome having elected Nicholas V., Felix himself proposes to resign the tiara, and thus terminate the scandal of the Church; accordingly he returns to his hermitage of Ripaille, in 1449; 139.

Amboyna, one of the Molucca Islands, possessed by the Dutch, iii. 105. Their commerce in spices, &c., which it was their system to engross to themselves, *ib.* The English East India Company sent ships to obtain cloves from the Spice Islands, and form an establishment, 1612, at Cambello, in Amboyna, *ib.* A treaty in London, 1619, with the Dutch, encourages a hope of participating in the profitable commerce, *ib.* The Dutch charge Captain G. Towerson, with nine Englishmen, and some Japanese, with a design to seize on the island; they torture the English and put them all to death, February 17, 1623; *ib.* ii. 18. On a remonstrance by the ministers of the infirm James I., the States of Holland apologize, and promise redress for so heinous an outrage, iii. 106.

AMBROSIUS, Aurelius, head of a Roman party opposed to Vortigern, about 440; i. 57.

America, for the history of the Revolution of this country—*see* George III. Remarks of Chalmers on the general results of the American war, § i. 568, 569. History of the United States, § iv. 526—558. War with England, 1812; 559—563.

America.—*Illustrations.* Port of Boston, &c., § i. 184. Plan of Boston, 185. Rhode Island, Long Island, &c. 190. American militia and minute men at Lexington, 212. The river St. Lawrence, and the great North American lakes, 221. American paper dollars, 255. Facsimiles of the signatures to the Declaration of Independence, July 4, 1776; 268. Group of Crow, Sioux, and Pawnee Indians, 307. Mohawk Indians, and their canoes, 393. The first coined money issued by the United States, 688.

Amersford, view of, § ii. 246.

AMHERST, general, embarks with Wolfe, 1758, for the island of Cape Breton, which he captured, iv. 603.

Amiens, treaty of, signed between England and France, March 27, 1802, § iii. 560*.

Anabaptists burned by Henry VIII., with the cruelty of slow fires, 1534; and fourteen Dutch anabaptists, for denying the real presence in the Eucharist, were, in May 1535, sent for example's sake to be burnt in various towns, ii. 386.

ANAGNI, John of, cardinal and papal legate, his assistance to Henry II.; he threatens to lay the kingdom of France under interdict, 1189; i. 478.

Ancrum Moor on the Teviot, 1544; total defeat of an English expeditionary force under Sir R. Evre, which had devastated the Scottish border, ii. 441.

ANDERSON, his pamphlet, entitled 'The Mystery of the New-fashioned Goldsmiths or Bankers Discovered,' printed in 1676; iii. 549.

Anderson's Place, Newcastle, the house in which Charles I. was delivered to the parliamentary troops, iii. 360.

ANDERTON, Henry, a celebrated painter of the seventeenth century, iii. 883.

ANDRÉ, major John, an accomplished and amiable officer on the staff of Sir H. Clinton, § i. 432. Por-

ANDRÉ, major— ·
trait of, *ib.* He undertakes to conduct the correspondence with Benedict Arnold, 1780; *ib.* He is seized by the Americans and executed, October 2, 1780; 435.

ANDRÉ, St., marshal, 1551, entertained by Edward VI. at Hampton Court, on occasion of bringing over the Order of St. Michael to Edward, an alliance being engaged in of the youthful king with Elizabeth, daughter of the French king, ii. 495. The marshal then visits the earl of Warwick (duke of Northumberland), *ib.*

Andredswold, the, or forest of Andreade, extending 120 miles in Sussex and its borders, i. 142. The main body of warriors of the great sea-king Hasting, 893, form a strong camp in the Anderida weald, whence they ravage the country, 162.

ANDREWS, Dr. Lancelot, translated from Chichester to the see of Ely, September 30, 1609; iii. 465. Made Bishop of Winchester, March 1619; 607. His answer to James I., when interrogated by him whether he might take his subjects' money without the leave of parliament, 606. His death, September 21, 1626.

ANGELO, or Michel Angelo Buonarotti, a most illustrious painter, sculptor, and architect, born March 6, 1474. Died February 17, 1563; iii. 570.

Angles, the, one of three celebrated Saxon tribes that invaded Britain, whence the later name of Anglo-Saxons, i. 139. A general emigration from Anglen of Holstein, to the east of Britain, about the year 600, and foundation of the state of East Anglia, 142.

Anglesey, island of, anciently called Mona. The Romans, under Suetonius Paulinus, enter the island, and destroy the Druids there dwelling, and their sacred groves, 59—61, i. 43, 61.

ANGLESEY, Arthur Annesley, earl of, member of the long parliament, iii. 670. Created April 20, 1661. He reproaches colonel Carew, a regicide, with the forcible exclusion of all the Presbyterian members in 1648: his death, 1686; 672.

Anglo-Saxon language, its original form similar to the Frisic, long spoken in Friesland, i. 139. The dialect of various tribes soon influenced by intermixture of races, 140. Manuscripts by Alfred the Great, translated from Latin into the vernacular language, and other works of that king, 165—167. Metrical specimens of, i. 182, 293—300, 612. Prose extracts, i. 296, 300, 611.

Anglo-Saxon king, his arms and accoutrements, and armour-bearer, i. 156.

ANGOULÊME, Charles, count of, eldest son of the duke of Orleans, espouses Isabella, widow of Richard II., 1406; ii. 19. Festivities at Paris, *ib.* Isabella, in 1408, died in childbed. Angoulême, his father being murdered, 1407, became duke of Orleans, and in 1409 marries Bona, daughter of the count of Armagnac, 20, 21. *See* Orleans.

ANGOULÊME, duke of, invests Rochelle, 1628, iii. 135.

ANGUIER, François, a sculptor of the 17th century, iii. 576.

ANGUS, earl of, *see* Umfraville.

ANGUS, Archibald Douglas, earl of, ii. 115. His plot, 1491, against the person of James IV., 304. At Flodden, 1513, he advised James not to give battle, 327. He left his sons and the Douglases to fight for their king, but he himself from old age retired, *ib.*

ANGUS, earl of, married queen Margaret, not long after the fall of her husband, James IV., ii. 349. Character of this young noble, *ib.* He armed his vassals, and Albany declared him a traitor at Stirling, 351. His daughter Margaret Douglas, born at Morpeth, (was grandmother of Mary of Scots,) *ib.* Angus forsook queen Margaret on her *accouchement,* returned into Scotland, and was re-

ANGUS, earl of—
stored in honours and lands by the Regent Albany, *ib.* In course of time, the forsaken queen took vengeance for this defection, *ib.* Feud betwixt Angus and the Douglases, and the other faction of Arran and the Hamiltons, 1518; 352.

Anjou, province of France, wars in, ii. 48, 55, 80. On Henry VI. espousing Margaret, daughter of René, count of Anjou, that province and Maine were ceded to count René, 1444; 81, 86.

ANJOU, Geoffrey Plantagenet, earl of, son of Fulk, marries Matilda, widow of Henry V. of Germany, and daughter of Henry I., 1127; i. 417. His wife quarrels with him, a reconciliation is effected, 1133, and Matilda bears him three children, Henry, Geoffrey, and William, 418. Geoffrey quarrels with Henry, his father-in-law, *ib.* Reduces Normandy; his eldest son, Henry, is acknowledged duke, 434. Matilda desires him to come to England, which he refuses, but sends his son Henry, *ib.* Prince Henry's promising character; he receives the honour of knighthood, 436. Geoffrey dies, and is succeeded by his son Henry, *ib.*

ANJOU, René of, (brother of Charles VII.'s queen,) negotiates with the English, ii. 59. He acquires Maine and Anjou, as the terms, ruinous to the English, of his daughter Margaret's marriage with Henry VI., 1444; 81, 86.

ANJOU, Henri, duke of, elected King of Poland, whence he returned, 1574, to mount the French throne, ii. 649. His suit for the hand of queen Elizabeth. *See* Henri III.

ANJOU, duke of, previously Alençon, a more favoured suitor than the first Anjou, ii. 649. In 1580, this young prince travelled in disguise to Greenwich, and the romance of this adventure charmed Elizabeth, 650. Ardent courtship; on Anjou's departure, the queen submitted the great question of her marriage to the lords of her council, *ib.* She shed tears on their not petitioning her to marry the French duke, a Catholic, *ib.* On his return to the Netherlands, he finds much trouble there, and after losing the best part of his troops, he flies to France, where he falls sick of a lingering illness, and dies June 1584, not without suspicion of being poisoned, 651.

ANKARSTROEM, a Swedish nobleman, assassinates Gustavus III., king of Sweden, March 1792; § iii. 49. He is executed, 50.

Annates, or first-fruits paid to the popes, abolished by Act, 1532; ii. 378.

ANNE (Boleyn), queen of Henry VIII. Maid of honour to Mary the king's sister, 1514; ii. 331, 363. She remained, after queen Mary's return to England, under protection of Claude, queen of Francis I., until 1524; 364. In 1527, she was maid of honour to Catherine of Arragon, *ib.* Her ingratitude to this indulgent mistress, *ib.* Lord Percy offered her marriage, which was prevented by royal authority, *ib.* Anne's inclination for the reformed doctrines, *ib.* King Henry declares his passion for her; she prudently refuses his advances, *ib.* The king's letters, 366, 371. Entertainment at Greenwich, masked ball, Henry's gallantry to her, 365. She was sent into Kent, having caught the sweating-sickness, 368. Her royal lover's fears ceasing with that fatal epidemic, he sent for Anne to his court, *ib.* The French ambassador's remark on this trait of Henry's character, *ib.* Anne was fully bent, 1529, on Wolsey's ruin, her uncle Norfolk, and also the duke of Suffolk, abetting and counselling her, 371. She received the title of marchioness of Pembroke, and repairing with Henry to Boulogne to meet Francis I., Anne gave a magnificent masque and ball to the two courts at Calais, 379. Her marriage took place at Whitehall, January 1533, Henry VIII. having no longer patience to wait for

ANNE (Boleyn)—
a divorce or dispensation from pope Clement, *ib.*
Portrait of Anne Boleyn: Holbein, *ib.* Popular
abuse of "Nan Bullen," 381. Her daughter, queen
Elizabeth, born, 383. The church prayers for
queen Anne and Elizabeth; anecdote, *ib.* On
the death of Catherine, Anne Boleyn is said to have
declared that " she was now indeed a queen," 390.
Report that queen Anne having discovered Jane
Seymour seated on the king's knee, the effect
of anger hastened her *accouchement,* *ib.* January
29, 1536, the queen prematurely gave birth to a son,
still-born, 390, 391. May 1, at an entertainment
at Greenwich, the king and queen Anne present,
lord Rochford and Norris were the challengers in the
lists, 391. Prompted by sudden jealousy at the gallant bearing of those young courtiers, or by the tales
of secret delators, Henry rose abruptly and quitted
for London, with but six attendants, *ib.* Next
morning as Anne Boleyn had taken boat at Greenwich, her uncle Norfolk, nevertheless her enemy,
and Cromwell met her, and told her that she was
charged with adultery, *ib.* She quickly arrived in
the Tower, her brother and Norris were already
confined there; soon also were added to the prisoners Brereton and Weston of the king's privy chamber, with Smeaton, a musician, *ib.* Anne's prison-
chamber was that in which she had slept the night
before her coronation; her pathetic discourse with
Kingston her custodian, *ib.* Aberration of mind, and
loud laughter, and *sudden insanity,* were remarked in
her conduct, *ib.* A Mrs. Boleyn, but her enemy,
Mrs. Cosen, and Mrs. Stoner, were her attendants charged to report every speech she uttered,
ib. Apology for Anne's free carriage acquired by
education in the French court, *ib.* Her eloquent
letter to Henry VIII., declaring her innocence, and
her knowledge of his intention to marry Jane Seymour, *ib.* She was conveyed to Greenwich to be
examined by the privy council; on her return she
told the lieutenant of the Tower she had been
cruelly handled by the council, and she cheerfully
made a great dinner, 392. Interrogatory, by the
council, of the five prisoners charged as guilty with
the queen; they all maintained her innocence and
their own; on a second examination, Mark Smeaton
confessed his guilt, *ib.* The indictment of the
queen, her brother, and the others; among the
averments they were charged with plotting to
murder the king, *ib.* Norris, Weston, Brereton,
Smeaton, condemned to be hanged, &c., *ib.* Noble
behaviour of Henry Norris: the king, unwilling he
should die, offered pardon if he would confess that
of which he was convicted; in reply he averred
that he believed the queen to be entirely innocent, *ib.* There was no precedent for the trial of
a queen; Henry chose 26 peers, Norfolk being
high-steward; the trial was held, May 15, in the
king's hall in the Tower, 393. Reasons for believing the unhappy Anne Boleyn entirely guilt-
less: a sacrifice to the new scheme of matrimony,
and to the apathy, or enmity, of the nobles who
judged her, *ib.* The queen condemned to be
burned or beheaded as the king should think fit, *ib.*
Her brother placed at the bar, on her removal, tried,
and condemned, *ib.* Her hope of a simple exile, and
even levity, gleamed through her despair and an-
guish, *ib.* May 19, Anne Boleyn was brought
on to the Green at the Tower, where she made a
gentle speech concerning the king, and submitted
herself calmly to the axe, 393, 394. Vivid picture
of the heartless and insensate conduct of Henry
VIII., on the day of his once most-loved queen's
death, 394. Retrospect of the conduct of her once
more powerful friend Cranmer: he was her confessor in the Tower, 393. His letter in her favour to the
king, seeking, as far as man dared, to turn him

ANNE (Boleyn)—
from this despotic act of cruelty, 394. His "Objections" to the legality of the queen's marriage, his
comportment in his ecclesiastical court, and the
declaration of illegitimacy of the princess Elizabeth,
were the conduct of a primate governed by events
beyond his power to control, 395. Cranmer's *want
of character* was one cause of the ruin of Anne
Boleyn, *ib.* The catholics believe the religion of
England to have been changed through Henry
VIII.'s marriage with Anne Boleyn, iii. 96.
ANNE of Cleves, (queen,) sister of the reigning duke
of Cleves, a protestant prince, ii. 412. Cromwell and
others having extolled her beauty, Henry VIII.
procured a miniature of her by Holbein, and fell
ideally in love, 413. Her portrait, *ib.* The monarch
privily obtained a sight of her at Rochester, on
her journey, and became disgusted, *ib.* His excessive rage at Cromwell and the rest, 414. He
tried to decline the marriage, but his council urged
matters of state policy, *ib.* The marriage, January
3, 1539; *ib.* He declared shortly after that life
would be a burthen in her society, *ib.* A divorce
took place, 415. Quiet submission of Anne, and
her humble letters, &c., *ib.* Report that she is delivered of a son, 420, *nota.* After the accusation of
queen Catherine Howard, the duke of Cleves proposes to Henry that he should take back to wife
his sister Anne, 421. She sat side by side with the
princess Elizabeth, when Mary made the grand procession through London, preparatory to her coronation, 507. She dies at Chelsea, 1557 ; 532.
ANNE of Denmark, queen of James I.; discontent of
the Scottish king respecting the crown jewels not
being forwarded to him for her attire, 1603 ; where-
fore he leaves his family in Scotland, iii. 3, 4.
She joins the king at Windsor Castle, 6. She was
crowned with king James, 25th July, in Westminster Abbey, 9. Portrait of the queen, 11. Her
fondness for dancing, dress, &c. 37. Her dissipation,
thoughtlessness, and extravagance, *ib.* Being ill,
she is much restored by a draught of the Elixir, or
panacea, concocted by Sir W. Raleigh, a prisoner
in the Tower, who made deep researches in chemistry, 73. Her death occurred soon after that
of Raleigh, for whose life she had warmly interceded, 80. Costume of this queen-consort, from
Strutt, 623.
ANNE, queen, 8 March, 1702—1 August, 1714 ; second
daughter of the duke of York. Marriage with
George, prince of Denmark, iii. 760. She discredits
the truth of the birth of a prince of Wales, 796.
Flies to the camp of the prince of Orange, 1688 ;
799. The English parliament votes her 50,000*l.*
per annum, iv. 19. On the disgrace of Marlborough, she quits the court, 36. Her accession to
the throne, 1702 ; 140. Her great seal before the
Union with Scotland, *ib.* 1702, she is proclaimed Queen, *ib.* The late king's ministry continued, *ib.* Her portrait, 141. Marlborough made
knight of the Garter, *ib.* Appointed captain-
general of all the English forces, and master of the
ordnance, *ib.* Prince George of Denmark becomes
lord high admiral and generalissimo, *ib.* Lady
Marlborough made mistress of the robes ; her two
daughters ladies of the bedchamber, *ib.* The earl of
Sunderland's pension continued, *ib.* The Tories
come into power, 142. Sir George Rooke appointed vice-admiral of England, *ib.* Marlborough sent
ambassador to the Hague ; is appointed to the chief
command of the allied armies ; he returns to England, 143. The earl of Rochester dismissed, *ib.*
War with France declared, May 4 ; 144. The
Commons vote the queen 700,000*l.* per annum for
life, *ib.* The name of the princess Sophia, Electress
of Hanover, introduced into the public prayers, as
next in succession to the throne, *ib.* Marlborough

C

ANNE, queen—

departs for Holland; places himself at the head of the army, *ib.* Description of the position of the allies, *ib.* He commences military operations, 144, 145. Venloo surrenders, 145. Ruremond and Stevenswaert taken, *ib.* Liege surrenders, *ib.* Marlborough captured on a canal, but liberated, *ib.* Rooke and Ormond make an unsuccessful attack on Cadiz, 146. They attack Vigo Bay; destroy the Spanish galleons and capture much booty, *ib.* Parliament meets, *ib.* The Occasional Conformity Bill passed in the Commons, but lost in the Lords, 147, 148. Marlborough raised to a dukedom, 148. The queen proposes to give him 5000*l.* a year during her life, 149. An annual revenue of 100,000*l.* settled on prince George of Denmark, *ib.* Lord Ranelagh, 1708, expelled the House of Commons, 149, 150. Litigation between the two Houses concerning lord Halifax, 150. Parliament prorogued, *ib.* Four high tories raised to the Peerage, in order to have a majority in the Upper House, *ib.* The two Houses of Convocation disagree, *ib.* The queen touches for the king's evil, 151. Marshal Villiers reduces the town of Kehl, *ib.* Various military operations, 153. The king of Spain (the archduke Charles) arrives in England, 154. Parliament meets, *ib.* The queen announces the intention to recover the monarchy of Spain from the house of Bourbon, and restore it to that of Austria, *ib.* Supplies are voted, and the army and navy increased, 155. The Occasional Conformity Bill again passed by the Commons, and rejected by the Lords, *ib.* The queen assents to the Land-tax Bill, *ib.* She informs the Commons of a plot in Scotland, 155–157. The Lords examine some parties; commit them to the custody of the black rod, who takes them out of the custody of the queen's messenger, but they are again given into his keeping, *ib.* The earl of Nottingham produces, by the queen's command, papers relative to Fraser's plot; the Lords are dissatisfied; continue their inquiry by committee, 157. The Commons address the queen. An Union of the kingdoms of England and Scotland proposed, *ib.* The case of Ashby v. White, on elections, determined by the court of King's Bench, 158. It is carried by appeal to the House of Lords. The judgment of the King's Bench reversed, *ib.* The Commons declare that the bringing the action is a breach of privilege in all parties concerned; and that all matters relative to elections belong to the House of Commons, *ib.* The Lords declare the decision of the Commons an unprecedented attempt upon the judicature of Parliament, and an attempt to subject the law to the will of the Commons, *ib.* The queen proposes that the first-fruits and tenths be given up for the augmentation of poor benefices, 159. The earl of Nottingham retires, 160. Harley made secretary of state, *ib.* Several other changes in offices of trust, *ib.* Inquiry into the condition and management of the navy, *ib.* The bill for recruiting the army, after a contest in the Houses, passes for a year, *ib.* The queen revives the order of the Thistle, 161. The Commons address the queen. The Scottish parliament assembles, *ib.* Settlement of the two crowns, 162. They pass a bill called the Scottish Security Bill for regulating the succession to the Scottish throne, and for disbanding the army. The queen gives her assent, 162, 163. Marlborough returns to England, 164. He rejoins the allied armies, *ib.* The battle of Schellenberg or Donawert, July 2, 1704; 167, 168. Battle of Blenheim, August 13; 170–172. Attempt to place the archduke Charles on the throne of Spain, 174. Admiral Rooke takes Gibraltar, 175. Sea fight off Malaga between the English and Dutch fleets under Rooke, and that of the French under the command of the count of Toulouse, *ib.* The manor of Woodstock, 1705, granted to the duke of

ANNE, queen—

Marlborough. The Commons grant money to pay off the incumbrances. The queen orders the erection of Blenheim House, 176. Admiral Rooke dismissed and Sir Cloudesley Shovel appointed, 177. The case of Ashby v. White again agitated; the burgesses of Aylesbury committed to Newgate; writs of Habeas Corpus are granted; a writ of error is removed to the house of Lords; the prisoners are placed in the custody of the Serjeant at Arms, *ib.* The Lords pass a resolution that appeal to courts of law is no breach of privilege, 178. Parliament prorogued, *ib.* Dissolved by proclamation, *ib.* Huy and Liege taken by the French, *ib.* Huy retaken by Marlborough, *ib.* The emperor Leopold dies, and is succeeded by his eldest son Joseph, *ib.* War carried on in Spain, 179. The earl of Peterborough takes Barcelona, relieves St. Matteo, and reduces Valencia, 179, 180. Parliament meets, 180. The queen's speech, 180, 181. A Regency Bill passed, 182. A naturalization bill passed extending to all the descendants of the Electress Princess Sophia, *ib.* Inquiry into the state of the church, 183. Mr. Cæsar committed to the Tower, *ib.* Parliament prorogued, *ib.* Marlborough leaves England, *ib.* Battle of Ramilies, May 23, 1706; 184. The French defeated by prince Eugene, between the Doria and the Stura, 185. Philip of Spain besieges Barcelona, but retreats on the appearance of the earl of Peterborough and vice-admiral Leake, 185. Lord Galway takes Madrid, 186. Commission opened for the Union of England and Scotland, 187. Names of the commissioners, *ib.* Cry of 'No Union' raised in Scotland, 188. Disturbances in Edinburgh, 191. The Treaty of Union passed by the Scottish parliament, 196. The last Scottish parliament rises, *ib.* Great seal of Anne after the Union of England and Scotland, 199. The act of Union, 1707, receives the royal assent, *ib.* The titles of the duke of Marlborough secured to his eldest daughter and the heirs male of her body; and then to his other daughters successively, and the heirs male of their bodies, 200. A pension of 5000*l.* a year settled upon him, his widow, and descendants, by Act of Parliament, *ib.* The last separate English parliament rises, *ib.* The duke of Marlborough and Charles XII. of Sweden meet, 201. Battle of Almanza, 202. Capture of Lerida, 203. Capture of Morella, Dec. 17; *ib.* Siege of Toulon; the Austrians gain possession of Naples, 203, 204. Sir Cloudesley Shovel wrecked off Scilly, 204. Intrigues in Scotland, 205. Louis XIV. cherishes the plan of exciting a civil war in Great Britain, *ib.* View of the palace of St. Germain, 206. The first parliament of Great Britain meets, 210. Privy council of Scotland abolished, 211. Both Houses address the queen to prosecute the war till the whole of the Spanish territories are restored to the house of Austria, *ib.* William Grey, 1708, hanged for high treason, 214, 215. Marlborough and Godolphin absent themselves from the council, 215. Harley is dismissed, 216. Parliament is informed by the queen of an intention in Scotland to reinstate the Stuarts, *ib.* The Habeas Corpus Act suspended, *ib.* A proclamation issued against the Pretender and his adherents, *ib.* The duke of Hamilton and twenty-one Scottish lords and gentlemen arrested, *ib.* Troops are marched into Scotland, *ib.* Sir George Byng sent with a fleet to Dunkirk, where the Pretender is ready to embark for Scotland, *ib.* He captures several ships, 217. Lord Griffin sent to the Tower, is condemned, but afterwards reprieved, *ib.* The Pretender returns to France, 218. None of the prisoners are executed, *ib.* Parliament prorogued, and afterwards dissolved, 219. Marlborough goes to the Hague, *ib.* Father O'Connor is sent from France to see if Ire-

ANNE, queen—
land is in a fit state for a rebellion, ib. The French
take Ghent, Bruges, Ypres, and invest Oudenarde,
ib. Battle of Oudenarde, 220. Lille surrenders
to Marlborough and Eugene, ib. Ghent, Bruges,
and several other places re-taken, ib. The island
of Sardinia taken by admiral Leake, 221. The
fortress of St. Philip in Port Mahon, taken by
general Stanhope and admiral Leake, ib. Minorca taken by the English, ib. The French gain
many successes in Spain, ib. Several Spanish galleons taken by commodore Wager, 222. Death of
prince George of Denmark, in October, ib. The earl
of Pembroke made lord high admiral, ib. Parliament meets, ib. A new treason act for Scotland
debated and passed, 226–228. An act of Grace
issued, 228. A scheme for invading Scotland agitated at Versailles, 228, 229. Heavy effects of the
Continental war on the subjects of the Palatinate,
229. Several bodies of emigrants from the Palatinate
settle at Blackheath; they are persecuted by the
English labourers and the French refugees, 230.
Large bodies of them shipped off for the colonies, ib.
Act passed for defining the privileges of ambassadors, in consequence of the Russian ambassador
having been arrested by a laceman for the sum of
100l., ib. The House of Lords resolves that no
peer of Great Britain shall vote for representative
peers for Scotland, 231. Eldest sons of Scottish peers
excluded from seats in the House of Commons, ib.
Calamitous condition of France, ib. Preliminaries
for a peace made at the Hague, 231–235. Tournay surrenders to Marlborough and Eugene, 235.
Battle of Malplaquet, 236. Parliament assembles,
ib. £6,200,900 voted for supplies, 237. Dr. Sacheverell preaches a violent sermon against the
ministry, ib. He is taken into custody and impeached, 238. His trial, 239—242. Is found guilty
of high crimes and misdemeanours; sentenced not
to preach for three years, and his sermons to be
burned by the common hangman, 242. The famous
Oxford decree burned by the common hangman,
243. The Whigs dismissed from office, 246. New
conferences for a peace holden at Gertruydenberg,
ib. Douay taken, 247. The campaign in Spain
commenced by general Stanhope and count Starenberg, ib. King Philip defeated near Almanara, ib.
Again defeated near Saragoza, ib. Saragoza surrenders, ib. General Stanhope takes possession of
Madrid, ib. King Charles enters Madrid, ib. Parliament meets, 248. General Stanhope taken prisoner by the duke de Vendôme, ib. Starenberg
retreats before Vendôme, ib. 1711, £350,000 voted
for building fifty new churches in the cities of London and Westminster, 250. A bill brought into
Parliament requiring property qualification for
members of parliament, ib. Mr. Harley is stabbed
by one Guiscard for proposing to lower his salary, ib.
Guiscard dies in Newgate of wounds received from the
swords of several lords present at his attempt, 251.
Proclamation issued ordering all Papists to remove
from London and Westminster, 252. Harley is
created earl of Oxford and earl Mortimer, ib. Death
of lord Rochester, ib. Marlborough's last campaign,
ib. Expedition to Quebec under Mrs. Masham's
brother, John Hill, ib. Bouchain taken by Marlborough, ib. Parliament prorogued, ib. The peace of
Utrecht, 253–256. The expedition to Quebec totally
fails, 257. Lord Raby created earl of Strafford, ib. Sir
Simon Harcourt made lord Harcourt and lord chancellor, ib. The duke of Hamilton created duke of
Brandon in the English peerage, ib. Scottish enthusiasm for the old Pretender, 258. Parliament
opens, ib. The duke of Brandon is refused his seat
as an English peer, ib. The Occasional Conformity
Bill passes both Houses, 259. The Commons charge
Marlborough with misappropriating the public

ANNE, queen—
money, ib. The queen dismisses him from employment, 260. 1712, twelve new patents of peerage signed, ib. The queen, by message, orders the
Lords to adjourn; the question is debated and
carried; the House adjourns, ib. R. Walpole committed to the Tower, and expelled the House of
Commons for corruption, 261. The House of Lords
re-assembles, ib. Toleration of episcopacy in Scotland, ib. Prince Eugene visits England, 262.
Ballads on prince Eugene's mother, ib. The Barrier
treaty, 263. Differences between England and the
States General, 263, 264. The congress opened at
Utrecht, 264. The ministry issues secret orders to
the duke of Ormond not to engage in any siege or
battle, 265. The queen announces to parliament
the terms of the intended peace, 266. Fleetwood,
bishop of St. Asaph, writes a preface to a book,
which is declared seditious by the House of Commons, and ordered to be burnt by the hands of the
common hangman, 267. Parliament adjourns, ib.
The duke of Ormond withdraws his troops, and
returns to England, 268. Dunkirk taken possession of by the English, ib. Marshal Villars obtains
several successes, 269. Lord Lexington is sent to
Madrid, 270. Philip, king of Spain, signs his renunciation of the French succession, ib. The duke
of Hamilton and Lord Mohun are both killed in a
duel, 271. Death of lord Godolphin, 272. The
duke of Marlborough retires to Brussels, ib. 1713,
the queen announces the completion of the Peace
of Utrecht, 273. Peace proclaimed, 274. A bill
for establishing a commercial intercourse between
England and France, lost in the Commons, 276.
The malt-tax extended to Scotland; lord Find-
later moves in the Upper House for leave to bring
in a bill to dissolve the Union, 277. His reasons
for it, ib. Parliament dissolved, ib. Several important changes in the court and cabinet, 278. The
monopoly of the Assiento granted to England, 279.
The Catalans subdued by king Philip, ib. Intrigues
for restoring the Stuarts, 280—282. Parliament
assembles, 282. The queen complains of the statement that the Hanoverian succession is in danger,
ib. Mr. Richard Steele expelled the House for
writing 'The Crisis,' 284. Lord Wharton moves
that the Protestant succession is in danger, ib.
The Lords agree to a vote proposing the issuing of
a proclamation, offering a reward for the apprehension of the Pretender in case he should land in Great
Britain or Ireland, 285. A writ demanded for sum-
moning the Electoral prince of Hanover to parliament, as duke of Cambridge, 285—287. The queen
writes to the Electoral prince, telling him not to
permit his son to come to England, 292. The
Electress Sophia of Hanover dies, 298. The Electoral prince of Hanover answers the queen's letter,
295. A proclamation issued for apprehending the
Pretender, 296. It is declared high treason to enlist,
or be enlisted, in the Pretender's service, ib. The
Schism Bill debated and passed, 296–298. Parliament adjourns, 298. The earl of Oxford dismissed,
299. The queen seized with apoplexy, 300. The
duke of Shrewsbury made Prime Minister, ib. A
messenger sent to hurry the arrival of the Electoral
prince, 301. Death of queen Anne, August 1,
1714, ib. Fac-simile of her autograph, 616. Coins
of this reign, 726, 727.
ANNE, czarina of Russia, dies 1740; iv. 441.
ANNE, of Bohemia, daughter of the emperor Charles
IV., marries Richard II., 1382; i. 790.
ANNE, lady, second daughter of Nevil, earl of
Warwick, 1470, married in France, by Edward,
son of Henry VI. and Margaret of Anjou, ii. 105.
Remarks of Comines on the marriages of Anne,
and of her sister Isabella, duchess of Clarence, ib.
Her marriage with the duke of Gloucester, 111.

ANNE, lady—
Suit of Clarence and Gloucester before king Edward in person, each royal duke pleading personally his right to the inheritance of Warwick, *ib.* Discontent of Gloucester that Anne has but a handsome marriage portion, and her sister Isabella the large estates, *ib.* Her coronation with Richard III., 1483, in Westminster Abbey, 124. Portrait of queen Anne, *ib.* They were again crowned at York, during Richard's progress; his reasons for this unusual repetition of the ceremony, *ib.* Her royal husband contemplated a new marriage with his niece, Elizabeth Plantagenet; his young son Edward, prince of Wales, whom he was on the point of marrying to the heiress of Edward IV., having recently died, 127, 128. Queen Anne sickened, and expired February 1485; 128.

ANNE, elder daughter of Francis II., Duke of Brittany; the duke of Orleans conceives the idea of obtaining possession of the duchy by marrying her, notwithstanding he was already married to one of the daughters of Louis XL, ii. 292. D'Albret, one of her suitors, attempts to carry her off by force, but she is rescued by the count of Dunois, and is subsequently protected by the people of Rennes, 295. She gives a reluctant consent to be married to Maximilian, and is affianced, by proxy, at Rennes, 296. Her accomplishments, 297. She is forcibly married by Charles VIII., in 1491, notwithstanding her former alliance, 298.

ANNEBAUT, the admiral of Francis I., in 1545, sent to invade Hampshire, ii. 442. Naval actions off Portsmouth, *ib.* The French armament withdrew to Brest, *ib.*

ANNESE, Gennaro, a blacksmith, raises a powerful rebellion in Italy against Philip IV. of Spain, iii. 395.

ANNIUS, or Nanni, his fabled history of England, i. 8.

ANSELM, abbot of Becco, consecrated to the see of Canterbury, December 1093; i. 406, 550. His dispute with the king, 550. He leaves his see, and sets out for Rome, 1098; *ib.* The pope threatens to excommunicate William, but is restrained by the earnest request of Anselm, 551. Anselm returns to England at the pressing invitation of Henry I., and assists at the marriage of Matilda, 406. The question concerning the investiture and homage of archbishop Anselm again renewed; pope Paschal II. decides in favour of the church, and Anselm returns to Rome, 551. It is decided that the bishops and abbots should do homage for the temporalities of their sees to the king, but the investiture with ring and crosier should not be insisted on; Anselm again returns to England, August 1106, and resumes the duties of his see, 552. His death, April 1109, in the 76th year of his age, *ib.*

ANSELM, chaplain to Richard I., accompanies the king in his expedition to the Holy Land: on their return they are driven on to the shore of Istria, and direct their journey through Germany, where Richard is detained, 1192; i. 502.

ANSON, commodore. His expedition in the South Seas; he enters the bay of Canton, November 1742; captures the Manilla galleon, iv. 473. Returns to England, June 1744; *ib.* Takes the command of the second Rochefort expedition, 1758; 601. His portrait, 689.

ANTONINUS, Pius, reign of, i. 47. Advance of Lollius Urbicus to the Clyde, 138; *ib.* Portrait of Antoninus from coins, 48.

ANTRIM, earl of, caught with the red hand in the province of Ulster, by general Monro, and imprisoned, but succeeds in making his escape, iii. 310. He undertakes to raise an army of Irish Catholics, and make a descent upon the Scottish coast, 1643; *ib.* Is again seized and cast into prison, *ib.*

Antwerp, city and commerce of. Description of its trade with England, &c., by L. Guicciardini, 1580 —1600; ii. 786. This great emporium was sacked in 1585, by the duke of Parma; about 6,000 of the inhabitants perished in the devastation of their city; and the commerce of the Spanish Netherlands was completely destroyed. The fishing trade removed to Holland; the woollen manufacture settled mostly in Leyden; the linen, removed to Haarlem and Amsterdam; and about a third part of the manufacturers in silk, &c., settled in England; Amsterdam now became what Antwerp had been, the grand emporium of Europe, 793, 794.

Appeals of arms and judicial encounters, ii. 247.
Appeals of treason abolished, 1399, 1 Henry IV., ii. 5.
APPIUS, colonel of a regiment of Hesse-Homburghers; his disgraceful conduct at the battle of Fontenoy, 1745; iv. 477.

Appleby, description of the fallen and decayed state of this ancient town, by Camden, in 1607; iii. 656.

Apprentices, description of, in the 17th century, iii. 634.

APSLEY, Henry Bathurst, baron—*see* Bathurst.

APULDORE, William, confessor of Richard II., beheaded by the insurgents of Kent, who had entered the Tower of London, during the king's absence at Mile End, June 14th, 1381; i. 787.

Aqueduct over the river Irwell, view of, § i. 577. The Chirk aqueduct completed about 1801; § iii. 670. The aqueduct bridge across the valley of the Dee, commonly called the Pont-y-Cysylte completed 1805; *ib.*

AQUINAS, St. Thomas, a favourite author of Henry VIII., ii. 333, 345, 366.

ARBUTHNOT, Dr. John, author of the Memoirs of Martinus Scriblerus, iv. 797. His death, 1735; *ib.*

ARCHER, John, racked, 1640. This is the last recorded instance of the use of torture in England, iii. 518.

Archers, ii. 260.

Archery, ii. 261, 870—872.

Architecture:—Service of, in the elucidation of history, i. 4. Erection of strong castles and fortifications, by Alfred, 167. Origin of Saxon architecture, &c., 307, *et seq.* Anglo-Saxon churches formed after the fashion of Roman basilicas, 311. View of the Basilica of St. Paul, Rome (supposed to have been founded by Constantine), after the fire in 1823; *ib.* Ground-plan of the church of Grisogono, at Rome, 312. Portico at Lorsch, *ib.* Cathedral of Worms, 313. Capital from the doorway of Mentz, *ib.* Description of the style of architecture of Ramsey Abbey, 313. Introduction of Norman architecture into England, exemplified in Westminster Abbey, as restored by Edward the Confessor, 314. Tower of Earl's Barton church, 315. Domestic architecture of the Anglo-Saxons; a Saxon nobleman's residence, 317. Military architecture of the Saxons, 318. Cathedrals, monasteries and churches in the Norman style enumerated and described, 614—633. Account of the munificent prelates who built our early cathedrals, 615. View of a Norman castle from an ancient drawing, 622. Conisborough Castle, 624. Keep of Richmond Castle, 625. Absence of sculpture in Norman architecture, 630. Early specimens of, 630, 631. Various changes of the Gothic, and introduction of the Decorated English style, 854. Examples of windows, 855. Specimens of the Decorated English style, 856—858. Tombs of archbishop Grey, 859, and of Aymer de Valence, 860. Monument of Hugh le Despenser, *ib.* Open carving in ornamental massive beams of wood, for great halls, without ceilings to the roofs;—1399, Westminster-hall;—in the two ensuing centuries, Eltham, Crosby-place, Christ Church, Oxford, Hampton-court, &c., ii. 225. Inferiority of the Romanesque architecture to the Grecian, 308, 601.

Architecture of the 15th century, ii. 222—233; of the 16th century, 841—851; of the 17th century, iii. 567—577; of the 18th century, iv. 735—751; § i. 631, 632; § iii. 731—740.

Architecture, the commencement of the 19th century eminently unfavourable to, § iv. 704.

Arcole, bridge of, Bonaparte's losses at the, Nov. 1796; § iii. 514.

Arcon, chevalier d', a French engineer, his unsuccessful attempt to take Gibraltar, 1782; § i. 492—495.

Arcot, royal palace at, § ii. 149.

Arden, executed by Elizabeth, as a traitor, on a false and unfounded charge of disaffection, ii. 654.

Ardern or Arden, John, an eminent English surgeon of the 14th century, i. 845.

Aremberg, count d', ambassador from Austria and the Spanish family, 1603, to James I., is opposed in his negotiations against the Hollanders, and meets with ill-success, iii. 7. Cobham's application to him, 1603, for 600,000 crowns, to support the cause of Arabella Stuart, but d'Aremberg does not seem implicated in the Bye or Main conspiracy, 9. Raleigh referred to La Rensy in this ambassador's service as better cognizant than himself of Cobham's intrigues, ib.

Argyle, earl of, takes up arms, 1578, to rescue James VI. from the hands of the regent Morton, ii. 652.

Argyle, earl of, declares himself head of the Covenanters, 1637; iii. 199. Is raised to the marquisate, 251. For a series of conflicts between him and the Lord of Montrose, see 337—340. Placed the crown on Charles's head at his coronation at Scone, 1651; 682. Sent to the Tower, 1661, as a regicide, 680. Beheaded at the Market Cross of Edinburgh, 682.

Argyle, earl of, iii. 680. Committed to Edinburgh Castle by the duke of York, 1681, and charged with treason, 736. Flies to Holland, 737. His estates forfeited, but afterwards given to his eldest son, ib. He lands a rebel band in the Western Islands, and declares James II. an usurper, 767. Is taken and beheaded, June 30, 1685; 769.

Arianism in Britain, i. 74.

Aristotle, his supposed mention of Ireland, i. 14.

Arkwright, Sir Richard, an English manufacturer, the inventor of that wonderful piece of mechanism, the spinning frame; he was born in the year 1732. In 1770, he obtained a patent for spinning with rollers, § i. 594. Difficulties and prejudice attendant on his invention, 595—597. He died in August 1792. Portrait of, 595.

Armada, the Spanish, illustration of, ii. 675. It set sail from the Tagus 29th May, 1588, and then consisted of about 130 vessels of all sizes; 45 of these were galleons and larger ships, 25 were pink-built ships, and 13 were frigates. They mounted altogether 2431 guns of different calibres. In addition to the mariners, they carried nearly 20,000 land troops, among whom were 2000 volunteers, of the noblest families in Spain, 674, 675. Description of the expedition, 675—678.

Armagnac, Bernard, the powerful count of, gives his daughter Bona in marriage to Charles duke of Orleans, 1409; ii. 21. His faction, styled the Armagnacs, opposed to the Bourguignons, 26. Invades the territory, 1414, of "Jean sans peur." duke of Burgundy, 27. His private wars, 28. His expedition, 1416, against Harfleur, unsuccessful, 35, 36. He governs in Paris in the name of Charles VI., 36. The duke of Burgundy retires into Flanders, ib. The dauphiness, daughter of that duke, is returned to her father's care, the Armagnacs being suspected of having poisoned the dauphin Louis, 36, 37. Armagnac is made constable of France, the preceding constable having been slain at Agincourt, ib. His severities at Paris; contests between the Armagnacs and Bourguignons,

Armagnac, Bernard— 1416; ib. Insurrections, free companies of foreign adventurers, cruelties of the count and his faction, 37. Death of the dauphin John, supposed by poison; disputes between the powerful count and the queen Isabella arise, 1417; ib. The queen joins the mortal enemies of the constable Armagnac; the duke of Burgundy marches again upon Paris; Henry V. lands, in August, 1417; 38, 40. The constable defends Paris, 40. He retains the old king and the dauphin Charles in his custody, and prepares a vigorous defence, ib. The count d'Armagnac is seized and imprisoned, the Parisians revolting from his party, 41. Many of his faction are massacred, even women and children, the count himself being taken from his prison and murdered, June 12, 1419; 42.

Armagnac, count of, 1417, son of the late constable, treats with Henry V., then carrying on the war in the French provinces, ii. 42, 48. Tanneguy-Duchâtel became the head of the Armagnac faction, the count being young, 42. Proceedings of the Armagnacs narrated, 44—48. The dauphin Charles being leagued with them, Tanneguy-Duchâtel murders the duke of Burgundy on the bridge of Montereau, 45, 46.

Armed Neutrality, the, 1780; § i. 419.

Armies, ancient British, i. 37. Standing, iv. 662—664.

Arminius, James, a Christian divine, and leader of the sect of Arminians, or Remonstrants, was born 1560, and died 1609; iii. 47.

Armorica, peopled by the Cymry, i. 8.

Armour, defensive, not used by the Britons, i. 36.

Armour, suits of, banners, &c., occasionally designed from monuments, i. 639, 640, 872—877; ii. 241, 857—870; iii. 625—627, 894.

Armstrong, Archibald, the famous court fool, goes to Madrid with prince Charles, 1623; iii. 94.

Armstrong, John, of Gilnockie, a border chief, hanged by James V., iii. 649.

Armstrong, John,'s poet and physician, author of the Art of Preserving Health, was born about 1709, and died in 1779; § L 607.

Armstrong, Sir Thomas, a Rye-house conspirator, iii. 740. Condemned and executed, 1684; 755.

Arne, Thomas Augustine, an eminent composer of the 18th century, who translated and set to music the opera of Artaxerxes; he died in 1778; § i. 635.

Arnold, Benedict, an American revolutionist, 1775; § i. 218. He makes an unsuccessful attack on Quebec, in which he is severely wounded, 222, 223. Portrait of, 279. He opens a secret communication with Sir H. Clinton, 1780, and agrees to deliver up West Point to the British, 431—437, 456.

Arran, earl of, a near relative of the royal family, revolted in 1516, and with his abettors, Glencairn, Lennox, and Mure, is overpowered by the regent Albany, who pardoned all but the Homes, ii. 351, 352. The earl and others of his family attempting vigorously to maintain the council appointed by Albany on his going into France, is expelled Edinburgh by Angus and the Douglases, 352, 353.

Arran, James Hamilton, earl of, assumed the regency of Scotland, December 1542, on the death of James V., and dispossessed David Beaton of that office, ii. 434. He was heir-apparent to the crown, a faithful guardian of the infant Mary of Scots, and was considered the head of the protestant party, 434, 435. Having imprisoned cardinal Beaton, he refused all applications of the Scottish lords for his release, and other their demands on affairs of religion, 435. Arran summoned a parliament at Edinburgh, 1543; ib. He requests the assistance of an English army, 436. Causes the treaties with England to be ratified by the nobles, ib. Fearing the exasperation of the Scots, he reconciles himself to

ARRAN, James Hamilton, earl of—cardinal Beaton, 437. He agrees to renounce his attachment to the reformed doctrines, and soon after publicly abjures his heresy in the Franciscan convent of Stirling, *ib.* He takes a solemn oath, as regent, to govern according to the advice of a new council formed by cardinal Beaton, *ib.* Angus and his party are accused of treason, *ib.* The earl of Hertford burns Edinburgh, but is forced to retreat, 440. Arran is gratified with the title of duke of Chatelherault; his brother, the primate of Scotland, called him a fool for resigning the government to the queen-dowager, Mary of Guise, when nothing stood between him and the crown but the life of a puling girl, 536, *note.* He heads the Congregation of the Lord, 548. Informs the queen-regent that she must dislodge the French army at Leith, 555. Suppresses the abbeys of Paisley, Kilwinning, and Dunfermline, *ib.* Marches upon Edinburgh, 557. Takes up arms against Mary queen of Scots on her marriage with Darnley, 581. Is acknowledged next heir to the throne after Mary, 583. Mary convokes a parliament in order to attaint him and the other rebel lords; but he negotiates with the queen, who promises him a pardon, *ib.* His absence in France, 604. His proxy at the coronation of James VI. protests against the proceedings, *ib.* All the Hamiltons keep away from Murray's parliament, 606. Arran returns from France and makes a faint effort in Mary's favour, 614. On Murray's death, 1570, he, with the earls of Argyle and Huntley, assumes the government as lieutenant of queen Mary; Elizabeth marches several armies into Scotland, and destroys the castles of the duke and the houses of all that bear the name of Hamilton, and thus reduces that great family, with nearly the entire clan, to the verge of ruin, 632.

ARRAN, earl of, son of the duke of Chatelherault, conveys himself secretly into Scotland, 1559; ii. 552. Declares James Hepburn earl of Bothwell a traitor, 558. And accuses him of a design to murder Lord James Stuart and Maitland; but upon investigation, the accuser being found insane, is committed to Edinburgh castle, 574.

ARRAN, James Stuart, earl of: this young man, who was second son of the lord Ochiltree, becomes a favourite of James VI., and recommends to the king the execution of the regent Morton, 1578; ii. 652, 653. He is thrown into prison by the earl of Marr, 654.

ARRAN, earl of, eldest son of the duke of Hamilton, expresses himself strongly for the recall of James II., iv. 2.

Arras, congress of, 1435; ii. 76. Articles of the treaty, between Philip of Burgundy and Charles VII., *ib.*

ARTHUR, fable of his Round Table, i. 23.

ARTHUR, nephew of Richard I. The king names him his heir, and opens a treaty with the king of Scotland to support his claims in case of necessity, i. 506. The settlement in his favour formally set aside, and John acknowledged Richard's successor, 507. On the death of Richard, 1199, the barons of Touraine, Maine, Anjou, and Brittany, proclaim Arthur their lawful sovereign, 515. He is supported by the French king, who declares war with John, and requires the surrender of all his French possessions, except Normandy, to Arthur, 516. Description of Arthur and his early life, *ib.* His claims deserted by Philip, 517. Arthur again assisted by Philip, *ib.* He besieges his grandmother Eleanor in the strong tower of the town of Mirebeau, 518. August 1, 1202, he is taken prisoner by John, *ib.* and first confined at Falaise, and afterwards removed to Rouen, *ib.* Supposed to have been murdered by his uncle John, April 3, 1203; 519, 520. Portrait of prince Arthur and Hubert de Burgh, 519.

ARTHUR, prince of Wales, son of Henry VII., his birth, ii. 287, 289. His marriage with Catherine of Arragon, daughter of Ferdinand of Spain, 310. The marriage ceremony, 1501, in St. Paul's, 312. His death, 1502, at Ludlow Castle, *ib.*

Articles, Thirty-nine, petition praying relief from subscription to the, 1772; § i. 123—125, 151, 152.

Artisans, group of, ii. 195.

ARTOIS, Robert of, his claim to the great fief of Artois; he excites Edward III. to declare war with France, i. 758.

ARTOIS, count d', uncle of Philip III. of France; he takes the command of the French troops at the commencement of the war with Edward I., and expels the English from nearly all their possessions on the continent, i. 712.

ARTOIS, count d', brother of Louis XVIII., his entry into Paris, April 12, 1814; § iv. 618°.

Arts, the Fine—*see* the disquisitions on "Literature, Science, and the Fine Arts," i. 118, 289, 603, 842; ii. 196, 813; iii. 360, 871; iv. 735. Reign of George III., § i. 604; § iii. 715; § iv. 696.

Arts and Manufactures, society for the encouragement of, instituted 1754; iv. 730.

Arun, the river, in Sussex, i. 103, 142.

Arundel Castle, Matilda received here by Alice, widow of Henry I., i. 438. View of, 429.

ARUNDEL, Edmund Fitzalan, earl of, 1301. Defeated by Sir James Douglas, 1317; i. 739.

ARUNDEL, Henry Fitzalan, earl of, 1543. Of Edward VI.'s council, 1547. He died, 1579; ii. 454.

ARUNDEL, Philip Howard, earl of, (son of the duke of Norfolk, beheaded in 1572,) becomes a convert to Catholicism; to escape imprisonment for his faith he resolves to quit his country, but is seized by Burghley on the coast of Sussex, and committed to the Tower, where he dies in a miserable condition, 1595; ii. 654.

ARUNDEL, Richard Fitzalan, earl of, 1375, impeached and beheaded, September 1397; i. 795.

ARUNDEL, Thomas, translated to the see of Canterbury, September 1396; banished 1398; restored 1399; i. 795. He declares Henry IV. to be unjustly named king of England, ii. 14. Persecutes the Lollards, 25. His death, February 1413. He is succeeded by Henry Chicheley, bishop of St. David's, *ib.* Visitation of the Universities of Oxford and Cambridge, iii. 163.

ARUNDEL—*see* Norfolk.

ASCHAM, Roger, tutor to queen Elizabeth, his portrait, ii. 813.

ASHBURNHAM, John, a firm royalist, 1642; iii. 293, 352. He flies into Holland, 364. Returns to England, 1647; 369, 371. His account of the first interview with Hammond, governor of the Isle of Wight, 376.

ASHLEY, Sir John, admiral of the blue, called to account in parliament for permitting the French ships under De Tourville to make their escape, but is honourably acquitted, 1692; iv. 38.

Ashridge, Bucks, the work of James Wyatt, 1808—14; § iv. 709.

ASHTON, chaplain to Robert Devereux, earl of Essex, 1601, persuades that condemned noble to write an ample confession, ii. 688.

ASKE, Robert, a gentleman of talent and enterprise, 1536, took the command of 40,000 insurgents in Yorkshire, ii. 399. The royal army compelled to retire south of the Trent, 400. The king's conciliatory letters to Aske and lord Darcy, *ib.* Captain Aske and divers of their leaders appeared to betray the common cause, and in some months, 1537, the malcontents dispersed to their homes, *ib.* Aske executed at York, 401, *note.*

ASKEW, Anne, her early marriage with Kyme, a neighbour of Sir William Askew, ii. 447. She resumed

ASKEW, Anne—
her maiden name and resorted to London for a divorce, ib. Their quarrel was a difference of religion, ib. She spoke boldly against the Romish dogmas, and introduced reformed books to Catherine Parr and her ladies, ib. Her recantation, 1546; urged thereto by Bonner, 448. She relapsed, was tried and burnt in Smithfield, ib.

ASOFF-UL-DOWLA succeeds his father, Sujah Dowla, as nabob of Oude, 1775; § ii. 133. Concludes the treaty of Chunar with Hastings, 1784; 169, 170.

Aspern, battle of, May 21 and 22, 1809; § iv. 411.

ASSER, the monk, a friend of king Alfred, his anecdotes of the monarch, i. 158, 166. His remark on the defeats of Hasting, the sea-king, and his expulsion from England by Alfred (897); 165. Is received with distinction at Alfred's court, the monarch being sedulously bent on improving his own education, 161, 166.

Assignats, French, of 1790; § ii. 444.

Assize, Grand, great importance of, as an improvement of the law introduced regno Henry II. by the advice of Glanville, i. 573. This mode of trial was not abolished till 1833; ib. note.

ASTLEY, Sir Jacob, a royalist major-general at the battle of Edgehill, October 23, 1642; iii. 297. Services in the royal cause, 316.

Aston, or Ashenden, Berkshire, signal victory, about 870, gained over the Danes, Ethelred and Alfred commanding the Saxons of Wessex, i. 154.

Astronomical instrument, Celtic, found in Ireland, (and explained by Sir William Betham), i. 122. Some of the Druidical circles were called the "Astronomers' circles," 123.

Astronomy, § iv. 703.

Athelney, isle of, fastness of the distressed Alfred in 878. Here a faithful band of warriors resort to him, i. 158, 166.

ATHELSTANE, A.D. 925, grandson of Alfred, succeeds Edward, king of Wessex, i. 168. Compels the Welsh to pay tribute, ib. He drives the British tribes back into Cornwall, ib. In 937 he gains the victory of Brunnaburgh over Olave the Dane, and his allies the Scots, and the ancient Britons from North Wales, Cumberland, &c. ib. He assumes the style of king of the Anglo-Saxons, 169. Splendour of his court, the resort of Louis d'Outremer of France, Haco the Norwegian, and the Celtic princes of Brittany, ib. His exalted character, laws, provision for the poor, patronage of letters, 170. He fosters a translation of the Bible into the vernacular language of his time, ib. His death in 940; he is buried at Malmsbury, ib. "Song of Victory," by this king, in Anglo-Saxon, with an English version, 297.

ATHELWOLD, a courtier of Edgar, weds through fraud the beautiful Elfrida, and is murdered in a wood, about 963; i. 173.

ATHOLE, Patrick, earl of, overthrew Walter Bisset at a tournament, 1242, and a few days after was found murdered; this excites a great disturbance in Scotland; suspicions fall on the Bissets; the king protects them from the violence of the people, but forfeits the lands of William Bisset, the head of the family, and banishes him into England; Bisset appeals to Henry to avenge him, which afterwards forms a pretext for that king to declare war with Alexander, i. 701.

ATHOLE, earl of, takes up arms, 1578, to rescue his young king James VI. from the hands of the regent Morton, ii. 652. Athole is shortly after poisoned at a banquet by Morton, ib.

Atomic Theory, the, announced 1808, by Dalton, and its development and illustration completed, 1814, by Wollaston, § iv. 704.

ATTERBURY, Dr. Francis, made bishop of Rochester, June, 1713; iv. 277. On the death of queen Anne, he proposes to proclaim the Pretender, 301. He

ATTERBURY, Dr. Francis—
is arrested and confined in the Tower, 380. A bill of banishment and deprivation passes against him, 1723; 381. He is conveyed on board a king's ship to Calais, 382. His death, 1732; 400.

Attorney-general, and King's solicitor, their offices, ii. 164.

Attorneys, statute passed 1455, restricting the number of, in Norwich, Norfolk, and Suffolk, ii. 195.

AUDHER, or Ohthere, regno Alfred, makes a voyage from the Baltic to the North Cape, i. 166.

AUDLEY, lord, 1459, defeated at Bloreheath, Shropshire, by Salisbury and the Yorkists, ii. 94. Audley slain, ib.

AUDLEY, lord, joined the Cornish insurrection, 1497; taken prisoner in the battle of Blackheath; he was beheaded, ii. 306.

AUDLEY, Sir Thomas, 1532, succeeded the learned More as chancellor, ii. 378. The chancellor assisted at the arrest, 1536, of queen Anne Boleyn, 391. Also at her trial, 393. He begs that two of the abbeys may be left standing in Essex, 405.

AUGUSTA, princess of Saxe Gotha, her marriage with her cousin Frederick, prince of Wales, 1735; iv. 491. On the death of the prince, 1751, she and her family are taken under the protection of the king, 567. Death of the princess-dowager, February 8, 1772, in the 54th year of her age, § i. 128.

AUGUSTINE and forty monks sent by Gregory the Great, 597, into England, i. 145, 230. Causes that conduced to the rapid success of this great mission: Bertha, a Christian princess (of Paris), the wife of the bretwalda, or chief ruler, Ethelbert, 231. Conversion of Ethelbert and the people of Kent, at the close of the sixth century, 145, 231. Advice of Gregory to Augustine; Pagan places of worship converted into Christian; ancient festivals maintained, but in honour of certain saints, 232. Deficient of ecclesiastics for converting all the Anglo-Saxon states, Augustine applies to those of the ancient church long established in Wales, ib. The Welsh clergy listen to the counsels of a hermit, being already jealous of the pre-eminence assumed by Augustine,—if the great missionary rise on their approach, they should obey him, 232, 233. At a conference with the Welsh bishops and the abbot of Bangor, the Roman prelate shows no such token of Christian humility, 233. Mutual dissatisfaction of these two branches of the primitive church, ib. Allegation of the irritated Augustine having prophesied the massacre of the monks of Bangor by Edilfrid of Northumbria, ib. Sebert of Essex converted, a Christian church erected in London, 604, ib. Redwald of East Anglia converted, who allows Christian and Pagan worship in the same temple, so that his people might make their election, ib. Augustine consecrates Justus and Mellitus as bishops, and appoints Laurentius to succeed him as primate, ib. Death of Augustine, 604, ib.

AUGUSTUS, improvements in Britain in the time of this emperor; he levies duties on exports and imports in Britain; receives tribute and presents thence, i. 105.

AUGUSTUS II., king of Poland, dies February, 1733; iv. 469.

AUMALE, Harcourt, count of, 1423, surprised an English convoy of oxen, from Anjou destined for Normandy; after a sharp rencontre he defeated the English troops with great loss, and John de la Pole remained his prisoner, ii. 56, 56.

AURENGZEBE, great mogul, born 1618. He seizes Surat and other factories of the English (about 1686), § ii. 20, and died in 1707; 23.

AUSTERLITZ, battle of, gained by the French over the allied armies of Russia and Austria, December 2, 1805; § iv. 177, 178.

AUSTRIA, Leopold, duke of, 1190, takes one of the

AUSTRIA, Leopold, duke of—
towers of Acre, and plants his banner upon it; king Richard tears it down, and casts it into the ditch, i. 499. He refuses to work at the fortifications of Ascalon, *ib.* Takes Richard prisoner when returning as a pilgrim through Germany, 503. The emperor Henry demands that he shall be delivered up to him, 503, 504.

AUSTRIA, the archduke of, sends d'Aremberg, 1603, to represent the Spanish interests at the court of James I., as to the affair of the United States of Holland, iii. 7.

AUSTRIA, Charles archduke of, receives the command of an Austrian army, 1797; § iii. 524. After receiving several terrible defeats on the Tagliamento, he retreats in admirable order towards Vienna, *ib.* He signs the peace of Leoben, April 18; *ib.* Defeats general Jourdan in several engagements, 1799, and drives him across the Rhine, 546. He loses the battle of Eckmuhl, and the French enter Vienna, May 13, 1809; § iv. 410. Battle of Aspern, in which the archduke gains a decided advantage over the French, May 21 and 22; 411. He is defeated at the battle of Wagram, July 6; 412, 413.

AUSTRIA, John archduke of, hazards an engagement with the republican general Moreau, December 2, 1800, at Hohenlinden, between the rivers Iser and Inn, is thoroughly defeated, and driven from the field with the loss of 10,000 men, § iii. 558. His campaign in Italy, 1809, and retreat to the valley of the Danube, § iv. 414—416. His portrait, 413.

AUSTRIA, Maria Louisa, archduchess of, daughter of the emperor Francis II. espoused Napoleon Bonaparte, emperor of the French, April 2, 1810; § iv. 458—461. Delivered of a son, March 20, 1811; 492. She is left regent of France by the emperor during his absence, 1814; but on the advance of the allies to Paris, she quits that city and retires to Blois, and shortly after puts herself under the protection of her father, the emperor Francis, 1814, 615*; 618*.

AUVERQUERQUE, M., a faithful servant of William III., iv. 139, 163, 166, 178, 184.

Avebury, Druidical temple of, i. 68.

Aversa, city of, opens its gates to count Daun, 1707; iv. 204.

AVIENUS, Festus, his interesting narrative of the Carthaginian voyage to Britain and Ireland, taken from the Punic records, i. 14.

Avignon, incorporated with France, 1791; § ii. 686.

AVISA, wife of king John, and daughter of the earl of Gloucester, i. 517.

AVISON, Charles, publishes, 1752, an essay on Musical Expression, iv. 764.

Avon, river in Hampshire, i. 142.

AVRANCHES, Hugh d', surnamed the Wolf, second earl of Chester, 1070; i. 376. His invasion of North Wales; he builds the castle at Rhuddlan, and subjugates Flintshire, *ib.* Prepares to go to Italy, with Odo, bishop of Bayeux, 385. He died, 1101.

Axe-heads, called Celts, of tin and copper, i. 104.

AYSCUE, sir George, forces the Barbadians to surrender their island to the English, March 1652; iii. 549.

BABINGTON, Anthony, head of the conspiracy known by his name. Executed as a traitor, 1586, with many of his accomplices, ii. 657.

BACON, sir Francis, born 1561; iii. 610. Author of the Inductive method of Philosophy, 611. In the Apophthegms, he gives an interesting anecdote of Elizabeth on her coronation, her wit and shrewdness, ii. 542. His warning counsel, 1600, to the earl of Essex, 684. His pleading on that noble's trial, 1601, although not so virulent as Coke against the earl, left dark spots on Bacon's own character, Essex. 687. Was himself abashed at a rebuke by Essex. 687. His closing speech on this trial, 688. Quotations from, and historical remarks by, ii. 286, 289, 291, 293,

BACON, sir Francis—
298, 307, 312, 498. Meets James I. on his approach to London from Scotland; he portrays the new king's style of speech and talent, 1603, in a letter to the earl of Northumberland, iii. 4. Knighted, July 1603, at Whitehall, with the other serjeants-at-law, 6. He was conspicuous in parliament, 1604, early displaying his character; a sycophant at Court; a bold and eloquent patriot in the House, 19. He defends the union of England and Scotland, 34. Is made lord keeper, 63. James on going to Scotland, leaves all power in his hands, 67. He abuses it, *ib.* His change on hearing of the king's return, 68. Made lord high chancellor, and baron Verulam, 70. Is created viscount St. Albans, 82. Impeached for corruption, *ib.* Sentenced to pay £40,000; be imprisoned in the Tower during the king's pleasure; made incapable of bearing office in the commonwealth, and forbidden to come within the verge of the court, 83. James remits the fine, and liberates him from the Tower after two days, *ib.* He retires to his house at Gorhambury, *ib.* His death, 1626; 611.

BACON, John, an eminent sculptor of the eighteenth century, § iii. 745.

BACON, sir Nicholas, keeper of the seals, 1558, first year of Elizabeth, ii. 543.

BACON, Roger, born at Ilchester, 1214; died 1292. His writings and character as a philosopher, i. 843.

Baconian Philosophy, iv. 767.

Badajoz, view of, surrenders to marshal Soult, March 11, 1811; § iv. 481. Invested by general Beresford, 486. Stormed by lord Wellesley, April 7, 1812; 504, 505.

BADBY, a Lollard, burnt for denial of transubstantiation, 1410; the prince (Henry V.) attempting in vain to move him to a recantation, ii. 146.

BAGNALL, sir Henry, marching into Tyrone, against the powerful O'Niel, 1598, was totally defeated by the rebellious earl, and slain, ii. 682.

Bahama Islands, the, captured by the Spaniards, 1782; § i. 490.

BAILLIE of Jerviswood, iii. 746. Executed 1684, for participation in the Rye-house plot. 755.

BAILLY, Charles, a servant of the queen of Scots, is seized at Dover, 1571, as he was returning from the duke of Alva, with a packet of letters, ii. 637, and tortured, 638.

BAIRD, sir David, retakes the Cape of Good Hope, January 8, 1806; § iv. 231.

BAKER, sir Richard, author of a Chronicle of the Kings of England, written while he was confined in the Fleet for debt, where he died, 1645; iii. 618.

BAKER, major, appointed joint-governor of Londonderry, 1689; iv. 16.

BAKER, a Romish priest, attends lord Lovat previously to his execution, 1746; iv. 553.

BALCANQUEL, Walter, publicly rebuked by James VI., January 1586, for preaching against the authority of bishops, iii. 442.

BALCARRAS, earl of, sent into Galloway, 1685, with a commission of fire and sword against the "resetters" of the rebels, iii. 770.

BALDWIN—see Flanders.

BALDWIN, archbishop of Canterbury, crowns Richard I., i. 483. He died at Acre, in Palestine, *circa* 1191.

BALDWIN de Bethune, a priest, accompanied king Richard in his journey through Germany, 1192; i. 562; but is arrested at Goritz, *ib.*

BALDWIN, a Jesuit, residing, 1606, in Spanish Flanders, iii. 29.

BALFOUR, Sir James, a chief conspirator in the murder of Henry Darnley, surrendered Edinburgh Castle to the regent Murray, 1567, stipulating immunity for his conduct, and receiving a pension and a large sum in cash, ii. 605.

BALFOUR, John, of Kinloch, kills archbishop Sharp, 1679; iii. 730.

BALFOUR, Sir William, lieutenant of the Tower, refuses to take a bribe of 22,000l., offered to him by the earl of Strafford, iii. 240. Removed by the king, 1641, from his office, 259, 317.

BALIOL, John, grandson of the eldest daughter of David, earl of Huntingdon, who therefore, according to the rule of descent as now established, possessed a clear right to the succession, as being the nearest relation of Alexander III., i. 707. Various competitors lay claim to the crown of Scotland; Edward addresses an invitation to the nobility and clergy to meet him at Norham, but nothing definite was determined, ib. In the meeting held on June 2, 1291, at Holywell Haugh, Bruce acknowledged Edward lord paramount of Scotland, and consents to ask and receive judgment from him, in that character; his example is followed by that of the other competitors, 708. Baliol was absent on the first day of the meeting, but on the 3rd of June the proceedings at Norham were terminated by an unanimous agreement, that a body of 104 commissioners should be appointed to examine the cause, and report to Edward; forty being named by Baliol, the same number by Bruce, and the remainder by Edward himself; on the 11th, the regents of Scotland made a solemn surrender of the kingdom into the hands of the English king, on condition that Edward should make full restitution in two months from the date of his award in the cause of the succession, ib. On the 17th of November, Edward gives judgment in the great hall of the castle of Berwick, "That John Baliol should have seisin of the kingdom of Scotland." On the 19th, the regents of Scotland and the governors of castles receive orders to surrender their respective trusts to the new king; and on the 30th, John Baliol is solemnly crowned at Scone, 710. The Scottish king being no longer able to endure the humiliating condition in which he was kept by Edward, on the 23rd of October, 1295, forms an alliance with the French king, who was then at war with England, and invades Cumberland, 713. On the 30th of March, a messenger delivers to Edward, who was then in Scotland with a large army, Baliol's solemn renunciation of his allegiance and fealty, ib. Edward carries every thing before him in Scotland, and Baliol basely lays down his kingly state, 714. The famous stone on which the Scottish kings had been wont to be crowned, is removed to Westminster; on the 28th, a parliament was held at Berwick, and many of the Scottish laity and clergy presented themselves to take the oaths of fealty, ib. Edward takes measures for settling the government of the conquered country, 715. Baliol is liberated from the Tower by Edward, and sent to his ancestral estate of Balilleul, in Normandy, where he lived till his death, 1314; 724.

BALIOL, Edward, king of Scotland, son of John Baliol, after being kept for some time in the Tower, was sent with his father to Normandy, 1299; i. 724. He returns to England; is joined by the lords Wake and Henry de Beaumont, 755. Raises a small army, and lands at Kinghorn, on the coast of Fife, August 1332; ib. Boldly throws himself between the two Scottish armies, commanded by the regent Marr and the earl of March, and encamps at Forteviot, ib. He crosses the river Earn, and surprises the army of the regent during the night; on the following day, he gains a complete victory over the regent at Duplin Moor, ib. Is besieged in Perth, by the earl of March, who commanded the other Scottish army, but his squadron destroys the Scottish fleet, ib. Crowned king of Scotland, at Scone, September 24, 1332; 756. December 16th, he is surprised at Annan by a body of horse, commanded by the young earl of Moray and sir

BALIOL, Edward—
Archibald Douglas, ib. Effects his escape into England, where Edward receives him as a friend, ib. Sir Archibald Douglas acts as regent, he comes to the relief of Berwick, which city was invested by a powerful English army under the command of Edward; May 19th, after a fatiguing march, Douglas comes in sight of Berwick; he rashly attacks the English, who were posted in a strong position on Halidon Hill, surrounded by marshes, and is killed; a dreadful slaughter of the Scottish army follows, ib. David Bruce, and his queen, Edward's sister, are conveyed to France. Edward Baliol again recovers the throne, openly professes homage and feudal service in its full extent to the king of England, and surrenders all the southern counties in perpetuity to Edward, ib. Baliol is again driven across the borders; Edward marches into Scotland, August 1335, is joined by Baliol at Perth, but meeting with no opposition returns, ib. Edward makes two other expeditions into Scotland, in 1336; ib. In 1338, Edward being fully occupied by his wars in France, Baliol is expelled from Scotland, 759. He has some grants made to him in the North of England, and is employed to watch and ward against the Scottish borderers, ib.

BALIOL, Joycelin, excommunicated by Becket, 1167; i. 452.

BALL, John, executed as a traitor, 1381; i. 789.

BALLANTINE, translated to the see of Aberdeen, 1634; iii. 478, note. Deposed, 484.

BALLS, § i. 644, et seq.

BALMERINO, lord—see Arthur Elphinstone.

BALTIC, arms and costume of tribes on the western shores of the, i. 139. Observations of early navigators on the shores of the Baltic, and also to the North Cape, recorded in Anglo-Saxon by king Alfred, 166, 167.

BALTIMORE, lord, Maryland granted to, by Charles I., iii. 540.

BAMBOROUGH, view of the rock and castle of, in its modern state, i. 147. The Danes, 993, took this fortress by storm, 176.

BAMPTON, Thomas de, one of the commissioners appointed to raise the poll-tax, 1381; the people of Fobbing, in Essex, refuse to appear before him when summoned, which commences the insurrection in Essex, Kent, Suffolk, and Norfolk, known by the name of the insurrection of Jack Straw, i. 785.

BANCROFT, Dr., prebendary of Westminster, elected to the see of London, April 21, 1597. His fulsome praise of James I., for the king's controversy, 1604, with the leading puritanical doctors, and professors of Oxford and Cambridge, iii. 17. Is promoted to the archbishopric of Canterbury, on the decease of Dr. Whitgift, 1604; he willingly deprives the non-conformists of all benefices in England, ib. His ideas of royal and episcopal authority, 41. He endeavours to defend his church from the reformers, and encourages the king in his prerogative course, 44. He addresses a long epistle to James against a 'bill in hand against pluralities,' ib. Encloses a copy of a bill against the proceedings of the High Commission Court, ib. Second letter to James, 45, 460, 463, 466. His death, November, 1610; 46.

Bank of England, founded 1693; iv. 692. Run upon the bank for specie, 1797; § iii. 516. Suspension of cash payments, 654–657, 663. View of the bank in 1785; 733. North-west view, § iv. 705. The bank recommences cash payments 1821, in consequence of Peel's Act passed in 1819; 670.

Bank of Scotland, set up 1695; iv. 694. Bank Royal founded 1727; ib.

Bankruptcies (18th century), § iii. 645–649, 663; (19th century), § iv. 666.

Bankrupts, statutes relating to, § iv. 642.

D

BANKS, Thomas, an eminent English sculptor, born 1735, died 1805; § iii. 744.

Bannockburn, battle of, fought June 23rd and 24th, 1314; i. 736—738. For a description of this battle, see Robert Bruce.

Banqueting-house, Whitehall, view of the, iv. 85.

BAR, duke of, the count of Marle, count of Dampierre, count of Vaudemont, and many other nobles who fell at Agincourt, 1415, enumerated, ii. 33.

BARBAZAN, an officer serving Armagnac, 1418; ii. 41, 48.

BARBER, 1683, a Rye-house conspirator, iii. 741. His deposition respecting the plot, 743.

BARBOUR, John, a Scottish historian and poet of the 14th century, i. 735, 851.

Barcelona taken by the earl of Peterborough, 1705; iv. 179, 180.

BARCLAY, John, author of the political romances of the Euphormio and Argenis, published in 1603 and 1621; iii. 616.

BARDOLF, lord, a participator in Percy, earl of Northumberland's latter rebellions, 1405; ii. 17. He flies to Edinburgh, ib. Re-enters Northumberland, 1408, with the earl, 19. They reach Knaresborough, are brought to action on Branham Moor, and defeated, ib. Bardolf dies of his wounds, and the great earl perishes in the battle, ib.

BARDOLF, lieutenant of Calais, 1415, fails in an attempt to succour Henry V., ii. 34.

Bards of Celtic nations, an important auxiliary class of the druidical priesthood, i. 63, 64. Their office was to sing the deeds of heroes and chieftains, 63. Grand costume of the Bards and Vaids, 65.

BARILLON, a minister of Louis XIV., iii. 716. List of bribes given by him to English members of parliament, and other persons of consequence, 727. Present at the death of Charles II., 761, 775.

Barking, William I. keeps his court here, 1066; i. 362.

Barking church, Laud, 1645, buried at, iii. 326.

Barnet, first battle of, fought February 17, 1461; ii. 97.
——, second battle of, fought April 14, 1471. The earl of Warwick is slain, ii. 108.

BARNWELL, Patrick, his counsels in 1540 for the better government of Ireland, ii. 428.

BARR, confederacy of, formed 1678; § i. 137.

BARRÉ, Isaac, an English gentleman who distinguished himself as a politician during the American war. His speech against the taxation, 1765; § i. 37. He receives a vote of thanks from the freeholders of Boston, 41. Portrait of, 89; 104, 109, 126. He is dismissed from the service, 1773; 151, 161, 163, 176, 238, 405.

BARRÉ, Luke de, a knight and a poet, made prisoner by Henry I., sentenced to be deprived of his eyes, i. 419. Intercession made by Charles the Good, earl of Flanders, to whom king Henry replied that Barré had satirized him, and this would be a wholesome warning to all satirizers, ib. Barré in presence of the torturers dashes his head against the wall, and dies, ib.

Barrier treaty, the, of 1712; iv. 263.

BARRINGTON, lord, made secretary-at-war, 1755; iv. 584. Resigns, May 1778; § i. 344, 379.

BARRINGTON, quoted, i. 577, 812, 814, 816, 820.

BARROW, Dr. Isaac, an eminent mathematician and divine, born in 1630, died 1677, in the forty-seventh year of his age, iii. 610, 803; iv. 780.

Barrows, representation of the principal forms of, i. 130. Contents of ancient British barrows, 131. Contents of Roman British barrows, 133.

BARRY, James, an eccentric and celebrated artist, born 1741, died 1806; § i. 627. His portrait, ib. His portrait of J. Wesley, iv. 617.

Bartholomew Fair, iv. 829, 830.

BARTOLOZZI, Francesco, an eminent engraver, born at Florence, 1728, and died at Lisbon in his 88th year, § i. 626.

BARTON, Elizabeth, the holy maid of Kent, executed at Tyburn, April 21, 1534, for prophesying the death of Henry VIII., ii. 384, 385.

Basil, council of, assembles 1431, and continues to sit till 1443; ii. 138.

Basilica of St. Paul at Rome, view of, after the fire in 1823; i. 311.

Basques and Bearnois, under Gaston de Foix, take Bayonne from the English, ii. 85.

Bass rock, with the prisons of the Covenanters, iii. 757.

BASSOMPIERRE, marshal de, iii. 125. He reconciles queen Henrietta Maria and Buckingham, 1626, ib. Leaves London, 127. Invests Rochelle, 135.

Bastia, view of, § iii. 400. Gallant conduct of the English seamen at the siege of, 1794; ib.

Bastille, attack on the, by the French Revolutionists, 1789; § ii. 384, 385.

BASTWICK, Dr., fined 5000l., pilloried and cropped, 1637; iii. 166. Whilst levying men for the parliament, he is taken by the king, and shut up in the gaol of York, 293.

BATES, a Turkish merchant, resists an import duty on currants, 1609; iii. 40. Is proceeded against in the court of Exchequer, ib. Several members of the House of Commons, 1610, declare the decision of the barons of the Exchequer concerning him illegal, ib.

Bath, a fashionable watering place, iv. 824.

BATH, Chandos of Brittany, created earl of, 1486; ii. 286.

BATH, Henry Bourchier, earl of, created 1636, died 1654; iii. 292.

BATH, John Granville, earl of, created 1661, died 1701; iii. 768.

BATH, William Pulteney, earl of, proposes a vote of censure for the orders sent by the ministers to the duke of Ormond, not to co-operate with prince Eugene, 1712; iv. 265. Becomes head of the Patriots, 1724; 386. Brings forward a motion beseeching the king to settle on the prince of Wales 100,000l. per annum, 1737; iv. 425. Is created earl of Bath, 1742; 459. He died, 1764.

BATHURST, lord, opposes the preparations making for war, 1727. He died, 1775; iv. 390.

BATHURST, Henry, earl of, 1775, becomes lord chancellor, 1771; § i. 109. Medal of, 528.

Battle Abbey, founded by William I. on the ground where the English had stood during the battle of Hastings, i. 358. Monks placed here from the great convent of Marmoutier near Tours, ib. View of Battle Abbey, 359. Here was deposited a roll containing the names of the Norman nobles who survived the battle of Hastings, ib.

BATTONI, Pompeo, the most eminent Italian painter of the 18th century, born at Lucca in 1708. His portrait of Augustus Henry, duke of Grafton, § i. 46.

BAVARIA, Louis of, letter to the duke from Henry VIII., 1521, recommending the punishment of Luther, ii. 345.

BAVARIA, electoral prince of, 1698, named by Charles II. of Spain as his successor, iv. 100. Immediately after he falls sick and dies, in the eighth year of his age, not without suspicions being entertained of his death having been occasioned by the intrigues of France or Austria, ib.

BAVARIA, elector of, Marlborough's campaign against the, 1704; iv. 166—173. He besieges the city of Brussels, 231.

BAVARIA, Maximilian Joseph, elector of, dies December 30, 1777; § i. 345.

BAXTER, Richard, iii. 490, 668. Quoted, 820. Declines the bishopric of Hereford, ib. He died at the age of 76 in the beginning of December, 1691; iv. 789.

BAYARD, a celebrated French commander, made prisoner, 1513, by king Henry VIII., ii. 323, 325. He falls in battle, 1524, in Italy, 358.

Bayeux Tapestry, a detailed account of this celebrated roll of linen, 214 feet long, worked in coloured worsteds, and delineating the career of Harold son of Godwin and victory of William of Normandy, &c., &c., i. 196, *note.* It is still preserved at Bayeux, *ib.* List of some of the chief historical and national illustrations transferred from it to this ' Pictorial History of England :'—Harold taking leave of Edward on his departure for Normandy, i. 196. Harold on his journey to Bosham, 197. Harold entering Bosham church, *ib.* His coming to anchor on the coast of Normandy, 198. His appearance at the court of duke William, *ib.* Harold's oath to William, 199. His interview with king Edward on his return, 200. Sickness and death of Edward the Confessor, 201. Funeral of Edward, 202. The crown offered to Harold by the people, 204. Coronation of Harold, *ib.* William giving orders for the Invasion, 207. Normans preparing arms and military implements for the Invasion, 208. Duke William's ships transporting troops, 209. Orders given for erecting a fortified camp at Hastings, 210. Cooking, and feasting, of the Normans at Hastings, 211. William of Normandy addressing his soldiers on the field of battle, 213. Battle of Hastings, 214. Death of Harold, 215.

BAYNAM, sir Edward, condemned for treason, 1601, after Essex's execution, purchased his pardon by large sums to sir Walter Raleigh, ii. 689.

Baynard's Castle, London, view of this ancient edifice, drawn in the 17th century, ii. 122. Petition of the Londoners presented to Gloucester at, 127. Private supper entertainment at, iii. 57.

Bayonet, the, invented in the reign of Charles II., iii. 895.

Bayonne, city of, surrendered, 1451, after an obstinate resistance, to Gaston de Foix, ii. 85.

BEAL, his portrait of Dr. Edward Stillingfleet, iv. 617.

BEALE, Mr. Robert, sent to announce to Mary the sentence of execution passed against her, December 6, 1586; ii. 663. He reads the death warrant, 668.

Bear-baiting, ii. 891; iii. 642.

Bear-garden, Southwark, iii. 904.

BEATON, cardinal David, successor to his uncle in the primacy, 1539, rendered the previous persecution of "heretics" in Scotland more appalling, and the Protestants disaffected to the king, ii. 431. He negotiated the marriage of the king with Mary of Guise, *ib.* His embassy, 1540, to Rome, 432. He is not averse to a war against Henry VIII.; result of this border warfare narrated, 433. On the death of James V. he produces a will appointing him guardian to the infant Mary Queen of Scots, and regent of the realm: Arran (Hamilton) declares this a forgery, and becomes regent himself, December 22, 1542. Beaton despatches agents to France to represent the danger of the queen dowager and her infant, and to beg for supplies to resist the encroachments of the king of England; Arran orders his instant arrest, and he is carried off to the castle of Blackness. Beaton had been recently appointed legate *a latere* for Scotland, and his influence with the clergy was unbounded; they shut up the churches and refused to administer the sacraments, &c., 434, 435. Henry demands his release, 435. Beaton recovers his liberty, but by what means is not clear, 436. He collects an army in the north of Scotland, *ib.* His proceedings with the nobles of Scotland, 437. In 1544, his renewed persecutions for religion had rendered him more unpopular, 440. He yet possessed great authority, and marched with Arran and Angus against the English at Leith, *ib.* George Wishart's opposition to the cardinal, 1545, 446. Marriage of a daughter of David Beaton, *ib.* The cardinal was murdered, 1546, in his castle of St. Andrew's by Norman Lesly and his confederates, 446, 747.

BEATON, James, catholic archbishop of Glasgow ; singular colloquy betwixt this prelate 1520, and Gawin Douglas, bishop of Dunkeld, ii. 352, 353. In 1528, Beaton aided James V. to escape from the Douglases to Stirling castle, 430. His death, 1539; 431.

BEATOUN, archbishop of Glasgow, sent as ambassador to the French court, 1599; iii. 450.

BEAUFORT, Henry, cardinal, second son of John of Gaunt by his third wife, Catherine Swynford, born before the marriage, but legitimatized by parliament, translated to the see of Winchester, March 14, 1405; ii. 52, *note.* His disputes with Humphrey of Gloucester, 57, 58, 70, 82. His great wealth; his design thereby to succeed to the papacy, 71. A crusade being preached by the pope against the Hussites of Bohemia, &c., the old cardinal decided on personally joining in it, *ib.* He levied 2250 English soldiers for his expedition, *ib.* At Paris, witnessing Bedford's difficulties, he resigned his army to the regent, 71, 150. Present at the execution of Joan of Arc; hearing her appeals for some other mode of death, he rises before the odious crime was perpetrated, and retired shedding tears, with some bishops who shared in his compassion, 77. At the coronation of Henry VI., 1431, in Paris, the old cardinal places the French crown on his head, *ib.* He indignantly quits the congress of Arras, so inimical to the interests of the English, 78. Joins in advising the king's marriage with Margaret of Anjou, and the cession of Anjou and Maine, 81. His last quarrel with Gloucester, and condemnation of the duchess (Eleanor Cobham) to perpetual imprisonment, on a charge of dealing by sorcery against the king's life, 83. He died, aged 80, March 11, 1447, and was buried at Winchester, 84. His chantry in that cathedral, *ib.* He bequeathed most of his property to charities, *ib.* In consequence, the Hospital of St. Cross, Winchester, was founded, and 4000*l.* given to debtors confined in London, *ib.*

BEAUFORT, Joanna, daughter of a duke of Somerset, and descended from Edward III., was espoused by James I. of Scotland, ii. 132.

BEAUFOY, Mr., endeavours, 1787, to obtain some mitigation of the disabilities inflicted on Dissenters, § iii. 561.

BEAUHARNAIS, Eugene de, only son of Alexander de Beauharnais, a French nobleman, and son-in-law of the emperor Napoleon, by whom he was made viceroy of Italy; in 1809, he gained many advantages over the archduke John, and most opportunely joined the French emperor before the battle of Wagram, § iv. 412, 414—416. His portrait, 414. In the Russian campaign of 1812, he commanded the Italian troops belonging to the grand army, and conducted the retreat with great skill, 589. In 1813 he successfully opposed the allies, 591, but on the downfall of the emperor Napoleon in 1814, lost his viceregal sway and retired to Munich, where he died in 1824; 623*.

BEAUMONT, Francis, a dramatic writer, born 1585, died March 1616; iii. 595.

BEAUMONT, French ambassador to Whitehall, 1603; his despatches, iii. 15, *note.*

BEAUVAIS, bishop of, taken prisoner by king Richard, 1197; i. 513. He takes the gallant Longsword earl of Salisbury prisoner, 526.

BECKET, Thomas à, sent as ambassador by Henry II. to the French court, i. 444. Henry commits to him, now chancellor of England, the conduct of the war in Toulouse, 445. He fortifies Cahors, takes three castles, and returns to Normandy to oppose the French there, *ib.* Is appointed to treat with the French king, 446. Early life of Thomas à Becket, 446, 552, 553. Made chancellor of England, preceptor to the prince, and warden of the Tower, *ib.* Becomes primate of England, May 27, 1162; 448, 554.

BECKET, Thomas à—

His consecration, from an ancient MS., 554. He lays claim to Rochester and other castles and several baronies, 1163; *ib.* Excommunicates William de Eynsford, but at the command of Henry absolves him, *ib.* Becket and the clergy sign a series of articles rendering the clergy subject to the civil courts for felony, at Clarendon, in Wiltshire, called the Constitutions of Clarendon, January 25, 1164; 449, 555. He is cited before the great council at Northampton, *ib.* Appears before the king with his pastoral staff; is renounced as primate by the bishops, October 11; 449, 450, 555. Accused of magic; his speech and departure from the council, 450. He leaves Northampton, and, travelling by night, disguised as a simple monk, flies to Gravelines, October 26; *ib.* Is reinvested by the pope with his archiepiscopal dignity, which he had surrendered into his hands, 451. His goods and possessions confiscated by Henry, and his relations and friends banished, *ib.* Becket excommunicates the supporters of the Constitutions of Clarendon, 452. He lands at Sandwich, December 1, 1169, and proceeds to Canterbury, *ib.* Excommunicates Ranulf and Robert de Broc, and the rector of Harrow, *ib.* Is reconciled with Henry, July 22, 1170, at a congress held on the borders of Touraine, 453. He excommunicates the archbishop of York and the bishops of London and Salisbury, 454. Is murdered in St. Augustine's church at Canterbury, December 29, 1170; 455, 456. This sainted archbishop of Canterbury, his tomb being broken open after the lapse of 400 years, was cited by Henry VIII. in 1539 to appear in Westminster Hall, ii. 402. Amount of gold and jewels taken on this occasion from Becket's shrine, 403.

BECKET's Crown, a chapel in Canterbury cathedral, view of, i. 556.

BECKFORD, alderman, portrait of, § i. 55. His speech on American affairs, 1769; 71, 80. Presents a remonstrance to the throne, 1770; 91. He entertains the members of the opposition at the Mansion House, 96. Presents a second petition, May 23; 97. His death, June 21, 1770; 98.

BECKWITH, endeavours to bribe his son-in-law, lieutenant Fowkes, to deliver up Hull to Charles I., iii. 282.

Bedarra, battle of, 1759; § ii. 78.

BEDE, the venerable, born about 675, some quotations from, i. 18—23, 229, 234. His writings in Latin; specification of his works, 290. Some account of his life, *ib.* His death, in 735, was fatal also for many years to history and learning, 305. His pupil, St. Cuthbert, has left an account of his last days, 290. *Illustration*—his birthplace, Jarrow, at the mouth of the Tyne, 291.

BEDFORD, John duke of, third son of Henry IV., attacks the rebels under Nottingham and Scroop, 1405, who surrender, ii. 17. Henry V., sailing from Southampton, appoints his brother regent in England, 1415; 28. The duke sails to the relief of Harfleur, 1416, and gains a great victory over a Genoese, Spanish, and French armament, 35. He escorts, 1422, queen Catherine to Harfleur, 50. Henry V., on his march south of Paris, finding the approach of death, resigned to Bedford the command of the army, *ib.* The king's dying instructions, 1422, to his brother, to Warwick, and others, *ib.* The parliament, violating the late king's wishes, declare the duke of Bedford regent or president of the council, and his brother Gloucester to be only protector of the realm and church in Bedford's absence with the armies, 52. His popularity as regent of France, 53. Nobles, and others, his companions in arms, 54. He meets the dukes of Brittany and Burgundy, 1423, in a congress; treaties, &c., *ib.* His marriage with Anne of Burgundy, *ib.* His victory of Crevant gained over Charles VII.'s forces and Scottish aux-

BEDFORD, John duke of—

iliaries, 1423; *ib.* *Illustration*—duke of Bedford before St. George, from the " Bedford Missal," 55. The regent, in 1424, granted plenary freedom to James I. of Scotland, who, returning home, prevented any more Scots going to France, 56. Bedford besieged Ivry; king Charles sent all his forces into Normandy for the relief of that fortress, *ib.* The French nobles jealous of Douglas and Buchan, their brave allies, this enabled the English to enter Ivry, *ib.* The regent Bedford marched upon Verneuil, then in the hands of the French, *ib.* He gained in 1424 the great battle of Verneuil, in which Buchan, Douglas and his son, with Narbonne, Tonnerre, and many chiefs, were slain; Alençon, de la Fayette, and other nobles, were made prisoners, *ib.* He beheaded Maucourt, Longueval, and others, 56, 57. The English had all dismounted, and stuck sharp stakes in the ground (chevaux-de-frize), a stratagem the regent had learnt from Henry V., his army being much inferior in numbers, 56. The regent married Anne, sister of Philip of Burgundy, which enabled him to prevent that prince for some years from leaguing with the dauphin Charles, 54, 57, 59. Bedford's reinforcements are diverted into Flanders by his brother Gloucester, 58. Beaufort and Gloucester's quarrel caused the regent to quit France, 1425, who, calling a parliament at Leicester, reconciled those two princes for a time only, *ib.* Paris being in the possession of the English, Orleans was the chief city of Charles VII., 60. The French were zealous to defend that fortress; the English laid siege to it, and the earl of Salisbury, repulsed in attempting to take the fortress by assault, was slain, 60, 61. The blockade, 61. Bedford sent sir John Fastolfe towards Orleans with a convoy of fish and provisions, *ib.* Fastolfe's victory, *ib.* Joan of Arc, the most formidable opponent of the English regent; her patriotic enthusiasm, 62. The earl of Salisbury slain in a reconnoissance, the earl of Suffolk succeeded him in his command, 61—67. The English retired from the blockade, 1429, to certain towns and castles on the Loire, 67. Suffolk captured in the fortress of Jargean, 68. Talbot retreating from the Loire was defeated at Patay and made prisoner, *ib.* Bedford, enraged at these sad reverses, disgraced Fastolfe for early withdrawing his division from the plain of Patay, *ib.* Being at length made sensible that Fastolfe's troops were panic-stricken, he restored that valiant captain, *ib.* Coronation of Charles VII. at Rheims, July 1429; 69. The regent was miserably neglected, in aids of men and money, by the English council, 70, 71. Beaufort having equipped 500 men against the Hussites of Bohemia, whom he intended, though old, to lead thither, reached Paris *en route*, 71. The cardinal, witnessing the destitution of the warlike regent, left him those troops, *ib.* The duchess reconciled the differences between her brother Burgundy and her husband Bedford, *ib.* Conference of those princes in Paris, solemn treaties read in public, and a statement of all the atrocities Charles had participated in, *ib.* Philip proved now but a weak and temporizing ally, *ib.* Normandy, in a state of insurrection, required Bedford's presence, *ib.* Returning to the defence of Paris with but a small army, Bedford pursued the French troops which marauded near the capital, *ib.* His letter to Charles VII. filled with taunts on his conduct, and challenging him to a personal combat: the French king, who had never evinced a ready courage, made no reply, 72. The two armies occupied good positions, and neither would quit its vantage ground, *ib.* Bedford was forced to march into Normandy to oppose Richemont's invasion, *ib.* The duke, 1429, once again marched into Paris, where his brother-in-law Philip joined him, 73. Bedford resigned the regency

BEDFORD, John duke of—
of France to the duke of Burgundy, and repairing to Rouen, maintained the English rule in Normandy, *ib.* The trial of the maid of Orleans, 74—76. Coronation of Henry VI., November 1431, in the cathedral of Notre Dame, 77. The duchess of Bedford died, 1432; *ib.* The regent's second marriage with Jacquetta, sister of the duke of Luxembourg, *ib.* This union, 1433, gives umbrage to Philip of Burgundy, brother of his late duchess, *ib.* Bedford resents his reproaches, and Burgundy makes peace with Charles VII., 77, 78. The regent's declining health, 78. The duke of Bedford died, 1435, at Rouen, and was buried in the cathedral. 79. His monument ; anecdote of Louis XI., 79, *note.*

BEDFORD, Jasper Tudor created duke of, 1485; ii. 282. *See* Pembroke.

BEDFORD, John Russell, earl of, privy-councillor and comptroller of the king's council, 1537; ii. 402, 423. Long known to history as lord Russell : he is sent, in 1549, to disperse a body of rebels, headed by one Humphrey Arundel, who had sat down to assault Exeter, but finding them in too great strength, he announces that he is ready to receive their complaints, 483. Afterwards, the rebels being on their march to attack the king's troops, Russell marches against them, and overcomes them at Fennington bridge, 485. Assisted by Lord Grey, of Wilton, he defeats the rebels in another engagement, and effected his entrance into the famished city of Exeter, *ib.* Assists in their suppression in Oxfordshire and Buckinghamshire, *ib.* Is created earl of Bedford January 19, 1550; 402, 469. He died 1554.

BEDFORD, Francis Russell, earl of, appointed by Elizabeth, 1566, as her proxy at the baptism of James I., ii. 639. At the command of his queen he petitions of Mary a pardon for the murderers of Rizzio, which she grants, 591. He died 1585.

BEDFORD, William Russell, born 1614, created earl 1641, and duke of, 1694, marries lady Anne Carr, iii. 62. He offers 100,000*l.* to Charles II. if he will pardon lord Russell, 748. He died 1700.

BEDFORD, John Russell, duke of, 1732, becomes secretary of state, iv. 557. He negotiates the treaty of Fontainebleau, 1762; § i. 22. He becomes president of the council, 1763; 28. He died 1771.

BEDFORD, Dr., 1714, author of a book on hereditary right, iv. 290.

BEDINGFIELD, sir Henry, appointed, 1554, constable of the Tower, is commanded to remove the princess Elizabeth to Woodstock, where he himself keeps severe watch over her, ii. 519.

BEDINGFIELD, confessor to James II. when duke of York, iii. 717.

BEDLOE, William, his depositions respecting the murder of sir E. Godfrey, 1678; iii. 721.

BEDYLL, Dr. Thomas, clerk of the council, 1533, his letter concerning Cranmer, ii. 381, *note.*

BEESTON, sir William, governor of Jamaica, 1699; iv. 97.

Behmenists, the, iii. 814.

BEHN, Mrs. Aphra, the Astræa of Pope, iii. 879.

BELESME, Robert de, 1100, earl of Shrewsbury, i. 408. Is besieged by Henry in Bridgenorth, and the citadel of Shrewsbury obliged to surrender ; all his lands in England confiscated ; permitted to return to Normandy, 409. Assists Robert, 410. The siege of Tenchebray being hard pressed by Henry, Robert comes to its relief, *ib.* He threw the English infantry into disorder, and had nearly won the victory, when De Beleame basely fled with a strong division of his forces, and left him to inevitable defeat, *ib.* As a reward for this service, Henry gives him a new grant of most of his estates in Normandy, *ib.*

Belgæ, doubtful if a German or Celtic race, i. 10. Historical allusions to the, 27.

Belgic colonies in south Britain, Celtic, i. 11.

BELHAVEN, lord, his speech in the Scottish parliament against the union of England and Scotland, iv. 194.

BELKNAPE, sir Robert, chief justice of the Common Pleas, sent into Essex to try the rioters who had refused to pay the poll-tax, 1381, but is compelled to flee ; his jurors are beheaded, i. 785.

BELL, Henry, (19th century) famous for his exertions in applying steam navigation to actual use, § iv. 683, 684.

BELLAMONT, lord, member of the privy council, exhibits articles of impeachment, 1693, against lord Coningsby and sir Charles Porter, lords justices of Ireland, for which he is dismissed, iv. 48.

BELLARMINE, cardinal, and the casuist Parsons, enter into controversy against James the First's publication, ' An Apology for the Oath of Allegiance,' 1606; iii. 33. The king, blind as usual with vanity, considers the triumph his own, *ib.* 95.

BELLASIS, lord, takes the command of Newark as governor, 1645; iii. 344. Receives orders from the king to surrender it, 354.

BELLASIS, Henry, son of lord Falconbridge, sent to the Fleet prison, 1640; iii. 217.

BELLIÉVRE, sent over to the English court by Henri III. to intercede for the life of Mary queen of Scots, iii. 664, 665.

BELLIÉVRE, M. de, iii. 359. Ambassador from France, implores Charles I. to accept the propositions offered by the parliament, but with no effect. He returns to France, *ib.*

BELLINGHAM, an insane merchant and Liverpool broker, shoots Mr. Percival in the lobby of the House of Commons, May 11, 1811; § iv. 499. Is tried and executed, 500.

Bellisle, taken by the English, 1761; § i. 9.

BELLIUS, Martinus, a fictitious name, assumed, as is supposed, by Sebastian Castalio, in a work published, 1553, denying the expediency of attempting to repress heresy by the civil power, iii. 807.

Bells, their introduction among the Anglo-Saxons, i. 316.

Belsize House, iv. 827.

Benares, view of, § ii. 125.

BENBOWE, admiral, dies at Jamaica, 1704, of wounds received in an action with Du Casse, iv. 160, *note.*

Benedictine monks, institution of, in the sixth century, i. 559. Portrait of a Benedictine monk, 560.

Benevolences, a mode of raising moneys for the kings, abolished by statute Ric. III., ii. 360.

BENNET, Gervas, a justice of Derby, gives the names of *Quakers* to the followers of George Fox, October 1650; iii. 810.

BENNET, John, published a set of madrigals, 1599; iii. 563.

BENNET, sir John, iii. 53. Judge of the prerogative court, impeached for corruption, 1621; 82.

BENTINCK, Lord William, envoy extraordinary and commander of the British forces in Sicily, 1811. Events in Sicily, 1806—1813, and establishment of a Sicilian constitution, § iv. 518—525. An Anglo-Sicilian force sent to the eastern coast of Spain, to oppose Suchet, 586. Lord William goes to Spain, June 17, 1813; 587. Returns to Sicily, takes the command of an army of 10,000 men, and lands in Upper Italy, to assist in expelling the French, 1814; 621*. Proclaims the independence of Italy, without authority from government, 622*, 623*.

BEORN, assassinated by Sweyn, his cousin, 1044; the latter, although not immediately degraded for this crime, sets out, 1052, in expiation, on a pilgrimage to Jerusalem, i. 189, 193.

BEORHTRIC, or Brihtric. in 795, king of Wessex, i. 150. Espouses the daughter of Offa, *ib.* Personal dangers of Egbert, competitor of Beorhtric, *ib.* Crimes of Eadburgha, the queen, *ib.* The king, in 800,

BEORHTRIC, or Brithtric —
dies of poison, *ib.* The nobles of Wessex decree,
that no future wife of their monarchs should share
the throne, or be styled queen, *ib.*

BEOWULF and Hrothgar, ancient Anglo-Saxon poem on
their feud, (*see* Cottonian Lib. Vitellius A. xv.) account of, i. 300. Extracts in Sharon Turner's History; also translations by Rev. J. J. Conybeare, *ib.*

BERENGARIA, daughter of the king of Navarre, her
journey from the Pyrenees to the Alps and Apen-
nines with her mother-in-law Eleanor, i. 493. Her
voyage from Sicily, 1190, attended by princess Joan,
sister of king Richard, 494. The fleet scattered in
a storm; her arrival at Limasol in Cyprus, *ib.* Her
marriage with king Richard, 495. She sets sail
with her husband, from Acre, October 1192; 502.

BERESFORD, marshal, a brave and skilful commander of
the British troops in the Peninsula ; he invests the
strong fortress of Badajoz, May 4, 1811; § iv. 486.
Gains the fiercely contested battle of Albuera, May
16; 487, 488. Wounded at the battle of Salamanca,
1812; 509. Attacks and carries the fortified heights
before Toulouse, with admirable skill, April 10,
1814; 606*, 607*.

Bergen-op-Zoom, view of, § iii. 475.

Berkeley castle, view of; Edward II. murdered here,
September 1327; i. 745.

BERKELEY, lord, acquitted, 1330, of having had any
part in the murder of Edward II., i. 755.

BERKELEY, Henry, earl of, his anger at the lavish
destruction of his game by queen Elizabeth, ii.
888. He died 1613.

BERKELEY, George, lord, entrusted by William III.,
1694, with the fleet for destroying Brest, which
undertaking entirely fails, iv. 48. Soon after,
he bombards and nearly destroys Dieppe and
Havre de Grace, 49. Bombards Dunkirque, Calais,
and St. Malo, and destroys the town of Grandeval,
58. He died 1698.

BERKELEY, sir John, iii. 389, 371. His account of his
interview, 1647, with Hammond, governor of the
Isle of Wight, iii. 376.

BERKLEY, sir William, killed in an action with the
Dutch, 1666, iii. 698.

BERKLEY, justice, iii. 180. Impeached for treason,
1640, and dragged from the bench with his ermine
on, but permitted to withdraw himself after having
been *forced* to give a *free* gift of 10,000*l.* for the
public service, 231.

BERKSHIRE, Thomas Howard, viscount Andover, earl of,
created February 1626; iii. 121. Curious anecdote
concerning him, relative to the election of Buckingham (1626) to the chancellorship of the University
of Cambridge, 122. He died in 1669.

BERKSHIRE, earl of, receives an extraordinary letter
from Charles I., 1642, which he produced to the parliament, iii. 274.

Bermondsey, view of the old monastery of, ii. 291.

BERNADOTTE—*see* Charles XIII.

Bernicia, kingdom of, in Durham, founded by Ida and
the Angles, who in 547 landed at Flamborough
Head, i. 142. It was then but a wild country, the
resort chiefly of the beasts of the forest, *ib.*

BERNINI, an architect and sculptor; Charles I. wishing
to possess a bust of himself by him, Vandyke
painted the well-known picture in which the king
is represented in three views; Bernini on receiving
the picture, pronounced the physiognomy to be that
of a man doomed to misfortune, iii. 576. Bernini
died 1680.

BEROLD, a butcher of Rouen ; the only person who
escaped from the Blanche-Nef, when prince William
and his sister were drowned, i. 415.

BERRI, the duke of, uncle to Orleans and Burgundy,
1407, endeavours in vain to reconcile those dukes;
takes them together to mass, and to receive the

BERRI, the duke of—
sacrament, ii. 20. But in a few days, Burgundy
causes the murder of Orleans, *ib.* Berri thereupon
joins his influence to the party of Charles of Orleans, and Bernard of Armagnac, 21. He sends the
archbishop of Bourges to Winchester to persuade
Henry V. against invading France, 28. His advice
to the French on the eve of Agincourt, 1415, the
old duke having full recollection of the evil of over-
confidence at Poictiers, 31.

BERTHA, sister or daughter of Charibert, king of Paris,
a Christian princess married to Ethelbert of Kent,
bretwalda of the Saxons, i. 145. Ethelbert and
some of his nobles converted by Augustine, dies in
616, but his son Eadbald and his people then return
to pagan worship, *ib.*

DERTHIER, M. de Sauvigny, executed by the French
Revolutionists, 1789; § ii. 394, 395.

BERTRAM, professor C., of Copenhagen, published in
1757 a MS. of Richard of Cirencester, declared to
be a geographical account of Britain by a Roman
general, i. 76.

Berwick-upon-Tweed, the town and castle taken by
Henry IV., 1405, who puts the governor, a son of
lord Graystock, to death, ii. 17. After many sieges,
the citadel and town were delivered over to the
English, 1482; 115.

BERWICK, James Fitz-James, duke of, natural son of
king James II., created March 19, 1687. Attainted,
1695. Accompanies his father in his departure
from England, iii. 802. Makes an unsuccessful
attack on marshal Schomberg, at Belturbet, iv. 23.
Retires to France in despair, 28. Comes to England
to promote an insurrection, 64. Enters Portugal,
and takes the town of Segura, 174. Gains the victory of Almanza, 202. Takes the command of an
army of 30,000 men, raised by the regent of France,
on the declaration of war by Spain, 355. Invests
Fuenterabia, *ib.* Takes the town and citadel of St.
Sebastian, *ib.* Over-runs Guipuscoa, 356. Enters
Catalonia, and makes an attempt upon Rosas, *ib.*
Is killed by a cannon ball, 1734, before the walls of
Philipsbourg, 414.

BEST, captain, succeeded in obtaining a charter, 1613,
from the Great Mogul, allowing the East India
Company to establish a factory at Surat, iii. 590.

BETHAM, sir William, Irish antiquary, quoted, i. 9, 11,
15, 16, 17, 22, 122.

Beverley, its flourishing condition attributed to the
privilege of paying no toll or custom in any port or
town of England, iii. 656.

BEVERN, prince of, mortally wounded at the battle of
Schellenberg, 1704; iv. 168.

BEWICK, Thomas, an eminent engraver on wood, of
the 18th century, to whom the merit of reviving
that art is due, § i. 633, 634; § iii. 751.

BEZA, Theodore, a divine of great eminence, and one of
the pillars of the church of Geneva, born June 24,
1519. Succeeds Calvin, 1563. Died 1605; iii. 65,
807.

Bible, translations of the, i. 808; ii. 712–716, 739.

Bible Society, British and Foreign, its revenues 1804
and 1820; § iv. 605.

BIDDLE, John, iii. 419, *note*, the father of English
Unitarians, receives a pension from the protector
Cromwell, 424.

BIDLOO, a Dutchman, physician to William III., iv.
137.

BIENFAIT, Richard de, justiciary of England, 1073;
i. 381.

BIGOD, Hugh, steward of Henry the First's household,
i. 421. He revolts and seizes Norwich Castle, 423.

BIGOD, Roger, 1087; i. 394, 409.

Billiards, iii. 641.

BILNEY, a man of learning, 1532, burnt in Smithfield,
for expounding the errors of popery : Henry VIII.

BILNEY—
commences the course of executing both catholics and protestants, under varying accusations, during the fluctuations of religion, ii. 378.

BILSON, Thomas, bishop of Winchester, iii. 64. His son knighted in consequence of his father's easy submission in the case of the divorce of lady Frances Howard, ib. 485. Bilson died 18th June, 1616. ·

BIRD, Francis, executed the monument to Dr. Busby, in Westminster Abbey, iv. 757.

BIRDE, William, a musician, regno Edward VI., iii. 561, 563.

Birmingham, formerly Bremicham, iii. 655.

Bishops, the petitioning, 1688; iii. 789—792. Medal struck in honour of the, 791.

BISSET, William, banished into England, by Alexander II., king of Scotland, it being supposed that he had been concerned in the murder of Patrick, earl of Athole, i. 701. He appeals to the English king Henry to avenge his cause, which afterwards forms a pretext for Henry to declare war with Alexander, ib.

BLACK, John, Scottish preacher, told king James VI. that matters of church ceremony ought to be left in liberty to each man's feeling, iii. 17.

BLACK, Joseph, a celebrated chemist and natural philosopher, discoverer of latent heat, born 1728. Died, December 6, 1799; § i. 623. His discovery of latent heat and fixed air or carbonic acid published 1755; iv. 786.

BLACKADDER, captain. This adherent of Bothwell, with four others, was executed for the murder of Darnley, June 1567; ii. 603.

Blackburn, iii. 666.

BLACKBURNE, Francis, a divine of the church of England, eminent for his theological writings, was born in 1705. He was distinguished as an extreme partisan of low church doctrine and politics, § i. 513. Collated to the archdeaconry of Cleveland, in 1750. Portrait of, 514. His confessional, ib. He died, August 7th, 1787.

Blackfriars bridge, view of, in 1839; § iii. 735. The architect of this beautiful bridge was Robert Mylne, who commenced the building in 1760, and completed it in the space of eight years, ib.

BLACKHALL, Dr. Offspring, elected to the see of Exeter, January 23, 1707. Died 1716; iv. 213.

BLACKMORE, sir Richard, a voluminous but commonplace poet; Pope assigns him the first place among the contending "brayers," at the games instituted by the goddess of the Dunciad, iv. 798.

BLACKSTONE, sir William, a celebrated English lawyer, and the most popular writer on the laws and constitution of his country, was born 1723, and died February 17, 1780. His summary of the provisions of the writ of Habeas Corpus, iii. 835. Quoted, i. 806, 810; iii. 844. His opinion on the case of John Wilkes, 1769; § i. 67, note. First volume of his Commentaries published 1765; 543.

BLACKWALL, styled the arch-priest, aged 70. reads to his congregation Paul V.'s breve forbidding to take the new oath of allegiance, iii. 33. Sent to jail, 1606, where, in six years, he dies, ib.

BLAKE, admiral, iii. 316, 414, 420. His death, 1657; 424.

BLAKENEY, general; he defends Stirling Castle, 1746, against the Young Pretender, iv. 521. Is besieged in Fort St. Philip by the French, and expects the assistance of admiral Byng, but being deceived in this he is forced to capitulate on honourable terms, 587. The king, however, is so well satisfied with his conduct, that he makes him an Irish lord, ib. note.

Bleaching, process of, § iii. 710. Introduction of chloride of lime or bleaching powder in the last

Bleaching—
years of the 18th century, by Mr. Tennant, of Glasgow, ib.

Blenheim, battle of, August 13, 1704; iv. 170-173. Blenheim House, view of, iv. 177, 747.

BLIGH, first points out the advantage of growing clover for cattle, in 1652; iii. 557.

BLINKHORNE, joins in a conspiracy headed by Waller, the poet, 1643, to deliver up London to Charles I., iii. 302.

BLOIS, Charles de, his claim to the duchy of Brittany, 1341, supported by the French king, i. 760. He is taken prisoner, and sent to London, where he is confined in the Tower, 769.

BLOIS, Henry de, cardinal, abbot of Glastonbury, brother to king Stephen. Consecrated to the see of Winchester 17th November, 1129. He founded the monasteries of St. Cross and Romsey. Died August 6, 1171; i. 615.

BLOIS, Peter of, his mission to Louis VII. 1175; i. 472. His character of Henry II., in a letter addressed to the archbishop of Palermo, 480. His character of Longchamp, 506. His valuable narrative of the foundation of the University of Cambridge, i. 606, 644.

BLONDEAU, Peter, a French artist, offers his services to the committee of state for the mint, in 1649; iii. 556.

Blood, circulation of the, discovered by Harvey, 1615; iv. 769.

BLOOD, colonel; he seizes the duke of Ormond, 1673, with intent to hang him at Tyburn, but an alarm being given makes off, firing a pistol at the duke, iii. 708. Next year he attempts to steal the crown, ib. The king pardons him, and grants him an estate in Ireland. worth 500l. a year, 709, and he becomes a royal favourite, 709, 777.

BLOUNT, sir Christopher, a catholic, married to Essex's mother, the countess dowager of Leicester, ii. 688, n. His step-son's rash insurrection, 1601, entailed the ruin of Blount, 684, 686. He was wounded, and made prisoner in London, defending the earl, 686. Beheaded on Tower Hill, March 1601. He exhibited firmness and constancy, 689.

BLOUNT, sir Thomas, sir Bennet Sely, Ferriby and Mandelein priests, executed 1401-2, for participation in the plot of the discontented peers to murder Henry IV. and his sons at a tournament at Oxford, ii. 7.

BLOUNT, sir Walter, accoutred in the armour with the device of Henry IV., who himself fought in private armour, was slain, 1403, at Shrewsbury, ii. 15.

BLUCHER, Gebharal Lebrecht von, an eminent Prussian general, born 1742. Distinguished himself by his successful retreat through Lubec, after the battle of Jena ; he takes the command of the Prussian army, 1813, and acts with great bravery at Lutzen, § iv. 591. Defeats marshal Macdonald at Katzbach, 593*, and enters Paris with the allied army, March 31, 1814; 615*. After the return of Napoleon from Elba, in 1815, he is again appointed to command the Prussian army ; on the 16th of June, after a day of severe fighting, is compelled to abandon his position at Sombref, and retire to Wavre, 633*. On the evening of the 18th he arrived on the field of Waterloo, and immediately commenced a hot pursuit, 637*. He died at Kriblowitz, September 12, 1819.

Blue-stocking clubs, origin of, § i. 648.

BOADICEA, widow of king Prasutagus, A.D. 59—61, resists the Romans, i. 43. Is scourged by Catus, and her daughters violated, ib. This queen of the Iceni, with the Trinobantes and other tribes, upon the destruction of the Druids of Mona and their grove, joins in a great insurrection, ib. They destroy Camalodunum and Verulamium, and expel the inha-

BOADICEA—
bitants of London with great slaughter, *ib*. Boadicea animates the Britons and fiercely assails Suetonius
in the field, but is totally defeated, 44. She poisons
herself, and the Romans massacre 80,000 of the
midland tribes, *ib*.
Board of Trade, William III. opposes a bill in Parliament to remodel the, iv. 62.
Bocland, i. 248.
BOETHIUS *de Consolatione Philosophiæ*, extracts from
king Alfred's version, into Anglo-Saxon, of this
work, which he admired, i. 296, 301, 302.
BOHADIN, the Arabian historian, quoted, i. 500.
BOHEMIA, John de Luxembourg, king of, killed at the
battle of Crecy, 1346; i. 768.
BOHUN, Eleanor, duchess of Gloucester, died 1399; in-
laid brass monument of, ii. 232.
BOLEYN, Mary, a daughter of sir Thomas Boleyn,
report of her having been mistress to king Henry,
previous to his courtship of her sister Anne, ii. 364,
note, 395.
BOLEYN, sir Thomas, created viscount Rochford, 1525,
father of queen Anne, ii. 363, 364, 368. Also earl
of Wiltshire, 374–376. *See* Rochford, and Wiltshire.
BOLINGBROKE, Paulet St. John, lord, votes against the
National Debt system, 1696; iv. 74.
BOLINGBROKE, Henry St. John, viscount, made secretary-at-war, iv. 160. Is deprived of office and succeeded by Mr. Robert Walpole, 216. Is raised to the
peerage by the title of baron St. John and viscount
Bolingbroke, 1712; 268. Sent in company with
Matthew Prior, as ambassador to Paris, to conclude
the peace begun to be negotiated at Utrecht, 269.
Dismissed from his office of secretary of state by
George I., 305. He flies to Calais, 307. Pledges
himself to the duke of Berwick to assist the Pretender, 310. The Pretender dismisses him from his
service, 327. Walpole gets his pardon passed under
the great seal, 1725; 382. He is put in possession of
his forfeited estates, 386. He returns to England
and fixes his residence at the family seat near Battersea, having broken up his connexion with the cause
of the Stuarts, 465. He dies at Battersea of a cancer
in the heart, 1751; 568. His portrait, 558, 797.
BOLINGBROKE, Henry of—*see* Henry IV.
BOLINGBROKE, Roger, a learned astronomer, with which
science astrology was interwoven in the middle ages,
ii. 83. Accused of conspiring to waste the king's
strength (Henry VI.), by necromancy, and with
counselling Eleanor duchess of Gloucester, 1441; *ib*.
He was drawn and quartered at Tyburn, *ib*.
Bombay, island, obtained by Charles II., 1663, as a
part of the dower of his wife the Infanta of Portugal,
and by him ceded to the East India Company, 1668;
§ ii. 19. View of, 20.
BONAPARTE, Jerome, brother of the illustrious Napoleon,
crowned king of Westphalia, 1807; § iv. 297.
BONAPARTE, Joseph, enters Naples and is crowned king,
February 15, 1806; § iv. 223, 224. His portrait, 326.
He is appointed by his brother to the throne of Spain
and the Indies, and resigns his kingdom of Naples,
July 7, 1808; 314. Spanish affairs, 314, *et seq.* Lord
Wellesley enters Madrid, 1812; 510: but soon after
retires to the frontiers of Portugal, 513—517. In
the spring of the following year, Wellesley again
enters Spain, and king Joseph takes his final departure from Madrid, 569. Battle of Vittoria, June 21,
1813. The united army under the command of king
Joseph and marshal Jourdan is defeated and entirely
dispersed, 570, 571. Narrow escape of king Joseph
from the city of Vittoria, *ib*.
BONAPARTE, Lucien, renders signal services to his
brother Napoleon, § iv. 28. He is appointed plenipotentiary at the court of Madrid, *ib*. His portrait,
29, 462.

BONAPARTE, Louis, brother of the great Napoleon, proclaimed king of Holland, June 5th, 1806; § iv. 240.
His portrait, *ib*. He resigns his crown and retires to
Bohemia, July 1, 1810; 462, 463.
BONAPARTE, Napoleon, present in an attack on La Ma-
dalena, January 22, 1793; § iii. 301. His portrait,
305. His skilful plan for forcing the English to
evacuate Toulon, *ib*. His Jacobinism, *ib*. He is
raised to the rank of brigadier-general of artillery,
410. Defends the Convention against the Parisian
mob in the émeute of October 5, 1795; 498. His
marriage with madame Josephine Beauharnais, 1796;
511. Is appointed to the command of the army of
Italy, 512. Gains the battle of Lodi, May 10; *ib*.
Gives orders to stop the insurrection of the city of
Pavia by massacre and plunder, 513. Sustains a
dreadful repulse from general Alvinzi at the bridge
of Arcole, 514. His hatred of the English and their
institutions, 525. Famous expedition to Egypt, 1798,
Battle of the Pyramids, 541. He takes Gaza with
10,000 men ; storms Jaffa, and massacres all the prisoners in cold blood, 547. After spending sixty
days before Acre, he is obliged to raise the siege,
and commences his retreat, May 21, 1799, burning
every thing behind him, *ib*. He re-enters Cairo,
June 14, *ib*. Gains the battle of Aboukir over the
Turks, July 25; 548. Returns to France, 549. Is
elected First Consul, *ib*. Writes to the king of England expressing a wish for peace, *ib*. His passage
over the Alps, 1800; 556. Makes a triumphant entry
into Paris, July 3; 557. The treaty of Amiens is
signed, by which England recognises the French
republic, and treats with Bonaparte as First Consul,
March 27, 1802; § iv. 3, 4. Bonaparte obtains the title
of President of the Cisalpine Republic, Jan. 26; 5 :
and procures the accession of Louisiana and Parma,
7. He abolishes the odious system of taxation,
and introduces order, thus causing national confidence to be restored ; from this time money was no
longer wanting for any of the necessary expenses
of the state, 16. Christianity protected in France
by order of the First Consul, 17. He removes from
the Luxembourg to the palace of the Tuileries, where
he holds splendid reviews and balls, and introduces
all the customs and amusements of the ancient kings,
18. The secret police re-organized, 20. Pope Pius
VII. sends Consalvi, the cardinal secretary of state,
and archbishop Spina, to Paris, to negotiate with
Bonaparte respecting the conditions and concessions requisite for the establishment of Roman
catholicism in France, 22, 23. It is proclaimed by
government the national religion. 23. General discontent excited in England by the proceedings of the
French government since the peace of Amiens, 43—70.
Recall of lord Whitworth, the English ambassador
at Paris. Declaration of war, 70. The English
seize all the ships of France and detain the people
on board as prisoners of war, *ib*. Bonaparte, in
return, seizes all the English subjects in France,
and treats them as prisoners, *ib*. He possesses himself of Hanover, and compels the Hamburghers and
others to close the Elbe and the Weser against the
trade of England, 71, 72. The duke d'Enghien,
grandson of the prince of Condé, enters France and
endeavours to raise disturbances. He is seized, and
shot, by order of Bonaparte, contrary to the treaty
of Baden, 1804; 109—117. Pichegru found strangled
in the prison of the Temple, April 6, 1804; 108—123.
Moreau is tried, found guilty, pardoned, and exiled,
122—129. The Imperial dignity is offered to Bonaparte by the people, and seconded by the municipality of Paris and the Tribunate, 130—134. The
haughty bearing of the First Consul, and the violation of the treaty of Baden, give umbrage to Russia
and Sweden, 136. Bonaparte sends his aide-de-

BONAPARTE, Napoleon—
camp, Caffarelli, to Rome, to engage the pope to come in person to Paris and crown him as emperor in Notre Dame, 137. Description of the emperor's coronation, December 2, 1804; 139—141. Creation of nobility, 141. The emperors of Russia and Austria unite with England in the war with France, 165. Napoleon is crowned king of Italy, at Milan, May 26, 1805; 166. Genoa is annexed to the French empire, June 4; 167. The French defeat the Austrians at Elsingen, and another army of 40,000 men surrender at Ulm, October 19; 172. The French army enters Vienna, and the emperor of Austria retreats to Moravia ; the Austrians are every where unsuccessful, 174, 175. A powerful Russian army comes to their assistance, but the emperor of France gains a complete victory over the armies of the allies at Austerlitz, December 2; 177, 178. The emperor of Austria sues for peace and signs a most humiliating treaty, December 26; 180. The attack of the French fleet on Dominica is unsuccessful, and it returns to Cadiz having lost two ships in the action with sir R. Calder, 181—186. The English gain a decisive victory off Cape Trafalgar, October 21, 1805; 188—195. The British and Russian forces having violated the kingdom of Naples, the French take possession of the country, and Joseph Bonaparte is crowned king, 223, 224. The Gregorian calendar restored by law in France, 236. Bonaparte bestows honours and rewards on his generals and favourites, 239. War with Prussia, 240. The French arms every where victorious, 241—250. Bonaparte gains a signal victory over the Russians and Prussians at Pultusk, December 26; 250, 251. Battle of Eylau, 291—293. Surrender of Dantzic, May 27, 1807. The battle of Friedland gained by the French, June 14; 295. Armistice between Russia and France at Tilsit, June 21; 296. Interview between Napoleon and Alexander on a raft in the river Niemen, followed by the treaty of Tilsit, June 25; ib. Jerome Bonaparte crowned king of Westphalia, 297. The French enter Portugal, 299. They take possession of Rome and the Papal States, 300, 301. Charles IV. of Spain resigns his crown into the hands of Napoleon, who appoints his brother Joseph king, July 7, 1808; 314. The French troops employed in the subjugation of Spain and Portugal, 314—334. Murat is appointed king of Naples, on the accession of Joseph Bonaparte to the Spanish throne, July 15; 314. Sir Arthur Wellesley arrives with a body of British troops in Portugal, August 1; 335. The English gain the battle of Vimiero, and the French evacuate Portugal, August 31; 338—342. Battle of Talavera gained by the British, July 27, 1809; 379–381. They retire to Portugal, 381—385. Take Flushing, Aug. 16; 390, 391. Napoleon gains the battle of Eckmuhl and enters Vienna, May 13, 1809; 410. Battle of Aspern; the French retire to the isle of Lobau, 411. Napoleon is joined by the corps of marshals Davoust and Eugene Beauharnais, 412. And again crossing the Danube gains the decisive battle of Wagram, July 6; 412, 413. Which is followed by the opprobrious peace of Schönbrunn, October 14, 414—417. Pope Pius VII. is taken prisoner and conveyed to Savona, July 5, 1809, and the Papal States united to the French empire, 416, 417. Bonaparte despatches marshal Massena with strong reinforcements to take the command of the army in Spain, and reduce Portugal, 441. Surrender of Ciudad Rodrigo, ib. Battle of Busaco, September 27; 444–446. Description of the lines of Torres Vedras, 448—451. The isles of Bourbon and France surrender to the English, and France is deprived of all her possessions in the East and West Indies, 457. Napoleon's divorce of the empress Josephine and marriage with the Austrian princess Maria Louisa, March 1810; 417, 436, 458—

BONAPARTE, Napoleon—
461. The kingdom of Holland united to the French empire, 463. The year 1810 is considered the meridian splendour of the French empire, when its emperor gave law to 80,000,000 of people ; after which its final downfall fast approached, 464. Badajoz surrenders to marshal Soult, March 1811; 481. Massena defeated by lord Wellesley at Fuentes de Onoro, May 5; 484, 485. Massena is recalled, 486. Battle of Albuera, May 16; 487, 488. Birth of Napoleon, the emperor's son, March 20; 492. Events in the interior of France, 492-496. Dispute with the emperor of Russia, and preparations for the Russian campaign, 495. Ciudad Rodrigo and Badajoz surrender to the English, 503–505. Battle of Salamanca, July 22, 1812 ; lord Wellesley enters Madrid, August 12; 510. Napoleon having collected a vast army of above 400,000 men, crosses the Niemen and invades the Russian dominions, June 24, 1812; 564. The Russians gradually retreat, 564, 565. But some partial engagements are fought at Mohiloff and Witepsk, 566. The bloody battle of Borodino fought; the French enter Moscow, Sept. 14; 566. The city takes fire and is almost reduced to ashes ; the *Grande Armée* begins its retreat, October 19; 567. The sufferings endured by the French army during the retreat were extreme; only 12,000 men of this once vast and invincible army reached Lithuania, 157,000 having perished, and 193,000 being taken prisoners, ib. Having accompanied the remains of his army back to Poland. Napoleon sets off to Paris, December 18; ib. The French suffer a complete defeat at Vittoria, June 21, 1813; 570. King Joseph takes refuge in Pamplona, which is shortly after invested by the Allies, 573. The emperor sends marshal Soult to take the command of the French army, 575. The French army suffers severely in its attempts to relieve Pamplona, and in the battles of the Pyrenees, 576–579. Marshal Soult retires to his entrenched camp at Bayonne, November 10, and lord Wellington enters France, 583, 584. Disastrous state of affairs in France, 588, 589. A proposition for peace is refused by the emperor Napoleon, 591. Prussia joins the emperor Alexander ; Berlin and Dresden evacuated by the French, ib. Prince Eugene Beauharnais checks the advance of the Allies, ib. Battles of Lutzen and Bautzen gained by Napoleon, May 1813; ib. The Allies withdraw from Leipzig and Dresden, 592. A general armistice agreed upon, June 5; ib. England joins the coalition with Russia and Prussia, June 14; ib. Austria remains neutral, and prince Metternich endeavours to mediate a general peace, ib. The armistice expires, August 10, and Austria joins the coalition, 593*. Bernadotte takes the field, and co-operates with the Allies, ib. Napoleon gains many advantages over the Austrians and Prussians at Dresden, ib. Battle of Leipzig, October 16 and 18, in which the French army is entirely defeated, 593*, 594*. Bonaparte retires with the remainder of his army across the Rhine, and repairs to Paris, 594*. Disputes with the legislative assembly; they are dismissed, 596*. General discontent prevails throughout the south of France, and Holland revolts, 597*. Soult is defeated at Orthes and Toulouse, which lord Wellington enters on the 12th of April, 1814; 604*-608*. Whilst these events were passing in the south, the allied army advanced to the frontiers of France, 610*. Napoleon dreading the consequences of an appeal to the people and levy *en masse* fails in procuring a sufficient force, 611*. Murat joins the Allies and defeats Eugene Beauharnais in Italy, 610*. Blucher defeated at Brienne, January 29; 614*. Napoleon suffers a defeat at La Rothière after a long and hotly contested battle, February 1; ib. He gains some advantages over the Austrians

E

BONAPARTE, Napoleon—
and Prussians at Montereau and Nangis, but the army of the Allies unites and marches on Paris, 614°, which they enter after a slight resistance offered by marshal Marmont, March 31; 615°. The allied sovereigns concert measures with M. de Talleyrand, for the immediate restoration of the Bourbons, 615°. The municipality of Paris, the French senate, and the *Corps Legislatif*, concur in the views of M. de Talleyrand, and pass a decree announcing that Napolean Bonaparte, in consequence of sundry arbitrary acts and violations of the *Constitution*, and by his refusing to treat with the Allies upon honourable conditions, had forfeited the throne and the right of inheritance established in his family; and that the people and the army of France were freed from their oaths of allegiance to him, 616°. The marshals of France announce to Bonaparte that it is the desire of the army that he should resign, *ib.* Napoleon signs a formal abdication at Fontainebleau, renouncing entirely, for himself and his heirs, the thrones of France and Italy, on condition that he should be permitted to retain the title of Emperor, with the sovereignty of the island of Elba, and a revenue of 6,000,000 francs, to be paid by France, Apr. 11, 1814; 617°. His journey to Elba; he embarks on board an English man-of-war, and lands at Porto-Farrajo, the capital of his new empire, May 5; *ib.* Louis XVIII. enters Paris; and a general peace is signed with the allied powers of Europe, 618°. Napoleon embarks for France with about 1000 followers and lands at Cannes, March 1, 1815; 628°. He proceeds to Dauphiny, where the people flock round his standard, and in all directions the troops sent to oppose him raise the cry of "Vive l' Empereur !" and join his standard, 629°. On the night of the 20th he arrives in Paris and enters the palace of the Tuileries, *ib.* He grants a constitution, and opens the two new chambers, 630°. Napoleon crosses the Belgian frontier with an army of about 125,000 men, and immediately commences active operations, June 14; the forces under Wellington at this time amounted to about 76,000 men, and those under Blucher to about 80,000; 631°. Napoleon compels the Prussians to retreat from Sombref and retire on WAVRE, but Ney is repulsed in his attempts to drive the English from Quatre Bras, June 16; 633°. Decisive battle of Waterloo fought June 18, 1815; 635°-637°. Bonaparte sets off to Paris, where he meets with great opposition from the Chambers, and signs his second abdication, June 22; 639°. Advance of the allied armies on Paris, 640°; which is entered, July 7; 642°. Louis XVIII. resumes the government of France, and Napoleon goes on board the Bellerophon at Rochefort, July 15; 642°, 643°. On the 31st he receives intelligence of the determination of the English government that he should be kept at St. Helena, 644°. He strongly protests against leaving England, but on the 7th of August quits the Bellerophon and goes on board the Northumberland, under sir George Cockburn, which had been appointed to convey him to St. Helena, 646°. His death, May 6th, 1821; 650°.
BONAPARTE, Napoleon Francis Charles Joseph, son of the emperor Napoleon, prince of the French Empire and king of Rome, born March 20, 1811; § iv. 492.
BONIFACE VIII., pope (Benedict Gaetano), elected December 24, 1294. Lays claim to the kingdom of Scotland as belonging of right to the Holy See. Died October 11, 1303; i. 719, 724.
BONNER, Edmund, his mission to Marseilles, 1533; his appeal, in the name of Henry VIII., from the pope to a general council, put an end to the conference then holding at Marseilles, ii. 382. Elected to the see of London, October 20, 1539. In obedience to a proclamation issued by Henry, Bonner, 1541, orders

BONNER, Edmund—
six great Bibles to be set up in different places of his cathedral of St. Paul's, with an admonition that they should be read quietly, suspended upon each of the pillars to which the books were chained, 715. He stands out against the new regulations made by Cranmer for the furthering of the Reformation, and is sent to the Fleet, 466. He is summoned before the council, 1549, reprimanded for his contumacy, and directed to preach at Paul's Cross to give proof of his orthodoxy; his sermon does not give satisfaction; sentence of deprivation is passed against him, Sept.1549, and he is consigned to the Marshalsea, where he remains a prisoner throughout the remainder of Edward's reign, 493. He is liberated by queen Mary on her entrance into London, 1553; 505. Gardiner growing weary of the persecution, his duties devolve on the sanguinary Bonner, who executes them with the utmost ferocity, 524. Not graciously received by Elizabeth on her accession, the sovereign recalling to mind his past severities, 539. Deprived again, May 30, 1559. Died September 5, 1569.
BONNIVET, admiral de, led the French royal army across the Alps into Italy, 1523, Francis I. giving up his design of leading them in person, and stopping at Lyons because of the treaty of Charles of Bourbon with the emperor, &c., ii. 356. His failure, 1524, before Milan, 358.
BONVILE, lord, 1454; ii. 92. Made prisoner by the Lancastrians, 1461, at Barnet, and beheaded, 97.
BOOTH, Sir George, royalist insurrection headed by, 1659; iii. 431, §18.
Boots, the, an instrument of torture, invented by archbishop Sharp, 1667; iii. 701.
Bordeaux, city of, the Bordelais sorry to hear of the deposition of Richard II., prefer to obey Henry IV. rather than submit to the heavy yoke of the French princes, 1401; ii. 8. Bordeaux attacked, 1451, by D'Orval; the citizens and garrison made a vigorous sortie, with severe loss, 85. Articles that if not relieved by a fixed day, 1451, the city should surrender, *ib.* Its fall, *ib.* In 1453, Talbot is invited by the nobles and citizens; he crossed over with a small well-equipped army, 91. The great English captain, and his son defending him, were slain by very superior forces at Châtillon, *ib.* One thousand English made prisoners there in the French intrenchments, which they had carried, *ib.* The small remaining garrison allowed to quit Bordeaux freely, *ib.* All Bordelais disinclined to French rule permitted to depart with the English, *ib.* So many availed themselves of the offer, that it was long before the city regained its population and commerce, *ib.*
Borderers, the, iii. 648.
BORN, Bertrand de, lord of Hautefort, a bard as well as a warrior; principal exciter of the revolts of the children of Henry II. He excelled in insinuation, elegance, and address, in versatility of talent and abundance of resource. His history, i. 471-475. He is taken prisoner by king Henry, but is pardoned, 475. He assists the French king against Richard, 513.
Borodino, battle of, 1812; § iv. 566.
BOSCAWEN, Edward, an excellent British admiral, born 1711. His service in India, 1747; § ii. 25. He is sent to the Gulf of St. Lawrence, 1755, to intercept a French fleet which was carrying reinforcements to the French Canadians, iv. 581. He gains a victory over M. de la Clue, commander of the Toulon fleet, off Cape Lagos, 606. Died 1761.
BOSCAWEN, Mr., advocates, 1681, the printing of the votes of the House of Commons, iii. 344.
Bosham, Harold's journey to, i. 197. Entering Bosham Church, *ib.*
BOSSUET, bishop of Meaux, James II. submits his declaration of 1693 to him as a case of conscience, iv. 63.

Boston, view of, § i. 42, 184, 185.

Boston Port bill, the, passed March, 1774; § i. 159-182.

Bosworth Field, king Richard III. slain in this battle, 1485; ii. 129.

Botanical garden at Oxford founded in 1632 by Henry Danvers, earl of Danby, iv. 787.

Bothwell Bridge, iii. 828, battle of, 1679; 730.

BOTHWELL, Ramsay, lord, favourite of James III., ii. 304. His agreement with Henry VII., for money, to seize James IV. and his brother, and deliver them up to him, ib. He was slain at Flodden in defence of his sovereign, 329.

BOTHWELL, James Hepburn, earl of, appointed by Mary of Guise a commissioner for settling border disputes, ii. 552. He sets upon the laird of Ormeston, 1559, who was carrying money from Berwick to Edinburgh, and plunders him; upon this the earl of Arran goes in force to seize him, but he being gone, Arran threatens to burn his house, and declares him a traitor, unless he return the money, 558. He is recalled to court, but Murray insisting on his trial, he flies to France a second time, where he remains till Murray's disgrace, when he is invited back by Mary, who gives him the command of all the Scottish marches, 586. During the murder of Rizzio, he in conjunction with the Earl of Huntley collects troops for the service of the queen, 588. He is wounded at Hermitage castle by an outlaw named Eliott of Park, 593. Mary goes to visit him, ib. He is suspected of a design against Darnley's life, 595. He told Melville (an English resident there), after the death of Darnley, that he saw the thunder come out of the sky, and burn the king's house, 596. Being generally accused of the murder of the king, he is brought to trial before the Justiciary Court, but in so hurried a manner that no prosecutor had time to appear, and no evidence against him being produced, he is acquitted, 597. Immediately after the rising of parliament he invites the members to a dinner, declares to them his purpose of marrying the queen, and procures them to sign a bond exculpating him from the late murder, and recommending the match, 598. Shortly after he forcibly seized Mary and carried her off to Dunbar castle, where he kept her five days, ib. A few days after the queen appears in the Court of Session, and informs them that she thinks it expedient to marry Bothwell, who is created duke of Orkney, and then married to her at Holyrood-house, 599. Strange divorce of Bothwell's former wife, ib. He leaves the queen in the midst of her danger at Carberry Hill, 1567; 601. The Privy Council after Mary's capture there offer a reward for his seizure; he seeks shelter in his dukedom of Orkney, but is denied admittance by his own keeper; he then threatens to scour the seas with a blood-red flag; the lords on this despatch a small fleet after him, but he flies to the coast of Norway, where he is seized by the Danish government as a pirate, and thrown into the castle of Malmoe, where he is said to have gone mad, and where he died about ten years after, 602, 603.

BOUCICAULT, marshal, the counts of Richemont, Eu, and Vendôme, the sires de Harcourt and Craon, among the noble prisoners taken, 1415, at Agincourt, ii. 33.

BOUFFLERS, marshal, iv. 33, 56; after a brave defence of Namur he capitulates, 1695; 58, 77, 78.

BOUGHTON, Joan, the first English female martyr, suffered 1494; ii. 698.

BOUILLÉ, marquess de. Tobago capitulates to, 1781; § i. 470: he becomes governor of Metz on his return from the American war; quells the insurrection at Nancy, 1790, and receives a vote of thanks from the Assembly for his promptitude, 513-516. He at-

BOUILLÉ, marquess de—tempts to co-operate with a large force in the king's flight to Varennes, 1791, but from some mismanagement in being too late, and finding the royal party recaptured, he addresses a letter to the National Assembly, menacing them with summary vengeance should any attempt be made on the life of the unfortunate Louis; for this threat he is sentenced to death par contumacy, 638-657. He enters the service of the Swedish king Gustavus, § iii. 48.

Boulogne, Henry VII., landing at Calais with a good army, invested Boulogne, 1492; ii. 298. Henry VIII. with a large army besieged the town, 1544; after two months it capitulated, and the English king made a triumphant entry, and having garrisoned the town, he burned down the church of Notre Dame, and returned to England much impoverished, 439.

BOULOGNE, Reynaud, earl of, with other barons determines, 1214, on the conquest of France, i. 526.

BOULTON, Matthew, born at Birmingham in 1728. Portrait of, § i. 580. He established the celebrated Soho works about 1762, and in 1774 the new steam-engine was there exhibited, 580, 587. This talented engineer raised the operation of coining to an almost perfect state of excellence, § iii. 687.

BOURBON, John, duke of, commander of a royal army of France, defeated and mortally wounded by the "Free Companions," 1364; i. 776.

BOURBON, duke of, his manifestos, 1400, on marching against the English in the south of France, ii. 8, 21. Present at the battle of Agincourt, 1415; 30. Is made prisoner, 33.

BOURBON, duke of, 1435, at the congress of Arras, ii. 78.

BOURBON, John, duke of, 1475; ii. 112.

BOURBON, Pierre de, lord of Beaujeu, ii. 292. His wife Anne dame de Beaujeu, daughter of Louis XI., ib. Charles VIII., 1483, fourteen years of age, placed by Louis under Madame Anne's tutelage, 292, 293, note.

BOURBON, Charles, duke of, constable of France, his dignity and great qualities, 1523; his loyalty to Francis I. long undisputed, ii. 356. Louisa of Savoy, mother of the French king, proposed that this prince should marry her, which Bourbon refused, ib. The king therefore heaped insults upon him, deprived him of his bâton of office, and caused a slavish parliament to sequestrate his fiefs, ib. Bourbon then treated with the emperor and with Henry VIII., ib. Articles of their convention against Francis, ib. The French king presented himself at the castle of his late constable, commanding him to join his army of Italy, ib. Bourbon escaped and joined an army of Charles V., ib. Failure of the common enterprise against France, ib. The emperor appointed Bourbon his lieutenant in Italy, in conjunction with Pescara, 1524; 358. They besieged Marseilles, and were forced to retreat, ib. Francis I. suddenly invading Lombardy, they reached Milan, reinforced the citadel, and retired to Lodi, ib. Bourbon pawned his jewels, raised 6000 men in Germany, and rejoined Pescara and Lannoy in Italy, 359. Defeat and capture of Francis I., 1525, at Pavia, ib. The constable's speech to his captive monarch, who betokened his anger and disgust, ib. The emperor, too poor to keep a disciplined army in Italy, employed partisan bands accustomed to live by plunder, 363. Their chiefs, Freundsberg and Bourbon, menaced Florence; and compelled to retire, they learn of the treaty betwixt Clement VII. and Lannoy, ib. Nevertheless Bourbon decided on plundering Rome to pay his forces, ib. May 6, 1527, the constable commenced the assault of the Christian capital, and was slain whilst mounting a scaling ladder, ib. Horrors of the sack of Rome depicted, ib.

BOURBON, James of, count of La Marche, 1405; ii. 18.

BOURBON, the cardinal of, 1475, brother of John ii. 112,

BOURCHER, Joan, condemned, 1546, for introducing heretical books at the court of Catherine Parr, ii. 448. She was not burnt till the reign of Edward VI., 448, 492. In 1550, Edward pathetically interceded with Cranmer to save her life, but in vain, she was consigned to the flames, 492.

BOURCHIER, Sir John, 1485; ii. 286.

BOURCHIER, cardinal Thomas, 1454, archbishop of Canterbury, and lord chancellor, ii. 147. He cites Reginald Peacock, bishop of Chichester, to answer certain charges of heresy, and Peacock after abjuration is imprisoned until his death, 147, 282. Bourchier dies, 1486; 700.

BOURGES, archbishop of, 1415, his conference with Henry V. at Winchester, ii. 28.

BOURNONVILLE, duke of, minister of Philip V. of Spain, 1726; iv. 391.

BOURNONVILLE, de, 1414, defends Soissons for the duke of Burgundy, ii. 27. Some English auxiliaries betray a gate to the Armagnacs, and the city is pillaged. Charles VI. being then with the royalist army, commands his execution, together with other knights, and many citizens, ib.

Bouvines, battle of, July 17, 1214; i. 526.

BOVES, Hugh de, head of a band of marauders, sent for by John after signing Magna Charta; he perished in a tempest, 1215, on his way from Calais to Dover, i. 530.

BOWLES, sir John, 1701, proposes Sophia, the Electress Dowager of Brunswick, as successor to William III., iv. 126.

Boxing, iv. 828.

BOYCE, William, an eminent musical composer of the 18th century; he died in 1779, at the age of sixty-eight, iii. 561.

BOYDELL, John, an English engraver, but more distinguished as an encourager of the fine arts, than on account of his own productions, born 1719. He engaged the first artists in the kingdom to furnish the pictures constituting the well-known Shakspeare gallery, but owing to reverses arising out of the French Revolution, he was obliged to solicit an act of parliament to permit him to dispose of that valuable collection by lottery; he died of inflammation of the lungs, December 1804; § iii. 741.

BOYLE, Mr. Henry, succeeds Robert Harley, 1708, as secretary of state, iv. 216.

BOYLE, Hon. Robert, born 1627; made considerable improvements in the air-pump; died 1691; iv. 779.

Boyne, battle of the, fought July 1, 1690; iv. 24–26.

BRABANT, Anthony, duke of, 1415, arriving at Agincourt, when the French had already suffered severe loss, heads a fresh charge, and is slain, ii. 32. His funeral rites, 34. His widow, Elizabeth of Luxembourg, remarried with John the Merciless, 57.

BRABANT, John, duke of, son of Anthony, an ungainly youth, married against her wish, but by dint of family persuasions, Jacqueline of Hainault and Holland, ii. 57. His low favourites, and savage conduct to Jacqueline, ib. She escaped from him, and lived at Windsor, ib. Obtaining a dispensation, she remarried with Humphrey of Gloucester, ib. Gloucester and his duchess seize all Hainault, 58. Brabant died, 1427; 59.

BRABANT, duke of, brother of the preceding, ii. 59.

BRACKENBURY, sir Robert, governor of the Tower, refused, 1483, to murder Edward V. and his brother Richard, ii. 125. He then had to give up the command of the Tower, and his keys, for twenty-four hours to sir James Tyrrel, sent by Richard III., ib. Slain at Bosworth Field, 129.

BRACKLEY, Thomas, viscount, lord chancellor, iii. 56, 60. Created baron Ellesmere, 1603, and viscount Brackley, Nov. 1616; 63. His death, March 15, 1617; ib.

BRADDOCK, major-general, defeated and slain, 1755, in an attempt to drive the French from the Ohio, iv. 582.

Bradford, iii. 655.

BRADFORD, Francis Newport, earl of, created May 11, 1694; made treasurer of the household, 1702. Died 1708; iv. 142.

BRADLEY, James, discovers, in 1728, the aberration of light, iv. 784; and in 1747, the nutation of the earth's axis, ib.

BRADSHAW, a brewer, elected for Westminster, iii. 730. He presides at the trial of Charles I., 1649; 390.

BRAGANZA, Catherine of, queen of Charles II. arrives at Portsmouth, May 20, 1661; iii. 685. Her portrait, 686. Titus Oates accuses her of consenting to a plot for murdering the king, 722.

BRAMANTE, Lazarus d'Urbino, a celebrated Italian architect, born 1444; he designed and commenced in 1513 the erection of St. Peter's at Rome; died in 1514; iii. 570.

BRANDENBURG, elector of, makes war with Louis XIV., 1674; iii. 712.

BRANDON, sir Charles, viscount Lisle, and duke of Suffolk. See Suffolk.

BRANDON, sir William, standard-bearer of Richmond at Bosworth, slain by the impetuous Richard III., in his attack on Henry, ii. 129.

Branham Moor, battle of, Feb. 28, 1402, ii. 19.

BRAOUSE, William de, refuses to send his son as security for his allegiance to king John; John gives secret orders to seize the whole family; they escape to Ireland, i. 522.

BREADALBANE, lord, iv. 45; committed to Edinburgh castle, 1695, for the massacre of Glencoe, 53.

BREAKESPEAR, Nicholas. See Adrian IV.

Breda, taken by the Spanish general Spinola, 1625; iii. 106.

Breda, declaration of, delivered to the House of Commons, May 1, 1660; iii. 431*.

BRENNER, sir Nicholas, lord mayor of London, is executed, 1388; i. 792.

BRENTFORD, Patrick Ruthven, earl of, repairs Edinburgh castle, 1639; iii. 207. Is forced to deliver up that fortress to the Covenanters, 1640; 219. Created earl of Brentford, May, 1644. He died, 1651.

Brenville, battle of, fought between Henry I. and king Louis, August 20, 1119; i. 413.

BRERETON, William, gentleman of the Privy Chamber, 1536, implicated in queen Anne Boleyn's presumed guilt, was sent to the Tower with others accused, tried, and beheaded, ii. 391, 392, 394.

Brest, action off, 1512; ii. 322. Sir Edward Howard, lord admiral, slain, 1513, in the harbour, ib. William III. attempts to destroy the arsenals and shipping at, iv. 48.

BRETEUIL, Eustace of, marries Juliana, an illegitimate daughter of Henry I. Inhuman treatment of Breteuil's children by Harenc with the permission of their grandfather, i. 414.

BRETEUIL, William de, treasurer to William Rufus. Attends the king, 1100, hunting in the New Forest, the evening of the death of Rufus, i. 402. Prince Henry and de Breteuil severally ride off in haste for Winchester, the first to seize on his brother's treasure, the latter to secure its safe custody, 404, 405. The royal treasurer boldly declares to Henry that he shall keep the money inviolate for his brother Robert, 405. The prince violently seizes the treasure and crown jewels, ib.

Bretigny, treaty of, 1360; ii. 28, 35, 44, 80.

Bretwalda, or Britwalda, the customary title of the lord paramount in the Heptarchy, having authority over the other Saxon kings, i. 144. Enumeration of the princes who held this title; a distinction that sometimes caused wars to secure it, 145, et seq.

BREWSTER, sir Francis, appointed one of the commissioners, 1699, for taking the account of the Irish forfeited estates, iv. 102.

BRIANT, Alexander, a seminary priest, apprehended, thrown into the Tower, and severely tortured, 1581; iii. 520.

BRICE, St.; on this festival, 13th November, 1002, the English massacre all Danes domiciled throughout the Anglo-Saxon territories (except where the Danes of the Danelagh, &c. formed the stronger population), i. 177. Neither age, sex, nor infancy, were spared, and Gunhilda sister of Sweyn perished, *ib*. The free quarters of their Danish guests everywhere devouring the daily provisions of the Anglo-Saxons, and the unbridled insults to wives and daughters, formed a sufficient apology for these comprehensive murders, no other remedy being available in the reign of the imbecile Ethelred, *ib*. The equally destructive retribution taken by Sweyn of Denmark (1003—1006); 177, 178. Famine ensues upon these dire atrocities, 178.

Bricks, known to the Anglo-Saxons, i. 315.

Bridgeham, treaty of, concluded between Scotland and Edward I., July 18, 1290; i. 707. Baliol releases Edward from this treaty, 1293; 712.

Bridgenorth, castle of, in Shropshire. It was in the siege of this castle that Hubert de St. Clair saved the life of Henry II. by receiving the arrow in his own breast, i. 442.

Bridges, erection of (18th century), § i. 576; § iv. 676—679.

BRIDGEWATER, John Egerton, earl of, created 1686, appointed to the command of the fleet, 1699; iv. 95. He prorogues parliament, 1700, the chancellor Somers being sick, 105. He died 1701.

BRIDGMAN, sir Orlando, iii. 517, 670, 672. Made lord-keeper, 1666; 703–706. Description of, by Roger North, 845.

Brigade, Irish, origin of the, 1691; iv. 34.

BRIGGS, Henry, an English mathematician; he died 1630; iv. 768.

Brighton, formerly Brighthelmsted, iii. 655.

BRIHTRIC, on occasion of a naval armament fitted out by the unhappy Ethelred to resist the Danish invasions, 1008, conspires against earl Wulfnoth, another commander, and with eighty ships pursues Wulfnoth with twenty, i. 179. Brihtric's ships are wrecked; Wulfnoth, who had been marauding on the coasts, as if he were a Dane, burns all the eighty ships; the rest of the king's fleet disperse, *ib*. This disaster induces a new army to land from the Baltic, called Thurkhill's host, *ib*.

BRINDLEY, James, an eminent engineer and mechanic, born in 1716. He effects great saving in the use of fuel for steam-engines, iv. 729. He successfully accomplished the duke of Bridgewater's canal, which was opened in July, 1761; § i. 577: and the Grand Trunk Canal was begun under his superintendence in 1766, although he did not live to see its completion. He died of hectic fever in 1772; 578. Portrait of, *ib*.

BRIOT, Nicholas, about 1628, introduces the process of coining by machinery, instead of the hammer, iii. 564, 578.

BRISSAC, colonel, committed to the state prison of Orleans, 1792, where he was massacred by the mob, in the dreadful month of September, § iii. 80.

BRISSOT, Jean Pierre, draws up a petition at the instance of the Jacobins, demanding the abolition of royalty in France, 1791; § ii. 667. Portrait of, § iii. 248. Head of the Girondists, 1793; 311. He is executed with twenty other leading Girondists, October 31, 1793; 353–357.

Bristol, slave-trade carried on at this sea-port town with Ireland in the eleventh century, i. 270.

BRISTOL, John Digby, earl of, created 1622; iii. 60. Ambassador at the court of Spain, 1623; 93. He is presented by Philip with a handsome set of plate, and an offer of money and honour if he chose to remain in his dominions; confident of a good reception in England he declines the offer, and returns to his country, but is forbidden to visit court, or to take his seat in parliament, *ib*. Explains his conduct at Madrid to several persons, 112. Claims his right to be heard in his defence, 119. Sent to the Tower, 123. Discharged from the Tower, 130. Recommends Charles to conclude a treaty with the Covenanters, 224. He died 1653.

BRISTOL, earl of—*see* Lord G. Digby.

Britain, i. 1, supposed to have been peopled from Celtic and Belgic Gaul, 118. The dialects of the Celts, the Belgæ, and the Britons, had but little difference, *ib*. The giants of Gogmagog, Albion, and Samothes, 3, 118. Trojan followers of Brut or Brutus, 8. Inland inhabitants of South Britain at the Roman invasion were the posterity of an early Celtic colonization, 11. Supposed to have been united to Gaul, *ib*. Derived from Brit, *ib*. Cæsar's two invasions of Cantium, 25–33. Signification of the title Britwalda, a king of one of the Saxon states of Britain, paramount above the other kings in the Heptarchy, 144.

Britannia, its derivation, i. 11.

BRITANNIA, earliest figure of, from a Roman coin, i. 48. On the coinage of Charles II. modelled after the court beauty Miss Stewart, duchess of Richmond, iii. 869.

BRITHNOTH, earl, of Danish descent, slain in battle in East Anglia, 991; the Danes receiving money from Ethelred to quit the kingdom, turn their prows towards the Baltic, i. 176. They carry the head of Brithnoth as a trophy, *ib*.

British Islands, original population and primitive history of the, i. 1, 118.

BRITO, Gulielmus, quoted, i. 641.

BRITO, Richard, one of the conspirators who murdered Becket, December 1170; i. 455, 456.

Britons, the, described as far as the obscurity of their early history permits, until the invasion of Cæsar, i. 1–24, 25. They had been constant allies of Cæsar's enemies, 25. They send an embassy to Cæsar, then in Gaul (A.C. 55), 27. The maritime tribes of Cantium bravely oppose the landing of Cæsar, 28. On their first defeat they give hostages, and conclude a hollow peace with the invader, 29. Witnessing the wreck of the Roman fleet, they resume courage, summon the inland tribes to their aid, form an ambush near the only field of corn still standing, and surround a legion sent to forage, *ib*. Cæsar marches to the succour of his foragers, and with difficulty rescues them, *ib*. They advance in force, horse and foot, to the Roman entrenchments, but are defeated, *ib*. They sue for peace, which Cæsar grants, and he departs for Gaul, hostages being promised, but few sent over to him, 30. In the year A.C. 54, Cæsar again lands without opposition, *ib*. The Britons are unable to maintain their stronghold or entrenched camp in the forests (near Canterbury), *ib*. Cassivellaunus (or Caswallon) elected chief of the confederate British states, 30, 77. Their gallantry in action, and victory, 31. They suffer a total defeat, and the tribes, for want of a sufficient principle of union, are discouraged, and retire to their several provinces, 32, 33. Cassivellaunus in vain opposes the passage of the Thames (at Coway Stakes, Chertsey), *ib*. Defensive war waged by this British commander to protect his own territory, 33. *Verulamium*, supposed to have been the capital of Cassivellaunus; an example of the character of a British town, 33, 77. Comparison with a modern town of Ceylon; also

Britons, the—

the mode of warfare of the Britons and of the Cingalese something similar, 33, 34. War chariots of the Britons, shield and spears, 32, 35, 44. Reflections on the wars between the British tribes and their Roman invaders, 36. Inferior materials of all their weapons, compared with the iron and steel of the Romans, 36, 91. Their cavalry, and infantry, war-chariots, and well-trained horses, 36. Often a foot-soldier accompanied each horseman, ib. Except the Druids, all Britons were trained to arms, ib. Strategy and evolutions, 37. Their cars and waggons employed as barricades both to their camps and on the battle-field, ib. Their chiefs were able to select the best positions, and excelled in all stratagems of war, ib. The constitution of their armies very defective, each clan was commanded by its head or chieftain, ib. All the clans of a state, or tribe, commanded by the native sovereign, ib. When several tribes coalesced, the chief commander was elected by those princes, ib. Jealousies among these often caused each clan to obey, exclusively, its own head, ib. The Roman legions implicitly obeying the recognised general were more manageable and effective, ib. After the departure of the Romans from Britain, the inhabitants were unmolested by foreign arms for nearly one hundred years, in which period they made considerable advances in civilization and the Roman arts, 36. No improvement in the political system of Britain, 39. Second invasion of Britain by the Romans, A.D. 43, under the emperor Claudius, ib. They offer no resistance at first, are defeated in the inland country, under Caractacus and Togodumnus, ib. Camalodunum, the chief city of the Britons, is taken, and Claudius returns to Rome, 40. Plautius recalled to Rome, ib. Ostorius Scapula arrives in Britain, ib. A line of forts erected on the Severn and Nene, ib. All Britons, south of the Tyne, submits to the Romans, ib. The Iceni take up arms, ib. Are defeated by Ostorius after a fierce engagement, ib. The Brigantes take up arms, but are defeated, 41. Ostorius marches against the Silures, they retire into the country of the Ordovices, ib. Their firm resistance; are at last vanquished, ib. Caractacus is taken prisoner, and conveyed to Rome, 42. The Silures gain a complete victory over the Romans; the prefect, with eight centurions and many soldiers, is slain, ib. Another advantage gained by the Britons, ib. Ostorius the Roman commander in Britain dies, ib. The Silures were first vanquished in the reign of Vespasian, by Julius Frontinus, ib. Paulinus Suetonius, A.D. 59-61, commander in Britain, 43. Anglesey, the seat of the Druids, taken, ib. While Suetonius was engaged in Anglesey, the Britons, provoked by the wrongs they suffered, take up arms, and, commanded by Boadicea, defeat the Roman legion which opposed them, take Camalodunum, the Roman colony, and lay it waste with fire and sword, ib. Suetonius returns and enters London, which he is obliged to evacuate; the Britons enter and put all the Romans there to the sword, ib. The inhabitants of Verulamium utterly annihilated, and 70,000 Romans slain, ib. The Britons defeated, Boadicea puts an end to her life by poison, 44. 80,000 Britons slain, ib. Suetonius leaves Britain, ib. Julius Agricola takes the command; Agricola's mild administration, 44, 45. Education of British youth, Roman customs and dress introduced, 45. The Romans advance into the north of Britain, ib. The Caledonians, to the number of 30,000, made a noble resistance under the command of Galgacus on the acclivities of the Grampian hills; but were at length defeated, 46. Agricola recalled, 47. Peaceful state of Britain for

Britons, the—

30 years, no mention of it being made by Roman historians, ib. Hadrian visits Britain, erects a new rampart, ib. Lollius Urbicus fixes the Roman frontier between the Clyde and Forth, ib. In the reign of Commodus the northern Britons again overrun the Roman provinces, 49. Clodius Albinus, the governor of Britain, disputes the empire with Severus; the best troops being taken from the island, the northern tribes desolate the Roman provinces, ib. Severus visits Britain, loses 50,000 men in his expedition into the northern parts, ib. He builds a wall of stone, and constructs the grand Roman military ways, ib. The Caledonians resume the war; Severus dies at Eboracum, 52. Caracalla's peace with the Caledonians and his return to Rome, ib. After the departure of Caracalla, Britain enjoys nearly 70 years of tranquillity, ib. The Scots from Ireland invade Britain, ib. Freedom of Rome imparted to the Britons, 52, 53. The Saxon pirates begin to ravage the coasts, 53. Carausius appointed commander of a strong fleet, ib. He obtains Britain, Boulogne, and the adjoining coasts of Gaul, with the title of emperor, ib. Britain a great naval power, assisted by the Scandinavian and Saxon pirates, under Carausius, ib. Allectus emperor of Britain, ib. Succeeded by Constantius Chlorus, ib. Constantine the Great began his reign at York, ib. In the fourth century the Frank and Saxon pirates ravaged the coasts of Britain, ib. The Picts, Scots, and Attacots, first appear in Britain, ib. The Saxons invade Britain, A.D. 367; 54. Maximus, a Briton, declared emperor of the Romans, ib. Takes all the best troops from Britain; defeats Gratian, but is afterwards vanquished by Theodosius, ib. Chrysantus defeats the Scots and Picts, ib. They with the Saxons again invade Britain, ib. The last remains of the Roman forces recalled, 55. Marcus chosen emperor of Britain, ib. Succeeded by Gratian, ib. Constantine, appointed emperor of Britain, aspires to the empire of the West, but fails, ib. Gerontius leagues with the Saxons, ib. Independence of Britain acknowledged, ib. The Roman municipal government of cities overthrown, ib. Civil wars, ib. Deplorable state of Britain, 56, 57. Roman and British factions, 57. Aurelius Ambrosius implores the aid of the Romans, ib. Religious controversy, ib. Vortigern called in the aid of the Saxons, following the example of the people of Brittany, ib. Civil war between Aurelius Ambrosius and Vortigern, ib. Hengist and Horsa, ib. Ancient British houses, their supposed structure, 98. Cæsar describes their towns as a portion of woodland, surrounded by a vallum and ditch, 99. Fortresses and entrenchments, or camps, 99—101. The tolman and rocking-stones, the Druidical temple of Stonehenge, attest a knowledge of the lever and mechanics, 101. Domestic furniture of the Britons, their civilization, &c., 101, 125. Handicrafts, basket-making, &c., 101. Their trade with the Phœnicians, and with the Gauls, 93, 101. Their agricultural implements, weapons, and war chariots, 101-104. Their sea-going vessels, &c., 102. Ancient canoes, found at North Stoke, on the Arun, Sussex, ib. Their knowledge of the working of metals, and the manufacture of weapons of bronze, 36, 91. Ancient British coins, 112. Armour and weapons, 128. Costume and ornaments, 127, 129. The skin painted by vitrium or woad with figures of animals, &c., an ancient tattooing, 129. The social condition of British tribes, customs, remarkable institution of their marriages, a sort of polygamy, and consequent arrangements as to paternity, 129. Commerce to the end of the Roman period: in grain, tin, lead, chalk, lime, cheese, horses, &c., 106. Cattle exported. British horses

Britons, the—
much esteemed at Rome, and the dogs reckoned of
superior merit to any known, *ib.* The Britons,
who had been marshalled by the Romans, before
their retirement to Rome, supposed to be possessed of
excellent swords and arms in the middle of the *fifth
century*, about the years 460 to 475; 140. They call
in the Jutes under Hengist to assist in repelling the
Picts and Scots, *ib.* Vortigern their king marrying Rowena daughter of Hengist, cedes Thanet to
the Jutes, 141. A war was soon waged by the
Roman faction still existing, and Britons upon the
Saxons for their encroachments, *ib.* The Saxons
ally themselves with the Picts and Scots, *ib.* Truce,
ib. The 'Triads and Bruts' of the Britons mention a feast at Stonehenge, where Hengist massacred
many Britons; an affair involved in doubt, 141,
142. First Saxon kingdom in Kent, 142. In 477,
Ella and his sons land their Saxons in Sussex, and
overthrew the Regni, driving them into the forest
of Andredswold, *ib.* He defeats confederate British princes, and establishes the kingdom of the
South Saxons, *ib.* Various Saxon states founded
betwixt the years 477 and 600; *ib.* During the successive Saxon encroachments, the Britons bravely
contest every portion of their native land, 450—
600; *ib.*
BRITTANY, Conan le Petit, duke of, also earl of Richmond in England. Henry II. confiscates his English property, i. 443; but afterwards affiances his
fourth son Geoffroy to Constance, the daughter of
Conan, 444. He resigns the government of Brittany, 452. He died in 1171.
BRITTANY, John de Montfort, duke of, implores the
assistance of England against the aggressions of the
French king Charles V., 1380; a considerable army
is raised and sent to his relief under the duke of
Buckingham, but the death of the French king
happening almost immediately, de Montfort concludes a treaty with Charles VI. and agrees to
abandon the interests of England, i. 784. Montfort
died, Nov. 1, 1399.
BRITTANY, John, duke of, born December 24, 1389;
ii. 21. Too late with his detachment for the battle
of Agincourt, 32. His alliance, 1423, with the
regent Bedford, 54. His secret treaty with Philip
of Burgundy, 54, 56. He declares in favour of
Charles VII., still called dauphin by the English,
1425; 58. His brother, the count of Richemont,
constable of France, 1425; *ib.* His defeats by Bedford's army obliged the duke to swear observance
to the treaty of Troyes, and to do homage to none
but the English king, *ib.* He died August 29,
1442.
BRITTANY, Francis II., duke of, ii. 126, *note.* The earls of
Richmond and Pembroke being driven on the coast,
are imprisoned by the duke, 126. Their danger of
being delivered up to Richard III. and escape, *ib.*
The duke of Orleans sought to marry his daughter
Anne of Brittany, 292. Civil war in Brittany, *ib.*
The French design to seize the duchy, *ib.* They take
Vannes and lay siege to Nantes, 1487; *ib.* Auxili-
aries of Francis, *ib.* He demands the aid of Henry
VII., who as mediator merely sends his chaplain
Urswick as ambassador, 293. The forces of Charles
VIII. continue their conquest, 293, 294. Sir
Edward Woodville and 400 English join duke
Francis's army, 294. Woodville was slain, 1488,
in a battle lost by duke Francis's generals, *ib.*
Orleans, then a refugee in Brittany, fell into La
Tremoille's hands, and was confined in the castle of
Bourges, *ib.* Treaty of Verger, 1488; 295. Death
of duke Francis, *ib.*
BRITTON, Thomas, a coalman, it was in his house
that the first periodical performance of music in
parts took place, iii. 887.

BRITTON, his opinion of the "peine forte et dure,"
quoted, i. 814.
Broad-cloths, manufacture of, iv. 711.
BROC, Ranulf de, his invectives against Becket; is ex-
communicated, i. 454.
BROC, Robert de, excommunicated by Becket, 1169;
i. 454.
BROKE, lord, sir Robert Willoughby, created 1486;
ii. 286.
BROKE, sir Richard, ravages the Scottish borders,
1544; ii. 441.
BROKE, captain of the Shannon frigate, which captured
the Chesapeake, June 1, 1813; § iv. 662*.
BROMLEY, sir Thomas, lord chief justice, ii. 500. His
dictation to a jury, case of sir. N. Throgmorton,
April 17, 1554; 518. Lord chancellor, 1579; 659,
660.
BROOKE, lord, together with lord Say, sets on foot a
great embarkation in 1637 for New England, but an
embargo is laid on the emigrant ships in the
Thames, iii. 182. He, together with lord Say,
refuses to take an oath tendered to him by
Charles I., 1639; 204. His house searched for papers, 218.
BROOKE, George, brother to lord Cobham, engages,
June 1603, in the conspiracy to seize James I. on
his way to Windsor, iii. 8, 9. Condemned at Winchester, November, the plague having delayed
the arraignment, 9. He was beheaded, December
5; 13.
BROTHERS, Richard, an insane fanatic, commences
his career as the apostle of a new religion, 1792;
§ iii. 588–591.
BROUNKER, lord, iii. 696; iv. 779. First president of
the Royal Society, published in 1653 his translation
of Descartes' Musicae Compendium, iii. 888.
BROWN, George, archbishop of Dublin, about 1535;
gave his support to a reform of the Irish church,
and acknowledged Henry VIII. as head of that
church, ii. 427. His letters, 1538, to the minister
Cromwell, *ib.* His complaints of the lord-deputy,
427, 428.
BROWN, Lancelot, a celebrated landscape gardener of
the 18th century, § iii. 733.
BROWN, Robert, founder of the Brownists (about
1580); ii. 745.
BROWNE, Mr. Samuel, a member of the House of
Commons, and one of the managers of the trial of
archbishop Laud, 1644; iii. 325.
BROWNE, sir Thomas, author of the 'Religio Medici,'
published 1642; iii. 578, 613.
Brownists, the rise of this third race of Puritans,
afterwards softened down into Independents, is
dated from 1581; ii. 745.
Broxley, abbot of, sent on a deputation to king
Richard in Germany, i. 509.
BRUCE, Robert, son of the Robert Bruce, who was
competitor with Baliol for the crown of Scotland,
and who was grandson of Henry of Huntingdon,
brother of William the Lion. His father had resigned to him the earldom of Carrick, which he had
obtained by his marriage with the countess of
Carrick, a short time before he joined Wallace, i.
715. It was in the last days of Baliol's reign that
the government confiscated the estates of the house
of Bruce and gave them to Comyn, earl of Buchan,
ib. On the approach of Edward, he leaves Wallace
and submits to the English, 716. Bruce is appointed to act in the name of Baliol, 724. He submits to Edward, and is permitted on the death of
his father, 1304, to take possession of all his estates
both in England and Scotland, 727. He makes a
private league with William de Lamberton bishop
of St. Andrew's, and on the 10th of February, 1306,
stabs Comyn at a private interview held in the convent of the Minorites at Dumfries, 728. He holds

BRUCE, Robert—
a meeting of his friends at Glasgow, and from thence rides to Scone, where he is solemnly crowned, March 27; *ib.* Edward sends a small force to oppose the insurgents, and prepares for an expedition in person; Bruce's forces are routed in the wood of Methven, and he retires into the fastnesses of Athole, 729. Being attacked by the Lord of Lorn on reaching the borders of Argyle, he flies to the isle of Rachrin, on the northern coast of Ireland, *ib.* All his friends are taken, and killed or imprisoned, his brother Nigel being hanged at Berwick, and his queen Marjory and her daughter taken prisoners and confined in England, where they remained for eight years, *ib.* He returns to the isle of Arran, 1307, and passing over to Scotland defeats an English force near Turnbury, *ib.* Bruce's two brothers Thomas and Alexander are attacked in Galloway by Duncan Mac Dowal, as they were bringing over 1100 adventurers from Ireland for the assistance of their brother, *ib.* Sent as prisoners to Edward, who executes them at Carlisle, 730. Sir James Douglas surprises Douglas castle, commanded by lord Clifford, *ib.* Bruce's forces increase, and he ventures to attack the earl of Pembroke at Loudon Hill, where, with great inferiority of numbers, he obtains a complete victory, May 10, 1307; *ib.* Three days after he defeats the earl of Gloucester, and then besieges both Pembroke and Gloucester in the castle of Ayr, *ib.* After this, Edward, who had been detained all the winter at Lanercost, by a serious attack of illness, proceeds to the village of Burgh-upon-Sands, where he expires, July 7; *ib.* After the death of Edward, the affairs of Scotland are neglected, and Bruce's power increases, but he is opposed by the earl of Richmond, who had been appointed guardian of Scotland on the return of Edward II. in 1307; besides a powerful faction of the Scottish nobility, who for the present supported the English interest, 734. Bruce avoids a general action, *ib.* He is taken ill in the spring of 1308; on the 22nd of May he gains the battle of Inverury, and shortly recovers, 735. The people of Aberdeen rise, storm the castle, and defeat an English force, which was marching against them, *ib.* Edward marches into Scotland, September, 1310, but returns in July, 1311, without achieving any thing, *ib.* Bruce ravages England as far as Durham; takes the castle of Perth, Jan. 1312; *ib.* Burns the towns of Hexham and Corbridge, and a great part of the city of Durham, penetrates as far as Chester, and then returns across the border; the four northern counties purchasing a truce from him by a payment of two thousand pounds each, 736. The castles of Roxburgh and Edinburgh surrender, March 1313. Edward summons all the military power of England to meet him at Berwick, on the 11th of June, and calls to his aid both his English subjects in Ireland, and many of the native Irish chiefs, composing a splendid army, exceeding a hundred thousand men; he also fits out a fleet to act in concert with his land forces, *ib.* On the 23rd, the English make their appearance at Bannockburn, where the Scottish army under the command of Bruce, consisting of about forty thousand men, was drawn up ready to receive them, *ib.* Their right wing being commanded by Edward Bruce, the left by Randolph, earl of Moray, the centre by sir James Douglas and Walter the Steward; the islanders, forming the reserve, were commanded by Bruce himself: on the 24th of June, the earls of Gloucester and Hereford led on the charge, supported by the main body of the army, formed in a long close column under the conduct of Edward himself, 737. Bruce directs sir Robert Keith to charge the English bowmen, who

BRUCE, Robert—
fly and spread confusion in all directions, *ib.* A general flight commences; the earl of Gloucester, the king's nephew, is slain, 200 knights, 700 esquires, and 30,000 of inferior rank perish in this battle, king Edward himself being hotly pursued for sixty miles, as far as the castle of Dunbar; twenty-two barons and bannerets, and sixty knights, were also taken prisoners, 738. Stirling castle immediately surrenders, and the earl of Hereford capitulates in Bothwell castle, *ib.* but is exchanged for the wife, sister, and daughter of the king of Scots, *ib.* The Scots again enter England, but fail in their assault on Carlisle and Berwick, 1315; *ib.* Edward Bruce, lands at Carrickfergus, May 25, 1315, with six thousand men. He defeats Richard de Burgh, earl of Ulster, at Coyners, September 10th; *ib.*: and Edmund Butler, justiciary of Ireland, January 26, 1316, and soon after gains a complete victory over Roger lord Mortimer, *ib.* He assumes the government of Ulster, and on the 2nd of May is crowned king of Ireland at Carrickfergus, *ib.* The king of Scots lands in Ireland; the Scottish army amounting to twenty thousand men advance to the south, but fail in their attempt to reduce Dublin, *ib.* and having proceeded as far as Limerick, succeed in making good their return to Ulster, 739. During the absence of Bruce, the English make several attempts to renew the war, but are successively defeated by sir James Douglas and the bishop of Dunkeld. *ib.* He returns and takes the important town of Berwick, March 28th, 1318; and follows up these successes by two invasions of England, *ib.* On the 5th of October, Edward Bruce is defeated and slain at Fagher, near Dundalk, and the Scots are expelled from Ireland. *ib.* Edward marches with a numerous army upon Berwick, but is repulsed, *ib.* The Scots invade England and ravage Yorkshire, *ib.* They gain the battle of Mitton, on the 21st of December; a truce for two years is agreed upon, *ib.* May 30, 1323, a suspension of arms for thirteen years is agreed upon, 741. After the death of Edward II., the Scots again invade England and penetrate into York; Edward III. marches against them with a large army, but they make good their return to Scotland with their plunder, under the command of the earl of Moray and lord James Douglas, 749. The English army returns and is disbanded at York, *ib.* A peace is concluded with England, and the independence of Scotland acknowledged; prince David, the only son of Bruce, is married to the princess Joanna, sister of king Edward, July 22nd, 1328; 751. Bruce dies at his castle of Cardross, June 7th, 1329, and is buried in the abbey church of Dunfermline, *ib.*
BRUCE, Robert, lord of Annandale, taken prisoner by the earl of Leicester, at the battle of Lewes, 1264; i. 685. Bruce and Hastings were the sons of David's two younger daughters, and therefore had an inferior claim to Baliol, who was grandson of his eldest daughter, i. 707. For the decision of his claim, *see* Edward I. He is made earl of Carrick by his marriage with that countess, 715. Family estates of the house of Bruce confiscated, *ib.* His death, 1304; 727.
BRUCE, Edward, brother of the great Robert Bruce, commands the right wing at the battle of Bannockburn, i. 737. Sets out on an expedition to reduce Ireland, and lands at Carrickfergus, May 25th, 1315, with 6,000 men, 738. Defeats Richard de Burgh, earl of Ulster, at Coyners, Sept. 10th, *ib.* Edmund Butler, justiciary of Ireland, Jan. 26th, 1316, soon after gains a complete victory over Roger, lord Mortimer, *ib.* Assumes the government of Ulster; on the 2nd of May is crowned king of

BRUCE,—
Ireland at Carrickfergus, *ib.*; is joined by his brother Robert, who comes over to Ireland to assist him, the Scottish army consisting of about 20,000 men, advances to the south, but fails in the attempt to reduce Dublin, *ib.* Having proceeded as far as Limerick, they succeed in making good their return to Ulster, 739. For a year and a half we have no mention of Ireland, but on the 5th of October, 1318, Edward Bruce engaged an English force at Fagher, near Dundalk, where he was defeated and slain, *ib.* After this battle all the Scots were expelled from Ireland, and it appears that the men of Carrick alone made good their escape to Scotland, *ib.*

BRUCE, David, only son of the great Robert Bruce, is married to the princess Joanna, sister of Edward the Third, when only five years of age, July 22nd, 1328; i. 751. On the death of his father in the following year, Randolph, earl of Moray, is appointed regent of Scotland, and guardian of the young king, 755. After his death, 1332, the earl of Marr was appointed regent. Edward Baliol, supported by English interest, lands in Scotland and obtains possession of the crown, *ib.* After various changes of fortune, David Bruce and his queen are conveyed to France, and kindly entertained by the French king in the Chateau Gaillard, 756. Baliol, who had been continually expelled, and as often restored by Edward, who was now occupied with his wars in France, 1338, is ejected from Scotland, 759. David, now in his eighteenth year, returns from France with his queen, and lands at Inverbervie, where he is received with enthusiastic joy, May 14th, 1341, *ib.* Edward forms a truce with him, which was prolonged till the end of the year 1344, *ib.* Whilst Edward is besieging Calais, David invades England with an army of 30,000 men, and takes the castle of Liddel; the English collect an army in Auckland Park, a battle is fought at Nevil's Cross, where the English gain a complete victory by means of their archers. David, although possessing great courage, was deficient in the military skill of his father, and after being twice wounded, and still disdaining to flee or surrender, is forcibly made prisoner by one Copland, a gentleman of Northumberland, who carried him off the field to his tower of Ogle, October 17th, 1346; 768. He is sent to London, and confined in the Tower, *ib.* Notwithstanding the captivity of their king, the Scots still preserve their independence, 771. While Edward is occupied on the continent the Scots again enter England, and retake Berwick; Edward returns, obtains supplies from his parliament, November 23rd, 1355, and in the January following recovers Berwick, and makes an expedition into Scotland, but is forced to return for want of provisions, the Scots all the while harassing his retiring forces, 772. The Scots agree to pay 100,000 marks as a ransom for their king, October 3rd, 1357; and in November Bruce returns to Scotland, 773. He proposes, in a council held at Scone, 1363, that Lionel, duke of Cambridge, Edward's third son, should be elected king of Scotland in the event of his dying without issue, but this proposal is rejected. On the death of Edward Baliol, he forms a secret agreement with Edward, that, in default of the king of Scots and his issue male, the king of England for the time being should succeed to the throne of Scotland, 774. The truce with Scotland is prolonged till 1371, in the February of which year Bruce dies, and is succeeded by his nephew, the Stewart of Scotland, who assumes the title of Robert II., 1371; *ib.*

BRUCE, James, minister of Kingsbarns, petitions against the new Book of Common Prayer, 1637; iii. 184.

BRUCE, Michael, an English gentleman residing at Paris. Lavalette having made his escape from prison the day before his intended execution, December 21, 1815, but not being able to leave Paris, informs Mr. Bruce of the imminent danger he was in, and requests his assistance, § iv., 654.* Bruce immediately solicits the assistance of Sir Robert Wilson and Captain Hutchinson, and accomplishes the arduous task of deliverance with complete success, but by the decision of a French jury they are imprisoned for three months, and on their return the two military gentlemen receive the censure of the Prince Regent, 656.*

BRUCE, Nigel, younger brother of Robert Bruce. He is compelled to surrender the castle of Kildrummie, and is sent in irons to Berwick, where he is hanged and afterwards beheaded, 1306; i. 729.

BRUCE, Robert de, a follower of the Conqueror, i. 375.

BRUCE, Thomas and Alexander, brothers of the great Robert Bruce, are defeated by Mac Dowal in Galloway, i. 729, and executed by Edward I. at Carlisle, 780.

BRUS, Robert de, the first to hold the office of " Chief Justice of the King's Bench." He was appointed in the 52 Hen. III.; i. 812.

BRUNSWICK, Prince Ferdinand of. Commanding an allied force, this prince resolved to wage battle for the defence of Hanover, and occupied a strong position at Minden, iv. 610. There he was assailed, July 31, 1759, by Contades and Broglie with a very superior army. After a long and severe fight, the French were repulsed from a field covered with their dead, 610, 611. Obstinate valour of the English infantry, 611. The English cavalry remained inactive, through the misconduct of Lord George Sackville, who refused to break the English line, when ordered to charge the French, 610. His previous discontents with Ferdinand, the general-in-chief, were well known, *ib.* Ferdinand gains the battle of Minden, *ib.*

BRUNSWICK WOLFENBÜTTEL, the duchess of, visited George II. in 1755, at Hanover, iv. 584. Desire of the king that the elder of her daughters should be espoused by his grandson Prince George, *ib.* The Princess-dowager of Wales opposed this union, *ib.*

BRUNSWICK, prince Francis of, slain at the battle of Hochkirchen, 1758; iv. 603.

BRUNSWICK, prince Albert Henry of, mortally wounded, 1761; § i. 8.

BRUNSWICK, duke of, killed at Quatre Bras, June 16, 1815, gallantly fighting at the head of his black hussars, § iv. 638.*

BRUTUS and his Trojan colony, i. 8. The name Britannia derived from, 11.

Brython, a colony from Llydaw (Bretagne), i. 9.

Bualth, prince Llewellyn, surprised and slain here by the earl of Mortimer, which effected the final conquest of Wales, i. 698.

BUCCLEUGH, Francis earl, protested against the act passed, 1649, abolishing the patronages of kirks, iii. 490.

BUCHAN, John Comyn, earl of, defeated with Mowbray, by Bruce, at the battle of Inverury, May 22, 1308; i. 735.

BUCHAN, earl of, a brother of Robert III., 1390, his violent disposition, ii. 131.

BUCHAN, earl of, second son of the regent Albany, 1417, conducts a large Scottish force to the assistance of the dauphin Charles, ii. 132. In 1421, La Fayette and Buchan surprised the duke of Clarence in Anjou, the duke is slain, but his bowmen coming up recover his body, and remain masters of the field, 48. He commanded the dauphin's armies, besieged Coane, and took La Charité, 50. Is slain, 1424, with most of the Scottish forces, in the battle of Verneuil, 56.

BUCHANAN, George, the poet and historian, born 1506; died 1582. Sits upon the commission appointed for trying the case of Mary queen of Scots and the earl of Murray, ii. 612. Portrait of, 813; iii. 38, 485.

BUCKHURST, lord, sent to Mary queen of Scots, 1586, to inform her of her sentence, ii. 663.

Buckhurst House, plan of, ii. 848.

Buckingham palace, by Inigo Jones, iii. 722.

BUCKINGHAM, Humphrey Stafford, duke of, ii. 88. Was wounded, 1454, at St. Alban's, 92. Slain in the retreat of the Lancastrians from Northampton, 1460; 95.

BUCKINGHAM, Henry Stafford, duke of, 1459. Joined Richard of Gloucester on his way to London, 1483; ii. 118. They secured the person of Edward V. at Stoney-Stratford, ib. They bent their knees to the young king, and escorted him to London, ib. Buckingham proposed the Tower as a safe residence for Edward until his coronation, 119. His speech at Guildhall, alleging that Edward and his brother were illegitimate, and proposing Gloucester for king, 122. Richard III. granted to the duke the inheritance of Humphrey de Bohun, on his claim by descent, with many other favours, 126. The duke still dissatisfied, ib. The duchess of Buckingham was sister of queen Elizabeth, and aunt of Edward V., ib. The duke countenanced the conspiracy to release the young king, but the princes were dead in the Tower, 124, 126. He proclaimed Henry of Richmond at Brecknock, 126. He was unable with his troops to cross the Severn; Richmond, with a fleet on the coast of Devonshire, finding no supporters there, sailed for St. Malo, ib. Buckingham fled, and falling into the hands of Richard III., was beheaded at Salisbury, October, 1483; 127, 343.

BUCKINGHAM, Edward Stafford, duke of, restored 1486, by Henry VII. to his honours and estates, ii. 286. He commanded the select guard of Henry VIII., 1513, in the battle of the Spurs, 323. His observation that the "Field of the Cloth of Gold" entailed ruin on the English nobles irritated Henry, who was already jealous of his descent from Thomas of Woodstock, and Edward III., 343. His possessions and popularity increased his danger, ib. His unlucky acquaintance with friar Hopkins, who had made some innocent predictions with success, ib. The carthusian, emboldened by repute thus gained, told Buckingham that his son Edward would succeed to Henry VIII., ib. Enmity, also, of Wolsey, accelerated the duke's ruin, ib. Henry was angry at the duke's number of retainers, and that sir William Bulmer had quitted his own service for the duke's, 344. Buckingham unsuspiciously accepted, 1521, an invitation to court, ib. Sir H. Marney boarded the duke's barge, and attached him for treasons, ib. Sir Charles Knevitt, his cousin Hopkins, &c., witnesses against him, ib. Arbitrary dictum of chief justice Fineux on the law of treason, ib. His condemnation, and reply to Norfolk, who pronounced sentence, ib. He declined to ask the king's mercy, and was beheaded on Tower-hill, 345. Lamentation of the people for his fate, ib.

BUCKINGHAM, George Villiers, duke of. He is installed James's cup-bearer, 1614; iii. 57; sworn a gentleman of the privy chamber, August 24, 1615; 58; made lord high admiral, warden of the cinque ports, master of the King's Bench Office, &c., 1616; 71; created earl of Buckingham, January 1617; marquess of Buckingham, January, 1618; and duke of Buckingham and earl of Coventry, May 1623; married Catherine Manners, daughter of Francis, earl of Rutland; is charged with corruption by Yelverton, 82; goes with prince Charles to Spain, under the assumed name of Thomas Smith, 91; stopped by a mayor at Canterbury, to whom he discloses himself, ib.; court of Spain surprised at the

BUCKINGHAM, George Villiers—
liberties he takes with prince Charles, 98; his embassy to Paris, to bring home Henrietta Maria, 109; declares love to queen Anne of Austria, ib.; goes to the Hague to pawn the crown jewels and plate, 114; wishes to proceed to Paris, but is informed by Richelieu that he cannot be permitted, his looseness of conduct having produced much disgust there, ib.; his insolence to Henrietta Maria, 115; Williams, the Lord Keeper, having offended him, loses his office, 117; he is charged by the earl of Bristol with divers crimes, 119; is impeached, 120; compared by sir J. Eliot to Sejanus, ib.; the chancellorship of the University of Cambridge conferred upon him, 121; he makes his defence in the House of Lords, 122; James writes to him to send back the queen's attendants to France immediately, 125; Bassompierre, the French ambassador, refuses to disclose to him his business, ib.; Buckingham reconciled to the queen by means of this ambassador, ib.; his violent desire to return to the French court, ib.; Bassompierre writes to tell him that the queen desires he would stay away, 127; he sets out on an expedition to retrieve the English honour lost on the Isle de Leon, ib.; his disgraceful return, 129, 133; stabbed at Portsmouth, by John Felton, 1629, 136; quietly buried at Westminster Abbey, 137; description of his expensive dress, iii. 629.

BUCKINGHAM, George Villiers, son and heir of the preceding, iii. 700. Kills the Earl of Shrewsbury in a duel, 897.

BUCKINGHAM, John Sheffield, duke of, third earl of Mulgrave, iv. 120. Created marquess of Normanby, May 10, 1694; duke of Normanby, March 9, 1703; and duke of Buckingham, March 23, 1703. Died, 1720. Description of, iv. 180, note.

Buckle manufacture, history of the, § iii. 686.

Building, progress of, in the reign of Elizabeth, ii. 889.

BULL, Dr., first professor of music at Gresham College, in the beginning of the sixteenth century, iii. 562.

Bullion, iv. 693.

BULOW, Baron, gaoler of Sophia Dorothea, wife of George I., iv. 394.

BULOW, a Prussian general. He commanded the combined army in the campaign against Bonaparte in 1814, and the following year he contributed to the victory of Waterloo, § iv. 636*.

Bunker's Hill, view of, § i. 216; battle of, fought June 17, 1775, ib.

BUNYAN, John, author of the Pilgrim's Progress. Born 1628; died 1688. His portrait, iii. 808.

BURBAGE, James, license (of plays) granted to, 1574; iii. 583.

BURCHELL, Dr. Robert, a Greek and Hebrew scholar, friend of Sir Walter Raleigh, iii. 72.

BURDETT, sir Francis, moves in parliament for the acquittal of Mr. John Jones; on account of his speech on this subject, which he printed in "Cobbett's Weekly Register," he is charged with a breach of the privileges of the House, and confined in the Tower, 1810; § iv. 429—432. His arrest causes riots and great excitement in the capital, 430—433. On the prorogation of parliament he is liberated, 435.

BURDETT, Thomas, accused of having recourse to magic to compass the death of lord Beauchamp, and executed 1477; ii. 114.

BURGH, Habert de, refuses to consent to prince Arthur's being blinded, when confined in the castle of Falaise, i. 520. He destroys a French fleet, August 23, 1217; 673. On the death of the earl of Pembroke, May, 1219, he is appointed regent in conjunction with Peter des Roches, bishop of Winchester, 675. Is disgraced and sent to the Tower, 1232, and his lands forfeited. He escapes into Wales, receives back his estates and honours, 1234, and is re-admitted into the king's council, 676, 677.

BURGH, Ulliac de, created, 1541, earl of Clanricarde, and called to the Irish parliament after the rebellion of O'Connor, O'Neil, Mac Murdo, &c., ii. 428.

BURGOYNE, John, an English general officer and dramatist, commands a force sent into Portugal, 1762, for the defence of that kingdom against the Spaniards, § i. 18. He lands at Boston with a considerable body of marines, May 1775; 214. Puts several nations of Red Indians under arms, 1777, and takes Skenesborough, 307, 308. Illustration of his attack on the American batteaux, 309; and of his encampment and retreat on the Hudson River, 312, 313, 316. *Illustration.*—Spanish troops surrendering to, 19.

Burgundians, their code of written law, promulgated early in the *seventh century*, i. 145.

BURGUNDY, Philip, duke of, uncle of Charles VI. of France. On the supposed murder of Richard II. at Pontefract, the duke invades the English part of Guienne, 1400, ii. 7, 8. His death, 17.

BURGUNDY, *Jean sans peur*, or the Fearless duke of Burgundy, 1406; sent to take Calais, fails, as his father Philip had formerly done, ii. 20. His disputes about the money he had drawn out of Flanders. Orleans, who had wasted the public money, destined for the war in Guienne, is unable to liquidate Burgundy's claims, who retired in anger to Flanders, *ib.* The people prefer of the two princes, the Burgundian, *ib.* This duke returns to Paris, appears perfectly reconciled to his cousin of Orleans, but soon employs bravoes to murder him in the street, *ib.* Burgundy obtains full possession of the government, and lawyers and priests extenuate his crime, as having delivered France of a tyrant and monster, *ib.* His territory, 1413, invaded by the Armagnacs, 27. The dauphiness, his daughter, 28. Being insulted, November, 1415, by Armagnac, constable of France, he marched to Troyes, and thence to Paris, which the Armagnacs prevented his entering, 36. Plot frustrated, *ib.* He ravages all France, 1416, betwixt his own territory and Paris, 37, 40. His interview at Calais with Henry V., with whom he signs a secret treaty of alliance, 37. He obtained a new but secret partisan, 1417, in queen Isabella; causes of this change stated, 38. He conducts her in triumph to Chartres, 40. He wages a cruel war against the dauphin, 42. His conferences with envoys of Henry V., 43. The duke, the queen, and princess, in great state, give a meeting to Henry near Meulan, 44. After some days they abscond, and league with the dauphin, who, alarmed by the courtly conferences yields to their own terms, *ib.* His reconciliation with the dauphin, and new family peace proclaimed, *ib.* Is invited to a conference with that prince, on the bridge of Montereau, 45. He boldly persists in making his appearance there, though well warned of intended treachery, *ib.* He is foully murdered on the bridge, and falls dead at the feet of the dauphin Charles, 46.

BURGUNDY, Philip the Good, duke of; when count of Charolais he sees to the funeral of his uncles slain at Agincourt, 1415; ii. 34. This duke signs a treaty with Henry V., as to his succession to the crown of France, 47. Henry V. and Burgundy take Montereau, whence the duke removes his murdered father's body to the cathedral of Dijon, 1420; 48. December, 1420, the two kings enter Paris in triumph; the three estates are summoned to a parliament; Philip demands justice on his father's murderers, *ib.* These were found guilty of high treason, though none were implicated by name in the accusation, *ib.* He entreats Henry V. to march, 1422, to the relief of his towns besieged by Buchan, general of the dauphin's army, 50. The English king dies in this expedition, 50, 51. He desires that Bedford should be regent of France, with counsels of duke Philip, 51. His sister Anne, of Burgundy,

BURGUNDY, Philip the Good, duke of— marries Bedford, 54. Congress, 1423, at Amiens, *ib.* His separate treaty with the duke of Brittany, *ib.* Upon the arrival of Gloucester with troops to secure Hainault, &c., the territories of his duchess Jacqueline, previously duchess of Brabant, and cousin of Philip, Burgundy challenged the English prince to single combat, 58. Gloucester fixed St. George's day for this duel, but the Burgundian refused to fight, *ib. See Jacqueline of Hainault* for the war betwixt these princes, which ended in duke Philip acquiring all her territories, 57—60. Nevertheless, it was many years before Burgundy broke his defensive treaty with his brother-in-law Bedford, 60. Duke Philip, cautious in his old age, turned from the Lancastrian cause, not being willing to quarrel with Edward IV., 1463; 100. He therefore sent queen Margaret, under an honourable escort to her father in Lorraine, 101. His death, 1467; 102, 103. Succeeded by Charles the Rash, or *le Téméraire*, 103.

BURGUNDY, Charles the Rash, duke of, 1467, succeeded duke Philip, ii. 103. He sent Anthony, Bastard of Burgundy to Edward IV. to solicit for him the hand of that king's sister Margaret, *ib.* Induced by the duke's vast possessions, and the commerce with Flanders, Edward, overlooking Warwick's actual commission as to the union of Margaret of York with Louis XI.'s. son, gave her to Burgundy, 103. Louis XI. was justly incensed at Burgundy's marriage, the duke having become Yorkist and his fierce enemy, 105. His enmity to Warwick for dethroning Edward IV., 107. He supplies that king, then in Holland, with ships and money, 1471; 108. Duke Charles was killed at the battle of Nanci, about 1476; 114. His immense possessions devolved on his daughter Mary, *ib.*

BURGUNDY, Margaret, duchess of, sister of Edward IV., and widow of Charles the Rash, ii. 289. Her court was long the safe refuge of all adherents of the house of York, *ib.* She sent (with the pretender Lambert Simnel) the brave Martin Swart, with 2,000 Germans, under the earl of Lincoln (her nephew), to Dublin, *ib.* These escorting Lambert Simnel into Yorkshire, were defeated at Stoke-upon-Trent and all of them slain, 290. She first dissembled, but finally acknowledged the new impostor, Perkin Warbeck, to be her nephew, Richard duke of York (murdered with Edward V. in the Tower), 299, 300. She sent him men and money, 1493, into Scotland, 305. Edmund de la Pole, son of the duke of Suffolk, fled to her court, 1504; 313.

BURGUNDY, Mary, duchess of, ii. 114. George, duke of Clarence, then a widower, 1476, offers her his hand, *ib.* Edward IV. prevents this union, *ib.* Louis XI. seized on most of her territories, 115. Being out with her hawks, February, 1482, Mary of Burgundy was thrown against the trunk of a tree, *ib.* Her death ensued in March, *ib.* Her children by the duke Maximilian, of Austria, were Philip, Margaret, or "Margot la gente demoiselle," and Francis, 116. The Flemings had respected the duchess Mary, but had no regard for Maximilian, *ib.* "Margot" was affianced at three years old to the dauphin, son of Louis XI., and immediately carried to the French court, *ib.* Charles VIII., having succeeded Louis, pretends an earnest desire to espouse Margot, until the very moment of his nuptials, 1491, with Anne of Brittany, 297. He then sent the Burgundian princess home to her father Maximilian, 298.

BURGUNDY, duke of, grandson of Louis XIV., and pupil of Fenelon, is said to have asked Louis why the Spanish succession should be preferred to the welfare of France, iv. 232. He dies in the spring of 1712, and is directly followed by his eldest son, a child six years old, 266.

BURK, Lord William, taken prisoner by the Scots near Coyners, 1315 ; i. 738.

BURKE, Edmund, a writer, orator, and statesman of great eminence, born January 1, 1730. Becomes M.P. for the borough of Wendover, 1765 ; § i. 39, 41. He proposes the repeal of the Stamp-tax, 45. Refuses a place at the Board of Trade, and goes over to Ireland, 1766 ; 48, 66, 67. Portrait of, 94 ; 104, 161, 179, 207. He, as agent for the colony of New York, presents a remonstrance, 1775, from the general assembly of that province, 209, 285. He makes a grand speech (1778) on the brutality of employing Indians in our warfare with America, 333. Introduces his plan of economical reform, 1780 ; 404, 414 ; which much retrenched, receives the royal assent in 1782 ; 484. His speech on the debts of the Nabob of Arcot, February 28, 1785 ; § ii. 184—187. He undertakes the impeachment of Warren Hastings, 1786-7 ; 192, 202, 226—241, 276—230. His opinions respecting the French Revolution, 447, 448, 451—455. He breaks with his intimate friend Fox on account of that gentleman's sentiments on this subject, 1791, 544—555. Joins with ministers in advocating war with France, 1792 ; § iii. 266. He publishes the two first of his celebrated " Letters on a Regicide Peace," 1796 ; 503.

BURLEIGH, sir William Cecil, lord, in 1547, served as judge-marshal in the invasion of Scotland by Somerset, ii. 459. Queen Elizabeth, on her accession, shows a decided preference for him, and immediately appoints him chief secretary of state, 539. His letter to the duke of Chatelherault, 551. Created lord Burleigh, 1571 ; 639. He gets into some disgrace for his share in the execution of the queen of Scots, 671, and for intriguing against the earl of Essex, 680. The death of this remarkable statesman occurred August 4, 1598 ; 681. Portrait of, 750.

BURLEY, sir Simon, a much-esteemed friend of Edward III. and the Black Prince. Seizes an industrious man at Gravesend as his escaped bondsman, on which the commons of Kent take up arms and demand his release, appointing Wat the Tyler their captain, i. 785. He was guardian to Richard II., and was executed at the instigation of Gloucester, 1388 ; 793.

BURLINGTON, Richard Boyle, earl of, 1704. A great patron of learning. He died, 1753 ; iv. 751.

BURNET, Dr. Gilbert, iii. 749, 803. Appointed preceptor to the young duke of Gloucester, only surviving child of the princess Anne, iv. 86. He urges some indulgence to the non-juring clergy, 620. Made bishop of Salisbury, March, 1689 ; 621. Impeached in the Convocation of the Lower House, holden in 1701, for his exposition of the Thirty-nine Articles, 641. Review of his works, 789, 790. Quoted, ii. 453, 457 ; iii. 477, 562, 690, n, 720 ; iv. 50, 113, 126, 163. He died 17th March, 1714.

BURNS, Robert, a celebrated Scottish poet. Born January 25, 1759. Died July 21, 1796 ; ii. 838 ; § iii. 726. His portrait, ib.

BURROUGH, Sir John, killed by a random shot, before the citadel of St. Martin, 1627 ; iii. 128.

BURTON, Latimer, iii. 124.

BURTON, Henry, fined 5,000l., pilloried, and cropped, for writing seditions books, 1637 ; iii. 166.

BURTON, Robert, author of the " Anatomy of Melancholy," died in 1640 ; iii. 614.

Bury, iii. 656.

BUSHELL, Captain, quells an insurrection in Glasgow, occasioned by a change in the malt-tax, 1724, in which nine of the rioters are killed. He is tried and condemned for murder by the lords of Justiciary, but pardoned and promoted in the service by the king, iv. 383.

BUSHER, Leonard, his tract vindicating religious toleration, printed 1614 ; iii. 807.

BUSHNELL, John, a sculptor of some eminence, regno William III., iv. 757.

BUTE, John Stuart, earl of, the favourite of the princess dowager of Wales. Court scandal alluded to by Waldegrave and Walpole, iv. 585. He is made groom of the stole to the young prince of Wales, 588. His favour on the accession of George III. to the throne. He is sworn a member of the privy council, 1760 ; § i. 2. Portrait of, 4. Description of, by earl Waldegrave, 5. His close intimacy with the princess dowager, ib., 24. He brings in the cyder bill, 25. Withdraws from office, April 8, 1763, ib., 44.

BUTLER, Edmund, justiciary of Ireland, defeated by Edward Bruce, January 26th, 1316 ; i. 738.

BUTLER, colonel, uncle to the earl of Ormond, detained in custody, 1642, by the House of Commons, iii. 270. The king explains his giving passports to him and other persons of good family, ib. The Commons reply that the rebels expect Butler to command one of their regiments, and that his brother was a rebel-general in Munster, 271.

BUTLER, Samuel, the witty author of " Hudibras," born 1612. Died 1680 ; iii. 875.

BUTLERS, family of the, settled in Ireland, ii. 289. Edward IV. causes penalties to be enacted against them, ib. Under their chief the earl of Ormond, they entertained for ages an inverate feud with the Fitzgeralds, of whom the earl of Kildare was chief, 425.

Buttons, manufacture of (19th century), § iv. 692.

Bye conspiracy, 1603, account of the, iii. 8. November 15, the trials at Winchester of those concerned, 9. November 29, their barbarous execution, 13.

BYNG, rear-admiral sir George, iv. 175. Despatched with several ships to Dunkirk, 1708, to intercept the Pretender, 216. He sails with the English fleet to the Mediterranean, 345. Gains the battle of Cape Passaro, 346. Prosecutes the war in Sicily, 358—363.

BYNG, admiral John, sails with a large fleet, October 14, 1755 ; iv. 582. Approaches Minorca, 586. An action is fought with the French, in which admiral West is engaged, but Byng is not, ib. Byng returns to Gibraltar without attempting the relief of Fort St. Philip, 587. He is placed under arrest, sent to England, and put in custody at Greenwich Hospital, ib. Is tried by court-martial and condemned to be shot, by the twelfth article of war, 590. Endeavours are made to save him, 590, 591. The Lords of the Admiralty issue a warrant for his execution, 591. A bill is introduced to absolve the members of the court-martial from their oath of secrecy, ib. The execution is respited for a fortnight, ib. The bill passes the Commons, but is thrown out by the Lords, 592. Byng is shot on board the Monarque, March 14, 1757, ib.

BYRON, George Gordon, lord, a poet of splendid genius, born January 22, 1788. Died, April 19, 1824 ; § iv. 701, 702. Review of his works, ib. His portrait, ib.

BYRON, sir John, lieutenant of the Tower, 1643 ; iii. 267. Royalist governor of the city of Chester, 310.

BYRON, admiral, 1778 ; § i. 348, 385.

CABAL ministry, the, engross the powers of the government, November, 1667. They form the Triple Alliance, and conclude the treaty of Aix-la-Chapelle, April, 1668, iii. 705, 706.

Cabochiens, faction, named from one Caboche, 1413, were the butchers of Paris ; their atrocities, ii. 26, 28. Repressed by the trade of carpenters, 27. The Cabochiens supported the duke of Burgundy against the Armagnac faction, 36.

CABOT (or Gabotto), John, a Venetian, settled at Bristol. He undertakes an expedition of discovery in the northern seas by permission of Henry VII.,

CABOT (or Gabotto), John—
and sails from Bristol in the beginning of May, 1497, accompanied by his son Sebastian; on the 24th of June they discover the coast of Labrador, in lat. 56°. After this he sails northwards, in hopes of finding a passage to India or China, and then returns to England, ii. 776.

CABOT, Sebastian, second son of John Cabot. He accompanied his father, in 1497, in his expedition to the north seas, in which the coast of Labrador was discovered, and in the two following years makes two more voyages to the American continent, ii. 776. For many years he remains at the Spanish court; and in 1517 is employed by Henry VIII., in conjunction with sir Thomas Perte, to make another voyage in the North Seas; in 1549 Edward VI. bestows on him a pension of 166l., 782.

CABRAL, Pedro Alvarez de, discovers the coast of Brazil, 1500, ii. 777.

CADE, Jack, his insurrection, 1450, ii. 87. Favourable to the cause of Richard, duke of York, then in Ireland, ib. The bold men of Kent encamp at Blackheath, Cade being their captain, 88. In reply to a message from the court he sends the complaint of the Commons of Kent, ib. He follows it by a document, in more decided terms, "The requests by the captain of the great assembly in Kent," ib. He demands that Richard of York, Exeter, Buckingham, and Norfolk, should be called in as advisers of Henry VI., ib. An army is sent to reply to these remonstrances, ib. Cade defeated a detachment of this force at Sevenoaks, and the commander sir Humphrey Stafford was slain, ib. Cade occupied the Surrey side of the river, demanded entrance to the city, which the Lord-Mayor granted, ib. He maintained discipline and forbade plunder, ib. He cites lord Say to Guildhall, and compels the mayor and judges to condemn that minister, ib. Say and Cromer, sheriff of Kent, beheaded, ib. Cade returned over London-bridge in good order each night, to Southwark, ib. The citizens resolved, with lord Scales, who had a force in the Tower, to prevent Cade from recrossing the bridge, 89. Part of the old structure was a draw-bridge; Cade had destroyed the chains, &c., ib. Contest by night on the bridge; the citizens were successful in keeping out the insurgents, ib. Redress of grievances promised; delusive pardon under the great seal to all who should return home, ib. Dissension among the rebels, ib. Cade accepted the pardon, and most of his men dispersed, ib. At Rochester this captain is terrified by the violence of some of the most disaffected, ib. He was proclaimed a traitor, and a reward offered by government for his apprehension, ib. Flying for the Sussex coast, Cade was overtaken by Alexander Iden, an esquire, and, after a combat hand to hand, was overpowered, July, 1450, ib. Iden received the reward 1000 marks, ib. Cade's head was stock up on London-bridge; many of his comrades were caught and executed, ib.

Caer Bran, circular stone wall and fortress of ancient Britons, on a hill in Cornwall, i. 100.

Caer-Caradoc, British camp on a lofty hill in Shropshire, near the confluence of the Teme and Coln, i. 41.

Caer Din, or Dinas, Welsh names for ancient fieldworks, or forts, generally on high mountains, i. 99, 100.

Caer Morus, a circular entrenchment at Cellan, Cardiganshire, i. 99.

CARMARTHEN, marquess of, covers the landing of some English troops in Cameret Bay, 1694, iv. 48.

Caernarvon Castle, view of, i. 699. Edward II. was born in this castle whilst his father was employed in the subjugation of Wales, ib.

CÆSAR, C. Julius, his expedition to Britain, i. 25. His motives explained by himself, and others sur-mised, 25, 26. Copper coin in the British Museum, with the profile of Cæsar, 26. British envoys sent across the Channel to offer him homage, and promise the submission of certain tribes, with whom he sends over Comius as his envoy, and to explore the country; the latter is loaded with chains on arrival, 27, 28. Cæsar, with two legions, sets sail from Portus Itius, or Witsand, near Calais, and attains the Dover shore (A.C. 55, August 26), 27. The transports, with the cavalry, fail to cross the Straits, 27—29. Cæsar seeks a safer landing, near Walmer and Sandwich, and, fiercely opposed by the natives, lands 12,000 legionaries, the aquilifer of the 10th legion being the first to dash ashore, ib. View of his landing, 28. Cæsar having defeated the maritime tribes, and received hostages, pardons the resistance of the Britons, 29. His eighty transports suffer irretrievable damage from the high tides at full moon, ib. The galleys, with his cavalry, dispersed, and forced back to the Gallic ports, ib. Dearth of provisions, consternation of the legionaries, and other results of this accident, ib. Being aware of the revived hopes of the Britons consequent on these unexpected difficulties, he diligently repairs his galleys, ib. A legion cutting some ripe corn, as foragers, is vigorously attacked; Cæsar supports it in person with two cohorts, and with difficulty rescues it from extreme peril, ib. He defeats the Britons, ib. Fires some villages, but accepts an offer of hostages, and sails for Gaul, 30. The breach of delivery of hostages serves as a pretext for his second invasion, ib. In the spring A.C. 54, Cæsar embarks at Portus Itius, in 800 vessels, bearing five legions, and 2,000 cavalry, in all 32,000 men, ib. Lands unopposed, and, marching to the vicinity of the present Canterbury, he takes the strongly-barricaded entrenchment of the Britons, ib. His fleet being again destroyed by shipwreck, he returns to the shores near Sandwich with all his forces, finds forty of his ships irretrievably lost, takes measures to construct a new fleet, and drags the best ships to his camp, ib. He marches against Cassivellaunus, posted near Canterbury, and repulses his attack, 31. He loses a tribune in battle, and suffers a defeat, ib. He sends out all his cavalry to forage, supported by three legions, and repels a very fierce assault, 32. His victory complete, the tribes disperse to their separate territories, ib. He pursues the discomfited Briton to his own possessions on the Thames, ib. Sustains a harassing warfare on the confines of Surrey, passing the river at Coway-stakes, near the present Chertsey, ib. He assails the capital fastness, or residence of Cassivellaunus (St. Alban's, or Verulamium, subsequently), and reduces it, 33. The Roman reserve on the coast (near Walmer) defeat the Kentish Britons, who attempt to surprise the fleet, ib. Cæsar grants peace to Cassivellaunus, takes hostages, and stipulates for tribute to Rome, ib. His admonitions to the British prince, ib. Cæsar finally quits the shores of Britain, establishing no forts, and taking all his forces into Gaul, ib. Character of his British war, reflections, and military remarks, 34—37. He informs Cicero of the results of the invasion of the island, and of the tribute imposed, 105. Importance of his conquests towards the civilisation of the people, by the introduction of the useful arts and the embellishments of architecture, ib., 135.

CÆSAR's narrative of his British expeditions, derived from his "Commentaries," i. 27—33, 102. Chief observations of the Roman invader, upon the warfare, religion, and customs of the Britons, 34—36, 59—77, et seq., 99, 104, 119, 125.

CÆSAR, Sir Julius, one of the commissioners appointed by James I. to consider the divorce of the earl of Essex, 1613, iii. 53.

CAJETANO, Cardinal, the pope's legate, examines Luther at Augsburg, by command of pope Leo, 1518; ii. 707.

Calais, town, harbour, and vicinity of; territory of the Morini, i. 27, 30. Siege of the town by Edward III., it surrenders Aug. 3, 1347; 768—770. *Illustration.* The citizens surrendering the keys to Edward, they receive pardon at the earnest request of queen Philippa, 770. View of Calais from the sea, ii. 535; besieged, 1435, by Philip of Burgundy, 79. His personal enemy, Gloucester, drives him from the siege, taking his artillery and baggage, 79, 80. Warwick appointed governor, 1454, and Calais thenceforward became his refuge and resort in adversities, 93, 94, 105. At length Warwick's lieutenant points the artillery against his ships: the earl sails from Calais to Normandy, and is most graciously received by Louis XI. and the admiral of France, 1470; 105. The citadel, town, and port taken in eight days by the duke of Guise, 1558, after it had been in the possession of the English for 211 years, 533—535. Grief and humiliation of the English at the conquest of the English pale by the French; the loss was not very important. Henry VIII. and Wolsey would have sold Calais, but for the national feeling, 535.

CALAMY, chosen by the Presbyterians to defend their cause, 1660; iii. 668. Declines the bishopric of Lichfield and Coventry, 820.

Calcutta, sold to the English by Azim Ooshaun, 1698; § ii. 21. View of, 44. Taken possession of by Suraju-Dowlah, 1756; 41—47. View of obelisk erected to the Englishmen murdered in the black-hole, 47. View of Calcutta, 95. View of the Council-house at, 114. Factory of, declared an independent presidency in 1707; iv. 723.

CALDER, sir Robert, captures two of the French ships commanded by Villeneuve, after a partial action, 1805; § iv. 186. On his return he is tried and reprimanded, ib.

CALDERWOOD, David, a distinguished preacher, exiled for life, 1617; iii. 66. Quoted, 436, 439, 450, 470.

Caledonia, the ancient name of North Britain, etymology of, i. 17. Original population of, Gothic, who migrated from Denmark, 23.

Caledonians, the, asserted by Tacitus to be of Scandinavian origin, i. 6. They settle in Scotland, 9. Agricola makes war upon them, 46; while he is advancing, they attack the new Roman forts, between the Forth and Clyde, ib.; and falling upon the ninth legion, fortified in a strong camp, nearly cut it to pieces, ib. They are defeated in a general battle, A.D. 83, ib. In Agricola's seventh campaign, they await his approach on the Grampian Hills, to the number of 30,000 men, commanded by the brave Galgacus, where they make a firm resistance, but are at last vanquished, A.D. 84, ib. Agricola withdraws his army, 47. The Caledonians, in the time of Hadrian, again attack the Roman frontiers, ib.; but are afterwards defeated by Antoninus Pius, Lollius Urbicus, and Severus, 47, 48.

Calendar, the French Revolutionary, came into use Oct. 1793; discontinued Dec. 1806; § iii. 377, 378.

Calico-printing, commenced in England towards the latter end of 1676; iii. 869; § i. 600; § iii. 694; improvement in the art, by the introduction of copper cylinders, about 1785; 710; progress of, during the nineteenth century, § iv. 694.

CALONNE, Charles-Alexander de, a French statesman, distinguished for his share in the transactions which preceded the Revolution. He was chosen as comptroller of the finances in 1783; but his conduct by no means justified the trust reposed in him, and in 1787 he was dismissed from office, § ii. 341. Portrait of, ib.

Calvinists, so named after the great reformer. They seize lands belonging to the archbishop of Prague

Calvinists—
and the abbot of Brunaw, iii. 80; they repair to the castle of Prague, and throw two zealous Catholics out of the window into the castle ditch, May 23, 1618, ib. Count Thurn addresses the people, ib.; the Calvinists flock to his banner. The palatine Frederick crowned by the Calvinists at Prague, November 4th, 1619; 81.

Camalodunum, taken by the Romans; i. 40; afterwards, being a Roman colony, assailed by Iceni and Trinobantes, when a Roman legion is cut to pieces, 43.

Cambray, congress held here in 1721; iv. 377.

Cambridge, University of, first institution of a school of science founded here by Gislebert in the twelfth century, i. 606; its rapid increase, &c., ib. King's College, founded, 1441, by Henry VI., ii. 198. *Illustrations*—Interior of King's College Chapel, 197; Doorway of King's College Chapel, 224. The University, after long hesitation and arguments, seals a declaration of the illegality of Henry VIII.'s marriage with Catherine of Arragon, 376. The University (1687) refuses to confer the dignity of M.A. on Alban Francis, a Benedictine friar, iii. 786.

CAMBRIDGE, Richard earl of, brother of the duke of York, conspires, 1415, to establish the earl of March on the throne, ii. 29. Henry V., after trial by the peers, orders him to be beheaded, that king being then about to invade France, ib. By Anne Mortimer, sister of Edmund earl of March, he left a son Richard, who succeeded as duke of York, and also inherited the royal claims of the house of Mortimer, 6, 89.

Camden, battle of, fought, August, 1780; § i. 426, 427.

CAMDEN, Charles Pratt, earl of, 1786. Tries the cause of John Wilkes, 1763; § i. 27. Declares general warrants to be illegal, 31. Is presented with the freedom of the city, 1764; 34. Is created baron Camden, 1765; 41. Portrait of, 51, 82. He is dismissed, 1770; 84. Accused of double-dealing by lord Sandwich, 90, 203. He presents a petition, 1775, from the British inhabitants of Canada, 210.

CAMDEN, the first who ventured to question the account of the Trojan population of Britain, i. 8, 11, 137; ii. 541. His Portrait, from an old picture, iii. 560. His "Britannia" first published in 1586; 616. His description of England, 656.

CAMELFORD, Thomas Pitt, earl of, created 1784; § i. 123.

Camera-obscura, the, invented by Baptista della Porta, iv. 764.

CAMERON, Dr. Archibald, iv. 547; executed as a traitor, June 7, 1753, for assisting the young Pretender, 579.

CAMERON, Jenny, confined in Edinburgh Castle, February 2, 1746; iv. 529.

CAMERON, Richard, founder of the Macmillanites in the eighteenth century, iv. 651.

CAMERON, a leader of the Covenanters, 1681; iii. 735.

CAMERON of Lochiel, joins the standard of the young Pretender, 1745; iv. 482.

CAMERON of Clunes, conceals the young Pretender at Glencoich, 1746; iv. 547.

Cameronians, the, burn the articles of the Union, 1706; iv. 193.

CAMMOCK, rear-admiral; he escapes from the battle of Messina with three of the Spanish ships, and captures some merchantmen, 1718; iv. 348. His dexterous attempt to obtain provisions from the governor of Tropea, 357.

CAMPBELL, Colin, a distinguished architect of the eighteenth century, iv. 751.

CAMPBELL, bishop of the Isles, deposed and excommunicated for not acknowledging the decrees of the Assembly of Montrose, passed in 1600; iii. 484.

CAMPBELL, captain, of Finab, lands with a number of emigrants at the Isthmus of Darien, iv. 98 ; he storms Tubucantee, *ib.*; and returns to Scotland, having lost all his men, 1699 ; 99, 326.

CAMPEGGIO, cardinal, 1528, legate conjointly with Wolsey, for the divorce of queen Catherine; conduct of the Italian, evasive and crafty, ii. 367—369. His return to Rome, without any sentence on the divorce pronounced, 1529. His room broken into at Dover, for the *decretal bull,* or other exhibits of the late suit, which surceased on the queen's appeal to Rome, 371.

Campes, treaty of, 1546, its provisions, &c., ii. 447, 457.

CAMPION, the Jesuit, racked by Elizabeth's order, and afterwards executed, ii. 654 ; iii. 519.

Campo Formio ; this celebrated treaty was concluded between Austria and France, October 17, 1797 ; § iii. 525.

CAMVILLE, Richard de, the government of Cyprus granted to him in conjunction with Robert de Turnham, by Richard I., 1190, i. 495.

Canadas, Lower and Upper provinces, important French colonies in North America. Left exposed to invasion in 1758, through the distresses of the French court. Lieut.-general Wolfe sailed up the St. Lawrence, June, 1759, to attack Quebec, which city he found to be almost impregnable, iv. 607. Defeat of Montcalm, death of Wolfe in the moment of victory, fall of Quebec, and conquest of both provinces, 608, 609.

CANALES, Marquis de, the Spanish minister residentiary in England, presents a memorial remonstrating against the settlement of Darien, 1699. iv. 98.

Canals, origin of navigable, in England, 1755, iv. 730. The Duke of Bridgwater's canal opened July 17, 1761 ; § i. 577, 578; § iv. 681, 682.

CANNING, appointed secretary for foreign affairs, March, 1807, § iv. 264. His dispute and duel with Lord Castlereagh, on Putney Heath, 1809, 424.

Cannon, specimen of ancient, i. 874. Descriptions of artillery used at an early period in England, France, &c., ii. 329, 330.

Canon law, five books of decretals published by order of Gregory IX., 1234, i. 803. A sixth part added by Boniface VIII., *ib.* Character and power of, &c., *ib.*

Canterbury, battles of the Britons with Cæsar, in the forest lands near the modern city of, A.C. 54, for the defence of Cantium, i. 30—33. This maritime province, called by the natives Cantirland, or Cantwaraland (whence both Kent and Canterbury remain as the local names), 77, 142. View of the ruins of St. Augustine's monastery at Canterbury, 558. Two Roman churches here, one of which was given to St. Augustine, by king Ethelbert, and dedicated as Christ's Church, 309. The eastern portion of this great structure was completed in the twelfth century, 615.

Cantii, a British tribe settled in Cantium, or Kent, their wars against Cæsar, A.C. 55, 54, i. 27—33, 77. *See* Kent.

CANUTE the Great, commands the fleet of Sweyn, his father, 1012, in the Humber, i. 179. Sweyn, of Denmark, being joined by all the Danish population of the "Danelagh," &c., marches triumphantly to the west, fixes at Bath, and receives homage as "full king of England," 179, 180. On his decease, at Gainsborough, 1013, his host proclaims Canute king of England, 180. War of the Danish monarch, and Edmund Ironside, called by the Saxon nobles to his father Ethelred's throne, *ib.* Pacification and partition, *ib.* Death of the brave Edmund, and suspicions attached to the royal Dane, probably unfounded, *ib.* Moderation of Canute, 1017 ; he calls a council of bishops and nobles, alleges that

CANUTE the Great—

Edmund in his treaty intended to reserve no right to the crown in favour of Ethelred's sons by Emma, *ib.* Canute receives the oath of allegiance from the English nobles, and promises a general amnesty, *ib.* He breaks the oath he had just taken, and puts to death many Saxon chiefs, banishing the rest of his enemies, 181. He puts to death Edmund's relatives and Ethelred's, the witenagemot being subservient to the tyrant, through fear, *ib.* Edwy, denominated "king of the churls," or peasants, a brother of Edmund, is outlawed and slain, *ib.* Canute sends Edmund and Edward, infant sons of Edmund Ironside, to Sweden ; the king of that country, not choosing to murder them, sends them to the king of Hungary, by whom they were reared in safety and honour, *ib.* Of these princes, Edward, marrying the daughter of the German emperor, was father of Edgar Atheling, Christina, and Margaret, *ib.* Canute wooes Emma of Normandy, widow of Ethelred, and that princess willingly married a new *king of England, ib.* Bearing a son to king Canute, she no longer shows the least regard for her sons Edward and Alfred, who remain in Normandy as exiles, *ib.* Ulterior consequences of this ill-assorted union, *ib.* He levies great sums arbitrarily, and his new subjects were also oppressed by the Danish chiefs, *ib.* Urging his rights over Norway and Sweden, as well as Denmark, he leads the Saxons to those distant expeditions, *ib.* The English fight valiantly for their Danish sovereign, *ib.* The Cumbrians and Scots, 1017—1019, maintained that the heir of Ethelred ought to ascend the throne, *ib.* Canute marches against them with a great force, and brings both Duncan of Cumbria, and Malcolm of Scotland, to reason, *ib.* Peace established in England, and its prosperous consequences, 182. The monarch now displayed a milder and more enlightened character, *ib.* He patronised bards, scalds, and minstrels, *ib.* His partiality for popular ballads, *ib.* Fragment of a ballad by Canute himself, *ib.* His visit to Ely, and the royal barge on the Nenne, *ib.* His devotion, he founds monasteries and churches, 182, 184. His pilgrimage to Rome, a staff in hand, and a wallet on his back, 1030 ; *narrative,* 182. Remarks, *ib.* Recrossing the Alps, he repaired to Denmark, and sojourned there some months, *ib.* Thence he addresses a letter, happily still extant, to Egelnoth, Alfric, other bishops, and to the English nation, *ib.* He declares therein his happy journey, and his having secured to his subjects free passage through divers states without payment of any tolls, *ib.* That he wants no monies raised by injustice, and requires all dues to the church to be instantly paid, 183. *Illustration.* Canute's reproof to his courtiers *(after Smirke),* the sea not obeying him, as they pretended it would, *ib.* The "King's Delf," a causeway from Peterborough to Ramsey, 184. His death, 1035, three years after his return, and sepulture at Winchester, *ib.* Silver coin of Canute, 180. Question whether Harold and Sweyn were his sons at all, or imposed on him by his mistress Alfgiva, 184. Canute said to have destined his real son, Hardicanute, to inherit Denmark ; Harold, to possess England ; and Sweyn Norway, *ib.*

CANUTE, son of Sweyn Estridsen, king of Denmark, came to England in the expedition commanded by Osbeorn, 1069, i. 371. He succeeds his father in the kingdom of Denmark ; his alliance with Olaf, king of Norway, and his father-in-law, Robert, earl of Flanders, for the invasion and expulsion of the Normans from England ; their united armament, calculated to amount to a thousand sail, 386. Delays of various kinds, Canute desists from the enterprise, 387.

CANYNGE, William, mayor of Bristol, a wealthy merchant, 1449; ii. 176. His ships and trade (under licence from Henry VI., and from the king of Denmark) to Iceland and Finmark, returning with fish, &c., *ib.* His monument in St Mary Radcliff, *ib.*

CAPEL, Lord Arthur, iii. 212, 281; beheaded in Palace-yard, 1649; 400.

CARACALLA, son of Severus, had served under his father's standard in Britain, but was anxious, 211, to return to Rome on account of Geta, his brother, left co-heir to the empire, i., 52. He ceded to the Caledonians the fertile lands so long contested for, as far as the line of the Solway and Tyne, *ib.* Seventy years of tranquillity ensued, *ib.* The Scots became more civilised, *ib.* Caracalla granted the privileges of Roman citizens to the provinces, inclusive of Britain, a great boon to the British subjects of the empire, 53.

CARACTACUS defeated by Aulus Plautius, A.C. 43; i. 39; commander of the British forces, 40; appointed commander of the Silures, 41. His animated address to the Britons, *ib.* They are defeated, but Caractacus escapes. *ib.* ; is taken prisoner, and conveyed to Rome, 42; appears in the presence of Claudius, *ib.* *See* Caradoc.

CARADOC, the supposed British name of Caractacus, i. 41. His camp of Caer-Caradoc, on a hill in Shropshire, *ib.*

CARAUSIUS, by birth either a Briton or Belgian, and supposed early in life to have been a pirate, is appointed by Diocletian and Maximian to repress the Saxon pirates and Scandinavians, who then first invaded Gaul and Britain, i. 53. Location in Belgium and the British islands of several colonies of Menapians, the nation to which Carausius belonged, *ib.* He defeats the Baltic pirates, and becomes wealthy by securing their ill-gotten booty, *ib.* The two emperors become jealous of their British commander, and give orders for his death, *ib.* Returning thereupon into Britain, the Roman legions 288, proclaim him emperor, *ib.* Being victorious over all the power the emperors of Rome could send against him, they ratify his government of Britain and the coast of Gaul, conceding to him the style and dignity of emperor in his province, *ib.* He equips a powerful fleet, mans it with Saxon and Scandinavian seamen, whom he had formerly chastised, and is complete master of the narrow seas, *ib.* Names of this *insular* emperor, *ib.* Gold coin of Carausius, *ib.* He was murdered, 297, at Eboracum by his declared friend and minister, Allectus, who succeeded to his power, *ib.*

Carberry Hill, surrender of Mary, queen of Scots, at, May 15, 1567; ii. 600, 601.

Cardiff Castle, view of, as it appeared in 1775; i. 411. Imprisonment of the unfortunate duke Robert, in this fortress, *ib.*

CARDONEL, Secretary to the duke of Marlborough, expelled from the House of Commons, 1712; iv. 261.

Cards, playing invented, 1391; at first painted splendidly by able artists, ii. 258. The invention of printing turned early to their production, *ib.* Law prohibiting their importation, *ib.* Old games, trump, primero, &c., *ib.* Gaming augmented by them to a ruinous extent, *ib.* Henry VII. enacts severe statutes against their use, 391.

CAREW, sir George, 1545, founders, with his crew, in Dudley's action with Francis L's admiral Annebaut, ii. 442.

CAREW, sir George, one of the council of war in 1596; ii. 680. The earl of Essex sails for England, and leaves the government of Ireland to him, in conjunction with the archbishop of Dublin, 1599; 684.

CAREW, sir Peter, rises in arms in Devonshire, to oppose the marriage of Philip II. with Mary of England, ii. 512.

CAREY, sir Robert, son of lord Hunsdon, is dispatched by Elizabeth, 1587, to make excuses to king James for the murder of his mother, ii. 571. On receiving the first intelligence of the death of his relative queen Elizabeth, posts to Edinburgh, where he arrives March 26, 1803, and announces this event to James VI. before the arrival of envoys sent by the English Council, iii. 2. His memoirs, 2, *note.*

CARGILL, Donald, a fanatic preacher in Scotland, condemned for rebellion and hanged, July 27, 1681; iii. 730, 735.

Caribbee Isles, the, conquered by general Monckton and admiral Rodney, 1762; § i. 17.

Carisbrooke Castle, Isle of Wight, view of this ancient fortalice, iii. 390.

CARLETON, sir Dudley, iii. 114. He describes the comfortable condition of the English in comparison with continental nations, 118. Is sent on an embassy to Paris, 1626; 125. Created viscount Dorchester 1628; died 1631; 136. His monument in Westminster Abbey, executed by sir George Hollis and Bernard Jansen, 576.

CARLETON, sir Guy, governor of Canada, examination of, 1774; § i. 170, 171, 218, 219. Portrait of, 256. Is appointed one of the Commissioners of Accounts, 1780; 405. Supersedes sir Henry Carleton, 1782; 488.

Carleton House, view of, § iii. 740.

Carlisle, view of this city, i. 398. Returning from his expedition against Malcolm Caenmore, 1092, William Rufus seized on this city, founded the Castle, and soon sent a colony of English from the south to occupy it and the adjacent lands, *ib.* View of Carlisle Castle, iv. 510.

CARLISLE, James Hay, earl of, created September, 1622; iii. 14, 57. His vast expenditure, *ib.* His embassy to France, 106. He receives a grant of the Caribbee Isles from James I. 540. He died, 1636.

CARLOS, Don, commands the Spanish forces in Italy, iv. 413. He enters Naples; the Spaniards conquer Sicily; he becomes master of the kingdom of the two Sicilies, May 10, 1734; 414; and is acknowledged king, 1735; 416.

Carnac, a great Druidical temple in Brittany, i. 68.

CARNAC, Major, arrives in India, 1763; § ii. 88.

CARNE, sir Edward, sent to notify to Pope Paul IV. the accession of queen Elisabeth, 1559; ii. 543.

CAROLINA Wilhelmina, daughter of John Frederic, margrave of Anspach, and queen of George II., born 1683; iv. 396. 100,000*l.* a year is settled on the queen for life, 399. The king leaves her regent during his absence, 403. Her portrait, 415. Her illness and death, November 20, 1737; 428, 429.

CAROLINE AMELIA ELIZABETH, second daughter of the duke of Brunswick Wolfenbüttel, and queen of George IV., to whom she was married April 8, 1795; § iii. 470.

CAROLINE MATILDA, youngest sister of king George III. Her marriage with Christian VII., king of Denmark, 1766; § i. 36, 128. This unhappy princess was hurled from her throne January 16, 1772, with the darkest imputations on her character, and confined in Cronborg Castle; the English king, by means of his ambassador, sir R. Murray, remonstrated and menaced, and finally induced the Danish court to permit her to quit the kingdom; she was removed to the Castle of Zell, in Hanover, where she died May, 10, 1775; 129, 180.

CAROLINE, Princess, third daughter of George II., her death, 1757; iv. 601, *note.*

Carpenter's Hall, Philadelphia, view of, § i. 187.

Carpets, in the seventeenth century, used for covering tables, the floors being matted or strewed with rushes, iii. 619. Art of making Brussels carpets introduced at Kidderminster, in 1745, from Tournay, iv. 811.

CARR, Robert, *see* Rochester.

CARRIER, one of the most bloody of the French Revolutionists, and inventor of the *mariages républicains*, § iii. 376, 377. He is brought to trial and guillotined by the Thermidorians, December 16, 1794, 455.

Carrighhill, subterranean chamber at, i. 97.

CARRION, a celebrated nun of the seventeenth century, iii. 98.

CARTERET, John, Viscount, his embassy to Russia, iv. 368. He arrives in Ireland as lord-lieutenant, and offers a reward of 300l. for the discovery of the author of 'The Drapier's Letters,' 385. He brings forward a motion, beseeching the king to settle upon the Prince of Wales 100,000l. per annum, 426. On the death of his mother, 1744, he becomes Earl Granville, 474. He died 1763.

Carthagena, unsuccessful attack on, by admiral Vernon and general Wentworth, 1741; iv. 452, 453. View of the bay of, 453.

Carthaginians, their voyages to Britain and Ireland, i. 14.

Carthusian monasteries. John Houghton, prior of the Charter-house, London; Webster and Lawrence, priors of those of Belval and Exham; Dr. R. Reynolds, a monk of Sion, and Hailes, vicar of Thistleworth, were hanged at Tyburn, 1535, with all the horrid concomitants of traitors' deaths, Cromwell being implacable in the persecution of monks; the chief allegation being a refusal to take the oath of the king's supremacy, ii. 386.

Carthusians. This order of monks introduced into England, 1180; i. 559. *Illustration* of a Carthusian monk, 560.

CARTWRIGHT, Dr. Edmund, inventor of the first power-loom, 1784; § iii. 697. His machinery for combing wool, 705.

CARTWRIGHT, Thomas, of Cambridge. His eloquent orations, declaring the Presbyterian church-government the only apostolical form, 1566; ii. 635. Influence of his writings, *ib.* His party agitate parliament by their measures for stricter religious reform, *ib.*

CARTWRIGHT, Thomas, bishop of Chester, 1686. Sancroft, archbishop of Canterbury, refusing to act in the ecclesiastical commission established by James II., he accepts the archbishop's place, iii. 786. He dies, April 15, 1689, neglected and destitute, in Ireland, iv. 620.

Cashel, Psalter of: bardic legends compiled, 850 to 900, by Cormac Mac Cullinan, bishop of Cashel and king of Munster, i. 303.

CASIMIR, duke, offers his hand to queen Elizabeth, ii. 575; enters the Netherlands with a powerful army, 1579; 650.

CASLON, makes great improvements in the English printing-type about 1720; iv. 733.

Cassano, battle of, April 27, 1799; § iii. 546.

Cassiterides, or Scilly islands, Phœnicians accustomed to export tin, &c. from the, i. 93, 104.

CASSIVELLAUNUS, chief of the confederated Britons, A.C. 54. Situation of his territories, i. 30. His valour, and former warfare with adjacent tribes, 31. He encamps in woods (near Canterbury), *ib.* He charges the Romans, and is repulsed, with mutual loss, *ib.* He issues suddenly from the forest, and routs a considerable portion of the enemy's force, *ib.* Comparison left on record of the mode of fighting of the light-armed Britons and the heavy-armed legionaries, 31, 32. The British general charges boldly the entire Roman cavalry, and endeavours to break through three legions formed in solid masses, but experiences a total defeat, 32. He fortifies with stakes the ford across the Thames (near Chertsey), but in vain oppos·s the passage of Cæsar, *ib.* His auxiliaries desert him, and Cassivellaunus, at the head of only a small army, continues a defen-

CASSIVELLAUNUS,— sive war, harassing the Romans, and always ready to retreat, 32, 33. He excites the four princes of Kent to attack Cæsar's reserve and fleet on the coast, but they are defeated, 33. Cassivellaunus, sues for peace, through the medium of Comius, king of the Atrebatians, which Cæsar grants him, stipulating for a payment of tribute, *ib.*

CASTALIO, Sebastian. *See* Martinus Bellius.

CASTAÑETA, commander of a Spanish expedition to Sicily, 1717; iv. 345.

CASTIGLIONE, prince of, taken prisoner by the Austrians, 1707; iv. 204.

CASTLEHAVEN, earl of, his mention of the Rebellion in Ireland of 1641; iii. 254, 310.

CASTLEMAINE, Lady, mistress of Charles II., iii. 685, 706.

CASTLEMAINE, Roger Palmer, earl of, cause of his creation, iii. 685. His embassy to Rome, 1686; 785.

CASTLEREAGH, Lord, secretary-at-war, March, 1807; § iv. 264. His dispute and duel with Mr. Canning, 1809; 424.

Castles, construction of strong, throughout England, in the reigns of Henry I. and Stephen, i. 615.

CATALANI, Madame, the eminent vocalist, § iv. 720.

Cateau Cambresis, peace of, April 2, 1559; its articles, ii. 547. Both Scotland and England were parties in this treaty, *ib.*

CATESBY, Robert, a Catholic gentleman, who had once retracted, but returned to the Romish creed, iii. 20. Had engaged in Robert Devereux, earl of Essex's unfortunate insurrection, *ib.* His intrigues with France and Spain, *ib.* He imagines the destruction of king and parliament, 1604-1605, by gunpowder, and collects many daring coadjutors in the plot, 21. He first communicates with Thomas Winter, a gentleman serving in the Low Countries, who, repairing thither, brings to London Guido Fawkes, a soldier of good family, *ib.* The conspirators meet at Catesby's, *ib.* He imposes an oath of secrecy at a lone house in fields near Clement's Inn; he then imparts his plot, and they receive the sacrament from the Jesuit, Gerard, *ib.* He enlists some men of good family and estate in his nefarious plot, to their utter ruin, 23, 24. Is resolute that no attempt should be made to warn any catholic relatives or patrons of the danger in parliament, lest the plot should be abortive, 25. He charges Tresham with deceiving them, 25, 26. He and J. Wright set out, Nov. 4, to join Digby in the field, 27. Rookwood, and the now daunted conspirators, arrive at lady Catesby's, Ashby-Saint-Legers; the whole party ride thence to Dunchurch, where the conspirators are shunned by every one, . 28. Catesby essays to lead them towards Wales, to raise the catholics of those districts, *ib.* He, sheltering with his party in Holbeach-house, Stephen Littleton's, is severely burnt by a great explosion of powder they were drying near the fire, *ib.* Is attacked by sir R. Walsh and the *posse-comitatus* of Worcester, and, with several of his partners, dies in defending Holbeach, *ib.*

CATESBY, a captain and chief adviser of Richard III., 1485; ii. 128. His attainder, 284. His execution, *ib.*

CATHCART, William Shaw, earl; created viscount, November 3, 1807; his service in the bombardment of Copenhagen, § iv. 287—290.

CATHELINEAU, Jacques, an able commander of the Vendeans in the insurrection of 1793; § iii. 370; mortally wounded in the attack on Nantes, 374.

CATHERINE of France, 1414; her hand sought by Henry V., ii. 28, 38. Her beauty excites admiration in the English monarch, her suitor, 44. The betrothal and marriage of the royal lovers at Troyes, 1420; 47. She is crowned with pomp at Westminster, 1421, 48. The king about to undertake a campaign, to avenge the defeat and

G

CATHERINE, of France—
death of his brother Clarence by the party of the dauphin Charles, leaves her at Windsor castle, 1421; 49. Birth of her son (Henry VI.), December 6, 1421, 50. Queen Catherine, with a great train of English nobility, lands at Harfleur, May 21, 1422, ib. Splendid court of Henry and Catherine held in the Louvre at Paris, ib. Decease of her royal husband, 50, 51. She follows the procession, conveying the king's corpse from Rouen to Westminster, 51. Their son, aged nine months, 1422, succeeds to the English crown, 52. Weak disposition of her son, Henry VI., 80. Her marriage with Owen Tudor, a private Welsh gentleman, 80, 125. Her promising family by her second husband, from whom sprung the royal house of Tudor, ib. Catherine died 1437, and was buried at Westminster, by the side of Henry V., 80.
CATHERINE of Medicis, niece of Clement VII., her betrothal, 1533, to the duke of Orleans, son of Francis I., ii. 382.
CATHERINE, daughter of Ferdinand, king of Spain, married, in 1501, to Arthur, prince of Wales, ii. 312. His death at Ludlow, in 1502, ib. Dispensation obtained for the widow's marriage with prince Henry, brother of her late husband, 312, 317, 319. Henry VIII. and Catherine were crowned June, 1509; 319. Her portrait, by Holbein, ib. She is left regent in England, 1513, on the king invading France, 323. Her affectionate congratulation to him, in writing news of the victory at Flodden, 330. She accompanied the king, 1520, to Calais, to the interview with Francis I., 338. The king notwithstanding her gentle conduct, and forgetful of their mutual duties to their only remaining child Mary, resolved to divorce Catherine, 364. Interest taken in her welfare by Charles V., her nephew, 365, 367, 376. The English and some foreign universities declared her union with Henry illegal, 376. Archbishop Cranmer, holding his court at Dunstable, declared Catherine's marriage with Henry null and void (See Henry VIII.), 381. On the marriage with Anne Boleyn, measures were taken to persuade the repudiated queen to resign herself to the judgment passed, and assume the title of princess dowager of Wales, 381, note, 383. Catherine obstinately, and also with great proofs of sentiment and consideration for her own dignity, resists all messages to that effect, 380, 381, 383. Her popularity throughout England, and particularly with the monastic orders, irritated by Henry's and Cromwell's measures of suppression, 381. This queen obliterated with her pen the words princess dowager wherever they had been written by her chamberlain Mountjoy, in his "Report" to the king of his mission to his former royal mistress, 381, note. Her name omitted in the church office, and that of queen Anne substituted in the prayer, 383. Anecdote of the octogenarian canon Carsley of Wells, ib. In her final sickness, at Kimbolton, (where she died, January 8, 1536), Catherine asked to see her daughter Mary, but the harsh-tempered king refused, 390. Her death-bed farewell to her royal husband, requiring him to be a good father to the princess Mary, her letter declaring her still latent affection for him, ib. King Henry dropped a tear at its perusal, ib. Catherine's prosperous rival, queen Anne, is said to exult, not knowing how rapidly her own worse doom approached, ib.
CATHERINE PARR, Queen (widow of Neville lord Latimer), became, in 1543, the sixth wife of Henry VIII., ii. 438. Remarkable for learning and discretion, she was reputed to be a sincere Protestant, which repeatedly endangered her life, ib. Her portrait by Holbein, 439. Henry VIII. gives orders to chancellor Wriothesley to prepare articles of impeachment against her, but she adroitly escapes

CATHERINE PARR—
the coming storm, 447. She marries to Sir Thomas Seymour, 473; dies in child-bed, September 30, 1548, after giving birth to a daughter, 476.
CATHERINE II., empress of Russia, princess of Anhalt Zerbst, 1762—1796. This ambitious and remorseless woman was born in 1729, and married to the arch-duke of Russia, afterwards Peter III., in 1745; she became the mother of two legitimate children —Paul, born in 1754; and Anne, in 1757: the latter of whom died in infancy. Urged on by fear of designs which she suspected her husband of forming against her, and being supported by the people, she formed a conspiracy to frustrate his purposes, and secure to herself the sole rule. In July, 1762, her adherents compelled Peter to sign a formal abdication, he was sent to Robscha, and shortly after murdered, § i. 21, 22. Tragical fate of the Czar Ivan, 1764; 132, 133. The first Partition Treaty, 1772; 134—140. Insurrection in the Morea aided by Russia, 1770; 141—148. Armistice signed at Giurgevo between the grand visier and general Romanzoff, May 30, 1772; 147. Treaty of Kainarji, July 21, 1774; 148. Catherine issues her manifesto in favour of the Armed Neutrality, 1780; 421. Her letter to Mary Antoinette, 1790; § ii. 505. War with Poland, 1791; § iii. 41. She dies of apoplexy, November, 1796; and is succeeded by her son Paul, 544.
CATHERINE of La Rochelle, her pretended inspiration; she promised Charles VII., 1430, that he should obtain abundance of riches, ii. 73. Unlike Joan of Arc, she never fought in battle, but only preached to the rich to give money for the king's service, ib. Friar Richard supports her inspired exertions, and both of these impostors were hostile to the valiant and enthusiastic Maid of Orleans, ib. Success of her friend the friar's preaching; he induced many towns to surrender, 70.
Catholic Committee, the, § iv. 619.
Catholic Emancipation, Roman; the catholic claims, 1802—1820, frequently advocated in parliament, § iv. 615. Pitt, a zealous supporter of this cause, ib. That minister, in 1799, had proposed a system for an independent provision of the Romish clergy, and the Roman catholic hierarchy agreed that government should have a certain influence in the appointment to sees, ib. George III. being inflexible in refusing the Roman catholic claims, Mr. Pitt resigned office, January, 1801; ib. The emancipation cause remained dormant in parliament until 1805; ib.
Catholic Emancipation Bill, 1813; § iv. 623.
Catholics, Roman, conspiracies, 1603, against James I., formed by Watson and Clarke, priests, and others, as the Scottish monarch on his succeeding Elisabeth decided against any relaxation of the penal statutes, iii. 8. The House of Commons, 1604, press the king to enforce with severity the penal statutes against the papists, 19. Persecution in Lancashire, 1604; execution of jesuits and priests under 27th Elizabeth, 22. Case of Mr. Pound, 1605; ib. They are disabled from sitting in parliament, 721. Act passed, 1791, for relieving protesting catholic dissenters from certain penalties and disabilities, § iii. 578—582, 586.
CATINAT, marshal, approaches within three leagues of Turin, when he is checked by prince Eugene, 1691; iv. 33; invests the town of Aeth, 77; is driven to the line of the Oglio by prince Eugene, 1701; 129.
CATTERTHUNS, the White, and the Black, two strong hill forts in Angusshire, crowning the two peaks of a bifurcate mountain, i. 99.
CATUS, Roman procurator, cruelly chastises Boudicea, i. 43. His defeat at Camalodunum, and flight to Gaul, ib.
CAULIAC, Guy de, quoted, i. 845.

Cavalry, British, i. 36.

Cavalry, Roman, i. 38.

CAVENDISH, chamberlain of Wolsey, and his biographer, ii. 365, 374, 377.

CAW, king of Strathclyde, after a war with Kenneth Mac Alpin, marries his daughter, i. 217. His kingdom remained independent till 973, when it merged into a province of Scotland, 217, 218. Dumbarton was the ancient capital, and named Alcluyd, 289. Gildas, our earliest historian, who flourished about 500, and the bard Aneurin, were sons of a prince Caw, of Strathclyde, ib.

CAXTON, William, first English printer, was born in the weald of Kent, about 1412; ii. 202. Specimen of his printing, ib. Introduced to the notice of Edward IV., 121, 207. Enumeration of the principal works printed by, 202—204. Supposed to have died in 1491-2; 202. His "Chronicle of England," 1480, derived from the Latin of Douglas, monk of Glastonbury, 209.

CEAWLIN, king of Wessex, 568, was the second chief obtaining the high office of Bretwalda, or paramount lord of all the Saxons, i. 145. Ethelbert of Kent disputes this title, and wars occur between the Saxons and Ceawlin, who adds Sussex to his dominions, ib. About 589 this king dies, when Ethelbert becomes the Bretwalda, ib.

CECIL, sir Edward. See Wimbledon.

CECIL, sir Robert, son of the earl of Burghley, ii. 679, 681, 687. He opens a secret correspondence with the king of Scotland, 692. His able conduct, March, 1603, in proclaiming James I., and securing him the English crown, iii. 3. He takes counsel with Nottingham, Egerton, and others, at Richmond, before the decease of Elizabeth was bruited, ib. Prepares the proclamation of the accession of James; and on the same day, March 24, causes it to be signed by the lord mayor, the archbishop of Canterbury, and others, ib. He reads it to the people at Whitehall and Cheapside, and sends heralds to proclaim the accession of the Scottish king in the Tower, ib. His vigorous measures to repress the partisans of those personages of royal blood who had rival pretensions to the crown, ib. He sends 800 suspected persons to serve with the fleet, ib. Retains lady Arabella Stuart in his safe keeping, ib. He and other great men neglect, in their zeal, to make any stipulations with the expected king, either for the liberties of the people or the privileges of parliament, ib. He remits money to James I. for his journey from Edinburgh, ib. Hastens the interment of Elizabeth in Westminster Abbey, 4. His flattery as to James's horsemanship, ib. His crafty conversations with the new monarch, and success in the formation of a new cabinet, 4, 5. He is created lord Cecil (in course of time viscount Cranborne, and earl of Salisbury), 5. At his house of Theobalds he settles with James I. the first cabinet of that king: names of such as he sedulously excludes, ib. Former friendship between Cecil and Raleigh, converted, 1603, into jealousy and hatred, 7. Wish of the opposition not admitted of the council of the new king to overthrow this minister, 7, 8. Measures of sir Robert Cecil for punishing all accomplices in the "Bye" and the "Main" plots, 1603, 8, 9. His attempt separately to inveigle both Raleigh and Cobham into admissions of guilt; successful only with the base lord Cobham, 9, 10, note. He reproves sir E. Coke for his extreme rudeness to Raleigh on his trial at Winchester, 11. Shows some favour to sir Walter, 12. His candid exculpation in court of the lady Arabella Stuart, ib. Shows, at first, some leniency to Garnet in the Tower, 30. Is rewarded with the Order of the Garter for his active prosecution of all the recent conspiracies, &c., 32. Is supposed to have been privy to a false rumour of the

CECIL, sir Robert,—assassination of the king, 1605, with a view to the moral effect upon the House of Commons, reluctant to grant the subsidies, which they at length do, 33. Feast given by Cecil to Christian IV., king James, and the court, at Theobalds, 33, 34. His letter to sir C. Cornwallis, English ambassador at Madrid, inveighing against Philip's receiving the earl of Tyrone, 39. He succeeds to the post of treasurer on the earl of Dorset's death, still retaining his secretaryship, ib. On becoming treasurer, he finds the king's debts amount to 1,300,000l., and his ordinary expenditure exceeding his revenue by 81,000l.; he proposes a perpetual yearly revenue to be granted by parliament, and every grievance redressed, &c., 41. Reasons given by historians as having partly caused his death, 45. He retires from business to drink the waters at Bath, ib. His death at Marlborough, May 24, 1612, on his way back to court, ib. Dying speech to sir Walter Cope, ib. Remarks on his character, ib.

CELESTINE III., pope, elected 1191, died 1198; i. 513.

CELESTIUS, an Irish monk, disciple of Pelagius, whence the followers of the Pelagian dogma were often called Celestians; age in which they wrote, i. 124. St. Jerome's vituperation of these famous heretics, ib.

CELLIER, Mrs., the meal-tub, containing a plan of that plot, found in her house, iii. 732.

Celtic, distinctions between the, and the Germanic races, affords no evidence as to the early population of Britain, i. 6; supposed by sir W. Betham to be the same people as the Phœnicians and Gaels, 9.

Celts, warlike implements of the Britons; prodigious number of; their use and form, etc., i. 36.

CEORL, with the men of Devon, about 851, defeats the Danes at Wenbury, i. 152.

CERDIC, at the close of the fifth century, conquered the Isle of Wight and Hampshire, there founding the kingdom of Wessex, or West Saxons; i. 142.

Ceremonies, Master of the, 1603, first instituted at the court of Westminster, by James I. (Sir L. Lewknor appointed); iii. 7.

Ceylon, the British Triads relate that the Cymry came from Defrobani, supposed by some to be Taprobane, or Ceylon, i. 8, 9. Cingalese villages compared to those of Britain, A.C. 54; 33, 34. The island taken from the Dutch by sir Edw. Hughes, 1782; ♥ ii. 150.

Chain-shot, invention of, attributed to De Witt, iii. 698.

Chalgrove Field, battle of, June 18, 1643, in which the patriot Hampden is killed, iii. 304.

CHALLONER, having engaged in the poet Waller's conspiracy, is hanged near his own house, 1643; iii. 302.

CHALMERS, his derivation of Picts, i. 18.

Chamberlain, his office, i. 569.

CHAMBERLAIN, Robert, esquire to Henry V., his armour and effigy, ii. 241.

CHAMBERLAIN, Dr., an eminent obstetrical practitioner, present at the birth of the son of James II., James Francis Edward, Prince of Wales, iii. 793.

Chambers, subterranean, i. 97, 98.

CHAMBERS, Richard, fined 2,000l. for refusing to pay any further duty for a bale of silks than might be demanded by law, 1629; iii. 145.

CHAMBERS, sir William, an eminent architect of the eighteenth century, § i. 631. Portrait of, ib.

CHAMPNEYS, sir Thomas, mayor of London in 1534; ii. 850.

Chancellor, office of the, i. 569.

Chancery, account of the Court of, i. 574, 818; ii. 761. Origin and properties of the, § i. 533—537. Abuses in the, § iv. 645, 646.

Chantilly, view of, with march of the Provincial Federalists for Paris, 1790; § ii. 495.

CHANTREY, sir Francis, an elegant artist of the nineteenth century, § iv. 716. His portrait, 717.

CHAPMAN, George, a dramatic writer, born six or seven years before Shakspeare; he began to write for the stage about 1595; his productions, iii. 592.

Chapter-house, St. Paul's, from an old print, iv. 640.

CHARETTE. See Conterie.

Chariots, British war, effects of, their form, &c., i. 34, 35.

Chariots, in use among the Gauls at an early period, i. 35, 36.

CHARLEMAGNE, the emperor, about 790, protects Egbert, the fugitive prince of Wessex, at his court, i. 150. He permits, in 800, Eadburgha, the profligate queen of Brihtric, to reside in a convent; she was afterwards driven from France into Italy, ib. His letter to Offa, king of Mercia, the earliest commercial treaty with England on record, 266.

CHARLES I., king of England, born in Scotland, 1600, being the second son of James VI. and Anne of Denmark. On the death of his elder brother, prince Henry, 1612, he is created Prince of Wales, iii. 63. His romantic journey to Spain, in order to pay his court in person to the Spanish infanta, 90—98. He returns to England, 99. The proposed match is broken off, 100. He accedes to the throne on the death of his father, 1625, and is proclaimed king at Theobalds, 106. His attention to religion, ib. The great seal, 109. His marriage with Henrietta Maria, daughter of Henri IV. of France, ib. His portrait, 110. Parliament adjourns; it is appointed to reassemble at Oxford on account of the plague, 111. Domestic quarrels, 115. The king persecutes the English-born catholics, 116. Popish lords disarmed, ib. Coronation of the king, 1626, 117. Parliament opens, ib. Buckingham is made chancellor of the University of Cambridge, 121. The king summons a parliament, 129. He liberates seventy-eight gentlemen who had refused to contribute to a forced loan; frees the earl of Bristol, and restores Abbot to his former authority, 130; confirms the Petition of Right, 134; prorogues parliament, ib.; receives the news of Buckingham's death, 137; appoints the earl of Lindsey commander of the expedition to Rochelle, 138; summons the houses, 1629, to Whitehall, 139; determines to support Laud and the hierarchy, 141; dissolves the parliament, 142; commits several members of the House of Commons to the Tower, ib.; makes peace with France, 146; signs the treaty of peace with Spain, 147; renews a treaty with Gustavus Adolphus, 150. His journey into Scotland, 156; is crowned at Edinburgh, ib. Proclamation issued for the repair of decayed churches, 158. The king contributes 10,000l. for the repairs of St. Paul's, ib.; cherishes the plan of governing without parliaments, 161. Parliament is called, 169. Charles claims all Connaught as crown land, 170. The English cabinet proposes, on the death of the Palatine Frederic, that his eldest son, prince Charles Louis, should take possession of the island of Madagascar, and his brother, prince Rupert, should found a colony in the West Indies, 173. Charles rejects a treaty proposed by the cardinal Richelieu, a leading clause of which was the restitution of the palatinate to his nephew, ib.; invites his two nephews to England, ib. The earl of Arundel despatched to Germany, to treat about the restitution of the prince Elector, 174. The king issues a writ for levying ship-money, 176; appoints the new service-book to be read in all Scottish churches, 182; sends down orders for removing the term and the council of government from Edinburgh to Linlithgow, 185; summons the earl of Traquair to London, and reproves him sharply, 186; draws up a commission for the marquess of Hamilton to reduce the Scots, 189. Preparations for invading Scotland, 192. The term restored to Edinburgh, 195. The king endeavours to sow dissensions amongst the Scottish nobles, 202. His journey to

CHARLES I.,—

York, 203. War with the Covenanters, 204. Amicable arrangement, 205. Both armies disbanded; Charles takes up his quarters in the town of Berwick, ib.; arrives in London, August 1, 1639, 206. He sends Loudon to the Tower, 207; demands from Oquendo, the Spanish general, 150,000l. for his safety, 208. Being urged by Wentworth, he reluctantly calls a parliament, 209. He produces the letter of the Scottish lords to the French king, 211; keeps sir John Elliot in prison till he dies, 212; summons the Houses to the banqueting hall, 213; persuades the Lords to hasten the Commons in granting the subsidies, 214; informs the Commons that the danger of the nation would be greatly increased if they delayed granting the subsidies longer, 215; sends Windebank to secure the speaker, 216; dissolves the parliament, ib. The king commits several members to prison, 217. Unjust proceedings to obtain money, 218. The mayor and sheriffs of London are cited to the Star-chamber, and four aldermen committed to prison, ib. The London apprentices attack Laud's palace, ib. The Covenanters resolve to enter England, 219. Charles makes lord Conway general of the horse, in place of the earl of Holland, 220. He publishes a proclamation, 1640, declaring the Scots, and all who assist them, traitors, ib. His hasty journey to York, ib. Conway is beaten, and flies to Newcastle, 221; thence to Durham; pursues his retreat to Darlington, where he meets with Strafford; they retreated to Northallerton, where the standard of Charles floated, 222. The king, Strafford, and Conway, fall back upon York, ib. The king receives lord Lanark who comes to negotiate peace, ib. Twelve English peers petition for a parliament, 223. The citizens of London sign a petition to the same effect, ib.; as also the gentry of York, 224. The king appoints sixteen English commissioners to act with eight Scottish commissioners about a peace, ib. He agrees to the petition of the Scots; allows them to levy 850l. per diem for the space of two months, and leaves in their possession Durham, Newcastle, and all the towns on the eastern coast beyond the Tees, with the exception of Berwick, 226. He opens in person the Long Parliament, November 3, 1640, ib. His speech, ib. He persuades the earl of Strafford to come up to the parliament, 230. He attempts to make a stand against the proceedings of parliament, 232; replies to the remonstrance of the Commons against popery, ib.; intercedes for John Goodman, a seminary priest, but gives him up at last to punishment, 233; confirms all the acts passed by the late Scottish parliament, 234; attends the earl of Strafford's trial, 235. He entertains several plans for that nobleman's escape, 240; calls both houses before him, and attempts to persuade them not to proceed severely against the earl, 241. The Lords pass the bill, abrogating the king's prerogative to dissolve parliament, 242. Charles summons his privy-council, and asks their opinions respecting the sentence of Strafford, 243. He signs the sentence of execution, ib. Promises instantly to disband the Irish army, 244; his letter to the Lords begging them to spare Strafford, ib. He passes the bill for putting down the High Commission Court and the Star-chamber, 247. The queen-mother, Mary de Medicis, arrives in England, ib. Charles agrees to disband his army at York, and to withdraw the garrisons he had thrown into Berwick and Carlisle, 248. Having named commissioners to take charge of the state during his absence, he goes to Scotland, 249. The earl of Holland having given notice to the parliament that he suspects intrigues between Charles and some of the Scots, they appoint commissioners to go into Scotland, and give them notice of whatever is there happening, ib. The king

CHARLES I.,—
attempts to get rid of lord Lanark, the marquess of Hamilton, and the earl of Argyle, 250. These noblemen, hearing of the plan, absent themselves from court, ib.; and the next day write to Charles, 251. He proceeds to the parliament-house with 500 soldiers; complains of the absence of the noblemen, and the vile slanders brought upon him, and urges a trial in parliament to prove his innocence, ib. The states propose a committee, the proceedings of which we know nothing; but a few weeks after, through the letters of the king and parliament, the noblemen return; Hamilton is made a duke, Argyle a marquess, ib. Meanwhile the English parliament, hearing of trouble there, and suspecting another Papists' conspiracy, order the Lord Mayor to secure the city of London, and the Justices of Middlesex and Surrey to obey such orders as the earl of Essex should give for ensuring the public safety, ib. The king attempts to corrupt the Scottish nobles, 252; he sends secret orders to the earls of Ormond and Antrim to secure the Irish army, and surprise the castle of Dublin, ib. The parliament obtains from the king an order for disbanding the army, but he still contrives by various artifices to keep it together, 253. The Irish rise, and butcher the Protestants without resistance; Clarendon says that 40 or 50,000 were murdered; Milton states it at 154,000; Sir J. Temple at twice that number; and Warner reduces it to 12,000; 254. Charles, still in Scotland, hearing of the massacre, desires the advice and assistance of their parliament; and having named the earl of Ormond lieutenant-general of his forces in Ireland, hastens to London, 255. The Commons present to him their 'Remonstrance of the State of the Kingdom,' 256. His answer to the petition, 257. He retires to Hampton-court, to prepare an answer to the Remonstrance, which had been printed by the parliament, 259. He removes sir William Balfour, lieutenant of the Tower, and appoints in his room colonel Lunsford, ib.; takes the keys away from him, ib.; removes the earl of Newport from the constableship of the Tower, ib.; impeaches five members of the House of Commons, 263; leaves Whitehall with his queen and children, and goes to Hampton-court, 265; waives his proceedings against the members for the present, ib. The civil war commences, 268. The king sends a message to the Commons, 270; their reply, ib. He marries his daughter Mary to the prince of Orange, 272; obtains permission for his queen to conduct the princess to Holland, ib. The Militia Bill tendered to Charles; he refuses to give his assent, 274. He orders that the prince of Wales should be sent to him to Greenwich. The houses refuse, alleging, amongst other reasons, the sickness of his governor, the marquess of Hertford, who, however, suddenly recovers, and delivers the prince into his father's hands, ib. The king proceeds to York, 277; attempts to gain possession of Hull, 278; and informs the parliament of his intention of going to Ireland, 279. Sir J. Hotham refuses the king admittance into Hull, ib. The royalists have recourse to stratagem to obtain the place, but are foiled, 282. The king issues a proclamation, forbidding the muster of any troops without his commands, 283. He receives the great seal at York from the lord-keeper, Littleton, 286; supply of arms from Holland, 288. Charles sends out commissions, enjoining all men to bring money, horses, &c., on the security of his forests and parks, 289. He writes to the Lord Mayor, forbidding contributions to be made for the parliament, 290; seizes Dr. Bastwick, and confines him in York gaol, 293; forms another plan for taking Hull, but it being discovered to the governor by one of his men, they fall on the royalist troops and put them to flight, ib. He fails in an attempt on the town of Coventry, 1642; 294. His letter to the earl of Newcastle, 296. Prince Rupert, nephew of the king, and a royalist, attempts to take Worcester, ib. The battle of Edgehill, Oct. 23; 297. Charles marches to Banbury, 298; proceeds to Oxford, ib; marches upon Reading, 299. The royalists attempt to take Brentford, ib. The king returns to Oxford, 300. The earl of Newcastle defeats the parliamentary army, under lord Fairfax, at Atherton Moor, June 30, 1643; 305. Battle of Newbury, Sept. 20; 307. The earls of Clare, Bedford, and Holland, desert to the king, but again return to the parliament, ib. The king sends the duke of Hamilton a close prisoner to the castle of Mount St. Michael: his brother Lanark escapes, and joins the English parliament, 309. The king maintains a correspondence with the confederated Irish parliament, 310; calls an anti-parliament at Oxford, Jan. 22, 1644; 312. Battle of Marstonmoor, July 2; 315. The parliament negotiates for peace, 1644; 326, 327. The king attempts to win over Whitelock and Hollis, 327. Conferences at Uxbridge, 1645; 329, 330. Colonel Windebank shot for a coward, 331. The king leaves Oxford, ib. Battle of Naseby, June, 14; 333. Rupert fortifies Bristol, 336. Letter of the Scottish clergy to Charles, 339. Montrose gains the battle of Alford, July 2; 340. Edinburgh surrenders. ib. The king takes Huntingdon by assault, Aug. 24; ib.. Prince Rupert surrenders Bristol, Sept. 11. The king commands him to resign his commission and to quit the country, 341. Battle of Rowton Heath, Sept. 23. The king loses 600 slain, and 1000 prisoners, ib. Battle of Philiphaugh; Montrose is defeated, ib. Charles escapes from Newark, and arrives at Belvoir Castle; proceeds to Oxford, 344. Negotiations with parliament, 345. The king escapes from Oxford, April 27, 1646, and throws himself upon the protection of the Scottish army, 350—352. He sends orders to Montrose to disband his forces, 354. Signs a warrant for the governors of Oxford, Lichfield, Worcester, and Wallingford, and to all other governors of towns, to surrender on honourable terms, 355. The Scots earnestly endeavour to make the king take the covenant, 356. His plans for renewing hostilities, 357. The parliament send their final propositions to the king at Newcastle; he refuses the conditions offered, July 23; 358, 359. Charles resolves to fly to the Continent, but is dissuaded by his worthless queen, 361. He is delivered up to the earl of Pembroke at Newcastle, Jan. 30, 1647; 362. Takes up his residence at Holmby House, Northamptonshire, 363. Colonel Joyce removes the king to Newmarket, 367: he is conducted to Windsor Castle, 369. Affecting interview with his children. ib. The officers of the army draw up their 'Proposals' for the settlement of the kingdom: they are refused by the king, 370, 371. The king receives letters advertising him of wicked designs against his life, 373. He flies from Hampton Court to the Isle of Wight, Nov. 10; 374—378. Parliament sends four propositions for the king to sign, Dec. 14; he refuses, 379. He endeavours to escape from the Isle of Wight, 1648; ib. Insurrectionary movements of the Royalists and Presbyterians, 381—383. The earl of Holland is defeated at Kingston-upon-Thames, July 5; he surrenders to Fairfax, 383. The prince of Wales arrives with a fleet in the Downs, but retires without performing anything, 383, 384. A treaty set on foot between the parliament and the king at Newport, 384. Petitions presented for justice on the king, 385. The king is removed to Hurst Castle, 386: conveyed from Hurst to Windsor Castle, Dec. 17-23; 388. Is put upon his trial before the high court of justice,

CHARLES I.,—
January 19, 1649; 390. He refuses to acknowledge the authority of the court, 391—393. Commissioners from the Scottish parliament protest against the proceedings, Jan. 25; 393. The king is condemned, Jan. 27; 394, 395. He is refused leave to speak after sentence, 395. The United Provinces send ambassadors to intercede for the king's life, but without effect, ib. The king entreats for the company of Bishop Juxon, and the society of the princess Elizabeth and the young Duke of Gloucester, which is granted, 396. His dying belief that he died the martyr of the people, 397. He is beheaded Jan. 30, 1649; ib. Illustrations.— The trial of the king, 390. Facsimile of his signature, 432.* Coins, 551—553. Writings attributed to the king, 607.

CHARLES II., May 29, 1660—February 6, 1685; born May 1630; baptized by Laud, bishop of London, who prays that "his father's graces may be doubled upon him," iii. 151. He appears in the Downs, 1648, with a fleet, 383; but makes no attempt to save his father, and after some time steers for the Dutch coast without firing a gun, 384. He sends to the parliament a carte blanche, signed and sealed, offering any conditions, provided only the life of his father were spared, 396. He is proclaimed king in Scotland and Ireland, February 1649; 401. David Leslie having been beaten near Dunbar by Cromwell, Charles flies to the highlands, August 31, 1650; 404. He collects another army, and marches to Worcester without molestation, 405; is defeated there by Cromwell, flies for his life, and escapes to France, September 3, 1651; ib. He offers to marry one of Cromwell's daughters, 425. Intends to enter England; but the plot being discovered, he defers his voyage, 431. Letters from Charles II. are read in the council of state, May 1, 1660; 431*. They are sent to the houses of parliament, ib. An answer is voted, and the terms offered by the king in the Declaration of Breda acceded to, ib. The navy declare for the king, May 8. Charles II. is proclaimed at the gate of Westminster Hall, 432*. The great seal, 662. King Charles and the dukes of York and Gloucester land at Dover, May 25, 1660; ib. Charles enters London, May 29; makes Monk a knight of the garter and privy-councillor; is addressed by both houses of parliament, ib. Measures taken for the prosecution of the regicides; a bill of indemnity is passed excepting many persons; tonnage and poundage are granted to the king for life, 665, 666. Portrait of the king, 666. Toleration in religion questioned, 667. Debate on the Thirty-nine Articles, ib. Archbishop Usher's scheme of union and church government, 668. The king publishes the Healing Declaration, October 25, 669. The trial of the regicides, 670—676. The duke of Gloucester dies of the small-pox, 677. The queen-mother, Henrietta Maria, arrives, ib. The marriage of the duke of York with Anne Hyde is publicly acknowledged, ib. The princess of Orange dies of the small-pox, 678. The convention parliament meets, ib. The bodies of Cromwell, Ireton, and Bradshaw are disinterred, hanged at Tyburn, and buried at the foot of the gallows, ib. Venner, a fifth monarchy-man, raises a riot in London, January 6, 1661; many rioters are killed, and others taken, 679. Cruel proceedings of the Scottish parliament, 681—684. The English parliament meets, May 8; 684. 60,000l. voted for the suffering cavaliers, ib. Parliament adjourns, ib. The Pension Parliament; a Conformity Bill passed; a hearth and chimney-tax granted to the king for ever, 685. Parliament prorogued, ib. The king marries Catherine of Braganza, and receives with her Tangiers, Bombay, a free-trade, and half a million sterling, ib. He insists on keeping his

CHARLES II.,—
mistress, the lady Castlemaine, to the great annoyance of the queen, 685—687. He sends back all the attendants of the queen to Portugal, 687. Sir Harry Vane executed, June 14; 689. Colonels Okey, Corbet, and Barkstead executed, 690. Mr. Lisle assassinated at Lausanne, ib. Act of Uniformity, 1662, by which 2,000 Nonconformists are turned out of their livings, 691. The king puts forth the Declaration of Indulgence, ib. Sells Dunkirk to France, 692. Parliament reassembles February 1663; 693. Deprecates the king's Declaration of Indulgence, ib. The Commons vote four subsidies, ib. Conspiracy of Farnley Wood, ib. The Triennial Act repealed, 1664, ib. The Conventicle Act passed, 694. Parliament prorogued, ib. The Conventicle Act used against the Presbyterians, ib. Archbishop Sharp re-establishes the High Commission Court, ib. Parliament re-assembles, 695. War with the Dutch, ib. The plague rages in the metropolis, 1665; ib. Success of the duke of York against the Dutch fleet, ib. The earl of Sandwich entrusted with the command of the fleet, 696. The court removes to Oxford, ib. The Five-mile Act passed, October, ib. The oath of non-resistance, ib. 1666. The plague disappears, and the court returns to Whitehall, 697. The English, under Monk, suffer in an encounter with the Dutch, 698; the Dutch retreat, ib. The great fire of London commences, September 2; 699. Parliament votes 1,800,000l. for prosecuting the war with the Dutch, 700. Appoints a committee to report on the growth of papistry, and another to examine the accounts of those who had received and issued money for the Dutch war, ib; this affair, however, is mismanaged, and parliament is prorogued, 701. An insurrection in Scotland, ib. Cruelties practised by those in power, ib. Negotiations opened at Breda between France, Holland, and England, ib. De Ruyter sails into the Downs, and does much execution to the English shipping, June 1667; ib. The sailors, who are starving by hundreds, refuse to fight unless they are paid, ib. Peace concluded at Breda, August, 702. Clamour in London for a parliament, ib. The king calls his old parliament together in July, after having raised an army of 10,000 men, without their consent, but dismisses them till October, without permitting them to transact any business, ib. The king requires Clarendon to surrender the great seal, which is given to Bridgman, ib. Clarendon is impeached by the commons, November 12; 705. The king urges him to fly, ib. He escapes to France, ib. The CABAL engross the powers of government, ib. Acts of the Cabal ministry, 1668, ib. The Triple Alliance formed between England, Holland, and Sweden, 706. Parliament meets, February, ib. Treaty of commerce with Spain, ib. Arrangements with the Nonconformists proposed, but broken off, ib. Parliament is adjourned, May 8; ib. The king captivated by two actresses, ib. He creates lady Castlemaine duchess of Cleveland, ib., note. Parliament assembles, February 14, 1670; ib. Charles opens the session with an escort of guards, 707. Parliament, after voting supplies, adjourns, ib. The king thinks of changing the religion of the land, ib. Louis offers assistance in men and money, on the condition that Charles shall make war on the United Provinces, etc., ib. Secret treaty concluded with France; the Dover treaty, ib. Parliament re-assembles, ib. Tax proposed to be laid on play-houses, ib. The Coventry Act passed, 708. Colonel Blood attempts to murder lord Ormond, ib. His attempt to steal the crown, 1671; ib. Persecution of the Nonconformists, 709. Charles, during the prorogation of parliament, shuts up the exchequer, ib. War declared with the Dutch, ib. United at-

CHARLES II.,—
tack of the French and English fleets on the Dutch, 710. Parliament meets, 1673, after a recess of a year and a half, *ib.* The commons vote 1,000,000*l.* for the prosecution of the war, 711; but fall with violence upon a declaration of indulgence which the king had issued during the recess, *ib.* The king recalls his declaration, and gives his consent to the Test Act; in consequence of which last the duke of York resigns his high admiralship, and Clifford his staff, *ib.* Parliament prorogued, November 4, *ib.* The Danby administration, *ib.* Parliament 1674, re-assembles, *ib.* The commons demand the punishment of several members of the Cabal administration, *ib.* A separate peace between England and Holland proclaimed in London, February 28; 712. Parliament assembles, April, 1675; *ib.* Is prorogued, 713. Vote passed by the Scottish parliament giving up the entire government of the church into the king's hands, *ib.* Charles makes a secret agreement with Louis, on condition of his giving him a pension of 100,000*l.* a year, and the aid of French troops, 1676; 714. The writ *de hæretico comburendo* abolished, 1677; *ib.* The commons vote 600,000*l.* for building new ships, *ib.* War with France proposed; the Commons refuse to supply the necessary money; parliament is adjourned; during the recess, Charles marries his niece, the elder daughter of the duke of York, to his nephew the prince of Orange, 715. Charles enters into a treaty with the States-General; Louis, in consequence, stops his pension, and employs it to bribe the English parliament, *ib.* Parliament meets, 1678; the king talks of a war with France, and a supply is voted for the maintenance of a fleet of ninety sail, and an army of 30,000 men, *ib.* Charles refuses to declare war, and carries on secret negotiations with Louis, *ib.* Suspicions are raised as to the use the king means to make of the army, *ib.* Charles makes another secret treaty with Louis, wherein he agrees to abandon the States-General and to dissolve parliament, for a large sum of money, 716. Parliament prorogued, *ib.* Charles makes a treaty with the States-General, which he never intends to keep, *ib.* Treaty concluded between the States and France, *ib.* The peace of Nimeguen, 717. The Popish Plot, *ib.* Murder of sir Edmondbury Godfrey, 719. Parliament re-assembles, October 21; 721. Several Catholic lords committed to the Tower, on the deposition of Titus Oates, *ib.* A bill passed disabling papists to sit in parliament, *ib.* Deposition of William Bedloe, *ib.* Letters from Coleman to father La Chaise, 723. Deposition of Prance, 724. The earl of Danby impeached, 726. Parliament dissolved, January 24, 1679, after having sat more than seventeen years, *ib.* Elections for the new parliament conducted 1679, with unusual heat, 728. Danby sent to the Tower, *ib.* Bill passed for excluding the duke of York from the throne, 729. *Habeas Corpus* Act passed, *ib.* Cruelties practised by Lauderdale on the Covenanters, *ib.* Executions of persons accused of joining in the Popish Plot, 730. A violent quarrel having fallen out between the duke of York and the duke of Monmouth, Charles sends the one to Holland and the other to Scotland, 731. Dangerfield, a profligate, pretends he has discovered a Presbyterian plot (1679) against the king's life, 732. He is found to be a cheat and remanded to Newgate; he then pretends he has discovered a popish plot (The Meal-tub Plot), *ib.* Parliament assembles, *ib.* Lord Stafford beheaded, December 29; 733. Various bills brought in, 1681, by the commons, *ib.* The king refuses to pass the bill for the exclusion of his brother, *ib.* He dissolves parliament, and appoints the next to meet at Oxford, *ib.* He concludes a treaty with Spain for the

CHARLES II.,—
maintenance of the peace of Nimeguen, which is afterwards broken off, *ib.* The king proposes that after his decease the powers of the crown should be vested in the princess of Orange, to which the commons will not agree, *ib.* He dissolves his fifth and last parliament, March 28, *ib.* Oliver Plunket, archbishop of Armagh, executed for treason, 735. William of Orange visits England, *ib.* Charles permits Louis to attack Luxembourg, *ib.* The Covenanters, under their leader Cameron, renounce Charles, *ib.* Many executions in consequence take place, *ib.* The duke of York, as king's commissioner, opens a Scottish parliament, 736. Lord Belhaven is imprisoned, for saying that the chief use of the Test was to bind a popish successor, *ib.* Argyle committed to Edinburgh Castle, *ib.*; is charged with treason, 737; flies to Holland, *ib.* James procures from the Scottish parliament an Act making it treason to maintain the lawfulness of excluding him from the succession, *ib.* He comes to England, *ib.*; in returning to Scotland, be narrowly escapes being drowned, 738. Courts of judicature established in Scotland, *ib.* The duke of Monmouth received enthusiastically by the people, *ib.*; he is arrested by order from the king, 739. Disputes about the election of sheriffs, *ib.* The Rye-house Plot, 740; it is betrayed to lord Dartmouth by one of the conspirators, *ib.* Monmouth and lord Russell seized for their concern in the plot, 745; Russell is committed to the Tower, *ib.* Lord Grey brought before the council, *ib.*; he escapes to Holland, *ib.* Lord Howard seized, 746. The earl of Essex, Algernon Sidney, and Hampden, sent to the Tower, 1683, *ib.* Trial of Russell, *ib.* Death of lord Essex, 747. Russell is condemned, 748; and executed July 31, 1683; 749. A judgment of *quo warranto* given against the city of London; the king allowed to regulate its government, 751. Charles signs the death-warrant of Algernon Sydney; he is beheaded on Tower-hill, December 8; 754. The duke of Monmouth is received back again at court, but after a few days flies to Holland, 755. Cruelties practised in Scotland, 756. Jeffreys attempts to obtain a surrender of the corporation charters, 757. Several catholic peers released from imprisonment, 758. The duke of York is re-admitted to the council, in defiance of the Test Act, *ib.* Halifax opens a secret correspondence with the prince of Orange, 759. George, prince of Denmark, marries the duke of York's second daughter, the lady Anne, July 24; 760. Lord Dartmouth destroys the fortifications, etc., at Tangier, *ib.* Charles falls down in a fit of apoplexy, February 2, 1685; *ib.* He makes his confession to Huddleston, 762. His death in the Romish faith, February 6; *ib.* *Illustrations.*—Charles II. and the English ambassadors at the Hague arranging the terms for his restoration, 494. The landing, 1660; 663. Fac-simile of the king's signature, 801. Coins, 868.

CHARLES the Bald, king of the Franks, (841—877), His daughter Judith, about twelve years of age, is espoused in the cathedral of Rheims by Ethelwulf, king of Wessex, in 854; i. 152. She is married, after that monarch's decease, by his son Ethelbald, 153. Is forcibly carried off from a convent at Senlis, whither she had retired, by Baldwin, grand forester of the Ardennes, *ib.* King Charles causes his bishops to excommunicate Baldwin, but the pope effects a reconciliation, and the nuptials take place in due form, *ib.* Baldwin is created earl of Flanders, *ib.*

CHARLES IV., (1322—1328), king of France, son of Philip le Bel, and brother of queen Isabella. He overruns some of Edward II.'s dominions, i. 742. Queen Isabella persuades Edward to permit her to

CHARLES IV.,—
go to Paris to make peace with her brother, the
French king, March, 1325; *ib.* Guienne and Poictiers are surrendered to France, *ib.* The queen
refuses to return; her connection with Mortimer
becoming known, Charles orders her to quit his
dominions, *ib.* She then takes shelter with the
count of Hainault, *ib.* Death of Charles, 1328; 757.
CHARLES V., (1364—1380), dauphin of France; after
the battle of Poictiers, in which king John was
taken prisoner, he is appointed lieutenant of France,
i. 773. The king of Navarre defies his authority,
and Stephen Marcel kills two of his counsellors,
774. Dreadful state of anarchy in France, 774, 775.
Charles holds the treaty of Bretigny in suspense,
776. The "Free Companions" defeat the royal
army, commanded by John de Bourbon, *ib.* On the
death of king John, April, 1364, Charles succeeds
to the French throne, and in 1367 invades Aquitaine,
777. Edward reassumes the title of king of France,
and sends reinforcements to the Black Prince in the
south, 778. The duke of Lancaster lays waste the
north-western provinces, the French being unwilling
to risk an engagement, *ib.* Charles regains some
towns and castles in the south, the Black Prince
prepares to take the field, and the dukes of Anjou
and Berri retreat with precipitation, *ib.* Limoges
betrayed to the French by the treachery of the
bishop and inhabitants, *ib.* The Black Prince retakes Limoges, massacres the inhabitants, and burns
the city to the ground; this was the last military
exploit of the prince, who then returns to England,
and soon after dies, *ib.* Charles supports don
Enrique in his claim to the kingdoms of Castile and
Leon, in opposition to John of Gaunt, who was
brother of the Black Prince, and had married Constance, daughter of Pedro, *ib.* June, 1372, the
Spaniards destroy the English fleet near Rochelle,
ib. The French avoid a general engagement, but
retake many towns under the command of their
consummate general, Duguesclin, 779. Thouars
surrenders, a truce is concluded, and the duke of
Lancaster returns to Engand, *ib.* By this truce,
which lasted till the death of Edward, Bordeaux,
Bayonne, and Calais were all that the English king
retained of his continental dominions, *ib.* The
English attempt to take St. Malo, but are obliged to
relinquish the siege, 783. The earl of Buckingham ravages France, 784. The king dies, 1379,
and is succeeded by his son, Charles VI., who was
then a minor, *ib.* Treaty concluded with Brittany, *ib.*
CHARLES VI., (1380—1422), king of France. Sends
John de Vienne, lord admiral of France, with a
small force to assist the Scots in their invasion,
1385; i. 791. Collects a splendid army of 100,000
men, including nearly all the chivalry of France,
and prepares a large fleet in the port of Sluys for the
invasion of England, in which he himself intended
to take a part, 1385; but being entirely in the power
of his intriguing and turbulent uncles, who oppose
this expedition, the army is disbanded, and the fleet
being dispersed by a tempest, many of the ships are
taken by the English, 791, 792. Imbecile, ultimately
mad, governed by his queen Isabella, Orleans, and
Armagnac, etc., ii. 7, 9, 13, 17, 20—22, 26—34.
His two eldest sons die suddenly, and the third was
long known as the dauphin Charles, 36, 37. His
queen's profligacy, 37. The king has one of her
lovers cast into the Seine in a bag, 38. He is at
length rescued from the power of Armagnac, who
governed Paris in his name and that of his brother
Orleans, 1418; 41. He signs the treaty, by which
Henry V., and not the dauphin, should succeed him,
47, 48. He outlived king Henry by a few months,
and dies 1422, in Paris, 54.
CHARLES VII., king of France, (1422—1461), became
dauphin at fifteen, by the sudden decease of his

CHARLES VII.,—
brother John, 1417, ii. 37. His crafty character, *ib.*
He forms a treaty with Isabella and Burgundy,
1418; but with the old king remains still in custody
of Armagnac at Paris, 41. He flies to Bourges
with Tanneguy-Duchâtel, 42. Assumes the title
of regent, and assembles a parliament at Poictiers, 1418; *ib.* His wars with Burgundy, *ib.* His
peace with "Jean-sans-peur," 44. He proposes a
conference with the duke at Montereau, 45. His
perjury, *ib.* Witnesses the atrocious murder of
Burgundy, which he had himself commanded, 46—
48. He retires to Languedoc, to his partizans and
troops, 48. In Henry's absence he besieged Chartres, 1421; but that king returning to avenge the
death of Clarence, the dauphin flies before him to
the fortress of Bourges, 49. Henry, dying 1422,
desired Bedford to make no peace with the dauphin
Charles, etc., 51. The dauphin, 1422, becomes king
by the death of Charles VI., and the voice of his
own party, 54. He was crowned at Poictiers, *ib.*
His army was defeated at Crevant, 1423; *ib.* He
receives auxiliaries from the duke of Milan, 55.
Charles, still mostly called the dauphin, and possessing the provinces of the south as his only secure
territory, sent his main army and Scottish troops to
Normandy, 1424, to the relief of Ivry, 56. His
generals were totally defeated at Verneuil, and
many nobles slain or taken by the English, *ib.*
Civil war; rebellion of many of his great nobles,
59, 60. Treaty with the king of Scotland, 60.
Vigorous measures for the defence of the city of
Orleans, *ib.* His neglect of Mary of Anjou, his beautiful wife, for his mistresses, and his total indolence,
must have ruined the new king, but for his excellent
captains, and the following romantic occurrences.
Charles's affairs were almost desperate, when Joan
of Arc, a young girl of the frontiers of Lorraine,
imagined she was commissioned by Divine *voices*
to restore her sovereign to dignity and power, 62
—64. The king observing the new enthusiasm
of his people and soldiery, sent Joan with a
convoy of provisions for the starving people of
Orleans, his best captains and some troops, to the
besieged city, 65. The English became unmanned
by superstitious fears, believing the maid to be of
the devil, 65, 66. The maid of Orleans gloriously
redeemed her promise of succouring that important
city; Joan was afterwards badly wounded, but took
the Tournelles from the besiegers, 1429; 67. The
king, in all perilous enterprises, kept aloof from
danger, 57, 67. The French victorious at Patay,
made Talbot prisoner, 68. Charles was at length
moved to lay aside his almost dastardly sloth, and
to traverse France, with Joan of Arc and a strong
body of cavalry, to Rheims, that she might fulfil her
second promise of his coronation, July, 1429; 69.
He refused her leave to return to her parents, 70.
Preaching of friar Richard, in the royal cause, of
beneficial effect, 69, 70. The towns opened their
gates, and Charles advanced through the Isle of
France towards Paris, 70, 71. His character
aspersed, 71. This king refused the personal challenge of the regent Bedford, 72. He occupied St.
Denis, but on the return of the English duke from
Normandy, he retreated to the Loire, 1429, and
wintered in the town of Bourges, 72, 73. In 1430
he advanced again from the south upon Paris,
where many conspired in his favour; but the
plot being discovered, the Bourguignons put them
all to death, 73. Defence of Compiègne by Joan of
Arc, who in a sortie was captured by the allied
forces besieging that town, 73, 74. Fearful disorders; the prince of Orange attacked the provinces
beyond the Loire, but was defeated by De Gaucourt
at the head of the royalists and free companies
under Villandrada, 74. The king's errant life with

CHARLES VII.,— his court and his mistresses, 77, 78. Negotiations at Arras; terms of alliance with the duke of Burgundy, who received absolution for this breach of preceding oaths, 78. Charles, by the dean of Paris, begged Philip's pardon publicly for his part in the murder of his father, ib. Paris submitted to Charles VII. and his ally Philip, 79. The duke of York succeeded Bedford in Normandy, 1435, ib. Talbot cleared that province of the French, took Pontoise, and threatened Paris, ib. Calais unsuccessfully besieged by duke Philip, 79, 80.

CHARLES VIII., (1483—1498) king of France, at fourteen ascended the throne, ii. 292. His sister Anne, wife of Peter of Bourbon, governed in the king's name, 292. Rebellion of Orleans, first prince of the blood, ib. In command of the Breton army, Orleans was totally defeated by La Tremoille, and sent a prisoner to Bourges, 1488; 294. The king, at twenty-one, took up the reins of government, and liberated d'Orleans, 297. His unfavourable exterior, and want of cultivation, ib. His breach of the contract to marry Margot of Burgundy, 297, 298. His duplicity, ib. He gained immediate and lasting possession of all Brittany (already indeed subdued by his troops), on his nuptials, 1491, with Anne of Brittany, ib. He countenanced Perkin Warbeck at his court, until he obtained king Henry's signature to the treaty of Estaples, 299. He marched into Italy, 1494, and seized Naples, but was forced, by a powerful league, to fight his way back to France, 311. His justice, charity, and devotion, ib. He expired, 1499, at the château d'Amboise, having struck his head by accident, ib.

CHARLES IX., (1560—1574) king of France, ascends the throne, December 5, on the death of his brother Francis II., ii. 563. He gives orders for the massacre of St. Bartholomew's day, 647. Dies a miserable death at Vincennes, May, 1574, in the twenty-sixth year of his age, 649.

CHARLES X., king of France (1824—1830.) Portrait of, § ii. 345.

CHARLES V., the emperor (1519—1558.) Treaty between his father the archduke Philip, and Henry VII., that when of suitable age he should espouse Mary, daughter of the English monarch, ii., 315, 331, 338. On the death of Ferdinand of Arragon, he became king of all Spain, 1516, as Charles I. of Spain, 336. The emperor Maximilian dying, Jan. 1519, Charles was elected emperor, as Charles V., 337. The new emperor courted the friendship of Henry VIII., and secured that of the ambitious Wolsey, 338. His visit to Henry VIII. at Dover Castle, when they inspected the gorgeous shrines, etc., of Canterbury cathedral, 1520; ib. The emperor's admiration of Mary, duchess of Suffolk, once affianced to himself, ib. He sailed for the Netherlands, and on the same day Henry VIII. and Catherine embarked for Calais, ib. Wars of the emperor and king Francis, 345, 346, 356. Charles revisited Henry and the queen, his aunt; was installed a Knight of the Garter at Windsor, and embarking at Southampton sailed with his great fleet for Spain, 348. He appoints a diet of the empire to meet at Worms, on the 6th of Jan., 1521, expressly for the purpose of putting down the new opinions entertained and preached by Luther, and the great reformer accordingly presented himself before them to defend his doctrines and his conduct, 707. The emperor took a generous interest in the cause of his aunt, Catherine of Arragon, 365, 367. Negotiations between Charles V. and Clement upon the basis of the pope's opposition to the divorce, 368. The emperor, 1535, expressed to Eliott, ambassador at his court, his admiration of the character of Sir Thomas More, and his reprobation of the cruelty of his arbitrary

CHARLES V., the emperor,—execution, 389. He resigns in favour of his son, 1558, and chooses for his retreat the monastery of St. Just, near to Placentia. It is related of him, that finding he could never make two clocks to go exactly alike, he deplored the pains he had taken, and the blood he had shed, in order to make all mankind think and believe in one way, 531. He dies about two years after his resignation, ib. Elizabeth solemnizes a grand funeral for him in Westminster Abbey, 541.

CHARLES VI., emperor of Germany, ascended the throne, 1711, died, Oct. 20, 1740; iv. 440.

CHARLES II., king of Spain, (1665—1700) a sickly boy, ascends the throne, 1665; iii. 707. Makes war with Louis XIV., 711. Names the young electoral prince of Bavaria his successor, who dies in his eighth year, iv. 100. In consequence of this, Charles names Philip, duke of Anjou, 110. Death of this king, 1700; ib.

CHARLES III., king of Spain (1759—1788) ascends the throne, 1759; § i. 10. Declares war with England, 1761; 13. His ambassador quits London, 380. The king offers his good offices as mediator between England and America, 1779; 383.

CHARLES IV., king of Spain (1788—1808.) Ruinous state of Spanish finances, 1794; § iii., 407. War with France, ib. The measures of this weak and imbecile monarch excite general discontent, § iv., 303. Disputes with his son Ferdinand, 304, 305. His intended flight to the Spanish possessions in South America; he is prevented by the people, March 17, 1808; 305. He signs his abdication in favour of his son Ferdinand, March 19; 306. Declares to Napoleon that his abdication was forced upon him, ib., and resigns his crown into his hands, 313.

CHARLES XL, king of Sweden, succeeded to the throne 1660, died 1697; iv. 78.

CHARLES XII., king of Sweden, succeeded to the throne 1697. Visited by Marlborough, who endeavours to bring him over to the English interest, iv., 201. Is beaten at Pultava by Russian serfs, 333; and killed before the fortress of Frederickshal in Norway, Dec. 11, 1718; 349.

CHARLES XIII., (1809—1818.) Bernadotte, king of Sweden, born 1778. His pacific inclinations towards England 1811; § iv., 491 Bonaparte treats him as a vassal of France, 563. He resists the oppression, and signs a treaty with the emperor Alexander, 1812; 564. Treaty of peace with England, 568. Large subsidies granted to Bernadotte to defray the expense of his army, 593*. He joins the allies, and renders signal service at the great battle of Leipzig, Oct. 16 and 18, 1813; ib. defeats the Danes, and occupies Holstein and Sleswig, 598*. Advances into Holland, 1814; 619*. Norway united to Sweden by the consent of the allies, 620*.

CHARLES JOHN XIV., king of Sweden, (1818—1844.) His service under the French in India,1783; § ii. 156.

CHARLES LOUIS, prince elector, son of the palatine Frederick, brother of prince Rupert, and nephew to Charles I. Invited to England by the king, 1635. After remaining nearly two years in England the king gives the two brothers 10,000l., and allows them to make war in whatever manner they should think fit. They throw themselves into Westphalia, and gain several trifling advantages; but are driven from the siege of Lippe, and their retreat is intercepted by Hatzfeldt. Some time after, whilst attempting to pass through France in disguise, Charles is arrested by Cardinal Richelieu, and shut up in the castle of Vincennes, iii. 173, 174.

CHARLES, second son of the emperor Leopold I., proclaimed king of Spain on the death of Charles II., 1700; iv. 154. His visit to England, ib. Is conveyed to Portugal in the English fleet, 174.

E

CHARLES EDWARD STUART, the young Pretender. Sails from France 1744. Is met by the channel fleet; retires; his fleet is dispersed by a hurricane, iv. 471. He returns to Paris, ib. Embarks for Scotland at Nantes, July 2, 1745; 480; sails on board the Doutelle, in company with the Elisabeth. They are engaged by the Lion, an English ship. The young Pretender lands in Scotland with noblemen and gentlemen. The seven men of Moidart, 480, 482. Portrait of the young Pretender, from a French print, 481. Another portrait, in Highland costume, 483. Four companies of regular troops are taken by the Highlanders, 483, 484. The young Pretender raises his standard, and publishes his father's proclamations, 484. Sir John Cope puts himself at the head of the royal troops near Stirling, ib. The rebels begin their march southward, ib. The council of regency offer a reward for the young Pretender, 485. Cope arrives at Dalnacardoch, and the next day at Dalwhinnie; thence having altered his course he reaches Inverness, 486. Charles Edward reaches Blair Castle, ib. He enters Perth, 487. Reaches Dunblane, 488. Crosses the ford of Frew, 489. Quarters his troops at Linlithgow, ib. He enters Edinburgh, and causes his father to be proclaimed, 491, 492. Cope marches from Dunbar, 493. Battle of Preston Pans; the royal army is routed, 495, 496. The Duke of Cumberland arrives from Flanders with a large body of troops, 503, 504. The rebels blockade Edinburgh Castle, 504. General Guest, governor of the castle, bombards the town, 505. Several Highland gentlemen join the Pretender at Edinburgh, ib. He issues various proclamations, 507. Appoints Lord Strathallan to command in Scotland, and marches south, 508. Crosses the Esk, and occupies Reddings in Cumberland, 509. Lays siege to Carlisle, ib. The town and castle surrender, ib. He enters Carlisle, 510. Arrives at Penrith, 511. The rebel army reaches Preston, ib. They reach Wigan, part enter Manchester, ib. The royal army lies at Newcastle-under-Wade, and at Lichfield under the duke of Cumberland, 512. The rebel army crosses the Mersey near Stockport, ib. Enters Macclesfield, 513. Enters Derby, ib. The old Pretender is proclaimed, 514. A council of war is held, 515. The rebel army commences retreat, 516. The royal army advances after them, ib. The young Pretender leaves Manchester, 517. Arrives at Lancaster, ib. Lord John Drummond with the advanced guard is attacked by the people between Penrith and Kendal, ib. The rebel army lies at Penrith, ib. The royal army advances to Kendal, 518. A skirmish takes place near Clifton Moor, ib. The rebels re-enter Carlisle, and leave it defended by 200 men, 519. They cross the Esk and return to Scotland, ib. The garrison at Carlisle surrenders, 519, 520. The rebels besiege Stirling Castle, 521. Charles encamps at Falkirk, 522. Battle of Falkirk, 522—524. The royalist army reaches Edinburgh, 525. The siege of Stirling Castle continues, 527. The Duke of Cumberland places himself at the head of the royalist army, 528. He enters Stirling, 529. The Duke of Cumberland arrives at Aberdeen, 531. The rebels take Fort George, Fort Augustus, and gain various other successes, 531, 532. A ship containing money for the Pretender is seized, 533. The royal army reaches Nairn, ib. The battle of Culloden, 535—539. Flora MacDonald secures the Pretender's flight as far as Mugstole, 543, 544. He goes to the island of Rasay, 545. Flora MacDonald is captured, 1746; ib. The Pretender embarks at Lochnanuagh, 548; reaches Morlaix, in Brittany, and proceeds to Paris, ib. Various executions, 548—551. He solicits aid from Ferdinand VI., king of Spain, but is denied, 558. His younger brother is made a cardinal, 559. The Pretender is

CHARLES EDWARD STUART,—
forcibly driven from France, 560. Present at the coronation of George III., 1761; ib. § i. 13. He caused his first child, by his mistress, Mrs. Walkenshaw, to be christened by a non-juring clergyman, 14. His marriage with Louisa Stolberg, a young German lady, of a very noble house, 1773, who afterwards procures a legal separation on account of his brutality, § ii. 310. His death, January, 31, 1788; his Divine hereditary right descends to his brother Henry Benedict, the cardinal, 310, 311.
Charlestown, America, view of, in 1779; § i. 391.
CHARLETON, Charles, lord Howard of, impeached by Denzil Hollis, 1642, iii. 288.
CHARLETON, Dr., impugns the opinion of Inigo Jones that Stonehenge was a Roman temple, dedicated to Cœlus, iii. 574.
CHARLOTTA AUGUSTA, eldest daughter of king George III. Her marriage with Frederick William, hereditary prince of Wurtemberg, May 18, 1797; § iii. 517.
CHARLOTTE SOPHIA, of Mecklenburg-Strelitz, second daughter of the late duke, married to king George III., September 8, 1761; § i. 6. Portrait of, ib. Act passed for the settlement of her dowry, 1762; 15.
CHARNOCK, enters into a plot for assassinating William III., 1696; iv. 64. He is executed as a traitor, March 11th, 68.
Charter House. Proclamations, 1603, by James I., at the, iii. 5. The governors refuse to admit a papist without the oath, 786.
Charters: Confirmation of the Great Charter and the Charter of the Forest (which latter had been granted in 1224) by Edward I., in the thirteenth and twenty-fifth years of his reign, i. 812, 813. Three knights appointed in every shire to punish all such as violated these Charters, 813.
CHASTELAR, a crazed French poet, etc., courted Mary Queen of Scots, ii. 585. She at first laughed at him, but as he persevered he was tried and executed by the queen's command, ib.
CHATEAUNEUF, L'Aubespine de, resident French ambassador at the court of queen Elizabeth; he negotiates in favour of the persecuted queen of Scots; to silence him he is accused in taking part in a new plot to assassinate the English queen, ii. 564. After the execution of Mary, Elizabeth publicly apologises for her harsh treatment to him, 671.
Châtelet, Prison of the, pulled down in 1802; ii. 388.
CHATELHERAULT, duke of, (see James Hamilton, earl of Arran.)
CHATHAM, William Pitt, earl of, begins to rise into eminence, iv. 434. He resigns his place in the household of the prince of Wales, 475. He marries lady Hester Grenville, 582. Is dismissed by the king, 583. He returns to court, 596. Devises a plan for securing North America, 598. His interview with the new king on the death of George II. Oct. 25, 1760; § i. 2. He resigns the seals of secretary, 1761; 11. Portrait of, 12. He denounces the treaty of Fontainebleau, 1762, as derogatory to the honour of England, 23, 27. Takes part with Wilkes in the privilege question, 30, 35, 40. His eloquent speech against the taxation of America, 42, 43, 45, 46. Is raised to the peerage (at his own desire) by the title of earl of Chatham, July 29, 1766, and becomes lord privy seal, 47. He refuses to transact business on pretence of illness, 1767; 57; resigns his office, 1768, which lord Bristol accepts, 63, 64, 79, 81, 86, 87, 89, 91. He seconds a motion for inquiring into the expenses of the civil list, 1770; 94, 95, 97, 104, 117. He declares himself, 1771, a convert to triennial parliaments, 118. He expresses his dislike of the Royal Marriage Bill to lord Shelburne, 1772; 127, 152, 162, 179, 194, 195. His provisional bill for settling the troubles in

CHATHAM, William Pitt, earl of,—
America, 1775; 199, 200. He recalls his son, lord
Pitt, who was serving in America against the revolutionists, 1776; 252, 293, 319, 323. He appears in
the House of Lords for the last time, April 7, 1778,
and makes an affecting and admirable speech, 340.
Death of this great orator, May 11, 1778; 341. Parliament votes 20,000l. for the payment of his debts,
and an annuity of 4,000l. to his heirs, 342. His
monument in Westminster Abbey, 343.
CHAUCER, Geoffrey, generally styled the father of
English poetry, was born 1328, and died at the
advanced age of 72; i. 851. Character of his poetry,
ib.; ii. 52, note.
CHAUVELIN, M., French ambassador at the court of
London, receives notice to quit, January 24, 1793;
§ iii. 279.
Cheapside, with the procession of Mary de Medicis on
her visit to Charles I., iii. 246.
CHEKE, sir John, the Greek scholar, a tutor of Edward the Sixth, ii. 453. Sent to the Tower, 1553, by
Queen Mary, 504. He obtains Mary's permission to
travel on the continent for a limited period; but on
his return, between Brussels and Antwerp, he is
arrested by a provost-marshal of king Philip, and
conveyed to the Tower of London, where he signs
three ample recantations, 530. This not being
deemed sufficient, he is forced to assist bishop Bonner in condemning the Protestants to the stake, ib.
He dies, at the age of forty-seven, of shame, remorse,
and affliction, ib.
Chemistry, iv. 786.
CHENEY, sir John, slain by the hand of Richard III.
at Bosworth-field, August 22, 1485; ii. 129.
CHENEY, sir John, created a knight-banneret by
Henry VII., October 28, 1485; ii. 282. He died
1496; ib.
Cherbourg, city and port of, assailed by sea and land,
1450; ii. 85. The English surrender, ib.
Chester, the county palatine, 1536, received by enactment the full benefit of English laws, having been
hitherto in an anomalous state, ii. 425.
CHESTER, Gherbaud, earl of, appointed about 1073,
to the command of a strong body of troops to defend the provinces in the north-west, i. 375; created
earl, 1086. He returned to Normandy, 376.
CHESTERFIELD, Philip Dormer Stanhope, lord,
created 1726. He threatens a suit in chancery
touching the will of George I., but is silenced by
20,000l. from the court, iv. 394; is deprived of his
white staff for opposing Walpole's excise scheme,
409. He goes over to Avignon to procure letters
to the principal Jacobites, urging them to exert
themselves against Walpole, 454. Is made lord-
lieutenant of Ireland, 1745; 475; and secretary of
state, 554. He resigns, 556. Introduces the Gregorian calendar into England, 1751; 569. He died
1773. Quoted, § i. 48, 53.
Chevy Chase (Otterburne,) battle of, August 15, 1388;
i. 793.
CHEYNEY, sir Thomas, privy councillor, 1547; ii. 454.
CHEYTE SING, nabob of Benares, arbitrarily arrested
1781, by Hastings, who was in great need of
money for the preservation of India. His subjects
fly to arms, and the English governor refusing to
accept any excuse from Cheyte Sing for this occurrence, the unfortunate prince takes refuge among
the rajahs of Bondilcund, where he dies, § ii. 164
—167.
CHICHELEY, archbishop of Canterbury, 1414; punishes
the Lollards, ii. 26, 146. His death in 1443;
147.
CHILD, sir Josiah, portrait of, iii. 852. His " New Discourses on Trade," published 1668; 854.
CHILDE, sir Richard, a wealthy trader, 1716; iv. 335.
CHILD, Dr. William, a musician of the 17th century,
iii. 566.

CHILLINGWORTH, William, an eminent divine, and
writer on controversial theology, born at Oxford,
1602; died January, 1644; iii. 610.
Chippenham, a strong town of the Saxons, i. 158.
Chivalry, its spirit declined gradually from the reign
of Edward III., and in the period between 1399 and
1485 fell rapidly into desuetude. It finally closed in
the occasional holding of tournaments at the courts
of potentates, and in judicial encounters or appeals
of arms in charges of treason, etc., ii., 247, 251.
Causes of this important change in national manners, 249.
CHOLMONDELEY, George earl, receives the privy seal,
iv. 468; is dismissed, 475; raises a regiment to
serve against the young Pretender, 1745; 503.
CHOLMONDELEY, Hugh earl, created, 1706. Objects
to the peace of Utrecht, 1713, and is removed
from his office of treasurer of the household; he died
1725; iv. 273.
CHRISTIAN IV., king of Denmark, spends a month at the
court of James I. in 1606; his handsome reception,
great feasts, etc., iii. 33. Both kings incapacitated by
wine, a common sin at the festivals of the time, ib.
The royal Dane said to have insulted the countess of
Nottingham, ib.
Christian Knowledge, Society for promoting, founded
1699; § iv. 605.
CHRISTIANA, second sister of Edgar Atheling, and
abbess of Wilton, or, as others say, of Rumsey;
Maud or Margaret, afterwards queen of Henry I.,
was brought up by her, i. 406.
Christianity, its introduction into Britain in the early
Roman period, i. 73. Persecution under Diocletian,
74. Constantine favourably inclined towards Christianity, ib. Arianism in Britain, ib. Mission of
Augustine and forty monks into England (see Augustine), 145. Conversion of Ethelbert, king of Kent,
his queen Bertha having been reared a Christian in
France, 145, 231. After his death, his son Eadbald
and his subjects relapse into paganism, 145, 233. Redwald, king of East Anglia, and Sebert of Essex,
converted, 233. St. Paul's, the first church built in
London, 604, ib.
CHRISTINE, Madame, second daughter of France, proposed as a wife for Henry prince of Wales, by the
queen regent of France, 1611; iii. 51. James opens
negotiations respecting her, 63.
Christmas festivities, ii. 355, 892.
Chroniclers, list of, in the thirteenth and fourteenth
centuries, i. 847.
Chronometer, the, for ascertaining the longitude at
sea, invented by John Harrison about 1741; § i.
602, § iii. 688.
CHRYSANTUS, lieutenant of Theodosius, about 390;
partially repressed the Pictish forays, i. 54.
Chun Castle, plan and section of, i. 99. Description
of this dun or fortress of the Britons, 100.
Chunar, treaty of, concluded, 1781, between Asoff-ul-
Dowla, nabob of Oude, and Warren Hastings, § ii.
169, 170.
Churches. The pagan temples of the Saxons in Britain
turned into Christian places of worship, i. 232. St.
Paul's, the first church built in London on the site
of the Roman temple of Diana, 233.
CHURCHILL, Charles, a poet and satirist of great tem-
porary fame, born in 1731; is said to have written
in the "Briton," a newspaper set up by the earl of
Bute in 1763; § i. 26, note. List of his poetical
works, 607. He died November 4th, 1764.
CHURCHILL, George, brother of the duke of Marlborough, iv. 142, 164, 170, 172.
CHURCHILL, Captain, iii. 738; announces to Louis
XIV. the accession of James II., 1685; 765.
CIBBER, Caius Gabriel, a sculptor of considerable eminence; he executed the bas-reliefs on the London
monument, and the two figures personifying raving
and melancholy madness which surmounted the

CIBBER, Caius Gabriel,—
gateway of the Old Bethlehem Hospital, and are now in the hall of the modern building, iii. 884.
CICERO, Marcus Tullius. His epistles to Atticus, quoted, i. 105.
CICERO, Quintus, serves under Cæsar in Britain, i. 105.
Cider Bill, the, 1763; § i. 25. Partially repealed, 1766; 46.
Clederholm, iv. 201.
Cingalese village, i. 34.
CIPRIANI, Giovanni Baptista, an eminent painter, born in Tuscany, 1727; died at Chelsea, 1785; § i. 626.
Cistercians; this order of monks introduced into England, 1128; i. 559. Illustration of a Cistercian monk, 560.
Ciudad Rodrigo, view of the fortress of, § iv. 442. Its surrender to the French, 1810; 441. Taken by the English, January 19th, 1812; 503.
Civilization, progress of, independent of the genealogical connection of nations. i. 5, 6. Irish civilization connected with that of the east, 13. Advanced state of British civilization at the period of Cæsar's invasion, 34.
CLANRICKARD, earl of, his death, 1638; iii. 170.
CLAN RONALD, mortally wounded at the battle of Dunblane, November 13, 1715; iv. 318.
CLARE, Roger, earl of, 1151. Becket demands of him the castle and barony of Tunbridge, 1163; i. 448.
CLARE, Robert Nugent, viscount, created 1766; § i. 53.
CLARENCE, Thomas Plantagenet, duke of, second son of Henry IV.; created earl of Albemarle and duke of Clarence, July 9, 1411. He was sent with a fleet, in 1403, to take revenge on the French, for their bitter naval attack on the English during the rebellion in Northumberland, ii. 15. He burns some French towns, and puts many of the people to death, ib. He lands in Normandy with an army, 1412; is refused money promised by some of the French princes; plundered the country, and traverses Maine and Anjou, an English division from Calais occupied also a part of Artois, 21, 22. Orleans repairs to his head-quarters; carried moneys to the English prince, who received him courteously, 22. Clarence, ceasing plunder, marches with 8,000 men through Guienne, and enters Bordeaux, ib.; was wounded at Azincourt, 1415, but saved by king Henry's personal valour, 33. Present at Meulan, 44. He marches into Anjou from his government of Normandy, 1421; 48. Is defeated and slain, 1421, by the dauphin's forces under La Fayette, and the Scotch auxiliaries under the earl of Buchan, 48, 49. The French losing their dread of the English arms, Henry V., lands at Calais, 12th of June, to avenge in some degree this disgrace, 49.
CLARENCE, George duke of, brother of Edward IV., ii. 99, 101. Dislike of the queen Elizabeth to this nearest male heir to the crown, 104. The duke, 1469, married, at Calais, Isabella, daughter of the earl of Warwick, 104. The king wrote to Clarence and Warwick to come over to his aid in the suppression of the rebels of Yorkshire, ib. They delay, and do not arrive before Edward had lost, at Edgecote, 5,000 men, together with their commander, the earl of Pembroke, ib. Clarence and Warwick suspected of abetting the insurrection; find the king disconsolate at Olney, ib. They shut king Edward up in Middleham castle; the army compels Warwick to free the king from such captivity, ib. Amnesty, even to the insurgents; family compact, Edward to love George of Clarence as formerly, ib. Fresh jealousies as to Clarence and Warwick; they are entrusted with some forces against insurgents in Lincolnshire, 1470; ib. The king marching with a royal army, came up first with the insurgents, whom he totally defeated, 105. Edward then openly declared against his brother George, who

CLARENCE, George, Duke of,—
fled across seas with Warwick and his family and friends, ib. Sailing into Calais, for the first time, Warwick was kept out of the town by his faithless Gascon lieutenant, who had declared for Edward IV., ib. His ships being at anchor, Isabella, duchess of Clarence, was delivered of a son, ib. Dilemma in which the duke was placed, betwixt allegiance to his brother, and regard for his father-in-law, 104, 106. Political remarks, 105, 106, 108. He deserts Warwick, mounts the white rose, and goes over to his brother Edward, near Coventry, 1471; 108. On the eve of the battle of Barnet, he sent to Warwick to offer his mediation, ib. Conduct of Clarence in the action at Tewkesbury, 109. Gloucester marrying the lady Anne, sister of Isabella, duchess of Clarence, demanded to share the estates and revenues of the earl of Warwick; Clarence defends the suit before the king, 111. Edward IV. adjudged the bulk of the property to George of Clarence, ib. Hence the fatal jealousy entertained of Clarence by Richard of Gloucester, ib. Clarence attends the king at the interview with Louis XI. on the bridge of Picquigny, 112. His duchess Isabella died, 1476; 114. The duke proposes to marry Mary of Burgundy, successor of Charles the Rash, ib. The king, jealous of Clarence's ambition, causes this negotiation to fail, ib. Burdett, one of the duke's household, and Stacey, a priest, condemned for devising the death of lord Beauchamp by magic, etc., ib. Clarence spoke in council on this unjust execution of his servants, ib The duke sent to the Tower, ib. Edward personally accuses his brother, 1478, in parliament, for treason, dealings with the devil, etc., ib. Clarence's speech, not extant; for the king permitted nothing obnoxious to himself to remain on the rolls of parliament, ib. The duke condemned to die, 7th February, 114, 115. Observations on the popular belief that he was drowned in a butt of Malmsey, 114. Suspicions fell on his brother Gloucester, ib.
CLARENCE, Isabella, duchess of, a daughter of Nevil, earl of Warwick, married, 1469, at Calais, ii. 104. She gave birth to a son in the harbour of Calais, 1470; 105. The rebellious lieutenant of the earl with difficulty allowed wine to be sent on board, ib. The fugitives land at Harfleur, and are treated with much gallantry by the French admiral and by Louis XI., ib. She obtains the chief share of her father's possessions; her sister Anne, duchess of Gloucester, a good marriage portion, 111. Her death, 1476; 114.
Clarendon, Constitutions of, a series of articles rendering the clergy subject to the civil courts for felony, signed by Becket and the clergy, January 25, 1164; i. 449, 555, 556. Their modification or repeal at the great council held at Northampton, 1176; 557.
Clarendon House, from a print of the period, iii. 704.
CLARENDON, Edward Hyde, earl of, created April 20; 1661. He maintained that to print the " Remonstrance " without the consent of the peers was illegal, iii. 256, 287, 480, 524, 653. He returns from exile with Charles II., 1660; 653, 686, 690. His description of the fire of London, 699, note, 702. Charles II. demands the great seal from him, 703. He is impeached, ib. Urged by the king, he flies to Holland, where he dies, 1674; 705. His portrait, 830. He proposes to destroy all public documents connected with the period of the commonwealth, ib. His arbitrary proceedings gave rise to the Act of Habeas Corpus, 835. Quoted, iii. 44, 90, 115, 136, 158, 178, note, 204, 205, 217, 219, 220, 285, 490, 693, 697.
CLARENDON, Henry Hyde, earl of, 1674. He proposes that James II. should be nominally left on the

CLARENDON, Henry Hyde,— throne, and a Protestant regent appointed during his life, iv. 4. He died 1709.

CLARENDON, Henry Hyde, earl of, 1723. Declaims against the Hanoverian troops in England; he died 1753; iv. 517.

CLARENDON, Sir Roger, natural son of the Black Prince, executed 1402; ii. 11.

CLARGES, Dr., M.P., 1660; iii. 431*.

CLARKE, Dr. John. He established a Baptist church at Newport, in America, about the middle of the 17th century, iii. 808.

CLARKE, Dr. Samuel, a celebrated divine and philosopher, born in 1675. His opinions respecting subscription to the Thirty-nine Articles, § i. 513. His "Scripture Doctrine of the Trinity," published 1712; 515. This work was censured by a convocation of clergy in 1714; iv. 646. His portrait, 617.

Clas Merddin, a name of Britain, i. 8.

CLAUDE, queen, wife of Francis I. (she was daughter of Louis XII. by Anne of Brittany), ii. 332, 364. Mary, widow of Louis XII., and duchess of Suffolk, left Anne Boleyn under the protection of Claude, but that queen died in 1524; ib.

CLAUDIAN the poet, quoted, i. 19.

CLAUDIUS, march of the emperor through Gaul to Britain, to the succour of Aulus Plautius, A.C. 43, i. 39. Claudius was at the taking of Camalodunum, received the submission of the Trinobantes, and returned to Rome, 40. His triumph, ib. Coins of Claudius, ib. His portrait from a copper coin, ib. Caractacus brought before Claudius, 42. Claudius meditates the relinquishing of Britain, 43.

CLAYDON, a currier of London, Turmin, and lord Cobham were burnt, 1415, for lollardism, ii. 147.

CLAYPOLE, lady, Cromwell's daughter, iii.; 425.

CLEMENT VII., Giulio dei Medici, elected pope, Nov. 19, 1523; ii. 357. He increased Wolsey's authority as papal legate, with permission for him to reform certain monasteries, ib. This pope sometimes resists the generals of Charles V., at other times he is compelled, 1526, to sign disadvantageous treaties, 362, 363. Yet his treaty with the viceroy, Lannoy, could not save Rome from sack, pillage, and slaughter, by the adventurers who formed the army of Bourbon, 363. Guicciardini's narrative of their atrocities, ib. Clement VII. escaped into the castle of St. Angelo, ib. He capitulated through famine, was forced to sign a treaty with Charles V. that he would oppose the divorce of Catherine, his aunt, 366. The pope escaped from Rome to Orvieto, and a French army under Lautrec marched into Italy, to his relief, 366, 367. He empowered Wolsey to decide on the divorce, and to grant Henry VIII. a dispensation to marry, 367. At Wolsey's desire, 1527, the pope appointed an Italian (Campeggio) as legate, conjointly with the English cardinal, for the trial of the divorce, but warned Henry that this would embarrass his cause, ib. Clement receiving an embassy from the English king, signed, though reluctantly, a decretal bull, which promised to confirm the decision of his two legates, 367, 368, 371. The pope was dangerously ill, 1529, giving thus a hope of the papacy for Wolsey; Clement recovered, 371. He concluded a favourable treaty with Charles V., revoked the commission to the two legates, and entertained Catherine's appeal, 370, 371. His conference at Marseilles with Francis I., and ambassadors of Henry VIII., 381,382. Union of Catherine de Medicis, his niece, with the duke of Orleans, second son of Francis I., arranged, 1533, but both sons of that king were still in the hands of Charles V. as hostages, 382. Clement referred the appeal of Catherine of Arragon to a consistory of the cardinals, and on their nearly unanimous decision, the pope gave judgment that her marriage with Henry

CLEMENT VII., Giulio dei Medici,— VIII. was valid and indissoluble, 384. Henry and his parliament had at this moment broken off all submission to the popes, ib. Clement died Sept. 26, 1534.

CLEMENT XIV., Pope, (John Vincent Anthony Ganganelli,) portrait of, § i. 522. Elected May, 19, 1769; ib. Issues a bull, July 21, 1773, for the suppression of the order of the Jesuits, ib. He died Sept. 22, 1774.

CLEMENT, Jacques, a fanatic monk of the order of the Jacobins, assassinates the French king Henri III., 1589; ii. 672.

CLEMENT, one of the judges of Charles I., seized by the convention parliament, iii. 664; and executed as a regicide, Oct. 17, 1660; 676.

CLEMENTINA, Princess, grand-daughter of John Sobieski, king of Poland, marries cardinal Alberoni. She is detained by the emperor, at the desire of the English government, in the castle of Inspruck, iv. 352; but escapes in the guise of a servant-maid to Bologna, 355.

CLERAMBAULT, commanded at the village of Blenheim, and was drowned in the Danube at the flight which followed that memorable battle, 1704; iv. 172.

CLERK, John, bishop of Bath and Wells, nominated 1523; his letter to Cromwell, 1533, exculpatory of old Dr. Carsley, a canon residentiary. He died 1540; ii. 383.

CLERMONT, count of, 1409; ii. 19.

CLERMONT, duke of, 1757; iv. 598.

CLERMONT, counsellor of Charles the dauphin of France, killed by Stephen Marcel, 1358; i. 774.

CLEVELAND, duchess of, mistress of Charles II., iii. 725, 762.

CLEVER, a schoolmaster, attempts an insurrection, 1556; he is taken prisoner, and executed at Bury St. Edmund's, ii. 531.

CLEVERLY, his illustration of the defeat of the Dutch fleet by Blake, Dean, and Monk, iii. 415.

CLEVES, duke of, a prince of the Protestant Confederacy, 1538; ii. 412, 416.

CLIFFORD, Thomas, lord, on the side of the red rose, falls, 1454, in the great defeat at St. Alban's, ii. 92.

CLIFFORD, John, lord, award to be paid by Warwick to, for his father's death, ii. 93. He overtook the youngest son of Richard duke of York, 1460, after the Lancastrian victory at Wakefield, 96. Though Rutland was but a young boy, he stabbed him to the heart, ib. He died, 1461.

CLIFFORD, Thomas, created baron Clifford of Chudleigh, 1672, lord treasurer; he resigns this office on the passing of the Test Act, iii. 711. His death, 1673, ib.

CLIFFORD, sir Robert, and W. Barly, secret agents of Henry VII. in Flanders, 1492—1494, learn all the family history of the pretender Warbeck, and communicate the names of his partisans in England to the king, ii. 300. Executions, imprisonments, etc., ensue, 300, 301.

CLINTON, Edward, lord, 1517, commanded the fleet in Somerset's Scottish expedition, 1547; ii. 459, 464. He died, 1584.

CLINTON, general sir Henry, lands at Boston, with a considerable body of marines, May, 1775; § i. 214. Portrait of, 217, 262, 422. He is superseded by sir Guy Carleton, 1782; 488.

CLIVE, Robert, lord, born 1725. Portrait of, § ii. 33. He takes possession of Arcot, 1751; 30. Retakes Calcutta, 1757; 48, 49. Gains the battle of Plassey, June 21, 1757, and raises Meer Jaffier to the musnud of Bengal, 59, 60. Clive accepts a Jaghire of 30,000l. per annum, 1759; 75. He sails to England, February, 1760; 79. Files a bill in Chancery against the Court of Directors, who attempted to deprive him of his Jaghire, 83. He reaches Calcutta, May

CLIVE, Robert, lord,—
3, 1765 ; 84. His reform of abuses in the government of India, 91—94. He quits India for the last time, January, 1767 ; 94. Committee of investigation appointed, 1772; their partial proceedings against Clive, who under the morbid influence of a diseased mind and body, dies by his own hand, November 22, 1774, in his forty-ninth year, 104 —113.

CLOOTZ, Jean Baptist, a Prussian baron, better known during the revolutionary scenes in France as Anacharsis Clootz, was born in 1755. His life, § ii. 491, 492.

Closter Seven, Convention of, signed by William duke of Cumberland, September, 1757 ; iv. 597.

Cloth-market, Leeds, as it appeared in 1600, from a print in the king's library, iii. 529.

CLOTWORTHY, sir John, iii. 237, 254, 326 ; is accused by the army, and obtains leave of absence and the speaker's passport to quit the kingdom, 1647 ; 369.

Clover, introduced from the Netherlands in the reign of Elizabeth, ii. 806.

Clubs, Political, iii. 898.

CLUTTERBUCK, one of the lords of the treasury, 1741; iv. 448.

Coaches, ii. 887 ; iii. 864 ; iv. 815.

Coal, increase of its use on the diminution of the woods, ii. 191, 806.

Coal-gas, first employed for illuminating the streets and buildings, in 1792, by Mr. William Murdoch, a Cornish engineer, § iv. 688.

Coal-mining, extension and improvement in, from the general introduction of the steam-engine about the middle of the eighteenth century, § i. 583.

Coal-tar, origin of the manufacture of, about 1779 ; § i. 589.

Coalition ministry, the, 1782 ; § i. 498.

CORBET, lieutenant-colonel, a parliamentary officer, 1648 ; iii. 386, 391.

COBHAM, Eleanor, duchess of Gloucester, ii. 59, 83. (See Humphrey duke of Gloucester.)

COBHAM, lord, sir John Oldcastle, so called in right of his wife, 1413 ; ii. 25. Considered the head of the Lollards and Wycliffite reformers, is condemned for heresy by archbishop Arundel, ib. King Henry who, when prince of Wales, had been his intimate friend, tries to persuade him to a recantation, 25. He escapes from the Tower to a safe refuge in Wales, ib. Insurrection of the reformers in London; Cobham repairs thither, again flies towards Wales, but is brought back prisoner, circa 1417. Hanged and burned as a rebel and heretic, 38, 147.

COBHAM, lord, an object of jealousy, 1603, to Sir R. Cecil, iii. 5. Was implicated with Raleigh, and Grey of Wilton, in the conspiracies of that year to seize the person of James, and overthrow Cecil, 7. Cobham and Raleigh are tried for the "Main Plot," after the priests and other conspirators had been convicted of the "Bye Plot," 8, et seq. Questioned by the Council, he betrays Raleigh, alleging that he was the instigator of the two plots, 9. The indictment charged Cobham with applying to d'Aremberg for a large sum to advance the pretensions of Arabella Stuart, 9, 10. Raleigh's indignation at the baseness of Cobham, relative to his letter addressed to himself in the Tower, produced by Coke on the trial, 10. Arraignment of Cobham and Grey of Wilton before a commission of their peers, by whom they are condemned, 12. Although his behaviour was dastardly during the trial, he evinced some firmness when brought to the scaffold ; whereon, after divers strange proceedings he is told by the sheriff of his reprieve, 14. Arguments founded on Cobham's confession militate (at a day then distant) against the life of Raleigh, 14, 15. His boldness on the scaffold caused many to suppose he had been made aware of the king's intention to commute the

COBHAM, lord,—
capital penalty into imprisonment, 15. Cobham in a few years was suffered to stray from the Tower, his mind having suffered by imprisonment, ib. His estates sequestrated, he finds a miserable refuge in the Minories, where he died, as is thought, of starvation, 1619, the great Raleigh having been then recently beheaded, ib. Copy of lord Cobham's letter on the day before Raleigh's trial, 10 note.

COBHAM, Richard Temple lord, created, 1718. He forces the garrison of Vigo to surrender, October 1719. He died 1749 ; iv. 356.

COCHRANE, sir Alexander, the Danish West India islands surrender to him, 1807 ; § iv. 290. He directs the attack on the French flotilla at Boulogne, 1809 ; 409. Admiral of the English expedition to Washington, 1814 ; 669.*

COCHRANE, sir John, 1685 ; iii. 769. 770.

COCHRANE, a favourite of James III., ostentatiously displays his power and magnificence, ii. 136. Is seized by the earl of Angus, 1482, and hanged over the parapet of the bridge of Lauder, ib.

COCHRANE, colonel, 1641 ; iii. 251.

Cock-fighting, ii. 891.

COCKAYNE, alderman, obtains by patent, 1608, the exclusive right of dyeing and dressing all woollen cloths, iii. 536.

COCKBURN, sir George, captain of the Northumberland, in which Napoleon sailed for St. Helena, August 7th, 1815 ; § iv. 646.*

COEHORN, a celebrated engineer, 1695 ; iv. 56, 152.

CŒUR, Jacques, a French merchant, celebrated for his opulence and loyalty, ii. 177. Confiscation of his property, 178. He died in 1456, ib.

Coffee, introduced into England by Edwards, a Turkey merchant, in 1652 ; iii. 548.

COIFI, high-priest of the Anglo-Saxon paganism; his spirited conduct at Godmundham, 627, in a council or witenagemot assembled by Edwin, king of Northumbria, i. 285. Coifi after the boldest speeches, calls for a horse and arms, he hurls a lance within the inclosure of a heathen temple, no lightning nor earthquake ensue, ib. The chief idol is then destroyed, the edifice razed to the ground, and the king and his Northumbrians, already well prepared by Paulinus, are baptized, ib.

Coinage, regno George III., § i. 572 ; § iv. 717.

Coining, process of, ii. 796. Machinery at Soho brought into operation in 1783 ; § i. 589. The first coining-mill impelled by the power of steam, 1788 ; § iii. 687. Disgraceful state of the coinage during the 18th century, 751.

Coins and medals furnish an illustration to true history, i., 4, 26. Ring-coins of the early Britons, 110, 111 ; ancient British, 112 ; of Cunobeline, 125. Silver coin of Offa, 150 ; of Egbert, 151 ; of Ethelwulf, 152 ; of Alfred the Great, 167 ; of Canute, 180 ; of Carausius, 53. Gold coin, bearing a fine profile of Constantine the Great, ib. Form and value of Saxon coins, 271, et seq. ; 837, 838.

Coins of the early Norman kings, specimen of, i. 594, 595.

Coiner at work, i. 594. Disquisition on the value, purity, or depreciation of English coins, from Edward III. to Richard III., ii. 184, 185. Perkin Warbeck's groat, 305. Coins of the 15th and 16th centuries, 797—803. Gold and silver coinage of queen Elizabeth, 803. Gold and silver coronation coins of Jac. I., 1603, with the quarterings and mottoes as commanded by the king, iii. 4. Coins of the 17th century, 549—557, 868.

COKE, sir Edward, ii. 686, 767. As attorney-general he becomes the public prosecutor of Raleigh, 1603, for the conspiracy called the "Main," iii. 10. He displays personal rancour against sir Walter, and uses the most vindictive and intemperate language, 10, 11. Employing the co-plot, the "Bye," as a

COKE, sir Edward,—
  plea against this prisoner, not indicted for that intended violence to the king, he is rebuked wittily by
  Raleigh, and this pleading challenged as contrary to
  forms of law, 10. Cecil, in court, rebukes Coke as
  too harsh, 11. He is commissioned with Dr. Hone, by
  the house of peers to demand a conference, 1604,
  with the Commons, 18. Chief-justice Popham, Coke,
  and others, examine Guy Fawkes, 29. Sir Edward
  Coke's speech against Garnet, on the jesuit's trial,
  March 1606; 31. His declination from the royal
  favour, 55. He is ordered to investigate the
  poisoning of sir T. Overbury, 58. Takes out 300
  examinations, ib. Reports that Frances Howard
  had employed sorcery to incapacitate her husband,
  and win the love of Rochester, &c., &c., ib. Is
  hated by the king, 62. Receives his supersedeas, 63.
  Committed to the Tower, 88. Denounces newly
  invented offices and useless officers, 112. Charles
  makes him a sheriff, 117. Superseded in his office
  by sir Harry Vane, 209. His death, 212.
COKE, sir John, secretary of state, 1629; iii. 146.
COKE, Roger, quoted iii. 318, 857.
COKE, Mr., solicitor-general at the trial of Charles I.,
  iii. 390. Executed as a regicide, 676.
Colchester Castle, remains of, from an original drawing, iii. 383.
Colebrook-dale, iron bridge at, completed 1779; § i.
  586. View of the, ib.
Colechurch, Peter of, architect of the first stone bridge
  across the Thames at London, 1176; i. 615.
COLEMAN, iii. 523, 719. His letters relative to the
  popish plot, 723. He is executed, 1678; 724.
COLERIDGE, a poet of considerable eminence, born in
  1772, died 1834; § iv. 698, 699. His portrait, 698.
COLET, dean, founder of St. Paul's School, 1509; ii.
  815.
COLIGNI, admiral, a leader of the Huguenots, ii. 570,
  573. Was murdered at the massacre of St. Bartholomew's day, 1572; 646, 647.
COLLEGE, Stephen, a joiner, executed as a traitor,
  1681; iii. 734.
Colleges, foundation of, ii. 814, 815.
COLLIER, Jeremy, 1696, a non-juring clergyman, iv.
  69.
COLLINGWOOD, Cuthbert, born 1748; greatly distinguishes himself at the battle of Trafalgar, October 21, 1805; and on the fall of lord Nelson, takes
  the command of the fleet, as senior officer; is created
  baron Collingwood, of Caldburne and Hethpoole,
  November 20, 1805; § iv. 194. His death, March,
  1810; 408. His monument, ib.
COLLINS, William, a distinguished modern poet, born
  about 1720; died in a miserable condition, 1756;
  § i. 607.
COLONNA, a powerful Roman family, ii. 357, 358,
  362.
COLOREDO, Count, governor of Milan, 1719, iv. 362.
COLUMBA, St., born in Donegal, passed into Caledonia,
  563, and converted the Pictish king, Brude II., i. 229.
  His followers, the Culdees, and their tenets, 229,
  244. Columba settled in Iona, one of the Hebrides,
  and founded his monastery, named I Columb Kill,
  which became a seminary and early seat of Christianity, 229. Illustration, the monastery of
  Iona, 228. Two Latin lives of Columba; one by
  Cuminius, who succeeded him as abbot of Iona, in
  657; the other by abbot Adomnan, in 679, are
  extant, 290.
COLUMBANUS, St., preached Christianity to the Gauls
  and Germans, and died, 615, at the monastery of
  Bobbio, in Italy, which he had founded, i. 289, 290.
  Account of his writings, 290. He did not leave the
  seat of learning in Ireland until he had reached
  fifty, ib.
COLUMBUS, discovery of America by, ii. 775. He
  sailed on his memorable voyage, from the bar of

COLUMBUS,—
  Saltes, near Palos, in Andalusia, August 3, 1492,
  and reached the island of San Salvador on the 12th
  of October. He afterwards discovered Cuba, and
  other of the West Indian islands; and on the 15th
  of March, 1493, he again landed at Palos. On the
  25th of September following, Columbus sailed from
  Cadiz, on his second voyage, from which he returned to the same port, June 11, 1496. He sailed
  on his third voyage, May 30, 1498; 776.
COMINE, Robert de, (1069), sets out from York with a
  small army of 1200 lancers, and advances to Durham, which he enters, but on the following morning
  is attacked by the English, and only two of the
  Normans escape, i. 370.
COMINES, merit of his "Memoirs," from 1464 to 1498.
  His style, ii. 209. His narrative of the mission of
  Garter, king at arms, to demand the French crown
  of Louis XI. Interview of that herald with the
  French monarch, 111. Of the interview on the
  bridge of Picquigny, between Edward IV. and
  Louis, 112. His account of Richard III. and Richmond, 126, note, 128. He was a partisan of Orleans
  (Louis XII.), 1483; 292, note.
COMIUS, a steady adherent of Cæsar, i. 26. He was
  king of the Atrebatians, a tribe of Belgæ, in Artois,
  27. Cæsar sends him as envoy into Britain. The
  Britons load him with chains, 28. He is released,
  29. Comius negotiates a peace for Cassivellaunus,
  and Cæsar quits Britain, 33.
Commerce, regulations respecting, i. 824—836. Prohibition of the exportation of wool, and the importation of manufactured woollen cloth, 1261. Its effects
  on the community, 826. The mariners' compass
  introduced into Europe towards the end of the
  twelfth century; generally used by navigators soon
  after the middle of the thirteenth, 830. A very
  curious description of the fleet employed by Edward
  III. at the siege of Calais, containing the comparative
  number of ships furnished by the principal commercial cities of England, and the number of seamen,
  831. Specimen of some ships in the time of Richard II., ib. A valuable document preserved in
  the exchequer gives the value of exports for the
  year 1354, at 212,338l. 5s., paying customs to the
  amount of 81,846l. 12s. 2d., and imports at 38,383l.
  16s. 10d., 832. Exportation and importation of
  corn regulated, and forbidden without a special
  license from the king, ib. Coals mentioned in an
  order of Henry III., in 1245; regulations respecting,
  etc., ib. Exportation of coals to France, 1325;
  834. Description of the Scottish trade at this period;
  the flourishing state of Berwick before its capture
  by Edward I., in 1296; 835, 836. Irish trade, 836.
  Fifteenth century: commerce and productions of
  Europe, ii. 170—174. Bills of exchange, and
  banks, 172. English mercantile laws, ib. Venetian merchants, 173, 174. Excellence of English
  wool, 173. The English trade with the cities
  of Flanders, 174. Wealth and influence of English
  merchants, 175. General prosperity of commerce
  throughout the seventeenth century, iii. 852.
Commerce, French council of, founded, 1700, iv.
  697.
Commercial treaties (eighteenth century), § iii. 652.
Common Prayer, book of, substituted for the Latin
  Mass Book, November, 1548, ii. 731, 732.
Commons, rights of commonage, and laws appertaining
  thereto, in Anglo-Saxon times, i. 351.
Commons, House of. Many important details are
  referred to under the general word Parliament.
Commonwealth, the. Charles I. opens the long parliament, November 3rd, 1640; iii. 226. Lenthall is
  chosen speaker of the lower house, ib. A committee of grievance appointed by the commons,
  227. The punishment inflicted on Burton, Bastwick
  and Prynne declared to be illegal, and damages

Commonwealth, the,—
awarded, 228, 229. Land is impeached for high treason, December 18, and committed to custody by the house of lords, 229. Strafford is impeached, and sent to the Tower, 230. Wren, bishop of Ely, is ordered to give security in 10,000l., to answer the judgment of parliament, ib. Windebank and Finch impeached, 231. Six of the judges are ordered by the House of Lords to find bail to abide the decision of parliament for their judgment regarding ship-money, ib. The triennial bill passes, January, 1641; 232. Plans for securing regular parliaments, ib. Parliament votes money for the payment of the Scottish army, 234. The commons resolve that the clergy shall be incapable of acting in any civil court, ib. Strafford's trial commences, March 22, 1641, 241. The king summon both houses before him, and proposes that Strafford should be tried for misdemeanour, ib. Bill passed for preventing the dissolution of parliament without the consent of both houses, 242. The royal assent is given to the bill of attainder against Strafford, May 10; 244; and that unfortunate nobleman is beheaded on Tower-hill, May 12; 245. Several officers of state resign; the earl of Leicester is made lord-lieutenant of Ireland, 246. The commons grant tonnage and poundage, and vote six subsidies; pass bills imposing a poll-tax for paying the army; and procure the abolition of the star-chamber and high commission court, 247. Thirteen bishops are impeached by the commons, 248. The king proceeds to parliament, August 10; 249; the parliament appoints a commission to watch his proceedings, ib. He meets the Scottish parliament, 249, 250. General Leslie is created earl of Leven, 252. An insurrection breaks out in Ireland; the protestants are massacred, 252—254. Measures for suppressing the insurrection, 255. The king commences his return to London, ib. The remonstrance on the state of the kingdom, presented to the king, December 1. Both houses resolve never to tolerate the popish religion in Ireland, 257. The "Remonstrance" is printed, 258. Balfour, lieutenant of the Tower, is removed by the king, and and colonel Lunsford appointed in his stead, 259. The commons resolve that he is unfit for that office, ib. The houses surrounded by tumultuous assemblies, 260. The thirteen bishops who had been impeached, having again taken their places, remonstrate to the king against all acts done in their absence, 261. The two houses pronounce the remonstrance a breach of privilege; the commons accuse twelve of them of treason; they are seized, and ten of their number committed to the Tower, ib. The commons send an address to the king praying for a guard, and bring arms into the house, 262. The king's answer, January 3, 1642; ib. Lord Kimbolton, Hollis, Haslerig, Pym, Hampden, and Strode, are accused of high treason, 263. The king attempts, but unsuccessfully, to obtain possession of their persons; the house adjourns, 263, 264. The commons establish a permanent committee at Guildhall. The king proceeds to the common council, and demands the five members, 265. The king issues a proclamation charging Kimbolton and the five members with high treason, ib. The royal family remove to Hampton Court, 266. Colonel Lunsford is committed to the Tower for raising troops for the service of the king, 267. The attorney-general Herbert is committed to the Fleet, ib. The Scottish commissioners offer themselves as mediators between the king and his parliament, 268. Petitions complaining of the delay in putting down the insurrection in Ireland, 269. Lord Digby is impeached by the commons, 272. Marriage of the princess Mary with the prince of Orange, ib. The royal assent given to a bill for excluding

Commonwealth, the,—
bishops from the House of Lords, and another for impressing soldiers for Ireland, ib. The queen and princess Mary embark for Holland, February 23; ib. The Militia bill passed by both houses, 274. The king refuses to permit the prince of Wales to come to London, ib. The parliament resolves to put the kingdom in a state of defence, 275. The king removes to Newmarket, and refuses his assent to the militia ordinance, 275, 276. The lords lieutenants are ordered to call out the militia by authority of parliament alone, 277. The king organizes a government at York, 277, 278. The parliament petitions for the removal of the stores from Hull to London, 278. Hull is taken possession of for the parliament, ib. The king issues a declaration for the collection of tonnage and poundage, 279. Sir J. Hotham refuses to admit the king into Hull with a guard of 300 men, April 23; The king proclaims him a traitor, ib. The parliament requires every one in authority to put the militia bill into effect, 283. The Scottish parliament remonstrate against the king going over to Ireland, 284. Lord-keeper Lyttelton sends the great seal to the king, and shortly after goes himself to York, 287. Parliament summons nine peers to appear at Westminster; they refuse to attend, 288. A Dutch ship runs ashore laden with military stores, June 2; ib. The parliament attempts, unsuccessfully, to treat with the king, ib. The nine peers are impeached by the commons; they are adjudged by the lords to be incapable of sitting as members of the house, and to be imprisoned during pleasure, ib. The earl of Essex is appointed captain-general of the army, July 12; 290. Negotiations between the king and parliament, 292. The king's forces endeavour to surprise Hull, 293. Charles issues a proclamation for all persons capable of bearing arms to meet him at Nottingham, ib. He erects his standard on Nottingham Castle, August 25; ib. He attempts to gain possession of Coventry, 294. The parliament refuses to treat with him, 295. He reaches Shrewsbury, September 20, and causes money to be coined there, 296. Battle of Edgehill, October 23; 297, 298. The king proceeds to Oxford; marches to Reading, 299. Prince Rupert attacks Brentford, but is repulsed; the royal army retreats to Oxford, 299, 300. Parliamentarian commissioners treat with the king at Oxford, March 1, 1643; ib. The queen returns to England, 301. Essex takes Reading, ib. The commons impeach the queen of high treason, 302. The poet Waller and others are detected in a conspiracy to betray the leading commonwealth-men into the hands of the king, ib. Robert Yeomans and George Bourcher are hanged at Bristol for conspiracy, ib. Hampden is mortally wounded at the battle of Chalgrove field, June 18; 303, 304. The royalist earl of Newcastle defeats Fairfax at Atherton Moor, June 30; 305. Sir J. Hotham and his son are committed to the Tower, July 15, for plotting to deliver up Hull to the king, ib. The royalists take Gainsborough and Lincoln, and defeat sir William Waller at Devizes, ib. The two Hothams are beheaded on Tower-hill, January, 1644; ib. Prince Rupert takes Bristol, 306. The royalists besiege Gloucester, September 3, 1643; ib. The earl of Falkland is slain at the battle of Newbury, September 20; 307, 308. The earls of Bedford, Clare, and Holland, go over to the king, but shortly return to the parliament, 308. The solemn League and Covenant of England and Scotland, 309. The national synod for settling the government of the church of England meets at Westminster, 311. Pym dies, and is interred in Westminster Abbey, ib. The parliament is summoned at Oxford, January 22, 1644; 312. Charles retreats from Ox-

Commonwealth, the,—

ford to Worcester, 314. Battle of Marston Moor, July 2; 315. York surrenders to the parliamentarians, July 15; ib. Successes of the royalists, 317, 318. The king marches from Cornwall; second battle of Newbury; the king retreats to Oxford, 318,319. The Self-denying Ordinance is introduced, December 9, by which members of parliament are excluded from command in the army, 322; passed in the Commons, but rejected by the Lords, ib. Fairfax is appointed general-in-chief of the parliamentarian army, 323. Alterations in the Self-denying Ordinance, ib. It is passed in the Lords, April 3, 1645; 324. Fairfax takes the command of the army at Windsor, ib. Laud is tried in the House of Peers, March, 12, 1644; his impeachment is abandoned in the ensuing October, and an ordinance of attainder passed against him by the Commons, 325. Laud is beheaded, January 10, 1645; 326. The parliament negotiates for peace, 326, 327. Conferences of peace held at Uxbridge, 329. Battle of Naseby, June 14; 333, 334. Montrose defeats the Covenanters, February 2, and gains several other advantages, 338—340. The battle of Alford gained by Montrose, July 2; 340. Glasgow taken by Montrose; Edinburgh surrenders, ib. The king takes Huntingdon by assault, August 24, ib. Lord-keeper Lyttelton dies at Oxford, August 27; ib. Prince Rupert surrenders Bristol, September 11; 341. Battle of Rowton Heath, September 23, ib. Battle of Philiphaugh, ib. The king escapes from Newark, and proceeds to Oxford, 344. He negotiates with parliament, 345. Escapes from Oxford, April 27, 1646; 350; and throws himself upon the protection of the Scottish army, 352. Oxford surrenders to the parliament, 355. The two princes Rupert and Maurice leave England, ib. The garrisons, with the exception of those in the north, fall into the possession of the parliamentarians, 356. The parliament sends final propositions to the king, at Newcastle, July 23rd, which the commissioners vainly entreat him to accept, 358, 359. The commons determine that England has no longer need of the Scottish army, 359; and vote them 400,000l. for their services, 361. Episcopacy is declared to be for ever abolished, and the bishops' lands are put up to sale, 362. The king is delivered up at Newcastle to the earl of Pembroke, January 30, 1647; ib. He is conducted to Holmby-house, 363. The disbanding of the army voted, 366. The soldiers refuse to disband without payment, etc., ib. A force from the Independents, headed by Joyce, remove the king, June 3; 367, 368. Conference between Cromwell, Fairfax, and the king, 368. The army marches towards London; demands the purgation of parliament, and formally accuses eleven of the members, 369. The king is removed to Windsor Castle, ib. Disputes between the Independents and Presbyterians; the parliament is surrounded by a disorderly rabble, and the speaker and many of the members flee to the army for protection; the residue of the houses elect lord Willoughby temporary speaker, and forbid the army to advance, ib. Fairfax advances to Hounslow Heath; the citizens hearing of his approach sue for a pacification, which he grants upon conditions, ib. Suppression of the Presbyterian party; several of the most intolerant are accused of treason, 370. Ireton and other officers draw up "Proposals" for the settlement of the kingdom; the king refuses to accept them, 370, 371. The friendly intentions of Cromwell towards the king alienate the affections of his army, 372. Lilburne and Wildman, two adjutors, form a plot to assassinate Cromwell, ib. The king receives continual notices of wicked designs upon his life, and, guided by his fears, flies from Hampton Court to the Isle of Wight, November 10;

Commonwealth, the,—

374,378. The levellers determine to take away Cromwell's life, but are checked by his prompt conduct, 378. [From this time Cromwell and Ireton were forced to join in the republican spirit of the army, and to be cold to the royal cause.] The parliament sends four propositions to the king, December 14, which he refuses to sign, 379. The army promises to protect the parliament, 1648; 381. A committee of safety for the commonwealth, ib. Insurrectionary movements in favour of the king suppressed by the army, ib. A Scottish army crosses the borders, but is defeated by Cromwell at Preston, and Hamilton and Langdale are captured, 382. Mutinous spirit in the navy, 383. The earl of Holland is defeated at Kingston-upon-Thames, and surrenders to Fairfax, ib. Colchester surrenders to Fairfax; he causes sir Charles Lucas and sir George Lisle to be shot, ib. The prince of Wales appears in the Downs, but retires without firing a gun, 383, 384. A treaty conducted between the parliament and king at Newport, 384. Petitions are presented for justice on the king, 385. The army demands that the regal office shall be elective, 386. The king is removed to Hurst Castle, November 30; ib. The Commons declare against the imprisonment of the king by the army, 387. Colonels Pride and Rich surround the house with troops, and the Presbyterian members are arrested, ib. The Rump, consisting of fifty Independents, is formed, 388. The king is removed to Windsor Castle, ib. The Commons declare their authority supreme, and the ordinance for the trial of the king passes, January 6, 1649; 389. The king is brought before the High Court of Justice, January 19; 390. He refuses to acknowledge the authority of the court, 391. The Scottish commissioners protest against the proceedings, 393. The king is condemned, January 27; 393—395, and beheaded January 30; 396, 397. The House of Commons prohibits, under pain of high treason, the prince of Wales to be proclaimed king or chief-magistrate of England, 398. Votes the abolition of the House of Lords; that the office of royalty shall be abolished, and that the late king's statues shall be taken down, and a suitable inscription set up in their place, 399. An executive council of state appointed, ib. Blake, Dean, and Popham appointed to command the fleet, 400. Hamilton, Holland, and Capel, are beheaded in Palace-yard, March 9, ib. Charles II. is proclaimed in Scotland, 401. Cromwell goes to Ireland, August 15, and, after several months, succeeds in suppressing the rebellion, ib. Montrose proceeds to Scotland with a foreign force, in favour of Charles II., 1650; 402. He is defeated at Invercarron, and hanged at Edinburgh, ib. Cromwell is appointed commander-in-chief of all the parliamentary forces; he invades Scotland, June 29; 403. The battle of Dunbar, August 31; Charles flies to the highlands, 403, 404. He marches into England, 1651. Battle of Worcester, September 3; Charles goes to France, 405. The union and incorporation of Scotland and Ireland with England, 406. Van Trump sails up the channel with a Dutch fleet, May 19, 1652; ib. Blake beats the Dutch, under De Ruyter and De Witt, off Plymouth, September 28; 407. Van Trump gains a victory over Blake in the Downs, November 29, ib. Blake engages Van Trump, February 18, 1653, for this and the two succeeding days, and gains a victory, ib. A committee of the House adopt the resolution of bringing into the parliament a number of Presbyterians, under the name of Neutrals, 409. Cromwell, hearing they are about to pass the bill, marches to the House with a file of musketeers and dissolves the Long Parliament, April 20; 410, 411. He summons the "Little Parliament," July 4; 412. They vote the abolition of

I

Commonwealth, the,—
the High Court of Chancery; dissolve, and surrender their trust into Cromwell's hands, 413. A council of officers appoint him lord-protector, ib. He is proclaimed, December 17; 414. Blake defeats the Dutch fleet, July 31, 1653, and Van Tromp is killed, 415. The brother of the Portuguese ambassador is tried for murder, and beheaded on Tower Hill, July 10, 1654; 416. Gerrard and Vowel are also executed for a plot to assassinate the protector, ib. The Scots refuse to acknowledge the commonwealth, ib. General Monk quells an insurrection in Scotland, ib. The parliament attends the protector in the Painted Chamber, September, 1654; 416; 417. Debates concerning the legislative power, 417—419. The parliament is dissolved January 22, 1655; 419. A plot is formed for setting the prince of Wales on the throne; the conspirators seize Salisbury, but are routed at South Molton, and several are executed, ib. The protector divides England and Wales into eleven districts, 420. Jamaica is taken by the English, 1655; Cromwell interferes with the duke of Saxony in favour of the Waldenses, ib. Treaty of alliance between England and France against Spain, ib. A new parliament called, September 17, 1656; Syndercombe, a republican officer, engages to assassinate the protector, ib. The parliament offers the title of king to Cromwell, and urges the appointment of two Houses, 1657; 421. He refuses the regal style, but agrees to recall the House of Peers, ib. Harrison, and other fifth monarchy-men, sent to the Tower, ib. The protector is inaugurated in Westminster Hall, June 25; 423, 424. Blake's death, 424. Charles II. offers to marry Cromwell's daughter, 425. Parliament meets January 20, 1658; sixty peers summoned to take their seats in the Upper House, 425, 426. Parliament dissolved, February 4; another conspiracy for the restoration; Dr. Hewit and sir Henry Slingsby are beheaded, 427. Success of the English arms abroad, ib. The protector dies of a bastard tertian ague, September 3rd, having declared his son Richard his successor, 427. Parliament meets, January 27, 1659; 429. The army divided into three factions, ib. The Lambertians draw up a petition setting forth their want of pay, etc., ib. The Quakers second the motion, 430. Parliament is dissolved, April 22, ib. Fleetwood, Lambert, and the council of general-officers publish a declaration, inviting the Rump to return to the exercise and discharge of their trust, ib. They meet, and pass a declaration to secure the liberty of the people without protectorate, kingship, or House of Peers; the protector retires to Hampton Court, and soon signs his demission in form, ib. Henry Cromwell, lord-lieutenant of Ireland, submits to parliament, ib. Insurrectionary movements in favour of a Restoration, 431. The Rump is suppressed, ib. General Monk secures Berwick, 432. The Rump resume, 429*. Monk advances, January 1660, and agrees to the restoration of Charles, 430*. Act passed dissolving the parliament, ib. The new parliament meets, April 25; the peers are restored, ib. Letters from Charles II. are read in parliament, one of them to the Commons contains the Declaration of Breda, 431*. The terms offered by the king are acceded to, and king Charles II. is proclaimed at the gate of Westminster Hall, May 8, 1660; 432*. Coins of the Commonwealth, 555.
Comnena, Anna, quoted, i. 640.
Company, the African, founded 1672; iii. 867.
Company, East India, see East India Company.
Compiegne, besieged by Philip of Burgundy and sir John Montgomery, 1430. The maid of Orleans threw herself into the beleaguered fortress, ii. 73. In a sortie she was wounded and made prisoner, 73, 74. Marshal de Boussac arriving, compelled the besiegers to retire, 74.

Compton, lord William. See Northampton.
Compton, Henry, bishop of London, 1675; suspended, 1686; iii. 786, restored, 1688; 796. He conducts the princess Anne to the camp of the prince of Orange, harnessed, a drawn sword in his hand, and pistols at his saddle-bow, 799. In the inquiry as to the state of the church in 1705, he stands up for the doctrine of passive obedience, 183. His death, July 7, 1713; 277.
Comyn, John, taken prisoner at the battle of Lewes, i. 685. Chosen one of the regents of Scotland, 724. He defeats Segrave at Roslin, February 24, 1303; 725. Submits to Edward at Strathorde, and receives full pardon, ib. February 10, 1306, Bruce and Comyn have a private interview in the convent of the Minorites at Dumfries, where, after a passionate altercation, Bruce stabs Comyn, 728.
Conan, a powerful burgess, engages to deliver up Rouen to William II., 1090. He is taken and condemned to perpetual imprisonment, and afterwards thrown from the battlements by prince Henry, i. 396.
Conciergerie, Paris, view of the, § iii. 349. Cell in the, where Marie Antoinette was imprisoned, 1793; 350.
Concini, marshal D'Ancre, murdered by Vitry, a captain of the body-guard, by the order of Louis XIII., iii. 63.
Condé, prince of, chief leader of the Huguenots, ii. 570, 571, 573, 621. He is taken prisoner at the battle of Jarnac, 1568, and shot in cold blood by Montesquiou, 626.
Condorcet, John, marquis de, portrait of, § ii. 688. He takes an active part in the French revolution, 1791; 688, 709; § iii. 243. Takes poison, in order to avoid execution by the guillotine, March 28, 1794; 367.
Conduit erected in Leadenhall-street, 1665; iii. 866.
Confession, Auricular, ii. 397.
Conflans, John de, killed by Stephen Marcel, February 22, 1358; i. 774.
Conflans, M., commander of the Brest fleet. He is beaten in Quiberon Bay in an engagement with Sir E. Hawke, 1759: iv. 606.
Conflans, M., surrenders Masulipatam to the English, March 1759; § ii. 71.
Conformity Bill, the, passed 1661; iii. 685. Upwards of 2000 ministers refused to conform, on St. Bartholomew's day, and were thrust out of their livings, 690, 824.
Conformity Bill, the Occasional, passed, 1702; iv. 147, 155, 259.
Congreve, a dramatic writer, died in 1729; iv. 799.
Coningsby, lord, present at the battle of the Boyne, 1690; iv. 24. He abuses his power of lord-justice of Ireland, 1693; 48.
Connaught, claimed by Charles I., as having fallen to the crown, through the forfeiture of a rebel in Edward IV.'s time, iii. 170.
Conrad, marquis of Montferrat and prince of Tyre; his right to the kingdom of Jerusalem, i. 496, 497. Supported by the Genoese. Civil war of the Christians in Acre. He is expelled by king Richard, and retires to his strong city of Tyre, 499. Is acknowledged king of Jerusalem by Richard, but murdered in the streets of Tyre, while preparing for his coronation, by two of the assassins, 500. Richard unjustly accused of being the instigator of his murder. Count Henry of Champagne marries his widow, and succeeds to his claims, ib.
Constable of England, office of the, i. 568.
Constable, Sir William, 1645; iii. 323.
Constance, Council of, 1418, enacts that synods should be held regularly for the government and reformation of the church, each, before dissolving, appointing the time and place for the meeting of its successor, ii. 138.

CONSTANCE, of Castile, wife of Louis VII., i. 444. Her death, 1160; 446.

CONSTANTINE, the Great, 306; declared emperor, at York, or *Eboracum*, i. 53. A campaign against the nations north of the wall of Severus, remains in obscurity as to all details, *ib.* Profile of Constantine, from a gold coin, *ib.* He quits Britain with a number of native youths, as recruits for his armies at Rome, *ib.* His transfer of the seat of empire from Rome to Byzantium seriously affected the condition of Britain, by the increased distance, *ib.* Peace flourished until the death of Constantine, 337; but under his immediate successors, barbarian nations pressed sorely upon the Romans and Britons, *ib.*

CONSTANTINE, namesake of the great emperor, elected in Britain, 407; i. 55. He evinced martial talents and made conquests on the continent, *ib.* A vast number of Britons slain in his cause, *ib.* Scots, or Attacotti, serve under him in Spain, where he established his son Constans, *ib.* Fall of Constantine, 411, *ib.*

CONSTANTINE, king of the Picts, 791; i. 217.

CONSTANTINE II., succeeded his uncle, Donald III., king of Scotland, i. 218. The Picts, who had been finally subdued by his father, Kenneth III., rebelled and wrested from the monarchy the districts of Sutherland, Caithness, Ross, the Hebrides, and Orkney islands, *ib.* The Norwegian chiefs called over by the Picts, long governed the northern counties, *ib.* After a long contest with the Danes, Constantine is said to have been put to death by them, after his defeat at Crail, in Fife, 881; or to have died in 882; 219.

CONSTANTINE III., and his ally, Anlaf the Northumbrian, 937, were routed in the field of Brunanburgh, where the Scottish king's son fell in battle, i. 219. Constantine assumed the cowl, 944; and was abbot of the Culdees of St. Andrews, *ib.*

CONSTANTINE IV. slain in battle, 994; i. 220.

CONSTANTINE, an associate of William Tyndal, ii. 712.

CONSTANTIUS CHLORUS, Roman emperor, 291; has Britain allotted to him in the then frequent division of the empire, i. 53. Allectus defeated and slain by the troops of Constantius. This emperor died at *Eboracum*, 306; and his son Constantine the Great, being present at his decease, commences his reign at York, *ib.*

Constitution, Government, and Laws, in the successive periods of our history:—Political divisions, government and laws of the Britons, before the conquest by the Romans, i. 76, 82. Of Roman Britain, 84. Of the Saxon period (449 to 1066), 246. From 1066 to 1216; 562. From 1216 to 1399; 809. From 1399 to 1485; ii. 155. From 1485 to 1603; 750. From 1603 to 1660; iii. 495. From 1660 to 1689; 829. From 1688 to 1760; iv. 658. Reign of Geo. III.—From 1760 to 1785; § i. 528. From 1785 to 1802; § iii. 600. From 1802 to 1820; § iv. 631.

Constitutional Queries, the, iv. 562.

CONTADES, marshal, defeated by prince Ferdinand of Brunswick, at the battle of Minden, 1759; iv. 610.

CONTERIE, M. Charette de la, a leader of the Vendeans, 1793; § iii. 371. Portrait of, *ib.* He is taken prisoner March 23, by the republican general, Travot, and shot the 29th of the same month, himself giving the word to fire, 489.

CONTI, prince de, a candidate for the crown of Poland, 1697; iv. 77. He routs the army of the king of Sardinia, near the town of Coni, 474.

Conventicle Act passed, March 16, 1664; iii. 694.

CONVERSANO, William count of, son of Geoffrey, who was nephew of Robert Guiscard, the founder of the Norman dynasty in Naples, and one of the powerful Norman barons in Italy. He entertained duke Robert, on his return from the Holy Land, and gave to him his daughter Sibylla in marriage, together with a large sum of money as her dowry, 408.

Convocations of clergy, iv. 639—648.

CONWAY, general, supports Pitt in his speech against the American taxation, 1764; § i. 33. He is deprived of all his employments, both courtly and military, *ib.* Is named one of the secretaries of state, 1765; 40. Receives a vote of thanks from the freeholders of Boston, 41. Coincides with Pitt, 1766, in condemning the taxation of America, 43. Expresses a strong desire to resign, 1767; 57, 67, 72, 238. Portrait of, 83.

CONYERS, sir John, 1641; iii. 259.

CONYERS, Mr., M.P. 1701; iv. 122.

COOK, sir Anthony, a preceptor of Edward VI., ii. 453. His learned daughters, *ib.*

COOK, Shadrach, a non-juring clergyman, 1696; iv. 69.

COOK, sir Thomas, M.P., 1695; iv. 52.

COOK, William, publisher of the first English newspaper, 1640; iii. 615.

COOK, captain, a musician of the 17th century, iii. 885.

Cookery of the 17th century, iii. 639.

COOPER, Anthony Ashley. *See* Shaftesbury.

COOPER, Samuel, an excellent miniature painter, born 1609, died 1672; iii. 569. His portrait of Richard Cromwell, 428.

COOPER, Alderman, compelled to proclaim the young pretender, 1745; iv. 514.

COOTE, sir Eyre, defeats the French, under general Lally, 1758; and conquers the whole of Arcot, iv. 609. He reduces Pondicherry, 1761; § i. 9. Takes the command of Fort St. George, 1780; § ii. 148. His death, April 26, 1783; 155.

COPE, sir John, commander-in-chief for Scotland, 1745; iv. 484. His march after the young pretender, 485, 486. He is brought to trial by court-martial, 1747; and acquitted, 553.

COPE, sir Walter, the earl of Salisbury's dying speech to, 1612; iii. 45.

Copenhagen, bombarded by the English fleet, under admiral Gambier, Sept. 7, 1807; § iv. 287—290.

Copenhagen, battle of, April 2,1801; § iii. 551*—553*.

COPLEY, Anthony, a Catholic of fortune and character, inveigled by Clarke and Watson to join in the plot of June, 1603, and condemned at Winchester, iii. 8, 9. Is banished, together with Markham and Brookesby, 15.

Copper, ii. 811; iv. 733. Copper coinage first appeared in 1613; iii. 554. Copper manufactures (18th century), § iii. 680.

COPPOCH, Thomas, made bishop of Carlisle by the young pretender, 1745; iv. 514. Taken prisoner, 520.

Coracles, British, delineation of the light boats so called, i. 56.

CORBET, colonel, executed as a regicide, 1661; iii. 690.

CORBOIL, William, archbishop of Canterbury, 1123. Crowns king Stephen, December 26, 1135. He died Nov. 21, 1136; i. 422.

CORDAY, Charlotte, assassinates the tyrant Marat, July 13, 1793; § iii. 335; for which she is brought to the guillotine, July 17, 338.

Cordeliers, Club of, instituted 1790; § ii. 483.

CORITON, M.P., 1629; iii. 142.

Corn, law permitting the exportation of, without royal license, passed, 1394; iv. 698.

Cornwall, its independence, by reason of its extreme position and natural barriers, i. 142. In 470, a body of 12,000 (Cornish and Devonshire) Britons, under subsidy of Anthemius of Italy, sail up the Loire, *ib.* Establishing themselves in Berry, they behave cruelly and insolently, and are cut to pieces by the Visigoths, against whom they had been hired by Anthemius, *ib.* In 809, king Egbert invades the Britons of Cornwall, and after some severe actions reduces them to a nominal obedience, 152. In 834, the Cornish and Devon-men join the

Cornwall,—
    Danish invaders, desirous of throwing off the Saxon
    yoke, *ib.* These confederates totally defeated by
    Egbert at Hengsdown-hill, *ib.* The Cornish-men,
    1497, overtaxed, took up arms, ii. 306. Their
    progress from the west to Blackheath, *ib.* Their
    defeat, *ib.* Their gallantry in action, *ib.* Lord
    Audley beheaded, *ib.* Joseph the blacksmith, a
    ringleader, and Flammock, executed at Tyburn,
    307. All the rest pardoned, *ib.* They joined Per-
    kin Warbeck in great force, assaulted Exeter with-
    out success, and marched to Taunton, 308. The
    adventurer taking secretly to flight, the Cornish-
    men submitted, *ib.* Some ringleaders were hanged,
    and the rest dismissed to their homes, *ib.*
Cornwall, the Constantine Tolman, a vast raised
    stone in, depicted, i. 101.
CORNWALL, Richard, earl of. Sent to Guienne
    with an English army, 1225, to the relief of the
    Albigenses, i. 675. Innocent IV. offers him the
    crown of the Two Sicilies, which he declines, 680.
    He is elected king of the Romans in 1256, and
    crowned at Aix-la-Chapelle, 681. He concludes a
    reconciliation between the English barons and his
    brother, Henry III., 683. His son Henry is slain
    by Simon and Guy de Montfort, when returning
    through Italy, having accompanied his cousin
    Edward to the Holy Land, 688. Death of Richard,
    December 1971, *ib.*
CORNWALL, captain. death of, 1744; iv. 472.
CORNWALLIS, Charles, marquess. His service in
    America,1776; § i. 278. Portrait of, *ib.* He gains
    the battle of Camden, 1780; 426. His march from
    Wilmington, 1781; 456—458. He is attacked in
    York Town by an overwhelming force, and obliged
    to capitulate, 460—464.
CORNWALLIS, sir Charles, English ambassador at
    Madrid, 1608-9; iii. 39.
CORNWALLIS, sir Thomas, 1554, one of Mary's coun-
    cillors, sent to Ashridge to arrest the queen's half-
    sister Elizabeth, on Wyatt's insurrection, ii. 515.
Coronation chair in Westminster Abbey, removed by
    Edward I. from Scone; beneath the seat is the cele-
    brated "Stone of Destiny," i. 219.
Corraniad, the, from Pwyll Settle, on the Humber, i. 9.
CORREGGIO, Antonio Allegri da, one of the greatest
    and most original of painters, born 1494, died 1534;
    iii. 567.
CORRICHIE, battle of, October 28, 1562; ii. 575.
Corsica, right of sovereignty over given to France from
    Genoa, 1768; § i. 64. Corsica annexes itself to
    Great Britain, 1794; § iii. 398.
COSENS, master of St. Peter's, Westminster, impri-
    soned 1640; iii. 139, 229.
COSPATRIC, commander of an English army against
    William I., 1069; i. 372. Submits, and is appointed
    governor of Northumberland, 375. William de-
    prives him of his earldom of Northumbria; he
    flies to Scotland, where Malcolm Caenmore gives
    him a castle and lands, 379.
COSSIM ALI MEER, becomes nabob of Bengal on the
    deposition of Meer Jaffier in 1760; § ii. 85. He
    takes up arms against the English, 1763, and loses
    the battle of Geriah, 87. Orders the execution of
    150 Englishmen taken at Patna, 88. Seeks the pro-
    tection of Soujah Dowla, nabob of Oude, *ib.* Flees
    to Rohilcund, 89.
Costume, various notices of, i. 92, 104. Anglo-Saxon,
    144, 156, 159, 174. Of the twelfth century, 636,
    637. 866—872. Fifteenth and sixteenth centuries,
    ii. 856—861. Seventeenth century, iii. 892—894;
    iv. 801—808. Eighteenth century, § i. 675—678;
    § iii. 760—766. Nineteenth century, § iv. 723—
    726.
COTES, Roger, a mathematician, died 1716; iv. 782.
COTTINGTON, Francis, lord, appointed, 1623, to accom-
    pany prince Charles to Spain, iii. 91. Created, July

COTTINGTON, Francis,—
    1631, 153. Chancellor of the exchequer, 162. He
    resigns his place of master of the wards, 247. He
    died 1653.
Cotton manufacture, importance of, in the eighteenth
    century, § i. 593—597; § iii. 691—698. Improve-
    ments made by Arkwright in the, § i. 595.
COTTON, sir John Hynde, made treasurer of the
    chamber in the royal household, 1744; iv. 475.
COTTON, sir Robert, draws out a pardon for the earl
    of Somerset, 1615; iii. 58. Applauds the parlia-
    ment for censuring Buckingham, and compares his
    conduct with that of Somerset, 112, 391.
COTTON, Mr., a Boston clergyman 1652; iii. 808.
COURCY, Robert de, slain in battle, 1157; i. 443.
COURCY, dame de, conveys to France news of Richard
    II.'s death, the recital of which so deeply affects
    king Charles, that it brings on a fit of insanity,
    ii. 7.
Court-a-street chapel, view of; here the maid of Kent
    uttered her prophecies, ii. 718.
COURTEN, sir William, an opulent merchant, founds
    a colony on the island of Barbadoes 1624; iii. 538.
    He obtains a charter, 1635, to trade for five years
    to Goa, Malabar, China, and Japan, 541.
COURTENAY. See Earls of Devonshire.
COURTENAY, William, bishop of London, 1375. His
    trial of Wicliffe, 1377; i. 780. The duke of Lan-
    caster supports Wicliffe and causes a riot in Lon-
    don, *ib.* Courtenay was translated to Canterbury
    January 1381. and died July 31, 1396.
Courtship, iv. 813—815.
COUTANCE, Geoffrey of, 1087; i. 394.
Covenant, National; the Presbyterians frame. and sub-
    scribe to the, March 1, 1638; iii. 186. Somewhat
    liberalised, it is received in England under the
    name of the Solemn League and Covenant, 1643;
    309. Renewed, 1666; 701.
Covenanters; some account of their proceedings will
    be found under Leslie, their leader. They renew
    the covenant, 1666; iii. 701; are so barbarously used
    by Lauderdale, 1674, that they take swords to their
    prayer-meetings, 729. They take Glasgow, but are
    routed by the duke of Monmooth, 730; they rally
    round Cameron, 1681; 735; are defeated, and
    several executed, *ib.*
Covent-garden theatre, erected 1809; § iv. 707; view
    of, 708.
Coventry Act, the, passed 1670; iii. 708.
COVENTRY, sir John, having made a remark, 1670,
    in the House of Commons upon the king's amours,
    he is set upon by some of the guards on his return
    home, and severely maimed; in consequence of
    this the Act, called the Coventry Act, is passed,
    making cutting and maiming a capital offence,
    iii. 707, 708.
COVENTRY, sir Thomas, the lord-keeper, 1626; iii.
    117, 144, 175.
COVERDALE, Miles, and his associates, completed the
    first English version of the Bible, ii 405, 713.
    Notwithstanding the king's orders, in 1536, that
    every parish should possess a printed copy, there
    were no funds left in 1540, to reward the learned
    translator, nor to pay Grafton the printer; thus the
    copies were necessarily at a high price, 405. The
    bishop's letter from Paris, to Cromwell. 405, *note.*
    Supposed to have assisted Tyndal in the translation
    of the New Testament. Coverdale was appointed
    bishop of Exeter, August 14, 1551; he was deprived,
    and imprisoned by queen Mary, 1553, and after-
    wards banished; after her death he refused to return
    to his bishopric, and lived privately until he attained
    his 81st year, 509.
COWELL, Dr., a high churchman, 1610, patronised by
    Bancroft and the king, iii. 41. His Interpreter, *ib.*
    His View of the Coronation oath, *ib.* He is impri-
    soned by the parliament, *ib.*

COWLEY, Abraham, a poet of great merit, born 1618; died July, 1667. Review of his works, iii. 578, 604, 875.

COWPER, William, earl, created baron Cowper of Wingham, 1706; iv. 180. He reads the first speech of George I. in parliament, 306. Is created viscount Fordwich and earl Cowper, 1718. Died, 1723; 344.

COWPER, William, a distinguished modern poet, born November, 1731; died, April, 1800; § iii. 715. His portrait, ib. Review of his style, and claims to merit as an original genius, 715-718.

Cox, Dr., preceptor of Edward VI.; Burnet's account of, ii. 453.

COXE, archdeacon, memoirs of, iv. 32, note.

CRABTREE, William, an astronomer, and friend of Samuel Horrocks. He died, 1641; iv. 768.

Cradle of James I., iii. 622.

CRADOC, sir Matthew, married the lady Catherine Gordon, widow of Perkin Warbeck, ii. 310. Their tomb and epitaph at Swansea, ib.

CRAGGS, James, sent by the council, at the approaching death of queen Anne, to hasten the journey of the elector to England, iv. 301. His death by small-pox, 1721; 376.

CRAIG, the colleague of Knox, publishes the banns of marriage between Mary of Scotland and the earl of Bothwell, ii. 599.

CRANFIELD, Lionel, created earl of Middlesex, 1622, iii. 71. Treasurer, 86. His statement relative to the force necessary for recovering the palatinate, ib. Censures Buckingham's conduct, 101. Is impeached, fined, and excluded from parliament, 103. He died, 1645.

CRANMER, Thomas, tutor in the family of Mr. Cressy; at supper there with Drs. Gardiner and Fox, the discourse broached was Henry VIII.'s divorce from Catherine, ii. 375. His opinion that holy doctors seeking authorities from Scripture, might settle the question, without further reference to the pope, ib. The king being told of this, commands Cranmer to draw up his opinion in writing, and it was quickly printed, ib. He was appointed a chaplain to Henry, and sent to reside with the earl of Wiltshire, father of Anne Boleyn, ib. His ulterior motives as to the reformed doctrines surmised, ib. This ecclesiastic was sent with the earl of Wiltshire on a mission, to repair, if possible, the dissension with the emperor and the pope, 376. Gaining no grace with Clement nor with Charles, Boleyn proceeded to France to the universities, etc., and Cranmer at length quitted Rome for Germany, ib. Here Cranmer overtly entangled himself between the two religions, by marrying the niece of the Protestant pastor Osiander, 377. On his return, 1532-3, he was tempted by Henry VIII. to accept the archbishopric of Canterbury, becoming the *Catholic* primate, notwithstanding his having deeply imbibed the Lutheran tenets, 380. He received the pallium from Clement VII., taking the oaths of canonical obedience to the pope, by the king's command, notwithstanding Henry's own assumption of supremacy, ib. He pronounced the marriage of Henry and Catherine null, and confirmed that of the king with Anne Boleyn, (see Henry VIII.) 380, 381. He crowned queen Anne at Westminster, 381. Cromwell, as the king's "Vicar-general," had in convocations, etc., a precedence over the primate, 390. Cranmer's letter to Henry VIII., showed his wish to serve or save queen Anne, whose merits in religious matters he recalled to the king's mind, 395. By royal command he drew up his "Objections" to her marriage, as void from the very first, and consequently to the legitimacy of Elizabeth, ib. Two days before the queen's execution, he gave judgment, in his ecclesiastical court, in favour of

CRANMER, Thomas,— the king's demand, ib. The archbishop deplored the complete waste of the monastic property; there was also a popular outcry; Henry VIII. then desired that some of the surplus should go for religious purposes, 405. Act to establish new bishoprics, deaneries, etc., ib. Six bishoprics, Westminster, Oxford, Peterborough, Bristol, Chester, Gloucester, were almost penuriously endowed, ib. The primate condemned Lambert the schoolmaster to the stake, for denying the real presence, 406, 410. Cranmer's covert opinions were nevertheless the same as those of the German reformers, and of the martyr, John Lambert, who appealing to the king, was, after a solemn disputation, 1538, burnt, 407. He accuses queen Catherine Howard to the king, 417. Subsequent persecutions of Protestants by this primate, 448. The Catholic party attempted the primate's overthrow, but the king's regard for him averted the peril, 1543; 438. Cranmer receives an order for the use of English prayers, June, 1544, immediately before Henry's last expedition to Boulogne, 438, 728. Cranmer attended, in 1547, the dying Henry, 451. Was one of sixteen executors of Henry VIII., 1547; 454. In the time of Edward VI., the primate promoted the Reformation by safe degrees, though much impeded by the Catholic prelates, 465. His ecclesiastical measures, ib. The Reformation promoted, | Edward VI., by several acts of parliament, that for the giving all chantries, colleges, and free chapels to the crown, was opposed by Cranmer, 467. He published a short English catechism, 468. He signs the warrant for the execution of sir Thomas Seymour, a thing forbidden by the canon law, 479. He attempts to prove to Edward VI. the necessity of signing the deathwarrant for Joan Boucher, who was condemned as a heretic, but all his arguments are of no avail: at length the young king signs the warrant, though with tears in his eyes; he tells Cranmer that he must answer for it to God, since it was only done in submission to his authority, 493. Shortly after Von Paris, a Dutchman, is burnt; obloquy cast on Cranmer through these proceedings, ib. He is arrested by queen Mary, and committed to the Tower, on a charge of treason, 507. Is pardoned for his treason, but detained in the Tower, on a charge of heresy, 509. Brought to trial for heresy, 525. He recants, 527, but is nevertheless brought to the stake and burnt opposite Baliol College, denying the pope and all his doctrines, March 21, 1556; 528, 735. His portrait, 696.

CRANSTOUN, colonel, killed at the battle of Malplaquet, June 12, 1709; iv. 236.

CRAVEN, lord, sails to Holland with the princes Charles Louis and Rupert, 1637, and a force for the recovery of the Palatinate; they are defeated; Charles Louis is captured, and sent to the castle of Vincennes, iii. 174.

CRAVEN, William, earl of, 1769, moves for an address to the throne, praying an increase of seamen, 1770; § i. 91.

CRAWFORD, earl of, agrees to seize lord Lanark, the earl of Argyle, and the marquess of Hamilton, 1641, and convey them to a ship lying in Leith Roads, or in case of their resistance to kill them, iii. 250. The Scottish parliament gives orders for his arrest, 251.

CRAWLEY, justice, argues in favour of ship-money, 1637; iii. 180.

Crecy, battle of, gained by the Black Prince, August 26, 1346; i. 765—768.

Crespi, treaty of, 1544, ratified by Charles V. and Francis I., ii. 439.

CRESSET, secretary to the princess dowager, 1748, iv. 567.

CRESSY, Mr., supper at his house, 1529, whereat Drs.

CRESSY, Mr.,—
Gardiner and Fox remarked the merit of the family tutor, Thomas Cranmer, ii. 374. A felicitous remark by the tutor, on the divorce, led to station and fortune, 375.

Crevant, victory of the English, 1423, over the French and Scots at, ii. 54.

Crevelt, battle of, 1758, iv. 603.

CREW, sir John, created, 1661; committed to the Tower, 1640. He died 1679, iii. 217.

CREW, sir Randolph, chief-justice of the King's Bench, 1626, iii. 123.

CREW, sir Thomas, iii. 55, 57, sent on a commission to Ireland, 1621; 88.

CREWE, Nathaniel, bishop of Durham, a member of the Ecclesiastical Commission Court, 1686, iii. 786, takes the oath to William III., 1689; died 1722; iv. 619.

CRICHTON, laird of Brunston, communicates to Henry VIII., in 1545, the projects of Beaton for the defence of Scotland, ii. 445, 446.

CRICHTON, lord Sanquhar, executed, regno James I, for the assassination of a fencing-master, who had thrust out one of his eyes, iii. 38.

CRICHTON, sir William, chancellor to James I. of Scotland, ii. 134, 135.

CRILLON, duke de, takes the island of Minorca, 1782; § i. 471, 477.

Crime (nineteenth century), § iv. 731.

Criminal legislation, § iv. 638.

Criminals conducted to prison and death, ii. 169.

CRISPIN, William, count of Evreux, 1119; i. 413.

CROFT, Elizabeth, 1554; her pretending to be a "spirit in the wall" a device against the Catholics, then all-powerful; punished only by an open confession at Paul's-cross, and being obliged to expose Miles and Hill, clergymen, with others, her confederates, ii. 519.

CROFTS, sir William, 1643; iii. 302.

CROKE, justice; he decides against the legality of ship-money, 1638; iii, 181. His portrait, 830.

CROMPTON, Samuel, inventor of the mule-jenny, about 1776; § i. 597.

CROMWELL, Henry, second son of Oliver, iii. 416, 679.

CROMWELL, Oliver, born April 25,' 1599; member for Huntingdon; his first speech, iii. 140. He embarks in 1637 with his kinsman, John Hampden, and a number of emigrants in shipping on the Thames, to join the "pilgrim fathers" in America, 182. Doubts as to the authenticity of this account, ib. Cromwell sits for the town of Cambridge, 212; takes a commission as colonel of horse, 291; exhibits charges against the earl of Manchester, who in turn accuses him, 319. The lord-chancellor of Scotland proposes to proceed against him as an incendiary, 320. His speech in the House of Commons, desiring that the war may be conducted with greater speed, 321; employed in the army pro. tem.; his successes, 331; made lieutenant-general, 332. Fac-simile of a portion of a letter from Cromwell to Lenthall, announcing the victory of Naseby, 335. He leaves London, having heard of a private resolution to secure him, and arrives at Triploe Heath, 368; is forced to join the republican party in the army, and side against the king, 378. He entertains notions of investing himself with the royal dignity, 408. Dissolution of the Long Parliament, 410. The Little Parliament, 412. Cromwell made lord-protector, 1653; 413. His portrait, from a painting by Vandyke, ib. Death of his mother, 419; note. His great seal for Scotland, 422. He refuses to give one of his daughters in marriage to Charles II., on account of his loose character, 425. He represses with suitable vigour a plot to take away his life, 427; nominates his son Richard Cromwell as his successor, ib. His death by a bastard tertian ague, September 3, 1658. Fac-simile of his signature, 432*. Coins, 556.

CROMWELL, Oliver,—
CROMWELL, Richard, proclaimed protector, 1658; iii. 427. Portrait [of, from a miniature by Cooper, 428. He signs his demission, 430. Parliament undertakes to pay his debts, ib. Fac-simile of his signature, 432*. Prynne desires his execution as a regicide; but after living on the continent some time, he is allowed to retire quietly to Cheshunt, 666.

CROMWELL, Thomas, earl of Essex, son of a blacksmith of Putney, ii. 377. He was clerk in a factory at Antwerp, and acquired modern languages, ib. As a trooper, he followed the constable Bourbon to the sack of Rome, ib. His commercial pursuits at Venice, ib. Returning home, he studied law, and became Wolsey's solicitor, ib. The cardinal makes him his agent in the foundation of his colleges, also in suppressing monastic houses, ib. As a member of the House of Commons his talents were conspicuous, ib. Cavendish relates the conduct of Cromwell at Esher on his master Wolsey's disgrace, ib. Reflections as to his real intentions in repairing to court, ib. He quickly acquired the confidence of Henry VIII., ib.; advises the king to declare himself supreme head of the church, which advice being followed, Cromwell is sworn of the privy-council, ib. He declared next that the body of the clergy were guilty of a præmunire, by having acknowledged Wolsey as legate, 377, 378. The convocation paid 100,000l. on this account, as a fine. 378. Cromwell insisted on their avowing Henry VIII. to be supreme head of the church; which the majority, after long debate, did, with a certain reservation of meaning, ib. The king's outbreak of temper in reproof of Cromwell as to this limitation, ib. By this new minister's advice the king rejects propositions by pope Clement for a reconciliation, ib. Parliament, under the absolute guidance of Cromwell, 1532, abolished the annates, or first-fruits payable to the pope, and abrogated the authority of the clergy in convocation, ib. Cromwell's persuasions to the vacillating Henry not to renew relations with Rome, 383. He carried bills through parliament, March, 1534, which abolished the papal power in England; and received the royal assent, 384. Cromwell's cruel persecution of monks and friars, especially the superiors of monasteries, commenced 1535, the Carthusians being among the first put to a cruel death, 386. King Henry appointed Cromwell "royalvicegerent," vicar-general, and chief commissary over all ecclesiastical affairs, 390. He took precedence of even Cranmer in the convocations, ib. His "report" on the state of the religious houses, ib. Cromwell, in conjunction with the archbishop, endeavoured to persuade Fisher, bishop of Rochester, and sir T. More, fully to submit to Henry VIII., and thus save their lives, 385. This minister obtained an Act, 1536, suppressing religious houses which had not 200l. a year revenue, realising thereby to the king 100,000l., besides 32,000l. a year, 396. Further allusions to his administration, 399, 403, 405, 407, 410, 414. Cromwell, in 1539, not being able to obtain sufficient proof against the old countess of Salisbury and others, for a criminal information, obtained the assent of the judges that parliament might pass a bill of attainder without any previous trial, and execution of the accused thereupon take place, 409. The suppression of Glastonbury Abbey; letters to Cromwell from his agents therein, 411. Execution of abbot Whiting, 412. King Henry having negotiated for a new matrimonial union with several princesses, and failed, Cromwell extolled to his royal master the reported beauty of Anne of Cleves, a sister of the Protestant duke, 412, 413. King Henry conferred the garter on this great minister, and created him earl of Essex, 414. Wriothesley and Sadler were made secretaries of

CROMWELL, Thomas, earl of Essex,—
state, to disburden the new earl of part of his multi-
farious labours, *ib.* Cromwell was in hopes that his
great Protestant scheme would meet success. Bishop
Gardiner preached at Paul's-cross against the
heresy of justification by faith: a friend of Cromwell's, a Dr. Barnes, from the same pulpit, intem-
perately inveighed against this leading Catholic
prelate, *ib.* This bitter but interesting dispute
accelerated the fall of Henry's trusty minister, 414,
415. Henry's disgust at his fourth marriage, and
his sudden love for Catherine Howard, niece of the
lay-leader of the Catholics, Norfolk, sealed Essex's
doom, 415. The ruin of this minister was concealed
by Henry VIII. till the moment to strike. Cromwell, as " vicar general," was prosecuting Catholics
on the oath of supremacy, and domineering, uncon-
scious of the plot against himself, when, in June,
1540, he was charged at the council-board with
treason, and transferred to the Tower, *ib.* The summary process of an attainder without a trial, which
he had first devised, against the aged countess of
Salisbury etc., was resorted to against himself, *ib.*
His letters to the king, crying for " mercy," were
backed by a letter from Cranmer, in his friend's
behalf, *ib.* He was declared by his peers a manifold
traitor and detestable heretic, *ib.* On the 28th of
July, Cromwell was beheaded, and on the 8th of
August following, Catherine Howard was declared
queen, 417. His portrait, 750. Stow records that
this earl, having built a mansion in Throgmorton-
street, and finding it pressed upon by a house in the
rear, caused the said house to be loosened from its
foundations, placed upon rollers, and backed twenty-
two feet into a garden belonging to the father of the
antiquary, who, in common with the owners of the
adjoining gardens, lost his land, without notice and
without compensation, 850.
CROMWELL, lord, Yorkist, falls in Edward IV.'s victory at Barnet, 1471, ii. 109.
Crosby-place, Bishopsgate, the protector Gloucester
resided, 1483, in that fine mansion, ii. 119.
CROSBY, a Jacobite spy, committed to prison, 1694;
iv. 64.
CROSBY, lord-mayor, committed to the Tower, 1771;
§ i. 116.
CROWLE, a lawyer, reprimanded at the bar of the
House of Commons, 1751; iv. 563.
Crown lands. By the fifteenth century, a great
alienation of the territorial districts acquired by
the conquest had taken place, under grants by
William I. and his successors, ii. 165. Crown lands
are declared inalienable in England and Wales,
1702; iv. 677.
CROY, sire de, with eighteen knights, under oath to
take king Henry alive or dead at Agincourt, i.
33. Henry V., struck by one of these with a mace,
staggered and fell on his knees, *ib.* His soldiers
close up, and kill the eighteen knights, *ib.*
Croydon, this monastery was burnt in 1091, with
its splendid library consisting of 900 volumes,
i. 610.
Croyland, abbey of, founded 716, by Ethelbald, king
of Mercia, i. 310. View of Croyland bridge, with
the Saxon sculpture of St. Ethelred, 377.
Crusades, general passion for, throughout Europe,
excited by the preaching of Peter the Hermit, the
bulls of pope Urban II., and the council of Clermont, i. 400. Robert, duke of Normandy, and
many others, join the, 401. Crusades, in 1428,
against Zisca and the Hussites proclaimed by
Martin V., ii. 150. Pope Pius II. preached a
Crusade against the Turks, who had recently taken
Constantinople, *ib.*
Cudgel-playing, single-stick, and quarter-staff, ii. 261.
CUDWORTH, Dr. Ralph, iii. 578, 610. An opponent
of Hobbes's system of philosophy. He published

CUDWORTH, Dr. Ralph,—
his " Intellectual System of the Universe," 1678;
881.
CUFFE, secretary to the earl of Essex, 1601, excites
his noble master and partisans to the insurrection
at Essex-house, London, ii. 684. Nature of his
counsels, 684, 685. This secretary, with the earl's
steward Merrick, suffered the cruel penalty of
traitors, at Tyburn, 689.
CUJAVIA, bishop of, proclaims Augustus elector of
Saxony, king of Poland, 1697; iv. 77.
Culdees of Scotland, opposed to St. Augustine and
the tenets of Rome, i. 229, 244.
CULEN, king of Scotland, 965; i. 219. Assassination
of his predecessor Duff, at Forres, *ib.* Violence to
the daughter of his relative, the king of Strathclyde; war with that state; Culen fell in battle
(south of the Forth), 970; 220.
Culloden or Drummossie Moor, view of, iv. 534;
Battle of Culloden fought April 16, 1746; 535—
539. Order of battle, 537.
CULLUM, sir T., a long extract from his history of the
parish of Hawsted in Suffolk, relating to husbandry
in the reign of Edward III., i. 838, 839.
Cultivation, or farming among the Anglo-Saxons, i.
276; *et seq.*
CUMBERLAND, William Augustus, duke of, created
1708. He arrives at Holyrood-house to conduct
the war against the young Pretender, 1746; iv.
527. His severities cause him to be named *the
Butcher,* 541. The commons vote him an additional 25,000l. per annum, *ib.* Being beaten by
Marshal D'Etrée, he is led to sign the disgraceful
capitulation memorable by the name of the Convention of Closter-Seven, September 7, 1757; 597.
He resigns all his commands, 600. His name is
struck out of the liturgy, 1760; § i. 3. His death,
1765.
CUMBERLAND, Henry Frederic, duke of, brother of
king George III., created 1766. Is brought to a
crim. con. trial, 1770, by the earl of Grosvenor, § i.
196. His private marriage with Mrs. Horton, 1771.
From this and the similar actions of his brother,
the duke of Gloucester, emanated the Royal Marriage Act, *ib.*; 198, 250. Cumberland died, 1790.
CUMBERLAND, Richard, a dramatic writer, born 1732.
His embassy to the courts of Lisbon and Madrid,
1780; § i. 440. His death, 1811; § iii. 715.
CUNNINGHAM, bishop of Aberdeen; baptizes prince
Henry, son of James I., iii. 445.
Currants, introduced from Zante, 1555; ii. 806. Such
was the avidity with which this delicate fruit was
used, that the Greeks, shortly after its introduction,
supposed that the English used it either for the
processes of dyeing, or for fattening hogs, 882.
CURSON, sir Robert, 1504; ii. 313, 314.
CURWEN, J. C., endeavours, 1816, to procure the revision, if not total extinction, of tithes, § iv. 600.
CURWEN, Dr., 1532, preached in reply to friar Peto's
sermon, before the king at Greenwich, ii. 381, 382.
Curwen was made a bishop, 382.
CUSACKE, sir Thomas, in 1541, counsels Henry VIII.
on the affairs of Ireland, just erected into a kingdom, ii. 428.
Custom-house, as it appeared before the great fire,
from a print by Hollar, iii. 527.
Customs duties (eighteenth century), § iii. 629.
Custrin or Zorndorf, battle of, 1758. 20,000 Russians
are left dead on the field, iv. 603.
CUTHBERT, St., his narrative of the last hours of his
learned master, the venerable Bede, i. 290. He
asks alms of Alfred in Athelney, 158. Receives
half the loaf and wine that Alfred still possessed,
159. He evades, but appears in the following night
to the distressed king, and, on being interrogated,
declares who he is, and that he is diligently employed in Alfred's service, *ib.*

Cutlery, § iv. 691.

CUTTS, lord, leads on the English to the capture of Namur, 1695; iv. 58.

Cymry, said to have first peopled Britain, and Armorica or Bretagne; their migration from the south, etc., i. 8. They settled on the east coast of Scotland, 216. Sailed to the western shores of England, and obtained a dominant power with the Celtic Britons of Wales, *ib*. The language of the early Welsh became chiefly Cimbrian, *ib*. The kingdom of Cumbria (Cumberland), a territory belonging to Strathclyde, received its name from them, *ib*. 219. The residence of the wizard Merlin, and the bard Aneurin, 216. The language spoken in that Scottish kingdom was also the Cimbric Welsh, *ib*. The population of *regnum Cumbrense*, Strathclyde, or Raged, is supposed to have been the same amalgamation of Celtic Britons and Cymry which still occupies Wales and Cornwall, 22, 23.

CYVELIOCH, Owen, leader of the clans of Powisland, 1165. His war with the English, i. 451.

DACRE, lord, at Flodden Field, under the earl of Surrey, ii. 328. He recognized the body of James IV., which was transferred to the monastery of Sheen, near Richmond, 329. His intrigues with discontented Scottish nobles, in furtherance of the design of Henry VIII. virtually to govern in Scotland, 350, 353; *note*. His bribes, 354.

DACRE, Leonard, the representative of the Dacres of Gillsland, takes up arms in the cause of the queen of Scots; Elizabeth sends orders to the earl of Sussex to arrest him; Dacre raises 3,000 English borderers, is defeated by lord Hunsdon, escapes across the borders, and passes over to Flanders, ii. 631.

DACRE, Randall of, his intrigues in Scotland, 1493; ii. 305.

D'ADDA, the pope's minister, 1686; iii. 786, 788.

DAGWORTH, sir Thomas, commander of the English army in Brittany, takes Charles de Blois prisoner, June 18th, 1347; i. 768.

DAHL, Michael, a Swedish painter; he came to England in the year of the revolution, and died in 1743; iv. 753.

D'AIGUILLON, duke 1758; iv. 602.

DALBIER, colonel, 1642; iii. 298, 324.

DALKEITH, castle of, surrendered to the Covenanters by Traquair, 1639; the regalia, crown, sceptre, and sword, falling into their hands, are triumphantly carried to Edinburgh Castle, also in their possession, iii. 203.

Dalriada, a district of the north-east of Ireland, i. 18. Carbry Riada, a chief of Antrim, *ib*, 217. The Scoti, who had settled there, sailed over to Caledonia, about the beginning of the sixth century, and founded Dalriada, a district of Ulster, 217. The Dalriadic kingdom in Argyleshire, 18. The roving Scoti are said partially to have settled on the west coast of North Britain, in the third century, 217. These Scoti were reinforced in the sixth century by the immigration of Lorn, Fergus, and Angus, sons of Erck, prince of Dalriada, *ib*. Contest between this new population, viz., the Scots and the old Picts of Caledonia, 217. Achaius, the lineal descendant of Fergus, married Urgusia, sister of the Pictish monarch, Constantine, who reigned in 791, *ib*. History of the line of Scottish monarchs, 217—222. In 973, Kenneth III. acquired the entire country, by his victory over the Pictish king Dunwallon, and it finally obtained the name of Scotland, 218.

DALRYMPLE, sir David, lord-advocate, is disgraced, 1711; iv. 258.

DALRYMPLE, sir Hew, after the battle of Vimiera, he arrives in Portugal to take the chief command of the army, and concludes the convention of Cintra, by which the French agree to evacuate Portugal, Aug. 31, 1808; § iv. 339—342. A court of inquiry ap-

pointed to examine the commanders of this expedition, sir Hew Dalrymple, sir Harry Burrard, and sir Arthur Wellesley; the court returns answer that they had acted wisely and honourably throughout the whole campaign, 342, 343. Sir Hew Dalrymple receives a severe reprimand in his Majesty's name, and during the war is not permitted to resume his post as commander at Gibraltar, 342. After the termination of the war, in 1814 he was created a baronet, in testimony of the royal approbation of his services 343.

DALRYMPLE, sir John, iv. 7, privy to the massacre of Glencoe, 1693; 44.

DALTON, announces the atomic theory, 1808; § iv. 704.

DALZIEL, perpetrates cruelties on the Covenanters, 1666; iii. 701.

Damfront, its citizens appoint prince Henry their governor, 1091, when he was reduced by his brother William II. to poverty, i. 398.

DAMPIER, William, a celebrated English navigator, born 1652; iv. 96, 431. His portrait, 689.

DANBY, Thomas Osborne, earl of, made lord-treasurer, 1674, and becomes in effect prime minister, iii. 696, 711, 712, 717. He is impeached, 1678; 726. A bill of attainder passes against him, and he is committed to the Tower, 728, 729. He died in 1712.

Danelagh, or Dane-law, territory set apart for the Danes. Wars with Alfred of Wessex, i. 876—878. Guthrun, a Danish king of this population, repeatedly overruns the hereditary dominions of Alfred, who lies concealed awaiting a fair opportunity for throwing off the yoke, 157—160. Route of the Danes at Ethandune (878), 160. Guthrun baptized; his people devote themselves to agriculture and industry, submit to more civilised laws, *ib*. Alfred draws a demarcation betwixt the two territories, leaving the east side of England, with Northumbria to the Danes, *ib*. Loyalty of Guthrun and his baptised Danes, 160, 161. Long period of peace, and its benefits, 162. In 890, King Guthrun dies, *ib*. When Alfred had to contest with the overwhelming fleets and warriors of the great pirate Hasting (in 893), the population of the Danelagh broke their oaths of fidelity, and, in a mass, aided the pagan invaders, 162—165. The Danes choose Ethelwald, nephew of the great Alfred, for king, 168. Defeat of the Danish army, and Ethelwald slain, 905, by the army of Wessex, under king Edward, *ib*. That monarch reduces the Danish towns betwixt the Thames and Humber, and constrains all the Danelagh to do him homage, *ib*. The northern tribes, settled in the Danelagh, remain quiescent in the contest that raged, 981—993, on the invasion of Ethelred's dominions by powerful Danish hosts, under Sweyne, or gradually join the northern pirates, who soon after established the Danish monarchy in England, 176. *See* Sweyn, and the other Danish kings of England. The Northumbrians and inhabitants of the Danelagh do not submit to William. *See* Edwin and Morcar. They supplicate the assistance of Sweyn Estridsen, king of Denmark, 371.

Danes, the, a Scandinavian race, i. 138.

Danish warriors, their arms and costumes, i. 151. These fierce piratical tribes, called Norsemen or Danes; by the French and Italians, Normans and Normanni, were native to Denmark, Norway, Sweden, and the Baltic coasts, 154. They were of Scandinavian origin and Teutonic descent, and bore resemblance to the cognate tribes of Saxons, whom they afterwards miserably oppressed in England, *ib*. The Normans exhibited some diversity of character, by reason of their long occupation of the plains of France, from the barbarous Norwegians of the northern fastnesses, whose only profits consisted in

Danes—
plunder and devastation, *ib.* The cruelties of Charlemagne, in 772—803, upon the pagan Saxons of the Rhine, supposed to have been the exciting impulse that called the Scandinavian races from their homes during the ninth century, 154. Their fleets described, and the localities on the Baltic whence they drew their warlike contingents, 154, 155. The northern monarchs received their tribute out of all plunder, on the return to Norway, 155. Inured to arms and the sea from boyhood, each head of a family possessed a *chiule,* keel, ship or boat, *ib.* Their great physical vigour, perseverance, and courage, *ib.* Nature of the Scandinavian literature in the *eighth century, ib.* Their superstitions, *ib.* The conversion of the Anglo-Saxons, a chief cause of the enmity of the pagan tribes, *ib.* They possessed good steel for their weapons, *ib.* The double-bladed axe and mace, *ib.* They were excellent bowmen, and the Anglo-Saxons, having neglected archery, derived their subsequent fame as archers through their long contests with the Northmen, *ib.* Their great knowledge of castrametation often rendered their intrenchments in England impregnable, *ib.* When oppressed by a superior and well-disciplined force in the field they esteemed it no dishonour to betake themselves to their fleet, if they could embark a good booty, *ib.* They long avoided coming to any general action, their object being to alarm all the coasts, and oblige each Anglo-Saxon district to watch chiefly its own defences, *ib.* Their first solicitude at any landing was to seize the horses of the country, for the sake of rapidity in their forays, *ib.* No treaty or oaths could ever bind this perfidious race, 155. They received gold from the Kentish men, on condition of leaving them to live in peace, yet soon ravaged that kingdom, *ib.* One chief often laid the charge of a breach of truce to another horde, *ib.* Their possession of Thanet gave them free access to all the shores of Essex, Kent, etc., *ib.* They conquered Northumbria, from the Tweed to the Humber, retaining that territory, *ib.* They were often established in Norfolk, Suffolk, Nottingham, Lincoln, Cambridge, and rebuilt the city of York, *ib.*—(For their battles, conquests, and defeats, see the names of places and kings.)

DANGERFIELD, discovers the Meal-tub plot, iii. 732. Brought before the King's Bench by James II. 766. Severe sentence passed upon him, 777. He is struck in the eye with a cane, by Mr. Robert Frances, which occasions his death, *ib.*

DANIEL, Samuel, iii. 600. Author of a history of England, published in 1618; 614.

DANTON, George James, a great actor in the scenes which succeeded the French revolution, portrait of, § ii. 483. Head of the Cordeliers, 1790; *ib.,* 532. Incurring the enmity of Robespierre, is guillotined, together with most of his party, April 5, 1794; 416—425.

DANVERS, sir Charles, or Davers, a close friend of the earl of Southampton, condemned for the insurrection of Essex-house; beheaded in March 1601. He died like a brave man, implicating no one, ii. 689.

DARCY, lord, a leader of the "Pilgrims of Grace," or Yorkshire malcontents, in 1536, together with the lords Latimer, Neville, and Lumley, ii. 399. Henry VIII. sent promises of immunity to the northern nobles and gentry, if they would but prove *lukewarm* in the cause of the vast insurgent masses, 399. Darcy and other leaders declined, through a very natural fear, to wait on the king, 400. He was beheaded, 1537, on Tower-hill, lord Hussey at Lincoln, while Aske and a multitude of persons were put to death in Yorkshire, 401, *note.*

Darent church, heads of windows at, i. 316.

Darien Company, established 1699, remonstrances of the, iv. 106, 107.

DARMSTADT, prince of Hesse, assists Rooke in the capture of Gibraltar, 1704; iv. 175. Aids the earl of Peterborough in the capture of Barcelona, 179. Is killed in the attack on the castle, 1705; 180.

DARNLEY, lord, James Stuart, commands the Scottish auxiliaries in the battle of Crevant, 1423; is defeated by Salisbury and Suffolk, wounded, and made prisoner, ii. 54, 55.

DARNLEY, lord Henry Stuart, eldest son of the earl of Lennox by the lady Margaret Douglas, daughter of the queen-dowager Margaret, sister of king Henry VIII. by the earl of Angus, ii. 578. Elizabeth permits him to go to Scotland; he waits upon Mary at Wemyss Castle, where he is courteously received, 579. He seeks the countenance of David Rizzio, the queen's favourite, 580. He marries Mary, his first cousin, 1565; *ib.* He *is said* to have made arrangements for assassinating the earl of Murray, 581. Created earl of Ross and duke of Rothsay; is proclaimed king at the Market-cross of Edinburgh, and the next day, July 28, 1565, married to the queen according to the Catholic ritual, *ib.* His debauched manners soon estrange the queen from him, and drive his father from the court, 584; this coldness he attributes to the queen's admiration of Rizzio, her secretary, 585. He enters into a league with some of the nobles for murdering this unfortunate man, and signs a document by which he takes the conspirators under his special protection. (For an account of the murder of the Italian secretary, *see* Rizzio.) He protests before the council that he had never consented to this proceeding, 588. On the earl of Morton receiving a pardon, Darnley quits Stirling Castle for Glasgow, 592. He accompanies the queen to Edinburgh; but the physician thinking it imprudent for him to reside in the crowded palace of Holyrood, he retires to a lonely but airy house, called the Kirk-a-field. It was generally suspected that the earl of Bothwell had some design against him, and the earl of Orkney warned him of his danger. On the night of February 10, 1567, the city was shaken by a violent explosion; the house of Kirk-a-field was found utterly destroyed, and the body of Darnley and that of his valet under a tree at some distance, bearing no marks of violence, 595.

DARTMOUTH, George Legge, lord, created 1682; Keyling discovered the Rye-house plot to him, 1683; iii. 741. He is sent with a squadron to Tangier, to demolish the mole and fortifications there, 1683; 760. He died, 1691.

DARTMOUTH, William Legge, lord, created 1711; made secretary of state, 1710; iv. 245. He died, 1750.

DARTMOUTH, William Legge, earl of, 1750. Portrait of, § i. 172. He died 1801.

DARWIN, Dr. Erasmus, a physician and poet, born December 12, 1721; published his "Botanic Garden" about 1781. He was author of several other publications, principally agricultural. He died suddenly, April 18, 1802; iii. 601, § iii. 718. His portrait, *ib.* Criticisms on his style, 718—720.

DASHWOOD, sir Francis. *See* lord Despencer.

DASHWOOD, sir James, moves for the repeal of the Jews' Naturalization Bill, 1753; iv. 580.

DAS MINAS takes several places in Castile, 1704; iv. 174.

DAUBENEY, Giles, lord, his creation, 1486; ii. 286. He defeated the Cornish insurgents at Blackheath, 1497; 306. Engaged also at Taunton, 308. He died 1507.

DAUBENEY, William, 1494, beheaded, ii. 300.

DAUN, count, the city of Capua opens its gates to, 1707; iv. 204. Averra does the same. *ib.* The magistrates of Naples present the keys of the city

DAUN, count,—
to him, *ib.* He is removed from the government, 360.

D'AVAUX appointed by Louis to accompany king James to Ireland, as ambassador extraordinary, 1689; iv. 11.

DAVENANT, Dr. Charles; states the current price of land in England, in 1666, to have been from fourteen to sixteen years' purchase, iii. 657. His portrait, 852. His discourses on trade, 855, iv. 791, 792.

DAVENANT, sir William, attempts to persuade Charles I. to accept the propositions offered by the parliament; and making use of foolish arguments, the king, indignant, drives him from his presence, iii. 359. He returns to France, *ib.*; exhibits entertainments of declamation and music at Rutland-house, 599. He introduces moveable scenery upon the English stage, 901.

DAVID, younger brother of Edgar, king of Scotland, and son of Malcolm III. Edgar, at his death, bequeathed to him the dominion of Cumberland when Alexander I. succeeded to the throne, i. 538. On the death of his brother Alexander, he became king, April 27, 1124; *ib.* Before he came to the throne he married Matilda, daughter of Waltheof, earl of Northumberland, and widow of Simon de St. Liz, earl of Northampton, *ib.* He attends at the great council of Henry I. in 1127, and swears fealty to Matilda and the infant Henry, *ib.* He declares war against Stephen according to the agreement of 1127, *ib.* His incursion into England; Stephen grants the lordship of Huntingdon and the Castle of Carlisle to him, 423, 540. He invades England with a numerous army, and overruns the country between the Tweed and the Tees, at the instigation of Robert earl of Gloucester, *ib.* Description of the Scottish army before the battle of Northallerton, 425, 541. *See* Northallerton. After the battle the Scots retreat, and rally within the walls of Carlisle; when having collected his scattered troops, David re-assumes the offensive by laying siege to Wark Castle, 426, 541. In the following year a peace is concluded, by which the Scots are left in possession of Cumberland and Westmoreland; and Henry, the king's eldest son, who had accompanied him in this expedition, is invested with the earldom of Northumberland, *ib.* He joined the cause of prince Henry, afterwards Henry II., when he came over to England in 1149, and bestowed on him the honour of knighthood, *ib.* He invaded England with his son Henry, and advanced as far as Lancaster, but retired without risking a battle, *ib.* He died on the 24th of May, 1153, *ib.*

DAVID, brother of Llewellyn, prince of North Wales. On Edward's first invasion of Wales, he assisted him, was knighted, and made an English baron, i. 697. He aids his brother Llewellyn in the second war with Edward, and takes the Castle of Hawardine by surprise, 1282, *ib.* Llewellyn leaves him to carry on the war in North Wales while he advances into the south, where he is surprised and slain by the earl of Mortimer, in the valley of the Wye, 698. After the death of Llewellyn, he wandered for six months, a free man, over his native wilds, but at last was betrayed, and, together with his wife and children, is carried in chains to the castle of Rhuddlan, and afterwards condemned as a traitor; thus ended the royal line of the ancient kingdom of Wales, 699.

DAVIES, sir John, condemned, 1601, for treason; was imprisoned, and finally pardoned, ii. 689, iii. 40. He was solicitor and attorney-general of James I., and author of several poetic works. He died in 1626; iii. 602.

DAVIES, lady, widow of sir John Davies, fancied that the spirit of Daniel was in her, iii. 157. Brought to the Star-chamber by Laud, *ib.*

DAVIES, Mary, a mistress of Charles II., iii. 706.

DAVIS, John, a navigator of the 16th century, ii. 790.

DAVISON, Alexander, fined and imprisoned for defrauding the government, April, 1807; § iv. 256, 257.

DAVISON, John, an able Presbyterian minister of the 16th century, iii. 445, 448.

DAVISON, William, minister from Elizabeth to the Netherlands, 1577; ii. 649. He presents the death-warrant of Mary queen of Scots to Elizabeth for signature, 666. Delivers the warrant to Burghley, to be forwarded to the commissioners, 667. The English queen, in pretended anger for what he had done in obedience to her own orders, condemns him to pay a fine of 10,000*l.*, and to be imprisoned during her pleasure; this poor secretary suffered miserably from want and sickness, as he was left in confinement during the seventeen years to which Elizabeth's reign was drawn, 671.

DAVY, sir Humphrey, his chemical experiments, 1800, etc., § iv. 704. His portrait, *ib.*

DAWES, sir William, consecrated to the bishopric of Chester, February 8, 1708. Translated to York, 1714; iv. 213.

DAY, George, bishop of Chichester, elected April 1543; deprived and imprisoned, 1551; restored by queen Mary, 1553. He died, 1556; i. 493.

DAY, John; receives a patent, 1634, granting to him the sole privilege of vending a price-current for fourteen years, iii. 544.

Dead, prayer for the; for parents and family, etc., ii. 397, 716.

DEAN, general, killed in an engagement with Van Tromp, 1653; iii. 414.

DE BROGLIE, marshal, his expedition, 1741, against Maria Theresa, empress of Germany, iv. 450. He retreats to the banks of the Neckar, 465. Is driven across the Rhine by prince Charles of Lorraine, 467.

Debt, National, history of the, iv. 685—687.

DE CASTRIES, M., a French commander, 1727; iv. 615.

DECKER, Thomas, a dramatic writer of the 17th century, iii. 593, 594.

DEERING, sir Edward, 1640; iii. 227. Compares modern episcopacy to papacy, *ib.* He deserts to the king, but returns and throws himself on the mercy of the parliament, 310, 491.

DEFOE, Daniel, supposed to have been the author of the Legion petition, iv. 124. Secretary to the English commissioners appointed to treat about the Union with Scotland, 1706; 187. His eminence as a political writer, 798, 799.

Defrobani, supposed to be Tabrobane, or Ceylon, i. 9.

De hæretico comburendo, writ, abolished, 1677; iii. 714.

Deira, kingdom of, founded about 550, by Saxon adventurers between the Tees and Humber, a long and savage war with the Britons on the Humber ensuing, i. 142.

Deities, Gaulish, i. 69.

DE LA CLUE, M., commander of the Toulon fleet; he is beaten in an engagement with admiral Boscawen, 1759, whilst attempting to form a junction with the Brest fleet, iv. 606.

DELAVAL, sir Ralph, vice-admiral of the red, 1692; iv. 37, 38.

DELAWARE, Charles West, lord, 1628. He died, 1687; iii. 367.

D'ELBŒUF, marquis, 1560; ii. 554, 560.

Delhi, view of, § iv. 204. Victory gained here by lord Lake, September 1803; 81.

DELL, secretary to archbishop Laud, iii. 506.

DELORGES, marshal, French ambassador, congratulates James II. on his accession, iii. 765. Invests Heidelberg, and takes it by storm, 1693; iv. 41. Attempts to force the passage of the Neckar, but after several repulses retreats into France, 42. Is again beaten by the prince of Baden, 1694; 49.

DELVIN, lord, 1642, about to set off for Ireland by the king's warrant to depart, is kept in custody, with some friends, by the House of Commons, iii. 270.

DENBIGH, William Fielding, earl of, created 1622. He died 1643; iii. 71.

DENDY, serjeant, proclaims the trial of Charles I., January 9, 1649; iii. 389.

DENHAM, baron, issues an order, 1633, against church-ales and revels on the Lord's day, in Somersetshire; for this he receives a severe reprimand from the archbishop, iii. 160, 603.

Denmark and Jutland, early Scandinavian population of, i. 140.

Denmark, king of, solicits the hand of queen Elizabeth by his nephew the duke of Holstein, 1560, who, though he failed in procuring that, obtained for his uncle a yearly pension and the Order of the Garter, ii. 562.

DENMARK, George, prince of, marries Anne second daughter of James II., 1683; iii. 760. He deserts to the prince of Orange, 1688; 799. On the accession of his wife to the throne, 1702, he is named generalissimo and lord high-admiral, iv. 141. His portrait, 143. The queen obtains for him a yearly allowance of 100,000*l.*, 149. He died October, 1708; 222.

DENMARK, queen of. See Caroline Matilda.

DENNY, sir Anthony. In 1547 he announced to Henry VIII. that the physicians considered his recovery hopeless, ii. 451. Appointed one of his executors by Henry VIII., 454.

DERBY, earl of. See Henry, duke of Lancaster.

DERBY, lord Stanley, earl of, 1485, ii. 282. (See Stanley).

DERBY, James Stanley, earl of, baron Strange, 1628. He makes an attempt to gain Manchester, 1642; a skirmish ensues, and one man is slain. This, according to May, was the first blood shed in the civil war, iii. 292. Became earl of Derby, 1642. August 1651, a band of royalists under his command was met by Cromwell on his route to attack Charles II. at Worcester, and cut to pieces, 405. Flying from that fatal field, September 3, he was made prisoner; tried by a court of military officers, he is beheaded, October 15, in his own town of Bolton, *ib.*

DERBY, Charles Stanley, earl of, thrown into prison for conspiring with royalists, 1659. He died, 1672; iii. 431.

Derbyshire. The lead mines worked in the Roman time, evidenced by pigs of lead marked Domitian, Hadrian, etc., i. 117.

DEREHAM, Francis, accused by archbishop Cranmer of criminal conversation with queen Catherine Howard, ii. 417. He is executed at Tyburn as a traitor, December 10, 1541; 420.

DERMOND MAC MURROGH, king of Leinster, 1140, seizes seventeen of his nobility and puts out their eyes, i. 429. He carries off Dergorvilla, the wife of Tiernan O'Ruarc, 1153; 460. He is worsted by O'Ruarc, and forced to fly. He acknowledges himself vassal of HENRY II., 1167. Henry grants him protection; he comes to England; engages with Richard de Clare, earl of Pembroke, Maurice Fitzgerald, and Robert Fitzstephen, to aid in his restoration; he returns to Ireland, 461, 462. Is defeated by Roderic and O'Ruarc, and accepts part of his territory as O'Ruarc's vassal, 462. He heads an English and Irish army, and besieges Wexford, which surrenders, 1170; *ib.* Fitzstephen overcomes the district of Ossory, *ib.* Mac Murrogh is acknowledged king of Leinster, 463. Maurice Fitzgerald arrives from England; Dublin is reduced, *ib.* Raymond le Gros lands in Waterford; he defeats the inhabitants, 464. The earl of Pembroke lands near Waterford; the city is attacked and taken; he marries Eva, daughter of Mac Murrogh; Dublin is taken; Meath is overrun, *ib.* The English slaves

DERMOND MAC MURROGH,— in Ireland are set at liberty, 465. Proclamation of Henry for the return of the English, *ib.* Ireland is taken by the Danes; they attack Dublin but are defeated, *ib.* Mac Murrogh dies, 1170, and Strongbow assumes the title of king of Leinster in right of his wife, *ib.*

DE RUYTER, a Dutch admiral, iii. 407, 698. He appears in the Downs and does much damage to the English shipping, 1667; 701. He repulses the combined fleets of England and France in three engagements, 711. Dies of a wound received off Messina, 1676; 714.

DERWENTWATER, James Ratcliff, third and last earl of, beheaded on Tower-hill, February 24, 1716; iv. 329.

DESBOROUGH, Cromwell's brother-in-law, iii, 422, 432.

DESMOND, earl of, his rebellion against Henry VIII. in the south of Ireland, ii. 349.

DESMOND, earl of, assassinated, 1583, by Kelly of Moriarty, who cuts off his head and sends it to the English queen, ii. 652.

DESMOND, George Fielding, earl of, 1622; iii. 71.

DESMOULINS, Benoit Camille, one of the ruling demagogues during the French revolution. Was born, 1762; § ii. 380. His speech in the Jacobin club, concerning foreign invasion, 1789; 532.

DESPARD, Edward Marcus, an officer in the English army. He served in America, in 1779, and afterwards acted as engineer in Jamaica; in 1783, he was appointed commander of the settlements on the Mosquito shore, but being suspended, he arrived in England in 1790. He was arrested in 1794, but was afterwards released on his own recognizance; being a second time arrested in 1802, and charged with forming a conspiracy against the life of the king, he was tried by an extraordinary commission,. February 7, 1803, and being found guilty was executed, together with seven of his accomplices, § iv. 44—48. His portrait, 44.

DESPENCER, lord Le, created earl of Gloucester, but in 1399 compelled to resume his older title, 1 Henry IV., ii. 5. Conspiring to murder the new king at Oxford or Windsor, the plot was betrayed, and the people of Bristol, capturing him and Lumley, strike off their heads, 6, 7.

DESPENCER, sir Francis Dashwood, lord, 1751; iv. 562, 591. He promises to call for a revisal of the Mutiny Act, 1760; 613. Resigns the chancellorship of the exchequer, 1763; § i. 25. Is made lord-lieutenant of Buckinghamshire, 27.

DESPENCER, Hugh, son of an Englishman of ancient descent; first introduced at the court of Edward II. by the earl of Lancaster; he became the king's favourite after the death of Gaveston, i. 740. The barons are provoked on account of the honours bestowed upon him and his father by the king, *ib.* They take up arms and destroy the castles of the Despencers. The earl of Lancaster marches on London, and the Despencers are banished by parliament, August 1321; *ib.* In October they return, *ib.* Lancaster is surprised at Boroughbridge, taken prisoner, 1322, condemned and executed, 741. In a parliament held at York, the attainders of the Despencer family are revoked, and the father made earl of Winchester, *ib.* He sends large presents to the French king, 742. Edward is deserted by all his barons, and flies, accompanied only by the two Despencers, and the chancellor Beldock, 743. The elder Despencer takes refuge in Bristol, surrenders, and is immediately executed as a traitor, *ib.* The younger Despencer accompanies the king, but they are driven on the coast of South Wales, after tossing about for many days in a tempestuousness, 744. He is taken and executed as a traitor at Hereford, 1385, *ib.*

DES ROCHES, Peter, a Poietevin by birth; on the death of the earl of Pembroke, 1219, he is appointed

DES ROCHES, Peter,— regent in conjunction with Hubert de Burgh; but a quarrel having arisen concerning the surrender of castles, he leaves England on pretence of making a pilgrimage to Jerusalem, and many of the foreign adventurers follow him out of England, i. 675. He returns to England, and the disgrace of Hubert follows his arrival, 676; but he soon renders himself odious to the nation, and Henry is forced to banish him, 1232; 677.

D'ESTRÉES, a French admiral, 1672; iii. 710.

DE TORCY, M., 1698; iv. 87.

Dettingen, battle of, fought June 16, 1743; iv. 466.

Devizes, castle of, i. 427, 433.

DEVON (or less correctly Devonshire), Thomas Courtenay, earl of, 1454, his feud with lord Bonvile, ii. 92. Beheaded, 1461, after the Lancastrian defeat at Towton, 99.

DEVON, earl of, 1469, beheaded after the battle of Edgecote, ii. 104.

DEVON, Edward Courtenay, earl of, created October 28, 1485; ii. 282; committed to the Tower, 1504; he died, 1509; 313.

DEVON, Henry Courtenay, earl of, 1511; created marquess, 1525; beheaded 1539; ii. 408, 505, 510, note;

DEVON, Edward Courtenay, earl of (son of the marquess of Exeter, who descended from Edward IV.), imprisoned at fourteen years old, ii. 505, 510, note; liberated by Mary, on her accession, 510; with his title of earl she restored to him his father's forfeited lands, ib. His high character and handsome person for a time inclined the queen to marry him; Courtenay bestowed his thoughts more upon Elizabeth, ib. He thus became a cause of jealousy between the royal sisters, ib.; is arrested at the same time with the princess Elizabeth, 1554, on suspicion of being privy to sir T. Wyatt's rising in Kent, 515. He protests his innocence, but is immured in the Tower, ib.; thence he is transferred to Fotheringay Castle, and vigilantly guarded, 519. Some account of his death, 1556, at Padua, 521. The ancient family of Courtenay, the present earl of Devon, etc., ib., note.

Devonport, iii. 655.

DEVONSHIRE, William Cavendish, earl of, impeached 1642; died 1684; iii. 288.

DEVONSHIRE, William Cavendish, duke of, receives the confession of sir John Fenwick, 1697; iv. 74. He votes against the Bill of Attainder passed against Fenwick, 76. He died 1707.

DEVONSHIRE, Georgiana, duchess of, a strenuous supporter of Fox; portrait of, § ii. 301.

D'EWES, sir Symonds, an English antiquary and statesman, born 1602; knighted by Charles I.; visited Prynne when in prison, 1634. On the rupture between the king and parliament, he adhered to the latter. He was expelled from parliament in 1648, and died in 1650; iii. 155.

DEWINT, Peter, an excellent painter in water-colours, of the nineteenth century, § iv. 712.

DE WITT, John, a Dutch statesman, born 1625; iii. 208, 407. Invention of chain-shot attributed to; 698, 710; is chosen pensionary of Holland, 710., is murdered at the Hague, 1672, ib.

DIEPENBECK, a pupil of Rubens, iii. 569.

DIGBY, lord George, son of John, earl of Bristol, created 1653; iii. 216, 227; speaks vehemently against the Commons proceeding with a bill of attainder against the earl of Strafford, 240; collects troops for the service of the king against his parliament at Kingston-upon-Thames, 267. The Commons draw up a charge of high treason against him, 272. His favour with the king, 341. He determines to march into Scotland to the assistance of Montrose, but is defeated before he gets to Carlisle, and obliged to take ship for Ireland instead of Scotland, 342. His portfolio taken by the enemy, ib. He died, 1676.

DIGBY, sir Everard, a large Catholic landholder of Rutlandshire, having a young wife and two children, is over-persuaded, by Catesby, to join the plot for blowing up king and parliament, Michaelmas, 1605, to advance 1,500l. for its furtherance, iii. 24. He agrees to collect his Catholic friends on Dunsmore-hill, Warwickshire, as on a hunting-party, on 5th November, ib. Catesby and John Wright, 3rd November, are desired to take horse, and join Digby at Dunchurch, 27. Percy, Rookwood, and others, find him surrounded by Catholic gentlemen, who seeing the palpable discomfiture of the chief plotters, steal away from the hunt, 28. He rides with the rest to the borders of Staffordshire, where they post themselves at Holbeach, but Digby quits them at that house, ib.; is captured near Dudley, 28, 29. He, alone, pleads guilty, 29. He suffers the cruel and ignominious sentence, January 30, 1606, in St. Paul's-churchyard, 30.

DIGBY, sir John. See Bristol.

DIGBY, sir Kenelm, a Catholic gentleman; he collects money from the Catholics for the service of the king, 1640; iii. 218; is a frequent guest at the table of the protector Cromwell, on account of his literary merits, 424, 568.

DIGGES, sir Dudley, a patriotic member of the House of Commons, 1613; iii. 55. He publishes a tract, entitled, "The Defence of the Trade," 1615, in reply to the author of the "Trade's Increase," who had attacked the East India Company, 536. The king sends him on a commission to Ireland, 1622; 88. One of the eight managers for the House of Commons in the impeachment of Buckingham, 1626; 120. The king seizes him and confines him in the Tower, but he is released after a few days, 121, 132. Being made master of the Rolls, 1629, he deserts his former friends, 145.

DIGGES, Leonard, a mathematician, etc. He died, 1574; iv. 766.

DIGGES, Thomas, publishes, in 1573, a tract upon Parallaxes, iv. 766.

DILLON, lord, 1643; iii. 310.

DINGHAM, Mrs., imported into England the art of making starch, about the middle of the 16th century, ii. 884.

Diodorus Siculus, quoted i. 15.

DIONYSIUS PERIEGETES, denominates Ireland, Ouernia and Bernia; England Alouion and Albion, i. 21.

Dissenters, the, generally reject the toleration offered by James II., and stand by the Episcopal church; iii. 788. Partial repeal of the penal code against Dissenters, 1778; § iii. 561. Disabilities inflicted upon, 564. Question of the repeal of the Test and Corporation Acts, 573. Act for the relief of, 1812-13; § iv. 615.

DIVES, sir Lewis, 1642; iii. 271.

Diving-bell, the, iii. 870. First applied, 1779, in submarine building operations, § iii. 672.

DIVITIACUS, prince of the Ædui, i. 65. His learning and spirit of divination, being himself a Druid, ib.

DOBSON, William, the most successful of the scholars of Vandyke. He died in indigence, at the age of thirty-six; iii. 569.

DODINGTON, George Bubb, iv. 421—424. His engagements with the earl of Bute, 1760; § i. 4. Portrait of, ib. He died about 1762, having been raised to the peerage by the title of baron Melcombe, about a year before, 20, 21.

DODWELL, Henry, a nonjuror, attempts to make William III. imprison him, iv. 32. He assumes that there is no validity in baptism, unless performed by a clergyman episcopally ordained, 645.

D'OISEL, a French general, 1560; ii. 559—561.

DOLEMAN, colonel, 1653; iii. 407.

DOLLOND, John, invented the achromatic telescope, 1758; iv. 784.

Domesday-book, importance of this survey, under

Domesday-book,—
William I., i. 391. Specimen of, 587. Contents of, 578, 579. Explanation of terms used in the, 579, 580.

Dominica, island of, surrenders to lord Rollo and sir J. Douglas, 1761; § i. 9. View of Rosean, 10.

Dominican friars. This order was instituted by St. Dominic de Guzman, and formally established by Honorius III., 1216; i. 803. Illustration, 804.

DONALD III., king of Scotland, reigned till 863; i. 218.

DONALD IV., king of Scotland. His victory at Collin, near Scone, over the Danes, for the possession of the "Stone of Destiny," which Kenneth Mac Alpin had transferred to Scone from Argyleshire, (893, et seq.) i. 219. More Danes landing from Ireland, Donald was slain in battle near his capital of Forteviot, ib.

DONALD VI. (Bane), king of Scotland, brother of Malcolm III., seizes the crown of Scotland, but is expelled by Duncan in 1094, after reigning a few months, i. 538. He obtains the assassination of Duncan by Malpedir, and again becomes king, 1095, ib. In 1098, being defeated by Edgar Atheling, is imprisoned and blinded, ib.

DONALD, accuses the marquess of Hamilton, 1630, of raising troops to usurp the crown of Scotland, iii. 150.

DONNE, Dr. John, a poet, and dean of St. Paul's. He died in 1631; iii. 603.

Donnington Castle, iii. 307.

DONOP, Count, mortally wounded, 1777, in storming the American redoubt at Mud Bank ; § i. 304.

Donoughmore, the round tower of, i. 13.

DOPPING, Dr., Protestant bishop of Meath, 1690 ; iv. 14.

DORISLAUS, Dr., iii. 390. Resident minister of the Commonwealth in Holland, assassinated, 1649, by six masked royalists, 402.

DORSET, John de Beaufort, marquis of. See Somerset.

DORSET, Thomas Gray, marquis of, created 1475, son of Elizabeth Woodville, by sir John Gray. Dorset, Cheney, St. Leger, Sir T. Montgomery, and lord Howard, annuitants, as well as Edward IV., of the French court, ii. 113. Custodian of the Tower for Edward V., 118, 119. He proclaimed Henry VII., or, Richmond, at Exeter, 126. Richard III. offers a price for the heads of Buckingham, Dorset, and their abettors, ib. Dorset fled to Brittany, 127. His attainder reversed, 1 Henry VII., 283. The king redeems him from his position abroad as hostage, 286. The marquis sent to the Tower, and his mother Elizabeth, queen-dowager, confined at Bermondsey, being suspected in regard to the young pretender Simnel, 288. He was liberated, 291. He died, 1501.

DORSET, Thomas Gray, marquis of, 1501. Sent by Henry VIII., 1512, to recover Guienne; was frustrated by the separate wars of Ferdinand the Catholic, ii. 321. His army, tired of inactivity on the Bidassoa, at length insisted on returning to England, ib. He died, 1530.

DORSET, Thomas Sackville, earl of, author of the tragedy, entitled, "Gorboduc," iii. 581. He was created lord Buckhurst in 1567, and earl of Dorset in 1604. Became lord treasurer to James I.; was stopped in the streets by the servants of the household for their wages. He died in 1608; 39.

DORSET, Edward Sackville, earl of, speaks in favour of sir F. Bacon in the House of Commons, 1621; iii. 83. Became earl of Dorset in 1624. Threatens John Felton with the rack, 1628 ; 137. His address to Prynne, 155. He died in 1652.

DORSET, Lionel Cranfield, earl of, 1706. Made warden of the Cinque Ports, and constable of Dover Castle, 1708. Created duke of Dorset, 1720. Lord-lieutenant of Ireland, 1730 and 1750. He died, 1763; iv. 223.

Dort, Synod of, gives a definitive judgment against Conrad Vorstius, 1619 ; iii. 48.

Douay, capitulates to Marlborough, 1710; iv. 247. Surrenders to marshal Villars, 1712; 269.

DOUGLAS, family of. See also the earls of Angus.

DOUGLAS, lord James, surprises Douglas Castle, commanded by lord Clifford, i. 730. Takes Roxburgh Castle by assault, March 7, 1313; 786. Commands the centre of Bruce's army at the battle of Bannockburn, 737. His skill and bravery, ib. Gains two victories over the earl of Arundel and sir Ralph Neville, during the absence of Robert Bruce in Ireland, 739. Commands an expedition in England, ravages Yorkshire, and gains the battle of Mitton, ib. An armistice, for thirteen years, is agreed upon between England and Scotland, 741. After the murder of Edward II. the Scots again invade England, and penetrate into York. Edward III. marches against them with a large army, but they return safe to Scotland with their plunder, under the command of the earl of Moray and lord James Douglas, 749. He crosses the river, and surprises the English camp, penetrating even to the tent of king Edward; and after having killed many of the English, returns safe with his few followers to the Scottish army, 750. The English forces return to York, where they are disbanded, ib. Peace is concluded with the Scots, and the independence of Scotland acknowledged, 751. Douglas is killed by the Moors in Spain, 1331, whilst carrying the heart of his illustrious master to the Holy Land, 755.

DOUGLAS, earl, commander of the Scottish forces at the battle of Chevy-chase, where he fell, August 15, 1388; i. 793.

DOUGLAS, earl. He marches with a gallant army, 1402, across the border into Northumberland, ii. 11. His booty hampers his soldiers on their return, ib. Is intercepted by the Percies, but posts himself on Homildon Hill, ib. He hesitates long to charge Hotspur; but on a great part of his men being killed by the English archers, he listens to the advice of Swinton, a knight, ib. Is wounded in the eye, totally defeated, and made prisoner, ib. List of noble Scots who fell, or were made captive, ib. Popular belief that the dispute between Henry IV. and the Percies related to these prisoners, 13. The earl is liberated by Hotspur, and speeds to raise his vassals, ib. He returns to Hotspur's camp in force, ib. His gallantry at Shrewsbury, 1403; 14. Flying, on witnessing the fall of Hotspur, he falls over a precipice, and is captured, 15. Is honourably treated, being a foreign knight, and not a rebel, ib. Is neglected by the regent Albany, 49.

DOUGLAS, Archibald, earl of, conducts a reinforcement into France, to join Buchan in the service of the dauphin Charles, 1418 ; ii. 132. He and his son James, the earl of Buchan, and the chief portion of the Scotch soldiery, were slain, 1424, in the battle of Verneuil, gained by Bedford, 56.

DOUGLAS, William, fifth earl of, seized in Edinburgh Castle, when on a visit to James II., by Crichton and Livingston, 1440, and executed at seventeen years of age, together with his younger brother, ii. 134, 135.

DOUGLAS, William, eighth earl of. His vast possessions in the south of Scotland; his family and feudal adherents, and his personal character, render him nearly as powerful as James II., ii. 135. At length induced to visit him in Stirling Castle, a hot argument ensued, and the king, then but sixteen, smote Douglas in the throat with his poniard, 1452; some courtiers came in and despatched the great earl, ib.

DOUGLAS, James, ninth earl of, brother of William, who was murdered, 1452, by James II. in Stirling Castle, ii. 135. He vowed vengeance against the rash monarch, and continued, with all his house, in

DOUGLAS, James,—
rebellion until James's death in the siege of Roxburgh, *ib.*
DOUGLAS, sir Archibald, surprises Edward Baliol at
Annan, and makes him fly to England, i. 756. He
acts as regent of Scotland for the young king David,
and marches to the relief of Berwick, which was
invested with a strong English army, commanded
by the king in person, May 19, 1333; *ib.* After
a fatiguing march, he incautiously attacks the
English army, posted in a strong position on Halidon
Hill. After a gallant charge the regent is killed,
and the Scots are defeated with great loss, *ib.*
DOUGLAS, Archibald, concerned in the murder of
Darnley, ii. 553.
DOUGLAS, Catherine, keeps the door closed against
the murderers of James I., of Scotland, till the
bone of her arm is broken, ii. 134.
DOUGLAS, Gawin, bishop of Dunkeld, 1518. His wit
in addressing archbishop Beaton, ii. 352. His
poetry, 353.
DOUGLAS, George, a bastard of the Angus family,
stabs David Rizzio, 1566, with the king's dagger,
ii. 586.
DOUGLAS, John, rector of the University of St. Andrews, presented to the see soon after the violent
death of archbishop Hamilton in 1570; iii. 436.
DOUGLAS, Robert, chaplain to the earl of Leven, 1644;
iii. 316.
DOUGLAS, sir Robert, falls at the battle of Steinkirk,
1692; iv. 37.
DOUGLAS, sir William, the first noble who joined
Wallace, 1297; i. 715. He lays down his arms and
submits to the English, 716.
DOUGLAS, William, procures the escape of Mary,
queen of Scots, from Lochleven Castle, 1568; ii.
606.
DOUGLAS, sheriff of Teviotdale, an officer of the
Covenanters, 1640; demands the gates of Newcastle
to be opened to him, iii. 222.
DOUGLAS, general, 1690; iv. 25.
DOUN, lord, dies of wounds received in battle, 1760;
iv. 615.
Dover, view of the port and castle of, i. 27. Julius
Cæsar's fleet appears off (A.C. 55), 26. Town and
castle taken by William I., 360. Eustace of Boulogne,
1051, intending to take ship at this port, proudly
entered the town, clad in mail, on his charger, and
his retainers similarly equipped, 189. One of the
French men-at-arms, selecting his night's quarters
with insolence, is refused entrance by the burgher,
whom the soldier wounds with his sword, *ib.* The
foreigner was killed. Eustace collects his knights,
forces the townsman's door, who is murdered at his
own hearth, *ib.* The count of Boulogne and the
French were then driven from the port with great
slaughter. He returns to the king, his brother-in-
law, and makes formal complaint of the men of
Dover, 189, 190. (For the great political results
of this violence, *see* Edward the Confessor, Eustace,
and Godwin.) Henry VIII. and the emperor
Charles V. at Dover Castle, 1520; ii. 338, 339.
Henry VIII., about 1525, at a great expense, erected
the first pier at Dover, 781.
DOVER, Henry Carey, earl of, created 1628. Impeached by the Commons, 1642. He died 1668;
iii. 288.
DOVER, James Douglas, duke of, *See* Queensbury.
DOWLAND, John, a celebrated musician, supposed to
have died in Denmark, 1615; iii. 563.
DOWNES, John, one of the commissioners on the trial
of Charles I., iii. 393.
DOWNIE, captain, killed in the harbour of Plattsburg,
September 1814; § iv. 671*.
DOWNING. He obtains possession of three parliamentarians who had fled to Holland, and they are exe-
cuted as regicides, 1661; iii. 690.

DOWNTON, captain, sails, 1614, with the first fleet
fitted out on account of the East India Company
as one united body, iii. 530.
DRAKE, sir Francis, obtains a commission, 1570;
ii. 656. In the course of three expeditions he
plunders the Spanish towns of Nombre de Dios and
Carthagena, and nearly all the towns on the coast
of Chili and Peru, and destroys and takes a
vast number of Spanish ships, returning from
each voyage with immense booty, *ib.* He is dispatched with a fleet, April 1587, to destroy all the
Spanish ships he can find in their own harbours,
672. Success of his mission, *ib.* He serves against
the Invincible Armada, 673. His letter to Walsingham, 676, 678. On his expedition to set Don
Antonio on the throne of Portugal, he repairs to
Coruña, where he takes four ships of war, and burns
the lower town, 678. Death of this famous man,
28th January, 1596; 680. Portrait of, 771. His
circumnavigation of the globe, 789, 790.
DRAKE, sir Francis, a conspirator in the Rye-house
plot, iii. 740.
Drama, the, ii. 877—880; iii. 579—599.
Dramatists of the eighteenth century, § i. 604—611.
DRAPER, colonel William, captures Luconia and the
surrounding isles, 1762; § i. 16.
DRAYTON, Michael, a voluminous poet, born 1563,
died 1631; iii. 586, 600.
Dreux, battle of, 1562; ii. 571.
DREUX BRUÉRE, receives a large tract of land from
William I., a relation of whom he marries, and kills
in a fit of passion, i. 374.
DRING, Robert, his residence the first Quaker's meet-
ing-house, 1654; iii. 811.
DROGHEDA, lord, one of the commissioners for taking
the account of the Irish forfeited estates, 1699; iv.
102, 104.
DROUET, Jean Baptist, his prominent part in the capture of Louis XVI., June 1791, in his flight to
Varennes, § ii. 642.
Druids, priesthood of the Celtic nations, established
especially in Britain; their extreme influence with
the population, i. 25. They confer the character of a
Holy island on Britain, and especially on Mona, 25, 26,
61. Druidism, and political station of its numerous
priesthood, described by Cæsar, etc., 59; their
tenets, doctrines, and philosophy, 61. Worship of
the sun, etc.; fire-worship, 121. Heathen divinities, 60. Temples, blocks of stones arranged in
circles, isolated altars of the fire-worship, rocking-
stones, Tolman of Cornwall, and similar vestiges of
Druidical rites, 61, 101. Sacred groves, of which
none now remain in England, 43, 61. Origin of
the epithet Druid, 61. Group of Arch-Druid and
Druids, 64. Arch-Druid in full judicial costume,
83. Disquisition on the learning of this priesthood;
of their written alphabet, 119. Their cultivation
of eloquence, of which the allegorical type was
Hercules Ogmius, 120. Poetry and music, *ib.* To
their theology were intimately conjoined law,
ethics, medicine, cosmogony, and astronomy, 120—
122. Civilisation of Celtic tribes consequent on
their influence, 123. Apology for their deceptions,
errors, and superstitions, *ib.*
DRUMMOND, James, joins the standard of the young
Pretender, 1745; iv. 487.
DRUMMOND, William, a graceful poet, born 1585;
died 1649; iii. 602.
DRUMMOND, of Bochaldy, comes over to Edinburgh,
February 1742, to assure the Jacobites of aid from
France, iv. 469.
DRURY, sir Drew, a fanatical Puritan appointed by
Elizabeth, 1586, to take charge of the queen of
Scots, ii. 658.
DRURY, sir William, destroys the castles of the duke
of Chatelherault, and the houses of the Hamiltons
generally, 1570; ii. 632.

DRURY, a priest, 1606, executed, iii. 33.

DRYDEN, John, the poet, born 1631; iii. 877. A guest at the table of Cromwell, 424. He writes with great violence against the Reformation and established church, 785. Portrait of, 871. Review of his works, 877, 878; iv. 788. He died, 1701; iii. 877.

Du Bartas, translated by Joshua Sylvester in 1605; iii. 585, 601.

Dubienka, battle of, gained by Kosciuszko over the Russians, July 17, 1792; § iii. 45.

Dublin, view of, *regno* Charles I., iii. 253.

DUBOIS, abbé, minister of state to the regent duke of Orleans, iv. 332. His death, August 1723; 383.

DUCKWORTH, sir John; his unsuccessful expedition to the Heilespont and Bosphorus, 1807; § iv. 273 —279. He takes Alexandria, but this expedition also proves unsuccessful, 279—281.

DUDLEY, sir Andrew, brother of Warwick (later the duke of Northumberland), captured the *Lion*, a Scotch man-of-war (1547); ii. 458.

DUDLEY, lord Edward, abandoned the castle of Ham in the English pale, 1558, after the capture of Calais and Guisnes by the duke of Guise, ii. 535.

DUDLEY, lord Guildford, fourth son of the duke of Northumberland, marries in May 1553, the lady Jane Grey, ii. 499. (*See* Jane Grey, Northumberland, Suffolk.) His trial and condemnation, together with the lady Jane, and his brother Ambrose, 509. They are consigned, however, as prisoners to the Tower, 509, 510. After the quelling of Wyatt's insurrection, 1554, the queen commands the execution of lady Jane Grey and her husband, to the great regret of the nation, 517, 518.

DUDLEY, John, viscount Lisle, high-admiral in 1545; ii. 442. One of Edward VI.'s guardians (1547); 454, 455. *See* John Dudley, duke of Northumberland.

DUDLEY, sir Robert. *See* Leicester.

Duelling, an effect of the cessation of the ancient chivalrous combats, ii. 869; iv. 819.

Duels of the seventeenth century, iii. 621—626. Duel between the duke of Buckingham and the earl of Shrewsbury, 897.

DUFAY, keeper of the king's garden at Paris, discovered the opposite exhibitions of electricity before 1739, and also showed that bodies similarly electrified repel, and those dissimilarly electrified attract, each other, iv. 785.

DUFF, succeeded Indulf on the Scottish throne, 961; but after defeating Culen, son of Induif, at Duncrub, Duff was assassinated, 965, at Forres, i. 219.

DUGDALE, one of the witnesses against Lord Stafford, 1680; iii. 732.

Du GUESCLIN; this consummate general made constable and commander of the armies of France, by Charles V. In the old age of Edward III., the French under his direction regain all their possessions on the continent, i. 779. He prevents the earl of Lancaster from taking St. Malo, 783.

Duke or Dux, a Roman military dignity, i. 90. The first English duke was Edward the Black Prince, who was created duke of Cornwall, 1337; 882.

DUMONT, an accomplice with De Grandval in the plot for assassinating William III., 1692; iv. 37.

DUMOURIEZ, Charles François Duperier, a Girondist and French general of great military talent, born January 25, 1739. He becomes minister for foreign affairs, 1792; § iii. 53. His portrait, *ib.* He resigns, 88. Gains the battle of Valmy, September 20, 1792; 182; attacks and takes the town of Breda, February 17, 1793; 285. He breaks with the Convention, and expresses his intention of re-establishing, with some modifications, the constitution of 1791; 286—288. He openly raises the

DUMOURIEZ,—

standard of revolt, and attempts to surprise Lille, 288; takes possession of the persons of four deputies of the Convention, who were afterwards exchanged (November 1795) for the princess royal, 289. Some of his troops mutiny, and attempt to take him prisoner, 290. A price is set on his head by the Convention; and finding himself wherever he went on the Continent an object of suspicion, he arrived in London, June 14, but almost immediately received an order to quit the kingdom; he then took refuge in Hamburgh, where he remained for several years, and, in 1805, obtained permission to reside in England, where he obtained a pension from the government, and died at Turville-park, March 1823; 291.

Dunbar Castle, view of the ruins of, i. 714; iii. 404.

DUNBAR, earl of, endeavours to quiet the murmurs of the Presbyterian clergy, 1606; iii. 65, 466.

DUNBAR, William, an early Scottish poet of considerable merit, born about 1465. He wrote many pieces, serious and comic, in which he discovered poetic genius, and great force and richness of description. Died about 1536; ii. 838.

DUNBAR, archbishop of Glasgow; his battle with cardinal Beatoun, about precedence in a procession to the cathedral, iii. 544.

Dunbarton, Castle of, in the hands, 1639, of the Covenanters, iii. 203.

DUNBARTON, lord, routs the earl of Argyle, near Glasgow, 1685; iii. 769.

Dunblane, battle of, fought Nov. 13, 1715; iv. 319.

DUNCAN, Adam, created viscount, October 30, 1797, for his victory gained over the Dutch admiral de Winter, off Camperdown, October 11, 1797; § iii. 522. He died, 1804. Monument in St. Paul's, *ib.*

DUNCAN, illegitimate son of Malcolm III. He lays claim to the crown of Scotland, and, by the aid of William II., succeeds in driving Donald from the throne, 1094; but is assassinated in 1095 by Malpedir, earl of Mearns, i. 538.

DUNCOMB, sir Sanders, obtains a patent, 1634, for letting sedan chairs to hire, iii. 544:

DUNDEE, viscount. *See* Graham of Claverhouse.

Dunfermline Abbey (Fife), view of, the burial-place of the illustrious Bruce, i. 752.

DUNFERMLINE, earl of, 1639; iii. 205.

DUNGARVON, lord, 1643; iii. 277.

Dunkirk, view of, iii. 692. Sold by Charles II. to France for 5,000,000 livres, *ib.*

DUNMORE, lord, governor of Virginia, proclaims freedom to all the slaves who would repair to his standard and bear arms for the king, 1775, and at the same time issues a proclamation, declaring martial law throughout that colony, § i. 224, 225. Makes a final effort to retrieve the king's affairs in Virginia, 1776, 264.

DUNNE, sir Daniel, one of the commissioners appointed, 1613, to try the divorce of the earl of Essex, iii. 53.

DUNNING, Richard, his plan for the management of the poor, 1685; iv. 844, 845.

DUNOIS, count of, his generalship and valour under the designation of the Bastard of Orleans, 1428; contributed to the expulsion of the English, ii. 62, 66, 71. He invaded Normandy, 1449, took fortresses, and, aided by a revolt at Rouen, drove out Somerset from that city, 85.

DUNSTABLE, John of, inventor of figurate harmony, iii. 561.

DUNSTAN, St., was abbot of Glastonbury, 945, at the accession of Edred; i. 170. His insolent deportment to Edwy and Elgiva at their coronation feast, 171. He is charged with peculation by that youthful king, and deprived of his places, *ib.* His abbey given by Edwy to the secular clergy and

DUNSTAN, St.,—
married priests, *ib*. Dunstan was the chief supporter of monks who adhered to the vow of celibacy, 172, 174, 243. His flight to Ghent, 172, 243. On his return he became archbishop of Canterbury, and proved a wise and vigorous minister in Edgar's reign, 172, 243. He placed Edward the Martyr, and afterwards young Ethelred, on the throne, 174, 176. His clerical measures, 242, 244. Penances, 244. His birth noble, 240. His early life, divine manifestations, etc., 241. His accomplishments; perils at the court of Athelstane, etc., *ib*. His cell at Glastonbury, and temptation by Satan, *ib*., 242. His portrait, 243. A synod held, in which the floor of the chamber fell, and his adversaries were overwhelmed, 244. His death, about 988; *ib*.

Duntocher Bridge, on the line of Graham's Dyke, i. 48.

DUPLEIX, Joseph, a distinguished French commander in the East Indies, becomes governor of Pondicherry, 1742. His service there against the English, § ii. 23, *et seq*.

Duplin-moor, victory gained here by Edward Baliol, August 1332; i. 775.

DU QUESNE, a French general, 1672; iii. 710.

Durham, view of, i. 373. Taken possession of by the Normans, 372. The bishopric suppressed, 1553, by Act of Parliament, and two new dioceses created in its place, one comprehending the county of Durham, the other that of Northumberland, ii. 499. The former bishop, Tunstall, deprived by a new court created for this especial purpose, a bill of pains and penalties against him having failed in parliament, *ib*. The suppressed bishopric erected into a county palatine, united to the crown by Edward VI., destined as a regal appanage for the ambitious Northumberland, *ib*.

Durham Cathedral, founded by William de Carilepho, 1093, view of the nave of, i. 621.

DURIE, John, a minister of Edinburgh, attacks the episcopal office, 1575; iii. 438. He is summoned before the council for having publicly justified the Raid of Ruthven, 441. Is convicted, 1605, by a slavish jury, of high-treason, and after a rigorous confinement the sentence of death is commuted into perpetual banishment, 64.

DUROC, general, the favourite aide-de-camp of the emperor Napoleon, slain in an engagement with the allies, May 23, 1813; § iv. 592.

DURST, a victorious Pictish king, son of Erp, i. 216.

DURY, general, slain at St. Cas, 1758; iv. 602.

DUVENNSERDE, Baron de Wassenaer, 1714; iv. 290.

Dyeing, regulations concerning, ii. 809. Improvement in the art of, towards the close of the 18th century, § iii. 710.

EADBALD succeeds his father Ethelbert, *anno* 616, as king of Kent, i. 145. He marries his father's young widow, which scandal being reproved by churchmen and others, he and his people abjure Christianity, so recently established by Augustine, 145, 233. Laurentius then persuaded the king to put away his step-mother; and Eadbald and his people return to the Christian fold, 145.

EADBURGHA, daughter of Offa, the king of Mercia, i. 150. Beorhtric, of Wessex, marries her, *ib*. That king, prompted by this cruel princess, is guilty of acts of ferocious tyranny, *ib*. Death of the king by poison, and the queen supposed to have intentionally administered the chalice, is expelled the kingdom, *anno*, 800, *ib*. She resides in a French convent, by permission of Charlemagne, but her vicious life causes her expulsion, *ib*. She afterwards begs for her bread, in the city of Pavia, in Italy, *ib*.

EADMER, monk of Canterbury, appointed bishop of St. Andrews, in Scotland, 1120; i. 539. He resigns his bishopric and returns to England, *ib*. His

EADMER,—
letter to king Alexander asking his permission to return, *ib*.

EANRED, king of Northumbria, submits, in 825, to Egbert, i. 151.

EARLE, sir Walter, idle rumour of a new plot with gunpowder against parliament, in 1641, reported by him to the House of Commons, iii. 242, 264.

EARLE, Mr., acts, 1645, in conjunction with Milton, as secretary for the English parliament, iii. 329.

Earl's Barton, view of the church, i. 315.

Earthenware, considerable quantities of this commodity were imported from the continent up to 1760, from which period the improvements of Wedgwood may be dated, iv. 734.

East-Anglia, kingdom of, founded by a warlike immigration from Anglen in Holstein, about the end of the sixth century, i. 142. These Angles, under the appellatives of the Southfolk and the Northfolk, gave name to Suffolk and Norfolk, *ib*. They dig a vast and deep ditch, as a defence to their frontier, in continuation of the natural bulwarks of marshes and meres; known afterwards as the "Giants' Dyke," or "Devil's Dyke," *ib*. This territory subdued by Egbert, is placed under a viceroy, 800; 150.

Easterlings, the, were in part merchants, and their ships often freebooting privateers; they chase the dethroned Edward IV. to the coast near Alkmaar, and would have captured him, but for Grutuse, stadtholder of those districts, rescuing the English fugitives, 1470, 1471; ii. 107.

East India Company, the, incorporated 1579; established 1600. The town of Madras was ceded to them in 1643, and the island of St. Helena in 1651. In October, 1657, a new charter was granted to the Company for seven years, after they had actually, in despair of obtaining the protection of the government, put up bills in the Royal Exchange offering their property and their privileges, such as they were, for sale, iii. 547. Different factories of the Company, 547, 548. They are re-incorporated by Charles, April 3, 1661, with the full confirmation of all their ancient privileges, and other important additional rights, 861. Examination into the state of the Company, 1767; § i. 54. Demands of the Company, *ib*. Their charter prolonged on certain conditions, 1769; 73. Its growing importance, 125. Select committee appointed, 1772, to examine into the state of the Company, 148. Review of its condition during the 18th century, 563—566, 569. The United East India Company formed, 1698; § ii. 22. Renewal of the charter for twenty years, 1793; § iii. 663. View of the old East India House, Leadenhall-street, § ii. 102. View of the state of the commerce of India, 1677. Increase in the territory of the, in 1801 and the following years, § iv. 672.

Eaton Hall, Cheshire, built early in the nineteenth century, by William Porden, § iv. 710.

EBOLT, duke of, 1734; iv. 414.

Ecclesiastical Commission, the, established by James II.; iii. 785.

Ecclesiasticus, book of, and the Apocrypha, discussed, 1604; iii. 16.

EDEN, sir Frederick, quoted, iii. 659, 660.

EDERA, father, a Jesuit of great credit at the court of Vienna, 1697; iv. 78.

EDGAR, brother of king Edwy, endowed by that youthful monarch with a royal *appanage*, probably Mercia, in 955; i. 171. His succession at fifteen to the English throne, in 958-9; 172. Dunstan's wise and enlightened administration, *ib*., 173. The young king possessing the regard of the Danes of East-Anglia and Northumbria, established separate earldoms in their states, 172. His well-trained fleets keep off the sea-kings in their marauding attempts, *ib*. He visits his provinces annually, *ib*. He cultivates the friendship of his nobles, holds

EDGAR,—
courts of justice and appeal, and feasts during these
royal progresses, 173. Celibacy of clerks enforced,
and married clergy expelled from all abbeys, cathedrals, etc., 172. His assumed titles of Basileus, or
emperor of Albion. 173. Is called "the Pacific," *ib.*
Eight crowned kings said to have plied the oars
of his barge on the river Dee, *ib.* He commutes
the Welsh tribute to the delivery of 300 wolves'
heads annually, thereby extirpating that ferocious
animal, *ib.* He reforms the coinage, *ib.* Profligacy of his court, *ib.* The king's mistress Wal-
freda, *ib.* Hearing of the exceeding beauty of
Elfrida, daughter of earl Ordgar, the king sends
his favourite Athelwold to ascertain this matter, *ib.*
Deceived by his envoy, who himself weds Elfrida,
ib. Edgar himself repairs to Ordgar's castle, in
Devonshire; Athelwold being murdered in a wood,
the royal nuptials then take place, *ib.* Murder of
Edgar's eldest son, *ib.* The lustre of the race of
Alfred was afterwards eclipsed under Ethelred, son
of Edgar and Elfrida, *ib.* The king dies, aged
thirty-two, and is buried at Glastonbury, which
abbey he had magnificently endowed, *ib.* His second
son, Edward the Martyr, succeeds to Edgar in 975; 174.
EDGAR, Atheling, grandson of Edmund Ironside, and
his sisters Christina and Margaret, i. 181. Is proclaimed king by the Witan, 1066; 360. Goes on a
deputation to William, 361. William confirms to
him the earldom of Oxford, 362. He flies to Scotland with his mother and sisters, and is received
with great honour and kindness by Malcolm Caenmore, then king of Scotland, 369. Joins the Northumbrians, and Osbeorn the Danish commander,
371; they take York, and slay 3,000 Normans; here
he is supposed to have assumed the royal title, and
exercised the rights of sovereignty, *ib.* The English, deserted by their Danish allies, fight bravely in
York, but are vanquished, and Edgar Atheling flies
a second time to Scotland, 372. Receives an advantageous offer from Philip, king of France, but is
prevented from going there by a storm, 379. Sends
a message to the conqueror, requesting a reconciliation, *ib.* William promises to him honourable treatment, *ib.* He goes to Normandy, and has an apartment allotted to him in the palace of Rouen, and a
pound of silver a day, 380. Edgar Atheling and
duke Robert bring about a treaty between Malcolm
Caenmore, king of Scotland, and William Rufus,
by which Edgar is permitted to return to England,
where he received some court employment, 398. He
is taken prisoner by Henry, at Tenchebray in Normandy, where he had been residing with duke
Robert; is sent over to England and allowed to
go at large, his niece having obtained for him a
small pension; he passes the rest of his life in an
obscure but tranquil solitude in the country, and
after this we hear no more of him, 411.
EDGAR, son of Malcolm III., and nephew of Edgar
Atheling, obtains the kingdom of Scotland in 1097,
by the assistance of Edgar Atheling and William
II., i. 538. His character, *ib.*
EDGECOMBE, captain, joins Byng in his expedition to
Minorca, 1756; iv. 586.
Edgecote, battle of, fought July 26, 1469; ii. 104.
EDGECUMBE, lord. *See* Mount Edgecumbe.
EDGECUMBE, Richard, created Baron Edgecumbe,
1742; iv. 460.
Edgehill, battle of, fought October 23, 1642; iii. 297.
EDGITHA, daughter of king Edgar, by the nun he had
carried off from Wilton Convent; herself afterwards
a nun in the same monastery, i. 175. Dunstan, in-
censed at the base murder of Edward the Martyr at
Corfe Castle, by his step-mother, desires to pass
over young Ethelred's title to the crown, and offers
it to Edgitha (979), *ib.* This timid but prudent
nun refuses the royal dignity, *ib.*

EDILFRID, king of Northumbria, slays a vast number
of the old Britons, and defeats the Scots, i. 145.
This Saxon prince, persecuting prince Edwin, is
himself attacked by Redwald, king of East Anglia,
about 621, and is slain in action, 146, 234. His
massacre of the abbot and monks of Bangor, 233.
Edinburgh, view of St. Giles's and the Old Tron
church, *regno Car. I.*, iii. 182. As it appeared
during the early part of the seventeenth century,
184. Market Cross at, 682. View of the parliament house and square at, iv. 191. Condition of,
837—840. Treaty of, 1560; ii. 561, 562. Bishop
of, nearly killed by the multitude, 1637, for preaching at St. Giles's kirk after the new liturgy had
been read there, iii. 183.
EDITHA, daughter of earl Godwin, her great accomplishments, gentle character, and beauty, i. 187.
Ingulphus, of Croyland, records her many virtues,
and her studies. *ib.* Becomes the queen of Edward
the Confessor, about 1042, who, fearing and hating
her powerful family, totally neglected Editha, *ib.*
On the expulsion of Godwin and his sons from
England, the king treats his still virgin wife cruelly,
seizes her dower, and all her property, 191. He
confines her in the monastery of Wherwell, of which
his sister was abbess, 1044, 1045, *ib.* On her
father's triumphant return, 1052, Editha is recalled
to the court, and treated with honour, 193. Present
at the consecration of Westminster Abbey, 1065,
re-built by Edward, 203. After the battle of Hastings she takes refuge in the city of Exeter, 366.
When Exeter surrenders to William, she escapes to
Bath, and finding no safety there flies to the small
islands at the mouth of the Severn, accompanied by
several ladies of rank, and thence passes over to
Flanders, *ib.*
EDMONDS, sir Thomas, an intriguing diplomatist, 1603,
under patronage of Cecil and Shrewsbury, iii. 15.
Ambassador at Paris, 52. Recommences, in the
name of prince Charles, the matrimonial treaty begun for his brother, *ib.* 140.
EDMUND, Atheling, in 940 succeeds his brother
Athelstane, i. 170. His courage, *ib.* His epithet
of "the Magnificent." His taste and improvements, *ib.* Anlaf or Olave, recalled from Ireland,
leads the Northumbrian Danes against him, and
conquers all the country north of the "Watling-
street," *ib.* The king expels king Dunmail, of
Cumbria, whose isolated British tribe, long settled in
Cumberland, had rebelled, 946, *ib.* Edmund grants
their principality as a fief to Malcolm of Scotland,
ib. He deprives the sons of Dunmail of their eyes,
ib. Such cruelties and maimings hitherto uncommon
with the Anglo-Saxons, *ib.* The banished robber
Leof, in 946, intrudes at a banquet of king Edmund,
ib. The incensed monarch seizes the outlaw by
his hair, struggles to eject him, but is himself
poniarded by Leof, *ib.* His interment at Glastonbury, *ib.*
EDMUND, *surnamed* Ironside, elected king, 1016 to 1017,
on the death of Ethelred, i. 180. He was a natural son
of king Ethelred, *ib.* He twice relieved London,
besieged by Canute, and fought five pitched battles
with various results, *ib.* He proposes single combat to Canute, which is refused, *ib.* The royal
Dane in his turn proposed to share the kingdom,
the south to be Edmund's portion, *ib.* Both armies
applaud this accommodation, and the treaty is perfected, *ib.* King Edmund, within two months, died
suddenly, and some mystery was said to envelop his
decease, *ib.* Canute succeeds to the kingdom,
1017, *ib.* His brother Edwy murdered by Canute,
181. His infant sons, Edmund and Edward, sent to
the king of Sweden to dispose of, Canute probably
intending their death, *ib.* The Swedish prince,
however, consigns them in safety to the king of
Hungary, out of reach of the Danish tyrant, *ib.*

L

EDMUND, *surnamed* Ironside,—

Edmund died without issue; Edward, who is sent for by Edward the Confessor to return home, dying in London suddenly, some suspicion of poisoning attached to Harold, 181, 195. Edward the Atheling, designated also Edward the Outlaw, left Edgar Atheling, Margaret, and Christina, *ib.*

EDMUND, prince, second son of Henry III., is declared by his father king of Sicily, 1253 ; i. 680.

EDMUND, brother of Edward I., sent to negotiate with the French king, i. 711.

EDNOTH, an English nobleman, defeats the two sons of Harold and their Irish pirates, who had landed and plundered the country near Bristol, but is himself slain in the battle, i. 365.

EDRED, in 946, succeeds his brother Edmund the Atheling, i. 170. His severe malady and debility, *ib.* Dunstan and Torketul, *ib.* Is invaded by the Northumbrian Danes and the sea-kings of the Hebrides ; by Eric and the princes of Denmark, Norway, etc., *ib.* Successes of Edred's armies. The territory of Northumbria acknowledges the English monarch, and the Danes of that land allowed no king, but only an earl to govern them, *ib.* The perpetual rebellions of that Danish population of Britain, with their allies, the plundering sea-kings, arose, from a wish to subvert the Anglo-Saxon monarchy, *ib.* The mental qualities of Edred remain a matter of doubt, *ib.*

EDRIC, a man of ambition and talent, raised from a low estate to the favour of Ethelred, 1008; is promoted to high offices, and receives the hand of the king's daughter, i. 178, 179. His brother Brihtric, 179.

EDRIC, surnamed the Forester, visits William at Barking, i. 362. Shuts the Normans up within the walls of Hereford, 365. Takes the town of Shrewsbury, but is unable to take the castle, 375. On the arrival of William at Chester, 1073, Edric submits, and is received into favour, *ib.*

EDUCATION, iii. 632; iv. 814—818.

EDWARD the Elder, king of Wessex, 901, succeeds his father Alfred, i. 168. His cousin Ethelwald, a competitor for the throne, is constrained to fly to the Danelagh, and being crowned by the Danes makes war upon Edward, *ib.* Edward, son of Alfred, routs Ethelwald, son of Ethelbald, in 905, when Ethelwald falls on the field, *ib.* Valour of king Edward. In 911 he totally defeats a Danish army on the Severn, *ib.* His celebrated sister Ethelfleda, widow of Ethelred of Mercia, in 912, assumes the government of that kingdom, *ib.* Edward, however, possesses himself of London and Oxford, and Ethelfleda maintains her authority over the rest of Mercia, *ib.* In 920, on his sister's decease, he seizes all Mercia, builds forts, and ultimately reduces the Danelagh, north of the Humber, to acknowledge his supremacy, *ib.* He receives homage from the Scots, the Welsh, and the ancient Britons of Cumbria and Strathclyde, *ib.* His death in 925, *ib.*

EDWARD the Martyr, about his fifteenth year, 975, succeeds his father Edgar, i. 174. His rights are disputed by Elfrida, who claims the crown for her son Ethelred, six years of age, *ib.* This dispute occasions fresh contests between Dunstan, with the celibate monks, and the secular and married clerks, *ib.* Edward is crowned, under the protection of the still powerful Dunstan, *ib.* Elfrida confederates with Alfere, of Mercia, and many of the nobles, 175. Out hunting in Dorsetshire, 978—979, the king quits his company, to visit at Corfe Castle his half-brother Ethelred and Elfrida, *ib.* She receives him with civility at the gate ; Edward will not dismount, and drinking to his brother's and her health he is stabbed in the back by one of her attendants, *ib.* He faints, is dragged through the woods

EDWARD the Martyr,—

entangled in the stirrup, and is found dead by his company, *ib.* The foulest deed, says the Saxon Chronicle, committed since the Angles came into Britain, *ib.*

EDWARD (the Confessor), son of king Ethelred and Emma of Normandy, resides many years at the Norman court, i. 180, 188. This prince (afterwards, from his devoutness, called ' the Confessor'), on Canute's death lands at Southampton, 1035. His mother Emma raises the population near Winchester, her residence, in favour of her son, Hardicanute, 184. His escape to Normandy, *ib.* A letter, purporting to be from queen Emma, but by some deemed a treacherous forgery, was then sent to invite her Saxon sons to come over and dispute the crown with the usurper Harold, *ib.* (*See* Alfred, son of Ethelred and Emma.) Edward, having been previously recalled from exile by his half-brother Hardicanute, and treated with honour and regard, he succeeds to the throne, 1042, without opposition, 186. The Danes submit to the Saxon king, Canute's line being extinct, 187. Earl Godwin maintains the right of Edward, and eventually exiles such Saxon councillors who made any resistance, *ib.* Doubtful tradition that William of Normandy, then fifteen years of age, threatened vengeance if this son of Emma of Normandy were not elected, *ib.* King Edward hates Godwin, on account of the murder of prince Alfred, but the crafty nobleman in elevating him to the throne, had secured for himself a wider government and increased honours, *ib.* Nuptials of king Edward and Editha, the beautiful daughter of Godwin, but never consummated by the monarch, who had an antipathy to all of that powerful family, *ib.* He subsequently persecuted his queen ; and also, for the same cause, the death of Alfred, his own mother Emma, *ib.* Edward holds a council at Gloucester; proceeds to Winchester, where queen Emma held her court, and sequestrates her treasures and chattels, 188. The queen-mother died, 1052, at Winchester, *ib.* Magnus, king of Denmark, 1043, intended an invasion, but Edward having a powerful fleet, and the Danes in England being quiescent, this danger was dissipated, *ib.* The king's character of exceeding mildness, but with occasional displays of vigour, *ib.* As usual in such instances, his personal authority is but small, and he is exposed to the ambition of his too powerful vassals, *ib.* Earl Godwin, and his six sons, possess full jurisdiction over the south, from Lincolnshire to the Land's End, *ib.*, and earl Siward and Leofric the north, *ib.* Edward's influence lay chiefly in the balance of these authorities. He abolished Danegeld, and reduced taxation, *ib.* He restored the Saxon laws, and governing with justice and mildness acquired popularity, *ib*; but living at the Norman court from the age of thirteen until twenty-seven, his predilections, habits, and language were essentially Norman-French, *ib.* Introduced the use of a "great seal" to his deeds, appointed Normans to bishoprics, and many offices, 189 ; banishes, 1044, Sweyn, a son of Godwin, and recalls him, *ib.* Edward's sister Goda, wife of Eustace the count of Boulogne, *ib.* The king is visited, 1051, by his brother-in-law, Eustace of Boulogne, *ib.* Sanguinary quarrel of that French prince at Dover, *ib.* Preparations for a civil war by the great earl, who refused to put the men of Dover to military execution at the infuriated command of the Saxon king, 190. Godwin delays to strike, listening to the negotiations of Edward, *ib.* This saves king Edward for a time, as the levies of Godwin and his sons could not be held together; not so with the king's thanes and forces, which daily increased their numbers, *ib.* The great earl summoned to

EDWARD the Confessor,—appear, flies down the Thames with his wife and sons to Flanders, 191. The king's extreme joy at being clear of the tutelage that Godwin had hitherto kept him in, *ib.* Edward sends queen Editha to a cloister, *ib.* The English were astonished at the sudden downfall of so great a family, *ib.* Edward giving more favour, if possible, to Normans, desires to have duke William for a guest (1051—1052), who hastens to Dover to gratify the Saxon monarch, 191, 192. At Canterbury, at the court of Edward, everything he found wore already a Norman aspect, and the most respectful attention was paid to William, who arrived with a magnificent retinue, 192. Warm reception of the duke by Edward, and royal present on departure; their consultations unknown, *ib.* Triumphant return, 1052, of earl Godwin and his sons; the king unable to resist his influence with the English people, who flocked to the earl's standard, 192, 193. Edward secures his crown only by discarding all Norman favourites, the Saxon council, or Witan, desiring their exile, *ib.* Godwin's death, *ib.* It occurring at, or soon after, a feast at the king's board, an ill-avouched tradition is extant that the king was again reproaching him with the death of Alfred, 194. Reasons for not crediting the fables of credulous chroniclers, *ib.* Edward becomes feeble in his age, *ib.* Harold, young and comely, is less obnoxious to the old monarch than was his father, but inherits his estates and power, with even increased popularity, *ib.* Earl Algar, son of Leofric, obtaining East-Anglia on Harold's exile, is dispossessed by Harold, *ib.* Algar rebels rather against Harold than the king; account of this contest, *ib.* (*See Algar.*) Death of Algar, 1059, who left Morcar and Edwin, *ib.* Death and history of the great earl Siward, whose earldom (in the minority of Waltheof) is entrusted to Tostig; this causes civil dissensions, to distract the aged Edward, 194, 195. His contemporaries, Duncan of Scotland and Macbeth, 194. The Welsh, reduced to submission, themselves decapitate their king, Griffith, 1063, and Harold presents that sad trophy, and the rostrum of that prince's ship, to Edward, 195. The Saxon king, and his Witan or assembly, enact that any Welshman taken in arms east of Offa's Dyke, shall lose his right hand, *ib.* King Edward contemplates a pilgrimage to Rome, to which the Witenagemot offers opposition, as the king is without offspring, 195. This king was long suspected of an intention to bequeath his realm to his cousin, duke William, but the Normans being held in detestation by his Saxon subjects, turned his thoughts to a more national succession, *ib.* Urged by his Witan and council, he sends ambassadors to Henry III., of Germany, requesting the return of Edward, son of his half-brother Edmund Ironside, *ib.* Speedy arrival of the Saxon prince with his family, *ib.* Death of Edward the Outlaw in London (whither he had been accompanied by his son, Edgar Atheling, and the rest of his family), under suspicion of foul play, probably groundless, *ib.* The feeble character of Edgar Atheling reduces the Confessor to new perplexities in the regulation of the succession, 196. His will in favour of William of Normandy, 196, 201. Harold takes leave of the Confessor, visits Bosham church, in Sussex, and arriving at William's court, promises, upon a solemn oath, to assist the Norman duke to mount the English throne, 198, 199; Death of Edward the Confessor, January 5, 1066; 200—203. His funeral, 202. His shrine in Westminster Abbey, *ib.* His great seal, 203. His character, *ib.* His code of laws compiled from those of Ethelbert, Ina, and Alfred, *ib.*

EDWARD I. (November 20, 1272—July 7, 1307.) Prince

EDWARD I.,—Edward marries Eleanor daughter of Alphonso, king of Castile, 1253; i. 680. He takes the oaths to the Provisions of Oxford with great reluctance, 682. Takes part with the barons, 683. Veers round to the court, and makes himself unpopular by calling in a foreign guard, *ib.* Leicester marches to London, and prince Edward flies to Windsor Castle, 1263, *ib.* A short reconciliation effected between the king and his barons, *ib.* Edward takes active measures against the barons, 1264; 685. Is taken prisoner at the great battle of Lewes, *ib.* The earl of Gloucester concerts a plan for releasing the prince, and is joined by him at Ludlow, where the royal banner is raised, the prince having sworn to respect the Charters, and govern according to law, 686. He takes the command of the forces; his military sagacity, *ib.* He surprises Simon de Montfort, son of the great earl of Leicester, near Kenilworth, *ib.* Leicester advances to Evesham, with the hope of meeting his son's forces, *ib.* He is surrounded by the royal forces, commanded by prince Edward, and having failed in an attempt to force the road to Kenilworth, he, together with his son Henry, and one hundred and eighty barons and knights, is slain in the battle of Evesham, 687. Prince Edward and his cousin Henry take the cross, 1267; 688. He is proclaimed king, November 20, 1272, while absent in the Holy Land, *ib.* A regency appointed, *ib.* His great seal, 689. His portrait, from a statue in the choir of York Minster, *ib.* His stay at Acre, and capture of Nazareth, 690. The emir of Jaffa opens a correspondence with Edward, under pretence of embracing the Christian religion, *ib.* His messenger attempts to stab him while in his tent with a poisoned dagger, but Edward seizes him and despatches him with his own weapon, *ib.* A skilful English surgeon pares away the sides of the wound, and some precious drugs sent by the master of the Templars, stop the progress of the venom, *ib.* A truce concluded with the sultan for ten years, 691. Edward returns through Italy, and is kindly received by the pope, *ib.* He continues his journey through France, and spends a short time at Paris, *ib.* The count of Chalons challenges him to meet him at a tournament, a fierce combat ensues, the count is dismounted and the French beaten, 692. Edward sends word to England to prepare for his coronation, *ib.* On the 2nd of August, 1274, he lands at Dover, after an absence of more than four years, *ib.*; and on the 19th is crowned with his wife Eleanor in Westminster Abbey, 693. Impositions on the unfortunate Jews, *ib.* In 1290, Edward commands all their property to be confiscated, and themselves to leave the kingdom, on pain of death, *ib.* Many wise and just laws enacted, 694. He attempts to recover such parts of the royal domain as had been encroached upon, and examines the titles by which the great men held their estates, *ib.* (For the history and conquest of Wales at this period, *see* Llewellyn.) After the death of Llewellyn, Edward remained more than a year in Wales, dividing the country into shires and hundreds, and restoring order and tranquillity, 699. He published a proclamation, offering peace to all the inhabitants, giving them at the same time assurances that they should continue to enjoy all their lands, liberties, and properties as they had done before, *ib.* He appointed other wholesome regulations, lightened the taxes, and when his second son was born in the castle of Carnarvon, he promised them that he should be their prince, *ib.* The Welsh chiefs, form the expectation that this "Prince of Wales" would have the separate government of their country, Alphonso, his elder brother, being then alive, *ib.* After the subjugation of Wales, Edward spends three years on the continent, being

EDWARD I,—

engaged as umpire to settle a dispute between the kings of France, Arragon, and the house of Anjou, respecting the island of Sicily, 700. Edward agrees with the regency of Scotland, upon a marriage between his eldest son and the princess of Scotland, daughter of Eric king of Norway, and Margaret, daughter of Alexander III.; this treaty was concluded July 18th, 1290, but the princess was taken sick on her passage, and, landing on one of the Orkney islands, died there, in her eighth year, 707. Various competitors lay claim to the crown of Scotland, Edward addresses an invitation to the nobility and clergy to meet him at Norham, but nothing definite was determined, ib. In the meeting held on the 2nd of June, 1291, at Holywell Haugh, Bruce acknowledges Edward lord paramount of Scotland, and consents to ask and receive judgment from him in that character; his example is followed by that of the other competitors, 708. Baliol was absent on the first day of the meeting, but on the 3rd of June, the proceedings at Norham were terminated by an unanimous agreement, that a body of 104 commissioners should be appointed to examine the cause and report to Edward, forty being named by Baliol, the same number by Bruce, and the remainder by Edward himself. On the 11th, the regents of Scotland made a solemn surrender of the kingdom into the hands of the English king, on condition that Edward should make full restitution in two months from the date of his award in the cause of the succession, ib. On the 17th of November, Edward gives judgment in the great hall of the castle of Berwick, "that John Baliol should have seizin of the kingdom of Scotland." On the 19th the regents of Scotland, and the governors of castles, receive orders to surrender their respective trusts to the new king, and on the 30th Sir John Baliol is solemnly crowned at Scone, 710. Marriage of his daughter Margaret with Henry, count of Bar, ib. Philip summons Edward, as duke of Aquitaine, to appear at Paris after the feast of Christmas, and answer for his offences against his suzerain; Edward sends his brother Edmund to negotiate, who surrenders Gascony for forty days, as a mark of satisfaction to the French king, 711. Philip refuses to restore Gascony, and pronounces a judgment of forfeiture, because Edward had not presented himself as a vassal ought, ib. War commences with Philip, but Edward is detained for some time in England by a revolt of the Welsh, ib. The count d'Artois takes the command of the French troops, and expels the English from nearly all their possessions on the continent, 712. Humiliating condition of the Scottish king, ib. On the 23rd of October, 1295, Baliol forms an alliance with the French king, and invades Cumberland, 713. On the 30th of March, a messenger delivers to Edward Baliol's solemn renunciation of his allegiance and fealty, ib. Edward carries everything before him in Scotland. and Baliol basely lays down his kingly state, 714. The famous stone on which the Scottish kings had been wont to be crowned is removed to Westminster. On the 28th a parliament was held at Berwick, and many of the Scottish laity and clergy present themselves to take the oaths of fealty, ib. Edward takes measures for settling the government of the conquered country, and appoints as governor John de Warenne, earl of Surrey, 715. (For the farther history of Scotland, see WALLACE.) In 1294 the English parliament is compelled to grant a tenth on lay property, and a half on the incomes of the clergy, August 28, 1296, Edward outlaws the clergy, and seizes their goods, for opposing his demands, 719. General discontent of the higher portion of the people; the earls of Hereford and Norfolk, with a great part of his army, refuse to leave England, ib.

EDWARD I,—

Edward leaves for France, the war is injudiciously managed, a truce with Philip for two years is agreed upon, and Edward returns, 1298; 721. He is obliged to grant another confirmation of the two Charters, and a full confirmation of the important statute called, "De Tallagio non Concedendo," passed in a parliament held by prince Edward, September, 1297; ib. He attempts to introduce a new clause into the Charters, but is obliged to re-confirm them in their old form, ib. He marries Margaret of France, and the prince of Wales is contracted to Isabella, daughter of Philip le Bel, 723. Edward collects an army, and lays waste Annandale, 724. Boniface VIII. claims Scotland as of right belonging to the holy see, ib. Segrave, the governor of Scotland, appointed by Edward, is defeated at Roslin, 725. Peace of Montreuil, ib. Edward commands another expedition, and advances as far as Lochendorb; all Scotland submits to him, and the great men receive a full pardon, with the exception of some who are banished for a certain number of years, ib. On the 22nd of April he besieges the castle of Stirling, which surrenders, July 20; 726. Wallace is taken prisoner, conveyed to London and executed as a traitor, ib. Bruce crowned at Scone, March 27th; 728. Is defeated in the wood of Methven, and his wife and daughter taken prisoners and confined in England; he makes his escape to the island of Rachrin, 729. Bruce's brother Nigel surrenders the castle of Kildrummie, and is executed as a traitor by Edward at Berwick, ib. Bruce returns to Scotland, and gains some victories; his two brothers, Thomas and Alexander, are taken prisoners, and executed at Carlisle, 730. His forces increasing, he ventures to attack the earl of Pembroke at London, where he gains a complete victory, May 10th, 1307; three days after he defeats the earl of Gloucester, and besieges them both in the castle of Ayr, ib. Edward expires at the village of Burgh-upon-Sands, July 7, 1307, and on the 27th is buried at Westminster, 781. Coins of this reign, 837.

EDWARD II., (July 8, 1307—January 20, 1327.) Edward, son of Edward I., married to Isabella, daughter of Philip le Bel, 1299; i. 723. He receives the order of knighthood, 726. Death of Edward I. at Burgh-upon-Sands, July 7, 1307; 730. Edward II. is acknowledged king at Carlisle, July 8; ib. He displaces all the ministers of his father, and permits his favourite Gaviston to return, ib. His portrait, 731. His great seal, ib. Funeral of his father at Westminster Abbey, July 27; ib. He marries Gaviston to his niece Margaret de Clare, and gives him the great earldom of Cornwall, ib. He sails for France, leaving Gaviston regent of England; and, Jan. 25, 1308, marries Isabella of France, at Boulogne, 732. On the 25th of February he is crowned at Westminster, ib. The barons petition against Gaviston; he is banished, but appointed governor of all Ireland; he is soon after recalled by Edward, and permitted to remain in England by a parliament which was held at Stamford, ib. The barons refuse to attend a parliament summoned to meet at York, October 1309; 733. They meet at Westminster, and appoint a committee of ordainers, 1310, ib. Edward marches into Scotland, September, 1310; ib. Gaviston is banished in a parliament held in August, 1311, and all the grants made to him by Edward recalled. It is also enacted that parliament shall be holden at least once every year, ib. In December Gaviston again returns, and his honours are re-granted by Edward, ib. Edward prepares an army at York to oppose the barons, ib. The earl of Lancaster, who headed the barons, falls suddenly upon the royal party at Newcastle; Edward and Gaviston make their escape, ib. The queen falls into the hands of

EDWARD II,—

the barons, who treat her with all respect, *ib.* Gaviston is besieged in Scarborough Castle, and on the 19th of May, 1312, surrenders, on capitulation, to the earl of Pembroke; he is conveyed to Warwick Castle, where he is condemned by the barons present, *ib.*, and executed at Blacklow-hill, contrary to the capitulation, 734. A reconciliation effected between the king and his barons, *ib.* Bruce obtains many advantages by the neglect of the English government; he gains the great battle of Inverary, May 22nd, 1308; 735. September, 1310, Edward marches into Scotland, but returns, having accomplished nothing. July, 1311. Bruce invades and ravages England as far as Durham, *ib.* January, 1312, Perth Castle taken by Bruce, *ib.* The castles of Roxburgh and Edinburgh surrender, 1313. Bruce ravages England as far as Chester, and burns the towns of Hexham, Corbridge, and a great part of Durham, 736. Edward summons all the military power of England to meet him at Berwick on the 11th of June, and calls to his aid both his English subjects in Ireland and many of the native Irish chiefs, composing a splendid army exceeding a hundred thousand men; he also fits out a fleet to act in concert with his land forces, *ib.* On the 23rd the English make their appearance at Bannockburn, where the Scottish army, under the command of Bruce, consisting of about 40,000 men, was drawn up ready to receive them, *ib.* On the following day the great battle was fought, which restored the independence and honour of the Scottish nation, 737. In this battle, the earl of Gloucester, the king's nephew, perished, with 200 knights, 700 esquires, and 30,000 of inferior rank, king Edward himself being hotly pursued for sixty miles as far as the castle of Dunbar; twenty-two barons and bannerets, and sixty knights, were also taken prisoners, 738. Stirling Castle immediately surrenders, and the earl of Hereford capitulates in Bothwell Castle, *ib.* The earl is exchanged for the wife, sister, and daughter of the king of Scots, *ib.* The Scots, under the command of Edward Bruce, invade Ireland and gain many victories there, but fail in their attempt on Dublin, *ib.* During the absence of Bruce, who had gone over into Ireland to assist his brother, the English make several attempts to renew the war, but are successively defeated by sir James Douglas and the bishop of Dunkeld, 739. Bruce takes the important town of Berwick, March 28, 1318, and follows up these successes by two invasions of England, *ib.* On the 5th of October he is defeated and killed at Fagher, near Dundalk, and the Scots are expelled from Ireland, *ib.* Edward marches with a numerous army upon Berwick, but is repulsed, *ib.* The Scots invade England and ravage Yorkshire, *ib.* They gain the battle of Mitton, and on the 21st of December a truce for two years is agreed upon, *ib.* After the death of Gaviston, Edward chose Hugh Despenser for his favourite; the barons take up arms and destroy the castles of the Despensers, 740. The earl of Lancaster marches upon London, and occupies the suburbs of Holborn and Clerkenwell, *ib.* Both the Despensers are banished in parliament, August, 1321; *ib.* In October they return to England, *ib.* Lancaster and his party are surprised and defeated at Boroughbridge by sir Simon Ward and sir Andrew Harclay, 1322; 741. He is taken prisoner, condemned, and executed as a traitor, *ib.* In a parliament held at York the attainders of the Despenser family are reversed, and the father made earl of Winchester, *ib.* A suspension of arms for thirteen years is agreed upon between England and Scotland, May 30, 1323; *ib.* Roger Mortimer effects his escape from the Tower, *ib.* Charles IV., king of France, overruns some of Edward's conti-

EDWARD II,—

nental dominions, 742. Queen Isabella persuades the king to permit her to go to Paris to settle the disputes which had arisen between him and the French king, her brother, March, 1325, *ib.* Guienne and Poictiers are surrendered to France, *ib.* The queen refuses to return, her connection with Mortimer becomes notorious, Charles orders her to quit his dominions, *ib.* She takes shelter with the count of Hainault from the feigned anger of her brother, *ib.* The prince of Wales goes to France, and is affianced by his mother to Philippa, second daughter of the count of Hainault, *ib.* Isabella and the prince of Wales land at Orewell, September 24, and are joined by both the king's brothers and most of the barons, 743. The Londoners refuse to follow Edward to the field; the king flies, accompanied only by the two Despensers and the chancellor Baldock, *ib.* The elder Despenser takes refuge in Bristol; he surrenders, is condemned and executed, *ib.* The prince of Wales is declared guardian of the kingdom by a general council of the prelates and barons, September 24, 1325; 744. The king takes ship, but is driven on the coast of South Wales, where, after having spent some time in the woods, Despenser and Baldock being taken, he surrenders up himself, *ib.*; is confined in Kenilworth Castle; his favourite Despenser is executed as a traitor at Hereford, *ib.* A parliament is summoned at Westminster, in the king's name, January 7, 1327, and on the following day it is determined that Edward should be deposed, and the prince of Wales proclaimed king, *ib.* On the 20th of January, 1327, a deputation of all the nobility and the representatives from the counties and boroughs assemble at Kenilworth, when sir William Trussel, as speaker, makes known to Edward that he is no longer king; he resigns his crown, and thanks the parliament for not having overlooked the rights of his son, *ib.* Edward, prince of Wales, is crowned at Westminster under the title of Edward III., 745. Edward is removed to Berkeley Castle, *ib.* In the following September (1327) murdered, and buried in the Abbey of Gloucester, 746. Coins of this reign, 837.

EDWARD III. (January 25, 1327—June 21, 1377,) prince of Wales, son of Edward II. and Isabella, goes over to France and joins his mother, 1325; i. 742. Is affianced to Philippa, second daughter of the count of Hainault, *ib.* Prince Edward, with his mother, lands at Orewell, Sept. 24th, 743. He is declared guardian of the kingdom by a general council of the prelates and barons, Sept. 24th, 1325; 744. A parliament is summoned at Westminster, in the king's name, January 7th, 1327; and on the following day it is determined that Edward II. should be deposed, and the prince of Wales proclaimed king, *ib.* On the 20th of January a deputation of the nation assembled at Kenilworth, and made known to Edward II. that he was no longer king, *ib.* January 24th, Edward III.'s peace is proclaimed, and on the 29th he is crowned at Westminster, 745. A regency is appointed, 745, 748. Edward II. is murdered in Berkeley Castle, September, 1327; 745, 746. The order of Templars abolished, 747. Portrait of Edward III., 748. His great seal, *ib.* The attainders, passed in 1322, against the great earl of Lancaster, are reversed; and the immense estates of the Despensers confiscated, *ib.* Queen Isabella and Mortimer monopolize nearly the whole power of government, 749. The Scots, under the command of the earl of Moray and lord James Douglas invade England, and penetrate into York; Edward collects a large army of 60,000 men, and marches against them, *ib.* They avoid a battle, the English are worn out with delay, *ib.* The Scots return with their plunder, and the

EDWARD III.,—

English forces, having suffered considerably in skirmishing, retire to York, and are disbanded, 750. Philippa, of Hainault, arrives in England, is received in London with great pomp, and on January 24th, 1328, is married to Edward, at York, 751. A peace is concluded with the Scots, and their independence acknowledged ; prince David, the only son of Robert Bruce, is married to the princess Joanna, sister of king Edward, July 22nd; ib. Bruce dies at his little castle of Cardross, June 7th, 1329, ib. Mortimer is created earl of March, the regency is displaced, and the power of Mortimer and the queen increases, ib. Lancaster opposes the unconstitutional impositions of Mortimer, ib. He is joined by the earls of Kent and Norfolk, the young king's uncles, but they soon abandon him, and he is compelled to ask pardon in a humiliating manner, and to pay an immense fine, 752. The earl of Kent is persuaded that his brother Edward II. is still alive, and confined in Corfe Castle ; he forms a plan for his deliverance, but is taken, accused of treason, and executed, ib. Young Edward forms a plan with lord Montacute to assert his authority, ib. Edward the Black prince is born at Woodstock, ib. The young king holds a joust in Cheapside, ib. Mortimer obtains a knowledge of the plan formed by Edward and lord Montacute, and informs the council of it, 754. The governor of Nottingham Castle admits Montacute by a secret subterraneous passage, Mortimer is dragged out of the castle, and committed to safe custody; ib. Edward issues a proclamation, informing his lieges that he had now taken the government into his own hands, and summons a new parliament to meet at Westminster on the 26th November, 1330; ib. Mortimer is condemned by his peers as a traitor, ib., and executed November 29 ; 755. The queen-mother is deprived of her enormous jointure, and shut up in her castle or manor-house at Risings, where she passed the remaining twenty-seven years of her life in obscurity, ib. Edward Baliol invades Scotland, ib.; is crowned at Scone, September 24th, 1332; compelled to fly, Edward assists him, and gains the battle of Halidon Hill, 756. He surrenders to Edward, for his services, all the south of Scotland, and does homage to him for the remainder, ib. Baliol is again expelled from Scotland, ib. (For Edward's expeditions into Scotland, see BALIOL.) Edward lays claim to the French throne in right of his mother, although Philip had reigned more than seven years, and his right had also been confirmed by the peers of France, the assembly of Paris, and the States-general, and Edward himself had twice done him homage for his continental dominions. 757. Philip threatens to fall upon Guienne, if Edward did not immediately banish from England Robert of Artois, 758. Edward sends a commission to the earl of Brabant and others, to demand the French crown as his right, October 7th, 1337; ib. He prepares for the invasion of France, and lands at Antwerp, July 19th, 1338; ib. He grants many commercial privileges to the Flemings and Brabanters, ib. Enters France with 15,000 men, and lays siege to Cambray, September, 1339, ib. Advances to Peronne, but being deserted by his allies, and having spent all his money, he retires to Ghent, ib. Assumes the title of king of France, and quarters the French arms, ib. Returns to England, and, having obtained fresh supplies, sets sail on the 22nd of June, 1340; 759. Gains a splendid naval victory at Sluys, and destroys the French fleet, June 24th, ib. He is joined by all his allies, and advances to the borders of France, with an army of 200,000 men; is again in want of money, and obliged to relinquish his project, after challenging the French king to single combat, ib. He returns

EDWARD III.,—

to England, displaces his ministers, and imprisons three of his judges, ib. The archbishop of Canterbury, who was president of the council of ministers, retires to Canterbury, refuses to appear at the summons of the king, and appeals to the protection of Magna Charta, ib. David, king of Scots, now in his eighteenth year, returns from France, with his queen, and lands at Inverbervie, where he is received with enthusiastic joy, May 14th, 1341, ib. John III., duke of Brittany, dies, and leaves a disputed succession, ib. John de Montfort is supported by the English king, and the people of Brittany; Charles de Blois is supported by Philip VI. of France, ib. Montfort is taken prisoner, ib. His wife heads his party, she is besieged in the castle of Hennebon; the English, under the command of sir Walter Manny, come to her relief, and compel the French to raise the siege, 761. Edward sails to Hennebon with 12,000 men, and performs some exploits there; a truce is concluded, and Edward returns, 1341 ; 762. Philip causes great disgust throughout France, and all the lords of Brittany take up the English cause, on account of the execution of Oliver de Clisson, and twelve other knights, without trial, ib. The earl of Derby gains many victories over the French in Guienne; James Von Artaveldt, governor of Flanders, Edward's old ally, is killed, 763. Edward lands near Cape la Hogue, July, 1346; ib. Takes many towns, burns St. Germain, St. Cloud, and Neuilly, and penetrates to the suburbs of Paris; he crosses the Seine at Poissy, 764; is hard pressed by the French army, commanded in person by Philip; he crosses the Somme at the ford of Blanche-Tague, and defeats sir Godemar du Fay, who defended the opposite bank, with an army of 12,000 men, ib. He takes up a strong position near Crecy, where he awaits the attack of Philip, who commanded a powerful army of eight times his number of men, 765. Disposition of Edward's army before the battle, ib. Description of the battle of Crecy, which was gained August 26th, 1346; 765—767. Death of the king of Bohemia, his crest and motto adopted by Edward the Black prince, 766. Edward returns towards the north, and lays siege to Calais, ib. David invades England with a Scottish army of about 30,000 men ; he takes the castle of Liddel, ib.; the English collect an army in Auckland Park, ib.; a battle is fought at Nevil's Cross, when the English, by means of their 3,000 archers, gain a complete victory, and take the king of Scots prisoner, who, twice wounded, and disdaining to flee or surrender, was forcibly made prisoner by Copland, a gentleman of Northumberland, and conveyed to his tower of Ogle, October 17th, 1346; ib. David is confined in the Tower, ib. Charles de Blois is taken prisoner, June 18th, 1347, whilst besieging Roche-Derrien, by sir Thomas Dagworth, which puts an end to the French interest in Brittany, 768, 769. He is confined in the Tower, 769. Calais surrenders, and at the earnest entreaties of Philippa, the six burgesses are pardoned, 769, 770. Princess Margaret is born at Calais, ib. A truce concluded between England and France; the French attempt to recover Calais; the parliament reluctant to grant the king more supplies, 771. Edward gains a brilliant victory over a large Spanish fleet, within sight of Winchelsea, ib. The plague sweeps off one-half of the whole population of England, 1348 ; ib. Philip dies, and is succeeded by his son John; the truce with France prolonged, ib. Prince Edward again opens the campaign in the south of France, 1355; he plunders and burns many of the richest towns of France, but the king is unsuccessful in his expedition in the north, ib. The Scots enter England, and retake Berwick; Edward returns, and obtains supplies

EDWARD III.,—
from his parliament, November 23rd, 1355; 772. He purchases all Baliol's rights to the Scottish throne; in the January following recovers Berwick, and makes an expedition into Scotland, but is forced to return for want of provisions, the Scots harassing his retiring forces, *ib.* The Black Prince conducts another expedition into France, and penetrates as far as Berri; the great battle of Poictiers is fought, king John and his son Philip are taken prisoners, September 19th, 1356; 772, 773. The prince returns to Bordeaux, with all his prisoners, meeting no opposition, 773; he concludes a truce of two years with the dauphin Charles, who was now lieutenant of France, *ib*; returns to England, and enters London in triumph, with his royal captives, king John and prince Philip, April 24th, 1357; *ib.* The Scots agree to pay 100,000 marks as a ransom for their king, October 3rd, 1357, and in November Bruce returns to Scotland, *ib.* He proposes, in a council held at Scone, 1363, that Lionel, duke of Cambridge, Edward's third son, should be elected king of Scotland in the event of his dying without issue, but this proposal is rejected, 774. On the death of Edward Baliol he forms a secret agreement with Edward, that, in default of the king of Scots and his issue male, the king of England for the time being should succeed to the throne of Scotland, *ib.* The truce with Scotland is prolonged till 1371, in the February of which year Bruce dies, and is succeeded by his nephew, the Stewart of Scotland, who assumes the title of Robert II., 1371; *ib.* Dreadful state of anarchy in France, *ib.* The French people unanimously refuse to ratify the conditions agreed upon between Edward and king John; Edward goes over to France with a great army, 1359, and lays siege to Rheims, but the winter season and the strength of the place baffle his efforts, and he is compelled to raise the siege and retire to Burgundy, 775. The French fleet takes and plunders Winchelsea, Edward marches upon Paris, and on the last day of March, 1360, encamps before that capital; the Dauphin wisely declines a battle, and Edward not being strong enough to besiege Paris, is compelled to retire towards Brittany, for want of provisions, *ib.* He encounters a dreadful tempest of thunder and lightning near Chartres, which acting powerfully on his religious fears he determines to make peace with France, *ib.* The treaty of Bretigny is signed, in which Edward renounces his pretensions to the crown of France, and his claims to Normandy, Anjou, and Maine, but reserves to himself Guienne and Poictou, with the cities of Calais and Guisnes, *ib.* King John is sent to Calais to ratify the treaty, which the two kings mutually swear to observe, October 24th. King John is set at liberty, and Edward returns to England, October 25th, *ib.* The duke of Anjou dishonourably breaks his parole and repairs to Paris; the French king being unable to perform the conditions of the treaty returns to London, hoping to obtain some modifications of its articles; he is kindly received by Edward, but soon after dies at the Savoy Palace, April, 1364; 776. Charles V. succeeds his father in the kingdom of France, *ib.*; Pedro IV., surnamed the Cruel, king of Castile, is expelled from his kingdom, *ib.* The Black Prince and his brother defeat don Enrique, and reinstate Pedro on his throne, April 3rd, 1367; 777. Having contracted heavy debts, and a malady, from which he never recovered, the Black Prince retires to Guienne, *ib.* Don Enrique returns, stabs Pedro, and again takes possession of the throne, *ib.* Charles breaks the treaty of Bretigny, and invades Aquitaine, 1367; *ib.* Edward re-assumes the title of king of France, and sends re-inforcements to the Black Prince in the south, 778. The duke of Lancaster

EDWARD III.,—
lays waste all the north-western provinces, the French being unwilling to risk an engagement, *ib.* Charles regains some towns and castles in the south, *ib.*; the Black Prince prepares to take the field, although in a very bad state of health, and the dukes of Anjou and Berri immediately retreat, *ib.* Limoges is betrayed to the French by the treachery of the bishop and inhabitants, *ib.* The Black Prince retakes Limoges, massacres the inhabitants, and burns the city to the ground, *ib.* This was the last military exploit of this famous warrior, who then returned to England, and soon after died, *ib.* John of Gaunt, duke of Lancaster, who had married Constance, daughter of king Pedro, takes the command in the south, *ib.* Pedro, shortly after his restoration, having been stabbed by his bastard brother, don Enrique, the duke of Lancaster lays claim to the kingdoms of Castile and Leon, in right of his wife, who was the king's eldest daughter, *ib.* Don Enrique is supported by the French king, *ib.* In June, 1372, the Spaniards gain a complete victory over the English fleet near Rochelle, commanded by the earl of Pembroke, the military chest is lost, containing 20,000*l.*, *ib.* The French, under the command of their consummate general, Duguesclin, carefully avoid coming to an engagement, but retake many towns and castles; Thouars surrenders, 779. A truce concluded between England and France, the duke of Lancaster returns, *ib.* By this truce, which lasted till the death of Edward, all that the English king retained of his continental dominions was Bordeaux, Bayonne, and Calais, *ib.*; the Black Prince supports the measures of the Commons, and several of the ministers are removed and imprisoned, *ib.* Unpopular measures of the duke of Lancaster, *ib.* Edward becomes enamoured of Alice Perrers, *ib.* Act passed, forbidding women to be guilty of maintenance, *ib.* The Black Prince dies, June 8th, 1376, and is buried in Canterbury cathedral, *ib.* His son, Prince Richard, is acknowledged by parliament heir to the throne, 780. The duke of Lancaster's influence in parliament; sir Peter de la Mare, speaker of the House of Commons, is arrested; William, of Wickham, bishop of Winchester, is deprived of his temporalities without trial, and dismissed the court, 1376; *ib.* The duke of Lancaster, and lord Percy, marshal of England, support Wycliffe, and threaten violent measures against the bishop of London, which causes a general riot, *ib.*; the Londoners plunder the Savoy Palace, *ib.* A general poll-tax granted by parliament, *ib.* The last public act of Edward was to publish a general amnesty for all minor offences, *ib.* His death, June 21st, 1377; 781. Coins of this reign, 837.

EDWARD IV., (March 4, 1461—April 9, 1483.) Report of sir Edward, earl of March, approaching London, 1452, with a Welsh force, intimidated the queen Margaret's party. His father, Richard, a prisoner, was set free, ii. 90, 94, 95. In 1461, on the fall of Richard, duke of York, at Wakefield, the earl of March succeeded to his father's titles, 96. He increased his forces by his Welsh adherents, and marched against queen Margaret, *ib.* At Mortimer's Cross he routed Jasper, earl of Pembroke, with great slaughter, *ib.* He beheaded Owen Tudor, taken in battle, whose son, Jasper (uncle of Henry VII.), escaped from the field, *ib.* His great general, Warwick, defeated in the first battle of Barnet, 97. Henry VI., forgotten in his tent, released by Margaret, 1461; *ib.* Edward, "late earl of March," denounced as a traitor, *ib.* So many Lancastrians were slain at Mortimer's Cross, that when York effected his junction with Warwick and the earl's broken forces, he was stronger than the Lancastrians, *ib.* The Londoners, and people south of the Trent, exasperated by the devastations com-

EDWARD IV.,—

mitted by Margaret's northern soldiery and the borderers, favour the cause of Edward, ib. London had been threatened by queen Margaret; some of her cavalry plundered its northern suburbs, but are repelled from the gates by the citizens, ib. February 25, 1461, duke Edward was welcomed in London; the men of Kent, Essex, and adjacent districts, flock in to admire this "flower of chivalry," ib. Lord Falconberg, at a review of troops in St. John's-field, and the bishop of Exeter, a brother of Warwick, address the spectators on the just title of Edward, ib. Some of the people shout for king Edward, ib. A council of lords, spiritual and temporal, declare that Henry, by breaking the agreement of 1460, had forfeited his crown, which therefore remained, as his just right, to the heir of York, 98. No parliament was sitting to be referred to, 97. March 4, 1461, Edward rode at the head of an immense procession to Westminster, and in his twenty-first year seated himself on the throne, and was proclaimed in the city, 98. Portrait and great seal of Edward IV., 98, 99. He and Warwick gained the victory at Towton, 1461; 99. At York he removed his father's and brother's heads from the gate of the city, ib. Reaching Newcastle, and confident in the loyalty of his captains, Edward left his army for the south, ib. His coronation at Westminster, ib. His parliament, all Lancastrians being absent, is obedient to him, and he was the idol of the Londoners, ib. His brothers George and Richard, created dukes of Clarence and Gloucester, ib. A Scottish army defeated before Carlisle by Montague, ib. Margaret of Anjou driven back from Durham, ib. Act declaring the three Henrys usurpers, and revoking all grants by them, 100. Bills of attainder passed against king Henry, and all the remaining princes and nobles, his partisans, ib. Edward was enabled by such great forfeitures to reward his brave adherents most royally, ib. The attainders of sir Richard Percy and Somerset reversed by parliament, upon condition of the surrender of Bamborough and Dunstanburgh to Warwick, ib. Queen Margaret visits Burgundy, Brittany, and France; the two first gave her aid in money, ib. Promising Calais to Louis XI., he granted her a considerable sum, and 2,000 men raised by De Brezé, seneschal of Normandy, ib. Some Scottish borderers join her on landing in Northumberland; miserable failure of these ill-assorted allies, ib. They re-embark with great loss; a storm wrecks her fleet, men, money, and stores on the coast, ib. Queen Margaret and De Brezé reach Berwick in a fishing-smack, ib. Alnwick Castle capitulated to Warwick, ib. Alnwick given to sir John Ashley, 1463, ib. Sir Ralph Gray, who expected that castle and honour, from Yorkist became a violent Lancastrian, ib. Lord Montague's victories, 1464, at Hedgley-moor and Hexham, 101. Somerset, De Roos, and Hungerford beheaded, after the latter victory, ib. Henry VI. after a long concealment in the northern wilds, is taken at Waddington Hall, 1465, and lodged in the Tower, ib. King Edward, at this time, appeared firmly seated on the throne, ib. The confiscations accruing from the civil war enrich Edward, 165. His marriage with Elizabeth Woodville, 1464; 101. Coronation of queen Elizabeth at Westminster, 25th May, 1465; 102. Discontent of the Nevils and the nobles, at the rapid advancement of the Grays and Woodvilles, ib. The king sends Warwick to negotiate the marriage of Margaret of York with a son of Louis XI., 1467; 103. The earl honourably entertained in France, returned, followed by French envoys, ib. The hand of Edward's sister was, however, bestowed on Charles, duke of Burgundy, to the great satisfaction of the English, ib. The king's danger in the Yorkshire

EDWARD IV.,—

and Lincolnshire rebellions, 1469, 1470; 104. His fears from the first of these; Warwick coming tardily to his assistance from Calais, ib. King Edward shut up by the earl in Middleham Castle; is restored to the army, which evinced indignation at the outrage on royalty, ib. His victory at Erpingham over the Lincolnshire men, 1470; ib. Warned of danger when at a feast given by George, archbishop of York, at his manor in Hertfordshire; the king quits abruptly, and, riding all night, reached Windsor Castle, ib. Flight of Warwick to France, where he treats with Margaret of Anjou, June 1470, and with Louis XI., 105. Lady Anne Nevil married to Edward, prince of Wales, as a condition of Warwick's supporting the house of Lancaster, ib. A lady, belonging to the duchess of Clarence, was sent over by Edward IV. on a secret mission to the royal duke, 106. Her complete success, evidenced by Clarence's subsequent loyalty to his brother, ib. Warwick's landing in Devonshire, September; the people everywhere joining his standard, king Edward embarked, with three small ships, for Holland, 106, 107. His danger from the Easterlings, merchant-pirates, 107. The lord de la Grutuse protected his landing, furnished clothing, and sent word to Charles the Rash, ib. The queen, her mother Jacquetta, and all her family, took sanctuary, ib. Act of Settlement, and restoration of Henry VI., 107, 108. Assisted by Charles of Burgundy, 16th March, 1471, king Edward landed at Ravenspar, 108. His duplicity; he declared at York that he only sought the recovery of that dukedom, and the estates thereto belonging, ib. Crossing the Trent, and joined by the people, he resumed his royal title, ib. Near Coventry his brother Clarence joined him with colours flying, ib. Edward enthusiastically received in London, ib. Within two days he marched to attack the Lancastrians at Barnet Common, ib. He gained a complete victory; Warwick and Montague among the slain; no quarter given, ib. Edward, Clarence, and Gloucester, 4th May, 1471, gave the Lancastrians a final defeat at Tewksbury, 109. Narrative of the foul murder of the prince of Wales in the king's tent, ib. Henry VI. again in the Tower; his pertinacious queen was at length captured in this great battle, and immured for five years, ib. Somerset and many knights having taken sanctuary at Tewkesbury, Edward, sword in hand, violated that asylum, but for a few days was resisted by a priest bearing the sacrament, ib. Those victims were dragged from the altar and beheaded, 109, 110. Margaret of Anjou was ransomed by Louis XI., 110. Attempt of Thomas Nevil to rescue Henry VI. from the Tower, ib. Edward's triumphant return, 21st May, at the head of his army, to London, ib. On the following morning, Henry VI. was found lifeless in the Tower; a contemporary chronicler says murdered, ib. Fate of the remaining Lancastrian nobles, ib. The king decides the dispute of his brothers respecting the inheritance of the earls of Warwick and Salisbury, 111. He contracts an alliance with Burgundy and Brittany, 1475; ib. He claims the crown of France, ib. Louis XI. bribed the herald, Garter, ib. Edward landed at Calais, with a fine army, 22nd June; his ally, Charles the Rash, having wasted his resources in some expedition, joined the English king with but few men, 112. Jealousy of the Flemish against the English, ib. Edward lay at Peronne inactive, and treated with the French king, who freely bribed the English courtiers, ib. The two kings held an interview on the bridge of Picquigny across the Somme, ib. Description, ib. A treaty, sworn by both monarchs, ib. Edward invited by Louis XI. to Paris; pleasantries, etc., ib. Articles of the treaty; a high ransom for Margaret

EDWARD IV.,—

of Anjou; a large annuity to be paid to Edward IV.; the peace to be for seven years; free-trade, and the dauphin to marry a daughter of Edward IV., so soon as marriageable, 112, 113, 115. Discontent of Gloucester and of the nation, 113. Trade prospered, and England was happy and tranquil, ib. Causes of the quarrel betwixt Clarence and his royal brothers; narrative of his trial, 16th January, 1478, king Edward in person making the accusation in parliament, 114. Condemnation of the duke, and mode of his death, ib. Remorse of Edward; he seeks solace in pleasures, ib. Comines notices the comeliness of the king, but mentions his corpulence, ib. King Edward sent Gloucester, 1480, against the Scots, 114, 115. He treats at Fotheringay, 1482, with Albany, brother of James III., 115. Berwick ceded to the English, ib. Gloucester returned to England, 115, 117. King Edward so greatly incensed at Louis XI. (for the affiancing of Margaret, the infant daughter of Mary of Burgundy, to the dauphin), that vexation aggravated the symptoms of his malady, 116. Death of Edward IV., 9th April, 1483; ib. His tomb in the royal chapel at Windsor, ib. His character, love of the chase, and luxurious pleasures, 114, 116, 121. Illustrations: King Edward and his court, 243. Male costume, ib. Female attire, 244.

EDWARD V. (April 9, 1483—June 25, 1483.) His accession, ii. 116. His portrait, 117. Great seal, ib. His autograph, 130. He was at Ludlow castle with his uncle Rivers, 117. His uncle Gloucester moves towards the south from the Scottish borders with the duke of Buckingham, 117, 118. His apparent loyalty and moderation, ib. He sware fealty to the young king at York, causing the gentry to follow his example, 118. Queen Elizabeth wrote to Rivers to bring Edward V. to London, under an escort of 2,000 horse, ib. Ambition of the queen-mother, ib. Altercations at the council, ib. Hastings and Buckingham violently opposed the queen, ib. The lord-mayor and chief citizens rode to Hornsey-wood, to do reverence to Edward V., 119. His entry in state into London, ib. Was lodged at the bishop's palace, but a council being summoned, was removed, on the motion of Buckingham, for safety to the Tower, ib. His brother Richard sent to him, to the same confinement, 121. Allegation of the illegitimacy of these young princes, 121, 122. Their cruel uncle, with apparent reluctance, assumed the crown, 122. Foul murder of these princes, by their uncle Richard's command, 124, 314. Insurrection on their account, 125, 126. Representation of the mode of their death, the perpetrators being sir James Tyrrel, Dighton, and Forest, 125. Tyrrel, on viewing the bodies, causes them to be buried in the Tower at the stair-foot, under a pile of stones, 125, 314. Tyrrel beheaded, 1504, for aiding the earl of Suffolk, 313, 314.

EDWARD VI. (January 28, 1547—July 6, 1553.) Portrait of, ii. 452. Born October 12, 1537. His education in the reformed religion, his early proficiency in Latin, etc., 453. It is agreed in the Treaty of Greenwich that he shall espouse Mary, queen of Scots, 436. His accession, January 28, 1547; the death of king Henry being some days kept secret, parliament assembled pursuant to adjournment, his first council, 453, 454. Great seal of, 452. Delineation of Edward and his council, 764. Character of the young king, by William Thomas, author of the "Pilgrim," 453, 454. His proclamation, and reception in the Tower by the nobility and council, 454. Of the late king's sixteen executors, the earl of Hertford seeks for chief power during the minority of his nephew Edward, 454, 455. A privy-council appointed; list of the king's guardians and of the council, 454. Creations of nobility

EDWARD VI.,—

in 1547; 456. Coronation of the king, ib. Norfolk and Pole excepted from the general pardon to all state offenders, 457. Edward Seymour, duke of Somerset (earl of Hertford), after opposition by the chancellor Wriothesley, is declared guardian of Edward VI., and protector of the realm, independent of the council, ib. The earnest desire of Henry VIII. that his son Edward should espouse Mary, queen of Scots, is imparted to the Scottish council, which evades the question, 457, 458. Hostilities ensue, and the Scottish ship Lion is captured by sir A. Dudley, 458. Death of Francis I., and fears of the Protestants that Charles V. would obtain therefrom a paramount power detrimental to the reformed religion, ib. Henry II., son of king Francis, forms a close alliance with the Scots and the earl of Arran, ib. Arran, being joined by a French fleet and auxiliary force, reduced the castle of St. Andrew's, ib. The army of Edward VI., under the protector Somerset, entered Scotland, 1547; journal of this invasion by W. Patten, 459 et seq. Battle of Pinkey, at Salt Preston; the Scottish army is routed and the camp plundered, 460—464. The fleet takes the island of Inchcolm, and the town of Kinghorn, and ravages the coast, 464. Leith is fired, ib. Lord Clinton takes Broughty Castle, ib. Hume Castle taken by Somerset, 465. The English army re-crosses the Tweed, ib. Visitors are appointed to inspect the dioceses throughout England; a copy of the Bible in English is ordered to be deposited in every parish church; various other regulations are made, 465, 466. Bonner and Gardiner are committed to the Fleet for objecting to the new injunctions, 466. Parliament assembles, ib. The Act of Henry giving proclamations the force of laws, with many other statutes of the same reign, is repealed, 466, 467. The election of bishops by congé d'élire is abolished; the sacrament is ordered to be administered to the laity; all chantries, colleges, and free chapels are vested in the king, 467. An extreme law is passed for the punishing of vagabonds, and for the relief of poor and impotent persons, 467, 468. The council issues an order prohibiting the carrying of candles on Candlemass-day, of ashes on Ash-Wednesday, or of palms on Palm-Sunday, 468. It is commanded that all images shall be removed from churches and chapels, and that all rich shrines with the plate belonging to them be seized for the use of the king, ib. A new office for the administration of the Lord's Supper is set forth, ib. Cranmer publishes an English catechism, ib. The Act of General Pardon restores Gardiner to liberty; he is brought before the council, and discharged; but soon afterwards committed to the Tower, 468, 469. The queen-dowager of Scotland applies for assistance from France; she offers the infant queen in marriage to the dauphin, 469. Lord Gray of Wilton, enters Scotland with a powerful army; he takes the town of Haddington and fortifies it, and burns Dalkeith and Musselburgh, ib. A squadron, conveying an army of French and Germans, arrives at Leith; the force consists of about 6,000 veterans, under the command of D'Esse D'Espanvilliers; aided by this force, Arran attempts the recovery of Haddington; the convention of estates ratifies the treaty with France, ib. The infant queen goes on board the French fleet at Dunbarton; she is conducted to St. Germain-en-Laye, and contracted to the dauphin of France, then a child of five years of age, she being but a few months older, ib. Haddington remains unreduced; an attempt to relieve it meets with success, but a second attempt, under sir Thomas Palmer, has a different issue, 469, 470. Haddington is relieved by the earl of Shrewsbury, 470. Shrewsbury, with his army, sets

M

EDWARD VI.,—

off to seek the Scots and French; but having come in sight of them, commences a march back to England, firing Dunbar in the retreat, *ib.* Lord Clinton lands at several places, but is repulsed, *ib.* Lord Gray makes an inroad into Scotland, and wastes Teviotdale and Liddesdale for the space of twenty miles, *ib.* D'Esse makes an unsuccessful attempt on Haddington, *ib.* Parliament assembles, *ib.* The plague in London, *ib.* An Act passed, permitting the marriage of the clergy, 471. An Act establishing the use of the Reformed Liturgy, and another touching abstinence from flesh in Lent, etc., passed, *ib.* Quarrel of the earl of Hertford and his younger brother, sir Thomas Seymour, related, 471, 472. Marriage of sir Thomas Seymour with Catherine, the queen-dowager, 473. Charges of the council against him, 473—475. The young king is kept very short of money by the protector, 475. The queen-dowager dies, after giving birth to a daughter, 476. Seymour, the lord-admiral, is committed to the Tower for high treason, 478. Cranmer signs the warrant for the admiral's execution, in opposition to the canon law, 479. The execution, 480. Popular tumult and confusion, 480—488. The rebels besiege Exeter, 483, 484. They are defeated by lord Russel at Fennington-bridge, 485. The lords Russel and Grey raise the siege of Exeter; the rebels of the west are executed, *ib.* Insurrection of Robert Ket, in Norfolk; the Tree of Reformation, 485, 486. The marquess of Northampton marches against Ket; he is driven out of Norwich by the rebels; lord Sheffield is killed; Northampton retreats to London, 487. The earl of Warwick defeats the Norfolk rebels, at Dussingdale; Ket and the principal insurgents are executed, *ib.* Disagreement between the Scots and French, 488. The Scots recover Fortcastle and Broughty-castle, 1549, by force of arms, 489. The English evacuate Haddington, *ib.* Sir W. Paget is sent over to Germany to propose the renewal, with some modifications, of the treaty made with the late king, *ib.* Fall of Somerset occasioned by the earl of Warwick; he is charged with treason, and committed to the Tower, 489—491. Parliament assembled, *ib.* Acts passed for the prevention of unlawful assemblies, against prophecies, and for repealing the law against vagabonds, *ib.* A bill of pains and penalties passes against Somerset; he is fined, and deprived of his offices, *ib.*; released from the Tower; he receives a royal pardon, *ib.* Warwick is made lord high-admiral, and great master of the household, *ib.* Peace concluded between England and France, the principal condition of which was the surrender of Boulogne, *ib.* Joan Boucher is burned in Smithfield, *ib.* Von Paris, a Dutch surgeon, burnt, 493. Obloquy cast on Cranmer by these executions, *ib.* Bonner is consigned to the Marshalsea, *ib.* Ridley is made bishop of London, *ib.* Gardiner, Heath, and Day are deprived, *ib.* John Hooper is nominated bishop of Gloucester, 493; committed to the Fleet, *ib.*; becomes bishop of Worcester, 494. The lady Mary, the heiress presumptive to the throne, objects against further changes in religion, *ib.* When the statute for the uniformity of worship is passed, in 1549, Mary is informed that her chaplains could not be permitted to say mass even in her private chapel, *ib.*; through the interposition of her uncle, the emperor, it was agreed that the law should not be enforced in her case for the present, *ib.* The agitation is renewed; it is rumoured that she designs to quit the kingdom, on which a fleet is sent to prevent her escape, *ib.* She appears personally before the council, *ib.* The emperor threatens to declare war if this indulgence is not granted, *ib.* The chief officers of

EDWARD VI.,—

her household are committed to the Tower, *ib.* The late protector and the earl of Warwick are apparently reconciled, 494, 495. Somerset takes secret measures for recovering his former office, 495. The marquess of Northampton is sent to Paris, to demand for Edward the hand of Henry's eldest daughter Elizabeth, *ib.* The marshal St. André brings Edward the order of St. Michael in return for that of the Garter, which had been sent to Henry, *ib.* The sweating sickness rages in London, *ib.* Somerset is charged with high treason, and committed to the Tower, *ib.* Several other lords are apprehended, *ib.* An indictment is presented and found against Somerset by the grand jury at Guildhall, 496. He is tried by the peers in Westminster-hall, found guilty of felony only against the earl of Warwick (now Northumberland,) but is beheaded on Tower-hill, 496—498. Sir Miles Partridge, sir Ralph Vane, sir Michael Stanhope, and sir Thomas Arundel, are executed as accomplices of the duke, 498. Parliament assembles, *ib.* Acts are passed, 1552, for enforcing the use of the Book of Common Prayer, for amending the law against treason, for the relief of the poor, for legalizing the marriage of priests, and various other purposes, *ib.* Parliament dissolved, *ib.* Parliament assembles, 499. The bishopric of Durham is suppressed and two new dioceses are created in its stead, *ib.* Durham is erected into a county palatine, *ib.* Declining state of the king's health, *ib.* Lord Guildford Dudley is married to the lady Jane Grey, lady Catherine Dudley to the Lord Hastings, and lady Catherine Grey to the lord Herbert, *ib.* Northumberland persuades the king to name the lady Jane Grey his successor, 500. The king orders the crown lawyers to draw up a bill entailing the crown on lady Jane Grey, *ib.*; on their representation that it would subject them to the pains of treason, Edward promises to give them, under the great seal, both a commission to perform the Act, and a pardon for having performed it, *ib.* This instrument is duly signed by the lords of the council, *ib.* Death of king Edward, July 6, 1553; *ib.* His signature, 695. History of religion during this reign, 729—734. Coins of Edward VI., 800. Fac-simile from the journal of this king, 822.

EDWARD ATHELING, son of Edmund Ironside, is sent for by king Edward and the Witan, i. 195. Arrives in London, where he dies, 1063, *ib.*

EDWARD, the Black Prince, eldest son of Edward III., born at Woodstock, June 1330; i. 753. He commands the English army, under Edward III., at the battle of Crecy, August 26, 1346; 765—767. Takes the crest and motto of the king of Bohemia, who was slain in the battle, 768. Prince Edward opens the campaign in the south of France, 1355, and burns many of the finest towns, 771. He makes another expedition into France, and penetrates as far as Berri; the great battle of Poictiers is fought, wherein king John and his son Philip are taken prisoners, September 19, 1356; 772, 773. The prince returns to Bourdeaux with all his prisoners, without meeting any opposition; he concludes a truce of two years with the dauphin Charles, who was now lieutenant of France; returns to England; and enters London in triumph with his royal captives, king John and prince Philip, April 24, 1357; 773. The Black Prince and his brother, the duke of Lancaster, reinstate Peter the Cruel, who had been expelled from his kingdom of Castile, and gain a complete victory over Don Enrique, April 3, 1367; 777. The French king Charles V. invades Aquitaine, and Edward again resumes the title of king of France, 778. The prince receives reinforcements, and again carries on the war in the south of France; the dukes of Anjou

EDWARD, the Black Prince,—
and Berri retreat with precipitation, *ib.* Declining
state of the prince's health; Limoges is betrayed by
its inhabitants to the French; the prince re-takes
Limoges, massacres its inhabitants, and burns the
city to the ground; this was the last military exploit of the Black Prince, who returns to England,
and dies, June 8, 1376, much regretted by the
nation, leaving a son named Richard, who was born
in 1366; *ib.* His burial in Canterbury cathedral,
778, 779. His effigy, 780.
EDWARD, son of Henry VI. and queen Margaret,
1453, created prince of Wales, ii. 92. Escapes with
his mother into Scotland, 95. Act of the Succession,
96. Queen Margaret and prince Edward rescue
Henry VI. in his tent, 1461, on the Lancastrian victory at Barnet, 97. At the chateau of Amboise,
Warwick was reconciled with queen Margaret,
young Edward being present, under the protection
of Louis XI., 1470; 105. This prince then married
the lady Anne, second daughter of the earl, *ib.*, 106;
on Edward IV.'s victory at Tewkesbury, 1471, the
captive prince of Wales was conveyed to the victor's
tent, 109. The prince (in his eighteenth year),
made a manly and direct reply to Edward IV., who
thereupon struck him on the mouth with his gauntlet,
ib. Young Edward was immediately despatched, *ib.*
EDWARD PLANTAGENET, prince of Wales, ii. 127. Act
of Parliament, declaring him heir-apparent to the
crown, *ib.* At eleven years of age his father, Richard III., sought to marry him to the princess Elizabeth, daughter of Edward IV., *ib.* Sudden death of
prince Edward, at Middleham Castle, *ib.*
EDWARDS, Richard, a dramatic writer of the 16th
century, iii. 584.
EDWARDS, Thomas, one of the commission of delegates appointed, 1613, to try the divorce of the earl
of Essex, iii. 53.
EDWARDS, a Turkey merchant, 1652, introduces
coffee into England, iii. 548.
EDWIN, an exile in his youth, is persecuted and pursued by Edilfrid the reigning monarch of Northumbria, i. 234. He repairs to the court of Redwald,
in East-Anglia, who, in fear of Edilfrid's power,
deliberates whether to surrender the fugitive to the
envoys of the Northumbrian, *ib.* Edwin refuses,
though warned of danger, to fly, and sits down at
the palace gate, *ib.* A mysterious agent there visits
him at night, who demands of the deserted prince
whether he would be *guided* at a future day in matters that concerned his welfare, by him who should
secure safety and dominion to him, *ib.* Edwin consents, and "*Paulinus*" placing his hand on the
prince's head, as a token on a future repetition of
imposing his hand, whereby the exile might recognise his now unknown visitant, *ib.* Redwald,
meantime boldly takes arms in Edwin's cause, marches against Edilfrid, who falls in the battle, *ib.* Edwin
becomes king of Northumbria, and after his adversity reigns with consummate wisdom, *ib.* He becomes Bretwalda of the Saxon confederacy, 621,
146, 235. Raises his northern kingdom to a
superiority over the states of the Heptarchy,
146. His queen, Edilberga, a Christian, was daughter of Ethelbert, king of Kent, *ib.* He allows her
the free exercise of the faith in which she had been
reared; Paulinus convoys her to Northumbria, 234.
Edwin is converted by this missionary in an extraordinary manner, 146, 234. Narrative, by the venerable Bede, of the occasion and solemnity of the
token of recognition repeated by Paulinus, and of
the effect on the open-hearted monarch, 235. Great
social improvement of the Northumbrians by their
adoption of the Christian faith, 146. Interesting
details of the assembly of king, nobles, and priests,
to discuss the relative merits of Christianity and the
old Paganism, 627, which council was held at God-

EDWIN.—
mundham, 235. Coifi, high-priest, requests that
Paulinus should give an account of the new faith, *ib.*
The impressiveness of the missionary's discourse
has its immediate effect, *ib.* Coifi is the first to assail
a temple and the chief idol, which are demolished, *ib.*
Great power of king Edwin; he adds the Isles of
Man and Anglesey to his dominions, 146. Keeps
excellent police and order throughout his states, *ib.*
The Scots and Picts acknowledge his supremacy,
ib. The pope, in 625, styled him *rex* Anglorum,
ib. Paulinus, archbishop of York, baptizes 12,000
in one day in the river Swale, 235. On king
Redwald's death, the Northumbrian Edwin is offered
the crown of East-Anglia, but refuses it in favour
of Eorpwald, son of Redwald, *ib.* Confederacy
against him in 633, Penda, Saxon king of Mercia,
and Cadwallader of North Wales, give him battle
on the banks of the Trent, when Edwin, in 634, is
slain, 146, 147, 235. The Welsh and Saxon confederates commit an indiscriminate massacre after their
victory, 147. Christianity suffers on Edwin's fall,
the archbishop Paulinus retires into Kent, and
the Northumbrians become apostate, until the succession of Oswald, 235.
EDWIN, son of Algar, and brother of Morcar, is defeated with Morcar by Hardrada and Tostig, 1066;
i. 208. They are appointed to the command of the
Saxon forces against William, 360. He goes with
Edgar Atheling on a deputation to the Norman, 361.
William promised Edwin, earl of Mercia, one of his
daughters in marriage, but afterwards refuses, and
insults the suitor, on which Edwin and Morcar withdraw to the north, and collect their forces, 368, but
are defeated near where the river Ouse falls into the
Humber, the rest of the army retreat to York, but
are driven from thence, and fly to Scotland, where
they are favourably received, 369. Edwin submits
a second time to the Conqueror, and is restored to
his paternal estates, 375. He hears of William's
intention to seize his person, and attempts to escape
to the Scottish border, but is betrayed and slain,
1073; 376.
EDWY, son of Edmund the Atheling, in 955 ascends
the Anglo-Saxon throne, at fifteen years of age,
i. 171. He grants to his brother Edgar a portion
of his kingdom to govern, on condition of acknowledging Edwy's supremacy, *ib.* Power of Dunstan and the ecclesiastics, *ib.* His marriage with
his kinswoman Elgiva, *ib.* Edwy retires from
a banquet he gave his nobility, along with his queen,
to an inner apartment, being young, and not relish-
ing the deep potations then customary, *ib.* Odo,
archbishop of Canterbury, a Dane, desires the
king's return to the banqueting-hall; Dunstan violently fulfils this behest of the primate, enters the
inner apartment, insults the queen, threatens her
mother, Ethelgiva, with an ignominious death, and
thrusts the king back to the festive hall, *ib.* Dunstan, the abbot, having been treasurer to the late
king Edred, is charged with peculation by Edwy, *ib.*
The king sequestrates the abbot's property, dismisses
him from his places at court, the monks of Glastonbury are expelled, and that abbey is filled with secular clergy, *ib.* Dunstan flies to Ghent, 172. Edwy
continues to substitute married clergy for the
monks under vow of celibacy, in many abbeys, *ib.*
This proceeding alienates from him, Odo of Canterbury, and the stronger party in the religious dissensions of that age, *ib.* The Northumbrians and Mercians, probably urged by the archbishop, himself a
Dane, rise and establish Edgar as independent sovereign of all England north of the Thames, *ib.*
Dunstan triumphantly returns, *ib.* The archbishop's
retainers seize Elgiva, sear her face with hot
irons to destroy her beauty, and she is carried
away a captive to Ireland, *ib.* She escapes thence

EDWY,—
(the scars having become cured or effaced), to rejoin Edwy, *ib.* Is recaptured near Gloucester, and cruelly mutilated, *ib.* Her death, *ib.* Edwy dies of grief in 958, aged nearly nineteen, *ib.* His epithet of Edwy the Fair, *ib.*

EFFINGHAM, Thomas Howard, earl of, 1763; his remarkable speech respecting America, 1775; § i. 210.

EGBERT, son of Alchmund, his claim to the throne of Wessex superior to that of Brihtric or Beorhtric, 795; i. 150. His flight into Mercia to king Offa, *ib.* He resides in the court of Charlemagne, *ib.* In the year 800, on the death of Brihtric by poison, he returns and is made king of Wessex by the thanes and people, *ib.* He defeats the Mercians at Ellandum in Wiltshire, and conquers that territory, *ib.* He places *reguli*, or petty kings, in Kent and East Anglia, and in 825 obliges Eanred, king of the Northumbrians, to do him homage as vassal, 150, 151. Unites the entire heptarchy under his rule as Bretwalda, but is content with the style of king of Wessex, 151. Wales acknowledges its dependence, *ib.* In 832, the Danes land in Sheppey, on the shore of the Thames, and sail again with plunder, 151, 152. They return in 833, give battle to Egbert at Charmouth, in Dorsetshire, and set sail, 152. The Danes form an alliance with the Britons of Cornwall and Devonshire, 834, *ib.* Egbert totally defeats them at Hengsdown-hill, *ib.* His death in 836, *ib.* Buried at Winchester, *ib.* Insecurity of the extensive kingdom he had acquired, evident at his decease, *ib.*

EGBERT, archbishop of York, his "Excerpta," 785—766; i. 266. His valuable library, described by Alcuin, 307.

EGERTON, lord-keeper, supports sir Robert Cecil in proclaiming king James I., March 24, 1603; iii 3. His address, at the head of the late queen's council, to king James, at Theobald's, 5, 463.

EGLANTINE, Fabre d', an orator in the Cordelier Club, 1790; § ii. 484.

EGMONT, count of, minister sent by Philip, prince of Spain, 1554, previously to his nuptials with Mary I., assaulted by a mob, ii. 519.

EGMONT, lord, supposed to have been the author of the "Constitutional Queries," 1751; iv. 562.

EGREMONT, Thomas Percy, lord. *See* Northumberland.

EGREMONT, Charles Wyndham, earl of, 1750; died August, 1763; § i. 27.

ECREMONT, sir John, 1489; joining the northern insurgents, fled to the duchess of Burgundy's court. ii. 296.

EINSIEDEL, general, is forced to abandon Prague, November, 1744; iv. 474.

El Arish, treaty of, concluded between the Turks and French, January 24, 1800; § iii. 555*.

ELCHO, lord, is defeated by Montrose at Tippermuir, 1645, iii. 337.

ELCHO, lord, a follower of the young Pretender, iv. 520. Present at the battle of Culloden, 1746; 538.

ELDON, John Scott, earl of, created, 1821; his eminence in legal learning, § iv. 642.

ELEANOR, daughter and heiress of William, IX. earl of Poictou and duke of Aquitaine, i. 438. She married Louis VII. of France, in 1137; and having gone to the Holy Land with her husband, was accused of immodesty at the court of Antioch, 439. In 1152 a general council of prelates being summoned at Baugenci-sur-Loire, a divorce, which both parties voluntarily agreed to, was permitted by the council, on the plea that they were cousins, and within the prohibited degrees, *ib.* Her marriage with Henry, duke of Normandy, and afterwards Henry II. of England, 439, 440. Henry and his queen crowned at West-

ELEANOR,—
minster, December 19, 1154; 440. Being jealous of her husband, she attempts to escape to the French court, but is seized and kept in confinement till the death of Henry, 468. She was momentarily reconciled with her husband, and released for a short time, 475. On the death of Henry, in 1189, her son Richard appoints her regent of England; her kind and mild government, 482. Richard adds to her estates the lands formerly possessed by Matilda and Alice, on his departure to the Holy Land, 486. She arrives at Brindisi with the young Berengaria, daughter of the king of Navarre, and Richard's intended wife, 493. After delivering the young bride to Richard, she returns to England, 494. Is besieged in the strong tower of Mirebeau by her grandson, prince Arthur, but relieved by king John, who raises the siege and takes Arthur prisoner, 518.

ELEANOR, queen of Edward I., daughter of Alphonso, king of Castile, i. 680; accompanies the prince in his expedition to Palestine; the report of her sucking the poison from his wound stated to be false, 690. Her portrait, 692. Her coronation in Westminster Abbey, 1274; 693.

ELEANOR, second daughter of Henry II., marries Alfonso the Good, king of Castile, i. 480.

Election, subject of, § iv. 631.

Elections, bribery at, iv. 677.

Electricity, experimenters on, iv. 785.

ELFRIC, or Ælfric, archbishop of Canterbury, 995 to 1005. His "Canons" mention seven orders of clergy in the church, i. 244. His Homilies; extract from the preface (Anglo-Saxon of the reign of Canute,) i. 300.

ELFRIDA, daughter of Ordgar, earl of Devonshire, deceived into a marriage with Athelwold, envoy from king Edgar, who had been sent to ascertain if her beauty equalled the report, i. 173. On the king's approach, her husband requests her to conceal as much as possible her charms, *ib.* To this she by no means consents, and Athelwold is shortly after found murdered in a wood, *ib.* Her union with Edgar; in process of time their son Ethelred, an imbecile youth, mounts the throne, *ib.* She resides in Corfe Castle, Dorsetshire, rearing her son Ethelred, then aged six (975); 174, 175. She declares Edward, called the Martyr, by Edgar's first wife, to be illegitimate, and collects a powerful party in favour of her own son, *ib.* She receives (978, 979), king Edward, who in hunting calls unattended at the castle gate, with much show of kindness, 175. Nevertheless, whilst he is drinking a cup of wine in her and Ethelred's presence, Edward receives his death-wound in the back from one of her household, *ib.*

ELGIVA, the beautiful, espoused by king Edwy, shortly after his accession, in 955, their relationship being within the prohibited degrees of kindred, i. 171. Her cruel persecution by archbishop Odo, and Dunstan, abbot of Glastonbury, 171, 172. Her face is seared; and soon afterwards, at about seventeen years of age, she is a second time seized, mangled and hamstrung, in Mercia, by myrmidons of the exasperated archbishop, 172. The king, broken-hearted, dies in the following year, 958; *ib.*

ELIBANK, lord, 1751; iv. 563.

ELIOT, sir Gilbert. *See* Minto.

ELIOT, sir John, one of the managers for the House of Commons in the impeachment of Buckingham, 1626; iii. 120. Is sent to the Tower, 121; liberated, *ib.* Is imprisoned for not contributing to a forced loan, 123. He denounces Arminianism, 141; is summoned before the privy council, 143; fined and imprisoned, 144, 181, 211. He dies a prisoner in the Tower, November 27, 1632; 212.

ELIOT, Thomas, receives the great seal from the lord-

ELIOT, Thomas,—
· keeper Littleton, and takes it to York to the king, 1642; iii. 286.
ELIOTT, general George Augustus, governor of Gibraltar; his brave defence of this important place, 1782; § i. 490, 495.
Elixir of life, a supposed medicament, ii. 208.
Elizabeth Castle, Jersey, view of, § i. 386.
ELIZABETH WOODVILLE, queen of Edward IV., 1464; ii. 101, 102. Soliciting the king for the reversal of the attainder of sir John Gray, her first husband, Edward became enamoured of her, and married her, keeping it secret for some months, 1464; ib. Discontent of Warwick, Clarence, etc., at this unequal marriage, 101. Her coronation at Westminster, 102. Magnificent feasts and tournaments, ib. Her portrait, ib. Elizabeth's relatives, the Grays and Woodvilles, sought titles and high fortune, ib. Her father created earl Rivers, ib. The heiress of the duke of Exeter, whose hand had been sought by Warwick, was conferred upon her eldest son, Thomas Gray, ib. Five of the great nobles or their heirs were induced to marry the queen's five sisters, ib. Consequent unpopularity of Elizabeth, ib. She accompanied the king to Rouen, 1467, where were Louis XI. and Warwick, 103. Joust in Smithfield between her brother, Anthony Woodville, now lord Scales, and the Bastard of Burgundy, ib. Her measures, on the accession of her son Edward V., prompted by fear of Gloucester, 1483; 118. Her grief on hearing of the king falling into the duke's hands, and her brother being sent to Pontefract, 118, 121. She seeks the Sanctuary at Westminster with her younger son Richard, and her daughters, ib. Her interviews with Rotherham, archbishop of York, 119. False charges against the queen's relations, ib. Some of them beheaded, 121. The prelate, commissioned by the protector, persuaded Elizabeth to deliver her young son Richard to him, and she did so by constraint and in tears, 121. Buckingham, her sister's husband, and a strong party, planned the release of her sons, not knowing that they had been smothered, 125, 126. They set up the title of Henry Tudor, earl of Richmond, and should they succeed they proposed he should espouse the princess Elizabeth (which Henry VII. did after gaining the crown), ib. The queen, and all her remaining relatives, joined in this design, 126, 127. Nevertheless this widow, flattered by Richard III., quitted sanctuary, and consented that prince Edward should marry her eldest daughter Elizabeth, 127. Accession of Henry VII., new scope for her ambition, 1485; 261. On her daughter's marriage with Henry, 1486, she is allowed no dower, but lived on a moderate maintenance, 285, 287. Henry VII. and his council imprisoned Elizabeth, from suspicion, 288, 291.
ELIZABETH, daughter of Edward IV., and styled heiress of the house of York, ii. 127. Compact by Yorkist chiefs, 1483, who set up the Lancastrian prince, Henry Tudor, against the usurper Richard III., that Richmond should marry Elizabeth, 125, 127. Her mother, queen Elizabeth, had joined in this plot, 126. The princess and the widowed queen listened to the promises of Richard; quitted sanctuary for the court, and agreed to the nuptials of the heiress of York with Edward prince of Wales, 127. The son of Richard III. dying suddenly at Middleham Castle, in his eleventh year, defeated this union, 1484; ib. King Richard then resolved himself to marry her, and meanwhile she lived entirely at court with Anne, wife of the usurper, 128. Reflections on the disgraceful conduct of the mother and daughter, ib. Richard dissuaded from the plan by Ratcliffe and Catesby, his trusty captains, ib. He confined her at Sheriff-

ELIZABETH,—
Hutton, 281. She is escorted with ceremony, 1485, to London, and lodged with her mother, ib. Although king Henry VII. was jealous as to intrigues with the late usurper, he espoused Elizabeth Plantagenet, 18th January, 1486; 285. He allowed her no influence, and she was queen but in name, ib. She kept her court at Winchester, 287. Gave birth to Arthur, prince of Wales, 287, 289. Elizabeth at length was crowned, November 1487, at Westminster, 291. The queen died in childbed, 1502, soon after the death of her eldest son Arthur, 312. Her portrait, from the tomb in Henry VII.'s Chapel, Westminster, 285.
ELIZABETH (November 17, 1558—March 24, 1603;) the last sovereign of the house of Tudor, born September 7, 1533; ii. 383. On the execution of her mother, queen Anne Boleyn, she was declared to be illegitimate, 395. Her sorrow on the decease of Henry VIII., 454. Immediately upon Wyatt's rebellion, January 1554, the princess Elizabeth, and Courtenay, earl of Devon, were arrested by Mary's command, 515. Southwell, Hastings, and Cornwallis, lords of the council, with an armed force, convey her by easy stages from Ashridge-house, Bucks; Elizabeth pleading severe illness, ib. At Highgate she was met by numerous cavaliers, who dared to show this token of respect, and all the people commiserated her, ib. Strictly examined before the council, she is permitted to return to Ashridge Manor, ib. Upon renewed charges of her being directly concerned both in Wyatt's and Carew's insurrections, she was removed, March 15, to Hampton Court, ib. Gardiner, the chancellor, and many of the council there charged her openly with treason; the princess declared her innocence, ib. The earl of Sussex and another peer arrive to convey her by water to the Tower, ib. Sussex permits her to write to the queen, charging himself with her letter, and a reply if obtainable, 515, 516, 517. Elizabeth's letter here printed, 516. The barge proceeds with the royal prisoner to the Tower, stopping at the "Traitors' Gate," 517. Reluctance of the princess to ascend the stair, on one stone of which she sat down; her reply to the lieutenant of the Tower, etc., ib. Her constant fears of execution renewed, especially on the appointment of sir H. Bedingfield as lieutenant, 517, 519. Mary, having no design against her sister's life, committed her to Bedingfield's vigilant custody, who conveyed his prisoner from the Tower to Woodstock, 519. She is summoned to Hampton Court to congratulate the queen on her supposed approaching delivery, which delicate business she adroitly manages, 524. She professes to Mary to believe the Roman Catholic doctrines, 529. She refuses the marriage offers of the duke of Savoy, and of prince Eric, son of the king of Sweden, ib. Her accession, November 17, 1558, hailed with acclamations in parliament, 539. Proclaimed in front of Westminster Hall, and at the Cross in Cheapside, ib. Public rejoicings, ib. She heard of her sister's death when at Hatfield; gives a gracious reception to some lords of Mary's council who attend her, ib. Appoints sir William Cecil principal secretary of state, ib. November 23, quitting Hatfield, she met the bishops coming to acknowledge their allegiance, ib. She presented to them her hand to kiss, omitting only bishop Bonner, ib. At the foot of Highgate-hill, the lord-mayor and whole estate of London attended to escort her to the city, ib. She dwelt in the Tower until December 5, and then removed to Somerset-house, ib. Argument as to her first intentions with regard to religion, 539, 541. The Catholics had lost much of their influence, ib. Her Great Seal, 540. The queen's Portrait, from a painting by Zucchero, ib. Funeral of Mary in Westminster Abbey, 13th De-

ELIZABETH, queen,—
cember, 541. Grand funeral service for the emperor Charles V., took place also at Westminster, *ib.* Elizabeth's views as to the maintaining of the Catholic religion or advancing the reformed were for but a short time left doubtful, for Christmas day, 1558, she left the chapel after Gospel, whilst the priest was robing for high-mass, *ib.* January 12th she proceeded in a barge to the Tower, and thence, amid a city pageant, to Westminster, *ib.* Delineation of her procession to Hunsdon-house, 542. Her coronation, January 15, 1559, by Oglethorpe, bishop of Carlisle, *ib.* The Catholic interest having taken alarm, no other prelate would perform that ceremony, *ib.* Interesting record by friar Bacon of the queen's reply, on being requested by a courtier, on her inauguration, to release the Evangelists and St. Paul from the bonds of an unknown tongue, *ib.* Elizabeth then authorised reading the Liturgy in English, forbad all preaching at Paul's Cross, and other measures ensued, *ib.* English refugees, for religion's sake, return in numbers, but their tenets were acquired from Zuinglius and Calvin (not Anglican, as established by Edward), 543. She notified her accession to Paul IV., who arrogantly replied she was illegitimate, *ib.* Elizabeth met her parliament, 25th January, which now, aware of her wishes, re-establish religion as it was in her brother's reign, *ib.* Her prejudice against married priests, *ib.* Dishonourable conduct of Elizabeth towards Dr. Story, 544. The Commons address her in regard to her marriage, *ib.* Her brother-in-law, king Philip, offers her his hand, *ib.* Parliament dissolved; the churchmen are advised to conform themselves to the late statutes; the bishops, headed by Heath, refuse, *ib.* Bonner, and all the bishops excepting Kitchen, bishop of Llandaff, refuse the oath of supremacy, 545. Pensions are reserved for those who quit their benefices on account of religion, *ib.* Acts of supremacy and uniformity, *ib.* Form of the oath of supremacy, *ib.; note.* Sir Edward Waldegrave and his lady are sent to the Tower, 1561, for hearing mass, 545. Persecution by the Protestants, 546. Elizabeth orders that images, etc., be destroyed, but that walls and glass windows be preserved, *ib.* Monastic establishments broken up; whole convents of monks and nuns are transferred to the continent, and many of the dispossessed clergy are conveyed to Spain, *ib.* Heath, Bonner, and Tuberville are committed to prison, *ib.* Death of Bonner, 547. England is included in a general treaty, signed at Cateau Cambresis, 1559; *ib.* Mary and her husband quarter the royal arms of England with their own, and assume the style of king and queen of Scotland and England, *ib.* Mary of Guise summons the reformed clergy to meet at Stirling, *ib.* Knox encourages the destruction of all religious houses in Scotland, 548. The Scottish reformers form themselves into a general league, styling themselves the "Congregation of the Lord," *ib.* Henry II. dies, and is succeeded by his eldest son, under the title of Francis II., 549. A French army lands at Leith, *ib.* Sir Ralph Sadler is appointed a privy-councillor, and commissioned to settle matters on the Scottish borders, 550, 551. The queen-regent of Scotland appoints commissioners to meet Sadler, 551. Meeting of the commissioners, 554. The French fortify Leith, 555. They send a great seal into Scotland for Mary, with the arms of France, England and Scotland engraven on it, and this insult Elizabeth never forgave, *ib.* Chatelherault desires the queen-regent to remove the French from Leith; she refuses, 556. The lords of the Congregation, together with Chatelherault, suppress the abbeys of Paisley, Kilwinning, and Dumfermline, *ib.* The lords of the Congregation, with the duke of Chatelherault and his son, the earl of

ELIZABETH, queen,—
Arran, at their head, march upon the capital; the queen retreats to Leith, 557. They call a parliament, and deprive the queen-regent of her authority, *ib.* Lord Bothwell sets upon the laird of Ormeston, who was conveying money from Berwick to Edinburgh, and takes possession of the whole, 558. Knox excites disgust in the English by advocating the Calvinistic discipline, *ib.* Arran besieges Leith; is defeated at Restalrig; evacuates Edinburgh, and flies to Stirling; the queen-regent re-enters Edinburgh, 559. Elizabeth concludes a treaty at Berwick with the lords of the Congregation, to last during the marriage of Mary with the French king, and a year after, *ib.* The French army ravages the county of Fife, *ib.* An English fleet appears in the Firth of Forth; D'Oisel mistakes it for a French fleet, under D'Elbœuf, and wastes his powder in firing a general salute, *ib.* On perceiving his mistake, D'Oisel commences a dangerous retreat; he reaches Edinburgh, where he finds the queen-regent in a dying state, 560. He then throws himself into Leith, which is assailed by land and sea, *ib.* The queen-regent dies in Edinburgh castle, 561. The treaty of Edinburgh; Leith is surrendered by the French, *ib.* A separate treaty is concluded between England and France, recognising the right of Elizabeth to the English crown, and agreeing that Mary shall not use the arms of England, 562. The duke of Finland arrives in England to negotiate a marriage between Elizabeth and his brother Eric, king of Sweden, *ib.* The duke of Holstein to negotiate in the same matter for his uncle, the king of Denmark, *ib.* The Scots proceed to settle their religion, *ib.* They declare the authority of the Roman church an usurpation; pass a declaration, renouncing the tenets of that church, and disowning the authority of the pope, 563. Mary refuses to ratify the treaty of Edinburgh, and denies her assent to the statutes passed against the Romish religion, *ib.* Francis II. of France dies; he is succeeded by his brother Charles IX.; Mary is harshly used, and thereupon retires from court to Rheims, *ib.* Mary requests Elizabeth to grant her a safe conduct to cross the seas into Scotland, and to allow her to pass through England if absolutely necessary; this Elizabeth refuses, *ib.* Mary's spirited reply to sir Nicholas Throgmorton, 564. Elizabeth receives a deputation from the Lords of the Congregation, *ib.* Mary embarks at Calais, arrives at Leith; John Knox undertakes her conversion, 565. Mary removes from Edinburgh to Stirling; she is forced to issue proclamations of banishment against monks and friars, 566. The Presbyterian clergy preach against the mass, dancing, etc., *ib.* The town-council issues a proclamation, banishing priests, monks, etc.; the privy-council, indignant at this assumption of authority, suspends the magistrates, *ib.* Mary attempts to soften the intolerant spirit of Knox, *ib.* The Scottish reformed ministers are ill-paid; lamentations of Knox on this account, 567. The queen's chapel at Edinburgh is broken into, and the altar defiled; two of the rioters are indicted; on this Knox writes circular letters to the faithful, charging them to come up to Edinburgh and protect their persecuted brethren; he is summoned before the privy-council, and acquitted, 568. Mary sends Maitland, of Lethington, to negotiate at the English court; fruitlessness of the mission, *ib.* Elizabeth pays off the crown debts, regulates the coinage, and increases the naval force, *ib.* The lady Catherine Grey marries the earl of Hertford; they are both committed to the Tower; their marriage is declared unlawful, and the fruit of it illegitimate, 569. Arthur and Edmund Pole are brought to trial for high treason; they confess to the indictment, are condemned, but pardoned by the queen, *ib.* Par-

ELIZABETH, queen,—
liament makes enactments against prophecies and prognostications on coats of arms, 570. France the seat of confusion and anarchy, *ib.* The prince, of Condé, chief leader of the Huguenots, applies to Elizabeth for assistance, *ib.* Elizabeth sends an army, under sir Edward Poynings, to take possession of Havre, and to aid the French Protestants; Rouen is taken by the French, *ib.* The king of Navarre is mortally wounded, *ib.* Lord Lisle is restored to the title of earl of Warwick, and sent with a reinforcement to Havre, *ib.* The Huguenots, under Condé and Coligni, are defeated at Dreux; Elizabeth sends further aid, 571. Parliament assembles; the Commons petition the queen to marry; the duke of Wirtemburg offers her his hand, *ib.* A remarkable law is passed, entitled " An Act of Assurance of the Queen's Royal Power over all States and Subjects within her Dominions," *ib.* Statute against conjuration, 572. Parliament is prorogued, *ib.* The duke of Guise is assassinated by Poltrot; a pacification is concluded between the French Protestants and Catholics, *ib.* Warwick receives orders to defend Havre; it is vigorously besieged; a pestilence invades the town; the earl of Warwick is wounded; the town capitulates, 573. Warwick brings the plague into England; it occasions great mortality; London is attacked by pestilence, scarcity of money, and dearth of food, 574. Earthquakes in divers places, *ib.* The peace of Troyes, *ib.* The earl of Arran is found to be mad, and is secured in Edinburgh Castle, *ib.* The queen confers upon the lord James Stuart the earldom of Marr, *ib.* Sir J. Gordon engages in an affray with the lord Ogilvie, *ib.* Mary goes on a royal progress to the north; the Gordons hold out the castle of Inverness against her; an entrance is forced, and the captain of the garrison is put to death, *ib.* It being found that lord Erskine had a legal right to the earldom of Marr, Stuart gives up that claim, and persuades his sister to give the greater earldom of Murray, *ib.* The earl of Huntley, to whom the latter earldom belonged, summons his vassals to defend his title with the sword; a fierce battle is fought at Corrichie; the earl of Murray gains a complete victory, and Huntley is thrown from his horse into a morass, and smothered, 575. Huntley's son is executed, *ib.* The Scots are anxious for the marriage of Mary; difficulty in selecting a proper husband; Elizabeth proposes sir Robert Dudley, *ib.* She creates him earl of Leicester and baron of Denbigh, 576. It is rumoured that this earl had murdered his wife, in the hope of obtaining Elizabeth's hand, *ib.* Mary reverses the attainder of the earl of Lennox, 579. The earl of Leicester and Henry lord Darnley are rivals for Mary's hand, *ib.* The estates of the kingdom recommend Mary's marriage with Darnley, 580. The French and Spanish ambassadors complain that Elizabeth sets a fatal example by countenancing the rebels of the Scottish queen, 582. The Commons petition the queen to marry, 590. Orders are sent to sir Nicholas Throgmorton not to attend at the coronation of James VI., 604. *(For a full account of the Scottish queen, see " Mary, queen of Scots.")* Elizabeth intrigues with the earl of Murray, 612. She offers to Mary to become mediator; Mary accepts the offer, and the famous commission meets at York, *ib.* Proceedings of the commission, 612—616. Maitland, of Lethington, suggests a marriage between Mary and the duke of Norfolk, 614. Elizabeth declares that Mary shall never be restored to the throne of Scotland, if Murray can make good his accusations, *ib.* The earl of Murray produces a silver box full of *original* love-letters from Mary to Bothwell, tending to prove her the murderer of her husband, 615. Elizabeth refuses to admit Mary

ELIZABETH, queen,—
into her presence, though she grants that favour freely to Murray; Mary protests strongly against such proceedings, *ib.* The bishop of Ross presents to Elizabeth a striking defence on the charges against Mary, 616. Elizabeth advises Mary to remain quietly in England, and leave the affairs of Scotland in the hands of those who held them; this Mary naturally refuses to do, *ib.* Elizabeth assures Murray that he may go safely back to Scotland, gives him 5,000*l.*, and publishes a proclamation for him to satisfy jealousies in Scotland, containing everything he could desire; Mary represents the unfairness of these proceedings, 616, 617. Elizabeth sends orders to lord Scrope to remove the captive queen with all haste to Tutbury, 618. Report of sir Nicholas White's observations on Tutbury-castle to Cecil, 618, 619. Elizabeth negotiates with France a marriage between herself and the young duke of Anjou; she writes a history of England and Scotland for the last ten years, to be shown to the French king, 619. Unhappy state of Philip II.'s dominions, 620, 621. The prince of Condé lays a plot for surprising the French king, Charles IX.; Elizabeth sends Condé money and advice, and it is asserted that sir Henry Norris was deeply implicated, 621. Battle of St. Denis, 622; the constable Montmorency is slain in this battle, *ib.* English money sent to the assistance of the Huguenots, *ib.* Sir Henry Norris demands the restitution of Calais; the French chancellor refuses the demand, alleging that by treaty Elizabeth was to forfeit all claim to that town if she committed hostilities upon France; and that Elizabeth had brought herself within the scope of that clause by taking possession of Havre, *ib.* Elizabeth, 1567, dispatches the earl of Sussex on a marriage embassy to Vienna, *ib.* The lady Mary Grey marries Martin Kays, of Kent, serjeant-porter at court; for this Elizabeth confines them in separate prisons, 623. The duke of Norfolk proposes to marry the queen of Scots, 623, 624; the secret is betrayed to Elizabeth by Wood, the agent of Murray, 624. Maitland flies from Edinburgh to the northern mountains, *ib.* Elizabeth severely reprimands the duke of Norfolk; he retires to Kenninghall, 624, 625. Paris, a Frenchman, is executed by Murray, on a charge of having been concerned in the murder of Darnley, 625. Murray forwards all the duke of Norfolk's letters to the English queen, *ib.* Elizabeth invites the duke of Norfolk to court; he obeys the summons, but when he had reached St. Albans, he is arrested by Edward Fitzgarret, and thrown into the Tower, 626. The bishop of Ross is committed to prison, *ib.* Elizabeth permits her subjects to enlist for the service of the French Huguenots, and amongst those who went was Walter Raleigh, *ib.* Battle of Jarnac; the Prince of Condé was taken prisoner, and shot in cold blood by Montesquieu; the Huguenots are again defeated at Moncontour, *ib.* Elizabeth seizes a Spanish squadron of five sail, carrying stores and money for the payment of Philip's army in the Low Countries; the duke of Alva retaliates by seizing the goods and imprisoning the persons of all the English merchants he could find in Flanders, *ib.* The French government remonstrates against the supplies sent to the Huguenots, and seizes the English merchandise in Rouen, 627. The counties of York, Durham, and Northumberland betray symptoms of insurrection, 628. Dr. Nicolas Morton comes from Rome with the title of apostolical penitentiary, *ib.* Mary establishes a correspondence with several noblemen, *ib.* The earl of Northumberland heads an insurrection; the insurgents march to Durham, and celebrate mass in the cathedral; they retreat to Raby Castle, and take Barnard Castle, 629. Mary is hastily removed to

ELIZABETH, queen,—

Coventry, ib. Many of the insurgents seek the protection of the border clans, 630. The earl of Northumberland is betrayed by Hector Græme, of Harlow, and confined in the castle of Lochleven, ib. The earl of Westmoreland, and several others, retire to the Spanish Netherlands, ib. Numerous executions take place; the number of offenders is so great that all the poorer sort are given over to martial law, ib. The countess of Northumberland escapes to the Scottish borders, leaving her children in great poverty, ib. Elizabeth issues a proclamation of pardon, and "a Declaration of the Queen's proceedings since her reign," ib. The earl of Sussex is commanded to arrest a Catholic gentleman named Leonard Dacre; who flies, and raises 3,000 English borderers, but is defeated in a desperate battle, and escapes to Flanders, 631. Hamilton, of Bothwell-Haugh, murders the regent Murray, 631, 632. The duke of Chatelherault with several others assume the government, as Mary's lieutenants, 632. Elizabeth sends two armies into Scotland; their destructive raid, ib. The earl of Lennox is sent down as regent of Scotland, he lays siege to the castles of the earl of Hume; sir William Drury is sent to co-operate with Lennox, who lays waste the vale of the Clyde, and destroys the castles of the duke of Chatelherault, and the houses of all that bear the name of Hamilton, and thus reduces that great family, with nearly the entire clan, to the verge of ruin, ib. Pius V. procures John Felton to affix a bill of excommunication to the gates of the bishop of London's town residence, ib. Felton is executed as a traitor, 633. Conspiracy for seizing Leicester, Cecil, and Bacon; the conspirators are executed, ib. Parliament assembles, ib. Several anti-Catholic bills passed, ib. Persecution of Puritans, 634. Elizabeth's religious principles, ib. She infringes the privileges of Parliament, 635. Subscription to the Thirty-nine Articles is rigorously exacted, ib. It is reported that the hand of the queen of Scots is sought by the duke of Anjou; Elizabeth to prevent this enters into negotiations, pretending to offer herself as a bride, 636. Anjou declines the match for various reasons, and the queen then proposes for his younger brother the duke d'Alençon, 636, 637. The French king had desired that Mary might live with him in France, but this was forgotten in the marriage prospects, 637. One Charles Bailly bringing letters from the duke of Alva to the queen of Scots, is arrested at Dover, ib.; these letters cause fresh suspicions to fall on the duke of Norfolk, and hasten his trial, 638, 639. Popular excitement; general fear of the duke of Alva in England, 639. Alarm excited by a plot for murdering some of the privy-council; Mather and Barney are executed, and Herle, who had disclosed it, receives a pardon, 640. Trial and execution of the duke of Norfolk, 640—644. General cry for Mary's execution, 644. The earl of Northumberland is sold to Elizabeth by Morton, and beheaded at York without trial, 645. Lennox surprises Dunbarton Castle; Hamilton, archbishop of St. Andrews, is hanged at Stirling without trial, ib. The earl of Huntley, lord Claude Hamilton, and Scot of Buccleugh, assemble 500 men, and take possession of Stirling; they are attacked by the earl of Marr, and forced to fly; but one of the Hamiltons shoots the regent Lennox through the head; the lords on this nominate the earl of Marr regent, 645, 646. Treaty with France concluded, 646. Charles IX. offers the hand of his sister to the young king of Navarre, nominal head of the Huguenots; the marriage is celebrated with great pomp at Paris, ib. Coligni, at the earnest invitation of Charles, comes to court; he is wounded by a dependent of the duke of Guise, 646, 647. The massacre of St. Bartholomew's, in which the admiral

ELIZABETH, queen,—

Coligni and 30,000 individuals perish, 647. Elizabeth hardly notices this atrocious deed in her negotiations with France, 648. An outcry is raised in England for the immediate execution of Mary; Elizabeth sends Killegrew down to Edinburgh to persuade the earl of Marr to execute Mary in Scotland, if she should send her there; but this negotiation falls to the ground through the honour of the regent, ib. Morton is chosen regent, the earl of Marr having died at a banquet which Morton had invited him to, ib. Kirkaldy, after a long siege, surrenders Edinburgh Castle; and is barbarously hanged by Morton, 649. Elizabeth sends assistance to the Huguenots, ib. Death of Charles IX., 1574; ib. Henry, duke of Anjou and king of Poland, ascends the French throne with the style of Henry III.; he detects a conspiracy to murder him, in which his brother the duke d'Alençon is deeply implicated; Alençon escapes from court, and levies troops in conjunction with Henry king of Navarre; Elizabeth offers herself as mediator, ib. Henry III. places himself at the head of a Catholic league, ib. The prince of Orange succeeds in establishing the independence of Holland and Zealand, ib. The duke of Alva is recalled and succeeded by Zuniga, commendator of Requesens, ib. The prince of Orange offers the sovereignty of Zealand and Holland to Elizabeth, ib. Requesens dies, and is succeeded by John of Austria, ib. Elizabeth assumes an offensive and defensive alliance with the Orange party; the jewels and plate which had been pledged by Mathias of Austria to the states of Holland, are sent to England, and on this Elizabeth advances 50,000l. for present exigencies, ib. The Dutch are defeated at the battle of Gemblours; Cassimir marches to their assistance with a powerful army, and Anjou follows with 10,000 men, 650. The latter renews his suit to Elizabeth with rare ardour, and gains a great ascendancy over her by means of Simier his envoy, who accuses the earl of Leicester of having privately married the widow of the late earl of Essex; for the first time the favourite finds his mistress implacable, he is severely reprimanded and confined at Greenwich, ib. The duke of Anjou arrives at Greenwich, having travelled thither in disguise; Elizabeth submits the question of marriage to the parliament; they are not unanimous in the approval of it, ib. The states of the Netherlands elect the duke of Anjou their sovereign; he raises the siege of Cambray, puts his troops into winter-quarters, and hurries over to England; the queen tenderly informs him she could never marry, ib. One Stubbs, of Lincoln's-inn, writes a pamphlet charging the queen with degeneracy from her former virtue; he, the publisher, and the printer are condemned to lose their right hands, and to suffer imprisonment, 651. Anjou departs England; the queen attends him as far as Canterbury; he finds the Netherlands in a dangerous condition, and after witnessing the loss of most of his troops flies to France, where he falls sick and dies, June, 1584, ib. Troubles in Ireland; Shane O'Neil is assassinated, and his lands vested in the English crown, 1568. Walter Devereux, earl of Essex, undertakes, 1573, to subdue and colonise the district of Clan-huboy; he dies at Dublin, 1576, ib. Gregory XIII. embarks 600 troops and 3,000 stand of arms to touch at Lisbon and take on board Fitz-Morris, an Irish exile, and then to proceed to Ireland, ib. Stukely, to whom this expedition was entrusted, offers his services to Sebastian, king of Portugal, and instead of going to Ireland proceeds to Africa to fight the Moors, who slew him, Sebastian, and all his host at the battle of Alcazar, ib. Fitz-Morris lands with a few soldiers in Ireland; and in the following year, 1580, an Italian officer, in the pay of the pope, arrives

ELIZABETH, queen,—
with 700 men and some arms and money, but they are assaulted both by sea and land in an unfinished fort, and San Guiseppa, after resisting three days, surrenders; the rights of war are not recognised, and they are all massacred, 651, 652. The earl of Desmond who had lain concealed for three years, is killed, 1583, by one Kelly, of Moriarty, who sends his head to Elizabeth, 652, which is fixed upon London bridge, ib. A convention of the Scottish nobility declare, 1578, that James, who was in his thirteenth year, is of proper age to govern by himself; Morton retires to Lochleven Castle, but three months after contrives to obtain possession of the young king; the earls of Argyle and Athole raise an army to rescue their sovereign, but the English ambassador interferes, and a hollow reconciliation takes place; shortly after Morton poisons the earl of Athole. Esmé Stuart, lord of Aubigny, arrives in Scotland, and, together with James Stuart, second son of lord Ochiltree, becomes a favourite of the young king, 652, 653. James Stuart, now earl of Arran, induces James to proceed against Morton; Elizabeth collects troops on the borders to intimidate the young king, who sends to inquire whether she wishes for peace or war; Elizabeth, on this, abandons her creature to his fate, who dies by the "Maiden,"—an instrument which he himself had introduced, 653. Spain and Rome send money to James, to enable him to assist his mother, ib. The earl of Gowrie invites James to his castle at Ruthven; the unsuspecting king accepts his invitation, and finds himself a close prisoner, 654. The government of the state falls to the earl of Marr and several others; Arran is thrown into prison, and Lennox (Esmé Stuart) flies to France, where he dies, ib. James soon recovers his liberty, resumes the exercise of his authority, and pardons all concerned in the raid of Ruthven, ib. Increase of torture in England, ib. The Penal Code is enacted in all its rigour against the Catholics in England: Arden suffers the death of a traitor; Somerville commits suicide; Campion the jesuit is executed; Philip Howard, earl of Arundel, is thrown into the Tower; the duke of Northumberland destroys himself; and Francis Throckmorton is executed at Tyburn, 654, 655. Parliament assembles, 1584; 655. Severe enactments against Roman Catholics, ib.; Dr. Parry who condemns one of these cruel bills is committed to the Tower; and afterwards executed on a charge of treason, 655, 656. The Catholics draw up a petition vindicating their loyalty, 656. Richard Shelley, who presented it, is committed to prison, and dies in confinement, ib. The Protestant Association is formed, ib. Drake, in the course of three expeditions, without any declaration of war being made with Spain, plunders the Spanish towns of Nombre de Dios and Carthagena, and nearly all the towns on the coast of Chili and Peru, taking an immense number of Spanish ships, ib. The earl of Essex takes the command of the army in the Netherlands, ib. The States, thinking to please Elizabeth, name him governor-general of the Low Countries and declare his authority absolute, ib. Anger of the queen at these proceedings, ib. Incapability of the arrogant earl, ib. Sir Philip Sydney is killed in an attack on Zutphen, ib. Babington's conspiracy, 1586; many of the conspirators are executed, 657; Elizabeth issues a commission to try Mary, 658. Sadler is superseded in the charge of Mary by sir Amyas Pawlet and sir Drew Drury, Puritans and friends of Leicester, ib. Mary's cabinets are broken open, and her papers, money, and jewels taken from her, ib. She is removed to Fotheringay, ib. Elizabeth charges her with being accessory to the Babington conspiracy; this Mary denies, 658, 659. Mary refuses

ELIZABETH, queen,—
to come to her trial, but at last consents, 659, 660. The commissioners assemble in the presence-chamber of Fotheringay Castle, 660; Mary's defence to the charges brought against her, ib. The commissioners adjourn the assembly and appoint it to re-assemble, at the Star-chamber in Westminster, 662. The commissioners assemble, ib.; sentence is pronounced against Mary, ib. On the same day the judges put forth a declaration that the said sentence did not derogate from the title of James king of Scots, who remained in the same right as if it had never been pronounced, ib. The parliament demands the instant execution of the sentence; Elizabeth's reply, 662, 663. Sentence of death is proclaimed, 663. Mary's last letter to Elizabeth, 664. Henri III. sends over Bellièvre as a special ambassador, to intercede for Mary's life, ib. L'Aubespine de Chateau-neuf, the French resident ambassador, is accused of participating in a plot to assassinate the English queen, and his secretary is thrown into prison, 664, 665. Coldness of James to the fate of his mother, 665; he sends Keith, a pensionary of England, to negotiate with the English queen, ib.; her inflexible conduct, 665, 666; she signs the death-warrant, but intimates to Davison that if possible she should desire Mary rather to be privately murdered, 666, 667. The death-warrant is read to Mary, 668. Execution of the queen of Scots, 671. Davison, to whom Elizabeth herself had given the death-warrant, is committed to the Tower, ib. The queen pretends wrath against Burleigh, who retires to his own house, but Davison is made the scapegoat, being condemned to pay a fine of 10,000l., and to be imprisoned during the queen's pleasure, ib. He lived in sickness, poverty, and confinement during the seventeen years to which the remainder of Elizabeth's reign was drawn out, ib. Sir Robert Carey is sent to James to make excuses for Mary's murder, ib.; the Scots are so infuriated that the king has to send troops to protect the messenger, ib. Elizabeth makes a public apology to L'Aubespine for the harsh treatment he had received, and endeavours to disarm the resentment of France, ib. Henri III. (December, 1588), secretly distributes forty-five daggers to as many assassins in the castle of Blois; the duke of Guise, who had been invited as a guest, was murdered at the door of the king's chamber, 672; on the morrow his brother the cardinal was assassinated in the like manner, ib.; the Catholics became more formidable than ever, ib.; the pope launched a sentence of excommunication, ib.; the doctors of the Sorbonne released the subjects from their oath of allegiance, and a few months after, as Henri was laying siege to his own capital, he was assassinated by a jacobin monk, named Jacques Clement, ib. Elizabeth opens negotiations with Spain, ib.; Leicester is recalled from the Netherlands, and the Hollanders set up prince Maurice of Orange in his stead, ib. While the queen continued to negotiate, sir F. Drake, with a fleet of thirty sail, is ordered to destroy all the Spanish ships he could find in their own harbours, which commission he ably executes, ib. Philip makes extensive preparations for the invasion of England; danger being imminent, Elizabeth calls a great council of war; the royal navy at this time only amounted to thirty-six sail, but merchant ships are fitted out by the people and armed for war; lord Howard of Effingham lord admiral; the number of ships collected was 191, of seamen 17,400; the Thames is fortified under the direction of Giambelli, an Italian deserter, and a great camp is formed at Tilbury Fort, 672, 673. Elizabeth reviews the army at Tilbury Fort; her speech, 674. The Armada appears July 20, 1588, drawn up in the form of a crescent, and measuring from horn to horn

N

ELIZABETH, queen,—
seven miles, 675. Description of the battle, 675—678.
Sir William Fitzwilliam, the lord-deputy, butchers
the unfortunate Spaniards shipwrecked on the Irish
coast, 678. The earl of Leicester falls sick, and dies
at Cornbury, Oxon, September 4, 1588; ib. Robert
Devereux, earl of Essex, becomes chief favourite,
ib. Expedition of the English, 1589, to place Don
Antonio on the throne of Portugal, 678, 679. Essex
marries the widow of sir Philip Sydney; he passes
over to France, 1591, with an army of 4,000 men
to assist Henry of Navarre, who on the death of
his predecessor was opposed by the French Catholic
league; he applies to Elizabeth, who sends him
20,000l., and some troops; in 1593, he embraces the
Catholic faith, but gives an enlarged toleration to
the Hugnenots, 678, 679. Persecution of the Catholics in Ireland, 679. A Jew and two Portuguese
are executed, 679, 680. The archduke Albert takes
Calais from Henri IV., 680. A fleet, under the
lord Howard of Effingham, sails for the Spanish
coast, ib. Essex, who commanded the land force,
compels Cadiz to capitulate, ib. The inhabitants pay
12,000 crowns for their lives, but everything they
possess is plundered, ib. Burleigh who had done his
best to undermine Essex, is himself driven from
court, and Essex is made master of the Ordnance, ib.
Philip prepares a new Armada, with the hope of
placing his daughter on the English throne; Elizabeth fits out a counter expedition, which fails, 680,
681. Spain intimates a desire to include England
in a general peace, 681. Henri IV. signs with
Philip the treaty of Vervins, ib. Essex withdraws
from court, ib. Deaths of Burleigh and Philip of
Spain, ib. Execution of Squires, who was accused
of a design to poison the queen, ib. Henri concludes a peace with Spain; he publishes the Edict
of Nantes, 682. Valentine Thomas, who had been
committed to prison for felony, deposes that James VI.
had hired him to assassinate the English queen, ib.
When James came to the English throne he hanged
this miserable man, ib. The earl of Tyrone defeats
sir Henry Bagnall, at Blackwater, ib. Sir John Norris
dies of grief, ib. The earl of Essex leaves for Ireland; he appoints the earl of Southampton general
of the horse; the queen compels him to revoke this
appointment, 683. Essex, distressed for want of
troops, leaves the government of Ireland to the archbishop of Dublin and sir George Carew, and hastens
to London, 684. Elizabeth receives him unkindly
and commits him to free custody, ib. Essex resolves on violent measures, 684—686. He is committed to the Tower, 686. Thomas Lee, a soldier
of fortune, is hanged as a traitor, ib. Trials of the
earls of Essex and Southampton, 686—688. Sentence
of "guilty" is pronounced against both, 688. Essex
is beheaded privately in the Tower, 689. Woodhouse, Cuffe, Merrick, sir C. Danvers, and sir C.
Blount are executed, ib. The Gowrie conspiracy,
690, 691. James sends the earl of Marr and Mr.
Robert Bruce as special ambassadors to London,
691. Their instructions, 692. Cecil intrigues with
the Scottish king, ib. Many grievous monopolies
are revoked, 692, 693. Don Juan D'Aguilar lands
at Kinsale with 4,000 Spanish troops, the lord-lieutenant Mountjoy shuts them up within their lines, 693.
The earl of Tyrone advances to the assistance of his
friends with 6,000 native troops and 400 foreigners,
but is repulsed, and defeated with great loss, ib.
D'Aguilar capitulates on honourable terms and is
allowed to return to Spain, ib. Famine reduces
the Irish to great extremities, and Tyrone, upon
promise of life and lands, surrenders to Mountjoy at
the end of 1602; ib. Elizabeth finds a new favourite in the earl of Clancarty, ib. Beaumont, the
French ambassador, informs his court that Elizabeth sinks rapidly from disease, ib. She is con-

ELIZABETH, queen,—
strained by her council to grant a pardon to the
earl of Tyrone, ib. She is said to have named
James as her successor, 694. This celebrated queen
expired at Richmond palace, at 3 A.M. March 24,
1603; ib.; iii. 2. Immediate measures taken by
her ministers and others for proclaiming James,
king of Scotland, as her successor, 3 et seq. Order
of the late queen's funeral in Westminster Abbey,
which was hastened, as Cecil perceived reluctance
in James to be present thereat, 4. Tomb of, ii. 694.
Her signature, 695. History of religion during this
reign, 737—749. Account of the revenue, 769.
List of monopolies, ib. Gold and silver coins of,
803. Fac-simile of Elizabeth's translation of a
Dialogue in Xenophon, 823.
ELIZABETH, czarina of Russia, 1741—1762. A powerful enemy of Frederick the Great, § i. 20.
ELIZABETH, daughter of James I. The powder-con-
spirators of 1605, designed to proclaim this princess,
in case of the destruction of her brothers, iii. 22, 25;
she is affianced to Frederick V., count Palatine, 52.
Solemnization of the nuptials, their grandness and
expense, ib. The gentlemen of the Middle Temple
and Lincoln's Inn exhibit an entertainment, ib.
Styled Queen of Hearts, on account of her misfortunes, 85.
ELLA, or ÆLLA, and the Saxons, land at Withering
in the isle of Selsey, in 477; i. 142. He subdues
the Regni, disperses the British forces, and founds
the kingdom of the South-Saxons, now Sussex, ib.
Extent of the Saxon acquisitions in the year 500, ib.
He was the first Bretwalda among the Saxon chiefs,
145. His death, about the year 510, ib.
Ellandun, or Elyndome, in Wiltshire, the Mercians
defeated by Egbert at, 800; i. 150.
ELLENBOROUGH, Edward Law, lord, an eminent common-law judge of the nineteenth century, § iv. 547.
His portrait, ib.
Ellesmere, baron. See Viscount T. Brackley.
ELLIS, sir Henry; his introduction to Domesday-book,
quoted, i. 580. His Collection referred to, iii. 4.
ELMHAM, Thomas de, prior of Linton, author of a life
of Henry V., ii. 208.
ELPHINSTONE, Arthur, afterwards lord Balmerino,
joins the standard of the young Pretender, 1745;
iv. 505. Is tried, and executed as a traitor, August
18, 1746; 549, 551.
ELPHINSTONE, William, an eminent merchant of the
fifteenth century, ii. 183.
ELPHINSTONE, bishop, founds the university of Aberdeen, ii. 183.
Eltham palace, open wooden roof of the great hall,
delineation, ii. 225.
ELWES, or Elvis, sir Jervis, made lieutenant of the
Tower, 1613; iii. 53. Is summoned into James
the First's presence, and questioned about the death
of sir T. Overbury; he convinces the king that he
was poisoned, 58.
Ely, fortified camp at, formed by the Saxon chief
Hereward, i. 376, 377, 378.
Ely Place, Holborn, palace of the bishop of Ely, ii. 120.
The protector, Gloucester, requested strawberries
from Ely gardens, of the bishop, 1483, ib.
EMMA, sister of Richard II., duke of Normandy, i.
177. Her nuptials with king Ethelred, 1002, to
whom she bore Edward, Alfred, the lady Goda, and
other children, 180, 181. Notwithstanding subsequent invasions of Normandy by the Saxon monarch,
when at length he is compelled to fly from the
victorious and vindictive Sweyn (1013), the royal
emigrants are hospitably received by Richard II.,
180. That duke rears his sister's sons at his court,
where Edward (afterwards the Confessor) imbibes
that love of Norman society, which clouded his
future reign, 181. Richard sends ambassadors to
Canute to urge the right of the Saxon prince, 1017; ib.

EMMA, sister of Richard II.,—

Emma, the "Flower of Normandy," again secures the hand of a king of all England, marrying Canute the Great, to whom she bore a son, Hardicanute, *ib.* She soon contemns her children by the imbecile Ethelred, and leaves them, ill-provided, in exile, *ib.* After Canute's decease, 1035, she conjointly with earl Godwin governs the south of England, in the protracted absence of Hardicanute, fixing her court chiefly at Winchester, 184. Although Harold Harefoot, another half-brother of Hardicanute, had usurped most of the kingdom, queen Emma raises the country about Winchester against her son Edward, who had landed with a small force, and was on his way to her for aid, *ib.* He retires with difficulty to Normandy, *ib.* Emma's next son, Alfred, is inveigled into England by a treacherous invitation in his mother's name, and perishes by a cruel death at Ely, 184, 185. (*See* ALFRED.) Emma of Normandy had the blame of this atrocity set to her account, and with Godwin and Harold was never forgiven it, 185. Hardicanute, 1040, treated Harold Harefoot's remains with indignity, 186. Godwin pacified the wrathful king, by a magnificent present of a ship, manned and fitted in a gorgeous style, *ib.* But it remained to the last of the half-brothers, Edward the Confessor, to punish his suspected mother, and draw an exemplary vengeance down on the once-powerful Godwin, 188, 190—192. Edward deprives his mother of all dower, and, hurrying to Winchester, seizes her treasure and goods, 188. Queen Emma died at Winchester, 1052, in the tenth year of Edward's reign, *ib.* Traditiona, *ib.*

EMMETT, Robert, son of Dr. Emmett, the court physician of Dublin. An emissary of Bonaparte, he encourages the rabble of Dublin, 1803, to rise and attack the castle; but finding them unruly and turbulent, he retires, § iv. 73—75. He is tried, and executed, 76.

EMMETT, one of the Association of United Irishmen, 1798, and brother of the preceding, banished for treasonable designs against the government, § iii. 532, 533.

EMPSON and Dudley, ministers employed by Henry VII. in extorting moneys from the people, 1503; ii. 313, 314. The modes of their extortions described, *ib.* Their court of commission, *ib.* Their spies, *ib.* They accumulate wealth for themselves, *ib.* Their execution, 1510, on Tower-hill, 320.

Enclosure Act, passed in 1710; iv. 729.

ENGELBERT of Nassau, monument of, assigned to Michel Angelo, iii. 575.

ENGHIEN, Antoine-Henri de Bourbon, duke d', son of the duke de Bourbon, and grandson of the prince of Condé; he was born at Chantilly, August 1772. In 1804, whilst endeavouring to excite disturbances in France against the consular government, he is taken, and shot by order of Bonaparte, in violation of the treaty of Baden, § iv. 109—117.

Engraving, iii. 577, 578; iv. 760, 761; § iii. 749—751; § iv. 717, 718; revival of the art of engraving on wood towards the close of the eighteenth century by Thomas Bewick, § i. 632—634.

ENRIQUE, Don, count of Trastamara, lays claim to the kingdom of Castile, i. 776; is defeated by Edward, the Black Prince, and Pedro the Cruel is restored, 1367; 777. Pedro goes to Guienne, July, 1367, *ib.* Don Enrique gains a victory over him, *ib.* A conference is arranged, in which Pedro is stabbed by his bastard brother, Don Enrique, who again takes possession of the throne, and is supported by the French king, *ib.* John of Gaunt, duke of Lancaster, and brother of the Black Prince, lays claim to the kingdoms of Castile and Leon in right of his wife, 778. The English fleet is defeated by the Spaniards, 1372; *ib.*

ERASMUS, born 1467; died 1536; his visit to England, his observations, etc., ii. 145, 329, 338, 385. His writings, and those of Cardinal Pole, spread their indignant opinion of sir Thomas More's execution throughout Europe, 389. Erasmus attempted to expound the Greek Grammar of Chrysoloras in the public schools at Cambridge; but his lectures were nearly unattended, and a storm of clamour was raised against him. His New Testament was actually proscribed by the authorities of the university, and a severe fine was denounced against any member who should be detected having the book in his possession, 816.

ERASTUS, a German divine of the sixteenth century, and founder of the sect of Erastians, iii. 493.

ERATOSTHENES, Ireland unknown to, i. 14.

ERCENWINE, in 527 to 529, lands to the north of the real estuary of the Thames, possesses himself of the flats on the eastern shore, and, extending his advantages into the country, founds the kingdom of the East-Saxons, or Essex, i. 142.

ERESBY, sir Antony, a parliamentarian, 1642; iii. 277.

ERIC, son of Hengist, establishes the Kentish, or first Saxon kingdom, in England, about 470; i. 142.

ERIL, Melzi d', appointed by Bonaparte vice-president of the Cisalpine Republic, January, 1802; § iv. 5.

Erin, properly Eire, pronounced Iar, signifies the land of the extreme west, i. 16.

ERIZZO, Venetian ambassador at Paris, 1696; iv. 69.

Erpingham, Rutland, 1470, the formidable army of Lincolnshire insurgents totally defeated by Edward IV. in person, ii. 104. The king sends the leaders to the block, 105.

ERPINGHAM, sir Thomas, his gallantry at Agincourt in command of the archers, 1415; ii. 32.

ERROL, earl of, a popish lord, lenity of James VI. to, iii. 444, 452.

ERROL, earl of, a Jacobite, 1707; iv. 206.

ERSKINE, Rev. Ebenezer, founded the Associate Presbytery, in the early part of the eighteenth century, iv. 649.

ERSKINE, sir Henry, represents the want of a militia in Scotland, 1760; iv. 613.

ERSKINE, John, the laird of Dun, 1571; iii. 436, 454.

ESCALONA, duke of, lord chamberlain to Philip V., king of Spain, his dispute with the cardinal Alberoni, iv. 342. He is banished, 343.

ESCOIQUIZ, the canon, § iv. 308. At Bayonne, in 1808, Napoleon addressed his conversation relative to the royal family of Spain to this canon, who with Pedro Cevallos were Ferdinand's ministers, 309. Eloquent arguments adduced by Escoiquiz, in reply to the emperor, 309—311.

ESPAÑA, Don Carlos de, a brave Spanish commander, he faithfully commanded the army under his care, and fought at the battles of Vittoria and the Pyrenees, 1813; § iv. 570, 576—583.

ESPEC, Walter, present at the battle of Northallerton, 1138; i. 424.

Essays, periodical, revival of, *regno* George III. § i. 611—616.

ESSE, d', D'Espanviliers, commander of the foreign auxiliaries, 1548, sent to Leith by Henri II., joined the earl of Arran in a protracted siege of Haddington, which was relieved by the earl of Shrewsbury with a strong army, ii. 469, 470. The allies posted at Musselburgh declined battle, which the English offered, 470. Shrewsbury, burning Dunbar, retired to England, on which D'Esse, a brave general, nearly took Haddington by surprise, prevented only by a French deserter firing a cannon at the gate the French were entering, *ib.* D'Esse fortified himself in Leith, *ib.* The Scots complain generally against the insolence of D'Esse and his soldiers, 488. Serious fray between some of his men and the citizens of Edinburgh, *ib.* He is recalled, *ib.* the command

Esse, d', D'Espanviliers,—
of the French forces in Scotland being given to Marshal Termes, 489.

Essex House, from Hollar's view of London, 1647; ii. 685.

Essex; about 527 the Saxons land on the low grounds, and soon found the kingdom of the East-Saxons, i. 142: Hasting, and a great force of Danish invaders, occupy Essex, 163. His entrenched camp at South Showbury, 163, 164.

Essex, Arthur Capel, earl of, created 1661. Lord-lieutenant of Ireland, 1672. He gives up his office of lord treasurer, 1679; iii. 731. He takes part in the Rye-house plot, 740. Is seized and lodged in the Tower, 746. Reported to have committed suicide, 1683; but there is a doubt whether he did not fall either by the hand of the king or duke of York, 747.

Essex, Henry de, hereditary standard-bearer; he accompanied king Henry in his expedition into Wales in 1157; and at the dreadful slaughter near Coleshill Forest, threw down the banner and fled. Six years after this he is accused by Robert de Montfort of treason; he appeals to arms, and is vanquished: however the king remits the consequent punishment of death, and appoints him to be a shorn monk in Reading Abbey, i. 443.

Essex, Henry Bourchier, earl of. His service, 1513, in Henry VIII.'s campaign in France, ii. 323. Friar Elstow's reply to the earl, 1533; 382. He died in 1539.

Essex, Robert Devereux, earl of. Commands the troops in the expedition, 1596, to the Spanish coast, Howard of Effingham being admiral, and the earl having a council of Raleigh, Carew, and others, on account of his youth. ii. 680. The admiral takes or burns a considerable fleet in the harbour of Cadiz, after a severe fight, ib. Essex lands, exacts a ransom for the lives of the citizens, besides vast plunder of property and merchandise, ib. He desires to remain in Cadiz and the Isla de Leon, with his army, but is overruled by his council, ib. He destroys both fortifications and city, the armament returning with triumph to England, ib. The Cecils intrigue against the favourite; Raleigh claims the merit of the success at Cadiz, ib. The young commander of the troops retaliates, by a declaration that he would have intercepted the treasure-ships at Terceira, but that the ministry had thwarted his project, ib. Burghley fell into disgrace with the queen for some time, and Essex triumphs at court, ib. Of an open character, he comes to settled terms of amity with the Cecils, ib. Indignant at his enemy Cobham being appointed warden of the Cinque Ports, and not Sir Philip Sidney; the queen pacifies him by making him master of the Ordnance, ib. Entrusted, 1597, with the command of an armament against Spain, Philip II. again preparing a great invasion of England; the earl is driven back by a tempest, 681. He sets sail once more, makes some valuable prizes, takes Fayal, Flores, and other islands of the Azores, which the English could not retain, ib. He is very ill-received by Elizabeth, dissatisfied by his small success, ib. He then secludes himself at Wanstead, but the queen relenting in the earl's absence, creates Essex Earl-Marshal, ib. Occasion of Elizabeth giving him a box on the ear in anger, 1598: he impetuously clapped his hand to his sword-hilt, swearing through resentment, and secluded himself at his house at Wanstead, ib. He accepts the government of Ireland, but reluctantly, being warned of the sinister designs of his enemies at court, 683. Having made his friend Southampton general of the horse, he is commanded to revoke that earl's appointment, ib. Receives other rebukes from the jealous temper of his sovereign, ib.

Essex, Robert Devereux, earl of.—
His army, few in number, and left purposely ill-appointed and inefficient, he complains to ministers, and receives some reinforcements, ib. Essex then, 1599, September, marches into Louth, where he meets Tyrone and all his forces, 683, 684. No battle ensued, but a personal conference of the two chiefs is followed by an armistice, 684. Receiving further reproofs in the despatches, he commits his government to the archbishop of Dublin and sir George Carew, and speeds without permission to court. ib. He hastens to Elizabeth's chamber, kneels before her, and entertained hopes of having regained favour, ib. Later in the day the queen exhibited much anger of reproof, and to sir John Harrington she declared her deep resentment against her former favourite, ib. The earl, in free custody, is called before the council, and spoke with discretion and calmness, ib. He consults the great sir F. Bacon. Remarkable reply of that lawyer of talent, ib. His countess and physician are not permitted to visit Essex, ib. His despondency; his desire for rural retirement from public affairs, ib. After eight months' durance he obtains liberty, May 1600, but not to appear at court, ib. A renewal of his monopoly of sweet wines is refused, ib. Sarcasm by Elizabeth on this head, ib. Rendered desperate, under ill counsels of his secretary Cuffe, the earl is persuaded to endeavour the forcible removal of sir R. Cecil, ib. Many lords and gentlemen join him in Essex-house, in the Strand, (see delineation of it,) 685. Egerton, lord-keeper, the chief-justice Popham, and others, repair to the earl's house to demand the cause of so menacing an assemblage, 685. Essex alleges a plot of Cobham, Raleigh, etc., against his life, ib. The lords from court advise him to submit his grievance to Elizabeth, who would redress the same with justice, ib. On a clamour in Essex-house that the earl was in danger in this conference, Essex bolts those great lords in an inner apartment as prisoners, but for their safety, ib. He then, followed by noble friends and armed adherents, rushes with his sword drawn into the city, ib. Despite his great popularity with the Londoners, not any of them answered to his appeal for taking up arms for "the queen," and to save his life from his enemies, 685, 686. He next attempts to retire homeward, but is opposed by a party stationed by the bishop of London, 686. A skirmish ensued, ib. Essex escapes by boat to his house, which he fortified; Egerton, Worcester, Popham, etc., having been set at liberty before his return, ib. He is therein besieged by a large force, with artillery planted opposite, ib. He surrenders to the lord-admiral, and Essex and Southampton committed to the Tower, ib. February 19, 1601, they are tried by twenty-five of their peers, Buckhurst, lord-steward on the trial; lords Cobham, Grey, and others, he had already termed his enemies, being of the number of his judges, ib. Essex demands if he might challenge those peers, and the chief-justice gives an adverse reply, ib. The indictment supported by Yelverton, Coke, and Francis Bacon, ib. Essex declares that he had simply acted in self-defence, and desired to remove the queen's evil advisers, naming Raleigh and Cobham, ib. Cobham himself, and subsequently Coke, replies to this allegation as to personal enemies, 687. Firmness and talent of Southampton in his defence, and reply by Coke, ib. Essex replies with acerbity to sir F. Bacon, alleging that lawyer's duplicity as to sir R. Cecil, the minister, and Cecil was himself declared to have spoken favourably of the Infanta's title to the succession, in conversation with sir Wm. Knollys, 687, 688. Cecil, who had been concealed in court, rose and demanded to vindicate himself, ib.

Essex, Robert Devereux, earl of,—
Essex defends his conduct in religion, 688. The peers take the opinion of the chief-justice and chief-baron on the guilt of treason, as far as supported by the evidence, ib. Verdict of guilty against both earls, ib. Essex implores for the life of Southampton, (which was subsequently spared,) ib. He refuses to ask the queen's mercy, but is fully prepared for death, ib. Account of his ample confession; said to implicate James VI., ib. Story of the ring, and of Elizabeth's hesitation, considered, ib. His execution, February 25, 1601, aged thirty-three, 689. Reasons for its privacy, the Tower being kept close, ib. His character, by Camden, ib. His great literary talent acknowledged by Bacon, ib. Execution of sir C. Blount, who had married Essex's mother, the widow of the favourite Leicester, ib.

Essex, Robert Devereux, earl of, son of the preceding earl, restored 1603. He is married to the lady Frances Howard, iii. 52. Her vicious conduct; she procures a divorce from him, 1613; 53. Essex is made lord-chamberlain, 1641; 247. The king, a few days after his departure from Whitehall, 1642, lays his commands upon him to attend at Hampton Court: 286. Essex excuses himself, by saying that by the king's own writ he was obliged to assist in parliament; in consequence of this the king demands his staff of office, ib. On ill terms with Cromwell, 319. Medal struck in honour of, 515. He died in 1646.

Essex, Thomas Cromwell, earl of, minister of Henry VIII., beheaded August 1540. See Cromwell.

Essex, Walter Devereux, earl of. created 1571; raised a small army, 1573, to subdue and colonise Claneboy, in Ireland. ii. 651. He fought gallantly, but for want of support failed in the enterprise, ib. He died poor, 1576, in Dublin, ib. His widow became the third wife of the earl of Leicester, 651, note.

Essex, William Parr, earl of, created 1543. See Northampton.

Essex, countess of. See lady Frances Howard.

Estaples, peace of, 1492, between Henry VII. and Charles VIII., ii. 299. Renewed by Louis XII. 311.

Ethelbald, son of Ethelwulf, conspires, about 855, against that monarch, i. 158. His jealousy excited as to his youngest brother Alfred, and other causes of the rebellion against his absent father, ib. The old king, being repugnant to an odious war, resigns the fairest portion of Wessex to Ethelbald, ib. In 857 the latter succeeds Ethelwulf, ib. He marries his father's queen, Judith of France, ib. Supposition, that on account of that princess's very tender age, Ethelwulf had only raised her to his throne, but never consummated the marriage, ib. He dies in 859, and the brief sway he held in Wessex was supposed to be a just vengeance for this incest, ib. See Judith.

Ethelbert, king of Kent, i. 145. As descendant of Hengist, he contests the dignity of Bretwalda with Ceawlin, but does not acquire it until 593; after the death of that king of Wessex, he espoused Bertha, sister or daughter of Charibert, king of Paris, to whom he granted the free exercise of her religion, she being a Christian, 145, 231. King Ethelbert and his courtiers are converted by Augustine, and other monks, sent by Gregory the Great, ib. His baptism; the pagan temples converted into churches, 203, 232. His code of laws (written) ib. Account of some other codes (of the Burgundians and of the Longobardi) which, at a later period, were introduced into England, 145. His long and prosperous reign; his death in 616; ib. Account of his young widow, ib. (See Eadbald.) Historical painting by Tresham, 231.

Ethelbert, successor of his brother Ethelbald, i. 158. The Danes overrun all England, burn Winchester, and form the Isle of Thanet into a permanent establishment, as the Saxons had also originally done, ib. Dying in 866, or 867, he is succeeded by his next brother, Ethelred, ib.

Ethelfleda, daughter of Alfred, espouses Ethelred, ealderman of Mercia, and, becoming a widow in 912, she wisely rules over that state, i. 162, 168. She expels the Danes from Derby and Leicester, 168. She marches into Breccanmere (Brecknock), and captures the Welsh king's wife, ib. Her praise by Ingulf, ib. Decease of the lady Ethelfleda in 920; ib.

Ethelnoth, archbishop of Canterbury, his conduct at the coronation of Harold Harefoot, i. 185.

Ethelred I., son of king Ethelwulf, in 867, succeeds his brother Ethelbert, i. 153. He is compelled to give battle on constantly recurring occasions to the Danes, with various results, ib. The Mercians and Northumbrians, etc., desert his camp, leaving the Wessex-men to contest singlehanded, 154. Nine yarls or earls and a Danish king, with vast hosts, perish by the sword, but fresh armaments of northmen land on the coasts throughout the reign of Ethelred, ib. Prince Alfred in most of these battles accompanies his brother to the field, ib. Alfred bears the brunt of the Danish attack at Aston or Ashenden, until Ethelred arrives with his division, having been detained at mass, ib.; Ethelred, in 871, dies of wounds, and Alfred mounts the throne, ib. Ethelred, long harassed by the barbarous sea-kings, leaves but the semblance of regal power, and a precarious authority to Alfred, the last of the sons of Ethelwulf, ib.

Ethelred II. surnamed the Unready, son of king Edgar by Elfrida, his second wife, i. 173. By her influence with Alfred, ruler of Mercia, and many nobles, she being daughter of the powerful earl Ordgar, she claims the crown for Ethelred (975), in opposition to Edward, elder half-brother, of Ethelred, but unsuccessfully, as Edward, called the Martyr, is maintained on the throne by the power of Dunstan, 174. Elfrida causes Edward to be murdered in her presence and Ethelred's, at Corfe Castle, 175. Her son, but ten years of age, had no participation in this guilt, and is crowned by the primate Dunstan, 979, ib. Reluctance of Dunstan on this occasion, 175, 176. The pusillanimity of the youthful monarch offers a hope to the Danish princes to renew with success, after a long cessation, their invasions of England, 176. Sweyn leads the first fleets to explore the condition of the coasts, ib. The Danes, (981,) plunder Southampton, and carry its people into slavery, ib. Chester and London are taken, and the western coasts, to the Land's End, everywhere assailed, ib. Ethelred having banished Alfric, son of Alfere of Mercia, is constrained to call that earl home, ib. The sea-kings, 991, ravage the country about Ipswich and Maldon, gain a victory, in which earl Brithnoth, of Danish descent, but loyal to the Anglo-Saxon monarchy, is slain, ib. Ethelred purchases their departure, ib. He mans and equips a fleet in the Thames, ib. Earl Alfric, entrusted with the command, traitorously deserts on the eve of a naval action, carrying many ships with him to the Danes, ib. Ethelred puts out the eyes of Elfgar, son of the powerful traitor, ib. Bamborough Castle, 993, stormed by a Danish host, ib. The populations of the Danelagh and Northumbria remain neutral, or frequently join the new horde of invaders, 980—1000, ib. The king often recurs to payments of gold and silver to Danes and Norwegians, who sail home, but only for short seasons, 176, 177. The ruinous impost of Danegeld becomes permanent, 177. Ethelred threatening to invade Normandy, the pope mediates, and Ethelred,

ETHELRED II.,—
being a widower, 1002, espouses the sister of Richard II., Emma, styled the " Flower of Normandy," *ib.* In the year of these nuptials, the domiciled Danes are massacred, on the festival of St. Brice, *ib.* Fresh invasions by the powerful king of Denmark, 1003—1006 ; 178. Richard II. of Normandy, notwithstanding Emma's marriage, maltreats the English in his dominions, *ib.* King Ethelred sends troops into Normandy, who are defeated, *ib.* The English king, by means of new burthens, builds a powerful fleet, 1008 ; but this last hope is frustrated by shipwreck, and the fleet burned by the traitor Wulfnoth, 178, 179. Martyrdom of archbishop Alphege, 179. At length Sweyn conquers the kingdom, and is acknowledged by all as king, 1013. He dies suddenly at Gainsborough, 179, 180. Ethelred, Emma, and their sons are hospitably received by Richard II. duke of Normandy, 180. His return is called for by his people, 1013, *ib.* The war is fiercely waged by Canute, and Ethelred dying, 1016, is succeeded by his natural son Edmund, surnamed Ironside, *ib.*

ETHELRED, a noble, espousing Ethelfleda, the daughter of Alfred, is created by the monarch earl or ealderman of the Mercians, i. 162. He leads the citizens of London against the Danes in Essex, Alfred being engaged in the west, 163. He besieges and takes Benfleet, a fortified post, with gold, silver, horses, etc. for booty, *ib.* He there makes captives, the wife and two sons of Hastings the invader, and presents them in London to the king, on his return, *ib.* His death in 912, when his widow, the high-spirited Ethelfleda, governs the Mercians, 168.

ETHELWALD, son of Ethelbald, the brother of King Alfred, disputes the throne of Wessex with his cousin Edward, in 901; i. 168. He retires from Wimburn into the Danelagh, north of Humber, where he is chosen king by the Danes, *ib.* His fierce wars with Edward, son of Alfred, who overthrows him in 905, *ib.* Ethelwald is slain, and the Danes conclude peace with Wessex, *ib.*

ETHELWOLD, abbot of Abingdon, his translation of the rule of St. Benedict, from Latin into Saxon, a contemporary manuscript of which is preserved in the Cotton collection, Tiberius, A. III. i. 301.

ETHELWULF, in 836, succeeding his father Egbert, resigns his former government of Kent to Athelstane, i. 152. Mercia rebels against this new king of Wessex, *ib.* The Scandinavian pirates plunder the coasts of Wessex and Kent, and pillage Canterbury, Rochester, and London, *ib.* Ethelwulf, in 851, assembles a congress of his thanes and bishops, *ib.* Success of their measures, *ib.* Barhulf, king of Mercia slain, *ib.* Ethelwulf, his son Ethelbald, and the army of Wessex, defeat the Danes at Okeley in Surrey, with greater slaughter than had hitherto been inflicted on them, *ib.* The Danes also defeated by the subregulus of Kent, Athelstane, at Sandwich, *ib.*, and by Ceorl, and the men of Devon, at Wenbury ; so that England was for some time cleared of the marauders, *ib.* This king said to have punished the Welsh for their inroads, *ib.* Leaving his kingdom in a state of peace, in 853, the king visits Rome, and resides there a year, *ib.* In 854, he espouses Judith, daughter of Charles the Bald, in the cathedral of Rheims, *ib.* His affection for his youngest son Alfred, who, accompanying Ethelwulf to Rome, was anointed (in prospect of his future fortunes) by the pope, 153. The eldest surviving son, Ethelbald, joins some powerful nobles and prelates in a plot to dethrone the absent king, *ib.* The discontent consisted in his having seated Judith by his side as queen, contrary to the law made on the expulsion of the wicked Eadburgha, *ib.* Also, the anointing of Alfred at Rome, *ib.* Osburgha, the former wife

ETHELWULF,—
of Ethelwulf, supposed to have been alive at this period, *ib.* Not desirous of a civil war, he resigns the west and richer portion of Wessex to Ethelbald, *ib.* In 857 (*anno regni* 21), the old king dies, and is succeeded by his sons in priority of birth, until, in 871, the crown devolves on the great Alfred, 153, 154.

ETHERIDGE, a dramatic writer (17th century), iv. 788.

Eton College, views of, ii. 196.

Etymologies, and derivations of names of places, etc., having some local interest worthy of remembrance, i. 11, 16, 17, 19, 61, 77, 92, 99, 138, 142, 144.

Eu, William, count of, a relation of William Rufus, joins in the conspiracy which was formed in 1095 for placing Stephen, count of Aumale, on the throne ; he challenges his accuser, is vanquished, and has his eyes torn out, i. 400.

Eucharist, the, as defined by the Bloody Statute, 1539, ii. 410.

EUCLID, first English translation of, published in 1573, professedly by the famous John Dee, but generally believed to have been the performance of sir Henry Billingsley, iv. 766.

EUDES, of Champaign, grants of king William to, he marries a half-sister of the Conqueror, i. 374.

EUGÈNE, prince, checks the approach of Marshal Catinat, 1691, who had advanced within three leagues of Turin, iv. 33. Threatens Lyons, 37. Defeats the Turks at the battle of Zenta, 1697 ; 77. Gains several advantages over Catinat and Villeroy, 129. Becomes the confidant of Marlborough, 164. Engages the duke of Vendôme at Cassano, 179. Wounded at the battle of Malplaquet, 1709; 236. Visits England, 262.

EUGENIUS IV., pope (Gabriel Condulmier, cardinal bishop of Sienna), elected March 1431. Arranges a grand European congress, which assembled at Arras, 1435. Died February, 1447; ii. 78.

EUSTACE, count of Boulogne, marries Goda, sister of Edward the Confessor, i. 189. His character, *ib.* His visit, 1051, to his brother-in-law; observing Normans to be in so great favour at Edward's court, he learned to contemn the Saxon subjects, *ib.* Returning homeward, he puts on his coat of mail, exchanges his palfrey for his war-charger when within a mile from Dover, *ib.* He rides into the town, with his retinue in armour also, and they select the best houses for the night, *ib.* One of his men wounds a citizen, who was forbidding him to cross his threshold, and the Frenchman is slain, *ib.* Eustace leads his knights to the townsman's house, which is forced, and the master of it murdered at his hearth, *ib.* The count and his Frenchmen gallop through the town with drawn swords, doing much injury, 189, 190. The burghers, after a fierce conflict, slaying nineteen of the foreigners and wounding more, drive back count Eustace and the rest, who are not permitted to embark, 190. The count repairs to Edward at Gloucester, who promises him ample redress against the burghers of Dover, *ib.* Edward gives orders to Godwin to punish the men of Dover with military execution, which the great earl refuses, *ib.* (*See* Godwin.) William I., being in Normandy, 1067—1068, the insurgents of Kent invited Eustace to their assistance, who, landing at Dover, a bold attack on the castle was repulsed, 365. Eustace re-embarked, but most of his soldiery were destroyed, *ib.* Takes part with Robert, and is besieged by William in the castle of Rochester, 395.

EUSTACE, prince, eldest son of Stephen. His father having been taken prisoner and confined in Bristol castle, his uncle Henry desires Matilda to put him in possession of his patrimonial estates, who insultingly refusing, Henry deserts her cause, i. 431. He leaves his father and goes into Cambridgeshire to

EUSTACE, prince,—
  get up a war on his own account, but is seized with
  a frenzy, of which he dies, 1152; 437.
Eutaw, battle of, fought September 8th, 1781; § i.
  467—469.
EVELYN, sir Ralph, 1645; iii. 323, 431, 704.
Evesham, view of the ruins of the monastery of, i.
  686. Battle of, fought between prince Edward and
  the great earl of Leicester, August 4th, 1265, in
  which the latter is killed, ib.
Evora, battle of, 1663; iii. 706.
EVRE, sir Ralph, 1543, ravaged the Scottish borders;
  destroyed, in 1544, the abbey of Melrose, but was
  totally defeated at Ancrum Moor and slain, ii. 441.
EWART, a distinguished preacher, suspended and im-
  prisoned, 1617; iii. 66.
EWER, colonel, made governor of the Isle of Wight,
  1648, on the recall of Hammond, iii. 386.
Exchange, the, built by sir Thomas Gresham, 1566;
  ii. 787. View of the, 788.
Excise scheme, the, 1733; iv. 407.
Exe, river, a Danish fleet destroyed by Alfred's ships
  off its mouth, 876-7; i. 157.
Exeter, city of. In 876-7, Guthrun the Dane is
  blockaded therein and capitulates, marching off to
  Mercia, whence he re-issues next year in force, i.157.
  The citizens agree to pay tribute to William I., but
  refuse to be his vassals, 351. William refuses these
  terms, the city is besieged for eighteen days, but at
  length capitulates and receives a Norman garrison,
  366. View of the city, iii. 782.
EXETER, Gertrude, marchioness of, imprisoned 1539,
  but pardoned by Henry VIII., ii. 408.
EXETER, Henry Courtney, marquess of, grandson of
  Edward IV., created 1525; arraigned with lord
  Montacute, brother of cardinal Pole, and their estates
  confiscated; in 1539 they were beheaded, ii.
  408, 505. His son Edward Courtney, long a prisoner in the Tower, was liberated by Mary I.
  on her securing the throne. (See Courtney), 505,
  510, note.
EXETER, Henry Holland, duke of, 1446, escapes with
  Somerset from Towton, 1461; ii. 99. Was left for
  dead on the field of Tewkesbury, 1471, being found
  living by his men, they conveyed him to sanctuary
  at Westminster, 109, note. In a few months, his body
  was discovered on the sea, near Dover, ib., 110.
EXETER, John Holland, duke of. See earl of Huntingdon.
EXETER, John Holland, duke of, invents the instrument of torture called the rack, regno Henry VI.,
  iii. 519.
EXETER, Thomas Beaufort, duke of, 1421, governor
  of Paris, ii. 49, 88. He died 1426.
EYNSFORD, William de, excommunicated by Becket,
  i. 448.
EYRE, Mr. Justice, 1690; iv. 22.
FABRICIUS, Philip, member of the council of Bohemia, 1618; iii. 30.
FABYAN, Robert, his "Concordance of Histories," ii.
  209.
FAGEL, the Dutch minister; in 1686, he refuses to
  seize English rebels who might have taken refuge in
  the United Provinces, as James II. demanded, iii. 771.
FAGG, sir John, 1675; iii. 839.
FAIRFAX, Edward, an eminent translator of ancient
  poetry at the commencement of the 17th century,
  iii. 602.
FAIRFAX, sir Thomas, a distinguished commander,
  and leading character in the civil wars which distracted England in the 17th century, iii. 322, 332,
  note, 366, 370, et seq.
FAIRLY, bishop of Lismore or Argyle, deposed about
  1600; iii. 484.
FAITHORNE, William, an eminent engraver of the 17th
  century. He died in 1691; iii. 884. His portrait
  of Milton, 871.

Falaise, castle of, prince Arthur confined here, i. 518.
FALCONBERG, lord, at a review in St. John's field,
  London, 1461, with George bishop of Exeter, a
  brother of Warwick, addressed the numerous spec-
  tators, proposing duke Edward for their king, which
  was consented to, ii. 97.
FALCONBERG, sir John, 1405; ii. 17.
FALCONBRIDGE, lord, 1405, beheaded at Durham, ii. 17.
FALCONER, sir James, 1704; iv. 162.
FALCONER, William, an English poet and writer on
  naval affairs, author of "The Shipwreck," published
  1762. Was born about 1730, and lost at sea about
  1769; § i. 608.
FALKES, John, accused of heresy about 1498; ii. 700.
Falkirk, first battle of, July 22, 1298; i. 718; second
  battle, Jan. 17, 1746; iv. 522—524. View of
  Falkirk, 525.
FALKLAND, lord, his house at Tew frequented by J.
  Hampden, iii. 178. Mortally wounded at the battle
  of Newbury, Sept. 20, 1643; 308.
Falkland Islands, dispute concerning the, between
  England and Spain, 1770; § i. 102, 110, 111.
FALMOUTH, Charles Berkely, earl of, created 1664.
  Is killed in battle, 1665; iii. 695.
FANELLI, Francesco, a sculptor in metal of the 17th
  century, iii. 576.
Faneuil Hall, Boston, view of, § i. 76.
FANSHAWE, sir Richard, a poetical translator of the
  17th century, iii. 602.
FARMER, Antony, 1687. iii. 786.
FARNESE, Alexander, prince of Parma, 1579; ii. 650,
  651.
Farnley Wood, insurrection at, 1663; iii. 693.
FARRANT, Richard, gentleman of the chapel to
  Edward VI. iii. 562.
FARRINGDON, Hugh, abbot of Reading, hanged and
  quartered with two of his monks near their abbey,
  1539; ii. 412.
FASTOLFE, sir John, a brave captain serving, 1422, in
  France, ii. 54. He commands in the transport of
  a great convoy from Paris to Orleans, 61. His
  passage opposed by an army of French and their
  brave auxiliaries the Scots, ib. Fastolfe gains the
  victory; John Stewart, constable of Scotland, and
  his son William, fighting side by side on foot, fall
  in this battle, ib. Called the battle of Herrings,
  being Lent, much of that fish was in the convoy, ib.
  The English captain arrived triumphantly before
  Orleans, ib. Charles VII. sick at heart on hearing
  of this catastrophe, ib. Exasperation of the brave
  Joan of Arc on hearing that Fastolfe was convoying
  more stores and provisions to Orleans, 66. After
  the raising of the siege, he effected a junction with
  Talbot; they were defeated by Alençon and the
  Maid: Talbot, Hungerford, and Scales, prisoners,
  68. Fastolfe at first disgraced for retreating, excul-
  pated himself successfully, ib. He leaves his estate
  of Caister to the Paston family. It is, however,
  claimed by the duke of Norfolk; legal proceedings
  in consequence of this claim, 276.
Fasts, observance of Lent, fish days. Statute of
  Edw. VI., 1549, against the late total neglect of
  fast days. Regulations, ii. 471.
Fatimites, their splendid library, consisting of 100,000
  manuscripts, i. 603.
FAVRAS, marquess de, trial and execution of, by the
  French revolutionists, 1789, § ii. 439.
FAWKES, Guy or Guido, a soldier of fortune in the
  Low Countries, of good family, accompanied Thomas Winter to London, being yet ignorant of the
  Gunpowder Plot, 1605; iii. 21. He described all
  his partners in guilt as having been of good family,
  22. He boldly guards the cellar occupied for the
  powder, 23, 26, 27. Sent to Flanders to see William
  Stanley. He being in Spain, Fawkes communicates
  with Captain Owen, 23. Suffolk, lord-chamberlain,
  and Mounteagle inspect the cellar, speak to Fawkes,

FAWKES, Guy,—
and *seem* to depart unsuspicious, 27. This bold traitor is surprised by sir T. Knevett and soldiers, at two in the morning, Nov. 5, looking out of the door he had unbarred, *ib*. His examinations, 22, 27, 29. His reply to king James, 27. Is severely tortured in the Tower, 29. His hand-writing, *ib*. Jan. 31, 1606, is executed near St. Paul's, 30.

FAY, sir Godemar du, a great Norman baron, endeavours to prevent the passage of Edward III.'s army across the Somme, at the ford of Blanchetaque, 1346; i. 764.

FEATHERSTONE, William, gives himself out (1555) to be Edward VI. He is seized, and committed to the Marshalsea as a lunatic, ii. 522. Is afterwards whipped through Westminster and banished into the north, *ib*. Still spreading abroad that Edward was alive, he is again apprehended and executed at Tyburn, *ib*.

Fel Ynis, a name of Britain, mentioned in the Welsh Triads, i. 8.

FELTON, John, a gentleman of property, executed as a traitor, Aug. 8, 1570, for affixing a bull of excommunication to the gates of the bishop of London's town residence, ii. 632, 633.

FELTON, John, stabs the marquis of Buckingham, Aug. 23, 1628; iii. 136. Hanged at Tyburn, 188.

FENWICK, sir John, iv. 68, seized as a participator in the Invasion Plot, June 1696; 74. His confession, 74, 75. Bill of attainder passed against him, 76. He is beheaded on Tower-hill, Jan. 28, 1697, *ib*.

FERDINAND II. Emperor of Germany, his death, 1637. Succeeded by Ferdinand III.; iii. 174.

FERDINAND II. (the Catholic), king of Spain, 1474–1516, and Isabella of Castile, ii. 310. Their fourth daughter, Catherine, married to Arthur prince of Wales, 312. Afterwards, by the pope's dispensation, to his brother (Henry VIII.), 312, 317. Death of Queen Isabella, 314. Their daughter, wife of Philip of Austria, inherited Castile, and with Philip, called, in her right, king of Castile, visited Henry VII. at Windsor, *ib*. On Philip's death, king Henry VII. proposed to espouse her, which (as she was insane for the loss of her husband) Ferdinand, her father, peremptorily refused, 314, 315. His daughter Catherine crowned at Westminster with Henry VIII., 1509; 318. He enticed Henry, full of military ambition, into a war against Louis XII., 320. Paralysed the efforts of Dorset against Guienne, by insisting upon a prior attack on Navarre, 321. He conquered Navarre from d'Albret, *ib*. Concluded a peace with Louis XII. which recognised his acquisition of Navarre, and thus seceded from his league with England, 323. His death, 1516. Succeeded in the Spanish monarchy by Charles V. (who was Charles I. of Spain), 336.

FERDINAND VI. king of Spain. Ascended the throne 1751, died 1759 of hypochondria, iv. 553; § i. 10.

FERDINAND VII. king of Spain, (1806–1834.) Disputes with his father, Charles IV. § iv. 303–305. He is proclaimed king on the abdication of the latter, March 19, 1808; 306. Ferdinand's election is declared illegal, and contrary to the will of Charles IV., who resigns his crown into the hands of Napoleon, 313. Napoleon appoints his brother Joseph king of Spain and the Indies, July 7, 1808; 314. Wars in Spain, 315 *et seq*. After a captivity of five years and a half in France, Bonaparte makes overtures for the restoration of Ferdinand, 602°—604°. He is liberated, and returns to Spain, 605°. Agrees to permit the French marshal Suchet to retire without opposition, *ib*.; The Cortes refuse these conditions, and refer the case to lord Wellington, who commands that the French should not be permitted to quit Spain except as prisoners of war, 606°. Ferdinand takes the

FERDINAND VII.,—
government of Spain into his own hands and imprisons some of the members of the Cortes, 625°.

FERDINAND IV., king of Naples, succeeded, 1759. Being deprived of his continental possessions, he retires to Sicily, under British protection. Events in Sicily, 1806—1813. Establishment of a Sicilian constitution by lord W. Bentinck, § iv. 518—525.

FERGUSON, Dr. Adam, refused a passport by Washington, 1778; § i. 357.

FERGUSON, James, the great philosopher, was the son of a day-labourer, and learned the elements of science whilst employed as a farmer's boy. He died in 1776; iv. 785.

FERGUSON, a Presbyterian preacher, fled with the earl of Shaftesbury to Holland; but, after his death, he returns privately to Scotland, where, fearing lest he should be tortured, he hides himself in a prison, 1685; iii. 756. He gives information respecting Fraser's plot, 1703; iv. 156.

FERGUSON, colonel, a royalist American officer, defeated and slain, 1780; § i. 427.

FERQUHARD, earl of Strathearn, attempts to seize Malcolm IV., 1159; i. 543.

FERRAND, earl of Flanders, refuses to follow Philip in his expedition to England, 1213, and withdraws his forces. Philip besieges Gheat. Ferrand, supported by the English fleet, (which burns the French fleet at Damme,) compels Philip to retire, i. 525, 526. He enters the confederacy against France, 1214, is taken prisoner at the battle of Bouvines, 526.

FERRAR, Robert, bishop of St. David's, appointed 1548; is committed to prison by queen Mary, 1554; ii. 509; and burned in his own diocese, March 30, 1555; 523.

FERRARS, George, M.P., arrested for debt while in attendance on the House, 1543. From this case originated that rule of Parliament which exempts members to this day from arrest, iv. 665, 666.

FERRERS, earl, revolts against Henry II., 1174; i. 470.

FERRERS, lord, slain, 1485, on the side of Richard III., at Bosworth, ii. 129. His attainder (*i. e.*, for his lands,) 284.

FERROUR, John, his letter to James I., 1603; iii. 2., *note*.

Festino, s, § i. 643.

Festoons, iv. 746.

Feudal system, institution and form of, i. 563, *et seq*.

Feudal tenure, i. 254. Parliamentary inquiry, 1604, into its incidents, etc., particularly the royal wardships therefrom resulting, iii. 19.

FEUILLADE, duke de la, invests Turin, 1706, but is driven by prince Eugene to the borders of Dauphigné, iv. 185.

FEVERSHAM, Lewis de Duras, earl of, throws a detachment of troops into Bridport, 1685; iii. 772, 779, 781. He died 1709.

FIELD, Dr., bishop of Llandaff, impeached, 1621, for bribery in the Chancery Court, iii. 82.

FIELDING, Henry, a novelist, eminently distinguished for humour and knowledge of the world, born April 22, 1707; died at Lisbon, October 8, 1754; § i. 605.

FIENNES, colonel John, 1645; iii. 336, 423.

FIENNES, Nathaniel, 1641; iii. 249, 265, 305.

FILMER, Henry, burnt, 1543; ii. 728.

FINCH, sir Heneage. *See* Nottingham.

FINCH, sir John, speaker of the House of Commons, 1626; iii. 132; created baron Finch, of Fordwich, April, 1640; made lord-keeper, 210. His speech at the opening of the long parliament, 226, *note*. He is proceeded against by the House of Commons, 231. He petitions to be heard for himself at the bar of their House, *ib*. His ingenious speech, *ib*.; is voted a traitor, and his impeachment carried up to the Lords, *ib*. He flies to Holland, *ib*. He died 1660.

Fines, Statute of, 4 Henry VII., ii. 751.

FINNIT, sir John, 1617; iii. 64.

Fire-arms, manufacture of, § iii. 685; § iv. 690.

FIREBRACE, sir Basil, receives a bribe of 40,000l., 1695, from the East India Company, iv. 52.

FIRMIN, Mr. Thomas, his proposals for employing the poor, 1678; iii. 910.

FISH, Simon, author of "The Supplication of Beggars," first printed in 1524; ii. 717.

FISHER, bishop of Rochester, appointed 1504. His cook, R. Rose, attempted to poison the bishop, 1530; sixteen of the household died thereby, though Dr. Fisher escaped the poison, ii. 378, note. The cook was boiled in a cauldron in Smithfield, ib. This good and learned prelate was recommended by the countess of Richmond to her grandson, Henry VIII., for his counsellor, and the young king was highly friendly to him, 385. He was charged, 1534, as was likewise sir Thomas More, with having heard the Maid of Kent's prophecy of the king's death, ib. The bishop defended himself on this charge, yet was condemned for misprision by the peers, and compounded with the crown, ib. This preliminary prosecution was designed to terrify Fisher into an approval of Henry's recent conduct; but as he justified himself therein, he was, in a fortnight, called to answer a more fatal persecution, ib. The bishop, as well as sir Thomas More, consented to take the oath of allegiance to the offspring of queen Anne Boleyn, to the exclusion of the princess Mary, but not to the doctrinal points involved in the oath, ib. They were condemned for misprision of treason, to pass the residue of their lives in the Tower, and their property was forfeit, ib. This prelate, aged seventy-six, experienced great severities, ib. He was next tried, 1535, for declaring that the king in spiritual matters could not be the head of the church, 386. A cardinal's hat arriving for him from Rome, Henry said he would take care that he had not a head on which to wear it, ib. He was beheaded, 1535, his head stuck up on London-bridge, his body buried at Barking, ib. Reflections, ib. On the execution of More, the body of Fisher was brought to the Tower, where they were placed in one grave, 389, note.

FISHER, captain, concerned in a plot for assassinating William III., iv. 65; discloses the affair to lord Portland, Feb. 11, 1696; 66.

Fisheries, most productive upon the coast of the British islands, iii. 528. Northern fisheries, 535. Fisheries (eighteenth century), § i. 558—560, 568; § iii. 639—642.

Fishing at an early period after the conquest was a source of considerable riches, i. 599, 600. Importance of both salt-water and river fish in Lent, etc., 1419—1453; ii. 191.

FITZALAN, Thomas, son of Robert, earl of Arundel, archbishop of Canterbury; his return from exile, with Bolingbroke. His persecution of the Lollards, 1413; 25, 26. Cites Oldcastle to his court, ib. Dies 1414; succeeded by archbishop Chicheleley, 26; 140.

FITZ-ERNEST, Robert, slain in attempting to seize the English standard at the battle of Hastings, i. 215.

FITZGERALD, Lord Edward, son of the duke of Leinster, becomes a leader of the Irish revolutionists, 1796; § iii. 503. His marriage with Pamela, natural daughter of Philippe Égalité, duke of Orleans, and Madame de Genlis, 529. His embassy to France, 1798, to procure a body of troops to assist the insurrection in Ireland, 531. He is apprehended by the government, May 19th, and, after a vain struggle with the officers, receives a wound of which he died, June 5, 1798; 533.

FITZ-HAMON, Robert, 1100, a baron supporting Henry I., i. 409.

FITZHERBERT, Anthony, a distinguished lawyer of

FITZHERBERT, Anthony,—the 16th century, author of the Grand Abridgment, and Natura Brevium, ii. 768.

FITZHERBERT, Mrs., her connexion with the prince of Wales (George IV.), 1786; § ii. 204, 219.

FITZ-JOHN, Eustace, slain in Henry the Second's invasion of Wales, i. 443.

FITZMORRIS, 1579, ii. 651.

FITZNICHOLAS, Ralph, his mission from king John, 1209, to the Emir al Nassir, i. 522. Abbot of St. Alban's, 523.

FITZ-OSBERT, William, commonly called Longbeard. He undertakes to lay the complaints of the people before Richard I., i. 512. His harangues at St. Paul's-cross. Is hanged at Smithfield, 1196, ib.

FITZ-OSBORN, Emma. See Roger, earl of Hereford.

FITZ-RALPH, Richard, archbishop of Armagh, 1357, ii. 196.

FITZ-ROBERT, William, only son of duke Robert and of Sibylla; when only five years old he falls into the hands of Henry (Robert, his father, being taken prisoner), who commits him to the charge of Helie de St. Saen, a Norman noble, i. 412. Not relying on the fidelity of Helie, Henry endeavours to surprise his castle and take possession of the young prince, but Helie flies with his young charge, and they are favourably received and entertained at the neighbouring courts, ib. William Fitz-Robert gains many friends, Louis engages to grant him the investiture of Normandy, and Fulk, earl of Anjou, to give him his daughter Sibylla in marriage, ib. General league formed against Henry in favour of Fitz-Robert, ib. Henry attacked at every point along the frontiers of Normandy, ib. After two years Henry puts an end to the war by a skilful treaty, the marriage between William and Sibylla is broken off, and his interests overlooked, ib. His cause again taken up, but relinquished, 413, 416. Louis gives his queen's sister in marriage to William, and with her, as a portion, the countries of Pontoise, Chaumont, and the Vexin, and soon after confers on him the earldom of Flanders, 417. Fitz-Robert dies, 27th of July, 1128, of a wound received under the walls of Alost, ib.

FITZ-STEPHEN, William, his description of London and its commerce in 1174, i. 589. Quoted, 642, 668.

FITZ-STEPHEN, captain of the "Blanche-Nef," in which prince William and his sister perished (1120), i. 414, 415.

FITZURSE, Reginald, one of the four knights who murdered à Becket; he gave the first stroke, i. 455, 456.

FITZWALTER, Robert, appointed by the barons in 1215, to be their general, i. 528. Excommunicated by the pope, 531.

FITZWATER, lord (John Ratcliffe), 1494, a partisan of Perkin Warbeck, pardoned, but imprisoned in Calais, ii. 300. Corrupting his keepers, he was beheaded, ib.

FITZWILLIAM, sir William, mentioned, in a letter, that Elizabeth, December, 1558, after her sister's funeral, declined to hear mass on Christmas day, ii. 541. Lord deputy-lieutenant of Ireland, he sends his marshal to massacre the Spanish sailors, who had been shipwrecked on the Irish coast after the destruction of the Armada, 678.

Five-mile Act, the, passed October 1665, iii. 696.

FLAMSTEED, John, appointed astronomer-royal, 1676. He died, 1719; iv. 782.

FLANDERS, Baldwin, grand-forester of the Ardennes, became first earl of Flanders by carrying off the young princess Judith (previously wife of Ethelwulf, king of Wessex), and marrying her, about 860; i. 153. Their son, the second earl, married Elfrida, daughter of Alfred the Great, ib. Gracious reception, 1051, of earl Godwin, by Baldwin, earl of Flanders, 191.

FLANDERS, Baldwin, earl of, assists William Fitz-Robert, i. 412. Dies of a wound received at the siege of Eu (1118), 413.

FLANDERS, Guy, count of, concludes a treaty of marriage between his daughter and Edward I., 1294. Philip le Bel jealous of any close union between England and Flanders sends him and his wife prisoners to the Tower in the Louvre, i. 790. By the remonstrances of a papal legate he is liberated, on condition of Philippa being given into his custody, ib. The count enters into a league with the English king. Edward, 1298, wishing to return home, makes peace with Philip, and leaves Guy to his fate. Brave conduct of the Flemings; they successfully contend with the French king, 723. Guy dies, and is succeeded by his son Robert, 724. A peace is concluded with France, ib. Robert is set at liberty, and enters on the possession of Flanders, ib.

FLANDERS, Philip, earl of, assists prince Henry against his father, 1173; i. 468.

FLANDERS, Robert, earl of, 1082 to 1085, engages to join Canute his son-in-law with six hundred ships, for the invasion of England, i. 386.

Flannels, manufacture of, § iii. 705.

FLATMAN, Thomas, a painter and poet of the 17th century, iii. 883.

FLAXMAN, John, an eminent sculptor, born 1755, died 1826; § iii. 746—749.

FLEETWOOD, sir William, 1625; iii. 117.

FLEETWOOD, William, bishop of St. Asaph, elected May, 1708. Author of a preface to a small volume of sermons; it is declared seditious and condemned to be burned by the hands of the common hangman, 1712; iv. 267. Translated to Ely, 1714. He died 1723.

FLEMING, sir William, iii. 263. He attempts to corrupt the earls of Leven and Calendar, 1645; 340.

FLEMING, a Scottish pirate, gives information of the approach of the Spanish Armada, ii. 675.

Fleta, quoted, i. 817.

FLETCHER, Andrew, lord-justice clerk of Scotland, 1787; iv. 419.

FLETCHER, Giles, a poet, and cousin of the dramatist. He died, 1623; iii. 600.

FLETCHER, John, a dramatic writer. Born 1576. Died 1625; iii. 594, 595.

FLETCHER, Phineas, a poet, and cousin of the dramatist, died 1650; iii. 600.

FLETCHER, Richard, bishop of London, died, 1596, from the immoderate use of tobacco, which he took to smother his matrimonial cares, ii. 885, note.

FLETCHER, lord-advocate, 1661; iii. 681.

FLETCHER of Saltoun, 1681; iii. 736, 771—773, 794; iv. 162, 194.

FLEURY, cardinal, becomes prime minister of France, iv. 391, 416. Dies at the advanced age of ninety, 1743, and is succeeded by count d'Argenson and cardinal Tencin, 464.

Flodden Field, Sept. 9th, 1513; admirable position of James IV. on Flodden Hill, with the river Till in his front, ii. 327. The earl of Surrey finding this hill impregnable, manœuvres betwixt the Scots and their own country, ib. The earl marches on Branxton, to occupy a similar hill, ib. James burnt the huts and litter on Flodden Hill, and under cover of the smoke hurried to seize the heights of Branxton, ib. Lord Lindsay of the Byres, lord Huntley, and Archibald Douglas, the old earl of Angus, counsel king James not to give battle, ib. Each army, about 30,000; 328. The English ordnance silenced the Scottish cannon, ib. Huntley and Home put the English right, under sir Edmund Howard, to flight, ib. Those Scottish nobles, after an obstinate contest, retreat with their spearmen, being charged by Dacre, the lord-admiral Howard, and sir Edmund, ib. The earls of Crawford and Montrose resist a furious onset, ib. The earl of Surrey advanced at the head of the English centre, ib. James IV., with the

Flodden Field,—
Scottish centre, rushed to the encounter, and a tremendous fight ensued, ib. Bothwell brought up the reserve, and victory seemed to favour the Scottish king, ib. The earl of Huntley urged Home to support the king with the remnant of the left wing; Home totally refused, thinking he had done enough, ib. Lennox and Argyle led up the right wing to the melée, ib. The archers of sir Edward Stanley galled the highland clans so dreadfully that they threw away shield and target, ib. Rushed with their claymores and axes against the English line, each man individually singling out his foe, ib. The English formed into squares, and the highlanders were overpowered and slaughtered, ib. Lennox and Argyle slain, ib. James IV. and his noble phalanx surrounded by Surrey, Stanley, the lord admiral, and others, ib. The Howards resolved to give no quarter, ib. James IV. fell mortally wounded close to the earl of Surrey. The Scotch long defended his body, and in various quarters maintained a vigorous resistance, 329. They retreated in good order, lord Home carrying off a rich booty and many prisoners, ib. The English horse pursued for four miles, ib. Surrey suffered too severely to cross the Tweed, ib. He transported the corpse of James IV. to the monastery of Sheen, near Richmond, ib. Names of the Scottish lords who fell at Flodden, ib.

FLORENCE, duke of, offers one of his daughters to James I., as a wife for his son prince Henry, iii. 51.

FLOWERDEW, John, 1549; ii. 485.

FLOYDE, Edward, a Catholic, and prisoner in the Fleet for debt, 1621; iii. 84. He rejoices at the success of the Catholic arms against the king of Bohemia, ib. The Commons attempt to punish him, but that being out of their prerogative, the lords undertake, ib. Sentenced, ib.

FOOGE, Captain, 1643; iii. 290.

FOIX, Gaston de, seizes Beziers, ii. 59. He enters Bayonne, 1451; 85, 91.

Folcland, i. 248.

FOLEY, Mr. Paul, chosen speaker of the House of Commons, 1695; iv. 51.

FOLIOT, Gilbert, formerly, (1148), bishop of Hereford, i. 448, but now (1174) of London. He proposed to throw the body of à Becket into a ditch, or hang it on a gibbet. His speech to the people on occasion of Henry II.'s doing penance at the tomb of à Becket, 470, 471. He died 1187.

Fontainebleau, treaty of, between England and France, 1762; § i. 22, 36.

Fontenoy, battle of, 1745; iv. 477, 478.

Fonthill, view of; § iii. 738.

Fonts, Norman-English, i. 552, 553.

FOOKES, sir Henry, severely hurt in dispersing a popular assembly, 1607; iii. 37.

Fools, dance of, ii. 257. Court fool and buffoon, 262.

FORBES, Duncan, lord president, iv. 420. He acquaints lord Milton with his plan for reconciling the Highlanders to the English government, and making them loyal subjects, 499. His patriotic exertions, 531. Is neglected by the government, 542. His death, December 10, 1747; 543.

FORBES, admiral, refuses to sign the death-warrant upon admiral Byng, 1757; iv. 591.

FORBES, brigadier, 1758; iv. 603.

Forbin, 1708; iv. 216.

FORD, John, a dramatic writer of the seventeenth century, iii. 594, 597.

FORD, Thomas, an excellent musician of the seventeenth century, iii. 566.

FORD, colonel, defeats the marquis de Conflans, and takes Masulipatam, 1759; iv. 610.

Forest, New, description of, i. 387—389. Richard, second son of William the Conqueror, was here gored to death by a stag, 387; and Richard, son of

Forest, New,—
duke Robert, likewise shot by an arrow while hunting in this forest, 401.

Forest, Henry, burned at St. Andrew's, by cardinal Beaton, about 1528. One of the archbishop's attendants, John Lindsay, advised that the victim should be burned in a cellar; for the smoke, said he, of Master Patrick Hamilton hath infected all those on whom it blew, ii. 747.

Forest, a friar, 1539, burnt in Smithfield. A miraculous crucifix and image, named David Darvel Gatheren, being removed from South Wales to serve as the fuel, in allusion to a prophecy that it should burn a forest, ii. 403.

Forgery, statutes concerning, § iii. 612.

Forojuliensis, Titus Livius, a Latin chronicler, invited to England by duke Humphrey, ii. 208.

Forres, ancient obelisk sculptured with figures at Cruden, near, i. 221.

Forster, sir John, a warden of the English borders, 1566; ii. 594.

Forster, Mr., raises a rebellion in Northumberland, 1715; iv. 312.

Fortescue, sir John, chief-justice under Henry VI., ii. 111. His eminence as a lawyer, ib., 163, 517. Edward IV. reversed his attainder, and employed him, 111. Quotations from, 253.

Fortescue, sir John, 1603, signs the proclamation of the accession of James I., together with Cecil and many others, iii. 3. Sir John was elected for Buckinghamshire, 1604. Neither he nor his competitor, sir F. Goodwin, permitted to sit, case of privilege, 18, 19.

Forth, view of the, iv. 488.

Fortifications, sieges, strategy. Illustrations; Siege of a town, (Harleian MS., 4379), ii. 246. Breaching-tower, cannon, etc., ib. Movable tower of archers, 248. Storming of a town, ib.

Foster, Mr. justice, 1660; iii. 672, 688.

Fotherby, Martin, pays 3,500l. for his bishopric of Salisbury. Elected 1618. Died 1620; iii. 71.

Fotheringay Castle, view of, ii. 659.

Foulon, M. de, executed by the French revolutionists, 1789; § ii. 393.

Fowkes, lieutenant, the royalist party attempt to bribe him, 1642, to let them enter Hull, iii. 282. He informs the governor of the plot, ib.

Fowler, sir David, fined 5,000l., regno Charles I., for dissuading a friend from compounding with the commissioners of knighthood, iii. 525.

Fox, Charles James, an eminent statesman, born January 13, 1748. He takes the ministerial part against Wilkes, 1770; § i. 83. Is made one of the junior lords of the Admiralty, in the place of sir Percy Brett, 88, 113, 123. He becomes a temporary convert to Whig principles, and resigns his post in the Admiralty, 1772; 127. He is dismissed from the Treasury, 1774; 161, 168, 179, 290, 399, 408. He states his causes for moving for the dismissal of the earl of Sandwich, 1780; 441. Delivers an impressive speech upon the vice of gaming, 443, 446. He becomes one of the secretaries of state, 1782; 482. He resigns, on the death of the marquess of Rockingham, in July of the same year, 485. The Coalition ministry, 498. He introduces his famous India bills, 1783; 502, 504. Portrait of, § ii. 2. Dispute concerning his Westminster election, 2—4. His liberal opinions respecting the French revolution, 451, cause a painful rupture with his friend Burke, 544, 555. Attentions paid to him by the empress Catherine, § iii. 7. He strenuously advocates parliamentary reform, 1792; 15. Opposes the war with France, 260, 283, 565. His visit to France, and interview with the first consul, § iv. 14, 15. He opposes the renewal of war, 48, 51; but on becoming secretary of state for foreign affairs, February, 1806, he acquiesces in the views of the

Fox, Charles James,—
Grenville party, 208. He opposes the plan for raising the income-tax to ten per cent., but the ministers are reluctantly compelled to adopt it, 215. Through the able support of Mr. Fox, a bill is passed for the future abolition of the slave-trade, 216, 217. During the summer his health rapidly declined, and on September 13th he expired, only a few months after his great rival, Pitt, 251, 252.

Fox, Dr. Edward, bishop of Hereford (1535), the chief supporter of Cranmer, ii. 367, 375. His death, 1538; 725.

Fox, George, founder of the sect of Quakers, born 1624; iii. 809.

Fox, Henry. See Holland.

Fox, John, the martyrologist, born 1517, died 1587, interferes on behalf of several German Anabaptists, whom Elizabeth had condemned to the flames, but his supplication is sternly rejected, ii. 746. His Acts and Monuments are displeasing to Laud, who orders that no more copies are to be printed, iii. 166. His portrait, from an anonymous print, 433.

Fox, Richard, successively bishop of Exeter, Bath and Wells, Durham and Winchester, a confidential minister of Henry VII., ii. 286. His embassy to James III., 1487; 291, 301. He demands of James IV. the surrender of Perkin Warbeck, which the Scotch king refused, 1490; 305. Concludes the treaty of marriage between James IV. and the princess Margaret, 311. He directed the pageants and feasts on the celebration of the marriage of prince Arthur and Catherine of Spain, 312. Appointed secretary and privy-seal, 1509, first year of Henry VIII., 320, 323. His struggle with the earl of Surrey for superiority in the council induced him to bring Wolsey into Henry's notice, and that ambitious churchman supplanted both in the royal favour, 333. He died 1528.

Fox, commodore, takes forty French ships, 1747, richly laden from the West Indies, iv. 555.

Foy, or Fowey river, iii. 317.

Frances, Mr. Robert, gives a mortal wound to Dangerfield, for which he is executed, 1685; iii. 767.

Franche-Comté, ceded to France by Spain at the peace of Nimeguen, 1678; iii. 717.

Francis I., king of France (1515—1547). When count of Angoulême he commanded a French force of cavalry against Henry VIII., ii. 325. Assisted at the nuptials of Louis XII. and Mary, sister of Henry VIII., supporting the crown above her head during that ceremony, 332. Accession of Francis I. January 1515, ib. His queen, Claude, daughter of Louis XII., by Anne of Brittany, 332, 364. He renewed the alliance with Henry VIII., 334. Marched with a great army into Lombardy, to recover the duchy of Milan from Sforza, ib. He gained the battle of Marignano, in person, against the brave Swiss mercenaries of the duke, 334, 335. He thus secured the temporary possession of Milan, 335. Henry VIII., 1519, proposed an interview with Francis, near Calais, which was for a time prevented by state affairs on the death of the emperor Maximilian, 336, 338. He conciliated the favour of Leo X., left Charles of Bourbon to govern Milan, and returned home, 336. His alliance with Henry VIII, 1518; ib. The French king sought to be elected emperor, and a lasting rivalry ensued between him and the successful competitor Charles V., 337. War betwixt Francis and Charles V., 345, et seq. The French king seized English ships and goods in all his ports; war commenced against Henry VIII., 348. Surrey's unsuccessful campaign: the duke of Vendôme avoided a battle, but harassed the small invading army, 349. Suffolk's ineffective campaign, 355. Francis sends Bonnivet with his army into Italy, 1524, and himself stopped short at Lyons, for the defence of France, 358. Ill success

FRANCIS I.,—
of that commander, and death of Bayard, *ib.* The French king appeared before Milan, which city was afflicted with the plague: he then besieged Pavia, *ib.* He continued the siege obstinately, 1525; the Imperialists attacked him in force, and Francis, wounded and utterly defeated, surrendered himself to the viceroy Lannoy, 359. Anecdotes relating to the royal captive, *ib.* Plans of Henry VIII. to invade France, become king, etc., *ib.* He soon concluded a treaty with the French regency, for the sake of moneys, as Charles V. had made a truce with Francis himself to secure ulterior advantages, 360. Francis, at his urgent request, was removed from the castle of Pizzeibitone to the Alcazar of Madrid, 359, 361. Negotiations, the emperor insisting on the restoration of Burgundy as his inheritance, which the French king long refused, 361. Francis abdicated in favour of the dauphin: his health suffered grievously in prison, *ib.* January 14, 1526, the Concord of Madrid was signed: enumeration of its articles, *ib.* Secret protest, *ib.* His exclamation of joy on reaching France, *ib.* Henry's embassage to him whilst at Bayonne, *ib.* Their alliance against Charles V., *ib.* The Venetians and other Italian states join in it, 362. Refusing to fulfil the treaty with the emperor, Francis retained Burgundy, and Clement VII. absolved him from his oaths, 361, 362. Negotiations for his espousing Mary, daughter of Henry and Catherine, and for Henry's marrying Renée, daughter of Louis XII., 364. Reception at Amiens, 1527, by Francis, of Wolsey, whose display as ambassador was splendid, 365. Articles of the treaties then concluded, 365, 366. Francis sent Lautrec with an army into Italy to the tardy relief of Clement VII., 366—368. Surrender of this army at Aversa, 368. In 1528 the French herald, Guienne, carried a defiance to the emperor; reply of Charles V., 367. King Francis, in 1532, entertained Henry VIII. at Boulogne, and then repaired with him to Calais; where, at a masked ball, Francis was partner to Anne Boleyn, 379. Francis sent a fleet to convey Clement VII. to Marseilles, 1533; a conference on the affairs of the Gallican and Anglican churches there held, both Henry and Francis being desirous of a settlement of the church, 379, 380. Before the pope returned to Rome, he arranged that his niece Catherine de Medici should marry Orleans, the second son of king Francis, *ib.* Mission of the bishop of Paris to London, and next to Rome, on the matter of church reconciliation, 383. Emotion of the French monarch at the execution of sir Thomas More: he told the English ambassador that his master should banish *such* offenders, not put them to death, 389. Henry VIII. returned a hard-hearted reply, *ib.* Coalition of Charles V. and the English king against Francis, 1543; 438. Henry in person took Boulogne, 439. The emperor signed the treaty of Crespi with the French, on which king Henry returned home, *ib.* In 1545, Francis I. resolving to re-conquer Boulogne, collected a powerful fleet; actions of his admiral Annebaut off Portsmouth, 442. Failure of his armament for the invasion of England, *ib.* His treaty (of Campes) with Henry in 1546, stipulating for the restoration of Boulogne, etc., 447, 457. His death, 1547, at Rambouillet, soon after that of Henry his rival, 458. His sword, supposed to have been the same worn at the catastrophe of Pavia, was delivered, 1808, by king Ferdinand to Murat at Madrid, as a present to the emperor Napoleon, § iv. 307, *note.*

FRANCIS II. (1559-1560), king of France, and husband of Mary queen of Scots, dies December 5, 1560, and is succeeded by his brother Charles IX., ii. 563.

FRANCIS I., Emperor of Germany, and husband of

FRANCIS I.,—
Maria Theresa (1745—1765.) His election to the throne, iv. 479.

FRANCIS II., emperor of Germany, (1792—1835,) born 1767, succeeded 1792, § iii. 39, 402. On the establishment of the Confederation of the Rhine in 1806, he ceased to be emperor of Germany, and became hereditary emperor of Austria, under the title of Francis I. His portrait, § iv. 179. For his wars with the French, *see* Bonaparte. He died 1835.

FRANCIS, sir Philip, arrives at Calcutta, 1774, as one of the members of the new council, § ii. 131. His continual disputes with the governor-general, Warren Hastings, 132, *et seq.* Supposed to be the author of Junius's Letters, 135, *which see.* He is named one of the committee for preparing articles of impeachment against Hastings, 1787; 236. Portrait of, *ib.* His death, 1818; § iii. 715.

Franciscan friars. This order founded by St. Francis of Assisa, and formally established by Honorius III., 1223; i. 803. Illustration, 804.

Frankfort, battle of, 1759; iv. 611.

FRANKLIN, Benjamin, an American philosopher and statesman of great celebrity, born at Boston, New England, 1706. Improved the Leyden jar into the electrical battery, iv. 785, and invented lightning-conductors, 1752; 786. He arrives in England, 1764, as agent for Pennsylvania, to deliver the sentiments of that province respecting the stamp-tax, § i. 35. Portrait of, 154. He is deprived of his place as postmaster-general for America, 1774; he died 1790; 159, 187.

FRANKLIN, sir Thomas, postmaster-general, 1714; iv. 301.

FRANKLIN, an apothecary, accused by sir Edward Coke, 1615, of having sold poison to Mrs. Turner, wherewith to take away the life of Overbury, iii. 58. He pleads not guilty, 59.

Franks, the, of Teutonic descent, and like the other northern cognate tribes issued from Scandinavia, i. 138.

FRASER, sir Simon, suffered as a traitor in London, 1307, for assisting Bruce, i. 729, 756.

FRASER, general, falls in battle against the Americans, 1777; § i. 313.

FREDERIC WILLIAM I., king of Prussia, 1713—1740; iv. 440.

FREDERIC II. (the Great) king of Prussia (1740—1786), ascends the throne of Prussia, iv. 440. He invades the territories of the empress Maria Theresa, 441. Enters Bohemia and captures Prague, 473, but is compelled to relinquish his conquests by prince Charles of Lorraine, 474. He gains the battle of Hohen Friedberg, June 3, 1745; makes himself master of nearly all Saxony, and drives the elector into Poland; hereupon he is declared a rebel by the Aulic Council, 589. The "Seven years' war" begins, *ib.* He gains the battle of Rossbach, November 3, 1757, *ib.* Defeats 90,000 Austrians and Imperialists with 30,000, at the battle of Lissa, December 5, 1757; *ib.* He gains the battle of Custrin or Zorndorf, in which 20,000 Russians are left dead on the field, 603. He is defeated by count Daun, in the battle of Hochkirchen, *ib.* He defeats general Wedel, in the battle of Zullichau, 611. He is defeated by marshal Laudon, at the battle of Frankfort or Kunerdorf, in which he loses nearly all his artillery, half of his generals and officers of distinction, and above 18,000 men in killed and wounded, *ib.* Gains the battle of Torgau, 1760,—the last in which he commanded in person, § i. 7. Portrait of, 21. He takes Schweidnitz, gains the victory of Freyberg, and drives the Austrians into Bohemia, 1761; 22. His death, August 17, 1786. He is succeeded by his nephew, Frederic William, § ii. 207.

FREDERIC WILLIAM II., king of Prussia (1786—1797). His accession to the throne on the death of his uncle, Frederic the Great, August 17; § ii. 207. He despatches the duke of Brunswick to the assistance of the prince of Orange, 1787, who is soon settled in his full powers as stadtholder, 242—246. Commercial treaty with Poland, 1790; § iii. 33. He marches an army into that unfortunate country, 1793, and compels the Diet to consent to a new partition, whereby Russia obtained a territory containing a population of more than three millions and a half, and Prussia a territory containing nearly one million and a half of inhabitants, together with the navigation of the Vistula and the port of Dantzic on the Baltic, 292, 293. He takes Mayence, July 22, 1793, and gains other advantages over the French, 294. Concludes a separate treaty with the Convention, April 5, 1795; 475.

FREDERIC WILLIAM III., king of Prussia (1797—1840.) born 1770. (For his wars with France, see Bonaparte). He enters Paris with the allied army, March 31, 1814; § iv. 615°.

FREDERIC IV., king of Denmark (1699—1730,) utters an insolent speech in reference to the power of William III.; iv. 107: the English king sends admiral Rooke against him, who scours the Baltic and bombards Copenhagen; Frederic is forced to beg for peace, 108.

FREDERIC VI., king of Denmark, and duke of Holstein, born 1768, succeeded 1808. Defeated by Bernadotte, and compelled to conclude an armistice with the allies, 1813; § iv. 598°. Holstein and Sleswig occupied by the Swedes, ib. Norway allotted to Bernadotte; its union with Sweden, 620°.

FREDERIC II., king of the Two Sicilies, dies 1250, in a state of excommunication, leaving a legitimate son, prince Conrad; i. 580. Innocent IV. declares the kingdom forfeited to the Holy See, in consequence of the position of the late king, ib. Conrad maintains his rights with an army, and the haughty pontiff offers the crown to whoever will accept of it, ib.

FREDERIC V., Count Palatine, proposed husband of the princess Elizabeth, daughter of James I., arrives in England to receive his bride, October 16, 1612; iii. 51. He evacuates Bohemia, 39; lives with his wife and family at the Hague on a Dutch pension, ib. His death at Mentz, 1632; 173.

FREDERIC, prince of Wales, and son of George II.; joy of the English people on his visiting England, iv. 402. He marries Augusta, princess of Saxe-Gotha, 1736; 421. Gives his first vote in parliament, 434. His death, March 20, 1751; 565.

Freemen, description of, i. 661.

French language, early, termed "the Romance" both in speech and writings, i. 188.

Freyberg, battle of, 1762; § i. 22.

Friedland, battle of, gained by the French, June 14, 1807; § iv. 295.

FRIEND, sir John, a devoted Jacobite, executed at Tyburn, 1696, for being concerned in the Invasion-plot, iv. 67, 69.

FRITH and HEWET, (the former a young man of learning and piety, condemned for his book against the doctrine of purgatory, for his opinions on transubstantiation, etc.), were burnt, 1534, in Smithfield, ii. 386.

FAITHRIC, abbot of St. Alban's; his bold answer to William the Conqueror, who demanded why he attempted to stop his advance into England, i. 361.

FRIXELL, William, 1632; iii. 544.

FROBISHER, Martin, the celebrated navigator; portrait of, ii. 771; 627. His voyages of discovery, 789. He died in 1594, of a wound received in an attack upon a fort near Brest, ib.

FROISSART, the chronicler; observations of, and events narrated by, i. 749, 849; ii. 7.

FRONTINUS, Julius, anno 75—78; subdued the Silures, in Britain, i. 44.

Fruit; several fruits introduced to English cultivation, from abroad, in the sixteenth century, ii. 806.

FRY, Mr., his account of the first appearance of the Habeas Corpus Act, iii. 334.

FULK, earl of Anjou, promises to give his daughter Sibylla in marriage to William Fitz-Robert, son of Robert, duke of Normandy; the marriage alliance is broken off; i. 412, 413. He gives his daughter Matilda to William, only son of Henry I., ib. His wars with Henry, ib. After the death of prince William, Fulk demands back his daughter, together with her dower; Henry sends back the young lady, but refuses to restore the money, 416. The war in favour of Fitz-Robert is renewed, but the earl of Anjou once more abandons the cause of his intended son-in-law, and a peace is concluded, ib. His departure for the Holy Land, 1126, and abdication of the government of Anjou in favour of his son, 417.

Fullanham, now Fulham-on-the-Thames, i. 161.

FULLARTON, captain, his courageous and praiseworthy conduct in India, 1783; § ii. 156—163.

FULTON, Robert, famous for his exertions (at the commencement of the nineteenth century) in introducing the powers of steam to the purposes of navigation, § iv. 682, 683. His portrait, 683.

Funeral, monks at a, ii. 267.

Furniture, specimens of, i. 634, 864; iii. 617—619, 622, 889—891; iv. 808—811; § iv. 723.

FUSELI, Henry, an eminent historical painter of the eighteenth century, born about 1739, died 1825; § iii. 742.

Fyvie Castle, iii. 338.

GABRIEL, a courtier who attended Charles I. in his expedition to Spain in 1623; iii. 94.

Gael, its orthography uncertain, i. 18.

Gaeta, city of, surrenders to the Austrians, 1707; iv. 204.

GAGE, lord, 1739; iv. 434.

GAGE, Mr. George, dispatched as an agent of James I. to the Vatican, 1622; iii. 89.

GAGE, colonel,.1639; iii. 201, 420.

GAGE, general, lands at Boston, May 13th, 1774, as governor, § i. 181, 184, 211. The Americans declare him, 1775, to be disqualified from acting in that capacity, 214. He issues a proclamation in the king's name, offering a full pardon to all who should lay down their arms, with the exception of Samuel Adams and John Hancock, 215. His dilatory and neglectful conduct, 215, 216.

GAGES, count de, 1745; iv. 479.

GAINSBOROUGH, Thomas, a celebrated English painter, born 1737, died August 2, 1788; § i. 629.

GALDRIC, king Henry's chaplain, takes duke Robert prisoner, 1106, for which he is promoted to the bishopric of Llandaff, but is slain by the people, i. 412.

GALILEO, a celebrated philosopher, mathematician, and astronomer, born at Pisa, 1564; discovered the satellites of Jupiter, 1608; died January 1642; iii. 611.

GALKE, secretary to the Hanoverian embassy in 1713; iv. 278.

GALLAS, count, 1719; iv. 360.

Galleys of the Romans, from coins in the British Museum, i. 30. Model at Greenwich Hospital presented by lord Anson, 31. Construction of the Roman galleys, 165. Of those of the Saxon invaders, of the Danish sea-kings and pirates, 162, 165. Navy of Alfred the Great, 162—165.

GALLOWAY, Patrick, a fanatic preacher, dissuades James I. from extending clemency to the chief conspirators in the Powder Plot, 1603, although some lords of council recommended examples of mercy, iii. 13. The king's indignant reply as to Galloway's cruel prompting, ib.; 468.

GALWAY, lord, iv. 49. Letter of the earl of Sunderland to, 134. He crosses the frontier of Estremadura, 1705, and takes Valencia, De Alcantara, Alvuquerque, and invests Badajoz, at which place a shot carries off his hand, 179. He takes possession of Madrid, 1706; 186: is defeated on the frontier of Estremadura, 236.

GAMA, Vasco de, a Portuguese navigator; his voyage to India, 1497; ii. 777.

GAMBIER, James, lord, created November 9, 1807, admiral of the British fleet in the bombardment of Copenhagen, September 7, 1807; § iv. 287—290, and in the attack of the French flotilla at Boulogne, 1809; 409.

GAMBLE, Mr., chaplain to the famous Monk, 1660; iii. 430*.

GAMEL, son of Quetel of Meaux, 1073; i. 374.

Games, rural and manly; bowling-hall, ii. 259. Club-ball, ib. Trap-ball, 260. Archery encouraged by laws, 260.

Gaming; with cards, ii. 258, 260; with dice; ancient dice-box delineated, 260.

GARDENER, the recorder of London, 1634; iii. 163.

Gardening, art of, commenced in the reign of Elizabeth, iii. 557.

Gardens and orchards of the Anglo-Saxons, i. 283.

GARDINER, STEPHEN, bishop of Winchester, his mission (with Dr. Fox), to Clement VII., 1528; their instructions, ii. 367. On his return from Rome, he conducted the cause of the divorce, as counsel for Henry VIII, 369, Secretary to Henry VIII.; he mentions Cranmer to the king, 375. Becomes bishop of Winchester, 1531. He was counsel for the king in Cranmer's court at Dunstable, 1533, on the divorce, 380. At Marseilles, Gardiner and Bryan, envoys to the solemn conference on church affairs, had not received powers to conclude anything from their undecided master; and Bonner's appeal to a council proved that nothing definitive was intended, 382. Liberated, 1548, by the general pardon, on Edward VI.'s accession, he was soon committed to the Tower; making no concession, he was deprived of his see, and remained long a prisoner, 468. He stands out against the new regulations of Cranmer for furthering the reformation, and is consigned to close imprisonment in the Fleet, 466, 493. He is made chancellor by Queen Mary, 506, 511. Being of a less sanguinary disposition than many, he grows weary of presiding in the court of Inquisition, and withdraws; his duties devolve on Bonner, 524. His death; he is succeeded as chancellor by Heath, archbishop of York, 526. His portrait, 696.

GARDINER, Mr., counsel to the earl of Strafford, 1641; iii. 239.

GARDINER, colonel, killed at the battle of Preston-pans, 1745; iv. 497.

GARGRAVE, sir Thomas, quoted, ii. 645.

GARLAND, condemned as a regicide, 1660, but not executed, iii. 674, 675.

GARNET, Henry, superior of the Jesuits in England, 1606, is arrested in Hendlip-house, Worcester, and confined in the Tower, iii. 30. Oldcorn, or Hall, found concealed with Garnet in the secret chamber at Hendlip, now becomes his fellow-prisoner, ib. Oldcorn, and two men-servants, are subjected to torture, but confess nothing, ib. The lieutenant of the Tower places them in adjoining cells, and, cautioning them to be careful, shows a door of communication, 31. Forset a magistrate, and Locherson a secretary to Cecil, are so placed as to hear all conversations, ib. 32. Details of the two jesuits' conversations, 31. Garnet acknowledges himself in a certain degree cognizant of Catesby's conspiracy; who put a question of expediency to him, as to destroying some innocent Catholics, together with many bitter enemies of their faith, ib. Garnet's

GARNET, HENRY,—
reply thereto, ib. His trial, which both the king and lady Arabella Stuart listen to, ib. May 3, 1606, Garnet is executed, 32.

GARRARD, lord mayor, 1709, denies that he ordered the printing of Dr. Sacheverell's sermons, iv. 238.

GARRICK, David, the most eminent actor ever produced by the English stage, born 1716, died January 20, 1779; § i. 609. Portrait of, ib.

GARTH, sir Samuel, an eminent physician, poet, and man of wit. He died in the height of literary and medical reputation, June, 1718; iv. 798.

GASCOIGNE, George, a poet, died Oct. 7, 1577; iii. 583, 585.

GASCOIGNE, lord chief-justice, his high character, 1405; ii. 17.

Gascony, wars of the English to retain possession of this province, ii. 8, 19.

GASCOYNE, sir William, treasurer to cardinal Wolsey, ii. 372.

GASSE, count de. See marshal Matignon.

GASSION, M. de, a lieutenant-general at the battle of Ramilies, May 23, 1706.

GATES, sir John, executed, 1553; ii. 506.

GATES, general, a gallant American officer, 1777; § i. 313, 316.

Gatheren, David Darvel; name of a crucifix in South Wales, ii. 403.

GAUDEN, John, elected to the see of Exeter, 1660; translated to Worcester, 1662, in which year he died. He was the author of the Eikon Basiliké, iii. 607.

Gaul, Cæsar's conquest of, i. 25.

Gaulish hut, as sculptured on the Antonine column, i 98.

Gauls, the, said by Cæsar to have been frequently assisted by auxiliaries from Britain, i. 25, 102. Their trade with Britain, 101. Their extensive potteries, 103. Their woollen fabrics, and dyeing with woad, etc., 104. The Druids, their sacrifices, etc., 60. Worship of heathen divinities, ib.

GAULTIER, Abbé, proposes the peace of Utrecht to France, iv. 253.

GAUNT, Elizabeth, burned at Tyburn, 1685; iii. 783.

GAUR, dynasty of, established by Mohammed styled the Gaurian, (who was assassinated in 1206,) and wholly terminated in 1289; § ii. 17.

GAVISTON, sir Piers, a knight of Gascony, the great favourite of Edward II., by whom he is made earl of Cornwall, i. 730—734. For his life, see EDWARD II.

Gawdy, queen Elizabeth's serjeant; his speech at the trial of Mary queen of Scots, ii. 660.

GAY, John, born 1688, author of a considerable quantity of verse, and above a dozen dramatic pieces. He died, 1732; iv. 797.

GED, William, an inhabitant of Edinburgh, discovers the art of stereotyping in 1725; iv. 733.

GELL, sir John, this gentleman and his brother were the only two of any note in Derbyshire who took part with the Parliament against Charles I., iii. 291.

Gembloura, battle of, 1581; ii. 650.

GEMINUS, Thomas, the earliest English copper-plate engraver (16th century), iii. 577.

Geneva, the church of; allusion to its festivals by James I., iii. 15.

GENLIS, Madame, her flight from Paris, 1793, § iii. 267.

Genoa; F. Doria commanded the galleys in the siege of Naples, 1528; a dispute ensuing, he abandoned Lautrec, the general of Francis I., ii. 368. Andrea Doria and the Genoese then joined the emperor, ib.

Genoese carracks defeated by the duke of Bedford, 1416, at Harfleur, ii. 35.

GENTILESCHI, Artemisia, daughter of the following, famous for her talents in painting; she passed the greater part of her life at Naples, and died in 1662; iii. 569.

GENTILESCHI, Horatio, an Italian painter, born 1563;

GENTILESCHI, Horatio,—
invited to England by Vandyke. He died in 1647;
iii. 569.
GEOFFREY, younger son of Geoffrey Plantagenet, earl
of Anjou, and brother of Henry II., lays claim to
Anjou and Maine, i. 442, 443. The citizens of
Nantes confer on him the government of their city,
443. He dies in 1158, and Henry claims the city
of Nantes as hereditary property, ib.
GEOFFREY, Prince, third son of Henry II., does homage to the French king for Brittany, i. 452. He
flies to France, 468; tries his fortune in Brittany,
470. Is reconciled to his father, who assigns him
two castles in Brittany, 471. Assists in the war
against his two brothers, Henry and Richard, 1183;
474. Demands the earldom of Anjou; is refused
by his father; he flies to the French court and prepares for war, 475, 476. Is killed at a tournament,
1186, and buried by the king of France, 476.
GEOFFREY, natural son of Henry II., his affection and
unwearying attentions to his father, he was present at his death, 1189; i. 479, 481. Was made
bishop of Lincoln when very young, 481, and subsequently chancellor, when he constantly accompanied the king; in his dying moments, Henry
expressed a wish that he might be made archbishop
of York, ib.; which dignity he afterwards obtained,
485. Geoffrey, who had been expelled from England, returns and lands at Dover, contrary to the
express injunction of the regent Longchamp, is
seized and confined in Dover Castle, from which he
is soon released; goes to London, and attends the
council of earl John, 507.
GEOFFREY of Monmouth, an English chronicler, says
Britain was peopled by the Trojans, i. 8, 11.
GEOFFREY, bishop of Coutance, 1073; i. 381.
Geology, iv. 787.
GEORGE, the, illustration of, from the original print
by Hollar, iii. 398.
GEORGE I. (Aug. 1, 1714—June 11, 1727,) Great Seal
of, iv. 302. Eighteen peers named by the elector
of Hanover take upon themselves the temporary
administration of affairs, according to the Regency
Bill, ib. Marlborough makes his triumphant entry
into London, 1714, ib. Joseph Addison appointed
secretary by the lords justices, ib. Claimants for
the honours and emoluments of office, ib. Portrait of George I., 303. The houses of parliament
meet on Sunday the day of the queen's death, according to an important provision in the Act of
Regency, 304. Supplies voted, ib. Upon the news
of Anne's death, the Pretender leaves Lorraine
with the intention of embarking for Great Britain,
but is prevented by Louis XIV., ib. George I.
departs for England, ib. Ministerial arrangements,
305. The Pretender's manifesto, asserting his right
to the throne of Great Britain, ib. Parliament dissolved, ib. The new parliament assembles, 306.
Bolingbroke flies from England, ib. The papers,
instructions, etc. relating to Ormond's withdrawing
the troops from the allies, and to the treaty of
Utrecht, referred to a select committee, 307. Sir
Robert Walpole presents the report to the House, ib.
Proceedings thereon, ib. Lords Bolingbroke and
Oxford impeached, ib. The duke of Ormond impeached, ib. Matthew Prior impeached, and
sent to close custody, 308. Lord Strafford impeached, ib. The duke of Ormond flies to
France, ib. Oxford is committed to the Tower,
ib. Bolingbroke and Ormond intrigue in France
for the restoration of the Stuarts, 309, 311.
Death of Louis XIV., 311. Lord Stair demands of
the duke of Orleans, regent of France, the seizure
of several ships fitted out for the service of the
Pretender, ib. The standard of the Pretender
raised at Brae Mar, by the earl of Mar, 312. He
issues a declaration, calling on the people to arm,

GEORGE I.,—
and assumes the title of lieutenant-general to king
James, ib. Several Scottish lords apprehended and
sent to Edinburgh Castle, ib. Mr. Forster raises a
rebellion in Northumberland, ib. Sir Richard Vivian
is sent in custody to London, 313. General Pepper
arrests several suspected persons, ib. The earl of
Derwentwater joins Forster ; they march to Warkworth, and are joined by lord Widdrington ; Forster proclaims the pretender; they march to Morpeth,
ib. The pretender proclaimed at Moffat by lord
Kenmure, ib. Forster attempts to take Newcastle,
but fails; he marches to Hexham, ib. Kenmure
joins Forster near Rothbury ; they march to Kelso,
ib. The duke of Argyle and general Whetham
prevent any successful attempt by the insurgents in
Scotland, 314, 315. Mackintosh and Forster arrive
at Penrith; march to Kirkby Lonsdale, proclaiming
the pretender, 316. The insurgents march to
Lancaster ; they are joined by the Roman Catholics;
they advance to Preston, ib. General Wills marches
against them ; they lay down their arms; lord
Derwentwater, Widdrington, Kenmure, and other
lords are taken; Mackintosh, Forster, and several
others are captured; the insurrection in England
suppressed, 317. The battle of Dunblane; the
insurgents under the earl of Mar are routed by the
duke of Argyle ; the battle of the Stuarts, called
" The Restoration," is taken, 317—319. The pretender leaves St. Malo and embarks at Dunkirk, 321.
Lands at Peterhead, ib. Goes to Fetteresso; is
joined by Mar, general Hamilton, and several other
Jacobites, ib. Removes from Fetteresso to Kinnaird,
322. Makes his public entry into Dundee, ib. Arrives at Scone, ib. A reward of 100,000l. offered
by the English government to any one who should
seize him dead or alive, 323. He orders the burning
of all towns between Perth and Stirling, 324. The
duke of Argyle and general Cadogan advance and
survey the roads leading to Perth, ib. The royal
army reaches Tullibardine, 325. The pretender
evacuates Perth, and proceeds to Dundee, ib. Perth
occupied by the royal troops, ib. Argyle follows the
pretender ; the insurgents retreat to Montrose, ib.
The pretender sails for France, ib. Argyle enters
Aberdeen ; many prisoners are taken, 326 ; and
executed by martial law, 327. The earls of Derwentwater and Kenmure are beheaded on Tower
Hill, 328, 329. A bill, enforcing the laws against
papists, 329. The Septennial Bill passed, 330, 331.
Act passed, disabling persons from sitting in Parliament who held pensions from the crown, 331. Parliament prorogued, ib. The king goes to Hanover,
ib. Treaty between the king of England and the
duke of Orleans, 332. Treaty between George I.
as elector of Hanover, and Frederic king of Denmark, 333. Sir John Norris appears in the Baltic,
to overawe Charles XII. of Sweden, ib. Charles,
indignant at the conduct of the English cabinet (for
he was already beset by many enemies) puts himself
in communication with the Jacobites, and engages
to back the pretender with 12,000 veteran Swedes,
ib. Peter the Great marches an army of Muscovites
into Mecklenburg, ib. George proposes to crush
the Czar immediately, ib. A division takes place in
the cabinet, 334. The French treaty is signed at
the Hague, 337. The king returns to England, ib.
The treaty is signed at the Hague for Holland, and
becomes the " Triple Alliance," ib. Count Gyllenborg, the Swedish ambassador, arrested by order of
the privy-council, 338. Parliament meets, ib. The
German ministry is formed, 339. The earl of Oxford tried for high treason, and acquitted, 339, 340.
Several lords and gentlemen freed, in consequence
of an Act of Grace, 340. War between Spain and
Austria, 341. The Spaniards conquer Sardinia,
342. The prince of Wales is ordered to quit

GEORGE I.,—

St. James's, 343. Parliament assembles; Mr. Shippen is committed to the Tower, 344. The Mutiny Bill passes, ib. James Shepherd executed for high treason, ib. Parliament prorogued, ib. Death of Addison, ib. Formidable Spanish armament, ib. The English fleet, under sir G. Byng, sails for the Mediterranean, 345. The Quadruple Alliance, ib. The city of Messina falls into the hands of the Spaniards, 346. Battle off Cape Passaro, 346, 347. Charles XII. of Sweden killed before Fredericksbal, 349. Parliament meets, 350. Lord Stanhope brings in a bill for strengthening the Protestant interest, 351. A bill introduced into the Upper House to limit the creation of peers, 351, 352. Parliament prorogued, 352. The king appoints a council of regency and goes to Hanover, ib. Spanish soldiers and arms landed in Scotland, 355. The Spaniards and Highlanders are defeated at Glenshiel, by general Wightman, 354. Fuentarabia surrenders to the French, 355. The Spanish shipping at Santona destroyed by the French and English, ib. St. Sebastian taken by the duke of Berwick, ib. The French make great conquests in Spain, 356. The citadel of Vigo taken by lord Cobham, ib. Sir George Byng prosecutes the war in Sicily, 358—363. The siege of Messina, 361—363. Philip of Spain accedes to the Quadruple Alliance, 365. The queen of Sweden throws herself on the protection of England; sir John Norris is dispatched to the Baltic with eleven sail of the line to her assistance, 368. The sovereign prince of Mecklenburg suspended from his government by the Aulic Council, ib. The king returns from Hanover, ib. Parliament assembles, ib. A bill passes the House of Lords, limiting the peerage, ib.; it is thrown out in the Commons, 370. The South-Sea-Company Bill passed, 370—372. The king is reconciled to the prince of Wales, 372. The king departs for Hanover, ib. The funds of the South-Sea-Company rise from 130 to 300, ib. The South-Sea stock rises to 1,000 per cent., 372, 373. Proclamation issued by the council of regency, forbidding the formation of companies, 373. Immense speculations formed, ib. The prince of Wales becomes a governor of the Welsh Copper Company, ib. The South-Sea stock falls, ib. The scheme sinks to nothing; consequent general panic, 373, 374. Parliament meets, 374. The directors of the South-Sea-Company are ordered to lay their accounts before parliament, ib. A bill passes, transferring part of the stock to the bank, and part into the stock of the East India Company, 375. Four members of parliament, directors of the company, expelled the House, and their papers seized, ib. A violent debate takes place in the House of Peers; the earl of Stanhope is suddenly taken ill in the House, and dies, ib. Report of the secret committee on the South-Sea scheme, ib. Ainslable is confined in the Tower, 376. Sunderland is accused and acquitted, ib. The property of the directors is confiscated, ib. Walpole is made first lord of the Treasury, ib. His bill for remedying the South-Sea scheme receives the royal assent, 377. Treaty of peace signed between Great Britain, France, and Spain, ib. Congress held at Cambray, ib. Parliament prorogued, ib. Parliament meets, 378. Is dissolved, ib. Sudden death of the earl of Sunderland, ib. The earl of Nottingham brings a bill into the House of Peers for the suppression of blasphemy and profaneness, ib. Death of the duke of Marlborough, 379. His body is deposited in Westminster Abbey, and afterwards removed to Blenheim, ib. New plot to restore the pretender; a camp is formed in Hyde-park, and several other precautions taken, 380. Lord Orrery and the duke of Norfolk sent to the Tower, but shortly after liberated, ib. Bishop Atterbury sent

GEORGE I.,—

to the Tower, ib. The pretender issues a declaration from Lucca, calling on George I. to resign the throne, 381. Parliament meets; the Habeas Corpus Act suspended, ib. Parliament orders the pretender's declaration to be burned by the hands of the common hangman, ib. Walpole brings in a bill for raising 100,000l. on the real and personal estates of all papists, which is afterwards extended. to all non-jurors, ib. Mr. Layer executed for enlisting troops for the pretender, ib. Bills of pains and penalties passed against several persons, ib. A bill of banishment and deprivation passes against bishop Atterbury, ib; who is conveyed to Calais, 382. The king goes to Hanover, ib. Bolingbroke is pardoned and returns to England, but shortly afterwards goes back to France, ib. Death of the abbé Dubois, 383. Death of the regent duke of Orleans, ib. The king returns to England, ib. Parliament meets; supplies voted; the standing army is raised to 18,200 men, 383, 384. The protections given by ambassadors, etc. restricted, 384. Parliament prorogued, ib. Wood's copper coinage creates much disturbance in Ireland, ib. Dean Swift employs his caustic pen against the coinage, and publishes his "Drapier's Letters," ib. The printer is indicted, but the grand jury ignore the bill, 385. A riot in Glasgow about the malt-tax, ib. Parliament meets; the standing army is continued, ib. The lord chancellor is impeached, fined for corruption, and sent to the Tower, 385, 386. Lord Bolingbroke is restored to his seat in parliament, 386. Don Louis succeeds to the Spanish crown on the abdication of king Philip, 387. His death, ib. Death of Peter the Great, 388. A treaty concluded at Vienna between Spain and the emperor, ib. A treaty concluded at Hanover between Great Britain, France, and Prussia, ib. Parliament meets, 389. Supplies voted, ib. Parliament prorogued, ib. The Russian ports blockaded by sir Charles Wager, ib. Admiral Hosier goes on an expedition to the West Indies, and sir John Jennings to the coast of Spain, ib. Parliament assembles; 26,000 soldiers and 20,000 seamen voted, 390. M. Palm, the Russian ambassador, ordered to quit the kingdom, ib. The British resident at Vienna recalled, ib. Death of the widow of Peter the Great, ib. Preliminaries of peace signed between England, France, Holland, and Russia, 391. The king of Spain accedes to them, ib. Rippenda, the prime-minister of Spain, dragged by force from the house of the English ambassador at Madrid, ib. The king sets out for Hanover. He is seized with a fit of apoplexy, and dies on the road to Osnaburgh, 11th June, 1727; 392. His signature, 616. Death of Sophia Dorothea of Zell, wife of George I., 393. Coins of this reign, 727.

GEORGE II. (June 11, 1727—October 25, 1760.) His conduct relative to his father's will, iv. 394. Great Seal of, 395, 615. He is proclaimed, 396. Portrait of, ib. A civil list of 830,000l. per annum settled on the king for life, and 100,000l. on the queen, 399. Parliament dissolved, ib. Intrigues of the pretender, 399, 400. Bishop Atterbury dies in Paris, 400. Death of the duke of Wharton, at the convent of Poblet, 401. Parliament assembles, ib. The Commons address the king for an account of the secret service money, 402. The congress of Soissons, ib. Frederic, prince of Wales, arrives in England, ib. Parliament assembles, ib. They pass resolutions for the preservation of Gibraltar and Minorca, 403. It is declared by the Commons a breach of privilege to publish their debates in a newspaper, ib. 115,000l. voted for a deficiency in the civil list, ib. Parliament prorogued, ib. The king goes to Hanover, and appoints queen Caroline regent during his absence, ib. The lines of San Roque or the Campo, constructed by the Spaniards, ib.

GEORGE II.,—

The treaty of Seville, Nov. 9, 1729; ib. Parliament opens, Jan. 1730; 404. A bill passed, prohibiting loans to foreign states without the license of the king, ib. The Pension Bill passed by the Commons, but rejected by the Lords, ib. The Charter of the East India Company is prolonged to 1766; ib. A bill passes, ordaining all pleadings and processes in the courts of law to be in English, 405. Sir Robert Sutton expelled the House of Commons for peculation, 1731; ib. The Salt-tax revived, ib. Parliament prorogued, ib. The duke of Lorraine visits England, ib. Parliament assembles, Jan. 1732; 406. Pulteney is struck out from the list of privy-councillors, ib. Parliament prorogued, ib. The king departs for Hanover, leaving his queen regent, ib. The Pragmatic Sanction ratified, ib. Persecution of the Protestant inhabitants of the archbishopric of Saltzburgh; many of them take refuge in England, and emigrate thence to the colony of Georgia, ib. Walpole takes half a million from the Sinking Fund for the service of the current year, 407. Introduces his scheme for excise duties, ib.; the bill passes the committee, 408; but is withdrawn, 409. Death of Augustus II., king of Poland, 1733; ib. The prince of Orange marries the princess royal, ib. Stanislaus is elected king of Poland; Augustus III. is also elected; Stanislaus flies to Dantzic, where he is besieged by the Russians; Augustus III. is proclaimed, 410. Parliament assembles, Jan. 1734; ib. A bill for repealing the Septennial Act rejected, 410—413. Parliament dissolved, 413. Don Carlos enters Naples, 414. Sicily is conquered by the Spaniards, ib. Don Carlos becomes master of the Two Sicilies, ib. The duke of Berwick is killed before Philipsburg, ib. Parliament meets, 415. The army and navy is increased, and a subsidy voted to Denmark, 1735; ib. Bolingbroke goes to the continent, ib. The king appoints queen Caroline regent, and goes to Hanover, ib. Don Carlos is acknowledged king of Naples and Sicily, 416. Sir John Norris is sent to the assistance of the Portuguese with a fleet of twenty-one sail, ib. The king returns from Hanover, 417. Sir Joseph Jekyll brings in the Gin Act, 1736; ib. Bill for repealing the Test Act lost in the Commons, ib. Bill for the benefit of the Quakers lost in the Lords, 418. Parliament prorogued, May 26; ib. The king goes to Hanover, ib. A riot takes place in Edinburgh, on the execution of Wilson for robbing an excise-officer, ib. Captain Porteous fires on the mob, whereby nine persons are wounded, ib. He is condemned for murder, but respited by order of queen Caroline, then acting as regent, ib. A mob attack the Tolbooth, hang Porteous, and then retire quietly to their homes, 419. Parliament assembles, 420. The corporation of Edinburgh fined 2,000l. for the relief of captain Porteous's widow, 1737; ib. The Scottish clergy are compelled to read a proclamation from the pulpit, calling on the people to bring the murderers of the captain to justice. ib. Lord Carteret and Mr. Pulteney move that 100,000l. per annum be settled on the prince of Wales, 425, 426. The princess of Wales is delivered of a daughter at St. James's palace, July 31, 426. The king forbids the residence of the prince of Wales at St. James's, 427. Death of queen Caroline, 428, 429. The princess of Orange, after the death of her mother, arrives in England, but is peremptorily sent back to Holland by the king, 429. Parliament assembles, 1738; 430. Captain R. Jenkyns, said to have lost an ear through the brutality of the Spaniards, is ordered to attend the House of Commons, 431. Debates on the right of search exercised by the Spaniards, 432. Parliament prorogued, 433. A convention is signed at Madrid, 1739; ib. Parliament meets, ib. The prince of Wales gives his first vote

GEORGE II.,—

in parliament, 434. Debates on the convention, 434, 435. Sir W. Wyndham takes leave of the House, 435. Walpole asks for a subsidy of 250,000 dollars per annum, for three years, for the king of Denmark, 436. Bill for facilitating the importation of wool from Ireland, ib. Parliament prorogued, ib. Cardinal Fleury offers the mediation of France, to prevent a war between Great Britain and Spain, ib. War with Spain, 1739; 437. Parliament assembles, 438. The Commons address the king, 1740, that no treaty should be entered into with Spain until they relinquish the right of search, ib. Supplies; upwards of four millions are voted, 439. Parliament prorogued, ib. Porto-Bello captured by admiral Vernon, ib. The king goes to Hanover, ib. Death of Frederic William, king of Prussia, May 1740; he is succeeded by Frederic the Great, 440. Death of the emperor Charles VI., Oct. 20, ib. He is succeeded by Maria Theresa, whose title is guaranteed, in conformity with the Pragmatic Sanction, by all the powers of Europe except Bavaria, ib. Parliament assembles, 441. The king of Prussia enters Silesia at the head of 30,000 men; Breslau, Namslau, and Ohlau, open their gates to him, ib. Maria Theresa, queen of Hungary, applies for advice and aid to king George, ib. Death of Anne, the czarina of Russia; she bequeaths her crown to Ivan, grandson of her elder sister, who is set aside by the Russian nobles, and the princess Elizabeth, daughter of Peter the Great, is placed on the throne, ib. Riots in England, owing to the high price of bread, ib. Parliament assembles, Death of sir William Wyndham, ib. Sandys moves an accusation against Walpole, 1741; 442—444. Walpole's defence, 445—447. He obtains a subsidy of 300,000l. for the queen of Hungary, 448. Parliament prorogued, ib. The king goes to Hanover, ib. Battle of Molwitz, 449. The town of Brieg surrenders to the king of Prussia, ib. The king of France sends the marshal de Belleisle to conclude an alliance with Prussia, ib. Sweden declares war with Russia, 450. Marshal Maillebois moves upon Hanover, ib. Devotion of the Hungarians to Maria Theresa, 451. The city of Prague taken by the Elector of Bavaria, ib. He is crowned as Charles VII., ib. The court of Vienna makes several concessions to Frederic, on his pledging his word not to attempt anything more against Maria Theresa, ib. In disregard of this truce, marshal Schwerin takes the town and fortress of Olmutz, ib. The French army is driven out of Austria by Khevenhöller, who pushes on into Bavaria, and obliges the Bavarian army to abandon Bohemia and hasten to the defence of their own country, ib. Ill success of the English forces, 451, 452. Tierra Bomba taken by the English, 452. Unsuccessful attack on Carthagena, 452, 453. Parliament assembles, Dec. 4, 454. Pulteney, seconded by Walpole, moves for an inquiry into the state of the nation, 455. Walpole prevails on the king, 1742, to offer the prince of Wales an addition of 50,000l. a year, and the payment of all his debts, provided he would cease opposing the measures of government, ib. Parliament assembles, 456. Walpole's last speech, ib. He tenders his resignation to the king, Feb. 1, ib. He is created earl of Orford; a pension of 4,000l. per annum is conferred upon him, and a patent of rank for an illegitimate daughter, 457. Lord Wilmington is made first-lord of the Treasury, 458. Changes in the cabinet, ib. Disputes for preferment, 459. Pulteney is created lord Bath, ib. Lord Limerick moves for a secret committee to inquire into the administration of sir Robert Walpole, 460. Report of the secret committee, 461. Sir Robert Goodschall moves for a repeal of the Septennial Act, ib.

F

GEORGE II.,—

500,000*l.* granted to the queen of Hungary, and more than 5,000,000*l.* voted for carrying on the war, *ib.* Parliament prorogued, July 15, 1742, *ib.* Treaty of peace concluded between Maria Theresa and the king of Prussia, through the mediation of England, *ib.* 16,000 men sent as auxiliaries to the house of Austria in Flanders, 462. Treaty between Maria Theresa and Frederic king of Prussia, *ib.* Commodore Martin threatens to bombard Naples, *ib.* Admiral Matthews destroys five Spanish gallies in the French port of St. Tropez, *ib.* The Spaniards fall upon Georgia, but are defeated with much loss by general Oglethorpe, 463. Parliament assembles, Nov. 16; *ib.* Supplies voted, 464. Parliament prorogued, *ib.* George departs for Germany, *ib.* Death of cardinal Fleury, 1743; *ib.* Bolingbroke returns to England, 465. De Broglie retreats to the banks of the Neckar, *ib.* The earl of Stair retreats before the duke de Noailles, *ib.* Battle of Dettingen, June 27, commanded by George in person, 466. Defeat of Noailles and de Broglie, 467. He signs, at Worms, an important treaty with Austria and Sardinia, *ib.* Death of Wilmington, who is succeeded by Pelham, *ib.* The king returns to England, *ib.* Parliament assembles, 468. Strong debates concerning the continuance of the Hanoverian troops, *ib.* The king informs the Houses that he has received undoubted information that the Pretender's eldest son had arrived in Paris, and was preparing an invasion, *ib.* The Habeas Corpus Act suspended, 469. Bill attainting the sons of the Pretender in case they should attempt to land, *ib.* A subsidy of 200,000*l.* is granted to Sardinia; 300,000*l.* is allotted to Austria; on the whole near 10,000,000*l.* is voted, *ib.* Parliament prorogued, *ib.* The Penal Laws are enforced against Roman Catholics and Non-jurors, *ib.* Association of Scottish Jacobites, *ib.* The French collect a large body of veteran troops, under Marshal Saxe, for the service of the Pretender, 470. The Old Pretender signs a proclamation, appointing his eldest son, Charles Edward, his regent and *alter ego, ib.* The Young Pretender reaches Paris, 1744; *ib.* The French fleet, under Roquefeuille, arrives off Dungeness, but the commander, terrified by the sight of the English fleet, bears away for the French coast, 471. Several French ships with their crews, lost, *ib.* The Young Pretender returns to Paris, *ib.* 6,000 Dutch troops landed at Gravesend to assist the English, *ib.* War declared between France and England, 472. Admirals Matthews and Lestock engage the Spanish fleet in the Mediterranean, *ib.* Matthews accuses Lestock of having misbehaved on the day of action, and sends him home to England for trial, *ib.* Matthews is recalled, and subjected, in conjunction with Lestock, to a court-marshal, *ib.* Lestock is honourably acquitted, and Matthews declared for ever incapable of serving his majesty, *ib.* Commodore Anson captures the *Manilla* galleon, 473. Frederic the Great, in disregard of his treaties, enters Bohemia with 60,000 men, and captures Prague, but is forced to retreat by prince Charles of Lorraine, *ib.* The prince de Conti defeats the king of Sardinia near the town of Coni, 474. Don Carlos compels the Austrian general, prince Lobkowitz, who had threatened to take Naples, to retreat behind the Po, *ib.* Deaths of the dowager-duchess of Marlborough and the countess Granville, *ib.* Lord Granville (the former lord Carteret) is dismissed, 475. Chesterfield is made lord-lieutenant of Ireland, *ib.* Pitt resigns his place in the household of the prince of Wales, *ib.* Various other ministerial changes, *ib.* An increased subsidy is voted to the queen of Hungary, 476. A new subsidy granted to the Elector of Saxony, and 8,000*l.* for the Elector of Mayence, *ib.* The Qua-

GEORGE II.,—

druple Alliance, 1744, *ib.* The Elector of Bavaria dies, *ib.* His son opens negotiations with Maria Theresa, *ib.* Death of sir Robert Walpole, *ib.* Marshal Saxe, at the head of 76,000 men, invests Tournay, *ib.* Battle of Fontenoy, May 11, 1745, in which the duke de Grammont is killed, 476—478. Battle of Hohen Friedberg, June 3, 479. Francis, husband of Maria Theresa, is elected emperor, *ib.* Victory of Soor, *ib.* George signs a convention at Hanover, guaranteeing to Prussia the possession of Silesia, *ib.* Unsuccessful campaign of the Allies of England in Italy, *ib.* Don Philip makes a triumphant entry into Milan, *ib.* The Young Pretender embarks for Scotland in the *Doutelle*, accompanied by the *Elizabeth*, 480. He is engaged by Captain Brett, *ib.* Arrives safely in Scotland, 481. Cameron of Lochiel swears to take up arms in his service, 482. A body of English, under the command of captain John Scott, are taken prisoners by the Highlanders, 483, 484. Tullibardine erects the standard of the Pretender at Glenfinnin, 484. Sir John Cope, commander-in-chief for Scotland, puts himself at the head of his troops, *ib.* The Regency offer a reward of 30,000*l.* to any one who should seize the Young Pretender, 485. Cope's march, 485, 486. The Young Pretender stays two days at Blair Castle, 486. He enters Perth, 487. James VIII. is proclaimed through Angus and Fife, *ib.* James Drummond and lord George Murray join the Pretender, *ib.* A reward of 300,000*l.* is offered to any one who should seize George, Elector of Hanover, 488. The Pretender reaches Dunblane, *ib.* His army is quartered at Linlithgow, 489. Dastardly conduct of two regiments of Cope's dragoons, *ib.* The Pretender summons Edinburgh, 491. Lochiel, with 800 Highlanders, takes possession of the city, 492. Cope forms his army in line of battle at Preston-pans, 494. Battle of Preston-pans, 495, 496. Letter of the justice-clerk to the marquess Tweeddale, 497, 498. Duncan Forbes communicates to lord Milton his plan for securing the loyalty of the Highlanders, 499. The Forty-second regiment of Highlanders is raised, 500. George, hearing of the success of the Pretender, arrives in London, 501. Preparations in London for fear of the Pretender, 501, 502. Prompt conduct of Dr. Herring, archbishop of York, in raising troops, 502. Parliament assembles, Oct. 18, 1745; *ib.* Foreign troops come over to England, 504. The Pretender blockades Edinburgh Castle, *ib.* Lord Ogilvie, Gordon of Glenbucket, and lord Pitaligo, join the Pretender, 505. Council of State of the Young Pretender, 508. He begins his march into England, *ib.* Carlisle surrenders, 509. View of the house in which the Pretender lodged at Derby, 513. Colonel Kerr drives before him a small body of the duke of Kingston's horse, and seizes captain Weir, *ib.* The Pretender enters Derby, Dec. 4; 514. He begins his retreat from Derby, 516. The lawyers form themselves into a regiment, under lord chief-justice Willes, to guard the royal family at St. James's in case of danger, 517. A skirmish takes place between the duke of Cumberland and the Highlanders, near Clifton Moor, 518. The Highlanders get back into Scotland, 519. Carlisle surrenders to the duke of Cumberland, 519, 520. Lord John Drummond lands at Montrose, and attempts to establish a military levy, 520. The people of Edinburgh resolve to defend the city, 521. The rebels besiege Stirling Castle, *ib.* Battle of Falkirk, Jan. 17, 1746; 522—524. Linlithgow palace burnt to the ground, 526. The duke of Cumberland arrives in the Scottish capital, 527. He puts himself at the head of the army, 528. The Highlanders retreat from Stirling, *ib.* A considerable number of the rebels deliver themselves up, 529. Ministerial re-

GEORGE II,—

volution, 530. Charles takes Fort George, 531; and Fort Augustus, 532. Desertions to the royal army, 533. The rebels agree on a night attack, 535. Battle of Culloden, April 17, 1746; 536—539. The Commons vote 25,000*l.* per annum to the duke of York, 541. Death of Duncan Forbes, 543. Flora Macdonald aids the escape of Charles Edward, 544. She is carried as a prisoner to London, 545. The Pretender arrives in Paris, 548. Severities exercised on the prisoners, *ib.* Lord Cromartie is pardoned, *ib.* Earl Kilmarnock and lord Balmerino are executed, 550. Trial of lord Lovat, March 1747. 551; his execution, 553. Sir John Cope is brought to trial by court-martial, and honourably acquitted, *ib.* Act of Indemnity passed to the rebels, *ib.* Act for disarming the clans and restraining their national garb, *ib.* Heritable jurisdictions abolished, *ib.* Battle of Roucoux, 554. Death of Philip V. of Spain, *ib.* Lord Chesterfield succeeds lord Harrington as secretary of state, *ib.* Parliament assembles, *ib.* Habeas Corpus Act suspended, *ib.* 100,000*l.* added to the queen of Hungary's subsidy, 555. The allies are beaten by marshal Saxe, at Lauffeld, *ib.* The fortress of Bergen-op-Zoom taken by the French, *ib.* Successes of the British navy, *ib.* Preliminaries of a peace at Aix-la-Chapelle, 556. Parliament assembles, *ib.* 13,000,000*l.* voted, *ib.* Parliament prorogued, *ib.* Several articles of the peace of Aix-la-Chapelle, 1748; 558. Louis XV. binds himself to exclude the Stuarts from France, *ib.* The Young Pretender solicits aid from Spain, *ib.* His brother enters the Romish church, 559. The Young Pretender is driven from France, 560. His father, the Old Pretender, dies, *ib.* Officers on half-pay are subjected to martial law, and it is enacted that all members of a court-martial shall be bound by oath not to disclose any of its proceedings, unless required by act of parliament, 1749; *ib.* Reduction of the forces, *ib.* Parliament prorogued, 561. The king goes to Hanover, 1750, *ib.* A British colony settles in Nova Scotia, *ib.* Settlement in the Gulf of Mexico, *ib.* Commercial treaty established with the court of Madrid, *ib.* Parliament assembles, 562. The Constitutional Queries, 1751, are burned by the hangman, 563. Gibson, and Alexander Murray, brother of lord Elibank, are confined in Newgate, *ib.* Death of Frederic, prince of Wales, March 20; 565. The princess of Wales throws herself on the protection of the king, 566. George, Frederic's eldest son, is created prince of Wales and earl of Chester, and a household settled for him, 567. A Regency Bill passed, May 8, 1751, *ib.* Death of the prince of Orange, 568. Death of the queen of Denmark, *ib.* Death of lord Bolingbroke, *ib.* The duke of Bedford resigns and lord Holderness obtains his place, *ib.* The Gregorian calendar is adopted in England, upon the motion of lord Chesterfield, 569. The journals of parliament printed, 572. Parliament prorogued, *ib.* Disagreements, 1752, in the household of the prince of Wales, 572—576. Pelham introduces a bill for the naturalisation of foreign Jews, 577. Hardewicke's Marriage Act; marriage by banns or license introduced, 578. Mr. Potter introduces a bill for establishing a general register of the population, which is thrown out by the Lords, 579. The Sloane Library and Museum, the Harleian MSS., and Montague-house purchased by the Government, 1753; *ib.* Dr. Archibald Cameron executed as a traitor, for his share in the rebellion of 1745; *ib.* Parliament assembles, *ib.* The bill for naturalising the Jews is repealed, 580. Death of Mr. Pelham, March 6, 1754; *ib.* A body of Indians fall upon major Washington, whilst erecting a little fort on the Ohio, and he is compelled to capitulate, 581. Dissensions between the French and English in the

GEORGE II,—

East Indies, *ib.* Parliament assembles; Admiral Boscawen is sent, 1755, with a good fleet towards the Gulf of St. Lawrence, to intercept a French fleet which was carrying reinforcements to the French Canadians, *ib.* Captain Howe captures two French ships of the line, 582. Sir E. Hawke goes on a cruise with eighteen ships of the line, *ib.* Admiral Byng puts to sea with twenty-two ships of the line, *ib.* Major-general Braddock is defeated, and slain in an attempt to drive the French from the Ohio, *ib.* Louis XV. concludes an alliance with the house of Austria, *ib.* Parliament assembles, 583. Pitt is dismissed by the king, *ib.* Fox is made secretary of state, 584. Pitt is made chief of the Leicester-house faction, *ib.* The duchess of Brunswick Wolfenbüttel pays George II. a visit at Hanover, with her two daughters, *ib.* The king desires that the elder of them should be espoused by his grandson, prince George, *ib.* The princess-dowager opposes this union, *ib.* Her affection for the earl of Bute; court scandal alluded to by Waldegrave and Walpole, 585. Abilities of Murray, the attorney-general, *ib.* Enormous supplies voted, *ib.* The Russians join the French and Austrians against the king of Prussia, *ib.* Admiral Byng is despatched to the Mediterranean to protect Minorca, 1756; he finds the English flag floating over the fortress of St. Philip, though the French flag was seen on other points, 586. Rear-admiral West attacks the French with spirit, and drives several of their ships out of the line, Byng keeps aloof, and West, being unassisted, is forced to veer round and permit La Galissonière to escape, 586, 587. Byng judges it impossible to assist Fort St. Philip, and sails back to Gibraltar; general Blakeney gallantly holds out till the beginning of July, when he is forced to capitulate, 587. On the news of Byng's retreat, admirals Hawke and Saunders take the command in the Mediterranean, *ib.* Byng is sent prisoner to England, *ib.* General rage of the people against him, *ib.* Fox resigns, October, on the appointment of Murray, the attorney-general, to be lord chief-justice, *ib.* The duke of Newcastle resigns the premiership, and is followed by chancellor Hardwicke, who had held the seals nearly twenty years, 588. Pitt is made secretary of state, *ib.* Change in the ministry, *ib.* King Frederic takes possession of Dresden, blockades the Saxon army at Pirna, defeats two Austrian armies, compels the Saxons to fly everywhere and surrender, and drives their elector into Poland, 589. He is declared a rebel by the Aulic Council, *ib.* Commencement of the Seven-years' war, *ib.* Trial of admiral Byng; he is sentenced to be shot, according to the twelfth article of war, 590. Letter of Voltaire to Byng, 590; *note.* The admiral is shot, on board the *Monarque*, March 14, 1757; 592. Plan of a new ministry, 593. Lord Temple and Pitt are dismissed, 593, 594. The new administration, 596. Pitt offers Gibraltar to Ferdinand, king of Spain, in exchange for Minorca, 597. He plans a descent on France, *ib.* The duke of Cumberland is beaten by the marshal D'Estrées, and led to sign the Convention of Closter-Seven, by which the electorate of Hanover is left in the hands of the French till peace should be concluded, and the Hanoverians, Hessians, and Brunswickers are dispersed into distant cantonments, under the obligation of not taking up arms again during the war, *ib.* Frederic is defeated by count Daun in the battle of Kolin, *ib.* General Haddick lays Berlin under contribution, *ib.* Marshal Lehwald forces general Apraxin to evacuate Prussia, *ib.*; and drives the Swedes out of Prussian Pomerania, taking 3,000 of them prisoners, 598. Frederic drives marshal Soubise and the prince of Hildbourghausen before him, *ib.* He gains the battle of Rossbach, Nov. 3, 1757, in which 30,000

GEORGE II.,—

French, and 20,000 imperial troops make a disgraceful and precipitate flight before five Prussian battalions and a few squadrons, ib. The Hanoverians and Hessians resume their arms in spite of the Convention of Closter-Seven, ib. The French set fire to Zell, ib. Battle of Breslau, ib. Frederic gains the victory of Lissa, December 5, 1757, in which he, with 30,000 men, defeats 90,000 Austrians and Imperialists, takes 24,000 prisoners on the field, 15,000 in the retreat, and 17,000 in the city of Breslau, ib. Pitt devises a plan for securing North America, ib. Whilst Clive is reducing Angria, Sujah-u-Dowlah takes Calcutta, and barbarously throws his prisoners into the Black Hole, 1756; 599. Clive reduces Calcutta, takes the city of Hooghly, with the military stores, and compels Sujah-u-Dowlah to sign such articles as he dictates, ib. Clive drives the French from Chandernagore, defeats Sujah-u-Dowlah at the battle of Plassey, and puts the ally of the English, Jaffier Ali Cawn, in his place, ib. The duke of Cumberland, on his return to England, resigns all his commands, 600. Factions in Ireland, ib. Riots in England on account of the new Militia Bill; Woburn Abbey narrowly escapes destruction, ib. Parliament meets Dec. 1; ib. A subsidy of 670,000l. per annum is voted to Frederic to carry on the war, 601. New taxes are laid upon houses and windows, ib. Lord Tyrawley accuses lord George Sackville of avoiding services of danger, ib. Death of the princess Caroline, 601; note. Pitt fits out a large naval and military force against the coast of France, 1758; 601. Lord Anson takes the command of this unfortunate expedition, ib. The attempt is repeated; prince Edward embarks as a volunteer, 602. General Bligh lands in the Bay of St. Lunaire, ib.; his men are beaten by the duke d'Aiguillon, ib. Admiral Boscawen embarks for Cape Breton; he takes the city of Louisburg, which he names Pittsburg, in honour of that minister, 603. General Abercrombie is repulsed with loss at Ticonderago, ib. Brigadier Forbes and colonel Bradstreet take Fort Duquesne on the Ohio, and Fort Frontenac on the St. Lawrence, ib. The Indians make treaties with the English, ib. Guadaloupe, Deseada, Marigalante, Goree, and Fort Louis are taken from the French, ib. Admiral Pococke defeats admiral d'Apché, ib. Count Fermor bursts into Prussia, and forces the inhabitants to swear allegiance to the czarina Elizabeth, ib. Frederic obliges the Russians to retire from the siege of Custrin, ib. He is defeated by marshal Daun in the battle of Hochkirchen, in which marshal Keith and prince Francis of Brunswick are killed, ib. Prince Ferdinand of Brunswick gains a complete victory over the count of Clermont, near Crevelt, Nov. 23, ib.; 12,000,000l. voted, ib. Dr. Shebbeare is sentenced to be confined in the pillory, ib. Sentence of death as a traitor is passed upon Dr. Florence Hensey, but he is pardoned on condition of leaving England for ever, 604, 605. A bill for extending the Act of Habeas Corpus is lost, 605. Anne, princess-royal of England, and dowager of Orange, dies, ib. Duties are laid upon sugar and other dry goods, 606. An invasion from the French being apprehended, the militia are called out, ib. Admiral Rodney bombards Havre-de-Grace, and does considerable damage to the French, ib. Admiral Boscawen, 1759, sends three ships of the line into the outer harbour of Toulon against some French ships, ib. The attacking ships being injured he descends to Gibraltar in order to refit, ib. M. de la Clue, commander of the Toulon fleet, sails down the Mediterranean, with intent to join the Brest fleet, ib. Boscawen falls upon him off Cape Lagos, ib. Clue is mortally wounded, and his ship, the

GEORGE II.,—

finest in the French navy, strikes its flag, ib. Sir E. Hawke gains a victory over the Brest fleet, commanded by M. Conflans, in Quiberon Bay, ib. M. Thurot, a daring adventurer, takes, and plunders Carrickfergus; he is boarded by captain Elliot, and, fighting bravely, falls covered with wounds on his deck; after his death, Elliott takes the ships and carries them as prizes into the Isle of Man, 607. The Canadas being left exposed to attack, through the disorders in France, Pitt resolves on a scheme for their conquest, ib. George selects general Hopson, but Pitt procures the promotion of lieutenant-general Edward Wolfe, ib. Scheme of the campaign, ib. General Wolfe's army is landed on the Isle of Orleans, in the St. Lawrence, by admiral Saunders, ib. A storm endangers the fleet; the French send down fire-ships and rafts, but both dangers are escaped, 608. Strength of Quebec by its natural position, and by military art, ib. Position occupied by the French commander, Montcalm, with 10,000 troops, ib. Amherst and Prideaux not having joined Wolfe, he determines to attack the French lines alone, ib. He crosses the Montmorenci to assail the French; his grenadiers are repulsed by a heavy fire of artillery, ib. He calls a council of war, ib. Concerts with admiral Saunders a plan for scaling the heights of Abraham, 609; the effort proves successful, and the French sentinels are taken by surprise, ib. Montcalm advances in too great a hurry to permit the French to bring up their artillery, ib. The French and Canadians open an irregular fire before they get in musket range, ib. The English reserve their fire till the enemy are close, and then pour in a terrible discharge, ib. In less than half an hour the French begin to waver, ib. Wolfe is twice seriously wounded, but he stands cheering his men till he is brought to the ground by a musket-ball in his breast, Sept. 13, 1759; ib. Montcalm and his second in command are mortally wounded, ib. Five days after Wolfe's death Quebec capitulates, and the remnant of the French army of Canada retires to Montreal, ib. Colonel Coote defeats the French under general Lally, and conquers the whole of Arcot, 610. Colonel Ford takes Masulipatam, ib. Prince Ferdinand of Brunswick gains the battle of Minden, ib. Misconduct of lord George Sackville, ib. He writes for leave to resign his command, and returns to England to face a court-martial, 611. Frederic of Prussia defeats general Wedet in the battle of Frankfort or Kunersdorf, where he loses nearly all his artillery, half his generals and officers of distinction, and above 18,000 men in killed and wounded, ib. Parliament assembles, ib. Lord Temple asks the king for a vacant Order of the Garter, which he had promised to the marquess of Rockingham; dispute, in consequence of this application, ib. 15,000,000l. are voted for supplies, 612. Trial of lord George Sackville, 1760; 612, 613. A bill for establishing a militia in Scotland is rejected, 613. Enlargement in the Qualification Act, 613, 614. M. Levi besieges general Murray in Quebec, 614. Montreal, the last stronghold of the French in Canada, capitulates, and the Canadas fall into the hands of the English, ib. The Austrians gain a victory over the Prussians, near Glatz, ib. They reduce the greater part of Breslau to a heap of ruins, ib. A Russian and Austrian army takes Berlin, and commits dreadful havoc there, but retreats on the approach of Frederic, 615. The hereditary prince of Brunswick is defeated at Corbach, ib. He takes the city of Cleves, and invests Wesel, but is compelled to retreat before M. de Castries, ib. The French overrun Hesse, ib. Death of George II., October 25, 1760; 615, 616. Signature of, 616. Coins of, 728, 729,

GEORGE III., eldest son of Frederic Prince of Wales (October 25, 1760—January 29, 1820,) on the death of his father is created prince of Wales and earl of Chester, iv. 567. Disposition of his household, ib.; disagreements in it, 572—576. No immediate change was made in the ministry on the accession of this king, Oct. 25, 1760; § i. 2. The name of the duke of Cumberland is struck out of the Liturgy, 3. George meets his parliament, Nov. 18, 1760; ib. Influence of the earl of Bute, 3, 4. Nineteen millions of supplies voted, 1761; 4. Important change in the commissions of the judges, 5. Mr. Legge is dismissed from the chancellorship of the Exchequer, and lord Barrington put in his place, ib. Lord Holderness resigns the office of secretary of state, which is given to the earl of Bute, ib. (This was the commencement of that series of incessant ministerial changes which so curiously distinguished the first ten years of this reign.) Parliament is dissolved, March 21; ib. Court scandal respecting the princess-dowager and the earl of Bute, 5, 24. The king marries Charlotte Sophia of Mecklenburg Strelitz, September 8, 1761; 6. General refinement in the court, ib. Prussian affairs, 7—9. Belliale taken by the English, 9. Pondicherry surrenders to colonel Coote, ib. The island of Dominica is reduced, ib. Declining state of France, ib. Preliminaries of peace between France and England, 9, 10. Death of Ferdinand VI. of Spain, 1759; 10. Pitt resigns his office of secretary, 11, and lord Temple follows his example, ib. Declaration of war between Spain and England, 12, 13. Parliament assembles, November 6; 13. Coronation of the king and queen, September 22, at which the Young Pretender was present, ib. Settlement of the queen's dowry, 15. Havanna capitulates to the English, August 13, 1762; 15. 16. Manilla carried by storm, October 6; 16. Martinique and other places surrender, 17. War between Spain and Portugal, which latter is assisted by the English, 17, 18. Unfortunate expedition against Buenos Ayres, 19. Death of the czarina Elizabeth, January 5, 1762; 20. Close alliance between Russia and Prussia, ib. Lord Bute becomes prime-minister, ib. Revolution in Russia; death of the czar Peter, July 6, 1762. Catherine II. ascends the throne, 21, 22. Negotiations for peace with France; the treaty of Fontainebleau, 22. Parliament assembles, November, 25; 23. Pitt denounces the treaty as derogatory to the honour of England, ib. Treaty of Hubertsburg, February 15, 1763; 24. The Cyder Bill, 25. Bute resigns, April 8th, and is followed by Fox and several others, ib. Prosecution of John Wilkes, editor of the "North Briton," 25, 26. Death of lord Egremont, 27. The duke of Bedford becomes president of the council, and lord Egmont is placed at the head of the Admiralty, 28. Wilkes is wounded in a duel by Mr. S. Martin, 29, 30. Riot, occasioned by the burning of the "North Briton," 31. Parliament meets, January 19, 1764; 32. The case of Wilkes is strongly agitated, 32—34. Grenville proposes the taxation of America. The Stamp Act, 34. Attack of the Indians on the colonists, 1763, 1764; 34, 35. The provinces of New England pass strong resolutions against the proposed taxation, 35. Benjamin Franklin arrives in England, ib. Parliament assembles, January 10, 1765; 36. The approaching marriage of the princess Caroline with the prince royal of Denmark is announced by the king, ib. Resolutions on American taxation, 37. The king gives his assent to the Stamp Act, 22nd March, 1765; ib. The king is attacked with that fatal malady which finally incapacitated him for the duties of government, 37, 38. The Regency Bill; the queendowager's name is excepted, but finally restored, 38, 39. Popular assembly in London, 39. The king treats with Mr. Pitt, who refuses to act, 40. The

GEORGE III.,— duke of Newcastle forms a new ministry, July 15, 1765. General Conway is made one of the secretaries of state, ib. Justice Pratt is elevated to the peerage by the title of lord Camden, 41. The marquess of Rockingham becomes premier, ib. Excited state of America; the colonists form associations against the importation of British manufactures until the Stamp Act should be repealed, ib. Parliament assembles, January 14, 1766. Pitt's eloquent speech against the taxation of the colonies, 42, 43; he is supported by general Conway, 43; further debates on this subject, 44, 45. The Stamp Act is repealed, 45, 46. Partial repeal of the Cyder Act, 46. The question of general warrants is resumed, ib. Pitt is created earl of Chatham, 47. The new ministry, 48. The marquess of Rockingham retires, ib. Parliament assembles, November 11, 1766; 50. Embargo laid on the exportation of wheat and flour, ib. Chatham's first speech in the House of Lords, 50, 51. Lord Edgecumbe resigns by desire of the king, 52. Sir Edward Hawke is appointed first lord of the Admiralty, 53. Debates on the Land-tax, 1767; 54. Examination into the state of the East India Company, ib. Inert conduct of Chatham, ib. Grenville proposes to levy 400,000l. on America for the support of troops, 56; proposed articles of taxation, 57. General Conway and lord Northington express their desire to resign, ib. Proposed arrangements for a new ministry, 58. Charles Townshend dies of a putrid fever, September 4, 1767; 59. The chancellorship of the Exchequer is entrusted, pro tem., to lord Mansfield, ib. Parliament meets, November 4, 1767; the duke of Grafton's administration, 59, 60. Parliament prorogued 10th March, 1768, and dissolved March 12; 60. Wilkes is returned for the county of Middlesex, 60, 61. Parliament meets, May 10; 61. Sir John Cust is elected Speaker, ib. Parliament prorogued, May 21; the standing order for the exclusion of strangers from the Houses was strictly enforced, ib. Wilkes is seized and imprisoned; riot occasioned by this procedure, 61, 62. His outlawry is reversed, but he is at the same time fined and sentenced to be imprisoned for two years, 62. Chatham begs to resign, 63; and the earl of Bristol becomes lord privy-seal, 64. Lord Shelburne resigns, ib. General Paoli, chief of the Corsicans, applies for succour to England, ib. Parliament assembles, November 8, 1768; 65. Further proceedings in respect of Wilkes, 66—70. American affairs; dispute on the Statute of the 35th Henry VIII. concerning Treason, 70—72. Parliament refuses to receive a petition from the people of New York, March 14, 1769; 73. The Charter of the East India Company prolonged, ib. Disturbances in America; the Mutiny Act, ib. The Convention request the inhabitants to furnish themselves with arms, 74—76. The Virginia Association, 77. Parliament rises 9th May, 1769; 78. Discontent in London, ib. "Junius's Letters," ib. Turbulent state of Ireland; the military establishment is increased in that country, 80. Parliament assembles, January 9, 1770, ib. Speech of Charles James Fox, 83. The lord-chancellor Camden is dismissed, and the honourable Charles Yorke, who had received the great seal, commits suicide, 84. The marquess of Granby resigns, 84, 85; various other resignations, 85. Remarkable speech of the earl of Chatham, 86. Death of sir John Cust; sir Fletcher Norton is elected Speaker, 87. Committee on the state of the nation formed, January 25, 1770; 87, 89. The duke of Grafton resigns the premiership, ib. Lord Frederic North undertakes the management of the state, ib; other ministerial changes, ib. Debates concerning the increase of seamen in the royal navy, 91. The earl of Chatham accuses the king of insincerity, ib. Petitions and remonstrances

GEORGE III.,—

from the city and county of Middlesex to the king, 91—93. Bill for regulating the trial of controverted elections, 1770; 93. Ministerial bill for repealing American taxes and duties, 95. Alderman Beckford presents another petition at St. James's, May 23, 1770; 97. Contentions between the military and the people at Boston, 98—102. Disputes with Spain concerning the Falkland Islands, 102, 103. Deaths of the marquess of Granby and Mr. G. Grenville, 1770; 104. Parliament meets, November 13, ib. Prosecution of the printers and publishers of "Junius's Letters," 106. Disputes concerning the holding of parliament with closed doors, 107. Lord Weymouth resigns the seals of secretary of state, which are given to lord Sandwich, 108. Mr. Harris, British minister at the court of Spain, recalled, ib. Thurlow becomes attorney-general, and H. Bathurst baron Apsley, lord-chancellor, 109. Termination of the dispute with Spain announced, 1771; ib. Further prosecution of printers and publishers; the lord-mayor, Crosby, and alderman Oliver, are committed to the Tower, 112—117. The practice of publishing parliamentary debates in newspapers established, 117. Chatham declares himself a convert to triennial parliaments, 118. Parliament prorogued, May 8, 1771; ib. Death of the earl of Halifax, June 8; the duke of Grafton becomes lord privy-seal, 119. Nomination of governor and preceptors for the king's eldest son, prince George, 120. Wilkes is elected sheriff, ib. Parliament meets, January 21, 1772; 121. It is made a standing order, that no bill should be permitted to pass the House whereby capital punishments were decreed, unless the same should be previously referred to a committee of the whole House, ib. Committee of Supply, 122. Petition against the Thirty-nine Articles negatived by a large majority, 123—125. Affairs of the East India Company, 125. The Royal Marriage Act, occasioned by the private marriages, etc., of the dukes of Cumberland and Gloucester, 126, 127. Parliament prorogued, June 10, 1772; 127. Fox becomes a temporary convert to Whig principles, and resigns the Admiralty, ib. Death of the princess-dowager of Wales, February 8, 1772. Caroline Matilda, queen of Denmark, and sister of George III., is confined in Cronborg Castle, with the darkest imputations on her character, 128, 129. Through the mediation of the English king, who, by means of his ambassador sir Robert Murray, alternately remonstrated and menaced, the Danish court is finally induced to agree that she should be permitted to quit the kingdom, whence she is conveyed to the Castle of Zell, in Hanover; she did not long survive her misfortunes, and died May 10, 1775, in the twenty-fourth year of her age, 130. Sudden revolution at Stockholm, 1772; 131. Tragical fate of the czar Ivan, 132, 133. History of Poland, 134—141. The confederacy of Barr, 1768; 137. Insurrection in the Morea, 1770, assisted by the Russians and English, 141—148. Battle of Tchesmé, 143. Marriage of the dauphin (Louis XVI.) with the Austrian archduchess Marie Antoinette, 1770; 145. The sultan solicits the mediation of Frederic of Prussia to obtain a peace with Catherine, ib. First Treaty of Partition signed at St. Petersburg, August 2, 1772, ib. Armistice signed at Giurgevo between general Romanzoff and the grand viaier, May 30, 1772; 147. Russia concludes a separate treaty with the Tartars of the Crimea, ib. The treaty of Kainarji signed, July 21, 1774, between the grand vizier and prince Repnin, 148. The English parliament assembles, November 26, 1772, ib. Select committee appointed to examine the state of the East India Company, 148, 149. Examination, 1773, of the state of the Island of St. Vincent, 149. Lord Howe presents a petition from his brother-officers, praying

GEORGE III.,—

for a trifling increase of half-pay, 149, 150. Colonel Barré is dismissed from the service, 151. Bill for the Relief of Protestant Dissenters, 151—153. The wife of the duke of Gloucester is delivered of a daughter, 1773; 153. The Americans institute a committee of correspondence, ib. Burning of the Gaspee schooner, 1772, by the Rhode Islanders, 154, 155. Destruction of tea at Boston, 156. Parliament assembles, January 13, 1774, ib. 20,000 seamen voted, as in the preceding year, 156. Grenville's Controverted Election Act passed, ib. American affairs, 156—252. Benjamin Franklin is dismissed from his place of post-master general for America, 1774; 159. The trade of Boston is removed to New Salem, ib. Bill for the better regulating of government in the province of Massachusetts Bay, 160, 161. Colonel Barré condemns the violent language used by the Houses against America, 161. Fox disagrees with the Government, and again turns patriot, ib. Bill for the quartering and better regulating the troops in the colonies, 162. Speech of Chatham concerning America, ib. Bill for making more effectual provision for the government of the province of Quebec, in North America; examinations, Mr. Mansfield counsel for the merchants of London, general Carleton, governor of Canada, and divers others, 164—174. Disputes concerning the boundary-line of Canada and New York, 1774; 179. The duke of Gloucester votes against ministers, 180. General Gage, the new governor, lands at Boston, May, 13, 1774; 181. The Virginians appoint the 1st of June as a day of fasting, etc., 182. The Assembly of Massachusetts meets for the last time at Boston, ib. Desertion in the British army, 184. Meeting of delegates held, notwithstanding a proclamation of the governor forbidding it, 185. Delegates to the General Congress, 187. The provincial congress of Massachusetts, 189. Parliament dissolved, September 30, 1774; 192. Wilkes is elected lord-mayor, ib. Reduction in the British navy, 193. Strangers and members of the House of Commons are admitted to the debates of the House of Lords, at the motion of the duke of Manchester, 194. Gibbon, the historian, sits in parliament, 1774, for the borough of Liskeard, ib. Alarming news from America, 1775. Debates thereupon, 194—398. Lord North's bill for cutting off the trade of New England, 203, 204. Conciliatory propositions in respect to America, 205—209. Burke, as agent for the colony of New York, presents a remonstrance from the general assembly of that province, 209. Petition from the British inhabitants of Canada, 210. Encounter between the inhabitants of the town of Concord and the English, 211—213. The provincial congress of Massachusetts resolves on the establishment of an army of 30,000 men, 214. The Americans declare general Gage to be disqualified from acting as governor, ib. Generals Howe, Burgoyne, and Clinton arrive at Boston from England, May, 1775; ib. Carelessness of the English commanders, 216, 217. Battle of Bunker's-hill, June 17, 1775; 216. Attack of the provincials upon Canada, 217. The forts of Ticonderoga and Crown Point are taken by Ethan Allen, 217, 218. Benedict Arnold, Allen, Montgomery, and others, make an unsuccessful attack on Quebec, 219—224. Lord Danmore, governor of Virginia, proclaims freedom to all slaves who would repair to his standard, and bear arms for the king; and at the same time issues a proclamation declaring martial-law throughout that colony, 224, 225. The town of Norfolk is reduced to ashes, 225. Congress appoints George Washington commander-in-chief, appoints a committee of safety for New York, and addresses a letter to the lord-mayor and livery of London, 227.

GEORGE III.,—
Some account of the life of Washington, 230—234. Proclamation issued for repressing rebellion in England, August 23, 1775. Petition of Congress laid before the king by Richard Penn, 235. General Conway expresses his abhorrence of the idea of conquering America by force, 238. The duke of Grafton is deprived of office, and lord George Germaine is made secretary for the colonies and intrusted with the management of American affairs, 1775; 242. Lord North brings in a bill for enabling the king to assemble the militia in cases of actual rebellion, ib. The Constitutional Society, 243. Lord Mountstuart brings in a bill for establishing a militia in Scotland, ib. Examination of Mr. Penn, 245. Resignation of lord Howard of Effingham, 248. Foreign troops engaged for serving against the Americans, 249. Chatham withdraws his son lord Pitt from the American service, 252. Parliament prorogued, May, 1776; ib. Trial of the duchess of Kingston, 253—255. American affairs, 255—282. Unsuccessful attack upon Quebec, 255, 256. Washington makes an attack on Boston, and forces Howe to evacuate the town, 259—261. Ill success of the government party in North Carolina, 261. Progress of the revolution, 264. The Convention of Virginia draws up a Declaration of Rights, May 15, 1776; 265. Twelve of the thirteen states of America vote in favour of the Declaration of Independence, 266. Facsimile of the signatures to this declaration, signed July 4, 1776; 268. Lord Howe attempts to open a communication with Washington, 270. Battle on Long Island, 271—273. Washington evacuates New York, September 12; 274. Lord Howe makes a second attempt at pacification, 275, 276. The Creek and Cherokee Indians invade Virginia and the Carolinas, 281. Parliament assembles, October 31, 1776; 282. Debates on American affairs, 282—287; 45,000 seamen voted, 286. Parliament adjourned, December 13; 287. Trial of John the Painter, or James Aitkin, the incendiary, 287—290. Bill for enabling the Admiralty to grant letters of marque and reprisal against the Americans, 1777; 290. Bill for the detention of persons suspected of treason or piracy, ib. Increase in the king's private revenue, 291. American affairs, 295—319. Fierce conflict between the English and the Americans, Jan. 1777; 296, 297. Action at Brandywine, 302. General Howe crosses the Schuylkill, September 22, 303. General Carleton sends over his resignation, 306. Burgoyne puts under arms several nations of Red Indians, ib. The Americans evacuate Ticonderoga, 307. Burgoyne's attack on the American batteaux, 308, 309. Expedition against Bennington, 310, 311. Siege of Stanwix Fort, 311. Battle at Still-water, ib. Burgoyne's retreat on the Hudson's River; general Fraser is slain, 313—315. Burgoyne capitulates to general Gates, at Saratoga, 316. Attack on forts Montgomery and Clinton, 317, 318. Parliament assembles, November 18, 1777; 319. Debates on American affairs, 319—328; 60,000 seamen voted, 328. Parliament receives official notice, March 17, 1778, of a treaty of amity and commerce between the French king and the Americans; the British ambassador at Paris is recalled, 335. Measures for the relief of Ireland, 338. Bill for the relief of the Roman Catholics, ib. Burgoyne, who had returned to England, speaks in justification of his conduct in the American war, 339. Chatham appears in the House of Lords for the last time, April 7, 1778, and speaks eloquently against the independence of America, 340. Death of this great orator, May 11, 1778; 341. 20,000l. is voted for the payment of his debts, and an annuity of 4,000l. upon his heirs, 342. Session of parliament terminated, July 7, 344.

GEORGE III.,—
Lord Barrington, the secretary at war, resigns, ib. Death of Maximilian Joseph, elector of Bavaria, December 30, 1777; 345. War between the emperor Joseph and Frederic the Great; treaty of Teschen signed, May 13, 1779, ib. Several French ships taken by the English, 347. Engagement between admiral Keppel and count d'Orvilliers, 347, 348. Disgraceful infraction of the Convention of Saratoga, 348. Distressed condition of Washington's army, 349; he is forced to press men into the service, 351. The Congress at York Town proposes another irruption into Canada, to be headed by the marquess Lafayette, ib. Dissipation in the English army in America, 353. Expedition for the destruction of American shipping in the upper part of the Delaware, 1778; 355. General Howe prepares for his departure to England, 356, 357. Clinton evacuates Philadelphia, 358, 359. Washington makes an unsuccessful attack on the English rear, 359, 360. Sullivan commences the siege of Newport, 361. Colonel Campbell takes possession of the town and fort of Savannah, 364. The Wyoming incursion, 366. The French take the island of St. Dominica, 1778, and the English in return take St. Lucie, 368—370. Governor Johnstone opens a private correspondence with several members of Congress, 371. The English commissioners issue a manifesto offering pardon, etc., October 3; 374. Parliament assembles, November 25, 1778; 375. Admirals Keppel and Palliser are tried by court-martial, and acquitted, 1779; 377, 378. Volunteer associations in Ireland formed, in imitation of the Americans, 380, 381. The Spanish ambassador quits London, 381. Inquiry into the conduct of affairs in America, 381. The Indemnity Bill, 382. Charles III. tenders his offices as mediator between England and America, 383. Meditated attack by the combined fleets of France and Spain on Gibraltar, 384, 385. Action between d'Estaing and vice-admiral Byron, 385. Colonel Campbell takes possession of Augusta, the principal town of Upper Georgia, 1779; 387. Major-general Tryon takes possession of Newhaven, and gains several other advantages, 389. The British take possession of Fort Lafayette and Stoney Point, 390. The French and Americans make an unsuccessful attack upon the Savannah, 390—393. Don Bernardo Galvez makes an irruption into West Florida, 396. Adventures of Paul Jones, 396—398. Thurlow is elevated to the chancellorship, 1779; 398. Parliament assembles, November 25, 1779; 399. Irish affairs, 400, 401. Debates concerning the public expenditure, 401—403. Petitions concerning a reform in parliament, 403. Burke's plan of economical reform, 404. The Board of Trade abolished, March 13, 1780. Debates concerning the Pension List, 405, 406. Commissioners of accounts appointed, 405. Contractors excluded from the House of Commons, 406. Debates concerning some repeal of the penal laws against Romanists in Scotland; riots in Scotland thereupon, 409—411. Popular meeting, headed by lord George Gordon; the great London riots, 411—417. Parliament prorogued, July, 1780; 418. Naval success of sir George Rodney, ib. The battle of St. Vincent, ib. The Armed Neutrality, 419. The English exercise of searching neutral ships, 419—422. American affairs, 422—439. Charlestown surrenders to sir H. Clinton, 1780; 423. Persecution of the royalists in North Carolina, 425. The battle of Camden, August, 1780; 426, 427. Discontent in Washington's army, 429. A French armament arrives at Rhode Island, July 13, 1780. Engagement between Rodney and admiral de Guichen, 430, 431. Benedict Arnold opens a secret correspondence with general Clinton; major André,

GEORGE III.,—

who conducted it on the part of the British, is seized by the Americans, and executed, 431—435. Articles agreed on between the United Provinces and the United States, 1778; 437, 438. Henry Laurens, an American agent, is seized and committed to the Tower, 438. The English ambassador at the United Provinces is recalled, and the Dutch ambassador in England demands his passports, December 29, 1780; 438, 439. Negotiations with Spain respecting the cession of Gibraltar, 439—441. Parliament dissolved, September 1, 1780; 441. Parliament assembles October 31, ib., and adjourns December 6, 442. Letters of marque and reprisal granted against the Dutch, ib. Burke reproduces his scheme of economical reform, Feb. 15, 1781; ib. Act, amending a clause in the Marriage Act of 1751; 445. Parliament prorogued, July 18, 1781; 446. Attack of the French on the Island of Jersey, ib. Reduced state of the Gibraltar garrison, 447. Mutiny in Washington's army, ib.—449. Negotiation of Washington with the French court, 449. General Arnold (now a British officer) seizes Richmond, the capital of Virginia, and burns it to the ground, 450. Lafayette is entrusted with the defence of Virginia, 451. Successes of general Phillips, ib. Battle of Guilford, March 15, 1781; 453, 454. March of lord Cornwallis from Wilmington, 456—458. Death of general Phillips, ib. Action between general Graves and count de Grasse, 459. Arnold takes possession of New London, September 1781; 460. Preparations for reducing lord Cornwallis in York Town, ib. Attack on the town, 461—463. Cornwallis proposes terms of capitulation, 463, 464. Colonel Brown is forced to capitulate and deliver up Augusta to the Americans, 465. General Greene makes an attack on Ninetysix, but is forced to raise the siege, 465, 466. Execution of colonel Hayne, 467. Battle of Eutaw, September 8, 1781. Colonel Washington is taken prisoner, 467—469. Rodney captures the Dutch island of St. Eustatius, 469. Tobago capitulates to the Marquess de Bouillé, 470. Captain Johnstone takes several rich prizes in Saldanah Bay, ib. Attack on Minorca, under the duke de Crillon, 471, 472. Engagement between sir Hyde Parker and admiral Zouttman, 472. The emperor Joseph II. declares his accession to the Armed Neutrality, 1781; 473. Parliament assembles November 27, 474. Debates on the American war, 476. Laurens is exchanged for general Burgoyne, 477. Parliament adjourns, December 20, ib. Minorca is captured February 5, 1782, ib. Parliament reassembles, ib. Inquiry into the ill success of the naval forces, ib. Resignation of lord G. Germaine; he is created viscount Sackville, 478. The House addresses the king for peace with America, 480. Lord North resigns, 481. The marquess of Rockingham becomes premier, 482. The new ministry, ib. Burke's plan of economical reform passes the Houses, 484. Separate treaty concluded with Holland, ib. Death of the marquess of Rockingham, July 1, 1782; 485. William Pitt becomes chancellor of the Exchequer, ib. Other changes in the administration, ib. Parliament prorogued July 11. Action between Rodney and admiral de Grasse, 486, 487. Rodney is raised to the peerage, 488. Execution of captain Joshua Huddy by the royalists, ib. Sir H. Clinton is superseded by sir Guy Carleton, who makes advances for peace, 489. Disordered state of Washington's army, 489. The Bahama Islands are captured by the Spaniards, 490. Bombardment of Gibraltar: admirable sortie made on the Spanish lines by general Eliott, 490, 491. The chevalier d' Arcon's plan for capturing the Rock, 492—494. Lord Howe's fleet arrives at Gibraltar, 494. Partial action with the combined fleets of France and Spain,

GEORGE III.,—

495. The Americans sign separate preliminary articles of peace with England, November, 30, 1782, being convinced of the duplicity of the French court, 496. Parliament meets, December 5, ib. Preliminaries of peace signed at Paris, January 20, 1783; 497. Conditions of the treaty in regard to America and France, 497, 498. Truce with the Dutch, 498. Parliament re-assembles, ib Coalition between lord North and Mr. Fox. Lord Shelburne resigns, 499. ministerial interregnum, 499, 500. The Coalition Ministry, 500. The Stamp Duty, 1783; ib Relief afforded to the American royalists, 501. The Quakers petition for the total abolition of the slave trade, June 17, 1783; ib. Separate establishment for the prince of Wales, ib. Parliament prorogued, July 16, ib. Preliminary articles of peace with the Dutch, signed at Paris, September 2, ib. Definitive treaties with France, Spain, and America, signed at the same place September 3, ib. Parliament re-assembles November 11 : the prince of Wales takes his seat in the House of Peers, as duke of Cornwall, 502. Fox introduces his India bills, 502—504. The king demands from Mr. Fox and lord North their seals of office, December 18, which terminates the Coalition, 504. The new ministry : Pitt is appointed first lord of the Treasury and chancellor of the Exchequer, 504, 505. Parliament adjourns till January 12, 1784; 505. The Mutiny Bill voted, March 8, 508. Parliament is dissolved, March 25, and the new parliament convoked, May 18; ib. Reduction of the duty upon tea, and proportionate raising of the Window-tax, 509. Act, restoring the Scottish estates forfeited on account of the rebellion of 1745, June 30; ib. The Appropriation Bill, ib. The king prorogues parliament, August 20, 1784; ib. Parliament assembles, January 25, 1785; § ii. 2. Dispute concerning the election of Mr. Fox, 2—4. State of Ireland : meeting of the National Congress at Dublin, 4—6. The Irish Trade Bill, 6. Pitt's project of the Sinking Fund, ib. Taxation on servants, 7. Parliament adjourned, and afterwards prorogued to December 1 ; ib. Reduced state of the Dutch, ib. The Barrier Treaty broken by the emperor Joseph, 8. An imperial army of 60,000 men enters the Netherlands: treaty concluded for maintaining the indivisibility of the empire and the rights of the Germanic body, July 23, 1785; 9. The Dutch conclude a close alliance with France, 10. Parliament re-assembles, Jan. 24, 1786; 12, 191. Burke recommends the impeachment of Warren Hastings, February 17; 192, 195. Pitt brings under consideration the national debt and his new sinking fund, March 29, 13. Inquiry into the woods and land revenues belonging to the crown, 15. Impeachment of Warren Hastings, late governor-general of Bengal, 16, 196. Parliament prorogued, July 11; 16, 202. View of Indian affairs, 16, 191. Margaret Nicholson attempts to assassinate the king, August 2, 202. Intimacy of the prince of Wales with the duke d' Orleans, 203. His connexion with Mrs. Fitzherbert, 204. Subject of his debts, 203 - 207, 218—223. Death of Frederic the Great, king of Prussia. August 17, 1786, and accession of his nephew Frederic William, 207. Disturbed state of Holland, 207—209. Treaty of commerce and navigation between France and England, signed at Versailles, 209. Parliament assembles, January 23, 1787; ib. The House meets in committee, to take into consideration the late treaty, 211—216. Pitt introduces his celebrated plan for consolidating the various duties upon articles in the Customs and Excise, 218. Abuses in the Post-office 223—225. Impeachment of Warren Hastings (continued) 226—241. Parliament prorogued, May 30, 1787; 241. Affairs of Holland, 241—254. Parliament

GEORGE III.,—

meets, November 27; 252. Lord Howe resigns, 1788; 255. Indian affairs, 255—258. Resolutions for improving the passage of slaves, 258—260. Impeachment of sir Elijah Impey, late chief-justice of Bengal, ends in nothing, 260—275. Trial of Warren Hastings, at Westminster-hall commences, February 13, 1788; 275—280. Parliament prorogued July 11, 281. Derangement of the king's mind, 282. Examination of the physicians by the privy-council, 283. Parliament re-assembles, December 4, ib. Debates concerning the appointment of a regency, 1788, 1789, 284—293. The prince of Wales accepts the regency, 294. Debates on the Regency Bill, 294—298. The king is declared to be convalescent, April 17, 1789; 299. A committee from the Irish parliament presents an address to the prince of Wales, requesting him to take upon himself the regency of Ireland as his right, 299, 300. Repeal of the Shop-tax, April 1789; 303. Procession to St. Paul's, April 23, on occasion of his majesty's recovery, ib. Proceedings respecting the slave-trade, 304. Lord Sydney resigns, ib. Trial of Warren Hastings, (continued) 305—309. Parliament prorogued by commission, August 11, 309. Death of the Young Pretender, Charles Stuart, January 31, 1788; 310. The Turkish war, in 1789; 311—819. Death of Abdul Hamet, April 7. Discontent of the Swedish nobles; their league with Russia, 319—322. Animosities between the emperor Joseph and his Hungarian subjects, 322, 323. The troubles in the Austrian Netherlands break out afresh, 1789; cruelties of general Dalton; the university of Louvain is cleared at the point of the bayonet; preparations for a similar attack on the college of Antwerp; the abbeys of Brabant sequestrated, 392—328. View of the moral and political state of France previous to the Revolution, 328—337. The French Revolution, 337—447. The Revolution Society opened in London, November 4, 1789; 449. Parliament assembles, January 21, 1790; 450. Opinions of Burke and Fox on the revolution, 451—455. Increase in the salary of the speaker of the House of Commons, 455, 456. Two vessels, navigated under the British flag, seized at Nootka Sound, by a Spanish officer, 457. The Spanish government makes satisfaction, 465. Debates on the slave-trade, 466. Trial of Hastings, (continued) 1790; 466—469. The king closes the session of parliament, 469. The earl of Westmoreland is appointed lord-lieutenant of Ireland, ib. Death of the emperor Joseph II., February 20, 1790; and accession of Leopold II., 470, 471. Anarchy in the Netherlands, 472, 473. Treaty of peace concluded between Sweden and Russia, August 14; 475. Storming of Ismael, 475, 476. The French revolution, (continued) 477—532. The Belgic revolution suppressed, 1790; 532—536. War with Tippoo Sahib, 537, 538. Parliament assembles, November 26; 538. Dissolution of friendship between Fox and Burke, occasioned by their different views of the French revolution, 1791; 544—555. Debates on the slave-trade, 555, 556; on the law of libel, 556—558. A finance committee appointed, April 8; 558, 559. The trial of Warren Hastings (continued); he is declared "Not Guilty," 558—569. The Birmingham riots, 581—586. The French revolution, (continued) 591—729. Parliament assembles, January 31, 1792; § iii. 1. Definitive treaty concluded between the emperor and the Ottoman Porte, ib. Animated debate in the parliament concerning the interference of England in favour of Turkey, 1—8. Marriage of the duke of York, 8. Debates on the slave-trade, 9—11. Massacres in the Island of St. Domingo, 9. Act for the better regulation of the Police of the Metropolis, 11. Bill for inclosing parts of the New Forest in Hamp-

GEORGE III.,—

shire, ib. Bribery at elections, 12. Grievances petitioned against by the royal burghs in Scotland, ib. Debates on the rotten boroughs in England; parliamentary reform, 14. Royal proclamation for preventing seditious meetings and writings, May 21, 1792; 16. The prince of Wales speaks in the House of Lords, for the first time, 18. Information filed by the attorney-general against the publication of Paine's "Rights of Man," ib. Bill for repealing certain laws affecting Dissenters, ib. The Unitarian petitioners, 19. Fox's Libel Bill passed, 21. Parliament prorogued, June 15; ib. Republican meetings in different parts of England, 22, 24. The chancellor Thurlow dismissed; lord Loughborough appointed his successor, 27. Death of the earl of Guildford, August 5; Pitt becomes warden of the Cinque Ports, ib. Sketch of the war in India, 27—33. Exploits of lord Cornwallis; attack on Seringapatam, 29, et seq.—Tippoo consents to the terms proposed by the English, 31, 32. Surrender of his two eldest sons to lord Cornwallis, 32. Lord Macartney's embassy to China, 1792; 33. Revolution in Poland, 34—47. Proposed alliance between Prussia and Poland, 35. Resolutions of the Polish diet; they declare the crown hereditary, and nominate the Elector of Saxony to succeed Stanislaus Augustus, 35, 37. The king accedes to the new constitution, May 3, 1791; 36. Treaty of Jassy concluded between Russia and Turkey, August, 1791; 38. Death of the emperor Leopold, March 1, 1792. He is succeeded by his son Francis II. (who, in 1806, became hereditary emperor of Austria, under the title of Francis I.) Act of Confederacy signed at Targowicz by several Polish magnates, inviting Russia to re-establish the old constitution, 39. Protest of the empress Catherine to the diet at Warsaw, 39—41. A Russian army enters Poland, May 18; 41. Answer of the diet, ib. Frederic William refuses to lend his assistance against the invasion, 42. Mission of count Bukaty to London, 43. The English parliament prorogued, June 15; 44. Timidity of the Polish king, ib. Battle of Dubienka, July 17, 1792; 45. Stanislaus signs the Act of the Confederation of Targowicz, July 25; 46. Swedish affairs, 47—50. Plans of Gustavus for invading France, and reinstating the royal family, 48. He is shot at a masked ball, by Ankarstroem, a Swedish noble, and expires twelve days after, March 29; 49, 50. The French revolution, (continued) 50—255. Execution of Louis XVI., January 21, 1793; 255. Visible grief in London at this tragical occurrence, 256. Meeting of the English parliament, December 13, 1792; ib. The militia called out, December 1; ib. Spread of revolutionary principles in England, 257. Riot in Manchester, 264. Lord Grenville introduces an Alien bill, on account of the immense quantity of French daily repairing to England, 265. War declared between France and England, 267. Statement of several facts and reasons tending to prove that the choice of war or peace no longer rested with the British government, 269—285. Chauvelin, the French minister, receives orders to quit England, January 24, 1793; 279. The Convention grants letters of marque against the English, ib. The Charter of the East India Company renewed, May 24; 281. Bill for preventing all traitorous correspondence with the king's enemies, 282. Parliament prorogued, June 21; 285. The French revolution, (continued) 285—292. Frederic William marches an army into Poland, takes possession of Thorn and Dantzic, and compels the diet to ratify a fresh partition, which made over to Russia a territory containing a population of more than three millions and a half, and to Prussia a territory containing nearly one million and a half of inhabitants, together with the naviga-

Q

GEORGE III,—
tion of the Vistula, and the port of Dantzic on the Baltic, 1793; 292, 293. Capture and evacuation of Toulon, 1793; 302—309. Tuscany agrees to break off all intercourse with the French Republic, and to unite with the grand European coalition, 310. The pope closes his ports against French shipping, and the grand-master of the knights of Malta expels all French agents from that island, 311. The French revolution, (continued) 311—361. The British parliament meets, January 21, 1794; 381. Volunteer forces of horse and foot are levied in every county, and the militia is augmented, 382. Trial of English and Scottish revolutionists, 383— 392. The British Convention, 387. The Suspension Bill passed, 1794; 391. Proceedings on the slave-trade, 392. Parliament prorogued, July 11; ib. Lord Howe's victory of the 1st of June, 392— 396. Success of the British forces in the West Indies, 397. Corsica annexes itself to the British crown, 398. Bastia capitulates to lord Hood, May 11; 400. Nelson loses an eye at the siege of Calvi, 401. Sir Gilbert Eliot appointed viceroy of Corsica, ib. Prussia subsidized, 402. Unsuccessful campaign of the allies in the Netherlands, 402—407. No quarter granted to English and Hanoverian troops by the Convention, 405. The whole of Austrian-Flanders and Brabant fall under the dominion of France, ib. Ruinous condition of the Spanish finances, 407. The army of Italy demands of the Genoese a safe passage through their country, which they are forced to permit, notwithstanding the neutrality of their Republic, 410. The French become masters of the valley of Tanaro, ib. The fortress of Saorgio capitulates, 411. The French revolution, (continued) 413—456. The empress of Russia demands the reduction of the Polish troops to 15,000 men; the Poles determine once more to try the fate of arms, and choose the celebrated Kosciusko for their leader, 456, 457. They gain several advantages, and drive the Russians out of Warsaw, 460; an allied army of Prussians and Russians endeavour to retake that city, but are compelled to raise the siege, ib.; the insurrection becomes general, and almost the whole of Great Poland falls into the possession of the insurgents, ib. Kosciusko is defeated at Macsiewice by count Fersen, wounded, and made prisoner, 461. Savaroff leads up his army to Praga, which he storms, November 4; ib.; allows no quarter to the inhabitants, and fires the city, ib.; the people of Warsaw, fearing similar treatment, send a deputation to the barbarous Russian, who enters the city, November 6; ib. The last Partition Treaty was finally settled, October, 1795; 462. Stanislaus Angustus was compelled to sign a formal act of abdication; he afterwards retired to St. Petersburgh, where he died, February, 1798; ib. The duke of Portland receives the order of the Garter, and the office of third secretary of state, ib. Government prosecutions of conspicuous members of political societies, 462—465. Parliament assembles, December 30, 1794; 465. Sheridan moves to bring in a bill for the repeal of the suspension of the Habeas Corpus Act, 466. Loan of 4,000,000l. to Austria, 467. Supplies for the year 1795; ib. Alarming state of Ireland, 469. Marriage between prince Augustus, duke of Sussex, and lady Augusta Murray, 1793, in defiance of the Royal Marriage Act, ib. The king institutes a suit of nullity in the Arches Court of Canterbury, ib. The prince of Wales forms an intimacy with lady Jersey (formerly Miss Twysden), and abandons Mrs. Fitzherbert, 1794; 470. His unfortunate marriage, April 8, 1795, with the princess Caroline Amelia Elizabeth, second daughter of the reigning duke of Brunswick Wolfenbüttel, ib. Dearness of provisions, 471. Settlement of the revenue of the prince

GEORGE III,—
of Wales, 472. The session of parliament closed by the king in person, June 27, ib. The duke of York returns to London, December, 1794; 473. Inefficiency of the medical staff and commissariat of the English army, ib. The democrats of Amsterdam mount the French cockade, and give an enthusiastic reception to the republican general, Pichegru, who made his entrance January 20, 1795; 474. The fortress of Bergen-op-Zoom is betrayed, by its garrison, to the French, ib. Cape Town surrenders to major-general Clarke, September 23, and by the end of this year, or the beginning of 1796, all the places the Dutch held in the Island of Ceylon, with Malacca, Cochin, Chinsura, Amboyna, and Banda, were taken possession of with scarcely any resistance, 475. The king of Prussia concludes a separate treaty with the French, April 5th, ib. Definite treaty of Peace between Spain and France, signed July 22, 1795; 476. The grand duke of Tuscany concludes a treaty with the National Convention, 477. Separate treaties between Great Britain, Russia, the Emperor of Germany, and the Dey of Algiers, ib. Victory of vice-admiral Hotham over the French fleet, commanded by rear-admiral Pierre Martin, March 13, 1795; 478. The French gain possession of St. Eustatius, 480. Energy of Victor Hugues in preaching republicanism to the negroes, ib.; his system succeeds completely in St. Lucie, ib. The English troops are overpowered, ib.; such of the British who escaped death are shipped off the island, and the tri-coloured flag is erected triumphantly, ib.; the flame of rebellion spreads to Grenada, Dominica, and St. Vincent, but after a fierce struggle is extinguished, ib. Pichegru makes an attempt to reduce Mayence, but sustains a terrible defeat by general Clairfait, 480, 481. Manheim surrenders to general Wurmser, November 22; 481. The whole of the Palatinate, and the country between the Rhine and the Moselle, is recovered by the united efforts of Clairfait and Wurmser, ib. Successes of the French on the side of Italy, ib. Public enlistment of men in the city of Genoa for the French army, 482. Admiral Hotham quits the command of the fleet, and is succeeded by sir Hyde Parker, ib. Hostility of the Corsicans towards the English, 483. Campaign of the French army of Italy under Massena, ib. Death of La Roche Jacquelin, January 28, 1794; 484. Peace of La Vendée signed February, 1795; 485. Fatal expedition to Quiberon, 486—489. Charette, the Vendean chief, is taken prisoner, and shot March 29, 1796; 489. The war of La Vendée expired with the death of Charette, ib. According to general Hoch's own statement, it cost the lives of 100,000 Frenchmen; and not a fifth part of the whole male population of the country was left alive, ib. The French revolution, (continued) 489—500. Death of the Dauphin (Louis XVII.), June 8, 1795; his eldest uncle took the title of king, and was proclaimed Louis XVIII., at the head of the emigrant army of the prince of Condé, 496. Scarcity of provisions in Great Britain, 500. Meeting of the London Corresponding Society, October 26; 501. The king, on his way to the House to open the session, October 29, was hissed and fired at, ib. Stringent measures are adopted, by which the tranquillity and domestic enjoyment of the subject are placed in danger, 502. Burke publishes the two first of his celebrated "Letters on a Regicide Peace," 503. The Directory issues a severe decree, prohibiting the admission of English goods into any part of France, or of the French dependencies, ib. Lord Malmesbury's first embassy to Paris unsuccessful and disgraceful, 504. Spain declares war with Great Britain, October 8; 505. General Abercrombie regains possession of St. Lucie, ib. The Batavian

GEORGE III.,—

republicans make a bold effort to recover possession of the Cape of Good Hope, *ib.* The English evacuate Corsica, October 14, 1796; 506. United attack of the French armies on Germany and Italy, 510. Success of the Austrians under the Archduke Charles; the republican general, Jourdan, is completely defeated at Amperg, and Moreau commences his famed retreat through the Black Forest, 511. Bonaparte receives the command of the army of Italy; he gains many advantages, and compels the king of Sardinia to sign a peace ruinous to that country, 512. General Beaulieu defeated at Lodi, May 10; *ib.* The city of Pavia given up to plunder, 513. Tuscany overrun, *ib.* Bonaparte sustains a severe repulse from general Alvinzi at the bridge of Arcole, 514. Termination of the third Italian campaign of 1796; 515. The new parliament assembles, October 6; *ib.*; augmentation of the national force, *ib.* The Loyalty Loan, *ib.* Run upon the Bank of England, 1797; the privy-council prohibits the directors from issuing any cash or specie to private persons, and bank-notes became the legal tender until 1819, when Sir R. Peel carried his well-known bill, 516, 517. General mutiny of seamen at Portsmouth and Sheerness, 517—522. Richard Parker is tried and executed, 522. Parliament prorogued July 20, *ib.* Battle off Cape St. Vincent, Feb. 14, *ib.* Sir John Jervis is made Earl St. Vincent, and Nelson a knight of the Bath, *ib.* Admiral Duncan's victory off Camperdown, October 11, *ib.* Nelson makes an unfortunate attack on Santa Cruz, in the Island of Teneriffe, which ends in the loss of his right arm, and in the lives of 200 of his men, 523. Reduction of the Island of Trinidad, *ib.* Strange expedition of the French to the English coast, *ib.* Moreau recovers Fort Kehl, *ib.* Preliminaries of a peace between Austria and France signed at Leoben, April 18, 524. The doge and senate of Venice resign, *ib.* Genoa democratised, and the government re-modelled on the French fashion, 525. Lord Malmesbury's second mission to Lisle, *ib.* Venice ceded to the emperor by the treaty of Campo Formio, after having maintained itself as a republic for 1400 years, 525, 526. The French Revolution, (*continued*) 526, 528. Parliament re-assembles, November, 2, 1797; 528. Rebellion in Ireland, 1798; the Alien Bill is revived, and the suspension of the Habeas Corpus Act prolonged, *ib.* Parliament prorogued, June 29, *ib.* Proceedings of sir Edward Fitzgerald and other leaders of the Society of United Irishmen, 529—533. Grattan brings a bill into the Irish parliament for the entire emancipation of the Catholics, 530. The insurgents receive great loss at Vinegarhill, June 21, 533. 900 French troops of the line land at Killiala, 534. Minorca surrenders to general Stuart, *ib.* The English evacuate St. Domingo to Toussaint l'Ouverture, *ib.* The French enter Berne, and treat Switzerland as a conquered country, 536. Bravery of the Nidwalders, 537. The Belgians break into insurrection, 538. Turbulence of the Roman democrats, *ib.* General Berthier marches to Rome, and prepares to bombard the city. The terrified cardinals sign a capitulation, 540. Pope Pius VI. refuses to acknowledge the Roman republic, and being driven from his power takes up his residence in a convent of the Augustinian monks in Siena, *ib.* Popular insurrections in Piedmont, *ib.* Bonaparte embarks in his expedition to Egypt, May 19, 1798; *ib.* He captures Malta, June 11; *ib.* Lands at Alexandria, June 30; 541. Gains the battle of the Pyramids, July 21; *ib.* Battle of the Nile, August 1; 542, 543. The Sultan declares war against France, 543. The people of Cairo burst into insurrection, September 22, which is put down by a dreadful mas-

sacre, *ib.* Nelson is created baron Nelson of the Nile, and of Burnham Thorpe, November 6, 1798 ; *ib.* The Island of Gozo capitulates to the English, 544. Parliament assembles, November 20 ; *ib.* Death of the empress Catherine, November 1796. She is succeeded by her son Paul, who enters into a close alliance with Great Britain, *ib.* Pitt introduces the Income-tax, *ib.* The king recommends to parliament the union of Ireland and England, 1799; *ib.* Parliament prorogued, July 12 ; 545. Alliance between Russia and Austria, *ib.* Attempt of general Mack to drive the French out of Italy, *ib.* The French general Championnet takes possession of Naples, January 31 ; royalty is abolished, and the kingdom converted into a republic, under the name of Republica Partenopea, *ib.* Battle of Cassano, April 27 ; 546. Cardinal Ruffo, with the assistance of lord Nelson, recovers the Neapolitan kingdom, 547. The papal government is re-instated, and Pius VI., having died in August, a new election takes place, which was not completed until March 1800, when Pius VII. was raised to the pontificate, *ib.* Combined attack of the Russians and English on the French in Holland, *ib.* The duke of York is appointed commander-in-chief, *ib.* Siege of Acre, 547, 548. Battle of Aboukir, between the Turks and French, July 25, 1799; 548. Bonaparte returns to France, *ib.* The constitution of France is again changed, 549. Proscription of the ardent republicans, *ib.* Bonaparte becomes first consul, *ib.* He writes to the king of England expressing a wish for peace, *ib.* Tippoo Sultaun proposes an alliance with the French republic, to drive the British out of Hindustan, 1797 ; 550. Jacobin Club established at Seringapatam, *ib.* The earl of Mornington dispatches general Harris into the Mysore country, which he enters March 5, 1799 ; *ib.* Seringapatam is stormed and captured, May 4 ; *ib.* Tippoo is slain in the action, and two of his sons are taken prisoners, *ib.* Parliament assembles, September 24, 1799 ; *ib.* Act for facilitating the reinforcement of the army, *ib.* Renewal of the suspension of the Habeas Corpus Act, 1800. Hadfield, a maniac, attempts to shoot the king, May 15; 553. Amendment of the Insanity Bill, *ib.* Scarcity of corn ; regulations respecting the sale of bread, *ib.* The plan of the union is approved by the Irish Parliament, 554. The Act of Union receives the royal assent, July 2 ; 555. French campaign against Austria, *ib.* Bonaparte enters Milan, June 2 ; *ib.* Battle of Marengo, 556. Triumphant reception of Bonaparte by the Milanese, 557. He returns to Paris, July 3 ; *ib.* Campaign of the French army on the Upper Rhine, *ib.* Battle of Hohenlinden, December 2, 1800; 558. Treaty of Luneville signed February 9, 1801; *ib.* Malta surrenders to the British, *ib.* The Island of Goree taken by sir Charles Hamilton, 559. Unfortunate expedition to the western coasts of France, *ib.* The scarcity of grain continues, *ib.* Parliament meets November 11, *ib.* Supplies voted for three lunar months, *ib.* Proclamation issued concerning the royal style, titles, etc., to be used as appertaining to the crown of Great Britain and Ireland. The old title of king of France is judiciously relinquished, 560. The Imperial Parliament is opened by commission, Jan. 22, 1801; *ib.* In consequence of the king's determined opposition to Catholic emancipation, which Pitt had led the Romanists to expect, that minister thinks proper to resign, after an administration of seventeen years, 561 —549*. The king experiences an attack of his former malady, 547*. Sir John Mitford is elected speaker, *ib.* The Addington administration, 549*. Continuation of the Act for the Suppression of Rebellion, and for the suspension of the Habeas Corpus Act in the United Kingdom, *ib.* Parliament pro-

GEORGE III,—

rogued by commission, July 2; *ib.* The czar Paul breaks his faith with England, and orders the English shipping in the harbour of Narva to be burned; above three hundred British vessels are seized, and the captains and crews put in irons, 550*. Battle of Copenhagen, April 2, 1801; 551*. Nelson is raised to a viscountcy for his splendid services, 553*. The insane emperor Paul is murdered by his officers, March 24, and his son Alexander succeeds to the throne, *ib.* Sir Hyde Parker is recalled and Nelson appointed commander-in-chief; in a very short time he returns to England for the benefit of his health, 554*. The treaty of El Arish concluded between the French and Turks, 555*. Improvement in the education of English officers, 556*. Battle of Alexandria, March 21, 1801; 557*, 558*. Sir Ralph Abercrombie dies of his wounds, March 28; 558*. The French quit Egypt, 559*. The court of Madrid declares war against Portugal, and a Spanish army commanded by Godoy, the prince of peace, invades the Portuguese provinces; but the treaty of Olivenza is soon adjusted, *ib.* The French invest Almeida, and menace Lisbon and Oporto, *ib.* Definitive treaty concluded at Madrid, *ib.* Preliminaries of peace between England and France, signed, Oct. 1, 560*. Peace of Amiens, March 27, 1802; *ib.* Treaty of Amiens signed March 27, 1802, by which England recognizes the French Republic, and treats with Bonaparte as first consul, § iv. 3. Disadvantageous terms of this peace. It is strongly opposed by lord Grenville and Mr. Windham, 5—10; 990,052*l.* granted by the House of Commons for clearing the civil list debts, 12. Debates on the prince of Wales's claim as duke of Cornwall, 11—13. The new parliament meets on the 16th of November, 1802. The speech from the throne does not afford any hope of peace, 42. Mr. Charles Yorke, secretary-at-war, moves the army estimates; he states the number of regular troops, necessary to be kept up for the ensuing year, at 129,000 men: the number of men for the navy fixed at 50,000; 43. On the king's message, announcing his having recalled lord Whitworth, the ambassador at Paris, 10,000 more seamen were granted, and measures adopted to defend the country, May 16th, 1803; 49. An act for raising an army of reserve, 51, 52. Attempts made in both Houses to censure the conduct of ministers, 51. A bill passed, enabling the king to raise a levy *en masse,* in case of invasion, 52. An insurrection having broken out in Ireland, Acts were passed to suspend the Habeas Corpus Act in that country, and to try the disaffected, 53. On the 12th of May, lord Whitworth quits Paris, and war commences, 70. The English seize French ships, and make those on board prisoners of war, *ib.* Bonaparte seizes the English subjects in France, *ib.* He possesses himself of Hanover, and compels the Hamburghers and others to close the Elbe and the Weser against the trade of England, 71, 72. Ireland shows great inclination to revolt. The rabble of Dublin, headed by Robert Emmett, commit many outrages, and falling on the carriage of lord Kilwarden, the chief-justice, as he was returning to Dublin Castle, they murder him and his nephew, 73—76. Emmett is tried and executed, and the Irish revolt suppressed, 76. Success of the English at sea, and capture of the French dependencies, 77. Splendid victories of lord Wellesley and general Lake in India, 1803; 78—87. The volunteer corps, exceeding 300,000 men, inspected and reviewed, 87. Parliament meets Nov. 22, and passes acts to suspend the Irish Habeas Corpus Act, and to continue the Martial-law Bill, 88. Feb. 14, 1804, the king's illness is formally announced, but the uneasiness is soon relieved by

his re-appearance in public, 88, 89. The ministers become more and more unpopular. Addington is compelled to resign May 12, and is succeeded by Mr. Pitt, May 18; 89, 90. A bill for regulating the slave-trade is postponed after the second reading, 98, and one for raising an additional force passed, 99. Bonaparte is crowned emperor of France, Dec. 1, 1804; 130—141. His letter to George III recommending peace, 141. Jan. 1805, Mr. Addington is created viscount Sidmouth, and unites with Mr. Pitt to strengthen his administration, 147. Lord Melville is impeached by the House of Commons, and convicted of using the public money for private purposes, 150—164. Addington resigns, 165. Russia and Austria unite with England in the war with France, *ib.* Proceedings on the continent. Bonaparte crowned king of all Italy, 165—177. Battle of Austerlitz gained by the French, Dec. 2; 177, 178. The emperor of Austria concludes a most humiliating peace with France, Dec. 26; 179, 180. Villeneuve escapes the vigilance of Nelson, and sails to the West Indies, 181. Lord Nelson gains a splendid victory over the combined fleets of France and Spain, off Cape Trafalgar, in which the English admiral is killed, Oct. 21st, 1805; 188—196. Success of the British arms in India, 199—203; and treaties of peace with Scindia and Holkar, 204, 205. Parliament meets, Jan. 21, 1806. Death of Mr. Pitt, Jan. 23; 206. Lord Grenville is appointed first-lord of the treasury, and Mr. Fox secretary of state for foreign affairs, Feb. 4; 208. An attempt is made to conclude peace with France, but without success, 210—213. The admission of lord Ellenborough into the cabinet gives great offence, 213. This administration was at first popular, but their majorities rapidly decline, *ib.* Army regulations, and repeal of the Additional Force Bill occupy the attention of the ministry, 213, 214. The supplies for the year announced to amount to nearly forty-nine millions, of which eighteen were to be raised by loan and nineteen by war-tax, 215. The Income-tax is raised to 10 per cent., *ib.* A resolution is passed for the gradual abolition of the slave-trade, 216, 217. Lord Melville is impeached, but acquitted, 217, 219. Examination into the conduct of the princess of Wales, 220—222. The French conquer Naples, and Joseph Bonaparte is crowned king, 223, 224. Continental affairs, 224—231. The Cape of Good Hope retaken by the English, Jan. 8; 231. Buenos Ayres captured by sir Home Popham, July 2; but shortly after retaken by the Spaniards, *ib.* American affairs, 232—235. Success of the British arms at sea, 236, 237. Severe laws enacted by Bonaparte against the importation of English manufactures, 238. Continental affairs. The Prussians are everywhere defeated, and the French arms victorious, 241—250. Battle of Pultusk gained by the French, 250, 251. Death of Fox, Sept. 13, 1806; 251, 252. Parliament is dissolved, but again meets, Dec. 19; 252. The negotiation with France debated, Jan. 1807; 254, 255. Liberal supplies voted, 255. The bill for the abolition of the slave-trade brought into the House of Lords by lord Grenville, and passed after warm debate; it received the royal assent, March 25, 1807; 257—259. The ministers again agitate the Catholic question, notwithstanding his majesty's opposition to the measure, and in consequence are compelled to resign, 259—264. Appointment of the new ministry, with the duke of Portland at its head, 264. Lord Eldon takes his place as speaker of the House of Lords, but nothing important occurs, and parliament is dissolved, 265, 266. The new parliament meets, June 22; 267. The second expedition against Buenos Ayres, under General Whitelocke, is most disgracefully conducted and defeated, 267—271.

GEORGE III,—

Sir John Duckworth's unsuccessful expedition to the Hellespont and Bosphorus, Feb. 1807; 273—279. Expedition to Egypt unsuccessful,279—281. Curaçoa taken by the English, Jan. 1, 1807; 285. Lord Cathcart and admiral Gambier bombard Copenhagen ; terms of capitulation are signed, Sept. 7, and the English take possession of the Danish fleet, 287—290. The Danish West-India islands surrender to the English, 290. Continental affairs, 290—301. Our neglect in not sending sufficient supplies to our allies on the continent compels the emperor Alexander to sign the treaty of Tilsit, July 7, 1807; 296. Parliament opens, Jan. 31, 1808; the speech from the throne announces the hostile policy of Russia, and the serious differences that had arisen with the United States of America, 301. Supplies for the year 1808, and increased war establishment,302. Spanish affairs; Joseph Bonaparte is declared king of Spain, July 7, 1808; 314. The French troops take possession of Spain and Portugal, 314—334. Sir Arthur Wellesley is appointed commander of a British force, to assist the patriots of the peninsula, and lands with about 10,000 troops at Figueira in Portugal, Aug. 1, 334, 335. Battle of Vimiera gained by sir Arthur Wellesley, Aug. 21; 338. Convention of Cintra; the French evacuate Portugal, 338—342. The commanders of this expedition are tried by a board of inquiry and honourably acquitted, 342, 343. Sir John Moore appointed to the chief command of the British forces in Spain, 343. Battle of Corunna gained by the English ; their brave commander, sir John Moore, is killed, 344—363. The conduct of the duke of York, as commander-in-chief, occupies the attention of parliament, 364—369. The English determine to continue the war in Spain and Portugal, 371. Sir Arthur again resumes the chief command, 1809; 372. Soult is compelled to quit Oporto and retire to Spain, May 11, 1809; Battle of Talavera gained by sir Arthur Wellesley, July 27, 379—381. The English retire to Portugal 381—385. Military preparations; fortification of Torres Vedras, 386—389. Preparations in England for the invasion of Holland, 389. The English take Flushing, Aug. 16, 390, 391. Operations in the south of Italy, 394—401. The Ionian Islands captured by the English, 1809, 1810; 402. Treaty of peace with the Ottoman Porte, Jan. 5, 1809; ib. Events in Turkey, 402—406. Death of lord Collingwood, 407, 408. Continental affairs, Napoleon's war with Austria ; battle of Aspern, May 21 and 22; 411. The archduke Charles defeated at the battle of Wagram, July 6, 412, 413, which is followed by the peace of Schönbrunn, 414, 417. Changes in the ministry, 426, 427. Parliament meets, Jan. 23, 1810. The attention of parliament is occupied in inquiring into the conduct and policy of the expedition to the Scheldt, during which all strangers are excluded, 428. A vote is carried, approving of the ministers' conduct in that affair, but the clearing of the gallery gives great dissatisfaction, and John Gale Jones and sir Francis Burdett are imprisoned, but liberated on the prorogation of parliament,428—436. Supplies voted, 436. An address, soliciting the king to prevail on the other powers of Europe to abolish the slave-trade, ib. A bill for parliamentary reform laid before the House, but rejected, 437. Events in Spain, 438—457. Cadiz garrisoned by an army of about 25,000 British and Spanish troops, 439, 440. Napoleon determines on the reduction of Portugal, 441. Ciudad Rodrigo surrenders to the French, ib. Battle of Bassco gained by lord Wellesley, September 27, 1810; 444 —446. His retreat towards Lisbon, 447, 448. Description of the lines of Torres Vedras, 448—451. The isles of Bourbon and France taken by the

GEORGE III,—

English, 457. Events in France, 458—464. Holland united to the French empire, 463. Death of the princess Amelia, and return of the king's mental malady, 465. Debates in parliament respecting a regency, 465, 466. A bill passes both Houses limiting the powers of the regency, which is accepted by the prince of Wales on the terms proposed, Jan. 11; ib. The king dies at Windsor Castle, Jan. 29, 1820; 678°. Private character of George III. and his queen, § iii. 755. Illustrations—Great seal, purse, and chancellor's mace, § i. 2. Portrait of the king at the time of his accession, 6. The coronation ceremony, 13.

GEORGE IV., (January 29th, 1820—June 26th, 1830,) born 1762; appointment of his governor and preceptors, 1772 ; § i. 120. His separate establishments, 1783; 501. He takes his seat in the House of Peers as duke of Cornwall, 502. Portrait of, § ii. 202. His intimacy with the Whig leaders, Fox and Sheridan, 1786; ib.; and with Philippe, duke d'Orleans, 203. His debts, 203—207, 218—223. His connection with Mrs. Fitzherbert, a member of the Roman Catholic church, 204, 219. The prince accepts the regency, 1789. in the restricted form offered to him by the parliament, 294. His first speech in the House of Lords, 1792; § iii. 18. He forms an intimacy with lady Jersey (formerly Miss Twysden), who supplants Mrs. Fitzherbert, 1794; 470. His marriage with his cousin, the princess Caroline Amelia Elizabeth, second daughter of the reigning duke of Brunswick Wolfenbüttel, April 8, 1795, ib. Settlement of his establishment, 470—472. He again accepts the office of regent, January 11. 1811; § iv. 467; and retains Perceval as first lord of the treasury, 472. His installation and speech on the opening of parliament, 472, 473. On account of the universal depression of commerce, a committee is appointed to inquire into the state of the national currency, 473, 474. Debates respecting the Suspension Act, 475, 476. Badajos surrenders to marshal Soult, March 11, 1811; 481. Massena defeated by lord Wellesley, at Fuentes de Onoro, May 5; 484, 485. Investment of Badajos, 486. General Beresford gains the fierce battle of Albuera, May 16; 487, 488. The island of Java, and all the Dutch East India settlements surrender to the English, 492. Birth of Napoleon's son, ib. Events in France, 492—495. Parliament opened by commission, January 7, 1812. Sir Francis Burdett moves an address, stating the grievances of the nation, which is negatived, and the usual address, after some remarks passed, 495, 496. Settlement of the king's household, 496. Inquiry into colonel M'Mahon's appointment, 496, 497. Murder of Mr. Perceval, May 11, in the lobby of the House of Commons, by Bellingham, 499; who is tried and executed, 500. Ministers resign; the earl of Liverpool is appointed first lord of the treasury, and Mr. Vansittart, chancellor of the exchequer, 501, 502. Serious riots in Lancashire, Cheshire, and Yorkshire, 502. A bill passed to preserve the public peace, ib. The strong forts of Ciudad Rodrigo and Badajos surrender to the English, 503—505. Victory of Salamanca, July 22, 1812; 508. Lord Wellesley enters Madrid, August 12; 510. The English again retire to Portugal, 513—517. Events in Sicily, 517—525. History of the United States of America, 526—559. War with England, 1812; 559—563. Bonaparte's Russian expedition, 1812; 564—567. Parliament assembles, Nov. 24, and votes 100,000l. for the war in Spain, and 200,000l. for the relief of the sufferers in Russia, 568. Lord Wellesley enters Spain, and gains the battle of Vittoria, June 21; 570. King Joseph retires to Pampiona, 573. This city is invested by the allies, who occupy the passes of the

GEORGE IV.,—
Pyrenees, *ib.* Marshal Soult is sent to take the command of the French army, 575. Battles of the Pyrenees, 576—579. San Sebastian and Pamplona surrender, 583. Lord Wellington enters France, and drives Soult from his strong position on the Nivelle, Nov. 10; 563, 584. Soult retires to his entrenched camp at Bayonne, and attacks the English at St. Jean de Luz, but is repulsed, 584. Whilst these events were taking place in the Peninsula, Napoleon refuses the proffered peace, and Prussia joins the emperor Alexander, 591. Berlin and Dresden are evacuated by the French, *ib.* Prince Eugène Beauharnais checks the advance of the allied army, *ib.* Napoleon gains the battles of Lutzen and Bautzen, May, 1813; *ib.* The allies retire from Lutzen and Dresden, 592. A general armistice agreed upon, June 5, *ib.* England joins the coalition with Russia and Prussia, June 14, *ib.* Napoleon refuses all overtures for peace, and the armistice expires, Aug. 10; 593°. Austria joins the coalition, *ib.* England furnishes large subsidies to the allies, *ib.* Napoleon gains some advantages over the Austrians and Prussians at Dresden, *ib.* Battle of Leipsic, in which the French are defeated with great loss, 593°, 594°. Napoleon retires with the remainder of his army across the Rhine, and repairs to Paris, 594°. General discontent prevails throughout the south of France, and Holland revolts, 597°. Parliament opens, Nov. 4; 599°. General rejoicing, on account of the success of the allies and improved state of the British commerce, *ib.* Vote of supplies for the year 1814; 600°. Early in February lord Wellington again commences the campaign, and compels Soult to abandon his fortified camp at Bayonne, and cross the Gave d'Oléron, 604°. Gains a complete victory at Orthes, and the allies enter Bordeaux, *ib.* Battle of Toulouse; the French retire, April 10; 606°, 607°. The English army enters the city, April 12; and in the afternoon Wellington receives information of the entry of the allies into Paris, and Bonaparte's abdication, 608°. Soult and Suchet conclude an armistice, 608°, 609°. Whilst these events are passing in the south of France, the allies cross the eastern frontier, 610°. Napoleon gains some advantages over the Austrians and Prussians, but is defeated at La Rothière. Feb. 1, 1814; 614°. The allied armies, having formed a junction, meet with little opposition, and march on Paris, which they enter on the 31st of March, 614°, 615°. The French government consents to the restoration of the Bourbons, and the establishment of a national constitution, 616°. Napoleon signs his abdication at Fontainebleau, April 11, and retires to Elba with the title of emperor, May 5; 617°. The Prince Regent conducts Louis XVIII, who had been residing in England since the revolution, to London, 618°. Louis embarks at Dover, April 24, *ib.* Accepts the constitution which had been framed by the provisional government, and enters Paris, May 3, *ib.* A general peace and amity signed with France, May 30, by which the boundaries of France are restored as they existed in January, 1792, but with considerable augmentations, *ib.* Provisions of the peace of Paris, in which England engages to restore to France all the colonies and dependencies which she held in 1792, with the exception of Tobago, St. Lucie, and the Isle of France, 619°. Continental affairs, 619°—625°. Lord Wellesley is created duke of Wellington, and the sum of 500,000*l.* is voted in parliament for the purchase of an estate, 626°. The Great Congress of Vienna assembles, and the duke of Wellington repairs thither, January, 1815, *ib.* Bonaparte returns from Elba; the allied powers of Europe form a general league for his expulsion, and for the

GEORGE IV.,—
support of the balance of power in Europe, March 13; 627°. The duke of Wellington is called upon to assist in drawing up a grand plan of military operations, by the allied powers of Europe, *ib.* His report on the defences of Belgium, *ib.* Napoleon crosses the Belgian frontier, and compels Blücher to retire from Sombref to Wavre, June 16; and on the 18th the decisive battle of Waterloo is gained by the duke of Wellington, 635°—637°. The English and Prussian armies enter Paris, July 7; 642°. Napoleon embarks at Rochefort, on board the *Bellerophon,* and sails for England, 644°. On the arrival of the *Bellerophon* at Torbay, captain Maitland receives instructions not to permit any communications with the land, but immediately to sail round to Plymouth Sound, where, on the 31st, Napoleon receives the unwelcome news of his destination for St. Helena, 644°. Death of Napoleon, May 6, 1821; 650°. Louis XVIII. signs a treaty with the allies, Nov. 20, 1815, by which but little alteration is made in the territory of France, but he consents to support 150,000 men of the allied armies in France for five years, and to pay 700,000,000 of francs to assist in defraying the expenses of the allies, 661°. Great Britain gains the sovereignty of the whole island of Ceylon, 662°. History of the war, 1814, 1815; 662°—676°. Peace concluded with America, Dec. 24, 1814; 662,° 677°.
Georgia, colony of, established by general Oglethorpe in 1732; iv. 722.
GERARD, a foreigner, persecuted for his religious tenets, 1166; his trial at Oxford, i. 557.
GERARD, a suspected Jesuit, 1604, 1605; iii. 21. On the arrest of Garnet, he and Greenway escape to the continent, 30.
Gerberoy, castle of, duke Robert's residence on the confines of Normandy, besieged by the Conqueror, i. 384. In a sally, Robert and his father, both clad in mail, with the visors of their helmets down, not recognizing each other, waged a fierce personal contest, *ib.* The king was wounded and unhorsed; his voice being recognized by his son, Robert fell on his knees for pardon, mounted him on his own horse, and conducted him out of the *mêlée,* *ib.* William relinquished the siege of Gerberoy in despair, and retired to Rouen, *ib.*
GERE, sheriff of Yorkshire, organises an insurrection, 1663; iii. 693.
GERMAINE, lord George. *See* Sackville.
Germanic tribes, their contests with the Romans; they occasionally ravaged Italy, until checked by Cæsar's arms, i. 26.
GERMANUS, bishop of Auxerre, about 442, led the Britons, to the shouts of Hallelujah, against some invading Picts, who were cut to pieces, i. 57.
Germany, Protestants of, 1300—1450, derived some of their tenets from the Albati or Bianchi of Italy; some from Wycliffe's writings: the early reformer, Walter Lolhard, was burnt for heresy at Cologne, 1322; and later, John Huss was burnt in 1415, by the Council of Constance, ii. 141. Henry VIII, who had pronounced the reformed tenets damnable, negotiated gladly, in 1535, for their aid, 389.
GERMINE, Thomas, present at the trial of Williams, bishop of Lincoln, 1634. iii. 164.
GERONTIUS, and other British chiefs, treacherously call in Saxons, Picts, etc., to oppress the Britons, 411—420, i. 55.
GERRARD, executed, 1654, for having engaged with several others to murder Cromwell and proclaim Charles II., iii. 416.
Gheriah, reduction of the pirates (Angria) at, 1755; § ii. 38. Battle of, 1763; 87.
GHEST, Laurence, burned *regno* Henry VII. for his opinions respecting the sacrament, ii. 699.
Ghisni, dynasty of, established at the beginning of the

GHIZNI,— tenth century by sultan Mahmood, and in less than 200 years subverted, § ii. 16, 17.

GIAMBELLI, Federico, an Italian deserter from the Spanish service, fortifies the Thames against the invincible Armada, ii. 673.

GIB, rev. Adam, 1742; iv. 656.

GIB, John, groom of the bedchamber to James I., carries, 1603, but almost too late, the reprieve to Winchester Castle for Grey, Cobham, and Markham, iii. 14.

GIBBON, Edward, an eminent English historian, born in 1737. Member for the borough of Liskeard, 1774; § i. 194, Died, January 16, 1794; 621, 622, § iii. 715. Portrait of, § ii. 621. Quoted, i. 262, 263, 560, 603.

GIBBONS, Grinling, a sculptor of high class. He died 1721; iii. 884.

GIBBONS, Orlando, an admirable musician of the sixteenth century, iii. 566.

GIBBS, James, an architect of the eighteenth century. Review of his principal works, iv. 748, 749.

Gibraltar, view of the bay and straits of, § i. 471. View of the Rock of, 491.

GIFFORD, Henry, a staunch adherent of Henry I., was appointed bishop of Winchester by that prince immediately on his accession. He died, 1129; i. 405.

GIFFORD, Walter, archbishop of York, i. 406. On the death of Henry III. appointed one of the guardians or regents of the kingdom, 688. He died 1279.

GILBERT, English (or Anglicus), flourished in the thirteenth century, the first English writer on medicine whose works have been printed, i. 845.

GILBERT, sir Humphrey, step-brother of sir Walter Raleigh, perished at sea 1583; ii. 791; iii. 538.

GILDAS, an ancient British historian, quoted, i. 56, 228. His history, 289. He relates that there were twenty-eight cities in Britain in his days, 347. Names of these cities given by Nennius, 348.

Gildhall, the German; the merchants of Cologne paid thirty marks to the crown in 1220 for the legal possession of this hall, i. 834. This hall is not to be confounded with the Steel-yard, ii. 179.

GILES, Dr., rector of Chinnor, attends the patriotic Hampden in his last moments, iii. 304.

GILL, Thomas, an ingenious Birmingham manufacturer, famous for his improvements in sword-cutlery, 1786; § iii. 684.

GILLESPIE, rev. Thomas (eighteenth century), in conjunction with the rev. T. Boston, founds the body still subsisting under the name of the Relief Synod, iv. 651.

Gilly-flower, the, introduced about 1567, by the Flemings who settled in Norfolk, ii. 806.

Gin Act, the, passed 1736; iv. 417. Revised 1743; 464.

GINCKEL, general, his services at the battle of the Boyne, 1690; iv. 26. Gains the battle of Aghrim, 1691; 33, 34. Invests Limerick and forces it to capitulate, 34. Is created baron Aghrim and earl of Athlone, ib. Invests Namur, and after a severe contest takes possession of it, 56—58. Destroys a vast magazine at Givet, ib.

Gingee, view of, § ii. 28.

GIOVACCHINO, a celebrated seer, his interview with king Richard, i. 492.

Gipsies, statute of Henry VIII. against, ii. 759.

GIRALDUS CAMBRENSIS, quoted, i. 12, 586, 695.

GISLEBERT, professor of theology, very skilled in philosophy and the sciences; he followed his fellow-monk Joffrid to England, who, when he became abbot of Croyland, sent him with three other monks to his manor of Cottenham (twelfth century), and having hired a public barn at Cambridge, Gislebert there lectured on philosophy and the other primitive sciences, i. 606. The number of his scholars rapidly

GISLEBERT,— increased, and he established a regular school, which afterwards became the University of Cambridge, ib.

GLADESDALE, sir William, altercation between him and Joan of Arc, 1429; ii. 66.

GLADSTANES, Mr. George, archbishop of St. Andrew's, iii. 451; his death, 1615; 466.

GLAMORGAN, Edward Somerset, earl of. See Worcester.

GLANVILLE, Ranulph de, he takes William the Lion, of Scotland, prisoner, 1174; i. 471. Is made lord-justiciary of England and regent of the kingdom, 484. He resigns his high office of his own will, and departs to the Holy Land, 485. He possessed at the same time both the office of high justiciary and that of dapifer, 568. The work, entitled "Tractatus de Legibus et Consuetudinibus Angliæ," the oldest English law-book extant, is usually attributed to him, 568, 574. The introduction of the "grand assize," instituted in the reign of Henry II., is ascribed to him; this form of law was not abolished till 1833; 573.

GLANVILLE, serjeant, iii. 120; chosen speaker of the House of Commons, 1640; iii. 212.

GLAS, rev. John, founded a new sect of Independents in the beginning of the eighteenth century, iv. 651.

GLASGOW, the university founded, 1450; ii. 199.

Glass, manufactured, 676, by artisans imported by abbot Biscop; used in the religious edifices of the Anglo-Saxons, York Cathedral, Wearmouth, etc., i. 310. Rarity of glass vessels in the early Saxon period, 325. Glass lamps mentioned by Bede, ib. English glass greatly improved about 1670, by foreign artists brought from Venice, iii. 869. This article remained free until 1746, when a duty was imposed upon the materials used in the manufacture, and additional duties were levied on foreign glass, iv. 734. Flint-glass first manufactured in England about 1557, and plate-glass about 1773; § i. 592. Duties, etc., on glass, ib. English glass-works successfully imitated in France under the auspices of Marie Antoinette, § iii. 691.

Glastonbury Abbey; Dunstan, abbot, i. 170—242. Endowed by king Edgar, who was entombed there, 173. Illustration: ruins of Glastonbury, in 1785; 242. Narrative of the spoliation and suppression of this wealthy abbey, 1539, addressed by Pollard, Moyle, and Layton, to Cromwell, minister of Henry VIII., execution of abbot Whiting, etc., ii. 411, 412.

Glee Club, the, established 1787; § iii. 754.

GLENCAIRN, earl of, joins the confederacy against Mary Queen of Scots, upon her marriage with Darnley, ii. 581. Destroys the queen's chapel at Holyrood, 603.

Glencoe, view of, iv. 44. Massacre of, 1692; 46.

GLENCO, Macdonald of, refuses to take the oaths to king William III., but afterwards complies, iv. 45.

GLENDOWER, Owen, formerly an esquire to Richard II., his affectionate remembrance of his royal master, ii. 9. He retires on that king's deposition to his district of Glendourdy, and his neighbour Grey de Ruthyn seizes a part of his inheritance, ib. Henry IV. being then in Scotland, the Welshman, 1400, rebels, 10. He maintains his lineal descent from the last of the Welsh princes, ib. Glendower's education at English universities and inns of court, enabled him to astonish the mountaineers, who considered him as a magician, 10, 164. He recovers his lands by force, and captures some of Grey's retainers, 10. He is outlawed, yet declares his sovereign right to the principality, and the Welsh take an oath of allegiance to him, ib. The Welsh throughout England abandon their concerns and retire home, ib. They carry with them arms, ib. The House of Commons informs the king that all Welsh

GLENDOWER, Owen,— students at universities had departed for Wales, *ib.* Henry IV., in 1401, marched into Wales, but Glendower avoiding close battle, frustrated three inroads by the English king, *ib.* In 1402, Glendower defeats his enemy Grey de Ruthyn, and carries him off captive, 11. In another great victory he captures sir Edmund Mortimer, *ib.* Henry IV., forming his army into three divisions, scours all Wales, yet never could find Owen Glendower; he concluded, agreeably to the common opinion, that the Welsh prince was a necromancer, and, completely foiled, he quits Wales, 11, 12. The Welsh acknowledge Owen to be the true descendant of Llewellyn, and their triumph is great, 12. Hotspur deceived in his expectation of Glendower effecting a timely junction with him, 13, 14. Prince Henry sent into Wales repeatedly defeats him, 15, 17. The *necromancer* or Welsh prince, supposed to have repaired to Paris, 1405, cunningly obtains from the French princes a considerable army of auxiliaries, who land in Milford Haven, 17, 18. Having advanced with his allies as far as Worcester, his farther progress is stayed before that city, by the king and prince, 1406; 18. He retreats to Wales, followed by the king, to whom he gives a severe check on the borders, *ib.* The French allies sail for their own ports, *ib.* His troops, under Scudamore and Rhees-ap-Dhu, are cut to pieces in Shropshire, and those leaders executed, *ib.* His subsequent career little intelligible from the records, *ib.* His son Meredith, *ib.* This hero and patriot died in freedom, as supposed after the battle of Agincourt, but the facts of his death and sepulture are uncertain, *ib.*

GLENGARRY, a brave Highlander at the battle of Dunblane, 1715; iv. 318.

GLENHAM, sir Thomas, governor of Oxford, 1646; iii. 355.

GLENLYON, Campbell of, massacres the Scots at Glenco, 1692; iv. 46.

Glenshiel, battle of, 1719; iv. 354.

Gloucester, from an old print, iii. 306.

GLOUCESTER, Robert earl of, illegitimate son of Henry I., i. 416. Dispute of priority with Stephen, *ib.* His resolution to promote the pretensions of his half-sister Matilda, 423. Takes the oaths of fealty and homage to Stephen (1137); and gains possession of his vast estates in England, *ib.* Plans an extensive insurrection, and sends a letter of defiance to Stephen, *ib.* King David invades England with a numerous army, at the instigation of Robert (March, 1138); *ib.* Not being supported by Robert and Matilda, who had promised to put themselves at the head of their party in England, a peace is concluded, 426. Gloucester lands in England with Matilda (1139); 428. While Stephen is besieging the castle of Lincoln, Gloucester advances by rapid marches with an army of 10,000 men, when a battle is fought in front of Lincoln (February 2, 1141), in which Stephen is taken prisoner and confined in Bristol Castle, 430. Gloucester is besieged with Matilda in the royal castle of Winchester, by Henry bishop of Winchester, and, whilst covering Matilda's escape is made prisoner, and soon after exchanged for king Stephen, 433. He lands in England with prince Henry, and is joined by Matilda near Wallingford, who had escaped from Oxford Castle where she was besieged by Stephen, 435. In the following month he defeats king Stephen at Wilton, *ib.* His death, 1147; *ib.*

GLOUCESTER, Richard de Clare, earl of. His quarrel with the earl of Leicester, 1259. His party gains the ascendency, and Leicester withdraws into France, i. 683. He is succeeded by his son, who becomes the friend of the earl of Leicester, *ib.* He died, 1261.

GLOUCESTER, Gilbert de Clare, earl of. On the death of his father, joins the earl of Leicester, and in March, 1263, calls his retainers and confederates together at Oxford, i. 683. He concerts a plan for releasing prince Edward, who escapes, and joins him at Ludlow, where the royal banner is raised, the prince having sworn to respect the charters and govern according to law, 686. After the battle of Evesham, Gloucester quarrels with the king, and once more takes up arms, 687. He submits, and receives full pardon, *ib.* In the absence of Edward I. in Palestine, he is appointed one of the guardians or regents of the kingdom, 1272; 688.

GLOUCESTER, Thomas Plantagenet, duke of, formerly earl of Buckingham, made duke of Gloucester, 1385; i. 791. He follows the plans of his brother the earl of Lancaster, and heads an opposition in parliament, 792. He is appointed head of the regency, 1386; *ib.* Which regency is declared illegal, 1387. The duke enters London with a large army, and the favourites of Richard take to flight or are imprisoned, *ib.* The "wonderful parliament" confirms the impeachments, and the duke of Gloucester causes the execution of sir Simon Burley, and three other knights, 793. The battle of Chevy Chase is gained by the Scots, August 15th, 1388; *ib.* In a great council held in May, 1389, Richard assumes the government, and Gloucester is banished from the council, 793, 794. Gloucester's brother Lancaster returns from his expedition in Spain, and again introduces him at court, 794. He is artfully arrested by Richard and sent to Calais, where he dies, 1397; 795.

GLOUCESTER, Humphrey, duke of, youngest son of Henry IV., attends the conferences near Meulan, between Henry V. and the queen of France, etc., 1420; ii. 44. The dying king desires that he should be regent or protector of England, 1422, the duke of Bedford regent of France, 51. The parliament denied the right of the late king to appoint a regent without their concurrence, 51. They appoint him protector of the realm and church, with a salary, during Bedford's absence, *ib.* He marries, 1434, Jacqueline, the heiress of Hainault and Holland, wife of the duke of Brabant, who had fled from her husband's brutality into England, 54, 57. Dispensation for her marriage with Gloucester, 57. He conducts Jacqueline to Mons, with a small English army, 58. Gloucester accepts the challenge to single combat sent him by his wife's cousin Philip of Burgundy, furious at an English prince acquiring an inheritance in Flanders, *ib.* Philip does not fight the personal duel, but wages war against Gloucester in Hainault, although his alliance with Bedford is still many years maintained, *ib.* Gloucester returned to England, 1425, for money and troops, *ib.* His dissensions with Beaufort threaten a civil war, 57, 58. Bedford quits his important command in France to reconcile these jarring interests, 58. In a parliament at Leicester, 1425, he makes his brother and the bishop shake hands, *ib.* Beaufort still incensed, resigned the seals, *ib.* The duke sends archers and money to Zealand for his duchess Jacqueline's assistance, 59. The council and Bedford prevent his sending her further aid, *ib.* Gloucester informed that Martin V. had declared their marriage null and void, marries Eleanor, daughter of lord Reginald Cobham, *ib.* Upon the death of Bedford, 1435, the duke of Gloucester acquires extended power as president of the council, 79. He foolishly perverts the English resources in troops and money, to his quarrel with Burgundy, *ib.* He challenges Philip to decide the contest at the head of their armies before Calais, *ib.* Philip deserts his artillery, and disperses, 80. Gloucester follows the duke into his territories, proclaiming himself earl of Flanders,

GLOUCESTER, Humphrey, duke of,—
as forfeited by Philip's treachery to the English, *ib.* He resists the cession of Anjou and Maine, on the marriage of Margaret of Anjou to the weak-minded Henry, 81. Breach of this popular duke with the new court party, and with Margaret, 82. His bitter quarrel with Beaufort, *ib.* His duchess (Eleanor Cobham) accused of conspiring, with astrologers and necromancers, against the king's life, 1441; 83. The waxen image, for this purpose, explained, *ib.* The duke silently endures these gross insults; his duchess condemned to penance, in London, and sent as a prisoner for life to the Isle of Man, *ib.* Parliament summoned, 1447, to meet at Bury St. Edmund's, *ib.* Gloucester quits his castle of Devizes to attend in his place, *ib.* Next day he was arrested for high treason, *ib.* He was found dead in his bed, February 28, *ib.* Observations of historians on his death, the credence being that he was foully murdered, *ib.* Cruelty to five of his retainers, accused of planning his duchesses escape: when half-hanged, their pardon is produced by Suffolk, and they were restored to animation, 83, 84. His estates confiscated, and divided among Suffolk, his family and partizans, 84. The duchess, on account of her conviction, could obtain nothing of his lands or chattels, *ib.* The good duke Humphrey left no legitimate children, *ib.* His personal friends laboured strenuously in parliament to clear his memory, *ib.*

GLOUCESTER, Henry Stuart, duke of, youngest son of Charles I., created earl of Cambridge and duke of Gloucester, 1659. He died of the small-pox, 1660; iii. 677.

GLOUCESTER, William, duke of, only surviving child of the princess Anne, elected knight of the garter in his seventh year, iv. 72, *note;* in his eighth year confided to the care of the earl of Marlborough and bishop Burnet, 85, 86. He dies, July 30, 1700, aged eleven, 112.

GLOUCESTER, William Henry, duke of, younger brother of king George III., created 1764; his private marriage with the widow of the late earl of Waldegrave about 1766; § i. 126, 180, 250. He died 1805.

Gloucestershire, jurisdiction of Wales over, iii. 48.

GLOVER, Richard, author of the epic poem of "Leonidas," born in 1712, appears to have written in "The Briton," a newspaper set up by the earl of Bute in 1763; § i. 26. He, as manager in behalf of the West-Indian merchants, is heard by the House of Commons 1775; 207.

GLYNNE, Mr., 1641; iii. 237, 261, 369.

GODDARD, colonel, his active conduct in India, 1779; § ii. 142, *et seq.*

GODFREY, sir Edmondbury, a magistrate of Westminster, iii. 718. Is murdered, October 18, 1678; 719.

GODFREY, Mr., killed at the siege of Namur, 1695; iv. 56.

GODOLPHIN, Sydney, earl of, iii. 759; betrays William's project of destroying the shipping, etc. at Brest to Louis XIV.; iv. 48. On the accession of queen Anne he is entrusted with the sole management of the finances, with the title of lord high treasurer, and becomes in reality prime-minister and arbiter of everything in the council, 112, 142. He advises the queen to pass a bill of supply, to which was tacked a considerable portion of the Security Bill, 163. Deprived of office, 245. His death, 1712; 272. Portrait, 658.

GODSCHALL, sir Robert, brings forward a motion for repealing the Septennial Act, 1742; iv. 461.

GODWIN, earl, rise of this Saxon, originally a cowherd, to a preponderating power in the kingdom, i. 187. He supports the claim of Hardicanute, being himself the most powerful ally of queen Emma, who had

GODWIN, earl,—
no love for her sons by her first marriage with Ethelred, *ib.* He governs the south in Hardicanute's name, against Harold I., who maintains his rule, 1035, over the north of the kingdom, *ib.* Is accused, conjointly with the queen-mother and the usurper Harold, of the death of Alfred, younger son of Ethelred, 184—186. Character of the great earl, considered in relation to the prince's death, 185. His magnificent present to conciliate Hardicanute, who ascended the throne in 1039, and consequent restoration to the duties of minister and ruler, 186. Godwin mainly contributed to the elevation of Edward, son of Ethelred, to the throne, 1042; but the Saxon king ever hated the earl for the tragical death of Alfred, 186—187. He banishes those Saxon nobles who opposed Edward's succession, 187. The king marries the earl's daughter, Editha, *ib.* Names of the six sons of Godwin; extent of the governments of this great Saxon family, comprising all the south from Lincolnshire to the end of Cornwall, 188. Godwin's rivals in delegated power, the earls Leofric and Siward, govern all Mercia and Northumbria, *ib.* Earl Godwin is opposed to the Norman courtiers of king Edward, 188, 189. The English people annoyed by the introduction of Norman prelates, manners, dress, and the use of the French language at court, look to Godwin as their national patron, 189. The crimes of Sweyn, second son of the earl, 1044, entail much disgrace on this great family, *ib.* Affray of Eustace of Boulogne, 1051, with the citizens of Dover, causes the English to rely on Godwin's protection, 189, 190. The Saxon earl is required by the king to inflict military execution on the people of Dover, 190. This cruel mandate is disobeyed by the great earl, who demands that the magistrates of the sea-port town should be heard in the king's courts, *ib.* Godwin is summoned to appear at Gloucester before the court, now virtually Norman; he declines; confiscation of his estates is threatened, *ib.* The earl, with his sons Harold and Sweyn, marches upon Gloucester and demands of the king to deliver over Eustace and his retainers to the national justice, *ib.* King Edward negotiates for some delay, which Godwin, to his own ruin, consents to, *ib.* The earls Siward, Leofric, and Ranulph, march to the king's rescue, the royal forces exceeding, by their contingents, the strength of Godwin's army, *ib.* The armies drawn up for fight alike refuse to commence a civil war, *ib.* Godwin and his sons are summoned to Westminster, they repair to Southwark with some armed retainers, and demand safe conduct in appearing before the Witenagemot and returning, 191. The king is obdurately firm in this quarrel of his French relative, and refuses a guarantee, *ib.* The great earl, his wife and sons, fly by night into Flanders; two of them, Harold and Leofwin, into Ireland, *ib.* Their lands and chattels are confiscated, their governments are granted to others, some being foreigners, *ib.* Meantime, the visit of William of Normandy to England, and the favour and arrogance of all foreigners increasing at the court of Edward, the Saxon people were ready for a change, 192. Godwin, by the summer of 1052, had collected ships, and landing on the south coast, was well received, *ib.* The garrison and men of Hastings declare for his cause, and a simultaneous rising ensues, *ib.* The earl is joined off the Isle of Wight by Harold and Leofwin from Ireland, lands some forces at Sandwich, and ascends the Thames to Southwark, 193. The Norman prelates, Robert and William, cut their passage forth of London, with some armed retainers, and embark in an open boat from the Ness on the Essex coast, *ib.* All the foreigners prepare for flight, *ib.* The Witenagemot declares

GODWIN, earl,—
Godwin innocent of the late dissensions, and the foreign adventurers guilty, *ib.* Outlawry is therefore pronounced against the Normans and French, *ib.* Of all Godwin's family, Sweyn alone, for his former crimes, is subjected to banishment, *ib.* Editha is received with honours as queen at her husband's court, *ib.* Godwin being at Windsor, soon after the apparent reconciliation, at the king's board, falls speechless and dies, 193, 194. A rumour is chronicled, that Edward the Confessor, again reproaching the earl as to Alfred, caused this; but the anecdote is considered doubtful, *ib.*
GODWIN and EDMUND, sons of Harold, their unfortunate adventures, i. 365—367.
GOLDSMITH, Oliver, an eminent poet and miscellaneous writer, author of "The Vicar of Wakefield," "The Deserted Village," etc., was born 1731, and died April, 1774; § i. 607.
Gomarists, a sect sprang from Gomarus, professor at Leyden, their hate of Vorstius, iii. 48.
GONDOMAR, count of Monterey, the Spanish ambassador, 1618; his pleasantries, iii. 73, 102.
GOODMAN, John, a seminary priest, 1641; iii. 232.
GOODMAN, concerned in the Invasion-plot, 1697; iv. 68, 76.
GOODWIN, sir Francis, his election, 1604, declared void, iii. 18.
GOOR, general, killed at the battle of Schellenberg, July 2, 1704; iv. 167.
GORDON, duke of, surrenders Edinburgh Castle, iv. 16; he favours the Pretender, 1708; 207.
GORDON, lord George; his activity in the great London riots, 1780, supposed to be the consequence of insanity, § i. 410—417. He renounces Christianity and becomes Jew, 1786; § ii. 218 *note*; and dies in Newgate, 1793; *ib.*
GORDON, Jane, duchess of, a zealous Pittite, 1789. Portrait of, § ii. 301.
GORDON, sir John, engages in an affray in the public streets of Edinburgh with lord Ogilvie; he is placed under arrest, but soon escapes, and flies to his father in the highlands, where he complains that he had been treated with severity, ii. 574. He is beheaded at Aberdeen, 1562, after the death of his father, the earl of Huntley, at the battle of Corrichie, 575.
GORDON, lord Lewis, raises a regiment for the service of the Young Pretender, 1745; iv. 520.
GORDON, of Earlstone, implicated in the Rye-house Plot; condemned, but afterwards the council wanting depositions from him, execution is deferred, that he may be tortured and made to confess, 1683; iii. 756.
GORE, sir John, arrested, 1659; iii. 431.
GORGES, sir Ferdinando, 1601; ii. 686.
GORGES, brigadier, 1706; iv. 186.
GORING, sir George, a companion of James I., iii. 64.
GORING, colonel, iii. 217—267. He agrees to deliver up Portsmouth to king Charles, 1642; 291, 317. Rises in arms for the king, 382. Is committed to close prison, 383. His life saved by the speaker's casting vote, 400.
GORTON, spreads Antinomian doctrines in Massachusetts, 1643. He is sentenced to imprisonment, iii. 308.
GOETZ, Baron, Voltaire's description of, iv. 337. Is executed, 1718; 349.
GOSNOLD, captain, 1602; iii. 533.
Gospel, Society for the Propagation of, in Foreign parts, incorporated, 1701; § iv. 605.
GOSSON, Stephen, his severe attack on music, iii. 566.
Goths, the, i. 138.
GOUGE, Dr. 1643; iii. 309.
GOURDON, Adam, a most warlike baron; he did not submit to Henry III. after the decisive battle of Evesham, but maintained himself in the woods of

GOURDON, Adam,—
Hampshire, i. 687. In a battle fought near Alton, Gourdon was vanquished in single combat by prince Edward, who generously spared his life, 688.
GOURNEY, Thomas, and William Ogle, murder Edward II. in Berkeley Castle, i. 745. Gourney is arrested in Spain, and killed, 755.
GOUVION, M., aide-de-camp of the commandant-general Lafayette, procures intelligence concerning the flight of the royal family from Paris, 1791; § ii. 631.
Government. *See* Constitution.
GOWAN, a Covenanter, hanged, 1681; iii. 682.
GOWER, lord. *See* Stafford.
GOWER, John Leveson, earl, created, 1746; made keeper of the Privy-seal, 1742; died, 1754; iv. 462.
GOWER, John, portrait of, i. 851. His monument at St. Saviour's church, Southwark, 852.
GOWER, sir John Leveson, impeaches the earl of Portland, 1701; iv. 120. He died, 1709.
Gowrie conspiracy, the, 1600; ii. 690, 691; iii. 451.
GOWRIE, William, earl of, a son of the murderous Ruthven, seizes the person of the young king James VI., ii. 654; he is beheaded, 1584; 690.
GOWRY, earl of, escape of James VI. from his violence, August 5, 1600; iii. 6.
GREME, Hector, of Harlow, betrays the earl of Northumberland to the regent Murray, 1569; ii. 630.
GRAFTON, Augustus Henry Fitzroy, duke of, 1757. Portrait of, § i. 46. Resigns his office of secretary of state, 1766, *ib.* Grafton's administration, 1768; 60. He resigns the premiership, 1770'; 87. Becomes lord privy seal, 1771; 119, 239.
GRAFTON, Henry Fitzroy, duke of, natural son of Charles II., created, 1675. Leads an attack against the duke of Monmouth, 1685. Married Isabella, daughter of H. Bennet, earl of Arlington, and died, 1690; iii. 774.
GRAHAM, George, bishop of Orkney, abjures episcopacy, iii. 206, 484.
GRAHAM, Patrick, bishop of St. Andrew's, is imprisoned on various charges in the Castle of Lochleven, where he dies, 1478; ii. 154.
GRAHAM, sir Richard, attends Buckingham and prince Charles on their way to Spain, iii. 91.
GRAHAM, sir Thomas. *See* Lynedoch.
GRAHAM, of Claverhouse, viscount Dundee, iii. 757. He falls in an engagement with Mackay, near the Pass of Killiekrankie, 1690; iv. 16.
GRAMMONT, duke of, iv. 465; slain at the battle of Fontenoy, 1745; 477.
Grampound, Cornwall, a borough of wealth and importance in 1621; iii. 177.
GRANBY, John Manners, marquess of, his services under prince Ferdinand of Brunswick, 1761; § i. 7. Portrait of, *ib.* Is placed at the head of the English army, 1766; 48, 83. He resigns, 84, 85. His death, October 19, 1770; 104.
GRANDVAL, M. de, shot for conspiring against the life of William III., iv. 37.
GRANGE, Kirkaldy of, conducts Mary Queen of Scots to the insurgents at Carberry-hill, ii. 601. On the death of Murray he puts the duke of Chatelherault in possession of Edinburgh Castle, 632. Having sustained a siege of thirty-four days, he surrenders Edinburgh Castle to sir W. Drury on a promise of favourable terms; Elizabeth, however, delivers him over to the vindictive regent Morton, and this magnanimous Scot perishes as a traitor, 1573; and with him the last remnant of Mary's party in Scotland, 649.
GRANT, John, of Norbrook, near Warwick, a mansion walled and moated, iii. 23, 28. Of a moody disposition, through religious persecution; he joins, 1605, in the Gunpowder Treason, 23. He perishes with

GRANT, John,—
his associates in guilt, January, 1606, at St. Paul's churchyard, 30.

GRANT, John, in 1662, calculated the population of England and Wales at about six millions and a half, iii. 654.

GRANT, sir William, an eminent lawyer of the eighteenth and nineteenth centuries, born 1754; died, May 25, 1832; § iv. 644. His portrait, ib.

GRANT, colonel, mortally wounded in an attack on Carthagena, 1741; iv. 453.

GRANTMESNIL, this family made hereditary seneschals of England, by William the Conqueror, i. 568.

GRANTMESNIL, Alberic de, son of Hugh de Grant-mesnil, excites Robert against his brothers, i. 383.

GRANTMESNIL, Hugh de, earl of Norfolk, and brother-in-law to William, returns to Normandy, i. 370, 394.

GRANTMESNIL, Yvo de, a supporter, 1100, of Robert of Normandy, i. 408.

GRANVILLE, John, earl. See viscount Carteret.

GRATTAN, his famous speech on Catholic Emancipation, 1808, § iv. 617.

Gravelines, battle of, 1558; ii. 537.

GRAVES, admiral, his action with the count de Grasse, 1781; § i. 459.

GRAY, John de, appointed to the see of Canterbury by king John, in opposition to Stephen Langton, i. 521. The government of Ireland entrusted to him by John, 523, 559.

GRAY, sir John, slain in the second battle of St. Alban's, 1461, and his estates confiscated, ii. 101. His widow Elizabeth, 1464, implored Edward IV. to reverse the attainder, ib. The king married the widow. See Elizabeth, queen of Edward IV.

GRAY, lord Leonard (son of the Marquis of Dorset), in 1535, suppressed the Irish rebellion of lord Thomas Fitzgerald and his five uncles; sent them to Henry VIII. in London, where, in 1537, those nobles were beheaded, ii. 426. He was appointed lord-deputy, ib. Recalled, and beheaded, June 28, 1541, on Tower hill, ib.

GRAY, sir Ralph, 1463, a Yorkist, seeing that Alnwick was conferred on sir John Ashley, became a violent Lancastrian, ii. 100. Made prisoner shortly after the battle of Hexham, 1464, he was degraded from his knighthood by Edward IV., drawn on a hurdle to the scaffold, and beheaded, 101.

GRAY, lord Richard, 1483, with earl Rivers, met Gloucester at Northampton, on the part of the young king, Edward V., ii. 118. They were courteously received, and accompanied Richard and Buckingham to Stoney-Stratford, ib. The duke there finding the young king within his grasp, suddenly sent Rivers, Gray, Vaughan, and Hawse under guard to Pontefract, ib. They were beheaded, 121.

GRAY, Thomas, a distinguished English poet, author of the famous "Elegy," published in 1751, and "The Bard," 1757, was born in 1716, and died July 30, 1771, § i. 607.

GRAY, lord, severely wounded at the battle of Pinkey, 1547; ii. 461.

Greek language, first publicly taught, 1512, in England, by William Lilly, master of St. Paul's-school, ii. 815. Encouragement of the new studies by the munificent Wolsey, ib. General opposition to the study of this language in England, 816.

Greek Testament, first edition of the, given to the world, contained in the Complutensian Polyglot, ii. 816.

GREENE, Robert, a dramatic writer; he died in 1592; iii. 578, 586.

GREENHILL, John, a painter of the 17th century, iii. 883.

GREENWAY, an Englishman, killed in an affray, 1654; iii. 416.

Greenwich, treaty of, executed, 1543; ii. 436.

GREG, William, a clerk in the office of Harley, secretary of state, detected in a traitorous correspondence with Chamillart, the French minister, and hanged for high treason, 1708; iv. 214.

Gregorian Calendar, the, introduced into England, on a motion by lord Chesterfield, in 1751; iv. 569.

GREGORY the Great, sends Augustine and forty monks, 597, into England, to convert the Anglo-Saxons, i. 145. Anecdote of his remarking, previously to his elevation to the papal dignity, some youthful slaves from England offered for sale at Rome, which conduced to this mission, 230.

GREGORY VII., Hildebrand, Pope, elected April 22, 1073. When archdeacon of the church of Rome he favoured the invasion of England by William I., i. 206, 207. He declares that kings and princes are but the vassals of St. Peter and his successors, 549. William I. peremptorily refuses to do homage for the possession of England, ib. Gregory died May 25, 1085.

GREGORY IX., pope, elected March 19, 1227, orders the five books of Decretals, constituting the Canon-Law, to be published, 1234; i. 803. He died August 21, 1241.

GREGORY XI., elected December 30, 1370. He restored the papal government to Rome, its ancient seat, ii. 137. His death, 1378; a schism, and two-fold election of popes, ib.

GREGORY XIII., elected May 13, 1572; sent, in 1579, some troops to succour the Irish; but Stukely, the commander, landed with 600 men in Africa, and was slain with Sebastian of Portugal at Alcazar, ii. 651. Fitz-Morris landed in Ireland with his small detachment, ib. In 1580 an Italian, serving Gregory, landed with 700 men, and a provision of arms and money, in aid of Desmond, but they were cut to pieces by Raleigh and others in Kerry, Spenser, the poet, being in the English camp, 652. Reflections on this carnage, ib. This pope died April 10, 1585.

GRENTMESNIL. See Grantmesnil.

GRENVILLE, George, treasurer of the navy, is dismissed, 1755; iv. 584.

GRENVILLE, George, portrait of, § i. 23. He becomes premier, 1763; 26, 28. Proposes the system of American taxation, 1764; 34, 44, 56, 67, 69. His Bill for Regulating the Trial of Controverted Elections, 1770; 93, 95. His death, November 13, 1770; 104. In 1774 his Controverted Election Bill was rendered perpetual, 156.

GRENVILLE, James, resigns his seat at the Board of Trade, 1755; iv. 584.

GRENVILLE, sir Richard, a relation of sir W. Raleigh, colonises the Island of Roanoak, 1585; ii. 791; iii. 538.

GRENVILLE, William Wyndham, lord, created 1790. His first speech in the House of Peers, § ii. 339. He opposes the preliminaries of the treaty of Amiens, § iv. 5. His able speech after the signing of the peace, 7—9. On the death of Mr. Pitt, he is appointed first lord of the Treasury, and his friend Mr. Fox secretary for foreign affairs, Feb., 1806; 208. An attempt is made to conclude peace with France, but without success, 210—213. The admission of lord Ellenborough into the cabinet gives great offence, 213. This administration was at first popular, but their majorities rapidly decline, ib. Army regulations, and the repeal of the Additional Force Bill occupy the attention of the ministry, 213, 214. The supplies announced for the year amount to nearly forty-nine millions, of which eighteen were to be raised by loan, and nineteen by War-tax, 215. The Income-tax is raised to 10 per cent., ib. A bill passed for the future abolition of the slave-trade; is warmly supported by Mr. Fox, 216, 217. Lord Melville is impeached, but acquitted, 217—219. Examination into the conduct of the princess of Wales, 220—222. The new parliament

GREVVILLE, William Wyndham,—
assembles on the 19th of December, 252. The bill for the Abolition of the Slave-trade is brought into the House of Lords by lord Grenville, and after warm debates passed; it received the royal assent, March 25, 1807; 257—259. The ministers again agitate the Catholic question, notwithstanding his majesty's opposition to the measure, and in consequence are compelled to resign, 259—264.

GRESHAM, sir Richard, 1539, lord mayor, ii. 403.

GRESHAM, sir Thomas, born 1519, portrait of, by sir Ant. More, ii. 771. He built the Royal Exchange, 1566; 787, 788. Founded the civic college known by his name, originally established in his house in Bishopsgate-street, on the site where the Excise-office now stands, 788; iv. 769. He died 1579; ib.

GREVILLE, sir Fulke, made chancellor of the Exchequer 1614; iii. 55.

GREY DE RUTHYN, lord, seizes the lands of Owen Glendower, ii. 9. The Welshman recovers them by arms, 10. In 1402, he defeats Grey in battle, and makes him his prisoner, 11. This captive baron is ransomed, paying 10,000 marks to the Welshman, 13.

GREY, lady Catherine, second daughter of the duke of Suffolk, 1553, married to lord Herbert, son of the earl of Pembroke, ii. 499, 568. She was sister of lady Jane Grey, and upon her execution had a similar claim to the crown, 499. Her mother, Frances, duchess of Suffolk, was the elder daughter of Mary, sister of Henry VIII., by Charles Brandon, duke of Suffolk, ib. Lord Herbert divorced lady Catherine, on the ruin of the house of Dudley, 568. About 1560, lady Catherine's clandestine marriage with Hertford (son of the Protector Somerset) was divulged to Elizabeth, who had soon after her accession restored him to his earldom, 569. Although pregnant, the countess of Hertford was kept a close prisoner in the Tower, and the earl summoned from the continent to answer for his conduct, ib. He avowed his marriage, and was also sent prisoner to that fortress, ib. Warner, the keeper, being indulgent to these illustrious victims, a second child was the result of their imprisonment in the same domicile, ib. The unhappy countess died in captivity, 1567; ib. Hertford, endeavouring legally to vindicate his children's legitimacy, was imprisoned for nine years longer, ib. The zealous Protestants preferred the line of Suffolk above Mary of Scots, and certain even of Elizabeth's ministers suffered some disgrace on this account, ib. Indeed, though bastardized by Elizabeth, the two children of this really lawful marriage were the nearest in succession to the English crown after Mary, 617, note.

GREY, lady Jane, statement of her descent from Henry VII., and of her claim to the crown, consequent on the Acts passed by Henry VIII., declaring Mary and Elizabeth, his daughters, illegitimate, ii. 499. Her mother, Frances, duchess of Suffolk, resigns her own right of succession to lady Jane on her nuptials with the lord Guildford Dudley, May, 1553; 499, 500. The descendants of Margaret Tudor by James IV. of Scotland, were not recognised in the will of Henry VIII. as having title to the English crown, 499. Northumberland, exercising a decided influence over the dying Edward VI., alarms him as to the extreme peril to the Protestant religion if his elder sister Mary should ascend the throne, 500. Edward then makes a formal instrument, declaring Jane Grey his successor, ib. Montague and Bromley, justices of the Common Pleas, and the crown lawyers, at first resist drawing out this will of Edward, but Northumberland compels them to perfect it, ib. The Great Seal affixed to it, ib. On the young king's death, 6th July, 1553, the lord-mayor and chief citizens are summoned by the

GREY, lady Jane,—
council to Greenwich, apprized of Edward having expired, and made to swear allegiance to queen Jane, by the terms of the will, 500, 502. On the 10th July, she was conveyed to the Tower by water, and publicly received as the new sovereign, 502. Many nobles, with their adherents, immediately resorted to Mary; troops raised by order of Northumberland went over from the party of Jane to that of the Catholic princess, and some of the fleet declared for her also, ib. Names of the chief opponents of queen Jane and of Northumberland, 503. The command of the forces is offered to the duke of Suffolk, Jane's father, but she expresses her reluctance at his assuming it, and Northumberland himself leads his partisans to the attack of Mary's army, who had been on her side proclaimed as queen, 12th July, at Norwich, ib. Northumberland, on quitting the metropolis, earnestly solicits the council to stand firm to the cause of their sovereign the lady Jane, who he declared had had the crown forced upon her, and had not sought it, ib. The Londoners witness the march of Northumberland's forces through the city in silence; the duke regards this as an unfavourable omen, ib. Queen Jane's cause advocated with zeal and eloquence by Ridley, bishop of London, at Paul's-cross, ib. The Council, Cecil, Cranmer, etc., persuaded the duke of Suffolk to permit their leaving the Tower, where all consultations had as yet been held, ib. Arriving at Baynard's Castle, the house of the earl of Pembroke, the Council declared for queen Mary, ib. They summoned the lord-mayor and aldermen to ride with them "into Cheap," where Garter proclaimed Mary, 504. Te Deum chanted in a procession to St. Paul's, ib. Lady Jane Grey deposed; she expresses her joy at being relieved from the queenly station, ib. Northumberland, totally dispirited, proclaims the lady Mary at Cambridge, July 20, 1553; ib. Jane, after personating a queen for ten days only, is kept as a prisoner in the Tower, ib. The duke of Suffolk, now released from the Tower, obtains the royal pardon, ib. On the 13th November, lady Jane and her husband, lord Guildford Dudley, together with his brother, lord Ambrose Dudley, and Cranmer, were condemned for high treason, 509. The queen, observant of the nation's sympathy for the youth and merit of the Dudleys and Jane, is satisfied with sending them back to the Tower as prisoners, ib. Some indulgences shown to them in the state-prison, 510. Unhappily, the duke of Suffolk, father of Jane, joins in sir T. Wyatt's insurrection, and also two of his brothers, January, 1554; 512. Queen Mary, conceiving the strongest fears of lady Jane, signs the warrant for her and her husband's execution, 517. On the 12th February, 1554, lord Guildford Dudley was beheaded on Tower-hill, and the lady Jane on the green within the Tower, 517, 518. Her calm and modest behaviour, 518. Her character and virtues, ib. The duke of Suffolk, her father, also beheaded, 23rd February, ib. Portrait of lady Jane Grey, 517.

GREY, lady Mary, youngest sister of Jane Grey, her marriage with Martin Kays, serjeant-porter, ii. 623. Queen Elizabeth immediately confined them apart, until the death of lady Mary, ib.

GREY, of Wilton, William, lord; he assists in quelling the rebellion of 1549; ii. 485. Is apprehended on a charge of participation in the duke of Somerset's rebellion, 495. Assists in blockading Leith, 1560; 560. He died 1562.

GREY, of Wilton, Thomas, lord, 1593; not selected by Cecil to join in the first ministerial cabinet of James I., gives way to discontent, with other leading men of whom Cecil was jealous, 1603; iii. 5, 7. This young noble was a chief beloved by the Puri-

GREY, of Wilton, Thomas, lord,—tana, 8. He promises 100 horsemen for seizing the king on his way to Windsor, June 24, 1603, but fails to supply them at the place of meeting, *ib.* He is found guilty by a commission of thirty peers, 12. His manly bearing during trial, and speech before sentence passed, 12, 13. Brought to the scaffold, he is taken away and locked in a cell, under some pretence, by the sheriff, 14. Re-conducted, like Cobham and Markham, to the scaffold ; the king's reprieve, after many obstacles by the way, arrives, *ib.* He is consigned to the Tower of London, where he dies, 1614, Cobham being permitted to escape, 14, 15.

GREY, of Groby, lord. *See* Earl of Stamford.

GREY, lord (Ford), admitted into the Rye-house Plot, 1681 ; iii. 740, 772. Is pardoned on mercenary accounts, 779.

GREY, sir Thomas, of Heton, beheaded at Southampton, 1415 ; ii. 29.

GRIBELIN, Simon, a native of Blois, engraved the first complete set of the cartoons (eighteenth century), iv. 760.

GRIFFIN, lord, 1688, captured in the *Salisbury*, one of the Pretender's ships, by sir George Byng. 1708. Execution is awarded against him, but he is reprieved by queen Anne, and dies a prisoner in the Tower, 1710 ; iv. 217.

GRIFFITH, king of Wales, supports the cause of his son-in-law, Algar, i. 194. His troops take Hereford and defeat earl Radulph, a Norman, and nephew of Edward the Confessor, *ib.* Harold drives his rival Algar back to Wales, which he invades, *ib.* On the death of Leofric, earl Algar again uniting with Griffith, 1057, obtains all his father's territories, *ib.* By his death, 1059, the Welsh princes are left exposed to fresh invasions by Harold, 195. Rees, brother of the Welsh king, taken prisoner, is put to death by command of Edward, *ib.* Harold commences, 1063, a severe warfare against the Welsh, not only on their coasts, but gains repeated victories over them in their mountains, *ib.* Reduced to despair, the turbulent British race decapitate king Griffith, and send his head to Harold, *ib.* Griffith's half-brothers consent to pay tribute, and swear fealty to Edward, *ib.*

GRIFFITH, son of Owen Glendower, made prisoner by prince Henry in the battle of Grosmont, 1405 ; ii. 17.

GRIG, (or Gregory), a powerful king of Scotland, lauded by the monkish chroniclers, he ruled in conjunction with Eocha prince of Strathclyde, i. 219. They were dethroned, 893, *ib.* And Donald IV. son of Constantine II., mounted the throne, *ib.*

Grignan, brigade of, iv. 172.

GRIMANI, Marco, papal legate, arrives in Scotland, 1543 ; ii. 437.

GRIMBALD, an eminent scholar, invited to England by Alfred the Great, i. 305.

GRIMOALD, Nicholas, a poet of the sixteenth century, iii. 582.

GRIMSTON, Harbottle, his speech in parliament, 1640 ; iii. 212, 227 : elected speaker of the House of Commons, 1660 ; 430*.

GRINDAL, Edmund, succeeds Parker in the primacy of Canterbury, 1575. He recommends to Elizabeth that milder measures be taken against the Puritans, for which he is confined to his house, and suspended from his ecclesiastical functions, ii. 744. He dies in 1583, and is succeeded by Dr. Whitgift, 745.

Grisogono, plan of the church of, i. 312.

GROSTÊTE, Robert, an eminent cultivator of mathematical science, elected to the see of Lincoln, 1234 ; died, 1253 ; i. 843.

GROTIUS, Hugo, the great publicist, wrote his " Mare Liberum," 1634 ; this treatise was answered by Selden, 1636 ; iii. 174. He died, 1645.

GROUCHY, a French marshal, sent by Napoleon to watch the movements of the Prussians, June 17, 1815 ; § iv. 633*, 638*.

GROVE, captain, executed, 1655 ; iii. 419.

GROVE, accused, 1678, of being engaged in a conspiracy to murder Charles II., iii. 717.

GRUDSHILL, sir Robert ; his effigy in Hoveringham church, Notts, ii. 241.

GRYMBALD, an eminent Norman, abbot of St. Alban's, to whom the education of Henry Beauclerc was intrusted by his father. i. 604.

Gualior, a strong Mahratta fortress taken by captain Popham, 1780 ; § ii. 144. View of the fort, 145.

GUALO, the pope's legate, i. 531. Crowns Henry III. in the church of St. Peter's, Gloucester, 671.

Guelphs, the, 1705, commence that close alliance to the Whig party which was scarcely interrupted, till several years after the accession of George III., iv. 182.

GUERICKE, Otto von, a natural philosopher of the seventeenth century, famous as the inventor of the air-pump ; was born in 1602, and died in 1686 ; iv. 779.

GUEST, general, iv. 489 ; governor of Edinburgh Castle, during its blockade by the Young Pretender, 1745 ; 504.

GUIDO RENI, a very celebrated painter, born at Bologna in 1575. He acquired immense wealth, which he as quickly dissipated in gaming. In his advanced years he was reduced to paint for his immediate wants ; he died in a melancholy condition at the place of his birth in 1642 ; iii. 567.

GUIDO, of Arezzo, his improved scale of musical notation, about 1030 ; i. 633.

Guienne and Gascony, wars of the English and French in, ii. 8, 19, 20, 85.

GUIENNE, William, earl of Poietiers, and duke of, zealous to join the first crusaders in Palestine, offered his dominions on mortgage to William Rufus, but the king's accidental death intervened, i. 401.

GUILDFORD, Francis North, earl of, becomes chancellor of the Exchequer, 1767 ; § i. 59. Portrait of, *ib.*, 83, 86 ; he died, 1790 ; § iii. 27.

GUILDFORD, Frederic, lord, son of the preceding, premier, 1770 ; § i. 88. Description of this nobleman, *ib.* He brings a bill into parliament, March 1774, for removing the customs, courts of justice, and all government offices from Boston to New Salem, 159. Medal struck in honour of, 201. His bill for cutting off the trade of New England, 203—206, 333, 474, *note*, 479. He resigns, 1782 ; 481. Re-appointed premier, 1783. The Coalition Ministry, 498, 504. His death, August 5, 1792 ; § iii. 27.

Guilford, battle of, fought, March 15, 1781 ; § i. 453, 454.

GUILFORD, lady, and other attendants of Mary (sister of Henry VIII.), dismissed 1514, by Louis XII. on his marriage with that princess, ii. 331.

Guillotine, the, voted to be the instrument of capital punishment by the National Assembly of France, March 20, 1792 ; § iii. 55.

Guinea, first struck in 1662, so named from Guinea, whence the gold was brought, iii. 867. Coins of this denomination recalled 1816, and *sovereigns* issued, § iv. 673.

GUISCARD, marquis de, stabs Mr. Harley with a penknife, 1711 ; iv. 250. He dies in Newgate of wounds received in the scuffle, 251.

GUISE, Mary of, queen of James V. of Scotland, iii. 644.

GUISE, duke of, an uncle of Mary queen of Scots, his influence in the reign of Henri II. of France, 1547 ; ii. 458. He takes Calais, after it had been in possession of the English for 211 years, 533—535, and Guisnes, 535. He obtains possession of the young

GUISE, duke of,—
Fronch king, Charles IX., 570. His wars with the Huguenots, *ib.* He solicits aid from Philip II., *ib.* Gains the battle of Dreux, 571. Is assassinated, February 24, 1563, by Poltrot, a Huguenot, 572.

GUISE, cardinal of Lorraine, brother of the duke, 1547; ii. 458.

GUISE, general, heads an unsuccessful attack on Carthagena, 1741; iv. 452.

GUIZOT, M., interesting historical remarks and deductions of; i. 246, 256, 355, 563, 575; iii. 497, 499, 509.

GUNDULPH, consecrated bishop of Rochester 1077. The most able architect of his time; he founded the Cathedral and Castle of Rochester, 1077, and built the Tower of London, i. 615. Trial of his suit, in 1078, by jury, 572. He died March 8, 1108.

Gunpowder Plot, for blowing up the Parliament-house, king and royal family, peers and commons, 1605, instigated in the first instance by Catesby, and attributed to a faction chiefly of Papists, who suffer in due course the penalties of the law, iii. 20—32. The Catholics were maddened by the more rigorous enforcement of penal statutes, 8, 12, 17, 19, 20. Robert Catesby, a wealthy Catholic of good family, contriver and instigator, 1604, of this treason, 20. Catesby first engages Thomas Winter, an officer who served in the Low Countries, and was an agent of English Catholics in Spain, 21. Winter repairs to the Netherlands, and hears from the Spanish ambassador that no clause of *toleration* could be obtained in the late treaty between James I. and Spain, *ib.* He leads into England Guido Fawkes, a soldier of fortune, who was not yet acquainted with the treason contemplated, *ib.* Thomas Percy, eager to forward any conspiracy; his brother-in-law, John Wright, famous as a swordsman, *ib.* Their oath of secrecy; Catesby divulges his entire scheme; the Jesuit Gerard gives them the sacrament, *ib.* View of the conspirators' house at Lambeth, 21, 22. Percy, a gentleman pensioner, takes a house, the rear of which touched the lower portion of the parliament-house, 22. The conspirators labour hard to break through the wall to obtain a communication, *ib.* Parliament is prorogued to the 7th February, *ib.* Robert Kay, a Catholic, *ib.* Christopher Wright, 23. January, 1605, the conspirators enlist John Grant, a gentleman possessing a moated mansion, near Stratford-on-Avon, gloomy of disposition, as he had been persecuted in Elizabeth's reign, *ib.*; also Robert Winter, closely allied to Grant, *ib.* Bates, servant of Catesby, admitted to the secret, *ib.* They meet in February to proceed with their operations, and experience an alarm, *ib.*; this was from Bright, coal-merchant, selling off his stock. Percy takes his now vacant cellar, immediately under the House of Lords, *ib.* They place thirty-six barrels of powder, faggots, billets, stones, and bars of iron therein, 23, 24. Fawkes sent to Flanders to tempt sir William Stanley and captain Owen, in which he meets not much prospect of success; he returns in August, *ib.* "The Conspirators," from a print published at the time, 23. The Vault beneath the old House of Lords, 24. September, 1605, sir Edw. Baynham sent to Rome, to gain favour of the Vatican, when the blow should have been struck, *ib.* Prorogation until 5th November, *ib.* Plan (on the destruction of James I. and prince Henry) to seize the persons of prince Charles and the princess Elizabeth, 22. Sir Everard Digby, of Drystoke, accedes to the plot, gives a large sum of money, and promises to be ready on the 5th November, with numerous Catholic friends, invited to a hunt on Dunsmore Heath, 24. Ambrose Rookwood, of an ancient family, and still wealthy, having suffered fines and persecution, also joins, *ib.* Francis Tresham was a third wealthy accession to the conspiracy, but Catesby

Gunpowder Plot,—
repented sorely at having admitted him, and not without cause, 24, 25. The meeting at White Webbs, a lone house, near Enfield Chace, 25, 26. The scheme, originally too comprehensive in the ruin to be dealt, fails, to the confusion and death of all the conspirators, 25. The desire of some of them to save Catholic relatives or patrons of either House, was irrepressible, *ib.* Tresham requires that warning should be given to lords Stourton and Mounteagle, who had married his sisters, *ib.* Kay wants to save lord Mordaunt, *ib.* Letter delivered to Mounteagle, at supper at Hoxton, *ib.* Fac-simile thereof, 26. Lords Suffolk and Mounteagle, 4th Nov., descend to the cellars of the House, and there finding Fawkes on watch, question him, but depart, 27. At 2 A.M. November 5, Fawkes unbars the door, and steps out to look around, when he is instantly seized by soldiers stationed ready, *ib.* His examination before the king at Whitehall, 22, 27. Flight of the conspirators towards Dunchurch, 28. They occupy Stephen Littleton's house at Holbeach, on the borders of Stafford, and he being cognizant of their guilt, 7th Nov. escapes into a wood with Robt. Winter, *ib.* Sir Richard Walsh, with the *posse comitatus* of Worcester, attacks all in the mansion; Catesby, Percy, and both the Wrights, are therein shot, stoutly defending themselves; Thomas Winter badly wounded; Rookwood, wounded previously by an explosion of damp gunpowder, which struck the daring conspirators with much horror, is made prisoner: Digby, Littleton, Bates, and all the rest, captured in their flight, or surrender at Holbeach, 28, 29. They are lodged in the Tower, as also Tresham, who remained some days at liberty in London, 29. Torturing of Guido Fawkes, who will not confess, *ib.* Bates confesses under such ordeal; Tresham declares that Garnet and Greenway, priests, were concerned in 1602 with Catesby in a treasonable correspondence with Spain, *ib.* Tresham expires of disease, 23rd December, after solemnly retracting, by writing, all he had said against the jesuits above-named, *ib.* The trial delayed till 27th Jan., 1606, in the wish to add the priests, Gerard, etc., sir Wm. Stanley, and Owen, *ib.* Digby alone pleads guilty, *ib.* Nothing occurs in the evidence to implicate the Catholic gentry, or even any priests, *ib.* The cruel penalty against convicted traitors is rigorously executed on Digby, Robert and Thomas Winter, Grant, Bates, Rookwood, Keyes, and Guido Fawkes, at the west end of St. Paul's churchyard, on 30th and 31st January, 30.

Gunpowder; idle report of an intention to blow up the parliament which had prosecuted and condemned Strafford, 1641; iii. 242. The report spreading to the city, the citizens and train-bands, under colonel Mainwaring, hasten to defend parliament, *ib.*

Guns, manufacture of, established at Birmingham about the beginning of the 18th century, § iii. 685.

GUNTER, Edmund, an eminent mathematician, born 1581, inventor of the logarithmic scale still known by his name, of the sector, and of the surveyor's chain; he was also author of several works, and of the terms 'cosine,' 'cotangent,' etc. He died 1626; iv. 768.

GUNTER, major, is slain in the battle of Chalgrove-field, June 18, 1643; iii. 304.

GURDUN, Bertrand de, shot king Richard in the shoulder at the siege of Chalus, 1199, whilst fighting for Vidomar, viscount of Limoges, who had found a treasure in his domains, and refused to deliver it up to the king, i. 514. The king, when dying, sent for him, pardoned him, and ordered a hundred shillings to be given to him; but he was flayed alive and hanged by Marchadee, after the king's death, *ib.*

GURTH (brother of Harold II.), 1042—1052; shares in his father Godwin's power, prosperity, and adversity, i. 188, 191, 194. His advice to Harold not to be present in person at the battle of Hastings, 212. He was himself there slain, 215.

GUSTAVUS ADOLPHUS, king of Sweden, succeeded his father Charles IX. in 1611. He invaded Germany, June, 1630; iii. 146. Gained the battle of Leipsic, Sept. 7, 1631, against Count Tilly; he was afterwards opposed by Wallenstein, who commanded the imperial army, in an action which took place on the plain of Lutzen, Nov. 16, 1632, when the Swedes were victorious, but their heroic leader fell, 173.

GUSTAVUS III., king of Sweden, (1771—1792.) War with Russia, 1789, § ii. 316, 473, 474. Invasion of Sweden by the king of Denmark, 316. Defection of the Swedish nobles, and loyalty of the Dalecarlians, ib., 319—321. Treaty of peace between Sweden and Russia, signed August 14, 1790; 475. His exertions in favour of the royal family of France, 637. His plans for invading France, and reinstating the royal family, § iii. 48. He is shot at a masked ball by Ankarstroem, a Swedish noble, and expires twelve days after, March 29, 1792. 49, 50.

GUTHRUM, a Danish king, in 876, capitulates in Exeter to king Alfred, abandons Devonshire and all Wessex, and leads his forces into Mercia, i. 157. He prepares a new war, and on the first day of 878, he appoints a rendezvous for his warriors; they surprise Alfred in Chippenham, that king making his escape with difficulty, when Guthrun conquers Wessex, 158. Alfred constrained to conceal himself on the moors, and finally in Athelney, from the scouts of king Guthrun, ib. Total overthrow of this Dane at Ethandune, 878; 160. He repairs to Alfred's camp, and is baptized, with many of his people, ib. New laws, and civilization in the Danelagh, ib. His territory defined by treaty, ib. He and his Danes long remain faithful to the English monarch, their great ally, 160, 161. Death of king Guthran in 890, in a time of peace and prosperity, 162. In 893 the Danes of the Danelagh rebel against Alfred, and afford vigorous assistance to the sea-king Hasting, 162—164.

GUTHRY, bishop of Murray, deposed, iii. 484; hanged at Edinburgh, 1661; 682.

GUY, count of Ponthieu, takes Harold prisoner, who is released by Duke William, i. 197.

GUY, secretary of the treasury, accepts 200l. for expediting the payment of arrears due to a regiment, and is in consequence sent to the Tower, 1695; iv. 51.

Gwyddyl, the, settle in Scotland, i, 9.

GWYN, Nell, a public actress, and mistress of Charles II., iii. 706.

GWYNNED, Owen, king of the Welsh; he fought against Henry II., i. 443, 451.

GYLLENBORG, Count, the Swedish ambassador at St. James's, iv. 337; is arrested by order of the Privy-council, 1717; 338.

HAAK, Mr. Theodore, suggests the institution of the Royal Society, 1645; iv. 773.

Habeas Corpus, writ of, found in operation at an early period of the English law; it came into frequent use regno Henry VI. From this period its progress can be distinctly followed. It is difficult to say at what period it first began to be used against the crown; the earliest precedents cited are regno Henry VII. The first case in which the nature of this writ was thoroughly discussed was in 1627. Its further progress, and Blackstone's Commentary on the Act, iii. 834, 835.

HACKER, colonel, a parliamentarian, commissioned to conduct Charles I. to the scaffold, iii. 396. Hacker suffers execution, 1660, as a regicide, 676.

Hackney-coaches introduced, 1625, into London, iii. 543. Their build, ib. Licenses, and number permitted, 544.

HACO, king of Norway; the earl of Ross and other northern chiefs invade the Hebrides, 1263, which were under the dominion of Norway; Haco prepares an expedition against Scotland; he is at first very successful, but in the autumn his ships are destroyed by the storms, and many of his men are slain at the battle of Larga. He retires to Orkney, and expires on the 15th of December; i. 704, 705. The Hebrides, the Isle of Man, and all the other islands belonging to Norway, are made over in full sovereignty to Scotland, 705.

HACO, nephew of Harold, and hostage at William's court, i. 197; is restored to liberty and returns to England, 199.

Haddenrig, in Teviotdale; the powerful Douglas faction defeated here by Huntley and Home, who commanded the forces of James V., ii. 433.

HADDICK, general, lays Berlin under contribution, 1757; iv. 597.

HADDINGTON, John Ramsay, viscount, partiality of James I. for, iii. 37. Is married to the daughter of the earl of Sussex, ib. Created earl of Holderness, 1621, ib. He becomes jealous of sir Philip Herbert, the English favourite, and strikes him with his whip on a race-course at Croydon, about 1607, ib. Haddington is sent to the Tower for a short time, 38, 71.

HADDOCK, Robert, medical practitioner at Oxford, 1604, reported to preach in his sleep; the fellows of New College accustomed to listen to him in these perorations, iii. 20. James I. sends for him to court, and causes divers lords to sit up with him, to hear this man preach asleep, which he performs as was his wont, ib. The king detects the imposture, and dismisses the preacher, under promise not to do the like, ib.

HADFIELD, a maniac, attempts to shoot the king in Drury-lane theatre, May 15, 1800; § iii. 553.

HADLEY, John, supposed to be the inventor of the useful instrument known by his name (eighteenth century), iv. 784.

HADRIAN, profile of the emperor, from a copper coin, i. 47. He landed in Britain, 120, the Caledonians having attacked the entire frontier, ib. He did not contest the long-disputed territory north of Agricola's wall, but constructed a strong rampart from the Solway Frith to the German Ocean, known as Hadrian's wall, ib.

Hague, view of the, § ii. 12. Treaty of the Hague, signed, March 1609; iii. 48.

HAILES, lord, quoted, i. 708, 709.

HAINAULT, count of, entertains queen Isabella; his second daughter Philippa is affianced to the prince of Wales, 1325; i. 742.

HAINAULT and HOLLAND, the count of (William of Bavaria), 1416, visits the courts of Henry V., ii. 35. He was brother-in-law of "Jean sans Peur," duke of Burgundy, 36. His daughter Jacqueline succeeds on count William's death, 57.

HAINAULT, Jacqueline of, being very young when she inherited, her uncle, John the Merciless, bishop of Liege, invaded Holland, ii. 57. John, duke of Burgundy arranged this quarrel, and put a stop to a cruel warfare, ib. She is compelled by her family to marry the duke of Brabant, a feeble youth of fifteen, whom she despised, ib. She was much older, being his godmother, and beautiful, the puny duke was entirely led by low favourites, ib. She commissions her half-brother the Bastard of Hainault to punish the chief of those minions, whom he kills in bed, ib. The duke of Brabant exiles all the ladies of the duchess Jacqueline, ib. In 1421, she sought an asylum at Windsor, and was honourably entertained by queen Catherine, ib.

HAINAULT, Jacqueline of,—
She becomes enamoured with Gloucester, and the duke proposes marriage, *ib.* Martin V. refuses to annul her marriage with Brabant, and give her the requisite dispensation, *ib.* The rival pope, Benedict XIII., grants the dispensation to re-marry, *ib.* Gloucester espouses Jacqueline; the affair of her continental inheritance eventually involves the English in trouble, 57, 58. In 1424, the duke and duchess of Gloucester landed with 6,000 men at Calais, attacked the duke of Brabant, and assembled the estates of Hainault at Mons, 58. Philip of Burgundy endeavours to drive Gloucester out of Hainault, even paying officers and soldiers who had served his personal enemy Charles VII., *ib.* After braving the rage of Burgundy for eighteen months, Jacqueline consents to the duke's return to England for money, etc., *ib.* In her husband's absence her chief cities are entered by duke Philip, the citizens of Mons deliver her over to Burgundy, who closely imprisons her in his palace at Ghent, 1425; *ib.* She escaped in male attire from her prison, and collected a strong party in Holland, 59. Her subjects there, willing to defend the rights of their countess, also fought for their own liberties against the duke of Burgundy, *ib.* Gloucester sends her money and some archers, *ib.* The English archers land in an island of Zealand, fight gallantly against duke Philip, but are driven to their ships, *ib.* Jacqueline evinces heroic courage in battles and in sieges, *ib.* Bedford and the English council prevent Gloucester from sending his duchess further succour, *ib.* Martin V., at length fully acknowledged for pope, declared her marriage with the English duke null and void, *ib.* Gloucester thereupon re-married with Eleanor Cobham. *ib.* Jacqueline's first husband, Brabant, died, 1427, *ib.* Her fleet, under William de Brederode, defeated by Philip with the assistance of ships of Amsterdam, 60. Abandoned by her partisans, she reluctantly, by treaty, 1428, declared her cousin of Burgundy her heir, resigned the government of her provinces to Philip, and reserved for her maintenance the revenues of a few places only, *ib.*

HALE, sir Matthew, 1654; iii. 416. He recommends that some definite agreement should be made with Charles II. prior to his restoration, 431*, 706. He assumes the population of England and Wales to be seven millions, 1670; 654. His portrait, 830. Description of, by Roger North, 845. His History of the Common-Law of England, quoted, i. 569, 574, 811, 818.

HALES, sir Edward, lieutenant of the Tower, demands fees of the petitioning-bishops on their leaving the Tower, which they refuse, 1688; iii. 791, 800.

HALES, Mr. John, a theological controversialist, iii. 178, 610; his death, 1656, *ib.*

HALES, sir Robert, treasurer of England; beheaded by the Kentish rioters, June 14, 1381; i. 787.

HALES, sir Thomas, one of the members for Kent, 1701; iv. 122.

HALES, attorney-general, filed bills in the King's Bench, 1529, against Wolsey, ii. 371. Judge Hales supported boldly the title of Mary I. to the crown, 510. He was, shortly, treated cruelly in prison, as a remonstrant against religious persecution, 1553, and lost his reason, *ib.* After liberation, he drowned himself, *ib.*

HALFDEN, or HALFDANE, in 875, regulates affairs in Northumbria, he carries war into Cumberland, Westmoreland, and the kingdom of Strathclyde, i. 157. He locates his followers in Northumbria, where they intermarry with the mixed population of Anglo-Saxons and the old Danish inhabitants, *ib.* His conquests, and those of three other Norse kings, include Cambridge, Mercia, and East-Anglia,

HALFDEN, or HALFDANE,—
ib. They embark and carry the war into Wessex, *ib.*

Halidon-hill, battle of, July 13, 1333; i. 756.

Halifax, iii. 655.

HALIFAX, Charles Montague, earl of, auditor of the Exchequer, dispute of the two Houses about him, 1703; iv. 150. He died 1715. His portrait, 858.

HALIFAX, George Savile, earl of, 1679; iii. 733, 740; he carries on a secret correspondence with the duke of Monmouth and the prince of Orange, 759; deprived of office, 783. His portrait, 830; dissatisfied with the office of privy seal, which was restored to him by William III. iv. 18, he retires from office, 19; his witty tract about elections, 59; his death, 1695, *ib.*

HALIFAX, George Montague, earl of, 1739. He died June 8, 1771; § i. 119.

HALL, Arthur, M.P., 1580; case of, iv. 668, 669.

HALL, Joseph, iii. 491, successively bishop of Exeter and Norwich, expelled by the Long Parliament; died in 1656, from imprisonment and poverty, 608. His portrait, 803.

HALL, rev. Robert, of Leicester, an eloquent preacher, his portrait, § iv. 615.

HALL, Timothy, bishop of Oxford, consecrated, 1688. Died 1690; iv. 620.

HALLAM, Mr., historical observations, etc., of, i. 574, 575, 803, 810, 811, 885; ii. 156; iii. 254, 586 *note*, 606, 613.

HALLEY, Edmund, author of numerous papers in the Philosophical Transactions, and of a catalogue of the southern stars, died 1742; iv. 783. He predicted the return of the comet known by his name, and suggested the observation of the transit of Venus, with the view of determining the sun's parallax, 784.

HAMILTON, lord Claude, younger son of the duke of Chatelherault, assembles 500 men, to avenge the death of archbishop Hamilton, and takes the town of Stirling; he is obliged to fly before the earl of Marr, but one of the Hamiltons, determining that the regent Lennox should not escape, bids him remember the archbishop, and shoots him through the head, 1571; ii. 645, 646.

HAMILTON, duke of, leads 6,000 men into Germany, 1630; iii. 150. His favour at court, *ib.* Receives an order from Charles to reduce the Scots to order, 189. The citizens of Edinburgh request him to repair to Holyrood-house; they demand the establishment of the Covenant, 190. He departs from Holyrood, July 4, 1638; 191; and, after having obtained instructions, returns, Sept. 17; 192. Foreseeing a rupture at Glasgow, he advises Charles to hasten his warlike preparations, 193. Urges the lords of the session to sign the king's "Confession of Faith," 195. His speech to the assembly, *ib.* His un-Scottish letter to the king, 196, *et seq.* He dissolves the assembly, 198. Returns to England to direct the preparations against the Covenanters, 199. Lord Kerr and the earl of Montrose charge him with treason; the parliament declares him innocent, 350. He is raised to a dukedom, 1641; 251. Sent a prisoner by Charles to the castle of Mount St. Michael, in Cornwall, 309. Having obtained his liberty, he renews his loyalty to the king, 361. He crosses the border at the head of 10,000 foot and 400 horse, 382. Is captured at Uttoxeter, *ib.* Beheaded in Palace-yard, 1649; 400.

HAMILTON, lord Basil; the Darien Company commissions him to present a petition to William III; the king refusing to receive him, he attempts to force the memorial into the king's hands, but is roughly repulsed, iv. 106.

HAMILTON, duke, opposes torturing in Scotland, iii. 756. Is appointed president of the Scottish Con-

HAMILTON, duke,—
vention of Estates, iv. 7. He reads the act of the Convention, declaring James to have forfeited the crown, 8. Lord high commissioner for Scotland, he refuses his assent to several bills proposed by the parliament, 1690; 43. Refuses, in the name of the parliament to appoint who should be the successor after the death of Queen Anne, 162. He opposes the union of England and Scotland, 191. His correspondence with the court of St. Germain, 195. Suspected by the Jacobite leaders of holding a secret correspondence with the court of London, 207. Strongly suspected by the government of endeavouring to bring back the Pretender, and in consequence arrested, 1708; 216. Appointed to go to France to negotiate the Peace of Utrecht, 271. Is killed in a duel with lord Mohun, who also falls, 1712, ib.

HAMILTON, sir Charles, takes possession of the island of Goree, 1800; § iii. 559.

HAMILTON, sir George, a Catholic, having a warrant granted him, 1642, by Charles I. in Scotland to pass into Ireland, is stayed by order of the House of Commons, and kept in custody, iii. 270. They allege that both colonel Butler's father, and Hamilton's father and brother are in rebellion, ib. The king assures them that no suspicion could attach to George Hamilton, and that Butler was uncle of lord Ormond, a good Protestant, 270, 271. Reply of the Commons, that all Hamilton's brothers are dangerous Papists, and had been bred up in the armies of Spain, 271.

HAMILTON, Gerard, prophesies the revolt of America, 1767; § i. 57.

HAMILTON, sir John, opposes the acts of the Perth Assembly, 1621; iii. 470.

HAMILTON, Mr. John, minister at Newburn, petitions, 1637, against reading the Book of Common Prayer, iii. 184.

HAMILTON, sir Patrick, 1518, slain in a contest with the faction of Douglas, earl of Angus, ii. 352; iii. 647.

HAMILTON, Patrick, abbot of Ferne, and first martyr of the Reformation in Scotland, was burned, Feb. 29, 1528. This young man was nearly related to the king, his father being brother to the earl of Arran, and his mother sister to the duke of Albany. James Beaton, the cardinal, to give the sentence the greater authority, caused it to be subscribed by all who were of any estimation in St. Salvator's College, amongst whom was the earl of Cassillis, a child thirteen years old, ii. 747. His death fatal to the interests of the Catholic church, ib.

HAMILTON of Bothwell-Haugh, made prisoner while fighting for Mary at Langside, 1568; he is condemned to death, ii. 632. His life is spared by the regent, but his property is forfeited, and his wife, who had recently been delivered, is turned out by night, half naked, into the fields, ib. The next day she is found frantic, ib. Hamilton vows revenge, ib. He engages an empty house at Linlithgow, where he lurks some time, and from which, shortly after, he shoots the regent, 1570; ib. Though hotly pursued, he escapes to France, ib. The subsequent history of this Hamilton is little known; but it appears that forty-nine years after this he found a quiet grave in the churchyard of a country parish of Ayrshire, ib.; note.

HAMILTON, archbishop of St. Andrew's, and natural brother of the duke of Chatelherault, ii. 646, note; hanged at Stirling by the regent Lennox without trial, 1570, 645; iii. 435. His death soon revenged, ii. 645, 646.

HAMILTON, bishop of Galloway, 1610; iii. 465.

HAMILTON, urges the Covenanters, 1679, to redress their grievances by the sword, iii. 730.

HAMILTON, colonel, second to the duke of Hamilton,

HAMILTON, colonel,—
1712, in the fatal duel with lord Mohun, iv. 271, 312, 321.

HAMILTON, surrenders Carlisle, which he held for the young Pretender, to the duke of Cumberland 1745; iv. 519.

HAMMOND, colonel, iii. 333. Lieutenant-general of the Ordnance, summoned to the bar of the House of Commons, 1647; 364. Governor of the Isle of Wight, 375. Is recalled, and colonel Ewer appointed in his place, 1648; 386.

HAMMOND, colonel Robert, nephew of the preceding, iii. 364.

HAMPDEN, John, born, 1594, of Saxon descent, iii. 177. He suffers for not contributing to a forced loan, 123. His landed property in Buckinghamshire, 177. His studies at Oxford, and in the Inner Temple, ib. His accomplishments, ib. His high character and handsome person, ib. He contemns such titles of honour as were to be purchased of James I., ib. His mother, Mrs. Elizabeth Hampden, ib. His marriage, in 1619, ib. In 1621 (and again in 1624) he sat as member for Grampound, 177, 178. He spoke briefly, seldom, and with modesty, yet evinced coolness of judgment and sagacity, 178. His intimacy with Selden, Wentworth, Pym, and Eliot, ib. In 1625 he was returned for Wendover, a borough near his paternal estates, in the first parliament of Charles I., ib. Was engaged much on the committees so important at that period, 177, 178. Death of his wife, 1634; 179. Member for Buckingham, 212. He takes a commission as colonel in the parliamentary army, 291. At the battle of Chalgrove-field, 1643, he leads on a party of horse, to prevent prince Rupert crossing Chiselhampton-bridge, 304. Is struck by two balls on the shoulder, and mortally wounded, ib.

HAMPDEN, accused of being concerned in the Ryehouse Plot, and fined 40,000l., 1684; iii. 755.

Hampton-court, iii. 64.

Hampton-court Palace, iv. 138.

HANCOCK, John, portrait of, § i. 189. His name excepted from a pardon offered by general Gage in the king's name, 1775, to all the revolutionary Americans who should lay down their arms, 215.

Hangings, paper and leather, invented early in the seventeenth century, iii. 618.

HANMER, sir Thomas, iv. 276. Chosen speaker of the House of Commons, 1714; 282.

HANOVER, Sophia, electress of, her letter to Mr. Stepney, iv. 112. Her name introduced in the public prayers, 144. Her death, 1714, supposed to have been occasioned by irritating letters from Queen Anne, 292.

Hanseatic League, the powerful, ii. 94. Their towns seventy in number, in 1475, when their commercial treaty with England was concluded at Utrecht, ii. 179. Illustration,—Wharf of the German merchants of the Steel-yard, Thames-street, ib. The Steel-yard Company was abolished, Feb. 22, 1552.

HARCLAY, sir Andrew, 1322; i. 741.

HARCOURT, Jacques de, his baronial castle of Crotoy, in Picardy; his inroads, 1421, upon the English in France, ii. 49.

HARCOURT, marquis d', agent of Louis XIV., 1700; iv. 108.

HARCOURT, sir Simon, created baron Harcourt, 1711; iv. 257. He died, 1727.

HARCOURT, Simon, earl of, appointed governor to the young prince of Wales, 1751 (George III.), iv. 567. He resigns, 573. He died, 1777.

HARCOURT, Mr., 1700; iv. 104.

HARDICANUTE, son of Canute by queen Emma; the kingdom of England is shared between him and his half-brother Harold, 1035; i. 184. Hardicanute remains long in Denmark, the habits of the Scandinavians being agreeable to him, ib. His mother

HARDICANUTE,—
and earl Godwin, her chief supporter, govern the south of England in his name, *ib.* Harold, in some time, adds the southern provinces to his own northern portion, *ib.* Archbishop Ethelnoth refuses to crown the usurper, 185. Harold Harefoot dying, the thanes repair to Bruges, 1040, and find Hardicanute preparing an armament, *ib.* He brings over with him the favourite companions of his revels and many Danish troops, 186. This system required arbitrary exactions and repeated danegelds, *ib.* The king's "hascarles," or household troops, collect these monies, *ib.* At Worcester they experience a formidable resistance; Turstane and Feader, the collectors, are slain, *ib.* That city was burnt in vengeance, and the vicinity laid desolate, *ib.* Hardicanute causes Harold's body to be thrown into the Thames, *ib.* Earl Godwin escapes the king's fury, by the timely present of a splendidly-adorned ship, manned by eighty warriors, gorgeously equipped, *ib.* Godwin, and Emma, relict of Canute, now govern in the king's name, who loved naught else but the table, *ib.* The king, at a marriage-feast held at Clapham, whilst pledging the bridegroom and company, falls senseless, with the wine-cup in his hand, 1042; *ib.* He dies without regaining speech, and was interred by the side of Canute at Winchester, *ib.*

HARDING, John, author of a "Metrical Chronicle of England," ii. 209.

HARDINGTON, Thomas, his mission to the Emir of Nassir, 1209; i, 522.

HARDRADA, Harold, king of Norway, at the instigation of Tostig invades England, 1066; i. 208. Hardrada and Tostig land their united forces at Riccall near York, *ib.* Are opposed by Morcar and Edwin, who are defeated, *ib.* They enter York, *ib.* Are attacked by Harold, *ib.* They draw up their forces at Stamford bridge; but are defeated after a long and fierce action; Hardrada and Tostig are slain, and most of the Norwegians perish, 209.

Hardwick-hall, ii. 849.

Hardwicke State-papers, iii. 14.

HARDWICKE, lord, quoted, iv. 93, 221.

HARDWICKE, Philip York, earl of, 1754, lord high chancellor, he introduces the bill known by the name of Hardwicke's Marriage Act, 1753; iv. 578. He resigns after having held the seals nearly twenty years, 1756; 588. He died 1764.

Hare Stone, Cornwall, i. 97.

Harfleur, town and fortress on the river Seine, capitulates, in 1415, to Henry V., arriving with his armament from Southampton, ii. 29. In 1416, the earl of Dorset, closely besieged by the French, is succoured by the duke of Bedford, who gained a splendid naval victory, 35. View of the present town, *ib.* Its importance to Henry V. when blockading Rouen, 1418; 39.

HARGRAVE, Mr., his tract on the origin and progress of the appropriation of parliamentary aids and supplies for particular services, iii. 842.

HARIOT, Thomas, the traveller and algebraist, iii. 72. He died in 1621; iv. 768.

Harlaw, battle of, July 24, 1411; ii. 132.

HARLAY, negotiator of king Louis at the treaty of Ryswick, 1697; iv. 78.

HARLEY, Edward, refuses to give his vote against sir Robert Walpole, 1741; iv. 444.

HARLEY, Thomas, his mission to the court of France, 1712; iv. 266.

HARLEY, Mr. *See* earl of Oxford.

HARMAN, sir John, 1666, severely wounded in an engagement with the Dutch, iii. 698.

HAROLD HAREFOOT, supposed illegitimate son of Canute, by Alfgiva daughter of the ealderman of Southampton; Canute leaves to him the kingdom of England; Hardicanute to have Denmark, 1035, i.

HAROLD HAREFOOT.—
184. Earl Godwin declared for the legitimate son, Hardicanute, and a civil war impended, *ib.* The Witenagemot summoned, decided on a partition. Harold to possess the north, *ib.* He also seizes the south of England, his brother being still absent, *ib.* Edward, elder son of Ethelred and queen Emma, invades England, but strongly opposed by his cruel mother, he withdraws to Normandy, *ib.* A treacherous letter induces Alfred, his younger brother, with 600 followers, to invade Harold's dominions, *ib.* The prince has his eyes put out, of which he speedily dies, 185. The odium of this atrocity was shared alike by Harold, Emma, and earl Godwin, *ib.* Harold becomes "full king;" narrative of his having placed the crown on his own head, Ethelnoth, archbishop of Canterbury, having refused to perform the ceremony, *ib.* His contempt for religion, *ib.* His fleetness on foot in the chase, which was his chief pleasure, *ib.* His death, 1040, he was buried at Westminster, *ib.* His body disinterred, decapitated, and cast into the Thames, by order of Hardicanute, for anger at the foul murder of Alfred, his half-brother, 186. Regained by Danish fishermen, the degraded remains were finally interred in St. Clement's cemetery near Temple-bar, *ib.*

HAROLD II.—He was eldest son of earl Godwin, and governed one of the provinces entrusted by Hardicanute and Edward to his powerful father, i. 188. On Godwin's flight, 1051, his son repairs to Ireland with Leofwin, 191. They return with reinforcements, 1052, and join the great earl off the Isle of Wight, 193. Harold succeeds to all his father's power and influence, 194. His former government of East-Anglia is bestowed by the court on his old enemy Algar, son of Leofric, *ib.* He accuses Algar of treason, who is exiled by the Witenagemot, *ib.* His arduous contest with this rival, who had taken Hereford with the aid of Welshmen supplied by his father-in-law Griffith, *ib.* Various success of Harold's enterprises, *ib.* The Welsh king, left exposed by Algar's death, 1059, is attacked in his mountain strongholds, 194, 195. Harold puts Rees, brother of Griffith, to death, 195. Combining with Tostig, he maintains a fleet, 1063, on the Welsh coasts, *ib.* He arms his troops with leather, instead of heavy armour, and defeats the mountaineers in all their fastnesses, *ib.* King Griffith had his head struck off by his subjects, who sent it in token of submission to the Saxon earl, *ib.* Harold returns in triumph, and presents his trophies to king Edward, *ib.* Supposed to have poisoned Edward Atheling, *ib.* His departure for Normandy, 196, 197. Is wrecked on the French coast near the river Somme, *ib.* Taken prisoner by Guy count of Ponthieu, and released by William, *ib.* Harold goes to Rouen, 198. His oath to William, 199. He returns to England, loaded with presents, *ib.* Marches against Morcar, who had been appointed earl by the Northumbrians, after the expulsion of Tostig, 200. Endeavours to persuade the Northumbrians to receive back Tostig; but as they refused, he consents to the appointment of Morcar, *ib.* Harold arrives in London, 201. Different opinions as to the person appointed by Edward for his successor, *ib.* Harold is proclaimed king by the people, 1066; 204. His coronation, *ib.* His popularity, and courteous behaviour, after this ceremony, 205. Hardrada and Tostig land in England; Harold marches to oppose them, as they had gained possession of York by the defeat of Morcar and Edwin, 208. He gains a complete victory, and Hardrada and Tostig are slain, 209. The Normans land, and Harold immediately sets out for London, *ib.* Where he is well received, *ib.* He mans 700 vessels to hinder William's escape, 211. He sets out for

HAROLD II.,—
the Sussex coast, but finding the Normans well prepared, he fortifies himself in an entrenched camp at Senlac, now Battle, ib. Night before the battle of Hastings in the two camps, 212. Description of the English camp at Hastings, 213. They are attacked in their camp; and suffer severely through impradently following the Normans, who feign flight, 213, 214. The English line in several points is broken, 215. Harold is struck by an arrow, and dies, ib. The English give way, and their standard is taken, ib.

HAROLD, son of Sweyn Estridsen king of Denmark, came to England in the expedition commanded by Osbeorn (1069), i. 371. His death, 386.

HARRACH, count, Austrian ambassador at the court of Spain, 1700; iv. 110.

HARRINGTON, lord, having accompanied the princess Elizabeth to the Rhine, claims on his return 30,000l. James I., having no money, gives him a grant for the coining of base farthings in brass, iii. 52.

HARRINGTON, sir James, iii. 863, author of the "Oceana," published, 1656; 612.

HARRINGTON, sir John, his surprise at the anger of Elizabeth on the return of Essex from Ireland, 1599; ii. 684. His description of a court pageant, iii. 627.

HARRIS, Mr. George, one of the conspirators in the Invasion Plot, 1696; iv. 66.

HARRIS, Mr. Howel, a companion and assistant of George Whitefield, iv. 654.

HARRIS, sir Thomas, engages in a plot for restoring Charles II., and endeavours to surprise Shrewsbury Castle, 1655, but is taken prisoner, iii. 419.

HARRISON, John, a most skilful mechanic, born in 1693. He is famed as the inventor of the chronometer for ascertaining the longitude at sea, and also of the gridiron pendulum, § i. 601. Portrait of, 602. He died March 1776; 603.

HARRISON, major, iii. 332, conveys Charles I. from Hurst Castle to Windsor, 388, 404. Imprisoned for joining in a conspiracy of the fifth-monarchy men, 421, 427, 671. Suffers as a regicide, 1660; 676.

HARSNET, an enemy of Abbot, archbishop of Canterbury, iii. 475.

HARTLIB, Samuel, a native of Poland and friend of Milton, iii. 424, he wrote several works on agriculture, 557. Cromwell, who encouraged the rural arts, granted him a pension, 558.

HARVEY, Dr. William, generally esteemed the discoverer of the circulation of the blood, regno James I., iii. 616, though this curious fact had been mentioned by Aristotle, Galen, Mondino, Berenger, by the famous Michael Servetus, and several others, iv. 769; the merit of demonstrating and establishing this fact is however indisputably due to our illustrious countryman, ib.

HASNAIN, battle of, gained, 1409, by the duke of Burgundy over his vassals, ii. 20.

HASELL, one of the conspirators who engaged to deliver up the city of London to Charles I. 1643; iii. 302.

HASELRIG, Hampden, Cromwell, and other discontents in 1637, said to have actually embarked for the North American colonies, but their ships detained by the king's mandate, iii. 182, 319, 426.

HASTING, a northern sea-king, or viking, in 893, leads a multitudinous fleet filled with a host of Danish warriors, and well provided with horses collected in Flanders, etc., against the Kentish coast, i. 162. His two fortified camps at Appledore near the Andredswold forest, and at Milton near Sittingbourne, ib. Each division of his Danes is confined to its entrenchments by Alfred's judicious position selected in the part of Kent intervening between the Danish strongholds, 163. Great strength of the English entrenchments; the Danes prevented from further forays are straitened for provisions, ib. Hasting pretends to sail, but simply

HASTING,—
crosses into Essex with his fleet, and chief forces, whither Alfred is unable to pursue him, ib. The baptised Danes of the Danelagh, who had been peaceable above seven years, join the newly-arrived pagan Northmen, ib. The division deserted on the Kentish shore by Hasting, break up their camp of Milton, and are hotly pursued by the English monarch, ib. He routs them at Farnham; the greater portion perish by the sword, or are drowned in the river, ib. The remnant skirt the Middlesex shore, and effect a passage into Essex, ib. They first find repose in the Isle of Mersey, but are unable to join their great leader Hasting, ib. Surrounded by Alfred, they are about to surrender through famine, when he is constrained by a diversion of Hasting's in the west to march upon Exeter, 163. The blockade of Mersey continued in his absence, ib. One fleet of Hasting's, lands the Danes in Devonshire, who besiege Exeter, ib. A second fleet circumnavigates the coasts of Scotland, and enters the Severn, where the Danes besiege an English fortress, ib. King Alfred repulses the army of Hasting before Exeter, and in the Severn, ib. Benfleet in Essex, a Danish fort, taken by the Londoners, with a rich booty, and also the wife and sons of Hasting, ib. They are liberated by Alfred, and sent back honourably to the sea-king, ib. Hasting fortifies himself, at Buttington on the Severn; his supplies cut off by Alfred; the Danes from hunger devour their horses, ib. Hasting endeavours to force his passage through the English lines; Alfred gains a decisive victory. 164. Reinforced in the Danelagh, Hasting seizes Chester; and blocked up there by land and sea, he rushes into North Wales, (895), ib. His strong camp at South Showbury, in Essex, 163, 164. In 896, he builds a fortress on the banks of the river Lea, 164. Alfred erects a fortress on either bank of the Lea, below the Danish camp, and, by cutting three channels from the Lea to the Thames, draws off most of the water from the former river, ib. This effects the ruin of the Danish fleet, which was left aground, and useless, ib. Its destruction by the Londoners, ib. The Danes force their way to the Severn, and raise an impregnable fortress at Quatbridge, near Bridgenorth, ib. In 897, the warlike Hasting finding only famine, and stout resistance, sails with his Danes to the river Seine, ib. Many of his troops betake themselves to the Danelagh and Northumbria, others sail to the rivers Schelde and Rhine, ib. Hasting, not finding the French king possessed of Alfred's wisdom, establishes himself in France, 165.

Hastings, in Sussex. William arrives at Bulverhithe, whence he proceeds to Hastings, and constructs there a fortified camp, waiting for the approach of Harold, i. 210. See Harold and William I. View of, from the Fairlight Downs, 212.

Hastings, battle of, (Oct. 14, 1066,) commenced by Taillefer, i. 213. Changes of the day, 214. William commands his archers to direct their arrows upwards, ib. Feigned flight of the Normans, ib. The English fortified encampment is entered, and their line broken, 215. Harold is slain, and the English standard taken, ib.

HASTINGS, lord, beheaded at Durham, 1405, for Northumberland's rebellion, ii. 17.

HASTINGS, lord, married to a sister of Nevil, earl of Warwick, partly mistrusted by Edward IV., 1470; ii. 106, 112, 113. A bitter enemy of the house of Woodville, which had engrossed places and power at court, 118. Apparent reconciliation effected by the dying Edward, 1483, between Howard, Hastings, and Stanley, with queen Elizabeth's relations, ib. Violence of Hastings in the council, ib. Remarks on his subsequent conduct, ib. He decides on up-

HASTINGS, lord,—
holding the cause of Edward V., 119. Narrative by sir T. More, of the summary execution of lord Hastings, 120, 121.

HASTINGS, sir Edward, a councillor of queen Mary, sent to fetch the princess Elizabeth from Ashridge to London, ii. 515.

HASTINGS, Warren, born 1732 or 1733. Is appointed governor-general of India, 1773 ; § ii. 16, 99, 102. Portrait of, 108. Beneficial effects of his government, 127. His exertions for enlarging the geographical knowledge of Asia, 128. Charges preferred against him by the new council of the East India Company, who opposed him in all his proceedings, 133, 135. Being in great need of money, he adopts the plan of *squeezing* the Rajahs ; arrest of Cheyte Sing, 1781 ; 164, 165. He concludes the Treaty of Chunar with Asoff-ul-Dowlah, the nabob of Oude, 1784 ; 169, 170 ; and accepts a present of 100,000*l.* from that prince, 173, 176. He resigns, 1784 ; 188, and embarks for England, February 1785 ; 189. He is graciously received by the king, 190. Burke produces charges against Hastings, 1787 ; 192—202, 226—241. His trial at Westminster-hall commences, February 13, 1788 ; 276—280, 305—309, 466—469, 559—569. He is declared " Not Guilty," April 23, 1795 ; 569. His retirement, 569—572. He is named one of the privy-council, 1814 ; 572. His death, August 22, 1818 ; *ib.*

Hats, notice respecting the manufacture of, ii. 194.

HATTON, sir Christopher, vice-chamberlain to queen Elizabeth, ii. 660 ; iii. 62, 584.

HATTON, Mrs., wife of sir E. Coke, iii. 59 ; her wealth, 68.

HATZFELDT, intercepts lord Craven and the Prince Elector in their retreat from the siege of Lippe, 1637 ; iii. 174.

Havanna, view of, § i. 15. Capitulates to the English, August 13, 1762 ; 16.

HAVERSHAM, John Thompson, lord, iv. 95. Proposes that queen Anne should invite over the Electress Sophia, heir-presumptive to the throne, to reside in England, in case of her death, 181. Speaks violently against the Union of England and Scotland, 196. Discourses on the state of the nation, 225. He died 1710.

HAWES, Stephen, a poet of the sixteenth century, and author of " The Pastime of Pleasure," first printed 1517 ; ii. 836.

HAWKE, sir Edward, the celebrated commander, iv. 582. In conjunction with admiral Saunders, he supersedes Byng in the Mediterranean, 587. Makes an unsuccessful attempt upon Rochefort, 597. He refuses to serve under captain Howe, 1758 ; 601. He gains a victory over M. Conflans, commander of the Brest fleet, in Quiberon Bay, 606. Appointed first lord of the Admiralty, 1766 ; § l. 53.

Hawking, i. 342 ; iii. 640.

HAWKINS, sir John, ii. 673, 680. Portrait of, 771. The Slave-trade was introduced in 1562 by this (afterwards) celebrated commander, 787.

HAWKINS, captain William, of Plymouth, traded, about 1530, to Guinea, for ivory, and made voyages to Brazil, ii. 780.

HAWKSBEE, Francis, published several works on electricity, and first detected the remarkable phenomenon of the production of light by friction, about 1707 ; iv. 785.

HAWKSMOOR, Nicholas, greatly distinguished himself as an architect in Anne's reign ; his principal works, iv. 749.

HAWLEY, general, iv. 520. His disgraceful conduct at the battle of Falkirk, 1746 ; 522. Hangs several of his soldiers, 527. He escapes a court-martial through the countenance of the duke of Cumberland, 553.

HAXEY, Thomas, preparing a bill or petition, which, after the allegation of other grievances, 20th Ric. II.,

HAXEY, Thomas,—
demanded that the excessive charges (caused by the number of bishops and ladies) for the king's household should be diminished ; Richard proceeded to parliament in anger, ii. 156. He sent for the peers to attend him, made the chancellor explain the affair, and declared he would maintain his prerogative, 157. The Commons surrender the untoward bill ; and its proposer, Haxey, is attainted and condemned to die, *ib.* The archbishop and prelates beg the custody of Haxey, he being a clerk, and thus his life was saved, *ib.* His attainder reversed, 1399, 1st Hen. IV., upon petition of the Commons, *ib.*

HAY, earl of Errol, of a Norman family, dating from the Conquest, i. 220. Time of the immigration into Scotland of the Hays, or De Hayas, and their acquisition of the lands of Errol, *ib.* Fable explanatory of the supporters to their arms, *ib.*

HAY, earl of Kinnoul, lord chancellor ; he died Dec. 16, 1634 ; iii. 477.

HAY, lord Charles, tried by court-martial, 1760, for criticising the conduct of his commander, lord Loudon, in America, iv. 613.

HAY, sir James. *See* Carlisle.

HAY, Mr., a servant of the Young Pretender, 1745 ; iv. 529.

HAYLS, a portrait painter of the seventeenth century, iii. 883.

HAYMAN, sir Peter, severely reprimands sir John Finch, 1629, for refusing to perform the duties of speaker ; for this he is summoned before the privy-council, iii. 141, 142.

HAYTER, Thomas, bishop of Norwich, 1749, named preceptor to the young prince of Wales (George III.), 1751 ; iv. 567. He resigns, 573. Translated to London 1761. Died 1762.

HEALE, king's serjeant, 1603, opens the pleadings against Raleigh, iii. 9.

Hearth-tax, voted in perpetuity to the king. March 12, 1662 ; iii. 685. Abolished by William III. 1689 ; iv. 10.

HEATH, Nicholas, bishop of Worcester, 1543 ; placed in confinement, 1550 ; ii. 493. On the death of Gardiner, he being then archbishop of York, is made chancellor, 526. On the death of queen Mary, 1558, he declares to both houses of parliament the accession of Elizabeth, 539.

HEATH, attorney-general, his charge against the earl of Bristol, 1626 ; iii. 119, 143.

HEATHCOTE, George, alderman, 1745 ; iv. 501.

HEATHCOTE, sir Gilbert, alderman, 1709 ; iv. 237.

HEBERT, a revolutionist and warm advocate of materialism, brought to the guillotine March 24, 1794, by Robespierre, § iii. 414—420.

Hebrides, the, become the residence of the Norwegian and Danish sea-kings, i. 170. *Illustration.*—Ruins of the monastery of Iona, or I-Column-Kill. Alexander, lord of the Isles, 1411, defeated by Marr at the battle of Harlaw, is compelled by the treaty of Lochgillip to acknowledge his vassalage to the king of Scotland, ii. 132. Is seized, 1427, in the parliament at Inverness, by James I., imprisoned two years, then liberated, 133. He rebels, and collects his retainers, *ib.* The king in person routs him near Lochaber ; Alexander throws himself on the royal mercy, *ib.* In 1431, his kinsman Balloch heads a new rebellion, James I. marches against him, and this chieftain is slain, *ib.*

HEDGES, sir Charles, secretary of state, 1701 ; iv. 112, 117, 142.

Hedgley-Moor, near Wooller, lord Montague defeated sir Richard Percy, 1464, at, ii. 101.

HEEMSKIRK, Dutch minister at Paris, *regno* William III., iv. 112.

HEGHAM, Richard, a heretic, *regno* Henry VII., ii. 700.

HEINSIUS, Grand-pensionary, a particular friend of William III., iv. 81, 164.

HELIE, lord of La Flèche, recognised by the inhabitants of Maine as their lawful chief, 1099; i. 401.

HELIE DE ST. SAEN, a Norman nobleman, married an illegitimate daughter of duke Robert, Henry commits to him the charge of William, son of duke Robert and Sibylla, 1106, and afterwards sends to surprise the castle, but he flies with his pupil, and they are favourably received at the neighbouring courts, i. 412.

HEMINGFORD, (properly Hemingburgh,) Walter, an English chronicler, of the thirteenth century, i. 520.

HENDERSON, Alexander, minister at Leuchars; refuses to use the Book of Common Prayer, 1637; iii. 184. His death, 1646; 357.

HENDERSON, Andrew, steward to the earl of Gowrie, 1600; ii. 691.

HENDERSON, Mr., a Scottish commissioner, 1643; iii. 309.

Hendlip House, Worcester, view of this old mansion, in which the Jesuit Garnet was found secreted, 1606; the seat of Thomas Abingdon, brother-in-law of lord Mounteagle, iii. 30.

HENGHAM, sir Ralph de, grand Justiciary, imprisoned and heavily fined by Edward I., i. 694.

HENGIST and HORSA, were Jutes, who, invited by Vortigern to his aid, in the year 449 led the Saxons into Britain, i. 57. They were closely followed by the Angles of Holstein; and the Proper Saxons, favoured by their maritime possessions in Holland and Belgium, became the most powerful of the invaders, 140. They were all Pagans, ib. Hengist and Horsa, as subsidiaries of the Britons, drove back the invading Picts and Scots, ib. Hengist's feast to Vortigern, British king, in the Saxon entrenchment at Thong-caster, Lincolnshire, ib. Rowena, daughter of Hengist, espoused by king Vortigern, 141. The Isle of Thanet acquired by Hengist, who fortifies it, 58, 141. A war ensues, ib. Feast of Stonehenge, where this leader is supposed to have put all the British chiefs present to death, with the exception of Vortigern, 141, 142. Eric, son of Hengist, founds the first Saxon kingdom of Kent, 142.

HENRIETTA MARIA, princess, iii. 93. Negotiations set on foot with France for her marriage with prince Charles, 1623; 106. She prepares to come to England, 107. Arrives at Dover, 1625; 109. Her first meeting with prince Charles, ib. Their quarrels, 115. Her portrait, ib. She watches the coronation of the king through a window at the palace gate, 117. Her unmanageable temper, 161. Her proclamation to the English Catholics, 201. She desires to leave England with her mother Mary de Medicis, but is refused by the parliament, 248. Professes she is much terrified lest the Commons should impeach her, 272. She arrives in Burlington Bay, and remains four months in York, 301. Sends arms and ammunition to the king at Oxford, 302. Is impeached, 1643, by the Commons of high treason, ib. She desires to go to Ireland, 357. Dissuades the king from going to France, 361. She marries Jermyn, with whom she had been living in the closest intimacy, soon after the execution of the king, 396. She arrives in England with a train of French nobles, 677. Her marriage with Philip, duke of Orleans, brother of Louis XIV., about 1660; 678.

HENRY, I. (August 5, 1100—December 1, 1135), son of William the first, offends his brother Robert, i. 383. His father bequeaths to him five thousand pounds' weight of silver; prince Henry lends Robert 3,000l., in return for which he receives the Cotentin country, which comprehended nearly a third part of the Norman duchy, 396. His dissensions with his brother Robert, ib. Besieged by his two brothers, Robert and William, in Mount St. Michael,

HENRY L.,—

397. Is obliged to capitulate, and obtains permission to retire into Britanny, 398. The inhabitants of Damfront invite him to take the government of their city, ib. He is reconciled with William, 402. On hearing of his brother's death, he immediately flies to seize the royal treasury, 1100; 403. He is acknowledged king by the Witan, at Winchester, 405. ·Is crowned king in Westminster-Abbey by Maurice, bishop of London; he promises to annul all the unrighteous acts that had taken place in his brother's time (5th of August, 1100), ib. His great seal, ib. Henry's Charter of Liberties and restoration of the Saxon laws, 405, 406. He marries Maud, daughter of Malcolm king of Scots, and of Margaret sister of Edgar Atheling; curious particulars attending the marriage, 406, 407. See Maud. Henry's popularity with the English nation, 407. His expulsion of favourites from his court, and imprisonment of Ralph Flambard, the obnoxious minister of the late king, ib. Robert, duke of Normandy, returns from the Holy Land, but delays much time in Italy and Normandy before he prepares to assert his right to England, 408. He lands at Portsmouth, where a treaty is entered into, 409. Robert gives up all claim to England, and obtains a yearly payment of 3,000 marks; the barons on both sides receive unconditional pardon, ib. Henry besieges Robert de Belesme, earl of Shrewsbury, ib. Brave conduct of his English troops; the earl is obliged to capitulate; his lands in England are confiscated, ib. Robert comes over to England to intercede for the unfortunate barons; is detained as prisoner, and obliged to purchase his freedom by renouncing his annuity of 3,000 marks, 410. William declares himself Protector of Normandy against the bad government of Robert, ib. He violates the Charter and promises made at his coronation, ib. Henry invades Normandy, and in the second campaign takes his brother Robert prisoner at Tenchebray, ib. Edgar Atheling taken prisoner at Tenchebray by Henry, who permits him to live in England without any restraint, and grants him a trifling pension, 411. Duke Robert kept as a prisoner in England, ib. He attempts to escape from his guard; is blinded by order of his brother, and confined in Cardiff Castle, where he died in 1135, after an imprisonment of twenty-eight years, ib. Henry gains full possession of Normandy, 412. William, only son of Sibylla and duke Robert, falls into his hands; he gives him in custody to Helie de St. Saen, a Norman noble; afterwards endeavours to take possession of the young prince, but Helie flies with his pupil, and they are favourably received at the neighbouring courts, ib. General league in his favour, ib. Henry is attacked at every point along the frontiers of Normandy, ib. His skilful treaty, ib. He proposes to marry his only son William to Matilda, daughter of Fulk, earl of Anjou, and his daughter Matilda to Henry V., emperor of Germany, ib. Checks some incursions of the Welsh, ib. Makes all the barons and prelates of England and Normandy swear fealty to prince William, 413. Maud, wife of Henry I., dies, 1118, and his chief minister, the earl of Mellent, ib. He assists his nephew Theobald, earl of Blois, in a revolt against the French king; Baldwin, earl of Flanders, dies; Fulk, earl of Anjou, bribed by Henry; the marriage between William and Matilda is effected, ib. After a chivalrous engagement between Louis and Henry, a peace is concluded by the intervention of the pope, 413, 414. Conditions of this treaty; the king embarks for England, 414. Circumstances attending the death of prince William and his sister, ib. View of the sinking ship, 415. William Fitz-Robert's cause again taken up after the death

HENRY I.,—

of Henry's son; peace concluded, Henry marries Adelais or Alice, daughter of Geoffrey, duke of Louvain, and niece to the reigning pope, 416. He causes his daughter ·Matilda to be acknowledged by the prelates and barons at Windsor, as heiress to his crown, ib. Her marriage with Geoffrey Plantagenet, 1127; 417. She quarrels with her husband; a reconciliation is effected; Matilda has three children, Henry, Geoffrey, and William, 1133; 418. Death of Henry, 1st December, 1135; ib. His character, 418, 419. Legend of a dream or vision seen by this king, 664, 665.

HENRY II. (Dec. 19, 1154—July 6, 1189.) Henry, eldest son of Matilda, daughter of Henry I. and Geoffrey of Anjou, acknowledged in Normandy as legitimate duke, i. 434. Lands in England, to assist Matilda, 1142; 435. Is placed in safety in the strong castle of Bristol, where his uncle, the earl of Gloucester, attends to his education, ib. He returns to Normandy, 1147; ib. Description of prince Henry, his promising character, 436. He lands in Scotland, and receives the honour of knighthood from king David, 1149; ib. This splendid ceremony, at Carlisle, was attended by crowds of nobles from all parts of England, Scotland, and Normandy, ib. On his return he is put in full possession of the government of Normandy, and succeeds to the earldom of Anjou by the death of his father, 1150; ib. He marries Eleanor, the divorced queen of Louis VII., 1152, and acquires with her the earldom of Poictou and the vast Duchy of Guienne, 436, 438—440. General alliance against duke Henry; the French king marches an army to the confines of Normandy, ib. Henry makes a truce with the king of France and sails to England; a peace is finally adjusted, on the 7th of November, 1153, by a great council of the kingdom, held at Winchester, in which it is agreed that Henry should succeed on the death of Stephen, 437. Stephen dies October 25, 1154; 438. Great seal of Henry II., ib. Henry and his wife Eleanor are crowned at Westminster by Theobald, archbishop of Canterbury, amidst the acclamations of the people, 440. Portrait of Henry II., ib. His reform of abuses, and appointment of the earl of Leicester grand justiciary, 441. All foreigners who had acted as mercenaries for Stephen and Matilda expelled the kingdom, ib. The ancient demesne of the crown determined by law to be sacred and inalienable, ib. Henry levels to the ground about 1,100 castles, to the inexpressible joy of the people, 442. He narrowly escapes at the siege of the castle of Bridgenorth, his life being saved by the self-devotion of Hubert de St. Clair, ib. He obliges Malcolm, king of Scots, to resign the counties of Northumberland, Cumberland, and Westmoreland, for the bonâ fide possession of the earldom of Huntingdon, which the Scottish princes claimed as descendants of earl Waltheof, ib. Does homage a second time to Louis VII. for Normandy and his other continental territories, ib. Compels Geoffrey, his younger brother, to relinquish his claims to Anjou and Maine, for a pension of 1,000 English and 2,000 Angevin pounds, 443. His expedition against the Welsh; he is defeated with great loss at Coleshill Forest; the Welsh resign the territory they had retaken from Stephen, and give hostages and do feudal homage for what they retain, ib. Henry lays claim to Nantes, ib. With consent from the French king, he affiances his eldest son to Margaret, infant daughter of Louis, and his then youngest son, Geoffrey, to Constantia, daughter of Conan, duke of Brittany, 444. Henry goes in person to Paris, ib. He lays claim to the great earldom of Toulouse, for which expedition he first levies a sum of money, in lieu of the presence and services of his vassals, both in Normandy and England, ib. He

HENRY II.,—

takes the town of Cahors, and marches upon the city of Toulouse, but the French king comes to its assistance, 445. Henry returns to Normandy, leaving Becket to conduct the war, a French force having made a diversion on the side of Normandy, ib. Becket also returns, ib. Peace concluded between Henry and Louis, 1160; 446. Louis VII. marries Adelais, niece of king Stephen, ib. The marriage-contract between prince Henry and Margaret, daughter of Louis, solemnized, ib. Thomas à Becket is made chancellor of England, preceptor to the prince, and warden of the Tower, ib. Theobald, archbishop of Canterbury, dies, and is succeeded by Thomas à Becket, 448. Becket lays claim to several castles, and excommunicates William de Eynsford, but afterwards absolves him, ib. Henry receives homage from Malcolm IV. at Woodstock, ib. Becket and the clergy consent to a series of enactments, called the Constitutions of Clarendon, from Clarendon in Wiltshire, the place of meeting, rendering the clergy subject to the civil courts for felony, 449. Becket is cited before the council of Northampton, and renounced as primate by the bishops, October 13, 1164; ib. He is accused of magic, and sentenced to imprisonment, but leaves Northampton, and, journeying by night disguised as a monk, escapes to Gravelines, ib. Is re-invested by the pope as archbishop, into whose hands he had surrendered that office, 451. Henry's vindictive banishment of all who were related to Becket, and confiscation of his property and goods, ib. Becket resides at the splendid abbey of Pontigny, ib. Henry commands in person a campaign against the Welsh, who for a long time had been successful, and one Norman castle after another had fallen, ib. He gains a victory on the banks of the Cieroc, but retreats with his army in great disorder, having suffered much from the war of elements, and in his rage commits great cruelties upon the hostages, ib. Accompanied by William, king of Scots, Henry passes over to the continent and reduces the country of Brittany, which had risen in insurrection, 1166; keeps his court at Mount St. Michael, Conan, duke of Brittany, having resigned his government to him: Henry reduces the turbulent barons, and affording law and prosperity to the country, governs in the name of Geoffrey and Constantia, 451, 452, 543. He orders a tax to be levied for the support of the war in the Holy Land, 452. Becket excommunicates all the supporters of the Constitutions of Clarendon, and several of Henry's favourites, ib. A peace is concluded with the French king, who had assisted the people of Brittany and Maine against Henry, ib. Henry's sons do homage for their several fiefs; marriage is agreed on between prince Richard and Alice, a daughter of Louis, ib. Becket lands at Sandwich, proceeds to Canterbury, and excommunicates Ranulf and Robert de Broc, and the rector of Harrow, 454. Prince Henry, eldest son of Henry II., is crowned, June 14, 1170, and receives homage from William, king of Scots, and his son David, 453, 543. A congress held July 22, 1170, on the borders of Touraine, when Henry and Becket are reconciled, ib. Becket sends into England letters of excommunication from the pope, against the archbishop of York and the bishops of London and Salisbury, 454. The excommunicated bishops appeal to the king, 454, 455. Becket is murdered in St. Augustine's, Canterbury; a full and very interesting history of this event, 455, 456. Reginald Fitzurse, William Tracy, Hugh de Norville, and Richard Brito, were the knights who left Normandy and perfected this conspiracy without either the knowledge or consent of the king; Fitzurse was the first to strike Becket, ib. Illustrations: Murder of Becket,

HENRY II.,—
from an ancient painting, 456. Henry's penance at his tomb, 456, 457. Henry's grief for the murder of Becket; he voluntarily, May, 1172, in a great council held at Avranches, at which two legates of the pope attended, swore, on the Holy Gospels and sacred relics, that he had neither ordered nor desired the murder of the archbishop, 458. He is absolved by the pope's legates, *ib.* Strongbow's proceedings in Ireland, from 1167 to 1170. *See* Ireland. Strongbow, earl of Pembroke, surrenders Dublin and other forts to the king, and holds the remainder in subjection to the English crown, 466. Henry lands with a large army at Crook, near Waterford, *ib.* He receives the submission of many princes and chieftains; all Ireland, except Ulster, is subjugated, 467. Hugh de Lacy is appointed governor of Dublin, *ib.* Henry sails from Wexford, and lands at Portfinnan, in Wales, *ib.* Prince Henry is again crowned, and his consort Margaret, daughter of Louis VII., is crowned with him, *ib.* He demands that either the government of England or that of Normandy should be delivered up to him, 468; on the refusal of which, he flies to France, 1172, to obtain assistance from the French king, *ib.* Richard and Geoffrey, the king's other two sons, go to the court of France, 1173, *ib.* Eleanor, Henry's queen, in like manner deserts him, but is retaken and imprisoned, *ib.* Prince Henry is acknowledged by Louis as sole king of England, *ib.* The three young princes swear that they will not make peace with their father without the consent of the barons of France, *ib.* Henry declares that England belongs to the jurisdiction of the pope, and submits the dispute to him, 469. War commences in Normandy; the rebels and invaders are repulsed, and a conference takes place between the kings of England and France, *ib.* The earl of Leicester insults Henry, *ib.* Richard de Lacy repulses the Scots and burns Berwick, 470. Prince Henry creates William of Scotland earl of Northumberland, *ib.* The powerful earl of Leicester having come over to England, is joined by Bigod, earl of Norfolk, *ib.* Leicester is taken prisoner by Richard de Lacy, *ib.* Louis again invades Normandy, and prince Richard commands the insurgents in Poictou and Aquitaine, *ib.* Henry returns to England, having taken prisoners his own wife and the wife of prince Henry, *ib.* He does penance at the grave of Becket, *ib.*; is scourged in the church, 471. The king of Scotland and sixty of his lords taken prisoners by Ranulph de Glanville; William, the Scottish king, is sent to Falaise, 471, 472. King Henry having subdued the revolt in England, leads his army into Normandy, where he raises the siege of Rouen, 471, 544. He is reconciled with his children, and peace restored, *ib.* A treaty is agreed upon at Falaise, and William of Scotland is released on doing homage to Henry: from this till 1189, Scotland figured only as a dependent province of England, 472, 544. Henry is again at variance with his eldest son; they are reconciled, 472. Dispute between the princes Henry and Richard, 473. They go to war with their father, 474. Henry submits to his father, but soon after falls sick at Château Martel and dies, June 11, 1183; 474, 475. The king takes Limoges by assault, and several other castles; he captures Bertrand de Born, but pardons him, 475. Prince Geoffrey is reconciled to his father, and queen Eleanor is released from her captivity, *ib.* Philip II., a young and active prince, succeeds Louis VII.; 476. Geoffrey goes to the French court and prepares for war, but is killed at a tournament, *ib.* Richard seizes his father's treasure at Chinon, heads another revolt in Aquitaine, submits to his father, *ib.* Henry and Philip engage to go on an expedition to the Holy Land, *ib.* Henry calls

HENRY II.,—
a great council at Gidington, to obtain the consent and co-operation of his vassals, *ib.* His extortion and violent measures against the Jews, *ib.* Suspicions as to the person of Adelais, the affianced bride of prince Richard, with whom it was reported that his father Henry was enamoured, 477. Henry refuses to give up Adelais to Richard and acknowledge him his successor, as requested by Philip, *ib.* Richard commits himself and his cause to king Philip, and does homage for his father's continental dominions, *ib.* Henry quits the assembly to prepare for war, *ib.* He remains supine, contenting himself with the exertions which were making in his favour by the pope's legate; the French king and prince Richard threatened with excommunication; another conference held at La Ferté-Bernard; Philip proposes the same conditions as in the former conference, which are again rejected by Henry, who proposes that Adelais should be united to John, whom he supposed to be dutiful to him, and declares his readiness to name him heir to his continental dominions; Philip refuses to consent to this proposal, and war is renewed; the pope's legate threatens to put the kingdom of France under interdict, which, however, Philip despises, and accuses the legate of partial and venal motives, 478. Prince Richard commands the people of Aquitaine, Poictou, and Brittany, and Philip attacks Henry in Anjou, *ib.* Henry solicits peace, and offers to resign himself to whatever terms Philip and Richard should propose; Philip and Henry meet on a plain between Tours and Azay-sur-Cher, a peal of thunder is heard in the cloudless sky, and the lightning falls between the two kings without hurting them; they again meet, and are in like manner separated; Henry being too ill to renew the conference, the conditions of peace are sent to his quarters for his signature; it is stipulated that he should pay twenty thousand marks to Philip, and Richard should be acknowledged heir to both England and Normandy, *ib.* Amazement of the king on hearing of the treachery of his son John; his death, 6th July, 1189, and burial at the Abbey of Fontevraud, 479. Character of Henry II., 479, 480. *Illustration* of this king banishing Becket's family, 667. Usual price of wheat in this reign, from Stow, 668.

HENRY III. (Oct. 28, 1216—Nov. 16, 1272.) Great seal of, i. 671. His portrait, 672. He is crowned at St. Peter's Church, Gloucester; does homage to the pope for England and Ireland, 671. Great council at Bristol; the earl of Pembroke chosen Protector, by the title of *Rector Regis et Regni*; Magna Charta revised, *ib.* Louis raises the siege of Dover Castle, 672. The Tower of London is given up to him, *ib.* He takes Hertford and Berkhampstead Castles, *ib.* Truce agreed on; Louis goes over to France to procure supplies, and leaves the government in the hands of Enguerrand de Coucy, *ib.* Preparations of Pembroke, *ib.* Louis narrowly escapes being made prisoner by Philip d'Albiney, 673. The earl of Pembroke lays siege to the castle of Mount Sorel, but is forced to retire, *ib.* The castle of Lincoln besieged by the count of Perche; the battle called the Fair of Lincoln fought, *ib.* Louis offers terms of accommodation, *ib.* A French fleet sails from Calais, but is totally destroyed by Hubert de Burgh, *ib.* Louis agrees to abandon his claim on England, 674. Terms of this agreement, *ib.* He sails for France, *ib.* A new charter is granted to the city of London; treaty of commerce concluded with Haco, king of Norway, *ib.* Eleanor, the queen-mother, re-marries to the count of La Marche, *ib.* Magna Charta re-confirmed by the young king, 674. The Charta de Foresta, 675 . Death of the earl of Pembroke, *ib.* Hubert de Burgh and Peter des

HENRY III.,—

Roches, bishop of Winchester, are appointed regents, *ib.* Pandulph resumes the legateship, on the departure of Gualo, *ib.* Henry is re-crowned by Langton, whom the pope had permitted to return to the kingdom, *ib.* His sister, Joanna, marries to Alexander, king of Scotland, *ib.* Henry is declared of age, *ib.* He summons a parliament to meet at Westminster; money is granted, on condition that he should ratify the two Charters, *ib.* Richard, earl of Cornwall, goes with an English army to Guienne, *ib.* Louis takes the cross against the Albigenses; a papal legate threatens the English with excommunication, if they raise obstacles to this holy war; a truce is agreed to, *ib.* Death of the French king; Louis IX., then in his twelfth year, succeeds to the throne, *ib.* War declared with France, 675. Henry lands at St. Malo, in Brittany, *ib.* Louis takes several towns from Henry; the latter returns to England covered with disgrace; Parliament refuses further supplies, *ib.* Hubert de Burgh is disgraced, and sent to the Tower; his lands are forfeited; he escapes into Wales; some time after, however, he receives back his estates and honours, and is readmitted into the king's council, 676, 677. Richard, earl of Pembroke, son of the Protector, is murdered, 677. Henry is forced to banish Des Roches, who had procured the disgrace of Hubert, *ib.* Henry marries Eleanor, daughter of the count of Provence, 678. The bishop of Valence is made chief minister, *ib.* The parliament refuses to grant supplies, *ib.* Henry sails from Portsmouth, and lands at the Garonne; he is defeated by Louis near Taillebourg, and again at Saintes; he flies to Blaye; truce for five years agreed on, *ib.* The parliament votes twenty shillings on every knight's fee, for the marriage of the king's daughter; the Jews are persecuted and plundered, 678, 679. Parliament refuses to grant supplies; Henry, to annoy them, establishes a fair at Westminster, to last fifteen days, during which all trading was prohibited in London; he likewise compels them to pay him 2,000*l.*; 679. Henry is forced to meet his parliament; the barons hold out the hope of a liberal grant, on condition of his consenting to a fresh and solemn confirmation of their liberties, *ib.* Description of the ceremony, 679, 680. Henry makes an expedition to Guienne, 680. Prince Edward marries Eleanor, daughter of Alphonso, king of Castile, *ib.* He enters into a project for raising one of his sons to the throne of the Two Sicilies, *ib.* He levies enormous contributions on the churches of England and Ireland, *ib.* Richard, earl of Cornwall, is elected king of the Romans, 681. Scarcity in England; parliament assembles at Westminster; the barons appear armed, *ib.* Simon de Montfort, earl of Leicester, marries Eleanor, countess-dowager of Pembroke, *ib.* He is banished the court, *ib.* The parliament, called the "Mad Parliament," meets at Oxford; a committee of government is appointed; it is enacted that four knights should be chosen by the votes of the freeholders in each county, to lay before the parliament all breaches of law and justice that might occur; that a new sheriff should be annually chosen by the freeholders in each county; and that three sessions of parliament should be held regularly every year, 682. Richard, king of the Romans, returns to England, 683. The earl of Gloucester becomes a rival to the earl of Leicester; the latter withdraws into France, but soon after returns to England, *ib.* Henry dismisses the committee of government; seizes the Tower and the Mint; the barons march upon the capital; prince Edward joins them; the king publishes a dispensation from the pope, absolving him from his oaths taken at Oxford, *ib.* Death of the earl of Gloucester; his son, the new earl, raises his retainers for Leicester,

HENRY III.,—

who march upon London; prince Edward, who had returned to the court, flies to Windsor Castle, and the queen takes refuge in St. Paul's, *ib.* The king and barons refer their differences to the king of France; the barons refuse to stand by the award; the civil war rages; the Jews are massacred and plundered throughout the kingdom by both parties, 684. The earl of Leicester takes the king, prince Edward, his eldest son, the king's brother Richard, John Comyn, and Robert Bruce prisoners, at the battle of Lewes, May 14, 1264; 685. Leicester concludes an agreement with the king at Lewes, and governs in his name, *ib.* His wise and mild administration, he summons the whole force of the kingdom to meet him in arms on Barham Downs, and takes the command of a fleet to prevent the landing of foreign troops, *ib.* The earl of Gloucester concerts a plan for releasing prince Edward, 686. He is joined by the prince at Ludlow, where the royal banner is raised, Edward having sworn to respect the charters and govern according to law, 686. Prince Edward takes the command of the royal forces, display of his military sagacity, *ib.* He surprises Simon de Montfort, the earl of Leicester's son, near Kenilworth, *ib.* Leicester advances to Evesham, with the hope of meeting his son's forces, *ib.* He is surrounded by the royal forces, commanded by prince Edward, and having failed in an attempt to force the road to Kenilworth, the royalists refusing to give quarter, he is slain together with his son Henry, and 180 barons and knights, 687. The king goes to Warwick, and is joined by his brother Richard and the other prisoners, taken by Leicester at Lewes, *ib.* A parliament assembles at Winchester, *ib.* The city of London deprived of its charter, *ib.* The war in many parts of the kingdom still continued, *ib.* The committee called the Dictum de Kenilworth, is appointed, *ib.* The earl of Gloucester, who had effected the restoration, quarrels with the king; he takes up arms and is joined by the discontented Londoners, alleging that the Dictum de Kenilworth,—a committee of twelve bishops and barons appointed to decide the cases of those who had opposed the king—was too harsh, *ib.* The earl of Gloucester submits, and receives full pardon, *ib.* November 18, 1267, the king, in parliament at Marlborough, adopts some of the most valuable of the provisions of the earl of Leicester, and enacts other good laws, 688. The country is reduced to a perfect state of tranquillity by these mild measures, *ib.* Prince Edward obtains the grant of a new charter, with the restoration of their liberties to the citizens of London, and a free pardon to a few nobles, who still lay under the king's ban, and in the month of July, 1270, sets out on a crusade, *ib.* The king dies on the 16th of November, 1272, and is buried in the abbey church of St. Peter's, which he had rebuilt from the foundation, *ib.* Coins of this reign, 837.

HENRY IV. (Sept. 30, 1399—March 20, 1413.) Henry of Bolingbroke made earl of Derby, 1385; i. 791. Receives the title of duke of Hereford 1397, having assisted in the impeachment of the earls of Warwick and the duke of Gloucester, 795. The duke of Norfolk challenges Hereford, Jan. 1398; Hereford is banished for ten years, and Norfolk for life, 796. Hereford returns to England and lands at Ravenspur, July, 1399; the Londoners receive him with great delight, and many of them join his army; he marches to the Severn, and is joined by the duke of York, who was then regent, the king having departed to take the field against the Irish, 797. He takes Bristol Castle; the earl of Salisbury, with part of the king's forces, lands at Conway; he is joined by some Welsh, but is soon deserted by all his men; Richard lands at Milford Haven with his

HENRY IV.,—
remaining forces, but is also deserted, and takes refuge in Conway Castle, which he is soon compelled to leave for want of provisions, *ib.* He is captured and taken to Flint, where he has an interview with Bolingbroke, and from thence is sent a prisoner to Chester, *ib.* While on his way to London he makes his escape at Lichfield, but is retaken, conveyed to London, and imprisoned in the Tower, 798. *Illustrations:* Meeting of Richard and Bolingbroke at Flint Castle, *ib.* Bolingbroke conducting Richard into London, 799. Parliament assembled for the deposition of Richard, *ib.* On the 30th of Sept., a parliament, summoned in the king's name, met at Westminster, where the resignation of Richard was read and accepted, and an Act of Deposition passed; as soon as this was finished, Bolingbroke was seated in the throne by the archbishops of Canterbury and York, 799, 800. Henry IV. (surnamed Bolingbroke) settled on the throne, 30th September, 1399; ii. 4. Portraits of Henry IV. and his second wife, Joan of Navarre, from the tomb at Canterbury, *ib.* His coronation, 155. He appoints to all vacant offices, new justices, etc., 4. Requiring the immediate aid of a parliament, he contrived to retain the old members, declaring that such measure should not be made a precedent, 4, 165. His Great Seal, 5. Royal banquet, *ib.* Thyrning, the justiciary, and other procurators, announce to Richard II. in the Tower, the people's acceptance of his abdication, and renounce fealty to him, *ib.* The calm reply of that prince, *ib.* Henry crowned, Oct. 13, in Westminster Abbey, *ib.* The House of Commons lends ready assistance to the usurping king, *ib.* Obnoxious acts repealed, *ib.* Attainder of Arundel and Warwick reversed, *ib.* The peers who had appealed to the duke of Gloucester called to account by the Upper House, *ib.* High words ensue, forty gauntlets cast on the floor; Henry calms this fierce dispute; appeals of treason in parliament abolished; reference to be had to the courts of law, *ib.* The dukes of Albemarle, Surrey, Exeter, marquis of Dorset, and earl of Gloucester, decreed to resume their previous titles, earls of Rutland, Kent, Huntingdon, Somerset, and lord le Despencer, and to resign the estates granted them by Richard II., *ib.* Badges or liveries of followers of the great nobles abolished, 6. The House of Lords, in reply to a royal message, decide to keep Richard II. fast in some castle, who is thereupon removed from one castle to another, *ib.* Henry's early popularity, *ib.* A faction of nobles desire his death, and the restoration of the abdicated king, *ib.* His leniency to the "lords appellants" unrequited, *ib.* Treasonable meetings in the apartments of the abbot of Westminster, *ib.* The turbulent barons invite Henry to a tournament at Oxford, Jan. 3, 1400, which he was inclined to accept, but is privately informed of the conspiracy, 6, 7. The lords surprise Windsor Castle 4th January; the king had left for London, and so escaped murder, 7. He returned next day towards Windsor, with a large body of Londoners, the refractory lords fly to arm their several retainers, *ib.* They proclaim king Richard, *ib.* Salisbury and Kent beheaded at Cirencester, Le Despencer and Lumley at Bristol, the earl of Huntingdon tortured and torn piecemeal by the tenantry of the duke of Gloucester, *ib.* Inquiry into the nature of Richard II.'s death in Pontefract Castle, *ib.* News of the deposition, and anxiety for the young queen, his daughter, affects the weak French king to such a degree as to bring on a fit of insanity, *ib.* Bourbon and Burgundy, simulating a desire for her safety, levy war in Guienne, 7, 8. To avert war Henry sends an embassy to France, and courteously receives the ambassadors from the French court, 9. Claim on him for queen Isabella's dower; he declines to pay the money,

HENRY IV.,—
but sends the widowed princess in safety to Calais, to the duke of Burgundy, who escorts her to her father Charles VL's court, *ib.* Hostilities of the French princes cease during this reign, *ib.* Henry marches against the Scottish king Robert, then sick, 1401; he menaces Edinburgh with an army of his barons and knights, doing feudal service in the field, but is without money or provisions, *ib.* David, earl of Rothsay, son of Robert, throws himself into Edinburgh, and the English king is constrained by want to re-cross the border, *ib.* His conduct generous and humane towards the invaded Scots, *ib.* Rebellion of Owen Glendower, who had been despoiled of some lands by lord Grey de Ruthyn, *ib.* The king outlawed Glendower, who then seised on Wales as a sovereign prince, and the people swore fealty to Owen; all the Welsh in England retired to their homes, 10. In 1401, 1402, king Henry thrice invaded the principality, but Glendower's military talent compelled him to withdraw, *ib.* Heralds arrive from Waleran, count of Liguy and St. Pol, with a declaration of hostilities (bearing date 10th Feb. 1402), by sea and land against Henry IV. for the murder of Richard II., *ib.* Many English still believed that Richard escaped into Scotland, and was levying an army, *ib.* Sir R. Clarendon and others executed for asserting the same, a severity that strengthened the belief, 11. The Scots invade England; they are defeated at Nesbit Moor, their commander Hepburn slain; a Scot (the earl of March) commanding the English, *ib.* Earl Douglas, at the head of a choice army, enters Northumberland, *ib.* He is totally defeated, 14th Sept. 1402, at Homildon Hill, by Hotspur and March, 11, 13. Henry IV. again invades Wales, as Glendower had gained victories recently, capturing the lord Grey and sir Edmund Mortimer, 1402; 11. Discomfited by tempests in the Welsh mountains, unable anywhere to meet Glendower's army, king Henry retreated, entertaining a full belief that this Welsh prince was a necromancer, 12. The English king challenged by the duke of Orleans, respecting the young widow queen Isabella; king Henry's replies, *ib.* Insurrection of the earl of Northumberland, its causes, 1402; 13. Bitter defiance addressed to Henry by the Percies, 14. The king in person, assisted by the prince of Wales, his son, gains the victory at Shrewsbury, July 21, where Hotspur fell in the field, Douglas was taken, etc., 1403; 15. He orders Worcester, Kinderton, and Vernon, to be beheaded on the field, *ib.* He graciously pardons Northumberland, without fines or penalties, *ib.* The French seize Jersey and Guernsey, land on the Isle of Wight, and burn Plymouth, 1403; *ib.* They capture a fleet of merchantmen, and plunder all English ships, *ib.* Thomas, duke of Clarence, the king's son, about 1405, sails to the French coast, burns the shipping and some towns, putting the people to death, *ib.* Henry's conciliatory transactions with parliament, not pressing too severely for aids, although he required money for the Welsh war, 16; also for the due defence of the coasts, *ib.* He proposed that he should resume all former grants, be prohibited from alienating crown lands without consent of parliament, and that he might appropriate certain portions of church property, *ib.* The nobles resist the resumption of grants, the archbishop of Canterbury successfully protected the church revenues, and Henry yielded, *ib.* An Act passed to suppress various pensions by Edward III. and Richard II., *ib.* The writs had forbidden any lawyers to be returned to this parliament, which met at Coventry, Oct. 6, 1404; *ib.* Lady Spencer contrives to liberate the earl of March and his brother, 1405, intending that Edmund Mortimer should be proclaimed in Wales, *ib.*

T

HENRY IV.,—

The young princes are retaken, ib. She accuses her brother, the duke of York, of being a party in designs against Henry's life, ib. York is kept near four years in prison, and then liberated, but his estates were sequestrated, ib. Ill-humour of the nobles and clergy, 17. New insurrections of Northumberland, Nottingham, and others, ib. The archbishop of York and earl of Nottingham beheaded at Pontefract, ib. Henry punished the citizens of York by fines, and suspension of their charters, ib. At Durham he beheaded the lords Hastings and Falconbridge, ib. He lays siege to Berwick, batters the citadel, and on its surrender he puts the governor to death, ib. He declines pursuing Northumberland to Edinburgh; he takes Alnwick, Cockermouth, and most of the earl's castles, ib. He reaches Wales by forced marches, to the succour of prince Henry, who had waged some severe campaigns, and in his victory at Grosmont had captured Griffith, son of Glendower, ib. The French princes had entertained Glendower hospitably, and resolved to send him over a considerable army, ib. Their first armament was frustrated by various causes, but in 1406, 12,000 French, under Montmorency, land at Milford Haven, and march upon Haverford-west, 18. The English fleet, sailing into Milford Haven, burn fifteen French ships, and putting to sea, intercept fourteen with ammunition and stores, and finally cut off all supplies, ib. Constitutional liberty progresses in this reign, 19. The demand for subsidies produces dissensions between king and parliament, 1407; ib. Northumberland, once more earnest to dethrone Henry, solicits the duke of Albany, who is more in the king's interest than the duke's, ib. The rebellious earl visits Glendower in Wales, but being joined by Scottish nobles inimical to Albany, the old Percy and Bardolf, 1408, enter Northumberland and surprise some castles, ib. Northumberland is slain in battle, ib. The French, with some Spanish ships, carry on a fierce war by sea, 1409; they also attack Gascony and Guienne, which provinces king Henry was too poor to succour, ib. Orleans, d'Alençon, and Clermont, waste their time in festivities at Paris, which affords a respite to the English, ib. In 1412, Henry sends his son Clarence to Normandy, who traversed Maine, Anjou, and Guienne, with 8,000 soldiers, and enters Bordeaux, 21, 22. The king in his last years had become suspicious and unhappy, with the gloomy recollection of his own remorseless career, 1412; 22. His constitution broke up, and he suffered from epilepsy and other maladies, ib. Remarks on his religious sentiments, ib. The wild courses of the prince of Wales had formerly given him pain, but he was relieved by that prince's valour and virtues, ib. Jealousy of his son's popularity, 23, 185. King Henry is seised with a fit, at his devotions in Westminster Abbey, 23. He expired 20th March, 1413, in the Jerusalem Chamber, ib. He was buried at Canterbury, by the side of his first wife, Mary de Bohun, the mother of all his children, ib. Delineation of his monument in the cathedral, ib. His character, 22, 23. Autograph of king Henry, 130. *Illustrations:* Henry IV. and his court, 238. Costume of his reign, 238, 239. His first parliament, 1399; 140. His dependence on parliament for aids, etc., 165. Amount of tonnage and poundage, custom dues, subsidies of a tenth or fifteenth, described, 166.

HENRY V. (March 21, 1413—August 31, 1422,) surnamed of Monmouth, is created prince of Wales, etc., 1399, and declared heir-apparent, ii. 6. Proposal that he should espouse the young widow of Richard II., declined by her father Charles VI., 9. He fought gallantly, 1403, at Shrewsbury, though severely wounded, until the victory was complete, 15. He gains some advantage in Wales, over

HENRY V.,—

Glendower, ib. And in 1405, several considerable victories, 17. The king and prince drive the Welsh and French allies from Worcester, 1406; 18. The prince reduces South Wales, and carries the war into the north of the principality, ib. His early wildness of character, alluded to, 22. His accession, 1413, undisputed and hailed with joy, 24. His Portrait and Great Seal, ib. He commands the removal of the body of Richard II. to Westminster Abbey, 25. Generously releases Edmund, earl of March, and restores to him his father's lands, ib. Invests the son of Hotspur with the possessions of the Percies, 25, 132. The Lollards cause disturbances, 25. King Henry endeavours to turn sir John Oldcastle (lord Cobham), his old friend, from joining the religious party of Wycliffe, ib. Failing therein, he makes him prisoner, and delivers him over to archbishop Arundel or Fitz-Alan, and Cobham is condemned to the flames, on the Statute *De Heretico Comburendo*, 25, 146. Cobham escapes from the Tower, ib. Insurrection of the Reformers repressed by the king in person, 25, 26. Executions, 26, 146. New Act of Parliament, 1414, against the Lollards; their lands and chattels sequestrated, 26. Henry V. suddenly, in 1414, asserts his right to the French crown, ib. Condition of the court of Charles VI., the Dauphin, the dukes of Burgundy and Orleans, and count of Armagnac, ib. Burgundy armed the butchers in Paris, called cabochiens, 1414, to support his authority, ib. Those butchers assumed power, wore a "white hood" as a revolutionary emblem, oppressed, imprisoned and murdered the richest citizens, ib. The Armagnac faction favour the claim of the English king, many Parisians adopt it also, ib. The butchers or "cabochiens" are expelled Paris by the carpenters, 27. The count d'Armagnac, father-in-law of the duke of Orleans, governs in Paris in a tyrannical and cruel manner, Charles VI. being imbecile, and the dauphin without power, ib. Orleans invested with supreme authority, ib. The dauphin demands aid from "Jean sans Peur," duke of Burgundy, his father-in-law, ib. That duke marched in 1414 to Paris, but was repulsed, ib. He is accused of the murder of his cousin the late duke of Orleans, and his possessions ordered to be seized, ib. The Armagnacs, taking Charles VI. along with them, invade Burgundy's territory, ib. Soissons is defended by De Bournonville, certain English fight in both armies, the city is betrayed, and frightful excesses committed, ib. Armagnac is repulsed before Arras, and returns to Paris, ib. A treaty ensues between the rival factions; the king being plainly insane, the dauphin secures possession of Paris, ib. Burgundy retires to his own territories, and Armagnac and the count of St. Pol wage private wars against their enemies, 27, 28. The people disgusted with twenty years of anarchy, look with hopes rather than fears towards the young English monarch, 28. Henry V. negotiates, sends his ultimatum, and arms, but also demands the hand of Catherine of France, ib. He announces to his council, 1415, his resolve to invade France for the conquest of "his inheritance," ib. Appoints Bedford, his brother, regent, ib. His conference, at Winchester, with the archbishop of Bourges, who was sent over by the duke of Berri, ib. He assembles his forces and a fleet at Southampton, ib. Plot of the earl of Cambridge, Scroop, and Grey, to establish the earl of March on the throne, 29. They are beheaded for this treason against king Henry, ib. The English anchor in the Seine, August 13, 1415; ib. Henry reduces Harfleur, but his army suffers severely by dysentery, ib. He directs his march with a small army upon Calais, ib. His challenge to the dauphin, refused by that prince, ib.

HENRY V.,—

He repulses the garrison of Eu in Normandy, *ib.* Narrative of his victory at Agincourt, his preparations on the eve of the battle, 30. He commands his soldiers to carry stakes, to be fixed by them on taking their ground during action, 31. Inferiority of the English in numbers, *ib.* The French occupy a bad position, and are oppressed by their vast number, *ib.* Advice of the duke de Berri, *ib.* The battle fought by the English on foot, *ib.* Reply of Henry to Walter Hungerford, *ib.* The constable of France unable to repress the rashness of the French princes, 32. An armistice proposed, Henry insists on his previous terms, *ib.* He commands the assault upon the French, who hesitated to attack, *ib.* Repulse of a charge of French horse under Messire Clignet, *ib.* The English charge furiously in their turn, slaying the constable, and duke Anthony of Brabant, *ib.* Henry V. saves the life of his brother Clarence; he is himself assailed by certain knights of the lord of Croy, and struck severely, but is rescued by his soldiers, *ib.* Alençon slays the duke of York, and strikes Henry V. on his helmet and crown, *ib.* The duke of Alençon's fall, *ib.* The king alarmed by a supposed reinforcement, marching under the duke of Brittany, orders his prisoners to be put to the sword, *ib.* He stops this carnage, *ib.* His speeches on the field, 33, 34. List of the French slain, and taken prisoners, 33. Interment of the French described, 34. Circumstances of Henry's return to Calais, *ib.* Enthusiasm of his people on his landing at Dover, and arriving in London, *ib.* The city pageant, described, 255. Henry's prudent councils and popularity, 34. Subsidy on wool granted him, *ib.* In 1416, Sigismund, the emperor elect, visits Henry V. in London, on a schism in the Roman church, *ib.* A French embassy, etc., fails, and for what reasons, 35. The French lay close siege to Harfleur, which is relieved by the duke of Bedford, who, sailing from Rye, gained a brilliant victory in the mouth of the river Seine, 1416; *ib.* September 1416, king Henry (with his guests Sigismund, and William of Bavaria, count of Holland,) repairs to Calais, and holds a congress attended in person by the duke of Burgundy, 35, 36. After some secret treaty with Burgundy, the king returns home, 36. The Lollards said to have invited the Scots into England, 1417; 38. Oldcastle, (lord Cobham) made prisoner on the borders of Wales, and condemned by the House of Lords to be hanged and burned, *ib.* The execution in London, *ib.* Henry having landed with a powerful army in August, 1417, took Caen, and other fortresses of Normandy, whilst the regent Bedford expels the Scots under Douglas and Albany, from before Berwick and Roxburgh, *ib.* The French court solicits peace, Henry V. demands the hand of Catherine, to be proclaimed regent, and declared the successor of Charles VI. on that king's death, *ib.* He reduces Cherbourg, Louviers, and Pont de l'Arche, 1418; 39. The Normans being averse to the English yoke, offer a brave resistance, but in vain, *ib.* The king crosses the Seine, and draws lines of circumvallation around Rouen, being master of the river also by his fleet, and his garrison of Harfleur, 40. Queen Isabella escapes from her confinement at Tours, and joins the duke of Burgundy, who takes Tours and Chartres, but in vain attempts Paris, *ib.* The duke of Lorraine made constable of France, the prince of Orange governor of Languedoc, 41. Excessive cruelties recorded, *ib.* The Parisians quit the party of Armagnac, and murder him and all of his faction in Paris, May, 1418; 41, 42. Tanneguy-Duchatel conveyed the dauphin Charles to the Bastille, and thence to Bourges,

HENRY V.,—

42. The duke of Burgundy and Isabella enter Paris in triumph, *ib.* The dauphin, with the title of regent, constitutes a parliament at Poictiers, and a civil war ensues, *ib.* Ambassadors from the dauphin, and from the duke of Burgundy, 43 ; also cardinal Ursini negotiates with Henry ; he declares his resolve to wear the French crown, *ib.* January 16, 1419, Henry entered Rouen in triumph, being master of all Normandy, *ib.* He marches on Paris, and near Meulan conferences ensue with great pomp between Burgundy and Isabella, and the English conqueror, 44. His admiration of the princess Catherine, his speech to Burgundy, he makes the treaty of Bretigny the basis of his claims, insisting on Normandy and other territories as independent possessions, before he should resign his claim to the crown, *ib.* The queen, Burgundy, etc., evade from the scene of these long conferences, and form an alliance with the dauphin Charles; meeting of Burgundy and that prince, June, 1419; 44, 45. Simulated reconciliation, yet Burgundy is murdered on the bridge of Montereau, in the presence of the dauphin, by his sanction and his chief officers, 45. His intrepid behaviour, though previously warned of danger, 45, 46. The dauphin's attempted exculpation, rejected with horror by the people and the Parisians, 46. Philip the Good, duke of Burgundy, arms to avenge his father's death, *ib.* He and queen Isabella then sought a close alliance with Henry V., who had already taken Pontoise near Paris, July, 1419; 47. Duke Philip and also Charles VI. sign the treaty on Henry's terms, *ib.* Eulogium, in the French parliament of Paris, on the virtues of the conqueror, *ib.* In May, 1420, Henry meets an honourable reception at Troyes, from the king, queen, and Burgundy, *ib.* The princess is immediately affianced to him, *ib* ; and the nuptials took place, 2nd of June, *ib.* The oaths taken to him as regent; gladly tendered by nobles and people, *ib.* He besieges and takes the city of Sens, 48. The regent Henry V. and Philip of Burgundy reduce Montereau; de Guitry obstinately held out in the castle; Henry V. hanged some prisoners in sight of the fortress, *ib.* The dauphin fled to the count of Armagnac in Languedoc, *ib.* Melun held out for four months, and capitulated in November, *ib.* December, 1420, the two kings and the queens of France and England, enter Paris, which was seriously suffering from famine, *ib.* The three estates ratify the treaty, and the murderers of John duke of Burgundy are attainted, *ib.* In 1421, king Henry arrived in London, and the coronation of Catherine took place at Westminster, *ib.* Royal banquet, *ib.* The king conducts Catherine through a part of England, *ib.* The duke of Clarence, governor of Normandy, and brother of Henry V., marches into Anjou, is defeated and slain, with great loss, by the dauphin's forces under La Fayette, and a Scottish auxiliary force under Buchan, 49. Consequences of this reverse, *ib.* Henry conducts his queen to Windsor Castle, whence he released James Stewart, king of Scotland, long a prisoner, *ib.* The Scottish king, and some of his nobles engage to follow king Henry, 1421, in his new campaign, *ib.* The English reinforcements landed, June 1421, at Calais, *ib.* King James of Scots besieges Dreux, and Henry, forcing the dauphin to raise the siege of Chartres, pursues that prince to Bourges, in Berry, *ib.* Disease and famine thin the English army, *ib.* Henry laid siege to the fortress of Meaux, defended by the ferocious chief called the Bastard of Vaurus, 49, 50. After a protracted siege, and the loss of lord Clifford, and the earl of Worcester who fell there, Henry carried

HENRY V.,—
the city, and hanged Vaurus on the elm-tree, on
which that captain of the late count of Armagnac
had executed so many victims, 50. May, 1422,
Henry meets his queen at Paris, and they hold a
splendid court in the Louvre, soon after the birth
of their son, Henry of Windsor, Dec. 1421, ib.
Although he was severely sick, king Henry marched
out of Paris to succour Philip of Burgundy, then
menaced by the advance of the dauphin and the earl
of Buchan, ib. His malady increasing, he resigned
the command to Bedford, and was carried in a
litter to the Bois de Vincennes, ib. His resignation,
his royal virtues, his love of Catherine, the daily
expectation of his being king of France, in title
as well as power, Charles VI. being also on his
death-bed, ib. He summons Bedford to him, gives
him counsels and instructions, commands him never
to make peace with the dauphin, so long as that
prince claims the crown, 50, 51. His desire that
his brother Bedford should be the regent of France,
and his brother Gloucester regent of England, 51.
August 31, 1422, this heroic monarch expired, ib.
Narrative of the transport of the body to Westminster, ib. His funeral; buried near Edward the
Confessor's shrine in Westminster Abbey, ib.
Character of this prince, 51, 52. His widow
Catherine wived Owen Tudor, and was grandmother of Henry VII., 125. Henry's autograph,
130. Curious record of the royal revenue, and
of its expenditure in this reign, 166. Gold and
silver coins for England and France, 185, 186.
Holinshed's account of Henry IV.'s suspicions
of his son as connected with the coinage of Henry
V., ib. Rich architectural style of this king's
chantry in Westminster Abbey, 231, 232. Music
in Henry V.'s reign, 233. Harps and drums,
ib. Song of the victory at Agincourt, 1415, and
other examples, 233—235, Illustrations; Tomb of
Henry V., 52. His chantry, 231. Henry V., and
his court, 239. Male attire of his reign, ib.
Female costume, 240. Henry's saddle, shield, and
helmet, 241. Tilting-helmet of this reign, 242.
HENRY VI., (Sept. 1, 1422—March 4, 1461,) born at
Windsor, 6th Dec., 1421; ii. 50. His accession,
1422, 52. Beaufort, bishop of Winchester, and the
earl of Warwick, appointed his custodians and
preceptors, ib. His Portrait, and Great Seal, 53.
Gloucester protector of the realm and church;
Bedford president of the council, and regent of
France, 52, 54. Proclaimed king of France, young
Henry is crowned at Paris, November, 1431; 54,
77. The arduous contest for defending the possession of France was conducted by Bedford, with
varying results of brilliant victories and sad defeats, 54—58, 70—80. The nuptials of Gloucester and Jacqueline of Hainault caused evil
consequences to the English cause in France, 57—
60. Rivalry of cardinal Beaufort and the king's
uncle Gloucester, 57, 58, 70. Salisbury laid siege
to Orleans, 60. This earl, mortally wounded, was
succeeded by Suffolk, 61, 65. The siege raised,
and Suffolk, occupying the neighbouring castles,
shut himself up in the fortress of Jargeau, 67.
He is there made prisoner, after a vigorous
assault by the Maid of Orleans, 68. Talbot withdrew the troops, but was totally defeated at Patay,
and taken prisoner, with some English lords and
knights, ib. Charles VII. crowned, July 17, 1429,
at Rheims, conducted thither by the enthusiastic
and valiant Maid of Orleans, 69. Bedford still
holds possession of Paris, 71. Joan of Arc burnt,
May 30, 1431, at Rouen, 76. Congress of Arras
attended by cardinal Beaufort, 78. It concluded
in a peace sworn betwixt Philip of Burgundy and
Charles VII., by the intervention of pope Eugenius, ib. Death of Bedford, the king's uncle, at

HENRY VI.,—
Rouen, Sept. 14, 1435; 79. Paris surrenders
to the French and Burgundians, April, 1436, ib.
The war carried into Normandy; the French
surprise Dieppe, ib. Richard, duke of York,
sent over with troops to replace Bedford, ib.
The duke of Gloucester sends word to Burgundy,
that he intends crossing to the relief of Calais, and
would offer him battle with his army before the
walls, ib. The alternative, that he would pursue
him to Flanders; disgraceful flight of Philip, with
his 30,000 men, leaving baggage and artillery at
Calais, 79, 80. The English prince, alleging the
treasons of duke Philip, styles himself earl of
Flanders, and pursues the duke into the heart of his
territories, ib. Ill effect of this enterprise, in
depriving the generals in Normandy, etc., of suc-
cours then most needful; but Gloucester's personal
power, being at length president of the council,
enabled him to pursue his private views, ib.
Gentle, devout, but weak character of Henry, 80.
Truce for two years with France, 1444; ib. The
earl of Suffolk negotiates a marriage between
Henry and Margaret of Anjou, 81. Suffolk and
Beaufort consent to resign Anjou and Maine to
her father René of Anjou, ib. Gloucester and the
nation protest against these proceedings, 81, 82.
Death, or murder, of Henry's uncle, the good duke
of Gloucester, 83. Normandy invaded, 1449; Rouen
taken by the French; Talbot delivered as an hostage, 85. In 1450, all Normandy submits to Charles
VII., ib. Bordeaux and Bayonne surrendered to
the French, ib. As Charles VI. ruined France, by
his imbecility and madness, so all our continental
possessions were lost by the weakness of the almost
imbecile Henry VI., 86. Fall of the duke of Suffolk,
1450; ib. The late minister and favourite beheaded
at sea, 87. Insurrection of John Cade and the men
of Kent; ib. Stated to have been designed for
the advancement of York to the throne, 87, 89.
Henry's incapacity inclined many of the people to
favour duke Richard, 89. York resigned his Irish
command, and, landing in England, 1451, visited
king Henry, 89, 90. Jealousy of Margaret and the
court on this occasion, 90. Somerset, head of the
younger branch of Lancaster, minister on the death
of Suffolk, ib. Each party takes up arms, 1452;
ib. Duke Richard took his oath in St. Paul's,
before the king and nobility, to be a loyal
and obedient subject, ib. Some nobles of Guienne
repair to London; Talbot, in his eightieth year,
sails with 5,000 men, and retakes Bordeaux,
91. The king's total incapacity entered on record
by the peers, and the duke of York appointed protector, 1454; ib. Talbot and his son were slain,
by superior armies, at Châtillon, ib. Birth of
Edward, prince of Wales, 92. In nine months,
Henry VI. regained memory, and about as much of
the reasoning faculty as he formerly possessed, ib.
The court claims for him the exercise of royalty,
and York immediately resigned, ib. Henry liberates Somerset; this and similar measures disgust
the nation, ib. The duke of York armed anew at
Ludlow; Warwick and other noblemen joined him,
ib. York gained the victory of St. Albans, May
22, 1454; ib. Somerset, Northumberland, and
Clifford, slain; king Henry, wounded, remains a
prisoner, ib. Respectfully treated by his captor,
ib. Henry met his parliament, improved in
health; the peers restore him, and York retires
to his estates, 1456; 93. Hollow reconciliation;
procession in amity to St. Paul's, 93, 94. Defeat
and death of lord Audley, at Bloreheath, 1459;
94. A general battle expected at the Yorkist
intrenched position beyond Worcester; Trollop,
marshal of duke Richard's camp, went over in the
night, with Warwick's veterans under his command,

HENRY VI.,—

to king Henry, *ib.* Parliament met at Coventry, attainted York, his duchess and sons, lord Clinton, Salisbury, his countess, and their son Warwick, November, 1459; *ib.* Warwick, with a powerful fleet, the sailors being all on his side, continues master of the channel, *ib.* The powerful earl lands in Kent, June, 1460, and conducts Edward, earl of March, to London, 95. Henry VI. made prisoner at Northampton, *ib.* Richard, duke of York, claims the crown in parliament, *ib.* Replies of the peers, *ib.* Compromise: Henry VI. to wear the crown during life, which was to descend to York and his heirs, to the exclusion of Edward, son of Margaret of Anjou, 96. New revolution effected by queen Margaret and the aristocracy, 1460; *ib.* York perishes in the battle of Wakefield, 30th December, *ib.* Salisbury flying, was beheaded, *ib.* The king is rescued from the hands of Warwick, 1461, by his victorious queen and son, after the first battle of Barnet, being found deserted in his tent, 97. His proclamation, denouncing Edward, "late earl of March," as a traitor, and asserting that the recent arrangement as to the succession had been wrung from him by force, *ib.* In March, 1461, the council declared that Henry, not adhering to the terms arranged in 1460, had forfeited the crown, and Edward IV. seats himself on the throne, 98. Henry VI. lay listless at York, but Margaret and Somerset gathered a powerful force of 60,000 horse and foot, *ib.* They were totally defeated at Towton, losing 28,000 men in the battle, 99. His queen uselessly parading him, in all her expeditions, Henry narrowly escaped capture near Durham, 99. Henry VI.'s total unfitness to reign, a virtual cause of the mass of the people and parliament acknowledging Edward by hereditary right of descent, *ib.* Act declaring the three Henrys tyrants and usurpers, recalling all grants made by them, 100. Attainder of Henry VI., queen Margaret, prince Edward, and the chief Lancastrians, *ib.* Present at Hexham; Henry escaped from that defeat, 1464; 101. King Henry lay long concealed among the moors of Lancashire, etc., no man thought of betraying him, *ib.* He was found, however, at dinner, in Waddington Hall, and taken by the men of Sir James Harrington, 1465; *ib.* Warwick lodged him in the Tower, but his life was respected, 101, 104. Reconciliation of Warwick (who was incensed at Edward IV., 1470, deceiving him with regard to his mission to Louis XI., for the marriage of Margaret of York) with queen Margaret of Anjou, 105. Prince Edward, son of Henry VI., marries Anne Nevil, second daughter of the great earl, 105, 106. Warwick landed in Devonshire, 106. The people flock to his standard, leaving Edward defenceless, 106, 107. Montague, Warwick's brother, proclaims Henry, 106. Edward sailed for Holland, and was there well received, 107. Warwick released king Henry from the Tower, and reinstated him on his throne, *ib.* A new Act of Succession, 107, 108, 114. King Edward, 1471, landed at Ravenspur, on the Humber, with a small army, 108. On crossing the Trent, the people flocked to Edward's standard. *ib.* At Coventry, the duke of Clarence deserted Warwick, and, mounting the white rose, went over, with all his division, to king Edward, *ib.* The Londoners receive Edward with enthusiasm, *ib.* He marches against the Lancastrian army, to Barnet Common; narrative of this decisive action, *ib.* Warwick, his brother Montague, and all the noble Lancastrians, fell on this fatal field, 109. Queen Margaret and her son landed at Plymouth, on the day of this battle of Barnet, *ib.* Henry VI. was again consigned to the Tower, *ib.* Margaret and the duke of Somerset were attacked at Tewkesbury, by the army of Edward, Clarence, and his brother Richard of

HENRY VI.,—

Gloucester, *ib.* Margaret of Anjou prisoner, 109, 110. The prince of Wales, aged eighteen, was murdered after the battle, in king Edward's presence, *ib.* Queen Margaret, after five years' captivity, was ransomed by Louis XI., and died in France, eleven years after her defeat at Tewkesbury, 110. The Bastard of Falconbridge made a desperate attempt to release king Henry, *ib.* Edward, 21st May, entered London, with a victorious army, and next morning king Henry VI. was found lifeless in the Tower, *ib.* Believed on all hands that he was therein murdered, *ib.* Miracles said to be wrought at his tomb in Chertsey Abbey, *ib.* Richard III. ordered the removal of his bones to Windsor; but when Henry VII. desired to entomb them at Westminster, they could not be found, *ib.* Autograph of Henry VI., 130. Coins of this reign, 186. *Illustrations:* Furniture of an apartment of the time, 236. Henry VI., and his court, 242. Male costume in his reign, *ib.* Female attire and head-dress, 244.

HENRY VII., (August 22, 1485—April 21, 1509,) title of the earl of Richmond, by his mother, Margaret Beaufort, great-grand-daughter of John of Gaunt, ii. 125. Henry was also grandson of Owen Tudor and Catherine of France, widow of Henry V., *ib.* Certain conspirators, who had risen to release Edward V. from the Tower, on his murder being divulged, resolved to set up Richmond, *ib.* They, being Yorkists, devised that, if successful, Henry should espouse the princess Elizabeth, daughter of Edward IV., and thus reconcile the factions of the royal houses, 126. His mother, the dowager-countess of Richmond, now lady Stanley, entered into the conspiracy, *ib.* Elizabeth, widow of Edward IV., and the marquis of Dorset, corresponded with the malcontents, *ib.* Buckingham discontented with Richard III., took the same course, which proved fatal to him, *ib.* Richmond's fleet appeared off Devonshire; finding no troops to support him, he again set sail for St. Malo, *ib.* Dorset and others, 1484, swore allegiance to earl Henry in Brittany, 127. Francis, duke of Brittany, intending to seize and deliver Richmond to king Richard III.; the exile, with much difficulty, escaped into France, 128. His armament at Harfleur, *ib.* Richmond well received by the French king, *ib.* Proclamation of Richard against the earl, and his followers, *ib.* Richmond landed at Milford-Haven, crossed the Severn, and led his forces, inferior in number, against Richard, 129. On the eve, and in the moment of battle on Bosworth Field, large desertions reinforce Henry, *ib.* Stanley joined Richmond, with 3,000 men, during the contest, *ib.* In a valiant attack by king Richard upon his rival, Henry's standard-bearer and others are cut down by the king's own hand, *ib.* Aiming a deadly thrust at Richmond, the usurper was knocked off his horse, and fell, covered with wounds, *ib.* His crown, battered and blood-stained, was placed on Henry VII.'s head by lord Stanley, *ib.* The numbers engaged in this decisive battle were inconsiderable, 130. On securing the crown, he incarcerated Edward earl of Warwick in the Tower, 281. His Great Seal, *ib.* Portrait of Henry VII., (from his monument at Westminster,) 282. He offered his standards on the altar in St. Paul's, *ib.* The great concourse in London; the fatal sweating sickness, *ib.* Henry VII. crowned and anointed by Bourchier, archbishop of Canterbury, and cardinal, 1485; *ib.* He appointed a number of chosen archers to attend upon his person, and named them Yeomen of the Guard, 283. His pretensions, right of conquest, etc., laid before his first parliament, 7th November, *ib.* Debates and provisoes thereon, *ib.* Such members of the Commons as had been attainted were

HENRY VII.,—
rehabilitated by an Act for that purpose, and
then took their seats, ib. Attainders reversed,
of the dowager-countess of Richmond, the dukes
of Bedford, Buckingham, Somerset, and many
lords, ib. The king "antedated" his coming to the
crown to the day *before* the battle of Bosworth, ib.
His motive was to attaint, for *high treason*, those
who fought against him, ib. Reflections on this
arbitrary Act, ib. Terms of this Bill of Attainder,
recital of the lords and knights whose lands and
chattels were thereby sought, 283, 284. The subservient parliament passes the Act, 284. Settlement
of the crown by Act of Parliament, ib. Act of
Bastardy against the children of Edward IV. annulled and burned, ib. Henry commands that all
records of his own attainder should be taken off the
file, ib. Various influences and motives of the
king stated, ib. His parliament humbly petitions
Henry to proceed in his marriage with the princess
Elizabeth, ib. Their union took place 18th January,
1486 ; 285. Dispensation by the papal legate, ib.
Innocent III. confirmed this dispensation ; terms
of the bull recited, 287. He sent his queen, and
her mother and sisters, with the countess of Richmond, to keep their court at Winchester, ib. The
king visited Lincoln, Pontefract, Nottingham, and
York, 286, 287. An insurrection suppressed in
this journey, 286. At York, Henry relaxed his
avarice, reduced an impost payable by that city,
287. He concluded a truce of amity with Scotland, and the two kings agreed upon a future
matrimonial alliance, ib. Birth of Henry's son,
prince Arthur, Sept. 20, 1486 ; ib. Panegyrics,
Henry claimed descent through the Tudors and
Cadwalladers from king Arthur, of the Round
Table, ib. A priest, named Simon, landed in
Dublin, with a beautiful boy, Lambert Simnel, pretending that he was the earl of Warwick, escaped
from the Tower, 287, 290. The credulous Irish
believed the imposture, the Anglo-Irish espoused the
cause, from dislike of the Lancastrian king, 287.
The memory of Richard, duke of York, still popular,
ib. The lord-deputy Kildare and the Irish people
recognised Simnel as the scion of York, ib. Pertur-
bation of the king, who called a great council at
Richmond, ib. His bad faith as to the first pardon
he had granted, procured him many enemies at
home, 287, 288. He published a new amnesty, free
from all exceptions, 288. The king and council
closely imprisoned Elizabeth Woodville, the queen-
dowager, in the monastery of Bermondsey, and sent
her son Dorset to the Tower, 288, 291. Bacon
supposed that she had furnished a minute account
of young Warwick, for the guidance of the impostor
Simnel, 288. Henry VII. exhibits the earl of Warwick throughout London, which satisfied the English of his identity ; but the Irish still pretended
Simnel was the true earl, ib. John de la Pole, earl
of Lincoln, sailed to Dublin, with two thousand
German veterans, supplied by Margaret, duchess of
Burgundy, 288, 289. Lambert Simnel crowned
there, 1487, as Edward VI., 289. Henry levies an
army, ib. Lincoln, having landed with Simnel
(styled Edward VI.) at the Pile of Foudray,
Furness, marched upon York ; but hearing of
Henry's approach, turned boldly to the south to
encounter him, 289, 290. Battle of Stoke, total
defeat of the rebel force by the earl of Oxford ;
Swart and all his Germans, Broughton, and the
earl of Lincoln slain in a gallant contest, 290. Lambert Simnel (son of a baker) remained Henry's
prisoner, ib. The king placed him in a menial
situation in his kitchen, ib. Henry's solemn thanks-
giving at the shrine of Our Lady of Walsingham, ib.
He diligently sought out all abettors of this plot,
granting pardon of life for ransoms, thus procuring

HENRY VII.,—
himself treasure on all occasions, 290. He became
unpopular, ib. Causes thereof, 291. He felt the
necessity of ordering the coronation of his queen,
ib. Henry was present at Westminster, at this
splendid ceremony, but secreted by a screen, ib.
He sent bishop Fox ambassador to James III.,
1487 ; ib. Affair of Brittany, which fell entirely
under the rule of Charles VIII., 292-298. Henry
VII. called on to succour Francis II. and the
Bretons, 1488, sends envoys ; he acts with great
duplicity, pretends to arm, for which parliament
furnished him a subsidy, which he adds to his
hoarded treasures, 293—295, 298. He sent Willoughby de Broke, with 6,000 men, to Brittany,
1489 ; but shortly recalled him, 295. Insurrection
in the north suppressed by the earl of Surrey, 296.
Execution of John à Chambre and others at York,
ib. King Henry talks of conquering France, and
invests Boulogne, 1492 ; 298. Peace with Charles
VIII., 299. Terms of this treaty, known as the
Peace of Estaples, ib. A fresh impostor, Perkin
Warbeck, pretended to be Richard duke of York,
son of Edward IV., ib. Warbeck landed in Cork,
1492, and was well received by many Irish ; but
Kildare, the deputy, was more circumspect than
in the affair of Simnel, ib. The adventurer repaired to the court of Charles VIII., who treated
him as the duke of York, ib. When king Charles
had alarmed Henry VII. by thus upholding a
rival, otherwise contemptible, the above treaty of
Estaples was ratified, ib. Charles then dismissed
Warbeck, as no longer useful, and the impostor
retired to the court of the duchess of Burgundy,
ib. She received and protected Warbeck, as if he
were the late young duke of York, her nephew,
ib. Henry's secret agents in Flanders sent him
details of the birth and life of the new pretender,
300. Philip, son of Maximilian, declined to oblige
the duchess of Burgundy to surrender Warbeck, ib. Henry seized many gentlemen of note,
as participators in the conspiracy, 1494 ; they were
all adjudged to die, ib. Sir Simon Mountford,
sir Robert Ratcliffe, and Daubeney, beheaded, ib.
The rest pardoned, ib. The priests concerned were
committed to the custody of their order, ib. Many
persons also fled, ib. Lord Fitzwater beheaded at
Calais, ib. The treacherous Clifford named sir
William Stanley, brother of lord Stanley, as a
sharer in the conspiracy, ib. Stanley made no
denial of being partly guilty, ib. He had saved
Richmond's life (Henry VII.) at Bosworth, ib. His
condemnation and execution, Feb. 15, 1495 ; 301.
His great wealth confiscated, and considered as the
reason of his not being pardoned, ib. Warbeck, with
a band of desperate men, landed near Deal, ib. The
people of the coast repel this invasion, ib. *All* the
captives, to the number of 169, were gibbetted, ib.
Henry's penury sometimes relaxed ; he gave a feast
to the serjeants-at-law, in Ely-place, ib. He created,
in 1494, twenty-three knights of the Bath ; grand
procession at Westminster, Henry and Elizabeth
wearing their crowns, and lord Harry, duke of York,
carried by the earl of Shrewsbury, ib. Warbeck
was well received, 1496, in Scotland, 301, 304, 305.
Last years of James III., 301—303. Dark plot to
seize James IV., fomented by Henry VII., 1490; 303,
304, 306. League of England, the pope, Venice, etc., to
prevent Charles VIII. from over-running Italy, 305.
Randall of Dacre, ib. The duchess of Burgundy
supplied Warbeck with men and money, ib. King
James and Perkin crossed the border, but finding
few partisans, were compelled by hunger to retreat,
306. Serious insurrection of the people of Cornwall, 1497 ; they marched in great force across the
west, and were defeated in the battle of Blackheath,
June 22, 306, 307. James IV., about to marry Mar-

HENRY VII.,—
garet, daughter of Henry VII., dismissed Warbeck with an honourable escort, 307. The adventurer landed, with a small force, in Whitsand-bay, and sent his wife, for safety, to Mount St. Michael, ib. He assumed the style of Richard IV., and was joined by numerous malcontents in Cornwall, etc., ib. He sat down before Exeter, with an irregular force of 10,000 men, ib. The earl of Devonshire, and many nobles and gentlemen defended that city with success, ib. After a vigorous assault, the pretender was forced to decamp, ib. He marched upon Taunton, and being opposed by the royal army, he fled by night, 308. Henry pardoned the Cornish insurgents, ib. He sent for lady Catherine Gordon, the pretender's wife, dismissed her to his queen's court, and treated her with honour, ib. He decoyed Warbeck from the sanctuary of Beaulieu, and exhibiting him in London, shut him up in the Tower; but soon permitted him to reside at court, in safety, ib. In six months, 1498, Perkin rashly escaped from court, and took sanctuary at Sheen, 309. He was put in the stocks at Westminster-hall, and in Cheapside, and read a paper of confession, ib. Sent to the Tower, he became the companion of the earl of Warwick, 1499, ib. Rumour that Warwick had escaped; Ralph Wilford, son of a cordwainer, pretended to be that prince, ib. Wilford executed, ib. Four of the gaolers conspired to murder sir John Digby, lieutenant of the Tower, and to convey Warwick and Warbeck to a place of safety; the plot discovered, ib. Warbeck condemned, and suffered at Tyburn, Nov. 23, together with O'Water, mayor of Cork, 310. Trial and execution of the earl of Warwick, Nov. 24, ib. Indignation of the people; Henry VII. endeavoured to shift the blame on Ferdinand of Spain, in the treaty of marriage of prince Arthur, ib. A plague in London, 1500; Henry retired to Calais, and held a conference with the archduke Philip, ib. He received some arrears, due by the treaty of Estaples, from Louis XII., 311. Marriage, Aug. 8, 1501, of James IV. and Margaret, eldest daughter of Henry VII., 311, 312. Marriage of Arthur, prince of Wales. Nov. 5, with Catherine, daughter of king Ferdinand, 1501; 312. Death of Arthur, 1502; ib. A dispensation obtained from Rome, that prince Henry might marry his brother's widow, ib. Death of the queen of England in childbed, 1503; ib. The king instantly seeks another wife, but was difficult on the question of money with one, ib. His avarice increasing with age, he more than ever required moneys from his subjects, ib. His most oppressive ministers were Empson and Dudley, lawyers, 313. Dudley speaker of the House of Commons, 1504; the parliament subservient to the king, ib. Discontents of the people, ib. History of Edmund de la Pole, ib. The king commissioned sir Robert Curson to the court of the duchess of Burgundy, to pretend disaffection, and gain from Pole and his brother a knowledge of their partisans, ib. Lord Courtenay, in consequence, committed to the Tower, ib. Sir James Tyrrel and sir John Windham beheaded, 313, 314. On the marriage of his daughter Margaret, and the knighting of his son Henry, the king obtained, by feudal customs, 30,000l. from parliament, 314. Henry called no more parliaments, but levied money arbitrarily, as benevolences, ib. His coffers full of treasure, ib. The archduke Philip, and his wife Joanna, queen of Castile, 1506, driven by a storm, landed at Weymouth, ib. They were put under honourable constraint, until the king's pleasure should be notified, ib. They repaired to Windsor, 315. Henry, magnificently attired, met the king of Castile (so styled in right of his wife), and conducted him to the castle, ib. He obliged Philip to sur-

HENRY VII.,—
render the person of the earl of Suffolk, then in penury in Flanders, ib. Treaty for Henry VII. to marry Margaret duchess of Savoy, Philip's sister, and a rich widow, ib. Also for a marriage between Mary, daughter of Henry, and Philip's son (afterwards Charles V.), 315, 331. The royal guests allowed to depart for Spain, 315. Philip dying in Spain, Henry proposed to marry his widow, queen Joanna, 316. That princess had become insane on the loss of her husband, ib. Dispute betwixt Henry VII. and her father, Ferdinand, 317. The king's maladies, 1509, became aggravated, ib. His conscience smote him sorely for oppressing his people, ib. He gave alms, and enlarged all prisoners for debt, under 40s., in the capital, ib. Empson and Dudley, however, continued to extort money from the wealthy citizens, ib. Sir William Capel, lord-mayor, and sir Lawrence Aylmer, a former lord-mayor, refusing to pay heavy fines, suffered imprisonment, ib. Alderman Hawes died of vexation pending a mock trial, ib. Henry himself kept the key of his treasures, at his manor of Richmond, ib. The king died, in his new palace there, 21st April, 1509, aged fifty-three, ib. State of Europe and of England in his reign, 317, 318. Character of Henry, ib. *Illustrations :* Interior of Henry VII.'s chapel, Westminster Abbey, wherein he was sepultured, 316. Henry VII. delivering to Islip, abbot of Westminster, a book containing the masses and collects for the souls of his father and relatives, and the provision allowed for thirteen beadsmen, 697. In 1494, the ninth year of this reign, the first English female martyr suffered; this was Joan Boughton, a woman of above eighty years of age, 638. History of religion during this period, 696—702. The archbishops of Canterbury during this reign were, cardinal Bourchier, who died 1486; John Morton, who died 1502; Henry Deane, who was only archbishop for a few months; and William Warham, 700. This king devoted much of his attention to the encouragement of trade, 771. His reign is memorable for the achievement of the passage to India by the Cape of Good Hope, and the revelation of America by the voyage of Columbus, 775. Coins, 797. His signature, 695.

HENRY VIII. (April 22, 1509—January 28, 1547.) Duke of York, 1495; ii. 301. Dispensation for his marrying Catherine, his brother Arthur's widow, 312, 317, 319. Henry knighted, 315. Proclaimed king, April 22, 1509, in his eighteenth year, 318. The people rejoiced at his frank disposition, so opposite to his father's cunning and duplicity, ib. His excellent abilities, and taste for learning and art, ib. He was crowned with queen Catherine, 24th June; 318. His portrait by Holbein, ib. His Great Seal, 319. His council of government appointed, 320. Empson and Dudley condemned, and after a year spent in the Tower, beheaded, Aug. 17. 1510; ib. The lesser oppressors fell victims to popular fury, ib. Henry's popularity, ib. He joins a coalition against Louis XII., ib. The young king sent heralds to Louis, to forbid his war against pope Julius II.; also to demand Normandy, Guienne, etc., ib. Henry summoned his first parliament, 1512, which voted him supplies for the expedition into France, with the hearty concurrence of the English nation, ib. He sent Dorset with a considerable force to recover Guienne, but the private views of his father-in-law Ferdinand prevented the English from even crossing the Bidassoa, and the army returned home, 321. Henry VIII. prepared a royal army, 1513, to land in France, in person, 321, 322. He confided to the earl of Surrey the conduct of an expected war with James IV., 322. Negotiations with Scotland, ib. Louis XII. equipped a powerful fleet; gained a victory over the English at Brest,

HENRY VIII,—
1512, and destroyed their finest ship, the "Regent"; but the French admiral Primauget is slain, ib, Sir Edward Howard sailed, 1513, and invited king Henry to join the fleet, who showed no desire to do so, ib. Rashness of Howard in boarding the French admiral in Brest harbour before his other galleys could come to his support, ib. He threw his insignia as lord-admiral overboard, and was slain with the other boarders, ib. His brother, Thomas Howard, lord-admiral, cleared the Channel of the French fleet, 323. Ferdinand of Arragon treated with Louis XII., and king Henry entered into an alliance, 1513, with Maximilian, now emperor, ib. Before embarking in his expedition against France, he caused the earl of Suffolk to be beheaded, who had been left for execution by Henry VII., ib. He left queen Catherine to govern the realm, and landed at Calais, 30th June, ib. Siege of Terouenne, 323, 325. The emperor Maximilian, with a small escort, joined the English camp, 325, 326, etc. Henry VIII. in person gained the Battle of the Spurs, capturing the bravest of the French captains, 323, 325. Engaged in the reduction of Terouenne, which was taken and utterly demolished; the king neglected to co-operate with a powerful Swiss army, and proved incompetent to the office of a general, 325, 326. Wolsey, being promised the vacant bishopric of Tournay, his royal master turned aside to besiege that town, 326. Henry VIII. entered Tournay in triumph, and having spent great sums in this campaign, he returned, in October, to England, ib. Narrative of the invasion of the English borders by James IV. with a strong, well-equipped army, ib. Surrey gained the victory of Flodden, Sept. 9, in which the Scottish king and his bravest nobility fell, 327, 328. Trophies won by the English in this celebrated fight, 329, 330. Catherine's letter to Henry VIII. on the fall of the Scottish monarch, 330. Queen Margaret appointed regent of Scotland during the infancy of James V., 331. Measures of Louis XII., in 1514, and his marriage with Mary, sister of Henry VIII., ib. The French king's reception of his young bride at Abbeville, ib. The young queen's letters, complaining of rude treatment, 331, 332. Death of Louis XII. 1st January, 1515; 332. Mary shortly after married Charles Brandon, duke of Suffolk, who soon became king Henry's favourite companion, ib. Wolsey made a cardinal, 1515; ib. History of Wolsey's rise to power and eminence, 333. (See Wolsey.) King Henry's early taste for learning met, in this favourite minister, a guide and learned associate, ib. Wolsey's genius for magnificent pageants, etc., eclipsing even the resources of bishop Fox in that line, also gained him the good graces of an extravagant monarch, ib. Henry appointed this English cardinal to be chancellor on the resignation of the seals by archbishop Warham, 334. His kingdom flourished greatly under Wolsey's administration, notwithstanding the arbitrary imposition of fines, etc., ib. Salutary regulation of magistrates and police, repression of thefts, etc., ib. Treaty between Henry VIII. and Francis I., ib. War of the Swiss and the French king narrated, 335. (See Francis I.) The emperor Maximilian tempted Henry by a hint of abdicating the imperial dignity in his favour, ib. Henry sent an embassy to negotiate with the emperor, and Dr. Tunstall, one of the envoys, detecting the fallacy, ingenuously apprises his master, 335, 336. A new treaty with Francis I. became the consequence of the German negotiation; the dauphin, when old enough, to espouse Henry's daughter Mary, the English king to restore Tournay on payment of a sum of money, and a pension to Wolsey in lieu of the revenues of that bishopric, 336. Proposed interview of Henry and Francis, interrupted

by the death of Maximilian, Jan. 1519, ib. Charles V. emperor, 336, 337. The English king commanded Wolsey to send his congratulations to Charles V., but keeps fair equally with Francis, 337, 338. Henry VIII. had reached Dover, for the interview with king Francis, when the new emperor paid an unexpected visit at Dover Castle, 338. Henry and Charles V. visited Canterbury Cathedral, and the splendid shrine of Thomas à Becket, ib. The emperor quitted England, and Henry with Catherine sailed for Calais, 1520; ib. Details of the interview between the English and French kings; "The Field of the Cloth of Gold:" Henry's temporary palace near Guisnes minutely described, 339, 340. Francis's pavilion being blown over, he made a castle at Ardres his quarters, 340. Wolsey's plenary power to consolidate a treaty, its articles; intermarriage, and pension to Henry if their children's union actually took place, ib. Honour of king Francis in not leaving the Scots at Henry's mercy, James IV. and the bravest of his army having perished to make a diversion in Francis's favour, ib. The meeting of the two sovereigns, ib. Splendid tournament, both monarchs engaging in the jousts, 341. Confiding visit of Francis, almost unattended, to Henry VIII. before he had risen, and whom he helped to dress, ib. This characteristic trait of the generous Francis led to familiarity in the royal society; balls, masquerading, etc., in which both queens took part, ib. Illustration: The Field of the Cloth of Gold, 342. Henry VIII. then went to Gravelines to visit the emperor Charles, who accompanied him to Calais; negotiations, etc., 343. Charles V. took leave of his aunt, queen Catherine, and Henry landed at Dover, both king and nobles having exhausted their purses, ib. Royal lineage of Edward Stafford, duke of Buckingham; the king, in 1521, sacrificed him on that account, and after a trial, this popular duke was beheaded on Tower-hill, 343—345. The Reformation, begun in earnest by Luther, 1517; 345. Wycliffe and the Lollards had prepared the English people for the radical reform in religion, ib. Cardinal Wolsey's first measures in this important matter, 1521, narrated, ib. Henry's letter to Louis of Bavaria, counselling him to burn Martin Luther and his books, ib. The king wrote his "Defence of the Seven Sacraments," and Leo X. conferred on him the title of Defender of the Faith, ib. Wolsey's mission as arbitrator between Charles V. and Francis I., 1521, war having commenced, and Leo X. taken the side of the emperor, 345, 346. Articles of the treaty, among which was one for the affiancing of Mary, daughter of Henry VIII., to Charles V., 346. 348. Reverses of Francis I.; death of Leo X., 346. The French king seized English merchandise in the ports of France, which led to immediate hostilities, 347, 348, Charles V. re-visited England; he was installed a Knight of the Garter at Windsor Castle, and Henry VIII. accompanied the emperor to Winchester and Southampton, 348. Their treaty, for the invasion of France, ib. The earl of Surrey, high-admiral, ravaged the coast of Brittany, ib. Wolsey levied a tenth for this war, and soon became unpopular, 349. Surrey's campaign a failure, Vendome harassing the invaders, but declining an action, ib. The earl of Desmond revolted, in Ireland, at the instigation of Francis I., ib. Henry's further transactions relative to Scotland, 349—352. His royal reception, 1516, of his sister Margaret, 351. Shrewsbury marches to Kelso, wasting the fertile district with fire, 1522, but repulsed by the borderers of Teviotdale and Merse, 353. Henry convened parliament, 1523, after a lapse of eight years, 354. A property-tax of ten per cent. granted for the wars in France, by the Commons,

HENRY VIII.,—
and the like rate by a convocation of the clergy,
355. Popular resistance, ib. Suffolk's campaign
in France, 1523; ib. On the capture of Francis I.
at Pavia, Henry claimed the French throne, and sent
an embassy to the emperor, 359. Preparations for
the invasion of France; arbitrary imposts; serious
insurrections; Wolsey rendered odious, 359, 360.
The concord of Madrid, 161. Henry sent Dr.
Taylor and sir T. Cheney to congratulate Francis I.,
in 1526, on his return to his dominions, ib. His
alliance with the French king against the emperor,
ib. Henry's misunderstanding with his favourite
Wolsey commenced in 1525; in the space of two
years the cardinal was disgraced and ruined, 362.
The king's reply to Martin Luther, ib. Mary
Boleyn and king Henry VIII., 364, note. Henry's
love for Anne Boleyn, 1527; 363, 364. His love-
letters, 366. Negotiations conducted by Wolsey
for a marriage between Henry VIII. and Renée,
daughter of Louis XII.; also for the princess
Mary marrying either Francis I., or his son
Orleans, 364, 365. Trial of divorce betwixt
Catherine of Arragon and king Henry, 364—367.
Referred to Clement VII., who appointed legates,
367. Henry VIII. submitted his own treatise on the
divorce to sir T. More, 366, 367. Clement VII.,
listening to the envoys Drs. Gardiner and Fox,
granted Henry a dispensation, and reluctantly
signed a decretal bull, 367, 368. Clarenceux and
Guienne, 1528, on the same day, defied Charles V.
in the forms of chivalry, for Henry and Francis,
367. The sweating-sickness, so fatal in 1528,
alarmed the king; he became devout, taking the
sacrament on Sundays with Catherine, 368. Arrival
of Campeggio, who delays the commission, and consulted only Clement's interest, who was again under
control of the emperor, 368, 369. The king, much
incensed with the pope and French king, requested
the legates to proceed with their commission; the
court met in the great hall of the Black-Friars,
May 31, 1529, and summoned Henry and Catherine to appear, 369. The king did so by proxy,
the queen personally; she appealed to the pope, ib.
The court again sat in June; speech of Catherine
(on her knees) to Henry; she never after re-ap-
peared in the trial, ib. Henry then made his own
speech, and exonerated Wolsey from having recommended the divorce, ib. Illustration, after Smirke,
of this scene, 370. The queen being pronounced
contumacious, Henry's counsel propounded their
arguments, and demanded judgment, ib. Campeggio's speech, adjourning the cause to October,
ib. Bickering between Wolsey and Suffolk, 371.
Clement revoked the legatine commission; and
entertained the queen's appeal, ib. Campeggio
returned home, receiving presents from Henry;
when at Dover, armed men broke into his chamber
to search for papers, ib. Details of the fall of
Henry's once favourite minister, Wolsey, and of
all the king's transactions therein, interspersed
with traits of character, 371—374. The king's
injunction to Cavendish at Hampton, regarding
the treasure of the deceased cardinal, 374. The
idea of Thomas Cranmer, at supper with the
family wherein he was tutor, to have the divorce
determined by doctors learned in Scripture, without
farther reference to Rome, delighted the king,
374, 375. Exclamation of the king, who adopted
the plan, and made Cranmer one of his chaplains,
375. Narrative of Henry's commissioners at
Oxford and Cambridge, the doctors and heads of
colleges at Oxford assenting to the divorce, the
juniors bold and refractory, ib. Both universities
declare the marriage of Catherine illegal, ib.
Opinions of foreign universities, 376. Henry
sent the earl of Wiltshire and Cranmer to
Rome, ib. Cranmer's marriage at Nuremburg, for
a time kept secret, 377. Henry finds a bolder
agent, Thomas Cromwell, son of a blacksmith;
romantic career of this enterprising man narrated,
ib. The king confirmed Cromwell as steward of
the lands of monasteries already seized by Wolsey,
ib. The king appoints Cromwell of his council,
his eloquence in the House of Commons being
conspicuous and bold; and his advice to Henry to
declare himself head of the Anglican church being
agreeable to the excited monarch, ib. The convocation, and all the clergy, accused as guilty of a
præmunire by having received Wolsey as legate,
mulcted in a large sum of money, 1532; 378, 709.
The king required that they should, in the deed
granting him this sum, designate him as supreme
head of the church and clergy of England; to
this they firmly demurred, except with a reservation, 378. His ebullition of temper, ib. More,
as chancellor, with peers spiritual and temporal,
went down to the Commons, and explained how
conscientiously Henry acted in repudiating his
brother's wife; the opinions of the universities,
foreign and at home, were read, and several learned
treatises, ib. Parliament prorogued, ib. Attempt
to intimidate Catherine of Arragon, she was transferred from Greenwich to Windsor; she settled at
Ampthill, ib. Her perseverance in maintaining her
title as Henry's wife, 378, 382, 390. Henry VIII
never declared himself a Protestant; his ill-defined
system of faith became a stumbling-block to his
subjects of all sects, 377, 378, 386. His bitter
persecutions commenced in 1532; he hanged
the Catholic clergy, monks, etc., and burnt the
Reformers, with little intermission till his death,
378, 386. Sir Thomas More, himself an active
persecutor of the Protestants, took umbrage at the
punishment of the Catholics, and the ill-usage of
the queen, 378. More pleaded age, and resigned
the seals, retiring to private life: sir Thomas
Audley made chancellor, ib. King Henry conducted Anne Boleyn, marchioness of Pembroke, to
Boulogne and Calais, to meet Francis I., 379.
Splendour of the entertainments, and of the two
courts, ib. In January, 1533, king Henry married
Anne Boleyn, at Whitehall, in great privacy, ib.
He sent the earl of Wiltshire to secure the friendship of Francis I., 380. In 1533, the king still
entertaining a respect for Rome in religious matters,
obtained a bull of consecration, and the pallium for
the new primate Cranmer, ib. The king soon
employed the primate in his great cause of matrimony, and was gratified by Cranmer's reply, that
he was superior to all law, ecclesiastical or civil,
ib. Acts passed to abolish appeals to Rome, also
to name Catherine not queen, but princess-dowager
of Wales, ib. She was cited by Dr. Lee to appear
at Dunstable before the court, consisting of the
primate, the bishops of London, Bath, Lincoln, and
others, appointed to pass a final judgment in her
cause, 381. Being pronounced contumax, her
marriage was declared null and void, ib. The
primate next held an ecclesiastical court at Lambeth, which declared the king's marriage with
Anne Boleyn lawful; and a private marriage
between this royal couple was celebrated again, ib.
Anne, now pregnant, was solemnly crowned, with
much magnificence, June 1, 1533, at Westminster,
by archbishop Cranmer, ib. Clement VII. excommunicated Henry VIII. and Anne, annulling also
the judgment given by Cranmer, ib. Lord Mountjoy
made report to Henry of his conference with
Catherine, who would never cede her right as queen;
the tide of popular opinion setting strongly in her
favour. Catherine expressed her desire that no
ferment or agitation should ensue on her account, ib.

HENRY VIII.,—

Friars Peto and Elstow reprove the king at Greenwich; he heard calmly Peto's audacious sermon, but they and their order, "the Observants," were banished the realm, 382. Henry VIII. showing an earnest wish for reconciliation with Rome, Clement VII., Francis I., the duke of Norfolk, etc., held a solemn conference at Marseilles, ib. This was put an end to by Bonner appealing from the pope to a council of the church, ib. An ill result attended this conference; the contract for the duke of Orleans to espouse Catherine de Medici, niece of Clement, ib. Violent persuasions, urging Catherine to descend from her royal station; Suffolk, Sussex, dean Sampson, archbishop Lee, and bishop Tunstall, all fail in their missions to Ampthill, 383 September 7, 1533, the birth of Elizabeth excited the deep vexation of her royal father, who had hoped for a prince, ib. The parliament, 1534, passed numerous bills of national importance, vesting in the king, as supreme head of the church, the appointing to vacant bishoprics, of deciding ecclesiastical causes, prohibiting all appeals to Rome, and all payments to the popes whatsoever, etc.; it likewise enacted that Henry's marriage with Anne Boleyn was lawful, that the princess Mary was illegitimate, and the succession was to devolve on the king's children by queen Anne, 384. The royal assent was given to the bills severing all ties with Rome, March 30, 1534; Cromwell had prepared them, and news of the decision of the consistory of March 23, on the appeal of Catherine, could not have arrived to cause the above Acts and Statutes, ib. Clement VII., awed by the power of Charles V., had referred that appeal to a consistory of the church, which declared the marriage of Catherine of Arragon with Henry lawful and indissoluble, ib. Affair of the so-called Holy Maid of Kent, Elizabeth Barton, afflicted with idiotcy and epilepsy, who prophesied that the king should die soon if he put away his first wife, 1534; she was sentenced, with six others, to be hanged, 384, 385. In its results this absurd prophecy led Henry VIII. to the commission of unpardonable cruelties, and several eminent men of virtue and honesty to the scaffold, whereby he became odious throughout Europe, 385—389. The king caused, 1535, the venerable Fisher, bishop of Rochester, to be tried for denying that he could be, in spiritual matters, the head of the church, 386. The aged prelate was beheaded, his head placed on Londonbridge, and his body buried at Barking, ib. The king's next great victim was sir Thomas More. (See More, 387—389.) Narrative of his execution, July 6; his head was placed likewise on Londonbridge, 388, 389. Europe resounded with hatred of this tyranny, 389, 401. Charles V. and Francis I. openly expressed their just indignation, 389. Popular exasperation was directed against queen Anne, as the cause of the violent deaths of More and Fisher, ib. Pope Paul III., considering bishop Fisher and sir T. More as martyrs in the cause of the church, cited king Henry to appear at Rome in ninety days personally, or by proxy, and in case of default declared his crown forfeit, his children by Anne Boleyn incapable of inheriting it, ib. This successor of Clement, enjoined all clergy, secular and regular, to quit England, absolved Henry's subjects from their allegiance and oaths, enjoining them to take up arms against him, and all Christian princes to make war upon him, until he should cease his rebellion against the church, ib. Paul nevertheless suppressed this bull for a season, ib. The king, menaced and irritated, although not a Protestant, now negotiated with the Reformers of Germany; he was joined by the French king, and he endeavoured to draw the young king of Scots

HENRY VIII.,—

into the same alliance, 389, 390. Henry, finding the active cares of "Supreme Head" a burden to himself in so serious a crisis, appointed the vigorous Cromwell his vicar-general, etc., with a separate department for church matters, 390. That minister was fully competent to this addition of duties, and as "royal viregerent" took precedence even of the primate in convocations, ib. He proposed to abolish certain abbeys, convents, etc., and to seize for the king their lands and chattels, Henry listening with much complacency, ib. Cromwell sends commissioners to all quarters, to inquire into the life and morals of all monks and nuns, to administer the oath of the king's supremacy, etc., (See Monastic Orders,) and send their reports to him, ib. Death of queen Catherine at Kimbolton, January 8, 1536, ib. She commended the princess Mary to Henry's paternal care, ib. Her dying letter to Henry drew some tokens of commiseration from the despotic king, ib. Anne Boleyn said to have exclaimed, that at length she was "indeed a queen," ib. Rumours existed also that she suspected Henry's attachment to one of her own maids of honour, Jane Seymour, ib. January 29, queen Anne was brought to bed prematurely of a son, still-born, 391. May 1, at a fête and tilting-match at Greenwich, wherein lord Rochford and Norris, groom of the stole, were the principal challengers, the king's temper was suddenly aroused, ib. He left the queen in the festal scene, and instantly departed with six attendants for London, ib. Next day her uncle Norfolk, chancellor Audley, and Cromwell met her on the Thames, informed her of an accusation of adultery, and lodged her in the Tower. (See Anne Boleyn for details and a narrative of her interrogatory and trial, 391—393). Execution of queen Anne, 394. The king, on the morning of her death, resolved to hunt in Epping Forest, ib. Being at breakfast, Henry heard the report of a distant gun, the signal to announce the execution; his exclamation of satisfaction; he engaged in the chase till evening, ib. On the morrow he married Jane Seymour, May 20, 1536, but he no longer commanded a coronation of a new queen consort, ib. Cranmer, who was supposed to be friendly to Anne Boleyn and her family, on her arrest had been commanded to keep house at Lambeth; his epistle to king Henry, 394, 395. The king enjoined the primate to declare the marriage with Anne Boleyn unlawful from the first, the condemned queen having confessed to a pre-contract with the lord Percy, that her death might be by the axe, not the stake, 395. The princess Elizabeth was declared illegitimate, equally with Mary, her half-sister, ib. Cranmer held his court at Lambeth, read his objections to the marriage, the divines were unanimous, and the primate solemnly pronounced judgment adverse to queen Anne and her daughter's rights, two days before the execution, ib. In June, the king caused parliament to settle the succession on the children he might have by queen Jane, and to grant also to him the faculty of bequeathing his crown; and these bills were enacted, ib. Henry perhaps had his natural son, the duke of Richmond, in contemplation; that noble, aged eighteen, to whom his royal father was most partial, died at this time, ib. His daughter Mary, subscribing to articles of submission propounded by Cromwell, had a suitable establishment, ib., note. He dissolved parliament, after it had sat by repeated prorogations, for six years, the king being angry at some resistance to the wholesale suppression of the small monasteries and convents, 396. Book printed against images, etc., ib. The king's religious sentences and awards, and his polemical turn dissatisfied now the Roman Catholic clergy and now the reformers, 396, 397. Henry

HENRY VIII.,—
reduced the sacraments to three—Baptism, the Lord's Supper, and Penance; forbad the worship of images, and abrogated many saints' days and holidays, 397. He ordered the Scriptures in English to be distributed, a copy for every parish church, and that the clergy should expound the church creeds in English, *ib.* He insisted on auricular confession, and that all who denied the real presence in the Eucharist should be burnt, *ib.* Puzzled in respect of purgatory, he permitted prayers for the dead, *ib.* The innovations, the Statute of Uses, imposts upon cattle and sheep, and a more heart-rending destitution to be witnessed everywhere, by reason of the suppression of monasteries, caused, in 1536, a formidable insurrection in Lincolnshire, *ib.* (For its suppression, *see* Brandon, duke of Suffolk, and Lincolnshire.) Popular fear of a spoliation of parish churches, *ib.* The bold statement of grievances being forwarded to the king, when Suffolk had bribed some of the leaders, and by temporising and promises caused dissensions among the rest, Henry sent to the *petitioners,* still formidable by numbers, his "Reply," arbitrary and contemptuous, *ib.* The "Pilgrims of Grace," in Yorkshire, are joined by divers lords *compulsorily;* Henry coins the plate in the Jewel-house, Tower of London, to send money to Suffolk, 399. The royal army at Doncaster grants an armistice, that the delegates might lay the northern petition of grievances before the king, *ib.* He sent them back with an elaborate written reply, 400. Winter approaching, the people became furious from privations; the army under Norfolk was compelled to retire south of the Don and Trent, *ib.* Great alarm lest the insurgents should march southward, *ib.* January 1537, at this crisis some of the leaders deserted the people, others were taken and sent to London, *ib.* Lord Darcy, in June, beheaded on Tower-hill; Aske executed at York, lord Hussey at Lincoln, etc., 400, 401; *note.* Henry's letter to Norfolk to take severe vengeance, and to hang the monks of Hexham and other monasteries, 401. Cardinal Pole, legate beyond the Alps, was furnished by Paul III. with extraordinary powers, and money for the English insurgent malcontents, 1537, *ib.* Henry requested king Francis to arrest Reginald Pole, and the emperor Charles refused him passage through his territory, *ib.* Surrey's mission, with others, to visit monasteries, etc., *ib.* The insurrection quelled, and Pole proclaimed a traitor; the cardinal returned to Rome, 402. Queen Jane delivered of a son, the prince Edward, October 12, 1537; *ib.* Twelve days afterwards, the queen died, *ib.* Idle report of the resort to the Cæsarean operation, refuted, *ib.*, *note.* Letters of bishop Latimer and the chancellor Audley, *ib.* With the sanction of an Act of Parliament, the king seized all abbeys and other religious houses, except a few, which by earnest petitions of the people were given up to representatives of the founders, 402—404. Under the pretence of preventing the worship of images, Henry next despoiled the shrines and altars, 402. He ordered "*Thomas Becket, sometime archbishop of Canterbury,*" to be cited to appear in court, to answer charges preferred against him; who not appearing, Henry graciously assigned him counsel, 402, 403. With all solemnity the court sat, June 11, 1539; the attorney-general pleaded for the crown, the counsel were heard for the defence, and the long-defunct prelate was convicted of rebellion and treason, 403. The sentence on him was, that his bones should be burnt, as an example, and the rich offerings at his shrine (his *personal property*) be forfeited to the king, *ib.* Amount of gold and jewels, *ib.* The Royal of France, a stone of great lustre, offered at the shrine of Becket in 1179 by Louis VII., was henceforward worn on his thumb by Henry VIII.,

HENRY VIII.,—
ib. Other shrines plundered; miraculous images and relics broken at Paul's-cross, *ib.* The king was next guilty of more deadly mockery, being induced to burn *Forest,* a condemned friar, instead of hanging (the constant punishment of Catholics), thereby to bring to pass a tradition respecting an old crucifix, that it should burn a *forest;* it was sent for from South Wales, and the execution took place in Smithfield, *ib.* Henry VIII. at length sequestrated the abbeys of the metropolis and adjacent counties, and shortly of all the kingdom; partition of the plunder, lands and goods, 1537—1540; 404. Images, Madonnas, mosaic pavements destroyed, *ib.* The libraries sold for waste-paper, the bells sent to foreign countries, the buildings converted to stables, *ib.* The promoters of the Reformation, at this early stage, would not or dared not speak for the conservation of anything; except that St. Alban's, Tewkesbury, Malvern, etc, being also parish churches, were saved, *ib.* A small portion of the proceeds of abbeys, etc., was allotted by the king to six new bishoprics; fourteen of the abbeys, were granted for cathedrals and collegiate churches, and some portion of land; the chapters being obliged to contribute towards maintaining the poor, and repairing the highways, 405. The fires of Smithfield, 1538; Anabaptists burnt, 406. King Henry's solemn argument in Westminster-hall with John Lambert, schoolmaster, who denied the *real presence* in the Eucharist; the result of the disputation being, that Lambert was burnt with peculiar atrocity, *ib.* King Henry had grown obese and bloated, could no longer resort to his once favourite field sports; and his early gay temper turned therefore to sour jealousy of his own subjects and of foreign powers, 406, 407. He was unprepared for war, 1538, 1539; and a powerful league of the pope, the emperor Charles, and Francis I., seemed to threaten him, 407. Paul III. now published the *bull* or fulmination against Henry VIII., hitherto kept in reserve; a truce for ten years was signed by Charles V. and king Francis at Nice, June, 1538; an active correspondence joined in by Reginald Pole, foreboded a crusade against the English monarch, *ib.* Henry, rendered timid in this emergency, is re-assured by the wise counsels of Cromwell, who speaks of forming a close alliance with the reformed princes of Germany, and tells him that no fleets are in preparation in Spanish or French ports, *ib.* Cromwell's letter to his master quoted, *ib.* Henry VIII, imbued with mortal hatred of cardinal Pole, ordered in 1538 the trial of his brothers, the lord Montacute and sir Geoffrey Pole, also of Courtney, marquess of Exeter (a grandson of Edward IV.), sir Edward Neville, etc., 408; when sir G. Pole, on a promise of life, pleaded guilty: his confession ruined the others, *ib.* Lord Herbert (cotemporary) writes, that he could never discover their offences; but as to the two peers, their royal descent sufficed; they were all executed, with the exception of Geoffrey Pole, *ib.* Henry next sent his near relative, the mother of cardinal Pole, to the block, 409. Her unavailing resistance, *ib.* The two great religious parties; missions from the German Protestants, sent home by the English king, without agreeing to any conciliation, etc., *ib.* Henry appeared at length to desire reconciliation with his Catholic subjects; he invested the duke of Norfolk with power above Cromwell's, desired Gardiner to preach at Paul's-cross, etc., *ib.* The Six Articles, shortly called the "Bloody Statute," passed, 1539; 410. Their enumeration, and immediate ill effects, *ib.* Pageant on the Thames, 411. Glastonbury despoiled of treasure; abbot Whiting executed, 411, 412. The abbots of Reading and Colchester hanged and quartered, 412. Hans Hol-

Henry VIII,—
bein's portrait of Anne of Cleves; other false reports of her beauty, caused the king to send over for that Protestant princess, 413. Cromwell's satisfaction (for reasons of religion) at this new marriage of Henry, ib. The king's extreme disgust; the divorce; resignation of the lady Anne, 413—416. Cromwell soon incurred the displeasure of Henry VIII., and was forthwith attainted and beheaded, 415—417. The king's marriage with Catherine Howard, 415. Dr. Barnes and others burnt as heretics; papists and protestants executed at the same time and place; an insurrection in the north, caused by the king's cruelties, suppressed, 417. The king's love for Catherine, who accompanies him on a royal progress, 1541, to the disaffected counties, 417. Henry's grief on their return, when Cranmer preferred allegations of her having been incontinent before marriage, ib. Further accusations against the queen, 417—422. A new parliament, 1542; trial of Catherine Howard; the queen (and also lady Rochford) beheaded in the Tower, 423. New enactment in the Bill of Attainder, ib. Remarks on Henry's religious principles, ib. Books published under the king's superintendence, for the settlement of religion: "The Bishop's Book," "The King's Book," etc., 424. By whom, and how the Scriptures might be read, ib. Influence of Gardiner and the Romish party increases, ib. Relaxation of persecution in the four last years of this reign, 425. Henry's political measures examined, ib. Condition of Wales and the Welsh, ib. In Ireland, the earl of Kildare, about 1523, lord-deputy, was unable to repress the factious spirit of the Butlers, ancient enemies of his family, ib. The earl was sent for to court, and imprisoned in the Tower of London, ib. Rumour that the king had put him to death, 1533, and consequent insurrection of his son, Thomas Fitzgerald, ib. Archbishop Allen, 1534, was murdered in presence of the Fitzgeralds, 425, 426. Fitzgerald submitted, his five uncles were captured, and, with their nephew the young earl, were beheaded, 1537, on Tower-hill, the earl having already died in prison, 426. Lord Leonard Gray, who conducted this Irish war for the king, was himself attainted, 1541, and beheaded, ib. Romantic history of the last scion of the Fitzgeralds; he fled to cardinal Pole at Rome, and was restored after Henry's death to the earldom of Kildare, 426, 427. State of church affairs in Ireland, 427. The religious houses, 427, 429. O'Connor rebelled, 428. O'Neil's rebellion, his country devastated by Henry's generals, ib. The English pale in its turn suffers by the O'Neils, O'Tooles, etc., ib. Submission of O'Connor, ib. Henry VIII. then designated Ireland a kingdom, 1541, and conferred titles on several native chieftains; O'Neil became earl of Tyrone, O'Brien earl of Thomond, etc., ib. Improvements, and salutary policy, 428, 429. Transactions on the Scottish border, 429. Albany returned with forces from France (1523), his power being insufficient, he retired once more to Francia, and marched with that king into Italy in the following year, ib. Regency of Margaret in Scotland, ib. Her quarrel with Henry VIII., her brother, 430. James V. assumed the government, ib. James Beaton, ib. Power of the earls of Arran, Angus, etc. 430—435. Cardinal David Beaton negotiates the second marriage of James V. with Mary of Guise, dowager-duchess of Longueville, 1538; 431. King James and this cardinal discontented the Scottish nation, by persecutions and the burning of heretics, ib. Henry VIII. had always interfered unjustly with his nephew James's rule, and at length resolved to seize on Scotland by force of arms, 432. King

Henry VIII,—
Henry's progress to York with his queen, ib. Norfolk's invasion, 1542, and retreat, 433. Death of James V., ib. Henry's ambition led him to propose, in 1543, arbitrary conditions for the affiancing of Mary of Scots with his son Edward, 434, 435. Treaty of Greenwich for this family alliance, 436. Causes of the failure of his scheme, 435, 437. Henry VIII. and Charles V. united, 1543, 1544, against Francis I., 438. Marriage of Henry with Catherine Parr, 1543, a Protestant, ib. Imminent peril of this sixth wife of Henry, on account of her religion, and also of Cranmer, ib. The reconciliation that ensued, by Catherine's prudence and submission, 447. Henry, in person, 1544, besieged Boulogne, and made a triumphal entry, 439. Causes of the emperor's abandoning the new alliance, ib. Return of the king, much impoverished, to England, ib. Remarks on this war, ib. Seymour, earl of Hertford, entered Edinburgh; but foiled before the castle, he marched to Berwick, 440. Henry's commission to this earl, his brother-in-law, ib., note. Scottish affairs, 441—448. The persecution of heretics in England renewed, 438, 447. His treaty of Campes with Francis I., 1546; 447. The king's malady, ib. Hertford (at the head of the Protestant interest) prevailed on the king to arrest Howard, duke of Norfolk, and his son, the poet Surrey, 448. The charges against Surrey, his trial, and eloquent defence, 449. His execution, 1547; 450. Attainder of Norfolk, 451. Henry's death, January 28, 1547; ib. This event took place but just in time to save Norfolk, who was however detained in the Tower, ib. The will of Henry VIII., 454. His character and temper, 453. Funeral of Henry, and state of the kingdom, 456. His signature, 695. History of religion during this reign, 701—729. Coins, 799. Henry's skill in music, iii. 561.

Henri II., king of France, (1547—1559,) on the death of Francis I., counselled by the family of Guise, aids the Scottish Catholics and Mary of Longueville, mother of Mary of Scots, 1547; ii. 456.

Henri III. (1574—1589.) On the decease of his brother Charles IX. in 1574, he quitted his kingdom of Poland, and ascended the French throne, ii. 649. The Huguenots detested the new king for his share in the St. Barthélemi, ib. Conspiracy detected, ib. Alençon, the king's brother, implicated; both brothers applied for aid to Elizabeth, ib. She became mediatrix, the Huguenots tolerated, and Alençon becomes duke of Anjou, ib. Henri III. became head of the Catholic League, and annulled the privileges of the Huguenots, 1577; ib. He sends over Bellièvre as a special ambassador to intercede for the life of the queen of Scots, 664. He secretly distributes forty-five daggers to as many assassins in the castle of Blois, to murder the house of Guise; a few months after, whilst besieging his own capital, he is assassinated by a fanatic monk, of the order of the Jacobins, named Jacques Clement, 672.

Henri IV. (1589—1610), as king of Navarre, he supported the persecuted Protestants of France, ii. 649. He marries the princess Margaret, 1572, sister of Charles IX. of France, 646. On the death of his predecessor, he finds himself opposed by the French Catholic League, he applies to Elizabeth, who supplies him with 20,000l.; 679. In 1593, to secure peace to his throne, he embraces the Catholic religion; anger of Elizabeth at this change, ib. He signs the treaty of Vervins, 681. He publishes the Edict of Nantes, 682. He commissions his favourite Rosni, 1603, to secure the interest of James I. for the States of Holland, iii. 7. He prepares to enter Juliers at the head of an army of 30,000 men, to support the claims of the Elector of Brandenburg, 1610, but is stabbed on the 14th of May, three days before that fixed for his departure, by Francis

HENRI IV.,—
Ravaillac, a friar of the order of the Jacobins, 48.

HENRY VI., (1190—1198), emperor of Germany, son of Frederic Barbarossa, demands that king Richard, who had been taken prisoner by Leopold, duke of Austria, should be delivered up to him, i. 503. His dislike to Richard for his assistance to Tancred, ib. His expedition into the south of Italy, and siege of Naples; during the heats of summer a malaria fever carried off a vast number of his men, and he himself falling sick, raised the siege of Naples and retreats, ib. His letter to Philip, stating the confinement of Richard, 5C9. General disgust of Europe at his doings; the pope threatens him with excommunication, ib. Richard brought before the diet at Hagenau, ib. Henry lays many and unjust accusations against him; he replies to all the charges, and leaves no suspicion of guilt in the minds of the diet, 510. Terms are agreed upon, and 70,000 marks raised for his ransom, ib. Richard agrees in this treaty to pay to the imperial court 100,000 marks of pure silver, and 50,000 marks to the emperor and the duke of Austria, ib. Death of the emperor, 1197; 513.

HENRY, son of David, king of Scotland, i. 423. His brave conduct at the great battle of Northallerton, 1138; 425, 541. Made earl of Northumberland, ib. He accompanies his father in his expedition into England, when he advanced as far as Lancaster, to assist prince Henry, afterwards Henry II., ib. He died 12th of June, 1152, a year before his father David, ib.

HENRY, prince, eldest son of Henry II.; contract of marriage solemnized between Henry, who was seven years old, and the daughter of Louis, the princess Margaret, 1160; i. 446. Prince Henry does homage to the French king, his father-in-law, for Anjou and Maine, 452. Crowned, 1170, during his father's lifetime, by the archbishop of York; he receives homage from William, king of Scotland, and his son David, 453, 543. Again crowned in 1172, with his consort Margaret, 467. He demands either the government of England or that of Normandy to be delivered up to him; on refusal of this request by his father, he flies to France, 1173, and obtains assistance from the French king, ib. He is acknowledged king of England by Louis, and a general assembly of the barons and knights of France, 468. He and his two brothers swear that they will not make peace with their father without the consent of the barons of France, ib. Louis invades Normandy, 1173; he is repulsed, and a conference takes place; the earl of Leicester insults Henry, and hostilities recommence, ib. Louis and prince Henry again attack Normandy, a powerful alliance being formed in his favour, 470. He promises William of Scotland the earldom of Northumberland; the Scots invade England, but are repulsed by Richard de Lucy, ib. The king returns to England, having taken prince Henry's wife prisoner, ib. Henry is reconciled to his father, and peace is restored, 471. Is again at variance, and again reconciled, 472. Henry and Richard make war against their father and prince Geoffrey, 1183; prince Henry submits, but soon after falls sick at Château Martel, and dies, June 11, 1183; 474.

HENRY, count of Champagne, nephew of king Richard, marries the widow of Conrad, 1191, and becomes possessed of her claim to the kingdom of Jerusalem, i. 500.

HENRY, son of Richard, king of the Romans, and cousin of Edward I., slain by Simon and Guy de Montfort, 1271, (sons of the great earl of Leicester), who had been banished from England after the battle of Evesham, i. 688.

HENRY, eldest son of James I., distinguished at the court of Windsor Castle, by his wit, affable carriage and devotion, 1603; iii. 6. Installed a knight of the Order of the Garter, ib. Some description of his character and pursuits, 49. His fondness for horses and martial exercises, ib. Picture of prince Henry and lord Harrington, 50. His aversion to swearing, 51. He takes a lively interest in the fate of the able and learned Raleigh, 73. For his instruction, that illustrious prisoner writes a "History of the World," completing the first part in 1612; ib. Prince Henry dying shortly afterwards, that great work remained unfinished, ib. Henry is seized with a dangerous illness at Richmond, 51. Recovering a little, he rides to Whitehall, to receive his proposed brother-in-law, the count palatine, ib. His illness increasing, he leaves St. James's abruptly; on the 2nd of November delirium ensues; he calls for sir David Murray, ib. Earnestly entreats that a number of letters in his closet should be burnt, 52. Raleigh sends him a cordial; his death, November 6, 1612, the effect of a putrid fever on a debilitated constitution, ib. Engraving and costume of prince Henry (from Drayton's "Polyolbion"), 623.

HENRY, younger brother of Stephen, created abbot of Glastonbury and bishop of Winchester by Henry I. 1129; i. 421. By his aid Stephen obtains possession of the royal treasury at Winchester, ib. Henry, now (1139) papal legate for all England, summons the king to answer for his violent proceedings against Roger, bishop of Sarum, and his two nephews, before the synod of bishops assembled at Winchester, 427. Henry acknowledges Matilda as queen, and wholly abandons his unfortunate brother, 430. He persuades the assembly of churchmen at Winchester, which he had convened, to ratify her accession, 431. He quarrels with Matilda, who refuses to restore his nephew prince Eustace to his patrimonial estates, ib. Matilda attempts to seize him at Winchester; he puts himself at the head of his armed vassals, and a thousand Londoners who had joined him, and besieges Matilda, with the earls of Gloucester, Hereford, Chester, and David, king of Scots, in the royal castle of Winchester, 433. Matilda and David make their escape, but the earl of Gloucester is taken prisoner, and soon after exchanged for king Stephen, ib. Henry summons a great ecclesiastical council at Winchester, in which Stephen a second time is declared king, and Henry endeavours to justify his conduct respecting Matilda, 434. He loses his great authority on the death of the pope, 435; and flies with his treasures to Clugny, 442. He died August 6, 1171.

HENRY, Patrick, the Chatham of America, his violent speech concerning the Stamp Act, 1765; § i. 41. Portrait of, 182, 187. He excites the Virginians to fly to arms, 224.

"HENRY's Primer, King;" or, Tracts on the Divine Offices, 1535, ii. 718. This manual shows the mixed religion as authorised at that date, by the king. It is half-Protestant; it contained the Litany in English, etc., ib.

HENSEY, Dr. Florence; he acts as a spy for the French ministry; sentence of death as a traitor is passed upon him; he receives the royal pardon, upon condition of leaving England for ever, 1758; iv. 604, 605.

HEPBURN, Mr. John, leader of the Cameronians, 1706; iv. 193.

HEPBURN, Mr., 1745; iv. 536.

Heptarchy, the, rendered wholly tributary to Egbert of Wessex in 825; i. 150, 151.

Heraldry, its rise, an early roll of arms of the reign of Henry III., i. 641.

HERBERT, lord, 1509, chamberlain, ii. 320. Laid siege to Terouenne, 1513; 323, 325. Considered as the biographer of Henry VIII.; his remarks and statements, 336.

HERBERT, Arthur, admiral. *See* earl of Torrington.

HERBERT, sir Edward (created baron Herbert of Cherbury, May, 1629), 1623, ambassador at Paris, receives private information of prince Charles and Buckingham being in that capital *incognito*, iii. 92. His interview with M. de Puisieux, secretary of state, on the subject, who promises not to impede the prince of Wales, then on his journey to Madrid, *ib.* Herbert sends after Charles, warning him to hold no communications with the Huguenots, *ib.* Is assured by De Luynes, 1625, that an overture for the hand of Henrietta Maria would be accepted, 106. Advises Charles I., 1640, to fortify York, and inveighs against a recent treaty with the Scottish commissioners, 225, 226. Attorney-general, 262. Committed to the Fleet-prison, 1642; 267. He died in 1648.

HERBERT, George, (a younger brother of the celebrated Edward, lord Herbert of Cherbury,) he was a poet, and author of the volume entitled "The Temple;" he died 1633; iii. 604.

HERBERT, sir Henry, deputy-master of the revels, 1625; iii. 595.

HERBERT, sir Philip. *See* earl of Montgomery.

HERBERT, Thomas, iii. 363, 388. His dream before the night of Charles I.'s execution, 396.

HERBERT, one of the managers of the House of Commons in the impeachment of the duke of Buckingham, 1626; iii. 120.

HERBERT, lord chief-justice, a member of the ecclesiastical commission, 1687; iii. 786.

HEREFORD, William Fitz-Osborn, earl of, seneschal of Normandy. He raises the siege of Exeter, i. 375. Dies a violent death in Flanders, 1070; 380.

HEREFORD, Roger Fitz-Osborn, earl of, son of William Fitz-Osborn, i. 380. Gives his sister Emma in marriage to Ralph de Gaël, contrary to the orders of William I., *ib.* Their marriage feast, 381. Fitz-Osborn and Ralph de Gaël conspire against the king, 1073; *ib.* Their scheme is betrayed by Judith, wife of Waltheof, *ib.* Gaël's attempt to cross the Severn is frustrated; he fortifies and garrisons Norwich Castle, leaves his bride, Emma Fitz-Osborn, to defend it, and passes over to Brittany, *ib.* Fitz-Osborn is defeated, and condemned to perpetual imprisonment, 382.

HEREFORD, Humphrey Bohun, earl of, constable of England; this great patriot takes part with the merchants and landed proprietors against the tyrannical and unlawful impositions of Edward I. In the end of February, 1297, when Edward had collected two armies, one to send into Guienne, the other into Flanders, the earls of Hereford and Norfolk, the marshal of England, refuse to quit the country; the marshal and constable withdraw, followed by 30 bannerets and 1,500 knights, leaving the king almost alone, i. 719. The constable and earl-marshal, in presence of the lord-treasurer and of the judges, forbid the officers of the Exchequer, in the name of the whole baronage of England, to exact payment of certain taxes which had been laid on without proper consent of parliament, and being supported by all the great trading towns, Edward is obliged to confirm the two charters, and the important statute called "*De tallagio non concedendo*," 721. In the full parliament the earls demand of Edward to ratify in person his recent confirmation of the charters, *ib.* Edward delays, but is at last compelled to grant the ratification so firmly demanded, 722. Death of this illustrious earl, 1208; *ib.*

Herefordshire, jurisdiction of Wales over, iii. 43.

Herefordshire Beacon, triple ramparted camp of the Britons on one of the Malvern hills, so named, i. 100. View of this remarkable vestige of ancient military science, *ib.*

Heresy, not punished with death, in England, until

Heresy,—the passing of the statute against the Lollards, *De hæretico comburendo*, 2 Henry IV., 1401, which was renewed and enforced by Henry V., ii. 140, 141.

HEREWARD, lord of Born, in Lincolnshire, having expelled the Normans from his patrimony, assisted others in doing the same, and establishes a fortified camp in the isle of Ely, where he raised the banner of independence, 1073; Morcar flies to him for protection, i. 376. William advances against Hereward, in which expedition the Normans being surprised in the bogs suffer some severe checks, 377. William cuts off all supplies by sea and land, *ib.*, and commences a wooden causeway across the bogs and rivers, which is burned by Hereward before completed, 378. After a blockade of three months, provisions becoming scarce, the monks of Ely guide the Normans through the bogs; the English are compelled to give way; Morcar and the bishop of Durham are taken, and confined to perpetual imprisonment; Hereward escapes, and is permitted to enjoy the estates of his ancestors, *ib.*

HERLE, discloses a plot, 1572, for murdering some of the privy-council, ii. 640.

HARMAN, succeeded, in 1046, as bishop of Winton, and as bishop of Shireburn, in 1050. He removed the see to Salisbury and founded a splendid library in that cathedral. He died before 1080; i. 604.

HERODOTUS, quoted, i. 13—15, 19.

HERRICK, Robert, author of a volume of poetry, published 1648; iii. 566, 604.

Herring fishery, 1400; ii. 191; 18th century, § iii. 639.

HERRING, Thomas, archbishop of York, his activity in raising soldiers against the Young Pretender, iv. 502. Translated to Canterbury, 1747; he died, 1757.

Herrings, battle of, fought at Rouvral, Feb., 1429; ii. 62.

HERSCHEL, sir William, his discoveries in astronomy, 1781, 1802, etc., § iv. 703, 704. His portrait, 703.

HERTFORD, Edward Seymour, earl of, uncle of Edward VI. (*see* Somerset.) He landed at Leith, and invaded Scotland, ii. 440, 448. Titles conferred on him by the king (1547); his elevation to supreme power as protector of the kingdom, 455, *et seq.* On the execution of the protector Somerset, his rival in power, Dudley, hitherto earl of Warwick, was created duke of Northumberland, 495.

HERTFORD, Edward Seymour, earl of, son of the protector Somerset, restored to the title of earl of Hertford, by Elizabeth, 1559; ii. 569. His marriage with Catherine Grey, great-grand-daughter of Henry VII., 1560, becoming known to queen Elizabeth, she sent them both to the Tower, although the countess of Hertford was pregnant, *ib.* The two children of the earl and countess were born in that prison, *ib.* The countess of Hertford, 1567, died a prisoner, and the earl was further detained for nine years in custody, *ib.* (*See* lady Catherine Grey.) He died 1621.

HERVEY, captain, 1756; iv. 586.

HEWET, Mr. Peter, commissioned to present a protestation of the clergy to the king, 1617; iii. 468.

HEWIT, Dr., beheaded by Cromwell, 1658; iii. 427.

HEWLET, condemned as a regicide, 1660, but not executed, iii. 673, 674.

HEWSON, colonel, a parliamentarian, 1658; iii. 425.

Hexham, St. Andrew's church at, founded, 674, by bishop Wilfrid, i. 310. Description of this great Anglo-Saxon structure, by Richard, prior of Hexham, *twelfth century*, when it still existed, *ib.* Battle of Hexham, May 15, 1464; ii. 101. View of Hexham, iv. 314.

HEYLIN, the biographer of archbishop Laud, quoted, iii. 158, 498.

HEYTHER, William, establishes a music lecture at Oxford, 1622; iii. 566.

HEYWOOD, Jasper, author of a series of translations of the tragedies of Seneca (16th century), iii. 584.

HEYWOOD, John, a dramatic writer of the 16th century, iii. 579, 584.

HEYWOOD, Thomas, a dramatic writer of the 16th century, iii. 594.

Hibernia, its derivation and meaning, i. 17.

HICKES, Dr. George, the Anglo-Saxon scholar, suspected of an inclination to popery, iv. 645.

HICKES, a Presbyterian preacher, present at the battle of Sedgemoor, iii. 780. He is executed, 1685; 781.

HICKFORD, secretary to the duke of Norfolk, 1571, his confession, ii. 638.

HIDE, David, supposed to have coined the name of Round-heads, iii. 260, note.

HIGDEN's "Polychronicon," with the translation of Trevisa, printed by Caxton, ii. 209.

HIGGINS, Francis, an Irish Protestant clergyman, declaims on the dangerous state of the church, 1709; iv. 237.

High-Commission-Court, origin of the, ii. 755; iii. 42, 694.

Highlands of Scotland, battle of Harlaw, July 24, 1411; defeat of Alexander, lord of the Isles, by Mar, ii. 132. This great chieftain totally overthrown by James I. of Scotland, 1429—1431; 133. The king, having executed many turbulent lairds at the parliament at Inverness, puts to death 300 Highlanders, in cold blood, as desperate robbers, ib.

Highlanders, Scottish, earliest occupants of North Britain, the descendants of a band of Irish who settled in Argyleshire in the third century under Carbry Riada, i. 18.

HILDEBRAND. See Gregory VII.

HILL, Abigail, cousin to the duchess of Marlborough. See Mrs. Masham.

HILL, colonel John, iv. 46. Makes an unfortunate expedition to Quebec, 1711; 257. He takes possession of Dunkirk, 1712; 268.

Hill Norton, in Warwickshire, assembly of Levellers at, 1607; iii. 36.

HILL, general sir Rowland, a skilful commander of the British troops in the Peninsula, § iv. 482. He defeats general Girard, 1811; 490. Carries, by a brilliant coup de main, the strong forts at Almaraz, and cuts off all communications between marshals Marmont and Soult, 1812; 505. He commands a division of the army at the battle of Vittoria, June 21, 1813; 570, 571. His brave conduct at the battle of St. Jean de Luz, December 13, 1813; 585.

HILL, accused of being concerned in the popish plot, and executed at Tyburn, 1678; iii. 725.

HILLIARD, Nicholas, a miniature painter of great talent (sixteenth century), ii. 854.

HILLSBOROUGH, earl of, appointed third secretary of state, 1767; § i. 59, 78.

HIMILCO, a Carthaginian navigator about a thousand years before our era, i. 14.

HINGSTON, John, organist to the protector Cromwell, iii. 567.

HIPPESLY, sir John, informs the king of the duke of Buckingham's murder, 1628; iii. 137.

History, evidences of genuine, derived from inscriptions, sculptures, edifices, and numismata, i. 4.

"History of the World," written by sir W. Raleigh in the Tower of London; the first part finished, 1612; the remainder, in consequence of prince Henry's death, and the illustrious author's release, although "hewn out," was left incomplete, iii. 73.

HOADLEY, Dr. Benjamin, portrait of, iv. 183, 617. He incurs the animadversion of the Lower House of Convocation, for a sermon preached before the lord mayor, 1705; 646.

HOBBES, Thomas, born 1588. He imagines the free use of the Scriptures to be an incentive to rebellion, iii. 498, 871. Review of his works, 880, 881; iv. 775.

Hochkirchen, battle of, 1758; iv. 603.

HODGES, Mr., writes a violent book against the Union of England and Scotland, at the time of that transaction, iv. 188.

HOGARTH, William, born 1697-8. His portrait of lord Lovat the morning before his execution, iv. 552. His portrait of Dr. B. Hoadley, 617. His portrait of himself, 735. Review of his principal performances, 755—757. His "London Lamp-lighter," 823. Hogarth died, 1764; 757.

Hohen Friedberg, battle of, June 3, 1745; iv. 479.

Hohenlinden, battle of, gained by general Moreau over the archduke John, Dec. 3, 1800; § iii. 558.

HOLBEIN, Hans: this eminent painter was born 1498, of a family of artists; both his father and his uncle were painters, and the latter is believed to be the Holbein who visited England regno Henry VII. He acquired the friendship of Erasmus in Basle. In 1526, he arrived in England with letters of introduction from Erasmus to sir T. More, who entertained him for three years in his house at Chelsea, ii. 852. Henry VIII. sends him into Flanders to draw the portrait of the duchess of Milan; on the failure of that negotiation, he was dispatched on the like errand to the lady Anne of Cleves. Holbein died of the plague, in 1554; ib. His portrait of Henry VIII., 318. Of Catherine of Arragon, 319. Of Anne Boleyn, 379. Of Jane Seymour, 394. Of Anne of Cleves, 413. Of queen Catherine Parr, 439. Of queen Mary, 501. Of cardinal Wolsey, 696. Of bishop Gardiner, ib. Of the protector Somerset, 750. Of Cromwell, earl of Essex, ib. Of lord Surrey, 813. Of sir T. More, ib. His portrait by himself, ib.

HOLBORNE, Robert, disputes the legality of ship-money, 1637; iii. 179.

HOLDER, Dr., author of a "Treatise on the Principles of Harmony," (17th century), iv. 763.

HOLDERNESS, earl of. See Odo.

HOLDERNESS, earl of. See Haddington.

HOLGATE, Robert, archbishop of York, committed to the Tower by queen Mary, ii. 509.

HOLINSHED, Raphael, the historian (regno Elizabeth), referred to, i. 3, 367, 368, 525; ii. 185, 687; iii. 615.

HOLKAR, Jeswant Rao, a Mahratta chief; he succeeded Maharow Holkar, soubah of Malwa, in the command of the Deccan, and in 1803 carried on a successful war against the Peishwa, who was obliged to take refuge among the English at Bombay, § iv. 78. His portrait, 79. Holkar commenced hostilities against the English in 1804, the result of which was a treaty, concluded Jan. 7, 1806, by which he gave up all his maritime provinces, 79—86, 199—205.

HOLKOT, Robert, author of the erroneous statement as to the intention of William I. to abolish the Saxon language; he lived in the fourteenth century, i. 611.

HOLLAND, embassy from the United Provinces to James I. in 1603; iii. 7. The States of Holland form a league with the kings of England and France, about 1610, to support the elector of Brandenburg in the succession of John, duke of Cleves, 48.

HOLLAND, William, earl of, commander of the English expedition in 1213, when the English fleet entirely annihilated that of the French at Damme, prepared for the invasion of England by Philip II., i. 525.

HOLLAND, John. See Exeter.

HOLLAND, Henry Rich, earl of, created 1624; iii. 114. He endeavours to procure the overthrow of Wentworth, 171. Resigns his office of groom of the stole, 1642; 268. He rises for the king, 1648; 383. Is beheaded in Palace-yard, 1649; 400.

HOLLAND, Henry Fox, lord, resigns his office of paymaster of the forces, 1763, and is raised to the peerage in the April of the same year, § i. 25, 26.

HOLLAR, Winceslaus, a native of Prague; is patronized by the earl of Arundel. Shortly before the civil war he was employed as drawing-master to prince Charles. His prosperity was fatally affected by the

HOLLAR, Winceslaus,—
downfall of the royal cause; he followed his patron to Antwerp, and returned to England in 1652, and engraved the illustrations of Dugdale's work, but was miserably paid; after the Restoration he was equally unfortunate; he died at the age of seventy, in absolute indigence, iii. 577. His print of the *George*, 398. Of the Custom-house, London. 527. Of London before the great fire, 545. Of the Pest-house in Tothill-fields, Westminster, 695. Of Oxford, 734.

HOLLIS, Denzil, a patriotic member of the House of Commons *regno* Charles I., iii. 141, 142, 144, 261, 337, 369. Created baron Hollis, April, 1661. He died, 1680; 727.

HOLLIS, sir Francis, youngest son of the earl of Clare, statue of, iii. 576.

HOLLOWAY, a Rye-house conspirator, condemned and executed, 1684; iii. 755.

Holmby-house, iii. 363.

HOLMES, sir Robert, detached by Charles, 1672, to capture the Smyrna fleet, iii. 709.

HOLMES, sir Thomas, destroys a great quantity of Dutch shipping, 1666; iii. 698.

HOLMES, an old republican officer, hanged at Dorchester, 1685; iii. 783.

HOLMES, major, concerned in a conspiracy for murdering William III., iv. 65.

HOLSTEIN-BECK, prince of, iv. 171. Mortally wounded at the battle of Blenheim, 1704; *ib.*

HOLSTEIN, duke of, offers an asylum to Conrad Vorstius, the Dutch divine; he arrived here 1622, but soon after died, iii. 48.

HOLT, sir Robert, his speech respecting the attack on sir J. Coventry, 1670; iii. 708.

HOLT, lord chief-justice, 1705; iv. 177.

Holwood-house, Hayes, Kent, the seat of the earl of Chatham, view of, § i. 85.

Holy days, or saints' days, the suppression of many of them, especially in harvest time, by Henry VIII. in 1536, a cause, among many discontents, of insurrections, ii. 397.

Holyrood-house, the ancient royal palace of Edinburgh, view of, ii. 557.

Holywood, Dumfriesshire, Druidical circle, and traditions of the grove of oaks, etc., i. 61.

HOME, a noble of the Scottish border. His successful charge, in conjunction with Huntley, upon sir Edmund Howard at Flodden, ii. 328. Home's refusal to bring his men again into action, weakens the forces of James IV., *ib.* The morning after the defeat, this refractory lord recrossed the Tweed in good order, with a large booty, 329. Being unpopular and discontented, he consents to lord Dacre's proposals, and to head the English faction, 350. Albany marches to suppress the discontents of the Scottish border, takes Home Castle; Home flying into England to Dacre, obtains an English force and seizes the tower of Blacater, near Berwick, 351. He accompanied queen Margaret and Angus into England, he returned across the border with that earl, and, submitting to Albany, both those powerful nobles were restored to their estates, *ib.* A new rebellion of many great lords; Home again heads the English faction, and, together with his brother, is taken, condemned, and beheaded, 352.

HOME, of Wedderburn, surprised De la Bastie, and riding to Dunse with that French commander's head on his saddle-bow, fixed it on the market-cross, 1518; ii. 352.

Homildon-hill, battle of, Sept. 4, 1402; ii. 11.

HONEYWOOD, colonel, severely wounded at Clifton Moor, 1745; iv. 518.

HONTHORST, Gerard, (known in Italy as Gherardo della Notte) an eminent painter of the seventeenth century, iii. 567.

HOOD, Samuel, viscount, reduces Bastia, 1794; § iii. 400.

HOOKE, colonel, a Jacobite agent in Scotland; his description of the readiness of Scotland to receive the Pretender, iv. 205.

HOOKER, Richard, a prose writer of the sixteenth century, ii. 836.

HOOPER, John. He is nominated, 1550, to the see of Gloucester, but refuses to receive consecration in the canonical habits, ii. 493, 741. He is committed to the Fleet for contumacy, 1551; 493. Afterwards he consents to be attired in the prescribed vestments at his ordination and when he preached before the king, or in his cathedral, or in any public place, but should be excused from wearing them on other occasions; in December following, his diocese is united to that of Worcester, but in 1552, another arrangement is made, and he becomes bishop of Worcester alone, on the suppression of the bishopric of Gloucester, 494. He is deprived by queen Mary, 1553, for having a wife, and other demerits, 509. Is burnt at Gloucester, Feb. 9, 1555, the year of the revival of old statutes against heresy, 523. The doctor, in Germany, had acquired puritanical doctrines, which first appeared in England on the accession of Edward VI., 741. Appointed to the see of Gloucester, 1550, he refused submission to the forms of consecration as then practised, *ib.* The king passes over this contumacy, and struck the obnoxious expressions out of the deed, *ib.*

HOOPER, Dr., attends on the unfortunate Monmouth in his last moments, 1685; iii. 777.

Hop-plant, its cultivation in England introduced, 1524, from the Netherlands, ii. 806.

HOPE, sir John, his brave conduct at St. Jean de Luz, December, 1813; § iv. 585. Is wounded in a sally of the French from Bayonne and taken prisoner, 609°.

HOPE, sir Thomas, leads on a body of lawyers against the royal forces at Newburn, 1640; iii. 221.

HOPE, M., Dutch minister at Vienna, 1699; iv. 101.

HOPETON, sir Ralph, signs a petition against church-ales, etc., 1633; iii. 151. Presents a petition from the parliament to the king, 1641; 257.

HOPKINS, sir William, a gentleman of the Isle of Wight, concerts a plan for the escape of Charles I.; iii. 385.

HOPKINS, the master witch-hunter, his proceedings, 1645-6; iii. 639. He is found guilty by his own ordeal, and subjected to the same penalty as his victims, *ib.*

HOPPE, Madame, wife of the Dutch minister in London, 1738; iv. 429.

HOPSON, admiral, present in an attack upon Vigo Bay, 1702; iv. 146.

HORN, count, wounded at the siege of Namur, 1695; iv. 58.

HORROCKS, Samuel, he first discovered, in 1639, the planet Venus on the body of the sun; and also anticipated, hypothetically, the view of the lunar motions which Newton afterwards showed to be a necessary consequence of the theory of gravitation, iv. 768.

Horse-racing, ii. 890.

Horses, ancient Britons well provided with; description of, i. 36. British horses were held in great estimation at Rome, 106.

HORSEY, Dr., chancellor of the bishop of London, is accused of participation in the murder of Richard Hunne, 1515; ii. 704.

HORSLEY, Samuel, elected to the bishopric of St. David's, 1788; opposes earl Stanhope's motion, 1789, for repealing several severe and almost obsolete laws respecting attendance at church, etc., § iii. 570, 581. His portrait, 572.

Horticulture: flowers, vegetables, hops, etc., that were introduced into England in the *sixteenth century*, ii. 806.

HORTON, Mrs., widow of Christopher Horton, esq., of Cotton Hall; her private marriage with the duke of Cumberland, 1771; § i. 126.

HOSIER, rear-admiral, goes on an expedition to the West Indies, 1726, but perishes, with a considerable part of his fleet, of the yellow fever, iv. 389.

HOSKINS, John, an eminent miniature painter of the seventeenth century, iii. 569.

HOSKINS, serjeant, poet and scholar, companion of Northumberland and Raleigh in the Tower; some account of this celebrated man, iii. 72.

Hospitallers, knights, the keeping of Messina entrusted to them and the Templars by king Richard, whose cause they espouse, i. 491, 495.

Host, representation of the passage of the, ii. 149.

HOTHAM, sir John, sent to the Fleet-prison, 1640; iii. 217, 267. He refuses to admit Charles I. into Hull with 300 men as a guard, the king thereupon declares him a traitor, 278. Having entered into a plot with his son to give up Hull to the king, he is hanged by the parliament, together with his son, 1644; 305. His motion for printing the votes of the House, 844.

HOTHAM, vice-admiral, gains a victory over the French under rear-admiral Pierre Martin, March 8-9, 1795; § iii. 478, 479.

HOUGH, John, bishop of Lichfield, 1699; translated to Worcester; he died, 1743; iv. 183.

HOVEDEN, quoted, i. 500, 583.

Howard Castle, iv. 747.

HOWARD, lord, ambassador to Louis XI., ii. 113. Took bribes from France, all Edward IV.'s courtiers being venal, 116. A supporter of Richard III. in his usurpation, 123. Created duke of Norfolk, 124. His son created earl of Surrey, ib. See Norfolk.

HOWARD, lord Thomas, 1513, succeeded his brother Edward as lord-admiral, ii. 323. He fought at Flodden, under the standard of his father, soon created duke of Norfolk for that decisive victory, 327. His insulting message to James IV., to which the Scottish king gave no reply, although he sent a chivalrous answer to Surrey, his father, ib.

HOWARD, lady Catherine, niece of the duke of Norfolk, ii. 414. Henry VIII. met her at a dinner given by Gardiner, bishop of Winchester, and was immediately enamoured of her, 415. He divorces Anne of Cleves, and marries Catherine, 416; ib. Portrait of queen Catherine, 416. The king's affection for his young wife, 417. Cranmer declares that before marriage the queen had led an abandoned life, ib. The king orders the arrest of all Catherine's accomplices and confidants, and puts them to the torture, ib. Cranmer undertakes the office of making her disclose her youthful irregularities, 1541; ib. The queen is driven to frenzy, 418. Instructions sent to Cranmer, ib. Examinations of divers persons, 419—423. Catherine is beheaded, 1542, protesting that she had been true to the king since she was his wife, 423.

HOWARD, lord Henry, undertakes the office of conducting the secret correspondence between James VI. and the English secretary Cecil, ii. 692.

HOWARD, Thomas, lord of Walden, lord chamberlain to James I., 1603; iii. 4.

HOWARD, lady Frances, married to the earl of Essex, iii. 52, sent home to her mother as being too young, ib. After four years, they going to live together, Essex discovers the coldness of his bride, ib. She is enamoured of Rochester, ib. Offers 1,000l. to sir John Wood to kill sir T. Overbury in a duel, 53. She sues for a divorce from her husband, 1613; ib. Her marriage with R. Carr, earl of Somerset, 54. Description of the fête, ib. She is implicated in the murder of Overbury, 60. Tried May 24, 1616, and pleads guilty, 61. Sentence of death pronounced, ib. James pardons her, 62. She retires to the country, and dies, 1632; ib.

HOWARD, lady Mary, committed on a charge of high treason, 1659; iii. 431.

HOWARD, lord, admitted into the secret of the Rye-house Plot, 1681; iii. 740. He is apprehended 1683, and brought before the council, 746. Whilst giving his witness against lord Russell, he hears of the death of the earl of Essex, 747.

HOWARD, sir Edward, lord-admiral, a son of the earl of Surrey, in 1513, attacked the fleet of Louis XII. in Brest harbour, ii. 321, 322. His daring character in action, 322. He boarded the French admiral followed only by a few seamen, ib.; the Frenchman cast his vessel loose from Howard's galley, ib. Seeing his death inevitable, he flung his gold chain and whistle into the sea, being the badges of his high office, and was slain with his men, before sir W. Sidney, Wallop, and Cheney, could come to his assistance, ib. The English fleet, disheartened by their gallant commander's death, made sail, ib.

HOWARD, Thomas. See earl of Berkshire.

HOWE, Richard, earl, a celebrated English admiral born in 1725. He presents a petition from his brother officers, 1773, praying for a trifling increase of half pay, § i. 149, 191. Blunders committed by this officer in the American war, 261, 276, 361. He sails with a small fleet to the relief of Gibraltar, 490. He resigns his place at the head of the Admiralty board, 1788, and immediately after was advanced to an earldom, § ii. 254. Receives a commission appointing him to the command of a fine fleet, June 22, 1790; 464. His unsuccessful attempt to come into action with admiral Truguet, 1793; 301, 302. He obtains the surrender of Toulon, 302. Gains the victory of the 1st of June, 1794; § iii. 392—396. He is commissioned by government, May 1797, to conciliate the sailors at Portsmouth, who had been driven into mutiny by harsh usage, which service he ably accomplishes, 520. His death, August 5, 1799; ib. Monument in St. Paul's, ib.

HOWE, general sir William, lands at Boston, May 1775; § i. 214, 297. Takes possession of Wilmington, 1777; 303. He departs for England, 1778; 357.

HOWEL, author of the "Londinopolis," published, 1657; iii. 546.

HOWIE, Mr. Robert, principal of the new college of St. Andrews, 1623; iii. 472.

HUBBA, a Danish king, landing in Devonshire is slain with his followers, about 877, and the raven banner of the Danes embroidered by the daughters of Lodbrog, fell into the hands of the Saxons, thus giving fresh hope and animation to Alfred, then in Athelney, i. 159.

HUBBERTHORN, Richard, an eminent Quaker; Charles II. grants him an audience, and promises to tolerate his sect, iii. 818.

HUBERT, an insane Frenchman, makes a voluntary confession of having caused the Fire of London, and is executed, 1666; iii. 699.

Hubertsburg, Treaty of, signed February 15, 1763; § i. 24.

HUDDLESTON, a priest, iii. 761, he had assisted Charles II. in his escape from Worcester, and confessed him at his death, 762. By order of James II. he published a relation of Charles's dying in the communion of the church of Rome, 764.

HUDDY, captain Joshua, execution of, April 12, 1782; by the American royalists, § i. 488.

HUDSON, chaplain to Charles I., 1646; iii. 350, 352.

HUDSON, his portrait of Dryden, iii. 871. Of Pope, iv. 731.

HUGH DE MONTGOMERY, succeeded as earl of Shrewsbury, 1094; enters into a conspiracy for placing Stephen count of Aumale on the throne, 1098. He died, 1098; i. 400.

HUGH, nephew of Aubert le Ribaud, governor of the district of Le Perche, assists prince Robert in his revolt against his father, 1077—1079; i. 383.

HUGHES, sir Edward, destroys the infant navy of Hyder Ali, 1781; § ii. 149. Takes possession of the island of Ceylon, 150. Engagements with the French admiral de Suffrein, 150—156. Assists in the defence of Gibraltar, 1782; § i. 494.

Huguenots, the, fly to arms under the command of the prince of Condé, the admiral Coligni, and others; the war rages from the banks of the Garonne to the banks of the Seine, and the shores of the British Channel, ii. 570. The duke of Guise solicits aid from Philip II.; the prince of Condé solicits the assistance of Elizabeth; the king of Navarre is mortally wounded at the siege of Rouen, 1562; ib. The Huguenots under Condé threaten Paris; a fierce battle is fought at Dreux, and the Protestants are defeated, 1562; 571. The duke of Guise is assassinated by Poltrot, a Huguenot, 1563, and on this a hollow treaty is concluded between the conflicting parties, 572. The French Protestants and Catholics unite to drive the English out of Havre, 1563; which is at length accomplished, 573.

HUGUES, Victor, his energy in preaching republicanism to men of colour. Its success exemplified in the insurrection at St. Lucie, 1795; § iii. 480.

HULL, iii. 655, castle of, temp. Charles I. ii. 278.

HUME, David, an eminent historian and philosopher, born 1711. Died August 25, 1776; § i. 619—621. Portrait of. 619.

HUME, sir George, afterwards earl of Dunbar, principal minister of James I. in Scotland, iii. 64.

HUME, sir Patrick, arrested for participating in the Rye-house plot, iii. 771.

HUMPHREY, Pelham, a musician of the seventeenth century, iii. 885.

HUNGATE, captain, concerned in a plot for assassinating William III., iv. 65.

HUNGERFORD, sir Thomas, speaker in the last year, 1377, of Edward III., i. 780.

HUNGERFORD, Mr., chairman of the committee on the Orphans' Bill, convicted of corruption, and expelled the House of Commons, 1695; iv. 51.

HUNNE, Richard, a merchant tailor, disputes with a parson, 1514, concerning a bearing-sheet; Hunne being sued in an ecclesiastical court, takes out a writ of præmunire against his pursuer; he is thrown into prison and soon after murdered; proceedings thereon, ii. 703—705.

HUNSDON, lord, 1559, Henry Carey, son of Mary Boleyn, and cousin of Elizabeth, created a peer with others, soon after that queen's accession, ii. 541.

Hunting, a sport much esteemed and practised by the Anglo-Saxons, and Normans, i. 341—343, 647. In the fifteenth century, hunting in inclosures introduced, ii. 255; iv. 831.

HUNTINGDON, David, earl of, and brother of the Scottish king, revolts against Henry II., i. 470; in 1124 he succeeded to the Scottish throne, by the title of David I.

HUNTINGDON, John Holland, earl of, half-brother of Richard II., created 1387. He murders John Latimer, 1384 (for accusing the duke of Lancaster of treason), besides one of the king's favourites, i. 791. Created duke of Exeter, 1397. In 1399, he was compelled to return to his old title, ii. 5. He invites his brother-in-law, Henry IV., to a tournament at Oxford, it being the intention of certain of the "lords appellants" to murder the newly established monarch, 6. He flies from Windsor Castle, which the conspirators had surprised, and is torn to pieces by the retainers of the duke of Gloucester whom he had injured, 7.

HUNTINGDON, George Hastings, earl of, created 1529. In 1536, sent, with other commanders, against the insurgents of Lincolnshire. He died, 1544; ii. 397.

HUNTINGDON, Henry Hastings, earl of, 1560. An object of Elizabeth's jealousy. He died 1595; ii. 618, note.

HUNTINGDON, countess of, head of the Calvinistic Methodists, after the death of Whitefield, in 1770; § i. 526. Portrait of, ib.

HUNTINGDON, Henry of, i. 589, 590.

HUNTLEY, earl of, his successful charge at Flodden, Sept. 1513. Sir Edmund Howard's division routed, ii. 328. He urged lord Home to renew the contest, and that they should lead the left wing of the Scots again to the mélée, to the rescue of the king, ib. This Home refuses to do, ib. Huntley then collected his own followers by trumpet, but before he could reach the centre, the king had fallen, ib., note. He marched off the field in safety, but his standard is said to have been taken by sir William Molyneux, ib.

HUNTLEY, earl of, taken prisoner by the English at the battle of Pinkie, 1547; ii. 463. Mary of Scotland having granted the earldom of Murray to her half-brother, James Stuart, Huntley to whom it had been previously granted, asserts his title by the sword; a fierce battle is fought at Corrichie in which he is totally routed, and in flying from the field is thrown by his horse into a morass, where he is smothered, Oct. 1562. His body is carried before parliament, and sentence of attainder passed upon it; and his son, sir John Gordon, is executed, 574, 575.

HUNTLEY, earl of, does his best to assist the queen during the murder of Rizzio, ii. 588.

HUNTLEY, marquis of, 1639, taking up arms for Charles I., in the north of Scotland, is routed by Leslie and Montrose, iii. 203.

HURRY or Urrie, a parliamentarian, deserts to the king, 1643; iii. 303.

Husbandry implements, iii. 558.

HUSK, general, 1746; iv. 522.

HUSS, John, preaches in Bohemia the religious doctrines and reforms first proposed by Wycliffe, 1428; ii. 71,; a crusade preached by pope Martin V. against his numerous followers, ib.; cardinal Beaufort conducting in person a small English army to join the crusaders against the Hussites, consents reluctantly to add his force to Bedford's army in Paris, ib. Huss is burned for heresy, 1414; iii. 80.

HUTCHINSON, captain Hely, assists in the escape of Lavalette, Jan. 1816; § iv. 654*, 656*.

HUTCHINSON, colonel, condemned as a regicide, 1660; iii. 666.

Huts, Gaulish, i. 98.

HUTTON, Matthew, archbishop of York, 1604, complains of James I. hunting, to the ruin of the standing crops, and neglect of public business, iii. 19. Cecil's letter in reply, 20. He sends the archbishop's letter and his own by the earl of Worcester to James, ib. Impression on the king's mind, and vexation, ib. Hutton died Jan. 1606.

Huy, captured by marshal Villars, 1705, and retaken by Marlborough the same year, iv. 178.

HYDE, Anne, daughter of the earl of Clarendon, delivered of a son six weeks after her marriage to the duke of York, 1660; iii. 677. She dies in the open profession of popery, 711.

HYDE, Mr. Edward, iii. 227. See Clarendon.

HYDE, sir Nicholas, made chief-justice of the King's Bench, 1626; iii. 123.

HYDE (son of the earl of Clarendon) made lord-treasurer, 1679; ii. 731.

HYDER ALLY, an Asiatic prince, an obstinate and formidable enemy to the English in Hindostan, in the latter part of the eighteenth century, § i. 73, 95—99. Portrait of, 97. His cruelty towards his dewans, 146. He dies, 1782, and is succeeded by his son Tippoo Saib, 154.

HYNDFORD, John Carmichael, earl of, his mission to Frederic the Great, 1741; iv. 449. He is insolently treated by the house of Austria, 572.

Hyperboreans, island of the, how far proved to be Ireland, i. 15.

IBERVILLE, M. de, 1716 ; iv. 332.

Iceni, their locality ; are defeated by Ostorius, i. 40 ; Boadicea, widow of king Prasutagus, 43. Her lands (Norfolk and Suffolk) invaded by Roman maranders, whom she resists, ib. Queen Boadicea and her daughters barbarously chastised by Catus, ib. Formidable insurrection of the Iceni and Trinobantes ; their successes and destruction of Roman colonies, (A. D. 60, 61,) they gave battle to Suetonius, and suffer an overwhelming defeat and massacre, 43, 44.

IDA, with his host of Angles, about 547, landed at Flamborough Head, and settled in the desert country between the Tees and Tyne, which acquisition took the name of the kingdom of Bernicia, i. 142.

Idel river, Nottinghamshire, battle betwixt two Saxon monarchs, Redwald and Edilfrid, on its banks, i. 146.

Iernis, name of Ireland in the Orphic poem, 500 years before Christ. This appears to be the earliest mention of Ireland ; also called Ierne in a work attributed to Aristotle, i. 14.

ILAY, earl of, made secretary of state for Scotland, 1724 ; iv. 385.

Images, worship of, in England, ii. 145, 396.

IMMYNS, John, established the Madrigal Society, 1741 ; iv. 763.

IMOLA, bishop of, 1486, papal legate, ii. 285.

IMPEY, sir Elijah, arrives at Calcutta, as chief-justice, 1774 ; § ii. 131. He pronounces sentence of death on Nuncomar, an intriguing Hindoo, for forgery, Aug. 1775 ; 137. His share in the business of Benares and Chunar, 174. He is appointed to the office of judge of the Sudder Dewaunee Adaulut; doubts as to the legality of his promotion, 177. He is recalled, 1782 ; 178. His impeachment, 1788, which ends in nothing, 260—275. His death, Feb. 1, 1812 ; 573.

INI, laws of, i. 203.

Inclosure Act, the, passed 1800—1 ; § iv. 634.

Inclosures, ii. 900.

Income-Tax, the, proposed by Pitt, 1798, and carried through parliament, 1799 ; § iii. 544. Plan of the, ib.

Independents,—These Nonconformists are a modification of the Brownists, the third race of Puritans, who sprung up about 1581; ii. 745.

India, embassy of Sighelm, bishop of Shireburn. to, in the reign of Alfred the Great, i. 266, 267. Pondicherry, the capital settlement of the French in the East Indies, taken by the English under colonel Coote, 1761; § i. 9. Establishment of the factory at Surat by the English, 1612 ; 16. Dynasties of Ghizni and Gaur, 16, 17. Timur or Tamerlane overturns the Afghan dynasty (end of the fourteenth century), 17. Island of Bombay ceded by Charles II. to the Company, 1688; 21. Azim Ooshaun sells Calcutta and other places to the Company, about 1698; ib. Death of Aurungzebe, 1707; 22. The Persians, under Nadir Shah, penetrate to Delhi, 1739, and massacre the Mohammedans and Hindus, ib. Labourdonnais, a Frenchman, takes Madras from the English, 1744; 23. Military operations of Dupleix, governor of Pondicherry, 23, et seq. Admiral Boscawen captures Pondicherry, 1748; 25. Siege of Devi-Cottah, 25, 26. Death of Nazir Jung, 28. Clive enters Arcot, 1751; 30. Siege of Arcot, 30—33. Successes of Dupleix, 36. Provisional treaty signed at Pondicherry between the French and English, December 26, 1754; 38. Geriah taken by admiral Watson, ib. Clive assumes the government of fort St. David, June, 1756; 39. Pacific rule of Aliverdy Khan, mussulman viceroy of the Great Mogul; his death in 1756, and succession of Suraj-u-Dowlah, his grandson, a cruel and effeminate youth, ib. Services of the merchant Omichund, ib. et seq. Suraj (the new viceroy) invests the English fort and factory at Cossimbuzar, 41. Takes Cal-

India,—
cutta, 1756; the tragedy of the Black Hole, 41—47. Expeditions of Clive, 48—59. Battle of Plassey, fought June 21, 1757; 59. Meer Jaffier is raised to the musnud of Bengal, 60. Death of Omichund, 61. Assassination of Suraj-u-Dowlah, ib. Count Lally arrives in India, April, 1758, with a French armament, 64. Capitulation of fort St. David, 65, 66. Conflans surrenders Masulipatam to the English, March, 1759 ; 71. Meer Jaffier opens a secret communication with the Dutch factory at Chinchura, 76. Battle of Bedarra, 1759 ; 78. Clive sails for England, Feb. 1760 ; Pondicherry is surrendered to colonel Coote, Jan. 1761 ; 81. Clive files a bill in Chancery against the Court of Directors, 83. He sails for the last time to India, and reaches Calcutta, May 3, 1765 ; 84. Meer Jaffier is deposed, and Meer Cossim Ali proclaimed nabob in his stead, 1760 ; 85. Ramnarrain, the governor of Patna, murdered by Meer Cossim, 86. Ellis takes the citadel of Patna, June 1763 ; Meer Jaffier re-instated on the musnud, 87. Battle of Geriah, between Meer Cossim and the English, August 2, 1763 ; ib. Massacre of 150 English, 88. Battle under the walls of Patna, ib. Sujah Dowla, nabob of Oude, who had taken Meer Cossim under his protection, is defeated by major Monro, October, 1764 ; ib. Death of Meer Jaffier, January, 1765 ; 89. Shah Alum is made governor of Allahabad and Corah, ib. Nujeem-ul-Dowlah, son of Meer Jaffier, appointed nabob of Bengal, but afterwards deposed, 90. Clive reforms many abuses in the management of Indian affairs, 91—94. Restrictions concerning double batta, 92. Origin of the fund for the support of disabled servants of the Company, 93. Clive departs from India for the last time, January, 1767 ; 94. Expeditions of Hyder Ali, the Mysorean, 95—99. Warren Hastings appointed second in council at Madras, March, 1769 ; 99. The city of Tanjore taken by the English, Sept. 16, 1773 ; 100. Inquiry into the conduct of lord Clive, 105. Bankruptcy of the Company, 1772; ib. Regulating Acts passed by parliament for the direction of East India affairs, 107. Warren Hastings is appointed first governor-general of Bengal, 1773 ; 108. Report of the select committee, 109—113. Clive, under the morbid influence of a diseased mind and body, puts an end to his life, Nov. 22, 1774 ; 113. Dreadful famine in India, 1770; 115. Mohammed Reza Khan, naib of Bengal, is arrested on divers charges, and conveyed to Calcutta, 1771; but being declared innocent, is acquitted, 116—120. Treaty of Allahabad, 121. Shah Alum takes the field with a numerous army, ib. He cedes Corah and Allahabad to the Mahrattas, 123. Devastations of the Senassie fakeers, ib. Negotiations between Hastings and the nabob of Oude, 1773; 125, 126. Beneficial effects of Hastings's administration, 127, 128. Invasion of the Rohilla country, 1774 ; 129. Change in the government of India, members of the new council; sir Elijah Impey one of the judges, 131. Continual disputes between the governor-general and the council, 132, et seq. Death of Sujah Dowla, 1775, and accession of his son, Asoff-ul-Dowla, 133. Island of Salsette seized by the English, 1773 ; ib. The council bring charges against Hastings, 1775 ; 135. Execution of Nuncomar, 137. Changes in the council, 140. Hazardous march of the English army from Calcutta to Bombay, 1778 ; 141. Taking of Gualior, a strong Mahratta fortress, 1780 ; 144. Cruelty of Hyder Ali towards his dewans, 146. Embarrassed state of the presidency of Madras, 147. Destruction of colonel Baillie's army at Conjeveram, ib. Flight of sir Hector Monro, 148. Sir Eyre Coote takes the command of fort St. George, ib. Destruction of Hyder's infant navy, 1781; 149. Lord Macartney lands at Fort St. George as governor of Madras, June 22,

India,—

1781 ; 150. Sir Edward Hughes takes the Island of Ceylon from the Dutch, ib. Arrival of M. de Suffrein with an army of veteran French troops, 1782; ib. Engagements between the French admiral (Suffrein) and sir E. Hughes, 150—156. Famine in the Carnatic, 153. Death of Hyder Ali, 1782, and accession of his son Tippoo, 154. General Mathews arrives at Bombay, 1783, and takes the command of the king's troops, ib. He is superseded, 155. Death of sir Eyre Coote, April 26; ib. Successes of colonel Fullarton, 156—161. Death of colonel Campbell, 163. Hastings, in great want of money, adopts the plan of *squeezing* the rajahs, 164, 165. The subjects of Cheyte Sing rise in arms, 165—167. Negotiations between Asoff-ul-Dowla, nabob of Oude, and the governor-general, 1784 ; the Treaty of Chunar, 169, 170. Tortures exercised upon Jewar Ali Khan and Behar Ali Khan, 171. Affairs of Fyzoola Khan, the last of the great Rohilla chiefs, 173, 174. The governor-general Hastings resigns, 1784; 188. Debates in parliament, 1788, concerning the establishment of royal troops in India without the assent of the Court of Directors, 255—258. War with Tippoo Saib; lord Cornwallis, the governor-general, besieges Bangalore, 1791; § iii. 28. Siege of Seringapatam, 29—33. Tippoo agrees to the terms proposed by the English, February 24, 1792; 31, 32. The definitive treaty signed March 15; 33. The Charter of the Company renewed, May 24, 1793 ; 281. Tippoo Sultaun is slain, May 4, 1799, in defending Seringapatam against the attack of general Harris, 550. The marquess of Wellesley turns his attention to the Mahratta states; they were then at war with each other, Holkar having defeated the Peishwa, § iv. 78. The Peishwa flies to Bombay, and sir Arthur Wellesley is sent by his brother to restore him, and succeeds, ib. Splendid victories gained by sir Arthur Wellesley and general Lake at Bokerdon, Delhi, and Laswarree, 79—84. The English arms in every part of India are victorious, and peace is successively made with all the native states, 84—86, 199—205. Judicious management of general Wellesley, and flourishing state of India, 86, 87.

INDULF, a Scottish king, was slain in battle with the Northmen in Banffshire, 961; i. 219.

Indulgence, Declaration of, Dec. 26, 1662; iii. 691.

Industry, history of the National ; manufactures, trade, and commerce. Of the Britons, under the Saxon Conquest (inclusive of Roman arts introduced by Cæsar's successors), i. 91—117. From 449 to 1066; 262. From 1066 to 1216; 584. From 1216 to 1399; 824. From 1399 to 1485; ii. 171. From 1485 to 1603 ; 771. From 1603 to 1660; iii. 527. From 1660 to 1688; 852. From 1688 to 1760; iv. 689. Reign of George III.: From 1760 to 1785; § i. 547. From 1785 to 1802; § iii. 628. From 1802 to 1820; § iv. 655.

Infantry, main strength of the British armies, i. 36. Charge of Roman infantry, 39.

INGLEBY, sir William, letter of James I. to the English councillors, on arriving, 1603, at Topcliff, the residence of, iii. 4.

INGULPHUS, monk of Croyland, citations from his History, i. 187, 257, 573, 609, 613.

INNES, Father, almoner to Maria d'Este, the Pretender's mother, iv. 208.

INNOCENT II., pope, elected February 15, 1130; his letter ratifying Stephen's title; he died Sept. 24, 1143; i. 422.

INNOCENT XII. (Antonio Pignatelli) pope, elected July 12, 1691. He advises Charles II. of Spain, to elect Philip duke of Anjou successor to his throne. He died Sept. 27, 1700 ; iv. 109.

Inquisition, the, first established at Rome by the advice of Paul IV., then cardinal Caraffa, a Neapo-litan, under the pontificate of Paul III. It obtained its greatest vigour during the pontificate of Paul IV. On the death of that odious pontiff in 1559, the Romans burned the tribunal of the holy office, liberated all prisoners for matters of religion, and razed the prisons of the Inquisition to the ground. The scene of its might was in Spain and Portugal ; whenever there was talk of introducing the tribunal into Naples, the Neapolitans rose in general insurrection and fought desperately with the Spaniards ; and the emperor Charles was forced to declare that he never had intended to establish the Inquisition, and never would, ii. 531, *note*.

Institutions and customs, no criterion of the lineage of a nation, i. 5.

Insurance, law of, § i. 537, § iii. 605, insurable property in Great Britain and Ireland, 714.

Insurance, Marine, earliest notice of (middle of the sixteenth century) ii. 786.

Intercursus Magnus, a mercantile treaty between England and the Flemings, about 1497 ; ii. 774.

Interest, reduced to six per cent, 1651; iii. 860.

Inverury, battle of, gained by Bruce, May 22, 1308 ; i. 735.

Iona, or I Columb Kill, a small island of the Hebrides. View of the ancient monastery, i. 221. Its abbots, 290. Considered as a seat of learning, St. Columba its founder, 220, 229, 290. The Culdees, 229, 244.

Ionian islands, captured by the English in 1809—1810; they were formed into a Republic under the protection of Great Britain by the peace of Paris, 1814 ; § iv. 402.

Ipswich, view of the gate-house of Wolsey's College at, ii. 814. Its foundation in 1509, and suppression on the cardinal's fall, 1529 ; together with Cardinal College, Oxford, 814, 815.

Ireland, disquisition on the many evidences of its primitive Celtic population, i. 12. The round towers said to be anterior to the first introduction of Christianity, ib. They prove an early civilization, probably derived from the east, 13. Ancient historians allude to the island under several names, 14, 15, 223. The Irish language a Celtic dialect, 15. Philological explanation of the name Eire or Erin, 16. Old traditions, 18. The Scoti, a name possibly connected with the Scythæ or Scythians of antiquity, occupied, about 200, the northern parts of Ireland, where their district was named Dalriada, 217. Carbry Riada, a Dalriadian, settled a colony of Scoti on the west coast of north Britain, ib. Erck, prince of Dalriada, ib. His sons Lorn, Fergus, and Angus, possessed themselves of the north of Caledonia, ib. History of the Scotic princes, their descendants, who finally made themselves kings over North Britain, and transferred thither the permanent name of Scotland, which had once designated Ireland, 217—223. The bardic account of the earliest settlers in Ireland looks to the date 600—500, n. c.; 223. Heber and Heremon, sons of Milesius, and their fabled Scotic followers, ib. Kings of all Ireland descended from Heremon, ib. Tacitus and Agricola alluded to, ib. St. Patrick overturned heathenism and Pagan worship in the island, in the early part of the fifth century; by his continued labours and preaching he firmly established Christianity, 223, 229. Leogaire MacNeil, reigned 428—463 ; he was the first Christian king, 223. In the reign of Donald III., the Danes or Norihmen, 748, made their first descent on the shores, ib. In 815 they established themselves in Armagh, ib. Turgesius, Norwegian king of Ireland, ib. Great massacre of the Danes, yet fresh invaders arrived and occupied the sea-board of the south and east, ib. Brien the Brave, king of Ireland, is killed by the Danes, 1014, at the

Ireland,—
battle of Clontarf, and is succeeded by Malachi, *ib.*
Death of Malachi, 1022, *ib.* Murtach, one of
the kings of Ireland dies, 1119; 459. Turlogh
O'Connor, called O'Connor the Great, king of Connaught, is acknowledged king of all Ireland, 1136,
ib. He divides Munster into two principalities,
after the battle of Moinmor, *ib.* Is succeeded by
Murtoch O'Lochlin as supreme king, 1156; *ib.*,
who is killed in battle, and succeeded by Roderick
O'Connor, 1166; *ib.* Dermond MacMurrogh,
king of Leinster, carries off Dergorvilla, the wife
of Tiernan O'Ruarc, 1153; 460. He is worsted by
O'Ruarc and flies his country, *ib.* He acknowledges
himself vassal to Henry II. of England, at Aquitaine,
1167; Henry grants him protection; he comes to England, engages with Richard de Clare, earl of Pembroke, called Strongbow, Maurice Fitzgerald, and
Robert Fitzstephen, for aid in his restoration; returns to Ireland, 461, 462. Is defeated, 1169, by Roderic and O'Ruarc, and accepts part of his former
territory as O'Ruarc's vassal, 463. He heads an English and Irish army, besieges Wexford, which surrenders, 1170; 462. Fitzstephen overcomes the district
of Ossory, *ib.* MacMurrogh is acknowledged king
of Leinster, 463. Maurice Fitzgerald arrives from
England, Dublin is reduced, *ib.* Raymond le Gros
lands in Waterford; he defeats the inhabitants,
464. Strongbow embarks at Milford Haven, with
a large force, and lands near Waterford; the city
is attacked and taken; Strongbow marries Eva, the
daughter of MacMurrogh; Dublin is taken;
Meath is overrun, *ib.* The English slaves in Ireland are set at liberty, 465. Proclamation of
Henry for the return of English, *ib.* Ireland
is invaded by the Danes; they attack Dublin, but
are defeated, *ib.* Dermond MacMurrogh dies, and
Strongbow assumes the title of king of Leinster in
right of his wife, *ib.* Lawrence, archbishop of
Dublin, causes a confederacy of native princes,
under the command of Roderick, to invest Dublin;
Strongbow cuts his way through the army of Roderick, which he routs, 465, 466. Fitzstephen is
besieged in Wexford, and surrenders, 466. Strongbow commanded by Henry to repair to Newnham;
he delivers up to the king Dublin and other forts, and
holds the rest in subjection to the English crown, *ib.*
Henry lands at Crook, near Waterford, with a large
army, 1171, and receives the submission of the
princes from all Ireland, except Ulster, 467. Hugh
de Lacy appointed governor of Dublin by the king
of England, who sails from Wexford and lands at
Portfinnan, in Wales, *ib.* General insurrection of
the Irish, 546. Ireland is acknowledged subject to
England, and the king of Ireland does homage,
1175; *ib.* The earl of Kildare, thrice lord-deputy
in the reign of Henry VIII., was finally called to
London, and imprisoned until his death, about
1534, of grief, caused by the unsuccessful rebellion
of his brothers, and of his son Thomas Fitzgerald,
ii. 425. Murder of Allen, archbishop of Dublin,
ib. Narrative of the daring rebellion of O'Connor
and the Fitzgeralds; execution of the latter,
425—427. Sequestration of monasteries, general
reform of the Irish church; archbishop Brown,
1538, repudiated all respects to papal authority, and
acknowledged the supremacy of Henry, 427. The
great rebellion, 1540, of O'Connor, O'Neil, and other
princes and chiefs, 428. The powerful chieftains
submit on receiving titles of nobility, and being admitted to the Irish Parliament, *ib.* In 1541, Henry
VIII. elevated Ireland, previously styled a lordship,
into a kingdom, *ib.* In the Irish rebellion of 1641,
50,000 Protestants are murdered, iii. 254. Change
in the Constitution of Ireland, § i. 539—543. Trade
with, 569—571. National Congress held at Dublin,
1784—5; § ii. 5.

IRELAND, Robert de Vere, duke of, receives the extraordinary grant of the whole revenue of Ireland,
from Richard II., 1385; out of which he was to
pay a yearly rent of 5,000 marks to the king,
i. 791. He makes his escape to the borders of
Wales, on the entry of Gloucester into London, and
receives letters from Richard, authorising him to
raise an army, and begin a civil war; he is defeated
by Gloucester, but escapes to Ireland, and thence to
Holland where he dies, 792.
IRELAND, William Henry, his Shakspere forgeries,
published 1795; § iii. 722.
IRELAND, father, executed 1678, on a charge of being
concerned in the Popish Plot, iii. 724.
IRETON, colonel, iii. 332, wounded at the battle of
Naseby, June 14, 1645; 333. He marries the
eldest daughter of Cromwell, 364. He dies in
Ireland, 419, *note.* His portrait, 495.
Irish brigade, the, iv. 171.
Irish chieftains, charge of, ii. 683.
Irish trade bill, the, 1785; § ii. 6.
Iron bridge at Colebrook Dale, completed 1779; § i.
586. View of, *ib.*
Iron manufactures, ii. 811; iii. 910; first furnace of
the Carron works blown, January 1760; § i. 584,
585. Sheffield and Birmingham manufactures, 587.
The Soho works established about 1762; *ib.*; § iii.
676—680; § iv. 689.
ISAAC, emperor of Cyprus; Richard I. of England in
his expedition conquers the island, and confines the
emperor in a castle at Tripoli, i. 495.
ISABELLA, queen of Edward II., and daughter of
Philip le Bel, of France, married at Boulogne,
January 25, 1308; i. 732. She persuades the king
to permit her to go to France, to settle the differences
which had arisen between him and her brother the
French king, March 1325; 742. Refuses to return,
and lays many charges against her husband, *ib.*
Her connection with Mortimer becomes notorious,
and she is ordered by king Charles to quit his
dominions, *ib.* She takes shelter with the count of
Hainault, from the feigned anger of her brother, *ib.*
Affiances the prince of Wales to Philippa, second
daughter of that count, *ib.* John Hainault, a young
brother of the count, takes part with Isabella, and
collects a small army, 743. The earl of Kent, the
king's own brother, the earl of Richmond, his
cousin, the lord Beaumont, and the bishop of
Norwich, all join the queen in the Low Countries,
though they had been sent by Edward as his trusty
ambassadors into France, *ib.* Orleton, bishop of
Hereford, effects a reconciliation between the Lancastrian party and the barons, who of late had
supported the royal cause, and raises a general
outcry against the personal vices of Edward, *ib.*
On the 24th of September they land at Orewell,
in Suffolk, with a small army, and are joined
by the earl of Norfolk with many other barons,
ib. The Londoners refuse to follow Edward
to the field; he flies, accompanied only by the two
Despensers and the chancellor Baldock, *ib.* The
elder Despenser is taken prisoner at Bristol, and
hanged as a traitor, *ib.* The prince of Wales is
declared guardian of the kingdom by a general
council of the prelates and barons, September
24, 1325; 744. He is crowned at Westminster,
January 29, 1327; 745. The parliament and
regency grant the queen 20,000*l.* a year, 1327; 748.
Queen Isabella and Mortimer monopolise nearly
the whole power of government, 749. Mortimer
is created earl of March, the regency is displaced,
and the power of Mortimer and the queen increases,
751. Lancaster opposes the unconstitutional impositions of the favourite, *ib.* He is joined by the
earls of Kent and Norfolk, the king's uncles, but
they soon abandon him and he is compelled to ask
pardon in a humiliating manner, and to pay an

ISABELLA, queen of Edward II., — immense fine, 752. The earl of Kent is executed for treason, 753. Young Edward forms a plan with lord Montacute for asserting his authority, ib. Mortimer is executed as a traitor, November 29, 1330. Edward takes the government into his own hands, the queen-mother is deprived of her enormous jointure, and shut up in her castle or manor-house at Risings, where she passed the remaining twenty-seven years of her life in obscurity, 755.

ISABELLA, queen of Richard II., and daughter of Charles VI. of France, ii. 7; still but ten years of age, at the time of her husband's deposition and death, ib. Her being left an unprotected widow in England, causes the French king great uneasiness. ib. Burgundy and Bourbon, on this occasion, governing for the imbecile Charles, attack Guienne, 7, 8. French embassy to demand this princess, and her dower, 9. Henry IV. unable to pay this obligation of his predecessor, 1401, proposes to unite her to Henry prince of Wales, which the French king Charles declines, ib. Isabella was safely conducted to Calais, with only her jewels, ib. Orleans, her uncle, 1402, challenges king Henry, in her cause, 12. Her marriage with Charles of Angoulême, eldest son of Orleans, 19. Festivities, ib. She became the duchess of Orleans in 1407; next year she expired in childbirth, 20, 21.

ISABELLA, queen of Charles VI. of France, cohabits openly with the imbecile king's brother d'Orleans, 1405, and they rule France in his name, ii. 17. Her grief for the assassination of d'Orleans by the duke of Burgundy's orders, 20. She retires to Melun, to form some plan of revenge, ib. Her depravity, 37. Her paramour Bois-Bourdon tortured by the king's order, and thrown in a bag into the Seine, 38. She is carried to Tours and kept prisoner, ib. The queen, through anger at the Dauphin and Constable, who had secured her treasure, leagues with the duke of Burgundy, 1417; ib. She escapes from her prison, and proceeds with Burgundy to Tours, etc., 40. Her proclamations, she has a Great Seal prepared, etc., ib. Her court, 41. A family peace, 1418, under the mediation of Martin V., ib. At Meulan, the queen, princess Catherine, and Burgundy, have a stately meeting with Henry V., which is interrupted after several days' conference, by her evasion with the princess, 44. She and Burgundy had meantime concluded a treaty with the dauphin, ib. She expired in Paris, 1435, in poverty and obscurity, 79.

ISABELLA, daughter of the count of Angoulême, wife of Hugh count de la Marche, i. 517. Marries king John, and is crowned at Westminster, ib. 674. On the death of the king, 1216, she returns to Guienne, and is remarried to the count of la Marche with great pomp, 674.

ISABELLA CLARA EUGENIA, Infanta of Spain, and daughter of Philip II.; her claim to the English succession through her descent from John of Gaunt, ii. 680. She marries the archduke Albert, 685.

Ismael, storming of, by the Russian General Suvaroff, December 1790; 30,000 inhabitants perished, § ii. 475, 476.

IVAN, the czar, son of Anne, grand-daughter of Peter the Great's elder brother, by Anthony Ulric of Brunswick; he was born in August 1740; on the death of his aunt Anne, he succeeded to the throne, but at the end of 1741, when he had reigned fifteen months, he was deposed by Elizabeth, and detained a state-prisoner, being carried about from one castle to another till 1764, when, an attempt at his release having been made by Vassili Mirovitch, he was murdered by his guards, § i. 132, 133.

JACKSON, Mr., English ambassador at Sweden, arrested by order of Charles XII., in retaliation of a similar arrest in England, iv. 338.

JACKSON, general, commander of the American forces at New Orleans, in which they repelled all the attempts of the English to gain possession of that town, and forced them to retreat, Jan. 1815; § iv, 675°. Elected president of the United States, ib.

Jacobin Club, the (formerly the Breton Club), obtained the name on taking possession of the Great Hall in the Convent of the Jacobins, 1789; § ii. 437. The Society is suppressed, Oct. 18, 1794; § iii. 453.

Jacobins, view of the Convent of the, § ii. 437. Reign of the, in France, 1790; 489, 599.

JACQUETTA, of Luxembourg, her marriage, 1433, with the regent, Bedford, ii. 77, 80, note. Death of the duke at Rouen, 1435; 79. Her second husband was sir Richard Woodville, 80, note, 102. She was visited at her manor of Grafton, Stony-Stratford, by Edward IV., 101. The young king then became deeply enamoured of her beautiful daughter, the widow of sir John Gray, ib. Edward's marriage with Elizabeth Woodville, May 1, 1464; 101. Sir Richard appointed lord high-constable, 102.

JAFFIER, Meer, a servant of Suraj-u-Dowlah, his services to the English, § ii. 55; et seq. He is made nabob of Bengal after the battle of Plassey, 1757; iv. 599, § ii. 61. He opens secret communications with the Dutch factory at Chinchura, 76. He is deposed, 1760, and Meer Cossim Ali proclaimed, 85. Is re-instated in his dignity, 1763; 87. His death, Jan. 1765, 89.

Jamaica, taken by the English, 1655; iii. 420.

JAMES I., king of England, was the son of Mary queen of Scotland by her cousin Henry lord Darnley. He was born at Edinburgh Castle, June 19, 1566. Ascended the Scottish throne, July 24, 1567; became king of England, March 24, 1603; his reign over both kingdoms terminated, March 27, 1625; ii. 588. His baptism, 589. His mother is made to sign a deed by which she resigns the crown in his favour, being then about fourteen months old, 604. Ceremony of his coronation; the earl of Murray is appointed regent during his minority, ib. The young king being in his 13th year, is declared of age, 1578. Morton, the regent, retires to Lochleven Castle, and soon contrives to gain possession of the young king; the earls of Argyle and Athole raise an army to his rescue, but the English ambassador interferes and makes up a reconciliation; the earl of Athole is shortly after poisoned by Morton at a banquet, 652. Esmé Stuart, lord of Aubigny, and brother of the earl of Lennox, becomes a favourite of the youthful James; but under him there was a minor favourite James Stuart, son of lord Ochiltree, whom James creates earl of Arran, and who persuades him to execute the earl of Morton, as a murderer of his father; several powers interfere in favour of the regent, who was generally deemed a sturdy Protestant, but, after all, he is abandoned to his fate, 652, 653. Money is sent to James from Spain and Rome, 653. The earl of Gowrie invites the young king to his castle of Ruthven, and makes him a close prisoner; the authority of the state then devolves on the earl of Marr and others; Arran is thrown into a dungeon, and Lennox escapes to France where he dies; James recovers his liberty, and formally pardons all concerned in the Raid of Ruthven, 654. His coldness to the fate of his mother; the king of France urges him to exert himself in her favour, and accordingly he sends over Keith, a pensionary of England, to intercede for her, 665. On first hearing of his mother's death, it is said this royal pedant burst into tears, and threatened to move heaven and earth for vengeance; but his mighty wrath soon evaporated, and he sat

JAMES I.,—
down quite contented with an increase of the pension which Elizabeth had long been paying him, and with a hope that his dutiful conduct would clear all obstructions to his succession to the English throne, on the death of its present occupant, 671. On receiving news of the death of the earl of Essex, he sends ambassadors to exculpate him to Elizabeth from any share in the late attempt, and to intrigue with her ministers, 691. Cecil undertakes to enter into a secret correspondence with him, which the lord Henry Howard undertakes to conduct, 692. James obtains an addition of 2,000*l.* to his pension, *ib.* He was proclaimed king of England, March 24, 1603, by the title of James I., iii. 2, 3. His portrait, after Vandyke, 2. He is apprised by sir Robert Carey of Elizabeth's death four days previous to the arrival of sir Charles Percy and Thomas Somerset, dispatched to him by Cecil and the council, *ib.* Until the arrival of these latter, James commands the secret to be kept, although some other officious messengers intervened, *ib.* Thirty-six signatures (some are named) to the Proclamation; Cecil, at the head of these personages, read it to the people at Whitehall, and at the High Cross in Cheapside, 3. Cecil sends heralds and a trumpet into the Tower there to proclaim James I., to the great joy and hopes of the state prisoners, *ib.* Account of the supposed claim of the descendant of Mary, duchess of Suffolk, sister of Henry VIII., to the English crown, 3, *note.* Doubts of the signature by that monarch to a will, by which he entailed the reversion of the crown on the heir of the houses of Suffolk, Somerset, and Hertford, *ib.* The title of lady Arabella Stuart considered by many as at least equal to that of James, she being an Englishwoman, and descended from Henry VII. equally with himself, 3, 9. Measures of Cecil to repress such rival claims, 3, 8. James receives remittances from Cecil for his progress from Edinburgh; he asks that Elizabeth's crown jewels should be sent to him for his queen, which the English council decline, 3, 4. (*See* Anne of Denmark.) On April 6th he departs without her for Berwick, 4. At Berwick he fired off a piece of ordnance with his own hand; he wrote to the English council to thank them for the money sent to him, and announcing his intention of a solemn entry into York, and a sojourn there, *ib.* He alludes to the ceremony of Elizabeth's interment, *ib.* Lord Hunsdon being ill, he appoints lord Howard de Walden his lord-chamberlain, *ib.* Travelling slowly, he reached Newcastle, April 13, whence he gave minute directions for a gold and silver coinage to be prepared, as customary, for the day of his coronation, 4, 552. His letter from sir W. Ingleby, at Topcliff, to certain of the council, shows his vexation, 4. He sojourns three days at York, where he confers with Cecil, *ib.* His ideas of the royal prerogative, *ib.* April 21, 1603, at Newark-upon-Trent, he issues his warrant to hang a cutpurse taken in the fact, who suffers death without trial, *ib.* Hunting at Belvoir Castle, and being an unskilful horseman, he is thrown; Cecil's flattering version of the accident, *ib.* The courtiers, on his nearer approach, flock to him : first impressions of the monarch on sir Francis Bacon, who describes his character, in a letter, *ib.* His features and awkward personal carriage, excite sarcasms from many, 5. Enumeration of the many knights made by king James during his procrastinated journey, *ib.*; a practice he continued, until within three months there were 700 new knights, also four earls and nine barons created, *ib.* May 3, the king receives the late queen's council, at Theobald's, the residence of Cecil, *ib.* His first cabinet formed, to which he adds four Scottish

JAMES I.,—
lords, and secretary Elphinstone, *ib.* Names of the new ministers, and of the disappointed aspirants; jealousy as to the employment of Scots, *ib.* May 7, the city corporation conduct him in state from Stamford-hill to the Charter-house, *ib.* His proclamations to suspend all monopolies recently granted, as well as the "royal protections" against suits at law, *ib.* His proclamation against killing of deer, and wild-fowl, *ib.* His language remarked as denoting a latent hatred and contempt of Elizabeth, 6. June, 1603, the king meets his queen Anne (Anne of Denmark), and all his children, except prince Charles, still in Scotland, *ib.* The eldest prince, Henry, by his sensible conversation and manners, pleases the court then held at Windsor Castle, *ib.* July 22, king James removes to Whitehall, and in its gardens he knights all the judges, serjeants-at-law, doctors of civil law, and many others, *ib.* His coronation, and queen Anne's, at Westminster, July 25, with a representation thereof from an old Dutch engraving, *ib.* The citizens of London, on account of the plague fearfully raging there, are forbidden access to Westminster, on this ceremony, *ib.* August 5, thanksgiving-prayers are offered up for the Scottish king's escape, three years antecedently, from the earl of Gowrie, *ib.* A fast commanded for each Wednesday, until the plague should cease, 6, 7. Special embassies relative to the Low Countries, Dutch provinces, etc., arrive from Holland, Austria, and Spain, also from Henri IV. of France, 7. James I. institutes a Master of the Ceremonies; sir Lewis Lewknor the first to fill the new office, *ib.* Tempted by Rosni to treat with Henri IV., he finds that he has no pecuniary resources for taking the field, and so resolves to live at peace, *ib.* Conspiracy to surprise the king on his way to Windsor, 1603, and by keeping him in the hands of a party of malcontents, to cause the downfall of Cecil, *ib.* In the state trials that ensued, two ramifications of this plot were investigated : one called the "Bye," for which Watson and Clarke, secular priests, Brooke, brother to lord Cobham, sir Griffin Markham, a Catholic, Anthony Copley, a Catholic gentleman, and others, were indicted; the "Main" plot, included sir Walter Raleigh, lords Grey of Wilton, and Cobham, 8, 9, *et seq.* (*See* the names of conspirators, for their several punishments, and participation in this treason). June 24, when the king was to have been seized, lord Grey's horsemen were not at the rendezvous, 8. Cecil meeting Raleigh on the terrace at Windsor, summoned him before the council in the castle, 8, 9. Sir Walter denies any knowledge of treasonable practice, and says that La Rensy, in d'Aremberg's service, might know something of Cobham's dealings with that ambassador, 9. Raleigh dismissed free, has the imprudence to warn Cobham, and this letter is intercepted by Cecil, *ib.* November 1603, the trials for the "Bye" Plot are holden at Winchester, when the two priests, and all arraigned under that accusation, are condemned, *ib.* Detailed account of the trial of Raleigh, 9. Execution of Rooke, and the priests Watson and Clarke, 13. James at this time shows mercy to Raleigh, also to Grey and Cobham, sending them to the Tower ; Markham and Brookesby, also condemned, he orders to quit his dominions, 13, 14. His messenger with the reprieve, sent at the latest moment to Winchester, arrives only just in time, 14. The strange proceedings of the sheriff, when Grey of Wilton, Cobham, and Markham were twice led to the scaffold, and the unusual courage shown by Cobham, gave scope for speculation that cannot now be rendered clear, *ib.* Perhaps James wished to show his sagacity, in procuring a new confession

JAMES I.,—

by lord Cobham in sight of the axe, many perhaps being incredulous as to the plot having ever existed, 14, 15. Religious parties: the Puritans and Presbyterians, 8, 15. The Roman Catholics, *ib.* James declares himself against toleration, 8, 12, 15. In his own country, forced to be subservient to the puritanical sect, he is (in England) zealous, in 1603, to enter into controversy against them, they having petitioned for a conference, 15. His speeches, 1590, at Edinburgh, in praise of the puritanical forms, *ib.* James changed the constitution of the Scottish church, 1598, by admitting certain of the clergy to seats in parliament, which was some approximation to an episcopalian church, 16. His " Basilicon Doron " characterised, *ib.*; in it he cautions prince Henry against Puritans, *ib.* Curious controversy, held at Hampton, January 14, 1604; king James and the Anglican prelates in argument with the reforming doctors, Reynolds, Sparks, Knewstube, and Chatterton, *ib.* Triumph of the king, who, though fond of polemics, orders that none shall speak to him of religion on his *hunting* days, 17. He orders all Nonconformist preachers to be expelled their churches; several of those who had presented the " Millenary Petition " carried before the Star-chamber, and, with many unlicensed preachers, imprisoned, *ib.* The king makes some slight alterations in the Book of Common Prayer and the church service, *ib.* He appoints Dr. Bancroft primate, on the death of Whitgift, the late archbishop, *ib.* His notion of the divine right of kings, and their supreme control of parliaments, given by him in his work long previously published, " On the True Law of Free Monarchies ; or, the Reciproque and Mutual Duty betwixt a Free King and his Natural Subjects," 18. Its doctrines, *ib.* His first parliament assembled, March 19, 1604; *ib.* It swarmed with Puritans, notwithstanding the king's commands to the electors, *ib.* Case of privilege: sir Francis Goodwin's election for Buckinghamshire; his return sent back to the sheriff, Goodwin having been outlawed; sir John Fortescue then elected, *ib.* The House of Commons declare Goodwin to be the representative; they refuse a proposed conference with the Lords, *ib.* James, " as an absolute king," compels the Commons to confer with the judges, in his and his council's presence, *ib.* Compromise ; both elections conceded to be void, 18, 19. Inquiries into monopolies, feudal tenure, and wardships to the king, and especially the abuses of purveyance, 19. Tonnage and poundage granted, *ib.* Statutes against Papists severely enforced, *ib.* July 7, prorogation, *ib.* James's predilection for hunting keeps him for long periods at Royston and Newmarket, to the detriment of public business (1604), *ib.* Facetious missive attached to the collar of the hound Jowler, *ib.* Letters of archbishop Hutton, Cecil, and Worcester on this immoderate following of the chase, 20. The king lets loose Cecil, " his little beagle," against the Puritans, who tormented him with petitions, *ib.* He investigated the case of the impostor Haddock, said to preach admirably when asleep, *ib.* The GUN-POWDER PLOT, 1604, 1605 ; 20—33. (*See* details under ' Gunpowder Plot,' and the names of the chief conspirators.) King James asks Guido Fawkes how he could entertain the thought of destroying his children, and so many innocent persons ; the reply, 27. Vulgar report that he was the first to decipher the mysterious meaning of the warning letter to Mounteagle, *ib.* Execution of Digby, Fawkes, Rookwood, and others, 29, 30. Capture, trial, and execution of Garnet, superior of the English Jesuits, 30—32. The king witnesses the trial from a closet, 31. Garnet executed, and many Catholics, for harbouring priests, and like offences, 32. Mordaunt, Montague, and Stourton arbitrarily fined in the Star-

JAMES I.,—

chamber, and imprisoned, on suspicion that they, being Catholic peers, intended to absent themselves, November 5th, from Parliament, as if cognizant of some danger, *ib.* Henry, earl of Northumberland, is fined 30,000*l.*, and sentenced to the Tower for life, on unfounded jealousies entertained by the king and Star-chamber, *ib.* Extreme penalties against Catholic recusants, *ib.* New oath of allegiance, renouncing the temporal power of the pope, or his right to meddle with English affairs, 33. Paul V. furbade Catholics by a *breve* to take such oath, *ib.* Drury, a priest, executed; Blackwall, aged 70, sent to gaol, wherein he dies, *ib.* The king publishes " An Apology for the Oath of Allegiance," and thinks that he has defeated the Jesuit Parsons, and Bellarmo, in a controversy on this matter, *ib.* His parliament sits again, January 21, 1606; they pass severer enactments against Catholic recusants ; the new oath of allegiance, 32. The king proposes to marry his son Henry to a Spanish princess, which gives great umbrage to Puritans and others, *ib.* The Commons present a list of grievances, the king evades all reply ; the House refrains from a subsidy, 33. A rumour is at this moment officiously circulated of the king's assassination at Oaking, Berks, *ib.* Surmise why the *bruit* was falsely spread ; the Commons grant subsidies, and parliament is prorogued to 18th Nov., *ib.* Arrival of Christian IV. of Denmark, brother-in-law of king James, July 1606, *ib.* Festivities, tilts, excesses in wine, *ib.* Next arrives the prince Vaudemont, a kinsman by the house of Guise, with a great retinue; and after festivities and hunts, departs, 34. Doctrines unpalatable to the Presbyterians broached, although James was devising an intimate union betwixt Scotland and England, *ib.* His wish to bring the Scottish kirk into conformity with the Anglican episcopal church, alienates all Scotland from even a political union (1606), *ib.* The English also were annoyed by James having lavished titles, offices, and money, on his Scottish followers, 35. Speeches in parliament violent against the Union, *ib.* In 1604, the commissioners of both countries had agreed to abrogate all hostile laws between the two kingdoms, to abolish border-courts and customs, *ib.* A decision in the courts of law extends the rights of naturalization to all Scots who were *post-nati*, or born after the king's accession, *ib.* Although the king was desirous of dictating an instant union, all the rest of the international relations were necessarily consigned to the action of time, *ib.* James rudely addresses parliament, threatens to abandon London, and make York or Berwick his royal residence, *ib.* Representations of the House of Commons, on this dispute, demanding liberty in their speeches in parliament, *ib.* The king replies with more complacency, *ib.* The Commons, about to read a petition sent to them against ecclesiastical abuses, are restrained by their Speaker, *ib.* Committee to search for precedents relative to royal messages touching petitions, *ib.* Both king and Commons concede a point in this matter, *ib.* Petition of English merchants, who had grievously suffered by the Spaniards, especially in the New World, 35, 36. A committee of the Commons report thereupon; demand a conference with the House of Lords; Cecil, now a peer, the chief speaker for the Lords, 36. The Commons are told that they have their own especial and local duties relating to the subjects each represents, but are not fit to examine or determine secrets of state, *ib.* The Commons give up the merchants' petition, and an outcry ensues, as James betrays a further leaning to Spain, *ib.* Prorogation, July 4, 1607, until November ; but this parliament did not meet again until February, 1610, *ib.* Rising of " Levellers " in the midland counties,

JAMES I.,—

May, 1607, who levelled all fences and hedges in recent inclosures of commons, ib. Otherwise the poor people committed no offence whatever, ib. They resist a charge by a military force, but are dispersed, and numbers slain, ib. Their leader, a madman, is executed, ib. Robert Carr becomes a favourite of the king, and receives the honour of knighthood, December 24, 1607; 38. Troops levied in England for the service of the Spaniards and the archduke Albert, 39. Poverty of the Crown, ib. Cecil is appointed treasurer, 1608 ; ib. Oppressive monopolies and taxes, 1609 ; 40. Parliament meets, February 14, 1610; the king summons both Houses before him at Whitehall; the Commons insist on the right of parliament to levy taxes, 40, 41. The Commons petition against the High Commission Court, and other grievances, 42. 200,000l. per annum granted to the king upon giving up the right of wardship, purveyance, and other privileges, 43. The bishops and clergy at Canterbury vote the king a subsidy of six shillings in the pound, 45. Private marriage between William Seymour and lady Arabella Stuart, contrary to the express command of the king; lady Arabella is committed to the Tower, and Seymour escapes to France, 46, 47. Lady Arabella dies mad in the Tower, September, 1615; 47. The king procures the exile of Vorstius from the Low Countries, 47, 48. Legate, an Arian, is burned in Smithfield, March 1, 1612; 48. Wightman burned for heresy at Lichfield, ib. Viscount Rochester is made a privy-councillor and knight of the Garter, 49. Carr is made lord-chamberlain, ib. Prince Henry falls sick and dies, November 6; 51, 52. The king prohibits any one to approach him in mourning, 52. The princess Elisabeth is married to the count palatine Frederic V., November 1, 1613; ib. The king exacts the old feudal aid for her marriage, ib. Gives lord Harrington a grant to coin base farthings in brass, ib. Sir Thomas Overbury is committed to the Tower, April 21, 1613; 53. The countess of Essex sues for a divorce; a commission of delegates is appointed by the king, ib. Sir T. Overbury dies in the Tower, September 24; 54. The marriage of the earl and countess of Essex is declared null and void, ib. Carr is created earl of Somerset, November 4; ib. Somerset and the countess of Essex are married at Whitehall, December 26. The order of baronets is created, 1611; peerages are sold, 54, 55. Parliament is assembled, April 5; the Commons demand a conference with the Lords on the right of the king to tax the subject; the Lords demand the opinion of the judges; the judges, headed by Coke, the chief-justice, refuse to give an opinion; the Lords decline the conference, 55. The king demands supplies, which the Commons refuse to vote unless their grievances should be redressed ; the king dissolves the parliament, June 7; 56. Five of the members of the late House of Commons are committed to the Tower, ib. Death of the earl of Northampton ; George Villiers appears at court; he gains the favour of the king, and is made royal cup-bearer, 57. Is knighted, 1615; 58. The king grants to Somerset a pardon for all treasons, felonies, etc., which he might hereafter commit ; chancellor Ellesmere refuses to put the great seal to it, ib. Somerset is committed to the Tower, ib. Examination into the death of sir T. Overbury; Weston, Mrs. Turner, Franklin, and Elwes, are tried for the murder, and hanged at Tyburn, 58, 59. The countess of Somerset is arraigned, May 24, 1616 ; she pleads Guilty, and is condemned to death, but pardoned, 61, 62. The earl of Somerset is brought to trial, and declared guilty, 61. Sir Edward Coke is disgraced, and Montague made chief-justice, 62, 63. Lord Ellesmere is created viscount Brackley, 63. Murder of Concini, marshal d'Ancre, ib. Villiers

JAMES I.,—

is created earl of Buckingham, January 5, 1617; ib. Chancellor Brackley resigns the seals, and shortly after dies, ib. Francis Bacon is made lord-keeper, ib. Several cautionary towns restored to the Dutch for 2,700,000 florins, 64. King James arrives in Scotland (June); he calls a parliament; an Act is prepared to declare that whatever should be determined by the king, with the advice of the bishops and clergy, relating to ecclesiastical affairs, should have the force of law; the clergy remonstrate; the parliament is dissolved, 66. James attends a great meeting of the clergy at St. Andrew's; Simpson, Ewart, and Calderwood, three of the remonstrants, are punished by the High Commission Court, ib. The king attempts to impose upon the Scottish kirk the ceremonies of the English church, ib. The matter is referred to a general meeting of the kirk ; ib. James returns to England, ib. On his way back he publishes his " Book of Sports," and appoints it to be read in the churches, 67. Lord Coke's daughter is married to sir John Villiers, 70. Coke is restored to the council-table, ib. Bacon is made lord-chancellor, January 4, 1618 ; ib. He is created baron Verulam, 70. Sale of peerages, 70, 71. Villiers is created marquess of Buckingham, made lord-high-admiral, warden of the cinque ports, etc., 71. The earl and countess of Suffolk are committed to the Tower, ib. They are brought before the Star-chamber and fined; recommitted to the Tower, and afterwards released, ib. Raleigh and his companions recover Guiana, November 13, 1617; 74. Disputes with the Spaniards; the town of St. Thomas is burned; captain Keymis shoots himself, 75. Sir W. Raleigh anchors at Plymouth, June, 1618; he is arrested and carried to London ; makes an unsuccessful attempt at escape ; is lodged in the Tower, 75, 76. He is examined by the privy-council, 77. Is brought to the Court of King's Bench to receive judgment for the treason committed in 1603 ; execution is granted, and Raleigh is beheaded in Old Palace-yard, October 29, 1618; 77—79. The Elector Palatine is made king of Bohemia, November, 1619 ; 81. Parliament meets, January 30, 1621. James asks supplies for the war in the palatinate, ib. The Commons vote the supplies; they attack the monopolists ; commit sir Francis Mitchell to the Tower ; the Lords adjudge him and sir Giles Mompesson to be degraded, fined, and imprisoned, 82. Yelverton is imprisoned for life, ib. Bacon is created viscount St. Albans, ib. He is impeached for corruption, ib. He is fined 40,000l. and committed to the Tower during the king's pleasure, 83. Edward Floyde, a Catholic, is severely punished, and committed to Newgate for life, 84. Bishop Williams is made lord-keeper, 85. The king abolishes thirty-six oppressive monopolies and patents, ib. Sir Robert Mansell sails to Algiers, burns some shipping, and returns home, ib. Parliament re-assembles, ib. The earls of Oxford and Southampton, and others, are committed to prison without trial, 86. The king reproves the Commons for questioning his commitments, and for objecting to the marriage of the prince of Wales with the infanta of Spain, 87. Parliament dissolved by proclamation, 1622; 88. Coke and sir Robert Phillips are committed to the Tower; Selden, Pym, and Mallery, to other prisons, ib. The king issues pardons for recusancy to all Catholics who should apply, 89. The prince of Wales and Buckingham proceed to Spain, 1623; 91. The king releases all the seminary priests and Jesuits from the London prisons, ib. Charles is received at Madrid by the royal family of Spain, 93, 94. King James offers to acknowledge the pope chief bishop on certain conditions, 95. He swears to observe whatever articles should be agreed upon in his name by prince Charles, 97. The infanta Donna

Y

JAMES I.,—
Maria adopts the style of princess of England, 98.
The prince and Buckingham land at Portsmouth,
October 5; 99. The prince refuses to marry the
infanta, 100. The earl of Bristol is commanded to
retire to his house in the country as a prisoner, ib.
Parliament assembles, February 19, 1624; the king
demands supplies to prosecute a war with Spain;
they are voted, to be applied by a parliamentary
committee; strict orders are issued against all Catholics, 102. The earl of Middlesex is impeached,
fined, and imprisoned, 103. The Spanish ambassador remonstrates with the king on the conduct of
Buckingham, 103, 104. Troops are raised for the
recovery of the Palatinate, 105, 106. Several Englishmen massacred by the Dutch at Amboyna, 105.
An embassy is sent to France, 1625, to negotiate a
marriage between the princess Henrietta Maria and
prince Charles, 106. The match is concluded, and
liberty of conscience promised to the Catholics, 107.
Declining health of the king; he dies at Theobalds,
March 27, 1625; the prince of Wales is immediately
proclaimed, 108 .Illustrations: The Great Seal, 86.
Procession to St. Paul's, 475. The king lying in
state in Westminster-hall, 108. Fac-simile of his
signature, 432*. Coins, 550.
JAMES II. (Feb. 6, 1685—Dec. 11, 1688), born Oct.
1633, and immediately created duke of York, iii.
279. After the capture of Oxford by the parliamentary army in 1648, James escaped, 381; note,
383. He encounters the Dutch fleet, under the
command of admiral Opdam, 1665; 695. Surrenders his office of high-admiral on the passing of
the Test Act, 1673; 711. The Exclusion Bills,
729. The Duke of York is made king's commissioner for Scotland, 738; he narrowly escapes being
drowned when returning to England in 1681; ib.
His cruel proceedings in Scotland, ib. 756. Accession of James II., 1685; he immediately calls
the council and addresses them, promising to support the government in church and state, 763.
He is proclaimed, ib. Attends mass in state, and
orders Huddleston, a priest, to publish a relation
of the late king having died in the Romish
faith, ib. Moral improvement in the court, ib.
Narrative of the Rye-house Plot, published
by command of the king, 765. Excise and
other duties levied, without authority of parliament, ib. Papists and Non-conformists discharged from prison by royal warrant, ib. The
king receives money from the French court, ib.
Scruples entertained concerning the Coronation
Oath; the opinion of the pope demanded, ib. The
coronation ceremony performed by Sancroft, archbishop of Canterbury, April 23, 1685; ib. Titus
Oates tried for perjury and severely punished, 766.
Dangerfield convicted of libel; fined, whipped, and
pilloried, 767. The Scottish parliament assembles;
customs granted to the king, ib. A rebel band
from Holland, headed by Argyle, lands in the
Western Isles, and proclaims James an usurper, ib.
Frances, a barrister, executed for murder, ib.
The king opens parliament, May 22; renews his
promises; the Commons vote him 1,200,000l. for
life, ib. The earl of Argyle lands in Scotland,
declares he comes to re-establish the Covenant;
he is routed by lord Dumbarton, near Glasgow,
769. Argyle is captured, and taken to Edinburgh Castle, June 2, ib.; beheaded, June
30. Richard Rumbald is tried and executed
as a traitor, ib.; 770. Sir John Cochrane condemned, but pardoned, 770. Cruelties committed
in Scotland, ib. The duke of Monmouth lands at
Lyme, June 4, declaring he comes to secure the
Protestant religion, and to deliver the country from
the tyranny of James duke of York, 771. He
assumes the title of king, June 20, 773; proceeds

JAMES II.,—
through several parts of the west, 773—775; he
is declared a rebel, 773. Battle of Sedgemoor, July
5, 1685; 775. Lord Grey and the duke of Monmouth are captured, 776. A Bill of Attainder
passes both Houses, 777; Monmouth is beheaded on
Tower-hill, July 15, 778. Cruelties committed by
lord Feversham and colonel Kirk, 779. Judge
Jeffreys is raised to the peerage, by the title of baron
Jeffreys of Wem, 780. Mrs. Alicia Lisle is tried
for harbouring two of the fugitives of Sedgmoor,
and beheaded, Sept. 3, 781. Death of the lord-
keeper North, ib. Jeffreys is made lord-chancellor,
ib. Hundreds of rebels are executed, and many
are sold as slaves, 781, 782. Cornish is tried at the
Old Bailey for the Rye-house Plot, and executed,
783. Elizabeth Gaunt is burned at Tyburn, and
Lindsay hanged on Tower-hill, ib. Lords Brandon,
Delamere, and Stamford, proceeded against for high
treason, ib. Halifax is deprived of office, ib. The
session of parliament opens, Nov. 9. John Kok is
committed to the Tower; both Houses address the
king to discharge all officers who refuse to take the
Protestant Test, 784. Parliament prorogued. Nov.
20, ib. Embassy from Rome received in London, 785.
Papists are openly admitted to all the offices of the
state, 1786, and 4,000 Protestant soldiers cashiered, ib.
Similar proceedings take place in Scotland and Ireland, ib. The king issues letters mandatory to the
English bishops, forbidding the clergy to preach on
controversial points, and establishing an ecclesiastical commission, ib. Sancroft refuses to act, 786.
Compton, bishop of London, is suspended, ib. Tyrconnel made lord-deputy of Ireland, ib. James attempts to deprive the princess of Orange of her right
to the succession, ib. The governors of the Charter-
house refuse to admit a papist without the Oath,
1687; ib. The fellows of Magdalen College refuse
to elect a papist their Master, ib. The king issues
a declaration of liberty of conscience, 787. Pechell,
the vice-chancellor of Cambridge, is suspended
by the Ecclesiastical-Commission Court, ib. The
king cites the fellows of Magdalen College before
him at Oxford, ib. The pope's nuncio is publicly
introduced at court, 788. James issues writs of
quo warranto against the charters of the proprietors and corporations in the Anglo-American
colonies, ib. He makes a pilgrimage to St. Win-
ifred's Well in Wales, ib. The king publishes a
new declaration, 1688, and commands the clergy
to read it in the churches, 789. Several bishops
petition the king against the measure, May 18, ib.
They are summoned before the council, June 8,
and committed to the Tower, 790. The bishops
are brought before the King's Bench, June 15, for
a misdemeanour, and are enlarged on their own
recognisances, 792. They are tried for censuring
the government, and giving their opinion about
affairs of state, June 29, ib. The queen is delivered
of a son, June 10, 793. Orders are issued for in-
serting the name of the prince of Wales in the Common Prayer-book, ib. The bishops are acquitted,
May 30, 1688; 792. A correspondence is opened
with the prince of Orange, 793, 794; he collects
large forces, 794. James attempts to appease the
Protestants, 796. The archbishop of Canterbury
and eight bishops wait on the king with a letter of
advice, Oct. 3; ib. The prince of Wales is baptized
according to the Romish rites, ib. The king calls
a council to prove the legitimacy of his infant son;
the archbishop of Canterbury, the marquess of
Halifax, and the lords Clarendon and Nottingham
refuse to sit at the table amongst papists, ib. The
prince of Orange embarks for England, Oct. 16,
but owing to stress of weather puts back into
Helvoet, ib.; he again sets sail, Nov. 1, and lands
at Torbay, Nov. 5, 798. James goes to the camp

JAMES II.,—
at Hounslow; several of his officers desert, 798, 799. He calls a council of war at Whitehall; the prince of Wales is sent to Portsmouth, 799. The king sets out for Salisbury, Nov. 19, but, fearing treachery, returns; Churchill and the duke of Grafton desert to the prince of Orange, ib. Prince George of Denmark and the duke of Ormond abandon the king, ib. The princess Anne proceeds to the camp of the prince of Orange, 799, 800. The prince of Wales is brought back to London, 800. The queen takes him with her to Calais, ib. The king commences his flight; he throws the great seal into the Thames; he is seized at the Isle of Sheppey, and carried to Feversham, ib.; his deplorable weakness of mind, 800, 801. Jeffreys is maltreated at Wapping; carried before the lord-mayor, and committed to the Tower, 801. A provincial council is formed; the prince of Orange is invited to London; James returns to London, invites the prince of Wales to a conference with him at Whitehall, which is declined, ib. The king attends mass, ib. Four battalions of Dutch guards and a squadron of horse are marched to Westminster, ib.; the palace is surrounded by guards, ib. Halifax requires the king to go to Ham-house, ib. James objects to the situation as unhealthy, and goes, by consent of the prince of Orange, to Rochester, 802. He embarks at the Medway, Dec. 23, and lands at Ambleteuse, Dec. 25, ib. He meets with a kind reception at the court of Versailles, iv. 11. Embarks for Ireland, 12; gives battle to the English fleet off Bantry Bay, ib. Forms a council of government, 13; repeals the Act of Settlement, ib.; his despair after the Battle of La Hogue, May 21, 22, 1692, 39; his commission to the Jacobites to make war on William, 70. He is seized with a fainting fit at the palace of St. Germain, and dies Sept. 16, 1701; 129.
Illustrations.—The Great Seal, iii. 763. Portrait of the king, 764. Fac-simile of the king's signature, 801. Coins, 868.
JAMES I., king of Scotland (April 4, 1406—February 20, 1437), son of Robert III., sent at twelve years old to France; is taken by the English, 1405. Henry IV. treats him kindly, but keeps him prisoner in Windsor Castle, ii. 19. There, with masters and books, and good society, he becomes an accomplished prince, ib. Romantic incidents during his captivity of nineteen years, ib. He becomes an excellent poet, on the model of Chaucer, ib. "The King's Quhair," 132. In 1423, Henry V. releases the royal captive, 49, 132. James with some of his nobles and knights follows Henry in his last campaign in France, 49. He besieges Dreux, which capitulates, ib. Is chief mourner at Henry's funeral, 51. Negotiation concluded at York, 1423, stipulating for the payment, by instalments, of 40,000l., incurred for his maintenance during eighteen years' captivity, 132. He is permitted to repair to his kingdom, ib. Feb. 24, 1424, he espoused at the church of St. Mary Overy, in Southwark, Joanna Beaufort, daughter of the duchess of Clarence and the duke of Somerset,—both parents descended from Edward III., ib. The royal couple are crowned at Scone, 133. A truce for seven years with England, ib. King James calls a parliament at Perth, inquires into the frightful disorders that had so long afflicted Scotland, and enacts numerous regulations for their correction, ib. He arrests Murdoch Stewart, duke of Albany, his sons Walter and Alexander Stewart, and twenty-six barons, attending a second parliament, 1428, ib. James presides at the trial of his near relations the Stewarts, who are condemned, May, 1428, ib. Albany, his two sons, and his father-in-law Lennox, aged eighty, are executed at Stirling, ib.

JAMES I., of Scotland,—
The king confiscates all their lands, ib. Having made this fearful example of feudal tyrants, he liberates the twenty-six great barons, ib. James yearly calls a parliament and legislates for the national improvement in agriculture, manufactures, commerce, internal police, and the defence of the realm against any foreign enemy, ib. The northern highlands showing no obedience to these wise laws, he calls a parliament at Inverness, 1427, and seizes fifty heads of the clans who were there attending it, many of them he brings to trial, and orders to be executed, ib. He slaughters, in cold blood, 300 Highlanders as robbers, ib. He determines to resume the lavish grants of crown-lands made by Albany, as these had impoverished the crown, 134; he strips, accordingly, some barons of estates they had enjoyed for many years, ib. He sends his infant daughter to France, 1435, to be betrothed to the dauphin (Louis XI.), and this measure involves him with the English government, ib. He broke the truce, 1436, and laid siege to Roxburgh, ib. Conspiracy against his life, ib. His queen, Joanna, came to his camp to apprise him of some danger; he raises the siege and returns home, ib. His suspicion is lulled, by no apparent danger, ib. Revels and Christmas festivities at Perth, ib. The chiefs of the plot were Robert Graham, Walter Stewart, earl of Athol, and his grandson Sir Robert Stewart, chamberlain of the household, ib. This latter it was planned to make king, as descended from Robert II., the legitimacy of Robert III. being impugned by those nobles, ib. February 20, 1436, the conspirators broke into the king's bed-chamber, yet conversing with the queen and her ladies, ib. Unarmed, James forced a plank of the floor, and dropped into a dark vault; Catherine Douglas held the door closed until her arm was broken, ib. Graham and the others, hearing some attempt of the king to quit the vault, discover the replaced plank, and descend, ib. James I. long resisted them, he received sixteen wounds, and was despatched by Graham, ib. All the above conspirators eventually paid the forfeit of their crime; they were put to death with tortures, ib. James I. perished in the thirteenth year of his actual reign, ib. Great depreciation of the value of Scottish coins at this period, 187.
JAMES II. king of Scotland (February 21, 1437—August 3, 1460,) crowned at six years of age, 1436; son of James I., ii. 134. Intestine confusion of the succeeding years, not elucidated by the records, ib. The chief personages in those troubles were Sir W. Crichton, Sir A. Livingston, and the house of Douglas, ib. As James approached manhood, he displayed his father's determination to become a king in real power, ib. William, fifth earl of Douglas, aged but seventeen, and his younger brother, were seduced to Edinburgh Castle, where the young king was residing, by Crichton and Livingston, ib. They were seized at dinner, 1440, and after a brief trial, executed, 135. When James II. undertook the reins of government, William, eighth earl of Douglas, was the most formidable noble of the realm, ib. James, wary and dissimulating, makes Crichton his chancellor, and confides especially in the counsels of his own cousin, Kennedy, bishop of St. Andrews, ib. James, in 1449, surprises the Livingstons in a family meeting of that house; he executes some of them, the rest made submission, but their faction was overthrown, ib. Douglas visits the king in Stirling Castle, 1452; ib. In the heat of dispute, the king, then but sixteen, plunges his dagger into the earl's throat, ib. James Douglas, the brother, and all the retainers of the family rebel, ib. Margaret of Anjou and prince Edward take refuge with king

JAMES II.,—

James, who, raising an army, 1460, marched towards England, ib. Besieging Roxburgh Castle, he is killed by the bursting of a cannon, ib. His son James, by his first wife Mary of Guelders, crowned, ib.

JAMES III. king of Scotland, (Aug. 3, 1460—June 11, 1488,) in his eighth year, ii. 135. The minority an era of turbulent agitations, ib. This prince's character indolent and irresolute; he was chiefly fond of study and privacy, ib. He commences the dangerous system of having favourites, and the powerful Boyds govern in his name, ib. The young king, 1469, is rendered jealous of the Boyds, dismisses them in anger, and causes the death of their chiefs, ib. His brothers, the duke of Albany and earl of Mar, possessed of more character than the king, are popular with the nobles, etc., ib. The king, 1480, charged Mar with a design, by aid of witchcraft, against his life, ib. The royal earl imprisoned; the mode of his death remains uncertain, ib. Albany flies to France, and returning, in 1482, styles himself king Alexander, and by treaty with Edward IV. consents to hold the crown as vassal to the English king, 136. Richard of Gloucester invades Scotland to support Albany, 114, 136. King James marches southward to oppose the invader, 136. At the Bridge of Lauder his favourite Cochrane, upon whom James had lavished riches and power, is seized by Archibald Douglas, earl of Angus, and, with others of the king's low favourites, hanged from the parapet, 115, 136. The king was shut up in Edinburgh Castle, and his forces disbanded, ib. Temporary reconciliation with his brother Albany; James released from custody, appoints him lieutenant-general of the kingdom, ib. A new revolution, and flight of Albany into England, ib. Peace concluded at Nottingham, Sept. 1484, to last for three years. His factious nobility, paid and encouraged by Henry VII., 301, 302. Bishop Fox sent to Scotland to negotiate certain royal marriages fails therein, 1487, ib. Rebellion of the duke of Rothsay and the southern barons, 302. The lords of the north of Scotland support the king's cause, ib. Temporary peace; the king soon forced to take the field, ib. His flight, June 18, 1488, on Lindsay's gray charger, out of battle, near Stirling, 303. James III. was thrown from his horse at the Brook of Bannock; traditions as to the mode of his death, ib.

JAMES IV. (June 11, 1488—Sept. 9, 1513,) duke of Rothsay, and his younger brother the marquess of Ormond; treaty for their marriage with two daughters of Elizabeth Woodville frustrated, 1487; ii. 302. The partiality of James III. for Ormond excites the suspicions of the barons, ib. Rothsay, aged 16, was induced to head an insurrection of the Scottish lords. The quarrel becoming aggravated, they proclaimed the prince, ib. Affair of Blackness, where some of their number were slain, ib. Treaty, whilst the two armies remained ready for battle, ib. The king makes concessions, and dismissed the northern forces that had supported him, ib. The barons took advantage of this imprudent measure of James III., and attacked the king and royalists at Little Canglar, near Stirling and Bannockburn, June 18, 1488; ib. The king flies on a war-charger given him by lord Lindsay, is killed by a fall, or murdered, 303. Remorse of James IV., ib. His coronation at Scone, ib. Revolt of lords Forbes, Lyle, etc.; their complaints stated, ib. Margaret Drummond, his beautiful mistress; ambition of her noble relatives, ib. James defeated the insurgents at Talla Moss, and suppressed the insurrection, ib. His clemency, ib. In time of peace with Henry VII. five English ships committed depredations in the Clyde, and damaged a Scottish ship of war, ib. Sir

JAMES IV.,—

Andrew Wood, of Largo, with the large men-of-war, "Flower," and "Yellow Carvel," captured the English fleet at Dunbar, after a gallant action, 303, 304. A second naval victory, 304. A plot of Bothwell, Buchan, and Tod, to seize and deliver to Henry VII. the persons of James IV. and his brother, now duke of Ross, 1490; ib. Henry granted them money, but the plot failed, ib. The earl of Angus, 1491, visited king Henry, and formed another dark conspiracy; also frustrated, ib. Hence James IV., in part informed of Henry VII.'s treachery, began to contemplate a war, ib. He chose to consider and receive Perkin Warbeck as the duke of York, entertained him royally, and gave him the hand of Catherine Gordon, daughter of the earl of Huntley, 304, 305. James summoned his lieges to meet him at Lauder, on the borders, 305. He would not come to any terms with bishop Fox and Wyat, ib. Concressault, ambassador from Charles VIII., well received by king James, ib. Bothwell and Buchan continue treasonably in Henry's pay; their attempt to corrupt young Ross, the king's brother, ib. Bothwell, still confided in by king James, sends to Henry VII. the names of Nevil, Lovel, Heron, etc., as partizans of Warbeck, ib. Articles of the treaty between James IV. and Warbeck, ib. Bothwell and Buchan make preparations to betray the army, 305, 306. James IV. declared war, and crossed the borders, 306. Address by Perkin Warbeck failed of inducing an insurrection in the north, ib. The army plunders, and the population becomes bitterly hostile to the invaders, ib. James, unable to procure any provisions, leads his forces home, ib. He recrossed the Tweed, 1497, and advanced to the Tees, but retired on the approach of Surrey with a powerful army, 307. Henry VII. offered him his eldest daughter, Margaret; the treaty was signed, 1497, but the nuptials did not take place until 1501, 1509; 307, 311, 312, 331. The Scottish king, too honourable to deliver up Warbeck, for whom he had made great sacrifices, gave him a ship to embark at Ayr, 307. Negotiations of West, dean of Windsor, commissioned to the Scottish court, 322. James sent a herald to Henry's camp in France, to declare war, 325. James IV., intending a diversion in favour of his ally, the French king, marched into England, August, 1513; 326. Norham Castle, Wark, and other strongholds, surrendered to him, ib. He rased Ford Castle, the seat of the Heron family, who were obnoxious to him, ib. Surrey, marching from York to Alnwick, sent Rouge Croix to defy the Scottish monarch to a general battle, 327. Reply of James, ib. The admiral, Thomas Howard, sent an uncourteous message, and James disdained to reply to him, ib. The king occupied a good position on Flodden Hill, ib. His old warriors, Angus, Lindsay, and Huntley, dissuade him from the fight, ib. Narrative of this great battle, in which king James and his chief nobility, in all 8,000, fell gallantly in the field, 327—329. The body of James IV. carried by the victorious Surrey to the monastery of Sheen, near Richmond, 329. Fond belief of the Scottish nation that James was not slain, ib. Artillery of the Scots described, 329, 330. Sword and dagger of James IV., and two knight's banners, 330. His will, 349. Queen Margaret wrote to her brother, Henry VIII. to show forbearance towards herself and infant prince, 331. She was appointed Regent; peace with England, ib. James passed a law requiring all barons and substantial freeholders to send their eldest sons to school at the age of six years, or nine at latest, iii. 643. Courtship of, 647.

JAMES V., of Scotland (September 9, 1513—December 14, 1542.) James V., the regency, during his

JAMES V.,—
minority, first conferred, 1513, on queen Margaret (*Tudor*), afterwards usurped by various of her enemies, ii. 331. Lord Dacre, agent of Henry VIII., endeavoured to persuade the queen to secure the persons of her sons, the minor king and the duke of Ross, and with them to repair to her brother's court, 350. Margaret refused to do so, ib. Dacre won over lord Home to the English views, and this spirit of treason among the Scottish nobility long continued, ib. The regent duke of Albany constrained the haughty Margaret to entrust both princes to him, and Fleming, Borthwick, and others, were charged with the care of them, 350, 351. Margaret, assisted by the earl of Arran, etc., gains possession of her son; he is proclaimed king, and invested with the supreme power when in his twelfth year, 430. The queen-mother disgusts the earl of Arran by taking another paramour, Henry Stewart, second son of lord Evandale, ib. The earl of Angus obtains possession of. the young king, ib. He consents to a divorce from Margaret, and she marries her young favourite, ib. James escapes from the Douglases, 1528, and throws himself into Stirling Castle, where he is joined by the earl of Arran, etc. ; he issues a proclamation, forbidding Angus or any of his house to approach his court, ib. His frank and generous disposition, ib. War on the borders of England and Scotland, ib. Treaty concluded (through the mediation of France) honourable to Scotland, 1534 ; ib. The king presides in person at the trial of David Straiton and Norman Gourlay, who are burned as heretics, 431. Henry makes him an offer of the hand of his daughter Mary, ib. James concludes a treaty of marriage with Marie de Bourbon, daughter of the duke of Vendôme, ib. He sails for France, where he is honourably received ; he is not pleased with the personal appearance of Marie, but is charmed with the princess Magdalen, daughter of the French king, whom he marries, ib. They land safely at Leith, but the queen dies of a rapid decline, ib. The king marries Mary of Guise, widow of the duke of Longueville, ib. Henry sends sir R. Sadler to James, to persuade him not to permit the bull of excommunication against him to be published in Scotland, 431, 432. James consents to meet Henry at York, where the English monarch waited for six days for the arrival of the Scottish king, but James came not, and Henry, furious at the insult, orders sir Robert Bowes to levy troops near the borders, and to the archbishop of York to ascertain the just title of the kings of England to the kingdom of Scotland, 432. James sends an embassy to deprecate his uncle's wrath, ib. Sir James Bowes, 1532, with a body of 3,000 horse, rushes into Teviotdale, 433. The earl of Huntley and lord Home gain a complete victory over the invading force, ib. The duke of Norfolk burns several towns and villages on the left bank of the Tweed, ib. James exhorts his troops to retaliate by making a raid into England ; they refuse, and he is forced to return to Edinburgh, ib. Battle of Solway Moss; the Scots are defeated, ib. James is broken-hearted, and sinks rapidly with a slow fever, ib. Mary of Guise had borne him two sons, but they had both died in infancy ; she was again *enceinte*, and it was hoped that the birth of a son would recover the king, but the queen was delivered of a daughter, the unfortunate Mary ; and James died seven days after her birth, December 14, 1542, foreseeing the dismal state of his country, and muttering with his last breath, " It came with a girl, and it will go with a girl." It is reported that a deputation of the clergy having applied to him for leave to persecute the Reformers, he, with great vehemence unsheathed his dagger, and drove them from his presence, iii. 644.

JAMES FRANCIS EDWARD, prince of Wales, son of James II., birth of, June 10, 1688 ; iii. 793. Reported to be a suppositious child, ib. Baptised according to the Romish rites, 796. Bill of Attainder passed against him, iv. 187. On the death of queen Anne he intends going to England, but is forbidden by Louis XIV., 304. He sets forth a manifesto, asserting his right to Great Britain, 305. He arrives at Dunkirk, 321. His portrait, 323. His Polish wife gives birth to a son, who, at a royal christening, receives the name of Charles Edward Louis Casimir, 379. His savage conduct induces his wife to shut herself up in a convent at Rome, 400. The Pretender signs a proclamation appointing his eldest son, Charles Edward, his regent and *alter ego*, 470.
JAMES, Francis, one of the delegates appointed, 1613, to try the divorce of the earl of Essex, iii. 53.
JAMIESON, George, the Scottish Vandyke, iii. 569. His portrait, by himself, is in the Florentine Gallery of painters ; he died in 1644, ib.
JANSEN, Bernard, a Dutch architect (17th century), iii. 576.
JANSEN, Cornelius, a Dutch painter (17th century), iii. 567.
JANSEN, Alderman, 1751; iv. 565.
Japhetic or Caucasic population of Europe, i. 10.
JARDINE, Mr., quoted, iii. 517, 519.
Jarnac, battle of, 1569 ; ii. 626.
Jarrow, View of, at the mouth of the river Tyne, i. 291.
Jassy, Treaty of, signed August, 1791 ; § iii. 38.
JAY, John, a father of the American revolution, § i. 183, 190, 266, 269.
JEFFERSON, Thomas, a distinguished American revolutionist, § i. 214. Portrait of, 266.
JEFFERYS, Mr., accompanies Charles XII. in the character of a volunteer, and reports to Marlborough everything done in the camp, iv. 201.
JEFFREY, William, severely punished, 1563, for affirming one John Moore to be Christ, ii. 572.
JEFFREYS, sir George, iii. 739, 740. His favour at court, 757. He attempts to stretch the limits of toleration to the Catholics, through private motives, 1684, but his attempt falls to the ground, 758. He advises James II. to collect the revenues without authority of parliament, 765. His bloody proceedings, 781. A member of the ecclesiastical commission, 786. His misgivings about prosecuting the petitioning bishops, 790. He is caught at Wapping, after the flight of James, 1688, in the disguise of a sailor, and committed, at his own request, to the Tower, 801. Description of, by Roger North, 845. He dies a prisoner in the Tower, April 19, 1689 ; iv. 22.
JEKYLL, sir Joseph, master of the Rolls, iv. 340, 406. He brings in the Gin Act, 1736; 417.
Jemappe, battle of, gained by the duke of Chartres, November 6, 1792 ; § iii. 187.
JENKINS, sir Leoline, secretary of state, iii. 741. Objects that printing votes of parliament is against the gravity of the House, 1681 ; 844.
JENKINSON, Anthony, agent for the Russia Company, 1557 ; ii. 785.
JENKINSON, Anthony, an English engraver, who flourished in 1562 ; iii. 577.
JENKYNS, captain Robert, brought to the bar of the House of Commons, 1738, where he accuses the Spaniards of having practised barbarities upon him, iv. 431.
JENNER, baron, with several others, receives a commission, 1687, for altering and new-modelling the statutes of the University of Oxford, iii. 787.
JENNINGS, sir John, goes on an expedition to the coast of Spain, 1726; iv. 389.
JENYNGS, Mrs. (duchess of Tyrconnel), *regno* Charles II., iv. 897.
JERMYN, lord Henry. *See* St. Alban's.

JERSEY, lord, appointed lord-chamberlain, 1700; iv. 106.

Jerusalem, City of, view of the walls and fortifications adjoining Ephraim Gate, i. 499. Intention of Henry V. and Philip of Burgundy to rescue Palestine, alluded to, 1422, ii. 51. Mission of De Lawnoy, who surveys the coasts of Egypt and Syria, 51, *note*.

JERVAS, Charles, an English painter of some reputation, but of little real merit; he died 1739, iv. 753.

Jesuits :—In the persecution in Lancashire, 1604, six Jesuits and seminary priests are executed, by 27th of Elizabeth, for staying within the realm, iii. 22. Jesuits concerned in the Gunpowder Treason, or punished immediately on its failure; Gerard, missionary, together with Greenway, escape, 21, 30. Henry Garnet, impelled by torture, makes confessions, 31. Arraigned, under the accusation of the learned Coke, he pleads that he did all in a priest's power to dissuade Catesby and the rest from the treason, yet could by no means reveal their confessions made to him, 31, 32. He was superior of the English Jesuits, and executed, May 3, 1606; 32. Oldcorn, Strange, and others, executed at Worcester, 31, 636. The Society of Jesuits was suppressed in Portugal, in September, 1759; in France, 1764; in Spain, 1767; with circumstances of peculiar cruelty: in the kingdom of the Two Sicilies and the dukedom of Parma, 1768; and finally, July 21, 1773, pope Clement XIV. issued his bull for the total abolition of the order, § i. 522.

Jewel-house in the Tower, from an original drawing, iii. 708.

Jews, the, carried on trade in England as early as 730; i. 266. Extortion and violent measures used against, by Henry II. (1188,) to obtain supplies for a war in the Holy Land; he procures 60,000*l.*, 476. Dreadful massacre of, at Lynn, Norwich, Stamford, St. Edmundsbury, and Lincoln, 504. They are attacked in York, fly to the fortress, and are received within by the governor, *ib.* The governor having gone outside the fortress, the Jews, fearing that he would permit the rabble to enter with him, refuse him admission, on which he orders the rabble to attack the castle, *ib.*; the Jews within, after a siege of several days, cut the throats of their wives and children, and then stab themselves, having first burned and destroyed all their valuable effects, 505. Persecution of, by John, 523; by Henry III., 584.

JOAN of Navarre, second wife of Henry IV., her portrait, ii. 4.

JOAN, daughter of Henry II., and wife of William II., king of Sicily, her magnificent dower, her supposed imprisonment by Tancred; her brother Richard demands her enlargement, and takes possession of the town and castle of Bagnara, which he puts her in possession of, i. 490. She receives the sum of about 20,000 oncie in compensation for her dower, 491; goes as companion to Berengaria, the young wife of her brother Richard; their arrival at Limasol, 494.

JOAN, sister of king Richard and queen-dowager of Sicily, marries the earl of Toulouse, 1197; i. 513.

JOFFRID, abbot of Croyland, sent to his manor of Cottenham, near Cambridge, the learned Master Gislebert, 1109, who first gave public lectures on science at Cambridge, and established the university there, i. 606.

JOHN, king of England, (May 27, 1199 – October 19, 1216,) youngest and favourite son of Henry II., who proposes to marry him, instead of Richard, to Adelais, and name him heir to his continental dominions, which Philip refuses, i. 478. King Henry dies of grief, on learning that John had joined his brother Richard in his unnatural rebellion, 479. John lands at Portsmouth with his brother Richard, now king of England, 482. Richard gives to him, besides the earldom of Moreton or Moretain, in Normandy, the earldoms of Cornwall, Dorset,

JOHN, king of England,—
Somerset, Gloucester, Nottingham, Derby, and Lancaster, 485. John attends at the great council in Normandy, *ib.* Sends a letter to his brother Richard, accusing Longchamp, chief justiciary of England, of ruining the kingdom, 506. Gerard de Camville claims the custody of Lincoln Castle, *ib.* Longchamp marches to London; but while he is besieging the castle, John puts himself at the head of a large army and takes the royal castles of Nottingham and Tick-hill, *ib.* Earl John is acknowledged successor to Richard, should he die without issue, 507. Geoffrey returns to England, and is imprisoned in Dover Castle, *ib.* John and the archbishop of Rouen take this opportunity to displace Longchamp, *ib.* They assemble a general council, and summon Longchamp to make amends to the archbishop, and answer for himself before the king's council, *ib.* Longchamp retires to the Tower of London; John enters London, and is proclaimed the chief governor of the whole kingdom, *ib.* The French king demands the princess Alice and her dower, 508. John goes to France, and does homage to king Philip for his brother's dominions on the continent, 1192; 509. Is betrothed to the princess Alice, *ib.* He takes Windsor and Wallingford Castles, and demands the crown in London, but is refused and defeated, *ib.* The French king invades Normandy, but is defeated by the earl of Leicester, *ib.* John's castle of Nottingham taken by Richard, 511. It is determined, at a great council held at Nottingham, that if John did not appear within forty days, all his estates in England should be forfeited, *ib.* He flies to France, and takes part with the French king; but when Richard lands in Normandy, he implores forgiveness, and is received into favour at the intercession of Eleanor, *ib.* Great Seal of king John, 514. His portrait, 515. Death of king Richard, April 6th, 1199, *ib.* John hastens to Chinon, and gets possession of his brother's treasures there, *ib.* He is inaugurated at Rouen on the 25th, *ib.* A great council is held at Northampton, and the prelates and barons swear fealty to John, *ib.* He lands at Shoreham on the 25th of May, and is crowned at Westminster on the 27th, *ib.* He receives the homage of the barons and prelates, *ib.* All the states on the continent, except Normandy, declare for Arthur; they are assisted by the French king; and William the Lion, of Scotland, threatens an invasion, 516. A treaty entered into with the French, who desert the cause of Arthur for the present, 517. John marries Isabella, wife of the count of la Marche, although he had already been married ten years to Avisa, daughter of the earl of Gloucester, *ib.*; is re-crowned with his new wife at Westminster, 1200, *ib.* He pays a visit to Paris, and is courteously entertained by Philip, *ib.* Philip again declares for Arthur, and assists the insurgents in Aquitaine, *ib.* Arthur is taken prisoner by John, when besieging the strong tower of Mirebeau, 518; is confined in the castle of Falaise, and thence removed to Rouen, 519; supposed to have been murdered by him, while, 519, 520. John permits the French and Bretons to advance into Normandy without opposition; their success, 520. He returns to England and demands supplies; the English nobles refuse to follow his standard out of England, 521. Rouen, Verneuil, and Château-Gaillard, taken by the French, 1204—5, *ib.* All Normandy, Brittany, Anjou, Maine, Touraine, and Poictou, surrender to the French, and acknowledge the authority of Philip; Aquitaine alone remaining to the English on the continent, *ib.* John lands with an English army at Rochelle, takes the strong castle of Montauban, and then marching to the Loire, burns Angers, *ib.* He lays siege to Nantes, *ib.* Flies to England, *ib.* A truce con-

JOHN, king of England,—
cluded for two years, through the mediation
of the pope's legate, 1207, *ib.* John's dispute
with the pope about the right of electing
bishops, *ib.* He appoints John de Gray to the see
of Canterbury; the pope refuses to consent to his
election, and appoints Stephen Langton, *ib.* He
expels and banishes the monks of Canterbury, 522.
England is laid under interdict, March 23, 1208, *ib.*
John receives the sentence of excommunication,
1209, and applies for aid to the Mahommedans of
Spain, *ib.* He collects a great sum of money, and,
on the 6th of June, 1210, lands in Ireland, 523.
Receives the homage of many chieftains; reduces
the castles of the revolted English there, and drives
Hugh de Lacy, earl of Ulster, and his brother
Walter, earl of Meath, out of Ireland, *ib.* He establishes English laws, and divides such part of the
country as was subject to the English into counties,
ib. He orders that the same money shall be current in both countries for the convenience of traffic,
and appoints John de Gray governor, *ib.* Exactions
and persecution of the Jews, *ib.* John prepares a
powerful army and invades Wales, penetrating as
far as Snowdon, 1211, when he returns, having
obtained tribute and hostages, *ib.* The Welsh rise,
1212; John hangs the hostages, *ib.* General defection of the English barons, *ib.* Pope Innocent pronounces the sentence of deposition against John,
1213; absolves his vassals from their oaths of allegiance, and invites Philip to invade England, *ib.*
Philip, by March, had prepared a large army for this
expedition, and a fleet of 1,700 vessels at Boulogne,
and other ports on the Channel, *ib.* John collects all
the vessels in his dominions, and prepares an army
of 60,000 men on the coasts of Kent and Sussex,
ib. The English mariners cross the Channel, take
the French squadron at the mouth of the Seine,
destroy the ships in the harbour of Fecamp, burn
Dieppe to the ground, and return in triumph, having
swept the whole coast of Normandy, the French
fleet at Boulogne not hazarding an attack, 524.
John encamps on Barham Downs; the pope's
legate, Pandulph, arrives, and persuades him to
consent to the election of Stephen Langton, to
restore the monks of Canterbury, and make full
satisfaction to the clergy and laity for the damages
they had suffered during the interdict, *ib.* On the
15th May, John swears fealty to the pope, and
surrenders his kingdom to him, *ib.* Peter the Hermit
hanged for predicting that John should be un-
knighted before three days, *ib.* The French invasion forbidden by the pope's legate, *ib.* The earl of
Flanders refuses to follow Philip to England, and
withdraws his forces. Philip besieges Ghent. Ferdinand applies for assistance to king John, 525.
John's fleet at Portsmouth, consisting of 500 vessels,
immediately makes sail for the coast of Flanders,
and entirely annihilates the French fleet at Damme,
the port of Bruges, although three times more
numerous than the English, *ib.* The English,
joined by the earl of Flanders, have a sharp action
with Philip, and retire to their ships, *ib.* Philip burns
the remainder of his fleet, lest it should fall into the
enemy's hands, and then hastens into France, *ib.*
John summons the barons to meet him at Portsmouth: they assemble, but refuse to follow him
unless he would perform his promises: the king
recalls the exiled bishops, and acknowledges Langton
as archbishop, 526. He sets sail, but his barons
refuse to accompany him, saying that the time of
their feudal service was expired, *ib.* The barons
hold a great council at St. Albans, and denounce
the punishment of death against all officers of the
king who should exceed their proper and legal
authority, *ib.* The king returns, and marching to
Nottingham lays waste the country: Langton

JOHN, king of England,—
remonstrates with him, *ib.* August 25, Langton
swears the barons, at an assembly held at London,
to maintain the charter of Henry I., *ib.* Cardinal
Nicholas, the pope's new legate, arrives, and John
again swears fealty to the pope, *ib.* A formidable
league formed for the partitioning of France, 1214,
between king John, Ferrand, earl of Flanders,
Reynaud, earl of Boulogne, and Otho, emperor of
Germany, *ib.* John commands the expedition in
Brittany, *ib.* The allies thoroughly defeated at the
battle of Bouvines, July 27th, *ib.* A truce is made for
five years between England and France, 527. John
returns to England, *ib.* On the 20th of November
the barons assemble at a great council held at St.
Edmundsbury, and swear to assert their rights, *ib.*
John goes to London, and shuts himself up in the
strong house of the Knights Templars; he postpones
the confirmation of the demands of the barons till
Easter, *ib.* John surrenders the right of election
to the pope, and takes the cross, 528. The barons
meet at Stamford, and then march to Brackley:
the king sends a deputation to them from Oxford,
ib., but refuses to grant their demands; the barons
then proclaim themselves "the army of God and
of holy church;" they elect Robert Fitz-Walter to
be their general, *ib.* They attempt to take Northampton Castle, but fail; are admitted by the people
of Bedford, and receive a deputation from London,
ib. They enter London, May 24, 1215, *ib.* The
lords and knights from all parts of England join the
national standard at London, *ib.* John despatches
a deputation to the barons at London, *ib.* Magna
Charta signed at Runny-mead, 15th of June, 1215,
ib. John sends to collect adventurers from the
continent, puts his castles in a state of defence, 529,
and at the head of his foreign troops quits Dover,
and besieges the castle of Rochester, 530. The
barons march from London to its relief, but are
obliged to retreat before his superior force, *ib.*
Rochester Castle surrenders; the barons are excommunicated by the pope, *ib.* Alexander, the young
king of Scotland, had joined the cause of the barons;
John marches to oppose him, and lays waste all the
country on his road, *ib.* The Scottish king retires;
and John, having advanced as far as Edinburgh,
returns, burning Haddington, Dunbar, and Berwick
on his way, *ib.* The English barons confined in
London send a deputation to France, offering the
crown to prince Louis, eldest son of Philip II., 531.
At the feast of Easter, Louis sets sail from Calais
with a numerous and well-appointed army, embarked on board 680 vessels, *ib.* The French land
at Sandwich; John, who commanded a numerous
army at Dover, flies before the French forces debark,
ib. Louis takes the castle of Rochester, and then
marches to London, where he is joyfully received,
and conducted, with a magnificent procession, to
St. Paul's; the nobles and citizens then swore fealty
to him, *ib.* He publishes a manifesto addressed to
the king of Scotland, and all the nobles not present
in London; the men of the north rise up in arms
against John, and his foreign mercenaries desert
him, *ib.* Louis marches to Dover, and lays siege to
the castle; the barons besiege Windsor Castle, but
raise the siege to oppose John, and then join Louis at
Dover, *ib.* Louis treats the English with disrespect,
and grants English estates and titles to his French
followers, *ib.* The viscount de Melun, reported to
have called to him, when dying, the English nobles,
then in London, and to have declared to them that
Louis had sworn to banish for ever all those who
had joined his standard, 532. Louis spends three
months in the siege of Dover, *ib.* The cause of
John brightens; he loses his treasures in crossing
the Wash, *ib.* He eats immoderately of some
peaches or pears, and drinks new cider at the

JOHN, king of England,—
  abbey of Swineshead, and on the following day is seized with a violent fever, *ib.*, of which he dies, October 18, 1216; 533. He appoints prince Henry, his eldest son, his successor, and orders his body to be buried at the monastery of St. Wulstan, *ib.*

JOHN L. of France (1350—1364), son of Philip VI., succeeds to the French throne, 1350; the truce with Edward is prolonged, i. 771. War again commenced in the south of France by Edward, the Black Prince. He devastates the country, and burns many of the finest towns in France, 1355; 771, 772. Battle of Poictiers; king John and his son Philip are taken prisoners, September 19, 1356; 772, 773. Dreadful state of anarchy in France, 774. The French people unanimously refuse to ratify the conditions agreed upon by Edward and king John; Edward goes over to France with a great army, 1359, and lays siege to Rheims; but the winter season, and the strength of the place, baffle his efforts, and he is compelled to raise the siege, and retire to Burgundy, 775. The French fleet takes, and plunders Winchelsea; Edward marches upon Paris, and encamps before that capital, March 31, 1360; the Dauphin wisely declines a battle, and Edward, not being strong enough to besiege Paris, is compelled to retire towards Brittany, for want of provisions, *ib.* He encounters a dreadful tempest of thunder and lightning near Chartres, which terrifies his imagination, and he determines to make peace with France, *ib.* The treaty of Bretigny is signed, in which Edward renounces his pretensions to the throne of France, and his claims to Normandy, Anjou, and Maine; but reserves to himself Guienne and Poictou, and the cities of Calais and Guisnes, *ib.* King John is sent to Calais to ratify the treaty, October 24, which the two kings mutually swear to observe; John is set at liberty, and Edward returns to England, October 25; *ib.* The duke of Anjou dishonourably breaks his parole, and repairs to Paris; the French king, being unable to perform the conditions of the treaty, returns to London, hoping to obtain some modification of its articles; he is kindly received by Edward, but soon after dies at the Savoy Palace, in London, April, 1364; 776.

JOHN, of Austria, illegitimate son of Charles V., a brave commander, and governor of the Netherlands, 1577; ii. 649. His early death, some report by assassination, 651; *note.*

JOHNSON, Samuel, fined and whipped, 1686, for writing an address to the soldiers, reminding them that they were freeborn Englishmen, iii. 786.

JOHNSON, Dr. Samuel, one of the most distinguished writers of the eighteenth century, born 1709; was touched for the king's evil by queen Anne; he published his "English Dictionary" in 1755; and died December 13, 1784; iii. 614; iv. 151, *note*; § i. 26, 615, 616. His portrait, 616.

JOHNSON, sir William, fails in an expedition against the French fort at Crown Point, 1755; iv. 582.

JOHNSTON, Archibald, 1649; iii. 485, 490.

JOHNSTONE, colonel Guy, 1775; § i. 219.

JOHNSTONE, sir Patrick, a commissioner for the Union of England and Scotland; his house furiously assailed by a Scottish mob, 1706; iv. 191.

JOHNSTON, sir William, induces the Indians of the Six Nations to join the British against the other Indians, 1764; § i. 34, 71, 108.

JOHNSTONE, of Warriston, uncle of bishop Burnet; he flies to France; is given up to Charles II. by the government, who sends him to Scotland, where he is tried, and hanged, 1661; iii. 683.

JOHNSTONE, governor, opens a *private* correspondence with several members of the American Congress, 1778; § i. 371.

JONES, Inigo, commences the restoration of St. Paul's; iii. 159, 546. Portrait of, after Vandyke, 560. His design for Whitehall, 571. Dies of grief, in 1652; 574. Buckingham Palace, by, 722.

JONES, John Gale, opposes the conduct of ministers in excluding strangers from the gallery of the House of Commons, 1810; § iv. 428, 429. He is arrested, and confined in Newgate till the prorogation of parliament, 436.

JONES, Paul (*alias* John Paul), his adventures along the English coast, etc., 1779; § i. 397. His service in the Russian fleet, 1788; § ii. 314, 497.

JONES, sir William, an eminent lawyer, scholar, and Orientalist, born September, 1746; died April, 1794; § iii. 725.

JONES, executed as a regicide, 1660; iii. 676.

JONSON, Ben, the famous dramatic writer, born 1574; died 1637; iii. 582, 592, 596.

JOSEPH I., emperor of Germany, death of, 1711; iv. 255.

JOSEPH II., emperor of Germany (1765—1790). He dissolves the Barrier Treaty, 1781; § ii. 7—9. He attempts reform in the Netherlands by force of arms, 1787, and alters the mode of study at the University of Louvain; the Council of Brabant remonstrate, and refuse to levy the subsidies until their grievances should be redressed; a deputation is sent to Vienna to lay their complaints before the emperor, who, being struck by the firmness of the deputies, for the present restores their privileges, 248—251. The emperor issues a declaration of war against the Ottoman Porte, February, 1788; 311. The troubles in the Austrian Netherlands break out afresh, 1789. Cruelties of general Dalton; the University of Louvain is cleared at the point of the bayonet; preparations for a similar attack on the College of Antwerp; the abbeys of Brabant are sequestrated; the patriots gain possession of Brabant and Flanders, 322—328. Joseph's death, February 20, 1790; he is succeeded by Leopold II., 470, 471.

JOSEPH EMANUEL, king of Portugal, (1750—1777.) Spain declares war against him, 1762; § i. 17—19.

JOURDAN, marshal, a skilful republican general; his wars in Germany, 1796; § iii. 511. He commands the French army at the battle of Vittoria, June 21, 1813; § iv. 570.

JOYCE, a cornet in Whalley's regiment, takes Charles I., from Holmby-house to Newmarket, iii. 367.

JUDITH, daughter of Charles the Bald, i. 153. King Ethelwulf, returning from his pilgrimage to Rome, 854, with his youngest son, prince Alfred, fell in love with the daughter of the king of the Franks, not twelve years of age, and solemnly espoused her at Rheims, having her crowned also as queen of Wessex, *ib.* His eldest son, Ethelbald, had prepared a rebellion against the old king's return, who ceded to him the best part of Wessex, and died in 857. Ethelbald then married the young widow, on a plea that Judith's marriage with his aged father had not been consummated, *ib.* The pope commanded his bishops in England to persuade Ethelbald to a divorce; but his reign lasted only two years, and Judith retired to a convent at Senlis, *ib.* Thence she was abducted by Baldwin of the Ardennes; king Charles was enraged, but was afterwards pacified by the pope, *ib.* Her new marriage was solemnized, and this her third husband created earl of Flanders, *ib.* She lived in a state of great magnificence, *ib.* By the nuptials of her son, the second earl of Flanders, with Elfrida, daughter of Alfred the Great, Judith became the ancestress, in course of years, of Matilda, wife of William the Conqueror, *ib.*

JUDITH, niece of William I., marries Waltheof, a powerful Saxon earl, i. 379. Being let into the secret of the conspiracy formed by Roger Fitz-

JUDITH, niece of William I.,—
Osborn and Ralph de Gaël, she betrays them, 381. Having conceived a passion for a Norman nobleman, she accused her husband, and obtained sentence of death against him, although it is supposed that he took no part in this conspiracy, 382. William insists on her marrying Simon, a Frenchman, a very brave soldier, but lame and deformed; on her refusal, he drives her from his presence, and she is compelled to live a wandering life, *ib.*

JULIANA, an illegitimate daughter of Henry I., married to Eustace of Breteuil; inhuman treatment of her children by Henry, i. 414.

JULIUS II., pope, elected November 1, 1503; ii. 320, 367. Validity of his dispensation for Henry VIII. to espouse his brother's widow is denied by the king's counsel on the suit of Catherine's divorce, 370. He died February 20, 1513.

Junius's Letters, § i. 78. Prosecution of the printers and publishers of, 1770; 106. Specimen of these atrabilious productions, 119, 120; 613—615. Supposed to be from the pen of sir Philip Francis, § ii. 135.

Jury, trial by, established, i. 572. Remarkable trial of sir N. Throgmorton, 1554; the jury returning a conscientious verdict of Not Guilty, are imprisoned, carried before the Star-chamber, and severely fined, ii. 518; iii. 839; iv. 677, 678. Rights of Jury, § i. 529, 530.

Justiciary, chief, office of the, i. 568.

JUSTUS, bishop of Rochester, consecrated by Augustine, i. 233. He retires from the anger of Eadbald, king of Kent, to Gaul, accompanied in his flight by Mellitus, *ib.* His recall, on the success of the primate Laurentius, 234.

Jutes, the, a Saxon tribe, i. 139. Their war with the Picts and Scots, 140. Led by Hengist and Horsa, they acquire Thanet, and fortify themselves therein, 141. Near the close of the *fifth century,* Eric calling over reinforcements of Saxons, extends Hengist's acquisition, and founds the kingdom of Kent, 142. The three first powerful bretwaldas of the Heptarchy were of this race, 144, 145.

JUXON, William, dean of Worcester, an old friend of archbishop Laud, appointed in 1632 clerk of the king's closet, iii. 160; bishop of London, 1633; 161; made lord high-treasurer, *ib.* His advice to Charles not to sign Strafford's death-warrant if it were against his conscience, 243. Charles demands his opinion whether he may conscientiously take the Covenant, 356. He attends the king in his last moments, who, presenting him with his George, utters the word "Remember," 397. He was translated to Canterbury, 1660, and died 1663.

Kainarji, Treaty of, signed by the grand-vizier and prince Repnin, July 21, 1774; § i. 148.

KALB, an American officer, slain at the battle of Camden, 1780; § i. 426.

KAYS, Martin, marries the lady Mary Grey; is imprisoned by Elizabeth for this offence, ii. 623.

KEENE, sir Benjamin, the British consul at Madrid, 1726, iv. 400. He concludes a commercial treaty at the court of Madrid, 561. Pitt instructs him to offer Gibraltar to Spain in exchange for Minorca, 596.

KEITH, sir William, governor of Berwick, nobly defends this town against a powerful English army, May 1333; i. 756.

KEITH, ambassador of James VI., of Scotland, 1586; ii. 665.

KEITH, marshal, killed in the battle of Hochkirchen, 1758; iv. 603.

KELLY, of Moriarty, assassinates the earl of Desmond, 1583; ii. 652.

KELLY, a non-juring clergyman, seized 1722, on suspicion of plotting the Pretender's return, iv. 380.

KEMP, John, cardinal, and archbishop of Canterbury, 1452; ii. 147. His death, 1454, *ib.*

KEN, Thomas, consecrated bishop of Bath and Wells, 1685; attends Charles II. in his last moments, iii. 762.; deprived for not taking the oaths to William and Mary, February 1691; 777.

Kendal, iii. 656.

Kenilworth, Castle of, the principal residence of the powerful family of De Montfort; it defies several royal armies, i. 686, 687. Its strength and extent of architectural works, ii. 289, 874.

KENILWORTH, Dictum de, 1265; i. 687, 688.

KENMURE, lord, beheaded on Tower-hill, February 24, 1716; iv. 329.

KENNEDY, Hew, younger brother of the earl of Cassilis, undertakes, 1602, to murder the laird of Auchindrane, iii. 643.

KENNET, Dr., compares the bill of the earl of Nottingham, 1721, for the suppression of blasphemy and profaneness to the establishment of a *Protestant Inquisition,* iv. 378.

KENNET, lord-mayor, 1780; his disgraceful conduct during the great London riots, § i. 413—417.

KENNETH MAC ALPIN, or Kenneth II.; a grandson of the Scottish king Achaius, succeeded Alpin in 836; i. 217. Uven, Pictish monarch was slain, 889, by the Danes, when Kenneth, in right of his grandmother Urgusia, claimed the vacant throne, *ib.* After a long contest, the Picts for a time submitted to the Scoti, 843, and Kenneth assumed the title of king of the Scots and Picts, *ib.* He next attacked Caw, prince of Strathclyde, made peace with him, and gave him his daughter in marriage, *ib.* Kenneth's wars with Danes and Saxons, 218. He died in Forteviot, his capital, 859, and his brother, Donald III., succeeded; on whose death Constantine II., a son of Kenneth Mac Alpin, succeeded to the throne, *ib.*

KENNETH III., son of Malcolm I., i. 218, 220. Defeated the Danes at Loncarty, near Perth, 220. He adds the territory of Strathclyde, 973, by conquest to the kingdom of Scotland, which had recently received that general appellation, 219, 220, 533. His character and abilities suited the crisis in which he came to the crown, 220. Under this prince the Dalriadian chieftains, by his victory over the last Pictish monarch, became possessed of all North Britain, 218, 220. He put to death Malcolm, son of his brother Duff, to break up the double line of inheritance of the crown, customary at that period, 220. He suppressed an insurrection in the Mearns, and put to death the son of the chieftain of the district, *ib.* Fenella, mother of that youth, murdered king Kenneth, 944, in her castle, for which deed she was punished with death, *ib.*

KENNETH IV., called the Grim, defeated Constantine IV. (son of Culen), who fell in the battle, i. 220. He was himself attacked, 1003, by Malcolm, prince of Cumberland, (son of Kenneth III.,) and fell in the battle of Monivaird, 221. His son, Boidhe, was father of a prince murdered by order of Malcolm II., *ib.* History of the lady Gruoch, daughter of Boidhe (the *Lady Macbeth* of Shakspeare). *ib.* The province of Lothian granted to him by Edgar, 533.

Kent (*Cantium*), the inhabitants of Cantium the most civilized portion of the British population, i. 10. Invasion of the Romans, B. c. 55, 54; 27—33, 77. The Kentish kings attempt to surprise the Roman camp and fleet. The Romans repulse the Britons with slaughter, and capture one of their princes, 33. Settlement of the Saxons and Jutes, under Hengist and Horsa, in Thanet, in the middle of the *fifth century,* i. 57, 58, 141. Eric, son of Hengist, first Saxon king of all Kent, 142. *Cantwara Land,* a name for Kent, *ib.* Hence the city of Canterbury took its name, 77. The White Horse, or ensign of Kent, 58. This kingdom submits to Egbert, king of Wessex, who appoints to its government a sub-king, 150. Augustine and Laurentius, in the

Kent.—
sixth and *seventh* centuries, convert the kings and men of Kent to the Christian worship, 145. Insurrection of the men of Kent, under John Cade, 1450 ; ii. 87, 88.

KENT, Edmund Plantagenet, earl of, son of Edward I., and uncle of Edward III., created 1321. He joins Lancaster in his opposition to the power of Mortimer, but soon deserts him, i. 751. Being persuaded that Edward II. is still alive and confined in Corfe Castle, he forms a plan for his deliverance, but is taken, accused of treason, and executed, March 19, 1330 ; 752.

KENT, Thomas Holland, earl of, created duke of Surrey, September, 1397. He was forced in 1399 to revert to his previous title, ii. 5. He conspires with some rebellious peers to murder Henry IV., and is beheaded at Cirencester, 1400; 7.

KENT, Henry Grey, earl of, served under Brandon, duke of Suffolk, 1536, in Lincolnshire, ii. 397. He died 1562.

KENT, Henry Grey, earl of, 1572, reads the death warrant to Mary queen of Scots, 1587. He died 1615 ; ii. 668.

KENT, James, an eminent English musician of the 18th century ; born 1700, died 1776, § i. 634.

KENT, William, an architect, born 1685. Observations on the Horse Guards, Holkham in Norfolk, and other of his works. His influence in introducing landscape-gardening. He died at Burlington House in 1748, and was buried at Chiswick, iii. 572; iv. 751.

KENT, Maid of, her prophecies ; she is put to death, 1534; ii. 717.

Kentish Petition, the, 1701; the petitioners committed to the Gate-house, iv. 122.

KEPPEL, Augustus, a celebrated English admiral, takes Bellisle, 1761, § i. 2, 59. He is brought to court-martial, 1778, for his engagement with count d'Orvilliers off Ushant, and honourably acquitted, 347, 348, 377, 378. Portrait of, 347.

KEPPEL, captain, desires a bill to release from their oath of secrecy the members of the court-martial who sat upon the trial of Admiral Byng 1757; iv. 591.

KER, Andrew, threatens to shoot Mary queen of Scots, 1566; ii. 587.

KER, John, of Kersland, his account of the religious sects in Scotland, iv. 652.

KEROUAILLE, mademoiselle, a mistress of Charles II. She became duchess of Portsmouth; Louis XIV. grants her, 1673, a French title and estate, iii. 707, 716. She asks Barillon, at the time of the king's death, to obtain a priest to whom he (the king) might confess, 761.

KERR, lord, charges the marquis of Hamilton with treason, 1641. Hamilton appeals to the parliament, which declares him innocent, and he compels Kerr to make an apology, iii. 250.

KERR, lord Robert, killed at the battle of Culloden, April 17, 1746, whilst fighting against the Pretender, iv. 538.

KERSLAND, laird of, complains to colonel Hooke, 1707, that he and another west-country laird had been ready to rise for the Pretender, but that the duke of Hamilton had stopped their proceeding, iv. 208.

KET, Robert, a tanner of Wymondham, heads a popular rising in 1549; ii. 485 : he and his brother are hanged in chains in Norfolk, 487.

Kew Palace, garden found of, § i. 3.

KEYLING, John, engaged in the Rye-house Plot, 1683, iii. 743.

KEYLING, Josiah, a salter, discovers the Rye-house Plot to lord Dartmouth, 1683; iii. 741, 742.

Keys of Dover Castle, ii. 810.

KEYS, executed at Tyburn, March 18, 1696, for engaging in the Invasion Plot, iv. 68.

KHEVENHÖLLER, drives the French army out of Austria, and obliges the Bavarian army to abandon Bohemia, 1741; iv. 451.

KILDARE, Thomas Fitzgerald, earl of, lord-deputy of Ireland, 1486, espoused the cause of the youthful impostor, Lambert Simnel, ii. 289. The earl testified more prudence, on the arrival of the adventurer Warbeck at Cork, 1492; 299. Kildare, in 1522, was a third time appointed lord-deputy, 425. Enmity of the Butlers to the house of Fitzgerald; their complaints laid before Henry VIII., in 1533, occasion the earl of Kildare's recall and committal to the Tower of London, *ib.*. Rebellion and execution of his son, Thomas Fitzgerald, and of the earl's five brothers, 425—427. The old earl died of grief in the Tower about 1534; 426.

KILDARE, Thomas Fitzgerald, earl of, being falsely informed that his father was beheaded, took up arms to avenge him, ii. 425. He surrendered to the forces of Henry VIII., and, 1537, was beheaded, 426.

KILDARE, Gerald Fitzgerald, earl of, the only scion of that noble family, escaped to the continent on the execution, 1537, of his brother, ii. 427. His adventures abroad, *ib.* He was well received by cardinal Pole at Rome, and there educated, *ib.* Pole, in the reign of Mary I., procured his restoration to his estates and honours, *ib.*

KILDARE, James Fitzgerald, earl of, also duke of Leinster, offers to raise and maintain a regiment at his own expense to serve against the Young Pretender; he died 1773; iv. 503.

Kildrummie Castle, view of the ruins of, i. 727. Bruce's queen and daughter take refuge here, 729. Bruce's brother Nigel compelled to surrender this castle, 1306; he is sent in irons to Berwick, where he is hanged and afterwards beheaded, *ib.*

KILMARNOCK, earl of, brought to trial as a traitor for assisting the Young Pretender, iv. 549, and executed, August 18, 1746; 550.

KILWARDEN, lord, chief-justice of Ireland, murdered by the Dublin rabble in 1803, § iv. 76.

KINCARDINE, earl of, represents, 1666, the dangerous consequences likely to ensue on account of the atrocities exercised against the Covenanters, iii. 694, 701.

KING, Gregory, his work upon the state and condition of England, iv. 841—844.

KING, John, bishop of London, elected September, 1611, died March 30, 1621; iii. 59.

KING, sir Peter, complains of the sermon of Dr. Sacheverell, preached before the magistrates, Nov. 5, 1709; iv. 237.

KING, captain, a servant of sir Walter Raleigh, iii. 76.

KING, an eminent chemist and physician, *regno* Charles II., iii. 760.

KING, executed at Tyburn, March 18, 1696, for participation in the Invasion Plot, iv. 68.

King's Bench, Chief-justice of the; this office was instituted in the 52nd Henry III., and was first held by Robert de Bruis, i. 812.

Kingston, St. Mary's Chapel at, i. 175.

KINGSTON, duchess of, (formerly Miss Chudleigh,) trial of, 1776 ; § i. 252—255. Entertainment given by, 1763; 642.

KINGSTON, lieutenant of the Tower, sent to Leicester Abbey to take charge of Wolsey, 1530; ii. 373. Celebrated message from the cardinal to Henry VIII., etc., 373, 374. Report of queen Anne Boleyn's various speeches to him, 1536, when in his custody, 391, 393.

Kinsale, from an old drawing, iv. 12.

KIP, John, a Dutchman, who arrived in England soon after the revolution ; he engraved a series of the palaces and mansions of England after the drawings of Leonard Knyff, iv. 760.

KIRBY, informs Charles II. of a plot to assassinate him, August 12, 1678; iii. 717.

KIRK, colonel; his savage conduct; he executes many of the prisoners taken at Sedgemoor, 1685; iii. 779; appointed by William III. to relieve the garrison of Londonderry, iv. 17.

KIRKALDY, William, laird of Grange, disaffected, and a pensioner of Henry VIII., joined other conspirators in 1546, and they murdered David Beaton at St. Andrew's, ii. 446.

KIRKMAN, Francis, a publisher, 1661, curious advertisement by, iii. 904.

KIRLE, Mr. Anthony, committed to the serjeant's ward, 1584, for having served Mr. Stepneth, a member, with a subpœna during parliament-time, iv. 666.

KIRTON, Mr., M.P., 1628; iii. 133, 140.

KITCHEN, Anthony, bishop of Llandaff, elected 1545; preserved his pastoral office for many years by a constant implicit obedience to the royal will and Acts of Parliament, ii. 545. In 1558, he was the only prelate consenting to take the Oath of Supremacy, ib. He died October, 1566.

Kits Coty House, a cromlech, near Aylesford, Kent, i. 63.

KNATCHBULL, sir Edward, M.P., 1714; iv. 285.

KNELLER, sir Godfrey, an eminent painter, born at Lubeck about 1648. He died in 1723, leaving his art in a low state of degradation, to which he had greatly contributed, iv. 752. His portrait of Charles II., iii. 666. Of James II., 764. Of bishop Burnet, 803. Of William III., iv. 6. Of queen Mary, 8. Of prince George of Denmark, 143. Of Dr. Tillotson, 617. Of Charles Montague, earl of Halifax, 658. Of lord-chancellor Somers, ib. Of Sidney, earl of Godolphin, ib. Of Locke, 735. Review of his works, 752, 753.

KNEVETT, sir Thomas, magistrate, and a party of soldiers, surprise Fawkes early on 5th November, 1605, at the door of the Gunpowder store, iii. 27.

Knighthood; king James I. (March to June, 1603,) confers the honour, in that short space, on about 700 persons, iii. 4, 5. He likewise knights at Whitehall, the judges, serjeants-at-law, and others, 6.

KNIGHTLY, Mr., searches the house of Mrs. Vaux, a Catholic, for munition, 1625; iii. 116.

KNIGHTLY, captain, concerned in a conspiracy for assassinating William III., 1696; iv. 65.

KNOLLES, Richard, author of the "History of the Turks," published in 1610; he is ranked by Johnson among the first English historians, iii. 614.

KNOLLYS, sir Francis, an agent of queen Elizabeth; complains of the charges incident on guarding the unfortunate queen of Scots, ii. 607, 610, 611.

KNOLLYS, sir William, 1601; ii. 687.

KNOWLES, sir Robert, traverses France from Calais to the walls of Paris, with an English army, 1373; i. 779.

KNOX, John, ii. 459. He preaches vehemently against the mass, and advocates the destruction of abbeys, churches, etc., ii. 548. He writes for money to secure the Protestant interests in Scotland, 554, 556. Disgusts the English by his Calvinistic principles, 558. His virulent conduct towards the queen of Scots, 566—568. He preaches at the opening of the regent Murray's first parliament, 606; iii. 186, 435, 437, 473.

Knyghton, Radnorshire, battle of, 1402; ii. 11, 13.

KNYGHTON, an English historian of the fourteenth century, i. 520.

KOCH, Christopher William, author of "Tableau des Révolutions de l'Europe;" his speech in the National Assembly, 1791, touching the proper measures to be pursued with the foreign princes who suffered the royalist emigrants to gather and arm in their territories, § ii. 721.

KOX, John, member for Derby, committed to the Tower, November 9, 1685; iii. 784.

KONIOSEGG, marshal, 1745; iv. 476.

KÖNIGSMARK, count Philip Christopher, murdered by order of the father of George I., for showing attention to that king's injured wife, Sophia Dorothea, iv. 392.

KÖNIGSMARK, count Charles John, brother of the preceding, iv. 392.

KOSCIUSKO, Thaddeus, an eminent Polish warrior, gains the battle of Dubienka, July 17, 1792; § ii. 45. Acts as generalissimo in the Polish insurrection of 1794, but is wounded and taken prisoner at the battle of Maciewice, Oct. 4, where he remained till the accession of Paul I.; § iii. 456—461. His portrait, 456.

Kunersdorf, battle of, August 12, 1759; iv. 611.

KUTUSOFF, a famous Russian general and minister of state, was born in 1745. He commanded against the Turks in 1791, and at the battle of Austerlitz, which, however, was fought contrary to his advice, Dec. 2, 1805; he had the principal direction of the allied armies; § iv. 177, 178.

KYD, Thomas, a dramatic writer of the 16th century, ii. 587.

KYD, captain, appointed, 1699, to the command of a privateer, to make war upon pirates. On reaching the American seas he himself turned pirate, was seized and hanged, 1701; iv. 102, 121.

KYME, Anne, commonly known as Anne Askew, second daughter of Sir W. Askew, obtains a divorce from her husband, assumes her maiden name and preaches the gospel according to the Reformed views, ii. 447. She is arrested and brought before Bonner, and induced to sign a recantation, ib. Her enthusiasm continuing, she is brought before the privy-council, and shortly after condemned as a heretic, 1545; 448. She is tortured before Wriothesley and Rich, who are said to have applied the instruments with their own hands, ib. Her execution, ib.

KYMER, Dr. Gilbert, a clerk and physician to Henry VI., ii. 208.

KYRIEL, sir Thomas, 1450, leads 3,000 men into Normandy to reinforce Somerset, ii. 85. He gallantly fought at Fourmigni against the count of Clermont, ib. A second army, under the constable of France, came up on his flank and rear, and Kyriel sustained a total defeat, ib. Made prisoner at Barnet, 1461; he was beheaded, 97.

LABÉDOYÈRE, tried and condemned for high treason by a court-martial on the restoration of Louis XVIII., August 19, 1815; § iv. 652*.

LABELYE, a Swiss, employed by the earl of Pembroke to erect Westminster-bridge, 1739; iv. 752.

LABOURDONNAIS, a Frenchman, takes possession of Madras, 1744; § ii. 23.

LA CHAISE, father, confessor of Louis XIV., iii. 719.

LACY, Hugh de, earl of Ulster, appointed governor of Dublin by Henry II., i. 467. Expelled from Ireland by king John, 1210; 523.

LACY, Gilbert de, receives a grant of the domain of Pontefract from William I. i. 374, 424.

LACY, Walter de, i. 381. Is concerned in the conspiracy formed in 1095, for placing Stephen, count of Aumâle on the throne of England, 400, 424.

LACY, Walter de, earl of Meath, expelled from Ireland by king John, 1210; i. 523.

Lady Place or Hurley House, vaults of, once the burying-place of the Benedictine friars. Here were meetings of those who desired the coming of the prince of Orange, iii. 794. View of, 795.

LA FAYETTE, marquis de, serves on the side of the Americans at the battle of Brandywine, 1777; § i. 301. Portrait of, 302, 351. He returns to France, 1778; 370. Arrives at Washington's head-quarters, 1780; 429, 457, 462, § ii. 362. Is appointed prévôt des marchands by the French revolutionists, 1789; 389, 424. He declares martial law in France, 1789; 438, 439, 488. Objects to any honorary titles being left to the royal family, 1790; 489. He resigns,

LA FAYETTE, marquis de,—
1791, but is persuaded to resume the command, 621.
He again surrenders his charge, Oct. 8, and retires
to his estates in Auvergne, 715, 716, 726. He is
formally denounced as a traitor by the Jacobin Club,
Jan. 2, 1792; § iii. 52.

LA GALISSONIÈRE, admiral, 1756; iv. 586.

LA HIRE, or Vignolles, a celebrated French knight,
1421; ii. 49, 56, 65, 68, 69.

La Hogue, battle of, May 19, 1692; iv. 38.

LAKE, Gerard, viscount, born in 1744. In September, 1803, he gained a great victory over the
Mahratta army, and the French general, Louis
Bourquien, on the plains of Delhi, and delivered
Shah Alum, whom they held in captivity, § iv. 81.
He afterwards triumphed over Scindiah and Holkar,
whom he compelled to conclude a treaty; and
returned to England in 1807, where he was created
viscount, and afterwards made governor of Plymouth. He died Feb. 21, 1808; 199—205.

LAKE, sir Thomas, made joint secretary of state with
sir Ralph Winwood, 1612; iii. 49.

LALLY, count, a veteran officer of Irish extraction, in
the service of France, arrives in India, April, 1758;
§ ii. 64. Reduces Fort St. David, 65, 66. Having
surrendered Pondicherry, Jan. 1761, he sails for
France, where he is thrown into the Bastille, and
afterwards beheaded in the Place de Grève, 81, 82.

LA MARCHE. See MARCHE.

LAMB, Charles, quoted, iii. 581, 586, 587.

LAMB, bishop of Brechin, 1610; iii. 465.

LAMBALLE, Marie Therese Louise de Savoie Carignan,
an amiable princess, born Sept 8, 1749. Appointed
superintendent of the household of Marie Antoinette,
queen of France. Murdered by the revolutionists,
Sept. 3rd, 1792, with circumstances of revolting
cruelty, § iii. 167.

LAMBE, Dr., physician of the duke of Buckingham,
murdered by the English rabble, 1628; iii. 135.

LAMBERT, John, schoolmaster, having suffered much
in prison for heresies, had yet the boldness to present to Dr. Taylor his reasons, in writing, for dis-
belief of the real presence of the Eucharist, ii. 406.
Cranmer, though mentally of the same opinion, condemned Lambert, who appealed to the king, ib.
Henry VIII. summoned the bishops and temporal
peers to Westminster Hall, 1538, in this religious
cause, ib., 724. Narrative of this celebrated argu-
mentation, 406, 407. Lambert was sentenced to die,
and burnt in Smithfield 407.

LAMBERT, colonel, a parliamentarian officer, iii. 365,
422, 432. Is condemned as a regicide, 1661, but
suffered to remain a prisoner in the Isle of Guernsey,
where he died, 690.

LAMBERTON, William de, bishop of St. Andrew's,
makes a league with Bruce, June, 1305; i. 728. He
is taken prisoner after the battle of Methven, 729.

Lambeth Palace and the Lombard's Tower. Illustration, ii. 147.

LAMONT, Dr, physician to Mr. Murray, M.P., who
was imprisoned in Newgate, 1751; iv. 564.

LA MOTTE, the French envoy, in vain endeavoured
to check the impetuosity of the highland clans at
Flodden, 1513, and was himself slain, ii. 328.

Lampeter, Cardiganshire, the castle taken, 1405, by
Henry prince of Wales, ii. 17.

LAMPLUGH, Thomas, Bishop of Exeter, iv. 619, is
elevated to the see of York, 1688; 622. His death,
May, 1691; ib.

LANARK, lord, secretary of state for Scotland, brother
to the marquess of Hamilton, presents the petition
of the Covenanters to Charles I., iii. 222, 268. He
escapes from the king and joins the parliament, 309.

Lancashire, iii. 656.

Lancaster, county, iii. 656.

Lancaster, the family colours of this house were white
and red, ii. 857.

LANCASTER, Thomas Plantagenet, earl of, cousin of
Edward II., supports the barons against the king,
and takes Gaviston prisoner at Scarborough, May
19th, 1312; i. 733. He decrees, with the other
barons in Warwick Castle, the death of Gaviston,
who is beheaded on Blacklow-hill, contrary to the
capitulation of Scarborough, 734. A reconciliation
effected between the king and his barons. ib. Lancaster marches upon London, and the Despensers
are banished, August, 1321; 740. The Despensers
again return, Lancaster is surprised and taken prisoner at Boroughbridge, and executed for treason,
1322; 741.

LANCASTER, Henry Plantagenet, earl of, raises a force
to oppose the oppressive power of Mortimer and
queen Isabella, 1329; i. 751. Is obliged to submit,
and pay an immense fine, 752. He died 1345.

LANCASTER, Henry Plantagenet, duke of, cousin of
Edward III., created 1351. He gains many victories
over the French in Guienne, 1345; i. 763. Assists
at the siege of Calais, 1347; 769. He died 1361.

LANCASTER, John of Gaunt, duke of, son of Edward
III., created, November 13, 1362. He assists his
brother, Edward the Black Prince, in restoring
Peter the Cruel to his throne, i. 776 Marries one
of the daughters of king Pedro, ib. Lays waste all
the north-western provinces of France, 778. The
command of the English possessions in the south is
left to him by his brother Edward, who returns to
England, ib. He advances his claim to the kingdoms of Castile and Leon in right of his wife Constance, daughter of king Pedro, which latter had
been stabbed by his bastard brother, Don Enrique,
who had now established himself in that kingdom,
ib. The English fleet, bringing supplies under the
command of the earl of Pembroke, after a fierce
engagement, is destroyed by the Spaniards near
Rochelle, and the military chest, with £20,000 in
it, is lost, ib. A truce is concluded with France;
John of Gaunt returns to England, 779. His unpopular measures, ib. His influence in parliament,
780. He supports Wycliffe, and threatens violent
measures against the bishop of London, which
causes a general riot; the Londoners plunder the
Savoy Palace, ib. On the accession of Richard,
1377, he retires in displeasure, at not being named
one of the regency, to his castle of Kenilworth, 782.
A French and Spanish fleet plunders the Isle of
Wight, and burns the towns of Hastings and Rye,
but meets with considerable resistance at Winchelsea, and suffer a severe repulse at Southampton by
the earl of Arundel, ib. An English fleet is fitted
out under the command of the earl of Buckingham,
which meets with little success, ib. Alice Perrers
is banished, 783. The duke of Lancaster is appointed commander of the fleet; he captures many
of the Spanish ships, takes possession of the town
and port of Cherbourg, and persuades the duke of
Brittany to cede to him the important town and
harbour of Brest, but fails in his attempt on St.
Malo, ib. While he is absent negotiating a peace
in Scotland, the rioters burn his palace of the Savoy,
786. He is accused of treason by John Latimer,
a Carmelite friar; Latimer is murdered, and Lancaster is reconciled to his nephew Richard, 1384;
791. July, 1385, he invades Castile, and gains
many battles; his daughter is married to the heir of
the king of Castile, ib. Lancaster is created duke
of Aquitaine for life, 1390; 794. He dies, December
1398, and Richard seizes his estates, 796. His third
marriage with Catherine Rowet; his three sons and
a daughter by her, previously to the marriage, are
rendered legitimate by Act of Parliament, ii. 52;
note. The issue of John of Gaunt reigned in
Spain for many generations, i. 791.

LANCASTER, captain James, sails from England, April
1601, in charge of the first adventure of the newly-

LANCASTER, captain James,—established East India Company; he returns to the Downs, September 1603; iii. 529.

Landau, plan of, with its fortifications, iv. 145.

Landen, battle of, fought July 29, 1693, in which king William was defeated, iv. 41.

LANDOIS, minister of Francis II., of Brittany, ii. 126. He enables Richmond to escape from a snare laid to deliver him to Richard III., 1483; ib. The duke was compelled by popular clamour to deliver up his minister to be tried for various offences, 292. He was tortured to confession, and hanged, ib.

Landrecy, siege of, 1712; iv. 269.

Land-tax Act, passed November 16, 1689; iv. 19. 155.

LANE, Mr., argues in favour of the earl of Strafford, on that nobleman's trial, 1641; iii. 239.

LANFRANC (abbot of Caen), the Italian archbishop of Canterbury, consecrated, August 1070, viceroy of England during William's absence in Normandy, i. 381. His letters to William, ib. He exacts promises from William Rufus, that he would govern according to law and right before crowning him as king, 392. Death of this great man, June 1089; 396. His history, and government of the see of Canterbury, 547.

LANGDALE, sir Marmaduke, iii. 332, captured by the Parliamentary forces near Widmerpool, 1648; 382.

LANGHORNE, a Jesuit, and famous Catholic lawyer, executed, 1679, for participation in the Popish Plot, iii. 730.

LANGLAND, author of the Visions of Pierce Plowman, regno Edward III., i. 851.

LANGLEY, sir Robert, foreman of the jury on the trial of the petitioning bishops, 1688; he pronounced the verdict of "Not Guilty," iii. 792.

LANGRISH, captain, 1642; iii. 263.

Langside, battle of, fought, May 13, 1568; ii. 607.

LANGTON, Stephen, appointed to the see of Canterbury by Innocent III., i. 521. King John determines to appoint John de Gray; dispute with the pope; England laid under interdict, 522. John submits, and Langton returns to England as primate, 1213; 526. He charges the king with the violation of his oaths, ib. Hastens to London, and persuades the barons at a council held there, to demand the confirmation of the liberal charter of Henry I., ib. He crowned Henry III., 675. Died, July 1228.

LANGTON, Walter de, bishop of Lichfield, elected, February 1296, lord-treasurer of England; deprived of his office, and thrown into prison by Edward II. He died, November 1321; i. 781.

Language, important advantages to be derived from, as affording positive evidence of the origin of the inhabitants of a country, i. 6, 7. Derivation of, 7.

LANIER, sir John, falls at the battle of Steinkirk, 1692; iv. 37.

LANNOY, viceroy of Naples for the emperor Charles V., ii. 359. Joins Pescara at Pavia, 1525, where Francis I., made prisoner, surrendered his sword to Lannoy, and was honourably treated, 359. His contest with Rome, Florence, etc., 362.

Lanterns of horn, said by Asser to have been the invention of king Alfred, i. 166. Form of an Anglo-Saxon lantern, 285.

LA PLACE, the great philosopher, assisted in the formation of the Republican Calendar, which came into use October 1793, and was discontinued, December 1806; § iii 377.

LA QUADRA, signs a convention at Madrid, January 14, 1739; iv. 433.

LA RABINIÈRE, a French naval commander, dies of his wounds at the battle of Solebay, 1672; iii. 710.

LATIMER, lord, expelled the king's council and thrown into prison, 1376; i. 779.

LATIMER, Hugh, bishop of Worcester, consecrated September, 1535. Preaches a sermon on the burning of Forest, a friar, who declared the oath of supremacy unlawful, ii. 403. As soon as the Six Articles, or the Bloody Statute was passed, 1539, Latimer resigned his see; he was shortly afterwards imprisoned for speaking against them, and remained in confinement till the king's death, 410, note. He was committed to the Tower by Mary I., 507. Condemned for heresy, and burned at the same stake with Ridley, October 16, 1555; 525, 526. His portrait, 696. Described the profits of a farmer or yeoman (his own father) in the reign of Henry VII., comparing them with the much-diminished advantages from the same holding in the ensuing reign, 803, 804. Specimen of his sermons, 831, 832.

LATIMER, John, a Carmelite friar, accuses the duke of Lancaster of treason, 1384; i. 791.

LA TREMOILLE, overruns Brittany, 1488; ii. 292. Defeats the Bretons and auxiliaries under the duke of Orleans, 294. Sir E. Woodville was slain, and Orleans (afterwards Louis XII.) was made prisoner, ib.

LATTEN, Mr., concerned in a plot for assassinating William III., 1696; iv. 65.

LAUD, William, archbishop of Canterbury, made bishop of St. David's, 1621, and prebendary of Westminster, iii. 117. Bishop of Bath and Wells, 1626; 123. Enjoins the preaching of the merits of lending or giving money without authority of parliament, ib. Translated to the see of London, July 1628; 134. Threatens John Felton with the rack, 138. His Arminianism, 139. Baptizes Charles II., 1630; 151. Installed in the archbishopric of Canterbury, 1633; 157. A cardinal's hat is offered to him, ib. Rumour of his being inclined to celibacy; he attempts to refute the charge, 159. He constructs the buildings at St. John's College, Oxford, sets up a Greek press in London, appoints a professor of Arabic at Oxford, and founds a hospital at Reading, 160. Named chief of the Board of Commissioners of the Exchequer, 161. Sends a chaplain to the factory at Delf, to establish the Anglican Liturgy, 162. Proceeds to reduce the French and Dutch refugees to conformity with the Anglican Liturgy, ib. Forbids the "Acts and Monuments" of Fox to be printed, and refuses new licenses to bishop Jewel's works, 166. Master of St. John's College, 177. His superstition and misgivings, 227. Accused by the House of Commons of high treason; the Lords sequester him from their House; he is committed to the Tower, 229. The parliament institutes proceedings against him, 324. He is condemned for high treason, 326. By his earnest desire the mode of execution is changed to beheading, ib.; note. He is executed, January 10, 1645, and buried at Barking church, ib. His portrait, 483.

LAUDERDALE, earl of; presses Charles I., 1647, to establish Presbyterianism, iii. 362, 471. He speaks, 1661, against the proposed Act Rescissory, 683. Archbishop Sharp accuses him to the king, 694. In 1663, Lauderdale published an Act of Grace, pardoning all offences against the Conventicle Act, 713. His portrait, 830.

LAUDERDALE, Maitland, earl of; his first speech in parliament, 1780, in support of Burke's Financial Reform Bill, § i. 443.

LAURENCE. See Lawrence.

LAURENS, Henry, American envoy to Holland, is seized, brought to London, and, after being examined by the secretaries of state, committed to the Tower, October, 1780; § i. 438.

LAURENTIUS, succeeds Augustine, 604, in the archiepiscopal church of Canterbury, i. 145, 233. He persuades Eadbald and the people of Kent, to return to Christian worship, which they had abandoned after the death of Ethelbert and Bertha, 145. Narrative of the miraculous adventure that befel Laurentius at Canterbury; his flagellation by

LAURENTIUS,—
St. Peter; and of the due impression made by the wounds from this scourging on the mind of the young king Eadbald, who returns forthwith to the bosom of the church, 233, 284.

LAUTREC, a general of Francis I., in Italy, ii. 366; his first successes, 1527; he laid siege to Naples, 368. His imprudent quarrel with his allies, the Genoese; Filippino Doria sailed away with his galleys from the bay, and Andrea Doria joined the emperor, ib. A malaria and plague ravaged the French lines; Lautrec perished, and his feeble army capitulated at Aversa, ib.

LAUZUN, count de, assumes the command of the Pretender's army in Ireland, 1690; iv. 24.

LAVALETTE, postmaster-general, under the emperor Bonaparte; he is condemned, on the restoration of Louis XVIII., in 1815, but succeeds in making his escape; § iv. 653*—656*.

LAVOISIER, the eminent chemical philosopher, guillotined, 1794; § iii. 426. His portrait, ib.

LAW, James, bishop of Orkney, becomes archbishop of Glasgow, 1615; iii. 466.

LAW, John, author of the South-sea scheme, flies from France, 1720; iv. 373.

LAWES, Henry, a musician, regno Charles I., iii. 566.

LAURENCE, Thomas, registrar to the archdeacon of Canterbury, 1534, accused of holding correspondence with the Holy Maid of Kent, ii. 385.

LAWRENCE, sir Thomas, an eminent painter, of the nineteenth century, received the commission to paint the Waterloo Gallery in 1817, and died in 1830; § iv. 713, 714.

LAWRENCE, archbishop of Dublin, causes a confederacy of native princes, under Roderick, to invest Dublin, about 1170; i. 465, 466.

Laws and religion, powerful evidences of the truth of history, i. 5.

Laws and government of the British nations previous to the arrival of the Romans, and until the Saxon conquest of Britain, i. 76—90.

Laws of the Anglo-Saxons: the first code of written laws promulgated by Ethelbert, king of Kent, and bretwalda of the Anglo-Saxon confederacy (close of the sixth century), i. 145.. He obtained the consent of the states to his kingdom to these laws, ib. They embodied much of the old German law, ib. Laws of Alfred the Great, 167. Code of Edward the Confessor compiled from the preceding, 203. Code of the Burgundians, early in the seventh century, a written law, 145. Written code of the Lombards, promulgated in Italy about 640; ib. Laws of Edgar and of Canute against pagan worship, etc., 244. Laws of James I., king of Scotland, 1428; ii. 133.

Laws. See Constitution, Government, and Laws.

LAWSON, Mr. James, 1582; iii. 441.

LAWSON, captain, his brave conduct in an action against Van Tromp, 1653; iii. 407. He, with other fifth-monarchy men, is arrested, and sent to the Tower, 1657; 421. He insists on the sitting of parliament, 1659; 429*.

LAWSON, vice-admiral, killed in an engagement with the Dutch, 1665; iii. 695.

Lawyers, distinguished, of the seventeenth century, iii. 844.

LAYER, tried for having enlisted men for the Pretender's service, and executed at Tyburn, 1723; iv. 381.

Lea, river, Hertfordshire. In 896, the Danes, under Hasting, erect a fortress on this river, near Ware, i. 164. Wise and prompt measures of Alfred to reduce them, after a contest of three years, ib. His two fortresses on the Lea, below that of Hasting, ib. He diminishes the volume of this once deep river, by transverse channels to the Thames, ib. The

Lea, river,—
Danish fleet thus left aground, falls a prey to the citizens of London, ib.

Lead, and lead-mines, of the British islands, i. 26, 92, 106, 117, 269.

Leaden manufactures, § iii. 683. Improvement in the manufacture of lead-shot, 1782, by Watts, a Bristol plumber, ib.

LEAKE, vice-admiral, 1706; iv. 185.

LEAKE, sir John, conquers the Island of Sardinia, September, 1708, and, in conjunction with general Stanhope, takes the fortress of St. Philip; thus the harbour of Port Mahon, and the whole of Minorca, fall into the hands of the English, iv. 221.

LEAKE, "His Historical Account of English Money," quoted, ii. 185; iii. 552.

Leather manufactures; § iii. 712.

Leathersellers' Hall, ii. 812.

LEBRUN, the French minister for foreign affairs, 1793; § iii. 282. Guillotined during the Reign of Terror, December 27, 1793; 361.

LECHMERE, Mr., impeaches James, earl of Derwentwater, of high treason, 1716; iv. 328. He advocates triennial parliaments, 330.

LE CLERC, the French chargé-d'affaires, 1618, gives sir Walter Raleigh a safe-conduct to the governor of Calais, iii. 76.

LE CROC, endeavours, 1567, to make an accommodation between the insurgents and queen of Scots at Carberry-hill, ii. 600.

Lectures, become a fashionable amusement in the middle of the eighteenth century; § i. 645.

LEDE, marquis of, iv. 342, makes overtures, 1719, to the count de Mercy and admiral Byng for evacuating Sicily, 364.

LEE, Dr. Edward, archbishop of York, appointed October, 1531, married privately Anne Boleyn (marchioness of Pembroke) to Henry VIII. at Whitehall, January, 1533; ii. 379. He cited Catherine of Arragon at Ampthill, to appear before Cranmer's court held at Dunstable, she declined to appear, and was declared contumacious, 381. Lee, and bishop Tunstall, endeavoured in vain to persuade Catherine to submission, after which she was left without attendants, 383, note Lee was compelled, 1536, to join the "Pilgrims of Grace," formidable insurgents in his province, 399. He died September 15, 1544.

LEE, Nathaniel, the dramatic poet, died 1691 or 1692, iv. 788.

LEE, Robert, lord-mayor of London, signs the Act of Proclamation of James I., 1603; iii. 3.

LEE, Thomas, executed at Tyburn, February 17, 1601; ii. 686.

LEE, William, invented the stocking-frame about 1589, but not receiving encouragement at home, he carried the improvement to France, ii. 810.

Leeds, view of the castle of, i. 740.

LEEDS, Thomas Osborne, duke of, created 1694, impeached for corruption, 1695; iv. 52. Dismissed from the presidency of the council, 1699; 95. He died, 1712.

LEEFDALE, a Dutchman, discovers a conspiracy against the life of William III., 1692; iv. 37.

LEETH, Robert, an English engraver, of the sixteenth century, iii. 577.

Legacies, imposition of Stamp-duty on the receipt of, § iii. 606.

Legate, the pope's, never very acceptable to the English people, even in the most Catholic times, ii. 511.

LEGATE, Bartholomew, tried as an obstinate Arian, and burnt March 18th, 1612, in Smithfield, iii. 48.

LEGENDRE, a violent French revolutionist, recommends to the National Assembly, 1792, the massacre of all refractory priests, § iii. 82.

LEGGE, chancellor of the Exchequer, opposes the ministry and speaks for war, November 13, 1755; he is dismissed, November 20; iv. 583.

Legion, number of men that constituted a Roman legion, equipment, etc., i. 37; cavalry of, 38.

Legion Memorial, the, presented to the House of Commons, 1701. Supposed to have been the production of Defoe, iv. 124.

Legislation, Saxon, i. 256, et seq.

LEHWALD, marshal, compels general Apraxin to evacuate Prussia, 1757; iv. 597.

LEIBNITZ, Godfrey William de, an eminent German mathematician and philosopher, born at Leipsic in 1646; died November, 1716; iii. 612.

Leicester—Illustration : Ruins of the Abbey, ii. 374. Scene, and Narrative of Wolsey's Death, 1529; 373, 374.

LEICESTER, Robert le Bossu, earl of, 1118; pronounces sentence of imprisonment against Becket, 1164. He died 1167; i. 450.

LEICESTER, Robert Blanchmains, earl of, 1167. His brave conduct in the Holy Land, i. 498; his return, 509. He defeats Philip, king of France, who had invaded Normandy during Richard's detention in Germany. He died 1190, ib.

LEICESTER, Simon de Montfort, earl of, 1236. He marries Eleanor, countess-dowager of Pembroke, a sister of Henry III., and sets himself forward as the enemy of foreign encroachment and foreign favourites, i. 681; he is banished the court, ib.; is entrusted with the government of Guienne, but hastily recalled and insulted by the king; he withdraws for a short time into France, but the king was soon reconciled, in appearance, and the earl returns to England, where his popularity increases daily, ib. He is appointed head of the Committee of Government, and procures the enactment of the "Provisions of Oxford," so called from the parliament which met at that place, 682. He drives the half-brothers of the king, and a numerous body of their retainers, out of the kingdom, ib. The earl of Gloucester starts up as his rival, and a violent quarrel ensues between these two powerful lords; Leicester withdraws into France; Gloucester would have reconciled himself with the king, but prince Edward seeing this, declares for Leicester, who returns, 683. Henry declares his intention to rule without the aid of the Committee of Government, and seizes the Tower and the Mint; Leicester departs to France, but on the death of the earl of Gloucester he returns, raises the banner of war, and, after taking several royal castles and towns, marches upon London, where the mayor and the common people declare for him, ib. A reconciliation being effected by Richard, king of the Romans, Leicester is again entrusted with the charge of the royal castles, 684. Civil war again commences, ib. Leicester takes the king, his brother the king of the Romans, prince Edward, John Comyn, and Robert Bruce prisoners at the battle of Lewes in Sussex, May 14th, 1264; 685. He concludes an agreement with the king at Lewes; governs in the king's name, ib. His wise and mild administration; he summons the whole force of the country to meet him in arms on Barham Downs, and takes the command of a fleet to prevent the landing of foreign troops, ib. The earl of Gloucester concerts a plan for releasing prince Edward, and is joined by him at Ludlow, where the royal banner is raised, the prince having sworn to respect the Charters, and govern according to law, 686. Prince Edward takes the command of the royal forces; display of his military sagacity, ib. He surprises Simon de Montfort, the earl of Leicester's son, near Kenilworth, ib. Leicester advances to Evesham, with the hope of meeting his son's forces, ib. He is surrounded by the royal troops, commanded by prince Edward, and having

LEICESTER, Simon de Montfort, earl of,— failed in an attempt to force the road to Kenilworth, is slain with his son Henry and one hundred and eighty barons and knights in the battle of Evesham, 1264; 687.

LEICESTER, sir Robert Dudley, earl of, third son of the earl of Warwick, 1550; married the daughter of sir John Robsart, ii. 495; note. Condemned to die as a traitor, 1554; 511. Created earl of Leicester, 1564. Becomes a favourite of Elizabeth, 575. She recommends him as a fit husband for Mary queen of Scots, 1562; ib. It is reported that he murdered his wife, in the hope of gaining Elizabeth's hand, 576. He accuses the earl of Norfolk of a plan to marry the queen of Scots, 624. He marries privately the widow of the late earl of Essex; is severely reprimanded for this by Elizabeth, and placed in confinement at Greenwich, 650. He takes the command of an army in the Netherlands, and induces the States to name him governor-general of the Low Countries, and to declare his authority absolute; anger of the queen at these proceedings, 656. Various plans being entertained by Elizabeth for the removal of the unfortunate queen of Scots, Leicester recommends the use of poison, 658. He is recalled from the Netherlands, and prince Maurice of Orange is put in his stead, 672. Elizabeth appoints him to the command of the land forces prepared for resisting the attack of the Invincible Armada, 674. He falls sick on his road to Kenilworth Castle, and dies at Cornbury in Oxfordshire, September 4, 1588. His Portrait, 750.

LEICESTER, Robert Sydney, earl of, 1626; made lord-lieutenant of Ireland, 1641, iii. 247; 389. He died 1677.

LEICESTER, Thomas Coke, earl of, 1744. He advises the duke of Newcastle to spare the life of lord Kilmarnock, 1746; iv. 550. He died 1759.

LEIGHTON, Alexander, Scottish Puritanical preacher, 1630; wrote "An Appeal to the Parliament; or, Sion's Plea against Prelacy," iii. 151. Sentenced in the Star-chamber, whipped, pilloried, ears cut off, nostrils slit, branded, 151, 152. Thrown into a dungeon; he was in ten years liberated by parliament, which beheaded both Land and the king, 152. Rushworth's remarks as to this victim, 152; note. He was father of archbishop Leighton, ib.

LEIGHTON, Dr. Robert, bishop of Dunblane, refuses to take the Oath of Supremacy, 1661; iii. 683. His Portrait, 803.

Leipzig, battle of, October 16 and 18, 1813; § iv. 593*, 594*.

LELY, sir Peter; this distinguished artist was a native of Westphalia, he came to England in 1643, and died, 1680; iii. 883. His Portrait of archbishop Usher, 433. Of Maria Beatrix of Modena, queen of James II., 768. Of the duke of Lauderdale, 830. Of George I. iv. 303. Description of his style of painting, 883.

LE MARCHAND, a sculptor of some note (seventeenth century); iv. 757.

LENNOX, earl of, opposed at Flodden Field, 1513, to sir Edward Stanley's division; falls in the battle, ii. 328, 329.

LENNOX, earl of, with many barons, rebelled in 1516, against the regent Albany, who defeated and then pardoned him, ii. 351, 352.

LENNOX, earl of, nearly related to the royal family of Scotland, is set up, during the infancy of Mary queen of Scots, as a rival to the earl of Arran, ii. 436. He throws himself into the English interests, 437. His eagerness for money, ib. He arrives from England with a fleet of eight ships, takes the Isles of Arran and Bute, plunders Kentire, Kyle, and Carrick, and returns loaded with booty to an English port, 1545; 441. He is driven from court through the insolence of his son Darnley, husband

LENNOX, earl of,—
of Mary queen of Scots, 584. He informs his
daughter-in-law of the intention of her husband to
go abroad, 592. He charges the earl of Bothwell
with the murder of Darnley, 596, 597. Elizabeth,
on the death of Murray, makes him regent of Scotland, 1571; 632.
LENNOX, Esmé Stuart, lord of Aubigny, duke of,
nephew of the preceding earl, becomes a favourite
of the youthful king James VI., 1578; ii. 652. The
Scottish king demands from Elizabeth the hand of
the lady Arabella Stuart for Lennox, who was
her cousin, iii. 46; 439. Lennox is driven into
France by the earl of Marr, where he soon after
dies, 654.
LENNOX, duke of; his patent for searching and seal-
ing new drapery, monopolies of wine, licenses,
duty on sea-coal, etc., voted a grievance by the
House of Commons, 1610; iii. 43.
LENNOX, duke of. See Richmond.
LENTHALL, a barrister, chosen as Speaker of the Long
Parliament, iii. 226, 429*, 526.
LENTULUS, Publius; his description of Christ, sent to
the senate of Rome, iii. 812.
LEO X., John de' Medici, pope, elected March 11,
1513. He supports the cause of Francis I. in his
war in Lombardy and Italy, ii. 336. In 1521, he
conferred the title of "Defender of the Faith" on
Henry VIII., 345. His alliance with Charles V.,
ib. Was head of the Italian League, and recovered
Milan, etc., from Francis I., 346. The pope's
triumph at Rome for these successes, 347. His
sudden illness and death, December 1, 1521; ib.
He instituted the sale of indulgences, 706.
LEOFRIC, earl. He supports Harold Harefoot in opposition to Hardicanute, i. 184. His power and territorial government in Mercia and the north of
England, 188. He marches to the assistance of
Edward the Confessor, 1051, at Gloucester, 190.
His son, Algar, 194. Death of the earl, ib.
LEOFWINE, one of six sons of earl Godwin, i. 188, 191,
193; he is slain at the battle of Hastings, October
1066; 215.
LEOPOLD I., emperor of Germany, 1658; iv. 33. He
dies, 1705, and is succeeded by his son, Joseph,
178. Bishop Burnet's description of him, ib.
LEOPOLD II., emperor of Germany, 1790—1792.
Ascends the throne on the death of Joseph II.,
February 20, 1790; § ii. 470. He attempts to
conciliate the Austrian Netherlands, 471—473.
Course and final overthrow of the Belgic Revolution, 532—537. Leopold engages to assist Louis
XVI. against his rebellious subjects, 1791; 638.
His death, March 1, 1792; § iii. 39.
LESLEY, Catholic bishop of Ross; his mission to Mary
of Scots, 1561, when about to return from France
to her kingdom, ib. 564. The Scottish Catholics
advised the young queen, by this prelate and historian, to land in the Highlands, and entrust herself
to Huntley for her safe establishment on her
throne; she declined, lest a civil war should ensue,
ib.
LESLIE, sir David, iii. 340. Charles I. offers him the
title of earl of Orkney, on condition that he will
espouse his cause and join Montrose, 354.
LESLIE, general, a leader of the Covenanters, takes
Edinburgh Castle, March 1639, iii. 203. The
Scottish army disbanded, 205. The Scots again
take up arms, and appoint Leslie commander-in-
chief, 219; he takes Edinburgh Castle, ib. Overcomes lord Conway, and crosses the Tyne, 220.
Brings down his artillery into Newburn town,
and compels the English to abandon their
breast-works, 221. His body-guard of Scottish
lawyers, ib. The gates of Newcastle are thrown
open to him, 222. He quits Newcastle to pursue
the royal forces, ib. Takes Durham, ib. Sends

LESLIE, general,—
lord Lanark, brother to the marquess of Hamilton, to present the petition of the Covenanters,
ib. Their list of grievances, September 1640; 223.
Sixteen English and eight Scottish commissioners
negotiate at Ripon, 226. Leslie is made earl of
Leven, 1641. He promises never more to take up
arms against the king, 252. The Commons vote
him a letter of thanks, etc., for refusing bribes from
sir William Fleming, 340.
LESLY, Norman, the master of Rothes, 1546; his
uncle, John Lesly, Kirkaldy of Grange, etc., conspired against cardinal Beaton, and murdered that
primate in his castle of St. Andrew's, ii. 446.
LESTOCK, admiral, subjected to court-martial by
admiral Matthews, and honourably acquitted, 1744;
iv. 472. He conducts an expedition to the coast of
Brittany, 554.
L'ESTRANGE; quoted iii. 667.
LE SUEUR, Hubert, an eminent foreign artist, arrived
in England about 1630. He executed the equestrian statue of Charles I. at Charing-cross, iii. 576.
Letters, revival of, in the western world, ii. 200—
222.
LEVER, Thomas; his description of the University of
Cambridge, regno Edward VI., ii. 819.
LEVESEY, sir Michael, overcomes the earl of Holland
at Kingston-upon-Thames, July 5, 1648; iii. 383.
LEVI, M., he succeeds general Montcalm in command of the French, 1760, and determines to make
a desperate effort to recover the French possessions,
iv. 614. He appears before Quebec; general Murray
marches out to attack him, but is defeated, and loses
nearly all his guns, ib. Levi brings up six frigates,
and commences the siege by land and water, ib.
His ships are destroyed by lord Colville, and he
decamps precipitately, leaving his artillery and
stores behind him, ib.
LEVING, sir Richard, iv. 102; committed to the
Tower, 1700; 104.
LEVINGSTONE, colonel, commander of the forces in
Scotland, 1693; iv. 46.
Lewes Priory, view of the ruins of, i. 684. A great
battle was fought here between king Henry III.
and the earl of Leicester, May 14, 1264, in which
both the king and his son Edward were taken
prisoners, 685. Treaty of, ib.
LEWIS, Erasmus, an active Jacobite, 1715; iv. 311.
LEWIS, M. P., accused by the army, June 15, 1647;
iii. 369.
LEWIS, Mr., gentleman of the horse to lord Fever-
sham, 1696; iv. 67.
LEWKNOR, sir Lewis, the first master of the cere-
monies, appointed 1603, on occasion of several
embassies to James I. at Whitehall, iii. 7, 92.
LEXINGTON, lord, sent on an embassy to Madrid,
1712; iv. 270.
Leyden jar, the, discovered, in 1745, by Cuneus and
Lallemand, iv. 785.
LEYDEN, John of, a mathematician of the 13th cen-
tury, i. 844.
LHUYD, Humphrey, a Welsh antiquary, i. 16, 21.
Libel, cases of, § i. 530—533; § iii. 613—621. Law
of, 556—566. Fox's Libel Bill passed 1792; § iii. 21.
Library, description of a, 17th century, iii. 630.
LICHFIELD, earl of, captain of the king's horse-guards,
killed before Chester, 1645; iii. 343.
LIGHTFOOT, Mr., counsel to the earl of Strafford on
his trial, 1641; iii. 239.
Light-house, erection of, at Plymouth, 1665; iii. 858.
Light-house, erected on the Eddystone rock by
Winstanley, in 1696, at the expense of the Trinity-
house, iv. 705. It was blown down, 1703, whilst
undergoing repairs, and Winstanley and all his
workmen perished. A new light-house, entirely of
wood, was soon after erected by Rudyerd, which
was burned down in 1755; it was succeeded

Lighthouse,—
by the present stone structure, the work of Mr. Smeaton, 705.
LIGNEVILLE, count de, 1719; iv. 360.
LIGON, his history of Barbadoes in 1647; iii. 548.
LIGONIER, colonel, present at the battle of Falkirk, 1746; iv. 523.
LILBURNE, John, cited to the Star-chamber, 1638, for publishing libellous books, and refusing to take an oath to answer the interrogatories of the Court, is adjudged to be contumacious, and sentenced to be fined, pilloried, etc., iii. 167. Having been liberated from the Fleet by the parliament, he is taken prisoner by Charles at Brentford, who threatens to proceed against him as a traitor, 302; but is prevented by the parliament, 303. His portrait, ib. He becomes a leader of the Adjutators, and forms a plan for assassinating Cromwell, 373.
Lime, in Kent, the Roman station Lemannæ, i. 90.
Limerick, view of, iv. 27. Invested by William III., 1690, who is obliged to raise the siege, 26. Capitulates on honourable terms to general Ginckel, 34.
LIMERICK, lord, he moves for a secret committee to inquire into the administration of sir Robert Walpole, March 9, 1742; iv. 460.
LINACRE, Thomas, an eminent physician and philologist, born about 1460, died 1524; iii. 820.
Lincoln, ancient Roman arches of Newport Gate, i. 116. Restoration of this gate a modern structure, ib. View of Lincoln, 430. State of in the 17th century, iii. 655. Battle of Lincoln, 1141, in which Stephen was taken prisoner by the earl of Gloucester, i. 430.
LINCOLN, John de la Pole, earl of, eldest son of John duke of Suffolk and Elizabeth, second sister of Edward IV. and Richard III., created March 1467; ii. 175, 288. He fell into the power of Henry VII., 1485, after the battle of Bosworth, but the king refrained from imprisoning him, 288. His high character caused the Yorkists to look up to him, ib. He resorted to the court of his aunt, the duchess of Burgundy, sister of Edward IV., 289. She supplied him with 2,000 German veterans, under Martin Swart. Lincoln and Lovel then embarked for Dublin, ib. Lambert Simnel having been crowned without opposition in the cathedral of that capital, as Edward VI., he landed in England, at Furness, supported by Lincoln, ib. They were joined by sir Thomas Broughton of Lancashire, ib. They marched on York, but were joined by none, 290. Lincoln bravely marched to meet Henry VII., and at Stoke was totally defeated by the earl of Oxford, commanding the king's vanguard, ib. Swart and all his Germans fell in this action, ib. Lincoln, Broughton, lords Thomas and Maurice Fitzgerald, were also slain, 1487. Lovel was drowned in the Trent, ib.
LINCOLN, John, instigates a serious tumult against foreign artisans, 1517; ii. 778.
LINCOLN, major-general, an American officer, 1779; § i. 387. Portrait of, ib.
Lincoln's-inn, description of its foundation by Mr. Reeves, i. 819.
Lincolnshire, insurrection of the commons of, 1470, suppressed by Edward IV. in person, ii. 104. The leaders sent to the block, ib. Formidable insurrection in, 1536. The duke of Suffolk and divers lords were sent to quell it, 397. The "Six Articles of Grievances," eloquently and respectfully stated, elicited a furious reply from the pen of Henry VIII., 397, 398. This year, eventful in royal agitations, the assembled masses loudly calling for redress, threw the king into a panic fear, ib. The duke of Suffolk sent with a great force against the rebels, ib. By promises of redress, time was gained, and dissensions sown among the Lincolnshire petitioners, ib. The result was the execution of "captain Cobbler,"

Lincolnshire,—
the leader, Dr. Makerel, a prior, and thirteen others, 398.
LINDESAY, Alexander de, a follower of Wallace, 1297; i. 715. He lays down his arms, 716.
Lindisfarne, or Holy Island, granted by Oswald, nephew of Edwin, about 638, to monks, for completing the conversion of the Northumbrians, i. 147. View of the abbey of, 146.
LINDSAY, lord (of the Byres), 1488, presented a gray charger to James III., ii. 303. He advised James IV. not to give battle at Flodden, 1513; 327.
LINDSAY, lord, 1638; iii. 186. A royalist; his disgust at the conduct of prince Rupert, 297.
LINDSAY, Alexander, an excellent navigator and hydrographer. He went on an expedition with James V. of Scotland, 1540, and drew from his observations the first known chart of Scotland and the adjacent islands, ii. 795.
LINDSAY, sir David, a witty poet, a favourite of the accomplished but unfortunate James V., ii. 638; iii. 644.
LINDSAY, Mr. David, minister of Leith, nominated to the see of Ross, about 1600; iii. 451. Deposed, 484.
LINDSAY, Mr. David, formerly under-secretary to James II.; is arrested, 1703, on suspicion of being concerned in Fraser's Plot, iv. 156. He is brought to trial for high treason, 1704; carried to Tyburn, and sent back to Newgate. He died in want in Holland, 161.
LINDSEY, Robert Bertie, earl of, created Nov. 1626. In 1628, on the assassination of Buckingham by Felton, Lindsey sails in command of the armament to La Rochelle, but returns with the dishonour of achieving nothing for the Huguenots, and that bulwark of Calvinism in France surrenders through famine, iii. 138. He died 1642.
LINDSEY, Montague Bertie, earl of, 1642; died 1666; iii. 696.
LINDSEY, Robert Bertie, earl of, brings into the Lords an intolerant bill, 1675, for the security of the Protestant religion. He died 1701; iii. 712.
Linen manufacture, in Scotland and Ireland, iv. 732; § i. 598; § iii. 703.
Lisbon, adventures of the fleet of king Richard here, when on its way to the Holy Land, i. 487.
LISLE, lord, eldest son of the earl of Warwick, marries the lady Anne, daughter of the duke of Somerset, June 3, 1551; ii. 495.
L'ISLE ADAM, 1418, a partisan of the duke of Burgundy, suddenly enters Paris, and secures the person of Charles VI., ii. 41. His subsequent career, 45, 73, 79.
LISLE, Mrs. Alicia, beheaded by James II. for giving shelter to two fugitives from Sedgemoor, iii. 780.
LISLE, sir George, a royalist officer at the battle of Naseby, iii. 333. Is shot by Fairfax, August 27, 1648; 383.
LISLE, sir John, Yorkist, 1471, falls in the great victory of Edward IV. at Barnet, ii. 109.
LISLE, Mr., a Commonwealth-man. Having fled to Switzerland for refuge, the Swiss refuse to give him up to the vengeance of Charles II., who desired his execution; the king therefore hires assassins, who murder him whilst in the act of entering a church, August, 1664; iii. 690.
Lissa, battle of, fought December 5, 1757. In this terrible encounter Frederic the Great, with an army of 30,000 men, defeats 90,000 Austrians and Imperialists, takes 24,000 prisoners on the field, 15,000 in the retreat, and 17,000 in the city of Breslau; the Austrians lost 130 pieces of cannon, 2,000 baggage wagons, their ammunition, and all their equipages, iv. 598.
Literary property, subject of, § i. 537—539.
Literature, Science, and the Fine Arts, at successive periods of our history, to A.D. 449; i. 118. From 449 to 1066; 289. From 1066 to 1216; 603. From

Literature,—
1216 to 1399; 842. From 1399 to 1485; ii. 196. From 1485 to 1603; 813. From 1603 to 1660; iii. 560. From 1660 to 1689; 871. From 1688 to 1760; iv. 735. Reign of George III. From 1760 to 1785; § i. 604. From 1785 to 1802; § iii. 715. From 1802 to 1820; § iv. 696.

Lithotomy, operation of, successfully performed at Paris, for the first time, in the year 1474, on a condemned criminal, ii. 208.

LITTLETON, sir Edward, solicitor-general, attempts to prove the legality of ship-money, 1637; iii. 179.

LITTLETON, sir Thomas, a judge of the Common Pleas, died in 1481; his simplicity and terseness in diction and matter, ii. 164. His "Tenures" in Norman French, ib. Parallel betwixt his style and the work of Coke, his commentator, ib.; iii. 727; iv. 92.

LITTLETON, Mr., implicated in the Essex-House affair, 1601; condemned, but surrendering his estate, and paying a heavy mulet, is thrown into the Queen's Bench, where he dies, ii. 689.

LITTLETON, lord-keeper, iii. 285. Sends the great seal to Charles at York, 286. His death, at Oxford, August 27, 1645; 340.

LIULF, a Saxon noble, married the widow of Siward, and mother of Waltheof, i. 384, 385. He complained to bishop Walcher de Lorraine of being robbed by that bishop's retainers, 1080, ib. Liulf, in consequence, was murdered, 385. The Northumbrians rose for vengeance, set fire to a church in which the bishop took refuge, and, on his coming out, put him to death, ib.

Liverpool, Litherpoole, or Lirpool, iii. 656.

LIVERPOOL, Charles Jenkinson, first baron Hawkesbury, created earl, June 1st, 1796. Under-secretary to the earl of Bute, 1761; § i. 5, 91.

LIVINGSTON, sir Alexander, a turbulent noble, 1440, aided by Crichton, seizes William, earl of Douglas and his brother, in Edinburgh Castle, and the Douglases are beheaded, ii. 134, 135. The Livingstons, holding a meeting of their family and clan, are surrounded by the troops of James I., 1449, and some of the chiefs tried and executed, 135. Their faction repressed, ib.

LIVINGSTONE, lady, appointed nurse to James I.'s eldest son, the prince Henry, iii. 445.

LIVY, the Roman historian, quoted, i. 35.

LLEWELLYN, description of the Welsh before their conquest by Edward I., from Giraldus, i. 595, 696. Llewellyn agrees upon a marriage with Elinor de Montfort; but while on her voyage from France to Wales, she is captured by four English ships, with her youngest brother, Emeric, and sent to Edward, ib. Llewellyn complains of this unjust seizure and detention of his bride during time of peace, ib. Hostilities commence, ib. Edward sets out in person, with a fine army, having matured his measures for the subjugation of Wales, 1277; 697. Llewellyn is reduced to extremities, and condescends to any terms that Edward should propose, ib. War again commences; David, brother of Llewellyn, who in the former war had assisted the English king, surprised and took the strong castle of Hawardine, March 22, 1282, belonging to Roger Clifford, the justiciary, who was taken prisoner, ib. A general insurrection ensued, and Llewellyn, joining his brother, laid siege to the castles of Flint and Rhuddlan, ib. Edward raises money by forced loans, and assembles a large army, and 1,000 pioneers, who cut down woods, and open roads into the fastnesses of Snowdon; Edward receives a complete check; but reinforcements continually crossed the Dee, or came up from the coast, and he procured the services of foreign mercenaries, who were well suited for mountain warfare, ib. After some protracted

LLEWELLYN :—
warfare, Edward is worsted, being obliged to fly for protection to one of his castles, leaving the lords Audley and Clifford dead on the field, 698. Llewellyn, elated by these successes, leaves his brother David to carry on the war in North Wales, and boldly turns towards the south to meet the new invaders, who were advancing from Pembrokeshire and Caermarthen, ib. Being surprised by the earl of Mortimer, near Bualth, in the valley of the Wye, Llewellyn is killed, November, 1282, and his head sent to Edward, ib.

LLOEGRWYS, a people of Gascony, who migrated to Britain, and gave their name to a great part of the country which was afterwards called Lloegris, i. 9.

LLOYD, Dr., his description of the body of sir Edmondbury Godfrey, who was murdered, October, 1678; iii. 720.

LLUYD, Humfrey, a Dutch engraver (sixteenth century), iii. 577.

LOBKOWITZ, prince, he threatens to attack the Neapolitan territory, but is driven behind the Po by Don Carlos, 1744; iv. 474.

Lochgillip, treaty of, 1411; ii. 132.

Lochleven Castle, view of, ii. 605. Account of sir William Douglas, the lord of this fortress, in which Mary Stuart suffered a harsh detention, after her surrender at Carberry Hill, 602. Her abdication, under threats of a violent death, 604. William Douglas, a mere youth, crossing the lake in a skiff to this strong castle, at night, released the queen, and delivered her to Seton, G. Douglas, and the Hamiltons, who escorted her to the town of Hamilton, 606. Solemn association of the nobility and prelates to maintain her rights, 607. Their total defeat at Langside, ib.

LOCKE, John, born 1632, died 1704; iv. 790, 791. His literary works, ib. Portrait of, 735.

Locks, manufacture of, an important branch of British industry, § iii. 685.

LODBROKE, or Lodbrog, the daughters of this brave but unfortunate Norwegian, embroider a magical banner of the raven, which is captured by the Saxons in Devonshire, 877; i. 159.

LODGE, Thomas, a dramatic writer, born about 1556. He was an eminent physician, and wrote a considerable quantity of other poetry besides his plays, iii. 587.

LODGE's 'Illustrations of British History,' quoted, iii. 2.

Lodi, battle of, May 10, 1796; § iii. 512.

LODONIA. See Picts.

LOE, Mr., counsel for the unfortunate earl of Strafford, 1641; iii. 239.

LOFTUS, sir Adam, chancellor, iii. 171. He buys the office of vice-treasurer for 6,000l., 1633; ib.

LOLHARD, Walter, founder of the Lollards, burned at Cologne, 1322; ii. 141.

Lollards, origin of the, ii. 140. Said to have acquired their religious doctrines from Wycliffe, 140, 141, 144. Walter Lolhard burnt at Cologne, 1322; his principles of reform adverse to Rome, 141. Petition of the Lollards to the English Parliament, in 1395; ib. In 1401, the statute De hæretico comburendo was passed to repress them, ib. Its provisions, 141, 142. The House of Commons having, by the years 1404—1409, imbibed strongly their principles, in reply to Henry IV.'s. demands for aid in his wars, propose a sequestration of church estates, 142. The House of Peers and the king support the dignified clergy, ib. Case of William Sawtre, who was deprived by archbishop Arundel, degraded for his new opinions, and burnt, 1401, in Smithfield, 143. William Thorpe, a priest, stoutly maintains a long argument in favour of the reformed doctrine of Wycliffe against archbishop Arundel, in 1407; Thorpe's own narrative quoted,

. Lollards,—
143—146. He was consigned to a dungeon, 146. Badby denied transubstantiation in 1410; condemned by archbishop Arundel, he was burnt in a tun, 146. Prince Henry (Henry V.) present at this execution in Smithfield, offered him pardon if he would recant; and on refusal, the prince commanded his immediate execution, *ib.* Accession of Henry V. in 1413, which does not stop the lamentable persecution, *ib.* Cobham, or Oldcastle, condemned for heresy, 1414; 25, 38; shortly after, Arundel dying, was succeeded by archbishop Chicheley, a more sweeping persecutor, 146. Cobham burnt, *ib.* In 1415 John Claydon burnt for having books called heretical, *ib.* Richard Turmin burnt, *ib.* The Lollards' Tower, built by Chicheley for their prison. View of Lambeth Palace, 147. Bishop Peacock, 1457, imprisoned for heresy, *ib.* Names of some learned Reformers, certain of whom, from fear and other motives, proved unsteady to the doctrines of their master Wycliffe, 144.
LOLLIUS URBICUS, his expedition into Caledonia, i. 47; builds a stone rampart, *ib.*
Lombards, or *Longobardi.* Their laws, reduced to a written code, were promulgated about 640; i. 145.
LOMBART, Peter, a native of Paris, and an excellent engraver; he came to England before 1564, and remained until after the Restoration, iii. 578.
LOMBE, John, proceeded to Italy, 1715, and clandestinely made drawings of a silk-mill; he erected the first silk-mill at Derby, 1719; iv. 731.
London, *Londinium.* Augusta, or Loudinium, pillaged by Scots in 367, who, arriving from Ireland carried away the inhabitants for slaves, i. 54. London in the Roman period. Paulinus Suetonius marches from the Menai to the relief of the rising city; retreats thence, followed by many of the inhabitants; the Britons exterminate the rest, 43. Defeat of Boadicea by Suetonius, 44. London, not a municipium, 86; its great trade and number of inhabitants, *ib.* The Londoners, under Ethelred, son-in-law of Alfred, besiege the Danish fortress of Benfleet, in Essex, and capture therein treasure, etc., also the sons of Hasting, the Dane, 894; 163. They capture, or burn, the Danish ships aground in the Lea, 896; 164. The see of London was founded, and a church built by king Sebert, 309. Influence of the city; deputation of the Londoners to Matilda for the liberation of Stephen, 435. No mention of commerce in the two charters granted to this city by William I., or in the charter of Henry I., except the clause declaring that all the men of London and their goods should be exempted throughout England from all tolls and customs, 585. Fitz-Stephen's animated description of London and its commerce, written in 1174; 589. The first stone bridge across the Thames was built, 1176, by Peter of Colechurch, 615. The citizens of London take part with the earl of Leicester against king Henry III., 684. Many of them are slaughtered at the battle of Lewes, where Henry was taken prisoner, 685. They are deprived of their charter, 687. Prince Henry obtains the grant of a new charter and the restoration of their liberties, 688. They refuse to follow Edward II. to the field against Isabella and the barons, 743. Influence of this city in the reigns of Richard I. and John, 810. The lord mayor, obliged to admit the Kentish-men under Cade, 1450, daily into the city, at length successfully defends the passage of London-bridge, ii. 88, 89. The civic procession to Westminster-hall, on the Thames, commenced 1453, John Norman, mayor, ii. 261. The Charter-house, the Black Friars, Grey Friars, White Friars, in London, suppressed, 1537—1540; as also the abbeys of Merton, Stratford, Lewes, Battle, Canterbury; so that by the year 1540 there were few monasteries left in England, the lands were

London,—
mostly granted to the courtiers of that period, 404. *Illustrations;* fifteenth century, the Tower and the City of London, 170. Hollar's print of the City before the Great Fire, iii. 545. The Great Fire of London, 1666, as it appeared from Southwark, 699.
Londonderry, view of the city, iv. 17.
LONDONDERRY, sir Charles Stewart, marquess of; sent as English envoy to the allied armies, 1813; § iv. 593*.
LONG, M.P., seized by the king, 1629; iii. 142. He is formally accused by the army, 1647; 369.
LONGBEARD.—*See* Fitz-Osbert.
LONGCHAMP, William, bishop of Ely, lord-chancellor and justiciary of England; consecrated December, 1189. He deprives Pudsey of the regency about 1189; i. 485. Appointed legate of England and Ireland, 505. He displaces the sheriff and governor of York for the late disturbance and massacre of the Jews there, and lays a fine on the richest of the citizens of York, *ib.* His dispute with Pudsey, 505, 506. His character, 506. Earl John's letter to his brother Richard, accusing Longchamp of ruining the kingdom, *ib.* Richard confirms his authority, *ib.* Gerard de Camville claims the custody of Lincoln Castle, *ib.* Longchamp marches to Lincoln, but while he is besieging the castle, earl John puts himself at the head of a large army, and takes the royal castles of Nottingham and Tickhill, *ib.* Earl John is acknowledged successor to Richard, in the event of his dying without issue, 507. Geoffrey, who had been expelled from England, returns, contrary to the commands of Longchamp; he is seized and imprisoned in Dover Castle, but is soon set at liberty. John, with the archbishop of Rouen, orders all the prelates and barons of the kingdom to assemble, and summons Longchamp to make amends to the archbishop of York, and to answer for the whole of his public conduct before the king's council, *ib.* Longchamp marches to London, but, not being joined by the citizens, who refuse to close their gates, he retires to the Tower, *ib.* They offer to him his bishopric of Ely, and the custody of three of the royal castles, but he refuses to commit any of the king's rights; he delivers up the keys of the Tower to John, and retires to Normandy, 508. He continues to hold his office, is employed in some important embassies by Richard, and dies, 1198, 511.
LONGLAND, John, bishop of Lincoln, appointed May 1520; writes to Henry VIII., 1530, respecting the sentiments of the University of Oxford on the question of Divorce, ii. 375, 376. He died May, 1547.
LONGSPEAR, William.—*See* earl of Salisbury.
LONGUEVILLE, duke of, taken prisoner at the battle of the Spurs, 1513, where he commanded. ii. 325. He informs Henry VIII. of negotiations between Louis XII. and the emperor Maximilian, 331.
LONSDALE, John Lowther, viscount, created 1696; is made lord privy-seal, 1699. He died, 1700; iv. 95.
Loo, § i. 644.
LOPEZ, Roderigo, physician to queen Elizabeth, is accused, 1594, of plotting against her life, ii. 679; he is executed, 680.
Lord, Congregation of the, ii. 548.
Lords, House of, view of the, § i. 164.
LORN, lord of, endeavours to take Bruce a prisoner, 1306; i. 729.
LORRAINE, cardinal of, uncle of Mary queen of Scots, ii. 583.
Lorsch, portico at, i. 312, 313.
LOSINGA, Herbert, consecrated bishop of Thetford, 1091. He removed the see to Norwich, April, 1094, and founded a Benedictine abbey there; he died July, 1119; i. 604, 615.

LOTHIAN, lord, iii. 352. He protests, January 25, 1649, against the proceedings instituted against Charles I., 393.

Lothians, the :—*Lodonia* long disputed between the Picts and Saxons of Bernicia, remained to the Pictish monarchy upon the battle fought at Dunnechtan, 685, by king Bridei against the Northumbrian Egfrid, i. 216. Formal cession of, by Eadulf the Dane, 221.

LOUDON, lord, is sent to London by the Covenanters, 1639; is seized and committed to the Tower for writing a letter signed "Au roi," iii. 207. When chancellor of Scotland, he endeavours to persuade Charles I., 1646, to accept the conditions offered by the parliament, 358.

LOUGHBOROUGH. Alexander Wedderburn, lord; made lord high-chancellor on the resignation of Thurlow, 1792; § iii. 27. He votes against the abatement of impeachment on the dissolution of parliament, 600. His portrait, *ib.*

LOUIS IV., named d'Outremer, king of France, 936 —954, finds an asylum in the court of Athelstane, i. 169.

LOUIS VI., king of France (1108—1137), kindly receives William Fitz-Robert, and promises to grant him the investiture of Normandy, i. 412. He bestows upon him his queen's sister, and with her, as a portion, the countries of Pontoise, Chaumont, and the Vexin, and soon after confers on him the earldom of Flanders, 417.

LOUIS VII., king of France, (1137—1180.) His marriage with and divorce of Eleanor, afterwards wife of Henry II., i. 439, 440. Receives homage from Henry II., 442. He affiances his infant daughter, Margaret, to Henry's eldest son, 444. He assists Raymond, earl of Toulouse, against Henry, 444, 445; marries Adelais, niece of king Stephen, and sister of the earls of Blois, Champagne, and Sancerre, 446; assists the people of Brittany and Maine against Henry, and receives Becket; a peace is concluded, and Henry's sons do homage for their several fiefs, 452. A marriage is agreed upon between prince Richard and Alice, daughter of Louis, *ib.* Prince Henry and his consort Margaret pay a visit to Louis, 467. Louis receives the young prince (who, having demanded of his father the government of England or Normandy, and being refused, had fled to Louis for assistance), and acknowledges him king of England in a great council of barons and bishops, 1173; 468. War commences in Normandy; the young prince's party is repulsed; a meeting takes place between the two kings, but is broken off, *ib.* Louis and prince Henry again attack Normandy, 1174; prince Richard leads the insurgents of Poietou and Aquitaine, 470. Henry II. lands his army in Normandy, where he raises the siege of Rouen, 471—544. He is reconciled to his children, and peace is restored, *ib.*

LOUIS VIII., king of France (1223—1226,) eldest son of Philip II. of France; the English barons, being hard pressed by John, send a deputation, offering to prince Louis the crown of England, 1215; i. 531. He accepts the invitation, and, at the feast of Easter, sets sail from Calais with a numerous and well-appointed army, embarked on board 680 vessels, *ib.* The French land at Sandwich; John, who commanded a numerous army at Dover, flies before the French land, *ib.* Louis takes the castle of Rochester, and then marches to London, where he is joyfully received and conducted, with a magnificent procession, to St. Paul's; the nobles and citizens swear fealty, *ib.* He publishes a manifesto, addressed to the king of Scotland and all the nobles not present in London; the men of the north rise up in arms against John, and his foreign mercenaries desert him, *ib.* Louis marches to Dover, and lays siege to the castle, *ib.*

LOUIS VIII,—
The barons besiege Windsor Castle, but raise the siege to oppose John, and then join Louis at Dover, *ib.* He treats the English with disrespect, and grants English estates and titles to his French followers, *ib.* The viscount de Melun, reported to have called to him, when dying, the English nobles in London, and to have declared to them that Louis had sworn to banish for ever all those who had joined his standard, 532. Louis spends three months in the siege of Dover, *ib.* The cause of John brightens; he loses his treasures in crossing the sands in the Wash, *ib.* He eats immoderately of some peaches or pears, and drinks new cider at the abbey of Swineshead, and on the following day is seized with a violent fever, *ib.*; of which he dies, October 18, 1216, and his son Henry is crowned, 533. On the death of John, after another attempt on Dover Castle, he raises the siege and returns to London, where the Tower is yielded to him; he takes the castles of Hertford and Berkhamstead, 672. A truce proclaimed; Louis goes over to France to procure supplies, and leaves the government in the hands of Enguerrand de Coucy, *ib.* On his way to the coast he narrowly escapes capture by Philip d'Albiney, who put himself at the head of a popular party in Sussex, 673. The mariners of the Cinque Ports cut off several of his ships; on this he lands at Sandwich, and burns that town to the ground; and after making another attempt on Dover Castle he marches to London, *ib.* The battle, called "The Fair of Lincoln," is fought, in which the French commander, the count of Perche, is slain, *ib.* Another fleet sails from Calais, but the whole is taken or destroyed by Hubert de Burgh, *ib.* Louis determines to evacuate England; the final terms settled, 674. He is so poor that he is obliged to borrow money from the citizens of London to defray the expenses of his journey home; he is escorted to the sea-side by the earl of Pembroke, and sails for France, *ib.* Louis, having succeeded his father Philip on the French throne, 1223, invades the continental dominions of the English, and takes Rochelle, 675. He takes the cross against the Albigenses; Richard, earl of Cornwall, is sent with an English army to their assistance, 1225. A papal legate threatens the English with excommunication if they raise obstacles to this holy war; in consequence of this a truce is agreed on, *ib.* Death of this king, *ib.*

LOUIS IX., king of France, (1226—1270.) He succeeds to the throne in his twelfth year, on the death of his father, i. 675. War declared with France; the French take several towns from Henry, 676. Louis endeavours to effect a reconciliation between the English king and his barons, 684. He sets out on a crusade, but turns aside to attack the bey of Tunis, 689. After taking the city of Carthage he is attacked by dysentery and dies, 690. On the arrival of prince Edward at Carthage he found more than half his army had perished, and that the survivors had made advantageous terms with the bey of Tunis, and had no intention of leaving for Palestine, *ib.*

LOUIS XI., king of France (1461—1483.) His wild expedition against the Swiss, ii. 84. His intrigues against his father, Charles VII., cause a civil war, *ib.*

LOUIS XII., king of France, (1498—1515.) Vexed at the power of Anne, sister of Charles VIII., and her husband, Peter of Bourbon, 1483, Louis, then duke of Orleans, took up arms on the accession of Charles VIII., ii. 292, 293. He fled to Brittany, 292. His purpose to marry Anne of Brittany fails, *ib.* He commanded the Breton army, 1488, for Francis II. of Brittany, 294. His signal defeat by La Tremoille, at Andouillé; he

LOUIS XII.,—
was made prisoner bravely fighting, and sent to the castle of Bourges, *ib.* Was set free by Charles VIII. 297. Louis XII. succeeds Charles 1498, and obtaining a dispensation from Alexander VI. divorced his wife Jane, and espoused the widow Anne of Brittany, 311. He renewed the treaty of Estaples, and agreed to pay the arrears due to Henry VII., *ib.* Louis laid claim to Milan, possessed himself of Lombardy, and occupied Naples, *ib.* Coalition against France, 1510; 320. Henry VIII. declared war against Louis, *ib.*—[For details, *see* Henry VIII.] King Louis, baffled in Italy by the power of the Holy League for the protection of Julius II., and in ill health, returned, 1513, to defend France against Henry VIII., 322. He determined on a naval warfare, *ib.* In an action off Brest, 1512, his admiral, Primauget, was blown up in his ship with 900 men, and king Henry's finest ship, the *Regent*, was also blown into the air with 700 men. *ib.* The French fleet was collected in Brest, and manned partly by Genoese, *ib.* Henry commissioned his admiral, Edward Howard, son of the earl of Surrey, to attack it, who sailed from Portsmouth, March, 1513. *ib.* Death of Howard in action, when Louis's fleet made some descents on Sussex, *ib.*

LOUIS XIII., king of France (1610—1643.) Son of Henri IV., succeeds to the throne on his father's death, 1610; iii. 49. His weakness of character, *ib.* compelled to lay siege to his own cities in France, 88.

LOUIS XIV., king of France (1643—1715.) invades Spanish Flanders, and threatens the independence of the United Provinces, iii. 706. He concludes the treaty of Aix-la-chapelle, 1668; *ib.* Agrees to aid Charles II. in making England a Catholic country, if he will assist him in his designs on Holland and Spain, 707. De Ruyter attacks the combined fleets of France and England, 710. Louis marches to the Rhine at the head of 100,000 men, under the command of Turenne, Condé, and Luxembourg, and overruns three of the provinces; but tired with the brave resistance of William of Nassau he returns to France, leaving Turenne to manage the war, *ib.* His intrigues with the king of England, 715, 717. He concludes the peace of Nimeguen with the States-General, 717. His extensive power, 760. He sends to James II. 500,000 livres, 765. He receives captain Churchill, who announced the accession of James II., seated and covered, *ib.* He imparts by letters to James positive information of the intended invasion of the prince of Orange, and offers to assist him with naval and military forces, 794. Lays siege to Mons in person, iv. 32. Returns to Versailles, 33. He takes Namur, 36. Offers proposals of peace to the English, which are rejected, 47. His death, 1715; 311.

LOUIS XV., king of France (1715—1774.) Marries Mary Leczinska, daughter of Stanislaus, the exiled king of Poland, iv. 387. Declining state of France during this reign, § i. 9.

LOUIS XVI., king of France (1774—1793.) Portrait of, § ii. 338. His marriage, 1770, when dauphin of France, with the Austrian archduchess, Marie Antoinette, § i. 145. Treaty between France and America, Feb. 6, 1778; 336, 346. The French king issues an edict, March 18, to seize all British ships in the ports of France, 347. View of the moral and political state of France previous to the revolution, 328, *et seq.* Management of the finances under Neckar and Calonne, 339—342. The Stamp-tax is enregistered in a *lit de justice*, 1787; 343. Dispute between the king and his parlement, 346. The duke of Orleans is commanded to quit Paris, 347. Seizure of d'Esprémónil and de Monsabert, members of the parlement, 348. Terrific hail-storm, July, 1788, which causes a scarcity of provision, 349. Terrible disorders in Paris, April, 1789; the

LOUIS XVI.,—
réveillon-mob, 353. Assembly of the states-general, May 4; procession to the church of Notre Dame, 354. Description of the complexion of this assembly, 355—364. Disputes between the different orders of the states-general, 365—369. Death of the young Dauphin, 366. The tiers-état constitute themselves the National Assembly, 369. Neckar resigns, July 11. Universal tumult in Paris, 381. Attack on the Bastille, 385, 386. Louis appears in the National Assembly, 389. Lafayette is nominated prévôt des marchands, that place being vacant by the murder of de Flesselles, *ib.* Marshal Broglie resigns, 390. The king enters Paris, July 17; his reception there, 391, 392. Murder of M. de Foulon, a counsellor of state, and his son-in-law, M. Berthier de Sauvigny, 393—395. Destruction of châteaux and churches, 398, 399. Cruelties practised by the revolutionists, 400. Destruction of title-deeds, *ib.* Resolutions of the National Assembly, Aug. 4, 1789; 404, 405. Abolition of tithes, 405. The resolutions are presented to the king, 406. The Declaration of the Rights of Man, 407, 408. Attempts of the assembly to frame a constitution, 409. Financial distress of the nation, 412. A Committee of Subsistence appointed, 415. The regiment of Flanders brought to Versailles, 418. Rising of the Dames de la Halle, 422. Attack on the palace of Versailles 427—432. Arrival of the royal family at Paris, 433, 434. Meeting of the National Assembly at Paris, 436. The Jacobin Club, 437. Martial Law declared by the assembly, 438. Exile of the duke of Orleans, *ib.* A revolutionary tribunal erected, 439. Trial and execution of the marquess de Favras, 439—441. The brother of the king is accused of conspiring against the people, but is acquitted, 440. Confiscation of church property, Nov. 2, 442. The memorable French assignats put in circulation, 444. (*Specimen of, ib.*) The parlements suspended from their functions, 445. Grand *émeute* in the Faubourg St. Antoine about bread, 446. The king comes down unexpectedly to the assembly and promises to observe the constitution that was being formed, 477, 478. Assassination of the vicomte de Voisins, 479. Federations on the Rhone, 480. Club of the Feuillants established, May 12, 1790; 482. The club of Cordeliers, 483. The National Assembly decree that instead of the sixty districts there shall be forty-eight sections, 485. Abolition of hereditary nobility decreed; reign of the Jacobins, 489, 490. Honours decreed to the conquerors of the Bastille, 491. The grand Fête of the Federation, 493—501. Criticisms passed upon it by the French journalists of the day, 501—503. Affability of Marie Antoinette, 504—507. The duke of Orleans is permitted to return, 1790; 410. Insurrection and mutiny of the troops at Nancy, 513—516. Neckar quits France, 518. The assembly pass a decree, prohibiting the political clubs from holding any intercourse with the army, 519. Debates concerning the erection of a High National Court, 520, 521. The duke of Chartres (*Louis Philippe*,) is introduced to the Jacobin Club, 522. The *Cercle Social* instituted by the abbé Fauchet, 523. An ecclesiastical commission appointed; civil oath imposed on the clergy, 1791; 590. Departure of two of Louis XVI.'s aunts from France, 603—605. Suppression of gaming-houses, 607. Destruction of the donjon at Vincennes, 609. Death of Mirabeau, April 2, 1791; 614. Death of the vicomte Mirabeau (younger brother of the preceding), 619. The king attempts a journey to St. Cloud, but is obliged by the people to return to the Tuileries, 620. The pope burned in effigy in Paris for excommunicating Talleyrand, 627. The king's flight is notified to the assembly by Alexandre Beauharnois, the president, June 21, 629. The houses of several foreign

Louis XVI,—

ambassadors threatened by the mob, 633. Account of the flight of the royal family, and their detention at Varennes, 637—651. Woeful effects of grief upon Marie Antoinette, 653. Declaration of the king and queen concerning their attempt at escape, 655. Menacing letter of general De Bouillé to the National Assembly, 656. *Emeute* in the Champ de Mars, July, 1791; 667—671. Resolutions for preventing similar occurrences, 671, 672. Open war declared between the Assembly and the Ultra-Jacobins, 672. Voltaire is disinterred by command of the Assembly, and reburied with much pomp at St. Geneviève, 675. The Assembly nominate eighty-eight preceptors for the young Dauphin, 676; vote that the constitution is finished, September 3; 680. The king gives his acceptation, September 13; 681. Law against clubs, 684, 685; against refractory priests, 686. Avignon incorporated with France, September 14; *ib.* Lives of several eminent revolutionists, 688—699. The new legislature open their session, October 1, 1791; 699. Proclamation concerning emigrations issued in the name of the king, 708. The king puts his veto on several of the resolutions of the Assembly, 711—713. Petition of several constitutional priests for leave of marriage to their order, 713. Lafayette surrenders his charge as commandant-general of the Parisian army, October 8, and retires to his estates in Auvergne, 715, 716. Pétion is elected mayor of Paris, 716. Resolutions concerning the dispersion of the emigrant forces on the frontiers, 721. *Emeutes* on account of the dearness of bread and sugar, 1792; § iii. 51. The Jacobins make a vow of abstinence from the latter article, 52. Breaking up of the ministry; Dumouriez, Rowland, etc., come into office, 53. General forging of pikes; invention of the guillotine, 55. The Assembly vote that men of colour, if free, shall enjoy the same liberty and equality as white men, *ib.* Discussion in the hall of the Jacobins as to the propriety of admitting the belief of a God, 56. War proclaimed against Francis II., 60—65. The fête of Liberty, 65—67. Flight of general Biron before a detachment of Austrian light cavalry, 69. Debates concerning the danger of permitting the king to keep his constitutional guard, 75, 80. Colonel Brissac is committed to prison, and afterwards (in September) massacred by the mob, *ib.* The abbé d'Anjou proposes to call a son of George III. to the French throne, 81. Legendre proposes to drown refractory priests, 82. 20,000 federates called up from the provinces to Paris, 83. Dumouriez resigns, 88. Attack on the Tuileries, 92—95. Louis petitions the assistance of the emperor of Austria, 99. The Assembly decree that the country is in danger, 102. The fête of pikes, 105—107. The duke of Brunswick commences his march from Coblents; his manifesto, 109—111. Arrival of the Marseillese band in Paris, 111. Their *émeute* with some grenadiers, 112. They demand the immediate dethronement of Louis XVI., 114. Attempt made to assassinate Marie Antoinette, 117. Proposed plans for the escape of the royal family, 117—120. Question of the forfeiture or déchéance of the king discussed, 120. Attack on the Tuileries, August 10, 1792; 127—139. The king and the royal family seek shelter in the Assembly, 134. The king is deprived of his functions, 141. The royal family are committed to the Temple, 144. Establishment of the tribunal of the 17th of August, 145, 146. Seizure of church ornaments, 149. Lafayette conveyed a close prisoner to the Luxembourg, 151. The duke of Brunswick takes Longwi, 152. Precautions for the security of Paris, 153. General massacre of prisoners commences, September 2, and lasts for several days, 155—177.

Louis XVI,—

Murder of the princess de Lamballe, an intimate friend of the unfortunate queen, 166. Massacre of lunatics in the Bicêtre, 168. Execution of marshal Maillé, 172. Verdun surrenders to the duke of Brunswick, 178. Battle of Valmy, September 20; 182. Retreat of the Prussians, 185. Lille bombarded by Saxe-Teschen, October, 186. Battle of Jemappe, November 6, 187. Tournay and other places open their gates to the French, and Flanders is voluntarily subdued, *ib.* Dumouriez enters Brussels, November 14; 188. Jacobin Club established in that city, *ib.* Liege surrenders, November 28; 189. General Custine invades Germany, and takes Spires, September 29, 1792; 190, 191. Mayence and Frankfort-on-the-Maine taken, *ib.* The National Convention meets in the Tuileries, September 21; 193. Robespierre and the most excessive Jacobins obtain the name of the Mountain, 194. The Convention decrees that royalty is abolished in France, 195. The Gironde demand a departmental guard, 196. Robespierre denounced, *ib.* Marat defends himself from several accusations, 199—201. Report of Roland, minister of the interior, on the actual state of Paris, 203. Committee appointed to inquire into the crimes of the king, 210. Debates as to the proper methods to be pursued in the trial, 210—216. Louis is brought before the Convention, 218—220. He is cruelly separated from his family, 219. M.M. Tronchet, Malesherbes, and Desèze become counsel for the king, 220, 221, 232. The banishment of Philippe Egalité proposed, 224, 225. Robespierre accuses the Girondists of plotting against the public tranquillity, 228. Louis appears at the Convention for trial, December 26; 232—235. He is condemned to death by a small majority, January 17, 1793; 244. Insults offered to the royal prisoner, 249. The sentence of death is officially communicated to the king, 250. His last interview with his family, 251, 252. He is conducted to execution, and guillotined in the Place Louis XV., January 21, 1793; 253, 254. His interment in the cemetery of La Madeleine, 255.

The French Revolution.—Breda and other towns capitulate to Dumouriez, § iii. 285. Disaffection of the Dutch garrisons, *ib.* The commissioners of the National Convention drive Belgium into revolt, 286. Dumouriez breaks with the French Republicans, and expresses his intention of re-establishing with some modifications, the constitution of 1791; 286—288. He raises the standard of revolt, 288, and seizes the persons of four commissioners of the Convention who were exchanged for the princess-royal in November, 1795; 289. Some of his troops mutiny and attempt to make him prisoner, 290. A price is set on his head, and general Dampierre takes to the command of the army; but dying shorly after, he is succeeded by general Lamarche, 291. The king of Prussia invests Mayence, which surrenders, July 22, 1793; 294. The duke of York bombards Valenciennes, which surrenders, July 28; *ib.* Quesnoy capitulates to the prince of Coburg, September 11; *ib.* General Jourdan compels Coburg to recross the Sambre, 295. The duke of Brunswick gains a victory over the French under Hoche, *ib.* The Austrians cross the Rhine, December 28; 296. The Spanish general, Ricardos, gains a complete victory over Dediers, *ib.*; makes an unsuccessful attack on the French at Perpignan, July 17; 297. Successes of general Kellerman over the Piedmontese, 299. The duke of Montferrat becomes master of the whole of Upper Savoy, but after a short time is obliged to abandon everything he had gained on the eastern side of the Alps, 299, 300. Admiral Truguet makes an unsuccessful attempt to conquer

The French Revolution,—
the Island of Sardinia, 300. Lord Howe sails from Spithead in search of the French fleet, July 14; 301. Attack on the French islands in the West Indies, 302. The English take possession of the French portion of the island of St. Domingo, ib. The French factories seized in the East Indies, ib. Toulon is delivered up to the English by the inhabitants, ib. Naples declares war against France, 304. Lyons surrenders to the Republicans, 305. Evacuation of Toulon, 306—309. Tuscany agrees to break off all intercourse with the French Republic, and to unite with the grand European coalition, 310. The pope closes his ports to French shipping, and the grand master of the knights of Malta expels all French agents from that island, 311. Fierce struggle between the Gironde and the Mountain, ib. Frightful disorders in the city of Paris, February 25; 312. Establishment of a new Extraordinary Criminal Tribunal, 314. Deputations from thirty-five of the sections demand the immediate expulsion of twenty-two leading Girondists, April 15; 319. Trial and acquittal of Marat, 320. Dissolution of the Committee of Twelve, 325. The Convention is surrounded by an armed force, who demand and obtain the expulsion of thirty-two leading Girondists, 327—334. Madame Roland is arrested and lodged in the abbaye, 330. Assassination of Marat by Charlotte Corday, July 13, 334, 335. Her trial and execution, 335—339. Funeral of Marat, 339—341. The Girondists and Royalists of Lyons put to death Chalier, president of the Jacobin Club of that town; Lyons is then bombarded, and a most dreadful vengeance is taken on the unfortunate inhabitants, 341—344. Increased number of executions at Paris, 344. Robespierre obtains a seat in the Committee of Public Safety, and the Reign of Terror commences, ib. Fête on the completion of the Edifice of Liberty, 346. Execution of general Custine, 346. Enactment of the Loi des Suspects, September 17; 347. Marie Antoinette is brought before the Revolutionary Tribunal, October 14; 348. The Dauphin is removed from the care of his mother, committed to the cruel charge of Simon, and made to sign a paper accusing the queen of unnatural crimes, ib. Execution of Marie Antoinette, Wednesday, October 16, 1793; 352. Execution of twenty-one noted Girondists, October 31, 1793; 352—357; of Philippe Egalité, duke of Orleans, November 6, 358, 359; of madame Roland, November 9; 359, 360; of Bailly, formerly mayor of Paris, November 10; 360; of general Houchard, Clavière, and Lebrun, 361. Flight of several fugitive Girondists, 362—368. Advantages gained by the revolution, 368. Insurrection of the Vendeans, 368—376. Atrocities of Carrier, 376, 377. Christianity denied, 377, 378. Formation of the Republican Calendar, which continued in use until 1806; 377, 378. Celebration of the Festival of Reason, 379. General pillage of churches, 381. Violation of graves, ib. Bastia capitulates to lord Hood, May 11, 1794; 400. The Convention orders that no quarter shall be given to British or Hanoverian troops, 405, 429. The whole of Austrian Flanders and Brabant falls under the dominion of France, ib. Successes of the army of Italy, 410. The fortress of Saorgio capitulates, 411. Strife between the Hébertists or Ultra-revolutionists, and the Robespierrists or Deists, 413; the former are seized and guillotined, 419, 420. Trial and execution of Danton and his friends, 423—425. Execution of Lavoisier, the chemical philosopher, and the princess Elizabeth, the amiable sister of Louis XVI., 426. The Cordelier Club dissolves itself, 427. The number of executions in the Place de la Révolution during the month of May reaches the amount of 324, ib.; frequency of suicide, ib.

The French Revolution,—
Festival to the Supreme Being, June 8, 1794. Robespierre officiates as pontiff, 430. Decree of the twenty-second Prairial, 432. Prophecies of Catherine Theot, 434. Animated speech of Robespierre against the doctrine of Materialism, 438. The Mountain loses its power in the Convention, and Robespierre, St. Just, Couthon, and the other leading members of their party, are outlawed and guillotined, June 28; 440—449. The party who effected this great change assume the name of Thermidoriens, 450. A large number of Nantese republicans are tried and acquitted, 452. The Jacobin Society suppressed, October 18; 453. Carrier is brought to trial and executed, December 16; 455. The police law is moderated, 456. The king of Prussia concludes a separate treaty with the French, April 5, 1795; 475. Peace with Spain, July 22; 476. The grand duke of Tuscany concludes a treaty with the National Convention, 477. Rear-admiral Pierre Martin is defeated by the English admiral Hotham, March 13; 478. The French gain possession of St. Eustatius, 480. Pichegru makes an attempt to reduce Mayence, but sustains a terrible defeat by general Clairfait, 480, 481. Manheim surrenders to general Wurmser, November 22, 481. Successes of the Republican forces on the side of Italy, ib. Public enlistment of men in the city of Genoa for the French service, 482. Successes of Massena, 483. Death of La Roche Jacquelin, January 28, 1794; 484. Peace of La Vendée signed, February, 1795; 485. Fatal expedition of the Royalists and English to Quiberon, 486—489. Charette, the Vendean chief, taken prisoner and shot, March 29, 1796; 489. The war of the Vendée may be said to have expired with the death of Charette; according to general Hoche's own statement, it cost the lives of 100,000 Frenchmen, and not a fifth part of the whole male population of the country was left alive, ib. Murders and massacres committed by the Royalists and Girondists upon the overthrown Jacobins, 489—491. Trial of Billaud, Collot, and Barrère, 492. Insurrection of the Faubourgs, 494—496. The galleries of the Convention are closed to the public, 496. Death of Louis XVII. in prison, June 8; his body, after being examined by the physicians, was buried without ceremony in the cemetery of Ste. Marguérite, ib. The eldest of the Dauphin's uncles now took the title of king, and was proclaimed as Louis XVIII. by the prince of Condé at the head of his emigrant army, ib. The Committee of Eleven present a new constitution for France; it settled the divisions of the kingdom, and enacted that the legislative body should consist of two chambers; a Council of Ancients, of 250 members, and Council of Five Hundred, one-third of which to be renewed every year; the executive was confided to a Directory of five. This constitution was approved, September 6, by the primary assemblies to which it was referred, and the elections took place, 496, 497. Attack on the Convention; the insurgents are dispersed by Napoleon Bonaparte, then a brigadier-general of artillery, 498, 499. The sister of the Dauphin (afterwards duchess of Angoulème) is exchanged for the Commissioners of the Convention in the hands of Austria, and delivered to the emperor. She arrived at Vienna, January 9, 1796; 500. The Directory issue a severe decree, prohibiting the admission of English goods into any part of France or of the French dependencies, 503. Lord Malmesbury's first unsuccessful and disgraceful embassy to Paris, 504. The English evacuate Corsica, October 14; 506. United attack of the French armies on Germany and Italy, 510. Jourdan is completely defeated at Amperg, and general Moreau accomplishes his celebrated retreat through

The French Revolution,—
the Black Forest, 511. Napoleon Bonaparte receives the command of the army of Italy; he gains many advantages, and compels the king of Sardinia to sign a peace ruinous to that country, 512. General Beaulieu defeated at Lodi, May 10; *ib.* The city of Pavia given up to plunder, 513. Tuscany overrun, *ib.* Bonaparte sustains a severe repulse from general Alvinzi, at the bridge of Arcole, 514. Termination of the third Italian campaign of 1796; 515. Battle off Cape St. Vincent, February 14; 522. Strange expedition of the French to the English coast, 523. Preliminaries of a peace between Austria and France signed at Leoben, April 18; 524. Lord Malmesbury's second embassy to Lisle, 525. The doge and senate of Venice resign, *ib.* Genoa democratised, and the government remodelled in the French fashion, *ib.* Venice ceded to the emperor by the treaty of Campo Formio, after having maintained itself as a republic for 1,400 years, 525, 526. The Montagnards and Jacobins make a terrible effort to recover their lost power, 526—528. Nine hundred troops of the line land at Killala, in Ireland, to assist the insurgents, 534. The French enter Bern, and treat Switzerland as a conquered country, 536. Bravery of the Nidwalders, 537. The Belgians break out into insurrection, 538. Turbulence of the Roman democrats, *ib.* The republican general Berthier marches to Rome, and prepares to bombard the city; the terrified cardinals sign a capitulation; pope Pius VI. refuses to acknowledge the Roman republic, and being driven from his power, takes up his residence in a convent of the Augustinian monks at Sienna, 540. Popular commotions in Piedmont, *ib.* Bonaparte embarks in his expedition to Egypt, May 19, 1798. He captures Malta, June 11; *ib.* Lands at Alexandria, June 30; 541. Gains the Battle of the Pyramids, July 21; *ib.* Battle of the Nile, August 1; 542, 543. The sultan declares war with France, 543. The people of Cairo burst out into insurrection, September 22, which is put down by a dreadful massacre, *ib.* The French general Championnet takes possession of Naples, January 31st, 1799; royalty is abolished, and the kingdom converted into a republic, under the name of *Republica Parthenopea*, 545. Battle of Cassano, April 27, 546. Cardinal Ruffo, assisted by lord Nelson, recovers the Neapolitan kingdom, 547. The papal government is reinstated, *ib.* Combined attack of the Russians and English on the French in Holland, *ib.* Siege of Acre, 547, 548. Battle of Aboukir, July 25; 548. Bonaparte returns to France, *ib.* Constitution of the year VIII.; Bonaparte is appointed First Consul, 549. Tippoo Sultaun proposes an alliance with the French Republic, 1797; 550. Jacobin Club established at Seringapatam, *ib.* The earl of Mornington despatches general Harris into the Mysore country, which he enters, March 5, 1799; *ib.* Seringapatam is stormed and captured, May 4; Tippoo is slain in the action, and two of his sons are taken prisoners, *ib.* French campaign against Austria, 555. Bonaparte enters Milan, June 2; *ib.* Battle of Marengo, 556. Triumphant reception of Bonaparte by the Milanese, 557; he returns to Paris, July 3; *ib.* Campaign of the French army on the Upper Rhine, *ib.* Battle of Hohenlinden, December 2; 1800. Treaty of Luneville signed, February 9, 1801; 558. Malta surrenders to the British, *ib.* George III. relinquishes the style of king of France, 560. The treaty of El Arish concluded with the Turks, 555°. Battle of Alexandria, March 21, 1801; 557°, 558°. The French quit Egypt, 559°. The court of Madrid declares war against Portugal; treaty of Olivenza, *ib.* The French invest Almeida, and menace Lisbon and Oporto, *ib.* The peace of Amiens concluded with

The French Revolution,—
England, March 27, 1802; *ib.*——For the continuation of the French Revolution, *see* Napoleon Bonaparte.

LOUIS XVII., anecdotes concerning this unfortunate prince, § ii. 420, 431, 504, 505, 640, 646, 676; § iii. 134, 142. He is imprisoned in the Temple, September 13, 1792; 144. Separated from the king, December 11; 217. His last interview with his father, January 20, 1793; 251. His consignment to the cruel keeping of Simon the shoe-maker, 249, 348. He is compelled to sign a paper, October 1793, accusing his mother of unnatural crimes; from that moment we are assured by his sister he never spoke again (he was then eight years old), 348. Death of this unfortunate prince, June 8, 1795. His body, after being examined by the physicians, was buried in darkness, without ceremony, in the cemetery of Ste. Marguérite, June 10; 496.

LOUIS XVIII. Stanislaus Xavier, (1814 — 1824.) Flies from Paris to Coblentz, June 1791, and takes a principal share in the organisation of the system of emigration. The Assembly decree, October 31, that he shall be required to re-enter the kingdom within two months, under penalty of forfeiting his eventual right to the throne, § ii. 710. He is proclaimed king by the prince of Condé at the head of the emigrant royalist army, on the death of the Dauphin, Louis XVII., June 8, 1795; § iii. 496. During the empire of Bonaparte he resided in England, but after the entry of the allies into Paris, in 1814, he was acknowledged king, and embarked at Dover, April 24; § iv. 618°. His public entry into Paris, May 3, *ib.* He accepts the Constitution formed by the Provisional Government, *ib.* A general peace and amity signed with France by the allied sovereigns of Europe, May 30, *ib.* This treaty secured to France the integrity of its boundaries as they existed in June 1792, but with considerable augmentations, *ib.* Bonaparte embarks for France with about 1,000 followers, and lands at Cannes, March 1, 1815; 628°. On his march to Paris he is everywhere joined by the troops sent to oppose him, and enters that city in triumph, March 20; 629°. Louis flies from Paris, and takes refuge in Lille, on the Belgian frontier, *ib.* In consequence of the battle of Waterloo, Louis re-enters Paris on the 8th of July, and quietly resumes the government, Napoleon having embarked at Rochefort on the 3rd, on board the *Bellerophon*, 642°, 643°. Execution of Labédoyère and Marshal Ney, 652°, 653°. Louis signs a treaty with the allies, November 20, 1815, by which France retains its former frontiers, with little alteration, and consents to support and pay 150,000 men of the allied armies for the space of five years, and to remit 700,000,000 of francs to assist in defraying the expenses of the allies, 661°.

LOUIS PHILIPPE, (ex-king of the French) introduced to the Jacobin Club, when duke of Chartres, by his father, the duke of Orleans, 1790; § ii. 522. Portrait of, § iii. 182. His flight from Paris, 1793; 291.

LOUIS, Don, mounts the Spanish throne, 1725, on the abdication of the king his father, but in seven months falls a victim to the small-pox, iv. 387.

LOUIS, the Dauphin (son of Charles VI.); his dispute with the duke of Burgundy, 1413; ii. 26, 28. Makes himself master of Paris, 27. Banishes several of the French princes, 28. His character, prodigal and rapacious, *ib.* He confines the dauphiness, a daughter of the duke of Burgundy, 1414, *ib.* His death, 1415; 36. His brother John, dauphin, 1417, dies suddenly, and Burgundy declared they had been poisoned, 37. Their brother Charles, dauphin.—*See* Charles VII.

LOUISA of Savoy, mother of Francis I., in love with the Constable Charles of Bourbon, who rejecting

LOUISA of Savoy,—
her hand was ruined, 1523; ii. 356. Francis's letter to the regent-mother after losing his liberty at Pavia, 1525; 359. The important treaty she concluded with Henry VIII. was ratified by Francis I., 360, 361.

LOVAT, Simon Fraser, lord, iii. 15. He persuades the body of Highlanders under the command of lord Murray, to desert to the viscount Dundee, 1690; iv. 15. Fraser's Plot, 1703; 155—157. Lovat is confined in the Bastille, 161. He takes up arms for the Pretender, 1716; 323. His trial, 1747; iv. 551. Portrait of, 552. He is executed, April 9, 1747; 553.

LOVE, alderman, refuses to take the sacrament, and is expelled the House of Commons, 1661; as he afterwards sat in the House, he must have conformed a little later, iii. 684.

LOVEL, Francis, viscount, fought for Richard III. at Bosworth Field, 1485; ii. 129. Took sanctuary, 284. His attainder, ib. Insurrection, in which Lovel fails, as Henry VII., well attended in his royal progress towards York, approached the insurgent force, 1486; 286. Lovel escaped to Flanders, ib.

LOVEL, sir Thomas, privy-councillor, 1509, constable of the Tower, ii. 320, 323.

LOVELACE, colonel Richard, an elegant writer of songs, etc. He died in 1658; iii. 604.

LOWE, sir Hudson, governor of St. Helena during Buonaparte's residence on that island, 1816—1821; § iv. 647°—650°.

LOWINGER, captain, a Dutch soldier of fortune, 1642; iii. 282.

LOWTHER, sir James (master of 40,000l. per annum), volunteers into the army, 1758; iv. 601.

LOWTHER, sir John. See viscount Lonsdale.

LUCAN. describes the Druids, their doctrines, and the sacred groves, i. 61.

LUCAS, lord, expresses a wish, on occasion of the murder of sir Edmondbury Godfrey, 1678, that all papists were expelled the court. iii. 721.

LUCAS, sir Charles, shot by Fairfax as a traitor, for espousing the royalist cause, August 27, 1648; iii. 383.

LUCAS, sir Jervas, governor of Belvoir Castle, 1645; iii. 344.

LUCAS, captain, joins in a plot for the restoration of Charles II., he is seized and executed, 1655; iii. 419.

LUCRETIUS, the poet, i. 105.

LUCY, Richard de, excommunicated by Becket, i. 452. He repulses the Scots, and burns Berwick, 470. Takes the powerful earl of Leicester prisoner, 1173, ib.

Luddites, the, their outrages, and destruction of machinery, 1811, 1812; § iv. 727.

Ludi, the, ii. 877—880.

LUDLOW, general, a Commonwealth-man; on the restoration of Charles II. he took refuge in Switzerland, where being secure from open violence, several attempts at secret assassination were made by the royalists, iii. 690.

LULLY, Raymond, a philosopher and alchemist, of the thirteenth century; he visited England, regno Edward I., and affirms that he performed the experiment of transmuting some crystal into a mass of diamond, i. 844. He made a strenuous effort to revive the Oriental tongues, and it was at his instigation that Clement VII., in 1311, published a constitution, ordering that professors of Greek, Hebrew, etc., should be established in the University of Paris, etc., 848.

LUMLEY, general, his prompt conduct at the battle of Schellenberg, 1704; iv. 167.

LUNDIE, colonel, appointed by William III. governor of Londonderry, iv. 16; the townspeople, fearing lest he should treacherously deliver up the town to the Pretender, depose him, ib.

LUNDIN, sir Richard, joins the standard of Wallace, 1297; i. 715, but almost immediately lays down his arms and makes submission to Edward, 716.

Lunéville, treaty of, concluded between the French Republic and the emperor of Germany, February 9, 1801; § iii. 558.

LUNN, a servant of Williams, bishop of Lincoln, sentenced to be fined, 1634; iii. 164.

LUNSFORD, colonel, a royalist officer, beaten at Newburn, 1640; iii. 221. He is sent to the Tower, January 1642, for raising troops for the king, 267.

LUPTON, Thomas, a dramatist of the sixteenth century, iii. 583.

LUTHER, Martin. This illustrious German Reformer was an Augustinian monk, and professor of philosophy in the newly-founded University of Wittemberg, when, in 1517, the Dominican friar Tetzel appeared in that city, as retailer, under commission from Albert, Elector of Mentz, and archbishop of Magdeburg, of the indulgences issued for sale over all Christendom by the reigning pope Leo X., ii. 706. Luther raises his voice against these indulgences, ib. He is summoned by Leo, July, 1518, to appear at Rome, though afterwards his case is appointed to be heard in Germany, and accordingly he makes his appearance at Augsburg before the legate, cardinal Cajetano, 707. He is protected by the Elector Frederic, ib. The emperor Charles V. appoints a Diet of the empire to meet at Worms, expressly to put down the new opinions, ib. Henry VIII. writes a book in confutation of Luther's opinions; this book is immediately answered by Luther, 708, 709. He cast aside his monastic habit, 1524, and the next year marries Catherine de Bohren, a nun, who had escaped from her convent, and relinquished her vows. He died at Eisleben, February 18, 1546. His opinion that it would be more lawful for Henry VIII. to have two wives at once, than to divorce Catherine of Arragon, 376.

Lutzen, battle of, Gustavus Adolphus killed at the, November 6, 1632; iii. 173.

Luxembourg, 1697, restored to Spain, iv. 79.

Luxembourg, View of the, § ii. 605.

LUXEMBOURG, Jaquetta of. See Bedford, duchess of.

LUXEMBOURG, James of. He came to Westminster, with a splendid retinue, 1464, to the coronation of his niece Elizabeth Woodville, daughter of his sister Jaquetta, ii. 101.

LUXEMBURGH, Walleran of, count of St. Pol and Ligny, brother-in-law of Richard II., sent heralds, 1402, to Henry IV., with a singular defiance in writing, for the murder of king Richard, ii. 10. Lands on the Isle of Wight, 15. See St. Pol.

LUYNES, duke de, minister of Louis XIII. after the murder of Concini, 1616; iii. 63, 106.

LYDGATE, John, ii. 210. His ballad, "The London Lickpenny," showing the manners of London in his time, 258.

LYLY, John, the Euphuist, and dramatic writer, sixteenth century, ii. 835; iii. 586.

LYNEDOCH, sir Thomas Graham, lord, gains the battle of Barrosa, in Spain, 1811; § iv. 483, 506, commands a division of the army at the battle of Vittoria, June 21, 1813; 571; recalled, to take the command of the British forces in Holland, 1814; 601°. Is repulsed with great loss in his attack on Bergen-op-zoom, 619°.

Lynne, iii. 655.

Lyon king-at-arms; Scottish herald, ii. 325.

Lyons, siege of, 1793; § iii. 342. Dreadful cruelties committed by the French revolutionists on the unfortunate inhabitants, 343.

LYTTELTON, Thomas, lord, 1773; § i. 194, 197, 203; is made Chief-justice in Eyre beyond the Trent, 1775; 242.

LYTTELTON, sir George, made chancellor of the

LYTTELTON, sir George,—
Exchequer, 1755; iv. 584. He is raised to the peerage, and retires into the country to write his "Dialogues of the Dead," 588. Quoted, i. 576, 582.

MACADAM, John London, his improvements in road-making, 1816; § iv. 675.

MACARTNEY, George, earl, lands at Fort St. George as governor of Madras, June 22, 1781; § ii. 150. His embassy to China, 1792; § iii. 33.

MACARTNEY, general, second to lord Mohun in the duel fought between that nobleman and the duke of Hamilton, November 15, 1712; iv. 271.

MACBETH, lord of the district of Mearns, in Ross, independent of the Scottish kings. By the murder of Duncan, king of Scotland, he gained the crown, i. 194. Battle near the hill of Dunsinane, 1054; young Siward or Osberne slain, ib. The lady Gruoch, of royal descent, fled to Macbeth's inheritance in Ross, 221. Their marriage, ib. They appeared friends of king Duncan, whose title had been denied by some of the princes, ib. Duncan assassinated, 1039, near Elgin, and not in Macbeth's Castle at Inverness, 221, 222. The lord of Mearns usurped the throne, 222. Several revolts in favour of Malcolm, son of Duncan, suppressed, ib. Macduff, the chief or marmor of Fife, rebels, and joined by earl Siward the Dane, brother-in-law of the murdered Duncan, attacks the usurper, ib. Macbeth's fortress on Dunsinane-hill, in Angus, near which he is defeated, 1054, ib. He prolongs the war among the Highland fastnesses, ib. His last refuge a fortress in a solitary vale of Aberdeenshire, ib. Macbeth slain, December 5, 1056, by Macduff and Malcolm, ib. His partisans set up Lulach, the son of lady Macbeth, as king; but he was slain in battle, April 3, 1057, by Malcolm III., ib. The lady Gruoch, queen of Macbeth, 221. She was descended from Kenneth the Grim, ib. Her first husband, Gilcomcain, chief of Moray, taking up arms to protect his wife's cause, was burnt, with fifty of his retainers, in his castle, by Malcolm II., ib. Lady Gruoch fled, with her infant son Lulach, into Ross, and there was espoused by Macbeth, ib.

MACCLESFIELD, lord; he speaks against the Abjuration Bill, 1690; iv. 21. Resigns the great seal, 385. Is impeached for abuse of his office, fined 30,000l., and imprisoned in the Tower till he should pay it, 1724; 386.

M'DONALD, colonel Æneas, accidentally killed by a M'Donald of Keppoch, 1746; iv. 526.

M'DONALD, Flora; she secures the flight of the young Pretender as far as Mugstole, 1746; iv. 543, 544. Her portrait, 545. She is carried to London as a dangerous rebel, ib.; but liberated after a year's confinement, 1747; 553.

M'DONALD, of Keppoch, killed at the battle of Culloden, April 17, 1746; iv. 539.

MACDOWAL, Duncan, defeats the two brothers of Bruce in Galloway, 1306; i. 729.

McGINNIS, joins in an insurrection in Ireland, October, 1641, and takes Newry, iii. 254.

MACHADO, Antonio Alvarez, one of the contractors of bread for supplying Marlborough's army, iv. 259.

MACHIAVELLI, principles of, ii. 318. "The Prince," by, 318, note.

MACK, general, surrenders an army of 30,000 Austrians, at Ulm, 1805; § iv. 174.

MACKAY, general, defeated by lord Dundee, 1689, near the Pass of Killicrankie, iv. 15. Present at the battle of Aghrim, July 12, 1691; 33. His gallant conduct at the battle of Steinkirk, 36; he falls in the thickest of the fight, 1692; 37.

MACKENZIE, sir George, author of several literary publications (17th century), iv. 789.

MACKENZIE, colonel Humberstone, his active service in India, 1783; § ii. 154. He dies of wounds

MACKENZIE, colonel Humberstone,—received in an engagement with some Mahratta pirates, 155.

MACKENZIE, sir John, holds the town of Inverness for the Pretender, 1715; iv. 323.

MACKEY, Mr., seizes the abbé Gaultier and Matthew Prior, who were returning privately from France, 1711, where they had been employed by the English government to make a secret treaty at the court of Versailles, iv. 256.

MACKINTOSH, sir James, quotations from, i. 168; iii. 780.

MACKINTOSH, of Borlum, a veteran soldier, 1715; iv. 315.

MACKWORTH, sir Humphrey, author of the "Memorial of the Church of England," 1705; iv. 183.

McLEAN, of Drimnin, killed at the battle of Culloden, iv. 539.

MACLEOD, of Assin, 1661; iii. 683.

McLEOD, of Rasay, fights for the Young Pretender both at Falkirk and Culloden, and affords him an asylum in his flight, iv. 545.

McMAHON, Hugh, reveals the design of the Irish insurgents to surprise Dublin Castle to Owen O'Connelly, 1641; iii. 254.

Macmillanites, another name for the Cameronians, iv. 652.

MACPHERSON, James, born 1738, died 1796, § iii. 724. His "Poems of Ossian," 1762, suppose the Highlanders to have been Caledonians of Celtic origin, and the Picts or Lowlanders the same; notwithstanding the marked distinctions between the two races, i. 18. Dr. James Macpherson also, in his "Dissertations on the Caledonians," agrees with his relative, ib. His observations on the commerce of the city of London, 591. Value of money in Scotland at the time of William the Lion, 592.

McVICAR, a Presbyterian preacher; his quaint prayer concerning the Young Pretender, iv. 504.

Macsiewice, battle of, October 4, 1794; § iii. 461.

MADDEN, sir F., his account of illuminated manuscripts of the twelfth century, quoted, i. 632.

MADOC, the brave leader of the Welsh, in their last struggle for liberty, before Edward I.'s departure for France, i. 711.

MADOX, an eminent English antiquary, quoted i. 567, et seq, 809.

Madras, View of, § ii. 24. Government buildings at, 35.

Madrid, View of, § iv. 511, entered by lord Wellesley's victorious army, August 12, 1812; 510.

Magdalen College, the fellows of refuse to elect Antony Farmer, a papist, for their master, 1687, and appoint Dr. Howe, iii. 786. The ecclesiastical commission insists on their electing Parker bishop of Oxford, but they refuse, 787. A commission is established to alter the statutes of the college; the fellows are incapacitated and expulsed, but large contributions are raised for them, and they suffer comparatively little inconvenience, ib.

Magdeburg; this rich and Protestant city was captured by Tilley and Pappenheim about 1629, and 30,000 of its inhabitants perished, iii. 147.

Magna Charta, signed June 15, 1215, i. 528. Its enactments, 576. Specimen of, engraved from the original copies, 577.

MAGNUS, king of Norway and Denmark, intending to invade Edward the Confessor's kingdom, is opposed, 1043, by an Anglo-Saxon fleet, and withdraws, i. 188.

MAGUIRE, Cornelius, baron of Inniskillen, together with sir Phelim O'Neal, enter into a plan for a general insurrection in Ireland, about 1641; iii. 252.

MAHMOUD II., sultan, 1809, § iv. 285. War with Russia, 405. The Russians defeated before Silistria, and compelled to retire, 405, 406.

Mahratta arms, group of, § ii. 32.

Mail-coaches, origin of, 1784; § i. 571; § iii. 645.

MAILLE, marshal, murdered by the French revolutionists, September 3, 1792; § iii. 172.

MAILLEBOIS, the French marshal, moves upon Hanover, 1741; iv. 450. He advances to the peninsula, 1745; 479.

Main Plot; Raleigh, Cobham, Grey of Wilton, etc., are tried, 1603, on this charge, iii. 8—14. Their estates confiscated, 15, 72. See James I., also Raleigh, Cobham, Grey.

Maine, people of, revolt against William. He defeats them with an English army, 1073; i. 379. Promises the province to his son Robert, 383. When duke Robert mortgages Normandy to his brother William, the inhabitants of Maine refuse to submit to his authority, 401. This province ceded (with Anjou) on the marriage of Margaret with Henry VI. to count René of Anjou, ii. 81, 84, 86.

MAINWARING, Dr. Roger, iii. 123. Obtains a bishopric, 1626; 124. Judgment obtained against, 1628; 134.

MAINWARING, colonel, 1641; iii. 242.

MAISTER, rector of Aldington, Bocking, Dering, Rich, Gold, and Risby, were hanged, 1534, with Elizabeth Barton, the Maid of Kent, for treasonably hearing her prophecy of Henry VIII.'s death, without duly reporting that poor idiot's illusion and proceedings, ii. 385.

MAITLAND, William, of Lethington, secretary to Mary queen of Scots, ii. 554, 559, 594, 612, 625, 649.

MAITLAND, general, an officer who distinguished himself at Quatre Bras, June 16, 1815; § iv. 635°.

MAITLAND, captain of the Bellerophon, a British ship of the line, renowned for the embarkation of the emperor Bonaparte at Rochefort, July 3, 1815; § iv. 643°. On the arrival of the Bellerophon at Torbay captain Maitland receives orders not to permit any communication with the land, but to sail round to Plymouth Sound, where, on the 31st, Bonaparte receives the unwelcome intelligence of his destination for St. Helena, 644°.

Majesty, a title of designation and address long confined to the emperors, in 1527 began to be employed in speaking of or to Henry VIII.; the style as to the English kings being, hitherto, your highness, or your grace, ii. 365, note.

MALACHI, king of Ireland, death of, 1119; i. 429.

MALCOLM I., cession to this Scottish monarch of Cumbria by Edmund, the Saxon king, on condition of his being ready to arm for the defence of the English territory, i. 219, 533. King Malcolm was assassinated in 953, 219.

MALCOLM II.; his victories over the Danes, i. 221. At Aberlemno, where are barrows and sculptures, ib. At Panbride, where he slew Camus the Dane, ib. At Cruden, where is Sueno's Pillar, closely sculptured, ib. He caused the grandson of Kenneth IV. to be murdered; he also defeated Gilcomcain, of Moray, who was burnt in his castle with his followers, ib. Cession of Lodonia, or the Lothians, 1020, by Eadulf, Danish earl of Northumberland, to Malcolm, ib. That territory had sometimes been called Saxonia, ib. Malcolm died in 1033, and his grandson Duncan mounted the throne, ib.

MALCOLM III., surnamed Caenmore, (1057—1093,) with the assistance of earl Siward, obtains the Scottish throne in the great battle fought with the usurper Macbeth in 1057, when Osberne, the son of earl Siward, is slain, and Siward dies, i. 194; 222. Malcolm Caenmore receives Edgar Atheling with his mother and sisters in a honourable manner, and afterwards marries Margaret, Edgar's sister, 369. He assists Edgar and the Northumbrians, 371, 372. After being defeated at York, Edgar Atheling returns to Scotland a second time, ib. William advances into Scotland, and receives the acknowledgment of Malcolm Caenmore, who nevertheless does not deliver up the English who had fled thither for protection,

MALCOLM III. :—
878, 534, 535. He advises to Edgar Atheling a reconciliation with William, 379. During the stay of William Rufus in Normandy, Caenmore invades England; William, on his return, collects a great force, and marches to avenge the insult; before the armies engage, duke Robert and Edgar Atheling bring about a peace; Caenmore, king of Scotland, acknowledges William as his lord; William sends for Caenmore to come to him at Gloucester, 398, 536, 537, and give hostages for his security; on Malcolm's arrival, Rufus requires him to do him homage, which he refuses as not being the practice of the kings of Scotland, and flies to the north, where he invades Northumberland, and is slain, together with his eldest son, Edward, having fallen into an ambush; his wife, Margaret, dies four days afterwards of grief, 1093; 399, 536, 537. Dimensions of the kingdom of Scotland in his reign, 533.

MALCOLM IV. (May 24, 1153—December 9, 1165.) grandson of David, king of Scotland, to whom he succeeds, May 24, 1153; i. 542. He obtains bonâ fide possession of the earldom of Huntingdon, as a descendant of earl Waltheof, 442, 542; goes with Henry II. to Toulouse, 445, 542; goes to Carlisle to be knighted by Henry, but disagrees with him and returns home, ib. He receives knighthood from Henry in France, ib.; returns to Scotland; his nobles attempt to seize him, ib. He routs the army of Somerled, thane of Argyle, who, together with his son, is slain, 543. He renews his homage to Henry at Woodstock, ib. His brother William is appointed regent, December 9, 1165. He dies at Jedburgh, and William succeeds him, ib.

MALCOLM, Alexander, author of a treatise on music, iv. 764.

MALET, William, commander of the Norman forces in York, 1069. He is besieged by the English, but William I. marches to his assistance, i. 370.

Malines, View of, § ii. 248.

MALLERY, Mr., committed to gaol, 1622; iii. 88.

MALLET, Robert de, promises to aid duke Robert with all his forces to obtain possession of England, 1101; i. 408.

Malmsbury, abbey of, founded by Roger, bishop of Sarum, in the twelfth century, i. 615.

MALMSBURY, James Harris, earl of, appointed ambassador to negotiate a peace with the French Republic, 1796. He arrived at Paris, October 22, and after vainly attempting to gain the desired end, was ordered to quit immediately, § iii. 504. His second useless embassy, 1797; 525.

MALMSBURY, William of, quoted, i. 589, 632, 687.

MALPEDIR, earl of Mearns, assassinates Duncan of Scotland, about 1095; i. 538.

Malplaquet, battle of, gained by Marlborough and prince Eugene, September 12, 1709; iv. 236.

Malta, island of, surrenders to major-general Pigot, September 15, 1800, after a blockade of more than two years, § iii. 558. View of, § iv. 401.

MALTHUS, Mr., his celebrated "Essay on the Principle of Population," published, 1798; § iii. 730.

MALTRAVERS, lord, marries a daughter of the duke of Lennox without the royal consent, 1626; iii. 119.

Malwood Keep, a hunting-seat in the New Forest, where William Rufus passed the night before he was killed, i. 401.

Man, isle of; royal standard hoisted in the, June, 1765; § i. 639.

Manchester, iii. 656.

MANCHESTER, Henry Montagu, earl of, created February, 1626. Lord privy-seal, 1630. He died, 1642; iii. 146.

MANCHESTER, Edward Montagu, earl of, accused of treason, 1642; iii. 263. His commission for recruiting the parliamentary army, 1643. He died, 1671; 306.

MANCHESTER, Charles Montagu, earl of, 1682. Created duke of Manchester, April, 1719. He died, 1722; iv. 106.

MANCHESTER, George Montagu, duke of, 1762; § i. 194.

MANCINI, Olimpia, mother of prince Eugene; her name insulted by the English rabble, 1712; iv. 262.

MANCINI, M., nephew to cardinal Mazarin, 1658; iii. 427.

MANDEVILLE, sir John, an English traveller of the fourteenth century, i. 845.

MANDEVILLE, William de. See earl of Albemarle.

MANDUBRATIUS, prince of the Trinobantes, (son of Imanuentius, put to death by Cassivellaunus,) i. 33. Cæsar reinstates him, ib.

MANLEON, Savaric de, stays king John from murdering D'Albiney, governor of Rochester Castle, on the surrender of that fortress, 1215; i. 530.

MANLEY, John, farms the post-office, 1652; iii. 552.

Manners and Customs of early races, corroborative of their true history, i. 5. History of Manners and Customs, in the early British era, and under the Roman rule, to A.D. 449; 125. From 449 to 1066; 323. From 1066 to 1216; 634. From 1216 to 1399; 864. From 1399 to 1485; ii. 236. From 1485 to 1603; 855. From 1603 to 1660; iii. 617. From 1660 to 1689; 889. From 1688 to 1760; iv. 801. Reign of George III. From 1760 to 1785; § i. 638. From 1785 to 1802; § iii. 755. From 1802 to 1820; § iv. 721.

MANNY, sir Walter, commands the English expedition in Brittany, and relieves Hennebon, 1341; i. 761, 762; assists Edward at the siege of Calais, and persuades him to have mercy on the men when it surrenders, 769.

MANOURIE, bribed by Raleigh when attempting to escape, 1618; iii. 76.

MANSEL, colonel, a Presbyterian officer accused by Dangerfield, 1679, of plotting against the state, iii. 732.

MANSELL, sir Robert, sails to Algiers, 1621; burns some shipping, and returns, iii. 85. Vice-admiral of England, 113. His anger at the fright of the members of parliament on the supposed Gunpowder Plot, May 5, 1641; 242.

MANSFELDT, count, general of the Elector Palatine, iii. 85. Collects troops in England, 1624; 106, 126.

MANSFIELD, William Murray, earl of, iv. 455, 585, 592. Chief-justice of the King's Bench, 1767; § i. 59. Alters the record of the indictment of Wilkes, 1769; 67, 82, 84, 94. Portrait of, 106, 248. His monument in Westminster Abbey, § iii. 749.

MANSFIELD, sir James, a distinguished lawyer, of the eighteenth century, is counsel for the merchants of London, 1774, who petitioned against the establishment of French law in Canada, § i. 169. Destruction of his property by the rioters of 1780; 417. Portrait of, 535.

Mansion-house, London, View of the, § i. 114.

Mantes, city of, taken and burnt, 1087, by William I., who there meets the accident that caused his death, i. 389.

MANTEUFEL, general, a Prussian officer, in the service of Frederic the Great, 1757; iv. 598, 611.

MANTON, Mr., chaplain at the inauguration of Cromwell, 1657; iii. 423. Accepts the living of Covent-garden, 820.

Manuscripts, illuminated, Gospel of St. John, i. 169.

MAR, earl of, third son of James II. of Scotland, he gains the battle of Harlaw, 1411; ii. 132. Accused by king James, his brother, of a design to destroy his life by witchcraft, perishes in prison, 135.

MAR, earl of, raises the standard of the Pretender, at Brae-Mar, September 1, 1715; iv. 312. His proceedings, 315—319.

MARAT, a French revolutionary journalist, 1790; § ii. 502, 521. His atrocious letter to Louis XVI., 529,

MARAT:—
530. Accuses Lafayette of being in league with the royalists, 1691; 610. Recommends to the French army, 1792, the massacre of all their generals, § iii. 71. Is nominated a deputy to the National Convention, 192, 199, 231. He votes the immediate death of the king, January 16, 1793; 243, 317. His trial and acquittal by the revolutionary tribunal, April 24, 320. He is assassinated by Charlotte Corday, July 14, 1793; 335. His funeral, 339, 434.

MARATTI, Carlo, a painter, of the seventeenth century; Villiers, duke of Buckingham, sends an invitation to him, but is unsuccessful, iii. 569. His portrait of the earl of Sunderland, 830.

MARBECK, John, burnt, 1544; ii. 728; iii. 562.

MARCEL, Stephen, provost of the merchants of France, kills two of Charles the Dauphin's councillors, February 22nd, 1358; i. 774.

MARCELLINUS, Ammianus, his mention of the Scots, i. 19; of the Druids, Vates, and Bards, 63.

MARCH, Mortimer, earl of. See Mortimer.

MARCH, Roger, earl of, declared successor to the crown, if Richard II. should die, 1385. He died 1398; i. 791.

MARCH, Edmund, earl of, confined at Windsor by Henry IV., 1399; ii. 6. See Mortimer.

MARCH, earl of, a disaffected Scottish baron, passes into England, where an English force marches under his command to Nesbit Moor, 1402; ii. 11. He defeats a Scottish army, slaying their leader, Hepburn, ib. Douglas enters England with a good army, but is totally routed by Hotspur (Percy) and this Scot, at Homildon Hill, ib. His lands near the borders are granted by Albany to Douglas, ib. In course of years Douglas loses influence with the Scottish regent, and March is restored to his honours and estates, 49.

MARCH, Edward, earl of, ii. 96, etc. See Edward IV.

MARCHE, count de la, robbed of his wife, Isabella, by king John, who marries her, and has her crowned as queen at Westminster, i. 517. He takes up arms against John, and is made prisoner, 517, 518. After the death of the king, he consents to receive back Isabella, and re-marries her with great pomp, 674.

MARCHE, Jaques de Bourbon, count de la, 1405; ii. 18, 48.

MARCHMONT, earl of, represents queen Anne in the General Assembly of the Kirk, 1702; iv. 140. Proposes an Act to exclude popish successors from the Scottish throne, 1704; 162. His answer to the speech of lord Belhaven, against the Union of Scotland, 195.

MARCUS, and afterwards Gratian, elected emperors, 407, and severally murdered by the refractory soldiers, i. 55.

MARE, sir Peter de la, speaker of the Commons, arrested, 1376; i. 780.

Marengo, battle of, June 14, 1800; § iii. 556.

MARESCHAL, William, i. 506. Is sent into England by John, on the death of king Richard, to secure the government till his arrival, 515.

MARGARET, sister of Edgar Atheling, flies to Scotland, 1068, and afterwards marries the Scottish king, Malcolm Caenmore, i. 369. Her life, by Turgot, her confessor, 537. Caenmore invades England, and is slain, together with his eldest son, Edward, having fallen into an ambush in Northumberland; this double calamity causes her death four days after, (16th November, 1093), 399.

MARGARET, daughter of Louis, married to Henry, eldest son of Henry II., 1160; i. 446. Taken prisoner by the king, 1174; 470.

MARGARET of Anjou. Portrait of, ii. 81. Negotiations for her marriage with Henry VI., ib. Popular prejudices against this queen, 82. Illustration of

MARGARET:—
the marriage ceremony, *ib.* Margaret is delivered of a son, 1453 ; he is recognised as Edward, prince of Wales, and earl of Chester, 92. After the battle of Northampton, Henry was taken prisoner, but Margaret and her son escape into Scotland, 95. The queen defeats the earl of Warwick at the battle of Barnet, February 17, 1461; 97. She, and her son, are forced to fly to Scotland after the battle of Towton, 99. She goes to France to solicit aid, returns with a small army into England, and takes Alnwick, Bamborough, and Dunstanburgh Castles ; but is obliged to fly before the earl of Warwick; a storm assails her ships, and she reaches Berwick in a fishing-boat, 100. She again sails from Scotland to solicit foreign aid ; Philip, duke of Burgundy, gives her some money, and sends her with a honourable escort to her father, in Lorraine, *ib.*, 101. She meets the earl of Warwick at the château of Amboise; he engages to restore the Lancastrian line, on condition that prince Edward should espouse the lady Anne, his second daughter, 105. She lands, with her son, and a body of auxiliaries, at Plymouth; her son Edward is brutally murdered at the battle of Tewkesbury, 1471, and she is taken prisoner, 109. She remains five years in captivity, being first confined in the Tower of London, afterwards at Windsor, and then at Wallingford ; she is ransomed by Louis XI., and dies in France, about eleven years after the battle of Tewkesbury, 110.

MARGARET PLANTAGENET, sister of Edward IV.; treaty for her marriage with a son of Louis XI., 1467 ; ii. 103. She was, however, married to Charles the Rash, of Burgundy, *ib.* See duchess of Burgundy.

MARGARET, daughter of Henry VII., married, 1501, 1502, to James IV., of Scotland, ii. 307, 311, 312. Her letter to Henry VIII., on the death of James IV. at Flodden-field, requesting his forbearance towards herself and their infant, James V., 1513; 331. She was appointed regent, and peace ensued betwixt the two kingdoms, *ib.* Her son, Alexander, duke of Ross, born after his father's fall in battle, 349, 350. His death in childhood, 351. By the queen's marriage with Douglas, earl of Angus, she forfeited the office of regent, 349. The new regent, Albany, demanding the custody of her sons, she haughtily closed the gate of Edinburgh Castle against him, 350. That duke, being supported by the nobles, compelled her to resign the care of those princes to him at Stirling Castle, 351. On the early death of Ross, the younger son, she alleged he had been poisoned, *ib.* She withdrew to Blacater Tower, then into England, and gave birth to a daughter, by her husband Angus, Margaret Douglas, (afterwards countess of Lennox, the mother of Darnley,) *ib.* She was welcomed, May, 1516, at her brother's court, with jousts, etc., in her honour, *ib.* Her anger at her husband Angus having left her when in childbed at Morpeth, *ib.* Reconciliation; Angus, with Arran and other lords, appointed as the council of state by Albany on going to France; she demanded that Angus should be declared regent, 352. Margaret holding her court at Edinburgh, he again quitted the queen, and withdrew to Douglasdale with a mistress, *ib.* She demanded a divorce, but Henry VIII. reproved her, and a new reconciliation was pretended, *ib.* She wrote to the duke of Albany, 1521, to return to Scotland; he did so, and resumed the executive government, 353. Dacre informed the English king that his royal sister passed not only the days but the nights with Albany, *ib.* The queen-mother, tired of her lover Albany, betrayed to Dacre his plan of invading Cumberland with 80,000 men, 354.

MARIA BEATRIX, of Modena, queen of James II., iii. 768.

MARIA-THERESA, queen of Louis XIV., iv. 100.
MARIA, infanta of Spain, iii. 93; takes the title of princess of England, 1623; 98. The marriage with prince Charles broken off, 100. She was married some years after to the king of Hungary, afterwards Ferdinand III., and lived to see Henrietta Maria driven a fugitive from England; to hear of the fatal fields of Marston Moor and Naseby, but not of Charles's death on the scaffold; she died in childbed, 1646; 395, *note.*

MARIE-ANTOINETTE, Joseph Jeanne de Lorraine, archduchess of Austria and queen of France, was born, November 2, 1755, and was married to the Dauphin, afterwards Louis XVI., at the age of fifteen ; portrait of, § ii. 354. The Maillard army attempt to assassinate her, 1789; 431. Her affable manners, 504. The flight to Varennes. June 1, 1791; 638—653. Effects of grief upon this unfortunate queen, 653; § iii. 117. She is separated from her children and friends; brought to trial, October 14, 1793, condemned to the guillotine, and executed, Wednesday, October 16; 348—352.

MARIGNANO, hard-contested victory of Francis I. at, 1515; ii. 334.

MARJORY, queen of Robert Bruce, taken prisoner after the rout of the Scottish army in the wood of Methven, 1306, and confined with her daughter in England, where she remained a prisoner for eight years, i. 729. She is exchanged with her daughter for the earl of Hereford, 738.

MARKHAM, sir Griffin, a Catholic, condemned for participation in the Bye Plot, 1603; iii. 8, 9. His hopes of pardon, 13. The king's messenger arrived with the reprieve for Raleigh, Grey, Cobham and Markham, at Winchester, just in time to save Markham's head, 14. He is banished, as also Copley and Brooksby, condemned for the same conspiracy, 15. Markham became a spy to sir Thomas Edmonds, the diplomatist, in the Low Countries, *ib.*

MARKHAM, sir Robert, proposes that on the death of Charles II. the prince of Orange should rule conjointly with the duke of York, iii. 733, *note.*

MARKHAM, William, bishop of Chester, named preceptor to the prince of Wales, (George IV.,) 1772; § i. 120; translated to the see of York, 1776; *ib.* He died, 1807.

MARLBOROUGH, earl of, obtains a grant of the Isle of Barbadoes from James, about 1605; iii. 538.

MARLBOROUGH, John Churchill, duke of, iv. 22; created, 1702. Disgraced, and prohibited from appearing at court, 1692; 36. Sent to the Tower, 37. Is admitted to bail, 39. He votes against sir John Fenwick, 76. The king appoints him preceptor to the duke of Gloucester, then in his eighth year, and the only surviving child of the princess Anne, 1698; 86. He is restored to his military rank and his place in the council, *ib.* Queen Anne makes him knight of the Garter, captain-general of the English forces, and master of the Ordnance, 1702 ; 141. He repairs to Nimeguen to assume the command of the army, 144. He takes Liege, October 29, 1702; 145. In his journey homeward, whilst descending the Meuse in a small boat, he is captured by a French partisan, but after plundering the boat they permit him to proceed, *ib.* The queen makes him a duke, 148. He gains the battle of Schellenberg, July 2, 1704; 167, 168 ; and the battle of Blenheim, August 13, 1704; 170—172. He meets for the first time prince Eugene, of Savoy, at Mondelsheim, 166. The emperor proposes to make him a prince of the empire, *ib.* He arrives at St. James's, carrying with him his prisoner the marshal Tallard, 173. He narrowly escapes death at the battle of Ramilies, May 23, 1706 ; 184. Receives a vote of thanks from both Houses, 200. Gains the battle of Oudenarde, July 11, 1708; 220. M. de Torcy attempts to bribe him, 235. His last cam-

MARLBOROUGH:—

paign, 252. He takes Bouchain, ib. Charged in the House of Commons with having misappropriated more than half a million of the public money, December 21, 1711; 259. He is dismissed from all his employments, 260. He retires to Brussels, where he remains till the death of the queen, 272. His correspondence with the court of St. Germain, ib. He arrives in England on the accession of George L, 301; is made commander-in-chief, and master-general of the Ordnance, 305. He expires at Windsor Lodge, June 16, 1722; 379. Is magnificently buried in Westminster Abbey, and afterwards removed to the chapel of Blenheim palace, ib.

MARLBOROUGH, lady, iv. 19. On the accession of queen Anne she is made groom of the stole, and mistress of the robes, and entrusted with the management of the privy purse; her two daughters are named ladies of the bed-chamber, 141. She resigns the golden key, 249. Her death, October, 1744; 474.

MARLOW, Christopher, a dramatist; he died in 1593; iii. 586.

MARMONT, marshal of the French empire, takes the command of the army in Portugal, 1811; § iv. 487. (Events in Spain, *see* Wellington.) Lord Wellesley gains the battle of Salamanca, in which Marmont is severely wounded, 508.

MARNEY, sir Henry, 1509, of Henry VIII.'s privy-council, ii. 320, 344.

Marquess.—The first English marquess was Robert de Vere, earl of Oxford; he was created marquess of Dublin for life in 1386; i. 882.

MARR, Donald, earl of, appointed regent of Scotland on the death of the great Randolph, earl of Moray, 1332; L 755. Marr is surprised at night by Edward Baliol, 1332, and many of his men are slain; the next day, hoping to take vengeance for the loss he had sustained, he engages in a disadvantageous position at Dupplin Moor, where he and 30,000 of his Scots are slain; the whole army of Baliol did not exceed 3,000, ib.

MARR, earl of, on the death of Lennox, 1571, be is made regent of Scotland, ii. 646. He refuses to have anything to do with a proposal made to him by Elizabeth, that she should send the queen of Scots to Scotland to be there executed, 648. He falls sick at the house of the chancellor Morton, where he had been invited to a banquet, and hastes to Stirling, where he died, October 1572, and was succeeded in the regency by Morton, ib.

Marriage Act, Royal, 1772; § i. 126. Precedent for this enactment, 6 Henry VI., ii. 80, *note*, 332.

MARRIOTT, doctor, advocate-general, examination of, 1774; § i. 172—174.

Marseilles, the Greek maritime colony *Massilia*, an emporium for tin of the Cassiterides, but chiefly purchasing of Phœnicians, and the northern Gauls, i. 26, 93. View of the modern city; § iii. 302.

Marseillese, march of the, composed, both words and music, by Rouget de Lille, an ardent Republican, in 1792; § iii. 112.

MARSH, bishop of Ferns, and afterwards bishop of Armagh, one of the first who treated the theory of acoustics methodically, iii. 888.

Marshall, or Mareschall, office of the, i. 569.

Marston Moor, battle of, gained by the parliamentary troops, July 2, 1644; iii. 315.

MARSTON, John, a dramatist of the sixteenth century, iii. 592.

MARTIN V., pope, Otho de Colonna, sends cardinals Ursini and St. Mark into France, 1417, to act as mediators, ii. 41. Henry V.'s reply to Ursini, 43. Martin V., elected November 11, 1417, by all the cardinals, and six deputies from the five great states of Christendom, 137. This formal solemnity put an end to the schism of two popes, etc., ib. Gibbon's

MARTIN V.,—

account of the great claim of the English to be heard at such elections, 138. Clement VIII., in 1429, makes a final submission to Martin as the real pope, ib. Martin V. convoked the council of Basil, 1431, which maintained the superiority of a general council even to the Roman pontiff, ib. Martin V. proclaimed, in 1428, the crusade against Zisca and the Hussites of Bohemia, 150. He named cardinal Beaufort captain-general of this crusade, who raised an army, and set out by way of Paris, 71, 150. The duke of Bedford being left by the council at home without sufficient strength in France, the cardinal patriotically resigned his troops to the regent, 71. Martin died, February, 1431.

MARTIN, sir Henry, 1647; iii. 363.

MARTIN, Henry, iii. 247. Condemned as a regicide, 1661; 672; but reprieved. 677. Establishes the paper called the "British Merchant," iv. 707.

MARTIN, commodore, threatens to bombard the city of Naples, 1742; iv. 462.

Martinique, surrenders to the English, 1762; § i. 17. View of Fort Royal at, 18.

MARVELL, Andrew, member for Hull *regno* Charles II., and author of a number of political satires, iii. 424, 605, 666.

MARY I. (July 6, 1553—November 17, 1558), daughter of Henry VIII. by queen Catherine, his first wife, ii. 364, 368. Question of her legitimacy, 364, 367. Parliament, in 1534, declared her illegitimate, and that the succession was lawfully vested in the children of Anne Boleyn, 384, 385. Catherine, on her death-bed, 1536, prayed Henry, in an affectionate letter, to show kindness to their daughter, 390. Mary's known affection for her mother, and attachment to the old discipline of the church, had caused her seclusion at Hunsden, nor would Henry permit her to have a parting interview with the dying queen, 395. The young princess subscribed humiliating articles of submission, 395, *note*. Mary then received a suitable establishment, without being restored in blood, 396. She wrote to Somerset against any further change in affairs of religion until the king, her brother, should be of age, 494. The Protector's reply to her epistle, ib. On the passing of the Statute for Uniformity, she is desired, 1549, not to have mass celebrated in her private chapel, ib. August, 1550, it being rumoured that this princess intended to quit the realm, ships were stationed to intercept her, ib. Her chaplains indicted, ib. March, 1551, Edward IV., in council, endeavoured, with his best learning, to dissuade her from obstinacy in this regard, but Mary was inflexible, ib. Charles V., by his ambassador, threatened war if his niece were finally denied to hear mass, ib. Cranmer persuades king Edward to indulge his sister; he reluctantly gave consent to the celebration in the solitary favour of the princess, ib.. Some of the Council attended on her at Copthall, in Essex. She totally refuses the new *service* in her house. Her speech regarding the young king, ib. Her great seal, 501. Her portrait ib. Northumberland summons her to attend Edward on his death-bed. On her way to the capital the earl of Arundel informs her that her brother is dead, and that Northumberland, who was plotting to place the lady Jane Grey on the throne, only wanted to make her a prisoner. On receiving this notice she changes her route, and retires to Suffolk, 502. Lady Jane is publicly received as queen, ib. Mary summons the nobility to her standard, ib. She is proclaimed at Norwich, 503. The duke of Northumberland undertakes the command of lady Jane's forces, ib. Ridley preaches at Paul's-cross, showing the right and title of the lady Jane, ib. The council declare for queen Mary, ib. The council take possession of the Tower for

MARY I.:—
her, *ib.* She is proclaimed at Cheap, 504. The duke of Northumberland proclaims Mary at Cambridge; he is arrested for treason, and committed to the Tower, *ib.* Queen Jane is likewise confined there, *ib.* The duke of Suffolk is made a state-prisoner, but he is soon afterwards discharged, and obtains the queen's pardon, *ib.* Elizabeth rides through London to receive Mary; her politic conduct, *ib.* Queen Mary enters London and liberates the duke of Norfolk, Gardiner, Bonner, and Tunstall from confinement, 505. Mary solemnizes the obsequies of her brother at the Tower, the dirge is sung in Latin, and a mass or requiem performed, but on the same day the body is buried in Westminster Abbey, and the service is performed in the Protestant manner by bishop Day, *ib.* The duke of Northumberland, the earl of Warwick, the marquess of Northampton, and several others, are arraigned for treason and condemned, *ib.* The duke of Northumberland, sir John Gates, and sir Thomas Palmer are executed, 506. Gardiner is made chancellor; the old Catholic service is sung in Latin in St. Paul's church, *ib.* Cranmer, Latimer, and several others are committed to the Tower, 507. The princess Elizabeth and lady Anne of Cleves ride side by side at the procession, *ib.* Mary is crowned with the usual formalities, 507, 508. Parliament assembles; high mass is celebrated, at which Taylor, bishop of Lincoln, refusing to kneel, he is thrust out of the House, 508. The queen is declared legitimate. All the statutes of the late reign, that in any way regarded religion, are repealed, *ib.* Gardiner summons a convocation to settle all doubts respecting the sacrament; the Book of Common Prayer is declared an abomination, and the immediate suppression of the Reformed English Catechism is called for, 508, 509. Many of the bishops conform, and many are deprived and sent to prison, 509. Cranmer is brought to trial for high treason, together with lady Jane Grey, lord Guildford Dudley, and lord Ambrose Dudley; they are condemned to suffer death as traitors, but they are all sent back to the Tower, *ib.* The attainder of the duke of Norfolk is reversed, 510. The queen issues an order that no one shall preach without a licence; Judge Hales, who had defended the queen's title with a rare courage, remonstrates; he is thrown into prison, where he falls into a phrenzy, and attempts suicide; he is at length liberated, but insanity had taken a firm hold of him, and he drowns himself, *ib.* Cardinal Pole is made papal legate for England, 511. Mary, without the consent of her council, promises solemnly to marry Philip, son of the emperor Charles; parliament petitions against this match, *ib.* Gardiner explains to parliament the conditions of the treaty, *ib.* Robert Dudley, son of the late duke of Northumberland, is condemned as a traitor, *ib.* Portrait of Philip, 512. Sir Peter Carew raises an insurrection in Devonshire against the Spanish match, *ib.* Sir Thomas Wyatt does the same in Kent, *ib.* The duke of Suffolk, who had been liberated from the Tower, flies to Warwickshire, and raises the people there, *ib.* The duke of Norfolk marches against sir T. Wyatt; the London trained bands desert to Wyatt, at Rochester-bridge; Wyatt marches to Southwark; retires to Kingston; marches to London; is met at Hyde-park by the royal forces; he surrenders, and is committed to the Tower, 512—514. Many of the rebels are hanged, 514, 515. Elizabeth is arrested and brought before the council, she protests her innocence, and is allowed to return to Ashridge, 515. Courtenay is committed to the Tower, *ib.* Elizabeth is again arrested, and sent to the Tower, 515—517. Lady Jane Grey and her husband are beheaded, 517, 518. Portrait

MARY I.:—
of the lady Jane, 517. The duke of Suffolk is tried for treason, and executed, 518. Execution of sir Thomas Wyatt, *ib.* Lord Thomas Grey and William Thomas executed, *ib.* Trial of sir Nicholas Throgmorton, the jury return a verdict of *Not* Guilty; they are threatened by the lord chief-justice, but continue firm; Throgmorton demands his acquittal according to law, but the lord chief-justice, sir T. Bromley, remands him to the Tower, and the jury are imprisoned and heavily fined, 518, 519. Elizabeth is removed from the Tower to Woodstock, 519. The earl of Devon is removed to Fotheringay Castle, *ib.* Dr. Pendleton narrowly escapes death whilst preaching papistry at Paul's-cross, *ib.* Elizabeth Croft plays the "Spirit in the Wall," *ib.* Philip, prince of Spain, arrives in Southampton water, *ib.*; his fear of being attacked by the people, *ib.*; his nuptials are celebrated at Winchester, with great pomp, 520. Parliament meets; continued jealousies of the English against the foreigner, *ib.* The Act of Supremacy repealed, *ib.* The pope confirms the abbey lands to their present possessors, *ib.* Cardinal Pole gives absolution to the parliament and people of England, 521. The old laws against heretics revived; statutes are enacted against seditious words; and it is made treason to imagine the death of Philip, *ib.* The earl of Devon receives permission to travel on the continent; he dies at Padua, 1556; *ib.* Mary mistakes the commencement of a dropsy for a sign of pregnancy; *Te Deum* is sung everywhere for the supposed infant, and parliament enacts many things concerning its education, *ib.* Tumults between the Spaniards and English at Westminster, 521, 522. William Featherstone counterfeits Edward VI.; he is executed at Tyburn, 522. Persecution of the Protestants, *ib.* Trial and execution of John Rogers, 522, 523. Bishop Hooper, bishop Ferrar, and Dr. Rowland Taylor are burned, 523. Laurence Saunders, and William Branch are burned, 524. J. Cardmaker, J. Bradford, T. Hawkes, J. Lawrence, Tomkins, Pigot, Knight, and Hunter, are burned, *ib.* Bishop Gardiner, being weary of these executions, his duties devolve on the ferocious Bonner, *ib.* Cardinal Pole endeavours to prove to Mary that the practice of persecution was not only dangerous to the government, but the scandal of religion, *ib.* Cranmer, Ridley, and Latimer, are brought to St. Mary's church to be examined, 525. Execution of Ridley and Latimer, 526. Philip goes to the continent, *ib.* Death of bishop Gardiner; the great seal is given to Heath, archbishop of York, *ib.* Philip, 1556, presses Mary for money; her unjust proceedings to obtain it, 527. Cranmer recants, *ib.*; but being, nevertheless, brought to the stake, he renounces the pope, 528. Amount of martyrdoms during this reign, *ib.* Cardinal Pole is installed archbishop of Canterbury, *ib.* The bones of Martin Bucer and Paul Phagius are burned at Cambridge, *ib.* The earls of Oxford and Westmoreland, and lord Willoughby, are censured by the council for religion, 529. Dissimulation of the princess Elizabeth, *ib.* She refuses the suits of the duke of Savoy and of the king of Sweden's son, Eric, *ib.* Death of sir John Cheke, 529, 530. Comparative insignificance of persecution in England compared to other countries, *ib.*; *note.* Increase of crime during this reign; a son of the lord Sandys is hanged for robbery, 531. A malignant fever, 1556, rages in London, and pestilence and famine in the country, *ib.* Conspiracy of Clever, a schoolmaster, *ib.* Charles V. resigns in favour of his son, Philip of England, *ib.* The pope, Paul IV., opens negotiations with the French; he sends the duke of Alva to take upon himself the government of Naples, *ib.* Troublesome state of Italy, 532. Philip,

MARY I.:—
1557, enters London, *ib.* Thomas Stafford, and a few others, land at Scarborough and surprise the castle; they are taken prisoners, and Stafford and some others, one a Frenchman, are tortured in the Tower, and afterwards beheaded; this is made a pretext for a war with France, which, at Philip's desire, is formally declared, *ib.* Death of the lady Anne of Cleves, *ib.* Philip gains a battle under the walls of St. Quintin, 533. Calais taken by the duke of Guise, after it had been in the possession of the English for 211 years, 533, 534. The castle of Guisnes surrenders, 535. The queen-dowager, Mary of Guise, assumes the title of regent of Scotland, 536. The nuptials of Francis, Dauphin of France, and Mary, queen of Scots, are celebrated, *ib.* Parliament votes supplies for recovering Calais; lord Clinton joins king Philip's squadron, with an English fleet, *ib.* The battle of Gravelines, 537. Death of queen Mary, November 17, 1558, *ib.*; cardinal Pole expires twenty-two hours after the queen, 538. Her funeral, 541. Her signature, 695. History of religion during this reign, 734—737. Coins of Mary, 801.
MARY, queen of William III., arrives at Whitehall, February 12, 1689; iv. 5. Proclaimed queen of England, *ib.* Her portrait, 8. She dies of small-pox, in the thirty-third year of her age, December 28, 1694; 50.
MARY of Guise, queen of James V.; ii. 412. Summons the reformed clergy to appear at Stirling, May 10, 1559; 547. She appoints commissioners to treat with sir Ralph Sadler to settle border disputes, 551. She implores lord Erskine to receive her into Edinburgh Castle, 560, where she dies, June 10, 1560, recommending to her half-brother, James Stuart, her child and their queen, 561.
MARY, queen of Scots (December 14, 1542—July 24, 1567,) daughter of James V. and Mary of Guise, born in December, 1542, a few days only before her father's decease, ii. 548. Her portrait, 549. Lamentations of the dying king, *ib.* Henry VIII., in 1543, negotiated with the Douglas party, and the lords whom he had captured on Solway Moss, for the custody of the infant Mary to be assigned to him, 434. Treaty concluded for that object, *ib.* Henry's design of uniting her to his son Edward, and also of uniting Scotland with England, narrated, 434, *et seq.* Cardinal Beaton, under a will of James V., had been appointed guardian of Mary, and regent of Scotland, 434. Arran (Hamilton), the heir-apparent to the crown, and leader of the Protestant party, immediately dispossessed Beaton of power, 1542—1543, and detained him prisoner, *ib.* State of the great Scottish factions during the childhood of Mary of Scots, explained, 435. The Scottish parliament favoured the scheme of marriage, but refused to send queen Mary to the English court, *ib.* In 1547, Mary, then five years of age, embarked in a French fleet, and was betrothed to the Dauphin Francis, who was a few months younger than her, 469. Accomplishment of their marriage, 536. Her husband, Francis II., dies, and is succeeded by her brother, Charles IX.; on this catastrophe Mary is harshly treated, on which she retires from court to Rheims, 563. She refuses to ratify the Treaty of Edinburgh, *ib.* She requests Elizabeth to grant her a safe-conduct to cross the seas into Scotland, and allow her to pass through England if absolutely necessary; this Elizabeth refuses, *ib.* Mary's spirited speech to sir Nicholas Throgmorton, 564. She embarks at Calais, 565; arrives at Leith, *ib.* Intolerance of the Reformers towards her, *ib.* Elizabeth demands Mary to lay aside *for ever* the arms and titles of England, 568. Mary goes on a royal progress to the North, 1562; her cold reception by the Highland clans;

MARY, queen of Scots:—
the castle of Inverness is held against her by the Gordons; the castle is entered by force of arms, and the captain put to death, 574. The queen confers upon her half-brother the earldom of Moray, *ib.* The battle of Corrichie is the consequence of this grant, 575. Suitors of queen Mary, *ib.* She consults Elizabeth upon the choice of a husband, who fraudulently proposes to her her own favourite, lord Robert Dudley, shortly afterwards the earl of Leicester, *ib.* Mary's subjects, growing weary of the long delays attendant on this proposition, point out Henry Stuart, lord Darnley, 578. He pays Mary a visit at Wemyss Castle, where he is courteously received, 579. He seeks to gain upon her affections through David Rizzio, the queen's private secretary, 580. The estates of the kingdom recommend the marriage, the lord Ochiltree alone refusing his assent, *ib.* Sir N. Throgmorton is sent by Elizabeth to Edinburgh, 1565, to declare her discontent at the projected match; he is unable to persuade Mary, who assures him that the affair had proceeded too far to be set aside with honour, *ib.* Throgmorton is ordered to intrigue with the earl of Moray, and other discontented Protestant lords, who begin to rumour that there would be no safety for the Protestant religion if the Catholic queen were permitted to have a Catholic husband, *ib.* Quarrel between Darnley and the earl of Moray, 581. The Assembly of the Kirk demand, by a formal Act, that the queen should conform to the Protestant faith, and abolish the Romish worship throughout the realm, *ib.* The earl of Moray, in conjunction with several others, lays an ambush to take Darnley, his father, and the queen, prisoners, *ib.* Darnley is created earl of Ross and duke of Rothsay, and proclaimed king at the market-cross of Edinburgh; the next day he is married to the queen, according to the Catholic ritual, in the chapel at Holyrood House, *ib.* The earl of Moray, the duke of Chatelherault, etc., fly to arms, 1565; Mary, clad in light armour, meets them at the head of a royal army; the lords instantly retreating, this campaign got the name of the Round-about Raid, *ib.* The lords fly into England, 582. Their curious reception by Elizabeth, *ib.* Mary convokes a parliament, for the purpose of attainting Moray and his associates; Chatelherault negotiates with the queen, and procures her pardon; Moray's friends then apply in his behalf, but the cardinal of Lorraine advises her not to pardon him, and she allows the proceedings to go on in parliament, 583. Mary joins the great Catholic Alliance, *ib.* She forbids Randolph her court, alleging that he takes part with the rebels of her country, 584. The insolence of Darnley drives his father, the earl of Lennox, from court, *ib.* Mary becomes weary of his society, *ib.* The case of Chastelar adduced as a proof against the probability of Mary's entertaining a criminal conversation with Rizzio, 585. The murderers of Rizzio, 586—588. The earl of Bothwell is recalled to court, *ib.* Description of the murder of the Italian secretary, 1566; probable reasons for this savage deed, 586, 587. Murray, and the other banished lords, present themselves at Holyrood House, pretending that they come to stand their trial, 587. Darnley abandons the murderers to their fate, *ib.* Mary relates her harsh usage to Murray, *ib.* Darnley protests before the council that he never consented to Rizzio's death, 588. Mary is delivered of a son, June 19, 1566; it is reported to Elizabeth, *ib.*; who is chosen godmother, 589. Performance of the ceremony, *ib.* This birth revives the spirit of Mary's partisans in England, *ib.* Mary presses Elizabeth to name her successor, and obtain from the parliament a recognition of her own rights, 590. She addresses a

MARY, queen of Scots,—
letter to the English Privy-council to the same effect, 591. Elizabeth takes the murderers of Rizzio under her protection, and instructs the earl of Bedford to plead to queen Mary in their favour at the baptism of her infant; Mary, at his request, grants them a free pardon, ib. Morton, Ruthven, and above seventy others, return to Scotland, ib. Darnley retires to Glasgow on hearing of the pardon of Morton, 592. He speaks of going abroad, ib. Bothwell is wounded at Hermitage Castle by an outlaw, 593. Mary, after eight days, goes to visit him, ib. This exertion brings on a dangerous fever, 594. She is wounded in the leg by the horse of sir John Forster, a warden of the English borders, ib. Darnley is attacked by the small-pox; on his convalescence, he is lodged in a lonely house, called the Kirk-a-field, 595. The earl of Orkney advertises him of his danger; it was suspected by many that the earl of Bothwell had some enterprise against him, ib. On the 10th of February, at midnight, the city is shaken by a violent explosion; the house of Kirk-a-field is utterly destroyed, and the bodies of Darnley and his valet are found lying in the garden, without any marks of violence on their persons, ib. The earl of Bothwell told Melville that he saw the thunder come out of the sky and burn the house; suspicion immediately falls upon this earl, 596. Reward offered for the apprehension of the murderers, ib. The earl of Lennox makes a formal accusation of Bothwell and others, ib. Hurried trial of Bothwell; he is acquitted, no prosecutor appearing, 597. Immediately after the rising of parliament, 1567, Bothwell invites the members to an entertainment in a tavern, and declares to them his purpose of marrying the queen, 598; he draws a bond from his pocket, recommending him as a suitable match for her majesty, which he procures to be signed by twenty-four peers, spiritual and temporal, ib. Four days after this Bothwell collects about a thousand horse, and lays in wait for the queen, who was then returning from Stirling Castle, whither she had been to visit her infant son; at the Foulbrigs he rides up to her, and takes her horse's bridle; and capturing besides several others, he carries them all as prisoners to Dunbar Castle, ib. A few days after Bothwell brings the queen back to Edinburgh Castle; Mary appears before the Court of Session, where she declares that though she had been carried off and greatly injured by the earl of Bothwell, yet she is disposed to forgive him and exalt him to higher honours, 599. Bothwell determines to have the marriage conducted in a strictly Presbyterian manner; Craig, the colleague of Knox, after some hesitation, publishes the banns, and then from the pulpit violently inveighs against the marriage, ib. Bothwell is created duke of Orkney, and united to the queen, ib. Melancholy condition of the queen; she calls for a knife to commit suicide, 599. As soon as the queen's honour is inseparably connected with Bothwell, Morton, Maitland, and the rest fly to arms; they attempt to seize the queen and Bothwell in Borthwick Castle, but they escape to the castle of Dunbar, 600; the confederates march upon Edinburgh, report that the life of the young prince is in danger, and assume the powers of government, ib. They call upon all the queen's people to join their standard, under pain of being deemed the murderers of the late king, ib. The queen summons her subjects, and marches towards Edinburgh, ib. On the 15th of June, 1567, she advances to Carberry Hill, and draws up her forces in order of battle. ib Whilst the armies were in this position the French ambassador, Le Croc, attempts a reconciliation, ib. Bothwell offers to prove his innocence by single combat, and the earl of Morton (a fit match) is

MARY, queen of Scots,—
said to have accepted the challenge; this bravadoing came to nothing, and only gave time for increasing the force of the confederates, 601. The queen treats with Kirkaldy of Grange, who (being himself deceived by the confederates) makes her fair promises, to which she assents, and Grange conducts her to the army of the Confederates, ib. When she reached the lines all this respect vanished, she is abused by the soldiery, and the next day conducted, under strong guard, to the castle of Lochleven, the stronghold of sir W. Douglas, uterine brother of the earl of Murray, 602. A reward is placed upon Bothwell by the Privy-council, he seeks shelter in his dukedom of Orkney, but is refused admittance by his own keeper; he then threatens to scour the seas with a blood-red flag, ib. The lords despatch a fleet after him, but he flies to Norway, ib. He is taken as a pirate by the Danish government, and thrown into the castle of Malmoe, where he is said to have gone mad, ib. He died about ten years after this, ib. The Hamiltons, etc., soon begin to devise measures for the protection of the queen, and insist that she ought to be restored to her liberty and her throne, upon equitable conditions, 603. The confederates assume the appropriate name of the Lords of the Secret Council, ib. They execute captain Blackadder, and four others, for the murder of Darnley, 1567; ib. Proceedings of the Assembly of the Kirk, 603, 604. Coldness of Elizabeth's behaviour towards Mary, 604. Mary is forced to sign a deed, resigning the crown in favour of her infant son, then fourteen months old, and appointing her half-brother regent during his minority, ib. Coronation of the child, ib. Murray is proclaimed regent, August 22, 605; he promotes Morton to the offices of chancellor, lord high admiral, and sheriff of the shires of Edinburgh and Haddington, 606. Murray assembles a parliament, from which all but his own partisans keep away; the Acts passed in 1560 against popery are revived, ib. Four obscure men are executed for assisting in the murder of Darnley, 1568; ib. Mary makes an attempt at escape, but is detected and carried back; shortly after, by the assistance of William Douglas, she succeeds in escaping from the castle, May 2, 1568, and is carried by lord Seton and a party of Hamiltons in triumph to Hamilton, 606, 607. An association for her defence is drawn up, and a force of 4,000 or 5,000 men enter the field, and move with her from Hamilton towards Dumbarton, 607. Murray could scarcely believe the possibility of his sister's escape; some of his friends advised him to retire to Stirling and avoid an encounter, but he knew his advantages, ib. Mary offered a free pardon to all save five, but the lords were not inclined to any composition, ib. The armies met May 14, 1568 at Langside, between Glasgow and Dumbarton, and attacked each other with desperate fury, fighting hand to hand, and locked together, ib. Mary remained on an adjacent hill, spectatress of the fight, which appeared to incline towards her side; but Morton, sweeping round with a large detachment, charged her friends in flank, broke them, and decided the day, ib. They flee in all directions; the queen, attended by a few friends, rides without stopping to Dundrennan Abbey, a distance of sixty miles, ib. She at last resolves on entering England, (as preferable either to throwing herself on the mercy of her subjects, or a flight to France,) notwithstanding her counsellors represented it to her as the most dangerous course of the three, ib. Lord Herries writes to Lowther, the deputy-captain of Carlisle, informing him of his queen's situation, and asking him if she might go safely to England, ib. He gives a doubtful answer, but says that if the queen found herself obliged to

MARY, queen of Scots,—
cross the borders, he would meet and protect her till his mistress's pleasure was known, *ib.* Mary arrives at Workington, in a state of complete indigence, *ib.* Some gentlemen give her a kind reception, and honourably conduct her to Cockermouth, *ib.* On the following day Lowther conducts her to Carlisle, and lodges her in the castle as a prisoner, *ib.* She complains to lord Scrope, that if Elizabeth did not mean to assist her, she might permit her to pass into France, as her case was by no means hopeless, and she should be able to procure assistance either from the Spaniards or French, 608. She sends lord Herries to plead her cause with Elizabeth, *ib.* She is carried, under strong escort, to Bolton Castle, July 16; she declares she will not move further into England unless force be used, 611. She writes to Elizabeth, 612. Elizabeth intrigues with the earl of Murray, *ib.* Mary accepts an offer made to her by the English queen to become mediator, and the famous commission for trying her case meets at York, October 4, *ib.* Proceedings of the commission, 612—616. Maitland, of Lethington, suggests a marriage between Mary and the duke of Norfolk, 614. Elizabeth declares that if Murray can make good his accusations against the queen, she shall never be restored to the Scottish throne, *ib.* The earl of Murray produces a box full of *original* love-letters from Mary to Bothwell, proving her the murderer of her husband; the authenticity of these letters Mary denies, 615, 616. Elizabeth advises Mary to resign her crown, and live quietly in England; this advice Mary refuses to adopt, 616. Elizabeth assures Murray that he may go back safely to Scotland, gives him 5,000*l.*, and publishes a proclamation for him to satisfy jealousies in Scotland. Mary represents these proceedings as unfair, 616, 617. Mary is removed, by Elizabeth's command, to Tutbury, February 3, 1569; 618. She opens a correspondence with the earl of Northumberland, the earl of Westmoreland, and several others, 628. Insurrection in her favour; she is removed to Coventry, 629. The English clamour for her execution, 644. She is removed to Sheffield Castle; insults offered to her by lady Shrewsbury, 644, 645. Her grief at the death of the duke of Norfolk, 645. Her papers and jewels are taken from her, 658. She is removed to Fotheringay Castle, *ib.* Thirty-six English commissioners are appointed to try her, *ib.* Elizabeth accuses her of being accessory to the Babington Conspiracy; this she denies, *ib.* Able defence of the Scottish queen to the charges brought against her, 660. The commissioners dissolve their assembly, and appoint it to re-assemble in the Star-chamber at Westminster, 662. Sentence is pronounced against Mary, October 25, 1586, and parliament demands its instant execution, 662, 663. Mary's last letter to Elizabeth, 664. Henri III. sends over Bellièvre as a special ambassador to intercede for Mary's life, *ib.* Coldness of James to the fate of his mother; he sends Keith, a pensioner of England, to negotiate with the English queen. 665. Her inflexible conduct, 665, 666. She signs the death-warrant, but indicates to Davison that she would much prefer Mary to be privately murdered, 666, 667. Mary calmly listens to the death-warrant, 668. Execution of this unfortunate queen, December 8, 1587. Her tomb in the south aisle of Henry VII.'s Chapel, Westminster Abbey, 670.

MARY, duchess of Suffolk, younger daughter of Henry VII., affianced to Charles of Spain, during the detention of his father Philip at Windsor, ii. 315, 331, 338. Henry VIII. was furious at hearing of Charles's intended marriage with another princess, Renée, the second daughter of the French king, 331. Louis XII., fifty-three years of age, had, in 1514, recently lost his queen, Anne of Brittany, *ib.*

MARY, duchess of Suffolk,—
The duke of Longueville, captive in England, proposed to Henry, that Louis XII. should espouse the princess Mary, beautiful and but sixteen years of age, *ib.* She was enamoured with Charles Brandon, afterwards duke of Suffolk, a favourite of Henry VIII., *ib.* Louis promised to Henry a million of crowns, in ten annual instalments, in liquidation of arrears under the treaty of Estaples, *ib.* The marriage ceremony took place, 1514, at Greenwich, Longueville being proxy for Louis XII., *ib.* Mary did not hasten to cross the sea, but the French king showed impatience at the delay, *ib.* Her royal brother escorted her to Dover, *ib.* Her meeting at Abbeville with king Louis, *ib.* He dismissed lady Guilford, Anne Boleyn, maid of honour, and all her English attendants, on the very next day, *ib.* Sir Charles Brandon, (viscount Lisle and duke of Suffolk,) remained as ambassador, and the duke of Norfolk, *ib.* Queen Mary wrote bitter complaints to her brother Henry, and demanded the restoration of her governess, lady Guilford, *ib.* Her coronation at St. Denis, 332. Grand reception of the young queen at Paris, *ib.* Tournament, at which Brandon carried off every prize, *ib.* December 1514, king Louis wrote to Henry VIII. expressing his happiness in this marriage, *ib.* January 1, 1515, this king, surnamed "the father of his people," expired from debility, *ib.* Henry VIII. sent Charles Brandon, duke of Suffolk, and others, to bring queen Mary home, *ib.* The young widow immediately married Suffolk, and wrote humble letters to her royal brother, *ib.* The king was wroth, but from affection for them both, he received them into favour, 332, 351. Mary's dower, 361.

MARY, princess, daughter of Charles I., married to the young prince of Orange, 1642; iii. 272.

MASANIELLO, a fisherman, heads an insurrection in Italy, 1648; iii. 395.

MASERES, Mr., attorney-general of Quebec, examination of, 1774; § i. 171, 172.

MASHAM, Mrs., a poor cousin of the duchess of Marlborough, and bedchamber-woman to queen Anne; she supplants the duchess in the royal favour, and lends great assistance to the Tory speaker, Mr. Harley, iv. 212.

MASON, Mr., secretary to the duke of Buckingham, 1626; iii. 121.

MASSENA, Andrew, prince of Essling, duke of Rivoli, and marshal of France, born 1758, distinguished for his services in the wars of the French Republic and of Bonaparte, for his eminent services at Essling and Wagram, 1809; created prince of Essling, § iv. 412, 413. He commanded the French army of Portugal in 1810 and 1811, but on account of the skill of his opponent, lord Wellesley, he was prevented from gaining any new laurels, 441—485. After the battle of Fuentes de Onoro, he was succeeded by marshal Marmont; when returning to Paris, he terminated his military career, and died at his seat at Ruel, April 4, 1817; 486.

MASSEY, colonel, governor of Gloucester, which place he bravely defends against the siege of the royalists, 1643; iii. 306. Is defeated by prince Rupert at Ledbury, 1645; 331. Is formally accused by the army, June. 1647; 369.

MASSINGER, Philip, a distinguished English dramatist, born 1584, died 1640; iii. 597.

MATTHEWS, general, his unworthy conduct in India, 1783; § ii. 155.

MATHIAS of Austria, jewels and plate pledged by him to the States of Holland, ii. 649. These were placed by the Dutch in queen Elizabeth's hands, for an advance of 50,000*l.*, *ib.*

MATILDA, queen of William I., publicly crowned, 1068, and assigned a large share of the confiscated territory, i. 365. She returns to Normandy, 370.

MATILDA,—
Her affection for her son Robert, 384. Her death, 1082 to 1085; 386.

MATILDA, queen; her marriage with Geoffrey Plantagenet, earl of Anjou, 1127; i. 417. She quarrels with her husband; a reconciliation is effected; her three children, Henry, Geoffrey, and William, 418. Geoffrey's dispute with Henry, *ib.* Stephen's determination to dispute the right of succession with Matilda, 421. He arrives in London, obtains the royal treasury, and is crowned king, 421, 422. General insurrection in Matilda's favour. (*See* Gloucester and David of Scotland, 423—426.) Matilda and Robert earl of Gloucester land in England, 1139. She is received by queen Alice, in Arundel Castle, 428. Joined by Alexander bishop of Lincoln, Nigel bishop of Ely, and many of the prelates and barons, *ib.* Stephen fails in his attempt upon her head-quarters at Bristol, 429. Bishop Nigel defeated, *ib.* While Stephen is besieging the castle of Lincoln, the earl of Gloucester arrives with 10,000 men; a battle is fought before Lincoln, in which Stephen is taken prisoner and confined in Bristol Castle, 430. Matilda is acknowledged queen by Henry bishop of Winchester, papal legate for all England, who wholly abandons his unfortunate brother, *ib.* She enters Winchester and takes possession of the royal castle, the crown, and treasury, *ib.* An assembly convened at Winchester to ratify her accession, 431. Deputation from the city of London for the liberation of Stephen, *ib.* Influence of this city, *ib.* Matilda enters London and makes preparations for her coronation at Westminster, *ib.* Her arrogant conduct; she quarrels with bishop Henry, *ib.* Is expelled from London by the citizens, and makes her escape to Oxford, 432. Attempts to seize Henry; he places himself at the head of his armed vassals and besieges Matilda in the royal castle of Winchester, whither she had summoned the earls of Gloucester, Hereford, Chester, and David king of Scots, 433. She escapes on the 14th of September, 1141, from Winchester Castle, and reaches the castle of Devizes in safety, but her half-brother, Robert, is taken prisoner and secured in Rochester Castle, *ib.* The earl of Gloucester exchanged for king Stephen; Henry summons a great ecclesiastical council at Winchester, in which Stephen a second time is declared king, and Henry of Winchester endeavours to justify his conduct with respect to Matilda, 434. Dreadful state of anarchy in England, *ib.* Prince Henry, eldest son of Matilda and Geoffrey of Anjou, acknowledged in Normandy as legitimate duke, 1142, *ib.* Matilda presses her husband Geoffrey to come to her assistance in England, which he refuses, but offers to send over prince Henry, 434, 435. Is besieged by king Stephen in the castle of Oxford, from which she makes her escape dressed in white, the ground being covered with snow, and joins the earl of Gloucester, who had landed in England with prince Henry, near Wallingford, 435. Stephen defeated by the earl of Gloucester at Wilton, *ib.* Matilda maintains her ground in the west, but her son Henry having returned to Normandy, and her brother Gloucester having died of a fever, she quits England and returns to Normandy, *ib.* Death of the empress Matilda at Rouen, 1167; 452.

MATILDA, daughter of Henry I., commonly designated as the empress Maud; married to Henry V. of Germany, when only eight years old, 1110; i. 412. Becomes a widow in 1124. On Christmas day, 1126, Henry I. caused his daughter to be recognised at Windsor, by an assembly of the bishops, abbots, and barons, as heiress to his crown, 416. Oath administered to this great council, *ib.* Aversion of the barons to the idea of a female sovereign, hitherto unknown in the English constitution, *ib.*. Disputes

MATILDA,—
for precedence betwixt Stephen, the king's nephew, and his illegitimate son Robert, decided in favour of Stephen, *ib.*

MATILDA, or Maud, the Good, daughter of Malcolm king of Scotland and of Margaret, sister of Edgar Atheling, sent, when very young, to England, and committed to the care of her aunt Christiana, Edgar Atheling's second sister, abbess of Wilton, or, as others say, of Rumsey, i. 406. Alan, lord of Richmond, wished to marry her, but died before he could obtain permission from William, *ib.* William de Garenne, earl of Surrey, was her next suitor, but Rufus refused to ratify the marriage, *ib.* Henry I. proposes to marry her, *ib.* Her disinclination to the match, *ib.* Many of the Normans assert that she had taken the veil, *ib.* Archbishop Anselm undertakes to question the maiden; the affair diligently inquired into, it is decided that Matilda had never taken the veil, and was not a nun, 406, 407. On the 11th November, 1100, her marriage with Henry was celebrated, and she was crowned queen with great pomp and solemnity, 407. Her death, 1118; 413.

MATILDA, daughter of Fulk, earl of Anjou. Her proposed marriage with William, only son of Henry I., i. 412. This marriage broken off, but afterwards carried into effect, 413.

MATILDA, or Maud, daughter and heir of Eustace, count of Boulogne, and of Mary of Scotland, sister to David, the reigning king, and to queen Maud, the first wife of Henry I., and wife of Stephen, earl of Boulogne, afterwards king of England, i. 421. Peace is concluded, by her intercession, between Stephen and her uncle David of Scotland, 426. She dies, 1151, and is buried at Feversham, 438.

MATILDA, eldest daughter of Henry II., married Henry duke of Saxony, Bavaria, Westphalia, etc.; from her is descended the present royal family of Great Britain, i. 480.

MATTHEWS, captain, an officer in the service of the duke of Monmouth, 1685; iii. 772.

MATTHEWS, admiral, he sinks five Spanish galleys in the French port of St. Tropez, 1742; iv. 462. His unsuccessful attack on the Spaniards, in the Mediterranean, 472. He is tried by court-martial, and rendered for ever incapable of service, 1744; *ib.*

MATUZOF, Andrew Artemonowitz, ambassador of Peter the Great. The case of this ambassador, who was arrested in London for debt, gave rise to the statute 7 Anne, c. 12, concerning the privileges of ambassadors, iv. 676.

MAULAC, Peter de, esquire of king John, supposed to have assisted him in the murder of prince Arthur, i. 520; afterwards made baron of Mulgref, *ib.*

MAUNSELL, sir Robert, in 1618 he sails to Algiers, to put a stop to the piracy carried on there, but returns home without effecting anything, iii. 537.

MAURICE, count, claimed to be duke of Gueldres; he proposed for the hand of lady Arabella Stuart, 1604; iii. 46.

MAURICE, bishop of London, consecrated Dec. 25, 1086. There being no archbishops then in England, this prelate consecrated Henry I., in Westminster Abbey, 1100, three days after the death of William Rufus, i. 405. He died Sept. 26, 1107.

MAURICE, a grocer, elected for Westminster, 1628; iii. 130.

MAUROLICO, Francis, a celebrated Italian mathematician, born at Messina, 1494; discovered the crystalline lens in the eye, iv. 764.

MAURY, John Siffrein, a modern French statesman and ecclesiastic, § ii. 480. Portrait of, *ib.* He advocates the rights and privileges of the king in the National Assembly, 496. He contends in favour of the clergy, 1791; 591.

MAW, Dr., urges the election of the duke of Buckingham as chancellor of the University of Cambridge, 1626; iii. 121.

MAXFIELD, Thomas, the first lay preacher employed by Wesley, iv. 654.

MAXIMILIAN I., the emperor (1493—1519,) son of Frederick III. His three children, when archduke, by Mary, duchess of Burgundy, ii. 116. Upon Mary's decease he was next a suitor for the hand of Anne of Brittany, 292. Elected king of the Romans, ib. He sends troops, 1487, to succour Francis II. of Brittany, ib. Charles VIII. breaks off the long-contemplated match with Margot of Burgundy, daughter of Maximilian, 116, 295, 297, 298. Henry VII. sends envoys to Maximilian and his son Philip, 295. Successes of the king of the Romans in Flanders, ib. He signs the treaty of Frankfort, 1489, with Charles VIII., 296. He was married by proxy to Anne of Brittany, ib. He loses this ambitious prospect, for Charles VIII., having conquered Brittany by his arms, marries the duchess Anne, who gave a reluctant consent, 297, 298. The French king sent Margot of Burgundy, under good escort, to her father, 298. Reflections, ib. Having received moneys from Henry VIII., by treaty, on becoming emperor, to join him near Calais with an army, Maximilian arrived nearly unattended in the English camp, 1513, and served as a volunteer under Henry VIII., 325. Battle of the Spurs, demolition of Terouenne, etc., ib. His sudden death, Jan. 1519. Francis, Henry, and Charles, all powerful monarchs, severally seek to be his successor, 335. Charles V. elected emperor, 337.

MAXIMILIAN, of Bavaria, an ambitious general of Gustavus Adolphus, iii. 146.

MAXIMUS, of British descent, provincial emperor in Britain, 382, repelled the Picts and Scots, i. 54. Popular in Britain, he attacked Gratian on the continent, with an army chiefly consisting of the most warlike of the Britons. Gratian defeated by him, ib. Theodosius defeated Maximus, and put him to death at Aquileia, 388, ib. Britain was left denuded of the flower of her nobility and youth, and became a prey to her marauding neighbours, ib.

MAXWELL, lord, 1542, escorted James V. to the castle of Caerlaverock, ii. 433. He invaded the border in Cumberland, ib. On Solway Moss the king's favourite, Sinclair, assuming the command, the clans, disgusted thereby, mutinied, were routed by some English cavalry, and Maxwell, with other Scottish chiefs were carried prisoners to Carlisle, ib.

MAXWELL, lord, being supported of papacy, is placed under the superintendence of Presbyterian ministers, 1602; iii. 452.

MAXWELL, James, gentleman-usher, 1640; iii. 216.

MAXWELL, John, a minister of Edinburgh, iii. 478; afterwards made bishop of Ross. Having been driven out of the country, at the general overthrow of episcopacy in Scotland, he obtained the bishopric of Killala in Ireland, and died, in 1646, archbishop of Tuam, ib., 484.

MAY, sir Humphrey, 1628; iii. 134; quoted 288, 858.

MAYNARD, governor of Goritz, and a relation of Conrad of Montferrat. Richard I. sends a page to Maynard to ask for a passport for Baldwin of Bethune and Hugh the merchant, who were pilgrims returning from Jerusalem. To forward his request the young man presented a very valuable ring, as a proof of his master the merchant's good will towards the governor. Maynard, much struck with the beauty and value of the ruby, exclaimed, " This is the present of a prince, not of a merchant;—your master's name is not Hugh, but king Richard; tell him, from me, that he may come and go in peace." i. 502.

MAYNARD, Mr. His report on ship-money, 1640. He manages, on the part of the House of Commons, in the trial of the earl of Strafford, 1641; iii. 237; quoted 320, 522. Is formally accused by the army, with several other members, June 15, 1647; 369.

MAYO, colonel, severely wounded, 1654; iii. 416.

Mazanderan, Pillar-temples of, their similarity to the Round Towers of Ireland, i. 16.

MAZARIN, cardinal, iii. 357, declared by the parliament of Paris an enemy of the public peace, 1649 ; 395. Obtains from the court of Saxony a solemn engagement to allow the Waldenses liberty of conscience and the restoration of all their ancient rights, 490, 427.

Meal-tub Plot, the, discovered by Dangerfield, a profligate man confined in Newgate; the notes and documents on which this sham plot was founded were discovered, 1679, in the house of Mrs. Cellier, a Catholic midwife, iii. 731, 732.

Meath and Caledonians, i. 126.

MEATH, earl of. See Lacy.

Medals, struck to commemorate the battle of the Boyne, iv. 25; battle of Oudenarde, 220; battle of Blenheim, 172; battle of Ramilies, 184; battle of Dunblane, 319; battle of Dettingen, 466; battle of Minden, 612; upon raising the siege of Londonderry, 18; to commemorate the able conduct of queen Mary, 28; to commemorate the flight of James from Ireland, 29; to commemorate the surrender of Lille, 222; to commemorate Vernon's capture of Porto Bello, 439; to commemorate Hawke's victory in Quiberon Bay, 607; in honour of John Wilkes, § i. 65; in honour of lord North, 201; to commemorate the evacuation of Boston, in 1776; 261; in honour of lord-chancellor Bathurst, 528; of lord Mansfield, 535; to commemorate the founding of the Royal Academy, 1768 ; 625.

MEDICI, Mary de, mother of Louis XIII., regent during his minority, iii. 49. Her system of politics, ib. Sends 10,000 men to join 4,000 English, who had landed on the continent, under sir Edward Cecil, ib. Her anxiety for peace, ib. She proposes a marriage between prince Henry and madame Christine, 1612; 51. Arrives in England, 1638, and obtains an enormous pension, and a monopoly on leather, from Charles I., 247. She desires a guard for her security; the subject is referred to a committee, who recommend that she should leave England, ib.; which she accordingly does, escorted by the earl of Arundel, and dies at Cologne, 248.

Medicine, practice of, in the fifteenth century, ii. 208.

MEDINA SIDONIA, duke of, commander of the invincible Armada, 1588; ii. 674.

MEDINA CELI, duke of, dispatched to Naples, 1625, to admit the imperial troops into that kingdom, iv. 109.

MEDINA, sir Samuel de, one of the contractors for bread to Marlborough's army, iv. 259.

Medway, Dutch fleet in the; burning of Sheerness, from a drawing of the period, iii. 702.

MELA, Pomponius, quoted, i. 36.

MELCOMBE, baron. See George Bubb Dodington.

MELDRUM, sir John, makes a sortie upon the king's forces, 1642, who were besieging Hull, iii. 293.

MELFORT, secretary of state to James II., iv. 14, 64. Disgraced, 116. Refused admission at the court of St. Germain, and imprisoned at the castle of Angers, iv. 117.

MELLENT, Walleran, earl of, i. 538.

MELLENT, Robert de, relative of Henry I., 1100, his chief minister, i. 409. His death; he was reputed to have been in his time the greatest statesman in Europe, 1118; 413.

MELLITUS, bishop of the East-Saxons, consecrated by Augustine, i. 233. King Sebert, of Essex, converted to Christianity, dying, his three sons declare

MELLITUS,—
    in favour of paganism, and expel the new bishop, *ib.* Mellitus resorts to Justus, bishop of Rochester, who is in like trouble with king Eadbald, the successor of Ethelbert, *ib.* Justus and Mellitus fly into Gaul, *ib.* Is recalled from banishment, 234.
Melun, on the Seine, taken, 1420, by Henry V., after a protracted siege, ii. 48.
MELUN, viscount de, when dying, informs the English, that prince Louis had sworn to banish all those who had joined him, as traitors, i. 531, 532.
MELVIL, Andrew, successor of Knox, iii. 64. His answer to some Scottish lords, 65. Committed to the Tower; released at the petition of the duke of Bouillon, *ib.* His death, 1620, at Sedan, *ib.*; 488, 441, 446, 448, 463, 464.
MELVIL, James, nephew of Andrew Melvil, iii. 65. Confined for life to Berwick; his death, 1614; *ib.*; 446, 463, 464.
MELVILL, Henry Dundas, viscount, created 1802; in 1805 he was impeached by the House of Commons, and convicted of using the public money for his private purposes, § iv. 150. In 1806, under the Grenville administration, he was again tried, but acquitted, 217—219.
MELVILLE, lord, his address to Charles I., iii. 156.
MELVILLE, lord, 1690; iv. 43.
MELVILLE, James, 1546, assisted in the murder of David Beaton, ii. 446.
MELVILLE, sir James, dispatched by Mary, queen of Scots, to Elizabeth, 1562, to make inquiries concerning her opinion respecting her marriage, ii. 575—579. He hastes to London to inform the English court of the birth of James I., 1566; 588. He flies from the anger of the earl Bothwell, 298. His testimony to the accomplishments of queen Elizabeth as a musician, iii. 564.
MELVILLE, sir Robert, earnestly intercedes in behalf of the queen of Scots, ii. 663, 668.
MÉNAGER, M., an expert diplomatist, 1711; iv. 255.
Mendicant Friars, statute respecting the, ii. 152. Simon Fish's "Supplication of Beggars," 1524, showing the amount of collections by the mendicant orders, a prohibited book, 717. Henry VIII., on reading the tract, recalled its author to England, 1526, *ib.* Shrewd remark by the king, *ib.*
Mentz Cathedral, capital from the doorway; of its style of architecture, i. 313.
MERCER, John, collects a fleet of Scots, French, and Spaniards with which he captures all the ships in the port of Scarborough, 1378. John Philpot, alderman of London, fits out a fleet at his own expense, recaptures the ships, and takes Mercer prisoner, i. 783.
Merchant Adventurers of London, Company of; this association incorporated by Royal Charter, 1505, under the name of "The Merchant Adventurers of England," can be traced back nearly to the beginning of the fourteenth century, ii. 774, 783, 784.
MERCY, count de, dangerously wounded at the battle of Alcantara, 1719; iv. 358. Messina surrenders to, 361; he is defeated at the battle of La Crocetta, 414.
MEREDITH, Mr., member for the county of Kent, 1701; iv. 122.
MERKS, Thomas, bishop of Carlisle, consecrated 1397; he was deprived, in 1399, and was afterwards vicar of Sturminster; and in 1404 became rector of Todenham. He died about 1499, i. 799; ii. 7.
MERRICK, sir John, enters the service of the parliamentarian army, 1642; iii. 291.
Mersey, isle of, Essex, a body of Danes routed by Alfred, here found a secure refuge, i. 163. Brook-ade of, *ib.*
MERTON, Walter de, appointed chancellor on the death of Henry III., 1272; i. 688.
MESCHINES, Renouf, first earl of Cumberland, 1073; i. 375.

Messina, revolts from the Spanish viceroy, 1676; iii. 714.
Metallic manufactures, iv. 732.
Methodism, origin of, in England, iv. 653—657; its growth in Ireland, 656.
Methodists, origin of this sect of the Reformed church; their first preachers, Wesley and Whitefield had studied the doctrines of the Moravians, and also the mysticism of William Law, etc.; iv. 653. The Wesleys, brothers, preached to the Indians in Georgia, 1785; and in 1739, Whitefield first preached in the *open air* to the colliers, near Bristol, and to great crowds in and near London, 653. Whitefield twice visiting America, was confirmed in the Calvinistic doctrines of election, etc., by the Puritans of the older colonies, and he adhered to that view of Christianity, *ib.*
Methuen Treaty, the, concluded between Portugal and England, 1703. The provisions were that England should admit Portuguese wine on payment of a duty one-third less than was paid upon French wines, and Portugal should admit English woollen cloths on the same terms as before they were prohibited, iv. 706.
METHUEN, sir Paul, moves for an address of condolence and congratulation to George II., 1727; iv. 399.
METHUEN, chancellor of Ireland, 1700; iv. 103.
Mezzotint, invention of, generally attributed to prince Rupert, but the claim unsupported, iii. 884.
MICHELBORNE, sir Edward, obtains a grant from James I. in direct violation of the Charter of the East India Company, iii. 529.
MICHELL, sir Thomas, obtains patents from James I.; proceedings against him, iii. 524.
MICKLE, the translator of Camoens, iii. 602.
Micklebar Gate, view of, iii. 287.
MIDDIMAN, Samuel, an admirable landscape line-engraver, (eighteenth century,) § iii. 750.
MIDDLEMORE, an agent sent by Elizabeth in 1568 to Scotland, to allay the farther danger of a civil war, ii. 610.
MIDDLETON, earl of, iii. 298, 416, 681. A commissioner for Scotland, *regno* Charles II.; he proposes a general Act rescissory, or an Act annulling everything done since the year, 1633; goes over to the continent, iv. 44.
MIDDLETON, Dr. Conyers, a learned and ingenious divine and polemical writer, born 1683, died 1750; § i. 611. Portrait of, *ib.*
MIDDLETON, sir Henry, sails on a commercial expedition to the East Indies, 1604; iii. 529. He again sets sail, 1610, but his ship was lost in Bantam-road, and he shortly after died of grief, 530.
MIDDLETON, Mr. Hugh, brought in the New River into the reservoir at Clerkenwell, 1609, after three years' labour, for which he was knighted by king James, iii. 547.
MIDDLETON, Mr., member for Sussex, 1641; iii. 242.
MIDDLETON, a dramatist, contemporary with Shakspere, (seventeenth century,) iii. 593.
Milan, duchy and city of, its sovereigns or rulers, contests for its possession, sieges, etc., ii. 334, 358.
MILAN, duchess-dowager of, rejected the offer of Henry VIII. to marry her, ii. 412. Her facetious reply, *ib.*
MILDMAY, sir Anthony, routs a body of Levellers at Newton, 1607; iii. 36.
MILDMAY, sir Henry, a parliamentarian officer, 1648; iii. 387. In action against De Witt, 1652; 407. Is confined to the Tower for life, 1661; 685.
Milesians, same as Scots, a Scythian colony, perhaps same as the Gael or Gauls, i. 15.
MILICZ, John, proceeded against by the pope, as a heretic, (end of the fourteenth century,) iii. 80.
Militia Bill, 1642; iii. 274.

Mills.—Hand-mill for corn, from an ancient manuscript, i. 600. Water-mills known on the continent before the end of the sixteenth century, *ib.* They existed in England before the conquest, *ib.*

MILL, Walter, an old infirm priest, and last of the Scottish martyrs, suffered at St. Andrew's, April 29th, 1558; ii. 747.

MILLAR, professor, quoted, i. 250.

Millenarians or Fifth-monarchy men, iii. 814; insurrection of, 818.

Millenary petition, the, presented April, 1603; iii. 455.

MILLINGATTI, father, confessor of James II., iv. 78.

MILTON, John, father of the poet, a composer of music, iii. 563.

MILTON, John, the English poet, born December 9, 1608. Became secretary for foreign correspondence during the Commonwealth, 1649; iii. 399. He assists Cromwell in his negotiation with the duke of Savoy in favour of the Waldenses, 420. Cromwell's partiality to him, 424. Returning from his travels to England, in 1641, he assisted the Puritans against the Established Church, in several publications, 609. Is committed to the custody of the serjeant-at-arms at the time of the Restoration, but escapes further punishment than being plundered and disqualified for the public service, 666. His portrait, 871. He died, November, 1674. Review of his works, 872—875.

Milton Gallery, the, § iii. 742.

Minden, battle of, gained July 31, 1759, by Ferdinand of Brunswick, commanding the Hanoverians, Hessians, and English, for the defence of Hanover, iv. 610. Marshal Contades and the duke de Broglie, flushed with recent successes, attacked with nearly double the allied force, but after a fierce engagement were defeated, 610, 611. Lord George Sackville received orders from prince Ferdinand to charge with the English cavalry, which he disobeyed, *ib.*—*See* Sackville.

Mines, notices of the English, i. 92. Lead-mines of Derbyshire, 117. Mines of iron and lead became, shortly after the Conquest, a source of considerable riches in England, 600. Improvements in refining and working metals, 601, 602.

Mining (eighteenth century,) § iii. 675. Improvements in the system of, during the nineteenth century, § iv. 686—688.

Minorca, island of, taken by the duke de Crillon, 1782; § i. 471, 477.

Minstrels, ii. 589.

MINTO, Gilbert Eliot, earl, appointed viceroy of Corsica, 1794; § iii. 401. He alienates the affections of the inhabitants, and quarrels with nearly all the English officers about him, 506. The Corsicans meet, 1796, in considerable force and concert measures for driving out the English, who evacuate the island, October 4, *ib.*

MINYARD, lord, 1642, iii. 270.

Miquelets, riotous proceedings of the, during the siege of Barcelona, iv. 180.

MIRABEAU, Honoré Gabriel Riquetti, comte de, famous for the political influence he exercised during the French Revolution, was born at Bignon, March 9, 1749. Portrait of, § ii. 356. Looseness of his manners, *ib.* He attempts to draw up a Declaration of the Rights of Man, by desire of the National Assembly, 1789, but gives up the task as hopeless, 406, 439. His interview with Marie Antoinette, 1790; he promises to use every effort for the preservation of monarchy, 507. His death, April 2, 1791; 612—614. His funeral attended by 100,000 persons, 616. Death of his younger brother the vicomte, 619. His remains are disinterred, 1794, and subjected to every indignity, § iii. 454.

MIREPOIX, M. de, French ambassador in England, recalled, 1755; iv. 582.

MIROVITCH, Vassili, having made an attempt to liberate the unfortunate czar Ivan, 1764, is executed, § i. 132, 133.

Mistletoe, the, sacred among the Druids, because growing on the oak, i. 63. Mode and time of their gathering it, *ib.*

MITCHELL, sir Francis, a patent monopolist, iii. 82. Condemned to lose his knighthood, to be fined and imprisoned, February 15, 1621, *ib.*

MITCHELL, James, a young Covenanter, attempts to assassinate archbishop Sharp, iii. 713. After a lapse of six years he is taken by Sharp and put to death, 1674; 729.

MITTON, colonel, a parliamentarian, storms Conway, 1646; iii. 356.

MOHAMMED ALI, nabob of Arcot, portrait of, § ii. 182. Resolutions, 1784, concerning his debts, 182—187.

MOHAMMED REZA KHAN, naib-dewan of Bengal, is arrested and brought to trial at Calcutta, 1771, but is finally acquitted, § ii. 116—120.

MOHUN, lord, killed in a duel with the duke of Hamilton, Nov. 15, 1712; iv. 271.

Moinmor, battle of, fought 1151; i. 459.

Mold, in Flintshire, gold breastplate found on a Briton's corpse in the cairn at, i. 128.

MOLESWORTH, captain, present at the battle of Ramilies, May 23, 1706; iv. 184.

MOLINAS, Don Jose, grand inquisitor, 1717, taken prisoner by the emperor, and confined in the castle of Milan, iv. 341.

Molwitz, battle of, fought April 10, 1741; iv. 449.

MOLYNEUX, William, a gentleman of Dublin, publishes a book, 1698, respecting the government of Ireland by an English parliament, iv. 81.

MOMPESSON, sir Giles, a patent monopolist, iii. 82. He flies beyond seas, *ib.* Sentenced to be degraded from the honour of knighthood, fined and imprisoned, *ib.* He is banished for life, 1621, *ib.*; 524, 534.

MOMPESSON, sir Richard, patent granted to, by queen Elizabeth, iii. 534.

Mona, island of, now Anglesey, resort of the Druids and the discomfited Britons, i. 43. Suetonius subdues and garrisons it, 43, 61.

Monasteries,—exhibiting the Norman architecture, founded by the barons and churchmen of the century and a half succeeding the Conquest, i. 614, *et seq.* Certain of them were reformed, and suppressed in 1525 by Wolsey, with the sanction of Clement VII., ii. 358, 362. More violent attacks on the monasteries by Cromwell, minister of Henry VIII., seizure of houses, lands, and chattels with recklessness and extreme cruelties, 381, 390. In 1536, parliament granted to the king and his heirs all the real and personal property of 380 lesser religious houses, 396. Fresh commissioners for the affair of those monasteries thus confiscated in a mass, and for the like designs against the remainder, were selected by Cromwell and Cranmer, and appointed by the king, *ib.* These agents were rewarded with grants of houses and glebe-lands, *ib.* The descendants of the founders and donors of lands claimed that the monastic tenants being expelled, the real property should revert in equity to them, the hereditary patrons and representatives, 397. A few houses were thus restored, 402. More religious houses, 1537, were seized, or the abbots terrified into a deed granting them to the king, *ib.* The prior of Henton's conscientious reply, *ib.* The prisons were crowded with priors and monks, who *rapidly* died therein, *ib.* Henry, with the full consent of Lords and Commons, at length confiscated all abbeys and religious houses, *ib.* Sequestrations, dissipation of chattels, waste, destruction; reflections, 404, 411.

Monastic orders, the. The monks and friars, 1533, boldly joined in the popular clamour against Anne Boleyn and Henry VIII., ii. 381. Cromwell instituted a visitation for the reformation of discipline in the English monasteries. He commissioned agents to visit every religious house, strictly to inquire of the morals of monks, friars, and nuns, to make all such renounce the authority of the pope, take the oath of supremacy, swear to the succession of the children of Henry and Anne Boleyn, 1535; 386, 390. Report compiled thereon for the king and parliament, ib. The monks were required to proclaim the pope to be antichrist in their chapels, as well as to take the oath of the king's supremacy; any reluctant juries were coerced to return a verdict of guilty by Cromwell; thus no hope of security existed, 386. Condemned as traitors, the Catholic clergy were hanged, often with the cruel additions to that mode of death, while Lutherans and other Protestants were burnt, ib. Popular commiseration, 1536, for the monks and starving nuns turned out on the world from which they had been sequestered, all small religious establishments being suppressed, and their property of all kinds granted by parliament to the king, 396. The Yorkshire insurgents restored the monks and nuns to their houses, 399. On the dispersion and punishment of the malcontents, the duke of Norfolk received the king's order to hang the monks of Sawley, Hexham, Newminster, Lanercost, and St. Agatha, 401. The earl of Surrey's commission to coerce all the monks and friars of the northern counties, ib.

Monastic Institutions' Bill, the, passed July 1800; § iii. 593.

MONCKTON, Robert, general, takes the fort of Beau Séjour, 1755; iv. 582; is dangerously wounded at the battle of Quebec, Sept. 12, 1759; 609. In conjunction with admiral Rodney he reduces Martinique, 1762; § i. 17.

Moncontour, battle of, October 1569, in which the Huguenots were terribly defeated, ii. 626.

Money, form and value of among the Anglo Saxons, i. 271, et seq.

Monghir, View of, § ii. 93.

MONK, general. See Albemarle.

MONKTON, Mr., M.P., 1701; iv. 114.

MONMOUTH, Henry Carey, earl of, 1639, impeached of high crimes and misdemeanours, 1642; he died, 1661; iii. 288.

MONMOUTH, James Fitzroy, duke of, 1663, natural son of Charles II., plans the attack on sir John Coventry, 1670; iii. 708. He attacks and routs the Covenanters, 730. The king sends him away to Holland, 1679; 731. He returns secretly to London, where he is hailed by the people, 732. He makes a progress through the kingdom, 1681; 738. The king issues a warrant for his apprehension; he submits, trusting to the writ of Habeas Corpus, 739. He participates in the Rye-house Plot, 740. Signs a paper acknowledging the plot, 1683, and thus makes his peace with the king, 754. He demands back the paper, 755. Flies to Holland, ib. Intelligence is received of his landing with an armed force, 769. The parliament attaints him as a traitor, ib. He lands at Lyme, June 4, 1685; 771. His declaration, ib. His flattering reception at Taunton, 773. Is declared a rebel, ib. He is totally defeated at the battle of Sedgemoor, July 5, 1685; 775. Is found concealed in a ditch, 776. His letter to the king, ib. He is beheaded on Tower-hill, July 15, 1685. His composed conduct on the scaffold, 778, 779.

MONMOUTH, Charles Mordaunt, earl of, created 1689. Is sent to the Tower, 1697; iv. 76. Succeeded as earl of Peterborough, 1697. His correspondence with the duke of Parma, 1719. He died 1735; 365.

Monopolies, Elizabeth revokes many grievous, ii. 692, 693. Enumeration of monopolies in 1601; 769. James I. on his accession, 1603, revokes those granted by Elizabeth until a reconsideration of the same: one of these granted an exclusive right to transport horn; one granted the exclusive privilege to Ede Schets of exporting ashes and old shoes; to sir Walter Raleigh the faculty to license taverns, and the sale of wines in the kingdom, iii. 5; oppressive monopolies, 40, 533. Monopolies of soap and starch, 151.

MONRO, sir Hector, defeats the Nabob of Oude in a decisive engagement, October 22nd, 1764; § ii. 88, 148.

MONROE, a leader of the Covenanters, iii. 204, 309.

MUNSON, lord, a distinguished Commonwealth-man, confined in the Tower for life, 1661; iii. 685.

MONSON, sir Thomas, chief falconer, 1615; concerned in the murder of sir Thomas Overbury, iii. 59, 60.

MONSON, sir William, quoted, iii. 535.

MONSTRELET, some historical remarks derived from his Chronicle, from 1400 to 1452; ii. 51, 60, 62, note; 209.

MONTACUTE, lord, assists Edward III. in asserting his right against the usurpation of his mother and her lover Mortimer, i. 753.

MONTACUTE, a Norman commander under William I., he repulsed the insurgents of Devonshire and Somersetshire, i. 375.

MONTACUTE. See Montague.

Montague House, built by Pouget, iv. 749.

MONTAGUE, lord Nevil, a Yorkist, brother of the great Warwick, defeated a Scottish army at Carlisle with much loss, ii. 99. He defeated sir Richard Percy at Hedgley Moor, 1464; 101. Gained the victory of Hexham; Percy was slain in the action, ib. Somerset, de Roos, Hungerford, sir Ralph Gray and others, prisoners, were beheaded, ib. Montague was rewarded with the titles and lands of the earls of Northumberland, 102. He neglected to suppress the Yorkshire insurgents, 1469; 104. Created marquis of Montague, he and archbishop Nevil, brothers of Warwick, remain at the court of Edward IV., and swear fidelity to him, 1470; 106. Nevertheless, Warwick having crossed the Trent, with a powerful army, the marquis and his troops declared for Henry VI., ib. The marquis ably and gallantly fights for his warlike brother at Barnet, 1471; they both fall in the field, 108, 109. Their bodies, exposed to the public in St. Paul's, were sepultured with their ancestors at Bisham Priory, Berkshire, 109.

MONTAGUE, Henry lord. See Pole.

MONTAGUE, sir Henry, chief-justice of the King's Bench, post of lord-treasurer sold to, 1618; iii. 71.

MONTAGUE, Dr. James, bishop of Winchester, 1616. He married Rochester duke of Somerset, and the lady Frances Howard, December 26th, 1613, being then bishop of Bath and Wells. He died, 1618; iii. 118, 167. 606.

MONTAGUE, Walter, 1628; iii. 138.

MONTAGUE, Mr. Wortley, proposes that sir Robert Walpole should be ordered to retire from the House, 1741, during the examination of his conduct, iv. 443.

MONTAGUE, a Catholic peer, fined by the Star-chamber, and imprisoned, 1605, under suspicion of his wish purposely to be absent from Westminster, 5th November, iii. 32; sent to disperse a body of levellers, 36.

MONTAGUE, general, his loyal reception of Charles II., 1661; iii. 432*.

MONTAGUE, ambassador at Paris, 1678; iii. 725.

MONTAGUE, chancellor of the Exchequer, concerts a scheme, 1696, which eventually leads to the National Debt, iv. 74; resigns his office, 103.

MONTAIGNE, George, bishop of London, elected 1621. He signifies the king's pleasure, 1626, to the University of Cambridge, that the duke of Buck-

MONTAIGNE, George,—
ingham should be elected chancellor; he died, 1628, being then archbishop of York, iii. 121.

MONTCALM, general, covers Quebec with an army of 10,000 men; Wolfe attacks him in his entrenchments, but is obliged to withdraw, iv. 608; he is killed September, 1759, in attempting to repulse Wolfe on the heights of Abraham, 609.

MONTECUCULI, imperialist general, 1677; iii. 714.

MONTEMAR, count of, Spanish general, 1734; iv. 413.

Montereau, bridge of; *Jean sans Peur*, murdered in a conference with the Dauphin Charles, ii. 45, 46. Henry V. and the new duke Philip, son of John, remove his body to Dijon the capital of Burgundy, 48. De Guitry defends the castle, 1420, and insults the English herald. Henry V. hangs some prisoners, and the citadel finally surrenders, *ib*. Chapel built at Montereau, and a stone cross erected on the bridge, in memory of John of Burgundy, 78.

MONTFORT, family of, earls of Leicester, and by marriage with the family of Grantmesnil, hereditary seneschals of England, till their attainder, when the office was given to Edmund, second son of Henry III., i. 568.

MONTFORT, John de, claims the duchy of Brittany; he comes over to England to solicit the protection of the king, 1341; i. 760. Returns and attends at the court of peers at Paris, *ib*. Repairs to London, and does homage for his duchy to Edward as lawful king of France, *ib*. Is taken prisoner, and confined in the Tower of the Louvre; his wife puts herself at the head of his party; she is besieged in the castle of Hennebon, *ib*. The English, under the command of sir Walter Manny, come to her relief, and compel the French to raise the siege, 761. De Montfort effects his escape, comes over to England, and shortly after dies, 762; his wife still carries on the war in Brittany, in right of his infant son; she is well supported by the English, and on the 18th of June, 1347, Charles de Blois, her rival, whilst besieging her in Roche-Derrien, is attacked and defeated by the English under the command of sir Thomas Dagworth; in this battle Charles was taken prisoner, sent to London, and confined in the Tower, which put an end to the French interest in Brittany, 768, 769.

MONTFORT, Robert de, accuses Henry earl of Essex of cowardice and treason, i. 443.

MONTFORT, Simon de. *See* Leicester.

MONTFORT, Simon de, son of the great earl of Leicester, is surprised and defeated by prince Edward at Ludlow, and escapes to Kenilworth Castle, i. 686. He maintains himself for a long time in the isles of Ely and Axholm, 687. Is banished with his brother Guy, and his mother the countess of Leicester, 688. As Henry, son of Richard, king of the Romans, was returning through Italy, he was murdered by Simon and Guy de Montfort, in a church, December, 1271; *ib*.

MONTGOMERY, Philip Herbert, earl of, a favourite of James I., created 1605. *See* Pembroke.

MONTGOMERY, Arnulf de, promises to assist Robert in his invasion of England, 1101; i. 408.

MONTGOMERY, sir James, 1693; iv. 43.

MONTGOMERY, Richard, a courageous American officer, § i. 219; he falls in an unfortunate attack upon Quebec, 1775; § i. 223.

MONTGOMERY, Roger de, i. 394. Takes part with Robert duke of Normandy, 1087, but is detached from the confederacy by a peaceful negotiation, 395.

MONTGOMERY, archbishop of Glasgow, 1584; iii. 441.

MONTMORENCY, marshal of Rieux, lands with a considerable army, 1406, in South Wales, to aid Glendower, ii. 18. Many of his ships are burnt in Milford Haven by an English fleet, which also intercepts

MONTMORENCY,—
stores and ammunition from France, and cuts off all supplies, *ib*. He burns Haverford West, but is repulsed by the garrison in the castle, *ib*. Takes Carmarthen, joins Glendower, and they advance to the gates of Worcester, *ib*. King Henry and the prince of Wales take post opposite to the allies for eight days, neither army would risk the attack, and the allies retreat to Wales, *ib*. Montmorency and de Hugueville embark their forces and desert Glendower, *ib*. He is slain in the battle of St. Denis, 622.

MONTMORENCY, duke of, lord-admiral of France, 1625; iii. 112.

MONTREUIL, madame de, 1538, purpose of Henry VIII. to marry her, ii. 412. He abruptly changed his mind, *ib*.

MONTREUIL, a French ambassador, iii. 346. He negotiates with the Scots, 1646, about their receiving Charles I., *ib*. He advises the king not to trust himself to the Scots, if any better conditions could be obtained, 348, 363.

MONTROSS, lord of, iii. 202, 330; a series of conflicts between him and the earl of Argyle, 337—340. He beats Baillie and the Covenanters; Glasgow opens its gates to him, and Edinburgh liberates the royalist prisoners, and sends delegates praying for the king's mercy; through this, and because the plague raged there, he forebore marching on to Edinburgh with his army, 340. He calls a parliament at Glasgow, is taken by surprise, and thoroughly beaten near Philiphaugh, 1645; 341. He escapes, *ib*. He receives orders from the king to disband his forces, 354. Is hanged at Edinburgh, May, 1650; 402.

Monument, the, on Fish-street-hill, iii. 700. Wren's first design for the, iv. 746.

MOORE, Mr. Arthur, M.P., 1700; iv. 103.

MOORE, John, an enthusiast, 1561; ii. 572.

MOORE, sir John, lord-mayor, 1681; iii. 739.

MOORE, sir John, born in 1761; on his return from Egypt he was created a knight of the Bath, and in 1808 was appointed to the command of the British troops in Spain, § iv. 343. Having advanced some distance into the interior, and meeting with little support from the Spaniards, he was obliged to retreat before a superior body of French troops, when having reached Coruña, and part of his forces having embarked on board transports to return home, an attack took place, January 16, 1809, when the general was killed by a cannon-ball, and was interred on the field of battle, the enemy having been defeated, 344—363. *Illustrations*:—His portrait, 346. View of Coruña, 358. His tomb, 360. His monument in St. Paul's, 363.

MOORE, Roger, a gentleman of Kildare, attempts to make the Irish help themselves, 1641, as the Scots had done, iii. 252.

MOORE, Thomas, a poet of the nineteenth century, remarkable for the beauty and elegance of his productions, § iv. 701.

MOORE, Mr., 1630; iii. 151.

MOORE, serjeant, said to have first contrived the species of conveyance, named *Lease and Release*, (seventeenth century); iii. 517.

MOORE, Mr., quoted, i. 14, 16, 20, 23.

Moravians, the, exertions made for their establishment in England and North America by count Zinzendorff, 1737; § i. 526.

MORAY, Randolph, earl of, nephew of the great Robert Bruce, taken prisoner at Methven, June 19th, 1306; i. 729. He takes Edinburgh Castle, March 14, 1313; 736. Commands the left wing of Bruce's army at the battle of Bannockburn, 737. His brave conduct, *ib*. He commands an expedition into England, and ravages Yorkshire, 739. He conducts another successful invasion, and returns laden with plunder, 749. On the death of Bruce, he is appointed regent of the kingdom of Scotland, and guardian of

MORAV, Randolph, earl of,— Prince David, 755. He dies suddenly, 1332, and is succeeded in the regency by Donald, earl of Marr, *ib.*

MORAY, sir Andrew, of Bothwell, he joins Wallace, 1297; i. 715, and continues firm to him when deserted by all the other nobles, 716.

MORAY, sir Robert, member of the Royal Society, 1666; iv. 776.

MORCAR. *See* Northumberland.

MORDAUNT, lord, a Catholic; desire of Keys the conspirator, 1605, to warn him from the parliament-house, November 5; iii. 25. Is fined and imprisoned for an intention so to absent himself, 32.

MORDAUNT, lord. *See* earl of Peterborough.

MORDAUNT, brigadier, 1746; iv. 540.

MORE, sir Antonio, a native of Utrecht, who having attained to great eminence in Spain, was sent to England to paint the portrait of Queen Mary, as the intended bride of Philip II. He remained in England the whole of that reign, and on the queen's death returned to Spain, ii. 853. His portrait of sir T. Gresham, 771; of sir Philip Sydney, 813.

MORE, sir George, lieutenant of the Tower, 1616; iii. 61.

MORE, Henry, an eminent English writer of the seventeenth century, iii. 578, 610.

MORE, sir Thomas, his character, and pleasant humour, ii. 354. Speaker of the House of Commons, *ib.* He wisely refused his opinion on the king's "Treatise of Divorce," 1527, his sentiments being adverse, 366. He became chancellor, in 1529, on the fall of Wolsey, 374. He went down to the Commons, with twelve peers, to show the righteousness of Henry's desire to be divorced from his brother's widow; he produced as exhibits the favourable opinions of doctors and universities; the Commons were desired, on returning home, to declare to all how just was the king's cause, 378. More took a melancholy part in persecuting the Protestants, *ib.* May, 1532, the chancellor retired to solitude and poverty, *ib.* His opinion as to the simple ignorance of the Maid of Kent, in reply to the king, who showed him her *sibylline* leaves, 384. He was himself shortly accused of a previous knowledge of her prophecies, etc., but was not tried for it, as was his friend, bishop Fisher, 385. He refused to take the whole of the new oath of allegiance, etc., willing to swear all that concerned the succession, but not to doctrinal points superadded to the oath, *ib.* Cranmer wished to favour More, by omitting from the oath the theological test, but the archbishop was overruled, *ib.* More, and the equally persecuted bishop Fisher, were condemned to the Tower for life, with forfeiture of their property, *ib.* His relations are kind to the ex-chancellor; his daughter, Mrs. Roper, piously attended to his wants, so that he suffered not the destitution of the bishop of Rochester, *ib.* On the condemnation of Fisher, the king resolved to bring More to the like severe account, 1535; 386. The four interrogatories put to More in the Tower, with his replies, 387. He was interrogated as to any communications with his fellow-prisoner, Dr. Fisher; his reply, *ib.* It was required of More to say if he would obey the king as supreme head of the church on earth; if he would recognise the marriage of Anne Boleyn as lawful, and declare that of Catherine unlawful; his answer, 387, 388. His affecting letter, declaring his weakness and dying condition, 388. More was deprived of writing materials, and Rich was sent to seize all his books, *ib.* After a year's incarceration, the ex-chancellor was led on foot from the Tower to Westminster-hall, and arraigned of high treason, *ib.* His hair had turned white, and he supported his frail body on a staff; but the mind was unbroken, and his judges feared the impression of his eloquence and wit, *ib.* The indictment, *ib.* He declined a conditional

MORE, sir Thomas,— offer of pardon; his clear exposition of the loyalty of his conduct, *ib.* The solicitor-general, Rich, deposed to certain words of More, who dilated upon the bad character of that lawyer as rendering him unworthy of belief, *ib.* More denied that he had sought to deprive the king of his title of supreme head of the church, that he had been *silent* thereon, *ib.* The judges, assisted by Norfolk and other great men, decided that such *silence* was treason; the jury then returned a verdict of Guilty, *ib.* More's final address to his judges, *ib.* Removed from the bar, his son fell on his knees in the hall, for his blessing, *ib.* He was led back on foot to the Tower,—the axe turned towards him; at the Tower Wharf his daughter, Roper, threw herself on his neck, to take a sad leave of this great and good man, 388, 389. He wept, as did also the people, 389. Narrative of his execution, July 6, 1535, fourteen days after the execution of bishop Fisher; his every speech proving the brightness of his talent, *ib.* His head was placed upon London-bridge, *ib.* Anne Boleyn, being known to favour the progress of reform in religion, shared the odium of these sad acts with the absolute king, as his secret adviser, *ib.* On the Continent, and at Rome especially, Dr. Fisher and More were considered as martyrs, *ib.* More's portrait, 813. Specimen of his "Dialogue concerning Heresies," 829. His fondness for music, iii. 562, 605. Remarkable quotations from sir Thomas More, ii. 120, 124.

MOREA, insurrection in the, 1770: § i. 141—148.

MOREAU, Jean Victor, born at Morlaix, in 1763, one of the oldest and most celebrated generals of the French Republic; he commanded with admirable skill both in Germany and Italy; his famous retreat through the Valley of Hell and the Black Forest, 1796; § iii. 511. On Bonaparte's return from Egypt, he entrusted him with the command of the armies of the Danube and the Rhine, and, after a series of splendid victories, he concluded the campaign by the battle of Hohenlinden, December 2, 1800; 558. He implicated himself in the conspiracy of Pichegru and Georges, for which he was brought to trial, found guilty, and sentenced to two years' imprisonment, and to bear the expenses of the suit, 1804, § iv. 122—129. He was, however, permitted to travel, on condition he would not return to France without consent of the government; in 1805 he embarked at Cadiz for America, but returned to Europe in the following July, 594*. Having joined the allies, he was severely wounded before Dresden, and died, September 1, 1813; *ib.*

Morella, capture of, December 17, 1707; iv. 203.

MORGAN, colonel, summons the marquess of Worcester, in the name of the Commonwealth, to deliver up Ragland Castle, 1646; iii. 355. He is despatched, with a body of troops by Cromwell, 1657, to join the French army under Turenne, 425.

Morini, a Gallic tribe near Calais, i. 27.

MORLEY, lord, a Roman Catholic, retires to the continent, 1570, to avoid persecution, ii. 633.

MORLEY, George, bishop of Winchester, 1662, described by Clarendon, iii. 178, *note.* His work on music, published 1597; 562. He speaks against Presbyterianism in the Assembly of 1660; 668. He vigorously supports an intolerant bill in favour of the Protestant religion, 1675. He died 1684; 712.

MORRICE, Mr., an intimate friend of general Monk, iii. 663.

MORSE, his statement respecting the ignorance of New England, iii. 808.

MORTAIGNE, earl of, taken prisoner by Henry at Tenchebray, 1106, and condemned to perpetual imprisonment, i. 410.

Mortemain, limited repeal of the Statute of, 1704; iv. 159.

2 D

MORTIMER, earl of, surprises Llewellyn in the valley of the Wye, 1282, cuts off his head, and sends it to Edward, i. 698.

MORTIMER, Roger, lord, defeated by Edward Bruce, 1315; i. 738; taken prisoner at Boroughbridge, 1322; 741; makes his escape from the Tower of London, where he was lying under sentence of death, and goes over to France, ib. His connexion with queen Isabella, 742. He takes the lead of the Lancastrian party, 743. A regency is appointed, and Edward II. imprisoned, 745, 748. He and queen Isabella monopolise nearly the whole power of government, 749. He is created earl of March, 1328; the regency is displaced, and his power and that of the queen increases, 751. Lancaster opposes his unconstitutional impositions, ib. He is joined by the earls of Kent and Norfolk, the king's uncles, but they soon abandon him, and he is compelled to ask pardon in a humiliating manner, and to pay an immense fine, 752. The earl of Kent accused of treason, and executed, 753. Young Edward forms a plan, with lord Montacute, to assert his authority, ib. The young king holds a joust in Cheapside, ib. Mortimer obtains a knowledge of the plan formed by Edward and lord Montacute, and informs the council of it, 734. The governor of Nottingham admits Montacute by a subterraneous passage; Mortimer is dragged out of the castle, and committed to safe custody, ib. Edward issues a proclamation, informing his lieges that he had now taken the government into his own hands, and summons a new parliament to meet at Westminster, November 26, 1330; ib. Mortimer is impeached, and executed as a traitor, ib. The queen-mother is deprived of her enormous jointure, and shut up in her castle at Risings, where she passed the remaining twenty-seven years of her life in obscurity, 755.

MORTIMER, Roger, earl of March, espoused Philippa of Clarence, daughter of Lionel, the elder brother of John of Gaunt, ii. 6.

MORTIMER, Roger, son of the preceding, governed Ireland, regno Richard II., where he was slain, ii. 6.

MORTIMER, Edmund, earl of March, 1898, son of the preceding. This Edmund Mortimer had a superior claim to Henry IV., ii. 6. He was confined by that usurper in Windsor Castle with a younger brother, ib. Being only nine years of age, his partisans were unable to support his title to the crown, 6, 16, 24, 25. The Percies rising in the north, 1402, assert his superior claim to the crown, 13, 14. Conspiracy to place him on the throne, 1415; 29, 89. He faithfully served the house of Lancaster in peace and in war, 89. He died without children, 1424; ib.

MORTIMER, Anne, the sister of Edmund, earl of March, married the earl of Cambridge, who in 1415 was beheaded by Henry V., ii. 89. Her son, Richard, duke of York, succeeded his paternal uncle, and eventually asserted his claim to the crown, 6, 89.

MORTIMER, sir Edmund, (uncle of the earl of March,) is defeated and made prisoner by Owen Glendower, 1402, at the battle of Knyghton, ii. 11, 13. Glendower gives him his daughter in marriage, 13. Mortimer's sister was the lady Percy, wife of Hotspur, ib.

MORTIMER, Hugh de, master of the castle of Bridgenorth, in Shropshire, at the siege of which Henry II. nearly lost his life. i. 442.

Mortimer's Cross, near Hereford, battle of, 1461, gained by Edward, duke of York; Owen Tudor, prisoner, with eight Lancastrian nobles, beheaded, ii. 96, 97.

MORTON, earl of, chancellor of Scotland, encourages Darnley in his insolent behaviour to the queen, ii. 584. He keeps the doors of the palace during the murder of Rizzio, 1566, to prevent any assistance coming to the queen, 587. He flies to the English

MORTON, earl of,—
marches, ib. Mary, at the petition of the earl of Bedford, pardons him, and he returns to Scotland, 591. Murray, when regent, restores him to the office of chancellor, makes him lord high-admiral and sheriff of Edinburgh and Haddington, 606. The temporalities of the archbishopric of St. Andrew's are granted to him, iii. 436, 437, 470. He basely sells the earl of Northumberland to Elizabeth, 1572; ii. 645. His great power in Scotland, 646. On the death of the earl of Marr, October, he succeeds to the regency, and hangs Lethington and the magnanimous Kirkaldy of Grange, 648, 649 1578, the young king is pronounced of age; Morton retires to Lochleven Castle, and gains possession of James, 652. On the recovery of his liberty, James arraigns the regent as a murderer of his father, and though intercession was made for him by several courts, by whom he was considered a sturdy Protestant, he is finally abandoned to his fate, and executed by the "Maiden," 1578, an instrument which he himself had introduced into Scotland, 653.

MORTON, John, elected to the bishopric of Ely, 1478; sent to the Tower, 1483; ii. 121, 126. He and bishop Fox, 1486, the chief advisers and ministers of Henry VII., 286. Morton appointed archbishop of Canterbury, 1486; 286, 306. His speech for a subsidy to enable Henry VII. to march to the aid of Francis of Brittany, 1488; 294. He became a cardinal, also lord-chancellor, his speech on trade and manufactures, 1487; 771, 772. His death in 1500; 310.

MORTON, Dr. Nicholas, arrives in England with the title of Apostolical Penitentiary, 1569; ii. 628, 767.

MORTON, bishop; his living sequestered, 1642; iii. 491.

MORTON, Mr., a laceman, 1709, obliges the Russian ambassador to find bail for 100l., which occasions the act defining the privileges of foreign ambassadors, iv. 230.

MORVILLE, Hugh de, one of the conspirators who murdered Becket. i. 455, 456.

MOSELY, Humphrey, publisher of the collection of Beaumont and Fletcher's plays, in 1647; iii. 598.

MOTTE, count de la, governor of Ghent in 1708; iv. 221.

MOULIN, Peter du, 1654; iii. 609.

MOUNT EDGCUMBE, George, earl of, created baron Edgcumbe, 1742. He resigns his treasurer's staff by express desire of the king. § i. 51, 52.

MOUNTAIN, Dr., dean of Westminster, preaches the sermon on occasion of the marriage of the earl of Somerset with the countess of Essex, 1613; iii. 54.

MOUNTEAGLE, lord, letter warning him of danger at the Parliament, November 5, 1605, leads to the detection of the Gunpowder Plot, iii. 25, 26. Allusions to this Catholic nobleman and his relatives, etc., 25, 27, 30.

MOUNTJOY, William Blount, earl of; his report, 1533, from Ampthill to Henry VIII., that Catherine of Arragon refused to be styled princess-dowager of Wales, and was resolved, being the lawful queen, never to injure her daughter Mary's rights by weak concessions of her own dignity, ii. 381. He was chamberlain to Catherine; some of his letters extant, 381, note.

MOUNTJOY, Charles Blount, earl of, created 1535, died 1545, ii. 679.

MOUNTJOY, lord, receives a patent, 1565, to work mines of copperas and alum, ii. 811.

MOUNTJOY, lord, successor of Essex in Ireland; blockaded d'Aguilar and his Spanish troops, 1601, in Kinsale, ii. 693. He routed Tyrone and his army, who attempted to surprise him, ib. D'Aguilar capitulated, and was permitted to embark for Spain

MOUNTJOY, lord,—
  with his troops and arms, ib. Tir Oen, or Tyrone, oppressed by a famine, surrendered to Mountjoy, 1602, on promise of his life and lands, ib.
MOUNTJOY, lord, confined in the Bastille, 1689; iv. 11.
MOUNTNORRIS, lord, vice-treasurer of Ireland, incurring Wentworth's displeasure, is sentenced by him, 1633, to be cashiered, publicly disarmed, and shot, iii. 171. The capital part of the sentence is remitted, but he is kept close prisoner, and treated with the greatest harshness, ib.
MOWBRAY, Philip de, is defeated by Bruce at the battle of Inverury, May 22, 1308; i. 735. Surrenders the castle of Stirling, after the battle of Bannockburn, June 23, 1313; 736, 738.
MOWBRAY, Robert de. See Northumberland.
MOWBRAY, Roger de, revolts in Yorkshire against Henry, 1174; i. 470.
MOYLE, Mr., M.P., 1641; iii. 242.
MOYLE, general, 1736; iv. 419.
Muggletonians, the, a sect fiercely opposed to the Quakers and Behmenists, iii. 814.
MUIR, Thomas, sentenced to transportation from Scotland for fourteen years for alleged sedition, 1794; § iii. 384—386.
Mulberry-trees,—James I. issues a proclamation concerning the planting of, 1608; iii. 558.
MÜLLER, John, an able trigonometrician (16th century), the inventor of decimal fractions, iv. 764.
Mummers, mummings, masqueradings, etc., called ludi, ii. 255.
MUNDEN, admiral, detached with a good squadron to intercept some ships in the West Indies, 1704, he comes in sight of Du Casse, but declines attacking him; he is in consequence tried by court-martial and acquitted, but the queen (Anne) cashiers him, iv. 160, note.
MUNGO, St., or Kentigern, a Christian bishop in Strathclyde, in the 6th century, supposed founder of the see of Glasgow, i. 229.
Municipia, Roman division of cities, i. 85.
MUNRO, colonel, slain at the battle of Edgehill, October 23, 1642; iii. 297.
MUNSTER, bishop of, an ally of king Louis, foiled at the siege of Groningen, 1672; iii. 710.
MURAT, Joachim, one of Bonaparte's most accomplished and successful generals, born March 25, 1771; in 1802 he governed the Cisalpine republic with the title of general, and in 1808, July 15, he was appointed by Napoleon king of the two Sicilies, after having for some time held the grand-duchy of Berg, § iv. 314. His portrait, 394. He retakes the island of Capri, and the rock of Scylla from the English, 395, 396. They destroy many of the villages on the coast, 396—401. His dispute with Napoleon. He is prevailed upon not to join the allies, 1813; 589. Appointed to command the French cavalry, ib. He returns to Italy, takes part with the allies, and defeats prince Eugene Beauharnais, 1814; 610*, 620*,—624*. After Napoleon's return from Elba, Murat, without waiting for instructions, immediately attacks the Austrians in Italy, but is defeated and compelled to fly from his own kingdom of Naples, 1815; 630*, 631*, 657*. He goes to Corsica, where he collects a small force and lands on the coast of Calabria, at Pizzo, October 8, 1815; 660*. Is taken by the fierce Calabrians and shot by order of king Ferdinand, October 13, 1815; 661*.
MURDOCH, William, a Cornish engineer, supposed to have been the first, 1792, who employed coal-gas for the purposes of illumination, § iv. 688.
MURRAY, James Stuart, earl of, prior of St. Andrew's, a natural son of James V.; the English having landed, 1548, in Fife, were repulsed with great loss at St. Monance by this prior, the residue regaining the fleet of the admiral Seymour of Sudley, ii. 470.

MURRAY, James Stuart, earl of,—
  Becomes principal leader of the Congregation of the Lord, 548. Mary confers upon him the earldom of Marr, 1562, but it appearing that lord Erskine possessed a legal claim to that earldom, he induces his sister to give him the much greater one of Murray; this greatly incenses the earl of Huntley, who had received, long before, a grant of this earldom, and he summons his vassals, being determined to defend his title by the sword; a fierce battle is fought at Corrichie, October 28, in which Huntley is totally defeated, and flying from the field is thrown from his horse into a morass and there smothered, 574, 575. On the marriage of Mary with Darnley, he became jealous of the latter, and was the first to fall from the queen's side, 580. He engages with Knox to extirpate the Romish worship, 581. He takes up arms against the queen, 1565, ib. Mary convokes a parliament to attaint him; his friends apply for a pardon in his behalf, which she was ready to sign, but her uncle, the cardinal of Lorraine, advised her against the measure, and she allowed the proceedings to go on in the parliament, 583. The next day after the murder of Rizzio, Murray presents himself at Holyrood, pretending that he had come to stand his trial; on the queen's informing him of the harsh usage she had sustained, he agrees to detach himself from the interest of the assassins, and aid her in bringing them to justice, but this he did only in appearance, 587. Before the trial of the earl of Bothwell came on for the murder of Darnley, Murray with much difficulty persuades her to let him depart for France, 597. He causes the queen to sign a deed resigning the crown in favour of her infant son, July 24, 1567, and appointing him regent during the minority, 604, 605. On becoming regent, he despatches a messenger to Denmark to announce his elevation, and to implore that Bothwell (detained a prisoner there) might be given up to him; the Danish government disregards this application, 603. He appears in person at the trial of Mary queen of Scots, 1568; 612. He produces a box full of original love-letters from Mary to Bothwell, in which she speaks of the approaching murder of her husband Darnley; Mary denies the authenticity of these letters, 615, 616. Elizabeth gives him every encouragement in his proceedings, 616, 617. He executes Paris, a Frenchman, 1569, on a charge of being concerned in the murder o. Darnley, 625. He accuses the earl of Norfolk of a plot to marry the queen of Scots, ib. He refuses to deliver up to Elizabeth a body of insurgent horse, who had entered into Liddesdale, 630. He is murdered by Hamilton, of Bothwell-Haugh, January 22, 1570; 632. Murray was a stern suppressor of the moss-troopers, iii. 649.
MURRAY, lord, son of the earl of Atholl, raises 1,000 Highlanders, 1689, to oppose the insurrection in favour of James, but they all desert to the opposite party, iv. 15.
MURRAY, lord George, joins the standard of the Young Pretender, 1745; iv. 487. Sole commander of the forces, 510. He represents the necessity of a retreat to Scotland, and offers to conduct the rear, 514. His skirmish with the duke of Cumberland, near Clifton Moor, 518. Further movements in. the service of the Pretender, 520—548.
MURRAY, Mr. Alexander, brother of lord Elibank, his imprisonment in Newgate, 1751; iv. 563, 564. He goes into voluntary exile, 565.
MURRAY, sir David, a confidential friend of Henry, eldest son of king James I., iii. 51, 52.
MURRAY, John, of Broughton, a member of the Secret Society of Jacobites, 1743; iv. 470. He turns evidence against his former associates, 1747; 551.
MURRAY, sir John, appointed to the command of the Anglo-Sicilian army in the east of Spain, § iv. 586.

MURRAY, sir John,—
He embarks his forces at Alicante, and lands them at Tarragona, which fortress he invests, June 3, 1813; 587. On the approach of a French relieving army, he precipitately embarks, leaving behind part of his artillery and stores, 588. At the close of the war he is tried by court-martial, but acquitted on admonition, *ib.*

MURRAY, Mungo, a confidential servant of Charles I., 1642; iii. 268.

MURRAY, sir Robert, forms a plan with Charles I., 1646, for his escape, iii. 362.

MURRAY, William; it is proposed by the Lords, 1642, that he, as an evil counsellor, should be removed from the person of the king, iii. 273, 362.

MURRAY, general, besieged in Quebec by M. Levi, 1760; iv. 614.

MURTACH, king of Ireland, death of, 1119; i. 459.

MURTOCH O'LOCHLIN, king of Ireland, killed in battle, 1066, and is succeeded by Roderick O'Connor, i. 459.

Museum, British, illustration of the public reading-room of the, iii. 616.

MUSGRAVE, sir Christopher, iv. 127. Opposes Marlborough's being raised to a dukedom, 1702; 148.

Music, English,—Improvement in the church music (1400—1500), Henry V. and the gentry of England performed; music was taught at the universities as essential to a polite education, ii. 233. Song on the battle of Agincourt, our first regular composition, *ib.* The music of it engraved, 234. Delineations of various performers, and of their instruments, 233, 235; iii. 561—567; specimens of, 563—566. Improvement in this branch of the fine arts between the revolution and the accession of George III., iv. 761—764. History of, during the reign of George III. § i. 634—637; § iii. 752—754; (nineteenth century) § iv. 718—720.

MUSKERRY, a volunteer of rank, killed in an engagement with the Dutch, 1665; iii. 695.

Muslins, manufactured in considerable quantities in Great Britain towards the close of the 18th century, § iii. 699.

MUSTAPHA, sultan, succeeds to the government of Turkey, on the deposition of his uncle Selim III., in 1807; § iv. 285. The treaty of peace with England, January 5, 1809; 402. He murders Selim, July, 1809, and is himself murdered by his brother Mahmoud, 424.

Mutiny Act, the, passed 1717; iv. 344. Description of, by lord Shelburne, in 1767; § i. 73, 508.

MYAGH, Thomas, an Irishman, charged with treason, and tortured, 1581; iii. 519.

MYLNE, Robert, architect of the most beautiful of modern bridges, Blackfriars, commenced in 1760, and completed in eight years, § iii. 735.

Mysorean cavalry, § ii. 162.

Mysteries, miracles, melodramas, etc., that preceded moralities, masques, and the regular drama, ii. 256, 257.

MYTENS, Daniel, an eminent Dutch artist of the 17th century, iii. 567.

Mythology of Scandinavia and the Teutonic tribes: Odin or Wodin, i. 138; Thor, 140.

NAIRNE, Miss, a Jacobite lady, accidentally wounded by a discharge of muskets on occasion of the Young Pretender's entering Holyrood-house, 1745; iv. 497.

Namur, surrenders to Louis XIV., June 30, 1692; iv. 36. View of, 55.

Nantes, inhabitants of, offer their city to prince Geoffrey, at whose death, in 1158, his brother Henry claims the government as hereditary property, and takes possession of the city, i. 443. Attack on Nantes by the Vendeans, 1793; § iii. 373.

Nantes, Edict of, published April, 1598, by which Henri IV. tolerated the Reformed religion and

Nantes, Edict of,—
worship, ii. 682. This Edict is revoked by Louis XIV., 1685; iii. 785.

NAPIER, Mr. David (19th century), his improvements in steam navigation, § iv. 685.

NAPIER, John, baron of Marchiston, distinguished as the inventor of logarithms, was born in 1550, and died April, 1617; iv. 767.

Naples, besieged in 1528, by French and Genoese. The French died of the plague; Lautrec falling a victim to malaria and grief, his army retreated to Averaa and surrendered, ii. 368. Taken possession of by the French and converted into a republic, January 23, 1799, under the name of "Republica Partenopea," § iii. 545. It was however recovered in the space of a few months by cardinal Ruffo and lord Nelson, 547.

NARES, James, an eminent English composer, of the 18th century, § i. 634.

Naseby, battle of, gained by the parliament, June 14, 1645; iii. 333. Obelisk at, from an unpublished lithograph, 334.

NASH, John, an architect of the 19th century, to whom we are indebted for Regent-street, the Regent's-park, and St. James's-park, § iv. 708.

NASSAU, Frederic prince of, (son of the prince of Orange,) arrives, 1603, at the court of James I., with Falcke, Barnevelt, and Brederode, to negotiate for his favour to the then infant States of Holland, iii. 7.

National Debt, scheme of, first proposed in 1696; iv. 74.

National Industry, history of the. *See* Industry.

National Manners and Habits of Scotland, iv. 833.

National School Society founded, 1811; § iv 605.

Navarre, kingdom of, united by Ferdinand the Catholic to the Spanish monarchy, 1512; ii. 321.

NAVARRE, king of, mortally wounded at the siege of Rouen, 1562; ii. 570.

Navigation, some tribes more addicted to than others, i. 6. Curious description of the number of ships furnished by the principal commercial cities of England to Edward III., at the siege of Calais. 331. Specimen of some ships of the time of Richard II., *ib.* Ships of war of the 15th century, ii. 177. *Illustration*:—Embarkation of Henry VIII., 1520, at Dover, 339. Shipping, during the early part of the 16th century, 780. Navigation, (18th century,) § i. 557, 558, 567, 568. Increase of inland navigation, § iii. 666, 669.

Navigation Act, (1651, 1652,) passed by the parliament, which, with other causes, led to immediate war between the United Provinces and the Commonwealth of England, iii. 496; iv. 162. Provisions of this Act, 496. Navigation Laws, iii. 857.

Navy-office, the, established by Henry VIII., ii. 780.

NAYLOR, James, an enthusiastic Quaker, apprehended at Bristol, December 1656, and severely punished, iii. 812, 813.

NEAL, Richard, iii. 55; bishop of Durham, 1617. He gives it as his opinion that kings may take the money of their subjects without the consent of Parliament, iii. 608. Commanded Dr. Alablaster to preach popery, 140. He died archbishop of York, 1640; 475.

NEALE, colonel, present at the battle of Chalgrove-field, June 18, 1643; iii. 304.

NECKER, James, a celebrated financier, twice minister of state in France, born at Geneva, 1732, died 1804. Portrait of, § ii. 338, 350, 379, 396, 518.

NEILE, sir Paul, delivers to the Royal Society, from the king, 1661, a proposition for finding two mean proportionals, iv. 774.

NEILE, bishop. *See* Neal.

NELSON, Horatio, viscount, a celebrated naval officer, born September 29, 1758. His gallant conduct at the siege of Bastia, 1794; § iii. 400. Loses an eye at

NELSON, Horatio, viscount,—
the siege of Calvi, 401. His portrait, 478, 505.
His energy during the evacuation of Corsica, 1796;
506. He is elected a knight of the Bath, 1797, for
his gallant conduct at the battle off Cape St. Vincent,
522. Loses his right arm in an unfortunate attack upon
Santa Cruz, in the island of Teneriffe, 528. Gains the
battle of the Nile, August 1, 1798; 542, 543. For
his services on this occasion he was raised to the
peerage, by the title of baron Nelson of the Nile
and of Burnham Thorpe, ib. He assists in recap-
turing Naples from the French, 1799. Sanguinary
vengeance taken by the Neapolitan court on the
Republicans, 547. His gallant conduct at the battle
of Copenhagen, April 2, 1801; 550*—553*. He is
raised to a viscounty, 553°; made commander-in-
chief, 554°. When hostilities commenced after the
peace of Amiens, he was appointed to command the
fleet in the Mediterranean, and for nearly two years
was engaged in the blockade of Toulon. On March
30, 1805, the French admiral Villeneuve escaped his
vigilance, and being joined by a Spanish squadron
from Cadiz, sailed to the West Indies, § iv. 181.
The English admiral hastily pursued them, and they
returned to Europe and took shelter at Cadiz, 181,
186. On the 19th of October, the French, commanded by Villeneuve, and the Spaniards by Gra-
vina, ventured again from Cadiz, and on the 21st
they came up with the English squadron off Cape
Trafalgar, 187, 188. An engagement took place, in
which a most glorious victory was obtained, at the
expense of the life of the English admiral, who was
wounded by a musket ball, and soon after expired,
188—195. Illustrations :—His Death, 192, and
Funeral, 197.
NENNIUS. See Ninian.
NERO, the emperor, i. 44.
NEUBURG, Maria Anne of, wife of Charles II. of Spain,
iv. 106.
NEVERS, count of, at Agincourt, ii. 33. His fall in
the battle, ib.
NEVILLE, sir Christopher, arbitrarily arrested, 1617;
iii. 86.
NEVIL, lord, deprived of his employments, 1376; i.
NEVIL, sir Francis, committed to the Tower, regno 779.
Charles I., for informing his Majesty of words
spoken in the House of Commons, iii. 264.
NEVIL, George, youngest brother of Warwick, made
archbishop of York, and chancellor, 1461; ii. 102.
His installation feast, 253. He became peace-maker,
1467, betwixt his elder brethren and the court,
103. 104.
NEVILLE, sir Henry, his speech in answer to a question
proposed to him by James I., iii. 43, 55.
NEVILLE, sir Ralph, defeated by sir James Douglas,
1318; i. 789.
New York, view of, from Long Island, § i. 271. Hos-
tility of this city to Congress, 1776; 274.
Newark Castle, from an original drawing, iii. 305.
NEWBURG, duke of, lays claim to the succession of
John duke of Cleves, about 1610; iii. 48.
NEWBURGH, William of, quoted, i. 593.
Newbury, Donnington Castle in the distance, from an
old print, iii. 307.
Newbury, battle of, fought, September 20, 1643; iii.
307.
Newcastle-upon-Tyne, founded by William the Con-
queror, i. 383. View of, 536. Considerable coal-
trade of, 1421, dues, etc., ii. 191. Esteemed by
Camden the glory of all the towns in Northumber-
land, iii. 656.
NEWCASTLE, earl of, defeats lord Fairfax, at Atherton-
moor, June 30, 1643; iii. 305.
NEWCASTLE, duke of, premier of England, resigns,
1756, iv. 588.
NEWCASTLE, Thomas Holles, duke of, created November, 1756. His grief at the death of George II. § i. 2.

NEWCASTLE, Thomas Holles, duke of,—
Portrait of, 20. He resigns, 1762, refusing any pension or compensation for the sacrifices he had made
out of his private fortune, ib.; and, in 1768, died
300,000l. poorer than when he came into office, ib.,
note.
NEWCOMEN, Thomas, an ironmonger of Dartmouth,
made several improvements in the steam-engine,
for which he took out a patent in 1705; iv. 778;
§ i. 579.
Newport, Rhode Island, view of, § i. 362.
NEWPORT, earl of, constable of the Tower, removed
from the post by Charles I. 1641; iii. 260.
Newspapers, English, the era of, commences 1640;
iii 615. Sunday Newspapers, their first appearance,
about 1780; § iii. 588.
NEWTON, sir Isaac; portrait of, iv. 735. His discovery
of the Binomial Theorem is assigned to 1664; 781;
his invention of fluxions to 1665; his demonstration
of the law of gravitation to 1666, though this was
not completed until 1682. His "Principia" was
published (at the expense of the Royal Society)
in 1687; his "Treatise on Optics" in 1704; and
along with it his tract "De Quadratura Curvarum,"
containing an exposition of the method of Fluxions,
ib. He died 1727.
NEWTON, Thomas, author of a translation of the
"Thebais," 1581; iii. 584.
NEY, Michael, a French marshal under Bonaparte,
born in 1769, made marshal in 1804, and in the
following year created duke of Elchingen; he
greatly distinguished himself in the Russian campaign, and was created prince of Moskwa in 1814.
He was one of the first of the imperial generals
who offered submission to the Bourbons. In 1815,
on Napoleon's return from Elba, he deserted with
all the forces under his command, and joined him,
§ iv. 629°, for which he was tried, and executed,
December 7, 1815; 652°, 653°.
NEYLE, bishop. See Neal.
NEYNOE, an Irish Catholic priest, attempting to escape
from arrest, is drowned in the Thames, 1722; iv. 380.
Nice, demolished by the duke of Vendôme, 1705; iv.
179.
NICHOLSON, Margaret, makes an attempt to assassinate George III., August 2, 1786; the Privy-
council having taken the opinion of medical men
that she was insane, she is committed to a lunatic
asylum, § ii. 202.
NICHOLSON, William, bishop of Carlisle, consecrated
June 1702, translated to Derry, in Ireland, 1718.
He laments the lenity of the English government
after the insurrection of 1715; iv. 548.
NICOLAS V., pope (Thomas de Sarzana), elected
March 6, 1447, distinguished as a patron of learning. He died March 24, 1455; ii. 199.
NICOLAS, an agent or solicitor in ecclesiastical causes.
His letter to Eadmer, bishop of St. Andrew's, i. 539.
He offers to undertake the defence of the indepen-
dence of the Scottish church at the papal court, ib.
NIGEL, bishop of Ely, and nephew of Roger, bishop
of Sarum, consecrated, October 1133. The king
orders his arrest; he prepares to defend himself in
the castle of Devizes, i. 427. Joins Matilda, 428;
builds a stone rampart among the bogs and fens on
the eastern coast; but being defeated by Stephen,
flies to Matilda's head-quarters at Gloucester, 429.
He died, June 3, 1169.
Nile, battle of the, August 1, 1798; § iii. 542, 543.
Nimeguen, View of, § ii. 209. Peace of, 1678; iii. 716.
NINIAN, bishop of Whithern, Wigtonshire, converted,
in 412, the Picts south of the Grampians, i. 229. He
died 432, ib.
NINIAN, or Nennius, a monk, escaped the massacre
in 613 at Bangor, in Wales, i. 289. His History of
the Britons, ib.
Nisi Prius, trials by, iv. 678.

NITHSDALE, lord, sentence of death passed on, January 19, 1716; iv. 328. He escapes from the Tower in disguise, February 23, ib.

NIVERNOIS, duke de, French ambassador extraordinary at the court of London, negotiates the treaty of Fontainebleau, 1762; § i. 22.

NOAILLES, duke de, 1694; iv. 49. George II. narrowly escapes being made his prisoner at the battle of Dettingen, June 27, 1743; 465. His generous treatment of the wounded English after the battle, 467, note. On the defeat of marshal de Broglie, by prince Charles of Lorraine, he returns in miserable condition to France, 467.

NOAILLES, count de, recommends to the National Assembly the abolition of liveries, 1790; § ii. 489.

NOLLEKENS, Joseph, a celebrated sculptor, born 1737, died 1823; § iii. 745.

Nomenclature, a trustworthy source of evidence as to the original population of a country; its durability, etc., i. 7.

Nonconformists, iii. 691.

Nonjurors, iv. 10.

Non-resistance, Oath of, iii. 696.

Nonsuch, palace of, ii. 844.

Nootka Sound, view in, § ii. 459.

Norfolk, town of, reduced to ashes, 1775, by command of lord Dunmore, § i. 225.

NORFOLK, Ralph de Gaël, earl of, marries the sister of Roger Fitz-Osborn, contrary to the orders of William, i. 380. Their marriage-feast, 380, 381. Fitz-Osborn and Ralph de Gaël conspire against the king, 1073; 381. Their scheme is betrayed by Judith, wife of Waltheof, ib. Norfolk attempts to cross the Severn, but is frustrated; he fortifies and garrisons Norwich, 1073, and leaving his bride, Emma Fitz-Osborn, to defend it, passes over to Brittany, ib. William attempts to seize him, but is frustrated by Philip, king of France, who forces him to raise the siege of Dol, 383.

NORFOLK, Roger Bigod, earl of, marshal of England, 1177; i. 719—722. See Humphrey Bohun, earl of Hereford.

NORFOLK, Thomas Mowbray, duke of, 1397; i. 795. Challenges the duke of Hereford, January 1398; 796. Is banished for life, and Hereford for ten years, September 16, ib. He died 1413.

NORFOLK, John Howard, duke of, ii. 113. 116, 123 Lord Howard created duke by Richard III., 1483; 124. Letter of Elizabeth, daughter of Edward IV. to the duke, 128. (See Elizabeth, queen of Henry VII.) Norfolk's fidelity to Richard III., and his valour at Bosworth Field, 129. He was slain, 1485; the action, ib. The act of attainder against Norfolk, Surrey, Ferrers, Lovel, etc., 284. Confiscations and forfeitures, ib.

Norfolk, Thomas Howard, created duke of; earl of Surrey, 1483; fought at Bosworth Field, where duke John, his father, was slain, 1485; ii. 129. Sent to the Tower by Henry VIII., 287. Released, 296. He suppressed an insurrection in the north, ib. Surrey's great victory at Flodden, 1513, whilst Henry VIII. was in France, 326—329. The king thereupon restored him to the ducal title, 330. He accompanied the princess Mary to Abbeville, on her marriage with Louis XII. 1514; 331. He shed tears in pronouncing sentence, 1521, against Edward Stafford, duke of Buckingham, an innocent and hospitable prince, 344. His government of Ireland popular, 1520; 348. Returning from his post of deputy, and appointed lord admiral, he accompanied Charles V. to the coast of Spain; he also devastated the French coasts, and burnt Morlaix, in Brittany, 1522; ib. He marched from Calais to the river Somme, burnt villages, but could not bring Vendôme to battle, 349. His harassed army suffered by dysentery, and he re-conducted it to Calais for the

NORFOLK, Thomas Howard, duke of,—
winter, ib. He destroys Merse and the Abbey of Jedburgh, 1523; 429. His death, 1524.

NORFOLK, Thomas Howard, duke of, succeeded, 1524. He quelled the Suffolk insurgents, who had threatened the life of their duke (Brandon), 1525, and Henry VIII. abandoned the arbitrary benevolences that gave his people offence, ii. 360. Gave a decided support, 1529, to the divorce of Catherine, 371; he and Brandon, duke of Suffolk, required from Wolsey the delivery of the Great Seal, 1529, under an order in the king's hand, 372. Norfolk was uncle of Anne Boleyn, by the marriage of his sister Elizabeth Howard with sir Thomas Boleyn, 363, 374. The duke became president of the council, 1530; 374. He was suddenly recalled from the conference at Marseilles, 1533, being a zealous Catholic, and the other English envoys proved to have no sufficient powers, 382. The duke commanded the royal forces in Yorkshire, but his army was not able to give the insurgents battle, the "Pilgrims of Grace" assuming a religious enthusiasm, and being commanded by some able leaders and divers of the northern nobility, 399. In conjunction with the earl of Shrewsbury, he secured the passages of the rivers, and arrested the progress of the insurgent masses at Doncaster, ib. The royal army compelled to retreat south of the Trent, 400. A truce and negotiations, 399, 400. The duke made promises, Suffolk bribed most of the leaders, and the insurgents dispersed to their homes, 400. The leaders were seized, sent to London and condemned, ib. The king's banner was unfurled as a token of martial law, June, 1537; Norfolk, by the special injunctions of Henry VIII., beheaded or hanged remorselessly the insurgents and the monks, 401. He is committed to the Tower, and excluded from the number of Henry's executors, 1545; 449. Is condemned, and an order despatched to the lieutenant of the Tower for his execution on the following morning, but the king dies in the intervening night, 451. His name is excepted from a general pardon granted to state offenders by Edward VI., 457. His attainder legally reversed by queen Mary, 1553; 510. He marches to oppose the insurrection of sir Thomas Wyatt, 1554, in which year he died, 513.

NORFOLK, Thomas Howard, duke of, grandson and heir, being son and heir of Henry Howard (eldest son of the last duke), who was attainted and beheaded vitâ patris, in 1547. See Surrey. Restored in blood and honours, 1553, and succeeded to his grandfather's dignities, 1554. He enters into a plan for marrying the queen of Scots, 1569; ii. 623, 624. The secret is betrayed to Elizabeth by the earl of Leicester; Elizabeth reprimands Norfolk for his offence; he retires to Kenning-hall, 624, 625. He is invited to court, but on his way thither is seized by Edward Fitzgarret, and committed to the Tower, 626. His humble submission to the queen, 638. He is tried and executed, June 2, 1572; 640—644. This eminent man was a pupil of Fox, the martyrologist, 641.

NORFOLK, Thomas Howard, earl of; earl marshal; restored in blood, 1603; iii. 117. Having offended Buckingham, he is shut up in the Tower, 119. The Lords demand his liberation, which the king, though ungraciously, grants, ib. Is confined again, 169. Despatched to Germany, 1637, to treat about the restitution of the Prince Elector, 174. Returns without effecting anything, ib. Created earl of Norfolk, 1644. He died, 1646.

Norham Castle, on the Tweed, built in the eleventh century by Ralph Flambard, i. 541. View of its ruins, 540. Surrendered to king David, 1138; 541.

NORMAN, John, lord-mayor, in 1453; he introduces the

NORMAN, John,—
 innovation of the lord-mayor's procession to West-minster, on the river, ii. 261.
Normandy; wars of Henry V. in this province, 1415—1419, which he finally conquers, ii. 29, 39, 43. Wars of Henry VI.'s generals in, 70, 72, 79, 84. Sir Thomas Kyriel totally defeated, 85. All Normandy fell into the hands of the French, 1450, *ib.*
Normans, origin of the, i. 138.
NORRIS, Henry, groom of the bedchamber; present, 1533, at the king's private marriage with Anne Boleyn, ii. 379. Norris and lord Rochford were the principals in a tilting-match, 1536, the king and queen both present, 391. Henry VIII. betokened a sudden jealousy, and quitted the fête in anger, *ib.* Norris and four others, chiefly of the court, were the next morning transferred from Greenwich to the Tower, all of them on charges of adultery with the ill-fated queen, *ib.* Norris said to have much admired the beauty of the queen, *ib.* The trial, the prisoners being also charged with plots against the king's life, 392. One of them, Mark Smeaton, confessed to his guilt, *ib.* Norris, Brereton, Weston, and Smeaton, sentenced to be hanged, etc., *ib.* Henry VIII. had been partial to Norris; he offered him a pardon if he would make confession, *ib.* This honourable man declared he believed the queen perfectly innocent, whereupon Henry exclaimed, "Hang him up then," 393. He was beheaded, 1536; 394. The earl of Abingdon, one of his descendants, 392, *note.*
NORRIS, baron, son of the above victim of king Henry's jealousy, was ennobled by Elizabeth. ii. 392, *note.*
NORRIS, sir Henry; Elizabeth sends him her "Ten Years' History," to show to the king of France, 1569; ii. 619. He is said to have been implicated in the attack of Condé on the French king, Charles IX., 621. He demands the restitution of Calais, 622. His intrigues with the Huguenots, 628.
NORRIS, sir John, grandson of Henry, executed on account of Anne Boleyn, was a brave commander in the service of Elizabeth, ii. 392, *note.* Commanding for the queen in the rebellion of O'Neil, or Tyrone, 1598, he failed in every attempt to suppress the Irish chief of Ulster, and died of excessive fatigue and grief, 682.
NORRIS, sir John, sails to the Baltic with eleven sail of the line, to the protection of the queen of Sweden, iv. 368. His unsuccessful expedition to Ferrol, 1740; 440.
NORTH, Francis, lord Guildford, born about 1640, was promoted to the office of solicitor-general in 1671, when he received the honour of knighthood ; was made attorney-general, 1673, the next year chief-justice of the Common Pleas, and in 1683 appointed lord-keeper, and raised to the peerage. He died, September 5, 1685; iii. 521. 522, 781. His "Philosophical Essay on Music," 1677; 845, 887.
NORTH, Francis, lord. *See* Guildford.
NORTH, Frederic, lord. *See* Guildford.
NORTH, lord, joins in an intended invasion of the Pretender, 1772; iv. 380; and afterwards conforms to the Romish faith, 400.
NORTH, sir Dudley, illegally appointed sheriff of London, 1681; iii. 739. Portrait of, 852.
NORTH, Roger, attorney-general of James II., iii. 521. His description of several eminent lawyers, 845—849. He died in 1733.
Northallerton, anciently Elfer-tun, great battle of, fought with David of Scotland, 1138, at which the ancient Saxon banners were used, and the Saxon saints invoked as before the Conquest, i. 424. Diligence of archbishop Thurstan in raising a sufficient army to oppose the Scots, *ib.* Description and picture of the great English standard there used, *ib.* English and Scottish armies before the battle, 425. Fierce engagement, and retreat of the Scots to Car-

Northallerton,—
 lisle; here David collects his scattered troops, and re-assumes the offensive, after which a peace is concluded upon very advantageous terms to the Scots, 426.
Northampton, Holy Well of St. Thomas à Becket, near, ii. 150. Battle of Northampton, 1460; 95.
NORTHAMPTON, William Parr, marquess of, created earl of Essex, 1543, and marquess of Northampton, 1546, a privy-councillor, *regno* Edward VI., ii. 454. He conducts a force of fifteen hundred horse against the rebels of 1549, and takes up his quarters at Norwich, which place he succeeds in clearing of the rebels, but the next day they forced their way back, drove out the king's troops, killing the lord Sheffield and many other gentlemen, and set fire to the city, 487. Northampton retreats to London, *ib.* Sentence is passed against him by Mary as a traitor, 505. Restored in blood but not in honours, 1558, and created marquess of Northampton, 1559. He died, 1571.
NORTHAMPTON, Henry Howard, earl of, 1604. Made lord privy seal, iii. 39. His death, June 15, 1614; 57.
NORTHAMPTON, William Compton, earl of, created August 2, 1618. Curious letter addressed to him by his wife, iii. 630. He died, 1630.
NORTHAMPTON, Spenser Compton, earl of, 1630. Impeached of high crimes and misdemeanours, 1642, in which year he died, iii. 288.
NORTHINGTON, Robert Henley, earl of, created May, 1764. Is made president of the council, 1766 ; § i. 48. Desires to resign, 57.
Northmen, or Norse tribes, the most celebrated of whom were the Normans, i. 9, 138.
NORTHUMBERLAND, Morcar, earl of, son of Algar; the Northumbrians appoint him earl, i. 200. Algitha, Morcar's sister, marries Harold, and becomes queen, 208. Morcar and Edwin are firm to the interests of Harold, but are defeated by Hardrada king of Norway and Tostig, near York, *ib.* They are appointed to the command of the Saxon forces, against William, 360. They withdraw towards the Humber, 361. Go on a deputation to William, *ib.* Take part with earl Edwin, 1068; 368. Are defeated by William, retreat to York, and thence fly to Scotland, 369. Morcar submits a second time to the Conqueror, and is restored to his paternal estates, 1073; 375. He hears of William's intention to seize him; his brother Edwin is slain, but he escapes to the camp of refuge in the isle of Ely, *ib.* Is condemned to perpetual imprisonment, 378. William, on his death-bed, releases his state prisoners, 389. Morcar and Wulnoth follow William Rufus to England, in hopes of having some of their possessions restored to them, but his first act was to imprison them in Winchester Castle, 392, 393.
NORTHUMBERLAND, Robert de Mowbray, earl of. This powerful earl of Northumberland possessed 280 English manors. Being commanded to appear at the feast of Whitsuntide he absents himself; William finding it impossible to besiege or blockade Bamborough Castle, builds another castle close to it, and leaves there a strong garrison, i. 400. Mowbray is decoyed from his safe retreat, and taken by the king's party, *ib.* His wife Matilda delivers up Bamborough Castle, *ib.* The conspiracy for placing Stephen, count of Aumale, nephew of the Conqueror, upon the throne, is discovered, *ib.* Mowbray is condemned to perpetual imprisonment, about 1095. He died, 1106; *ib.*
NORTHUMBERLAND, Henry Percy, earl of, 1377. At the coronation of Henry IV., 1399, he carried the sword worn by that prince when he landed at Ravenspur, ii. 5. He informs the House of Peers that Henry IV. desired Richard II. to live, and demands their counsels, which were to shut him up in a castle, 6. No grateful concessions by Henry were

NORTHUMBERLAND, Henry Percy, earl of,—
able to satisfy this haughty baron for his services,
13. The earl being ill, gives the command of the
insurgent forces to his son, Harry Hotspur, 1403,
ib. Declaration of the Percies against king Henry,
14. Their allies, *ib.* When marching with reinforcements towards Hotspur's camp, he is informed of
the fatal fight of Shrewsbury, and retreats to his
castle of Warkworth, 15. Compelled to surrender,
he presents a petition to Henry IV., who grants him
a plenary pardon, *ib.* Ungrateful for the king's
mercy, the old earl, 1405, again rebels; which
Henry avenges by the execution of certain great
men, and takes the citadel of Berwick, and all
Northumberland's castles, 17. The earl finds an
asylum at Edinburgh, *ib.* At the head of a Scottish
force he surprises some of his castles in Northumberland, 1408, and advances to Knaresborough, 19. Is
encountered at Branham Moor, Tadcaster, by sir
T. Rokeby, and slain, *ib.*

NORTHUMBERLAND, Henry Percy, earl of, the young
son of Hotspur, is exchanged, 1414, for lord Murdoch Stewart, son of the regent Albany, ii. 132.
He is restored to his ancestral honours by Henry
V., 25, 132. Slain at St. Alban's, 1454; 92.

NORTHUMBERLAND, Thomas Percy, earl of, created
baron Egremont, 1449; ii. 93. Slain at the battle
of Northampton, 1460; 95.

NORTHUMBERLAND, John Nevill, earl of, 1464; after
the victory of Hexham, Nevil, lord Montague is
invested with the estates and titles of the Percies,
ii. 102—104, 106. Slain, 1471, at Barnet, 108.

NORTHUMBERLAND, earl of, 1475, attended Edward
IV. at the conference of Picquigny, ii. 112. He
commanded the northern contingent for Richard III.,
at Bosworth, 129.

NORTHUMBERLAND, earl of, 1489, murdered by the
northern insurgents, ii. 296.

NORTHUMBERLAND, Henry Algernon Percy, earl of;
Anne Boleyn, maid of honour to queen Catherine,
preferred this noble, 1527, above other admirers, ii.
364. He offered her marriage, *ib.* The jealous
Henry VIII. discovered their passion, and Percy
was forced by his father Northumberland to marry
a daughter of the earl of Shrewsbury, *ib.* The earl
of Northumberland was commissioned to arrest
Wolsey for treason, at York, 1529; 373. Brought
up in the cardinal's household, he evinced feeling in
the performance of this duty, *ib.* The queen's pre-
contract to marry lord Percy, was the king's allegation for rendering his own marriage with Anne
Boleyn null from the beginning, 395. He died, 1537.

NORTHUMBERLAND, John Dudley, duke of, when
viscount Lisle, and admiral of England, 1544, landed
Hertford and his army at Leith, ii. 440. His action
with a French armament of invasion, 1545, under
Annebaut, an admiral of Francis I.; Dudley's
prompt fulfilment of Henry VIII's commands to
fight, 442. The result was the French fleet withdrew to Brest, and the English admiral to Portsmouth, *ib.* On the accession of Edward VI., he
was created earl of Warwick, but resigned the
office of lord-admiral to Thomas Seymour, 456.
He joined Somerset, 1547, in his invasion of Scotland, 460, 462. He is appointed to conduct an
army of 6,000 men against the Norfolk rebels, 1549;
487. He forces his way into Norwich, and the
next day falls upon the enemy, who were encamped
in a valley called Dussingdale, and achieves a
decisive victory, *ib.* Mounts into eminence on
the fall of the protector Somerset, 491; is created
duke of Northumberland, 1551; 495. Somerset
is beheaded for attempting the duke's life, 496, 497.
Northumberland sedulously labours to win the
affections of the dying Edward, 499, and persuades
him to entail the crown on his daughter-in-law, the
lady Jane Grey, 500. He summons the lord-mayor

NORTHUMBERLAND, John Dudley, duke of,—
and several aldermen, and causes them to swear
allegiance to the lady Jane, 502. He takes the
command of the lady Jane's troops, but hearing of
the proclamation of Mary in London, calls for a
herald, and proclaims queen Mary at Cambridge,
504; is arrested by the earl of Arundel, and lodged
in the Tower, *ib.*; is attainted and beheaded, 1553;
505, 506.

NORTHUMBERLAND, Thomas Percy, earl of, 1557; ii.
607, 608; heads an insurrection in favour of Mary
queen of Scots, 629. On the failure of the undertaking, he takes refuge amongst the Scottish borderers, but is betrayed to the regent by Hector
Græme, of Harlow, and imprisoned in Lochleven
Castle, 630. His countess escapes to the Scottish
borders, leaving her children in great distress, *ib.*
He is basely sold to Elizabeth by the chancellor
Morton, and beheaded at York without trial, July,
1572; 645.

NORTHUMBERLAND, Henry Percy, earl of, (brother of
the last earl,) is accused of conspiring to liberate
Mary, and to save the forfeiture of his lands shoots
himself, 1583; ii. 654. A doubt, however, may be
raised whether he was not assassinated, as a pistol
was not an instrument commonly left in the hands
of a state prisoner in the Tower, *ib.*, *note*.

NORTHUMBERLAND, Henry Percy, earl of. Letter of
Francis Bacon, describing the new king James I. to
this nobleman, 1603; iii. 4. The earl, amused with
some promise of favour at court, finds that Cecil
had dissuaded the king from employing him, 5;
said to have communicated with Rosny and Beaumont, ministers from France, 7. He takes no real
share in Cobham's conspiracy, 8. His agent and
distant relative, Thomas Percy, one of the most
zealous of the Gunpowder conspirators, 21—28.
Northumberland is accused of admitting his said
kinsman to be a gentleman pensioner, without exact-
ing the proper oaths, and of wishing to render himself chief of the Catholic party, 1605, 1606; 32;
fined 30,000*l.* by the Star-Chamber, and committed
to the Tower for life, 33. In the gloomy state-
prison he becomes the intimate friend of Raleigh;
and patronises, by means of his wealth, some men
of talent therein immured, 72. He enters into sir
Walter's alchemical and scientific projects, 73. He
died 1632.

NORTHUMBERLAND, Algernon Percy, earl of, 1632.
He sails with a fleet, 1636, and sinks some Dutch
vessels in the northern seas, iii. 174; declines the
office of commander-in-chief, *about* 1640; 220. He
died, 1668.

NORTHUMBERLAND, Hugh Smithson, earl of, created,
October, 1766; § i. 49. 50.

Northumbria, formed a powerful territory, about 617,
uniting all Bernicia and Deira, with extensive conquests by fresh hordes of Angles, Jutes, etc., betwixt
the Wash and the Humber, which included all Lincolnshire, and extended to the Frith of Forth, i.
142. The Saxon king, Edilfrid, slain, 146. Edwin,
bretwalda of the Saxons, (621,) and king of Northumbria, raises this northern kingdom to be the chief
and most powerful state of the Heptarchy, *ib.* In
825, Egbert the Great marches across the Humber
into the heart of Northumbria, and receives the
submission of king Eanred, but subjects him only to
a mild dependence, 150. Danes from Northumbria,
Norfolk, and Suffolk, (893—898,) aid Hastings
against king Alfred, 163. Their attack on the coast
being continued after the withdrawal of that sea-
king, the crews of all Northumbrian ships captured
in the three ensuing years, are hanged by the English
monarch, 165. The feeble Ethelred being assailed
by vast armaments, 994, conducted by Sweyn, king
of Denmark, agrees to treat, and buys them off
with money, 176. The Northumbrians either join

Northumbria,—
the invading Danes, or offer them no resistance, *ib.* Their firm opposition to William. *See* Edwin, Morcar, William, and Sweyn Estridsen.

Norwegians, the, of Scandinavian origin, i. 138.

Norwich, iii. 655. View of the Castle, i. 380. Cathedral church of, built by bishop Herbert Losing, who, in 1094, removed the episcopal see from Thetford, 615.

Nottingham Castle;—View of Mortimer's Hole, i. 754.

NOTTINGHAM, John Mowbray, earl of, joining in rebellion, 1405, with Northumberland and archbishop Scroop, he surrenders to prince John, son of Henry IV., and is beheaded at Pontefract, ii. 17.

NOTTINGHAM, Charles Howard, earl of, lord high admiral in 1587. Elizabeth, from motives of economy, in 1588, commanding him to lay up four of his largest ships, he nobly replied, that rather than that he would take upon him to disobey his mistress, and keep them afloat at his own charge, ii. 675. He sails, 1596, on an expedition against the Spanish coast, 680. March, 1603, joins in council at Richmond, with Cecil, Egerton, and others, for securing the English crown to James of Scotland, iii. 3. Accepts a pension, and retires from office, 71. He died in 1624.

NOTTINGHAM, countess of, (wife of the lord-high admiral,) insulted at Theobald's by Christian IV., of Denmark, 1606; iii. 33.

NOTTINGHAM, Heneage Finch, earl of, created May, 1681. Lord-chancellor; died 1682. Description of, by sir William Blackstone, iii. 844.

NOTTINGHAM, Daniel Finch, earl of. *See* earl of Winchelsea.

NOY, William, attorney-general, iii. 84, 152. Prepares with his own hand the writ for ship-money, and induces the king to demand seaport towns and inland counties to furnish ships for the service of the crown, 175. His death, August, 1634; *ib.*

NUCE, Thomas, translator of the "Octavia," 1566; iii. 584.

NUJEEM-UL-DOWLAH, son of Meer Jaffier, appointed to the sovereignty of Bengal, 1765, but afterwards deposed, § ii. 90.

NUN OF KENT, (Elizabeth Barton,) 1533; her supposed prophecies declared by sir T. More to be only the phantasies of a simple woman, subject to fits, ii. 384. She was deluded by vulgar admiration to consider herself a prophetess, *ib.* She predicted the death of Henry VIII., if he should divorce Catherine, and the time thereof, *ib.* She was hanged at Tyburn, with several of the clergy, and respectable men, who had conversed with her and not divulged the insane prediction, 1534; 385, 717. Dr. Fisher, bishop of Rochester, and sir Thomas More implicated, were soon after brought to account for this among other matters, 385. *View* of Court-à-street chapel, Aldington; scene of her inspirations and prophecies, 718. Fisher was convicted of *concealment* of this treason, and compounded with the crown, 385. He pleaded that he "well knew the Holy Maid had been admitted to an audience of the king," and that the Maid had told him that she had imparted her revelations and visions to Henry himself, *ib.*

NUNCOMAR, an intriguing Hindu, executed for forgery, August 5, 1775; § ii. 137.

Oaks, grove of, i. 62.

OATES, Titus, his depositions respecting the Popish Plot, September 28, 1678; iii. 718. He is brought before judge Jeffreys, charged with sundry libels, and fined 100,000*l.*; 758. Summoned to the King's Bench, 1685; severe sentence passed upon him, 766.

Oaths.—Forms of the oaths of allegiance and supremacy, iv. 660.

OBRIAN, one of the conspirators who assisted in maiming sir J. Coventry, 1670; iii. 707.

O'BRIEN, Murrock, 1541, created earl of Thomond, and summoned by Henry VIII. to sit in the Irish parliament, ii. 428.

O'BRIEN, Mr., quoted, i. 15.

Observatory, Royal, at Greenwich, founded in 1676 by Charles II., iv. 782. View of the, 783.

OCCAM, William, styled the Invincible, a Franciscan monk, and eminent logician; he died at Munich in 1347, i. 843.

O'CONNELLY, Owen, iii. 254; gives an account of the conspiracy of the Irish, 1641, to parliament, iii. 254; they reward him with 500*l.*, and an annual pension of 200*l.*; 255.

O'CONNOR, this Irish king, 1535, abandoned the fallen fortunes of the Fitzgeralds, and gave hostages to Skeffington, lord-deputy, ii. 426. His rebellion, in concert with O'Neil's, O'Brien's, O'Thole's, etc., 1540. His invasion of Kildare, and subsequent submission to Henry VIII.'s deputy, 428.

O'CONNOR, Ambrose, provincial of the Irish Dominicans, sent by the court of St. Germains in 1708, to survey the condition of Ireland, which mission he dexterously performs, iv. 218.

O'CONNOR, the Irish antiquary, quoted, i. 22.

Ocsakoff, siege of, 1788; § ii. 312, 313.

ODIN or WODIN, of Scandinavia, an ancient sovereign, whose valour and government conferring renown upon him, the rude and superstitious Teutonic tribes worshipped him as a god, i. 138. His residence, Sigtuna, betwixt Upsala and Stockholm, *ib.* Sigge, son of Fridulph, chief of the Asi, a Scythian tribe, emigrated, at the close of the Mithridatic war, to the Baltic, and conquered Scandinavia, 224. Reflections on his career, 225. He gave civilised laws to the northern tribes, but asserted he was the deity, Odin; his wife and children also deified, 224, 225. The Scandinavian mythology and tenets, 225—228.

ODO, earl of Holderness, joins the conspiracy, 1095, to place Stephen count of Aumale on the throne; his lands are confiscated, and he is condemned to imprisonment, i. 400.

ODO, archbishop of Canterbury; this prelate was by birth a Dane, i. 172. He opposes the marriage of clerks, and supports Dunstan in his system of church discipline, *ib.* He instigates a rising against king Edwy, whose brother Edgar is declared independent ruler of the country north of the Thames, *ib.* Question, whether Odo by the instrumentality of his armed retainers, or the rebellious Mercians, put Elgiva the queen to death, *ib.*

ODO, bishop of Bayeux, his command in the Norman army, i. 212, 214. Heads the expedition against Ralph de Gaël, earl of Norfolk, 381. His savage revenge on the Northumbrians for the death of Walcher de Lorraine, 1082 to 1085; 385. Endeavours to obtain the election to the papacy, and sets out for Italy, accompanied by a brilliant escort, *ib.*; but is stopped at the Isle of Wight by William, who seizes his treasures, and summons him before a Norman council; he is confined in a dungeon in his death-bed, 392. He persuades Robert to invade England, 394. Raises the standard of that prince in his old earldom of Kent, *ib.* Departs finally from England, 1087; 395.

OFFA, king of Mercia, and Bretwalda, i. 265. Letter of Charlemagne to the Saxon king, being an early English treaty, 266,

OGILVIE, an Irishman, defends Prague against the Elector of Bavaria and Marshal de Broglie, 1741; iv. 450.

OGILVY, a Jesuit, executed 1616, iii. 66.

OOLE, William, and Thomas Gourney, murder Edward II. in Berkeley Castle, September, 1327; i. 745.

OGLETHORPE, Owen, bishop of Carlisle, crowns queen Elizabeth in Westminster Abbey, January 15, 1558,

2 E

OGLETHORPE, Owen, bishop of Carlisle,—
none other of the prelates being willing to perform the service, ii. 542. He was deprived in
1559.

OGLETHORPE, general, founds the colony of Georgia,
about 1732; iv. 406. Defeats 4,000 Spaniards who
were marching on Frederica, the capital of his
colony, 463. Pursues the Young Pretender in his
retreat to Scotland, 518.

O'HANLAN, takes Tanderage, 1641; iii. 254.

O'HARA, brigadier-general, wounded at the battle of
Guilford, 1781; § i. 453, 454.

O'HARA, general, takes the command of the land forces
at Toulon, 1793, where he is wounded and made
prisoner, § iii. 305, 306.

OHTHERE, his voyage to the North Seas, related by
Alfred, i. 267.

Oileloth, manufactured in England, 1660; iii. 389.

Okeley, Surrey, defeat of the Danes, 851, by Ethelwulf, at, i. 152.

OKEY, colonel, a parliamentarian officer, 1659; iii.
429*. Flies to Holland, 1661, but is basely delivered up by the States, and executed as a regicide,
690.

OLAF, king of Norway, and son of Hardrada, furnishes
sixty ships to assist Canute in his intended invasion
of England, 1082 to 1085; i. 386.

OLAVE, king of Norway, and Sweyn of Denmark,
ravage, in 994, the south of England, i. 176. They
are bribed by Ethelred to withdraw, ib. King
Olave was baptised, according to the articles of the
treaty, 176, 177.

OLDCASTLE, sir John, ii. 25. See Cobham.

Oligarchies, Roman, i. 85.

Olivenza, treaty of, June, 1801; § iii. 559*.

Oliver, Isaac, a miniature painter, seventeenth century,
iii. 569.

OLIVER, Peter, son of the preceding, and also a miniature painter, he excelled his father, iii. 569.

OMFREVILLE, Robert d', a follower of the Conqueror, receives a grant of the forest of Riddesdale,
1073.

OMICHUND, an intriguing and wealthy Hindoo merchant, 1756; § ii. 39, et seq.

O'NEAL, Daniel, a royalist officer, his gallant conduct
at the battle of Newburn, 1640; iii. 221.

O'NEAL, sir Phelim, joins in the Irish insurrection of
1641; iii. 252, 253; and takes Charlemont and
Dungannon, 254.

O'NEIL, O'Nial, or O'Neal, ancient princes of Ulster
of this family, ii. 428. Joining O'Conner in rebellion, Hugh assaulted Dundalk, ib. O'Neil, often
styled in his country Tir-Oen, was the son of
lord Dungannon, and created by Henry VIII. earl
of Tyrone, 428, 682. Constitutes himself sovereign
of Ulster; collects his sept or clan, and retainers,
1598, and defeats sir Henry Bagnall at Blackwater,
who perished with most of his soldiers, 682. Essex
marches towards the north, 1599; his sorry, ill-
appointed army, through the devices of his personal enemies at court; O'Neil was too powerful
for this new lord-deputy, 683. An armistice ensues;
Tyrone entrusts the Irish demands to the earl of
Essex to forward to Elizabeth, 684. This done,
that chieftain leads his army homewards from
Louth, into the north, ib. O'Neil's attempt to
surprise Mountjoy, 1601, when blockading a Spanish
force that had landed at Kinsale, 693. He is defeated, his troops now suffered from famine, and the
earl, 1602, surrenders himself, ib. Tyrone having
incurred the suspicion of planning a new insurrection flies his country, and throws himself on the
protection of the Spaniards, who treat him as a
prince, iii. 39.

O'NEIL, Shane, is basely assassinated, and his lands,
comprising the greater part of Ulster, are vested in
the English crown, 1568; ii. 651.

ONSLOW, sir Richard, iv. 112; elected speaker of the
House of Commons, 1708; 234.

OPDAM, admiral, slain in a naval engagement off Lowes-
toffe by the duke of York, June 3, 1665; iii. 695.

Opera, Italian, (nineteenth century,) § iv. 719.

Oporto, View of. § iv. 374.

OQUENDO, the Spanish admiral, anchors near Dover,
1639; he is attacked and beaten by Van Tromp,
iii. 208.

O'QUIN. joins in the Irish insurrection of 1641, and
takes Mountjoy, iii. 254.

ORANGE, prince of, in the service of Philip of Burgundy, 1430, crossed the Loire, meeting with success,
in the south of France, ii. 74. Villandrada, a Spa-
niard, with his free companies, and Gaucourt with
king Charles's troops, totally defeated the prince of
Orange, and drove him back across the Loire, ib.

ORANGE, duke of, ii. 292, 296; was proxy for Maximilian of Austria in a secret marriage with Anne of
Brittany, that was annulled, 296—298.

ORANGE, prince of, establishes the independence of
Holland and Zealand, ii. 649. Offers the sovereignty
of Holland to Elizabeth, 1576; ib. Is named governor
of the Low Countries, 1587; 672. He sends Barnevelt,
Falcke, Brederode, and his son Frederick of Nassau,
1603, to James I., at the Scottish king's accession on
the demise of Elizabeth, to solicit aid against Spain
and Austria, in the struggle of the United Provinces,
iii. 7. Henri IV. of France, sends Rosny also to
Whitehall with gold, to support the interests of the
Hollanders, ib. James willingly accedes to a treaty
against the Spaniards, yet remains inactive for want
of resources to fulfil this engagement, ib. Is over-
matched by the general Spinola, 1624; 106. He
dies at the Hague, 1625; ib.

ORANGE, William Charles Henry Friso, prince of,
marries Anne daughter of George II., about 1747;
iv. 556.

ORANGE, prince of, deprived of the government, 1785;
§ ii. 11. The princess is attacked on a journey by
an armed party, 1787; she applies to her brother
the king of Prussia to redress the insult; he
despatches the duke of Brunswick with 30,000 men,
who settle the prince of Orange in his full powers
as Stadtholder, 241—245. The French take possession of Holland, and the Stadtholder retires to
England, 1795. After the battle of Leipzig, in 1813,
the inhabitants revolt, and the Stadtholder returns
and assumes the title of sovereign prince of the
United Netherlands, § iv. 597*, 598*. He offers a
new constitution, which is accepted by the Assembly
of Representatives at Amsterdam, March 28, 1814;
619*. England restores all the Dutch settlements
except the Cape of Good Hope, 620*.

Orange societies, established in England, 1813; § iv. 624.

ORDERICUS VITALIS, an historian contemporary with
William I.; i. 575, 583, 584, 613, 614.

ORDGAR, earl of Devonshire; his daughter, Elfrida,
married by king Edgar, i. 173.

Ordinance, the Self-denying, introduced, December 9,
1644, by which members of either House are excluded from command in the army, iii. 322.

Ordnance, England famous for the manufacture of, iii.
559.

O'REGAN, sir Teague, bravely defends Charlemont,
but is forced by famine to surrender to the Protestants, 1690; iv. 23.

ORFORD, earl of. See Walpole.

ORFORD, earl of. See admiral Russell.

ORKNEY, Elizabeth Villiers, countess of, mistress of
William III., receives a grant of the forfeited Irish
estates of the late king James, 1699; iii. 108.

ORKNEY, lord, pursues Villeroy after the battle of
Ramilies, May 23, 1706; iv. 185.

Orleans, city of, narrative of the siege and blockade
by the generals of the regent-duke of Bedford, 1428,
etc., ii. 60—67.

ORLEANS, duke of, brother of Charles VI., desirous of war with England, to avenge the injuries of Isabella, wife of the deposed Richard II., ii. 9. Burgundy, being more powerful, opposes this war, and a mortal enmity ensued between these princes, 1400, which did not terminate till the quarrel ended in the subversion of their power by Henry V., ib. Orleans challenges king Henry IV. to fight in single combat, or with a certain number on each side, 1402; 12. Replies of the king, ib. Orleans equips ships to harass the English, 15. His intrigues with Isabella, wife of Charles VI., 17. Orleans and the queen, in 1405, govern France, ib. He sends an army to Milford Haven to assist Glendower, 18. His son marries the widow Isabella, 19. What with the fêtes in Paris, and his heavy gambling, on his advance to the war in Guienne, he is entirely frustrated, 1409, and returns to Paris, cursed by the soldiery, without food or pay, 20. Is murdered in Paris, 1407, by assassins hired by the new duke of Burgundy, ib. His widow, the duchess of Orleans, is promised redress by Charles VI., who wept for his brother, but was totally without power, ib. Queen Isabella, at first brooding over her revenge, quits Paris, but Burgundy being all-powerful, she consents to a reconciliation, and the duchess dies of vexation, ib. The duke's children, 20, 21.

ORLEANS, Charles, duke of, 1407, succeeds his murdered father; demands justice against the duke of Burgundy, ii. 21. His first wife (when count of Angoulême) was Isabella, widow of king Richard II., 19. She died 1408; 20. The young duke next married, 1409, Bona of Armagnac, whose father, the powerful count, ever afterwards gave him his support, and the Armagnacs and Bourguignons long distracted France with their fatal quarrel, 21. The Armagnacs take up arms for the destruction of "Jean sans peur" of Burgundy, and many of the French princes and nobles league with the intrepid Armagnac in the cause of young Orleans, ib. His apparent reconciliation with Burgundy, ib. He pays a large contribution to the English duke of Clarence, 1412, 22. More formidable dissensions with Burgundy, 1414. (See Armagnac, who governs Paris in the name of Orleans,) 26. Orleans is made prisoner at Agincourt, 33. Being wounded, he refused sustenance, but was graciously consoled by the victor, 34. Remains a captive in England, 36, 51, 83, note. Illustration: This prince's captivity; the Tower and city of London, 170.

ORLEANS, bastard of, one of Charles VII.'s most gallant commanders, 1428; ii. 62, 66. Known later as the great count of Dunois. See Dunois.

ORLEANS, duke of, 1483; ii. 292. See Louis XII.

ORLEANS, duke of, contract for his marriage, 1533, with Catherine de Medici, ii. 382.

ORLEANS, Gaston, duke of, brother of Louis XIII.; iii. 129.

ORLEANS, Henrietta, duchess of, sister of king Charles II., poisoned, 1670; iii. 707.

ORLEANS, Philippe Égalité, duc d', portrait of, § ii. 347. He is confined to his château of Villars-Cotterets, 1787, for his opposition to the king, ib. Is exiled France by Lafayette, 1789; 438. Permitted to return, 1790; 510. Is accused by the marquis de Bouillé of having hired assassins to murder the royal family at Versailles, 512. Is nominated a deputy to the National Convention, 1792; § iii. 193. His renunciation of any claim to the throne, in 1791; 228. The Convention debates the expediency of banishing him from France, 228 —230. He votes for the death of the king, January 16, 1793; 243. Is himself guillotined during the reign of terror, November 6, 1793; 358.

ORLEANS, the Maid of; history of this enthusiast, whose valour, in its results, firmly established

ORLEANS, the Maid of,— Charles VII. on the French throne, ii. 62. Her illusion of Divine voices and injunctions, 63. et seq. Baudricourt and De Metz listen to her inspired proposal, that she should miraculously assist the king, whose hopes were at a low ebb, 63, 64. Caution of the king, and of learned doctors, before placing any confidence in this humble yet intrepid deliverer of France, 64. Her examination, and acute replies; she was unlettered, but knew that she should raise the siege of Orleans, and conduct the dauphin to Rheims to be anointed king, ib. Her standard, armour, and miraculously-discovered sword, 65. Her religious decorum and modesty, ib. Escorted by La Hire, Saintrailles, etc., a reinforcement of troops, and with a convoy of provisions, she approached Orleans by the river Loire, ib. The garrison made sorties against the besiegers, and Joan of Arc, with the provisions, safely entered the beleaguered city, ib. The English troops were struck with a superstitious dread of this holy maid, their dismay and despondency became uncontrollable, and the crisis had arrived which speedily deprived Bedford of the fruits of his victories, 65, 66. Joan severely wounded in an assault on the English works, 67. Recovering her senses, she continued to animate her followers, and took the Tournelles Fort, sir William Gladesdale, and all the knights being slain in its defence, ib. Suffolk and Talbot, May 8, 1429, raised the siege, and retired to Jargeau and adjacent castles, ib. The Maid of Orleans next rejoined Charles VII., urging him to prepare for the march to Rheims, as she should die within a year, 67, 68. She reduced Jargeau, where she was struck down into the ditch; but Suffolk fell into her hands; Talbot withdrew the garrisons, and retired upon Paris, 68. After Talbot's defeat at Patay, the Maid conducted Charles, with an escort only of horsemen, across provinces occupied by English and Burgundians, to Troyes, 69. The citizens shut their gates; Charles's followers, fatigued and famished, accused Joan of imposture, ib. The citizens, persuaded by friar Richard, an eloquent preacher, admitted Charles, ib. Joan of Arc, July 15, 1429, escorted him with triumph into Rheims, ib. His coronation and anointing, ib. Speech of the Maid of Orleans to king Charles, ib. Having fulfilled her inspired promises, she requested leave to retire to her humble home, 70. The ungrateful prince resolved to retain her in his camp so long as her fame and presence might serve him, ib. Successful campaign; the towns revolt from the Burgundians; narrow escapes of Joan from the English garrisons, the soldiery having resolved to burn her, ib. Charles VII., 1429, published a general amnesty, to induce the Parisians to open their gates, 72. The English garrison repulsed a serious assault, in September, ib. The Maid of Orleans was severely wounded, and, after repeated assaults, forcibly withdrawn by some of her companions in arms, ib. She broke her sword, the miraculous blade, in beating some disorderly soldiers, ib. Experiencing fresh taunts and insults, she hung up her armour at the shrine of St. Denis; but Charles again persuaded her to remain in camp, ib. The retreat to the Loire, 73. The royal army returned towards Paris, 1430, and Joan of Arc fought her way, with a reinforcement, into Compiegne, besieged by Burgundy, to whom Bedford resigned the regency, and by sir John Montgomery's division, ib. She headed a sortie, but whilst fighting with great courage, she was deserted by her soldiers, and made prisoner, ib. Her captor, the Bastard of Vendôme, sold her to John of Luxemburg, 74. Anecdotes, ib. Luxemburg sold the Maid to the bishop of Beauvais, who kept her incarcerated six months in strong castles, ib. This bishop of Beauvais carried her to Rouen

ORLEANS, the Maid of,—
reserving to himself the management of the trial, *ib.*
In 1431, the celebrated accusation of her having
dealt with the Devil as a sorceress or witch, took
place, amid great solemnity, 74, 75. Details of
Joan's trial and condemnation, superstitions and
political motives, reflections, anecdotes, 75—77.
Her execution, May 30; 76, 77. *Illustration:*
Monument of Joan of Arc, at Rouen, 76.

ORLETON, Adam, bishop of Hereford, appointed
April 7, 1317. Effects a reconciliation between the
barons and the Lancastrian party, i. 743. He
died bishop of Winchester, July 18, 1345.

ORM, or Ormin; his "Homilies," i. 301.

ORMOND, earl of, made lieutenant-general of the
forces in Ireland, 1641, by king Charles I., iii. 255.

ORMOND, duke of, recalled from the government of
Ireland, iii. 741, 759. He secures Dublin for
William III., 1690; iv. 26. Makes an unsuccessful
attack on Cadiz in conjunction with sir G. Rooke,
August 1702; 146. Obtains the military appoint-
ments of Marlborough on the disgrace of that noble-
man, 1712; 265. He flies to France, 1715; 308.
Takes the command of an army organized by the
cardinal Alberoni, for the purpose of invading
England, and enthroning the Pretender, 353.

Ornaments of China-ware first brought from Italy in
Elizabeth's reign, iii. 618.

OROSIUS, epitomised by king Alfred, i. 302.

Orphans' Bill, the, 1695; iv. 51.

ORPHEUS, story of, in Anglo-Saxon, by king Alfred,
with a version, i. 296.

ORRERY, earl of, his government in Ireland after the
Restoration, iii. 680.

ORRERY, Charles Boyle, earl of, editor of the "Greek
Epistles," published 1695, attributed to Phalaris,
tyrant of Agrigentum; contest which arose from
this publication, iv. 792.

ORTELIUS, Abraham, author of the "Theatrum Orbis
Terrarum," published 1570; iii. 577.

OSBALDESTON, master of Westminster School, sentenced to branding, pillory, etc., but escapes the
search of the officers, about 1633; iii. 165.

OSBEORN, brother of Sweyn Estridsen, king of Denmark, entrusted with the command of the expedition
to England; he enters the Humber, lands his forces
near the Ouse, 1073, and being joined by the
Northumbrians and some Scots, takes York and
cuts to pieces the Norman garrison to the number
of 3,000; i. 371. Is bribed by William to send no
more assistance to the Northumbrians, 372. On his
arrival in Denmark with the wreck of his fleet,
which had suffered much from the storms, he is
banished by his brother Sweyn Estridsen for his
corrupt and faithless conduct towards the English,
386.

OSBERNE, son of earl Siward, slain at Dunsinane,
1054; i. 194.

OSBURGHA, wife of king Ethelwulf, i. 153. Her sons
Ethelbald, Ethelbert, Ethelred, and the great
Alfred, successively reign in Wessex, 857—871;
153, 154.

OSSORY, lord, son of the duke of Ormond; his threat
to Buckingham, 1671; iii. 709.

OSTORIUS, Scapula, Roman prætor in Britain, A.D. 50;
i. 40; his success, *ib.* Erects forts and lines to
protect the Roman territory, *ib*; marches against
the Silures; they make a firm resistance, but are
vanquished, 41. Ostorius dies in his expedition
against the Silures, 42.

OSWALD, bishop of Salisbury. Disputes having
occurred towards the latter part of the Conqueror's
reign, between the Saxon monks of Glastonbury
and their Norman abbot Thurstan, concerning
uniformity in the public worship, this prelate com-
poses a church-service which becomes universal
throughout the realm, i. 549.

O'TOOLE, in 1540, joined in the rebellion of O'Connor
and other Irish chiefs, ii. 428.

Otterbourne, battle of, gained by the Scots, August
15, 1388; i. 793. View of the battle-field, *ib.*

OTTOBONI, the pope's legate in England; his exertions
in restoring peace between. Henry III. and his
subjects, i. 688.

OVERBURY, sir Thomas, courts the royal favourite,
Robert Carr, iii. 38, 49. Assists Rochester in
writing letters to lady Frances Howard, 53.
Threatens Rochester that he will raise an insuper-
able obstacle to the divorce from Essex if he
attempts to marry her, *ib.* Appointed on an embassy to the great duke of Russia, which he refuses
to undertake, *ib.* Rochester represents him as
insolent and disobedient, and he is consigned to a
dungeon, *ib.*; found dead, September 24, 1613; 54.

OVERKIRK. *See* Auverquerque.

OVERTON, makes an unsuccessful attempt in Scotland,
1655, to raise the country in the royal cause, iii.
420.

OWEN, sir John, a royalist, condemned 1649, but
ultimately spared, iii. 400.

OWEN, Nicholas, a confidential servant of the Jesuit
Garnet, commits suicide to avoid the tortures with
which he was threatened, iii. 520.

OWEN, Thomas, found guilty of high treason, *regno*
James I., for saying that the king, being excommunicated by the pope, might be lawfully deposed
and killed by any one, iii. 57.

OWEN, Dr., a Nonconformist, accused by the duke of
Monmouth, 1683, of being privy to his designs, iii.
754. Portrait of, 803. Vice-chancellor of Oxford,
817.

Oxford, plan of, with the lines raised for its defence
by Charles, from the old print by Antony Wood,
iii. 314. Print of, from a drawing by Hollar, 734.

Oxford, castle of, (fifteenth century), i. 682. View of
the tower of, 432. Matilda was besieged here by
Stephen, and the city burnt, 435.

Oxford, University of, earliest express mention of,
i. 306. Establishment of this school of science
in the twelfth century, 806; highly patronized by
Richard I., and recognized as an establishment of
the same kind with the University of Paris, *ib.*
Decrease of students from 30,000 to 6,000, in 1357;
ii. 196. Opinion of the University that the first
marriage of Henry VIII. was illegal; sealed declaration obtained after the display of a turbulent
spirit, as narrated to the king by bishop Longland,
375, 376.

Oxford Society, the, originated about the middle of the
seventeenth century, iv. 773.

OXFORD, countess of, mother of the hapless Robert de
Vere, duke of Ireland; she credits the renewed
report, 1404, of Richard II. being alive in Scotland,
for which she was shut up in close prison, ii. 16.

OXFORD, John de Vere, earl of, 1464, the only Lancastrian noble who escaped from the carnage at
Barnet, 1471; ii. 109. He then joined the earl of
Pembroke in Wales, *ib.* He was imprisoned
after the triumph of Edward IV., 110, and attainted,
1474. Released by sir W. Blount, he commanded
the advanced guard of Richmond at Bosworth,
1485, and sustained the vigorous attack of Norfolk,
129. His attainder reversed, 1 Henry VII., 283.
He and lord Danbeny defeated the insurgents, June
22, 1497, at Blackheath, 306. He pronounced judgment, as lord-steward, 1499, on the unhappy earl of
Warwick, 310. He died, 1513.

OXFORD, Henry de Vere, earl of, 1604. He died,
1625; iii. 68.

OXFORD, Robert Harley, earl of, created, 1711; iv.
49, 92, 135. Is elected speaker of the House of
Commons, 1701; iv. 112; and again chosen, 1702;
146. Becomes chief secretary of state, 1704; 160. Is
dismissed, 1708, and succeeded by Mr. Henry

OXFORD, Robert Harley, earl of,—
Boyle, 216. Is stabbed by Guiscard, a Frenchman, 1711. Created earl of Oxford and earl Mortimer, 1711; 252. Portrait of, 658. He moves for a bill for the further security of the Protestant succession, to make it high treason to bring any foreign troops into the kingdom, 1714; 284. The queen commands him to resign his treasurer's staff, 299. He is tried for high treason, 1717; 339. And acquitted, 340. He died, 1724.

Oxymuriatic acid, or chlorine, discovered, 1774, by Scheele, a celebrated Swedish chemist, § iii. 710. Its application in the process of bleaching, ib.

PACE, Richard ; his missions from Henry VIII. to the Diet of Frankfort, 1519 ; ii. 336. Allusions to Pace, 343, note.

PACE, sir Christopher, suggests, 1657, that the Lord-Protector should be desired to assume the name of king, iii. 421.

Paganism.—Roman and heathen temples in Britain, i. 72.

Pageant, account of a, exhibited before James I. and Christian IV. of Denmark, iii. 627. Scottish pageant at the baptism of James VI., 644.

PAGET, lord, dispatched to Carlowitz, 1698; iv. 92. His embassy to Hanover, 1714; 287.

PAGET, sir William, is sent over, 1549, to renew the treaty of peace with Germany which had been made in the reign of Henry VIII., ii. 489.

PAINE, Thomas, a celebrated political and deistical writer, born in 1737. In 1776, he produced his celebrated pamphlet, entitled "Common Sense," which was of considerable benefit to the colonial cause. Publishes his "Rights of Man" in 1791, 1792. The legislature of Philadelphia vote him 500l.; § i. 264, 265, 394, 395, 449; § ii. 447, 497, 578. His constant attendance in the hall of the Jacobins, 660. His portrait, 690. His opinion respecting the proper course to be pursued against Louis XVI., 1792; § iii. 213. He recommends that some mercy should be shown to the king, 243, 247. He is expelled from the Convention, June, 1793, and subsequently thrown into prison, 421. He is released by the Thermidorians, December, 1794.

Painting, i. 631; ii. 851—854; iii. 567—569; iv. 735, 752—757; § i. 623—630; § iv. 711—715.

PAKENHAM, general sir Edward; his endeavours to dislodge the American army from its position before New Orleans proves ineffectual; Pakenham is killed, and the English army retires, January, 1815; § iv. 673*, 674*.

Palais Royal, view of the, § ii. 482.

Palatinate, the ; ruined by the frequent wars on the Rhine; many of the Protestant Germans resolved to emigrate in a considerable body to other countries, where their industrious mode of life might obtain a securer reward, iv. 229. The "Palatines" who came to England, with the sanction of queen Anne, 1707, pitched their peaceable tents to the number of 5,000, on Blackheath, ib. Obtaining employment, a reduction of the English labourer's wages occasioned a popular clamour, 229, 230. The Tories increased, intentionally, the effervescence, and despite a severe winter and high price of wheat, refused all charitable assistance to those unhoused wanderers, 230. Some good and independent men, compassionating the emigrants, both Catholics and Protestants, continuing to arrive, relieved them, shipped numbers for North America, ib. The rest settling themselves in Ireland and some English counties, they ceased to form an isolated mass of immigrants, ib.

PALEY, William, a celebrated divine and philosopher, and author of many excellent works; born, 1743, died, May 25, 1805; § iii. 730. His portrait, ib.

PALGRAVE, sir Francis, on the Municipal Institutions of the Anglo-Saxons, i. 87, 248—257, 350, 351, 572, 575.

Pall-mall in St. James's-park, iii. 641.

PALLADIO, Andrea, one of the greatest classical architects in modern Italy, was born at Vicenza, 1518, and died in 1580 ; iii. 570.

PALLISER, sir Hugh; his trial by court-martial for disobedience, etc., 1779; § i. 347, 348, 377, 378, 442.

PALM, M., the German resident at London, is ordered to quit the kingdom, 1727 ; iv. 390.

Palm-Sunday, previously to the Reformation held as a religious festival throughout Europe, ii. 896—898.

PALMER, sir Geoffrey, an eminent lawyer of the seventeenth century, iii. 517, 688.

PALMER, John, the first projector of mail-coaches; his great plan of reform in the Post-office was adopted in 1784, when he was made the comptroller, with a salary of 1,500l. a year. He was suspended in 1792, and died in 1818 ; § i. 571.

PALMER, Roger. See earl of Castlemaine.

PALMER, sir Thomas, 1548; ii. 469 ; said to have accused the duke of Somerset of designing an insurrection, 495. He denied having made the statement, 1551; but was nevertheless placed in custody, 496. Executed as a traitor, 1553; 506.

PALMER, Mr., M. P., committed to the Tower, Nov. 23, 1641; iii. 256.

Pamplona, View of, § iv. 573 ; invested, ib. Surrenders Oct. 31, 1813 ; 583.

PANDULPH, the pope's legate, arrives in England, and persuades the king to consent to the commands of pope Innocent. John surrenders his kingdom to the pope, May 15, 1213 ; i. 524.

PANTALEON SA, brother of the Portuguese ambassador, is executed for murder on Tower-hill, July 10, 1654; iii. 416.

PANZANI, Gregorio, an envoy from the Vatican, courteously received by king Charles, 1638 ; iii. 167.

PAOLI, Pasquale de, begs the interference of England in behalf of Corsica, 1768; § i. 64. Is banished, 1769. Recalled to France, 1789, § iii. 394. His portrait, ib. Heads the Corsican insurrection of 1793; 399.

Paper, made of cotton, in common use in the 12th century, though no evidence exists that that manufactured from linen rags was known till about the middle of the 13th, i. 611 ; iv. 712. Paper manufacture, (18th century,) § iii. 713. Marbled paper, ib.

PAPILLON, nominated a sheriff of London, 1681 ; iii. 739.

Papists. See Catholics.

Paris, besieged by the Danes, 886—888 ; i. 162. Reign of Charles VI. Rivalry of the French princes for the government of the capital; Charles VI. being imbecile, discord, tumults, assassinations, sieges, and changes of masters, 1400, et seq. ; ii. 9, 13, 20, 28, 36, 38, 42, 46, 48, 50. Affairs of, in the time of Charles VII., 72, 73, 78. The Parisians rise, and the English garrison capitulates, 1436; 79. Paris entered by the Allies, March 31, 1814 ; § iv. 615*. Peace of Paris, and general settlement of Europe, May 30, 1814 ; § iv. 618*, et seq. View of, 630*.

PARIS, Matthew, the English historian, i. 522, 576. Portrait of, from a drawing by himself, 847.

PARIS, a Frenchman, executed on a charge of being concerned in Darnley's murder, 1569 ; ii. 625.

PARKER, sir Hyde, commander-in-chief at the battle of Copenhagen, April 2, 1801; § iii. 551*. He is recalled, May 5, 554*.

PARKER, Dr. Matthew, archbishop of Canterbury, elected 1559, his adventures with the rebels of 1549; ii. 486. His persecution of the Puritans, 635, 743. He recommends the execution of Mary queen of Scots, 648. He dies, 1575, and is succeeded by Grindal, 744.

PARKER, sir Peter, portrait of, § i. 263.

PARKER, Richard, hanged, June 30, 1797, for inciting the sailors at Sheerness to mutiny, § iii. 521, 522.

PARKER, Samuel, bishop of Oxford, consecrated 1686. James issues a mandate, 1687, to the fellows of Magdalen College to elect him master, which they refuse to do. He died, March, 1688; iii. 787.

PARKER, a Jacobite spy, committed to prison, 1694; iv. 64.

Parliament.—Form of holding parliaments in the early Norman period, i. 809, 810. A regular parliament was held in 1262; 810. Parliaments generally assembled for the imposition of taxes. In 1376-7, sir Peter de la Mare, speaker, being arrested, the Commons demanded, in right of Magna Charta, that he should be liberated or put upon his trial, 780. First parliament of Henry IV., 1399; ii. 140. Henry VI.—Indignant at the policy and behaviour of the minister Suffolk, 1450, the Commons impeached that duke, and he was exiled by the king beyond sea, 86. Henry VI. being found totally imbecile, York is declared Protector of the Realm, 1454, and the obnoxious minister Somerset, sent to the Tower, 91, 92. The infant prince Edward, 1453-4, created prince of Wales, 92, 96. The Commons, 1454, requested the peers to provide a protector, in case of the recurrence of the king's malady. The prelates maintained that by ancient custom this was their privilege, but the lay peers listened to the Commons. York was again declared protector, to act as such until discharged from the duty by the peers, 92. The peers reinstate king Henry, 93. Henry VII.—His first parliament met 7th November, 1485, the members of the Commons having been elected immediately after the decisive battle of Bosworth, 283. A question of the legality of the new Lower House was mooted; the new king himself and many of the elected members being under attaint, not yet reversed, reference was had to the judges of the land, ib. The decision was, that the actual possession of the crown removed prescriptively the royal attaint,—and that, as to the members under attainder by the two preceding sovereigns, they should not sit nor vote, till bills, reversing their several attainders, had passed, ib. First parliament of Henry VIII., 1512, voted supplies for the French war, 320. Subserviency of his parliaments from 1532, remarkable at the epoch of Henry's divorces, new marriages, etc., 378. The Commons voted supplies and subsidies, poll-tax, etc., for the French wars, 1512; 320, 321, 355. Wolsey repaired in state to the House of Commons, contrary to its privileges, to demand a property-tax; the members preserved an obstinate silence till he retired; afterwards the House granted ten per cent. on property, 354, 355. More, as chancellor, with twelve peers, spiritual and temporal, informed the Lower House of the justice of the king's desire to be divorced from Catherine of Arragon, 1532, and caused the opinions of twelve universities to be read, 378. Excepting in money-bills, the now frequent parliaments implicitly obeyed Cromwell and the court, ib. Elizabeth,—The Commons declared that Elizabeth had violated their *privileges*, 1567, by commanding the Puritan Strickland to absent himself, 655. The queen thought it prudent to yield, and the House thus maintained its privilege, ib. James I.—Election for Buckinghamshire, 1604, sir F. Goodwin and sir John Fortescue, iii. 18. Goodwin returned, though formerly an outlaw. His return was sent back to the sheriff, and Fortescue was returned; the House of Commons considered their privileges violated; they refused a conference demanded by the Lords, and enforced by a royal message, ib. The House appeared before the judges in the king's presence, when both elections were by a compromise declared void, and a new writ issued, 19. Statutes, attainders, trials, enactments, and debates,

Parliament,— 1604—1616, iii. 18—25, 32. The *Gunpowder Plot*, narrated, 20—33, etc. James's first parliament swarmed with Puritans; refractory spirit of the Commons; Buckinghamshire election; wardships, purveyance, monopolies, etc. 18, 19. The Commons complain, 1610, of the delay of law in granting writs of prohibition and Habeas Corpus, and of other grievances, 42, 43. Parliamentary privileges, iv. 665—669.

STATUTES.

1217. The Charter of Forests granted, i. 675. Confirmations of this Charter, 1224; 812, 813.

1224. The Charter of the Forest, 812, *note.* Confirmed by Edward I., 812.

1275. Statute of Westminster, the First, 816, 817.

1279. The Statute, entitled " De Viris Religiosis," was passed. The object of this law was to enforce and to extend a provision of Magna Charta, which prohibited all gifts of land to religious societies without the consent of the lord of the fee, 815.

1284. "Statuta Walliæ." By this Act Wales was in a great measure put on the same footing as England with respect to its laws and their administration, 813.

1285. A famous collection of laws passed in the 13th of Edward I., commonly known by the name of the Statute of Westminster the Second; its enactments, 815, 816. The Statute of Winchester passed. It contained some provisions for enforcing the ancient police, and also enacted that the people of the county should be answerable for the felonies done among them; that the walls of the great towns should be shut from sun-setting to sun-rising; and that the highways should be cleared of wood to the breadth of two hundred feet. 816, 817.

1290. The Statute, called " Quia Emptores," passed, 817.

1297. September. The important Statute, called " De Tallagio non Concedendo," passed, by which it was determined that no tallage or aid should be levied without assent of the peers, spiritual and temporal, the knights, burgesses, and other free men of the realm, 721. This Charter was confirmed, 1306, in more explicit terms, 813.

1300. An Act passed confirming the privileges of the Great Charters, and appointing three knights in every shire to decide on all cases respecting the infringement of these rights, and to punish the offenders, 813.

1305. The Act, "Ordinatio Forestæ," passed, 813.

1311. August. An Act passed, that parliament should be holden once every year; that the king should not leave the kingdom, or make war without the consent of the baronage; that parliament should appoint a guardian or regent during the royal absence; and that all the great officers of the crown, and governors of foreign possessions, should at all times be chosen by the advice and assent of parliament, 733.

1352. The Statute of Treasons passed. This is the most important statute of Edward III.'s reign, and defines the charges of treason, 820.

1363. Act ordaining that henceforth pleas should be held in the English tongue, and enrolled in Latin, 820. Acts for restraining the use of excessive apparel, ii. 272, 273.

1399. Appeals of Treason in parliament abolished; other Statutes, 5. Act to abolish badges of retainers of the nobles, 6.

1401. For the punishment of heresy, 140, 141.

1413, 1414. Statutes against the Lollards, etc., 25, 26.

1415. Subsidies on wool and leather, 34.

1459. November. Acts of attainder against the duke and duchess of York, their sons, Salisbury, his countess, Warwick and Clinton, 94. These acts of

Statutes,—
attainder were reversed, 95. Deliberations on the succession to the throne, at the demand of Richard, duke of York, 95.

1461. Act, declaring Edward of York's just title by descent, 99. This act declared Henry IV., Henry V., and Henry VI. to have been usurpers, and resumed all grants made by those three monarchs, 100. Bills of attainder passed against Henry VI., his queen and son, Somerset, Exeter, Northumberland, Devonshire, Nevil, Dacre, and a number of Lancastrian lords and esquires, ib.

1485. Acts, to relieve the members of the House of Commons from attaint, 283. To *antedate* Henry's reign by one day, that his enemies, in the battle of Bosworth, might be attainted for *high treason*, ib. To attaint Richard of Gloucester, John of Norfolk, and about thirty of the Yorkist leaders, 284. To settle the crown and the succession, ib. To revoke the Bastardy Act against the children of Edward, IV., ib. This latter act was burnt, and all persons commanded to destroy any copy thereof, ib. All records of Henry's own attainder removed from the Rolls, ib. Grant of tonnage and poundage for the king's life, ib.

1530. Statute against Egyptians, (Gipsies,) 759.

1531. The old Statutes of *Præmunire* were enforced against the clergy in a body for having acknowledged Wolsey as legate, 377, 378.

1532-3. Act for paving the streets of London, 781. Abolition of annates, or first-fruits to Rome, 378. Annexation to the Crown of the authority of the clergy in Convocation, 378. Declaring that Catherine of Arragon should be restricted to the title of dowager-princess of Wales, and that none should call her queen, 380.

1534. First-fruits and tenths annexed to the crown, 386. A new oath of supremacy to be taken by the bishops, 386. Act investing the king with power to *define and punish heresies,* ib.

1536. Act entailing the crown on king Henry's issue by Jane Seymour : also empowering Henry VIII., by letters-patent or by will, to name and appoint his successor, 395. Granting monastic houses, whose revenues did not exceed 200l. a year, with all their property, real or personal, to the king and his heirs, 396. Statute of Uses, 397.

1539. The Six Articles, or the Bloody Statute, passed, 410, 725, 730. Repealed, 1547, by Edward VI., 467.

1547. Act passed, ordaining that in the sacrament the cup be delivered to the laity as well as to the clergy ; as also an Act for putting an end to the election of bishops by *congé d'élire*, 467. In the same year a bill was brought in for making over to the Crown all chantries, colleges, and free chapels that yet remained unconfiscated, ib.

1549. Act permitting the marriage of clergy, 470, 471. This was followed by an act establishing the use of the reformed liturgy; and an enactment touching abstinence from flesh in Lent and other usual times, 471.

1552. Acts for enforcing the use of the Book of Common-prayer; for amending the law of treason; for observing fast days and holy days; for the relief of the poor; for legalising the marriage of priests, and legitimatising their children; besides several others relating to trade and manufacture, 498.

1571. Acts, declaring it high treason to claim a right to the succession of the crown during the queen's life. Enacting the pains of treason against all who should obtain or put in use any bull or instrument from the bishop of Rome; obliging all persons above a certain age to attend the Protestant church regularly; commanding every person who had left or might leave the realm, with or without license, to return in six months, after warning by

Statutes,—
proclamation, under pain of forfeiture of his estates, 633, 740.

1585. Act passed against Jesuits, 740.

1627. The writ of *Hubeas Corpus*, sued by the subject against the Crown, iii. 834. *Vide Habeas Corpus*.

1645. Act abolishing the Court of Wards and Liveries, 832.

1648. Act for the regulation of the officers of the navy and customs, 832.

1650. Act ordaining that all law-books shall be translated into the English tongue, 831. Act abolishing the *damna clericorum*, 831.

1652. Act abolishing the Court of Chancery, 832.

1653. Act establishing a register of marriages, births, and burials, 832.

1654. Act prohibiting cock-matches and duels, 832.

1660. Act giving a new establishing to the Post-office, 865.

1661. Act against tumults and disorders upon pretence of preparing public petitions, 833.

1662. Act for repairing the highways in London, 866. Act for sweeping the streets, 867. Act for lighting the streets, ib. Act requiring silk-throwsters to serve an apprenticeship of seven years, 869. Act prohibiting the importation of foreign bone-lace, etc., 870. Act reducing the labouring population of England to their ancient condition of *ascripti glebæ*, 906.

1663. Act regulating the Post-office revenue, 865.

1665. Act passed for encouraging the manufacture of linen cloth and tapestry, 869.

1678. Act prohibiting trade with France, 858.

1689. November 16. The Bill of Rights, iv. 19. Land-tax Act, ib.

1690. Act of Grace, 20.

1699. Act for the further preventing the growth of popery, 634.

1714-15. The Riot Act, § iii. 609.

1715. Act compelling all papists of the age of twenty-one years to register their names and estates, with the yearly rent, in books, to be kept by the clerk of the peace for every county, 636.

1716. Act regulating the lighting of the city, 855, 856.

1784-5. Act for the more easy and effectual sale of lands, etc., 605.

1792. Act for regulating the police of the metropolis, 11.

1797. Act laying additional duties upon articles of gold and silver plate, 687.

1797-8. Act for the administration of assets, 606.

1800. The Monastic Institutions Bill, 593—596.

1800-1. The General Inclosure Act passed, § iv. 634.

1801. Act disqualifying persons in holy orders to sit in the House of Commons, 596.

1802-3. "Lord Ellenborough's Act," concerning cases of capital felony, 640.

1806. May. The Limited Service Bill, passed. The Additional Force Bill repealed, and Mr. Windham's plan for limited service introduced by way of clause, in the Annual Mutiny Bill, 214.

1807. Bill for the Abolition of the Slave-trade passed, 257—259.

1811-12. Act for the relief of infant suitors in courts of equity, 635.

1811-12. Act on the subject of violations of the revenue laws, 639.

1812-13. Acts for the relief of Dissenters, etc., 615.

1814-15. The General Stamp Act, 636.

1819. Peel's Act passed, authorising the Bank of England to recommence cash payments in 1823; 670.

1834. The Veto Act, 608.

PARMA, duchess of, regent of the Netherlands for Philip II. of Spain, ii. 620.

PAROTT, sir James, sent on a commission to Ireland, 1622; iii. 88.

PARR, Catherine, (widow of lord Latimer,) became in 1543 the sixth queen of Henry VIII., although professing the Reformed religion, ii. 438. Her life menaced by the king on that account, was saved by her prudent submission, and a reconciliation took place, 438, 447.

PARR, William, earl of Essex. *See* Northampton.

PARRY, sir John, one of the commissioners appointed, 1613, to inquire into the divorce of the earl of Essex, iii. 53.

PARRY, Dr., executed as a traitor, 1585; ii. 655, 656.

PARSONS, sir William, one of the lords justices of Ireland, 1641; iii. 253.

PARSONS, a celebrated Jesuit, 1606; controversy on the new Oath of Allegiance, iii. 33.

Partition Treaty, the first, 1698; iv. 87—92. The second, 1700; 108 - 112.

Partition Treaty, the first, of Poland, signed at St. Petersburg, August 2, 1772; § i. 145. Final dismemberment of Poland between Prussia, Russia, and Austria, October, 1795; § iii. 462.

PASCAL II. pope, (Rainer abbot of S. Lorenzo fuori le mura,) elected August 13, 1099. The question concerning the investiture and homage of archbishop Anselm is referred to him; he decides in favour of the church, i. 551. Anselm again goes to Rome, 1103; *ib.* It is decided that the bishops and abbots should do homage for the temporalities of their sees to the king, but the investiture with ring and crozier should not be insisted on; Anselm again returns to England, August 1106. His death, 1109, in the seventy-sixth year of his age, 552. Pascal died the 18th or 21st of January, 1118.

PASS, Crispin, an engraver, settled in England in the seventeenth century; he executed numerous plates, iii. 577.

Passaro, Cape, battle off, August 11, 1718; iv. 346, 347.

Paston Letters, the, their great interest in elucidating the state of society, from 1440 to 1455, also in many historical questions, ii. 145, 275.

PASTON, John, his son, died, 1466; ii. 275.

PASTON, sir John, Lancastrian, at the field of Barnet, 1471; ii. 109, *note*, 275.

PASTON, sir John, in 1487, at the battle of Stoke; lived till 1503; ii. 275. His letter to his mother after the battle of Tewkesbury, 279.

PASTON, Margaret, ii. 145.

PASTON, sir William, knight, a justice of the Common Pleas, died 1444; ii. 275. Ancestor of the earls of Yarmouth, *ib.*

Patay.—The English defeated in this battle, 1429; Talbot, Hungerford, and Scales prisoners, ii. 68.

PATERSON, William,—The Bank of England founded principally through the exertions of, iv. 692.

PATERSON, proposes to make a Scottish colony on the Isthmus of Darien, 1695; iv. 54, 83. Sails from Leith Roads with 1,200 men, 95. Loses all his men by famine, etc., and on his return to Scotland becomes insane, 1699; 99.

Patna, view of, § ii. 56.

PATON, bishop of Dunkeld, enjoined penance by the Assembly, 1572, for not having executed sentence of excommunication against the earl of Athole and his lady, who were papists, iii. 438.

PATRICK, St., 422, converted the Irish to Christianity, i. 229.

PATTEN, his vivid description of the invasion of Scotland, 1547, by Edward, duke of Somerset, ii. 459—463.

PAUL III., pope, (Alexander Farnese, bishop of Ostia,) elected October 13, 1534; finding that Henry VIII. kept no measures of submission to the see of Rome, signed, August 30, 1535, a bull, containing many articles of punishment of the English

PAUL III.,—

king, yet reserved the bull for promulgation at a future season, (*see* Henry VIII.,) ii. 389. He cited Henry VIII. to Rome to answer for his evil actions, 1535; declared his treaties with Christian princes void, and absolved his subjects from their oaths of allegiance, *ib.* He appointed, in 1536, cardinal Pole to be legate beyond the Alps, 401. This pope having sent to Dr. Fisher, while in the Tower, a cardinal's hat, Henry exclaimed that Paul might send the hat, but he would not leave the bishop a head to wear it, 386. Paul died, November 10, 1549.

PAUL IV., pope (Giampietro Caraffa, archbishop of Chieti,) elected, May 23, 1555; the tribunal of the Inquisition first established by his advice, when cardinal Caraffa, under the pontificate of Paul III., 531, *note*. He opens negotiations with France on the accession of Philip II. to the Spanish throne, 531. Throws into prison Garcilasso de la Vega, who was the ambassador at Rome from king Philip, in his quality of king of England, 532. When Elizabeth notified to him her accession to the throne, he arrogantly replied that he looked upon her as illegitimate, and that she ought to lay down the government, and expect what he might decide, 543. He died, August 18, 1559.

PAUL V., pope (Camillo Borghese,) elected May 16, 1605. His bull, 1606, against the Oath of Allegiance tendered by king James to his Catholic subjects; he died, January 28, 1621; iii. 33.

PAUL I. (1796—1801,) emperor of Russia, son of Catherine II., by her husband Peter III., born 1754; § i. 22. Succeeds to the throne, November, 1796, on the death of the czarina, § iii. 544. Is murdered by his officers, March 24, 1801; 553*.

Paul's School, founded by dean Colet, 1509; the first celebrated master for the Greek language, 1512, being the grammarian Lilly, ii. 815.

Paul's Walk, *Illustration* of, iii. 637.

PAULET, sir Amias, some account of, 1514; ii. 333, 658, 668.

Pavia, sieges, battles, government, and various transactions, ii. 358.

Paving.—Act passed 1532, 1533, for paving the streets of London, ii. 781.

PEACHAM, Edmond, minister of the gospel, in Somersetshire, accused of high treason, iii. 56, and condemned August 7, 1615; 57; died in Taunton gaol a few months after, *ib.*

PEACOCK, or Pocock, Reginald, bishop of Chichester, 1450; his learning, zeal, and writings, patronised by Humphrey, duke of Gloucester, ii. 147. In 1457 he had to answer for certain heresies before cardinal Bourchier, 147, 148. He was no persecutor of the followers of Wycliffe, like the other prelates, 148. He denied the infallibility of the church, *ib.* He was condemned to die, but read his abjuration at Paul's-cross, and delivered his own books to be burnt, *ib.* He was confined in Thorney Abbey, where in three years he died, *ib.* Great merit of the few of his works that escaped the burning of the chief portion of his writings, *ib.*

PEACOCK, Samuel, warrant issued for his trial by torture, 1620; iii. 518.

Pearls, British, i. 26. The mussel producing the pearls of Britain and Caledonia described, mode of fishing for them, etc., 106, 107.

PECHELL, vice-chancellor of Cambridge, suspended by the Ecclesiastical Commission Court, 1687; iii. 736.

PECKHAM, John, a learned mathematician of the thirteenth century; made archbishop of Canterbury, March 1278, died, December 1292; i. 844.

PEDRO, IV., surnamed the "Cruel," king of Castile, driven from his throne, 1366, by Don Enrique, count of Trastamara, but restored by Edward the

PEDRO IV.,—
Black Prince, i. 776, 777. Two of his daughters are married to Edward's brothers, the duke of Lancaster and the earl of Cambridge, 776. He is stabbed by his bastard brother, Don Enrique, 1367, who seizes the government, 777.

PEELE, George, a dramatic writer of the 16th century. iii. 585, 601.

PELAGIUS, an Irish monk, some of his controversial writings extant, i. 124. His heretical opinions and doctrines, ib. His disciple Celestius, ib. They flourished about the year 400, ib.

PELHAM, Mr., alderman of Hull, 1642; iii. 279.

PELHAM. Mr., becomes first lord of the Treasury on the death of the earl of Wilmington, 1743; iv. 467. He introduces a bill for the naturalization of foreign Jews, 1753; 577. Dies suddenly, March 6, 1754; 580.

PEMBROKE, Richard de Clare, earl of, 1149, surnamed "Strongbow," engages to restore Mac Murrogh, king of Leinster, to his dominions, 1167; i. 461, 462. Embarks at Milford Haven with a large force, and lands near Waterford; the city is attacked and taken; Strongbow marries Eva, the daughter of Mac Murrogh; Dublin is taken, and Meath is overrun, 464. On the death of Mac Murrogh, Pembroke assumes the title of king of Leinster, 1170; 465. He routs the army of Roderick, who had invested Dublin, 465, 466. He delivers up Dublin, and other forts to the king, and holds the rest in subjection to the English crown, ib. He died, 1176.

PEMBROKE, William Marshal, earl of, 1189. Appointed one of king John's sureties, 1214; i. 527. Accompanies the king at Runnymede, at the signing of Magna Charta, ib. Marshal of England. After the burial of John he marches with the royal army and prince Henry to Gloucester, where Henry is crowned, October 28th, 1216; 671. He assumes the title of regent, ib. Lays siege to the castle of Mount Sorel, and defeats the count of Perche at Lincoln, May 20th, 1217; 673. After this battle the cause of the French prince declined, and on the 11th of September a peace was concluded, and Louis returned to France, 674. In May, 1219, this excellent protector died, and was buried in the church of the Knights Templars, 675.

PEMBROKE, Aylmer de Valence, earl of, appointed guardian of Scotland by Edward I., i. 728. Defeats Bruce at Methven, June 19, 1306; 729. He died 1323.

PEMBROKE, Jasper Tudor, earl of, 1452, uncle of Henry earl of Richmond; his defeat at Mortimer's Cross, Hereford, 1461, by Edward of York, ii. 96. His father, Owen Tudor, captured in the action, was beheaded, ib. Pembroke attainted, 1462; 100. Defeated at Edgecote, 1469; 104. He retired to the Continent, 1471; 110. Imprisoned far fifteen years by Francis II., duke of Brittany, together with his nephew, Henry Tudor, earl of Richmond, 110, 126. He was created by Henry VII., 1485, duke of Bedford, 282, and his old attainder reversed, 283. He died, 1495.

PEMBROKE, William Herbert, earl of, 1601. He died, 1630; iii. 146.

PEMBROKE, Philip Herbert, earl of, 1630, a favourite of James I.; created earl of Montgomery, 1605; is struck on a race-course at Croydon by the viscount Haddington, iii. 37. Courts Robert Carr, the new favourite, and by that means secures a continuance of favour to himself, 38, 146. Becomes earl of Pembroke on the death of his brother, 1630. He presents the final propositions of the parliament to king Charles at Newcastle, July 6, 1646. He died, 1650; 358.

PEMBROKE, Thomas Herbert, earl of, disperses a party of men assembled in the cause of the duke of Monmouth, 1685; iii. 774. Is made president of the

PEMBROKE, Thomas Herbert,—
council, 1699; iv. 95. Resigns both the presidency and the lord-lieutenancy of Ireland, 1708, and is made lord high-admiral. He died, 1733; 222.

PENDERTON, sheriff of London, 1603; iii. 3.

PENALVA, countess of, an attendant of Catherine of Braganza, queen of Charles II., is permitted to remain at court on account of indisposition of health, when all the queen's other Portuguese servants were dismissed, iii. 687.

PENDERGRAST, informs lord Portland, February 14, 1696, of a plot for assassinating William III. iv. 66.

PENDLETON. Dr., a Catholic, preaching at Paul's-cross, 1554, shot at and nearly killed, ii. 519. This instance of the desperation of many Protestants was accompanied by some extravagant demonstrations—a cat shorn as a priest, hanged on a gallows in Cheapside; also the "Spirit in the Wall," etc., ib.

Penitentiary House, Millbank, Act for the erection of, 1812; § iii. 613.

PENN, Thomas, petition of, 1774, in behalf of himself and his brother, John Penn, § i. 169.

PENN, vice-admiral, takes the important island of Jamaica, 1656; iii. 420, 696.

PENNINGTON, vice-admiral, petitions, 1625, not to be sent to serve against the Huguenots, iii. 112.

PENRUDDOCK, captain, executed 1655, for joining in a plot for the restoration of Charles II., iii. 419.

Pension Bill, the, 1730; iv. 404.

PENTHIÈVRE, count of, 1450, invaded Guienne; Bordeaux, Blaye, and Bayonne were taken from the English, ii. 85. He defeated old Talbot, at Châtillon, 1453, who fell in action, 91.

People, History of the Condition of the, to A. D. 449; or, eras of the Britons and of the Romans, i. 135. The Saxons, from 449 to 1066; 346. The English and Normans, from 1066 to 1216; 658. From 1216 to 1399; 882. From 1399 to 1485; ii. 268. From 1485 to 1603; 899. From 1603 to 1660; iii. 650. From 1660 to 1689; 905. From 1688 to 1760; iv. 841. Reign of George III., from 1760 to 1785; § i. 679. From 1785 to 1802; § iii. 767. From 1802 to 1820; § iv. 727.

PEPPER, general, arrives in Oxford, 1715, with an army, and arrests several persons suspected of being in the service of the Pretender, iv. 313.

PEPUSCH, Dr., publishes, 1731, a "Treatise on Harmony," iv. 764.

PEPYS, Roger, chief-justice in Ireland, iii. 506. In his youth he was a great Cromwellian, though after the Restoration he obtained preferment at court, 678, note. Quoted, 677, 678, note; 701, 704, et passim.

PERCEVAL, lord, expresses his intention, 1741, to move for a committee of accusation against the minister Walpole, iv. 456.

PEACHE, Marie, countess of, half-sister of prince William, i. 414.

PERCIVAL, right hon. Spencer, first lord of the Treasury and chancellor of the Exchequer, 1809—1812; shot by an insane merchant, named Bellingham, in the lobby of the House of Commons, May 11, 1812; § iv. 499.

PERCY. See Northumberland.

PERCY, Henry, denominated for his prompt valour Hotspur, taken prisoner at the battle of Otterbourne, 1388; i. 793. Totally defeats earl Douglas at Homildon-hill, Northumberland, 1402; ii. 11. The Scotch earl, receiving many wounds, remains captive in Percy's hands, besides many nobles, ib. Loss of the Scots on the battle-field, or drowned in the Tweed, ib. Hotspur's wife was sister of sir Edmund Mortimer, who had been made prisoner by the gallant Owen Glendower, 11, 13. In 1403 he marches, with confederates, against the king, whose army was in Shropshire, 14. He transmits the

Percy, Henry,—
defiance of the Percies to Henry IV., *ib.* Terms of this declaration, *ib.* Battle of Shrewsbury, 21st July, *ib.* Irresistible charge by Percy and Douglas, 15. They were unable to find the king, but slay sir Walter Blount and the earl of Stafford, who wore the royal arms, *ib.* They break through the king's line, which closes up, and Percy is unable to retire to his main body, *ib.* Hotspur being slain by an arrow, his army took to flight, *ib.* Account of the captives and slain, *ib.*

Percy, sir Charles, commissioned, March, 1603, to announce to James I., then in Edinburgh, his accession to the English crown, iii. 2.

Percy, sir Jocelyn, a papist, 1642; iii. 282.

Percy, Thomas, steward to his distant relative the earl of Northumberland, iii. 21. Takes the oath of secrecy from Catesby, and joins the Gunpowder Conspiracy, 1605; *ib.* Having an appointment about court, he is selected to hire a house adjoining the Parliament-house, 22. Also Bright's cellar, or coal-warehouse, under the House of Lords, a depository for the gunpowder, 23, 27. His wish to save the earl of Northumberland, 25. He departs, after Fawkes's arrest, for Dunchurch, the rendezvous of Digby's friends, 27, 28. The Catholic gentry invited for a hunting-party, abandon the company of all the conspirators, now so discomfited; Percy, Digby, Catesby, and Rookwood, escape to Grant's house of Norbrook, 28. Percy is wounded at Holbeach, and dies there, *ib.*

Percy, general, a royalist officer at the battle of Chalgrove-field, June 18, 1643; iii. 304.

Percy, bishop, quoted; i. 9, 10, 22.

Perkins, sir William, concerned in a conspiracy for William III., 1696; iv. 64.

Perpignan, View of the Gate of, § iii. 296.

Perrers, Alice, a favourite of Edward III. He makes her a grant of his late queen's jewels, 1376. An Act passes, forbidding women to be guilty of maintenance, 779. She is banished, 1377, after the death of the king, and all her effects are forfeited, 783.

Persia, its connection with Britain, i. 36.

Person, Anthony, burnt, 1543; ii. 728.

Perth, View of, iv. 316.

Perth, duke of, commander of the Young Pretender's army, 1745. Generally disliked by the Highlanders on account of his Romish tenets, iv. 510.

Pescara, an eminent general of Charles V., co-operating with Bourbon, retired across Lombardy before the French army, 1524; ii. 358. He totally defeated Francis I., 1525, and that monarch became his prisoner at Pavia, 359. Consequences of his great victory, *ib.*

Pest-house, in Tothill-fields, Westminster, from a print by Hollar, iii. 695.

Peter the Great, czar of Russia, 1685—1725. His death, iv. 388.

Peter III. becomes emperor of Russia on the death of his aunt, the czarina Elizabeth, January 5, 1762. His ardent admiration of Frederic the Great, with whom he concludes a treaty, March 16th; § i. 20. He introduces the Prussian discipline and uniform into his own army, and offends the clergy by building Protestant churches; and his remorseless wife Catherine, taking advantage of these circumstances, procures herself to be declared sole empress, 21. Peter is obliged to sign a formal act of abdication, and is shortly after murdered at Robscha, 22, 133.

Peter, surnamed the Hermit, preaches the Crusades, about 1096; i. 400. Predicts king John's death; is hanged, 1213; 524.

Peter of Capua, the pope's legate, mediates a peace between the English and French kings for five years, 1197; i. 513.

Peterborough, Henry Mordaunt, earl of, 1642. Is informed by Dr. King, 1685, of the sudden illness of Charles II., iii. 760. His death, 1697; iv. 179.

Peterborough, earl of. *See* Monmouth.

Peterborough, Charles Mordaunt, earl of, leads the forlorn hope at the battle of Schellenberg, July 2, 1704; iv. 167. Becomes earl of Peterborough on the death of his uncle, 1697; 179. Takes Barcelona, 1705; 179, 180. Presses the siege of Alicant, 1706; 186.

Peters, Hugh, an Independent minister and great advocate of Republicanism, employed by the Dutch, 1653, to try the inclinations of the Rump Parliament for a peace, iii. 407. Is charged, 1660, with having encouraged the soldiers in the execution of the king, and executed, 675, 676.

Pétion de Villeneuve, Jerome, an ultra-Jacobin French Revolutionist, elected president of the tribunal at Chartres, 1790; § i. 519. Portrait of, 674. His insolent conduct to the royal party in their return from the flight to Varennes, 1791; 649, 650. He is elected mayor of Paris, 716. He threatened, 1793, to pursue Robespierre to the guillotine, § iii. 318.

Petit Trianon, View of the Gardens and Palace of the, § ii. 417.

Petition of Right, 1628: iii. 131, 134.

Petitot, John, carried the art of enamel to its highest perfection; he was knighted by Charles I., iii. 569.

Peto, a friar of the order of Observants, 1533, preaching at Greenwich before Henry VIII., reproved the king for his marriage with Anne Boleyn, ii. 381. On the next sabbath, Dr. Curwen in a sermon at Greenwich inveighed against Peto, with a challenge to defend himself in argument, 382. Peto being absent, friar Elstow replied with spirit to Curwen, *ib.* The two friars, before the council, were threatened by Essex with being thrown into the Thames; they declared they feared not death, *ib.* They were banished with all their order, and Dr. Curwen became a bishop, *ib.*

Petre, sir William, 1547, secretary of state, ii. 454.

Petre, father, confessor of James II., iii. 783.

Petty, sir William, estimates the number of Protestants massacred in the Irish insurrection of 1641, at 37,000, iii. 254, *note.* Author of the "Political Arithmetic," published 1676; 855.

Pevensey Castle, William takes possession of, i. 392. Ruins of, 393. Odo besieged here by William, 1087; 394.

Peyton, sir Thomas, his effigy, ii. 247.

Peyton, lady, her effigy in Isleham church, Cambridgeshire, ii. 243.

Philadelphia, View of, § i. 226.

Philharmonic Society, the, formed 1813, § iv. 719.

Philip I., of France, (1060—1108.) Forces William I. to raise the siege of Dol, i. 383. Establishes Robert in the castle of Gerberoy, 384. William goes over to the continent to make war with him, 388; but in the burning of Mantes is bruised by his horse, and dies at Rouen, 1087; 389. Philip assists duke Robert against his brother William, who attempts to seize his duchy of Normandy; a treaty entered into at Caen, 397. William having broken the treaty of Caen, Philip comes to the assistance of Robert, but is bought off by William, who is obliged to return to England to oppose the Welsh, 1094; 399.

Philip II., of France, (1180—1223,) son of Louis VII., a young and active prince, agrees with Henry, 1188, to go on an expedition to the Holy Land, i. 476. Supports prince Richard against his father, 477, 478. His conference with Henry at Bonmoulins, and at La Ferté-Bernard; the pope's legate threatens him with an interdict, 478. He attacks Henry in Anjou, who solicits peace and offers to resign himself to whatever terms Philip and Richard

PHILIP II.,—should propose; Henry pays him twenty thousand marks, and renounces his sovereignty over the town of Berry, and appoints Richard his successor, ib. Expedition of Philip to the Holy Land, 486. He separates from Richard at Lyons, and takes the nearest way to Genoa, where he is again joined by Richard, ib. His doings at Messina, 490, 491. Dispute between the two kings; Richard refuses to marry the French princess Alice, but agrees to restore her dower, and to pay to Philip 2,000 marks per annum for five years, 493. His arrival at Acre, 495; which he takes. Philip returns home, 1191; 497. He accuses Richard of being the instigator of the murder of Conrad, 500. Demands that the princess Alice with her dower should be restored to him, and being refused prepares for an invasion of Normandy, 508; but is deserted by many of the French nobles who refuse to accompany him; the pope threatens him with excommunication, and he is obliged to renounce his enterprise, 509. The princess Alice is betrothed to John, ib. Philip invades Normandy, but is defeated by the earl of Leicester, ib. Richard lands in Normandy, and defeats Philip in several engagements, 511. A peace is agreed upon for five years at the mediation of Peter of Capua, 513. Philip declares war with king John, who had succeeded to the crown on the death of king Richard, 1199, and demands all his continental dominions except Normandy for prince Arthur, 516. Peace concluded, 517. He makes war on Normandy, 518. Death of Arthur, 519. Success of the Bretons and the French king; they advance to Radepont, 520. John returns to England and applies for assistance, the English nobles refuse to follow his standard out of England.—Rouen, Verneuil, and Château Gaillard taken by the French, 1204; all Normandy surrenders together with Brittany, Anjou, Maine, Touraine, and Poictou, Aquitaine alone remaining to the English, 521. John lands with an English army at Rochelle, and takes the castle of Montauban, and then marching to the Loire, burns Angers, ib. He lays siege to Nantes, proposes an accommodation, and flies to England, 1203; ib. A truce of two years agreed upon, ib. Philip is invited by pope Innocent to invade England and dethrone John, 1213; 523. He prepares a large army, and a fleet of 1,700 vessels, ib. John collects all the ships in his dominions, and the English mariners having crossed the channel, take the French squadron at the mouth of the Seine, destroy the ships in the harbour of Fecamp, and burn Dieppe to the ground. 524. The French invasion forbidden by the pope's legate, ib. The earl of Flanders refuses to follow Philip to England, and withdraws his forces; Philip besieges Ghent, on which Ferrand applies for assistance to king John, 525. John's fleet at Portsmouth, consisting of 500 vessels, immediately makes sail for the coast of Flanders, and entirely annihilates the French fleet at Damme, the port of Bruges, although three times more numerous than that of the English, ib. The English joined by the earl of Flanders, after a sharp action with Philip retire to their ships. Philip burns the remainder of his fleet lest it should fall into the enemy's hands, and then hastens into France, ib. A formidable league formed for the partitioning of France, 1214, between king John, Ferrand earl of Flanders, Reynaud earl of Boulogne, and Otho emperor of Germany, 526. The allies are defeated at the battle of Bouvines, and the power of Philip established, July 27, 1214; ib. A truce for five years between England and France, 527. The English barons confined in London send a deputation to Philip offering the crown of England to his eldest son, Louis, 1215; 531. For this expedition see Louis.

PHILIP III. of France, surnamed le Bel, (1270—1265.) Ascends the throne on the death of Louis IX., summons Edward I., as duke of Aquitaine, to appear at Paris, and answer for his offences against his suzerain. Edward sends his brother Edmund to negotiate, who surrenders Gascony for forty days, as a mark of satisfaction to the French king, i. 711. Philip refuses to restore Gascony, and pronounces a judgment of forfeiture, because Edward had not presented himself as a vassal ought, ib. The English king, being fully occupied with his wars in Wales and Scotland, neglects for a time his affairs on the continent. The count d'Artois, having taken the command of the French forces, the English are beaten in several encounters, and finally expelled from all the country, with the exception of a few maritime towns, 712. Philip seizes Guienne, 713. Edward forms a powerful alliance against him; but the war is badly managed, and the English king concludes a peace, 1295, for two years, 721, and afterwards marries Margaret, sister of Philip, and contracts the prince of Wales to Isabella, the king's daughter, 723.

PHILIP VI., of Valois, king of France, (1328—1350,) son of Charles of Valois, i. 757. Receives the homage of Edward III. for his continental dominions, both in 1329 and in 1331, ib. Edward sends a commission to the earl of Brabant and others, to demand the French crown as his right, October 7th, 1337, ib. Prepares for the invasion of France, and lands at Antwerp, July 19, 1338, ib.—(For the particulars of these wars, see EDWARD III.) Philip beheads Oliver de Clisson and twelve other knights without trial, 762. France again invaded by Edward, 764. Battle of Crecy, August 26, 1346; 765—767. Calais taken by the English, August 3, 1347; 769, 770. Philip dies, and is succeeded by John I., 1350; 771.

PHILIP II., of Spain, (1556—1598,) his character, ii. 511. His father, Charles V., proposed the prince of Spain, then a widower, as husband to Mary I. of England, 1553, a contract at first politicly kept secret, ib. January, 1554, a splendid embassy arrived from Spain, and Gardiner, lord-chancellor, announced to the lords, etc, the contemplated marriage, also to the lord-mayor, ib. The government to be entirely vested in the queen, but Philip to assume the style of king of England; articles as to settlement, inheritance, etc, ib. Portrait of Philip, from a painting by Titian, 512. Fears of the English of all parties, 511. Dread of a Spanish Inquisition, ib. The English rise in several places to oppose Philip's marriage with their queen, ib. He arrives in Southampton water, July 19, 1554; 519; passes over to the Continent, 526. He becomes king of Spain through the voluntary resignation of his father, Charles V., 1557; 532. Gains the battle of St. Quintin, 533. On the death of queen Mary, he offers his hand to Elizabeth, 544, and soon after marries the daughter of Henry II., of France, who had been affianced to his own son, warmly recommending to Elizabeth his cousin, the archduke Charles, of Austria, 547. He erects a tribunal in the Netherlands, after the model of the Spanish Inquisition 620. The prince of Orange and the counts of Egmont and Horn place themselves at the head of a confederacy formed in the spring of 1566, for putting down this institution; the duchess of Parma, who governed the provinces in the name of Philip, declares that the Inquisition shall be abolished, ib. The Protestants meet in their places of worship with arms in their hands; the duchess sets forth an edict against these proceedings; in Antwerp they set the regent at defiance, and destroy the images, etc., the Walloon provinces alone being quiet; Philip recalls the duchess of Parma, and dispatches the duke of Alva, who soon reduces the country to

PHILIP II., of Spain,—
obedience, 621. The prince of Condé renews a correspondence with the prince of Orange, and lays a plot for surprising the French king, Charles IX., at Monceaux, but he is saved by his Swiss mercenaries, ib. Philip sends a present of 12,000 crowns to James VI., 653. He animates his people with a desire of vengeance on Elizabeth for the execution of the queen of Scots; obtains from the pope supplies of money, and a renewal of the bull of excommunication against Elizabeth, and prepares the Invincible Armada, 1587; 672. His daughter lays claim to the English throne, by right of her descent from John of Gaunt, 681. His death, 1598. He is succeeded by Philip III., ib.

PHILIP III., of Spain, (1598—1621;) ii. 681. His embassy, 1603, to the court of James I., being then desirous of amity with the Scottish successor of Elizabeth, iii. 7. His death, 1621; 89.

PHILIP IV., of Spain, (1621—1665,) succeeds to the throne, iii. 89 His gracious reception of Charles, prince of Wales, and of Buckingham, March, 1623, at Madrid, after their adventurous expedition under disguise through France, 93 The king, then nineteen, was of a cheerful character, though weak, and upholding all the gravity of Spanish ceremony, 94. His visits to prince Charles, to whom his sister, the infanta Maria, was betrothed, (see Maria,) 93, 94; gives him apartments in his magnificent palace, 94.

PHILIP V., of Spain, (1700 - 1751,) duke of Anjou and grandson of Louis XIV., iv. 110. His letter to William III., dated from Buen Retiro, in the style of king of Spain, 119. He invests Barcelona by land, whilst the count de Toulouse bombards it by sea, 1706, but is scared by the appearance of the earl of Peterborough and vice-admiral Leak, 185; signs his renunciation of the French throne, 1712; 270; abdicates the Spanish throne in favour of his son, 1725; 386; but on that prince's death again takes the supreme command, 387. His death, 1751; 554.

PHILIP, archduke, son of Maximilian and Mary of Burgundy, H. 116; 300. His conference with Henry VII. near Calais, 1500; 310. He landed at Weymouth, 1506, through stress of weather, with Joanna of Castile, 314. The king and queen of Castile prisoners at Windsor Castle, 315. Treaty betwixt the two kings for certain royal marriages, ib. Festivities, and orders of knighthood conferred, ib. After three months of courtly constraint, Philip and Joanna sailed for Spain, ib. His early death in Spain, which caused Joanna of Castile to become insane through grief, 316.

PHILIPPA, queen of Edward III., second daughter of the count of Hainault, married at York, January 24th, 1328; i. 751. Her portrait, ib. She reviews the troops before the battle of Nevil's Cross, 768; persuades Edward to pardon the burgesses of Calais, 770.

PHILLIPS, sir Robert, his speech against the viscount St. Albans; lord-chancellor, 1621; iii. 82. Is committed to the Tower, 1622; 86. The king, fearing his abilities in parliament, names him as a sheriff, 1625; 117. He complains of the violations of the subjects' liberty, 1629; 139.

Philosophy, ancient, acquisitions of the Celtic nations in, i. 62. The Druids studied especially the processes and secrets of nature, 64.

PHILPOT, John, an alderman of London, i. 783. Fits out a fleet, at his own expense, to retake the Scarborough fleet, which had been seized by John Mercer, 1378; he succeeds in capturing the Spanish fleet, and taking Mercer prisoner, but, on his return, is reprimanded by the council of government, ib.

Phœnicians, originally a Persian colony supposed to have peopled Britain and Ireland, i. 9, 14, 15, etc.

Phœnicians,—
Their commerce with Britain and the Cassiterides, 16, 77. 91—101. They export tin and other metals from these islands to all quarters, yet conceal the real position of Britain, 93.

PICHEGRU, Charles, born in 1761, a celebrated French general; he was appointed in 1795, by the National Convention, commandant of Paris, that he might resist the designs of the Terrorists, which he successfully accomplished, § iii. 493. Elected president of the Council of Five Hundred, 1797; 526. Soon after he was accused of being concerned in a royalist conspiracy, and sent to Cayenne, 527; whence he made his escape to England; engaging in the schemes of the emigrants against the government of Bonaparte, he was seized and imprisoned, and on the 6th of April, 1804, he was found strangled in the Temple, § iv. 108—123. His portrait, ib.

Pic-nic supper, nature of a, § iii. 752.

Picquigny, near Amiens, treaty of, 1475; ii. 112, 115. Personal interview of Edward IV. and Louis XI. described, 112.

PICTON, sir Thomas, greatly distinguished at Quatre-Bras, June 16, 1815; § iv. 635*; and killed at Waterloo, June 18; 637*.

Picts, the, anciently Gwyddyl Ffieti, settle in Scotland, i. 9. Inhabited south of the Grampians, 18. The Scots colonizing the north of Caledonia, from their acquired provinces in the north of Ireland, were oftener allies than enemies of the older population; both Picts and Scots were probably Celtic, and from the north of Europe, 18, 19. Those south of the Grampian Hills converted in 412, by Ninian, 229. King Brude had been converted by St. Columba, ib. The Picts were originally Cimbrians, a remnant of the ancient Cimbri, who, having crossed the German Ocean, settled in Britain, under Hu Cadarn, and afterwards migrated from the east of Scotland, and settled in Wales, from whom the present Welsh are descended, 22. Their origin and history, 216. Their great king, Durst, son of Erp, ib. The south-east district, as far as the Forth, occupied by the Northumbrians, became debateable ground, ib. This district, called Lodonia, (the Lothians,) ib. In 685, Bridei (son of Beli) fought the battle of Dunneehtan with Egfrid of Northumbria, and secured that territory for the Picts, ib. Dunwalion, the last Pictish king, was defeated, 973, by Kenneth III., and fell in the battle of Vacornar, 218. The Picts soon became incorporated with the Scoti of Dalriada, and North Britain was thenceforth known only as Scotland, ib.

Pie-poudre, Courts of, regulated 1477; ii. 191.

PIERCE, William, 1632, bishop of Bath and Wells, a friend of archbishop Laud, iii. 218. He styled the Scottish war "bellum episcopale," 1640; ib. He died April, 1670.

PIGOT, sir Christopher, member for Buckinghamshire, is expelled by the Commons, November, 1606, and committed to the Tower, iii. 35.

Pigs.—The Anglo-Saxons possessed herds of swine, a chief portion of their flesh-meat, i. 277. The swineherd, and beating of acorns for fattening swine, ib. Their number in Middlesex, Hertfordshire, and Essex, ib. They formed an important item of goods and chattels, ib.

Pilchards, demands for in the Italian states, 1782; § iii. 639.

Pilgrims, and pilgrimages to Rome, etc., i. 182, 265, 266; ii. 145, 150. To the Virgin at Walsingham, Norfolk, and other images and shrines in England, 145. To the Holy Sepulchre at Jerusalem, 151.

PINDAR, sir Paul, gives 4,000l. towards the repair of St. Paul's Cathedral, 1631; iii. 158.

PINE, John, an eminent engraver, born in 1690; he executed the ceremonies of the Order of the Bath, and the tapestry of the House of Lords, which last

PINE, John,—
now survives only in his representation; he died
May 4, 1756; iv. 760.
PINKERTON, John, an investigator of the distinctions
between the Celtic and Gothic nations, i. 10.
Pinkey. battle of, September 10, 1547; ii. 460.
PIPEREL, or Peverel, William, entrusted with an extensive command at Northallerton, 1138; i. 424.
Pisans, the, support Guy, of Lusignan, in his claim to
the kingdom of Jerusalem, 1191; i. 499.
PITSLIGO, lord, joins the standard of the Young Pretender, 1745; iv. 505.
PITT, William. See Chatham.
PITT, William, second son of the preceding, born
May, 1759; he delivers his first speech in support of Burke's Financial Reform Bill, 1780;
§ i. 443. His sentiments on the American war,
446. He becomes chancellor of the Exchequer,
1782; 485, 499. He resigns, 1783; 500. Is appointed first lord of the Treasury and chancellor of
the Exchequer, 504. Portrait of, § ii. 5. He
brings under consideration the National Debt, and
his new Sinking Fund, March 29, 1786; 13. His
speech on the commercial treaty with France,
1786; 211. He introduces his plan, February,
1787, for consolidating the various duties upon
articles in the Customs and the Excise, so as to
convert them into single duties upon each article,
218. Becomes warden of the Cinque Ports, 1792;
§ iii. 27. Is declared the enemy of the human race
by the National Convention at Paris, August 7,
1793; 344. Introduces the Income-tax, 1799;
844. He resigns, March 14, 1801, after an administration of seventeen years, in consequence of the
aversion to Catholic emancipation, 561—549°, 565.
After his resignation, in 1801, for a time he supported the Addington administration, which concluded the peace of Amiens, in 1802; § iv. 5; and
then joined the opposition, and spoke on the same
side with his old antagonist, Mr. Fox, 51. The
new minister, having renewed the war, and being
unable to maintain his ground, resigns, May 12,
1804, and Mr. Pitt again resumes his office as
Treasurer, May 18; 90. Returning to power as a
war minister, he exerts all the energy of his character to render the arduous contest successful, and
succeeds in engaging the two great military powers
of Russia and Austria in a new confederacy, which
was dissolved by the fatal battle of Austerlitz, 165.
Mr. Pitt, whose state of health was previously
declining, was sensibly affected by this event; and
the parliamentary attack upon his old associate,
lord Melville, deeply wounded his feelings, 165,
208. A state of extreme debility ensued, which
terminated in death, January 23rd, 1806; 205, 206.
It is decreed in parliament that he should have a
public funeral, and that his debts should be paid
by the nation, 206—208. On the death of Mr.
Pitt, lord Grenville succeeded, and united with
Mr. Fox and his friends to form the new ministry,
206.
PITTARDO, lady of, apprehended on a charge of witchcraft, July, died in prison, December, 1649; iii. 489.
PIUS II., pope, (Æneas Sylvius,) bishop of Sienna,
elected August, 1458, proclaimed a crusade against
the Turks, whence having overthrown the Greek
emperor of Constantinople, menaced the south of
Europe, ii. 150. His description of the Northumbrians, 656. He died, August 15, 1464.
PIUS VI., pope, (John Angelo Braschi,) elected Feb.
15, 1775. Burnt in effigy by the French Revolutionists, 1791, for excommunicating Talleyrand, § ii.
622. His dominions are invaded by Bonaparte,
1796; he sues for peace, and obtains it by submitting to the exorbitant demands of the invaders, § iii.
513. Revolt of the democratic part of his subjects;
a body of French and Poles, under Dombrowski,

PIUS VI.,—
again invade the papal states, 1798, and the aged
pontiff being driven from Rome, takes up his residence in a convent of the Augustinian monks in
Sienna, where he died, August, 1799; 539, 547.
PIUS VII., pope, (cardinal Gregory Barnabas Chiara-
monte,) elected March 13, 1800; § iii. 547. He
sends Consalvi, his cardinal secretary of state, to
Paris, who grants many concessions to the French,
and the Roman Catholic faith is again established in
France as the national religion, § iv. 23. His portrait, ib. The French take possession of the Papal
states, 1808; 300, 301, which are united to the
French empire; and pope Pius is taken prisoner and
conveyed to Savona, July 5, 1809; 416, 417. He is
liberated and returns to Rome, January 23, 1814;
622°. Is restored by the Allies, and died August
20, 1823.
Place Bill, the, passed December 13, 1692; iv. 40.
Place d'Armes, Montreal, View of the, § i. 219.
Plague, the Great, of 1349, said by Dr. Mead to have
destroyed half the population of the European states
it invaded, ii. 268. Severe in London, 1500, Henry
VII. withdrew to Calais, 310. Rages in London,
1548; 470. The troops of Warwick, suffering
severely from sickness and mortality at Harfleur,
carried on their return to London, 1563, the pestilence; at the same time there was a dearth of
food in England, and alarming storms of light
ning exceeding past experience, 574. Raged in
1603, in London and its suburbs, iii. 6, 9, 18.
Fasts, and sermons of repentance, appointed in
August, for every Wednesday until that scourge
should abate, 6. It breaks out at Whitehall, 1625;
108; and is severe and aggravated, 110. The Great
Plague, 1665, in the course of five months, carries
off 100,000 souls, iii. 695, 697.
Plantation Trade, the, or the trade carried on with the
settlements of North America, rose into consider-
able importance towards the end of the seventeenth
century, iii. 863.
Plassey, battle of, gained June 23, 1757; § ii. 57—59.
PLATEN, countess, a German mistress of George I.,
iv. 309.
Plays, moral, common in Scotland in the sixteenth
century, iii. 645.
PLINY'S "Natural History," quoted, i. 63, 92, 117,
127.
Plough-Monday, ii. 893.
PLOWDEN, Edmund, publishes his "Commentaries,"
1571; ii. 767.
PLUMER, Mr., introduces a motion for repealing the
Test Act, 1736; iv. 417.
PLUTARCH, quoted, i. 14.
Plymouth, iii. 655. View of, iv. 280.
POCOCKE, admiral, gains a victory over the admiral
d'Apché, 1758; iv. 503.
Poitiers, battle of, gained by the Black Prince, September 19, 1356; i. 772, 773.
POICTIERS, Richard de, quoted, i. 473.
POICTIERS, William of, the Conqueror's chaplain, i.
363. His description of Winchester, ib.; of England, and the return of William to Normandy, 364,
584, 585, 613.
POIX, John de, surprised St. Germain-en-Laye,
whence Charles VI. with difficulty escaped, 1416;
ii. 37.
Poland, distracted state of this country during the latter
part of the eighteenth century, §.i. 134—147. The
confederacy of Barr, 1768; 137. The first Treaty
of Partition, signed at St. Petersburg, August 2,
1772; 145. Revolution in Poland, 1788—1792;
§ iii. 34—47. Proposed alliance between Prussia and
Poland, 35. Resolutions of the Polish Diet; they
declare the crown hereditary, and nominate the
Elector of Saxony to succeed Stanislaus Augustus,
35, 37. The king accedes to the new constitution

Poland,—

May 3, 1791; 36. Treaty of Jassy concluded between Russia and Turkey, August, 1791; 38. Act of Confederacy signed at Targowica by several Polish magnates, inviting Russia to re-establish the old constitution, 39. Protest of the empress Catherine to the Diet at Warsaw, 39—41. A Russian army enters Poland, May 18; 41. Answer of the Diet, ib. Frederic William refuses to lend his assistance against the invasion, 42. Mission of count Bukarty to London, 43. Timidity of the Polish king, 44. Battle of Dubienka, July 17, 1792; 45 Stanislaus signs the Act of the Confederation of Targowica, July 23; 46. Fresh partition of this unfortunate country, 1793, by Russia and Prussia, 292, 293. The empress of Russia demands the reduction of the Polish troops to 15,000 men; the Poles determine once more to try the fate of arms, and choose the celebrated Kosciusko for their leader, 456, 457. They gain several advantages, and drive the Russians out of Warsaw; an allied army of Prussians and Russians endeavour to retake that city, but are compelled to raise the siege; the insurrection becomes general, and almost the whole of Great Poland falls into the possession of the insurgents, 460. Kosciusko is defeated at Macziewice by count Fersen, wounded, and made prisoner, 461. Suvaroff leads up his army to Praga, which he storms, November 4, 1794, allows no quarter to the inhabitants, and fires the city; the people of Warsaw fearing similar treatment, send a deputation to the barbarous Russian, who enters the city, November 6; ib. The last Partition Treaty was finally settled, October, 1795. Stanislaus Augustus was compelled to sign a formal act of abdication; he afterwards retired to St. Petersburg, where he died, February, 1798; 462.

POLE, Arthur and Edmund, conspired with sir A. Fortescue to liberate Mary of Scots, and to crown her in England, ii. 569. They were condemned and pardoned by Elizabeth, who detained them some time in the Tower, 569, 570. This act of clemency was followed by enactments against false diviners, some having prophesied the queen's death to happen in 1561; ib.

POLE, Henry lord Montacute, brother of cardinal Pole, 1539, beheaded, ii. 408. Another brother, sir Geoffrey Pole, having confessed, was pardoned, ib.

POLE, John de la, brother to the duke of Suffolk, marching incautiously when encumbered with booty and numerous oxen, 1422, 1423. was surprised and defeated in Anjou, ii. 55. Taken prisoner, he was soon after exchanged, 56.

POLE, John de la, created duke of Suffolk, 1463. Espoused Elizabeth, second sister of Edward IV., ii. 175, 288. See Suffolk.

POLE, John de la, earl of Lincoln, son of the preceding, 1486; ii. 175, 288. See Lincoln.

POLE, Michael de la, created earl of Suffolk 1385; ii. 175. He became lord-chancellor, but, in the reform of Gloucester's parliament, his property was confiscated and he fled to France, about 1388; ib.; iii. 655.—See Suffolk.

POLE, Michael de la, son of the first earl of Suffolk, was restored before the dethronement of Richard II., ii. 175; he died 1415. His son Michael, earl of Suffolk, fell at Agincourt, 34.

POLE, Reginald, cardinal, son of sir Richard Pole, Margaret, countess of Salisbury, the daughter of George, duke of Clarence, the brother of Edward IV., ii. 401, 457, 510. Henry VIII. allows this young relative a pension to prosecute his studies in France and Italy, 401. The king, willing to promote him to the richest preferments, makes conditions that the young priest should defend his divorce, and the assumption of supremacy; Pole plainly refused, ib. A total quarrel ensued, ib.

POLE, Reginald, cardinal,—

From the north of Italy, Pole indignantly spread the infamy of the judicial murder of sir T. More, ib. In his "De Unione Ecclesiasticâ," he maintained the cause of Rome, ib. Invited, 1536, by Paul III. to the Vatican, he feared the worst consequences to his relatives, but in some time repaired to the pope, 401, 408. Receives a cardinal's hat for his services and talent, ib. Is appointed legate beyond the Alps with extraordinary powers, ib. Francis I., at the instance of king Henry, refused to see him, ib. At Cambray, he was ordered not to enter the territories of Charles V., ib. He was carrying money to the English rebels, but the northern insurrection had been suppressed, ib. His treasonable exertions on the continent against king Henry became notorious, 407, 408. Henry VIII. unable to secure his person, wreaked his vengeance on his family in England; his brother, lord Montacute, 1539, beheaded, 408. Another brother, Geoffrey Pole, making confession, was pardoned, ib. The rancour of the king desired the extermination of this family; his own near relatives, the aged and the young were sacrificed, ib. The young son of Montacute was attainted, incarcerated, and never heard of again, ib. Margaret, countess of Salisbury, aged 70, mother of Reginald Pole, was also attainted, and in 1540, after a year's imprisonment, was atrociously beheaded in the Tower, declaring her innocence of all treason, 409. (See Salisbury.) He is excepted from a general pardon to state offenders issued by Edward VI, 457. His high character, his eloquence and learning, 510. Rumour that his kinswoman, Mary I, intended, 1553, to bestow her hand on him, as he had not then taken priest's orders, ib. Alarm of Charles V. on this head, 511. His attainder under Henry VIII. not as yet reversed, ib. He had been raised to high employments by the pope, and attended the Council of Trent, 510. His retirement to a monastery on the Lago di Garda, 511. Is appointed legate to England, but delays his journey for a time, as the people were not prepared to receive him in that office, ib. He represents persecution to Mary as dangerous to government, and the scandal of religion, 524. His moderation caused him to be suspected of heretical notions, ib. Is installed archbishop of Canterbury, March 22, 1555, the day after Cranmer's death, 528. He expires at Lambeth, November 17th, 1558, twenty-two hours after queen Mary, 538.

POLE, William de la, duke of Suffolk, beheaded at sea, ii. 54—87, 175.—See Suffolk.

POLE, William de la, a wealthy merchant of Hull, lent a large sum to Edward III., ii. 175. He was employed in embassies, made a knight banneret, and chief baron of the Exchequer, ib.

Police, medical and criminal, want of at the beginning of the reign of George III. § i. 652, et seq.; § iii. 11.

POLIGNAC, cardinal, ambassador in Poland, 1696; iv. 72. Endeavours to secure the election of the prince of Conti to the Polish throne, 77. His negotiations in Holland, 1710; 246. He is banished from Paris by the duke of Orleans, 1718 ; 349.

Political economy, iii. 863.

POLLEXFEN, Mr., maintains gold and silver to be the only riches of a nation, about 1698: iii. 856.

Poll-tax, the causes much disturbance in England, 1378; i. 784, et seq.

POLO, Marco, his travels in Tartary and China, i. 845.

POLTROT, a Huguenot, assassinates the duke of Guise, February 24, 1563; ii. 572.

Polygars, group of, § ii. 157.

POMPONE, M., an eminent diplomatist and minister of Louis XIV., iv. 72, 87.

Pondicherry surrenders to colonel Coote, January, 1761; § ii. 81.

PONIATOWSKI, Joseph. commander-in-chief of the Polish forces, 1792; § iii. 45.

PONIATOWSKI, Stanislaus Augustus, king of Poland, 1764. His portrait. § i. 139. On the final dismemberment of Poland in 1795, he is compelled to sign a formal act of abdication at Grodno. He afterwards retired to St. Petersburgh, where he died, February, 1798; iii. 462.

PONSONBY, general sir William, killed at the battle of Waterloo, June 18, 1815; § iv. 637*.

Pont-y-Cysylte, an aqueduct bridge over the valley of the Dee, completed 1805; § iii. 670. View of, 671.

PONT, Robert, abbot of, his deputation to Richard, 1193; i. 509.

Pont-fract Castle, built by Gilbert de Lacy, regno William I., i. 374. Death of Richard II. in this fortress, 1400; ii. 7. View of the castle, regno Charles II., 8.

PONTEFRACT, Robert de, promises to assist duke Robert in gaining possession of the crown of England, 1101; i. 408.

POOLEY, an accomplice in the Babington conspiracy, 1586; he betrays the whole plot to Walsingham, ii. 657.

Poor, the, Edward VI. passes an extreme law for the suppression of mendicity, or as it was entitled, "for the punishment of vagabonds, and the relief of the poor and impotent persons," ii. 467, 468. Popular risings owing to the extinction of villenage, etc., 481. Severe enactments against pauperism, 904—907; iii. 659. Glimpses at the pauper population, 905—12. Estimate of the charges of, iv. 845—848. General state of the poor during the eighteenth century, ib.

Poor-laws, early noticed, 1609, as an incentive to idleness, iii. 659. The Act of 1662 constituted a new era in this branch of the national economy, 907. Important change in the management of the poor, regno George I., iv. 847. Poor-laws during the eighteenth century, § i. 686—688; § iii. 772.

Poor-rates, the earliest information that has been found with regard to the amount of, is in 1673; the sum then expended was estimated at about 840,000l. a year, iii. 908.

Poor-rates, nineteenth century, § iv. 730, 731.

POPE, Alexander, a celebrated English poet, born May 22, 1688; speaks in defence of bishop Atterbury, 1723; iv. 381. His portrait, 735. He plans and executes the first English garden, 752. He died May 30, 1744; 795. Review of his works, 794—796.

POPE, sir Thomas, founder of Trinity College, Oxford, 1554; ii. 819.

POPHAM, Andrew, a papist; James II. commands the governors of the Charter-house, 1687, to admit him without test or oath; but they resist the mandate, iii. 786.

POPHAM, sir Home, bombards Ostend, 1798; § iii. 534. Takes Buenos Ayres, July 2, 1806; § iv. 231.

POPHAM, sir John, 1603, assists in the proclamation of the Scottish king as successor to Elisabeth, iii. 3.

Popish Plot, the, declared by Titus Oates, September 28, 1678; iii. 717. Medal struck to commemorate the, 718. Depositions concerning the, 718—724.

POPOLI, duchess of, rescued, 1705, by the earl of Peterborough from the Miquelets, iv. 180.

POPOLI, duke of, recommends the invasion of Naples, 1717, to Phillip V. of Spain, iv. 341.

Population.—Assistance to be derived from the physical characteristics of nations in regard to the early population of a country, i. 5.

Population of England in the fourteenth, sixteenth, eighteenth, and nineteenth centuries, ii. 268, 903; § iii. 773; § iv. 729, 730.

PORTA, Giovanni Battista della, a learned Neapolitan, born in 1445, inventor of the camera-obscura, and author of several curious works; he died in 1515, iv. 764.

Portalegre, surrenders to the duke of Berwick, 1704; iv. 174.

PORTEOUS, John, hanged by the Edinburgh populace. September 7, 1736, for inhumanly firing on a mob, iv. 419.

PORTER, sir Charles, lord-justice of Ireland, 1693; iv. 48.

PORTER, Endymion, chosen by prince Charles to accompany him in his intended journey to Spain, 1623; iii. 91.

PORTEUS, Beilby, elected to the bishopric of Chester in 1776, translated to London, 1787; died 1808; § iv. 606. His portrait, ib.

PORTLAND, Richard Weston, first earl of, lord-treasurer, accused as an enemy of the nation by sir J. Eliot, 1629; iii. 141, 146. Created 1633. He died 1634; 161.

PORTLAND, Jerome Weston, earl of, 1634. Delivers a petition to the king, 1642; iii. 274. He (being governor of the Isle of Wight) is arrested by the parliament, 1642. He died 1662; 291.

PORTLAND, William Bentinck, earl of: Fisher discloses to him, February 11, 1696, a plot to assassinate the king, iv. 56. He arranges the preliminaries of Ryswick, 1697; 78. Enters Paris, February 27, 1698, to negotiate the first Partition Treaty, 86, 87. He resigns his offices, 1700; 106. Is impeached, 1701; 120. He died 1709.

PORTLAND, William, duke of, 1762. Receives the Order of the Garter, and the office of third secretary of state, 1794; § iii. 462.

PORTMAN, sir William, signs a petition, 1633, showing the mischief and profanity consequent on church-ales, etc.. iii. 161.

PORTOCARRERO, cardinal, archbishop of Toledo, and minister of Charles II. of Spain, endeavours to force that dying king, 1700, to name Philip, duke of Anjou, universal successor to the Spanish monarchy, iv. 109, note; 110.

PORTOCARRERO, don Vincente, arrested at Poictiers by order of Dubois, 1719; iv. 349.

Portsmouth.—The Roman build a fortress, Portus Adurnus, 250—300, against Saxon pirates, i. 90. View of the Fortress and Harbour of, ii. 800. Drawing of the House in which Buckingham, in 1628, was assassinated by Felton, iii. 137.

PORTSMOUTH, duchess of. — See Mademoiselle Keroualle.

Port-wine, first introduced into England about the middle of the seventeenth century, iv. 706.

Post, established by James I. for communication with foreign countries by letter. iii. 544. Post-office, and posts for many parts of England and Scotland, established, 1635; 544. Rates of postage, 545. The Post-office revenue at the accession of James II. amounted to 65,000l. per annum, 865. Great plan of reform in, suggested by J. Palmer, brought into operation, 1784; § i. 571, 572. Abuses in the, 1787; § ii. 223. Growth of the Post-office revenues during the interval between the war of the American and the war of the French revolution, § iii. 644.

Potato, the, came into general use in England about the middle of the eighteenth century, iv. 729.

POTTER, Dr. John, archbishop of Canterbury, 1737; iv. 418. Dispute concerning his nomination to the Regius Professorship of Divinity at Oxford, 1707; 213. He died 1747.

Potteries of the Gauls and Britons, i. 103.

Pottery, manufacture of (eighteenth century,) § i. 589—592. The first blue printed table-service made in England, 1780; 591. Manufacture of crucibles and earthen retorts, § iii. 690.

POULET, lord, subscribes a petition, 1633, showing the mischief and profanity consequent on church-ales, etc., iii. 161.

POUND, Mr., an aged Catholic, 1604, presented a petition complaining of his antecedent sufferings, iii. 22. Coke inveighs against him and all papists before the Star-chamber, ib. He is imprisoned, twice pilloried, and fined 1,000l., ib.

POWEL, Mr. Justice, his stout defence of the petitioning bishops, 1688; iii. 792.

Power-loom, first invented by Dr. E. Cartwright, 1784; § iii. 697.

POWIS, lady, sent to the Tower, 1679; iii. 732.

POYNINGS, sir Edward, comptroller, 1509, of Henry VIII.'s council, ii. 320, 323, 570.

POYNINGS, sir Thomas, 1545. gallantly preserved Boulogne from the attack of Francis I., ii. 442.

POYNTZ, commander of the English forces in the north, 1645; iii. 340, 354.

Præmunire, statutes of, some references to them, i. 807; ii. 371, 377.

Pragmatic Sanction, the, guaranteed, 1725; iv. 388.

PRANCE, a Catholic silversmith, arrested, 1678, on suspicion of being accessory to the murder of sir Edmondbury Godfrey, iii. 724.

PRATT, lord chief-justice. See Camden.

Prayer, Book of Common, review of, 1661; iii. 821. Names of the commissioners, 821, 822.

Preaching, extemporaneous, first practised, in 1739, by George Whitefield, iv. 653.

Preaching, lay, first practised by Thomas Maxfield, iv. 654.

Preston Tower, View of, iv. 496.

PRESTON, lord, 1685; iii. 767.

PRESTON, Thomas, a dramatic writer of the sixteenth century, iii. 583, note.

Prestonpans, battle of, September 1745; iv. 495, 496.

PRETENDER, the Old.—See James Francis Edward.

PRETENDER, the Young.—See Charles Edward Louis.

PREVOST, sir George, British commander in Canada; his disgraceful conduct and retreat from Plattsburg, September 11, 1814; § iv. 671*, 672*.

Price-current, printing of a weekly, 1634, for the use of commercial men, established, iii. 544.

PRIDE, colonel, a parliamentarian officer, iii. 333. He takes an active part in clearing the House of Parliament from Presbyterian members, 1648; 387, 422, 425.

PRIDEAUX, Mr., introduces a bill, January 19, 1641, for preventing the dangers arising from the long intermission of parliaments, iii. 231.

PRIESTLEY, Joseph, an eminent philosopher and dissenting divine, born March 1733. His library is burned by the Birmingham rioters, 1791; § ii. 585. Subscriptions raised for his relief, 588. He sends his son to France, 1792, to learn the principles of the French Revolution, § iii. 83, 389. He takes up his residence in the United States, 1794; where he died, February 6, 1804; § ii. 588.

PRIMROSE, sir Archibald, said to have first proposed the general Act Rescissory of 1661; iii. 683, note.

Prince's metal, invented towards the middle of the eighteenth century, iii. 870. Application for table furniture, § iii. 683.

Printers, marks of early English, ii. 825.

Printing, origin of, ii. 201—206. Three different towns contend for the honour of giving birth to this art shortly before the middle of the fifteenth century, 201. Printing practised in Germany thirty years before its introduction either into England or France, ib. Introduced into England, 1474; 202. Facts collected by Warton respecting libraries of the fifteenth century, 205. Printing type imported from Holland, iv. 733. Regulations concerning printing, § iii. 610. Revival of stereotyping by Mr. Tilloch, 1780; 714. Logo-

Printing,— graph abandoned, ib. Improvements in the printing-press during the nineteenth century, § iv. 694.

Printing-office, ancient Dutch, ii. 824.

PRIOR, Matthew, a distinguished writer of the eighteenth century, born 1664; iv. 797. Accompanies lord Portland on an embassy to Paris; his witty speech to a courtier there, iv. 86. Dispatched to France with the Abbé Gaultier, to begin the peace of Utrecht, 1711; 254. Sent with viscount Bolingbroke to conclude the same peace, 269. Is impeached and committed to close custody, June 1715; 308. He died in 1721.

PRITCHARD, Dr., asserts that the Teutonic and Celtic languages belong to the great family of Indo-European languages, etc., i. 11.

Prize-fights, iv. 828.

Procession, description of a royal, iii. 901.

Prophecies and predictions of Merlin, etc., ii. 258.

Prose fiction (eighteenth century,) § i. 604—611.

Protestant Association, the, instituted, 1585; ii. 656.

Protestantism, rival forms of, iii. 433—494.

Protestants. See Lollards, the followers of Wycliffe's new doctrine. James I. declares against toleration of Roman Catholics, 1603, and espouses the High Church party; the Protestant worship established by law, iii. 8, 12. 19.

Provinces, the United, send over ambassadors to intercede for king Charles's life, 1649; iii. 395.

Provision, price of, 1610; iii. 657. Ordinances passed for regulating the price of, 658.

PRYDAIN, Inys, name of Briton, i. 8.

PRYDAIN, son of Aedd the Great, i. 11.

PRYNNE, William, a barrister of Lincoln's-inn, brought into the Star-chamber, 1634, for publishing a libellous volume, entitled the "Histrio-Mastix," iii. 152. Is heavily fined, pilloried, burnt in the forehead, slit in the nose, and cropped, 154, 155. Is again punished, 1637, in an equally barbarous manner, 166. Is nominated by the parliament, 1643, to prepare evidence against his former persecutor, archbishop Laud, 324. He represents the danger likely to be incurred by the loose manner of the proposed restoration of Charles II., 431*. Portrait of, from an old picture in the Prynne family, 493, 567.

PTOLEMY, his mention of Ireland and Britain, i. 14, 20. His geographical remarks, i. 138.

PUCELLE, Gerard la, an eminent scholar, one of the first and most celebrated teachers of canon and civil law at the University of Paris; he lectured there from 1160 to 1177; i. 610. Was made bishop of Lichfield and Coventry, September 1183, and died January 1185; ib.

PUCKERING, serjeant, Speaker of the House of Commons, 1586, recommends the execution of the queen of Scots, ii. 662.

PUDSEY, Hugh, treasurer of York and archdeacon of Westminster, consecrated Bishop of Durham, December, 1153; appointed regent of England by Richard I., i. 485, 505. He is seized by Longchamp, bishop of Ely, 505. He died, March 3, 1194, aged 70.

PUISIEUX, M., principal secretary of state in France, 1623, promises to lord Herbert not to interrupt the prince of Wales on his secret journey to Spain, iii. 92.

PULAWSKI, general, slain at the siege of Savannah in 1779; § i. 393.

Puppet-shows, iii. 902.

PURBECK, viscount. See John Villiers.

PURCELL, Henry, an excellent composer of music, born 1658, died 1695; iii. 886, iv. 761.

Purgatory, doctrine of, ii. 397.

Puritans.—Introduction of puritanism from Germany, 1547—1550, into England, by Peter Martyr, Bucer, and Hooper, ii. 741. The Protestants, emigrating during the persecution by Mary, and returning

Puritans,—
after her decease, had acquired much of the doctrines of Zuinglius, and dissent in the Protestant Church of England ensues, ib. The Puritans are persecuted, 1567, by Elizabeth, 743. Their desire, 1603, for the establishment of a church similar to the kirk established by Knox, iii. 8. They draw up a "millennary petition," and demand a conference, 15, 17. James I., who in Scotland had found it convenient to speak in the views of the Puritans, attended by his bishops, held a Conference at Hampton, with four of the reforming preachers, 14th January, 1604, 16. He rudely denied their proposals of conciliation, and caused all Nonconformist preachers in England to be ejected, 16, 17. Spies were set to watch their secret conventicles, and numbers of preachers sent to prison by the Star-chamber. 17, 18. Many Puritans returned to parliament, 1604, despite James I.'s warning to electors against the choice of either Catholics or Puritans, 18.

PURVAY, John, a Reformer who abandoned the tenets of Wycliffe, 1400—1407, for a benefice from archbishop Arundel, ii. 144.

Purveyance for the royal table, etc. Investigation by the first parliament, James I., 1604, of the forced labour of men and horses, felling of timber by the royal purveyors, and other grievances, iii. 19. This inquiry suppressed, as premature, ib.

PUTNAM, general, an American officer, 1775. Portrait of, § i. 213.

PUTTENHAM, Webster, a writer of the 16th century, ii. 835.

PYKAS, John, his deposition, 1527, respecting the Scriptures in English which he possessed, ii. 712.

PYM, John, a noted parliamentarian, regno Charles I., born, 1584. One of the managers of the articles of impeachment against the duke of Buckingham, 1626, iii. 120, 139. Takes an active part in the impeachment of the earl of Strafford, 236, et seq. His death, December 8, 1643; 310. Portrait of, 495.

Pynsaint, Carmarthenshire, fine specimen of levels in Roman mines at, i. 117.

Pyramids, battle of the, gained by Buonaparte over the Mamelukes, July 21, 1798; § iii. 541.

Quadruple Alliance, the, concluded between the courts of Vienna, Paris, the Hague, and London, 1718; iv. 345, 476.

Quakers, origin and tenets of, iii. 809—818. (See George Fox.) Persecution of the sect, 809. The Quakers petition for the total abolition of the slave-trade, June, 1783; § i. 501. Bill for their relief brought in by serjeant Adair, 1796; § iii. 591.

Quatre Bras, battle of, June 16, 1815; § iv. 633*.

Quebec, View of, § i. 222. Battle of, September 1759; iv. 608, 609.

QUEENSBURY, James Douglas, duke of, iii. 767; iv. 106, 107, 156. His activity in punishing the Fraser's Plot conspirators, 1704; 162. He opens the last Scottish parliament that ever sat at Edinburgh, 1706; 187. Created duke of Dover, 1708. Died 1711; 231.

Quesnoy, invested by prince Eugene, 1712; iv. 267.

Quintain, an ancient English sport, i. 649. View of an ancient Quintain, now standing on the green of Offham, Kent, ib.

QUIROS, Don Bernardo de, Spanish ambassador at the Court of Holland, 1700; iv. 108.

RABY, Thomas Wentworth, lord.—See Strafford.

Rack, the, invented by John Holland, duke of Exeter, regno Henry VI., iii. 519.

RADNOR, John Robarts, earl of, 1679; iii. 318. Obtains the government of Ireland, 1667. He died, 1685; 705.

RAFAELLE, Sanzio, an eminent painter, born at Urbino, 1483. He executed the famous Cartoons, and died in 1520; iii. 567.

RAIKES, Mr., a printer of Gloucester, the House of Commons taking great offence at his publishing some of their reports, resolved, February 26, 1729, that it was a breach of their privilege to publish any account or minutes of their debates, iv. 403.

Railroads, progress of (18th century), § i. 576; § iii. 668; § iv. 679, 800.

RAINSBOROUGH, captain, assisted by the emperor of Morocco, destroys the shipping and town of Sallee, 1636; iii. 174, 370. He influences the army against the king, 1647; 371. Is murdered by three royalists, 1648; 385.

RAJAH SHITAB ROY, naib-dewan of Bahar, is arrested by Warren Hastings on various charges, 1771, and brought to trial at Calcutta, where he is declared innocent; he returns to Patna, but dies shortly after of a broken heart, § ii. 118—121.

RALEIGH, sir Walter, enlists in the service of the French Huguenots, 1569; ii. 626. Serves in Ireland, 1580, against San Giuseppa, 652. Obtains the lands of Anthony Babington, head of the conspiracy that goes by his name, by royal grant, 1586; 666, note, 676. Intrigues against the earl of Essex, 1596; 680. Joins an expedition against the Spaniards, 1597; 681. Allusion made to his policy and conduct on the accession of James I., March, 1603; iii. 3. Obnoxious to the Scottish monarch from the commencement of his reign; he was deprived of all his employments, except the government of Jersey, 5. His authority of granting licenses to taverns, and for the sale of wines in England, affected by the proclamation against monopolies, 5, note. He is deprived of the licensing and his captainship of the guards, 7. He engages, June 1603, in the "Main" Conspiracy, or was suspected by the government, 8. Interrogated before a secret council at Windsor, he exculpates himself, and is left at liberty, 9. His letter to Cecil, stating that La Rensy, in count d'Aremberg's household might know more of Cobham's intrigues, ib. His imprudent letter to warn lord Cobham of his danger intercepted, ib. His letter to Cecil, shown to lord Cobham, that nobleman declares that sir Walter had led him into the conspiracy, whereupon both are committed to the Tower, ib. The chief object appears to have been to obtain 600,000 crowns of Spanish money, under pretence of forwarding the claim of Arabella Stuart, 9, 15. The indictment against the "Main" Conspirators, sir Walter pleading Not Guilty, 9. Coke, attorney-general, in his pleading alleges the criminality of the "Bye," and Raleigh answers that he was simply indicted on the "Main," 10. Wit of sir Walter's replies to the vituperations of sir Edward Coke, ib. His impressive defence, displaying the powers of reason and eloquence, ib. Coke produces the letter of lord Cobham inculpating Raleigh, ib. Sir Walter asks that Cobham should be sent for and confronted with him, 11. Popham, chief justice, on Raleigh pleading that by the statutes of Edward VI. two witnesses are needful on indictments for treason, replies that such statute had been annulled by Philip and Mary, and that the trial was held by common-law, 25 Edward III., one witness sufficing, and the accusation and confession by confederates being full proof, ib. Cecil rebukes Coke in court for his violent language, ib. Verdict of Guilty reluctantly given by the jury, ib. Sir Walter throws himself on the king's mercy, 11, 12. His sentence, 11, 12, 72. He requests Suffolk, Devonshire, Howard, and Cecil to intercede that his death might be honourable, 12. Roger Ashton and a Scotsman announce this verdict to James I., and speak to him with admiration of Raleigh's defence, ib. Raleigh, under sentence to die on the Monday, witnesses from his prison window the preparations for the execution of Markham, Cobham, and Grey, 14. The reprieve. ib. Imprisoned during

2 G

RALEIGH, sir Walter,— many years in the Tower of London, *ib.* Raleigh in the Tower of London has, in the progress of years, the society of congenial minds addicted to learning and science, who were immured in those gloomy precincts: Henry Percy, earl of Northumberland, and serjeant Hoskins: their visitors were frequently Hariot, formerly mathematical tutor to Raleigh, and Dr. R. Burchill, 72. In Elizabeth's reign, sir Walter had conveyed his chief property, the estate and castle of Sherborne, to his eldest son, *ib.* A legal flaw in this deed of conveyance being discovered, chief-justice Popham declared it invalid, lady Raleigh obtaining audience of James, with her children also on their knees before the king, implores him not to deprive them of their patrimony, *ib.* James, however, bestows the estate on Robert Carr, his favourite. *ib.* Raleigh had obtained from Elizabeth the lands of Anthony Babington, *ib.* Solacing his poverty in prison, during thirteen years, Raleigh devotes himself to abstruse studies, chemistry, the discovery of the philosopher's stone, also to an elixir to remedy all diseases, 73. Queen Anne being very ill, fancied she received immediate relief from this elixir of Raleigh's, *ib.* Henry, prince of Wales, took great interest in sir Walter, *ib.* For the instruction of that prince Raleigh wrote and finished in the Tower, 1612, the first part of the "History of the World;" the remainder being sketched out, on prince Henry's decease remained incomplete, *ib.* Raleigh makes promise to the king, through secretary Winwood, 1614 to 1616, of procuring wealth from a gold mine in "El Dorado," or Guiana, South America, *ib.* The monarch fears a rupture thereby with Spain, and Gondomar the ambassador takes serious alarm, *ib.* Gondomar's remonstrances against any piratical enterprise, at length he offers no obstacle to a peaceful attempt to colonise the "Golden Land," 74. Raleigh neglects to obtain a pardon, 73. Bribe to the two uncles of George Villiers, the new favourite, *ib.* Untoward sarcasm of Raleigh on Carr, earl of Somerset, the grantee of the Sherborne forfeiture, being committed to the Tower for the murder of Overbury, *ib.* Sir Walter released from the Tower, *ib.* He, chiefly at his own expense and that of many of his own and wife's relatives (who accompany him) fits out a fleet of fourteen ships, 74. His memorial, *ib.* His commission as general and governor of the intended colony, *ib.* He hoists his flag in the *Destiny*, and sets sail March 28, 1617, *ib.* Inauspicious and stormy voyage, November 13, he reaches Guiana, *ib.* Sickness lamentably thins his crews, and the admiral afflicted with a severe calenture, remains at Trinidad with his fleet, *ib.* He hears of a Spanish fleet, and that the Spaniards had taken up arms in the interior to dispute the country with him, *ib.* His faithful captain Keymis, who served with him in 1595, and explored the gold or mine district, he dispatches up the Oronoco with five ships; instructions given by Raleigh, *ib.* Keymis posts himself between St. Thomas, a new town, and the mine; he loses many of his people in a night assault by the Spaniards, *ib.* Next day, Keymis in a vigorous action takes St. Thomas, *ib.* Walter Raleigh, son of the admiral, is slain whilst fighting with courage; the English, to revenge his death, burn St. Thomas, *ib.* Its governor, a relative of count Gondomar, is slain, *ib.* The only booty made was two ingots of gold, 75. Keymis descends the Oronoco and rejoins Raleigh, who fell into despair, and bitterly accuses Keymis of his ruin, *ib.* Keymis addresses his defence in a letter to the earl of Arundel, and finding his commander still reproaching him, shoots himself, *ib.* Mutiny in Raleigh's fleet; captains Whitney, Woolaston, and others desert with their ships, leaving Raleigh with only five vessels, *ib.* He refuses all solicitations to plunder, and refits his ships at Newfoundland, *ib.* He, however, held out to his daring seamen, by way of keeping down their mutinous spirit, a hope of intercepting the treasure galleons, *ib.* June 1618, he anchors at Plymouth, and hears of a proclamation out against his person, *ib.* Buckingham and his royal master promise the enraged ambassador Gondomar an exemplary punishment of the offender Raleigh, *ib.* His ships and goods confiscated, *ib.* His slaughter of Spaniards in a fort in Ireland, and on the coast of Guiana in 1595; his exploits with Essex in the Azores and Canary Islands, are alleged by the vindictive ambassador, whose relation had been slain at St. Thomas in the El Dorado expedition, *ib.* Aware of his personal danger, Raleigh returns to secure Arundel and Pembroke, who had become bound for his return, 75, 76, 79, *note.* His own relative, sir Lewis Stukely, vice-admiral of Dover, arrests him, 76. On his road to London he feigns madness and the plague, so that the king grants him to remain a few days at his house in London, *ib.* His friend captain King prepares a bark on the Thames for Raleigh's escape, *ib.* Le Clerc, *chargé d'affaires*, grants him a safe conduct to the governor of Calais, *ib.* Stukely, to whom he had given a diamond of price, betrays him in descending the Thames, and Raleigh is lodged in the Tower, *ib.* His examinations by archbishop Abbot, Bacon, and Coke, 77. Sir Thomas Wilson, placed as a spy near his person, can detect no guilt by his conversation, *ib.* In the King's Bench, to which Raleigh was taken by writ of *Habeas Corpus*, Yelverton demands a renewal of the sentence passed at Winchester fifteen years antecedently, 77, 78. Raleigh in vain pleads that the king's recent commission, with powers of life and death over his followers, and a high and honourable command, had virtually restored him and barred the old attainder, 78. Chief-justice Montague replied to the crown lawyers that execution is granted, *ib.* His parting with lady Raleigh in the Gate-house, Westminster, *ib.* His devotions, *ib.* A contemporary depicts his character and habits, *ib.* His comportment, and remarkable coolness, on the eve and morning of execution, 78, 79. He died, denying any share in procuring the death of Essex, 79. His remark on beholding the axe, *ib.* Regret for his death, 29th October, 1618, in the sixty-seventh year of his age, 79, 80. His "Essay on the Foreign Commerce of England," 527. His voyage to Guiana, 538. Portrait of, by Zucchero, 560. His "History of the World" first published, 1614; 614.

RALEIGH, Mr. Walter, accompanies his father in the El Dorado expedition, 1617, and is slain gallantly fighting at St. Thomas, on the Oronoco, iii. 74.

RALEIGH, lady, with her children, asks an audience of James I., and entreats him not to deprive them of Sherborne Castle and estate, but she implores in vain, iii. 72. She sells her own estate of Mitcham to supply sir Walter with money for his expedition to Guiana, 74. Her farewell on the eve of his execution; she informs him that the king had granted his body to her for sepulture, his reply thereto, 78.

RALPH, surnamed "Le Flambard," bishop of Durham, succeeds Lanfranc as chief minister, 1089; i. 396, 549. Is appointed royal chaplain, treasurer, and justiciary, *ib.* His fierce and arbitrary conduct, *ib.* He escapes from the Tower and goes to Normandy, 1101; 407. Excites duke Robert to invade England, 408. Delivers up the castle of Lisieux to Henry, and obtains the restoration of his English see, 410. He died 1128.

Ramilies, battle of, May 23, 1706; iv. 164.

RAMNARRAIN, the celebrated governor of Patna, murdered by Meer Cossim, 1763; § ii. 86.

RAMPENTON, Philip of, a learned Lollard, 1400—1407; when he became bishop of Lincoln he persecuted the Reformers, ii. 144.

RAMSAY, sir John. *See* Haddington.

Ramsey Abbey, description of, i. 313.

RANDALL, Edward, high marshal of Havre, introduces into London the plague of 1563; ii. 573, 574.

Ranelagh, iv. 825.

RANELAGH, lord, paymaster of the army, expelled the House of Commons, 1703; iv. 150.

RANULPH, or Ralph, a Norman, 1051, earl of Worcester, joins the army of Edward the Confessor against Godwin, i. 190.

RANULPH, bishop of Durham. *See* Ralph le Flambard.

Rastadt, taken by marshal Villars, 1707; iv. 204.

RASTELL, John, a law-writer and printer, *regno* Henry VIII., ii. 763.

RATCLIFFE, Egremont, joins an insurrection in favour of Mary queen of Scots, i. 569, ii. 629. He flies to the Spanish Netherlands, 630.

RATCLIFFE, sir Richard, a bold adherent of the protector Gloucester, ii. 128. Slain at Bosworth Field, August 22, 1485; 129.

RAVAILLAC, Francis, a friar of the order of the Jacobins, stabbed Henri IV., May 14, 1610; iii. 48. On the rack, he maintained that he had no accomplices, *ib.* Probability of his being a madman, *ib.* His horrible death, *ib.*

RAVENSWORTH, lord, acquaints Mr. Pelham, 1753, of the Jacobitism of the sub-governor of the prince of Wales (George III.,) iv. 574.

RAWDON, lord, a British officer commanding in America, 1780; § i. 426. Portrait of, 427, 456, 466.

RAY, volunteer, quoted, iv. 536.

RAYMOND, earl of Toulouse, acquaints Henry II. with the intentions of his wife and son, 1173; § i. 468.

RAYMOND de la Guerre, commissioned, 1416, by Armagnac, hanged all the Bourguignon nobles whom he could seize, ii. 37.

RAYMOND, lord, opposes the bill passed, 1731, for all pleadings and processes in the courts of law to be in English, iv. 405.

RAYNALDE, Thomas, published the first book with copper-plates, in 1540; iii. 577.

Reading, View of, from Caversham-hill, iii. 301.

Reading Abbey, built by Henry I., who was buried therein, 1135; i. 418. View of the ruins of, 419.

READING, Mr., announces the election of the duke of Buckingham, 1626, to the chancellorship of the university of Cambridge, iii. 122.

Reason, Festival of, celebrated in France, Nov. 10, 1793; § iii. 379, 380.

REAY, lord, accuses the marquis of Hamilton of raising troops to usurp the crown of Scotland, 1630; iii. 150.

RECALDO, Martinez de, appointed, 1587, vice-admiral of the Spanish Armada, ii. 674.

Recognition, bill of, 1690; iv. 21.

REDESDALE, John Freeman Mitford, baron, brings in a bill, 1791, for relieving papists from certain disabilities and penalties, § iii. 578.

REDVERS, Richard de, a powerful Norman baron, and steady friend of Henry I., i. 409.

REDWALD, king of East-Anglia, converted, 604, *et seq.*, yet permits the Scandinavian worship to be co-existent with the Christian worship in his dominions, i. 145, 233. About 617, he was elected Bretwalda of the Saxon states, *ib.* Edilfrid, king of Northumbria, having defeated the Scots, and slain many of the Britons, gives battle to the Bretwalda near the river Idel, Nottinghamshire, 145, 146. Redwald defeats him, and Edilfrid falls in this action, 146.

REES-AP-GRYFFITHS, king of South Wales; his nephew being murdered by a Norman baron, he makes war on the English, and for some time is successful, 1165; i. 451.

REEVES, Mr., quoted, i. 818—822. His description of the foundation of Lincoln's Inn, 819.

Reformation, the, by Luther, was begun in earnest, 1517; but Wycliffe had long before that prepared the English nation to receive the doctrines of the great reformer, ii. 345. History of this great moral and political change, 696—749.

Regency Bill, the, 1765; § i. 38.

Regiments, names of, as they still exist, given *regno* Charles II., iii. 895.

REGINALD, of St. Augustine's, Canterbury, elected by the monks to the primacy on the death of Hubert Walter, in 1205; but was afterwards, at their own request, set aside by the king, i. 559.

Relief Synod, the, founded by the Rev. Thomas Gillespie, 1752, in conjunction with the Rev. Thomas Boston, iv. 651.

Religion, B.C. 55 to A.D. 449;—Druidism, i. 59. Introduction of Christianity, 73. From A.D. 449 to 1066;—Saxon paganism, 224. Christianity, 228. From 1066 to 1216, history of religion continued, 547. From 1216 to 1399, religion in this period, 801. From 1399 to 1485, the Romish faith still the religion of the state; the Reformed doctrines received by many of the people, ii. 137. From 1485 to 1603, bitter persecutions, ending in that reaction by which the Reformed religion was established, 696. From 1603 to 1660, the Protestant Establishment, the Presbyterians, the Puritans, Independents, etc., iii. 433. From 1660 to 1689, Protestants, Catholics, etc.; the dissensions in religion that conduced to the English Revolution, 803. From 1688 to 1760, History of Religion (*continued*), iv. 617. Continuation of this essential portion of history, from 1760 to 1785; § i. 510. From 1785 to 1802; § iii. 561. From 1802 to 1820; § iv. 593.

REMINGTON, prepared for the duchess of Buckingham a remedy for the dying James I., which was supposed to have hastened the king's death, iii. 108.

"Remonstrance of the state of the kingdom," November 22, 1641; iii. 256. Some description of, *ib.*

RENÉE, daughter of Louis XII.; ii. 364.

RENNIE, John, constructor of Waterloo and Southwark Bridges, § iv. 676, 677. His portrait, 677.

Rental of England and Wales, in 1769, estimated at 16,000,000*l.*, § i. 573.

RESBY, John, burnt as a Wycliffite, in 1408; he, as far as is known, was the first person who thus suffered in Scotland, ii. 153.

Resumption Bill, the, 1700; iv. 105.

Revenue, account of the royal, *regno* William I.; i. 580—583. Statement by Sinclair of the income of the Norman line of kings, the Plantagenets, and the first of the Tudors, ii. 165. Rates of tonnage, poundage, customs, etc., *regno* Henry IV.; 166. Subsidies, a tenth or fifteenth of incomes, how levied. etc., *ib.* Modern history of the public revenue, iii. 849; iv. 682—685; § i. 544—546.

Revolution, French. *See* Louis XVI., and the emperor Napoleon Bonaparte.

REYNAUD, earl of Boulogne, enters the confederacy against France, and is taken prisoner at the battle of Bouvines, 1214; i. 526.

REYNOLDS, John, a leader of the levellers, iii. 36. Executed as a traitor, 1607; 37.

REYNOLDS, sir John, sent over to Boulogne, 1657, with a body of troops, to join the French army under Turenne, iii. 425. Is drowned upon the Goodwin Sands, 1658; 427.

REYNOLDS, sir Joshua, an eminent English painter, born 1723, died unmarried, 1792; § i. 624, 625. Portrait of, 625. His portraits of Georgiana, duchess of Devonshire, and Jane, duchess of Gordon, § ii. 301.

REYNOLDS, and SPARKS, Drs., with two other reforming preachers, hold controversy, 1604, with James I. and his bishops, respecting the subscription

REYNOLDS and SPARKS, Drs.,—
to the "Thirty-nine Articles," and such matters of religion as were in dispute, iii. 16. All Nonconformist preachers were then deprived, by the king's command, of their benefices, 17. Reynolds accepts the bishopric of Norwich, but is obliged to resign it, 820, 821.

Rhé, island of, taken by the Huguenots, 1625; iii. 107, 128, 135.

Rhode Island, settlement of Providence founded at, about 1635, by the Rev. Roger Williams, iii. 807.

Rice, origin of the cultivation of, in Carolina, iv. 721.

RICE, lord chief-justice of Ireland, 1690; iv. 11.

RICH, Robert, lord, impeached of high crimes and misdemeanours, 1642, by the House of Commons, iii. 288.

RICH, sir Nathaniel, sent on a commission to Ireland, 1622; iii. 88, 132.

RICH, sir Richard, solicitor-general, deposed as to private conversation he had had with the ex-chancellor More, 1535; two persons called to support Rich's evidence, though present in the room, refused to swear to More's words, which were perilous to the prisoner, ii. 388. More denied them, and spoke of Rich's infamous character, that his oath was not to be believed, ib. He became "chancellor of the Augmentations," 397. The Lincoln rebels, 1536, complained of him and Cromwell by name as upstarts, who, pretending service to the king, had sought their own gain and lucre, ib. Privy-councillor, 1547; 454. Created lord Rich, 456.

RICH, colonel, assists, 1648, in purging the parliament from its Presbyterian members, iii. 387. Marches against Charles, 1651; 404. He, together with other Fifth-monarchy-men, is sent to the Tower, 1657; 421.

RICH, a merchant, an admirer of the Quaker Naylor, 1656; iii. 813.

RICHARD I., (September 3, 1189—April 6, 1199,) second son of Henry II., does homage to the French king for Aquitaine; a marriage is agreed upon between prince Richard and Alice, daughter of Louis, i. 452. He quarrels with his father, and flies to the French court, 1173; 468. Leads the insurgents in Poictou and Aquitaine, 1174; 470. Is reconciled to his father, 471. Refuses to do homage to his brother Henry for the duchy of Aquitaine; war commences between them 1185; 473. Assists prince Henry against his father, 474. Goes to the French court, 1186; seizes his father's treasures at Chinon; heads another revolt in Aquitaine; submits to his father, 476. Takes the cross, ib. Suspicions as to the person of Adelais, his affianced bride, with whom it was reported that his father Henry was enamoured, 477. He does homage to king Philip for his father's continental dominions, ib. Success of the French king; a treaty put on foot which is afterwards broken off, the French king being true to Richard's cause, ib. Richard commands the people of Aquitaine, Poictou, and Brittany; and Philip attacks Henry in Anjou, who solicits a peace, and offers to resign himself to whatever terms Philip and Richard should propose, 478. Stipulations of this treaty; Richard appointed successor to England and Normandy, ib. Amazement of the king on hearing of the treachery of his son John; his death, July 6th, 1189, and burial at the abbey of Fontevraud, at which prince Richard was present, 479. Great seal of Richard I., 482. He imprisons Stephen of Tours, treasurer of Henry II., until he should deliver up the funds of the late king, ib. Sends letters into England for the enlargement of Eleanor, the queen-dowager, and appoints her regent in England; her mild and wise government, ib. Richard lands at Portsmouth, and takes possession of the royal treasury at Winchester, ib. Portrait of Richard I., from his tomb at Fontevraud, 483.

RICHARD I.,—
His first act as sovereign was to discard and persecute all those who had plotted against his father, even his most familiar friends, ib. His coronation at Westminster, September 3rd, 1189; description of this ceremony, ib. Destruction of the Jews in London, 484. Richard's preparations for war in the Holy Land; general sale of crown-lands and offices of the kingdom, 485. Richard receives 20,000 marks from the Scottish king, for which he is released from all obligations extorted from him during his captivity, and all the charters and documents of his servitude are given back, ib. A general council is held at Pipwell, in Northamptonshire, in which Hugh Pudsey, bishop of Durham, is appointed regent (Rector Regni) with William de Mandeville, earl of Albemarle, ib. Longchamp, bishop of Ely and chancellor of England, takes from Pudsey the regency, ib. The king confirms to his mother Eleanor all her estates, and adds to them those of Matilda and Alice, ib. Her share in the government, 486. Richard leaves England, and holds a great council in Normandy, 1190; arrangements for the government of the kingdom, and for obtaining supplies, ib. Mutual oaths of the kings of England and France, ib. They set out for the Holy Land; at Lyons the two kings separate, Philip taking the nearest road to Genoa, and Richard keeping his course by the valley of the Rhone, towards Marseilles, where his fleet was to be in readiness, ib. It not having arrived in time, he proceeds coastwise with some of his forces to Genoa, where he again meets the French king, ib. Laws enacted by Richard for preserving order in the fleet, 487. Adventures of his fleet before arriving at Marseilles; their stay at Lisbon, ib. Arrival of his fleet at Messina, with the army from Marseilles, 488. His journey through Italy, his stay at Naples and journey to Salerno; description of Salerno; his quarrel with the Calabrians, ib. His arrival with his fleet at Messina; he demands the enlargement of his sister Joan, and restoration of her dower; he forcibly takes possession of the town and castle of Bagnara, 490. His dispute with the people of Messina, ib. The city taken by storm; he commits the keeping of it to the Knights-Hospitallers and Templars, 491. Gaming among the pilgrim-soldiers prohibited, ib. Richard makes peace with Tancred, king of the two Sicilies, by which the magnificent dower conferred on his sister Joan by her husband is exchanged for the sum of 20,000 once, Richard receiving a like sum in compensation for all demands, ib. He affiances his young nephew Arthur to an infant daughter of Tancred, 492. His lavish expenditure, ib. He confesses his sins, and humbly receives penance, ib. His interview with the celebrated seer Giovacchino, ib. His visit to Etna; is met by Tancred, who gives him a letter affirmed to have been sent by the French king, in which Richard is accused of being a traitor, and offering to assist Tancred in driving him out of Sicily, 493. Richard gives the letter to Philip, and asks him if he knew it; the French king pronounces it a forgery, 1190, and accuses Richard of seeking a pretext for breaking off his marriage with the French princess, ib. Richard replies that his father Henry had cohabited with her, and therefore he could not marry her, but agrees to pay to Philip 2,000 marks a year for five years, and to restore the princess Alice, together with the fortresses received as her marriage portion, ib. He is permitted by Philip to marry whatever wife he chose, ib. His marriage with Berengaria, daughter of the king of Navarre, 493, 495. He sets sail for Acre; description of his fleet, 494. Is obliged to put into Rhodes; some of his ships wrecked on the island of Cyprus, and the mariners and crusaders barbarously plundered; he takes the

RICHARD I.,—
island, and imprisons the emperor Isaac, 495. Falls in with and attacks one of Saladin's large ships, 495. Enters the roadstead of Acre, ib. Assists in the siege of Acre; description of this dreadful siege, ib. His dispute with the French king, ib. Capitulation of Acre, after the loss of about 300,000 Christians, who perished in the siege, 496. The Saracens agree to restore the wood of the cross, to set at liberty 1,500 Christian captives, and to pay 200,000 pieces of gold, ib. Departure of Philip; he takes an oath not to molest any of the territories of the king of England, and leaves with him 10,000 men, 497. General massacre in the Christian camp of all Saracen prisoners, 1191; in revenge for which Saladin massacres all his Christian prisoners, ib. The army sets out for Jerusalem, ib. Richard attacks Saladin, whose army was greatly superior in number; he gains a complete victory at Azotus; Saladin retreats in great disorder, having lost 7,000 men; Richard advances to Jaffa without interruption, 498. He is persuaded to lose the summer in repairing the fortifications; his brave conduct, ib. He sets out from Jerusalem, but is obliged to retire to Ascalon, where he restores the fortifications, ib. He erects a chain of forts, and rebuilds the walls of Gaza, 499. His treasures are exhausted; general defection of the allies, ib. Conrad retires to Tyre, and opens a correspondence with Saladin, ib. Richard proposes an accommodation with Saladin, 500. Conrad murdered by two of the assassins in the streets of Tyre; Richard accused of being instigator of this murder, ib. The crusaders set out on their march to Jerusalem, 501; but finding that city strongly fortified, and a large force of the Saracens ready to oppose them, it is determined in a general council to be more advisable to besiege Cairo, ib. The French and Germans desert the standard altogether, ib. Richard retires to Acre, ib. Jaffa taken by the Saracens, ib. Richard arrives by sea with a small force, and puts the Saracens to flight, ib. On the next day, having been joined by the rest of his army, he gained the battle of Jaffa, 1192, which is esteemed the most brilliant that he fought, ib. A treaty concluded with Saladin, in which it is stipulated that the cities of Jaffa and Tyre, with all the castles and the country on the coast between them, were to be left to the peaceful enjoyment of the Christians; and full liberty of repairing to Jerusalem at all seasons was granted to the pilgrims of the west, ib. Richard refuses permission to the French to visit Jerusalem, as they had not assisted in procuring the benefits of the treaty, ib. He is prevented from visiting Jerusalem by a violent fever, 502. Richard sets sail from Acre, October, 1192, ib. His fleet, being scattered by a storm and some of the vessels wrecked, when within three days' sail of Marseilles, he changes his course for the Adriatic, and a storm drives him on the coast of Istria, ib. In the disguise of a pilgrim he crosses the Friuli Mountains, and proceeds inland to Goritz, ib. He sends a page to Maynard, the governor of that town, to ask for a passport for Baldwin of Bethune, and Hugh the merchant, who were pilgrims returning from Jerusalem, ib. The page presents a valuable ring to the governor as a proof of his master's good will, ib. Maynard discovered it was from king Richard, to whom he sent a message, ib. Richard alarmed, fled by night, and reached Freisach, where he was discovered by a Norman knight who however did not betray him, although a large reward had been offered for his detention, but warned him of his danger, and presented him with a swift horse, ib. Richard escapes with one knight and a boy, all the rest of his companions who had been able to keep up with him thus far were taken and thrown into prison, ib.

RICHARD I.,—
He enters Erperg, 1192, a village close to Vienna, and sends his boy into the city to buy provisions, where he excites attention by his plenty of money, and costly clothes, 503. He eluded inquiry by saying that his master was a very rich merchant, ib. Soon after he is seized and scourged, and being threatened with torture reveals the retreat of the king, ib. Richard is seized by Leopold, duke of Austria, who surrenders him to the emperor Henry VI., on conditions, 1193; 504. History of England during Richard's absence, 504; et. seq. General massacre of the Jews at Norwich, Stamford, St. Edmondsbury, Lincoln, and York, 504, 505. Longchamp displaces the sheriff and governor, and lays a fine on the citizens of York, 505. Richard confirms the authority of Longchamp, who had been accused by earl John of ruining the kingdom, 506. Gerard de Camville claims the custody of Lincoln Castle, ib. Longchamp marches to Lincoln; but while he is besieging the castle, earl John puts himself at the head of a large army, and takes the royal castles of Nottingham and Tickhill, 506. Earl John is acknowledged successor to Richard, should he die without issue, 507. Geoffrey, who had been expelled from England, returns contrary to the commands of Longchamp; is seized and imprisoned in Dover Castle, but soon set at liberty by Longchamp, ib. John, with the archbishop of Rouen, orders all the prelates and barons of the kingdom to assemble, and summons Longchamp to appear and make amends to the archbishop of York, and to answer for the whole of his public conduct before the king's council, ib. Longchamp marches to London, but not being joined by the citizens, who refuse to close their gates on earl John, he retires to the Tower, ib. Earl John is joyfully received in London, on taking a solemn oath that he would be faithful to his brother Richard, and maintain and enlarge the franchises of the city, ib. On the 9th of October, 1191, John is proclaimed, "The Chief Governor of the whole kingdom," ib. Walter, archbishop of Rouen, is appointed grand justiciary and chancellor in the place of Longchamp, 508. John promises to restore Longchamp on the receipt of 700l., to be paid within a week, but Walter and his ministers buy John off for 500l.; the French king demands the cession of princess Alice and her dower, and offers her in marriage to John, ib. The governor of Normandy refuses to make any restitutions before the return of his master, as contrary to the treaty of Messina, ib. Philip prepares for the invasion of Normandy, but many of the French nobles refuse to accompany him; the pope threatens him with excommunication, and he is obliged to relinquish his disgraceful enterprise, 509. Arrival of the news of Richard's departure from the Holy Land, ib. General disgust of all Europe at his imprisonment by the emperor, ib. The abbots of Broxley and Pont-Robert sent as deputies into Germany to give the king advice and consolation; the pope excommunicates Leopold duke of Austria, and threatens the emperor with the same sentence unless he immediately liberates Richard, ib. John goes to France, and does homage to king Philip for his brother's dominions, on the continent, 1192; ib. He takes Windsor and Wallingford Castles, and demands the crown in London, but is repulsed, ib. The princess Alice is betrothed to John, whom Philip engages to assist in obtaining possession of his brother's dominions by invading Normandy, while he overruns England; Philip enters Normandy, but is defeated by the earl of Leicester, ib. John is brought before the diet of the empire, 1193; 510. Terms agreed upon for his liberation; 70,000 marks are raised for his ransom, ib. In February, 1194, he is liberated, and on the 13th of

RICHARD I.,—

March lands at Sandwich, 510, 511. Proceeds to London, and receives the surrender of Nottingham Castle, 511. On the 30th of March, 1194, Richard holds a council at Nottingham, and is re-crowned with pomp at Winchester, ib. He prepares for war with Philip, and lands in Normandy, ib. Philip's military chest, together with the cartulary, the records, and the archives of the crown of France fall into Richard's hands, ib. Death of Leopold of Austria, ib. England afflicted with a famine, accompanied by the plague, 512. War again commenced with France, ib. Richard defeated in two engagements by the Bretons, 513. A peace agreed upon for five years between England and France, at the mediation of the pope's legate, ib. Vidomar, viscount of Limoges, having found a treasure in his domains, Richard demands that he shall deliver it up to him, 514. Vidomar offers him the half, ib. Richard besieges his castle of Chalus, and refuses any terms of capitulation, threatening to hang every one in it upon the battlements, ib. The castle is taken by assault, and all the men in it are butchered, with the exception of Bertrand de Gurdun, who in the siege had wounded the king in the shoulder with an arrow, ib. Richard, when dying, pardons Bertrand, and orders a hundred shillings to be given to him; but after the king's death he is flayed alive, and hanged by Marchadee, ib. Death of king Richard without issue, April 6, 1199, aged forty-two years, ib. He directed that his heart should be buried at Rouen, and his body at the feet of his father, at Fontevraud, ib.

RICHARD II. (June 22, 1377—September 29, 1399,) surnamed of Bourdeaux, son of Edward the Black Prince, i. 780. His Portrait, 781. His Great Seal, ib. His accession, 22nd June, 1377, 782. His coronation at Westminster, July 16. A regency is appointed, ib. A French and Spanish fleet plunders and wastes the Isle of Wight, and burns the towns of Hastings and Rye, but meets with considerable resistance at Winchelsea, and is repulsed with great loss at Southampton by the earl of Arundel, ib. An English fleet is fitted out, under the command of the earl of Buckingham, which meets with little success, ib. Alice Perrers is banished, 1377; 783. The duke of Lancaster is appointed commander of the fleet; he captures many of the Spanish ships, takes possession of the town and port of Cherbourg, and persuades the duke of Brittany to cede to him the important town and harbour of Brest, but fails in his attempt on St. Malo, ib. Berwick is taken by the Scots, but soon after retaken by the earl of Northumberland. John Mercer collects a fleet of Scots, French, and Spaniards, with which he captures all the ships in the port of Scarborough, 783. John Philpot, an alderman of London, fits out a fleet at his own expense, retakes the ships, and after a fierce engagement captures the Spanish fleet, taking Mercer prisoner; on his return he is reprimanded by the council of government, ib. The earl of Buckingham commands another expedition into France, and goes to the assistance of the Bretons. The French king dies, and is succeeded by his son, Charles VI., then a minor, 784. Peace is concluded between France and Brittany, ib. Parliament grants the king a new aid, 1378, in the form of a poll-tax of three groats upon every person above fifteen years of age, ib. Some parts of Kent and Essex refuse to pay the poll-tax, 785. The people of Fobbing drive away Thomas de Bampton, one of the commissioners, ib. Sir Robert Belknape, chief-justice of the Common Pleas, is sent into Essex to try the offenders, but the people rise, drive him away, kill the jurors, and appoint Jack Straw their captain, ib. The daughter of a poor man, named

RICHARD II.,—

Walter the Tyler, being insulted by one of the commissioners, her father kills him, ib. About the same time sir Robert Burley demands an industrious man of Gravesend as his escaped bondsman, on which the commonalty of Kent take up arms and demand his release, appointing Wat Tyler their captain, who enters Canterbury, and threatens to kill the archbishop, ib. He then marches towards London, and on the 11th of June, 1381, encamps at Blackheath with 100,000 men, ib. Richard and his ministers retire to the Tower, June 12; ib. The rebels destroy the Marshalsea, the King's Bench, and the mansion of the lord-treasurer at Highbury, ib. Walworth, the lord-mayor, admits them into London, where they burn the Savoy Palace, the Temple, the Priory of St. John at Clerkenwell, and demolish the prisons, ib. During the night of the 13th, London is involved in all the horrors of anarchy. On the 14th, the king promises to meet the rebels at Mile-end, where they appear before him with mild and respectful demeanour, and present four very moderate demands, which the king readily promises to grant, ib. While the king is absent at Mile-end the rebels of Kent, who had remained in London, enter the Tower, and behead the archbishop of Canterbury, the chancellor, sir Robert Hales, the treasurer, William Apuldore, and Legge, 787. The Kentish rioters, under Wat Tyler, reject the just Charter of Concessions granted to the men of Essex, ib. Wat Tyler is slain in Smithfield, Walworth, the lord-mayor, giving him the first blow, for being insolent to the king, ib. The lord-mayor advises Richard to persuade the rioters to follow him to the open fields, promising him that the citizens would arm and soon come to his assistance, 789. The king is joined by sir Robert Knowles, with 1,000 men-at-arms; the insurgents throw down their arms and fly, ib. The king having collected 40,000 horse, declares that the charters meant nothing, ib. The men of Essex make a stand, but are defeated with great loss, and a commission is appointed to try the chief offenders, ib. Philip Von Arteveldt takes the command of the democratic army of Flanders, and raises the siege of Ghent, 790. Richard marries Anne of Bohemia, daughter of the emperor Charles IV., 1382; 789, 790. The French and the aristocratic army of Flanders gain the battle of Rosebecque, and the illustrious Von Arteveldt is slain, 790. The bishop of Norwich raises an army in England, and invades Flanders, at the desire of the pope, ib. John Latimer accuses the duke of Lancaster of treason; Latimer is murdered, and Lancaster is reconciled to the king, 791. The French land an army in Scotland, 1385, and, being joined by the Scots, invade England, ib. Richard raises an army of 80,000 men, and compels them to retreat, ib. He burns Edinburgh, Perth, and other towns, but is obliged to return, having received information that the French and Scots were besieging Carlisle, ib. The princess of Wales, the king's mother, dies, 1385, ib. Henry of Bolingbroke is made earl of Derby; the earls of Cambridge and Buckingham are created dukes of York and Gloucester; Michael de la Pole is created earl of Suffolk; and Robert de Vere duke of Ireland, ib. Roger, earl of March, is declared successor to the crown, ib. The duke of Lancaster invades Castile, and gains many battles, ib. His daughter is married to the heir of the king of Castile, whose issue reigned for many years in Spain, ib. Charles VI., the young king of France, collects a splendid army of 100,000 men for the invasion of England, 1385, but this project is opposed by his uncles; the army is disbanded, and many of the ships prepared for this expedition are captured by the English, 791, 792. De la Pole,

RICHARD II,—
the earl of Suffolk, is expelled; the Commons sentence him to pay a heavy fine and to be imprisoned, 792. A regency is appointed, with the duke of Gloucester at its head, *ib.* Tresilian, the chief-justice, and some of the judges, declare that the commission of regency is illegal, 1387; and on November 17, the duke of Gloucester enters London with a large army, and all the favourites of Richard take to flight, or are imprisoned, *ib.* The "Wonderful Parliament" confirms the impeachments of the duke of Gloucester, 793. Sir Simon Burley, the lord-mayor, and three other knights, are executed, 1388 ; *ib.* The battle of Otterbourne, famous under the name of Chevy Chase, is gained by the Scots, August 15, 1388; *ib.* In a great council held in May, 1389, Richard assumes the government, and Gloucester is banished from the council, 793, 794. Lancaster returns from Spain, is created duke of Aquitaine for life, 794. He takes a leading part in the administration, and becomes exceedingly moderate and popular, *ib.* He negotiates a peace with France, *ib.* A truce with France and Scotland concluded for four years, *ib.* Queen Anne dies at Shene, June 1394, *ib.* Richard goes into Ireland with an army to suppress the insurrection of Irish chiefs there; they immediately submit, and no battle is fought, *ib.* Richard returns, and is well received by his subjects, *ib.* He goes to France and marries Isabella, daughter of Charles VI., October 1396, *ib.* Returns to England and artfully arrests the earls of Warwick and Arundel, *ib.* The duke of Gloucester is sent prisoner to Calais, and the archbishop of Canterbury is banished, July 1397, *ib.* The earl of Arundel is impeached, and beheaded September; Gloucester dies at Calais, and Warwick is imprisoned, 795. Bolingbroke is created duke of Hereford; the earl of Nottingham and John Holland are created dukes of Norfolk and Exeter, *ib.* The parliament votes the king a subsidy on wool for life, *ib.* The duke of Norfolk challenges Hereford, January 1398; 796. Hereford is banished for ten years, and Norfolk for life, *ib.* On the death of the great earl of Lancaster, December, 1398, Richard seizes his vast estates, and in May, 1399, sets out for a campaign in Ireland with a splendid fleet and retinue, 797. In the following July, Hereford returns to England and lands at Ravenspur, *ib.* The Londoners receive him with great joy, and many of them join his army, *ib.* The duke of York, who was left regent of England during the king's absence in Ireland, raises the royal standard at St. Alban's, *ib.* The regent's army is disaffected, and Hereford immediately sets out to meet him, *ib.* On arriving at the Severn a conference is proposed, when the regent joins his forces with those of Hereford, *ib.* They take Bristol Castle, and kill three of the members of Richard's council, *ib.* The earl of Salisbury, with part of the king's forces, lands at Conway, and is joined by some Welsh, but is soon deserted by all his men, *ib.* Richard lands at Milford Haven with his remaining forces, but is also deserted, and takes refuge in Conway Castle, which he is compelled to abandon for want of provisions, *ib.* He is captured and taken to Flint, where he has an interview with Bolingbroke, and from thence is sent a prisoner to Chester, *ib.* While on his way to London he makes his escape at Lichfield, but is retaken, conveyed to London, and imprisoned in the Tower, 798. On the 30th of September a parliament, summoned in the king's name, met at Westminster, where the resignation of Richard was read and accepted, and an Act of Deposition passed, *ib.* As soon as this was finished, Henry of Bolingbroke, duke of Hereford, and cousin of king Richard, rose, and was seated on the throne by the archbishops of Canterbury and York,

RICHARD II,—
799, 800. He is murdered at Pontefract Castle, ii. 7. After his death reports are circulated that he is still alive, and about to return at the head of an army to assert his rights, 10. *Illustrations*; Meeting of Richard and Bolingbroke at Flint Castle, i. 798. Bolingbroke conducting Richard into London, 799. Parliament assembled for the deposition of Richard, *ib.* Coins of this reign, 838.
RICHARD III. (June 26, 1483 — August 22, 1485 ;) created by Edward IV., duke of Gloucester, ii. 99. His gallant conduct, 1471, at Tewkesbury, 109. He persuades the lady Anne Nevil, widow of Edward prince of Wales, to marry him, 111. Their union, by permission of king Edward and the council, *ib.* He disputed her great possessions or revenue, with Clarence, before Edward, in person, *ib.* After hearing the eloquent arguments of both his brothers, the king adjudged a handsome portion to the lady Anne, and the estates to Isabella duchess of Clarence, the elder sister, *ib.* No real reconciliation ensued betwixt the royal dukes, *ib.* Suspicions that Gloucester advised the trial and death of Clarence, 114. His campaigns, 1480—1482, against James III., the treacherous Albany aiding the duke of Gloucester, 114, 115. Cession of Berwick to the English, 115. Return of duke Richard, 115, 117. He professed loyalty to his nephew, at York and other places, 117, 118. At Stoney Stratford, attended by Buckingham, he secured the person of Edward V., 118. He rode bareheaded into London before the young king, 119. Edward lodged in the state-rooms in the Tower, *ib.* Gloucester at the council-table appeared in a merry humour, 119, 120. He quitted the council-chamber in the Tower for an hour, and returned with an angry countenance, *ib.* His charge against queen Elisabeth, and Jane Shore, that they by sorcery had dried up his arm, *ib.* He gave a loud rap on the council-board, and the chamber was filled with armed men, 120. He arrested lord Hastings, and commanded his immediate execution, *ib.* Lord Stanley was wounded, but falling beneath the table was saved, *ib.*; but he was kept prisoner, 121. The protector present at the conclusion of Dr. Shaw's sermon on the illegitimacy of the young princes, which allegation was repeated by Buckingham, 121, 122. The proposition that Richard of Gloucester should be king, made at Guildhall, 122. The children of Clarence set aside by reason of that duke's attainder, *ib.* Deputation of the lord-mayor, and many of the nobility to the protector at Baynard's Castle, *ib.* Gloucester *reluctantly* accepted the crown, *ib.* Thus ended the nominal reign of Edward V., *ib.* Portrait of Richard III., 123. His great seal, *ib.* His speech in Westminster-hall, *ib.* His coronation with queen Anne, in Westminster Abbey, 124. He did not call a parliament, *ib.* His royal progress, and reception with acclamations, *ib.* To gratify his trusty adherents at York, he was again crowned there with queen Anne, *ib.* Murder of Edward V. and Richard duke of York, by order of Richard III., related by sir T. More, *ib.* Insurrection, 124, 125. Richard III., to daunt the insurgents, allowed the murders in the Tower to be divulged, 125. The conspirators, not expecting mercy if taken, resolved to set up Henry earl of Richmond, then in France, *ib.* That prince appeared off Devonshire with a fleet, but returned to St. Malo, 126. Richard's proclamation, *ib.* Buckingham, who had helped him to the crown, took up arms against him, with a Welsh levy, *ib.* The people near the Severn, fearing the indiscipline of such troops, broke down all bridges, and no fords were passable, *ib.* Buckingham fled, was captured, and at Salisbury Richard denied him an audience, 127. The duke beheaded in the market-

RICHARD III.,—
place, ib. King Richard then called his only parliament, ib. Bills of attainder, the king divides the
forfeited estates among his faithful adherents, ib.
His son Edward, prince of Wales, declared heir-
apparent by an Act of entail of the crown, ib.
Richard negotiates with queen Elizabeth, that his
son should marry Elizabeth daughter of Edward
IV., ib. The usurper's great dejection on the
death of the prince, 128. His resolve to espouse
his niece Elizabeth, intending to obtain a dispensation, ib. Sickness and death of queen Anne, Feb.
1485, ib. Reflections, ib. The princess Elizabeth
wrote to Norfolk to advance her marriage with the
king, declaring her great love for Richard III., ib.
His never-failing friends, Catesby and Ratcliffe, dissuade him from the marriage, ib. The king thereupon solemnly declared to the lord-mayor and a
great meeting convened by him in the Temple, that
he had never contemplated such an union, ib. He
wrote to that purport to his partisans at York, ib.
He negotiated with duke Francis of Brittany, for
the seizure of Richmond, who narrowly escaped
into a forest near Vannes, and thence to France, ib.
Bitter proclamation of king Richard, its allegations
against Richmond, ib. It called upon all his liege
subjects to arm in defence of their hearths, etc., ib.
Henry of Richmond had his armament ready at
Harfleur, ib. Some forced loans rendered the usurper
unpopular in London, 129. He trusted the sea-coasts
to officers, many of whom betrayed him, ib. Richard
raised his standard at Nottingham, where he was
joined by Northumberland, and his northern partisans, ib. Landing of Henry at Milford Haven, ib.
At Leicester Richard was joined by Norfolk, Lovel,
and Brackenbury, but lord Stanley did not come in,
ib. Lord Strange, son of Stanley, was in Richard's
camp under strong guard, ib. Artifice was requisite
to save Strange's life. Stanley with his forces had
sided for Richmond, ib.; he therefore advanced to
the field as if retreating before the invaders, closely
pursued, and was only to declare himself during
action, ib. Richmond crossed the Severn, was
joined by the Talbots and others, and marched
onwards with a force small in comparison of the
usurper's, ib. He received, however, numerous
deserters from the king's army, ib. At Bosworth,
August 22, 1485, Richard, wearing his crown, led his
army into the field, ib. In the commencement of the
fight more of the king's lords and their troops joined
Richmond's lines, ib. Lord Stanley appeared in
Henry's array of battle, ib. Norfolk charged the
advanced guard under the earl of Oxford, ib. The
king catching sight of Richmond, hoped to win the
day in a personal conflict with the invader, ib.;
he cut his way to Henry's standard, killing with his
own hand sir William Brandon and sir J. Cheney,
ib. Whilst aiming a deadly thrust at Richmond, he
was struck from his horse and despatched, ib. Stanley placed the blood-stained crown on the head of
Henry VII., ib. Observations and reflections, 129,
130. His autograph, ib. Richard's body interred
in the Grey Friars, at Leicester, ib. His reign had
lasted two years and two months, ib. His countenance and person described, ib. Coins of king Richard, 187. Act of Attainder passed against Richard,
late duke of Gloucester, and his partisans who fought
at Bosworth Field, 1485; 283, 284. The forfeitures
and confiscations chiefly reserved by the king, a
portion of them granted by Henry VII. to his
adherents, 284.
RICHARD, second son of William I., gored to death
by a stag in the New Forest, i. 387.
RICHARD, natural son of Robert of Normandy,
killed by an arrow accidentally in the New Forest,
some short time preceding the similar catastrophe
of the Red King, i. 401.

RICHARD, half-brother of prince William, perished in
the Blanche-Nef, 1120; i. 414.
RICHARD of Cirencester, a Benedictine, fourteenth
century, his writings alluded to, i. 76.
RICHARDSON, Samuel, a very distinguished English
novelist, born in 1689; died of apoplexy, 1761; § i.
605.
RICHARDSON, lord chief-justice, his speech against
Prynne's "Histrio-mastix," iii. 153. He issues an
order against church-ales and revels in Somersetshire, 1633; 160.
RICHARDSON, captain, saves the life of sir Patrick
Johnstone, 1706; iv. 192.
Richborough, in Kent, the site of the Roman maritime
station Rutupæ, i. 90.
RICHELIEU, cardinal bishop of Luçon, introduced
into the ministry, 1616, by the influence of the wife
of Concini, marshal d'Ancre. His eagerness to
defeat the match of Charles I. with Spain, iii. 106,
107. He applies to the English for assistance
against the French Protestants, 1625. His cold
reception of sir D. Carleton, 1626; 125. He
denies Buckingham admission to Paris, 1627; 114.
Constructs the Dyke around Rochelle, 135. Takes
Rochelle, 1628; 138. He died, 1642, aged 58.
RICHELIEU, duke of, he lands in Minorca with 16,000
men, 1756; iv. 586. Quits the service in disgust,
1757; 598.
RICHEMONT, Arthur, count of, brother to the duke
of Brittany, ii. 54. He marries a sister of John
duke of Burgundy, by the intervention of Bedford,
1423; ib. He became discontented with Bedford,
and returning to Brittany endeavoured to turn his
brother from the English alliance, 56. He persuaded
that duke to declare for king Charles; Richemont
had been made constable of France, and served
beyond the Loire, but Brittany was overrun by the
troops of the regent Bedford, 58. He seized
Charles's chief favourite, the Sire de Giac, who
was punished for his misdeeds by drowning, 58, 59.
The constable caused the new favourite Camus de
Beaulieu, to be murdered, 59. He recommended
George de la Tremoille to the king; who shortly
became so great a favourite, that the constable conspired with other chiefs to murder him also, ib.
Richemont was banished by Charles VII., and in
1428 headed a formidable revolt, and a civil war
ensued in Poietou, etc., ib. Recalled by the king,
at the wish of the royal army, 68, 69. His remarkable speech to the Maid of Orleans, 68. Was
present at the congress of Arras, 78. Repulsed,
1436, from the walls of Calais, 79, 80.
Richmond, in Yorkshire, View of; formerly granted
by William I. to Allen the Breton, i. 374.
Richmond Palace, ii. 841.
RICHMOND, John de Dreux, earl of, appointed governor of Scotland, 1307; i. 734. The Scots gain the
battle of Inverury, May 22, 1308; increase of the
Scottish power, 733. Richmond died about 1334.
RICHMOND, dowager-countess of, mother of Henry
VII., ii. 126. Her second marriage with lord
Stanley, ib. She entered into the plot for bringing
over Richmond from France, ib. Her attainder
reversed, 1 Henry VII., 283. She resides with
queen Elizabeth at Winchester, 287. She recommended the union of Henry VIII. and Catherine
of Arragon, 319, 320.
RICHMOND, Henry Fitzroy, duke of, a son of Henry
VIII. by Elizabeth Blount, widow of sir Gilbert
Tailbois, created, June 1525; ii. 364. Henry's
affection for this illegitimate son, having caused
both the princesses Mary and Elizabeth to be declared by parliament illegitimate, the king caused
an Act to pass giving him by letters-patent, or by
will, power to name his successor, 1536; he was not
then certain of any offspring by queen Jane, and
Richmond's prospects were hereby advanced, 395.

RICHMOND, Henry Fitzroy, duke of,—
The duke died at this time, 1536, aged 18, and the king grieved much for his loss, *ib.*

RICHMOND, James Stuart, duke of, third duke of Lennox in Scotland, iii. 169. Raised to the English peerage, 1641. He died, 1655; 249.

RICHMOND, Charles Lennox, duke of, natural son of king Charles II. Created August, 1675. He died, 1723; iii. 762.

RICHMOND, Charles Lennox, duke of, 1750. His speech, April 7, 1778, relative to America, hastens the death of the aged earl of Chatham, § i. 340, 341. He moves for an address, beseeching his majesty to reflect on the manifold distresses and difficulties of the country, 1779; 401. He died, 1806.

RIDER, sir Dudley, chief-justice of the King's Bench, dies, 1756, and is succeeded by Murray, earl of Mansfield, iv. 587, *note.*

RIDLEY, Nicholas, he throws the kingdom into a ferment by a Lent sermon, which he preached both against images and holy-water, ii. 731. He is transferred, 1550, from the see of Rochester to that of London, 493. He preaches eloquently on the right and title of the Lady Jane Grey, 503. He is committed to the Tower by queen Mary, 509; and brought to trial for heresy, 525. He is burned at the same stake with Latimer, October 16, 1555; 525, 526. His portrait, 696.

Rights, Bill of, passed, 1689; iv. 19, 660.

RILEY, John, a painter of original talent; he died, 1691; iv. 753.

RINUCCINI, the pope's nuncio in Ireland, 1646; iii. 357.

Riots, the great London, 1780; § i. 409—418.

RIPPERDA, a Fleming, prime-minister of Spain. Being dismissed, May 14, 1726, and, fearing both the people and the court, he takes refuge in the house of Mr. William Stanhope, the English envoy; but is dragged thence by force, and imprisoned in the castle of Segovia; he escaped out of the Tower, 1728, and, after several adventures, arrived in England; he left for Holland, 1731, and presently entered the service of Muley Abdallah, where he became a pacha; after an unfortunate expedition against Spain, he was forced to resign his command, and retired to the protection of the pacha of Tetuan, at which place he died, in 1737; iv. 391, 392.

RIVERS, sir Richard Woodville, earl, 1466, father of Elizabeth, queen of Edward IV., appointed treasurer in the room of lord Mountjoy. ii. 80, *note*; 101, 102. After the victory of Edgecote, gained by the Yorkshire insurgents over Pembroke, who was slain, 1469, they captured Rivers and sir John Woodville, took them to Northampton, and cut their heads off, 1469; 104. *See* Jacquetta, duchess of Bedford.

RIVERS, Anthony Woodville, married the heiress of lord Scales, and took that title, 1467; ii. 103. On the murder of his father, he succeeded as earl Rivers, 107. Edward V., thirteen years old, under his care at Ludlow Castle, 1483; 117, 118. At Stoney-Stratford, so soon as duke Richard found his nephew, Edward V., within his grasp, he arrested Rivers and lord Richard Gray, together with Vaughan and Hawse, favourite esquires of the young king, 118.. They are sent by Gloucester to Pontefract Castle, *ib.* There they were beheaded, 1483; 121. Rivers was accomplished, and patronised Caxton, introducing our first printer to Edward IV., *ib.* His encounter in tournament with the Bastard of Burgundy, 249.

RIVERS, John Savage, earl of, succeeded February, 1640; he was a Roman Catholic, and a royalist; he died 1654; iii. 292.

RIVERS, Richard Savage, earl of, 1694; arrives at Lisbon with a body of troops, 1706. He died 1712; iv. 186.

RIVET, John; the statue of Charles I. was sold to him by the revolutionists, for the worth of the metal, on the condition of his destroying it; he, however, hid it till the Restoration, when it was replaced, about 1678; iii. 576.

RIZZIO, David, comes to Scotland in the suite of Morata, the ambassador of Savoy. Though of low birth, he had been well educated, and was an excellent musician, ii. 585. Mary, queen of Scots, promotes him to the office of private secretary, but he is much looked down upon by the nobles, *ib.* On the 9th of March, 1566, he was savagely murdered by Darnley and Ruthven in the queen's presence, 586, 587.

Roads in Britain, constructed by the Romans, i. 117. Road-making during the eighteenth century, § i. 575. Improvements of Telford and M'Adam, § iv. 675.

ROBART, M., a servant of the duke of Leeds; on the trial of his master, 1695, he absconds, and thus renders the evidence against him incomplete, iv. 52.

ROBARTES, Richard, merchant of Truro, obliged to accept the title of baron Robartes, of Truro, 1625, and pay 10,000*l.* for it, iii. 70.

ROBARTS, John, lord. *See* Radnor.

ROBERT II., Stewart of Scotland, (1371—1390,) nephew of David Bruce, succeeds to the throne of Scotland, 1371; i. 774. A French army is sent into Scotland under the command of John de Vienne to assist the Scots in making an inroad into England, 791. Richard forces the Scots to retire, and burns Edinburgh, Perth, and other towns, 1385, but returns to England on hearing that the Scots were besieging Carlisle, *ib.* Robert II. dies, April 19, 1390, and is succeeded by Robert III., 794.

ROBERT III., (1390—1406,) his accession, 1390, as king of Scotland, ii. 131. His accomplishments, piety, and amiable nature, *ib.* Became king, aged above fifty, *ib.* His brothers, the earl of Fife, afterwards duke of Albany, and the earl of Buchan, *ib.* Albany guardian of the king and kingdom, *ib.* Their characters more fit for such times than the king's, *ib.* The king's eldest son, David duke of Rothsay, having many friends, is appointed regent, 1398, in lieu of Albany, *ib.* Rothsay repulses Henry IV. from Edinburgh, 9. He is imprisoned for a short time by king Robert, for dissipation of conduct, *ib.*; and starved by Albany in Falkland Castle, 19, 131. The king, under alarm, sought the safety of his young son James earl of Carrick, whom he embarked for France, but who is intercepted by the English, and carried to Windsor Castle as a captive, *ib.* Robert's generals defeated in England, at Nesbit Moor and Homildon-hill, 11, 131. King Robert retired to Rothsay Castle, in Bute, where he died, 1406, of grief, 19, 131. A parliament at Perth declared young James to be king, and continued Albany in the regency, 131.

ROBERT, eldest son of William the Conqueror, claims the government of Normandy, which his father refuses to grant, 1077-9; i. 383. Being provoked by his two brothers William and Henry, he attempts to slay them, *ib.* Flies to Rouen, but fails in his attack on the castle, *ib.* Is reconciled to his father, *ib.* Again demands the government of Normandy, and is refused, 384. He goes to the king of France, Philip I., who establishes him in the castle of Gerberoy, *ib.* William besieges the castle, but is obliged to relinquish the attempt; it was in this siege that Robert accidentally wounded his father, *ib.* A reconciliation is again effected, but Robert flies for the third time and never sees his father's face again, *ib.* William appoints Robert his eldest son as his successor in the duchy of Normandy, 389. Robert is absent at his father's death; he returns immediately to Normandy, and is joyfully received as duke in Rouen, 393. Is persuaded by Odo and

2 H

ROBERT, eldest son of William the Conqueror,— other Norman barons to lay claim to England, 1087; 394. A strong party of Norman barons in England favour his cause, ib. His plans frustrated by his foolish delays; William's wise measures; energy of the Saxon population in his cause, ib. Robert's party in England is extinguished; many of the barons being executed, others permitted to fly to Normandy, and their estates confiscated, 395, 396. William attempts to take from him the duchy of Normandy, 396. The king of France comes to his assistance; a treaty of peace is concluded at Caen, 397. Conditions of this treaty, ib. Robert and William besiege prince Henry in Mount St. Michael, ib. Robert and Edgar Atheling bring about a treaty between Malcolm Caenmore, king of Scotland, and William, by which Edgar is permitted to return to England, 398. William breaks the treaty of Caen; Robert returns to Normandy; William submits the matter in debate to the arbitration of the twenty-four barons, according to the treaty of Caen, who having decided in favour of Robert, William commences war, 399. His success, ib. Philip comes to Robert's assistance, is bought off by William, who is obliged to return to England, the Welsh having overrun Cheshire, Shropshire, and Herefordshire, and reduced the Isle of Anglesea, 1094; ib. Duke Robert, taking the cross, 1096, was one of the most valiant Christian princes in the first crusade, 400. He mortgaged Normandy to William Rufus for 10,000l., and set out for Palestine at the head of many of his knights and vassals, 400, 401. His son Richard was killed in the New Forest by a chance arrow, 401. Prince Henry hastening, on the death of Rufus, to Winchester to seize the royal treasure, 1100, the right of the absent duke Robert was nobly maintained by De Breteuil, the treasurer, but in vain, 404. Henry I., conscious of the oaths he had formerly taken to his brother Robert, reported that the latter had been elected king of Jerusalem, and would therefore not return to claim England, 405, 407. Robert returns from the Holy Land, after the capture of Jerusalem, 15th of July, 1099, having greatly distinguished himself there, and performed prodigies of valour, 407. Delays much time in Italy, and resides for some time at the castle of William, count of Conversano, in Apulia, a powerful Norman baron of Italy, whose daughter Sibylla he marries, and receives a large sum of money as her dowry, 408. Is joyfully received in Normandy, ib. He prepares for the invasion of England, ib. The greater part of the English navy deserts to him, 409. He lands at Portsmouth, a reconciliation is made, and a peace agreed upon, wherein Robert gives up all claim to England, and receives a yearly payment of 3,000 marks, and all the castles which Henry possessed in Normandy, with many other conditions, ib. Duke Robert comes over to England to intercede for the unfortunate barons; is detained as prisoner, and obliged to purchase his freedom by renouncing his annuity of 3,000 marks, 410. The treaty is broken by Henry, ib. Robert's inability at government, and deplorable state of Normandy, ib. Henry declares himself protector of Normandy against the bad government of his brother, ib. He invades Normandy, 1105, but is unable to complete the ruin of Robert in this campaign; in the following year he re-appears in Normandy with a more formidable army, ib. The siege of Tenchebray being hard pressed by Henry, Robert comes to its relief, ib. He throws the English infantry into disorder, and had nearly won the victory, when De Belesme basely fled with a strong division of his forces, a general panic spread; after a last and most brilliant display of valour, Robert was taken with four hundred of his knights, ib. Is kept as a prisoner in England, 1106;

ROBERT, eldest son of William the Conqueror,— 411. He attempts to escape from his guard, but is taken and condemned to be blinded by order of his brother, ib. He lived twenty-eight years after this, and died in Cardiff Castle in 1135, a few months before his brother Henry, ib.

ROBERT, archbishop of Canterbury, 1043, a Norman, i. 189. On the danger to all foreigners, caused by the affair of Eustace and the burghers of Dover, followed by Godwin's triumphant return, the archbishop flies, 193. With some armed retainers, he fought his way out of London, galloped to the Ness, on the Essex shore, and escaped in an open boat, 1052; ib. Supposed to have communicated to William the intention of Edward to appoint him his successor, 196.

ROBERTS, Lewes; his work on the trade of England, 1638; iii. 540.

ROBERTSON, William, a celebrated modern historian, born 1721; died June, 1793; § i. 621. Portrait of, ib.

ROBERTSON, a smuggler, sentenced to death; his escape through the self-devotion of his friend, Wilson, 1736; iv. 418.

ROBESPIERRE, Maximilian Isidore, born at Arras, 1759; recapitulation of his early life, § ii. 361, 362, 485, 497. He recommends to the National Assembly, 1791, to avoid war, 725. His eloquent speech against Atheism, § iii. 56. He is denounced by Brissot, 58. He defends himself against the charge of aiming at the dictatorship, 203. Threatens to bring Vergniaud to the guillotine, 1793; 329. Obtains a seat in the Committee of Public Safety towards the beginning of August, (the Reign of Terror dates from this period,) 344. He procures the celebration of the Festival to the Supreme Being, June 8, 1794, at which he officiates as pontiff, 430, 431. Declaims against the doctrine of Materialism, which was rapidly gaining ground in France, 438. He loses his power in the Convention, and, together with many other members of the Mountain, is brought to the guillotine, July 28, after an unsuccessful attempt at suicide, 442—449.

ROBINSON, John, consecrated bishop of Bristol, November, 1710; translated to London, March, 1713; he died 1723; iv. 277.

ROBINSON, sir Thomas, secretary of state, 1755; iv. 580. He is dismissed, 584.

ROCAFERTI, inquisitor-general in the time of Charles II. of Spain, iv. 110.

ROCHAMBEAU, Donation Joseph Marie de Vimeur, takes the command of the French expedition to St. Domingo, after the death of Leclerc, 1802; § iv. 38. Being compelled to evacuate the island, he was taken prisoner by the English, and did not return to France till 1811. He was killed at the battle of Leipsic, in 1813.

Rochdale, iii. 656.

ROCHE-JAQUELEIN, count Henri de la, a brave leader of the Vendeans, 1793; § iii. 370. Portrait of, ib. He is shot by a republican grenadier, Jan. 28, 1794; 484.

Rochelle, La, port of, in Brittany, (View drawn in 1650), iii. 129.

Rochelle, city of, invested by the duke of Angoulême and marshal Bassompierre, 1627; iii. 135. Taken by Richelieu, 1628; 138.

Rochester Castle, View of the keep of, i. 395. Its defence by Eustace of Boulogne, and bishop Odo, ib. Its surrender to William Rufus and his English army; the Norman knights who had defended it being allowed honourable conditions, ib.

Rochester Cathedral, founded by Gundulph, 1077; View of the west front of, i. 620.

ROCHESTER, Robert Carr, earl of, of the border family of Fernyherst, iii. 38. Description of his person, ib. Appears as page, 1606, to lord Dingwall, at a tilting-match at Westminster, his horse falling,

Rochester Castle, Carr, earl of—
breaks his leg; the king's attention to him; he undertakes to teach him Latin, and knights him, 1607; *ib.* He is created viscount Rochester, March, 1611; and member of the Privy-council, April, 1612; also, master of the Order of the Garter, 49. On the death of the earl of Salisbury, he becomes lord-chamberlain, *ib.* The post of secretary being vacant for some time, he does the duties of that office by means of sir T. Overbury, *ib.* He is suspected of having poisoned prince Henry, son of James I., 1612; 52. Notion absurd, *ib.* The countess of Essex becomes enamoured with him, *ib.* He is created earl of Somerset, 1613; 54. His marriage with lady Frances Howard, December 26, 1613; *ib.* Is implicated in the charge of the murder of Overbury, 60. Pronounced guilty, 1616; 62. Pardon offered to him; he retires to the country with his lady, on a pension of 4,000*l.* per annum, *ib.* He died 1645.

ROCHESTER, Lawrence Hyde, earl of, second son of the earl of Clarendon, iii. 419. Made president of the council, 1684; 759. Appointed to the government of Ireland, 759, 779. Member of the Ecclesiastical Commission, 786. Deprived of his employments, 1686, he receives a pension of 5,700*l.* per annum, *ib.* He raises a doubt as to the continuation of the parliament after the death of Mary, queen of William III., iv. 51. Made lord-lieutenant of Ireland, 1701; 112. Continued in his office by queen Anne, 142. His death, 1711; 252.

ROCHFORD, lady, beheaded, February 13, 1532; ii. 423.

ROCHFORD, lord, son of the earl of Wiltshire, (sir Thomas Boleyn.) This young noble, conspicuous in a tourney at Greenwich, in presence of queen Anne Boleyn, his *sister*, and Henry VIII., 1536, was immediately arrested, with other courtiers, on charges of incontinence with the queen, 391. His trial before a court of peers of the king's choosing, 393. Put to the bar, on the moment of the condemned queen being led off, Rochford was convicted on the same insufficient evidence, chiefly the *confession* of a musician (one of the accused,) tortured, and with a prospect of life, *ib.* Improbability of the guilt of any of the accused, the jealous and impetuous monarch anxiously awaiting the moment of the queen's execution, to marry Jane Seymour, 393, 394. Rochford's execution, 1536; 394.

ROCKINGHAM, Charles Watson Wentworth, marquess of, 1750. Portrait of, § i. 40. Is placed at the head of the Treasury, 1765; *ib.* He refuses an interview with Mr. Pitt, 1766; 47. Resigns, 48. He moves for an inquiry into the lamentable state of the kingdom, 1770; 86, 164, 202, 292. He becomes premier, 1782; 482. His death, July 1, 1782; 485.

RODERIC, invests Dublin, 1170; Strongbow routs his army, i. 465, 466.

RODNEY, George Brydges, baron, a gallant and successful naval commander, born 1717. Bombards Havre de Grace, 1759: iv. 606. Distinguishes himself in the reduction of Martinique, 1762; § i. 17. Gains the battle of St. Vincent, 1780; 418, 419. His action with admiral de Guichen, 430, 431, 469, 475. He is superseded by admiral Pigott, and raised to the peerage, with a pension of 2,000*l.* a year, 488. He opposes the measures projected, 1788, for alleviating the condition of slaves, § ii. 260.

RODOLPHUS, Glaber, quoted, i. 636.

ROE, sir Thomas, ambassador to the Indian emperor from the king of England, 1615; iii. 530.

ROGER, bishop of Salisbury; chief-justiciary and regent of England, 1135; i. 421. This magnificent prelate rebuilt the cathedral of Sarum, 426, 615. His strong castles, splendid mansions, etc., *ib.* He is arrested by order of king Stephen for a viola-

ROGER, bishop of Salisbury;—
tion of the king's peace, together with his nephew Alexander, bishop of Lincoln; Nigel, bishop of Ely, (who was also a nephew of Robert,) refuses to submit, and prepares to bid defiance to the king in the strong castle of Devizes; Stephen orders Roger and the bishop of Lincoln to be kept without food till the castle should be delivered up, which is accordingly done after they had been three days in a "fearful fast," 426, 427. His death, December, 1139; 428. This violent proceeding caused a quarrel between Stephen and his clergy, and commenced the civil war, 427, 428.

ROGER of Hoveden, quoted, i. 450, 476.

ROGERS, John, Mary's first Protestant victim, burned at Smithfield, February 24, 1555; ii. 523, 524, 725.

ROKEBY, sir Thomas, 1408, defeats Percy, earl of Northumberland, near Tadcaster; Percy falls in the fight, ii. 19.

ROLAND, Madame, born at Paris, 1754; guillotined, November 9, 1793; § ii. 695—699; § iii. 359, 360.

ROLLES, Mr., complains of his goods being unjustly seized, 1629, iii. 139.

ROLLO of Powhouse, 1745; iv. 521.

Roman and Greek writers, how far their works corroborate our knowledge of the early history of Britain, i. 4.

Roman Roads, the, afford valuable means of communication throughout the island, i. 49, 117.

Romance language, the origin of the French, as it incorporated the Roman or Latin largely upon the Frankish dialect of the Teutonic, i. 188.

ROMANO, Julio, a celebrated Roman painter, born in 1492. He exercised his talent both as a painter and architect, and died at Mantua in 1546; iii. 567.

Romans, the, invade Britain under Julius Cæsar, B.C. 55; i. 26—29. Cæsar's second invasion B. C. 54, narrated, 30—33. Roman galleys, 30, 31. Their temples in Britain, 72. Antiquities, 51, 72. Roman coins, 48. Their working of mines in Britain, 117. They built fortresses in the third century, on the south and east coasts of Britain, against the numerous Saxon pirates, 90. The "*Count of the Saxon shore*," as the commander of the nine fortified seaports was termed, held a court of justice with suitable officers appointed, *ib.* At the same time the governor of the fortified demarcation, Severus's wall, commanded about 15,000 soldiers, garrisoning thirty-seven castles, *ib.* He was styled the "*Dux Britanniarum*," and held his court in the north frontiers, similarly to the "*Comes Littoris Saxonici,*" above described, *ib.* The Romans introduce the arts of civilized life into Britain, 658.

Romans, Richard, king of the.—*See* Cornwall.

Rome.—Gregory the Great sends Augustine and forty monks to England to convert the Anglo-Saxons, about 597; i. 145. Remarkable instance of the pope's anointing Alfred, eight years of age, when at Rome with his father Ethelwulf, although but the youngest son of the king of Wessex; a jealousy thereby arising among the princes, his brothers, 153, 165. Impression of the magnificence of the papal city on the youthful Saxon prince, 155. Schism in the papal church, 1378, on the death of Gregory XI., ii. 137. Elections of rival popes, *ib.* The Lollards, both in England and on the continent, were opponents to the pretensions of the popes and Romish hierarchy, 1322—1401; 140, 141. The petition they laid before the House of Commons, 1395, containing the avowed creed of this important sect, bore against the whole system, doctrinal and institutional, of the Established Church, and, without mention of Rome or of Wycliffe, was a virtual denial of the *infallibility* of the popes, 141. The Act 2 Henry IV. enforced against them the punishment of heretics, 141, 142.

ROMILLY, sir Samuel; his humane exertions (*regno* George III.) to soften the severity of the Penal Code, § iv. 641.

Romney Marsh, the great armament of Hasting, in 893, lands at the mouth of the Limine, near this place, i. 162. Some of William's forces land here, and are assaulted and beaten by the people on the coast, in revenge for which William massacres the inhabitants and burns the houses, 359.

ROMNEY, Henry Sidney, lord, created, 1694; iv. 102. Appointed groom of the stole, 1700; he died, 1704; 106.

ROMNEY, George, a painter, born 1734, died 1802. His portrait of Edmund Burke, § i. 94.

RONJAT, a Frenchman, surgeon to William III., iv. 137.

RONQUILLO, Spanish ambassador, warns James II. not to fill his court with priests and confessors, iii. 788.

Rood of Grace, the, ii. 722.

ROOKE, sir George, iv. 42, 95. Made vice-admiral of England, 1702; 142. He makes an unsuccessful attack on Cadiz, 146. Takes possession of Gibraltar, 175. Comes into action with the count de Toulouse, off Malaga, *ib.* He is dismissed from the service, February, 1705; 177. His name erased from the Privy-council, 200.

ROOKWOOD, Ambrose, a Catholic gentleman of landed property in Suffolk, is persuaded by his bosom friend Catesby, to join in the Gunpowder Treason, iii. 24, 27. His repentance for this sin, 28. The trial, 29. His execution, 1606, with Fawkes and others, 30.

ROOKWOOD, concerned in a conspiracy for murdering William III., 1696; iv. 66.

Rope manufactures, § iii. 712.

ROPER, Mrs., daughter of sir Thomas More, 1534, her pious attention to her imprisoned father, ii. 385. His tender solicitude for her, 387. Her letters, urging him to submit to the king's will, *ib.* Mr. Roper, her husband's book, *ib.* Her parting with More on his way to the block on Tower-green, 388.

ROQUEFEUILLE, admiral, sails up the channel, 1744, to examine the state of the English guard-ships, iv. 471.

ROSAMOND, the Fair, her romantic history, i. 481, 482.

ROSEN, general, conducts the siege of Londonderry for James II., iv. 17, 23, 24.

Roses, Wars of the two; or civil war of Yorkists and Lancastrians, ii. 87, 92, 94, 96, 108, 130, 165.

ROSETTI, the nuncio, an attendant of the Queen of Charles I., 1641; iii. 232.

ROSNY, M. de, 1603, repairs to James I. to counteract the influence of d'Aremberg in the affairs of the Low Countries, iii. 7. *See* duke of Sully.

Ross, bishop of, his defence of Mary queen of Scots, 1569; ii. 616. He is committed to prison, October 11, having pleaded in vain his privileges as the ambassador of James VI., 626. Burleigh threatens him with the rack, 639.

Ross, major-general, takes Washington, August 24, 1814; § iv. 669. Killed in the attack on Baltimore, Sept. 12, 670⁰.

Rossbach, battle of, fought November 5, 1757, in which 30,000 French, and 20,000 imperial troops made a precipitate flight before five Prussian battalions and a few squadrons headed by Frederick the Great, iv. 598.

ROSSI, Charles, a sculptor of the nineteenth century; he executed the statue of the duke of Bedford in Russell-square, § iv. 715, 716.

ROSSITER, commander of the English forces in the north, 1645; iii. 340.

ROSSUS, John, of Warwick, a Latin chronicler, ii. 209.

ROTHERHAM (alias THOMAS SCOTT,) archbishop of York (translated from Lincoln, 1480,) and chan-

ROTHERHAM, archbishop of York—cellor, 1483; ii. 119. He carried to Elizabeth, widow of Edward IV., a friendly message from lord Hastings, *ib.* The queen's ominous reply, *ib.* He delivered the great seal to the forlorn widow then in sanctuary, *ib.* He repented of that rash step, sent secretly for the seal to be returned to him, and carried it to a meeting of the great nobility and gentry, as was 'customable,' *ib.* Is sent to the Tower by Gloucester, 121. Is liberated, 124. He died, May 1500.

ROTHES, earl of, iii. 156. Made chancellor of Scotland, 1664; 694.

ROTHES, earl of, 1704; iv. 162.

ROTHSAY, David, duke of, eldest son of king Robert III., and regent of Scotland, 1398; ii. 131. He protects Edinburgh against the feudal army of Henry IV., 1400; the English king, without money or provisions, retires across the border, 9; 131. His marriage with the daughter of Douglas discontents the earl of March, whose own daughter had been betrothed to this prince, 1402; 11. His dissipated conduct represented by his enemies, causes Robert to order his temporary confinement, 131. He is shut up in Falkland Castle, and supposed to have been starved by his ambitious uncle Albany, 19, 131.

ROUBILLIAC, Louis Francis, an eminent sculptor of the French school, settled in England *regno* George I.; his best work is the figure of Eloquence, in the monument of John duke of Argyll, at Westminster, iv. 758. Another admirable piece of sculpture is his statue of Handel, 763, *note.* He died, 1762; 758. His portrait, § i. 631.

Rouen, city of; Henry V. in 1418, besieges this important fortress, ii. 38, 39. Defences and state of the town, 39. The king's mode of reducing it by a complete blockade and ditches on the land side, his fleet from Harfleur commanding the Seine, *ib.* Iron chain across the upper part of that river, to prevent supplies, 40. Surrender of Fort St. Catherine, *ib.* The city, reduced by famine, opens its gates to Henry V., who behaved with the utmost humanity, and makes himself master of the whole of Normandy, 43. Is taken, 1449, by the count of Dunois, 85.

ROUEN, Walter, archbishop of, his attempts to assume the regency with pretended letters from king Richard, i. 506, 507. He is appointed by earl John grand justiciary and chancellor of the kingdom, 1192; 508. Lends John 500*l.* from the king's treasury, *ib.*

Rongemont Castle, Exeter, View of, i. 367.

ROUILLÉ, M. de, dispatched to Flanders by Louis XIV. to beg for a truce, 1709; iv. 232.

Round Table. King Arthur's festivities said to have been holden at Stirling, i. 23.

Round Towers, Irish, i. 13. Disquisition respecting the origin of these ancient edifices, and their use in tracing the progress of Celtic tribes, 12—17. O'Brien's theory respecting, 17.

ROUSE, Francis, appointed speaker of the House of Commons, 1653; iii. 412.

ROUSE, John, arrested, 1681; iii. 734.

ROUSE, a Rye-house conspirator; he dies, 1683, protesting his innocence, iii. 746.

ROUSE, Dr., chaplain to William III.; his sermon before the battle of the Boyne, iv. 24.

Rouvrai, battle of Herrings fought at, February, 1429; ii. 62.

ROWAN, Hamilton, a leader of the United Irishmen, 1794; § iii. 387, 530.

Rowe, general, iv. 170. Killed at the battle of Blenheim, August 13, 1704; 171.

ROWLEY, William, a dramatist, supposed to have died about the middle of the sixteenth century, iii. 593, 594.

ROWLEY, admiral; he bombards and burns several towns on the Genoese coast, 1745; iv. 479.

Rowton Heath, battle of, gained by the Parliamentary forces, September 23, 1645; iii. 341.

Roxburgh Castle, various sieges of, and events at, ii. 134, 135.

ROXBURGH, earl of, lord privy-seal, attempting to take home the bishop of Edinburgh, who had preached at St. Giles's kirk, after the new liturgy had been read there, 1638, was forced to order his footmen to draw their swords, iii. 183.

ROXBURGH, duke of, secretary of state for Scotland, is suspected by Walpole of encouraging the popular commotions there, and is accordingly dismissed, 1724; iv. 385.

ROY, a satirist of Wolsey, ii. 829, 830.

Royal Academy, the, founded 1768; § i. 625.

Royal Society, the; the origin of this institution traced to about the year 1645; iv. 773. History of, 773—777. Seal of, 775.

RUBENS, Peter Paul, the most eminent painter of the Flemish school, born 1577; he was engaged by Charles I. to paint the ceiling of the Banqueting-house at Whitehall, and received in England the honour of knighthood. He died at Antwerp, in 1640; iii. 148, 568.

RUDD, Anthony, bishop of St. David's, elected March, 1594; died March, 1615; remarkable speech of, iii. 460.

RUDING, Mr., quoted, i. 595.

RUDYARD, sir Benjamin, M.P., 1640; iii. 212. Denounces Episcopacy, 227.

RUDYERD, erected a lighthouse off Plymouth towards the beginning of the eighteenth century, which stood until 1755, when it was burned down, iv. 705.

RUE, De la, an accomplice in a plot for murdering William III., 1696; his relation concerning the attempt, iv. 66.

RULE, Dr., principal of Edinburgh College; his opinion respecting the obligation of the Scottish Covenant to conform England to Presbyterianism, iv. 193.

RUMBALD, Richard, a Rye-house conspirator, iii. 741. Is executed, June 30, 1685; 769.

RUMSEY, his depositions respecting the Rye-house Plot, iii. 744.

Runic Odes, admirably imitated by Gray, i. 300.

Runnymead, view of, i. 529.

RUPERT, prince, son of the Elector Palatine, and nephew of king Charles I., iii. 173. Surrenders his sword to Hatzfeldt, 1637; 174. He arrives in England, 1642, and attaches himself to the king, where his petulant temper does much mischief, 295. Created duke of Cumberland, 1644. View of his house at Barbican, ib. He assured Charles, 1645, that he could keep Bristol for four months; but after a few days having surrendered it, Charles commands him to resign all his commissions, and to quit the country, 341. Despising the king's orders, he comes to Newark to give an account to the king of his surrender, 343. Is cleared by Court-martial of treason, but not of indiscretion, ib. He and his brother, with sir R. Willis, and 200 horse, demand passes from the king, and get the leave of the parliament to go beyond seas, 1646; 344. He negotiates for peace with Cromwell, 416. Commands the English fleet in conjunction with Monk, 1666; 698. He died 1682.

Ruremond, surrenders to Marlborough, October 7, 1702; iv. 145.

RUSHOUT, sir John, 1746; iv. 530, 613.

RUSHWORTH, John, an industrious and useful historical collector, born 1607, died 1690. Quotations from, iii. 15, 264, 294, note, 517.

RUSSELL, Edward, admiral, misconduct of, iv. 34. He gains the battle of La Hogue, May 21 and 22, 1692; 37, 38. Is dismissed from the service, 40. Created earl of Orford, 1697; 77. He resigns his

RUSSELL, Edward, admiral,—offices both in the fleet and Admiralty, 1699; 95. He died 1727.

RUSSELL, William, lord, born about 1641; iii. 62. Inveighs against a standing army, 1678; 715. Is appointed a member of the Privy-council, 1679; 728. He carries up the Exclusion Bill to the House of Lords, 1680; takes part in the Rye-house Plot, 740. Is committed to the Tower, 745. Brought to trial, 746—749; and executed July, 1683; 750.

RUSSEL, lord. See Bedford.

RUSSEL, James, an accomplice in the murder of archbishop Sharp, May 3, 1679; iii. 730.

RUSSELL, Mr. John, his gradual rise to high dignity and wealth, 1537; ii. 402, 469. See Bedford.

Russia, first obtains weight as an European power under Peter I., 1685—1721; iv. 73.

RUTH, captain, iv. 11. Killed at the battle of Aghrim, July 12, 1691, 34.

RUTHVEN, Alexander, son of William, earl of Gowrie, who was beheaded in 1584; ii. 690.

RUTHVEN, Patrick. See Brentford.

RUTHVEN, lord, rises from a bed of sickness, 1566, to have a principal hand in the murder of David Rizzio, ii. 586. On his entering the queen's sitting-room armed, she commands him, on pain of treason, to quit her presence, but he totally disregards the injunction, ib. He had previously made Darnley sign a bond, taking him and his fellow-conspirators under his special protection; but after the deed was done Darnley disregards this agreement, and Ruthven is obliged to fly to the English marches, 587. Mary, at the petition of the earl of Bedford, pardons him, and he returns to Scotland, 591.

RUTHVEN, lord Grey of, impeached of high crimes and misdemeanours by the House of Commons, 1642; iii. 288.

Ruthven, raid of, August 1582; iii. 440.

RUTLAND, earl of, Edward Plantagenet, created February 1390. Created duke of Albemarle, September 1397; was constrained, 1399, on the advent of Henry IV. to the crown, to bear only his previous title, ii, 5.—See York. He was slain at Agincourt.

RUTLAND, earl of, aged thirteen, flying from Wakefield with his tutor, on his father, Richard of York, falling in that battle, is butchered by Clifford, 1460; ii. 96.

RUTLAND, Thomas Manners, earl of, created 1525, marched against the insurgents 1536; ii. 397. He died 1543.

RUVIGNI, a minister of Louis XIV. 1678; iii. 716.

RYCHARDES, Thomas, assumed to be the author of a play, entitled "Misogonus," the only copy of which is in MS., and is dated 1577; iii. 581.

Rye-house, the, from an old print, iii. 742.

Rye-house Plot, the, 1683; iii. 740—755.

Rymer, quoted, iii. 582.

RYSBRACH, John Michael, a statuary of great eminence, born 1694, died 1770. Amongst many admirable specimens of the art may be mentioned the monument of the duke of Marlborough, iv. 379, 758.

Ryswick, treaty of, signed September 20, 1697; iv. 78.

SAARBRUCK, prince of, iv. 144. His death, 1703; 152.

SACÆ, emigrate from Scythia, in the age of Cyrus, to Europe, i. 138. Their supposed descendants the Saxons, ib.

SACHEVERELL, Dr. Henry, his violent sermon against the ministry, November 5, 1709; iv. 237. He is taken into custody and impeached, December 15, 238. His trial, 239—242. He is found guilty of high crimes and misdemeanours, sentenced not to preach for three years, and his sermon to be burned by the common hangman, 243.

SACKVILLE, Edward. *See* Dorset.

SACKVILLE, George, viscount, enters into engagements with the Leicester-house faction, 1757; iv. 593. Refuses to submit to the commands of prince Ferdinand of Brunswick, 604, 610. He is tried by court-martial for misconduct at the battle of Minden, and rendered unfit for future service, April 3, 1760; 612, 613. He assumes the name of Germaine by Act of Parliament, 1770; § i. 108; *note.* Portrait of, 326. He resigns, 1782, and is created viscount Sackville, 478.

SACKVILLE, Nigellus de, rector of Harrow, excommunicated for wounding one of Thomas à Becket's horses, i. 454.

SACKVILLE, Thomas. *See* Dorset.

SACKVILLE, colonel, iv. 32. He informs Louis XIV., 1694, of the project of William III. for destroying the shipping at Brest, 48.

Sacramental Test, the, first imported into Ireland 1699, iv. 635.

Sacraments. Henry VIII. confined them to three,— Baptism, the Lord's Supper, and Penance, ii. 397.

SADES, Donatian, marquis de, born at Paris, 1740; died in the mad-house at Charenton, December 2, 1814; § ii. 608.

SADLER, sir Ralph, 1540, an adroit envoy, commissioned by Henry VIII. to pry into the sentiments and resolves of James V. of Scotland, ii. 431. His representations to James respecting the Scottish negotiations with Rome, 432. Failure of his mission, followed by war betwixt James and Henry, 1541—1543, *ib.* He is next commissioned, 1543, to reprove the earl of Angus and the Douglas faction, who had so long been in king Henry's pay and interest, 435. His support to Scottish malcontents, 443—445. A privy-councillor, 1547, to Edward VI., 454. On the persecution of Protestants by Mary he gives up his appointments and retires to the village of Hackney, where he remains till the accession of Elizabeth, 529. He is appointed to a seat in the privy-council by that queen, and is commissioned to settle certain disputes on border matters, 550, 551, 556. He is nominated one of the commission for trying the cause of Mary, queen of Scots, Oct. 1568; 612. He is sent down to watch the earl of Sussex, 629. Is appointed to take charge of the queen of Scots; but the English queen, not thinking him sufficiently severe, he is superseded by sir Amyas Pawlet and sir Drew Drury, 658.

ST. AIGNAN, duke de, the French ambassador at Madrid, understanding the design of cardinal Alberoni, 1719, to detain him prisoner, sets out secretly from Spain, and arrives safely in France, iv. 350.

St. Albans, *Verulamium;* its description as a British stronghold, B.C. 54, when taken by Cæsar, i. 33. The British allies, under Boadicea, massacre the Roman colony of, 43. Victory of Richard of York, 1454, at, ii. 92. The town and abbey plundered, 1461, by Lancastrians, 97.

ST. ALBANS, Henry Jermyn, earl of, iii. 240. His intimacy with the queen of Charles I. at Paris, 342. Created April 1660, dies 1683; 727.

St. Andrew's, see of; clerical and political disputes respecting the consecration of its bishops, 1107—1120, etc., i. 539. This see was erected into an archbishopric in 1471, by pope Sixtus IV. This measure was resorted to in consequence of the renewal, by Nevil, archbishop of York, of the old claim of his see to supremacy over the kingdom of Scotland, ii. 154. *Illustrations*; Views of the Ruined Cathedral, etc., 199, 748. Bishop Wardlaw, 1410, founded the university, 198. Bull of Benedict XIII. in 1413, *ib.* Charter, 1432, by James I., 199. Bishop Kennedy built the college in 1455, grammar-schools being established in the Scottish

St. Andrew's, see of ;—monasteries, 199. Murder of cardinal David Beaton, 1546, in the strong castle of St. Andrew's, 446. The castle surrendered to Arran and Leo Strozzi, commander of the fleet of Henri II., in 1547; 458.

St. Andrew's, castle of, ii. 748.

ST. ANDREW's, archbishop of, crowns Charles I. in Scotland, 1633; iii. 156. Lord-chancellor, 183.

St. Andrew's, New, iv. 96.

St. Antoine, Port, View of the, § ii. 422.

ST. AUBYN, sir John, speaks violently, 1742, against the introduction of Hanoverian troops into England, iv. 463.

St Bartholomew's day, massacre of, 1572; ii. 646, 647. In this massacre Coligni and 30,000 individuals lost their lives, *ib.*

St. Catherine Creed, church of, consecrated by Laud, 1631; iii. 158.

ST. CLAIR, Hubert de, saves the life of Henry II. at the siege of the Castle of Bridgenorth, by receiving the arrow in his own breast, i. 442.

ST. CLAIR, general, commands an expedition to the coast of Brittany, 1746, iv. 554.

St. Denis, battle of, 1567; iv. 622.

St. Edmundsbury, View of, i. 527. A great council of the barons held here in 1214, *ib.*

ST. ESTEVAN, count of, recommends to Charles II. of Spain the duke of Anjou as a proper successor, iv. 108.

St. Germain, View of the Palace of, iv. 206. It was here that the fugitive James II. found a refuge after his departure from England.

St. Giles's, Edinburgh, from an old print, iii. 183.

ST. GILLES, Raymond de, earl of Toulouse ; Henry II. lays claim to his earldom, but the French king comes to his assistance, i. 444, 445.

St. James's Palace, View of, iii. 42.

ST. JOHN, Oliver, fined, 5,000*l.* by the Star-chamber, 1614, for refusing to contribute to a forced benevolence, iii. 56. He disputes the legality of ship-money, 1637; 179.

ST. JOHN, lady, speaks in favour of the unfortunate Mrs. Lisle, 1685; iii. 780.

St. John's, on the Sorel, View of, § i. 259.

ST. JUST, Anthony, a barbarous French revolutionist, born 1768; § ii. 658. Recommends to the National Convention, 1792, the speedy execution of Louis XVI., § iii. 212, 224, 235. Impeaches twenty-two noted Girondists, 1793; 352. Is guillotined, together with Robespierre and many other members of the Mountain, July 28, 1794; 449.

ST. LEGER, married to the duchess of Exeter, Richard III.'s sister, was beheaded for the insurrection in favour of Henry of Richmond, on the failure at first of that enterprise, ii. 126.

ST. LOW, sir William, 1554, an officer in the princess Elizabeth's household, arrested for the rising of sir Thomas Wyatt, in which Elizabeth was supposed to be implicated, ii. 515. He is set at liberty, 521.

St. Lucie, island of, taken from the French, 1778; § i. 369. View of, *ib.*

St. Martin's Church, iv. 749.

St. Mary Woolnoth, Lombard-street, iv. 750.

St. Michael, mount of, in Normandy ; prince Henry besieged here by his two brothers, Robert and William, i. 397. View of, *ib.*

St. Paul's Cathedral, partly restored by Laud, 1631; iii. 159. Plan and elevation of the Portico of Old St. Paul's, with the plan of the portico of St. Martin's, drawn within, in order to give an idea of the scale, 573. Sir Christopher Wren receives a commission to furnish plans for re-building this formerly magnificent but then ruined church, iv. 736. He lays its foundation in 1765; 737. His first design and plan for this building, 743. Exterior and plan of St. Paul's, 744. Dome and choir of, 745.

St. Paul's Cross, 1620 ; iii. 476, 492.

St. Pierre, Eustace de, a rich burgess of Calais, and the first to offer himself to be delivered up to Edward, 1347, who promised that he would spare the men of Calais if six of the notable burgesses should be sent to him with the keys of the town and castle in their hands and halters round their necks, i. 769.

St. Pol, Walleran of Luxemburgh, count of Ligny and; his curious defiance to king Henry, he having married a sister of Richard II., 1402; ii. 10. He landed, 1403, on the Isle of Wight, but was repulsed, 15. His private wars, 28.

St. Quintin, battle of, 1557; ii. 533.

Saintrailles, Poitou de, a valiant French captain, 1421; ii. 49, 55, 56, 58, 60, 65, 69.

St. Stephen, church of, at Caen, View of, i. 390. William the Conqueror buried here, 391.

St. Stephen's Chapel, ii. 766 ; iii. 784.

St. Stephen's, Walbrook, interior of, iv. 740.

St. Vincent, John Jervis, earl, created, May 27, 1797, for his noble victory over the Spanish fleet, §. iii. 522. Becomes first lord of the Admiralty, 1801; 549*.

Saladin, sultan, his wars with the Crusaders and king Richard, i. 495. et seq. (See Richard.) Saladin sends to Richard during the battle of Jaffa two magnificent horses, seeing that he had been dismounted during the action, 501. He is defeated by Richard, who gains a decisive victory at Jaffa, 1192, and a treaty of three years is agreed upon by Saladin, who surrenders the whole country on the sea-coast from Jaffa to Tyre, including those cities, to the peaceful enjoyment of the Christians, and grants full liberty of repairing to Jerusalem to all the pilgrims of the west, ib.

Salads, etc., introduced from the Netherlands about 1524; ii. 806.

Salamanca, View of the city of, § iv. 508. Battle of, July 22, 1812; ib.

Salerno, king Richard's visit to, and description of this beautiful city, then celebrated for its School of Medicine, i. 488.

Salisbury, jurisdiction of Wales over, iii. 43. Cathedral of, rebuilt, 1107—1139, by the powerful and wealthy bishop Roger, i. 426, 615.

Salisbury, William Longspear, earl of, natural son of Henry II., and William earl of Holland, commanded the English expedition in 1213, when the English entirely annihilated the French fleet prepared by Philip II. for the invasion of England, i. 525. Is taken prisoner at the battle of Bouvines, 1214; 526. He died, 1226.

Salisbury, earl of, John de Montague. On Henry IV.'s accession, 1399, the earl remained free from punishment, ii. 6. He shortly joined in a plot with other refractory peers to restore Richard II., the conspirators, desiring to murder Henry, surprise Windsor Castle, 7. Apprised, probably by Rutland, son of the duke of York, the king fled to London and returned to Windsor at the head of the Londoners, ib. Salisbury beheaded by the burghers of Cirencester, 1400 ; ib.

Salisbury, Thomas de Montague, earl of, 1409. Served the regent Bedford, 1422, against the dauphin Charles, ii. 54. Gained the battle of Crevant, over Charles's generals, lord Darnley and marshal de Severac, 1423; ib. This brave earl, with but 9,000 men, blockades the populous city of Orleans, well prepared for defence with a good garrison, 1428; 60. Salisbury wounded, dies in a week, regretted as an excellent commander, 61. Was succeeded by Suffolk, ib.

Salisbury, Richard Nevill, earl of, 1442, joined the banner of Richard of York, at Ludlow, 1454; ii. 92. A short time lord-chancellor, 93. His quarrel with Percy, lord Egremont, ib. Marching from Middleham Castle, 1459, he totally defeated a Lancastrian army, under Audley who fell in battle,

Salisbury, Richard Nevill, earl of,— 94. New triumphs of his son Warwick, ib. The old earl and his brave son form an intrenched camp near Ludlow, but the defection of Trollop, who seduced all Warwick's veteran troops to desert, ruins the campaign of 1459; ib. Salisbury and his duchess being attainted, they are conveyed by Warwick to his safe fortress of Calais, ib. He shared in the great defeat at Wakefield, where Richard of York was slain, December, 1460; 96. Salisbury flying, was closely pursued, and beheaded at Pontefract Castle, with some others, ib.

Salisbury, countess of, Margaret Plantagenet, 1513, daughter of George duke of Clarence, ii. 401. By her marriage with sir Richard Pole she had for sons, the lord Montacute, cardinal Reginald Pole, and sir Geoffrey, 401, 408. The enmity of Henry VIII. towards the cardinal, led, in 1538, to lamentable results; lord Montacute was beheaded with others on vague charges; and, in 1539, Cromwell thought he had detected a correspondence with the cardinal, 408, 409. The countess Margaret, a boy the son of Montacute, and other persons were sent to the Tower, 408. Cromwell, for want of sufficient evidence to proceed to trial, demanded of the judges whether parliament might condemn persons accused of treason without a previous trial, 409. The judges assented, and a servile parliament passed the bill of attainder, ib. Lamentable circumstances of her execution in 1541; ib.

Salisbury, John of, quoted, i. 607—610, 633.

Salisbury, captain Owen, 1601, implicated in Essex's insurrection, designedly exposed his own life at a window of Essex-house, and was shot from the street, ii. 686.

Sallee, town of, destroyed by captain Rainsborough, 1636; iii. 174.

Salmon, rev. Thomas, proposed (seventeenth century) to reduce the clefs (in music) to one, but was opposed by Lock, an eminent musician of the day, and his improvement thus fell to the ground, iii. 887.

Salt, procured by evaporation, an important branch of industry in the early Norman period, i. 600 ; § iv. 692.

Saltoun, lord, his zeal for the Pretender, 1707 ; he advises colonel Hooke to be on his guard against the duke of Hamilton, iv. 207.

Sammes, Aylett, a writer of the seventeenth century, the first to suggest that Britain and Ireland were peopled from Phoenicia, i. 9.

Samothes, king, and the fabled giants of Britain, i. 118.

Sampson, dean, his interview with Catherine of Arragon, at Ampthill, ii. 383. He was counsel for Henry VIII. at Lambeth, 1536, on the case before Cranmer, of the nullity of Anne Boleyn's marriage from the beginning, and of the consequent illegitimacy of her daughter Elizabeth, 395. He assists in the trial of the priest, John Lambert, 406.

Sancroft, William, archbishop of Canterbury, consecrated January, 1678; iii. 764. Crowns James II., 765. Refuses to act in the ecclesiastical commission, 786. Absent at the first parliament of William III., iv. 3. He refuses to take the oath of allegiance tendered by the new king, and in consequence loses his office, February, 1691, 9. He died, November, 1693. Sanctuary at Westminster, from a sketch before its destruction in 1775; ii. 110.

Sancy, father, confessor to the marshal de Bassompierre, 1626; iii. 125.

Sanders, Mary, a Quaker, and servant of the Protector Cromwell, iii. 817.

Sanderson, sir Thomas, speaks in favour of war with Spain, 1739; iv. 434.

Sandilands, sir James, sent over to France, 1560, by the Scottish parliament to announce to queen Mary their manifesto against the church of Rome, ii. 563.

Sandown Castle, ii. 844.

SANDS, an accomplice in the attack on sir J. Coventry, 1670; iii. 707.

Sandwich, first landing of Cæsar betwixt Walmer and, i. 28.

SANDWICH, Edward Montague, earl of, dispatched, 1661, with a small fleet to take possession of Tangiers, and bring home Catherine of Braganza, iii. 685. He attacks a Dutch fleet at Berghen, in Norway, 1665, and is repulsed, 696. His vessel is blown up at the battle of Solebay, May 3, 1672, by a fire-ship, and he perishes together with his crew, 710.

SANDWICH, John Montague, earl of, 1729, made first lord of the Admiralty, 1748; iv. 557. Becomes secretary of state, 1763; § i. 28. His portrait, ib. 89, 94, 108, 193. Seriously wounded by the rioters of 1780; 413, 414. He died 1792; 441.

SANDYS, Edwin, bishop of London, 1570. His fear lest the zeal of the preachers against the massacre of St. Bartholomew's day might not square with the queen's diplomatic relations with France; his letter to Burghley thereon, ii. 647, note. He proposes that the queen of Scots should be executed, 648. He was translated to York, 1576, and died August, 1588.

SANDYS, sir Edwin, arbitrarily arrested, 1621; iii. 86.

SANDYS, colonel, falls in a charge against prince Rupert, 1642; iii. 296.

SANDYS, moves an accusation against sir Robert Walpole, 1741; iv. 442.

SANGALLO, Antonio, an eminent architect of the sixteenth century; he died in 1546; iii. 570.

SANMICHELI, Michael, a distinguished Italian architect, born at Verona, in 1484, and died in 1559; iii. 570.

San Roque, lines of, constructed by the Spaniards, 1729; iv. 403.

San Sebastian, taken by storm, 1813; § iv. 580, 583.

SANSUM, rear-admiral, slain in battle, 1665; iii. 695.

Saragossa, city of, surrenders, 1707, to the duke of Orleans, after a strange exhibition of superstition, without firing a shot, iv. 202.

Saratoga, Lake, View of, § i. 310.

SARSFIELD, general, iv. 33. Slain at the battle of Landen, July 29, 1693; 41.

Sarum, Castle of, enlarged and strengthened by bishop Roger, i. 427. View of the ruins of, ib.

SAUNDERS, Laurence, 1555, a learned and powerful preacher, burnt at Coventry, under the revived statutes against Lollards and heretics, ii. 524.

SAUNDERS, chief-justice, description of, by Roger North, iii. 848.

SAVAGE, sir John, slain before Boulogne, 1492; ii. 298.

Savannah, fort and town of, taken by colonel Campbell, 1778; § i. 364. View of, ib.

SAVARY, general, his mission to Madrid, 1808; whence he inveigled the new king Ferdinand VII. to set out for Burgos to meet Napoleon, § iv. 307. He urged the unwary prince on to Vittoria, and finally to Bayonne, ib. He commands his gendarmes to prevent the escape of Ferdinand and his brother Carlos, 310.

SAVERY, Thomas, constructs a steam-engine for draining mines, 1698. The merit of producing a vacuum by the condensation of steam is also his due, iv. 729.

SAVILE, sir Henry, provost of Eton College, published a magnificent edition of Chrysostom in 1612; iii. 616.

SAVILLE, sir George, demands a strict inquiry into the pension-list, 1780; § i. 405.

Savoy Palace, the, burnt by the rioters of 1381; i. 786. View of the ruins of, 787. View of in 1661; iii. 821.

SAVOY, duke of, retired to a hermitage, 1435; ii. 78.

SAVOY, duke of, his successes against the French, 1692; iv. 37. He makes a secret treaty with Louis XIV., and declares his intention of establishing a neutrality throughout Italy, 73. He negotiates with the emperor, 153.

Savoyard, Lombard, and German adventurers during the civil dissensions in France, 1416; commit therein the greatest excesses, ii. 37. The constable Armagnac takes vigorous measures to repress them, ib.

Saw-mills first used in England about 1763; § i. 601.

SAWTRE, William, rector of Lynn, was the first Lollard who was burnt, 1401, under the statute De heretico comburendo, ii. 142.

SAXE, marshal, natural son of Frederic Augustus II., king of Poland, iv. 469, note. He takes the command of 10,000 men for the service of the Pretender, 1744; 469, and on the failure of the expedition is sent into the Low Countries, 471. He invests Tournay, 476.

Saxon.—Observations on the Saxon Language, i. 292. Specimens of the, 293—301. Literature, 300 et seq. Education, 304. Manners and customs, 323, et seq. Household furniture and costume, ib. Military costume, 332. Anglo-Saxon weapons, 333. Children of the Anglo-Saxons, 337. Hunting and hawking, favourite sports among the Anglo-Saxons, 341—343. In-door sports, 342—345. Division of the race into three great tribes, 346. Statement of Holkot, a writer of the fourteenth century, that William I. endeavoured to abolish the Saxon language, proved to be false, 571, 611. Specimen of the Saxon language as spoken in England at the close of Stephen's reign, 611. Specimen of Saxon poetry, supposed to have been written in the time of Henry II., 612. General view of Saxon Literature; survey of the early histories of England, 613, 614.

Saxons, the, and Scandinavians, infested the coasts of Britain and Gaul, i. 288. They were repulsed by Carausius, who afterwards employed them, 53. The Saxon pirates in the third century so greatly infested the south-eastern coasts, that the Romans built there nine forts, under the command of the Comes Littoris Saxonici, and those shores were termed the Littus Saxonicum, 90. Officers of the warden of the Saxon coast, his courts, and list of the nine castles, ib. Meaning of this gentile name, 138. Origin of the Saxons, ib. Their tribes distinct, nevertheless all of them Teutonic or Gothic, ib. Those which invaded Britain, known as Saxons, Angles, and Jutes, having affinity in origin, and sharing in the new conquest, 139. District of Anglen, in Holstein, 139, 142. The Saxons Proper located in Westphalia, Friesland, Holland, and part of Belgium, 139. Similarity of the Anglo-Saxon to the ancient Frisic tongue, ib. Their weapons in the first century but rude, 140. In the fifth they had provided themselves with well-wrought blades, ib. In their earliest piracies their boats were small, and the upper parts of wicker, ib. Later their war-vessels were constructed well, long lofty, and fit for numerous crews, 140. They were a barbarous nation on invading Britain, their only arts being those of war and navigation, ib. Arms and costume of a Saxon military chief (from a Saxon illumination,) 144. Arms of an Anglo-Saxon king, and his armour-bearer, 156. The ascendant ruler, and most warlike among the kings of the heptarchy, obtained the office of Bretwalda, which gave him a paramount authority over the rest, 144, 145. Saxon princes and nobles addicted to pilgrimages to Rome, 152. King Ethelwulf accompanied thither by Alfred, when the young prince is anointed by the pope, ib. Winchester, the capital of Wessex, burned by the Danes, 153. They permanently establish themselves in Thanet,

Saxons, the,—
ib. The Danish power in England, 156, 157. Saxon arms and costume, ib. Revival of their nautical power under Alfred; victories over the Danes, 157, 158. The Danes overrun Wessex, 158, 165, 166. The history of the Saxons, after this period, will be found under their kings.

SAXTON, Christopher, (sixteenth century,) an engraver, to whom we are indebted for the first publication of county maps, iii. 577.

SAY AND SELE, James Fiennes, lord, an obnoxious minister of Henry VI., July, 1450, tried at Guildhall, and beheaded in Cheapside by John Cade's men, ii. 88.

SAY AND SELE, William Fienes, lord, 1451. Slain at Barnet 1471; ii. 109.

SAY AND SELE, William Fiennes, viscount, created, 1624; refuses to pay ship-money, 1637, and excites a general opposition in Warwickshire, to the arbitrary impost, iii. 181. Together with lord Brooke, he projects a scheme of emigration to New England, 1637; Hampden, Cromwell, and Haselrig embark, but are detained, with other emigrants, by the king's order, 182. The truth of this assertion denied by historical inquirers, ib. Say and Sele refuses to take an oath tendered to him by Charles I., 1639; 204. Is made master of the wards, 247. He died 1662.

Scalds and Bards of the Scandinavians and Celts, i. 228, 229.

SCALES, Thomas de, lord, 1418; governor of the Tower, 1450; resists the progress of Cade and the men of Kent, ii. 89. He died 1460.

Scandinavia, superstitious mythology of, i. 138, 224—228. (See Odin.) Powerful tribes of warriors issuing from the shores of the Baltic, 138. The Scandinavians ravaged the coasts of Gaul and Britain, together with Saxon pirates, and gained a competent knowledge of the British islands even in the Roman period, 53, 288, et seq.

SCHALKEN, Godfrey, an eminent painter, born at Dort, 1643, famous for his candle-light paintings; he died at the Hague, in 1706; iv. 753.

SCHAUB, sir Luke, 1723; iv. 383.

SCHEELE, a celebrated Swedish chemist, discovers oxymuriatic acid, or chlorine, 1774; § iii. 710.

SCHEEMAKERS, an artist, designed and executed the Horse-Guards, iv. 752, 758.

Schellenberg, or Donawert, battle of, gained by Marlborough, July 2, 1704; iv. 167, 168.

SCHEVEZ, William, archbishop of St. Andrew's, dies 1494; ii. 154.

SCHILTER, his assertion that the Celtic and Teutonic languages had a common origin, i. 10.

SCHOMBERG, marshal, iii. 128. He lands at Carrickfergus, August 13, 1689, with a large army of English, French, Dutch, Huguenots, and others, iv. 18. Takes Belfast, and several other places; he is brought to a stand by king James, 23; and falls at the battle of the Boyne, July 1, 1690; 26.

SCHOMBERG, duke of, son of the above, iv. 33, 174.

Schools.—Old St. Paul's School, founded 1509; ii. 815. King's School, Canterbury, founded 1542; 816. Westminster School, 817. Merchant Taylors' School, ib.

SCHROTTENBACH, viceroy of Naples, 1719; iv. 361.

SCHULENBERG, mademoiselle, mistress of George I., iv. 309.

SCHUTZ, baron, the Hanoverian resident in England, iv. 278. Demands of the lord-chancellor a writ of summons for the Electoral Prince, who had been created duke of Cambridge, April 12, 1714; 285.

SCHWARTZENBERG, prince, general of the Austrian army in the invasion of France, 1814; § iv. 613*.

SCHWERIN, marshal, iv. 449. He takes the town and fortress of Olmutz, 1741; 451.

SCHWICKELT, Mr., Hanoverian plenipotentiary at the court of Frederick the Great, 1741; iv. 450.

Sciacca, town of, taken by the Imperialists, 1719; iv. 364.

Science, progress of. See "Literature, Science, and the Fine Arts," i. 118, 289, 603, 842; ii. 196, 813; iii. 560, 871; iv. 735. Reign of George III. § i. 604; § iii. 715; § iv. 696.

Sciences, mathematical and physical, iv. 764—787; § i. 623.

Scilly Islands, resorted to by the Phœnician colonists of Gades (or Cadiz) for tin, etc., i. 92. Silura, the chief island of the Cassiterides, 93.

SCOT, Mr. William, 1607; iii. 464.

SCOT, a Commonwealth-man, executed as a regicide, July, 1660; iii. 676.

Scotland, History of Religion in; the Culdees and St. Columba opposed to the Roman see, i. 244, Manners and customs of, ii. 264—267. Regalia of, iv. 189.

Scots, the; both Highlanders and Lowlanders supposed to be Celtic, i. 18. Said by historians to have been, in 360, allies of the Picts; they are supposed to have immigrated from northern Germany into Ireland, 19. Scotia anciently meant Ireland, and not Albion or Caledonia, ib. The Scots came from Ireland, and settled in North Britain, 19, 20. Derivation of the name, 20. Scots, or Milesians, were, according to Irish tradition, a great nation who settled in Ireland at a very early period, and brought with them the Irish or Gaelic language, ib. Scots and Picts, their invasions of South Britain, 52—56. Disputes concerning the naturalization of the Scots, iii. 35. Domestic life of the, 646. Diet of the, 647. Courtship and marriage of the, ib. Funeral customs of the, ib.

SCOTT, sir Walter, laird of Buccleuch, 1544, assisted in the victory of Ancrum-moor over the Scottish malcontents, and a portion of the earl of Hertford's troops, ii. 441.

SCOTT, sir Walter, an excellent poet and novelist, born, August 15, 1771. Delicacy of his health in childhood; his marriage with Miss M. C. Carpenter, December, 1797. His "Lay of the Last Minstrel," appeared in 1805; his "Marmion" in 1808; and his "Waverley" in 1814. Author of many other well-known publications. He died at Abbotsford, September 21, 1832; § iv. 699, 700. His portrait, 699. Quotations from his poems, ii. 329.

SCOTT, a Jacobite, appointed, 1751, sub-preceptor to the young prince of Wales (George III.), iv. 567.

SCOTTI, marquess, intrigues against the cardinal Alberoni, 1720, and procures his ruin, iv. 365.

SCOTUS, DUNS, a royal visitation of the two universities, by commissioners of Cromwell's appointment, took place in 1535, when injunctions were issued abolishing altogether the reading of the works of the most subtle doctor, iii. 818. Consequent destruction of the copies of his work, ib.

Scrofula, touching for the, commenced in the time of Edward the Confessor, iii. 902.

SCROGGS, chief-justice, his partial conduct towards the victims of the Popish Plot, 1678; iii. 724.

SCROOP of Masham, Henry, lord, a favourite of Henry V., conspiring against the king, then at Southampton with his army, was tried and beheaded, 1415; ii. 29.

SCROOP, Richard, archbishop of York, 1398. Engaged in Northumberland's rebellion, 1403; ii. 13, 14. He joins in a new rebellion of the earl of Northumberland, 1405; appears accoutred with armour at Shipton-on-the-Moor, where the earl of Nottingham's troops were posted, 17. They are tempted to surrender to prince John, and are delivered to Henry IV. at Pontefract, ib. Chief-justice Gascoigne refuses to condemn them, for reason that

SCROOP, Richard,—
one was a prelate and not amenable to the lay courts, the other a peer, ib. One Fulthorp sentenced them to die, and Henry being inexorable, Scroop was the first mitred head that fell beneath the axe in England, 1405; ib. The pope excommunicated all concerned; Henry sent a justification of his conduct, and the pope, having then but little power in England, revoked his sentence, ib.

SCROPE, lord, despatched by Elizabeth, 1568, to visit the captive queen of Scots at Carlisle, ii. 608.

SCROPE, lady, the daughter of lord Hunsdon, communicates the decease of queen Elizabeth to her brother sir Robert Carey, iii. 2.

SCROPE, colonel, a parliamentarian officer; the earl of Holland surrenders to him, 1648; iii. 383. His name is set down in the list of regicides, 1660; 665: and he is condemned although he had surrendered under the royal proclamation, and had been regularly admitted to the king's pardon, 672. Is executed, October 16, 1660; 676.

SCUDAMORE, son-in-law of Glendower, and Rhees-ap-Dhu, enter Shropshire; their army is cut to pieces, and they are executed as rebels, ii. 18.

Sculpture of the Anglo-Saxons, i. 318. The horn of Ulphus, ib.

Sculpture, ii. 851—854; iv. 757—760; § i. 630, 631; § iii. 744—749; § iv. 715—717.

Scutage, levied by Henry II. in lieu of the personal services of his vassals, i. 444.

SEAFIELD, earl of, secretary of state for Scotland, 1699; iv. 97, 99, 106.

Seaton House, View of, iv. 494.

SEBERT, king of Essex, is converted, 604, by the influence of his uncle Ethelbert, Christian king of Kent, i. 233. On Sebert's death, his sons, 616, restore paganism, and banish Mellitus, ib.

SECKENDORF, marshal, enters Bavaria, 1744; iv. 473.

SECKER, bishop of Oxford, translated from Bristol, 1737; translated to Canterbury, 1758. He died, 1768; iv. 455.

Sedan-chairs, 1634, patent for, to sir Sanders Duncomb, iii. 544. Illustration of, from prints and paintings of the period, ib., iv. 823.

Sedgemoor, battle of, July 5, 1685; iii. 775.

SEDLEY, Catherine, mistress of James II., created countess of Dorchester, iii. 785.

SEDLEY, sir Charles, a poet of the seventeenth century; review of his works, iii. 876. He died 1701; his speech respecting finances, iv. 21.

Seekers, the, a religious sect, the followers of sir Harry Vane, iii. 814.

SEGRAVE, John de, made governor of Scotland by Edward I.; is defeated near Roslin by Comyn, February 24, 1303; i. 725.

SEGUIR, chancellor of France, recalls Nicholas Briot, a coiner, 1640; iii. 554.

Segura, town of, taken by the duke of Berwick, 1704; iv. 174.

SELDEN, the lawyer and antiquary, imprisoned, 1621, for differing in opinion with the king and bishops, iii. 86; again arrested, ib., 88, 129, 133, 138, 142. Quoted, i. 809.

SELIM III., nephew of Abdul Hamet, succeeds to the dominion of Turkey on the death of that prince, April 7, 1789. The Turkish ministry is dismissed, and the grand vizier, whose talents had been so beneficial to his country in the preceding year, is executed, § ii. 317. Battle of Tabac, 318. Siege of Orsova, 319. The Turkish Government prudently determined to train troops after the European mode, but before they succeeded, the Janissaries rose, gained the mufti to their party, and boldly demanded a new Sultan; Selim did not hesitate to resign, and was succeeded by his cousin Mustapha, 1807; § iv. 282—285. War with Russia; an English squadron under the command of sir John

SELIM III.,—
Duckworth, enters the Hellespont, and appears before Constantinople, but is compelled to retire with loss, 273—279. Selim is murdered by sultan Mustapha, July 28, 1809; 402.

Selsey, Isle of, i. 142.

SEMPIL, lord, 1602; iii. 452.

Senassie fakeers, ravages of in India, 1771; § ii. 123.

Seneschal, or Dapifer Regis, office of the, i. 568.

Sens, city of, taken, 1420, by Henry V., ii. 48.

SENTLOW.—See St. Low.

Sepoys, group of, § ii. 124.

Septennial Bill, the, passed, April 26, 1716; iv. 331.

SERLE, a gentleman in Richard II.'s service, hearing that Richard was not dead, but in Scotland, proceeds thither, 1404; ii. 16. He there finds a resemblance in Ward, the court-fool, whom he persuades to personate that prince; he forges Richard II.'s privy seal, entraps the old countess' of Oxford and many people into an absurd belief, ib. The countess's secretary hanged, ib. Serle avows he had himself a guilty share in the murder of Gloucester, at Calais, ib. He is drawn on a sledge from Pontefract to London, and is there executed, ib.

Serpent.—Superstitious worship and great Celtic or Druidical temples to the sun (fire, or Bel), and to the serpent, thus united in the pagan superstitions of Europe, i. 68. Pliny's account of the serpent's egg, a badge of the Druid priesthood, ib.

SERVETUS, burning of, at Geneva, in 1553, for his anti-trinitarian opinions; a controversy is occasioned by his death on the expediency of repressing heresy by means of the civil power, iii. 807; iv. 769.

SETON, Christopher, suffered as a traitor for assisting Bruce, 1306; i. 729.

SETON, Mr., of Pitmedden, one of the commissioners appointed, 1706, for settling the Union of Scotland, iv. 195.

Settlement, Act of, 1689; iv. 13, 19.

" Seven Sacraments, Defence of the," written by Henry VIII., ii. 345. Leo X., after reading this treatise, conferred by a bull the title of "Defender of the Faith" on the English monarch, ib.

Seven Years' War, the, iv. 589.

Severn, river.—Danish camp at Buttington; Alfred, with Saxons and North Welshmen, cuts off the supplies of the Danes, under Hasting, i. 163. Victory of Alfred, on the banks of this river, ib. The English king is obliged to respect the strong fort of Quatbridge; but Hasting, in 897, departs for France, and his followers disperse, 164.

SEVERUS, the emperor, 207, landed in South Britain, and passed the walls of Agricola and Hadrian, i. 49. He lost 50,000 men by fatigue in Durham, then a wilderness, and his northward march, ib. Made roads and constructed bridges on his route, penetrating further into North Britain than his predecessors, ib. From the Murray and Cromarty friths, he returned southward, and constructed a stronger wall on the line of Agricola's, between the Tyne and Forth, ib. Hadrian's wall, and Severus's re-construction of it, described, ib. Illustrations: Stone Wall of Severus, near Housesstead, Northumberland, 50. Roman sculptures found on this Line, 51. This wall, as seen above the Sand-stone Quarries, Denton Dean, near Newcastle-upon-Tyne, 52. Severus marched against the refractory Caledonians, 211, but died at Eboracum, ib.

SEXBY, colonel, presents the first manifesto of the Adjutators to the House of Commons, 1647, iii. 66, 427.

SEYMOUR, queen Jane, married in 1536, to Henry VIII., the day after Anne Boleyn's execution, ii. 394. Act of Parliament to settle the succession on the children that Henry might have by her, 395, 396. She gave birth, 1537, to a prince (Edward VI.,)

SEYMOUR, queen Jane,—
402. Refutation of some circumstances frequently reported as to her death, 402, *note.*

SEYMOUR, lord Henry, blocks up the ports of Spain along the coast of Flanders, 1587 ; ii. 673.

SEYMOUR, Mr. Edward, presents the impeachment of the earl of Clarendon at the bar of the Lords, November 12, 1667, iii. 705, 768.

SEYMOUR, sir Edward, 1689, one of the first to join the prince of Orange, iv. 3, 92, 160.

SEYMOUR, sir Francis, appointed sheriff, 1625; iii. 117, 130.

SEYMOUR, Mr. Portman, 1711 ; iv. 253.

SEYMOUR, sir Thomas, 1547, created lord Seymour of Sudley, and lord high-admiral, ii. 456. Relation of his quarrel with the earl of Hertford, 471, *et seq.* His character, 472. He marries Catherine Parr, queen-dowager of Henry VIII., 473. Is executed on Tower-hill, March 26, 1549; 480. His child by the lady Catherine; her penniless condition, *ib.*

SEYMOUR, William, son of lord Beauchamp, iii. 46. His acquaintance with lady Arabella Stuart; their private marriage, 1610; he is committed to the Tower, *ib.* He escapes in the disguise of a physician, 47. The vessel having set sail with his wife before he reaches it, he gets on board a collier, the captain of which agrees to land him on the coast of Flanders for 40*l.* ; his safe arrival, *ib.*

SFORZA, Maximilian, 1515, and his Swiss allies defeated by Francis I., at Marignano, ii. 334. His duchy of Milan submits to the French king, *ib.*

SHAFTESBURY, Anthony Ashley Cooper, earl of, created, April 3, 1672; appointed a member of the council of state, 1655; iii. 413. Assists at the trial of the regicides, 1660; 671. Lord chancellor, 1673; 711. Deprived of his office, *ib.* He is committed to the Tower, February 5, 1677; 714. A new council is formed with the earl of Shaftesbury at its head, 1679; 728. He is dismissed, 731. He presents a bill to the grand jury against the duke of York, as a popish recusant ; the judge discharges the jury, 1680; 732. He attends the Oxford parliament, 733. Is committed to the Tower, 1681; 734. Fearing for his life, he retires to his house in Aldersgate-street, and takes a part in the Rye-house Plot, 740. He flies to Holland, where he dies, 1683 ; *ib.*

SHAH ALUM, is invested with the government of Allahabad and Corah, § ii. 89. His negotiations with the Mahratta chiefs; he is carried in triumph to the palace of Aurengzebe, 1771; 121. Portrait of, 122. He cedes Corah and Allahabad to the Mahrattas, 123.

SHAKSPEARE, William, the most illustrious name in the history of English dramatic poetry, born at Stratford-upon-Avon, April 23, 1564. He died on the anniversary of his birth, 1616, having exactly completed his fifty-second year. Review of his works, iii. 588—592. Painting of, after the Stratford bust, 560. Burial-place and monument of, from an original drawing, 591.

Shakspeare Gallery, the, § iii. 741.

SHARP, John, archbishop of York, consecrated, July 1691, died 1714; iv. 183.

SHARP, archbishop of St. Andrews, iii. 683. Re-establishes the High Commission Court, 1664 ; 694. Attempts the ruin of lord Lauderdale, 701. He invents the instrument of torture called "The Boots," *ib.* Is murdered in his coach by James Russell and other Covenanters, May 3, 1679; 730.

SHAW, Edmund, lord-mayor, 1483; rode with the sheriffs and citizens to Hornsey-wood to receive Edward V., ii. 119. He waits on the Protector, with Buckingham and other nobles, who then accepted the crown, 122.

SHAW, Dr., brother of the mayor; his sermon at Paul's-cross, which alleged that the two princes

SHAW, Dr.,—
were illegitimate sons of Edward IV., that monarch having a wife (Eleanor, widow of lord Boteler) living when he married Elizabeth Woodville, ii. 121. His panegyric on Gloucester, *ib.* Buckingham, at the hustings at Guildhall, repeated, in the words of this sermon, the illegitimacy of the young princes, 122.

SHAXTON, Nicholas, bishop of Salisbury, elected February 1535; resigned his bishopric, 1539, on the passing of the Six Articles; long imprisoned, ii. 410 ; and, in 1546, condemned to the stake, 448. He saved his life by a recantation, and in vain persuaded Anne Askew to follow that example, *ib.*

SHEBBEARE, Dr., a reviewer and pamphleteer, set in the pillory 1758 ; iv. 604.

Sheen, priory of, near Richmond, ii. 309, 329.

Sheep; considered more valuable by the Anglo-Saxons for their wool than for their flesh, i. 277. Statement of their price at that period, *ib.*

Sheffield, iii. 655.

SHEFFIELD, John, marquess of Normanby. *See* Buckingham.

SHEFFIELD, Edmund, created baron Sheffield of Butterwicke, February 1547; he died 1548 ; ii. 456.

SHEFFIELD, captain, a parliamentarian officer, 1643; iii. 304.

Sheffield plate, first made in 1742 ; iv. 733 ; § i. 587.

SHELBURNE, earl of, appointed secretary of state, 1766; § i. 48. His description of the Mutiny Act, 1767; 73, 201, 203. Portrait of, 284, 343, 402. Is wounded in a duel with Mr. Fullarton, 1780; 406, 496. He resigns, 1783 ; 499.

SHELLEY, Richard, presents a Catholic petition to Elizabeth, for which he is committed to prison, where he dies, 1585 ; ii. 656.

SHEPHERD, James, executed by George I. as a traitor, 1718; iv. 344.

SHEPHERD, presents the first manifesto of the Agitators to the Commons, 1647; iii. 366.

SHEPHERD, his depositions respecting the Rye-house Plot, 1681; iii. 744.

SHERFIELD Mr., fined 500*l.*, 1631, for destroying a painted glass window, iii. 159.

SHERIDAN, Richard Brinsley, distinguished as a statesman, wit, and dramatist, born October 1751 ; chosen member for the borough of Stafford, 1780 ; § i. 443, 444. Becomes Secretary to the Treasury, 1783 ; 500. Portrait of, 610. His dramatic works, *ib.* Takes part in the impeachment of Warren Hastings, 1787 ; § ii. 227, 280. Moves for an inquiry, 1792, into the grievances petitioned against by the royal burghs in Scotland, § iii. 12. Attempts to palliate the massacres and atrocities committed in France, 1793; 382. Moves to bring in a bill for the repeal of the suspension of the Habeas Corpus Act, 1795; 466, 596. His death, 1816 ; 715.

Ship, form of a Saxon, i. 266. Ships of war of the fifteenth century, ii. 177. Medal exhibiting a first-rate ship of war, iii. 864. *See* Navigation.

SHIPPEN, Mr., committed to the Tower, November 1717; iv. 344. He refuses to give his vote against sir R. Walpole, and quits the House, followed by thirty-four of his party, 1741; iv. 444.

SHIRLEY, James, a dramatist, born about 1594; iii. 592, 597, 598.

SHIRLEY, Dr. Thomas, his appeal against sir John Fagg, 1675; iii. 839.

SHIRLEY, general, makes an unsuccessful attack on the French fort at Niagara, 1755; iv. 582.

Shooting-matches, iv. 827.

Shop-tax, Repeal of, April 1789; § ii. 303.

SHORE, Jane, portrait of, ii. 120. The Protector Gloucester accused her of wasting his arm by sorcery, 1483; *ib.* She had been one of the mistresses of Edward IV.; her money sequestered by Gloucester, who delivered her over to the Ecclesiastical

SHORE, Jane,—
Court, 121. She was condemned to do public penance, dressed in a kirtle, and carrying a taper, ib.
SHOVELL, sir Cloudesley, placed at the head of the Admiralty Board, 1693; iv. 41. Appointed to the command of the fleet on the dismissal of admiral Rooke, 1705; 177. He waits off the coast of Provence, with a combined English and Dutch fleet, to assist at the siege of Toulon, 203. Is wrecked off Scilly, October 22, 1707; 204.
Shrewsbury, battle of, July 21, 1403; ii. 15.
SHREWSBURY, Hugh, earl of.—See Hugh.
SHREWSBURY, John Talbot, earl of.—See Talbot.
SHREWSBURY, George Talbot, earl of, privy-councillor and steward, 1509; ii. 320. He served under Henry VIII., 1513, in the king's campaign in Picardy, 323. He laid waste the Scottish border, 1522, but his army was driven back to England, 353, 354. His house of Sheffield Park; Wolsey's delay there by sickness, 373. The earl, 1536, served against the Lincoln and northern rebels, 397—399. He died 1541.
SHREWSBURY, Francis Talbot, earl of, 1541. His expedition into Scotland, 1548; ii. 470. He died 1560.
SHREWSBURY, George Talbot, earl of, 1560. Superintends the execution of Mary queen of Scots, 1587; ii. 668. He died 1590.
SHREWSBURY, countess of, her harshness to the lady Arabella Stuart, iii. 46.
SHREWSBURY, Francis Talbot, earl of, falls in a duel with the duke of Buckingham, 1667; iii. 897.
SHREWSBURY, Charles Talbot, duke of, on the rejection of the Abjuration Bill he resigns his offices, 1690; iv. 22. Created duke of Shrewsbury, 1694; being accused by sir John Fenwick of treasonable practices, he begs leave to return the seals, which petition the king rejects, 75. He absents himself from parliament whilst the Bill of Attainder is being passed against Fenwick, 1697; 76. He resigns, 1699; 95. Is sent to Paris to conclude the peace of Utrecht, 272. He is made prime-minister by queen Anne when on her death-bed, 300. His death, 1718; 344.
SIBTHORPE, Robert, vicar of Brackley, a divine who obtained considerable notoriety in the time of Charles I., by his defence of the royal prerogative. He died in 1662; iii. 124.
SIBILLA, lady, illegitimate daughter of Henry I., and wife of Alexander I. of Scotland, i. 538.
SIBYLLA, daughter of William, count of Conversano, a powerful lord of Lower Apulia, marries duke Robert, who resided for some time at her father's castle, when on his way home from the Holy Land, i. 408. She dies and leaves an infant son, 1102; 410.
SIBYLLA, daughter of Fulk, earl of Anjou, promised by her father to William Fitz-Robert, son of the duke of Normandy; the marriage treaty broken off, and her sister Matilda given in marriage to prince William, son of Henry the first, about 1113; i. 412, 413.
SIDMOUTH, Henry Addington, viscount, created, 1805. He becomes premier of England on the resignation of Pitt, March, 1801; § iii. 549*. He favours the hope of maintaining peace with France. Treaty of Amiens signed, March 27, 1802; § iv. 3. Its provisions unfavourable to England, 5—10. He opposes a renewal of the war with France, 48. In both Houses censures are moved on the conduct of his administration, 51. His administration becomes more and more unpopular, and he is compelled to resign, May 12, 1804; 89, 90. He is created viscount Sidmouth, January 12, 1805; and supports Mr. Pitt in his administration, 147. He resigns his office, and joins the opposition, 165. He is appointed lord privy seal, on the death of Mr. Pitt, when lord Grenville and Mr. Fox formed the new administration, February 4, 1806; 208.

SIDONIUS, speaks of the delight that the early Saxons had in a life on the seas, i. 140.
SIGHELM, bishop of Shireburn, his embassy to India in the reign of Alfred, i. 267.
SIGISMUND, king of the Romans, and emperor elect, confers, 1416, with king Henry V. in London, on the schism in the church, the rival popes, etc., ii. 34. His mediation between France and England fails, 35.
Silbury Hill, in Wiltshire, i. 67.
Silk.—It is enacted in 1455 that no wrought silk be brought into England by way of merchandise for five years to come, ii. 193. An Act passed, 1504, to regulate the importation of foreign silk, 775. In 1562, the silk-throwsters united into a fellowship, 810. Silk manufactures, iii. 558; § i. 600; § iii. 707. Silk-mill, first erected at Derby in 1719, by the Messrs. Lombe, iv. 731.
Silures, the, supposed by Tacitus to have been of Spanish descent, i. 6. They were the fiercest and most obstinate enemies of the Romans, 41. Caractacus's address to the Silures, ib. They fight bravely, but are at last vanquished, ib. Caractacus, their commander, taken prisoner, 42. Ostorius, the Roman commander, dies in an expedition against them, ib.
SIMIER, presses the suit of the duke of Anjou to queen Elizabeth, ii. 650.
SIMNEL, Lambert.—See Henry VII.
SIMON, Thomas, maker of the beautiful coinage of the Commonwealth, iii. 578. Supposed to have died of the plague in 1665; ib.
SIMPSON, Cuthbert, tortures practised upon, 1558; ii. 735, 736.
SIMPSON, Thomas, an eminent mathematician, born at Bosworth, 1710; died, May 14, 1761; iv. 785.
SIMPSON, a distinguished preacher, convicted of seditious behaviour, suspended and imprisoned, 1617; iii. 66.
SINCLAIR, Oliver, a favourite of James V., assumed the command of the royal army on the borders of Cumberland, 1542, and was routed by a small English force, ii. 433.
SINCLAIR, bishop of Dunkeld, defeats an English force near Inverkeithing, 1317; for this action he received the name of the "King's Bishop," i. 739.
Sinking Fund, the, established 1717; iv. 720. Brought under consideration by William Pitt, March, 1786; § ii. 13; § iii. 624.
SIWARD, earl, of Danish origin, extent of his government, 1043, from the Humber to the Scottish border, i. 188. Applied to by king Edward, 1051, for succour against earl Godwin; he marches to join him, 190. Assists, 1054, Malcolm, prince of Scotland, against the usurper Macbeth, 194. His son Osberne falls near Dunsinane, ib. Siward returns from Scotland, and dies; anecdotes of his and his son's death, 194, 195. His popularity, 195.
Six Articles, the, regarding the Eucharist, Celibacy of Priests, Auricular Confession, etc., passed into a statute, 1539; Henry VIII. joining in the debate in support of the Romish observances therein, ii. 410. Pains and penalties provided for all who should contravene or not observe the "Bloody Statute," its subsequent name, ib. Reflections on this and other tyrannical, or unconstitutional enactments, 411.
SIXTUS IV. (Francis d'Albescola della Rovere,) elected August 9, 1471; this pope, in 1476, takes part with the Franciscans in the long-disputed question between them and the Dominicans respecting the conception of the Virgin Mary; he died, August 13, 1484; ii. 701.
Skating, winter sport of, ii. 261.
SKEFFINGTON, sir William, lord-deputy of Ireland, 1535, took the field against the rebels under Thomas Fitzgerald, ii. 426.
SKELTON, John, poet-laureate, regno Henry VIII.; specimens of his verse; he died, June 21, 1529; ii. 827, 837.

SKERRETT, colonel, bravely defends Tarifa, 1812; § iv. 505. San Lucar taken by storm, 510.

SKIPPON, sergeant-major, a parliamentarian officer, 1642; iii. 267. His gallant conduct, 1644; 317. Dangerously wounded at the battle of Naseby, June 14, 1645; 333, 365.

SKYRING, Mrs.; her enthusiastic reception of the Young Pretender, 1745; iv. 512.

SLANY, sir Richard, 1642; iii. 292.

SLAVATTA, Martinitz, member of the council of state at Prague, 1618; iii. 80.

Slave-trade; the English trade in negroes was commenced in 1562, by John Hawkins, (subsequently the famous naval commander,) ii. 787. The Quakers petition for the total abolition of the, June 17, 1783; § i. 501. They are ably seconded by Wilberforce and others, 1788; § ii. 258, 466, 535; § iii. 9. Mr. Wilberforce's Bill for the Abolition of the Slave-trade, is negatived by a division of 77 to 70, February, 1805; § iv. 150. A resolution passed for the gradual abolition of the slave-trade, 1806; 216, 217. After the death of Mr. Fox in 1807, the labours of Mr. Wilberforce were crowned with success, and an Act was passed for the Abolition of the Trade in Slaves by the subjects of Great Britain, which received the Royal assent, March 25, 1807; 257—259; 640.

Slaves; children of the Angles (or English) exposed for sale at Rome, i. 230, 269. Inhabitants of London in 367, carried into slavery, 54. It was a practice of the Danish sea-kings to carry off many Anglo-Saxons to sell as slaves, 981. Case of Southampton among others, 176. Laws forbidding the sale of Christians for slaves, 269. Bishop Wulfstan's account, 1060, of the regular sale of Saxons (from Bristol,) even by near relatives, to the Irish and the Ostmen of the Irish coasts, 270.

SLINGSBY, sir Henry, a parliamentarian officer, beheaded by Cromwell, 1658; iii. 290; 427.

SLOPER, colonel; his deposition respecting sir George Sackville, 1760, who was under trial by court-martial, iv. 613.

Sluys, naval victory gained here by Edward III., June 24, 1340; i. 759.

SMEATON, John, a celebrated civil engineer, born May 28, 1724. He erected the Eddystone Lighthouse, 1755. Died, September 8, 1792; iv. 705. His portrait, § i. 579.

SMEATON, Mark, musician, accused, in 1536, as well as four others, for criminal conversation with queen Anne Boleyn, ii. 391. He was treated, as of a less station than the rest, with more severity, so that at length he confessed, 391, 392. Although such evidence was important against the queen and the gentlemen who all maintained their innocence, the musician was tried, condemned, and executed, 392, 394. Even if his life were promised him, it was impolitic to let such a witness live, 394.

SMITH, Aaron, iii. 747.

SMITH, Adam, a distinguished writer on morals and politics; born, June, 1723; died, July, 1790; iii. 906. Profile of, § i. 623.

SMITH, Robert, an eminent divine and mathematician, born, 1689. Author of " The Harmonica," or the " Philosophy of Musical Sounds." He died in 1768; iv. 764.

SMITH, sir Sydney; portrait of, § iii. 308. His gallant and humane conduct at the evacuation of Toulon, 1793; 307—309. His services at the battle of Alexandria, 1801; 555°.

SMITH, sir Thomas, an eminent statesman, philosopher, and linguist, of the sixteenth century; born about 1512; died, 1577; ii. 636; iii. 517.

SMITH, William, pupil of Isaac Becket, brought the art of mezzotint to perfection. He died, October, 1618; iv. 760.

SMITH, colonel; his services in India, 1768; § ii.96; et seq.

SMITHFIELD, burning-place in, ii. 698.

SMOLLETT, Tobias, a writer of considerable reputation and varied powers, born, 1721; died, October 21, 1771; § i. 605.

Smyrna, English ships trading to, plundered by Corsairs, iii. 85; iv. 42.

SNATT, William, a non-juring clergyman, 1696; iv. 69.

Snowdon, View of, i. 698.

SOANE, sir J., an eminent architect of the nineteenth century; superintended the erection of Trinity Church, Marylebone, in 1824; the State-Paper Office in 1829; the Treasury Buildings at Whitehall, etc., § iv. 706. His portrait, ib.

SOBIESKI, John, king of Poland, died, 1696; iv. 77.

Soho, Boulton and Watt's iron-works, established at, about 1762; § i. 587. View of, 588.

Soissons, Congress of, June, 1728; iv. 402.

SOLIMAN, the Arabian merchant, mentions tea as the common beverage of the Chinese in 850; iii. 862.

Sombref, battle of, June 16, 1815; § iv. 633°.

SOMERLED, thane of Argyle, revolts against Malcolm IV., and is slain in battle, together with his son, 1164; i. 542, 543.

SOMERS, John, lord, a distinguished lawyer and statesman, born 1652. Counsel for the petitioning bishops, 1688; iii. 791. Appointed lord-keeper of the great seal, iv. 41. He effects a reconciliation between the princess Anne and William III., 51. He is created lord Somers, baron of Evesham, and lord-chancellor, 1697; 77. Letter of the king to, 89. He is accused by the Tories of being a pirate on the high seas, 102. He is again attacked, but comes off with greater credit than before, 105. He resigns the great seal, 1700; 106. Hearing the Commons are about to impeach him, 1701, he makes a speech at their bar, 121. The Commons beg the king to prohibit his appearance at court, ib. He is impeached, 125. The Lords dismiss the charges against him, 128. Quotations from a letter of his to the earl of Sunderland, 132. He becomes President of the Council, 1708; 222. His death, April, 1716; 331. His portrait, iv. 658.

SOMERS, sir George, a captain of the Virginia Company, supposed to have discovered the Bermudas in 1609; iii. 538.

Somerset House, View of, ii. 845.

SOMERSET, John de Beaufort, earl of, created marquess of Dorset, 1397; deprived of that title, 1399. Restored 4 Henry IV. He died, 1410; ii. 5.

SOMERSET, Edmund de Beaufort, earl of, a son of John of Gaunt, and legitimatized by parliament, on his parents' subsequent nuptials, declared capable of inheriting the crown, ii. 52. His military service, 1422, under Bedford, 54. The duke of York, being recalled from Normandy, Somerset succeeds to the command in France, 84. He writes to the council, that he had no military chest, insufficient forces, and that the Norman fortresses were dilapidated, ib. Is attacked by the armies of Charles VII., 1449; under the count of Dunois, 85. He defends Rouen with a small force, but the disaffection of the citizens causes the loss of that city, ib. Gallantry of Talbot in defence of Rouen, ib. Somerset retired into Caen, leaving Talbot as an hostage, ib. For want of adequate troops, he loses Caen, 1450, and all Normandy, ib. Unpopular both from this cause, and as succeeding Suffolk in queen Margaret's favour, 90. He is chosen as the opponent to Richard duke of York, ib. Somerset was the nearest male relation to Henry VI., ib. York visiting the king in his tent, was arrested by Somerset as a traitor, 91. Henry VI. incapable of his high duties, and idiotic, ib. Somerset is sent to the Tower, and York appointed Protector, ib. The king recovering his former degree of reason, is restored to his royal office, and

SOMERSET, Edmund de Beaufort, earl of,—
soon liberated Somerset, 1454; 92. A civil war
ensued, and Somerset was slain in the first battle,
at St. Albans, ib.

SOMERSET, Henry de Beaufort, duke of, 1455. Commanded the Lancastrians, in their fatal defeat at
Towton, 1461; ii. 98, 99. He escaped with the duke
of Exeter to York, whence he conveyed Henry VI.
and Margaret of Anjou, with prince Edward into
Scotland, ib. Warwick, as a condition on the surrender of Bamborough and Dunstanburgh, agreed
that Somerset, sir R. Percy, etc., should be restored
to their titles and lands, 100. Somerset, notwithstanding his submission to Edward IV., joined the
turbulent Percy in the north, 1464; 101. He remained a prisoner after the battle of Hexham, and
was beheaded with Hungerford and De Roos, ib.

SOMERSET, Edmund de Beaufort, duke of, commander
of the forces for queen Margaret, after the death of
the two preceding dukes, ii. 109. He imprudently
sallied from the Lancastrian intrenchments, whence
the Yorkists had been repulsed, in the battle of
Tewkesbury, 1471; ib. A part of the troops not
following his banner, he was driven in with dreadful loss, ib. He suspected treachery, and lord
Wenlock being one of those who remained in the
intrenchments, he clove that captain's head with his
battle-axe, ib. Margaret being taken, Somerset
fled to sanctuary in a church at Tewkesbury, with
many knights who had escaped from the field, ib.
King Edward broke into the church sword in hand,
and was only restrained by a priest bearing the
sacrament, casting himself between the victor and
the victims, ib. The king thereupon promised to
spare their lives, ib. Somerset in a few days was
dragged from the altar, and beheaded with sir H.
Audely, sir Gervis of Clifton, sir W. Gainsby, sir
W. Cary, sir H. Rose, sir T. Tresham, and others,
109, 110.

SOMERSET, Edward Seymour, duke of, (known as the
earl of Hertford until the accession, in 1547, of his
nephew Edward the Sixth.) In 1544, Hertford
landed at Leith, took Edinburgh, but was foiled
before the castle, ii. 440. He laid waste the country from that capital to the borders, was joined by
the partisans of the Douglas faction; opposed by
Arran and cardinal Beaton; he retired to Berwick,
ib. The campaign was continued by Lennox in
the English interest, but the army of Henry
VIII., and the Scottish malcontents were routed
at Ancrum Moor, 441. In 1545, Seymour again
invaded Scotland, burnt and laid waste the lands
beyond the border; destroyed Kelso Abbey, slew
the monks, ruined the abbeys of Melrose and
Dryburgh, and converted the country into a
desert; these cruelties compelled him to withdraw
his famishing army to England and disband it,
445. Account of his French and other auxiliaries,
ib. Hertford, considered as the head of the Protestant interest, persuaded Henry VIII. to order
the arrest of the Catholic nobles, Norfolk and
Surrey, 1546;—they were attainted, Surrey (the
poet) was beheaded January, 1547; narrative of his
trial; Norfolk (who had gained the battle of
Flodden Field) was saved from the block by the
king's death, 448—451. Hertford conducted the
youthful Edward to London, 454. His father's
executors recommended Hertford to Edward VI.
for his governor, during the minority, 455. The
king agreed thereto, and also gave his uncle a
thousand marks out of the estate of the imprisoned
Norfolk, ib. Seymour was created duke of Somerset, 1547, and named Protector of the kingdom, etc.,
456, 457. Being popular as the head of the
Reformation, he was styled by the people "the
Good Duke," 456. Somerset dismissed his rival,
Southampton (Wriothesley) from the office of

SOMERSET, Edward Seymour, duke of,—
chancellor, and from the council, 457. The duke
demanded of the Scottish government the conclusion
of the promised nuptials of Mary and king Edward,
458. Narrative of the Protector's fresh invasion,
1547, of Scotland, 459. After a severe and perilous
combat on Fawside Brae, near Preston Pans,
Somerset and Warwick defeated the army of the
regent Arran, with immense slaughter, 460—464.
Somerset marched on Leith, but soon turned homeward; took Hume Castle on the borders, and crossing the Tweed repaired to London, 464, 465. His
quarrel with his younger brother, sir Thomas Seymour, related, 471. His disposition, 472. His fall,
489. He is succeeded by the earl of Warwick, ib.
A Bill of Pains and Penalties is read against him;
he is deprived of all his offices; his personal property is forfeited, as also 2,000l. a year of his
revenue from his lands, 492. He is released from
the Tower; a pardon is granted to him, and he is
restored into favour, and sworn of the Privy-council; but this was the end of his greatness, ib. Apparent reconcilement between him and the earl of
Warwick; lord Lisle, Warwick's eldest son, is married to the lady Ann, one of his daughters, 495.
Somerset takes secret measures for recovering his
former office, ib. He is charged with high treason
and committed to the Tower, ib. He is executed
upon Tower-hill, January 22, 1552; 497.

SOMERSET, William Seymour, duke of, 1660; is made
governor to prince Charles, 1641; iii. 247. The
king nominates him lord-general of Cornwall, etc.,
1642. He died 1660; 292.

SOMERSET, Charles Seymour, duke of, 1678; dismissed
by queen Anne from the presidency, 1702, to make
room for the earl of Pembroke; he died 1748; iv.
142.

SOMERSET, earl of.—See Rochester.

SOMERSET, countess of.—See Frances Howard.

SOMERSET, Thomas, Esq., and sir Charles Percy, sent
by Cecil, to Edinburgh, 1603, to king James I.,
iii. 2.

Somersetshire, the Saxons of, bravely assist king
Alfred (874—878,) i. 156, 158.

SOMERVILLE, strangled in Newgate, regno Elizabeth,
for a supposed conspiracy, ii. 654.

SOPHIA DOROTHEA, of Zell, queen of George I.; her
portrait, iv. 352. Cause of her confinement in the
castle of Ahlen, 392, 393. Her death, November
13, 1726; 393.

SORBIÈRE, Samuel, a physician by profession, born at
St. Ambroise, 1615; he became historiographer of
Louis XIV.; his description of the Royal Society;
he died in 1670; iv. 775—779.

SOUBIER, a leader of the Huguenots, receives permission of the English king to levy men and ships to
assist the French Protestants; and in May, 1627, a
fleet of a hundred sail is fitted out, under the command of the duke of Buckingham, iii. 127, 136.

SOULT, marshal.—The strong fortress of Badajos
surrenders to him, March 11, 1811; § iv. 481.
Defeated in the fiercely-contested battle of Albuera,
May 16, by general Beresford, 487, 488. Lord
Wellesley enters Madrid, August 12, 1812; on
which marshal Soult is compelled to quit the blockade of Cadiz, and retire precipitately to Granada,
510. Marshal Soult is recalled, to oppose the Russian army, about to advance through Germany to
the banks of the Rhine, 1813; 569. After the victory at Vittoria, the English army immediately
advanced to the frontiers of France, 574. Marshal
Soult dispatched to take the command of the
army, and prevent the passage of the Pyrenees,
575. Battles of the Pyrenees, 576—579. San
Sebastian and Pamplona surrender, October 31,
1813; 583. Lord Wellington enters France, ib.
Marshal Soult is driven from his strong position on

SOULT, marshal,—
the Nivelle, November 10; 584. Attacks the British left at St. Jean de Luz, but is repulsed, *ib.* Retires to his entrenched camp at Bayonne, which he is compelled to abandon, and cross the Adour, February 27, 1814; 604*. He is defeated at Toulouse, April 10, and on the 12th the allied army, enters that city 606*—608*. In the afternoon of the same day, messengers arrive from Paris, and give information of the entry of the Allies, and the abdication of Napoleon, 608*. A convention is signed with Wellington, and hostilities concluded, *ib.*

South Sea Company, 1720; its origin and fall, iv. 370 —377, 714.

SOUTHAMPTON, Thomas Wriothesley, earl of, 1547. The baron Wriothesley, lord-chancellor, informed parliament, January 27, 1547, that Henry VIII. had passed the Bill of Attainder against Norfolk, ii. 451. One of sixteen executors named in the king's will, 454. From his personal ambition, he at first opposed the election of one of the executors to represent the whole body, the guardianship of young Edward being vested in their hands, 455. He represented the Catholic party, and Hertford the Protestant interest, 455, 457. He is created earl of Southampton, 456. Hertford, now duke of Somerset and lord-protector, jealous of Southampton's influence, disgraces him with the loss of office, *ib.*, 491. His death, 1550; 492.—*See* Wriothesley.

SOUTHAMPTON, Henry Wriothesley, earl of, 1581. He joins the earl of Essex in his rash plan of obtaining an audience from Elizabeth by force, 1601; ii. 685. He is committed to the Tower, and afterwards brought to trial, 686. He is declared guilty, 688; but is kept a close prisoner till the accession of James I., 1603, when he is released, restored to his title and estates, and taken into the sovereign's favour, 689. He died 1624; iii. 3.

SOUTHAMPTON, Thomas Wriothesley, earl of, 1624.— Deprived of his estate adjoining the New Forest, and almost reduced to poverty, iii. 150. His objections to a standing army, 679. He died 1667.

SOUTHCOTE, Joanna, an extravagant fanatic, belonging to the communion of the Wesleyan Methodists, born April, 1750; died December 29, 1814; § iv. 627— 629.

SOUTHEY, an eminent poet, of the nineteenth century, § iv. 699. His portrait, *ib.*

Southwark Bridge, commenced 1814; § iv. 677. View of, 678.

SOUTHWELL, sir Richard, and other councillors, arrested the princess Elizabeth, 1554, at Ashridge. *See* Elizabeth, ii. 515.

Sovereigns, contemporary.—The period from the Norman Conquest to the death of king John, A.D. 1066 —1216; i. 357. 1216—1399; 670. 1399—1485; ii. 3. 1485—1603; 280. 1603—1660; iii. 1. 1660 —1688; 661. 1688—1760; iv. 1. 1760—1775; § i. 1. 1760—1801; § ii. 1. 1760—1817; § iv. 1.

Sovereigns (gold coin) first issued 1816; § iv. 673.

Spain.—Splendid library of the Ommiades, consisting of 600,000 volumes; high state of learning in Spain; students accustomed to repair from every other country to study in these Arabic schools, i. 604. The emir al Nassir receives the embassy sent to him from king John, requesting his assistance, 1209; 522. Allusions to the Cortes, or Assembly of the States of, ii. 354. Embassies from Austria and Spain, 1603, to James I., on his accession, relative to Holland, iii. 7. Philip III., desirous of amity with the successor of Elizabeth, sends a regular ambassador to James's court, *ib.* Independence of Portugal recognised by Spain, 1668; 706.

Spalatro, golden gate of Dioclesian at, i. 308. Console from, 309.

Spanish troops of Charles V., excellence of the infantry serving in Italy, Naples, Flanders, etc., ii. 358.

SPARKES, Michael, a publisher, brought before the Star-chamber, 1634; iii. 152. •

Spectacles, iv. 828.

SPEED, John, an industrious antiquary, born about 1555. Quoted, i. 483, 484. His works, iii. 615. He died 1629.

SPENCE, secretary of the earl of Argyle; he flies to London, but is sent back to Edinburgh, where he is cruelly tortured, August, 1684; iii. 756.

SPENCER.—*See* Sunderland, and Marlborough.

SPENSER, Edmund, an English poet of great celebrity, born in 1553; author of the "Faerie Queen;" died, January, 1599; ii. 652, 813, 839; iii. 582.

Spices, commerce in, iii. 105. The Dutch in Amboyna, one of the Spice Islands, seize Capt. Towerson, 1619, with nine English, and put them to death, being jealous of England sharing in the trade of Amboyna, *ib.*

Spinning-mill, the, invented by sir R. Arkwright; the first mill of this kind worked by water was erected on the river Derwent in 1771; § i. 596.

SPINOLA, Ambrose, one of the most celebrated generals of his time; born in Spain, 1569. In the war produced by the disputed succession to the duchy of Cleves, he took Aix-la-Chapelle, Wesel, and Breda. He died in 1630; iii. 85, 105, 106.

SPINOLA, marques, defends Messina against the Imperialists, 1719; iv. 360.

Spires, capitulates to the French general Custine, September 29, 1792; § iii. 190, 191. Diet of, 1530; ii. 709.

"Spirit in the Wall," 1554; Elizabeth Croft prompted to this imposition, which was designed to spread seditious speeches against Mary and Philip, the mass, etc., ii. 519.

Sports, field, and rural or popular, i. 647—657, 876— 881; ii. 255—267, 889—898; iii. 642; iv. 852.

SPOTSWOOD, John, archbishop of St. Andrew's, born 1565. Raised to the office of chancellor of Scotland, 1635. He died, 1639; iii. 438, 443, 451, 453, 465, 467, 477, 484.

SPRAT, Thomas, bishop of Rochester, consecrated November, 1684; iii. 743, *note.* He published a narrative of the Rye-house Plot by command of James II., 765. Warrant issued against him, 1692; iv. 37. He is falsely accused by Robert Young of an attempt to bring back James II., 39. His death, May, 1713; 277.

SPREUL, a fanatic Scottish preacher, 1679; iii. 730, 786.

Spurs, battle of the, fought 1513; ii. 323—325. *Illustration,* 324.

SPURSLOW, Dr., an Independent minister, attends Hampden in his last moments, June, 1643; iii. 304.

SQUIRES, a soldier, executed, 1598, on his confession on the rack, that at the instigation of Walpole, a jesuit, he had designed to take Elizabeth's life by a subtle poison, ii. 681.

STACEY, a priest, accused of having recourse to magic to compass the death of the lord Beauchamp, and executed, 1476; ii. 114.

STAËL HOLSTEIN, Anne Louise Germaine Necker, Baroness de, a celebrated female writer, the daughter of Necker the French financier, born April 22, 1766. Her admiration of Mirabeau, 1789; § ii. 414, *note.* Her portrait, § iii. 51. She plans a mode of escape for the royal family, 119.

STAFFORD, Edmund, earl of, 1365. Slain 1403, in the battle of Worcester, ii. 15.

STAFFORD, William Howard, earl of, 1640. Accused by one Tuberville of having commissioned him to assassinate Charles II., 1680; iii. 732. Though the accusation was manifestly false, Stafford is condemned and executed, December 29, 1680; *ib.*

STAFFORD.—*See* Buckingham.

STAFFORD, sir Humphrey, defeated at Sevenoaks by Cade, 1451 ; falls in the action, ii. 88.

STAFFORD, Humphrey and Thomas, collecting some insurgents, 1486, were disconcerted by the flight of the chief rebel Lovel, ii. 286. Humphrey executed at Tyburn; Thomas Stafford pardoned by Henry VII., 287.

STAFFORD, John, archbishop of Canterbury, translated from Bath and Wells, by bull, dated May 15, 1443 ; cardinal and lord-chancellor. He died, 1452; ii. 147.

STAFFORD, Thomas, a refugee of rank in France, 1557, landed at Scarborough with thirty-two adventurers, and surprised the castle, ii. 532. They surrendered immediately to the earl of Westmoreland, ib. Put to the torture in London, they declared that Henri II., abetted their enterprise, ib. Stafford beheaded, 28th May, on Tower-hill, others hanged at Tyburn, ib. Queen Mary declares war against the French king, ib.

STAFFORD, Granville Leveson Gower, marquess of, created 1786. He refuses the office of secretary of state, 1766 ; § i. 47. He died 1803; 107, 400.

STAFFORD, George Gower, marquess of, 1803. English ambassador at the court of France; recalled, August 17, 1792; § iii. 273.

STAIR, lord, commissioned to draw up a test for the preservation of the Protestant faith, 1681 ; iii. 736, 770. Recommends the Union of Scotland, 1689; iv. 8. Throws up his commission, 1743; 467.

STAMFORD, Henry Grey, earl of, created 1628. Presents a petition to the king, 1642 ; iii. 280. Raises the militia in Leicester by command of the parliament, 293. He died, 1673.

Stamford-bridge ; here the great battle between Hardrada and Harold was fought, 1066; i. 209.

STAHL, George Ernest, a German physician and chemist, and founder of the phlogistic theory ; he was born at Anspach, October 21, 1660, and was one of the most illustrious medical philosophers of his age; his name marks the commencement of a new era in chemistry. He died at Berlin in 1734; iv. 786.

Stamp Act, the, 1814-15 ; § iv. 636.

Stamp Duties, § iii. 606—608.

Stamp-tax, the, proposed by the premier, George Grenville, 1764 ; § i. 34. It is strongly resisted by the Americans, 35. The king gives his assent to this tax, 22nd March, 1765 ; 37. It is repealed, March, 1766; 46, 553—555.

Standard, battle of the, 1138 ; the Scots defeated, i. 424—426, 541.

STANDISH, Ralph, one of the esquires of king Richard II.; he thrust his sword into the side of Wat Tyler, June, 1381; i. 788.

STANDISH, Dr., asserts the claims of the civil power in a debate before king Henry VIII.; his trial, ii. 704.

STANHOPE, James, earl of, assists the earl of Peterborough in the capture of Barcelona, 1705; iv. 180. In conjunction with count Staremberg, he takes possession of Saragoza, 248. Enters Madrid, September 21, 1710; ib. He is defeated and made prisoner by the duke of Vendôme at Brihuega, December 9; ib. Created viscount Stanhope, 1717; 340. Resigns the Treasury and chancellorship of the Exchequer to Sunderland and Aislabie, 344. His death, 1721; 375.

STANHOPE, Charles, earl, endeavours, 1789, to procure the repeal of several severe laws, which, though seldom called into action, remained in force on the statute book, § iii. 566—578. His portrait, 566. Brings forward a bill, June, 1812, "for the Relief of certain Members of the Church of England and others from the operation of certain unjust Penalties and Disabilities," § iv. 613. He died, 1816.

STANHOPE, colonel William, 1719; iv. 355.

STANHOPE, sir William, called to order by the Speaker 1747 ; iv. 557.

STANHOPE, Mr., English ambassador at Spain, recalled by William III., iv. 101. Acts as plenipotentiary to William throughout the Partition Treaties; instructions given to him, 1701 ; 117.

STANHOPE, dean, prolocutor of the Lower House of Convocation, 1706—1707; iv. 644.

STANLEY, Thomas, lord ; his marriage with the dowager countess of Richmond, mother of Henry, afterwards Henry VII., ii. 126, 300. Alarmed, 1483, at the first proceedings of the Protector Gloucester, 119. He was wounded in the Council-chamber in the Tower, at the moment of the arrest of Hastings, 120. Stanley sent to the Tower, 121. Richard III., on his coronation, received Stanley into favour, 124. He procured his wife's pardon, 127. He persuades Richard of his devotion to his cause, ib. Stanley not having joined Richard III. at Nottingham, wrote to plead his being ill, as the cause of delay, 129. Peril to his son, lord Strange, then a hostage in Richard's camp, ib. Early in the battle of Bosworth Field, Stanley, with 3,000 men, joined Richmond, at a moment when the usurper, already engaged, might not think of his son, and the youth's life was thus saved, ib. On Richard III. falling, in his bold attack on the person of Richmond, Stanley picked up the bruised crown, and placed it on the head of the victor, Henry VII., ib. Created earl of Derby, 1485 ; 282.—*See* Derby.

STANLEY, sir Humphrey, knight-banneret, 1485; ii. 282.

STANLEY, sir William, brother to lord Stanley, who placed the crown on Henry's head at Bosworth Field, executed, 1495, for Perkin Warbeck's plot, ii. 300.

STANLEY, sir Edward, a skilful English commander; he repulses the Highlanders at the battle of Flodden Field, September 9, 1513; ii. 328.

STANLEY, sir William, holding a command in Spanish Flanders, 1605, iii. 23. Guido Fawkes commissioned to him by the conspirators, can only consult with Captain Owen, Stanley being in Spain, 23, 24. The English council demand those two officers of the Spaniards by *extradition*, but meet a direct refusal, 29.

STAPLETON, sir Philip, sent into Scotland to watch the king, 1641; iv. 249. He leads a body of the Parliamentarian horse, at the battle of Edgehill, October, 1642; 298.

Star-chamber, Westminster, View of the edifice, iii. 143; origin of the name, ii. 752 ; *note*. It commits the leading Puritans and Nonconformists, 1604, to gaol, and spies beset the secret conventicles, iii. 17. Mr. Pound, an old gentleman, sentenced, as a Catholic, to prison and pillory, and a fine of 1,000*l*.; 22. Bills, 1641, to abolish the High Commission Court, and the odious Star-chamber, 247. Charles I. with reluctance consents to the destruction of those bulwarks of tyranny, ib.

Starch, art of making, imported into England from Holland by Mrs. Dingham, about the middle of the sixteenth century, ii. 684.

STAREMBERG, count, a general of high reputation, sent by the emperor of Germany to serve in Catalonia, 1708 ; iv. 221.

State Paper Office, the, erected, 1829, by sir J. Soane, § iv. 706.

Statutes.—*See* Parliament.

STAYLEY, executed at Tyburn, on a false deposition of Carstairs that he was concerned in the Popish Plot, 1678; iii. 723.

Steam.—Application of steam as a moving power, proposed by the marquess of Worcester in 1683 ; iv. 729. Savery's engine for draining mines, 1698 ; ib. Brindley effects great savings in fuel, 1756 ; ib. Watt commences his experiments on the power of steam in 1763; 730. The first really efficient steam-

Steam,—
engine constructed about 1711, under a patent obtained by Newcomen, § i. 579. Watt's improvements in 1765; 580, 581. Importance of this power in the extension and improvement of coal-mining, 583. Application of steam to the assistance of manufacturing industry, § iii. 674.
Steam-boats, invention of, by Livingstone and Fulton, at the commencement of the nineteenth century, § iv. 682—686.
Steam-carriage, model of, exhibited in France, 1758, or 1759, by John T. Cugnot, § iv. 680.
Steam-engine, application of to the purposes of navigation, § iv. 682—686.
Steel, cast, first manufactured about the year 1770, by a person named Huntsman, § iii. 683. Its extensive service in the formation of cutting instruments, ib.
Steel, Mr., attorney-general at the trial of Charles I., iii. 390.
Steele, sir Richard, born in Dublin, 1671; iv. 282. Expelled the House for libel, 282, 283. This author holds a distinguished rank as a comic dramatist and English essayist; he wrote the comedy of "The Tender Husband" in 1703; and in 1709, commenced the series of periodical papers, so celebrated under the title of "The Tatler;" in 1711, "The Tatler" was brought to a close, and succeeded by the still more celebrated "Spectator;" the "Guardian" was commenced in 1713. He died of a paralytic stroke on the 1st of September, 1729; 796.
Steel-yard Company, the; mention of this hof, 1475; ii. 179. The privileges of the Company were abolished by Edward VI., 783.
Steinkirk, battle of, 1692; iv. 36, 37.
Stekna, Conrad, together with Milicz and Janowa, opposed some of the fundamental doctrines of the Romish Church, in the middle of the fourteenth century; the pope proceeded against them as heretics, and they were compelled to seek refuge in Poland, iii. 80.
Stephen, (December 26, 1135—October 25, 1154,) Nephew of Henry I., by the daughter of the Conqueror, Henry's sister Adela, i. 416. Stephen's priority of claim to the crown of England acknowledged by the assembly at Windsor, 1126; ib. Great seal of Stephen, 420. His portrait, 421. His marriage with Maud, a princess of the Saxon line, ib. The great estate forfeited by Robert Mallet in England, and that of the earl of Mortaigne in Normandy, conferred on Stephen, ib. His great popularity both with the English and Norman barons, ib. He hastens to England, and is received in London as king, ib. Obtains the treasury at Winchester, ib. Is crowned December 26th, 1135; 422. Summons a great council of the prelates, abbots, and lay-barons at Oxford, and receives their oaths of allegiance, ib. Letter of pope Innocent II., ratifying his title, ib. His charter of liberties, ib. Is joyfully received in Normandy, ib. Louis VII. grants the investiture of this duchy to his young son Eustace, ib. Revolt of the earl of Exeter, ib. Scottish incursion, ib. Stephen gives to David the lordship of Huntingdon, and castle of Carlisle, 423. Robert earl of Gloucester takes the oath of allegiance, ib. General revolt of the barons, ib. Stephen's merciful treatment of the vanquished beyond all precedent, ib. Robert, earl of Gloucester, plans an extensive insurrection, and sends a letter of defiance to Stephen, ib. David invades England with a numerous army, and overruns the whole of the country between the Tweed and the Tees at the instigation of Robert, ib. Exertions of archbishop Thurstan to raise a sufficient army to oppose the Scots, 424. The names of the Saxon saints invoked, and the ancient Saxon ban-

Stephen,—
ners used, ib. Description and picture of the English standard at the battle of Northallerton, ib. The English flock around their ancient standards, 424, 425.—See Northallerton. After the battle of Northallerton the Scots retreat, and rally within the walls of Carlisle; when David, having collected his scattered troops, reassumes the offensive, by laying siege to Wark Castle, 426. In the following year a peace is brought about by the intercession of Alberic, the pope's legate, and Stephen's queen Maud, very advantageous to the Scots, who are left in possession of Cumberland and Westmoreland, and king David's eldest son, Henry, is invested with the earldom of Northumberland, ib. Stephen arrests Roger, the powerful bishop of Sarum, and his two nephews, for a violation of the king's peace, ib. Nigel, one of Roger's nephews, and bishop of Ely, refuses to submit, and prepares to bid defiance to the king in the castle of Devizes. The king orders that Roger, and his nephew Alexander, shall be kept without food till the castle should be given up, which surrenders after three days, 427. Henry, bishop of Winchester, the king's brother, now papal legate for all England, summons the king to appear and answer for these violent proceedings before the synod of bishops assembled at Winchester. The king appoints Alberic de Vere to plead for him, who shortly dismisses the assembly, appealing to the decision of the pope, 427, 428. Matilda and Robert, earl of Gloucester, land in England, 1139, are joined by Alexander and Nigel, 428. Matilda is received by Alice, widow of Henry I., in Arundel Castle, from which she is permitted by Stephen to depart safely and go to earl Robert, ib. Stephen fails in his attempt upon Bristol, now the head-quarters of Matilda and Robert, but defeats Nigel, 429. Lawless state of England; cruel treatment of the defenceless population, ib. Stephen lays siege to the castle of Lincoln, as Alexander, bishop of Lincoln, in alliance with the earls of Lincoln and Chester, had become very formidable, 430. The earl of Gloucester having arrived, by forced marches, with an army of 10,000 men, a battle is fought before Lincoln, in which Stephen is taken prisoner through the desertion of his troops, and confined in Bristol Castle, ib.—See Matilda. Exchanged for Robert, earl of Gloucester, 433. Acknowledged a second time as king, 1142; 434. Besieges Matilda in Oxford Castle, 435. She escapes and joins the earl of Gloucester and prince Henry, her eldest son; who, having been acknowledged duke of Normandy, had come over to her assistance, ib. The king defeated by the earl of Gloucester, at Wilton, ib. Matilda maintains her ground in the west; but prince Henry having returned to Normandy, and the earl of Gloucester having died of a fever, she quits England and retires to Normandy, ib. Stephen endeavours to curb the overgrown power of the nobility; he exiles archbishop Theobald, who lays the country under interdict, ib. A reconciliation is effected, ib. A general council is held at London, in which Theobald, archbishop of Canterbury, positively refuses to anoint Eustace, Stephen's eldest son, as his successor, ib. Promising character of prince Henry; he receives the honour of knighthood from David, king of Scotland, 436. Is put in full possession of the government of Normandy, and succeeds to the earldom of Anjou by the death of his father, 1150, ib. In 1152 he marries Eleanor, the divorced queen of Louis VII. of France, and acquires with her the earldom of Poictou, and the vast duchy of Guienne, ib. General alliance against prince Henry, ib. Henry makes a truce with the French king, and sails to England, when a peace is finally adjusted on the 7th of November, 1153, by

2 к

STEPHEN,—
the great council of the kingdom held at Winchester, in which it is agreed that Henry should succeed to the throne on the death of Stephen, 437. Death of prince Eustace, ib. Death of Stephen, October 25th, 1154; 438.

STEPHEN, count of Aumâle, nephew of the Conqueror, extensive conspiracy for placing him on the throne, 1095; i. 400.

STEPHEN of Tours, seneschal of Anjou, and treasurer to Henry II., thrown into prison by Richard I.; i. 482.

STEPNEY, Mr., a poet and politician of little eminence; the princess Sophia wrote a very curious letter to him, 1701; iv. 112, 113.

Stereotyping discovered, in 1725, by William Ged, iv. 733. Revived by Mr. Tilloch, 1780; § iii. 714.

STERNE, Laurence, a divine, and popular writer of great eminence, author of "Tristram Shandy," the "Sentimental Journey," etc., was born November, 1713, and died March, 1768; § i. 606.

STEUBEN, baron, a Prussian officer, engages, 1778, to teach the American troops the field-exercise of Frederick the Great; § i. 352, 457.

STEVENSON, an agent of the Scottish Company at Hamburgh, 1697; iv. 84.

Stevenswaert, surrenders to Marlborough, October, 1702; iv. 145.

STEWART, sir John, constable of Scotland, and his son, lord William, perish bravely fighting against Fastolfe, at the battle of Herrings, February, 1429; ii. 61.

STEWART, Walter, eldest son of Murdoch, duke of Albany, executed in front of Stirling Castle, 1428; ii. 133.

STEWART, colonel, imprisoned by the Scottish parliament, 1641; iii. 251.

STEWART, Dr., a royalist commissioner at the conference in 1648; iii. 329.

STIGAND, archbishop of Canterbury.—He was bishop of Winchester, and is generally considered to have succeeded Robert Gemeticensis in the primacy, in 1052, but he was never constituted so by any authority; question regarding his crowning of Harold, son of Godwin, 1066, i. 204. The cause of Edgar Atheling supported by Stigand and Aldred, 360. Stigand supplies the Atheling's place in the council, ib., and accompanies him on a deputation to William, 361. He was deprived, in 1069.

STILICHO, in his great contest for the defence of Honorius and the empire of the West, aided the Britons against the Saxon incursions, 395; i. 54. In 403, he was compelled, by the arms of Alaric, to withdraw his troops from Britain, and the Britons were left at the mercy of their northern enemies, 55.

STILL, John, bishop of Bath and Wells, born 1543, author of the play entitled "Ralph Roister Doister;" elected January, 1592; died February, 1607; iii. 580.

STILLINGFLEET, Edward, bishop of Worcester, born April, 1635, author of several curious works; consecrated October, 1689; he died March 27, 1699. His portrait, iv. 617.

STILLINGTON, Robert, bishop of Bath and Wells; formerly archdeacon of Taunton; lord-chancellor; elected to this see in January, 1466; he died May, 1491; ii. 284, 285.

Stirling Castle, View of, i. 717.

Stochach, Pass of, iv. 165.

Stock-jobbing, rise of, iv. 687, 688.

Stocking-frame, the, invented about 1589, by William Lee, ii. 810.

Stocking-looms, exportation of, prohibited, 1696; iv. 732.

Stocking-manufacture, § iii. 709.

Stockings of silk knit were first made in England in the reign of Elizabeth, ii. 867.

STODTHARDT, Charles Alfred, an artist and antiquary of great talent and research, born July 5, 1789; died May 28, 1821; his print of William III. landing at Torbay, iii. 798.

Stoke-upon-Trent.—Here the earl of Oxford totally defeated the earl of Lincoln, June 16, 1487, and Lambert Simnel remained prisoner, ii. 290.

Stone, the Broad, Nottinghamshire, iii. 697.

STONE, Andrew, appointed sub-governor to the young prince of Wales (George III.) iv. 567.

STONE, Nicholas, a statuary of some eminence in the reign of James I. and his son, iii. 575. The statue of sir Francis Hollis is considered his best performance, 576. He died in 1647, aged sixty-one, ib.

Stonehenge, great Temple of the Druids at, i. 68. Method of joining some of the great stones of this circle, 101. Transverse imposts, ib.

STORY, Dr., acted as royal proctor in the proceedings against Cranmer, ii. 543. In anger, like many of the Catholic party, at the preponderance of the Protestants, 1559, soon after Elizabeth's succession, he very rashly declared his sentiments, ib.; avowing that "he had advised the late queen to pluck down heretics of eminence; that instead of labouring only about little twigs, they should have struck at the roots," 543, 544. This speech having been reported as if Story had wished or counselled the death of the princess, before the close of Mary's reign, he retired to Antwerp, 544. Seized there by queen Elizabeth's desire, he was conveyed to England, and executed, ib.

Stour, river, near Canterbury, i. 30.

STOURTON, Edward, lord, a Catholic, 1588; iii. 25. Suspected of an intention to be absent from parliament, 5th November, 1605, is on that slight presumption of a guilty knowledge of danger, arrested, 32. Fined by the Star-chamber, and imprisoned, ib. He died, 1632.

STOW, John, author of the "Summary of the English Chronicles, 1565," and several other works, born 1525, died 1605; iii. 615.

STRABO, his account of Britain and Ireland, i. 14, 93.

STRAFFORD, Thomas Wentworth, earl of, first baron Raby. He first sat in the House of Commons in 1621, when John Hampden also was elected, for whom and whose principles he professed high regard, iii. 178. His bold eloquence contrasted with Hampden's coolness and modesty of speech, ib. Suffers for not contributing to a forced loan, 1626; 123, 130, 145. President of the north, privy-councillor, and viscount, 1633; 168. Created earl of Strafford, 1640; 209. Made commander-in-chief, 220. He is impeached of high treason, 1640; 230. Refused bail, and lodged in the Tower, 231. His trial, 235, et seq. He asks permission of the lieutenant of the Tower to see archbishop Laud, a prisoner like himself, but is denied, 245. Is attended by archbishop Usher on the scaffold; he makes a speech to the people, and is beheaded on Tower-hill, May 12, 1641; ib. His portrait, 495.

STRANGE, James, lord.—See Derby.

Strasburg, 1697, delivered up to the French, iv. 79.

STRATFORD, John, translated to the see of Canterbury, November, 1333. Refuses to appear at the summons of Edward III., and appeals to the protection of Magna Charta, i. 759. Lord-chancellor. He died, August, 1348.

STRATFORD, Nicholas, bishop of Chester, consecrated September, 1689. Died 1708; iv. 213.

Strathclyde or Reged, also called Regnum Cumbrense, formerly inhabited by the Picts or Cymri, who afterwards migrated to Wales, i. 23. Reign of king Caw, he concludes a peace with Kenneth MacAlpin, 217. Strathclyde lost its independence, 973, Kenneth III., king of Scots, having totally defeated Dunwallon, the last king at Vacornar, 218, 220. Just previous to this, Culen, son of the Scottish king

Strathclyde or Reged.—
Indulf, having violated a princess of Strathclyde, was slain in battle, 970; 219, 220.
STRAW, Jack, a priest, chosen captain by the men of Essex and the neighbouring counties in their insurrection in 1378; i. 785—787. His execution, 789. (For particulars, see *Richard II.*)
STRICKLAND, Walter, captain of Cromwell's guards, iii. 424.
STRICKLAND, Mr., commanded by Elizabeth to absent himself from the House of Commons, and to await the orders of her privy-council, with which he refuses to comply, and takes his seat in the House, 1571; ii. 635.
STRODE, Mr.; his speech in parliament respecting the assault of Lambeth Palace by the London apprentices, 1640; iii. 219.
STRONGBOW.—*See* Pembroke.
STROUD, one of the members of parliament arrested and imprisoned by order of Charles, 1629; iii. 142.
STRYPE's "Ecclesiastical Memorials," died 1737; ii. 453.
STUART, lady Arabella, first-cousin of James I., and daughter of the earl of Lennox, brother of Darnley, iii. 3. By birth in England, her claim to the crown, 1603, considered perilous to James's cause, who was a Scotchman born, *ib.* Sir Robert Cecil then held her in his safe keeping, *ib.* Lord Cobham, Raleigh, Brooke, and others indicted for a conspiracy to place her on the throne, June, 1603; the lady Arabella Stuart urged to write letters to foreign potentates, 9. Cecil declares that this accomplished lady laughed at Cobham's application to her, and sent his letter to the king, 12. Lady Arabella was in court when Raleigh was tried, and Howard, earl of Nottingham, attending her, declared in her name that she had had no dealings with the conspirators, *ib.* Her innocence generally acknowledged, *ib.* Her person secured by Cecil, 46. The king of Poland demands her hand, *ib.* Her acquaintance with William Seymour, son of lord Beauchamp; their private marriage; the lady Arabella is committed to the custody of sir T. Parry; while on her journey to Durham, she escapes, and attempts to reach France, but is seized and conveyed to the Tower; where she dies, September 27, 1615, in a state of insanity, 47.
STUART, Alexander, archbishop of St. Andrew's, natural son of James IV., slain in the battle of Flodden, September 9, 1513; ii. 329. Names of the Scottish nobles who fell with their king, *ib.*
STUART, sir John, gains a victory over the French at Maida, in Sicily, July, 1806; § iv. 253, 254.
STUBBES, Philip, author of the "Anatomy of Abuses," published about 1590; iii. 658.
STUBBS, John, a spirited lawyer, born 1541; publishes a pamphlet, charging Elizabeth with degeneracy from her former virtue; the queen orders the pamphlet to be burnt, and condemns the author, publisher, and printer, to lose their right hands, ii. 651.
STUDLEY, John, translated the "Medea" and "Agamemnon" in 1566; iii. 584.
STUKELEY; Gregory XIII. entrusts this officer with a body of troops for the assistance of Ireland; he, however, touching at Lisbon, offers his services to Sebastian, king of Portugal, and proceeds to Africa to fight the Moors, by whom he was slain, together with king Sebastian, and all his host at the battle of Alcazar, 1578; ii. 651.
STUKELY, sir Lewis, vice-admiral of Dover, arrests sir Walter Raleigh at his return in 1618; iii. 76.
STUTEVILLE, Robert de, taken prisoner at the battle of Tenchebray, July, 1106, and condemned by king Henry to perpetual imprisonment, i. 410.
STUTEVILLE, William de, left by king John to oppose the Scots who threatened an invasion when he departed for Normandy in 1199; i. 516.

STYRUM, count, mortally wounded at the battle of Schellenberg, July 2, 1704; iv. 168.
Succession Bill, the, passed 1701; iv. 126; 149.
SUCKLING, sir John, a minor but graceful and spirited poet; born 1609, he died in 1641; iii. 604.
SUDBURY, Simon, *alias* Tibold, made archbishop of Canterbury, May, 1375; lord-chancellor; beheaded by the rebels under Wat Tyler, June 14, 1381; i. 787.
SUDELY, lord, Lancastrian, 1454, wounded at St. Albans, ii. 92.
SUETONIUS, Paulinus, Roman governor of Britain, A.D. 59—61, slays many Druids and Britons in Anglesey, i. 43, 61. Destroys the sacred groves of the isle of Mona, *ib.* The great insurrection under Boadicea constrains him to retire across the Menai upon London, which city he was also obliged to abandon, 43. Is reinforced, awaits battle in a good position, repulses the army of Boadicea, and his troops devastate the country with fire and sword, 44. He quits his command, and returns home, *ib.* Quotations from. 26, 29, 36.
SUFFOLK, Michael de la Pole, earl of, a favourite of Richard II., created 1385; i. 791. He became lord-chancellor, was expelled from the king's council, and sentenced to be fined and imprisoned, 792. The earl of Gloucester enters London with a large army; Suffolk flies to France about 1388, where he soon after dies, *ib.*—*See also* Michael de la Pole.
SUFFOLK, Michael de la Pole, earl of, slain, 1415, at Agincourt, ii. 34, 175. His effigy on the monument at Wingfield, 241.
SUFFOLK, William de la Pole. earl and duke of, uncle of earl Michael who was slain at Agincourt, ii. 175. This earl succeeded his nephew as earl of Pembroke, 1446; was created duke of Suffolk, June, 1448. His services in France, 1422; 54. Salisbury being mortally wounded before Orleans, Suffolk continued the investment, 1429; 61, 175. His troops partake in the belief of the preternatural mission of Joan of Arc, 65. They bravely resisted the sorties of the French, led by the Maid of Orleans, 66. The works erected by Suffolk, the *tournelles, bastilles,* towers, and lines being taken by the followers of Joan, he raised the siege, 1429, 8th May; 67. The earl led off his troops in perfect order, garrisoned many castles on the Loire, and threw his main corps into Jargeau, a few miles off, to wait for Bedford, *ib.* That fortress was taken by the Maid of Orleans, and Suffolk fell into her hands, 68. He negotiated a truce for two years, 1444; 80. He married Alice, daughter of Thomas Chaucer, speaker of the House of Commons, 176. The terms of his treaty for Henry VI.'s marriage with Margaret of Anjou, disgusted the nation, 81, 66. Is created a marquis, 82, 175. Suspected, together with queen Margaret, of causing the murder of Gloucester, whose estates he seizes for himself and friends, 83, 84. Ill consequences of his ceding Maine and Anjou; Charles VII. breaks the truce and invades Normandy, 1449; *ib.* Popular indignation at the loss of Rouen and Bordeaux directs itself against the duke of Suffolk, the queen's chief adviser and favourite, 1449; 86. Impeached by the Commons, the Peers sent him to the Tower, *ib.* The charges, and his eloquent pleading on his trial, 1450; *ib.* The chancellor announces, that as Suffolk did not put himself on his peerage, the king banished him for five years, 87. The populace sought his life in London. *ib.* He sails on the appointed day for Calais, *ib.* The *Nicholas of the Tower,* a great ship of war, intercepts him, and orders him on board, *ib.* Communications held with some great personages at home, *ib.* A boat, with an executioner and block comes alongside, and Suffolk is beheaded at sea, 1450; 87, 175.
SUFFOLK, John de la Pole, duke of, created 1463; son of the unpopular duke William, was restored by

SUFFOLK, John de la Pole, duke of,—
Edward IV., ii. 175. He married Elizabeth Plantagenet, sister of that king, and died 1491, *ib.* Their eldest son John, created earl of Lincoln, declared by Richard III., his presumptive heir, died 1487, before his father, *ib.*, 313. Their daughter was betrothed to James IV., but the marriage did not take place, *ib.* Their second son Edmund, was an object of jealousy to Henry VII.; he was beheaded in 1513; *ib.*, 175, 313—315, 323.

SUFFOLK, Mary, duchess of, second daughter of Henry VII.; her prospective claim to the English crown, in preference to her elder sister Margaret queen of Scotland, by a will of Henry VIII., iii. 3, *note.—See Mary;* (also Brandon duke of Suffolk.)

SUFFOLK, Edmund de la Pole, earl of, 1491, claimed the honours and lands of the duke his father, but Henry VII. and his obsequious parliament refused him, ii. 313. Henry granted as a royal favour a scanty portion of the revenues, with the title of earl, *ib.* In a broil Suffolk committed a homicide, *ib.* Permitted to plead the royal pardon, he sought refuge with his aunt the duchess of Burgundy, *ib.* Induced by Henry to return, he attended the marriage of prince Arthur, and became involved in debt, *ib.* He takes his brother Richard de la Pole to the court of Burgundy, *ib.* Sir R. Curson, a crafty spy, set to learn what party he might have, and to gain his confidence, *ib.* In consequence his brother William de la Pole, and lord Courtenay, were confined in the Tower, *ib.* Tyrrel, who had been accused of the murder of Edward V. in the Tower, and sir W. Windham, are beheaded on a charge of aiding Suffolk's escape, in 1499; 313, 314. The earl became a needy wanderer in Germany, etc., 314. Surrendered, 1506, by Philip of Burgundy and Castile, he was sent prisoner to the Tower, 315. Henry VII., in his last moments, signed a warrant for Suffolk's execution, *ib.* Beheaded, 1513; 323.

SUFFOLK, Charles Brandon duke of; the princess Mary enamoured with sir C. Brandon, lord Lisle, ii. 331. His brilliant display at a tournament, 332. On the decease of Louis XII., 1515, the young queen married Brandon, *ib.* King Henry soon forgives his younger sister and Suffolk, 332, 351. Despite Brandon's chivalric qualities, he was foiled, 1523, in his French campaign, 355. His delay before the walls of St. Omer, 356. Crossed the Oise river, and approached close to Paris, *ib.* The Germans of Charles V. were in retreat before the duke of Guise, and the English army was surrounded by Vendôme and Tremoille, who cut off its communications with Calais, *ib.* Retreat of Suffolk without provisions, and in severe weather, *ib.* Sickness; the Flemings desert, and Brandon reached Calais in great distress, 357. Anger of Henry VIII., who had expected glorious results from this expedition; Brandon's head in danger, 357, 371. An odious impost causes his life to be menaced in Suffolk, 360. Brandon's exclamation against cardinals, in the hall of the Black Friars, 1529, and spirited reply of Wolsey, 371. Suffolk, lord-marshal, Norfolk, lord-president, etc., on the fall of the cardinal, direct the king's counsels, 374. The duke, with divers lords and prelates, argued with Catherine of Arragon, 1533, to submit more humbly to the deprivation of her royal dignity; the deserted princess pertinaciously maintained her rights, 383. Studying chiefly the arbitrary wishes of king Henry, he was one of the peers selected by the monarch for the trial of Anne Boleyn, 393. Brandon found the Lincoln and Yorkshire insurgents, of 1536, formidable, notwithstanding the king's forces entrusted to his command, 397. The duke gained time, and his army being of little avail, he negotiated with the rebels; he forwarded their "Articles of Grievances" to Henry; and receiving a liberal supply of money from the

SUFFOLK, Charles Brandon, duke of,—
king, then justly in alarm, he bribed the popular leaders of the great northern rebellion, 397—399. Captain *Cobbler*, a *fictitious* name, was leader of the Lincolnshire rebels; Robert Aske (a man of character) of those of Yorkshire and Durham, 398, 399. Various transactions, 416. Suffolk died, August 22, 1545.

SUFFOLK, Henry Grey, duke of, husband of Frances duchess of Suffolk in her own right, and father of lady Jane Grey, created October, 1551; ii. 499. His daughter queen Jane, unwilling that he should march in command of her forces, the duke could not coerce the council in London on the expedition of Northumberland, 503, 504. He was pardoned, 1553, by queen Mary, 504. He sat upon the trial of Northumberland, 505. Suffolk, with his brothers John and Leonard Grey, take arms, in conjunction with Wyatt, to prevent the nuptials of Mary and Philip, 1554; 512. His trial in Westminster Hall, and execution on Tower-hill, 518.

SUFFOLK, Frances duchess of, (eldest daughter of Mary Tudor, a sister of Henry VIII.,) ii 499. Marriage of her elder daughter, the lady Jane Grey, to lord Guildford Dudley, May, 1553, at Durham-House, Strand, *ib.* Also of the younger daughter, lady Catherine Grey, to lord Herbert, *ib.* The duchess of Suffolk, at the instance of Northumberland, transferred her right (as to the succession) to lady Jane Grey, 500.

SUFFOLK, Thomas Howard, earl of, created 1603. Becomes lord-treasurer on the death of Cecil, in 1612; iii. 49. He is charged with peculation, and thrown into the Tower, but afterwards recovers his liberty, 71. He died, May 28th, 1626.

Sugar-manufacture of the West Indies; introduction of the Otaheite cane, 1793; § iii. 712.

SUJAH, Dowla, nabob of Oude, concludes a treaty with Meer Cossim, the fugitive nabob of Bengal, § ii. 88. He is beaten in a decisive engagement by major Monro, 1764, ib. Throws himself on the mercy of the English, 89. Oude is restored to him, with the exception of Allahabad and Corah, *ib.* His negotiations with Warren Hastings, 1773; 125, 126. Corah and Allahabad sold to, 126. His expedition into the Rohilla country, 1774; 129, 130. His death, 1775; 133.

SULLY, Maximilian de Bethune, duke de Rosny, born December 13th, 1560. Sent by Henri IV. on an important mission to James I., 1603, on his arrival from Scotland at Whitehall, iii. 7. He died December 22, 1641.

Sulphuric acid, improvements in the manufacture of, 1749; § i. 600.

Sumptuary laws; expense of apparel limited according to rank, labour, etc., 1363; ii. 272.

Sun, Druidical worship of the, i. 68.

Sunderland, its obscurity in the time of Camden, iii. 656.

SUNDERLAND, Henry Spencer, 1643, slain at the battle of Newbury, September 20th, 1643; iii. 308. His portrait, 830.

SUNDERLAND, Robert Spencer, earl of, 1643; iii. 727, 759, 779, 785, 786. William III. admits him into his favour, iv. 47. He suggests a letter of reconciliation between the princess Anne and the king, 51. Is made lord-chamberlain, 77. Accused of being the principal promoter of the keeping up of a standing army, 1697; 80. He retires, 81. His correspondence with king William, lord Somers, and lord Galway, 131, 133, 134. On the accession of queen Anne, his pension of 2,000*l.* is renewed, 141. His death, 1702; 149.

SUNDERLAND, Charles Spencer, earl of, eldest son of Robert, who died in 1702. His marriage with Anne Churchill, second daughter of John first duke of Marlborough, 1701; iv. 130. Succeeds to the earl-

SUNDERLAND, Charles Spencer, earl of,—dom of Sunderland, 1702 ; 149. He strongly opposes a grant made to prince George of Denmark, *ib.* He is admitted into the government as one of the secretaries of state, 1707; 200. Deprived of office, 1710; 245. He exchanges his lord-lieutenancy of Ireland for the privy-seal, 1716 ; 335. He resigns the premiership, 1720, on account of the odium he had incurred by his participation in the South Sea scheme, 376. Dies suddenly, April 19th, 1722; 378.

Supremacy, Act of, revived in all its vigour by Elizabeth, ii. 545.

SURAJ-U-DOWLAH succeeds to the government of Bengal on the death of his grandfather, Aliverdy Khan in 1756 ; § ii. 39. Portrait of, and his ten sons, 40. He takes Cossimbuzar and Calcutta ; tragedy of the Black Hole, iv. 599 ; § ii. 41—47. Battle of Plassey, June 21st, 1757 ; 57—59. Suraj is assassinated by order of Meeran, son of the new nabob, Meer Jaffier, 61.

Surat, factory established at by the English, 1612 ; § ii. 16. View of, 17.

Surgery; its low consideration and condition in the 15th century, ii. 208. Lithotomy first successfully practised at Paris, 1474; *ib.*

SURREY, William de Warren, earl of, earl Warren in Normandy ; created earl of Surrey by William Rufus; he married Gunnora, daughter of William the Conqueror; William I. bestows on him twenty-eight villages, i. 374. Appointed justiciary of England, 381. He died in 1089.

SURREY, William de Warren, earl of, succeeded his father as earl of Surrey in 1089. He requested permission of William II. to marry Maud (daughter of Malcolm and Margaret, the sister of Edgar Atheling,) but was refused, i. 406. On the death of Rufus, 1100, he supports the title of duke Robert, 408. He died in 1135.

SURREY, John Plantagenet, earl of. Succeeded his father William as earl of Surrey in 1240. He escapes from the battle of Lewes, 1264 ; and lands in South Wales with a small force, to aid prince Edward, i. 686. His answer to the commissioners of Edward I., when commanded to produce the titles by which he held his estates, 694. Illustration, *ib.* He is appointed by Edward I. governor of Scotland, 1297; 715. Is defeated by Wallace near Stirling, September 4th, 1297; 717. He died in 1304.

SURREY.—*See* Norfolk.

SURREY, Henry Howard, earl of, eldest son of Thomas Howard, who succeeded to the dukedom of Norfolk in 1524. He incurs the displeasure of the king, and is sent to the Tower, December, 1545, on surmises of treason, and arraigned for having quartered in his escutcheon the royal arms of Edward the Confessor, to which he had an hereditary right, ii. 449. Notwithstanding an able defence, he is found guilty by a subservient jury, and six days after suffered the sentence of the law by decapitation on Tower-hill, January 19th, 1547; 450, 838. His portrait, 813. Specimen of his poetry, 830; iii. 562, 582.

Suspension Bill, the, passed, 1794 ; § iii. 391.

Sussex, or kingdom of the South-Saxons, founded in 477, i. 142.

SUSSEX, Thomas Ratcliffe, earl of, 1556. Despatched by Elizabeth on a marriage embassy to Vienna, 1567; ii. 622. His description of the archduke Charles, *ib.* He died, 1583.

SUSSEX, Augustus Frederick, duke of, sixth son of king George III., created November 7th, 1801. Contracts a marriage with lady Augusta Murray, 1793. The king institutes a suit of nullity, and the Ecclesiastical Court pronounces the ceremony to be void on the ground of the Royal Marriage Act, § iii. 469. The duke had two children, a son and a daughter, by this lady, *ib.*

SUTHERLAND, earl of, committed to the general surveillance of the Presbytery of Edinburgh, 1602, by order of the Assembly of Holyrood-house, iii. 452.

SUTTON, sir Robert, convicted of fraud and peculation, and expelled the House, 1731; iv. 405.

SUTTON's monument at the Chapter-house, iii. 576.

SUVAROFF, Alexander, count Riminsky, prince of Italisky, a field-marshal of the Russian armies, equally renowned for his desperate courage in battle, and his barbarity to the conquered; he was descended from a noble Swedish family, and born in 1730. His daring valour at the siege of Oczakoff, 1788; § ii. 312, 313, and sanguinary conduct at the storming of Ismael, 1790, where 30,000 of the inhabitants perished, 475, 476. Massacre of Praga, 1794; § iii. 461, 546. His *portrait*, 460.

Sweating sickness, its sudden attack in all parts of the kingdom, 1485; ii. 282. It was most severe in London, and its attack was generally fatal, *ib.* This disease afflicted London, May 1528, many of the people dying, 368. Henry VIII., in great fear, attended to all his religious duties ; but so soon as the epidemic had passed, he recalls Anne Boleyn to court, *ib.* Its fatal ravages in England, 1551; on the continent only the English, it is said, suffered, 495, *note.*

Sweden, site of the capital of the ancient chief Wodin, or Odin, at Sigtuna, on the Malar Lake, i. 138. Revolution in 1772; § i. 131.

SWEDENBORG, Baron Emanuel, founder of the sect calling themselves by his name; he professed to have received the first of his divine revelations in London, 1743, and died here in 1772 ; § i. 527.

Swedenborgians, Establishment of, in the 18th century, § i. 527.

SWEYN, prince of Denmark, exiled by his father, collects an adventurous band, and explores the English coasts, i. 176. He takes Southampton, 981, 191. Successes of the Danes, *ib.* Become king of Denmark, he invades England, 994, with Olave, king of Norway, *ib.* Treaty with Ethelred, stipulating for money to return home, 176, 177. His sister, Gunhilda, perishes in the massacre of the Danes, 1002; 177. King Sweyn collects a great armament, manned with choice warriors, to take exemplary vengeance, 178. Magnificence of his armada, *ib.* He lays waste the most fertile provinces, puts the population to the sword, and burns Norwich and other towns, 1003, 1004, *ib.* He returns in 1006, and his devastations are stopped only by a contribution of 36,000 pounds of gold, *ib.* He sails into the Humber, and takes formal possession of Ethelred's dominions, 179. He is joined by all the old Danish residents of Northumbria, etc., *ib.* Leaving his son Canute in charge of his fleet, he marches southward, takes Oxford and Winchester, but is repulsed from London by the brave citizens, and Ethelred, *ib.* He was acknowledged king of England, January 1013, and soon after died at Gainsborough, 180. His army proclaims Canute as his successor, *ib. See* Edmund Ironside.

SWEYN, second son of earl Godwin, 1044, was exiled for violating an abbess, i. 189. He causes his cousin Beorn to be murdered, *ib.* He is restored to his provincial government by Edward, *ib.* He and Harold collect a large force to assist Godwin, 1051, in his revolt, on the quarrel as to Eustace, count of Boulogne, 190. He accompanies the great earl in his expatriation, and, with all Godwin's family, forfeits his estates, 191. On the triumphant return of earl Godwin, 1052, Sweyn alone of all the sons is excluded from pardon, 193; not for the late civil dissensions, but for his early crimes, *ib.* He puts on a pilgrim's garb, and quitting Flanders walks barefooted to Jerusalem (which he reached,) that his devoutness might purify him from

SWEYN,—
his sins, *ib.* His death occurred in Lycia, on his return through Asia Minor, *ib.*
SWEYN ESTRIDSEN, king of Denmark, refuses to invade England, as proposed by Tostig, i. 208. But, after the battle of Hastings he determines upon a descent into England, 371. William, by means of Adelbert, archbishop of Bremen, endeavours to persuade him to renounce his project, *ib.* After three years, being earnestly solicited by the English emigrants, 1069, he prepares a fleet of 240 sail, with orders to act in conjunction with the king of Scotland and the Northumbrians, under the command of Osbeorn his brother, and his two sons, Harold and Canute, *ib.*: they sail up the Humber, and land at the mouth of the river Ouse, *ib.* Are joined by the Scots, Northumbrians, and all the men of the north, *ib.* They take York, after a siege of eight days, and slay the Norman garrison, to the number of 3,000 men, with the exception of William Malet, the governor, his wife and children, Guilbert of Ghent, and a few others, who were kept for ransom, *ib.* Malcolm Caenmore, king of Scotland, never arrived with his promised army, 372. The confederates unwisely remain in the north without any decisive action; the Danes retire to their ships in the Humber during the winter; William gains time to collect his forces, and succeeds in inducing Osbeorn, the Danish commander, by means of gold and other presents, to bear no more assistance to the Northumbrians, *ib.* Sweyn Estridsen banishes Osbeorn, his brother, on his return home with a shattered fleet, for his corrupt and faithless conduct towards the English, 386. Sweyn then assembles a second fleet for the assistance of the English confederates under Hereward, but on his arrival finds that William was provided with a maritime force sufficient to prevent his landing, and returns to Denmark, where he soon after dies, 1082—1085; *ib.*
SWIFT, Jonathan, an eminent English divine and politician, born, November 30, 1667. His portrait, iv. 735. Review of his works, 792—794. He determines to bequeath his fortune to build an hospital in his native country for persons afflicted with the calamity of madness, to which he himself fell a prey in 1742; 794. He died in October, 1745.
SWINTON.—He was the man of all Scotland most trusted and employed by Cromwell. He was attainted, 1661, but admitted to mercy, iii. 683.
Swiss, the.—Their valour in the war against Louis XII., 1513. Siege of Dijon by their army, ii. 325.
Switzerland, entered by the French, 1798. Fall of the Republic of Berne, § iii. 535.
Swords, made anciently of a mixture of copper and tin, i. 91. Modern improvement in the manufacture of, by Thomas Gill, 1786; § iii. 684.
SYDENHAM, Dr. Thomas, a celebrated English physician and medical writer, born 1624, died 1689; iv. 786.
SYDNEY, Algernon, a celebrated English republican and martyr to liberty, born about 1617. He was nominated a member on the trial of Charles I., but was not present at that crisis. After the Restoration he remained an exile for seventeen years, and returned to England, 1677, on a promise of pardon. He intrigues with Barillon, the French ambassador, to prevent war with France, iii. 727. He takes part in the Rye-house Plot, 1681; 740; and is committed to the Tower, 1683. His trial, 751—754. , He was executed on Tower-hill, December 8, 1683; 754. His sentence of attainder was reversed, and his execution declared murder, 1689; iv. 11.
SYDNEY, Henry, brother of the preceding, iii. 794.
SYDNEY, sir Philip, nephew to Leicester, the favourite of queen Elizabeth, perishes in an attack upon Zutphen, 1586; ii. 656, 657, 836. *Portrait* of, 813; iii. 582, 583, 602.

SYDSERF, bishop of Galloway, assists in drawing up a Liturgy and a book of Canons for the Scottish church; the latter was confirmed by letters patent, 1635; iii. 478. He was suspended, with many other bishops, by order of the Assembly of Montrose in 1600; 484.
SYLVESTER, Joshua, his metrical translation of Du Bartas, iii. 585, 601.
SYLVIUS, Æneas.—*See* Pius II.
SYLVIUS, Bonus, or Coil the Good, a British writer, alluded to by Ausonius, i. 124.
SYNDERCOMBE, undertakes to assassinate the Protector; but being discovered, to escape the punishment of treason he commits suicide, iii. 420.
Synod, National, meets at Westminster, 1643; iii. 311.
TAAFFE, lord, carries on a correspondence between the Irish Catholics and king Charles, 1642; iii. 310.
TACITUS, the historian, quoted, i. 6. 9, 16, 33, 43—47, 61, 72, 76, 106, 124, 223, 352. Criticism of M. Guizot on this celebrated writer's "*De Moribus Germanorum,*" i. 246.
TAILLEFER, a gigantic follower of duke William at Hastings, while leading the van he chaunts the ballads in praise of Charlemagne and Roland at Roncesvalles. Is the first to slay a Saxon, but he himself soon falls mortally wounded, i. 213.
TAILOR, Robert, a dramatic writer of considerable eminence; he was a contemporary of Shakespeare, iii. 593, 594.
Talavera, battle of, gained by the English, July 27, 1809; § iv. 379—381.
TALBOT, sir John, created earl of Shrewsbury, May 20, 1442, distinguished under Henry V., ii. 54. He was made lord-lieutenant of Ireland in 1446. He is defeated at Patay, and falls into the hands of the French, rashly and gallantly fighting, 68. He had been strongly advised by Fastolf not to give battle, as the soldiery were disheartened by their ill-success before Orleans, *ib.* Fastolf leads off his own division in safety, *ib.* He reduces, 1436, the revolted towns of Normandy, defeated the French near Rouen, took Pontoise in winter, and nearly surprised Paris, 79. In 1449 he valiantly aids Somerset in the defence of Rouen, but is left as an hostage in the hands of Dunois, 85. The nobles of Guienne repaired to London, irritated at the French rulers, the Bordelais being in open insurrection, 1453; 91. Talbot lands with 5,000 soldiers and entered Bordeaux, *ib.* Charles VII. laid siege to Châtillon, *ib.* Talbo', marching to relieve that fortress, cut to pieces a French division, and nearly carried the intrenchments, *ib.* Penthièvre came up with a fresh army, and Talbot, aged eighty, and his son, were slain, 1453; *ib.*
TALBOT, sir Gilbert, knight banneret, 1485; ii. 282.
TALLARD, Camille d'Hostun, duke de, | marshal of France, born Feb. 14, 1652. He was appointed to the French troops on the Rhine, 1702; iv. 89, 116. He reduces Treves and Traerbach, 151, 164. He surrenders to Marlborough at the battle of Blenheim, 1704; his son having been killed, and himself severely wounded, 172. He was conveyed to England, where he remained seven years, 173. On his return to France, in 1712, he was created a duke, and in 1726 appointed secretary of state. He died, March 3, 1728.
TALLEYRAND, Charles Maurice. nominated a deputy of the States-general, 1789; § ii. 363. Portrait of, 364. He is proscribed by the Convention, § iii. 276, *note.*
TALLEYRAND. M. de, prime-minister of the emperor Napoleon. In 1814 he coincided in the views of the allies for the restoration of the Bourbons, and was appointed member of the provisional government, § iv. 616*.
TALLIEN, John Lambert, a French Republican statesman, and ardent Jacobin, born, 1769. Head of the Société Fraternelle, 1791; § ii. 600.

TALLIS, Thomas, one of the greatest musicians of the sixteenth century; was born in the early part of the reign of Henry VIII., and died in 1585; iii. 561.

TAMWORTH, a dependent of the earl of Leicester, is sent down to Scotland by Elizabeth with a special mission, ii. 582. Not wishing to recognise Darnley as king, he did not apply for a pass, for the want of which he is arrested by Mary's authorities on his return homeward, ib.

TANCRED, grandson of the great Ruggiero, cousin to William the Good, and count of Lecce, chosen king of Naples and Sicily, and crowned at Palermo, i. 490. His dispute and treaty with king Richard I., 489—493.

TANFIELD, chief-baron, his opinion on certain curious points respecting the sale or conveyance of land, 18 James I., iii. 517.

TANKERVILLE, Forde Grey, earl of, created in 1695; he was made keeper of the Privy-seal in 1701, in which year he died, when his titles became extinct, iv. 112.

TANNEGUY-DUCHATEL, a brave but ferocious leader of the Armagnacs, 1418; after the murder of the constable, he becomes the chief of the faction, ii. 41, 42, 44.

Tanning, ii. 812.

TANUCCI, marquis Bernardo, an Italian statesman, born 1698; this able man retired from office at the age of eighty, and died four years afterwards, in 1783; iv. 413.

TARBES, bishop of, and his brother, viscount Turenne, 1527, on an embassy to Henry VIII., ii. 364. He inquires as to the legitimacy of Mary, daughter of Catherine of Arragon, with respect to her union with Francis I., or his son, ib. Fête at Greenwich, 365.

TARBET, lord, recommends the union of England and Scotland, 1689; iv. 8.

TATE, Nahum, an English poet, who flourished about the close of the seventeenth and the commencement of the following century; he was Poet-laureate to William III., and died August 12, 1715; review of his works, iii. 879.

TATE, Zouch, introduces the Self-denying Ordinance, December 9, 1644; iii. 322.

Tax, Roman, on pasture-ground, etc., i. 89. Saxon, 253.

Taxes, of the eighteenth century, § i. 545.

TAYLOR, Dr. Brook, a celebrated philosopher and mathematician, born at Edmonton, August 28, 1685; he died December 29, 1731; iv. 782.

TAYLOR, Jeremy, bishop of Down and Connor, an eminent divine, born 1613; iii. 491, 578. He died at Lisburne, August 13, 1667; 610. Portrait of, 433.

TAYLOR, John, bishop of Lincoln, June 18, 1552, refuses to kneel at the celebration of the mass, ii. 508; he is deprived, for thinking amiss concerning the Eucharist, March 20, 1553; 509.

TAYLOR, Dr. Rowland, rector of Hadleigh, Suffolk, is burned, 1555; ii. 523, 735. Anecdote concerning him, 523. Stone at Hadleigh to commemorate his martyrdom, 734.

TAYLOR, Dr., a Jurist, sent, 1526, with sir T. Cheney, to Francis I., to congratulate him on his return to his kingdom, ii. 361. Their advice, ib.

Tchesmé, battle of, 1770; § i. 141, 142.

Tea, introduced into England early in the seventeenth century, iii. 862. Mentioned by Soliman, the Arabian merchant, as the common beverage of the Chinese as early as 850; ib.

TEDDIMAN, sir Thomas; he is commanded by the earl of Sandwich to take the Dutch ships out of the fortified port of Berghen, but fails in this enterprise, 1665; iii. 696, 698, note.

Telicherry, View of, § ii. 158.

TEMPEST, Mr., engaged in a conspiracy for assassinating William III., 1696; iv. 67.

TEMPEST, his print of Westminster Hall and Abbey, iii. 766.

Templars, Knights, instituted 1118; i. 746. They deliver up the princess Margaret's dower to Henry II., 1160; 444, 446. Are expelled from France, 446. The keeping of Messina is committed to them by king Richard, 1190; 491. They espouse the cause of the king of France, 495. Portrait of a Knight-Templar in his mantle, 561. This order of knights abolished, 746. Cruelties inflicted on the order in France, 1310; ib. Without any cause, their lands are confiscated, and themselves imprisoned, throughout England, 747. Their lands given to the knights of St. John of Jerusalem, ib.

Temple, View of the Prison of the, § iii. 144, 233.

TEMPLE, Richard Grenville, earl, 1752. Resigns his office, 1761; § i. 11. Is dismissed from the lord-lieutenancy of Buckinghamshire, 1763, for taking part with Mr. Wilkes, 27, 47, 69, 84. Portrait of, 323. He is appointed one of the secretaries of state, 504.

TEMPLE, lord, signs the sentence of death upon admiral J. Byng, 1757; iv. 591. He speaks earnestly in favour of a revision of the Habeas Corpus Act, 605. Demands of the king a vacant Order of the Garter: dispute in consequence of this request; he resigns, but is persuaded to resume his office, on condition that he shall receive this mark of favour, 611, 612.

TEMPLE, sir John, Master of the Rolls, 1649; iii. 254, 389.

TEMPLE, sir William, born 1628, an able diplomatist in the service of the Cabal Ministry, by means of whom they open negotiations with the great De Witt to oppose the plans of Louis XIV., 1668; iii. 706, 712, 716. He died January, 1700.

Tenchebray, a strong fortress in Normandy; faithful attachment of its garrison to Robert, who is taken prisoner by his brother in attempting to raise the siege, i. 410.

TENCIN, cardinal de, his devotion to the interests of the Pretender, iv. 470.

TENISON, Thomas, archbishop of Canterbury, translated from the see of Lincoln, December, 1694; iii. 777; iv. 50. He is recommended by archbishop Tillotson to be placed in the ministry of St. Martin's, London, as "a strong-bodied man, and therefore fit to take care of so large a parish;" he is subsequently elevated to the archbishopric of Canterbury, iv. 638. He died in 1715.

Tennis-court, iii. 640.

Tenths and First-fruits, applied by queen Anne for increasing the revenues of poor benefices (Queen Anne's Bounty,) iv. 159.

TERMES, marshal, succeeds D'Esse in the command of the French forces in Scotland, 1549; ii. 489.

Terouenne, laid siege to, 1513, by lord Herbert, ii. 323. After gaining the battle of the Spurs, Henry VIII. appeared in person before the walls, 325. Capitulation of this important fortress, ib. By the advice of the emperor Maximilian, the town was burnt to the ground, 325, 326.

Teschen, Treaty of, signed May 13, 1779; § i. 345.

TESSÉ, René de Froulai, marshal of France, born about 1650; died May 10, 1725; iv. 179, 387.

Test Act, the, passed 1673; iii. 711.

TESTWOOD, Robert, burnt, 1543; ii. 728.

TETZEL, John, a fanatical monk of the sixteenth century, received a commission from the archbishop of Mayence to preach up the indulgences of Leo X.; died 1519; ii. 705.

Teutonic, common origin with the Celtic languages, i. 10. Its relation to the Greek and Latin, 11. No Teutonic settlements in Britain before the Saxons, in the fifth and sixth centuries, ib. Nations of the Teutonic race, 138.

Tewkesbury, battle of, 4th May, 1471, in which Edward IV. defeated queen Margaret, the duke of Somerset, and her French auxiliaries, ii. 109.

Thames, ford of the river, at Coway-Stakes, Chertsey; delineation of the spot where Cæsar made good his passage across the, B.C. 54; i. 32. Ercenwine landing within the estuary on the eastern shore, founds the kingdom of the East Saxons, 527—529; 142.

Thanet, isle of, i. 58, 141.

Theatrical representations, iv. 325, 326.

Thellusson Act, the, passed in the 39th and 40th Geo. III., for prescribing the accumulation of property, § iii. 603.

THEOBALD, earl of Blois, assisted by his uncle, Henry I., in a revolt against Louis, 1118; i. 413.

THEOBALD, abbot of Beceo, elected archbishop of Canterbury, December, 1138, joins with Henry, bishop of Winchester, and papal legate, in acknowledging Matilda, i. 430. Attends the council of Rheims against the express orders of king Stephen, and is exiled; he puts himself under the protection of Bigod, earl of Norfolk, and publishes a sentence of interdict against Stephen, and all who acknowledged his rule, 435. Reconciliation effected, ib. A general council is held at London, in which he positively refuses to anoint Eustace, Stephen's eldest son, as his successor, ib. Crowns Henry II. and his queen Eleanor, 440. His death in 1160; 448.

Theobald's, View of the Great Hall at, iii. 34. Feast given in 1606, by Cecil, at his house of, 33. James I. dies at, 108. Charles I. proclaimed at, ib.

THEODORE, archbishop of Canterbury, 668, landed by Bede for the excellence of his schools, imparting Greek and Latin, besides divinity, etc; i. 304.

Theodosian Code, i. 87.

THEODOSIUS, repelled the Scots from the south of Britain, about 370; repaired the southernmost wall and forts, and pursued the pirates as far as the Orcades, i. 54.

THEODOSIUS the Great, son of the preceding, defeated Maximus, his rival for the empire, who being of British origin, led the most warlike of the Britons to this distant contest, a loss which enfeebled Britain irrecoverably, i. 54. He put Maximus to death, 388; ib.

THEOT, Catherine, a French maniac, who prophesied the immediate appearance of the Second Advent, 1794; § iii. 434.

Theowes, a lower order among the Saxons; they possessed no political rights, i. 249.

Thermometer, the, invented at Florence in the early part of the seventeenth century, iv. 786.

THÉROIGNE, mademoiselle, a French revolutionist, 1789; § ii. 483; § iii. 132.

Thistle, Order of the, revived by queen Anne, iv. 161. Collar of the Order of, ib.

THOMAS, John, elected to the bishopric of Peterborough in 1748. Nominated preceptor to the prince of Wales (George III.,) 1752. He died bishop of Winchester in 1781; iv. 574.

THOMAS, Valentine, committed for a common felony, 1598, declared that James VI. had hired him to kill queen Elizabeth, ii. 682. Elizabeth communicates the matter to the Scottish king, (see James,) ib. She keeps Thomas a close prisoner; he is hanged by king James on his accession, ib.

THOMAS, William, the learned Clerk of the Council, 1547; his character of Edward VI. (in "the Pilgrim,") ii. 453. His "Works," published from a MS. in the Cottonian Collection, apologetic for all the actions of Henry VIII., 518; note. He was executed at Tyburn, soon after the death of lady Jane Grey, 518.

THOMOND, Murroch O'Brien created earl of, 1541; ii. 428.

THOR, his mighty "hammer," imitated by the Saxon club, bound and spiked with iron, i. 140.

THORNHILL, sir James, a distinguished painter, born at Weymouth, 1676. He was state-painter to Anne,

THORNHILL, sir James,—
George I., and George II., by the latter of whom he was knighted. He died in 1734, aged 58, leaving a son, and a daughter who was married to Hogarth, iv. 754.

THORPE, a priest, 1407, charged with heresy before archbishop Arundel, ii. 143. His narrative of the remarkable disputation the primate held with him, 143, 145. He was condemned to imprisonment, 146.

THORPE, lady de; her effigy in Ashwelthorpe Church, Norfolk, ii. 240.

Threshing-machine, first employed in Great Britain about 1710; iv. 729.

THROCKMORTON, Francis, tortured and executed by order of Elizabeth, ii. 655.

THROGMORTON, sir Nicholas, arraigned for participation in sir T. Wyatt's rebellion, 1554, was found Not Guilty, and reconveyed to the Tower by mandate of lord chief-justice Bromley, to answer other charges, ii. 518. Infringement of the right of fair trial in this remarkable case; the jury, who persevered in their verdict, notwithstanding intimidation and menaces by their chief-justice, are subjected to imprisonment and fines, ib.; 580, 603, 604.

Thule, the ultima, of ancient poets and geographers, i. 124.

THURKHILL's host, from the Baltic, invades Ethelred's dominions, his navy having been wrecked, 1009—1012, they accept bribes, but refuse to depart, i. 179.

THURLOE, John; acted as secretary for the English parliament, 1645, at Uxbridge, in the matter of the attempted treaty with Charles I., and with the Scottish parliament, iii. 329. Made secretary of State, 416. He discovers a plot of the Fifth monarchy-men, 421.

THURLOW, Edward, becomes solicitor-general, 1770; § i. 88, 109. He is dismissed from his office of chancellor, 1793; § iii. 27. He votes for the abatement of impeachment on the dissolution of parliament, 602. His portrait, ib.

THUEN, count, leader of the Calvinists, 1618; iii. 80.

THUROT, M., a daring adventurer; he takes and plunders the town of Carrickfergus, but is pursued and boarded by captain Elliot, and falls covered with wounds on his own deck, 1760; iv. 607.

THURSTAN, or Toustain, abbot of Glastonbury, i. 382, 549. Elected to the see of York, August, 1114, but not consecrated until October, 1119. His great exertions to raise a sufficient English army to oppose the Scots, 424. He resigned, January, 1139.

THYNN, Mr., murdered by count Charles John Königsmark, iv. 392.

THYNNE, serjeant, argues for the rights of the University of Oxford, June 21, 1634; iii. 163.

TICHBORN, lord-mayor, 1657, assists at the inauguration of the Protector Cromwell, iii. 423.

Ticonderoga, Fort of, View of the Ruins of the, § i. 218.

Tiernstein; view of the castle and town of, i. 503.

Tilbury Fort; delineation of, ii. 673. Queen Elizabeth's great camp there; defences constructed at Gravesend and on the shores of the Thames against the Spaniards, ib. The queen reviewed her troops at Tilbury, 674. Her harangue, ib.

TILBURY, Gervase of, quoted, i. 580, 581, 583.

TILDESLEY, sir Thomas, royalist-governor of Lichfield, commanded by the king to surrender his charge to the parliament, 1646; iii. 355.

TILLEUIL, Humphrey, warden of Hastings Castle, 1067; he returns to Normandy, i. 370.

TILLIERS, count de, an attendant of Henrietta Maria, queen of Charles I., 1626; iii. 126.

TILLOTSON, John, nominated archbishop of Canterbury, April, 1691. He began to publish his sermons in 1661, and died in 1694. Review of his works, iii. 749; iv. 790. His portrait, 617.

TILLY, count, compels the king of Denmark to cross the Elbe, August 27, 1626; iii. 123.

Tilsit, Treaty of, July, 1807; § iv. 296.

TIMUR, or Tamerlane, a Mogul Tartar, and one of the most celebrated of the Oriental conquerors, born 1335. He subjugates Hindustan, 1390, and thus overturns the Affghan dynasty, § ii. 17.

Tin of the Cassiterides, i. 26, 91, 92. Its employment by the Britons in the manufacture of weapons and tools, 104. Mines of lead and tin in Britain yielded abundantly during the Roman government, 106. Quantity of, produced in the eighteenth century, § i. 582, 583. Exportation of, commenced 1789; § iii. 643. Importation of Banca tin, 1787; 681. History of the Tin Trade, towards the close of the eighteenth and commencement of the nineteenth century, § iv. 688, 689.

Tinning, art of, introduced from Germany by Andrew Yarranton, in the seventeenth century, iii. 870.

TINTORE, Giovanni, archdeacon of Naples, attributes to John of Dunstable the invention of figurate harmony, iii. 560.

TIPPOO SAIB, sovereign of Mysore, and son of the famous Hyder Ally, to whom he succeeded in 1782; § ii. 154. Treaty concluded between him and the English, March, 1784; 163. Portrait of, 164. His embassy to Paris, 1790, to demand assistance on the condition of driving the English from India, 537. His cruel civil and military code, § iii. 28. War with the English; he is compelled to accept the terms proposed by them, 1792, and to deliver up his two eldest sons as hostages, 27—33. He demands the assistance of the French, 1797, to assist in expelling the British from Hindustan, 550. Jacobin Club organised in Seringapatam, ib. General Harris enters Mysore, March 5, 1799, and storms and captures the capital, May 4; in the defence of which Tippoo falls, ib.

Tithes, discussions on, 1816; § iv. 600.

TITIAN, Vecelli, one of the most distinguished of the great Italian painters, born in 1480. He generally lived in Venice, where he maintained the rank due to his genius. He died of the plague in 1576, at the advanced age of 96. His portrait of Philip II., of Spain and England, ii. 512; iii. 567.

TITUS, sir Silas, recommends the assassination of Cromwell, 1658; iii. 427.

Tobacco, extreme aversion of king James I. to this article, iii. 539. Importation of, iv. 702.

TOD, sir Thomas, conspires with Bothwell to seize James IV., ii. 304.

TOGODUMNUS, son of Cunobelinus, defeated by Aulus Plautius, 43; i. 39. Slain in battle, ib.

TOLAND, John, a writer of considerable note in political and religious controversy; he was born in 1669, and died, March, 1722. His considerations respecting the Belgæ, if of German or Celtic origin, i. 10. His view of the learning and religion of the Celts, 65; iv. 127.

Toleration, Presbyterian opinion of, iii. 311.

TOLLEMACHE, general, killed whilst bombarding Brest, 1694; iv. 48, 49.

TOMKINS, brother-in-law of Waller the poet, engages with him and others to seize the influential members of the Commons, in 1643, and is hanged in Holborn, iii. 302.

TONGE, Dr., 1678, presents to the king a roll of papers containing a full account of the Popish Plot, iii. 717.

TONSTAIN, surnamed the Fair, carries the Norman banner at the battle of Hastings, 1066; i. 213.

TOOKE, rev. John Horne, a person of considerable celebrity both in the literary and political world, born in June, 1736. He gets up a remonstrance to the king from the freeholders of Middlesex, 1770; § i. 93, 118. Is brought to trial for high treason, November 17, 1794, with several other conspicuous

TOOKE, rev. John Horne,— members of revolutionary societies in England; he pleads with much self-possession and acuteness, and is declared Not Guilty, November 22; § iii. 462, 463. His portrait, 463. Nominated member for Old Sarum, 1801; an attempt made to exclude him on the ground of ordination, § iv. 593—596.

TORCY, M. de, a French diplomatist, 1700; iv. 112, 116, 232.

Torgau, battle of, gained by Frederick the Great, November 11, 1760; § i. 7.

TORREGIANO, Pietro, an eminent sculptor of the Florentine school, entertained in England by Henry VIII. He executed the tomb of Henry VII. in 1519. He was of a fierce and ungovernable temper, and died in a dungeon of the Spanish Inquisition, ii. 853.

TORRINGTON, Arthur Herbert, earl of, created 1689. Naval action between him and the French fleet, iv. 12. Espouses the interests of James, 27. He died 1716.

Torture, discontinuation of, at the time of the Commonwealth, iii. 517. Abuse of in Scotland, 756.

Tory, origin of the term, iv. 679.

TOSTIG, a son of the great earl Godwin, i. 188, 191, 194. On the demise of Siward he governs Northumbria, Waltheof being too young to succeed to his father's government, 194. He excites the hatred of his new subjects, 195, 200. Assists Harold in the total defeat of Griffith, king of Wales, 195. Is expelled from his earldom of Northumbria, 200. Flies to Bruges, considering himself unjustly betrayed by his brother Harold, and opens a correspondence with William, ib. He ravages the Isle of Wight, 208. Does great harm on the coast of Lincolnshire, ib. Sails up the Humber, but is driven thence by Morcar and Edwin, ib. Invites Sweyn, king of Denmark, to the conquest of England, who being unwilling to undertake it, he then goes to Hardrada, king of Norway, who accepts the invitation and sails to England, ib. Tostig and Hardrada gain a victory over Morcar and Edwin near York, ib. He is slain, together with Hardrada, in the decisive battle at Stamford-bridge, 209.

Toulon, 1707, besieged by the duke of Savoy, iv. 203. Bombarded, and a great part of the city ruined, ib.

Toulouse, earldom of, claimed by Henry II., i. 444, 445.

TOULOUSE, count de, his unsuccessful engagement with admiral Rooke off Malaga, 1704; iv. 175. He bombards the city of Barcelona, 1706, 185.

Tournaments. Illustrations. The Lists, ii. 250. The Mêlée, 251. Field of the Cloth of Gold, 1520, (Hen. VIII. and Francis I.) 342. Tournaments patronised by James IV. and James V., iii. 645.

Tournay, town of, surrenders to prince Eugene, iv. 235. View of, 236.

TOURNEUR, Cyril, a dramatic writer of considerable note, and contemporary with Shakspeare, iii. 593. His works, 594.

TOURVILLE, count de, admiral of the French fleet; he engages admiral Russell, 1692; iv. 88.

Tower of London. A fortress erected in London by the followers of William, before he enters, on the site of the Roman castle, afterwards the Tower of London, i. 361. King Henry VI. often imprisoned here, ii. 107. Desperate attempt by Thomas Nevil, 1471, to release this king, 110. May 22, Henry found lifeless; Fabyan says stabbed by Gloucester, ib. Walpole, in his Richard III., says there is no sufficient proof of the deed, ib. George, duke of Clarence, condemned, 1478; perished in the Tower, 114. Edward V. lodged for safety in this fortress; the Protector Gloucester held a council therein, 1483, 119. His brother Richard confined with him, 121. The young princes murdered, 125. Edward Plantagenet, earl of Warwick, imprisoned

Tower of London,—
by Henry VII, 1485; 281, 287. Perkin Warbeck became his companion, and some of the gaolers conspired to set them at liberty, 1499; 309. Lord Courtenay committed to the Tower, 1504; 313. Cranmer sent to the Tower, 509. Condemned and respited, but recommitted for heresy, 13th November, 1553; *ib.* Lady Jane Grey and lord Guildford Dudley imprisoned and beheaded, 1553—1554; 509, 517. The princess Elizabeth committed to the Tower, and the earl of Devon, 1554, from whence they were removed to other castles, 515. Various prisoners confined in this fortress, 1603—1620; Raleigh, Henry, earl of Northumberland, and others, iii. 9, 72, 73. *Illustrations:*—The duke of Orleans in captivity; the Tower, 15th century; London-bridge, etc., ii. 170. The State-prison in the Tower, 516. The Tower, from a print of the Royal Antiquarian Society, and engraved from a Survey in 1597; iii. 76.

Towerson, Gabriel, is seized, with several others, by the Dutch about 1619, charged with a conspiracy to expel the garrison from Amboyna, and on this impossible charge mercilessly killed, iii. 105.

Towns, alderman, 1642; iii. 290.

Town or city, British, i. 99.

Town-house, Hague, iv. 31.

Townley, Mr. Francis, iv. 512, 519. Executed as a traitor on Kennington-common, 1746; 548.

Townshend, Charles, viscount, 1687; iv. 287. Is made lord-lieutenant of Ireland, 1717; 336. Resigns, after a severe contest with Walpole, 1730; 404. He died 1738.

Townshend, George, marquess of, becomes lord-lieutenant of Ireland, 1767; § i. 59.

Townshend, Charles, chancellor of the Exchequer, 1766; § i. 54, 57. Dies of a putrid fever, September 4, 1767; 59.

Townshend, Thomas, junior, portrait of, § i. 165. He desires some provision to be made in Canada for the Protestant religion, 1774; 175.

Township, Town, derivation of the word, and Anglo-Saxon institutions, i. 351. Its inclosed extent, similar to the manor of Norman times, was invested in the lord who possessed sovereign or seignorial jurisdiction over his sokemen or tenantry, *ib.* He could grant leases for lives, or in perpetuity as feuds, *ib.* His courts and town-reeve (or seneschal), *ib.* Villainage, tolls, and dues, *ib.* The tenants themselves sat as the township court, presided over by the tun-gerefa, (*all which institutions exist in most parts of England and Ireland at the present time,*) 351, 352.

Towton, great victory, 1461, of Edward IV. at, ii. 98, 99. Northumberland died fighting; earls of Devonshire and Wiltshire were beheaded, 99. The queen and prince, with their general Somerset, carried Henry VI. safely into Scotland, *ib.* Of the two armies 38,000 men fell in this dire battle, *ib.*

Tracy, William, one of the conspirators who murdered Becket, December 28, 1170; i. 455, 456.

Trade.—*See* National Industry.

Trade, Board of, appointed by king William, 1696; iv. 698. Abolished, March, 1780; § i. 404.

Tradition, testimony of, i. 4, 5.

Trafalgar, a decisive victory gained here by lord Nelson, October 21st, 1805, in which he is killed; § iv. 188—195.

Trafford, sir Cecil, a popish gentleman, commissioned by king Charles to take up arms, 1642; iii. 299.

Trajan's Column at Rome: *Illustrations* (Roman soldiery) from, i. 38, 39.

Traquair, earl of, lord-treasurer of Scotland, 1637; he issues a proclamation against Presbyterian meetings, on pain of treason, 1638; iii. 186. Is summoned

Traquair, earl of,—
up to London, *ib.* He presses the king, 1647, to establish Presbyterianism, and approve the Covenant, 362. This great man (according to Burnet) suffered afterwards such a reverse of fortune that he was forced to beg, and, as was believed, died of hunger, 480, *note.*

Traun, count, surrenders Capua, November, 1734; iv. 414.

Treason, ii. 757; iv. 669. Amelioration in the Criminal Code relating to the punishment of, 1813, 1814; § iv. 638.

Treasurer, office of the, i. 569.

Treating Resolution, the, passed 1677; § iv. 632.

Treby, recorder of London, pronounces sentence of death on lord Russell, 1683; iii. 748.

Trelawney, colonel, successor to colonel Kirk, 1685; iii. 780.

Tremoille, George de la, count of Guines; he threw Charles VII.'s favourite, M. de Giac, into the river, and then married madame de Giac, ii. 58. He became the king's chief favourite, escaping the daggers of some noble conspirators by never quitting the royal castle, 59, 68. His counsels, and power with the king, 69.

Trenchard, John, a Rye-house conspirator, 1681; iii. 740, 745.

Trenchard, John, born in 1669; author of "The History of Standing Armies," iv. 82. He died in 1723.

Tresham, Francis, son of sir Thomas Tresham; which latter had suffered for twenty years by grievous persecutions of the Star-chamber, iii. 24. Francis Tresham had been deeply implicated in Essex's insurrection, *ib.* Addicted to plots, he is concerned with the Gunpowder Conspiracy, 1605, and causes alarm to Catesby, the chief of that plot, 25. He requires a warning to be given to Mounteagle and Stourton, his relatives, to absent themselves from parliament, 5th November, *ib.* Letter, supposed from Tresham to lord Mounteagle, *ib.* Facsimile of this document, 26. He absconds from the meetings of the conspirators, but, October 30, returns to them, *ib.* His solemn oath of not being cognizant of the letter, saves him from their poignards, 26, 27. He does not fly with the rest on the capture of Fawkes; offers his service to the council to detect the conspirators, 27. He accuses fathers Garnet and Greenway of a traitorous correspondence, 1602, with Spain, by means of Catesby, etc., 29. He dies of severe illness in the Tower, December, 1605, having retracted his accusation against the Jesuits, *ib.*

Tresham, speaker of the House of Commons, when the duke of Suffolk was impeached, 1449, assassinated by partizans of queen Margaret, ii. 90.

Tresilian, chief-justice of England; he determines the Council of Regency to be illegal, August, 1387; i. 792. The earl of Gloucester enters London with a large army, and Tresilian is discovered, and executed, 1388; *ib.*

Trevisa, John de, a chronicler of the fifteenth century, ii. 209.

Trevor, sir John, iii. 705, 845; iv. 20. He accepts a bribe of 1,000*l.* for forwarding the Orphans' Bill through the House of Commons; and this being discovered, he, as speaker, is obliged to accuse himself, and is expelled, 1695; 51.

Triads, Welsh poetical Histories of Britain; their history of the first inhabitants, i. 8, 304.

Tribute, Roman, imposed on a conquered people, i. 89.

Trichinopoly, View of the Rock of, § ii. 27.

Triennial Act, passed 1641; iii. 232. Repealed 1664; 693.

Triennial Bill, the, passed in both Houses, 1692, but William III. refuses to give the royal assent to it, iv. 40. Royal consent obtained, 1694; 49.

Triers, Board of, appointed by Cromwell, March, 1653; iii. 494.

Trinity College, Cambridge, Library of, iv. 737.

Trinity House of Deptford, Corporation of, established by Henry VIII. in the fourth year of his reign, ii. 780.

Trinobantes, the people of Essex and Middlesex, i. 33, 77. This gentile name signifies "a powerful people;" not derived from Trinovant, New Troy, a fable, ib.

Triple Alliance, between England, Holland, and Sweden, 1668; iii. 706.

Triple Alliance, between England, France, and Holland, at the Hague, 1717; iv. 337, note.

Trojans, said by Geoffrey of Monmouth to have first peopled Britain, under the command of Brutus, a grandson of Æneas; the earliest writer to whom this fable can be traced is Tysilio, a Welsh priest, supposed to have lived in the latter part of the seventh century, i. 8.

Troyes, city of, marriage of Henry V. and Catherine of France at, 1420; ii. 47. Peace of concluded, April, 1564; 574.

Truguet, admiral, makes an unsuccessful attempt to conquer Sardinia, 1793; § iii. 300.

Trumbull, sir William, an English statesman, born 1636; he became secretary of state in 1695, which office he resigned in 1697; he died December 14, 1716; iv. 66.

Trussel, sir William, speaker of the parliament, or deputation of the nation, held at Kenilworth, January 20th, 1327; he makes known to Edward that he is no longer king, i. 744.

Tryon, governor of New York, 1775; § i. 230, 389.

Tuam, archbishop of, slain in a skirmish near Sligo, (about 1645,) iii. 345.

Tuberville, a royalist officer, 1645; iii. 344.

Tuberville, witnesses against lord Stafford, and procures his execution, 1680; iii. 732.

Tudor, the family colours of this House were white and green, ii. 857.

Tudor, Owen, espouses Catherine, widow of Henry V., ii. 80; 125. Their grandson, the earl of Richmond, slaying Richard III., mounts the English throne, 125. His son, Jasper, earl of Pembroke, being defeated, 1461, by Edward, duke of York, Tudor is made prisoner, and with eight noble Lancastrians beheaded at Hereford, 96.

Tuileries, View of the Palace of the, § ii. 435, 505. Attack on the, August 10, 1792; § iii. 136.

Tuke, sir Bryan, 1532, read in parliament twelve answers of universities touching Henry VIII.'s divorce, and produced books by learned doctors on this case, ii. 333.

Tull, Jethro, commences experiments in drilling and horse-hoeing in 1732; iv. 729.

Tullibardine, erects the standard of the Young Pretender at Glenfinnin, 1745; iv. 484.

Tunneling, eighteenth century, § iii. 671.

Tunstall, Cuthbert, bishop of Durham, translated from London, March, 1530; a negotiator of eminent talent; was sent to Maximilian, who pretended to offer the empire to Henry VIII.; Tunstall's dispatches home explained to the king the futility of that idea, ii. 335, 336. He is again dispatched to the emperor's court, 359. His report from Ampthill on the affair of Catherine of Arragon, 383. Appointed one of Henry VIII.'s executors, 1547; 454. Deprived in 1553; his see converted into two smaller dioceses, and the suppressed bishopric into a county palatine, 499. He is liberated by queen Mary on her entrance into London, 1553; 505. He died in November, 1559.

Turenne, Henry de la Tour d' Auvergne, one of the greatest captains of modern times, born at Sedan, September 16, 1611. After he had defeated the Imperialists at Mulhausen, and again at the more terrible battle of Turkheim, he was opposed by the

Turenne,—celebrated Montecuculi, and these rivals for glory were about to meet at Saltzbach, when Turenne was killed by a cannon-shot as he was examining the ground for raising a battery, July 27, 1675. He was honoured with a splendid funeral, and interred at St. Denys, among the sovereigns of France, iii. 710, 714.

Turgot, confessor of queen Margaret of Scotland, appointed, 1107, bishop of St. Andrew's, i. 538. Consecrated in 1109, by the archbishop of York, 539. His life of queen Margaret, 537.

Turkey Company, the, incorporated 1581; ii. 790.

Turkish soldiers of different corps, § i. 140.

Turlogh O'Connor, king of Connaught, acknowledged king of all Ireland, 1136; i. 459. After the battle of Moinmor, he divided Munster into two principalities, ib. His death, ib.

Turner, Francis, translated to the see of Ely, August, 1684, deprived for not taking the oaths, February, 1690; iii. 777.

Turner, sir James, commander of a body of troops quartered throughout Scotland, 1664, to force the people to respect the newly-imposed Episcopalian Liturgy, etc., iii. 694. He is seized by the Covenanters, 1666, who had risen in insurrection, 701.

Turner, Mrs., accused of procuring poison wherewith to kill sir Thomas Overbury, iii. 58. She pleads Not Guilty, 59. Her illicit amours, ib. Applies to Dr. Forman for a spell, ib. She is hanged at Tyburn, 1615, ib.

Turner, Mr., enumerates the total number of persons of all descriptions mentioned in Domesday Book to amount to 300,785; i. 350.

Turnham, Robert de, appointed governor of Cyprus by Richard I., i. 495.

Turnpike-roads, first established in 1663; § i. 574—576; § iii. 668. Improvements in, by Telford and MacAdam, § iv. 674—676.

Turton, baron, 1690; iv. 22.

Tweeddale, marquess of, represents to the king, 1666, that the severities against the Covenanters were excessive and dangerous, iii. 701.

Tweeddale, marquess of, lord high-commissioner for Scotland, is dismissed, 1698; iv. 62. He is re-appointed, 1704; 161.

Twiss, Dr., prolocutor of the National Synod, 1643; iii. 311.

Tye, Christopher, an eminent church composer, preceptor in music to Edward VI. He was organist of the Chapel Royal to Elizabeth; his freedom of language to that queen; he put the first fourteen chapters of the Acts into metre; he died about 1590; iii. 561, note.

Tyler, Wat, or Walter the, an inhabitant of the town of Dartford. One of the commissioners for collecting the Poll-tax, 1378, having offered an insult to his daughter, he knocks out his brains, i. 785. He is chosen captain of the band of Kentish rioters, and is slain in Smithfield by the lord-mayor of London, 785—787. Picture of his death, 788. (For the particulars of this rebellion, see Richard II.)

Tylesworth, William, burned in Amersham, 1506, his daughter being compelled to set fire to him with her own hands, ii. 699.

Tyndal, William, prints a translation of the New Testament at Antwerp, 1526, and afterwards other editions, ii. 712.

Tyrawley, lord, sent out to supersede general Fowke as governor at Gibraltar, 1756; iv. 587, 601.

Tyrconnel, disarms the Protestants in Ireland, 1686; iii. 785, 786. His death, iv. 34.

Tyrone, Con O'Neil, earl of, created in 1541, ii. 428, 682—684, 693; iii. 39, 172, 232. See O'Neil.

Tyrrel, sir James, master of the horse to Richard III., sent to London to put the two princes in the Tower to death, ii. 125. He employed Dighton and Forest, mur-

TYRREL, sir James,—
derers, ib. Tyrrel then entered the chamber to see they were dead, and buried them at the stairs' foot, ib. Historical engraving of the foul deed, ib. Employed at the court of Henry VII., 285. Beheaded in 1504, for having assisted De la Pole, earl of Suffolk, 313, 314. His supposed confession of the murder of Edward V. and his brother, examined, 314.

TYRREL, sir Walter, also called sir Walter de Poix, supposed to have accidentally shot William Rufus while hunting in the New Forest, August 1, 1100; i. 402. Escapes to France, and soon after departs for the Holy Land, 403.

TYSILIO, a Welsh priest, i. 8.

TYTLER, James, accused, 1793, of principles dangerous to the constitution of Great Britain, and not appearing to answer to the charges, is outlawed, § iii. 383.

ULF, Norman bishop of Dorchester, 1043, appointed by Edward the Confessor, i. 189.

ULPHUS, Horn of, a beautiful specimen of Saxon sculpture, i. 318.

ULRICA ELEANORA, sister of Charles XII.. of Sweden, ascends the throne on the death of her brother, 1719; iv. 349.

ULSTER, Hugh de, earl of. See Lacy.

ULSTER, Richard de Burgh, earl of, defeated by Edward Bruce near Coyners, September 10, 1315; i. 738.

UMFRAVILLE, Gilbert de, earl of Angus, refuses to deliver up the castles of Dundee and Forfar to Edward, 1291; i. 709.

UMFRAVILLE, sir Robert, sails on a plundering expedition to Scotland, 1410; ii. 182, 183.

Uniformity, Act of, articles of the, (1559,) ii. 545. See Conformity Bill.

Union, with Ireland, Act of, receives the Royal assent, July 2, 1800; § iii. 555.

Union, with Scotland, Treaty of, 1706; iv. 187. Chief provisions of the, 196.

Union Workhouses, Mr. Gilbert's Act for the erection of, 1782; § iii. 772.

Unitarian Petitioners, the, 1792; § iii. 19.

Universities of Europe; the twelfth century may be considered as properly the age of their institution, i. 605, 606. Many colleges founded in the thirteenth century, list of, 845. Foundations of, ii. 814. Curious account of the state of the University of Cambridge in the reign of Edward VI., 819.

Upnor Castle, iii. 701.

URBAN II., pope, (Otho, bishop of Ostia,) elected March 12, 1088. Receives and supports the claims of archbishop Anselm, i. 551. In the great council held at Rome at this time, excommunication is denounced against all laymen who should presume to grant investiture of any ecclesiastical benefice, and against every priest who should accept of such investiture, ib. This pope died, July 29, 1099.

URBAN VI., (Bartholomew Pregnano,) elected 1378; ii. 137. His use of torture even against cardinals, ib. They excommunicate this pope, and elect another, Clement VII.; most of the states, including England, countenance Urban in this great schism, ib. He died, October 18, 1389.

URSWICK, Christopher; his mission to Brittany and France, 1487; ii. 293, 294.

Uses, Statute of; its enactment a cause of complaint and insurrection, 1536; ii. 397, 755.

USHER, James, archbishop of Armagh, born January 4, 1580; i. 22. Advises James to follow the opinion of the judges in respect to the death-warrant of Strafford, iii. 243. Portrait of, by sir Peter Lely, 433. He leaves a scheme of union and plan of church-government, 668, commonly called his reduction of Episcopacy, 820. Principle of, ib. He died at Ryegate, in Surrey, March 21, 1656.

Utrecht, View of, iv. 257; § ii. 216. Preliminaries of the Peace of, executed, 1711; iv. 253—256. The queen announces that the treaty is signed, 1713; 273.

Uxbridge, View of the Treaty-house, in which the king's commissioners, and those of the English and Scottish parliaments assembled, 1645; iii. 328.

UZEDA, duke d', his mission to Innocent XIII., 1700, concerning the election of a successor to the Spanish throne, iv. 109.

Vails, abolition of the custom of, middle of the 18th century, § i. 641.

VAL, Ambroise Du, a sculptor of reputation regne Charles I., iii. 576.

VALENTINE'S day, St. (February 14,) practices of this festival, ii. 897.

VALLANCEY, Charles, an enthusiastic investigator of Irish antiquities, was born in 1721, and served for several years in a military capacity; he supposed the Irish to be a colony of Indo-Scythians. He died 1812; i. 15.

VALLANS, author of a dramatic composition in blank verse, published 1590; iii. 583.

Valmy, Battle of, September 20, 1792; § iii. 182.

VALOIS, Charles de, brother of Philip III. of France, i. 712.

VANBRUGH, sir John, an architect of eminence, and author of several comedies; he was born about 1672; iii. 573. His designs for Castle Howard and Blenheim-house, iv. 747. He dies 1726; 748. His principal works in architecture and literature, 748, 799.

VANDEPUT, sir George, 1751; iv. 563.

VANDERBANK, his portrait of Caroline, queen of George II., iv. 415. His portrait of sir Isaac Newton, 735.

VANDERDUSSEN, rear-admiral. He serves under Rooke, at the taking of Gibraltar in 1704; iv. 175, 232.

VAN DER GUCHT, a celebrated painter. His portrait of Pym, iii. 495.

VAN DER MEULEN, the celebrated battle painter; he came to England 1676; iv. 755.

VAN DER WERFF, a Dutch painter, born 1659, died 1722. His portrait of queen Catharine Howard, ii. 416. His portrait of bishop Ridley, 696.

VANDREUIL, marquis de, invested in Montreal by general Amherst, general Murray, and colonel Haviland, and forced to deliver up that last strong-hold of the French in Canada, 1760; iv. 614.

VANDYKE, sir Antony, a portrait-painter of peculiar eminence, born at Antwerp, March 22, 1598-9. The reports of the favour shown to the arts by Charles I. drew him to England, where he was at first disappointed in the expected introduction; but subsequently he received an invitation from the king, through sir K. Digby, with which he complied, and England was afterwards his principal abode. He received the honour of knighthood in 1632; and died of gout in 1641, at the age of forty-two, iii. 568. His portrait of James I., 2. Of Charles I., 110. Of queen Henrietta Maria, 115. Charles I. and armour-bearer, 225. His portrait of Oliver Cromwell, 413. Of archbishop Laud, 433. Of Wentworth, earl of Strafford, 495. Of Inigo Jones, 560.

VAN GHEST, the Dutch vice-admiral, killed at the battle of Solebay, 1672; iii. 710.

VAN OST, author of the equestrian statue of George I. in Leicester-square, iv. 760.

VAN RICHTEREN, count, one of the plenipotentiaries of the confederates at Utrecht, 1712; iv. 269.

VANSOMER, Paul, an eminent portrait-painter, born at Antwerp, in 1576, died 1621; iii. 567.

VAN TROMP, the celebrated Dutch commander, attacks and beats a large Spanish fleet, 1639; iii. 208. He sails up the Channel, but is worsted by Blake, 406. He faces Blake in the Downs, and

VAN TROMP,—
obtains a temporary advantage, but is again worsted, and returns humbled to Holland, 1653; 407. His death by a musket-ball, July 1653; 415.

VANE, sir Henry, supersedes Coke in the office of secretary, 1639; iii. 209. The king sends him with a message to the House of Commons, 1640; 215. His letter to secretary Windebank, 222.

VANE, sir Henry, a conspicuous character in the time of Charles I. and the Commonwealth; he was born about 1612. Being uneasy at home, on account of his religious opinions, he migrated to New England, and was elected governor of Massachusetts; being displaced he shortly returned, and was chosen to represent Hull, 1640; iii. 226. Took an active part against the earl of Strafford, 1641; 238. Obtained from the earl of Warwick a charter of incorporation for Massachusetts, 1643; 807. Was sequestered from his seat, 1659; 429°. Is brought to trial, 1661, as a regicide, 687, and executed, June 14, 690.

VARELST, an eminent Dutch painter of flowers; he met with encouragement at the court of king Charles II., iii. 883.

VARNEY, sir Edmund, knight-marshal and standard-bearer to king Charles I., iii. 95, 293. He perished at the battle of Edgehill, October 23, 1642; 297.

Vates, or Augurs, having a prophetic gift, and, like the bards, the chief poets of antiquity, i. 64. The vaids of Celtic nations a subordinate class of the Druidic hierarchy, 65. Their costume among the ancient Irish, ib. The ancient names Enhages, Eubates, and Ouates, designate these soothsayers, 63—65.

VAUBAN, Sebastian le Prestre, seigneur de, marshal of France, and the greatest engineer which that country has produced, was born May 1633, and died at Paris, 1707; iii. 714; iv. 48, 56.

VAUDEMONT, prince, of the house of Guise, 1606, visits his kinsman James I., iii. 34.

VAUX, lord George, 1595. Committed to the Fleet Prison, 1625, for striking a civil officer; he died 1661; iii. 116.

Vauxhall, as it appeared in 1751; iv. 826.

VAVASOUR, colonel, taken prisoner at the battle of Edgehill, 1642; iii. 297.

VELASCO, Don Louis de, governor of Havanna, slain, 1762, whilst defending that place against the attack of the English, § i. 16.

VELASCO, governor of the town of Barcelona, capitulates to the earl of Peterborough, 1705; iv. 180.

VENABLES, general, a Cromwellian officer, takes the island of Jamaica, 1556; iii. 420.

Vendeans, the, rise in insurrection against the tyranny of the French revolutionists, 1793; in the struggle thousands of lives are lost on both sides, § iii. 368—377, 484—489. The Peace of Vendée signed February, 1795; 485. The war, according to general Hoche's own statement, cost the lives of 100,000 Frenchmen, and not a fifth part of the male population of Vendée was left alive, 489.

Vendée, Peace of, February, 1795; § iii. 485.

VENDÔME, duke of, 1417, sent by the dauphin, Charles, to the Scottish regent, obtains a gallant and numerous army of auxiliaries, under Albany's son, the earl of Buchan, and the earls of Wigton and Douglas, iii. 132.

VENDÔME, duke of, a successful general of Francis I., king of France, ii. 349, 356.

VENDÔME, Louis Joseph, duke of, a distinguished French general, the great-grandson of Henri IV., was born in 1654; he served in Holland under Louis XIV., and afterwards was employed in Spain, where he took Barcelona, in 1697; iv. 73, 77. He was then sent into Italy, where he was very successful against the Imperialists, defeating prince

VENDÔME, Louis Joseph, duke of,—
Eugene, in 1706, at the battle of Cassano, 151. Was recalled from Italy, to take the command, instead of Villeroy, against the English and their allies, 185. He afterwards returned to Spain, where he died, at Tignaros, June 11, 1712.

Veneti, inhabitants of Vannes, in Brittany, i. 25. Description of their ships of war, and contest with Cæsar, 102. They received some military aid from Britain, ib.

Venice, carrying trade of the Venetians, ii. 172. Their ships admitted, 1409, to all English ports, 172, 173. This republic, after having maintained itself for 1,400 years, was ceded to Austria at the treaty of Campo Formio, 1797, by the French, who, partly by means of the troops under Bonaparte, and partly by stirring up the democrats of the republic to rebel against the Doge, gained possession of the state, § iii. 525, 526.

Venloo, surrenders to Marlborough, September 23, 1702; iv. 145.

VENNER, a wine-cooper, and Fifth-monarchy-man, iii. 421; raises a riot in London, 1661; 679.

VERE, Alberic, or Aubrey de, appointed by king Stephen to plead for him, when summoned by the synod at Winchester, 1138; i. 427, 428.

VERE, sir Francis, a celebrated English captain, born in 1554, was severely wounded at the battle of Nieuport, in 1600; he died in 1609, and was magnificently interred in Westminster Abbey, iii. 575.

VERE, sir Horatio (of Tilbury,) born in 1565; he served in the Netherlands, where he distinguished himself at the battle of Nieuport; was sent to Germany, 1620, with a body of troops, to assist the Elector Palatine; he died in 1635; iii. 81, 85.

Verneuil, Battle of, 17th August, 1424, gained by the regent Bedford over the French and Scots, ii. 56. The town of Verneuil surrenders to the English, 57.

VERNON, Edward, a distinguished English admiral, born 1684; he goes to the West-Indies with a squadron, 1739, and captures Porto Bello, iv. 430. His unsuccessful attack on Carthagena, 1741; 452, 453. He died October, 1757.

VERNON, sir Richard, beheaded, 1403, on the field of Shrewsbury, ii. 15.

VERRIO, Antonio, an eminent Neapolitan painter, invited to England by Charles II., iii. 882.

Versailles, View of the Palace of, § ii. 344, 383.

VERTUE, George, an eminent engraver and antiquary, born 1684; he died in 1756; iv. 760. His observations on painting, i. 631; iii. 577. Lord Orford has given a catalogue of his engravings, which amount to 500. His portrait of Dr. John Owen, 803. Of sir Dudley North, 852.

VERULAM, baron. See sir Francis Bacon.

Verulamium, or St. Alban's, on the site of the former capital of Cassivellaunus, i. 33. The Roman colony of, annihilated by Boadicea or her allies, 43.

Vervins, Treaty of, signed, 1597; ii. 681.

VESPASIAN, his command in Britain, under the emperor Claudius, i. 40.

Veto Act, the, passed, 1834; § iv. 608.

VETERI, general, the Abruzzi and the fortress of Pescara surrender to, 1707; iv. 204.

Vexin, le, a territory between the rivers Epte and Oise, i. 388.

VICTOR AMADEUS II., duke of Savoy and first king of Sardinia, born 1666, and succeeded his father, Charles Emanuel, in 1674; married Anna Maria, daughter of Henrietta Anna of England, sister of Charles II., 1684; was made king of Sardinia, 1718; iv. 345. He died in 1732.

VICTOR IV., anti-pope, 1159, is supported by the emperor Frederic Barbarossa in opposition to Alexander III.; he died April, 1164; i. 446.

VIDOMAR, viscount of Limoges; having found a treasure in his domains, Richard demands it; Vidomar

VIDOMAR, viscount of Limoges,—
offers him the half; Richard, on this, besieges his
castle of Chalus, 1199, and refuses any terms of
capitulation, threatening to hang every one of them
upon the battlements; it was in this siege that
Richard received his death-wound, by an arrow
shot by Bertrand de Gurdun; the castle was taken,
and every one in it butchered, i. 514.

Vienna, View of, § iv. 175.

VIENNE, John de, lord-admiral of France, sent with
1,000 men, and 40,000 francs in gold, to assist
the Scots in making an inroad into England, 1385;
i. 791.

VIGNOLA, or Giacomo Barozzio, a celebrated Italian
architect, born in 1507, executed many works of
importance; died in 1573, and was interred, with
great pomp, in the Pantheon at Rome, iii. 570.

VIGNOLLES, or the famous partisan La Hire, 1421;
ii. 49.

VILLADARIAS, general, sent to recapture Gibraltar,
which had been taken by admiral Rooke, 1704;
iv. 175.

VILLAHERMOSA, duke of, commander of the Spanish
confederates, 1678; iii. 717.

Villains, i. 660, 666.

VILLARS, Louis Hector, duke de, marshal of France,
born in 1653; reduced the town of Kehl, 1703; iv.
151. Is sent against the insurgents of the Cevennes,
1704; takes Rastadt, 1707; 204. Is wounded and
defeated at the battle of Malplaquet, 1709; 256.
Takes Marchiennes, 1712; 269. Refuses to take
the command of an army of 30,000 men, raised by
the regent of France, to serve against the Spaniards,
355. Died at Turin, June 17, 1734.

Villena, a town of Valencia, laid siege to by lord Galway and Das Minas, 1707; iv. 202.

VILLENEUVE, admiral of the Toulon fleet; he escaped
the vigilance of Nelson, in 1805, and sailed to the
West Indies; but after an inconsiderable action
with sir R. Calder, in which he lost two ships,
returns to Cadiz, § iv. 181—186. He is entirely
defeated off Cape Trafalgar by lord Nelson, October
21st, 188—195. Taken prisoner, and sent to England,
but was shortly liberated on parole, and allowed to
return to France; being prohibited from returning to Paris, he is said to have committed suicide,
196.

VILLEROY, bombards Brussels, 1695; iv. 56, 77.
Forms a plan with the marshal de Tallard, to force
the passage of the Rhine, 165. He loses the battle
of Ramilies, May 23, 1706; 185.

VILLIERS, lord Francis, brother of the duke of Buckingham, slain in a rising for the king, 1648; iii.
383.

VILLIERS, John, created viscount Purbeck, June,
1619; iii. 68. Becoming insane, is placed in confinement, where he dies, 1657; 70.

Vincennes, View of, § ii. 335.

VINISAULT, an English historian, quoted, i. 497, 500,
502.

VIRGIL, quoted, i. 63, 84.

Virginia Association, the, 1769; § i. 77.

Visigoths, possessions and wars of the, A.D. 470; i.
142.

VISSCHER, Print of the Great Fire of London, by,
iii. 599.

VITALIS, Ordericus, an historian of the twelfth century, i. 423.

VITRY, captain of the body-guard, murders Concini,
marshal D'Ancre, 1616; iii. 53.

Vittoria, battle of, June 21, 1813; § iv. 570, 571.

VIVIAN, cardinal, his character of Henry II., i. 479.

VLEIT, his print of Charles II. and the English ambassadors at the Hague, arranging the terms of his
Restoration, iii. 494.

VOERST, Robert de, a celebrated engraver of the
seventeenth century, iii. 577.

VOISINS, marquis de, assassinated by the French Revolutionists, 1790; § ii. 479.

VOLTAIRE, Marie Francis Arouet de, the most celebrated literary character of his age, born 1694, died
May 30, 1778. His interment at St. Geneviève, by
order of the National Assembly, 1791; § ii. 575.

VOLUSENUS, Caius, dispatched by Cæsar in a single
galley to explore the south shore of Britain, does
not venture to land, and returns to Portus Itius, near
Calais, i. 27.

VON ARTAVELDT, Philip, son of James Von Artaveldt,
commands the Flemish army, and compels the
French and aristocratic party to raise the siege of
Ghent, i. 790. He is slain at the battle of Rosebecque, 1382, which is gained by the aristocracy, ib.

VON ARTAVELDT, a brewer of Ghent, appointed
governor by the people of Flanders; he is slain in
a popular commotion, 1345; i. 763, 790.

VON PARIS, a Dutch surgeon in London, was burnt in
the reign of Edward VI., 1551, for denying the
divinity of Christ, ii. 493.

VON SAVIGNY, i. 564.

VORSTIUS, Conrad, an eminent divine of the Arminian
sect, born at Cologne in 1569, elected to the professorship of divinity at Leyden, vacant by the death
of Arminius, 1610; iii. 47. His book on the attributes of the divinity, ib. James I. sends to the
States to accuse him of heresy, ib. The Hollanders
return a cool and evasive answer, ib. James sends
again to tell them they must either give Vorstius up,
or forfeit his favour, ib. He is expelled from Leyden, 48. Conceals himself at Tergau; the synod
of Dort give a definitive judgment against him; he
is driven from Holland, and sentenced to perpetual
banishment; the duke of Holstein offers him and
his followers an asylum; he dies the same year,
1622; ib.

VORTIGERN, British king, opposed the Roman chief
Ambrosius, i. 57. He called in the SAXONS, 449, to
assist in repelling the Scots and Picts, ib. He gave
Hengist and Horsa the isle of Thanet as their home,
58. He was entertained towards the close of the
fifth century, by Hengist, at his residence of Thong-
Caster, 140. He espoused Rowena, daughter of the
Saxon chief, 141. He permits the Jutes to fortify
Thanet, ib. Dissensions subsequently arose, ib.
Vortigern said to have been deposed, and his son
Vortimer elected, ib. Massacre by Hengist, (sub-
ject to doubt,) the scene of the fatal feast being
Stonehenge, 141, 142. Vortigern alone spared by
the Jutish leader, 141.

VORTIMER, king, i. 141.

VOSTERMANS, Luke, a foreign artist, seventeenth century, iii. 577.

VOWEL, Mr., hanged at the Mews'-gate for plotting
against the life of Oliver Cromwell, 1654; iii.
416.

VROOM, Henry Cornelius, a Dutch painter, born at
Haarlem, 1566; designed the tapestry representing
the defeat of the Spanish Armada, which afterwards
decorated the walls of the House of Lords, and
perished in the fire of 1834; ii. 854.

WACHTENDONCK, general, takes the town of Caormina
by stratagem, 1719; iv. 360.

WACHTER, John George, a learned German antiquary
and linguist, author of "Glossarium Germanicum;"
he died in 1758; i. 10.

WADE, sir William, removed from the lieutenancy of
the Tower, 1613; iii. 53.

WADE, colonel, 1685; iii. 775. He arrests the Swedish
ambassador by order of the Privy-council, iv. 338.
His march after the Young Pretender, 1745; 512—
513.

WAGER, sir Charles, 1708, captures a Plate fleet, iv.
222. Blocks up the Russian ports, 1726; 389.

Wages, rate of, in the latter part of the fifteenth century, ii. 903, 904. In 1610; 658. In 1661; 912.

Wages, rate of,—
　During the eighteenth and nineteenth centuries, § i.
　680, 686; § iii. 769, 770; § iv. 727.
Wagram, Battle of, gained by the emperor Napoleon,
　July 6, 1809; § iv. 412, 413.
Wake, William, archbishop of Canterbury, born in
　1657. He endeavours to effect an union between
　the churches of England and France, iv. 394, 418;
　§ i. 513. Elected to the primacy, 1716. His death,
　January 24, 1737. Portrait of, ib.
Wakefield, Battle of, December 30, 1460; ii. 96.
Wakefield, Gilbert, a distinguished scholar and
　critic, born 1756, died September 9, 1801; § iii. 729.
Wakeman, sir George, physician to the queen, 1678;
　iii. 717, 730.
Wakes, the, ii. 897.
Walcher de Lorraine, bishop of Durham, 1080, an
　oppressor of the English, i. 384. His retainers mur-
　dered Liulf, a Saxon noble, 385. The Northum-
　brians driven to madness by this outrage, rose
　instantly for revenge, ib. The bishop agreed to
　meet them, for explanation, at Gateshead, but the
　people in great numbers carried secret arms, ib.
　Walcher, alarmed, sought refuge with his foreigners
　in a church; it was set on fire, and the bishop, issu-
　ing forth, was murdered, ib. One hundred Normans
　and Flemings perished with him, ib. The Conqueror
　commissioned Odo, bishop of Bayeux, to punish the
　Northumbrians, ib. This savage prelate marched
　against the people of that district, and was unop-
　posed in the field, ib. Entering the dwellings, he
　beheaded or mutilated all the men he could find, ib.
　A few wealthy inhabitants were spared on the sur-
　render of their lands and chattels, ib.
Waldegrave, sir Edward; he and his lady are com-
　mitted to the Tower, 1561, for hearing mass, ii. 545.
Waldegrave, James, lord, succeeded his father in
　1741. Is appointed governor to the prince of Wales,
　(George III.) iv. 574. Endeavours to create union
　in the royal family, 576. The king forces upon
　him the premiership of England, 595, and confers
　upon him the Order of the Garter, 596. He died in
　1763. His description of John, earl of Bute, § i. 5.
Walden, Roger, dean of York, appointed archbishop
　of Canterbury by Richard II., instead of Fitzalan
　or Arundel, who was banished; he is compelled, in
　1399, to resign the see upon Arundel's return in
　the train of Bolingbroke, ii. 140.
Wales, formerly possessed by a different race. The
　present Welsh proved to be the nation of the ancient
　Picts, who migrated from Scotland, i. 22. Wales
　was the resort of the Britons who were expelled by
　the Saxon invaders from the champaign counties of
　England, 216. The arrival in Cornwall, north and
　south Wales, of the Cimbrians of the north of
　Europe, is of uncertain date, ib. Landing from their
　previous settlements in Caledonia, that people
　obtained power with the Celtic Britons, implanted
　their own language, became so identified with the
　occupying race, that the name Cymry still remains
　to it, ib. (For the conquest of Wales by Edward I.,
　see Llewellyn.) Previously to 1536, the Principality
　of Wales had been governed in one portion by
　English laws, in another by the Welsh, the latter
　consisting of independent lordships; it was enacted,
　by Henry VIII., that both should receive the same
　laws as alike portions of the English realm, ii. 425.
　State of the country, ib.
Walker, Henry, a pamphlet writer, 1642; iii. 265.
Walker, sir Hovenden, dispatched in 1711, to make
　the conquest of Canada, iv. 257.
Walker, Robert, an eminent portrait-painter, much
　patronized by Cromwell, iii. 569.
Walker, a Presbyterian minister, 1689; iv. 16, 159.
Wallace, William, second son of a knight of ancient
　family, sir Malcolm Wallace, of Ellerslie, in Ren-
　frewshire. The first mention we have of him is in

Wallace, William,—
　May, 1297, when he is mentioned as the captain of a
　small band of marauders; in a short time we find
　him appearing as the national champion; the first
　person of note who joined him was sir William
　Douglas, i. 715. The united chiefs immediately
　marched upon Scone, the seat of government, ib.
　Ormesby, the justiciary, flies, and for a time all the
　neighbouring country falls into their hands, and
　the great men of Scotland once more crowded to the
　uplifted standard of freedom and independence, ib.
　Wallace was now joined by Robert Bruce, (son of
　the Robert Bruce who had formerly been a com-
　petitor with Baliol for the crown of Scotland,) who
　possessed the vast earldom of Carrick, ib. An army,
　commanded by sir Henry Percy and sir Robert
　Clifford, is sent into Scotland to oppose the insur-
　gents, but all the nobles at once lay down their
　arms and submit, no one having sufficient influence
　to take the command of the patriotic army, 716.
　Wallace withdraws to the north with the forces he
　still possessed, 717. His army continually increases,
　ib. He expels the English from the castles of
　Brechin, Forfar, Montrose, and most of the other
　strongholds north of the Forth, and was besieging
　the castle of Dundee, when he heard that an English
　army was advancing on Stirling, ib. He immediately
　marches to oppose it, and gains a complete victory
　over the earl of Surrey near Stirling, September 4,
　1297; the castles of Edinburgh, Dunbar, Roxburgh,
　and Berwick, surrender, and he is appointed
　guardian of the kingdom, and commander-in-chief
　of the armies of Scotland, in the name of king John,
　ib. An English army is collected at York, but
　having proceeded as far as Berwick, returns, 718.
　A peace for two years is concluded with Philip, and
　Edward returns to England, ib. Having collected a
　large army, he invades Scotland, ib. For a long time
　Wallace keeps from engaging with Edward, but the
　English king having found many obstacles in his
　advance, was returning, when the battle of Falkirk
　was fought, and the army of Wallace completely
　routed, July 22, 1298; ib. After this battle, Edward
　ravages Scotland, and in September returns to
　England, 719. After this a new regency is appointed,
　724. Wallace is outlawed by Edward, 725. Is
　taken, and conveyed to London, where he is executed
　as a traitor, 1304; 726.
Wallenstein, Albert, a celebrated German com-
　mander, born 1584; general of the emperor Ferdi-
　nand II. He was defeated in the battle of Lutzen,
　November, 1632; iii. 146, 173; and was murdered
　shortly after by Butler, an Irish colonel, 331.
Waller, Edmund, the poet, born in 1605. He un-
　dertakes, (1643,) with his brother-in-law Tomkins,
　Challoner, Blinkhorne, etc., to seize the persons of
　the leading members of parliament, and deliver Lon-
　don to Charles I., iii. 302. Their plot is betrayed
　to Pym; they are all found guilty at Guildhall,
　Tomkins and Challoner hanged, the rest reprieved,
　ib. The poet was confined one year in the Tower,
　when on payment of 10,000l. he was permitted to
　travel abroad, ib. Being accused by the army, he
　again obtains the speaker's leave to quit England,
　369. He died at Beaconsfield in 1687; 744. Review
　of his works, 875.
Waller, sir Hardress, accused, 1661, of being con-
　cerned in the murder of Charles I.; he pleaded
　guilty, and thus saved his life, iii. 671.
Waller, sir William, born in 1597, was an eminent
　military officer, who distinguished himself in the
　civil wars between Charles I. and the parlia-
　ment. The west of England was the principal
　theatre of his exploits; he was one of the members
　impeached of high treason by the army, and finally
　expelled the House of Commons. He died, Sep-
　tember 19, 1668; iii. 291, 307, 318,

Wallingford, View of the Thames at, i. 436. It was here that the treaty between king Stephen and duke Henry was concluded, 437.

Wallingford House, iii. 137.

WALLINGFORD, an English historian, who wrote in the twelfth or thirteenth century, quoted, i. 533.

WALLIS, Dr. John, a learned algebraist and geometrician, born 1616, died 1703; iii. 888; iv. 780.

WALLOP, sir Robert, confined to the Tower for life, 1661; iii. 685.

WALMODEN, countess of, mistress of George II., created baroness and countess of Yarmouth, iv. 429.

WALPOLE, Robert, (earl of Orford.) He was born August 26, 1676, and received his education at Eton and King's College, Cambridge; in 1700, he married Catherine, daughter of sir John Shorter, and in 1705, was appointed secretary-at-war; in the following year he was made treasurer of the navy, iv. 216. He is accused of corruption, and committed to the Tower, 261. On the accession of George I., a new Whig ministry was formed, and he is appointed paymaster of the forces, treasurer of Chelsea Hospital, and a privy-councillor, 305. He vehemently opposes the Mutiny Bill, 344. Declares loudly against the Quadruple Alliance, 350. In 1715, he displays so much energy and vigour in support of government during the rebellion, that he is raised to the important posts of first lord of the Treasury and chancellor of the Exchequer, 376. He informs George II. of the death of his father, 395. Tenders his resignation to the king, 456. Is created earl of Orford; a pension of 4000l. per annum is conferred on him, and a patent of rank for an illegitimate daughter, 457. He dies in 1756; 476. His portrait, 658.

WALPOLE, Horace, born 1718; succeeded to the earldom of Orford, 1791. His judgment on the style of Charles I.'s writings, iii. 607. His tragedy, entitled, "The Mysterious Mother," § i. 609. His portrait, 640. His death, 1797; 715.

WALSH, sir Richard, sheriff of Worcester, attacks Holbeach-house, in the king's name, and kills Catesby, two Wrights, Thomas Percy, wounding Rookwood and Thomas Winter, capturing the rest, 1605; iii. 28.

WALSH, a Jesuit, accused by Bedloe of being concerned in the murder of sir Edmondbury Godfrey, 1678; iii. 721.

Walsingham, chapel of our Lady of, pilgrimages to, etc., ii. 145, 289, 290. Miracles, 145. The image was the most celebrated in England, ib. The offerings maintained the monastery, etc., which dated from the twelfth century, ib. This image, with divers others from Ipswich, Worcester, etc., removed by Cromwell, minister of Henry VIII., to Chelsea, and burnt, ib. Henry seized the accumulated treasures, and dissolved the religious house of Walsingham, ib.

WALSINGHAM, sir Francis, an illustrious statesman, in the reign of Elizabeth; his first employment was that of ambassador to France, whence he returns, in 1573; ii. 636. His message to Catherine de Medici, after the massacre of St. Bartholomew's day, 648. Elizabeth commissions him to procure the destruction of the unfortunate queen of Scots, 658. He died April, 1590. Portrait of, 750.

WALSINGHAM, Thomas of, a Benedictine, of the abbey of St. Albans; author of a History of England, beginning at 1273, and extending to the beginning of the reign of Henry VI.; and of a History of Normandy, from the first acquisition of the duchy by Rollo, the Dane, ii. 208. Quoted, i. 832, 887.

WALTER, Hubert, elected bishop of Salisbury, 1188; He led the third body of pilgrims to Jerusalem, 1192. At the bishop's request, Saladin grants permission to the priests of the Latin church to have regular establishments at Jerusalem, Bethlehem,

WALTER, Hubert,— and Nazareth, i. 502. He was translated to Canterbury, 1193, and became lord-chancellor, 511, 515. He attempts to form an establishment of canons regular, in opposition to the monks of Canterbury, and proceeds to erect a splendid edifice at Lambeth, 557. Its completion is forbidden by Innocent III., 1198, and the building is destroyed, 558. His death, June 29, 1205; 559.

WALTHEOF, son of Siward, and other Saxon nobles, join the Danish invasion under Osbeorn, and the Northumbrians, 1073; i. 371. After having suffered many reverses whilst fighting for the Saxon liberty, he submits to the Conqueror; is made earl of Huntingdon and Northampton, and receives the hand of Judith, niece of king William, 375. William confers on him the confiscated earldom of Northumbria, 379. He attends the marriage of Emma Fitz-Osborn and Ralph de Gaël, which had been forbidden by William, 380. Roger Fitz-Osborn and Ralph de Gaël conspire against William ib. Waltheof lets Judith, his wife, into the secret, 381. He is supposed to have taken no decided part in this conspiracy, ib. Is betrayed and accused by his wife, 382; and executed, 1073; ib. His possessions given to Simon of Senlis, ib.

WALTON, Izaak, an ingenious and amusing writer, born August, 1593; he was the editor of several publications, and biographer of Dr. Donne and others; he died December 15, 1683; iii. 604, 606.

WALTON, colonel, a Parliamentarian officer, slain, 1643, at the battle of Edgehill, iii. 298.

WALWORTH, John, lord-mayor, admits the Kentish rioters into London, June 13, 1381; i. 786.

WALWORTH, William, a citizen of London, appointed by parliament to receive the moneys voted for the defence of the country, 1377; i. 783.

WANDESFORD, one of the managers appointed by the Commons to confer with the Lords respecting the impeachment of the duke of Buckingham, 1626; iii. 120.

Wanstead House, iv. 751.

WARBECK, Perkin, an impostor, who pretended to be Richard, duke of York, son of king Edward IV., ii. 299. See Henry VII.

WARBURTON, Dr. William, bishop of Gloucester, 1760; his violent speech against J. Wilkes, 1763; § i. 29. He died 1779.

WARD, John, (sixteenth century,) author of a set of twenty-eight madrigals, amongst which is the famous and unexcelled work, "Die not, fond man," iii. 566.

WARD, sir Simon, and sir Andrew Harclay, take the earl of Lancaster prisoner at Boroughbridge, 1332; i. 741.

WARD, the court-fool, personates Richard II., at the instance of Serle, 1404; ii. 16.

WARDLAW, Henry, bishop of St. Andrew's, 1410; ii. 198.

Wardships, royal, diminution in the profits accruing from this prerogative of the Norman dynasty, ii. 165. Allegation in parliament, 1604, that the king received the rents and profits of his wards until of age, and did not then account for the same, iii. 19.

WARENNE, Reginald de, a steady adherent of William II.; his opposition to duke Robert, 1090; i. 396.

WARHAM, William, translated to the see of Canterbury, 1504; ii. 319, 320, 323. He resigned the seals, 1515, and Wolsey succeeded him as lord-chancellor, 334. Letter from the aged prelate to Wolsey, warning him against any insensate occupation of France, 360. His death, 1532; succeeded by Cranmer, 380.

WARISTON, laird of, his letter to lord Johnston, 1639; iii. 202, 239.

WARNER, William, an English poet, of the sixteenth century, was an attorney of the Court of Common

Warner, William,—
 Pleas; he died suddenly, at Hamwell, Herts, March 9, 1609; iii. 600.
Warner, lieutenant of the Tower, 1561; ii. 569.
Warren, sir Peter, an English admiral, distinguished for his professional talents; he assists at the capture of the Isle of Breton, 1745; iv. 479. He was made M.P. for Westminster, and died in 1752; his monument in Westminster Abbey, 759.
Warren, William de. *See* Surrey.
Warton, John, fined and pilloried, 1638; iii. 167.
Warton, Thomas, a poetical and prose writer of some eminence, born 1728; died May 21, 1790; § i. 608.
Warwick Castle, Guy's Tower, View of, i. 784.
Warwick, Thomas de Beauchamp, earl of, 1369; attainted, 1397, when his honours were forfeited, but was restored in blood and honours in 1399; he died in 1401; i. 795.
Warwick, Richard de Beauchamp, earl of, succeeded 1401; created earl of Aumâle for life, 1417; sent by Henry V. to negotiate with Burgundy, etc., 1418; ii. 43, 44. A truce concluded, that Henry might confer with Isabella, queen of France, and with Burgundy, 44. He attends king Henry, 1422, on his death-bed, 50. This earl, and Beaufort, bishop of Winchester, appointed to the care of the person and education of Henry VI., 1422, then a child, 52. Serves under Bedford against the Dauphin, 54. On the recal of the duke of York, 1437, this earl was placed in the vacant command, 80. Death of Warwick, 1439, *ib.* *Depicted* as a pilgrim worshipping in the holy sepulchre, Jerusalem, 151. Effigy from his monument in St. Mary's, at Warwick, 245.
Warwick, Richard Nevil, the great earl of, son and heir-apparent of Richard earl of Salisbury. He married Anne de Beauchamp, and succeeded as earl of Salisbury in 1462. He espoused the cause of York and the White Rose, 1454; ii. 92. At the commencement of the civil war he joined duke Richard, *ib.* Battle of St. Alban's gained by the Yorkists, *ib.* He was governor of Calais, and attacked a Hanseatic fleet, and carried some of the ships into Calais, 94. He there collected an army of veterans, *ib.* He joins his father Salisbury and the duke of York at Ludlow, *ib.* His enemies designed to murder him, *ib.* Sir A. Trollop deserted with the veteran army to Henry VI.'s camp, and the Yorkists disperse, *ib.* The new duke of Somerset sent to supersede Warwick at Calais, but the garrison compelled him to retreat to Guisnes, *ib.* The mariners joined Warwick with the fleet, who became master of the Channel, *ib.* Parliament passes an attainder against the earl and his parents, the earl and countess of Salisbury, *ib.* He convoys them in safety to his stronghold of Calais, also young Edward, earl of March, *ib.* He captured two small fleets of the royalists, *ib.* York, being popular in Ireland, has there found a refuge, and Warwick sailed to Dublin, *ib.* He landed in Kent, 1460; the people, the archbishop, the lord Cobham, knights and gentry, flock to his standard, 94, 95. Warwick, Salisbury, and Edward earl of March, were welcomed in London as deliverers, 95. The great earl attacked the Lancastrian camp at Northampton, *ib.* Lord Grey de Ruthyn deserted to the Yorkists; Buckingham and other lords were slain, *ib.* King Henry was made prisoner; Margaret and young Edward reached Scotland, *ib.* Parliament repealed the attainders against York, Warwick, Salisbury, etc., *ib.* York then claimed the crown in parliament, *ib.* The earl of Warwick routed, 1461, at St. Alban's by queen Margaret, left the captive Henry VI. forgotten in his tent, 96, 97. Edward, duke of York, victorious at Mortimer's Cross, joined the earl and his defeated forces; they marched on London, where they were joyfully

received, 97. Edward proclaimed in London, 98. He led the van of king Edward's army towards the north, 1461; 98. The king and earl gained a decisive victory at Towton, 99. Warwick drove the auxiliaries of queen Margaret, commanded by the seneschal de Brezé, to the sea, 1462; 100. The earl retook Bamborough, Dunstable, and Alnwick, *ib.* Meeting Henry VI. under escort as a prisoner, in Islington, he again lodged him in the Tower, 101. Account of the house of Nevil, 102. Causes of Warwick's resentment against king Edward, 102, 103. Lingard denies that the marriage of king Edward was the exciting cause, 103, *note.* Account of his mission to Louis XI., 1467, regarding the marriage of Margaret of York with one of the French king's sons, 103. The earl reappeared at court, and was courteously received by king and people, *ib.* A storm was evidently rising, *ib.* He married his daughter Isabella to George of Clarence, 1469, at Calais, 104. Edward, unable to resist the Yorkshire malcontents, wrote with his own hand to the earl, archbishop Nevil, and the duke of Clarence, to hasten from Calais to his aid, *ib.* Tardy arrival of those personages, when Edward was near falling into the Lincolnshire insurgents' hands, 1469, *ib.* They shut the king up in Middleham Castle, but the army constrain Warwick to restore Edward to them, *ib.* Edward, jealous of the earl's conduct, turned openly against him and Clarence, 1470; 104, 105. They cross the sea, and Warwick's Gascon lieutenant of Calais drives them off, 105. Birth of Clarence's son in Calais harbour, *ib.* The fugitives are well received at Harfleur, and by Louis XI., *ib.* Reconciliation of queen Margaret and the great earl, *ib.* Marriage of Warwick's daughter, the lady Anne Nevit, to Edward prince of Wales, *ib.* Political reflections on these affairs, *ib.* Warwick's resolve to recover his estates, and be revenged on Edward IV., 106. He avoided the blockading fleet of Charles the Rash, and sailing from Havre, on its dispersion by a storm, he landed in Devonshire, 1470; *ib.* All men flocked to the earl's standard, and Edward IV. escaped to Holland, 107. Warwick released Henry from the Tower, in which five years previously he had shut him up, *ib.* Supposed Act of Settlement, its articles, *ib.* King Edward landed at Ravenspur, on the Humber, 1471; he found Clarence and Warwick in position near Coventry, 108. The royal duke, mounting the White Rose, led his division to his brother's lines, *ib.* Warwick, deserted by his son-in-law, retired, *ib.* He drew out his army on Barnet Common, *ib.* The duke of Clarence sent to Warwick, offering his mediation, the two armies being in line, *ib.* The earl's indignant reply, *ib.* Warwick had always fought on horseback, and when a defeat was evident, galloped from the field, *ib.* His brother Montague now persuaded him to fight on foot, *ib.* Both the Nevils fell in the battle, and a great slaughter of the Lancastrians took place, *ib.* The earl and marquis lay stripped in St. Paul's, that the people might see the fate of such turbulent nobles, and were afterwards removed to the family vault at Bisham Priory, 109.
Warwick, Ann de Beauchamp, countess of, wife of Richard Nevil earl of Warwick. She accompanied her husband, 1470, to Calais and Harfleur, ii. 105. Her destitution on the partition of the earl's estates between Clarence and Gloucester, the husbands of her daughters Isabella and Anne Nevil, 111.
Warwick, Edward Plantagenet, earl of, son of George duke of Clarence, ii. 281. Richard III. kept him prisoner in the manor-house of Sheriff-Hutton, *ib.* Henry VII., on the victory at Bosworth, immediately shut him up in the Tower, 281, 287. The impostor Lambert Simnel, a youth,

WARWICK, Edward Plantagenet, earl of—taught to personate Warwick, escaped from the Tower. (*See* Henry VII.) 1486 ; 287. Perkin Warbeck, being confined in the Tower, gained the confidence of the unfortunate Warwick, and they were accused of conspiracy, 309, 310. They were tried and condemned ; Warbeck executed at Tyburn, and Edward Plantagenet beheaded on Tower-hill, 1499 ; 310. Popular indignation at this savage deed, *ib.*

WARWICK, John Dudley, viscount L'Isle, created earl of Warwick, February, 1547; was made duke of Northumberland in 1551. *See* Northumberland.

WARWICK, Ambrose Dudley, earl of, created baron L'Isle, December 1561, and afterwards earl of Warwick ; goes with an English force to the assistance of the Huguenots, ii. 570. Is basely shot in the thigh by a French soldier at the siege of Havre, whilst standing in a breach during a truce, 573. He died in 1589.

WARWICK, Robert Rich, earl of, 1618. His assistance to the Presbyterians, iii. 365, 367, 383. He carried the sword of state before the Protector at his inauguration, June 26, 1657; 423. He died in 1658.

WARWICK, sir Philip, iii. 178. His "Memoirs" quoted, 220, *note ;* 241, *note ;* 245, *note ;* 331, 342, 391, *note.*

WASHINGTON, George, commander-in-chief, and first president of the United States of America, was born February 22, 1732, in Virginia, § i. 230. In 1755 he served in general Braddock's fatal expedition against the French, and retires from the service, 1758; 231. His *portrait, ib.* Signs the Virginia Association, 1769; 77. Is elected a delegate to the first General Congress, 1774 ; 187. Is appointed, by Congress, 1775, commander-in-chief of the American forces, 227, 232. When he took the command of the army he found the American affairs every way deplorable, but by his bravery, prudence, firmness, and soldierly abilities, he overcame every obstacle, and terminated this eventful war by the surrender of the British army under earl Cornwallis in 1781; 232, *et seq.* On the 14th of April, 1789, he was appointed president of the United States ; and at length, having steered the country during an unquiet period of more than seven years, he declined re-election and retired, 1796; § iv. 527—546. In the following year he was obliged to quit his retirement, and again take upon himself the management of public business, in consequence of some aggressions on the part of France, 547. His death, December 14, 1799, at Mount Vernon, in the sixty-eighth year of his age, 548.

WASHINGTON, colonel H., royalist governor of Worcester, 1646; iii. 355.

WASHINGTON, colonel, taken prisoner at the battle of Eutaw, September 1781; § i. 468.

Wassail-bowl, the, presented by Rowena to Vortigern, i. 141.

Watches of English make in great repute in France, (17th century,) iv. 733, § iii. 687. Exportation of parts of watches prohibited, iv. 733.

Watchmen, iv. 818.

Water-colouring, § iv. 711—715.

Waterloo, battle of, June 18, 1815; § i. 635*—637*.

Waterloo Bridge, originally the Strand Bridge, commenced 1811, by the late sir John Rennie, opened 1817; § iv. 676. View of, *ib.*

WATSON and CLARKE, secular priests, executed for the conspiracy, 1603, to seize king James I., iii. 8, 9, 13.

WATT, James, principally distinguished for his improvements in the steam-engine, was born in 1736. In 1765 he contrived his first engine, § i. 580 ; § iii. 673. His *portrait, ib.*

WATT, Robert, a citizen of Edinburgh, declared guilty of high treason, August 19, 1794 ; § iii. 463, 464.

WATTS, a plumber of Bristol, his improvements in the manufacture of lead shot, 1782 ; § iii. 683.

WAYNE, brigadier-general, an American officer, 1779 ; § i. 390. *Portrait of, ib.*

Wearmouth, monastery of, commenced 675, by bishop Benedict, i. 310.

Wearwell, Abbey of, i. 188, 191.

WEBSTER, John, a dramatic poet of the 17th century; his works are numerous, iii. 587.

Wedding, description of a, in the 16th century, ii. 887, 888.

WEDGWOOD, Josiah, an ingenious improver of the English pottery manufacture, born July, 1730. He produced the manufacture called Queen's ware, in 1763 ; § i. 590 ; and discovered the method of painting on vases without the glossy appearance of ordinary painting on porcelain,—an art which had been lost since the time of Pliny, 591. *Portrait of, ib.* He died Jan. 3, 1795.

WEELKES, Thomas, organist of Winchester college, *regno* James I., author of many excellent madrigals, iii. 566.

WELDON, colonel, a parliamentarian officer, 1645 ; iii. 331.

WELLESLEY, Richard Colley, marquis Wellesley, governor-general of India. Under his government great conquests and victories are gained by his brother Arthur and lord Lake, 1803—1806 ; § iv. 78 —89, 199—205. Mr. Paul brings charges against his management in India, before parliament, 1806 ; 223. A motion is again made to censure his conduct in the Indian administration, but lost, 1808 ; 302. He is sent ambassador to the Central Junta in Spain, but is unable to prevail with them to act in concert with the British troops, 385, 386. Is made secretary of state for foreign affairs, 1810; resigns 1812; 498.

WELLINGTON, Arthur Wellesley, duke of; he is sent by his brother, the marquis of Wellesley, and then governor of India, to restore the Peishwa, who had been driven from his dominions by Holkar, and succeeds, May 13, 1803; § iv. 78. He gains the battle of Argaum, November 29; 83, and takes the strong fortress of Gawil-Ghur by storm, *ib.* Battles of Bokerdon, Delhi, and Laswarree, gained by the British troops, 79—82. The English arms, under general Wellesley, are everywhere successful, and peace is successively made with all the native states, 84—86, 199—205. Wellesley is elected Knight of the Bath, 1804. His judicious management restores peace and prosperity to India, 86, 87. He leaves India, and returns to Europe, 1805; 87. Speaks ably in defence of his brother, the marquis of Wellesley, in the House of Commons, 223. Serves under lord Cathcart in the expedition against Copenhagen, September 7, 1807 ; 287—290. Vote of thanks for his able conduct in this war, 302, 303. Is appointed commander of the Spanish expedition, and lands at Figueira, in Portugal, not far from Lisbon, Aug. 1, 1808 ; 334, 335. Is attacked by general Junot at Vimiera, and gains a decided victory, August 21 ; 338. Sir Hew Dalrymple takes the chief command of the army in the Peninsula ; the convention of Cintra; the French evacuate Portugal, August 31, 338; 342. A court of inquiry appointed to examine the commanders of this expedition, sir Hew Dalrymple, sir Harry Burrard, and sir Arthur Wellesley ; the court declares that these generals had acted wisely, and that the expedition had reflected lustre on the British arms, 342, 343. Sir Arthur again resumes his office of chief secretary for Ireland, 343. He resigns his seat in parliament and again takes the command of the British forces in the peninsula, 372. Soult evacuates Oporto, and retires to Spain, May 11, 1809; 373. Sir Arthur gains the battle of Talavera, July 27, but is obliged to retreat, leaving many of his sick

WELLINGTON, Arthur Wellesley, duke of,—
and wounded behind him, 381—385. He is created
baron Douro of Wellesley, and viscount Wellington
of Talavera, in reward for this victory, 385. Military preparations in Portugal, and fortification of
Torres Vedras, 386—389. Marshal Massena is
appointed commander of the French army for the
reduction of Portugal, 441. Ciudad Rodrigo surrenders to the French, ib. Battle of Busaco gained
by lord Wellesley, September 27, 1810; 444—446.
His retreat towards Lisbon, 447, 448. Description
of the Lines of Torres Vedras, 448—451. After
passing the winter in Portugal the French commence their retreat towards Spain, closely followed
by the English, who take many prisoners, and compel them to abandon their baggage, March, 1811;
478. Badajoz surrenders to marshal Soult, March
11; 481. Massena, having received reinforcements
and provisions, again enters Portugal, intending to
relieve Almeida, but is defeated by lord Wellesley,
at Fuentes de Onoro, May 5; 484, 485. Massena is
recalled and Marmont appointed to succeed him,
486. The French retire to Salamanca, and Badajoz
is invested, ib. General Beresford gains the fierce
battle of Albuera, May 16; 487, 488. Ciudad
Rodrigo taken by storm, Jan. 19, 1812; 503. Lord
Wellesley is created earl of Wellington. Thanks
are voted in parliament, 504. Badajoz stormed,
April 7; 504, 505. The English army enters Spain,
June 13; 505. The French army defeated at Salamanca, and their commander Marmont severely
wounded, July 22; 508. Lord Wellington enters
Madrid with his victorious army, August 12; 510,
but again retires to the frontiers of Portugal, 513
—517. He is appointed commander-in-chief of the
Spanish armies, 569. In May, of the following
year, 1813, he again enters Spain, and the French
retire, ib. Battle of Osma, ib. The French army,
commanded by king Joseph and marshal Jourdan,
suffers a complete defeat in the memorable battle of
Vittoria, fought June 21; 570. Siege of Pamplona,
573. Lord Wellington occupies the passes of the
Pyrenees, ib. Marshal Soult is sent to take the
command of the French army, 575. He attacks the
English before Pamplona, on the heights of the
Pyrenees, but is repulsed, 576—579. San Sebastian
taken by storm, 580, 583. Pamplona surrenders
Oct. 31, 583. Lord Wellington enters France, ib.
Soult is driven from his strong position on the Nivelle, Nov. 10; 584. He attacks the British left at
St. Jean de Luz, but is repulsed, ib. He retires to
his intrenched camp at Bayonne, and the allies go
into winter-quarters, 585. Lord Wellington compels marshal Soult to abandon his fortified camp,
and cross the Gave d'Oléron, 604*. He gains the
battle of Orthez, and crosses the Adour, Feb. 27,
1814; ib. Bordeaux throws open its gates to
the allies, ib. The French army is defeated and
driven from the fortified heights before Toulouse,
April 10; 606*, 607*. Lord Wellington enters
Toulouse, April 12, and in the afternoon receives
intelligence of the entry of the allies into Paris, and
Bonaparte's abdication, 608*. Soult and Suchet acknowledge the provisional government established
by the allies, and conclude an armistice, 608*,609*.
Lord Wellesley is created duke of Wellington by
the prince regent, 625*. Takes leave of his army
at Bordeaux, June 14, 1814, and meets with an
enthusiastic reception in London, June 23; 626*.
Takes his seat in parliament, June 28. The sum of
500,000l. is voted, to purchase an estate for him,
ib. He proceeds to Paris, as English ambassador
there, ib. The great Congress of Vienna assembles,
1815, and the allied powers of Europe call upon
the duke, who was then at Vienna, to assist in
drawing up a grand plan of military operations, to
oppose Bonaparte, who had again entered Paris,

WELLINGTON, Arthur Wellesley, duke of,—
and been joined by the whole army of France,
627*. His report on the defences of Belgium, ib.
Napoleon crosses the frontiers with an army of about
125,000 men; the force under Wellington at that
time amounted to about 76,000, and the Prussians
under Blucher to about 80,000, 631*. The French
compel Blucher to retreat from Sombref and retire
to Wavre, but are repulsed in their attempts on
Quatre Bras, June 16, 1815; 633*. The duke of
Wellington gains the famous victory of Waterloo,
June 18, 1815; 635*—637*. Napoleon signs his
second abdication, June 22; 639*. The English and
Prussian armies enter Paris, July 7; 642*, and Na-
poleon embarks on board the Bellerophon, 644*.
Welsh, or Cymry, the, orthography of their lan-
guage, i. 19. Anciently possessors of the kingdom
of Strathclyde or Cumbria, south of Scotland, of
Pictish origin, 22, 23. Their immigration into
Wales was of a later period, 22. Pedigrees of
Welsh families ascend to the era of the kingdom of
Reged or Cumbria, 23. King Urien of Reged,
Arthur and the Round Table, the bards Aneurin and
Taliessin, the enchanter Merlin, surnamed Cale-
donius, all belong to traditions of the Picts and
Cymry of Scotland, ib. The Welsh invade England
under Algar, who recovers possession of his vast
earldoms, 194. Harold's second campaign and invasion of Wales; his successes, and capture of
Griffith the Welsh king, 195. The Welsh invade
and plunder England during William's absence in
Normandy, 1094—5; 399. His first expedition
unsuccessful, ib. His campaign in the following
summer equally so, ib. Erection of a chain of forts
between England and Wales, ib. Henry II. commands in person a campaign against the Welsh,
1163, who for a long time had been successful, and
one Norman castle after another had fallen. He
defeats them on the banks of the Cieroc, but retreats
with his army in disorder, and in his rage commits
great cruelties upon his hostages, 451.
Welsh, John, a Presbyterian minister, regno James
I., iii. 64, 448, 462.
Wenlock, lord, slain by the duke of Somerset at the
battle of Tewkesbury, May 4, 1471; ii. 109.
Wentworth, lady Henrietta, mistress of the duke
of Monmouth, who was executed 1685; iii. 769.
Wentworth, sir George, brother of the earl of
Strafford, who was executed in 1641; iii. 245.
Wentworth, sir John, a devoted friend of Carr, earl
of Somerset, 1615; iii. 59.
Wentworth, Paul, M.P., 1566; ii. 590.
Wentworth, Thomas. See Strafford.
Wesley, rev. John, born at Epworth, June 17, 1703.
In 1729 he associated himself with several friends
who met and read together divinity. In 1735 he
accepted an invitation of Dr. Burton, and preached
the gospel to the Indians of Georgia, iv. 653. In
1738 he commenced the systematic labours in England which have made him the Founder of Methodism, and in May, 1739, the first stone of a Methodist
Meeting-house was laid in Bristol, 655—657. He
died May 2, 1791, in the 88th year of his age. Portrait of, 617.
Wessex, or kingdom of the West Saxons, founded
about 500, by Cerdic, included Hampshire and
the Isle of Wight, i. 142. King Brihtric, 150.
Crimes of his wife, Eadburgha, ib. Reign of Egbert
the Great, who united all the states of the Heptarchy in 800—825; 150, 152. Alfred succeeds to
the throne of Wessex, but in great straits, from the
power and warlike habits of the Danes, 871; 154.
After the battle of Wilton, peace is often concluded, and the Danes evacuate Wessex, 157. This
kingdom falls into the power of the Danish king
Guthrun, 878; 158. Alfred reconquers it, 160.
West, Benjamin, a celebrated painter, born in 1738,

WEST, Benjamin,—
near Springfield, in Pennsylvania. In 1763 he
arrived in England, where he met with much encouragement, and executed many excellent works;
he died, March, 1820; iii. 572; § i. 627. His
painting of Cromwell dissolving the Long Parliament, iii. 411. Of the Death of Wolfe, 610. Of
the Landing of Charles II. at Dover, 663.

WEST, dean of Windsor, his mission, 1513, to James
IV., and report made to Henry VIII., ii. 322.

WEST, a Rye-house Conspirator, 1683; iii. 741.

WEST, rear-admiral, engages part of the fleet under
admiral La Galissonière, 1756; but not being properly assisted by admiral Byng, is forced to let the
ships escape; it was for this that admiral Byng was
shot, iv. 586.

Westminster Abbey, rebuilt from the foundation by
Edward the Confessor, and completed in 1065, a few
days before his death; i. 203. *Illustration*; His
funeral, and view of his shrine therein, 202, 314,
316. William I. crowned here, 361. Westminster
Palace, in the Norman style, 314. Windows at,
ib. Doorway, *ib.* Bishopric of, suppressed, 1550;
ii. 493. Hall and Abbey, from a print by Tempest, iii. 766. First stone of Westminster-bridge
laid, 1739, by the earl of Pembroke, iv. 752.

WESTMINSTER, Matthew of, i. 592.

WESTMORELAND, Ralph Nevil, earl of, and prince
John, overtake archbishop Scroop and Nottingham,
who lose their heads, 1405; ii. 17. Westmoreland
died in 1425.

WESTMORELAND, Charles Nevil, earl of, 1563, cor-
responds with Mary, queen of Scots, ii. 628. Heads
an insurrection in her favour, 1569; 629. Flies to
the Spanish Netherlands, 630.

WESTMORELAND, John Fane, earl of, 1774; appointed
lord-lieutenant of Ireland, 1790; § ii. 469. He
died 1842; 469, *note.*

WESTON, Francis, a gentleman in Henry VIII.'s
household, arrested for a guilty intercourse with
Anne Boleyn, and, together with that hapless
queen, and the others accused, 1536, was condemned
to a cruel death, ii. 391, 392. The drawing, hanging, etc., commuted to death by the axe, 394.

WESTON, Richard. *See* Portland.

WESTON, sir Richard, publishes an account of the
cultivation of turnips in Flanders, about 1652; iii.
557.

WESTON, accused of administering poison to sir T.
Overbury, iii. 58. He pleads Not Guilty, but afterwards confesses to the murder, 59. He is hanged
at Tyburn, 1615; *ib.*

WEYMOUTH, Thomas Thynne, viscount, 1751; severe
comments on by Wilkes, 1769; § i. 67. He resigns
the seals of secretary of state, 1770; 108. He died
1796.

Whale-fishery.—The English began to engage in this
species of maritime adventure in the reign of Elizabeth, ii. 793; § iii. 642.

WHALLEY, colonel, a Parliamentarian officer, relates
to the Lords the manner of the king's escape from
Hampton Court, November, 1647; iii. 375, 432.

WHARTON, Philip, lord, 1625; the king refuses to
grant him a commission, 1642; he died 1696; iii.
292.

WHARTON, Thomas, Marquess of, created 1715; opposes the Abjuration Bill, 1690; iv. 21. Proposes
a bill for establishing a council of regency in the
event of queen Anne's death, 1705; 152. Is made
lord-lieutenant of Ireland, 1708; 222. For the
cause of his promotion, *see* 223, *note.* His death,
1715; 335.

WHARTON, Philip, duke of, created 1718; makes a
violent speech, 1725, against the earl of Stanhope,
which so irritates that nobleman as to cause his
death, iv. 375. In 1726 he went abroad, attached
himself to the Pretender's service, and embraced

WHARTON, Philip, duke of,—
the Catholic religion; his loose manners, 400. Soon
after he received an order, under the privy seal of
England, commanding him, on his allegiance, to
return home. This letter he set at defiance; and was
attainted in 1728. His first wife having died in
England, he married Miss O'Byrne, whom he suddenly deserted; he fell sick at Lerida, and died in
the Bernardine convent of Poblet, May 31, 1731; 401.

WHARTON, Mr., comptroller, carries up the articles of
impeachment against the duke of Leeds to the House
of Peers, 1695; iv. 52.

Wheat, average price of, seventeenth century, iii. 557;
Eighteenth century, iv. 849, 850. Nineteenth century, § iii. 665; § iv. 655—666.

WHEELER, admiral, drowned at the Straits of Gibraltar,
1694; iv. 48.

WHETHAMSTEDE, John de, abbot of St. Albans, his
valuable " Chronicon " ii. 208. His libraries,
organs, pictures, etc., *ib.*

Whig, origin of the term, iii. 701; iv. 679.

WHITAKER, his derivation of Britannia, or Britain,
i. 11. Supposes the Scots were emigrants from
Britain, 20.

WHITE, John, with several other adventurers, emi-
grates to Virginia, 1587; unfortunate termination of
this adventure, ii. 792.

WHITE, Nicholas, master of the Rolls in Ireland, *regno*
Elizabeth, ii. 618.

WHITE, William, constable of Aylesbury, 1703; iv. 158.

WHITE, joins in a conspiracy, 1643, to deliver the
leaders of the parliament to the king, iii. 302.

WHITE, Mr., one of the Assembly of Divines, 1643;
iii. 309.

White-boys, of Ireland, § i. 79.

Whitehall, and adjoining buildings, with a royal
aquatic procession, iii. 759; iv. 784. This edifice,
in 1698, was burnt to the ground, with the exception of the Banqueting-house, 84.

Whitehaven, iii. 656.

WHITEHEAD, Paul, an indifferent English poet, born
January 25, 1710; he took a prominent part, 1751,
in exposing the harshness of parliament to Mr.
Murray; he died December 30, 1774; iv. 564.

WHITELOCK, Bulstrode, an eminent statesman and
lawyer, born, 1605. He was one of the managers
for the Commons in the impeachment of Buckingham, 1626; iii. 120. Was brought before the privy-
council, 1629; 142. Was chosen M. P. for Marlow, 1640, where he acted as a moderate anti-
royalist. In 1642-3, was one of the commissioners
appointed to treat with the king at Oxford, 320.
The king endeavoured to win him over to his side,
1645; 327. He opposed the designs of general
Monk, 429*, and narrowly escaped execution as a
regicide at the period of the Restoration, 665. He
died in January 1676.

WHITELOCKE, general, his disgraceful expedition
against Buenos Ayres, 1807; § iv. 267—271.

WHITFIELD, George, founder of the Calvinistic
Methodists, was born at Gloucester, December 16,
1714. Sensation produced in London by his
preaching. He made several voyages to America,
and died at New England, September 30, 1770; iv.
653. *Portrait of,* 617.

WHITFORD, bishop of Dunblane, 1635; iii. 478.

WHITGIFT, John, an English prelate, born in 1530,
succeeds Grindal in the primacy of Canterbury,
1583. Suspends many hundreds of the clergy for
refusing subscription to a new set of articles he
thought proper to issue. Cecil attempts, though
unsuccessfully, to mitigate their rigour, ii. 745. His
approval, 1604, of James's speech in conference
with the Puritans, iii. 17. His death shortly ensues,
and Bancroft succeeds to the primacy, *ib.*, 466.

WHITING, Richard, abbot of Glastonbury, 1539, excused attendance, but his vote taken by proxy as

WHITING, Richard,—
the court wished, ii. 411. His abbey suppressed in this session, ib. Pollard, Moyle, and Layton, inform their master Cromwell that money and plate had been concealed, and accuse the abbot and certain of his people of treason, ib. Abbot Whiting tried at Wells, ib. He was hanged and quartered on Tor Hill with his treasurers, Thorne and James, in view of his splendid abbey, 412. His head stuck up on the abbey gate, ib.

WHITTAKER, captain, 1704; iv. 175.

WHITWORTH, Charles lord, English ambassador at Paris, 1801—3; § iv. 49. His *portrait*, 62. He quits Paris, May 12, 1803; 70; and dies in 1825.

WHYTTINGTON, Richard, lord-mayor in the years 1397, 1406, 1419. He was the son of sir William Whytington, as is stated in the ordinances of his college of St. Spirit and St. Mary, ii. 176. His almshouses near Highgate, ib. His loan of 1,000l. to Henry IV., ib.; Norbury and Hende, London merchants, each lending to the king the sum of 2,000l., ib.

WHYTTINGTON, sir William, father of Richard Whytington, ii. 176.

WICKHAM, William of, consecrated to the see of Winchester, 1367. Was deprived of his temporalties, 1376, and dismissed the court, i. 780. The bishops petitioned that he should either be tried or liberated, ib. He died 1404.

WIDDERINGTON, sir Thomas, 1639; iii. 203.

WIDDRINGTON, William, lord, a Catholic, 1695; joins the Pretender, 1715; iv. 313.

Wight, Isle of, i. 42, 158, 193.

WIGHTMAN, Edward, convicted of heresy, was burnt 11th April, 1612, at Lichfield, iii. 48. This was the last of the fires of religion in England; the nation felt an irrepressible disgust, the bishops doubted the utility, and lawyers the legality, of these horrors, ib.

WIGHTMAN, general, gains the battle of Glenshiel, June 10, 1719; iv. 354, 525.

WILBERFORCE, William, born August 1759. Is returned for the borough of Kingston-upon-Hull in 1780; § i. 443. His friendship with William Pitt, 1783; 498. His exertions for the abolition of the slave-trade, 1788; § ii. 258, 466, 555; 1792, § iii. 9, 392; § iv. 98, 150. After the death of Pitt, in 1806, he so far succeeded as to induce the House to agree to a resolution for the gradual abolition of the trade, 216, 217. It was not, however, till 1807, during the short administration that followed on the death of Mr. Fox, that Wilberforce had the gratification to see his labours effectual to the extent of the abolition of the trade in slaves by subjects of Great Britain. After warm debates the bill passed both Houses, and received the royal assent, March 25; 257—259.

WILD, serjeant, presents charges of impeachment against thirteen bishops, in the name of the Commons, 1641; iii. 248. Opens an accusation against archbishop Laud, 1644; 325.

WILDMAN, major, an adjutator, in conjunction with Liburne, forms a plan, 1647, for assassinating Cromwell, iii. 373. Is seized by the Protector, 1655, for a similar attempt, 419. Joins in the Ryehouse Plot, 1681; 740.

WILFRID, bishop, glazes the windows of the cathedral of York, i. 310. Assists in the foundation of Wearmouth Monastery ib. Founds St. Andrew's, at Hexham, 674; 310.

WILKES, John, a political character of great temporary celebrity, born 1727; became member of parliament for Aylesbury in 1757; § i. 26. In his " North Briton " (a periodical paper) for April, 1763, he commented on the king's speech in such caustic terms, that a prosecution was determined on, and Wilkes being seized by general warrant was com-

WILKES, John,—
mitted to the Tower. Shortly after he was brought before chief-justice Pratt, who declared him entitled to a discharge, being a member of parliament, 27. His " Essay on Woman," 28. Is wounded in a duel with Mr. Martin, 30. His cause is again tried before justice Pratt, who now declares general warrants to be in themselves illegal, and Wilkes prosecutes the secretaries of state, and obtains damages, 31. Receives sentence of outlawry, 1765; 87. Retires to France, but afterwards, in 1766, returns to England, 49. He is returned for the county of Middlesex, 1768; 61. Is thrown into prison by government, ib. The outlawry against him is reversed, 62. Medal struck in honour of this *champion* of liberty, 65. Further proceedings respecting Wilkes, 66. He is expelled the House, 1769; 67. Is again returned for Middlesex, 68, 69. Is cited to the bar of the House of Commons, 1771. He refuses to attend, unless as member for Middlesex, 114, 117, 128, 153, 192, 202. Letter of Congress addressed to, 227, *note*, 234. He obtains the resolutions previously passed against him to be expunged from the journals, 1782; 483. He votes against the impeachment of Warren Hastings, 1787; § ii. 237. *Portrait of*, § i. 27.

WILKINS, Dr. John, bishop of Chester, born 1614; published a work, 1638, attempting to prove the practicability of a passage to the moon. He married Robinia French, sister to Oliver Cromwell, 1656; yet notwithstanding, through the favour of Buckingham, was, in 1668, promoted to the episcopal bench. He died November 19, 1672.

WILKINS. His collection of Saxon laws, i. 256.

WILKINSON, Mr., a favourite chaplain of Henry prince of Wales, 1612; iii. 51.

WILLES, lord chief-justice, heads a regiment of lawyers, 1745; iv. 517, 565.

WILLIAM I., the Conqueror (Dec. 25, 1066—Sept. 9, 1087.) Natural son of Robert, duke of Normandy, by Herleva or Harlotta, a girl of Falaise, mistress to Robert, born 1024; i. 191. His father, when William was seven years of age, goes on a pilgrimage to Jerusalem, ib. In reply to the Norman chiefs, who represented the detriment of the absence of their duke, he gives them his " little bastard" for their duke, 1033, to whom they swear true allegiance, 192. Robert died 1034, on his return towards home, ib. Some discontented relatives of the absent duke and other lords, levy war immediately against the Bastard, ib. William's partisans triumph ; the youth displays early attachment to martial exercises, and the day on which he first endued armour, and mounted without stirrup, became a festal anniversary, ib. His fondness for a fine stud, preferring horses of which the pedigree was known, ib. His character for indomitable spirit, pitiless revenge, and exceeding craft, ib. William and Harold competitors for the English throne, 196. Edward's supposed will, ib. William demands the release of Harold, who had been taken prisoner by Guy, count of Ponthieu, 197. Edward's death, and supposed appointment of William as his successor, 201. William's agitation when he heard that Harold had succeeded to the English throne, 205. His preparation for the invasion of England, ib. The great parliament or assembly convoked by William, at Lillebonne, ib. The debate which ensued, 206. The assembly breaks up in a general tumult, ib. William summons the members of the Assembly into his presence one by one, and obtains their consent to and assistance in the invasion of England, ib. His ban of war published in all the neighbouring countries; preparations for the invasion, ib. Arrival of the pope's bull, justifying the expedition, etc., 206, 207. He solicits the aid of the French king, Philip I., who refuses any direct assistance, 207 ;

WILLIAM I.,—

but is aided by other French princes, etc., *ib.* Three days after the battle of Stamford-bridge the Norman forces land in England, 209. 3,000 vessels at the mouth of the river Dive, *ib.* They set sail, but are detained for several days by a storm at Valery, near Dieppe, *ib.* William's soldiers murmur, 210. The spirit of the troops being revived, William crosses the sea with a prosperous wind, *ib.* They anchor off the coast of Sussex, and land without opposition, Sept. 28, 1066, *ib.* The army marches to Hastings, where William traces a fortified camp, *ib.* They quit Hastings and occupy an eminence opposite to the English, 212. Night before the battle in the Norman and English camps, *ib.* William's address to his troops, *ib.* Battle of Hastings commences, *ib.* The English attacked in their fortified camp, 213. William is supposed to be slain; the Norman troops commence a flight, 214. William and Odo succeed in rallying them, and the charge on the English camp is renewed, *ib.* William commands his bowmen to direct their arrows upward, which has great effect, *ib.* The Normans feign flight, and turn, *ib.* Many hundreds of English slain, *ib.* The Normans enter the fortified enclosure, and the English line is broken in several places, 215. Harold is slain and the English standard taken, *ib.* Great seal of William, 358. He builds Battle Abbey on the spot where the English had stood, *ib.* Some Norman reinforcements land at Romney, and are beaten by the people, 359. William returns from Battle to Hastings, having received reinforcements from Normandy; he marches to Romney, and having massacred the people there, advances to Dover, *ib.* He takes the castle and town with little or no opposition, *ib.* A dreadful dysentery breaks out in the Norman army, *ib.* William marches direct from Dover to London, without opposition, 360. The Saxon Witan assembled, and appointed Edgar Atheling king, *ib.* William arrives in London, 361. Sets fire to Southwark, *ib.* Departs from London, *ib.* Ravages Surrey, Sussex, Hampshire, Berkshire, and Hertfordshire, *ib.* Takes up a position at Berkhampstead to cut off all communication from the north, *ib.* Submissive deputations sent to him, *ib.* He marches towards London; passes through St. Alban's, *ib.*; and sends part of his army to build a fortress in the capital (the Tower of London), *ib.* Coronation of William, 361, 362. General confusion, *ib.* He keeps his court at Barking, *ib.* Mild and conciliating measures in the early part of his reign, 362, 363. William goes to Normandy, 364. Confides the royal power to his half-brother, Odo, during his absence, *ib.* Animated description of England by William of Poictiers, *ib.* Odo's oppressive rule in the absence of William, 364, 365. Partial insurrections of the English, 365. The men of Kent, commanded by Eustace, count of Boulogne, attempt Dover Castle, but are repulsed, *ib.* Edric the Forester shuts up the Normans in Hereford, 364—365. William returns to England and celebrates the festival of Christmas, 366. His kind reception of the Saxon nobles, *ib.* His proclamation to the citizens of London, *ib.* His second campaign in England, 1068, commences in Devonshire, *ib.* The city of Exeter holds out against him, but is taken after eighteen days, and favourable terms granted to it, *ib.* Godwin and Edmund, sons of Harold, are defeated by Earl Beorn, 366, 367. William makes himself master of Oxford, 367. He refuses to earl Edwin his daughter, whom he had before promised, 368. Edwin and Morcar withdraw to the north, and assemble their forces, *ib.* William immediately marches from Oxford, takes Warwick, Leicester, Derby, Nottingham, and Lincoln, 369. Arrives at the river Ouse, near the

WILLIAM I.,—

point where it falls into the Humber, where he finds Edwin and Morcar prepared to oppose him, *ib.* A fierce battle ensues, Edwin and Morcar are defeated, *ib.* York is taken and destroyed, *ib.* The Normans build a strong citadel here, *ib.* Aldred's reprimand, *ib.* Many of the English chiefs who had formerly adhered to William fall off, and many of his Norman nobility return to Normandy, *ib.* William, surrounded by great difficulties, sends his wife Matilda back to Normandy for safety, 370. He is greatly reinforced from the continent, *ib.* William Malet and his Normans being besieged in their fortress at York, William marches thither, raises the siege, lays the foundation of a second castle, leaves there a double garrison, and returns, *ib.* The Normans, under the command of Robert de Comine, advance to Durham, which they enter, but on the following morning they are attacked by the English, and only two escape, *ib.* The assistance of Sweyn Estridsen, king of Denmark, is supplicated by the Northumbrians and the English nation in general, 371. The Northumbrians open a correspondence with Malcolm Canemore, king of Scotland, *ib.* The Danish forces arrive with 240 sail, and enter the Humber, having sailed up as far as the river Ouse, *ib.* They land and are joined by the Scots, Northumbrians, and all the men of the North, *ib.* The English and their allies take York; 3,000 Normans are slain, *ib.* The English make no advance during the winter, and the Danes retire to their ships on the Humber, thus giving the Norman king time to collect his forces, 372. William bribes Osborn, the Danish commander, to lend no more assistance to the Northumbrians, 1073, and having collected his army, marches to York and defeats the English, who were deserted by their allies, Edgar Atheling escaping to Scotland, *ib.* He then lays waste all the country of the Northumbrians with fire and sword; the English army, commanded by Cospatric, retreating disheartened and disorganized, *ib.* Durham taken, *ib.* Deplorable state of England, 372, 373. William's danger on his return from Hexham to York, 373. General confiscation of English property, 373, 374. Norman oppression, 375. Cospatric, Waltheof, Morcar, and Edwin, submit to the conqueror the second time, and their lands are restored, *ib.* William's passage across the mountains; discontent of his troops, *ib.* He marches to oppose Hereward on the eastern coast, who had fortified the Isle of Ely, 377. After a blockade of three months by sea and land, the provisions becoming scarce, the monks of Ely betray the English camp, 378. Most of Hereward's followers are slain; Morcar and the bishop of Durham are condemned to perpetual imprisonment, but Hereward escapes, *ib.* William advances into Scotland and receives the homage of the Scottish king, *ib.* He first employs an English army in the recovery of Maine, 379. He promises honourable treatment to Edgar Atheling, *ib.* A conspiracy raised against him during his absence by Roger Fitz-Osborn and Ralph de Gaël, 380. Execution of Waltheof, 382. William's promise of giving up the government of Normandy to his son Robert, if he should succeed in his enterprise, 383. Robert claims the fulfilment of the promise, 1077—1079, which his father refuses to grant, *ib.* He attempts to slay his brothers, and is with difficulty prevented by William, *ib.* He then flies to Rouen, but fails in his attempt on the castle, *ib.* Is reconciled to his father, *ib.* Again demands the government of Normandy, and is refused, 384. He goes to the king of France, who establishes him in the castle of Gerberoy, *ib.* William besieges this strong castle, but fails in taking it, *ib.* It was in this siege that the Conqueror narrowly escaped being acci-

WILLIAM I,—
dentally slain by his son, *ib.* A reconciliation is again effected, which is but of short continuance, for Robert fled for the third time, and never saw his father again, *ib.* Liulf, an English nobleman, murdered by order of Walcher de Lorraine, bishop of Durham, and governor of Northumbria, *ib.* The Northumbrians revenge his death, but are savagely treated by Odo, bishop of Bayeux, 385. He attempts to go to Rome, with the hope of being elected pope, *ib.* Is arrested, accused, and imprisoned by the king, 386. Canute, king of Denmark, son of Sweyn Estridsen, prepares for the invasion of England and expulsion of the Normans. His armament was to amount to a thousand sail, *ib.* William's preparations to resist this armament, which never arrived, 387. He orders the sea-coast to be laid waste, so that the Danes might find no ready supply of food or forage, *ib.* The New Forest, *ib.* William summons all the chiefs of the army to meet him at Salisbury, and after having the second time exacted the oath of allegiance, sets out for Normandy with a large sum of money, intending a war with France, 388. He takes and destroys Mantes, 389. Is grievously bruised by the pommel of his saddle, and dies at Rouen, *ib.* He liberates all his state-prisoners before his death, *ib.* Leaves Normandy to his eldest son Robert, and England to William; to Henry he grants five thousand pounds weight of silver, *ib.* His death, September 9, 1087; *ib.* Is interred at Caen, in the church of St. Stephen, 390. Character of William, 391. Statue of at St. Stephen's, at Caen, *ib.* *Illustration*,—William granting lands to his nephew, the earl of Brittany, 566.

WILLIAM II., surnamed Rufus, (September 26, 1067—August 2, 1100,) second son of the preceding sovereign, was born in 1060. He insults his elder brother Robert, 1077, 1079; the consequence of which was the immediate revolt of that prince, i. 383. His father desires that he should succeed to the crown of England, 389. Great seal of William Rufus, 392. He leaves his father at the point of death, and sails to England to take possession of the crown, 1087; *ib.* He seizes the important fortresses of Dover, Pevensey, and Hastings, concealing his father's death, and takes possession of the royal treasury, *ib.* Is crowned king, by Lanfranc, the 26th of September, 1087; *ib.* His first act was to imprison the English whom his father had set at liberty when on his deathbed; Morcar and Wulnot are confined in the castle of Winchester, *ib.* The Norman state - prisoners re-obtain possession of their estates, 393. Dispute as to the rightful succession to the crown of England and duchy of Normandy, *ib.* Odo, bishop of Bayeux, excites Robert to invade England, 394; whose standard he, and other barons who favoured Robert's cause, raise in Kent, *ib.* English privateers, their important services, the attempt at invasion abandoned in consequence, *ib.* William proclaims his ban of war in the old Saxon form; his English army, with which he takes Pevensey and Rochester castles; Odo flies from England, 1087, *ib.*, 395. Robert's party extinguished; many of the barons are executed, and others permitted to escape into Normandy, their English estates being confiscated, 395, 396. Change in the king's conduct after the death of the primate Lanfranc, 396. William attempts to take from Robert the duchy of Normandy, 1090; *ib.* He arrives in Normandy; the king of France comes to Robert's assistance; a treaty of peace is concluded at Caen, 397. Conditions of this peace, *ib.* Robert and William besiege prince Henry in Mount St. Michael, *ib.* A peace concluded with Malcolm Caenmore, Edgar Atheling is permitted to return to England, 1091; 398. The war is renewed; Malcolm, together with his eldest son Edward, is slain by

WILLIAM II,—
an ambush, 1093; 399. The king having broken the treaty of Caen, war is again commenced between him and Robert, who is assisted by Philip, *ib.* William is obliged to return to England to oppose the Welsh, who had overrun Cheshire, Shropshire, and Herefordshire, and reduced the isle of Anglesea, 1094; *ib.* His unsuccessful campaign in Wales, *ib.* Extensive conspiracy in the north, by the powerful Norman barons, Robert Mowbray, earl of Northumberland, and William, count of Eu, with many others, who intended to place Stephen, count of Aumale, nephew of William the Conqueror, on the throne, 1095; 399, 400. Duke Robert engages in the crusades, and resigns the government of the duchy to his brother for the sum of 10,000*l.*; 400. The inhabitants of Maine refuse to submit to William, 401. He receives a slight wound while besieging a castle, and returns to England, *ib.* His feast at Malwood Keep, with many curious incidents relating to his last hunt in the New Forest, where he is supposed to have been accidentally shot by Sir Walter Tyrrel, August 1100; 402, 403. *Illustration :* The king falling from his horse, and the tree against which the arrow glanced, 402. His body found in the evening, and brought to St. Swithin's Church, at Winchester, in a charcoal-maker's cart, 403. Tomb of Rufus, *ib.* Stone in the New Forest, marking the site of the fatal oak-tree, 404. Character of this king, *ib.*

WILLIAM III, (February 13, 1689—March 8, 1702.) This king was the posthumous son of William II., prince of Orange, and of Mary, daughter of Charles I., king of England; was born November 14, 1640. The Dutch entrust him, 1672, with the supreme command of their forces, but bind him by an oath never to advance himself to the stadtholderate, iii. 710. Afterwards he is released from his oath, and takes upon him that office; he foils the bishop of Munster, an ally of Louis XIV., at the siege of Groningen, and beats the French in several attacks, *ib.* He marries, 1677, the elder daughter of the duke of York, 715. His patriotic conduct, 717. He takes Luxembourg, *ib.* He unites with the courts of Madrid and Vienna in urging Charles to take part in a league (against Louis XIV.) for the preservation of the independence of Europe, 760. Embarks for his intended invasion of England, but is obliged, through stress of weather, to put back into Helvoet (October 16, 1688); 796. He lands at Torbay, November 5; 798. *Illustration* of the landing, *ib.* He declines a personal conference with James, at Whitehall, and hastes him from England, 801. The crown in abeyance for two months, 1688; iv. 2. The House of Lords request the prince of Orange to undertake the administration of affairs, and to issue writs for a Convention, *ib.* The members of the House of Commons of Charles II., the aldermen and common-council present an address to the same effect, *ib.* The Convention meets in the Houses of Parliament, speakers elected, *ib.* Letter from William read in both Houses, *ib.* They petition him to take upon him the government of the kingdom, 3. The Commons vote that the king has *abdicated* the throne, 4. Clarendon proposes that the fugitive king should be nominally left on the throne, and a Protestant regent appointed during his life, *ib.* The Lords vote that the king has *deserted* the throne, *ib.* Final resolution of the Houses, 5. Mary arrives at Whitehall, *ib.* William and Mary proclaimed, *ib.* Great seal, 6. Portrait of William, *ib.* Scottish Convention of Estates meet, 7. The duke of Hamilton appointed president, *ib.* Proceedings of Dundee, *ib.* *Portrait* of Mary, 8. The Union of Scotland and England rejected, *ib.* The Convention votes that James has forfaulted his right to the crown, January, 1689; *ib.*

WILLIAM III.,—

List of William's first privy-council, 9, *note*. William makes his first speech to the Houses, 9. Oath of allegiance tendered, which the archbishop of Canterbury, and several other lords spiritual and temporal, refuse to take, March 1 : *ib.* Habeas Corpus Act suspended, 10. Supplies voted, *ib.* Hearth-tax abolished, *ib.* William proposes a repeal of the Test Act, but the measure is rejected, *ib.* A free toleration granted to all sects, except the Roman Catholic, 11. James meets with a kind reception at the court of Versailles, *ib.* Lord Mountjoy is sent to France, and, when arrived there, confined in the Bastille, 11, 12. James lands at Kinsale, March 12; 12. Château Renaud gives battle to Herbert, the English admiral, *ib.* List of James's council of government, 13. He repeals the Act of Settlement, *ib.* Is obliged to send his secretary of state, Melfort, out of Ireland, 14. Lord Dundee raises an insurrection in Scotland in favour of James; lord Murray's men desert to Dundee; general Mackay's troops are defeated by Dundee near the Pass of Killikrankie; Dundee is killed, 15, 16. James summons Londonderry in person, 17. It is bravely defended, and James draws off, but leaves general Rosen to conduct the siege, *ib.* His savage conduct, *ib.* He raises the siege, *ib.* General Mackarty defeated before Inniskillen, *ib.* Marshal Schomberg lands at Carrickfergus with 16,000 men, 18. Appointments at the English court, *ib.* Parliament opened, October 19 ; 19. The Bill of Rights, and the Land-tax Bill passed, November 16 ; *ib.* The princess Anne has 50,000*l.* a year granted to her by parliament, *ib.* The king's revenue settled for one year, *ib.* The Convention Parliament dissolved, 1690 ; *ib.* Parliament meets, 20. The king's speech, *ib.* Resolutions of the House of Commons, *ib.* Speech of sir Charles Sedley, 21. Supplies, *ib.* Abjuration Bill, *ib.* ; lost in the Commons, 22. Divers bills, *ib.* The queen is authorised to act during the king's absence, *ib.* The *quo warranto* judgment against the city of London reversed; a general pardon passed ; thirty-one persons are excepted, *ib.* Parliament prorogued, 23. William lands at Belfast, *ib.* Disappointments of James, *ib.* He marches from Dublin, 24. Crosses the Boyne, and takes up a position on the right bank, *ib.* William arrives on the left bank, is wounded by a cannon-ball, *ib.* Battle of the Boyne, July 1, 1690; 25, 26. Marshal Schomberg killed, 26. James embarks for France, *ib.* Drogheda surrenders, *ib.* William enters Dublin, *ib.* Various places surrender, *ib.* William lays siege to Limerick, *ib.* ; raises the siege, and returns to England, August 30, *ib.* The English and Dutch fleets engage the French off Beachy Head, 27. The earl of Marlborough lands at Cork, September 21 ; he and the duke of Wirtemberg besiege Cork and Kinsale, both surrender; the duke of Grafton is killed, 28. Louis recalls his troops, *ib.* Dreadful state of Ireland, *ib.* Marlborough returns to England, *ib.* The duke of Berwick goes to France, *ib.* The parliament opened, 29. The Commons vote 4,000,000*l.* for the support of the army and fleet, *ib.* ; and 800,000*l.* for building ships, 30. 1691, parliament adjourned, *ib.* William leaves for the Hague, but is obliged to return, *ib.* Makes a triumphal entry into the Hague, and is waited on by the confederate princes, *ib.* He complains of the divisions among the Dutch, 31. Encroachments of the French in Holland, *ib.* William leaves the Hague for Loo, March 5, 1691; *ib.* The French besiege Mons, 32 ; the town capitulates, *ib.* William returns to England, *ib.* Tillotson advanced to the archbishopric of Canterbury, and the sees of the non-juring bishops filled up, *ib.* The king embarks for Holland, May 1 ; *ib.* He returns to England, 33. Various military operations, *ib.* General Ginckel

WILLIAM III.,—

attacks Athlone, June 18 : *ib.* ; he passes the Shannon, and captures the town, *ib.* Battle of Aghrim, July 12 ; the French and Irish are defeated, 33, 34. Death of Tyrconnel, 34. Limerick besieged by Ginckel, *ib.* ; it surrenders, *ib.* An end put to the Irish war, *ib.* Ginckel created baron Aghrim, and earl of Athlone, *ib.* Parliament votes supplies for increasing the army and navy, 35. 1692, a Poll-tax Act passed, *ib.* Parliament prorogued, *ib.* Parliament assembles, *ib.* Admiral Russell tried for his misconduct, *ib.* The Commons complain of abuses and peculations amongst the servants of Government, *ib.* An increase in the army and navy, *ib.* 1692, a variety of bills passed, *ib.* Poll-tax laid on, *ib.* Parliament prorogued, *ib.* The earl of Marlborough disgraced, and prohibited from appearing at court, 1692 ; 36. The princess Anne leaves the palace and repairs to Berkeley-house, *ib.* William embarks for Holland, *ib.* Namur surrenders to the French, *ib.* Louis in triumph returns to Paris, *ib.* Battle of Steinkirk, *ib.* William is defeated, 37. De Grandval, a French conspirator, shot in the allied camp for attempting to assassinate William, *ib.* Lyons threatened by the duke of Savoy, *ib.* The French make preparations for invading England, *ib.* Several Jacobites taken into custody, *ib.* The earl of Marlborough confined in the Tower, *ib.* Battle of La Hogue, 38, 39. A number of Jacobites released, 39. Marlborough admitted to bail, *ib.* His name is struck out from the list of privy-councillors, *ib.* William returns from the Continent, *ib.* Parliament assembles, *ib.* Marlborough discharged, and exonerated by a Bill of Indemnity, 40. The Place Bill passed, December, 1692; *ib.* Admiral Russell dismissed, *ib.* A Bill for Triennial Parliaments passed both Houses, *ib.* The king refuses the royal assent, 41. Parliament prorogued, *ib.* Somers made lord-keeper, 1693 ; *ib.* William returns to the allied army, *ib.* He is defeated at the battle of Landen, July 29; *ib.* The French take Heidelberg, *ib.* The Smyrna fleet attacked, 42. The English and Dutch fleets beaten by the French, 43. Plots and conspiracies in Scotland, *ib.* Several bills proposed by the Scottish parliament are rejected by the duke of Hamilton and the king, *ib.* William consents to the abolition of Episcopacy in Scotland, *ib.* In the midst of a great ferment, Hamilton adjourns the parliament, *ib.* The massacre of Glencoe, 1692; 44—46. William returns from the Continent, 46. Changes in the offices of government, 47. Russell restored, *ib.* William rejects proposals for peace offered by Louis, *ib.* Parliament meets, *ib.* The English attempt to destroy the shipping, etc., at Brest, but through the treachery of Marlborough, and several other noblemen, the plan is discovered to the French, and the English are defeated, 1694; 48, 49. Dieppe and Havre-de-Grace bombarded by Berkeley, 49. Russell blockades Toulon, etc., *ib.* William arrives at the allied camp, *ib.* His proceedings, *ib.* He lands at Margate, *ib.* Parliament meets, *ib.* The royal consent given to the Triennial Parliament Bill, *ib.* Death of queen Mary, December 28, 1694; 50. William reconciled to the princess Anne, 51. 1695, The secretary of the Treasury, and sir John Trevor, speaker of the House of Commons, expelled for receiving bribes, *ib.* Bribes received from the East India Company by members of both Houses ; proceedings thereon, 51—53. Parliament prorogued, 53. The Scottish parliament assembles, *ib.* The massacre of Glencoe inquired into, 53, 54. Scottish Company on the Isthmus of Darien, 54. Parliament in Ireland, *ib.* Severe laws against Papists, 54, 55. William puts himself at the head of the allied army, 55. Death of the duke of Luxembourg, *ib.* Namur invested, July, 56. Brussels bombarded

WILLIAM III,—
by Villeroy, 57. Namur evacuated by the French, September 5; 58. William returns to England, October 20; ib. Lord Berkeley bombards Dunkirque, Calais, and St. Malo, and destroys the town of Grandeval, ib. Parliament dissolved by proclamation, 59. The king makes a progress to the north, ib. The new parliament assembles, November 22; ib. An address of thanks voted to the king, 60. Act for regulating trials in cases of treason and misprision of treason, ib. The king bestows on Bentinck, earl of Portland, four extensive manors in Denbighshire, which excites a great clamour, 61. The king, in consequence, recals his grant, but compensates Bentinck by another equally extensive, ib. Clamour raised against the Scottish Company, 1696; ib. The Commons impeach the Directors for misdemeanor, 62. Motion for creating a Board of Trade, ib. Intrigues of James, 63, 64. Design to assassinate the king, 65, 66. Apprehension, trial, and execution of the conspirators, 66—69. Habeas Corpus Act suspended, in consequence of the late attempt, 71. All Papists banished London and Westminster, ib. Bond of association signed, ib. Bill for the better security of the king, 72. Russell bombards Calais, ib. Parliament prorogued, ib. William arrives on the Continent, 73. Several successes, ib. Russia, under Peter I., enters the lists as an European power, ib. The duke of Savoy makes a secret treaty with France, and declares his intention of establishing a neutrality throughout Italy, ib. He heads the French army, and invests the fortress of Valencia, ib. Spain accedes to the neutrality, ib. The States-General accept overtures of peace from Louis, but they are altogether rejected by the emperor and the king of Spain, ib. Sir J. Fenwick, engaged in the Invasion Plot, arrested June, 1696; 74. He makes a confession, implicating many persons, ib. William returns to England, ib. Parliament opened, ib. Supplies are voted, ib. Money is proposed to be borrowed upon state counters, or Exchequer tallies, bearing interest, and secured upon supplies voted in succeeding sessions, ib. 1697, Admiral Russell lays the confessions of Fenwick before the Commons, 76. Fenwick is summoned, ib. The papers voted false, and an Act of Attainder brought in against him, ib. He is beheaded on Tower-hill, ib. The earl of Monmouth confined in the Tower, ib. Parliament prorogued, ib. Admiral Russell created earl of Orford, 77. Lord Somers, baron of Evesham, and lord-chancellor, ib. Sunderland, lord-chamberlain, ib. The king appoints a council of regency, and proceeds to the Continent, ib. Preliminaries of the Treaty of Ryswick arranged, 78. Treaty of Ryswick signed, September 20; 79. William returns to England, 80. The Commons pass a resolution for disbanding the army raised since 1680, December 3; 81. Sunderland retires, ib. Parliament votes 700,000l. per annum to the king for life, ib. Several Acts passed, injurious to Ireland, 81, 82. The Commons complain of the standing of the remaining portion of the army, 1698; 82. Parliament prorogued, ib. Dissolved, ib. Scottish parliament assembles, 83. The king entrusts the duke of Gloucester to the care of the earl of Marlborough and bishop Burnet, which occasions great displeasure to the Tories, 86. The Treaty of Partition, 86—92. The king returns to London, 92. Parliament opens, ib. Resolution passed for disbanding the army, 1698, except 7,000 in England, and 12,000 in Ireland, native subjects, 92, 93. The king requests that the Dutch guards may remain, 94. The Commons refuse, ib. The earl of Orford resigns his places, 1699; 95. Bill of Supply passed, with a clause for taking an account of the estates forfeited in Ireland, in order that they may be applied, ib. The king goes to Loo, ib.

WILLIAM III,—
Paterson sails from Leith Roads, with 12,000 men, for his intended colony at the Isthmus of Darien, ib. They reach the Isthmus, land at Acta, and establish New St. Andrew's and New Edinburgh, 96. The king issues a proclamation against the Scottish settlement at the Isthmus of Darien, April 1699; 97. The colonists are reduced to great necessity; the remainder embark for Scotland, 98. Captain Campbell and a new set of adventurers arrive there; they attack the Spaniards at Tubucantee and rout them, ib. The Spaniards besiege New St. Andrew's; Campbell capitulates, and returns to Scotland with a few remaining followers, 99. The Scottish Company remonstrate upon the conduct pursued in regard to Paterson and his followers, ib. Great seal of William III.; 100. The young Electoral Prince of Bavaria, who had been named by Charles II. of Spain as his successor, dies in his eighth year, not without suspicions being entertained of foul means used either by France or Austria, 100, 101. Charles II. writes a spirited remonstrance against the proceedings of the English court, 101. The English declare it to be insolent and seditious, and order the Spanish ambassador to quit England, ib. William returns to England, October, ib. Parliament assembles, ib. The Commons receive the report of the commissioners for taking the account of the Irish forfeited estates, 103. Lady Orkney's grant brought into question, 1700; 103, 104. Sir R. Leving committed to the Tower, 104. The Commons pass the Resumption Bill, and tack it to a money bill; the Lords amend it; the Commons reject the amendments; the Lords pass the Bill, 104, 105. Parliament prorogued, 105. Lord Somers is removed, 1700, and sir Matthew Wright made lord-keeper, 106. The government of Ireland offered to Shrewsbury, who, instead of accepting, resigns his office of lord-chamberlain, and departs for Italy, ib. Lord Portland resigns, ib. Lord Jersey appointed chamberlain, and lord Romney groom of the stole, ib. The king departs for Loo, ib. The Scottish parliament meets, ib. Petition from the Darien Company, 106, 107. Violent commotions in the Scottish parliament through continual adjournment, ib. The duke of Queensbury receives the Order of the Garter, 107. The marquess of Argyle raised to a dukedom, ib. Reduction in the English navy, ib. Admiral Rooke drives the Danish fleet into Copenhagen, 108. Frederick IV., king of Denmark, implores peace with England, ib. Treaty between Sweden and Denmark, ib. Charles II., of Spain, again consults about the succession, 108, 109. His death, 110. Louis dispatches his grandson Philip into Spain, to take upon him the government, ib. The second Partition Treaty, 1700; 108—112. Letters of William to the pensionary Heinsius, 110, 111. Death of the young duke of Gloucester, July 30, 1700; 112. Parliament assembles; R. Harley elected Speaker, ib. The king recommends a settlement of the succession, ib. The States-General abandon the Partition Treaty, 1701; 114, 115. A letter from lord Melfort to the earl of Perth, proposing measures for the restoration of James intercepted, and read in parliament, 115. In consequence of this letter parliament votes large supplies, 116. Instructions given to Mr. Stanhope, William's plenipotentiary, 117. Committee appointed for considering the two Partition Treaties, ib. Letter from the duke of Anjou, written in the style of the king of Spain, received and read in William's cabinet-council, 119. The earl of Portland impeached for negotiating the Partition Treaties, 1701; 120. Lord Somers, lord Halifax, and lord Orford impeached for having advised the signing of them, 121. The Kentish Petition, 122. The petitioners

WILLIAM III.,—
sent to the Gate-house, *ib.* The Legion Memorial presented to the House of Commons, 124. The impeachment of lord Somers carried up to the House of Lords, May 19, 125. His defence, *ib.* The Succession Bill passes, 126, 127. Lord Somers is acquitted, 127, 128. Lord Orford acquitted, and the charges against Portland and Halifax dismissed, 128. The Commons present a liberal money-bill to the king, *ib.* Parliament prorogued, *ib.* The king embarks for Holland, *ib.* The Second Grand Alliance signed at the Hague, September 7, 1701; 128, 129. War carried on by prince Eugene against Catinat and Villeroy, 129. James II. dies at St. Germain, September 16; 130. Parliament dissolved, *ib.* William writes to the earl of Sunderland, desiring to know from him the condition of affairs in England. 131. His answer, 131, 132. William returns to England, 133. Change in offices of state, 135. Parliament assembles, *ib.* The king's speech, *ib.* Supplies, 135, 136. A Bill of Attainder passed against James II.'s son, January 2, 1702; 137. Bill of Abjuration passed, March 7, *ib.* The king fractures his collar-bone, *ib.* He recommends to parliament, by message, the union of England and Scotland, *ib.* The royal assent given to the Attainder Bill, 138; also to the Abjuration and Malt-tax Bills, *ib.* Death of king William, March 8, 1702; 139. His autograph, 616. Coins of this reign, 725.

WILLIAM L, king of Scotland (1165—1214,) surnamed the Lion, succeeds Malcolm IV., i. 452. Accompanies Henry in his expedition into Brittany, 543. Does homage to prince Henry, 453, 543; who promises him all his predecessors had possessed in Northumberland and Cumberland, for his assistance against his father, 468, 543. Richard de Lucy repulses the Scots and burns Berwick, 470. The Scots again invade England; Hugh Bigod takes Norwich Castle, *ib.* Ranulph de Glanville takes prisoner William the Lion, with sixty of the Scottish lords; William is sent to Falaise, July 12, 1174; 471, 544; he is released on doing homage to Henry, *ib.* From this time till 1189, Scotland figured as a dependent province of England, *ib.* John Scot, elected bishop by the chapter of St. Andrew's, 544. William seizes the revenues, and orders the consecration of Hugh, 1178, *ib.* The pope, Alexander III., cancels the appointment, and confirms that of John Scot, who is consecrated, but afterwards banished by William, *ib.* The pope excommunicates William, and lays Scotland under interdict, 1181; he dies, and is succeeded by Lucius III., who reverses the decree, and appoints Hugh bishop of St. Andrew's, and John Scot bishop of Dunkeld, *ib.* Richard I. receives 20,000 marks from the Scottish king, for which he releases him from all obligations extorted from him during his captivity, and gives him back all the charters and documents of his servitude, 485, 545. William does homage to John for his English possessions, 545. Dispute between the two kings, *ib.* Death of William at Stirling, December 4, 1214; 545, 546. His Great Seal, 545.

WILLIAM, the Good, king of Sicily, history of; he died 1189; i. 489.

WILLIAM, prince, son of Henry I.; his proposed marriage with Matilda, daughter of Fulk, earl of Anjou, i. 412. This marriage treaty broken off by Henry, 413. Afterwards carried into effect, *ib.* Particular account of the death of prince William, 25th November, 1120; 414; and View of the sinking vessel, 415. His bad character, 416.

WILLIAM, natural son of Henry II., surnamed Longsword, married, 1189, the heiress of the earl of Salisbury, and succeeded to the .high titles and immense estates of that baron, i. 480, 481.

WILLIAM, a Norman, made bishop of London by Edward the Confessor, i. 189. He escapes, together with the primate Robert, but with much difficulty, to the Continent, 193.

WILLIAM, son of duke Robert. *See* Fitz-Robert.

WILLIAMS, sir Charles Hanbury, 1751; iv. 569.

WILLIAMS, John, an English divine and statesman, of some eminence, in the seventeenth century, was born March 25, 1582; became dean of Westminster, etc., 1620; iii. 71. James gives the seals to him, 85; and abolishes thirty-six patents and monopolies by his advice, *ib.* He refuses to issue a dispensation from Penal Laws to the Catholics, as being without precedent, 97. Censures Buckingham's conduct, 101. On the accession of Charles L, is ordered not to attend at the coronation, 1629; his name is erased from the privy-council; in 1636 (being then bishop of Lincoln) he is sentenced to be fined, and committed to the Tower, 164. Is released, 1640; made archbishop of York, 1641; 261. Committed to the Tower, *ib.* Quits the king's party, and, declaring for the parliament, puts a garrison in his house at Purin, and persuades the county not to pay contribution any longer to Conway, 356. Lord Byron, hearing of his revolt, sends a party to besiege him, *ib.* Colonel Mitton laid siege to Conway, *ib.* The archbishop, assisting in person, is wounded, *ib.* He died in 1650.

WILLIAMS, rev. Roger, born 1598, founded the first sect, in Massachusetts, that made universal toleration an article of its creed, iii. 807.

WILLIAMS, a papist, convicted of high treason, 1614; iii. 57.

WILLIAMSON, sir Joseph, one of the commissioners who negotiated and signed the first Partition Treaty, 1698; iv. 90, 120.

WILLIAMSON, clerk of the crown, 1628; iii. 134.

WILLIS, Mr. schoolmaster to the lord-keeper Guilford during his childhood, iii. 521.

WILLOUGHBY, William, first baron of Parham, created 1547; died 1574; ii. 456.

WILLOUGHBY, lord, of Parham, founds an English colony in Surinam, 1641; iii. 540. Presents to the king the parliament's justification of their late conduct, March 26, 1642; 277. Is elected temporary speaker, 1647; 369. Governor of Barbadoes, *regno* Charles IL, 549. He died 1666.

WILLOUGHBY DE BROKE, 1489, sent by Henry VII. with a small army into Brittany, ii. 295. This force is soon recalled, *ib.*

WILLUGHBY, Francis, a celebrated naturalist, born in 1635. He became a member of the Royal Society in 1662, and died in 1672; iv. 787.

WILLS, general, a distinguished officer, 1715; iv. 316.

WILMINGTON, Spencer Compton, earl of, created May 14, 1730; George II., on his accession to the throne, 1727, appoints him to draw up the Declaration to the Council; being unable, he begs sir Robert Walpole to perform that office for him, iv. 395, 405. On the resignation of sir Robert Walpole, he becomes first-lord of the Treasury, 458. He dies 1743, and is succeeded by Pelham, 467.

WILMOT, Robert, a dramatic writer of the sixteenth century, iii. 584.

WILMOT, commissary, his gallant conduct at the battle of Newburn, 1640; iii. 221.

WILSON, Alexander, provost of Edinburgh, disabled from holding any office in Great Britain, 1737; iv. 420.

WILSON, Richard, an eminent English landscape-painter, born 1714; died May, 1782; § i. 628, 629.

WILSON, sir Robert, his skilful command of the Portuguese troops in the war of the Peninsula, 1809; § iv. 382, 384. He assists the escape of the postmaster Lavalette, January, 1816; 654*, 655*.

WILSON, sir Thomas, celebrated by Johnson for the politeness of his style; he wrote in 1551; iii. 579. Specimen of his language, 832.

WILSON, Dr., chaplain to the bp. of London, 1626; iii. 121.

WILSON, a noted smuggler; his execution, at Edinburgh, 1736, for robbing a collector of the Excise, occasions much disturbance, iv. 418.

Wilton, battle of, fought against the Danes, by the army of Alfred, that monarch not being present, i. 157. Truce, and the restoration of Wessex to Alfred, 874; ib.

WILTON, Joseph, an eminent sculptor of the eighteenth century, § i. 631.

WILTSHIRE, James Butler, earl of, created July 8, 1449; succeeded, as fifth earl of Ormond, in Ireland, 1452. Lord-treasurer. Is made prisoner at Towton-heath, and beheaded, 1461; ii. 99.

WILTSHIRE, sir Thomas Boleyn, earl of, ii. 363. Created viscount Rochford, 1525; 364, 368; and earl 1529; 374. He was descended from a lord-mayor of London; espousing lady Elizabeth Howard, sister of the great duke of Norfolk, he came into place and power, 363. His mission to Clement, at Rome, 376. Charles V. declared him an interested party, ib. Boleyn's better success in France, ib. On his daughter's marriage with Henry VIII., he was again commissioned to Francis I., in case Charles V. should betoken extreme anger, 380. He died 1538.

WIMBLEDON, Edward Cecil, viscount, 1610; iii. 49. Is created lord Wimbledon, July 25, 1626; 113. He heads an unfortunate expedition to Spain, 1625, and is called before the council, 114. He died November 16, 1638.

WIMUND, his piratical descents upon the Scottish coast; after giving considerable trouble, he was taken, and deprived of his eyes, in 1151; i. 541, 542.

WINCHELSEA, Daniel Finch, earl of; earl of Nottingham, 1682. Succeeds to the title of Winchelsea, 1729. Delivers the report of the Committee on the Partition Treaties, 1701; iv. 117. Appointed secretary of state on the accession of queen Anne, and allowed to restore sir C. Hedges to office in the place of secretary Vernon, 142. He resigns, 160. Brings in a bill for the suppression of blasphemy and profaneness, 378. He died 1730.

Winchester, View of the City of, i. 363. Described by William of Poictiers, ib.

WINCHESTER, William Paulet, marquess of, formerly earl of Wiltshire, lord high-treasurer, 1537. Created marquess, October, 1551. He died March 10, 1572; ii. 402.

WINDEBANK, sir Francis, in the interest of archbishop Laud; appointed June 1632, secretary of state, iii. 160, 167, 169, 209. He fled 10th December, 1640.

WINDEBANK, colonel, shot for surrendering Bletchington-house, 1645; iii. 331.

WINDHAM, William, son of colonel Windham, born in 1750. He was educated at Eton, whence he removed to the University of Glasgow, and subsequently to University College, Oxford. He entered parliament in 1782, as member for Norwich, and sided with the opposition till 1782, when he followed the lead of Mr. Burke, and was appointed secretary-at-war, with a seat in the cabinet, which office he held till 1801; and in 1802 he greatly distinguished himself by his opposition to the ephemeral Treaty of Amiens, § iv. 7—9. His portrait, 9. In the administration of lord Grenville and Mr. Fox, in 1806, he held the post of secretary for the colonies, 208, in which capacity he carried his bill for limited service in the regular army, 214. His death took place, May 17, 1810, in consequence of a contusion of the hip.

WINDHAM, Mr., M.P., 1628; iii. 133.

Windsor Castle, captivity of James I. of Scotland at, during nineteen years, ii. 19. Birth of Henry VI. in the castle, whence he was denominated Henry of Windsor, 50, 52.

Windsor, palace of, iii. 731.

Winnowing-machine, introduced from Holland, in 1710; iv. 729.

WINSTANLEY, erects the first lighthouse on the Eddystone Rock, in 1696; and is drowned with all his workmen whilst repairing it in 1703; iv. 705.

WINSTON, Dr., 1642; iii. 287.

WINTER, Robert, joins his brother in the Gunpowder Plot, 1605; iii. 23. Grant, of Norbrook, a conspirator, had married their sister, ib. He and Littleton are betrayed during the general attempt at evasion, 29. He suffers the extreme penalty of the law, with the rest of the then survivors, none being pardoned, 30.

WINTER, Thomas, overcome with horror at Catesby's proposal of the Gunpowder Plot, but listens to his picture of the grievous intolerance, 1605, exhibited by James I. to the Catholics, iii. 21. He was a gentleman and a soldier, connected with English Catholic refugees in Spain, ib. His mission to the Low Countries, whence he returns with Guido Fawkes, whom he entrapped for this treason, ib. He watches the countenances of the Lords' Commissioners on the day of prorogation, and reports that the secret of the plot is unsuspected, 24. He remains steady to the plot, notwithstanding impending danger, 25—27. Is disabled by a wound; and then, standing by Catesby, they are both shot at the house called Holbeach, Staffordshire. Catesby expires there, 28. On trial, Winter pleads Not Guilty, 29. Executed in front of St. Paul's, London, 30.

WINTON, lord, condemned for high treason, March 15, 1716, but escapes from the Tower, iv. 329.

WINTZENRODE, captain, aide-de-camp of prince Ferdinand of Brunswick, 1760; iv. 613.

WINWOOD, sir Ralph, an able statesman, regno James I., born about 1564. He accompanied sir H. Neville in his embassy to France, 1599, in the capacity of secretary. Sent as envoy to the states of Holland, 1603, iii. 47. Knighted in 1607. Visits Holland on the theological business respecting Vorstius, 1609, ib. Is made secretary of state, 1614; 49, 56. Listens, in 1614, to Raleigh's propositions respecting El Dorado and supposed mines of gold, 73. James I., after long hesitation, and without granting a pardon, listens in turn to his secretary, and Raleigh sails, March 28, 1617; 73, 74. Winwood expresses his opinion that the countess of Essex and Somerset had caused sir Thomas Overbury to be poisoned, iii. 58. He died 1617.

Wire-mill, the first, erected (17th century) by a Dutchman, at Sheen, iii. 870.

WIRTEMBURG, duke of, offers his hand to queen Elizabeth, 1562; ii. 571.

WISE, Michael, an English musical composer, educated at the Chapel Royal soon after the Restoration. He stood high in the favour of Charles II., till his unhappy temper lost him the king's countenance; he was killed in a scuffle with a watchman, 1687; iii. 886.

WISEMAN, sir Richard, killed in a riot, 1641; iii. 261.

WISHART, George, one of the first martyrs to the Protestant religion in Scotland, ii. 445. His school for Greek, etc., at Montrose, ib. He preached, 1538, at Bristol, against worship of the Virgin, 446. He saved his life by a recantation, ib. He returned, 1543, to Scotland, and preached against the popish doings of Cardinal Beaton, and was himself protected from violence by armed disciples, ib. His converts destroy some monasteries, ib. His supposed prophecies, ib. In communication with the English party in Scotland, he was accused of conspiring against Beaton's life, ib. He was surprised at Ormiston-house by Bothwell, ib. Condemned by Beaton and a council of the bishops and abbots, he was burnt at St. Andrew's, March 2, 1546, ib. On his death the conspirators surprised the cardinal at St. Andrew's and murdered him, ib.

WISHART, Dr., principal of the University of Edinburgh, 1745; iv. 490.

WISHEART, Robert, bishop of Glasgow, joins Wallace, 1297; i. 715. Submits to the English, 716. Assists Robert Bruce, 728. Is taken prisoner at the battle of Methven, June 19, 1306; 729. Restored after the battle of Bannockburn, June 23, 1313; 738.

WITCH OF EYE, Margery Jourdayn, 1441, burnt in Smithfield, ii. 83.

Witchcraft.—Influence of this vulgar superstition over affairs of state, and the fate of princes and nobles, ii. 66, 68, 114, 120, 135. Belief in witches, iii. 638. Persecution of, eighteenth century, § i.; 662.

Witenagemot, manner of holding a; power, etc., i. 251—253. Edgar Atheling appointed king by the, after the battle of Hastings, 360.

WITHER, George, a Puritan poet, born June 11, 1588. Author of "Abuses Stript and Whipt," and many other satires, etc. He took an active part on the side of parliament when the civil war broke out. At the period of the Restoration he lost his property; and shortly after was committed to the Tower; when he was released is not recorded; he died, May 2, 1667; iii. 605.

WITHERINGS, Thomas, Post-office farmed out to, 1632; iii. 544.

WITLAF, king of Mercia, his charter to the Abbey of Croyland, i. 320.

Woad, *Isatis Tinctoria*, employed in staining the skin, and in dyeing, i. 104.

WODIN, of the Scandinavians, i. 138. *See* Odin.

WOLCOT, John, a humourist, poet, and satirist, author of the biting compositions published under the name of Peter Pindar; born 1738; died 1819; § iii. 724.

WOLFE, lieutenant-general James. The Canadas being left exposed to attack, through the sad state of Louis XV. and his monarchy, 1759, Pitt's scheme for their conquest was resolved on, iv. 607. General Hopson, a veteran, was chosen by George II.; but Pitt urging the *heroic* character of Wolfe as an omen of success, procured the command for that youthful protégé, of his own promoting, *ib.* Scheme of the campaign: Wolfe, arriving by sea, was to attack Quebec; Amherst to occupy Crown Point, Ticonderago, and fall down the St. Lawrence to Quebec, to join Wolfe; Prideaux, with his troops and Indians, to invest Niagara, besiege and carry Montreal, and join the 'main army at Quebec, *ib.* General Wolfe's army was landed, 30th June, on the Isle of Orleans, in the St. Lawrence, by admiral Saunders, *ib.* Next day, a storm endangered the fleet, the French sent down fire-ships and rafts, but both dangers were escaped, 608. Strength of Quebec, by its natural position, and by military art, *ib.* Position occupied by Montcalm with 10,000 troops, *ib.* Although Amherst and Prideaux were successful in their operations, they had not joined general Wolfe, and the latter resolved alone to attack the French lines, *ib.* Wolfe crossed the north channel of the St. Lawrence, and encamped on the Montmorenci, opposite to the marquis de Montcalm, *ib.* July 31, he crossed the Montmorenci to assail the French; his grenadiers, without waiting for the divisions of Townshend and Monckton, attacked the entrenchments, and were repulsed by a heavy fire of artillery, *ib.* September 2, he wrote of his great difficulties, his sufferings by fever, and of his having called a council of war, to his patron, Mr. Pitt, 608, 609. Alarm of that minister, 609. Wolfe concerted with admiral Saunders a plan for scaling the Heights of Abraham: owing to the inaccessible nature of which, the fortifications on that side of Quebec were the weakest, *ib.* This desperate effort proved successful, and the French sentinels, through the darkness of night, were taken by surprise, *ib.* Wolfe had now but 5,000 effective soldiers; one gun was hauled up

WOLFE, lieutenant-general James.—
by the seamen, and four guns, in a French battery, were seized on the summit, *ib.* The experienced French general perhaps too rashly consulted his innate valour, and, quitting his entrenchments, advanced in haste, without artillery, to attack the English crowning the heights, *ib.* The French wasted powder in advancing, but Wolfe drawing his men up in line near the outworks of the city, gave a murderous volley when the enemy was close upon him, and then continued a deliberate and destructive fire, *ib.* Twice seriously wounded, Wolfe stood obstinately in his front line cheering his soldiery, but was brought down by a musket-ball in the breast, *ib.* Dying (September 13, 1759,) he was informed that the French ran in all directions, and exclaimed that he died content, *ib.* General Monckton was dangerously wounded; Montcalm, and his next in command, mortally, *ib.* Townshend completed the victory; in five days after Wolfe's death in battle, Quebec capitulated, and the remnant of the defeated French retired on Montreal, *ib.* Grief of the English nation for the early fall of general Wolfe, *ib.* *Illustration:* Death of Wolfe, by Benjamin West, 610.

WOLLASTON, sir John, alderman of London, 1642; iii. 290.

Wollaton, Nottinghamshire, ii. 845.

WOLSEY, Thomas, born at Ipswich, in 1471, almoner of Henry VIII., and his chief favourite, 1513; ii. 323, 332, 333. He and bishop Fox follow the king's army in France, 323. Wolsey became, by the influence of the emperor Maximilian, bishop of Tournay, 327. His father, a substantial butcher, gave Thomas an education to qualify him for the church, 333. At Oxford, he taught the grammar-school attached to Magdalen (in his days of prosperity, he erected the tall Gothic tower of that college,) *ib.* Dorset, whose sons were among his pupils, procured Wolsey the living of Limington, *ib.* Dissipated in early life, he is said to have been put in the stocks, *ib.* Recommended by bishop Fox to Henry VII., he was made dean of Lincoln, and almoner, and sent on a mission to demand the hand of Margaret of Savoy, *ib.* Fox next introduced Wolsey to Henry VIII.; who shortly acquired more favour than his patron with the young king, *ib.* The new favourite flattered both Henry's taste for learning and for pleasures, *ib.* Appointed chancellor of the kingdom, 1515; his magnificence, splendid retinue, etc., 334, 336, 372. The cardinal's charity, liberality, and strict justice, rendered him popular, notwithstanding the weight of taxes and fines, 334. His patronage of men of learning, and promotion of scholastic foundations, etc., *ib.* His foreign policy not equal to the wisdom of his administration of home affairs, *ib.* His countenance being secured covertly by Francis I., Wolsey concluded a treaty between him and Henry VIII.; its provisions, 336, 338. Charles V. also granted him a pension on two Spanish bishoprics, and promised to make Wolsey pope, 338. On the doctrines of Luther acquiring great influence in Germany, etc., Wolsey commanded all men in England to deliver up heretical books; and that the bishops should affix on all church doors a list of the *heresies*, that people might read, and be thus warned against them, 345. Wolsey on the sudden decease of Leo X., renews his claim to be pope, 346. As Henry's representative at Calais, he signed, with Charles V., an offensive league against Francis I., but it became unpopular with the English, in the provinces, by loss of trade. His correspondence with the cardinal repair Commons, to ... wars; is received ...

WOLSEY, Thomas,—
breach of privilege, ib. The people resist payment of this grant, and Henry allowed the odium to rest upon Wolsey, 1523; 355. Death of pope Adrian, 1523; some cardinals voted for Wolsey, but Giulio de Medici was elected, 357. This pontiff, Clement VII., made Wolsey legate for life, with increased authority, and a commission that he might reform, or even suppress, certain religious houses, ib. Sums secured to the cardinal, 1525, by Francis I., for kind services, 361. Wolsey commenced the suppression of monasteries, 1525, intending the proceeds for the foundation of Christ's Church College, Oxford; the king's misunderstanding with the cardinal then first commenced, 358, 362. Luther wrote to Henry VIII. against Wolsey, and received a severe reproof from that monarch, 362. Wolsey's appeal to king Henry in favour of Clement VII., and the cardinals, on the sack of Rome, 1527; but his royal master was engrossed by his love for Anne Boleyn, 363. Splendour of Wolsey as ambassador to Francis I., 365. Treaties signed with the French king, 364, 365. Affairs of the church provided for until Clement VII. should be delivered from thraldom, 365. Letters from Wolsey to Henry VIII., 365, note. On his return, the cardinal found it a matter of prudence to aid his master in the intended union with Anne Boleyn, 1527; 366. He urged the pope to join Campeggio with him as legate, 367. Wolsey, in 1529, received assurances from Francis I., that he should be pope; Clement's death being prematurely reported, 369. The hearing of pleas for a divorce, at the Blackfriars, in London, ib. Wolsey's animated vindication of his brother cardinal and himself, when taunted by Suffolk in open court, 371. Wolsey's fall, the result of Anne Boleyn's resentment, the counsels of Suffolk and Norfolk, and the king's cupidity, who desired to seize his riches, and palaces of York-place, Hampton, etc., ib. Henry VIII. taking mistress Anne on a progress into Northamptonshire, Wolsey ventured to ride after the court to Grafton, ib. The king received him with cordial regard, ib. On the morrow, he ordered him to London; and Wolsey never again saw his royal master, ib. Attorney-general Hales, at Michaelmas, filed bills against him for having exercised the functions of legate, ib. Dejection of the fallen minister, he admitted his guiltiness, ib. He transferred his wealth by deed, to the king, on condition of retaining his dignity and emoluments in the church, 371, 372. Is ordered to quit his palace of York-place, 372. Resigns, by royal command, the Great Seal, ib. His jewels, plate, etc., ib. Wolsey's reply to his treasurer Gascoyne, ib. On the way to Esher, sir John Norris presented the cardinal with a ring from Henry's hand, and a kind message, ib. Having no property left fit to present in return, the cardinal sent his fool, as a gift to the king, worth 1,000l., for amusement, ib. Henry compassionates his old favourite's sickness and depression at Esher, ib. Cavendish narrates Cromwell's deportment, 376. Law proceedings: free pardon for the cardinal; the sees of York and Winchester alone left to him, but the latter diminished in its revenues, 373. After hopes of reconcilement of his master, and residence at Esher and Richmond, 1530, Wolsey received command to repair to his archbishopric, ib. His popularity in the north; kind reception at York by his clergy; appointed day for his instalment in his cathedral, ib. Arrested by the earl of Northumberland (arriving from the court,) on a charge of high treason, ib. His sickness at the earl of Shrewsbury's, at Sheffield, ib. The cardinal arrested for treason, 1529, at Cawood House, near York, ib. Wolsey's dying moments in Leicester Abbey, ib. His address

WOLSEY, Thomas,—
to Kingston, lieutenant of the Tower, 373, 374. The cardinal expired, aged 60, on 29th November, 1530, and was buried in the church of the monastery, 374. His portrait, 696. Chronology of the rise and fall of this remarkable man, 705—709.
Wolves' heads, a tribute paid by the Welsh kings to Edgar, which led to the extinction of that animal, anno 960; i. 173.
WOOD, sir Andrew, of Largo, a brave seaman of James IV., 1489, captured several marauding English ships, which infested the Scottish rivers and coasts, ii. 303. Stephen Bull, a London merchant, equips more ships, and not prevented by the crafty Henry VII., he sailed to the Forth, to take revenge, 304. Wood, after a long and severe engagement, captured Bull and his ships, ib. He presented Bull to king James, who, after serious remonstrance against such infringements of the peace, gave the English captain and all his men their liberty, ib.
WOOD, Anthony, an eminent English antiquary and biographer, born at Oxford, 1632, author of "Historia et Antiquitates Universitatis Oxoniensis," and "Athenæ Oxonienses." He died in 1695, and left his books and papers to the University of Oxford. Interesting observations and records by, i. 846; ii. 197. His plan of Oxford, iii. 314, 520.
WOOD, John, secretary to the earl of Murray, 1568; ii. 612, 624.
WOOD, sir John, offered by lady Frances Howard, 1613, 1,000l. to take away the life of sir T. Overbury in a duel, iii. 53.
WOOD, William.—George I. grants him a patent for coining farthings and halfpence for the kingdom of Ireland, 1724, which occasions much disturbance there, and gave rise to Dean Swift's famous "Drapier's Letters," iv. 384.
Wood.—Asp-wood for arrows, pattens, etc., ii. 191.
WOODES, Nathaniel, minister of Norwich, and author of a comedy, 1581; iii. 581.
WOODHOUSE; a young man hanged, 1601, for a rash speech against the queen's proclamation as to the insurrection of the earl of Essex. ii. 689.
Woodstock, ruins of the Royal Manor-house of, i. 481. Bower of, 482. Manor and honour of, presented to the duke of Marlborough, iv. 176.
WOODVILLE, Anthony, eldest brother of queen Elizabeth.—See Rivers.
WOODVILLE, sir Edward, and some adventurous adherents, fought for Francis II. of Brittany, 1488. Woodville slain, iii. 53.
WOODVILLE, sir John, 1469, a brother of Elizabeth, queen of Edward IV., taken by insurgents, with his father, earl Rivers, ii. 104. They were beheaded at Northampton by their captors, ib.
WOODVILLE, sir Richard, married Jaquetta of Luxembourg, widow of John duke of Bedford, ii. 80, note. Being father of queen Elizabeth, he was created earl Rivers, treasurer, and afterwards lord highconstable, 101, 102. Illustrious husbands found for his unmarried daughters, 102. Was beheaded, with his son sir John Woodville, by the Yorkshire insurgents, 1469; 104. See Rivers, earl of.
WOODWARD, Dr., prolocutor of the Lower House of Convocation, died February 13, 1702; iv. 642.
Wool, high price of, regno James I., iii. 658.
Woollen cloths. Of the ancient Gauls, i. 125. Increase of this manufacture in England, 1197; 601. This was one of the earliest incorporated trades. In the reign of Henry I. the weavers and fullers had guilds at Winchester and Oxford, as well as in London, 601, 602. The manufacture of woollens assumes importance as the great staple of the nation, ii. 192, 193. Shared in by the agricultural population, 802, 807. Restrictive statutes, 1551—1555, to protect the considerable towns in

Woollen cloths,—
their manufacture of this staple commodity, 807;
iii. 558; iv. 703. Woollen manufactures of the 18th
century, § i. 599, 600. Deterioration in British
wool towards the end of the century, 704. Welsh
manufactures, flannels, etc., 705, (19th century,)
§ iv. 693.

Worcester.—The Welsh, and their French allies, 1406,
approach the city, but are resisted by Henry IV.,
and compelled to retire, ii. 18. Battle of, September
3, 1651, in which Charles II. is routed by Cromwell,
iii. 405. View of this City, given from an old
engraving, ib.

Worcester, Thomas Percy, earl of, an uncle of
Henry Percy, joins him with a body of archers,
1403, previous to the battle of Shrewsbury, ii. 13.
Is taken prisoner, 15. Beheaded on the field; as
were lord Kinderton and sir Richard Vernon, ib.

Worcester, John Tiptoft, earl of, 1466; ii. 102. A
great patron of learning, 206. Beheaded, 107. He
drew up a code of laws for the regulation of the
tournament, 249.

Worcester, Edward Somerset, earl of; 1589, a companion of James I., 1604, in his field-sports, iii. 19.
He presents letters of archbishop Hutton and Cecil
to the king, and himself writes a letter relative
thereto, 20. He died 1628.

Worcester, Henry Somerset, marquess of, lord privy-
seal, 1629; iii. 138. Created 1642. His loyal
defence of Ragland Castle for the king, 1646; 355.
He died 1646.

Worcester, Edward Somerset, marquess of; his treaty
with the Irish papists, 1644, whilst earl of Glamorgan, iii. 345. He disbands his army after the surrender of Chester, 346. Succeeds to the title of
marquess, 1646; is said to have described and discovered the first steam-engine, iv. 777. He died in
1667.

Worcester, William of, a Latin chronicler, ii. 208.
Worcestershire, jurisdiction of Wales over, iii. 43.
Worde, Wynkyn de, an early printer, iii. 630.
Wordsworth, an eminent poet, at the close of the
eighteenth century, § iv. 697, 698.

Workhouses, iv. 846, 847.

Worms, Diet of, summoned. January 6, 1521, by the
emperor Charles V., to put down the new doctrines
preached by Martin Luther, ii. 707. Treaty of,
1743; iv. 467.

Worsley, entrance to the tunnel at, § i. 578.
Worsteds, manufacture of, ii. 193, 808. 809.
Wotton, sir Edward, 1547, (a guardian of Edward
VI.) ii. 454.

Wotton, Dr. Nicolas, 1547; ii. 454.

Wratislaus, count, ambassador extraordinary of
the emperor Leopold at the English court, 1700; iv.
112, 123. He informs Marlborough of the desire of
the emperor, 1704, to make him prince of the empire, 166.

Wren, sir Christopher, a celebrated architect and
mathematician, born, October 10, 1632; iii. 522; iv.
735. Elected to the Savilian professorship of
Oxford, 736. Receives a commission, 1663, under
the Great Seal, to furnish plans for the restoration of
St. Paul's Cathedral, ib. Names of several buildings executed by him, 737. He visits France, 1665;
738. Is appointed, 1667, deputy-surveyor and principal architect for rebuilding the city after the
fire of 1666; ib. Received the honour of knighthood, 1674; died February 25, 1723; public works
of this architect, 740. Parallel of some of his
principal towers and steeples, 741. His first design
for St. Paul's, 743. His first design for the Monument of London, 746.

Wren, Dr. Matthew, an eminent prelate, born 1585;
iii. 121. Translated to the see of Norwich, November, 1635; and, in 1638, to that of Ely, 163. Is
ordered, 1640, to give security in 10,000l. to answer

Wren, Dr. Matthew,—
the judgment of parliament, 230. Is committed to
the Tower, where he remained a prisoner till the
Restoration; his death took place in 1667; 504.

Wright, Christopher, 1605, joins in the Gunpowder
Plot, iii. 22. Is shot in Littleton's house, of Holbeach, in the assault thereof, by the sheriff of Worcester, 28.

Wright, John, a celebrated swordsman, engages,
1605, in the Gunpowder Treason, iii. 21. Also shot
in the defence of Holbeach, 28.

Wright, Michael, a talented painter, of the seventeenth century: he executed the portraits of the
judges in the Guildhall of London, iii. 883.

Wright, sir Nathan, made lord-keeper, 1700; iv.
106. Deprived, 160.

Wright, sir Robert, chief-justice, receives a commission, 1687, to examine and alter the statutes of
Magdalen College, iii. 787, 792.

Wriothesley, Thomas, his urgent letters to the
minister Cromwell, 1536, relative to the insurrections, ii. 399. His financial measures, 1545, having
succeeded Audley, as chancellor; his letter to the
council, etc., 442. Commanded to impeach Catherine Parr; and appearing to arrest her, Henry VIII.
sharply reproved him, 447. He assisted in the
torturing of Anne Askew, 448. He announces to
parliament the death of Henry VIII., 453. On the
accession of Edward VI., he was created baron,
453, 454. An executor of the will of Henry VIII.,
1547; 454. Resists the appointment of Seymour,
duke of Somerset, as protector of the realm, 455.
Is considered the head of the Catholic party, ib.
Created earl of Southampton, 456. Is deprived of
the Great Seal by the council, at the dictation of
Somerset, 1547; 457. His death, 1550; 492.

Wroth, sir Thomas, 1648; iii. 380.

Wulfnoth, earl, flies with twenty of Ethelred's ships,
1008, from the vindictive pursuit of Brihtric, who
also held a command, i. 179. Wulfnoth then plundered the southern coast, but, hearing of eighty
ships under Brihtric being wrecked, he returns,
and burns them, ib. Thus the royal fleet is dispersed, and the Danes again land in force, ib.

Wulfreda, a nun at Wilton, carried off by king
Edgar; Dunstan imposes a penance on the monarch,
i. 173.

Wulfstan, navigator.—His voyage round the Baltic,
committed to writing by king Alfred, i. 167.

Wulfstan, or Lupus, his Homilies, i. 301.

Wulstan, bishop of Winchester, the last bishop of
English descent, at the death of William I., i. 548,
549. Lanfranc and the synod at Winchester demand
his resignation, which he refuses, but lays his pastoral staff on the tomb of Edward the Confessor, ib.

Wulnoth, son of Godwin, and brother of Harold II.,
shares in his father's power and fortunes, i. 188, 191.
Is an hostage at the court of William, who releases
him on his death-bed, 389; he is immediately re-
incarcerated by William Rufus, 392.

Wyat, sir Henry, 1509, privy-councillor, ii. 320.

Wyatt, James, an eminent architect of the eighteenth
century, projected the Pantheon Ball and Concert-
room in Oxford-street, § iii. 737.

Wyatt, sir Thomas, rises in arms to oppose the marriage of Philip II. with Mary of England, 1554; ii.
512—514. Surrenders to sir Maurice Berkley,
514. Is committed to the Tower, ib.; and executed,
April 11, 1554; 518.

Wycliffe, John, a famous divine and theologian,
born about 1324. His preaching against the abuses
of the Catholic clergy, i. 780. Prosecuted in 1377
by the bishops, his cause was espoused by John of
Gaunt, and by lord Percy his friend, who attended
his trial in St. Paul's, before Courtenay, bishop of
London, ib. The powerful duke of Lancaster
threat violently insulted the bishop, ib. The Lon-

WYCLIFFE, John,—
doners rose in the cause of their prelate, and the storm was not allayed without extreme difficulty, ib. A priest, mistaken for the lord-marshal Percy, was slain; the duke's palace, the Savoy, was gutted, and they were glad to row themselves to a suburb out of danger, ib. The lord-mayor and aldermen repaired to Sheen, to an audience of the moribund Edward III., and submit to Lancaster's forgiveness, ib. The duke turned them out of office, and creatures of his own were appointed, ib.; Wycliffe is tried at St. Paul's before the bishop of London, 807. He dies of a paralytic stroke, October 31, 1384, at his rectory of Lutterworth, ib. His translation of the Bible, 806. Specimen of, ib. The great English Reformer's principles were carried out in Bohemia by the martyr Huss, against whose followers a crusade was preached, 1429; ii. 71. His disciples, the Lollards, persecuted in England, and many burnt under the statute Hen. IV. anno 1401; 140—147.

WYNDHAM, sir William, an eminent statesman, born 1687. Is reprimanded by the Speaker of the House of Commons, 1715; iv. 306. Is arrested, 312. His opposition to the measures of sir R. Walpole, 402, 410. His death, 1740; 441.

WYNDHAM. See Windham.

WYNTON, Andrew, a Scottish author of the 14th century, i. 851.

WYOMING, Vale of, from an original drawing, § i. 367.

XIMENES, cardinal, 1508, a Spanish minister of eminent talent, ii. 317.

Yarmouth, iii. 655.

YARRANTON, Andrew, introduces (17th century) the art of tinning plate-iron from Germany, iii. 870. His plan for supporting the poor, 909.

YELVERTON, sir Henry, an eminent English lawyer, born in 1566; iii. 40, 55. Created attorney-general, 1618. He files an information against sir Edward Coke, 68. Is charged with being partaker in the corruption of Mompesson, and Mitchell, and sentenced to be fined and imprisoned for life, 1621; 82. He was subsequently liberated and advanced to the bench, and died in 1630.

YELVERTON, sir William, a judge of the King's Bench, (15th century). Letter of, ii. 145.

YEOMANS, Robert. He, with his brother William Yeomans, agreed, 1643, to deliver the city of Bristol into the hands of the royalists; the plot is discovered, and they are both hanged, iii. 302.

Yeomen of the Guard instituted, 1485; ii. 283.

YNIOSA, a Spanish ambassador, regno James I., iii. 103, 105.

YONG, sir Richard, saves the life of king James, 1622, who had fallen into the New River, iii. 88.

YONGE, sir William, secretary-at-war, 1742; iv. 463, 563.

York, metropolitan see and city of, opens its gates to the Norwegian conqueror Hardrada, after the battle in which Morcar and Edwin were defeated near York, 1066; i. 208. The army of Edwin and Morcar retreat to York followed by the Normans, who enter the city, and destroy everything with fire and sword, 369. Cathedral of, founded by Edwin, 310. Its windows glazed by bishop Wilfrid, 669; ib. St. Peter's church at, damaged by fire, and rebuilt by Albert, 767; ib. View of York from the ancient ramparts, 368. Description of this city from Doomsday-book, 662.

York, house of, its title to the crown derived from Lionel, duke of Clarence, through the marriages of his daughter Philippa with Roger Mortimer, and subsequently of the lady Anne Mortimer with Richard earl of Cambridge son of Edmund, duke of York, ii. 6. The family colours of the house were murrey and blue, ii. 857.

York-place, a stately palace of Wolsey, ii. 372.

York Town, View of, § i. 461.

YORK, Edward Plantagenet, duke of, is compelled by Henry IV.'s first parliament to resign the title of duke of Albemarle, and resume that of earl of Rutland, ii. 5. Joining shortly after in the Tournament Plot of the lords at Oxford, for murdering Henry, he absconds from Oxford previous to the surprise of that castle, and is supposed to have betrayed the conspirators, 7. Is slain, 1415, by Alençon, Henry V., endeavouring to defend the prostrate duke, is also struck on his crown and helmet, and Alençon is slain by the soldiery, 33.

YORK, Richard Plantagenet, duke of, (son of the earl of Cambridge, beheaded at Southampton,) 1415; ii. 89. His secret views upon the crown of England, 79. Is sent to France to command the late regent's forces, 1436, Paris having just been lost, ib. His chief captain was Talbot, victorious near Rouen. ib. The duke, 1437, superseded in command by Warwick, 80, 89. York, on the demise in 1439 of that general, resumed the command, ib. He is recalled from France, but in 1449 sent as viceroy to Ireland, 84, 89. John Cade, 1450, assumed the name of Mortimer, as some relation to York, 87. This insurrection supposed to relate to the advancement of the duke of York, 87, 89. Richard inherited the titles of his grandfather and uncle, dukes of York, 89. Also by his mother, Anne Mortimer, countess of Cambridge, his claim to the throne of the Plantagenets was superior to that of Henry VI., ib. In 1449 he quelled a rebellion of the Irish, and became popular with all the English resident in that island, ib. In 1451 he resigned, and landed unbidden in England with a considerable force, ib. Richard visited the king in London, and then silently withdrew to his castle of Fotheringay, ib. The Court, suspecting him, sought to counteract him by Somerset, the nearest male relation of Henry VI., 90. He collected forces at his castle of Ludlow, Shropshire, ib. A royal army sent against him, which he evaded, and reaching London, found its gates closed against him, ib. The king came up with him at Dartford, and a negotiation being amicably come to, York disbanded his force, ib. He assured Henry that he had only wished to protect himself from evil machinations long devised against his person, ib. Attending the king without followers, in his tent, he was arrested by Somerset, ib. His release; he remained tranquil in his castle of Wigmore, ib. The infirmities of Henry increasing, York is recalled to the council, 1454; 91. Archbishop Kemp dying, a deputation of peers proceeded to Windsor to confer with the king, who could neither comprehend nor reply to them, ib. This total incapacity was entered on the records, and York was made Protector, ib. His great victory at St. Alban's; Somerset slain; the king, slightly wounded, remained prisoner, and treated with mildness, 1454; 92. The duke opened parliament, November, as the king's lieutenant, and was again appointed Protector, ib. His moderation, 93. In 1456 Henry attended parliament in person; the peers restored him to regal authority, and York resigned the protectorate, ib. He retired to his estates, and kept his retainers in readiness against dangers, ib. Terms of the pacification, ib. Conference of the duke with Salisbury and Warwick, 94. The latter earl went to Calais to embark his veteran soldiers, ib. Duke Richard joined on the Welsh marshes by Salisbury, 1459, ib. Salisbury's victory at Bloreheath over lord Audley, ib. Warwick joined his father and the duke near Ludlow, and formed an intrenched camp, ib. Sir A. Trollop, captain of the veteran army from Calais, betrayed Warwick's confidence, and deserted by night to Henry VI., marching up from Worcester, ib. The Yorkists thereby ruined for the remainder

YORK, Richard Plantagenet, duke of—
of the campaign, retreat in different directions, *ib*.
The duke and all his family attainted. Richard,
popular in Ireland, found safety there, *ib*. His son
Edward and Salisbury, find refuge in Calais, where
Warwick, by fortunate circumstances, was joined
by all the fleet, *ib*. Warwick landed in Kent, and
entered London with Edward, 95. Duke Richard
arrived from Ireland and demanded the crown, *ib*.
Firm replies of the peers, *ib*. Act of the Succession,
96. Duke Richard, 30th December, 1460, fell at
Wakefield, in the great battle gained by Margaret
and Somerset, *ib*. His young son, Rutland, stabbed
by the fierce Clifford, *ib*. Queen Margaret causes
duke Richard's head to be stuck on a gate at York,
ib. His character of moderation one cause of his
ultimate fall, the greatest of his enemies having
been repeatedly in his power, *ib*.

YORK, duchess of, widow of duke Richard, ii. 104.

YORK, Richard Plantagenet, duke of, created 1474; at
eleven years of age removed by queen Elizabeth to
the Sanctuary at Westminster, 1483; ii. 118. Gloucester sends prelates to demand the boy, and then
secures him, with his brother Edward V., in the
Tower, 121. The princes were murdered by their
cruel uncle's command, 124, 125.

YORK, James Stuart, duke of, created 1643; ascended
the throne as James II., 1685. (*Which see*.)

YORK, Edward Augustus, duke of, brother of king
George III., sworn a member of the privy-council,
1760; died 1767; § i. 2.

YORK, Frederick, duke of, created November 1784.
His marriage, 1792. Provisions made by parliament for a suitable establishment, § iii. 8. His
portrait, 291. He lands at Ostend, 1793, with a
small army, to co-operate against the French republicans, *ib*. Bombards and takes possession of
Valenciennes, July 28; 294, 402. His ill success
against the French in Holland, 1799; 547. His connection with Mrs. Ann Clarke, § iv. 364. He
resigns the office of commander-in-chief, 1809, after
having held it for fourteen years, 369. Is re-
appointed by the Prince Regent, 1811; 473.

YORK, sir Philip, attorney-general, supports Walpole
in his scheme for Excise duties, 1733; iv. 408.

YORKE, honourable Charles, accepts the Great Seal,
1770, and shortly after commits suicide, § i. 84.

YORKE, sir Joseph, English ambassador at the Hague;
recalled 1780; § i. 439.

Yorkshire.—The yeomen and others rise in great
force, 1469; ii. 104. At Edgecote they defeat Pembroke, who is slain, *ib*. They take Rivers and
Woodville, father and brother of the queen, and

Yorkshire.— ——
behead those noblemen, *ib*. Edward IV., at Olney,
in danger from the insurgents, is removed by
Clarence and Warwick to Middleham Castle almost
as their captive, *ib*. Strong suspicions of Warwick and the prince being the abettors of these
insurgents, and of the Lincolnshire-men, 1470; 104,
105. The too sudden innovations by Henry VIII.,
such as the suppression of monasteries, which left
the poor (heretofore chiefly relieved by friars and
monks) to form a more deteriorated class of *destitute
paupers*, convulsed, in 1536, the social condition of
the nation, 397—399. The great rising in the
northern counties, *ib*. "The Pilgrims of Grace;"
the archbishop and several lords joined the insurgents, possibly by constraint, 399. Suppression of
this great movement; executions; cruelties, 400, 401.

YOUNG, Dr. Edward, the celebrated author of the
"Night Thoughts," born 1681; died April 1765;
iv. 800.

YOUNG, Dr., dean of Winchester, 1623; iii. 472.

Zealand, ceded to Charles I., 1630; iii. 147.

Zeuta, battle of, 1697; iv. 77.

Zinc, manufacture of, § iv. 692.

ZINZENDORFF, count; *portrait* of, § i. 526. He gives
the Moravians an establishment on his estates in
Upper Lusatia; and in 1737 comes to England, and
makes arrangements for the introduction of Mora-
vianism both in this country and in North America,
ib. Death of, 1760; 527.

ZINZERLING, count, 1706; iv. 186.

ZISCA, celebrated commander of the Hussites of
Bohemia, 1428; crusade proclaimed by Martin V.,
etc., ii. 150.

Zorndorf, battle of.—*See* Custrin.

ZOUCH, John, lord, 1485, fought for Richard III., ii.
284.

ZOUCH, sir Edward, iii. 64. Proclaims king Charles I.,
1625; 108.

ZOUCHE, lord, sent with others by James I. to disperse
a popular assembly, 1607; iii. 36.

ZUCCHERO, an eminent Italian artist of the 16th cen-
tury. His *portrait* of the earl of Leicester, ii. 750.
Of Walsingham, *ib*. Of Mary of Scotland, 549. Of
Cecil, earl of Salisbury, iii. 495. Of sir Walter
Raleigh, 560.

Zullichau, battle of, 1759; iv. 611.

ZUMJUNGEN, general, besieges Messina, 1719; iv. 360.

ZUNIGA, commendator of Requesens, succeeds the
duke of Alva in the regency of the Netherlands,
ii. 649. He dies about 1576, and is succeeded by
John of Austria, *ib*.

London: Printed by William Tyler, Bolt-court.

Milton Keynes UK
Ingram Content Group UK Ltd.
UKHW021328111224
3609UKWH00031B/334

9 781022 789500